U. S. S. R.
Caspian Sea
Tehran
IRAN
PAKISTAN
Baghdad
Tigris
Euphrates
IRAQ
KUWAIT
Kuwait
Persian Gulf
Gulf of Oman
QATAR
UNITED ARAB EMIRATES
SAUDI ARABIA
Riyadh
OMAN
YEMEN PEOPLE'S DEM. REP.
Sea
YEMEN ARAB REP.
San'ā
Indian Ocean
Aden
Gulf of Aden
DJIBOUTI
SOMALIA
Addis Ababa
ETHIOPIA
0 100 200 miles
0 100 200 300 km
© carta, JERUSALEM

MIDDLE EAST CONTEMPORARY SURVEY

Volume One

MIDDLE EAST CONTEMPORARY SURVEY

Volume One
1976–77

COLIN LEGUM, Editor

HAIM SHAKED, Academic Editor

Jacqueline Dyck, Executive Editor

The Shiloah Center for
Middle Eastern and African Studies
Tel Aviv University

Holmes & Meier Publishers, Inc.
New York and London

Published in the United States of America 1978 by
Holmes & Meier Publishers, Inc
30 Irving Place
New York, New York 10003

and in Great Britain by
Holmes & Meier Publishers, Ltd
Hillview House
1, Hallswelle Parade
Finchley Road
London NW11 ODL

ISBN 0-8419-0323-9

Manufactured in the United States of America

Preface

The *Middle East Contemporary Survey* (MECS) is planned as an annual record and analysis of political, economic, military and international developments in the Middle East and its peripheral regions. The need for a record which meets both standards of contemporaneity and high scholarship prompted the Shiloah Center for Middle Eastern and African Studies at Tel Aviv University to consider complementing its respected *Middle East Record* (which has been published since 1962 and to date covers events up to 1970). The present inaugural volume of *Middle East Contemporary Survey* answers that need by providing scholars, diplomats, students and informed laymen with an up-to-date reference work recording the rapidly changing events in an exceptionally complex part of the world. At the same time, every attempt has been made to make use of the widest range of source material while maintaining the highest possible academic standards.

MECS is a joint publishing venture between the Shiloah Center and Holmes & Meier Publishers. The choice of Colin Legum as editor represents the serious wish of the sponsors and the publishers to establish MECS's reputation for objectivity. Most of the essays have been researched and written by the staff of the Shiloah Center; other contributions have been made by distinguished academics and experts mainly from the United States and the United Kingdom.

The material in this volume is arranged in two parts. The first comprises a series of essays which study developments relating to internal and external issues, both regionally and internationally. Subjects explored in detail include the Israeli-Arab conflict, inter-Arab relations, and the international dimension of the contending forces in the region. The second part comprises a country-by-country survey of each of the Middle Eastern entities, excluding the three North African states of Tunisia, Algeria and Morocco.

The period surveyed in this volume, unless otherwise specifically indicated, is generally from October 1976 to October 1977, but a number of chapters deal with events to the end of 1977 and even early 1978. The dramatic change in the Middle East situation, precipitated by the visit of President Anwar al-Sādāt to Jerusalem and the direct Egyptian-Israeli negotiations in November 1977, is analysed in the introductory essay, "The Middle East in Perspective," which covers major developments in the negotiating process up to January 1978.

One of the major difficulties in dealing with a region where no single country is unaffected by the policies of its neighbours is how to avoid too much repetition while at the same time achieving a comprehensive survey of the affairs of each country individually. Extensive cross-references have been used: readers will also find it useful to refer to the extensive "Chronology and Commentary on Political Developments in the Arab-Israeli Conflict," which provides a useful guide to dates and an explanation of key events during the period under review.

Acknowledgements

As editors we are indebted to a large number of contributors who have made this volume possible. First and foremost we acknowledge the work of the staff of the Shiloah Center for Middle Eastern and African Studies at Tel Aviv University whose individual contributions are separately acknowledged.

The economic sections of the countries surveyed in Part II, together with the accompanying statistical tables, have been prepared by Moshe Efrat and Ira E. Hoffman. The former is responsible for Turkey, Iran, Lebanon, Iraq, and North and South Yemen; and the latter for Sudan and Libya, as well as the statistical tables for Israel and the Gulf States. Ira Hoffman has also rendered invaluable services in proof-reading and, especially, in compiling the index. Avi Plascov has been a valued adviser in the area of his special research which is the Palestinians and Jordan. We also wish to acknowledge the information provided by the *Military Balance* of the International Institute for Strategic Studies (London), whose statistics have been used in the various chapters.

Jacqueline Dyck deserves a special place, having performed the exacting task of copy-editing as well as the usual functions of an executive editor.

Anita Gregory, who has worked as an editorial assistant and co-ordinator in London, and Jo Palmer our editorial secretary, have given valiant service.

Among those at the Shiloah Center who must be singled out for special thanks are Daniel Dishon who provided the Shiloah Center authors with invaluable advice; Edna Liftman, who has done wonders in co-ordinating the flow of material between Tel Aviv, London and New York; and the new Director, Elie Rekhess, who came in at a fairly late stage of our operation, but soon made his mark felt. Steven Frieder and Dennis Kurzon have been of great help to those in the Center whose native language is not English. Special thanks are also due to the Shiloah Documentation Center headed by Amikam Salant and Amira Margalith.

Finally, we would like to mention Max Holmes who, from the inception of MECS, has viewed this work not simply as another publishing venture, but more imaginatively, as a serious contribution towards widening knowledge and understanding of Middle Eastern affairs. We have also had the benefit of the advice and co-operation of Terry Walz, Associate Editor of Holmes & Meier, who has been a vital link between ourselves and the publishers.

C.L.
H.S.

Table of Contents

PART ONE

CURRENT ISSUES

The Middle East and World Affairs

The Arab-Israeli Conflict

Inter-Arab Affairs

Palestinian Issues

Middle East Economic Issues

PART TWO

COUNTRY-BY-COUNTRY REVIEW

List of Tables and Documents

Transliteration

The Arabic alphabet has been transliterated as follows:

b	for	ب	n	for	ن
d	for	ض،د	q	for	ق
dh	for	ذ	r	for	ر
f	for	ف	s	for	ص،س
gh	for	غ	sh	for	ش
h	for	ه	t	for	ط،ت
h	for	ح	th	for	ث
j	for	ج	w (or ū)	for	و
k	for	ك	y (or ī)	for	ي
kh	for	خ	z	for	ظ،ز
l	for	ل	’	for	ا،ء
m	for	م	‘	for	ع

In addition,

Long vowels have been distinguished from short ones by a stroke over the letters
The *hamza* is shown only in the middle of a word
The *shadda* is rendered by doubling the consonant containing it
The *ta marbuta* is not shown
The definite article is always shown as "al-" regardless of whether or not it is assimilated to the following letter
No distinction is made between the ordinary and emphatic d, s, t or z
Exceptions to the above are those Lebanese and North African personalities who have adopted a French spelling for their names

Abbreviations

ABEDA	Arab Bank for African Economic Development (or BADEA)
ACP	Africa, the Caribbean and the Pacific (Lomé Convention)
ADF	Arab Deterrent Force (in Lebanon)
AFESD	Arab Fund for Economic and Social Development (Kuwaiti-based)
AGOIC	Arabian Gulf Organization for Industrial Consulting
Aramco	Arabian-American Oil Company
CEMA	Council of Mutual Economic Assistance
CENTO	Central Treaty Organization
CIEC	Conference on International Economic Co-operation (North/South Dialogue)
cif	cost, insurance and freight
EEC	European Economic Community
EIB	European Investment Bank (EEC)
EL	Egyptian pound
ELF	Eritrean Liberation Front
ETCA	Economic and Technical Co-operation Agreement
EUA	EEC Unit of Account (or UA)
fob	free on board
GA	General Assembly (UN)
GDP	Gross Domestic Product
GNP	Gross National Product
IDF	Israel Defence Forces
IEA	International Energy Agency
IL	Israeli pound
IMF	International Monetary Fund
JP	Justice Party (Turkey)
KFAED	Kuwait Fund for Arab Economic Development
LAA	Lebanon's Arab Army
NA	National Assembly
NATO	North Atlantic Treaty Organization
nie	not included elsewhere
NSP	National Salvation Party
OAPEC	Organization of Arab Petroleum Exporting Countries
OECD	Organization for Economic Co-operation and Development
OPEC	Organization of Petroleum Exporting Countries
pa	per annum
PDFLP	Popular Democratic Front for the Liberation of Palestine
PDRY	People's Democratic Republic of Yemen (South Yemen)
PFLO	Popular Front for the Liberation of Oman
PFLP	Popular Front for the Liberation of Palestine
PFLOAG	Popular Front for the Liberation of Oman and the Arab Gulf
PLA	Palestine Liberation Army

PLO	Palestine Liberation Organization
Polisario	Front for the Liberation of Saquiet al-Hamra and Rio de Oro
RCD	Regional Co-operation for Development (Turkey-Iran-Pakistan)
RPP	Republican People's Party (Turkey)
SC	Security Council (UN)
SDRs	Special Drawing Rights (IMF)
Tapline	Trans-Arabian Pipeline
UAE	United Arab Emirates
UNDOF	United Nations Disengagement Observation Force
UNEF	United Nations Emergency Force
UNGA	United Nations General Assembly
UNRWA	United Nations Relief and Works Agency (for Palestine Refugees)
UNTSO	United Nations Truce Supervision Organization
YAR	Yemen Arab Republic (North Yemen)

List of Sources

Newspapers, Periodicals, Yearly, Irregular and Single Publications

Name (Place, frequency of publication)	*Abbreviation*	*Notes*
Al-Ahrām (Cairo, daily)		
Al-Akhbār (Cairo, daily)		
Akhbār al-Khalīj (Manāma, daily)		
Akhbār al-Yawm (Cairo, weekly)		
Ākhir Sā'a (Cairo, weekly)		
Al-'Amal (Tunis, daily)		Organ of the Socialist Dustūr Party
Amnesty International (London, irregular)		
Al-Anbā' (Beirut, weekly)		Organ of Junblāt's Socialist Progressive Party
Al-Anwār (Beirut, daily)		
The Arab Economist (Beirut, monthly)		
Arab Report and Record (London, fortnightly)	ARR	
Arabia and the Gulf (London, weekly)		
Die Arbeiter-Zeitung (Vienna, daily)		
Asian Profile (Hong Kong, bi-monthly)		
Al-Ayyām (Khartoum, daily)		
Baltimore Sun (Baltimore, daily)		
Al-Ba'th (Damascus, daily)		Organ of the Syrian Ba'th Party
Al-Bilād (Jedda, daily)		
Business Week (New York, weekly)		
Christian Science Monitor (Boston, daily)	CSM	
Commentary (New York, monthly)		
Cumhuriyet (Istanbul, daily)		
Daily Telegraph (London, daily)	DT	
Department of State Bulletin (Washington, weekly)	DSB	

Department of State Press Release (Washington, irregular)	DSPR	
Diplomat (Ankara, weekly)		
Al-Dustūr (London, weekly)		Pro-Iraqi. Originally a Beirut weekly reflecting the Iraqi Ba'th views. Closed down in Beirut by the Syrians (December 1976). Published in Paris (until July 1977), then in London
Economic and Political Weekly (Bombay, weekly)		
The Economist (London, weekly)		
The Egyptian Gazette (Cairo, daily)		
Ettela'at (Tehran, daily)		
Events (London, weekly)		Published in English by the owner of al-Ḥawādith, Beirut
Al-Fajr al-Jadīd (Tripoli, daily)		
The Financial Times (London, daily)	FT	
Foreign Affairs (New York, Quarterly)		
France Soir (Paris, daily)		
The Guardian (London, daily)		
Ha'aretz (Tel Aviv, daily)		
Al-Hadaf (Beirut, weekly)		Organ of PFLP
Ha-Olam ha-zeh (Tel Aviv, weekly)		
Al-Ḥawādith (Beirut, weekly)		Reflects views of PDFLP
Al-Ḥurriyya (Beirut, weekly)		
Information: European Economic Community (Brussels, irregular)		
International Financial Statistics (Washington, monthly)	IFS	Published by the International Monetary Fund
International Herald Tribune (Paris and Zürich, daily)	IHT	
Iran Economic Service (Tehran, weekly)	IES	
Issues and Studies (Taipei, monthly)		
Al-Ittiḥād (Haifa, twice a week)		Organ of Communist Party
The Jerusalem Post (Jerusalem, daily)	JP	

Al-Jihād (Tripoli, daily)		
Jordan Times (Amman, daily)		
Al-Jumhūriyya (Cairo, daily)		
Kayhān (Tehran, daily)		
Kayhān International (Tehran, daily)		English-language edition of the Kayhān
Los Angeles Times (Los Angeles, daily)	LAT	
Lugano Review (Lugano, bi-monthly)		
Ma'ariv (Tel Aviv, daily)		
Le Matin (Casablanca, daily)		
Al-Mawāqif (Manāma, weekly)		
The Middle East (London, monthly)		
Middle East Economic Digest (London, weekly)	MEED	
Middle East Intelligence Survey (Tel Aviv, fortnightly)	MEIS	
Middle East International (London, monthly)	MEI	
Mideast Markets (New York, fortnighly)	MM	
Middle East Record (Tel Aviv, yearbook)	MER	
The Military Balance 1977–78 (London, Yearly)		Published by the International Institute for Strategic Studies
Milliyet (Istanbul, daily)		
Monday Morning (Beirut, weekly)		
Le Monde (Paris, daily)		
Monthly Statistical Bulletin (New York, monthly)	MSB	
Al-Muḥarrir (Beirut, daily)		Pro-Iraqi, pro-PLO
Al-Mustaqbal (Paris, weekly)		Pro-Saudi
Al-Nahār (Beirut, daily)		Rightist
Near East Report (Washington, weekly)		
Newsweek (New York, weekly)		
New York Times (New York, daily)	NYT	
The Observer (London, weekly)		
October (Cairo, weekly)		

Outlook (Ankara, weekly)		
Petroleum Economist (London, monthly)		
Peking Review (Peking, weekly)	PR	
Pulse (Ankara, daily)		Summary of Turkish Press
Al-Qabas (Kuwait, daily)		
Quarterly Economic Review (London, Quarterly)	QER	Published by the Economist Intelligence Unit
Al-Quds (East Jerusalem, daily)		Known for favourable views towards Jordan
Rastakhiz (Tehran, daily)		Organ of Rastakhiz party
Al-Ra'y (Amman, daily)		
Al-Ra'y al-'Amm (Kuwait, daily)		
Rūz al-Yūsuf (Cairo, weekly)		
Al-Safīr (Beirut, daily)		Reflects Libyan views
Al-Saḥāfa (Khartoum, daily)		
Saudi Arabian Monetary Agency (Jedda, annual)	SAMA	Also biannual Statistical Summary
The Saudi Gazette (Jedda, daily)		Published by 'Ukkāz publishing house
Al-Sayyād (Beirut, weekly)		
Al-Sha'b (Algiers, daily)		
Shu'ūn Filastīniyya (Beirut, monthly)		Issued by the PLO Research Institute
Al-Siyāsa (Kuwait, daily)		
La Stampa (Milan, daily)		
The Sunday Telegraph (London, weekly)		
Sunday Times (London, weekly)		
The Swiss Review of World Affairs (Zürich, monthly)		
Al-Talā'i' (Damascus, weekly)		Organ of al-Sā'iqa, the Syrian-run organization belonging to the PLO
Al-Thawra (Damascus, daily)		
Time (New York, weekly)		
The Times (London, daily)		
Tishrīn (Damascus, daily)		

Trouw (Amsterdam, daily)	
'Ukkāz (Jedda, daily)	
United Nations Monthly Chronicle (New York, monthly)	
Al-Usbū' al-'Arabī (Beirut, weekly)	
Wall Street Journal (New York, daily)	
Washington Post (Washington, daily)	WP
Al-Watan (Kuwait, daily)	
Weekly Compilation of Presidential Documents (Washington, weekly)	WCPD
The White House Press Release (Washington, irregular)	WHPR
The World Today (London, monthly)	
Al-Yamāma (Riyadh, weekly)	
Al-Yasār al-'Arabī (Paris, monthly)	
Yediot Aharonot (Tel Aviv, daily)	
Die Zeit (Hamburg, weekly)	

News Agencies

Full Name	*Abbreviation*
Agence France Presse	AFP
Arab Revolution News Agency (Tripoli, Libya)	ARNA
Associated Press	AP
Iraqi News Agency	INA
Middle East News Agency (Cairo)	MENA
New China News Agency	NCNA
Qatari News Agency	QNA
Syrian Arab News Agency	SANA
The Saudi News Agency	SNA
Sudanese News Agency	SUNA
Telegraph Agency of the Soviet Union	Tass
United Press International	UPI

Radio Stations and Monitoring Services

(Radio stations known by the location of their principal transmitter are not listed—their names being self-explanatory.)

Name	*Abbreviation*	*Notes*
British Broadcasting Corporation	BBC	
Summary of World Broadcasts; the ME and Africa	SWB	
Daily Report: ME and Africa	DR	Monitoring reports of ME and African broadcasts published in English translations by the US FBIS.
(Washington: Foreign Broadcast Information Service).	FBIS	

Israel Broadcasting Authority	IBA	
R Cairo, Voice of Palestine	VOP	Run by PLO under the supervision of R Cairo
R of the Phalanges		Transmissions of the Phalanges Party, Lebanon
R Tripoli, Voice of the Arab Homeland		Libya Transmitter beaming to Arab states outside Libya.

Notes on Contributors

W.A.C. (IAN) ADIE, M.A. (Oxon). Formerly worked on Far Eastern affairs at the British Foreign Office. Senior Research Fellow at St Antony's College, Oxford. Senior Research Fellow at the Australian National University. Now Director of International Affairs Research Unit, Australia. Contributor since 1962 to such journals as *China Quarterly, Mizan, China Report, International Affairs. World Today*. On editorial board of *Asia Quarterly, Lugano Review, Asian Perspectives.*

ISRAEL ALTMAN Ph.D. in Islamic Studies (University of California, Los Angeles). Head of the Palestinian Organizations Section, Shiloah Center.

DAN AVIDAN, M.A. (University of California, 1975). Served as Research Fellow and Co-ordinator of the Near Eastern Research Unit, the Harry S. Truman Research Institute at the Hebrew University, Jerusalem. Presently a member of the research staff of the Shiloah Center, specializing on the Administered Arab Territories.

OFRA BENGIO, B.A. in History of the Middle East and English (Tel Aviv University). Joined the Research Staff of the Shiloah Center in 1967. Head of the Iraqi Section since 1969.

VARDI BEN-ZVI, B.A. in Arabic Language and Literature and Political Science (Hebrew University of Jerusalem, 1966). Head of the Inter-Arab Relations Section at the Shiloah Center.

URIEL DANN, B.A. in Modern History (London University, 1959); Ph.D. in History of the Muslim Countries (The Hebrew University of Jerusalem, 1966). Since 1966 has taught Middle Eastern history at Tel Aviv University; also Research Fellow of Shiloah Center. Published *Iraq Under Qassem* (Jerusalem, London and New York, 1969).

DANIEL DISHON (Hebrew University, Jerusalem, 1938–40). Editor *Middle East Record* and Senior Research Fellow at Shiloah Center since 1967. Specializes in the contemporary Middle East and inter-Arab relations.

MOSHE EFRAT B.Sc. M.Sc. (Tel Aviv University). Ph.D. candidate in Economics (LSE). Has written economic surveys in *Middle East Record* and in the quarterly "Hamizrah Hahadash" (New East). Recently published (in Hebrew): "The Palestinian Refugees: A Social and Economic Survey 1949–74".

MOSHE GAMMER, B.A. in Middle Eastern and General History (Tel Aviv University). Joined the Research Staff of the Shiloah Center in 1976, working in the Arab-Israeli Conflict Section.

GIDEON GERA, Senior Research Associate at the Shiloah Center. Presently completing a Ph.D. thesis on the Qadhdhāfī regime in Libya.

IRA E. HOFFMAN, B.A. M.Sc. (University of Michigan; the Hebrew University, Jerusalem; and the London School of Economics). Taught in the Department of International Relations, LSE. Presently working on his doctorate at the LSE on the subject of European Community relations with the Middle East.

YAIR P. HIRSCHFELD, Ph.D. with distinction (Tel Aviv University, 1977). Head of the Iranian Section at the Shiloah Center from 1976–77. As of 1977, faculty member in the Department of Middle Eastern and African History at Tel Aviv University.

BRIGADIER KENNETH HUNT, Deputy Director of the International Institute for Strategic Studies from September 1967 to October 1977. Now a Fellow of the Institute. Regular officer in the British army for c. 30 years. Among his published works are *NATO without France: The Requirements of Military Technology in the 1970s* and *The Alliance and Europe, Part II: Defence with Fewer Men*. Has worked extensively on security matters relating to the Middle and Far East for the Institute and made frequent visits there including many to Japan and Korea. Specialist Adviser to the Parliamentary Sub-Committee on Defence and External Affairs at the House of Commons. Now Director of the British Atlantic Committee.

ELIYAHU KANOVSKY, Associate Professor and Head of Economics Department at Bar Ilan University. Senior Research Fellow at Shiloah Center. Held Fellowships at various research centers, published books and articles on economic affairs in the Middle East.

GEOFFREY KEMP, Ph.D. in Political Science (Massachusetts Institute of Technology). Currently an Associate Professor of International Politics at the Fletcher School of Law and Diplomacy, Tufts University. Has written extensively on Middle East military affairs.

COLIN LEGUM, associate editor of the *Observer* and editor of *Africa Contemporary Record* since 1968. Published works include *Must We Lose Africa*? (1954); *Bandung, Cairo and Accra* (1958); *Attitude to Africa* (1953) with others; *Congo Disaster* (1972); *Pan-Africanism* (1962); *South Africa: Crisis for the West* (1964) with his wife; *The Bitter Choice* (1968) with his wife; *After Angola* (1976); *The Fall of Haile Selassie's Empire* (1976); *Vorster's Gamble for Africa* (1977); *The Year of the Whirlwind* (1977); *Conflict in the Horn of Africa* (1978).

ESTHER LIDZBARSKI-TAL, B.A. in History of the Middle East and Africa (Tel Aviv University); M.A. student. Head of Turkish Section at Shiloah Center since 1976.

MISHA LOUVISH, M.A. Hons (Glasgow University). Associated with the *Middle East Record* since its inception as English editor (1960), Associate editor (1961) and contributor (1968–71). Taught in Glasgow and Tel Aviv. Since 1949 has been engaged in studying Israel's development and culture. Editor of various publications, including *Here and Now, Facts about Israel* and *Israel Digest*. Worked and written for a number of newspapers, magazines and publications including *Jerusalem Post, Jewish Frontier* and *American Jewish Year Book*. Recognized as one of the foremost translators from Hebrew into English, he translated the maior speeches of all Israeli Prime Ministers from 1955–63, as well as most of David Ben-Gurion's essays and fiction by Nobel prizewinner S. Y. Agnon.

DAVID MORISON is Director of the Central Asian Research Centre and joint editor of *USSR and Third World*, a regular survey of Soviet and Chinese relations with the countries of Africa, Asia and Latin America. Contributor to *Africa Contemporary Record.*

AVI PLASCOV recently submitted his Ph. D. thesis on *The Palestinian Refugees in Jordan* at the School of African and Oriental Studies, University of London. Author of "A Homeland for the Palestinians?" published by *Survival* (The International Institute of Strategic Studies Bulletin, 1978).

ITAMAR RABINOVICH, Ph.D. (University of California, Los Angeles, 1971). Chairman and Associate Professor, the Department of Middle Eastern and African History; Senior Research Fellow at the Shiloah Center. Visiting Professor at the Norman Patterson School of International Affairs, Ottawa, Canada (1975–76). Fields of specialization: the modern and contemporary history of the Arab world with particular reference to Syria, Lebanon and inter-Arab affairs.

ROUHOLLAH K. RAMAZANI is Edward R. Stettinius Professor and Chairman at the Woodrow Wilson Department of Government and Foreign Affairs, University of Virginia. Associate Editor of *Journal of South Asia and Middle Eastern Studies*, Advisory Editor of the *Middle East Journal*, and consultant to the Rockefeller Foundation and Institute for Foreign Policy Analysis. Author of *The Middle East and the European Common Market; The Northern Tier: Afghanistan, Iran and Turkey; The Foreign Policy of Iran, 1500–1941: A Study of Foreign Policy in Modernizing Nations; The Persian Gulf: Iran's Role; Beyond the Arab-Israeli Settlement: New Directions for US Policy in the Middle East*; and numerous articles and reviews.

BERNARD REICH, B.A. in Government (City College, N.Y.), M.A. and Ph.D. in Foreign Affairs (University of Virginia). Professor of Political Science and International Affairs, and Chairman of the Department of Political Science at the George Washington University. Has also taught at Tel Aviv University and the US Defence Intelligence School. Has lectured at Foreign Service Institute; the Department of State; the National War College; the US Military Academy (West Point); in Jerusalem at the Hebrew University and in Egypt at the Nasser High Military Academy; the Diplomatic Institute of the Foreign Ministry; the Strategic Studies Center at *al-Ahrām*; and the International Symposium on the October War. Held at Fulbright Research Scholar Grant for Egypt in 1965 and a National Service Foundation Postdoctoral Fellowship for Israel in 1971–72. Consultant to the Department of State. Author of numerous articles on Middle East politics and US Middle East Policy. Has published extensively, his latest book being *Quest for Peace: US-Israel Relations and the Arab-Israeli Conflict* (New Brunswick, N.J.: Transaction Books, 1977).

ELIE REKHESS, M.A. in Middle Eastern and African History (Tel Aviv University). Head of Israeli Arabs Section, Shiloah Center. Since 1977, Director of the Shiloah Center. Published works include the politics of the West Bank and the Gaza Strip and the political trends of the Arab population in Israel.

YEHUDIT RONEN, B.A. in the History of the Middle East and Arabic (Tel Aviv University, 1971). Head of the Sudanese Section at the Shiloah Center.

DANKWART RUSTOW, Ph.D. (Yale 1951), is Distinguished Professor of Political Science at the City University of New York. Taught at Princeton University (1952–59) and Columbia (1959–70) where he was Professor of International Social Forces. Has also held visiting appointments at Yale, Harvard, M.I.T., Heidelberg, Torino, the London School of Economics and the University of Sussex. Among his earlier publications are *The Politics of Compromise* (1955), *A World of Nations* (1967), *The Cyprus Conflict and US Security Interests* (1967), *Philosophers and Kings: Studies in Leadership* (1968), *Middle Eastern Political Systems* (1971), and articles in many leading publications. He is co-author of *OPEC: Success and Prospects* (Council on Foreign Relations, 1976). Was Vice-President of the Middle East Studies Association of North America (1969–70) and the American Political Science Association (1973–74).

DAN SCHUEFTAN, B.A. in History of the Middle East and Africa (Tel Aviv University). M.A. student at the Arane School of History (Tel Aviv University). Specializes in the Arab-Israeli conflict and the Arab world. Has published articles on the Arab-Israeli conflict.

RAN SEGEV studied Middle Eastern and African History at Tel Aviv University. Joined the research staff of the Shiloah Center in 1977. Acting Head of the Egypt Section.

HAIM SHAKED, Ph.D. (School of Oriental and African Studies, University of London, 1969). Associate Professor for Middle Eastern and African History. Head of the Shiloah Center; Dean of the Faculty of Humanities, Tel Aviv University. Author of *The Life of the Sudanese Mahdi* and co-editor of *From Here to October: The ME Between 1967–1973.* Has also written numerous articles on the Middle East in general and on fields of specialization: Sudan, Saudi Arabia, Yemen and South Yemen. Co-editor of *Middle East Record*; Chairman, Editorial Board of the Shiloah Center Monograph Series.

SHIMON SHAMIR, Ph.D. (Princeton, 1960). Associate Professor of Modern History of the Middle East and Senior Research Fellow at Shiloah Center. In 1966, established at Tel Aviv University the Department of Middle Eastern and African History and the Shiloah Center, which he directed until 1971 and 1973 respectively. Held appointments at Harvard University (1968–69) and at University of Pennsylvania (1976–77). Has published books on the modern history of the Arabs and contemporary Egypt and various articles on Ottoman Syria and Palestine. Edited *USSR and the ME, Decline of Nasserism* and *Egyptian Intellectuals.* Has conducted several interdisciplinary field studies on Arab-Palestinian society.

ARYEH SHMUELEVITZ, Senior Research Fellow at Shiloah Center and in the Department of Middle Eastern and African History. Fields of interest: history of the Ottomans and the Persians, contemporary history of Turkey, Iran and the Persian Gulf Principalities.

BENJAMIN SHWADRAN, M.A., Ph.D. (Clark University). Taught Middle Eastern Studies in the New York School for Social Research; Professor of Middle Eastern Studies and Director of Middle East Institute, Dropsie University, Philadelphia; taught in Hofstra University, New York. Professor of Modern Middle East History at Tel Aviv University since 1973. Was editor of *Middle Eastern Affairs* and of the Council for Middle Eastern Affairs Press. Among his publications are *Middle East Oil and the Great Powers* (three editions); *Jordan, a State of Tension; The Power Struggle in Iraq; General Index Middle Eastern Affairs; Neft Hamizrah Hatikhon: Berakha Veiyum; Middle East Oil: Issues and Problems.*

ASHER SUSSER, B.A. in Modern Middle Eastern History and Political Science (Tel Aviv University, 1972). Head of the Jordan Section at Shiloah Center.

MICHAEL VLAHOS, B.A. (Yale University, 1973). Presently a Ph.D. candidate at the Fletcher School of Law and Diplomacy specializing in International Studies.

TAMAR YEGNES, B.A. in the History of the Middle East and Hebrew Literature (Tel Aviv University, 1977). Joined the Research Staff of the Shiloah Center in 1972 as Head of the Saudi Arabia, Yemen Arab Republic and the People's Democratic Republic of Yemen Sections.

HANNA ZAMIR, B.A. in the History of the Middle East and Arabic (Hebrew University, Jerusalem, 1968). Since 1967, Head of the Lebanese Section at the Shiloah Center.

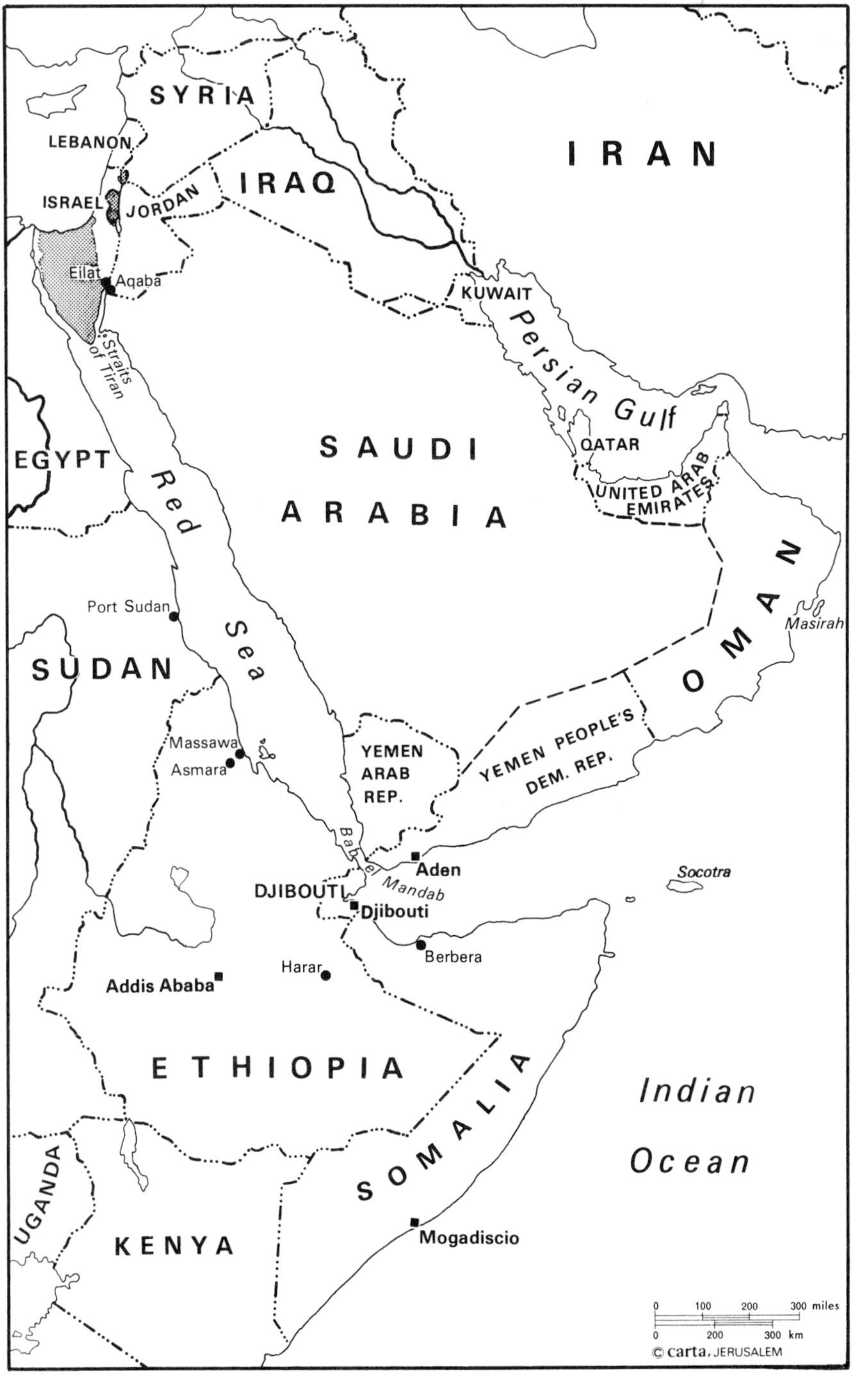
SYRIA
LEBANON
ISRAEL
JORDAN
IRAQ
IRAN
Eilat
Aqaba
KUWAIT
Persian Gulf
Straits of Tiran
EGYPT
SAUDI ARABIA
QATAR
UNITED ARAB EMIRATES
Red Sea
OMAN
Masirah
Port Sudan
SUDAN
Massawa
Asmara
YEMEN ARAB REP.
YEMEN PEOPLE'S DEM. REP.
Bab el Mandab
Aden
Socotra
DJIBOUTI
Djibouti
Berbera
Harar
Addis Ababa
ETHIOPIA
SOMALIA
Indian Ocean
UGANDA
KENYA
Mogadiscio
0 100 200 300 miles
0 200 300 km
© carta, JERUSALEM

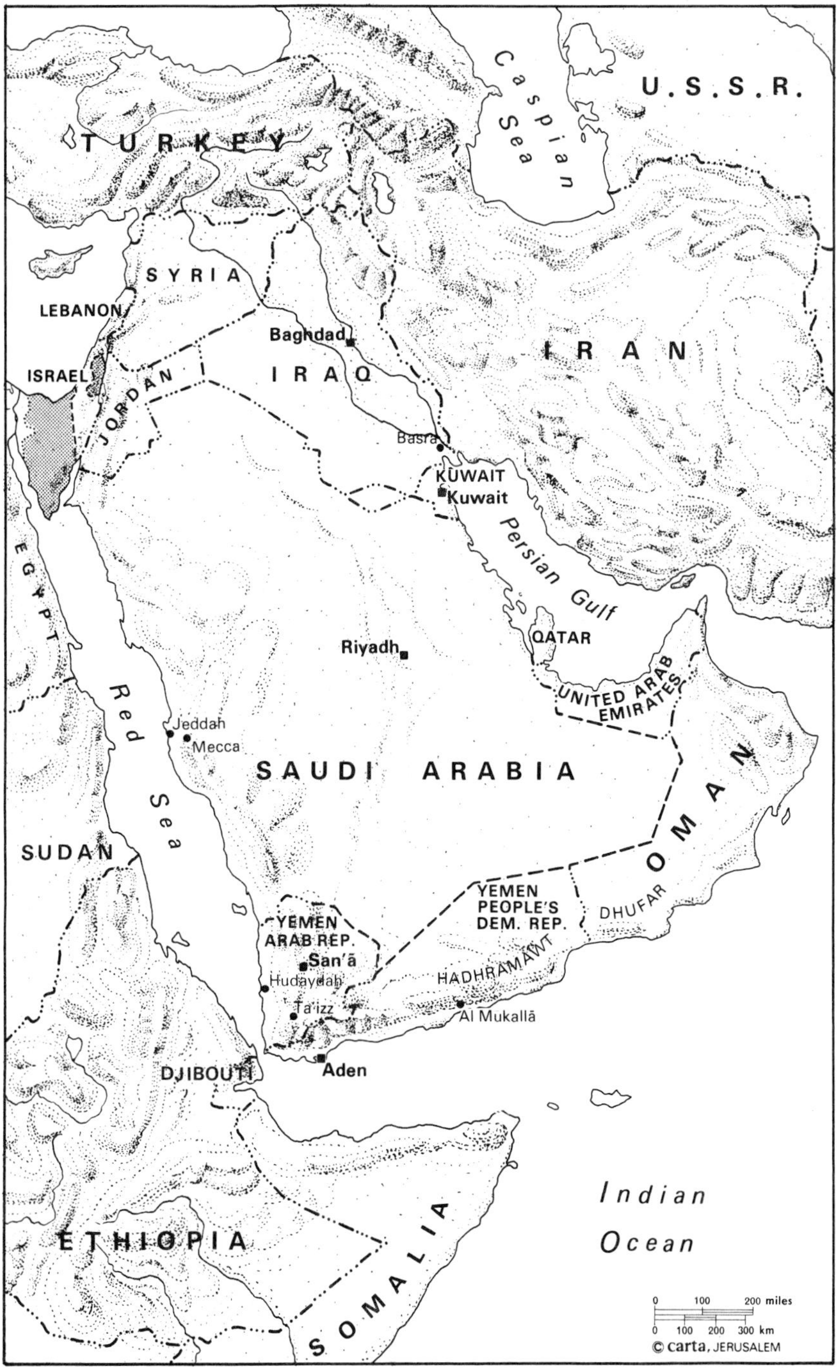

U.S.S.R.
Caspian Sea
TURKEY
SYRIA
LEBANON
ISRAEL
JORDAN
IRAQ
Baghdad
IRAN
Basra
KUWAIT
Kuwait
Persian Gulf
EGYPT
QATAR
Riyadh
UNITED ARAB EMIRATES
Red Sea
Jeddah
Mecca
SAUDI ARABIA
OMAN
SUDAN
YEMEN PEOPLE'S DEM. REP.
DHUFAR
YEMEN ARAB REP.
San'ā
Hudaydah
HADHRAMAWT
Ta'izz
Al Mukallā
DJIBOUTI
Aden
Indian Ocean
ETHIOPIA
SOMALIA
0 100 200 miles
0 100 200 300 km
© carta, JERUSALEM

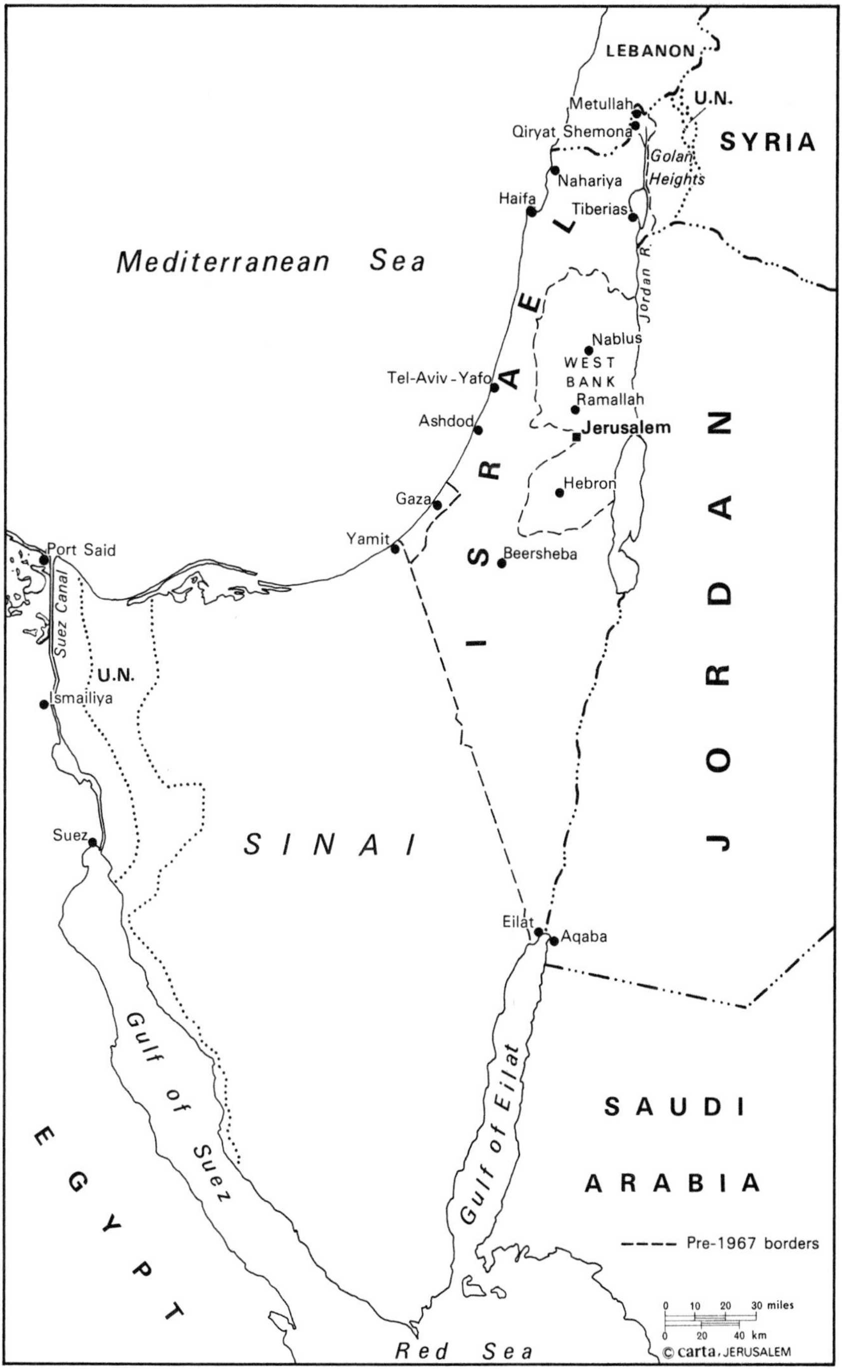
LEBANON
U.N.
SYRIA
Metullah
Qiryat Shemona
Golan Heights
Nahariya
Haifa
Tiberias
Mediterranean Sea
Jordan R.
Nablus
WEST BANK
Tel-Aviv-Yafo
Ramallah
Ashdod
Jerusalem
JORDAN
ISRAEL
Hebron
Gaza
Yamit
Beersheba
Port Said
Suez Canal
U.N.
Ismailiya
SINAI
Suez
Eilat
Aqaba
Gulf of Suez
Gulf of Eilat
SAUDI ARABIA
EGYPT
Pre-1967 borders
0 10 20 30 miles
0 20 40 km
Red Sea
© carta, JERUSALEM

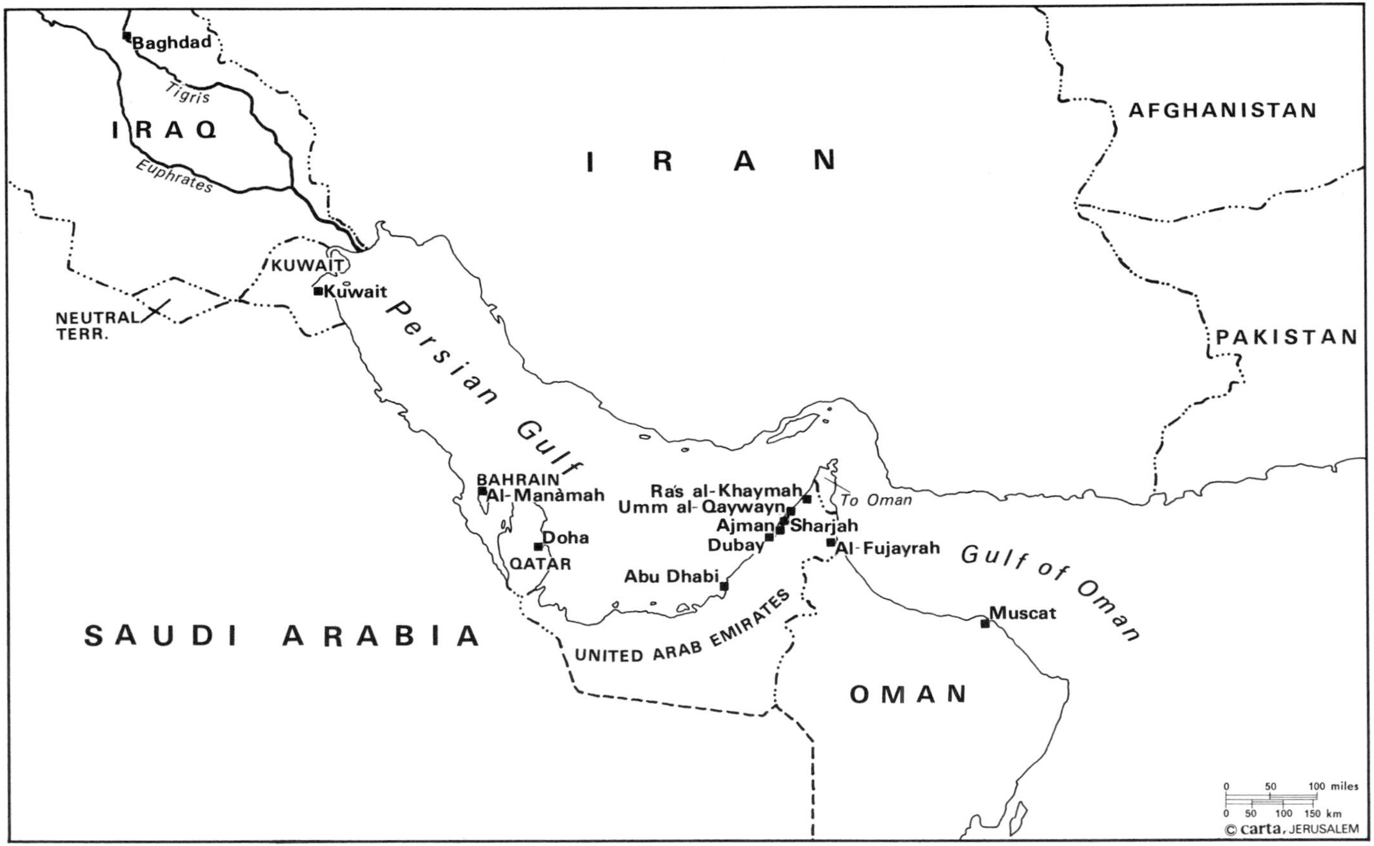
Baghdad
Tigris
IRAQ
Euphrates
I R A N
AFGHANISTAN
PAKISTAN
KUWAIT
Kuwait
NEUTRAL TERR.
Persian Gulf
BAHRAIN
Al-Manàmah
Doha
QATAR
Ras al-Khaymah
Umm al-Qaywayn
Ajman
Sharjah
Dubay
Abu Dhabi
To Oman
Al-Fujayrah
Gulf of Oman
Muscat
SAUDI ARABIA
UNITED ARAB EMIRATES
OMAN
0 50 100 miles
0 50 100 150 km
© carta, JERUSALEM

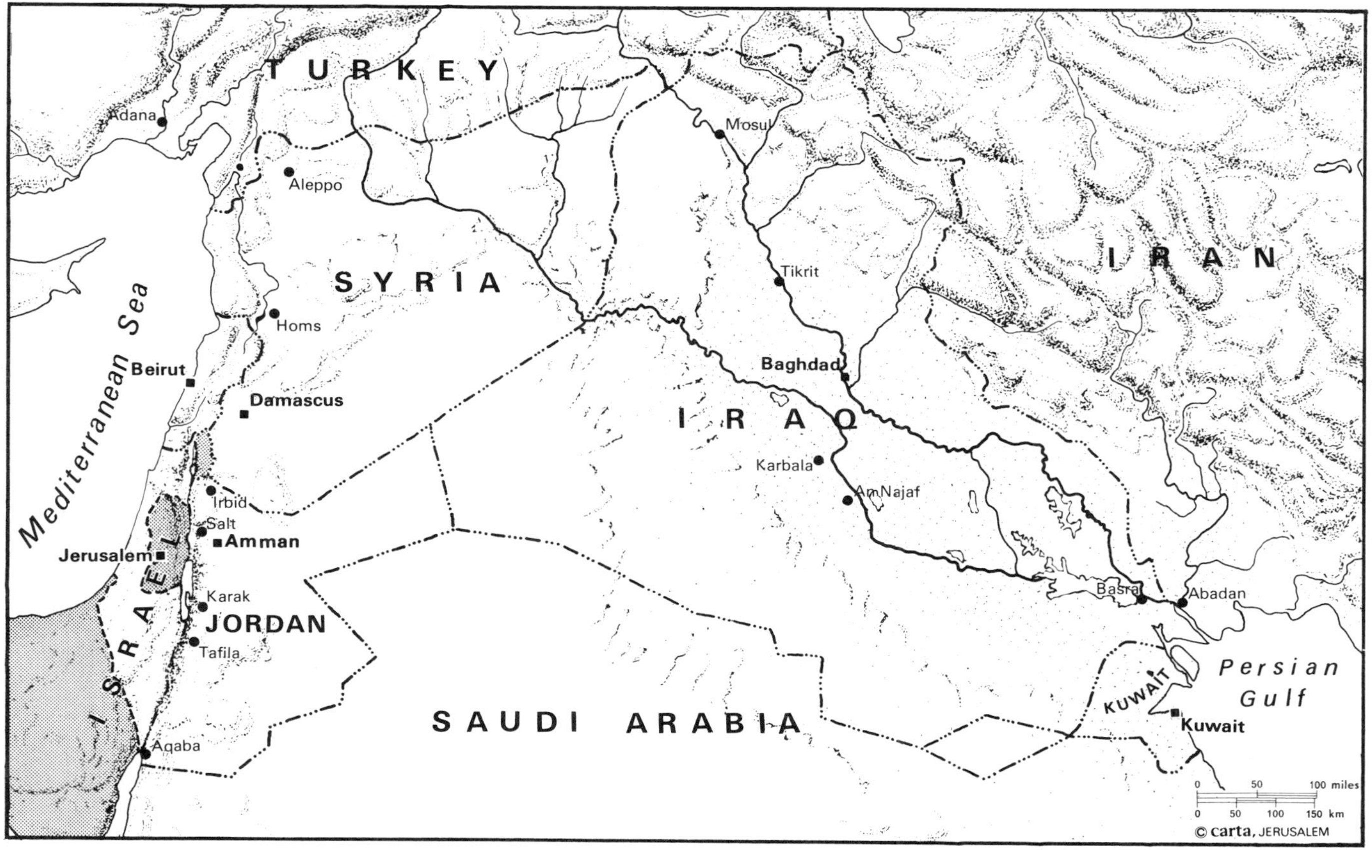
TURKEY
SYRIA
IRAN
IRAQ
JORDAN
ISRAEL
SAUDI ARABIA
KUWAIT
Mediterranean Sea
Persian Gulf
Adana
Aleppo
Mosul
Tikrit
Homs
Beirut
Damascus
Baghdad
Karbala
An Najaf
Irbid
Salt
Amman
Jerusalem
Karak
Tafila
Aqaba
Basra
Abadan
Kuwait
0 50 100 miles
0 50 100 150 km
© carta, JERUSALEM

PART I
Current Issues

The Middle East in Perspective: A Review of the Crucial Changes in 1977

DANIEL DISHON*

For the first time since 1948, the Arab-Israeli conflict decisively changed course in 1977, beginning with President Anwar al-Sādāt's announcement of 9 November that he would go to Jerusalem; his subsequent visit there from 19–21 November; the opening round of the Cairo conference (14–27 December); and the Ismā'īliyya meeting of President Sādāt and Prime Minister Begin on 25 and 26 December. In this essay, an attempt has been made to describe some of the major implications of this turn of events, to the extent that they could be perceived at the time of writing. The first part of the essay will also help to update the surveys in this volume, almost all of which cover an earlier period and were completed before Sādāt's initiative. The second part deals with trends in evidence in the Middle East throughout 1977 which were not, or only marginally, affected by Egypt's new approach.

EGYPT'S CHANGE OF COURSE: A PRELIMINARY EVALUATION

Egyptian policy towards Israel began to diverge from that of other Arab countries early in 1977. Cairo displayed a greater commitment to what came to be called "the political process" than did Damascus, its major prospective partner, and showed greater interest in accelerating the pace of the process than any of the other Arab states. A crucial aspect of Egyptian policy was the reliance it placed on the American role, both as mediator and as the one great power capable of bringing pressure to bear on Israel. Beginning with his visit to Washington in the spring, President Sādāt indicated a willingness to envisage some progress towards normalizing Israeli-Arab relations following a political settlement; whereas earlier, he had spoken only in terms of "ending belligerency."

In early 1977, Sādāt also seemed to come to regard the PLO as an obstacle to the speeding up of the political process (then still expected to culminate in the reconvening of the Geneva conference) and sought ways of circumventing its "veto power" over the course of political contacts. One way was to try to prevail upon the PLO to moderate its stance, but repeated efforts to achieve this were unsuccessful. Another way was to grant a pre-defined role to Jordan in the solution of the Palestinian issue. Sādāt had tentatively broached the subject as far back as the summer of 1974, but had subsequently dropped the idea and joined Arab ranks in supporting the pro-PLO Rabat resolutions of October 1974. However, he had reverted to the idea at the end of 1976 when he suggested a Jordanian-Palestinian link prior to the establishment of a Palestinian state, an idea he thereafter pursued consistently. In a third attempt to circumvent the PLO, Sādāt proposed, in August 1977, to have a "working group" of foreign ministers prepare for the Geneva conference. This would have relegated the question of PLO participation to a much later stage of the negotiations. However, Sādāt's proposal was speedily and thoroughly demolished by Syria, supported by Jordan and Saudi Arabia on this issue.

*In this essay, the author has drawn extensively on the expertise of his colleagues at the Shiloah Center and wishes to acknowledge his indebtedness to them.

Notwithstanding all these moves, there was no Egyptian deviation from the broad Arab consensus over the question of Palestinian self-determination as such, or over the insistence on a Palestinian state (even though linked to Jordan) as one of the "legitimate rights" of the Palestinians. Neither did Egypt differ from any other Arab state in the demand for total Israeli withdrawal from all the territories held since 1967. The points of divergence and convergence became clear after the drafting of the US-Israeli "Working Paper" of 5 October 1977 which Egypt, alone among the Arab states, considered a possible vehicle to get "things moving." These words, ironically, were spoken by Egypt's Foreign Minister, Ismā'īl Fahmī, who only a month later preferred to resign rather than accompany Sādāt to Jerusalem.

The above trends set Egypt apart to some extent from other Arab confrontation states, let alone the "rejectionists," but were not so radical as to foreshadow the spectacular turn of events in November 1977. Other more deeply-rooted aspects of Egypt's overall domestic and international situation need to be considered to explain the initiative. Clearly, it is not yet possible to establish the relative importance of the various factors which, in combination, prompted Sādāt to take his decision.

Egypt's dire economic circumstances, aggravated by the population explosion, was undoubtedly a major factor. A wide gap in the balance of payments, price inflation, supply difficulties, overt and concealed unemployment, the incipient disintegration of the infrastructure and of many public services were its principal characteristics. All of these problems go back 12 years or even further. However, the late 1960s and the 1970s saw a sharpening of three trends: a mood of passive acceptance was replaced by mounting public discontent; the leadership began to see the solution of economic, social and demographic problems (the latter mainly in the context of population dispersal) as vital for the regime's survival; and both the establishment and the politically conscious public came to link the country's economic ills with its wars against Israel as well as with its role in the overall Arab-Israeli conflict. Another factor was the growing concern about the cost to Egypt, both in human lives and in economic resources, of the wars against Israel. Egypt was the only Arab country which had fought in *all* Israeli-Arab wars, including the war of attrition in 1969–70, which had left a strong imprint on Egyptian society because of its duration, the deep-penetration bombings and the almost complete inactivity of the other Arab countries. The impact of Egypt's participation in the war in Yemen (1962–67), seen in retrospect as a pan-Arab venture which did not eventually benefit Egypt, added to these perceptions. The extension of conscription to the middle-class and professional strata after 1967 extended anxiety beyond those previously directly affected in the fighting, to include sectors of public opinion to which the leadership was more sensitive. Technocrats and intellectuals, in particular, were more keenly aware than before of the destructiveness of a new war and came to favour a de-escalation of the conflict, possibly even by means of a formal peace.

Another crucial set of considerations stemmed from the state of Egypt's armed forces which, unlike Israel's, were not appreciably stronger than in 1973. This led to a preference for achieving Egypt's national policy objectives by means less risky than the exercise of the military option. Although this option lost its former priority, it was not entirely excluded, either for the purpose of bolstering Egypt's negotiating position, or as an actual alternative in the case of political deadlock.

Another cluster of factors with a bearing on Sādāt's decision centred on the regime's desire to give higher priority to Egyptian rather than to Arab affairs. Three elements combined to strengthen this trend: the disillusionment with the Arab policies pursued during the period of 'Abd al-Nāsir, which had come to be regarded as "adventurist"; a growing pragmatism stemming from weariness with "messianic" revolutionary fervour and ideological commitment; and an increasing emphasis on the Egyptian, rather than the pan-Arab component of national identification. The disputes with Libya and other "rejectionist" states, the quarrel with Syria in 1975 and 1976, and the failure of Sādāt's attempts to make the PLO fall in line with Egypt's policies reinforced these trends. The contrast between Egypt's self-perception of having sacrificed so much for the Arab cause, and the often bitter aspersions cast on its all-Arab loyalty by its Arab critics, caused resentment and alienation. These were heightened by the feeling that the financial assistance granted to Egypt by oil-rich Arab countries was disproportionate, both to its own needs and to the wealth of the donors.

The deterioration in Soviet-Egyptian relations and the increasing Egyptian reliance on the US, also played their part. Pro-Soviet orientation would have improved Egypt's chances for strengthening its military option; co-operation with the US increased the prospects of maximal gains through the political process. At the same time, once the pro-American policy had begun to pay some dividends in the form of US economic assistance, a reversal to a militant policy would endanger that aid—thus again aggravating Egypt's economic problems. Both the emphasis on domestic reconstruction and the retrospective dissociation from Nāsirist tenets (including their strong anti-Western overtones) worked in favour of an American orientation.

Finally, there was the personality of Anwar al-Sādāt himself, whose own thinking clearly reflected many of the motifs just described. His predilection for grand gestures—shown on previous occasions—cannot altogether be discounted as a factor in what was obviously a highly personal decision. The reasons for its timing and course—the dramatic path to the Knesset—are not yet clear, but some of the considerations that weighed with him can be identified. For instance, a growing measure of US consideration for the Syrian point of view in preparing for the Geneva talks undoubtedly caused some pique on Sādāt's part, particularly at a time when Egyptian-Syrian rivalry was again becoming more prominent. The PLO, partly as a result of Syria's influence over it, slipped further away from Egypt. Not wishing to upset its relations with Syria, Jordan too declined to fall into line with the Egyptian idea of a Palestinian-Jordanian link, which it interpreted as unwelcome Egyptian pressure for a PLO-Jordanian reconciliation. Further, the US-Soviet joint statement of 1 October 1977 was received in Egypt with open disappointment and some anxiety: it seemed to accord the USSR that active role in regional affairs which Egypt had been trying to deny it since 1972.

The Egyptian appraisal of the combined effect of these developments was that the Geneva conference would probably not convene in 1977 or early 1978. Sādāt realized that Arab insistence on PLO participation would remain unacceptable to Israel. In September 1978, the second Sinai Agreement would run out, presenting Egypt with the choice of renewing it and losing face in the Arab world, or abrogating it and risking military tension in Sinai. The political process as hitherto understood was thus called into question. By contrast, the desire of the new Israeli government to establish direct contacts with Egypt was by now known to Sādāt. (The role of Romania in this respect has become public knowledge; other preparatory soundings are probably still to be disclosed.) Sādāt's publicly-stated impression of Begin's government as being "strong"—a good deal more so, in his view, than Rabin's—possibly also contributed to his decision to lift the political process to an altogether different plane.

IMMEDIATE RESULTS OF THE EGYPTIAN INITIATIVE

At a time when the ultimate outcome of the events of late 1977 and early 1978 are in no way predictable, the following evaluation of their immediate results can be made.

As regards Israeli-Egyptian relations, Egypt made Israel rather than the US its primary interlocutor for promoting the political process. Rather than using US leverage over Israel as the principal vehicle for political gain, Sādāt elected to address himself to Israel's government, its politicians and, most vigorously and directly, its people. For this purpose he could have no better platform than the one he chose—the Knesset in Jerusalem.

In doing so, Sādāt abandoned the longstanding Arab objection to direct talks with Israel. Security Council Resolution 242 had hitherto been regarded as "self-implementing" by those Arab states who accepted it. Resolution 338 had been interpreted as calling for talks between "the parties concerned" in the setting of an international, not an Arab-Israeli, conference. The meetings leading to the various disengagement agreement were defined, on the Arab side, as "military talks"—not as fully-fledged direct contacts. However, Sādāt's visit to Jerusalem and Begin's to Ismā'īliyya were precisely that: meetings at the highest level with no third party present. In the view of Sādāt's Arab critics, this exchange of visits as well as his participation in ceremonies at which Israel's flag was flown and its national anthem played, constituted a *de facto* recognition of Israel. Sādāt himself, however, repeatedly protested against this interpretation.

In his Knesset speech and on subsequent occasions during 1977, Sādāt spoke of Egypt's willingness to "really and truly welcome you [Israel] to live among us in peace and security"; he held out hope for a peace treaty presumed to contain most of those elements of normalization which, in the Israeli view, constituted "genuine peace." He also pledged consideration for Israel's security concerns. At the same time, it should be noted what Sādāt did *not* propose: he did not offer a separate Israeli-Egyptian settlement, and he did not, in 1977, speak in terms of a substantive compromise. The peace he offered was predicated on Israel's acceptance of total withdrawal and self-determination for the Palestinians. Direct negotiations should indeed be conducted, but they should concern the *modalities* of implementing the two basic Arab demands, not their *modification*. Sādāt's promise of "no more war" was, in all likelihood, applicable only to a situation in which Israel accepted that qualified view of what negotiations were to mean. The motif underlying this choice of words reflected something of Egypt's war-weariness; yet it would also serve Egypt well in winning over world opinion if the military option were to be revived at some future time.

THE IMPACT OF EGYPT'S POLICY ON ISRAEL

Israeli policy underwent important changes in the interval between the Jerusalem and the Ismā'īliyya talks. Its policy on Sinai, though not departing from that of former governments in the assessment as to which areas in Sinai were of most importance to Israel, became much more sharply defined. At its base was an attempt to combine the recognition in principle of Egyptian sovereignty over the entire area of Sinai with the preservation of an Israeli presence at the Rafaḥ approaches (including the settlements there), and identical or similar security safeguards at Sharm al-Shaykh. On the Palestinian issue, Prime Minister Begin's proposal for self-rule in Judea, Samaria and the Gaza Strip was a major departure both from his own earlier attitudes on the subject and from those of his predecessors since 1967. It was viewed in Israel, but not in Egypt, as a basic revision of national policies made in response to Sādāt's visit. As for the Golan Heights, Israel did not seem to regard Egypt as a negotiating partner to determine its future.

THE IMPACT OF EGYPT'S POLICY ON THE PLO

The PLO lost much of what it had gained since the 1973 war during the last two months of 1977. Sādāt disassociated himself from it, as did the US in his wake. Sādāt declared that, in joining the Tripoli group (see immediately below), the PLO had itself invalidated the Rabat decisions of 1974 which had granted it the status of "sole legitimate representative" of the Palestinians. His argument—which he did not spell out—presumably rested on the fact that another clause of the Rabat summit resolutions had referred, though rather guardedly, to the desirability of pursuing the political process. By coming out against this process, the Tripoli states had, in Sādāt's view removed themselves from the Rabat consensus in *all* its aspects. Sādāt caused further damage to the standing of the PLO by repeatedly referring to how it acted against its better judgement because of Syrian and Soviet pressures. Following the opening of the Cairo conference in December 1977, he said that by not attending it "the PLO had lost the opportunity of receiving recognition." Finally, he spoke of the inhabitants of the West Bank as the "genuine" Palestinians, contrasting them with the PLO leaders to be found in Beirut cafes and cabarets.

Thus, at year's end the PLO was effectively (if not yet permanently) removed from the main arena of Middle Eastern negotiations. Having lost Egyptian backing as well as its immediate chance for a dialogue with the US, and having failed during 1977 to find any common ground whatsoever with Jordan, its only supporters were now those Tripoli-group states who had themselves been relegated into subsidiary positions. There were indications of growing discontent with this state of affairs within al-Fath. the largest of the PLO's constituent organizations and Yāsir 'Arafāt's personal power base. By the end of 1977, however, no overt realignment of forces within the PLO had taken place.

THE IMPACT OF EGYPT'S POLICY ON THE ARAB WORLD

On the inter-Arab scene, Sādāt's moves produced a spectacular shift in the constellation that had existed earlier in the year. Syrian-Egyptian tensions, smouldering until mid-1977 and more marked from August onwards, now erupted into an open rift. Initiating what soon developed into a wider chorus of recrimination—charges of "treason" and accusations of seeking a separate deal—Asad tried to place Syria at the head of an anti-Egyptian Arab bloc. An anti-Sādāt conference convened in Tripoli (Libya) early in December 1977 but lost much of its effectiveness when Iraq (placing its long-standing private quarrel with Syria above the cause of forming an anti-Sādāt coalition) walked out of the meeting and proceeded to attack Syria for not having become genuinely "rejectionist." Syria continued the conference with Algeria, Libya, South Yemen and the PLO, who together formed what they called the "Front of Steadfastness and Opposition." Their joint resolutions were carefully phrased to convey both their rejection of Sādāt's new policies and Syria's desire not to close the door entirely against the possibility of joining the negotiating process—if and when it was expedient for her to do so. It was obvious from the start, however, that Syria's partners in the Front (all of them veteran "rejectionists") would not go along with Asad if he made any move to take up the political option he had struggled so hard to leave open for himself at the Tripoli conference. The Front thus had no valid common denominator and a rather low degree of cohesion. Other partners in the Front—Algeria, Libya and various PLO leaders—realizing that Iraq's walkout was a major factor of weakness in the new constellation, attempted to effect a Syrian-Iraqi *rapprochement*. But by the time the anti-Egyptian coalition reassembled in Algiers at the end of January 1978, Iraq still stood aloof.

Even more grievous for the Syrians than their failure to become the leader of a wide "steadfastness" bloc was the undoing of Jordan's "special relationship" with Damascus. While occasionally critical of Sādāt and sceptical of the likelihood of Egypt's policies succeeding, Jordan firmly declined to range itself alongside Syria. King Husayn's decision undid within a few days much of the effort invested by Asad over the four preceding years (of building up a Middle Eastern subregion centred on Damascus and embracing Lebanon, Syria, Jordan and the PLO). At the same time, it set back Syria's search for a military option against Israel capable of being exercised without Egyptian participation, which was to be based on an "Arab firing line" to envelop Israel's heartland from the Lebanese border down to the Gulf of 'Aqaba. Jordan continued to consult with Syria, but otherwise basically stayed on the sidelines, waiting to see whether any palpable benefit for specifically Jordanian interests in the West Bank and the Gaza Strip would result from the Israeli-Egyptian contacts. Meanwhile, Jordan joined with the other major group of Arab countries which had dissociated themselves from Sādāt's initiative—the group led by Saudi Arabia and Kuwait who called for "healing the rift" and for "restoring Arab solidarity." As was their wont, the Persian Gulf Emirates and North Yemen followed the Saudi lead. Oman, however, came out for Sādāt (possibly taking its cue from Iran), and South Yemen joined the Tripoli group.

Saudi Arabia itself had not clarified its attitude by the end of 1977. Its first reaction had been of hurt surprise. The Saudis felt that their position as inter-Arab arbiter had been challenged by Sādāt's unilateral decision and his failure to consult them. Their capacity to exercise a casting vote in Arab affairs depended on a modicum of co-operation between Egypt and Syria, which lapsed at a time of vocal dispute. Yet the Saudis could hardly join those who, like the Tripoli group, tried to "discipline" or "excommunicate" Egypt, partly because Sādāt's possible overthrow would almost certainly bring to power a regime less easy to deal with, and partly because they could not ally themselves with those Arab regimes which continued to criticize Saudi Arabia as "reactionary" and "subservient to US interests." The initial note of criticism, therefore, soon became muted. Some observers attributed the indecisiveness of Saudi policies in November and December to unresolved differences of opinion within the royal family; others saw it as the Saudi habit of holding their cards close to the chest. Whatever the reason, Saudi appeals for renewed Arab solidarity proved incapable of changing the course of events during the crucial weeks at the end of 1977—thus demonstrating the limits of Saudi power to manipulate other Arab countries.

The only positive development for Egypt in the inter-Arab arena was a further strengthening of Egyptian-Sudanese relations. President Numayrī gave Sādāt immediate and valuable political support, and Egyptian leaders (perhaps rather more emphatically than the Sudanese) stressed the fact that the inhabitants of the Nile Valley together constituted something like two-thirds of the entire Arab world, and therefore hardly needed the blessing of the rest.

Although Egypt was seemingly relegated to isolation within the Arab League in 1977, with only three of its 22 members (Sudan, Morocco, Oman) in Sādāt's support, in reality, it was Syria and Saudi Arabia who were the principal losers in terms of the immediate inter-Arab balance. Even from its ostensibly isolated position, Egypt was able to determine both the direction and the pace of events, putting the rest of the Arab states in the position of having to react rather than choose their own ground. While the Tripoli group decided only to suspend diplomatic relations with Egypt, it was Cairo which actually severed them and, disregarding Iraq's walkout from Tripoli, broke off relations with Iraq as well. Sādāt was thus able, at least in the initial stage, to dismiss his Arab adversaries as "pigmies," reject Arab "guardianship" over his policies, describe talk of Egypt being isolated as "idle," and assert, repeatedly and emphatically, that Egypt and Egypt alone was the key to peace or war in the region.

THE REPERCUSSIONS OF EGYPT'S POLICY ON THE GREAT POWERS

Sādāt's new approach also had an immediate effect on the position of the two great powers in the area. The US needed three weeks to evaluate the new turn of events and determine its own policy in response to it. Eventually, it threw its weight behind the Egyptians, even though it was clear that the Carter Administration regarded this as a risk to the pursuance of its declared aim of a comprehensive rather than a separate or interim settlement. The overall standing of the US as principal mediator in the Middle East underwent some modification during the last two months of the year. Its role in the strictly bilateral aspects of Egyptian-Israeli relations seemed diminished (the US was not co-opted to participate in the Israeli-Egyptian Military Committee), but with regard to the wider range of issues—particularly the Palestinian problem—its role remained a central one (as borne out by its participation in the Political Committee). More significantly, perhaps, the main US effort now came to be directed towards adding more participants to the Egyptian-Israeli negotiating process, first and foremost Jordan; towards mobilizing wider Arab support for Sādāt's policies, notably from Saudi Arabia and through it from other countries; and towards keeping a line open to Syria for possible future revision of the stand it adopted in November. By year's end, least had been achieved towards this last objective. Asad avoided meeting Carter during the latter's tour of Europe and Asia in December 1977 and January 1978, and Syria's media fell in line with the rest of the Tripoli group in adopting a strongly anti-American note. Yet, two months after Sādāt's initial announcement, the US appeared to be well on the road towards re-establishing itself as the only power capable of offering its good offices to Israel and the Arabs in an effective manner.

For the USSR, the chain of events that started in November 1977 proved a mixed blessing. Following closely on the joint Soviet-US statement of 1 October—which had signalled the imminent re-entry of the USSR into the process of preparing for the Geneva conference—Sādāt's move in effect excluded Moscow from what was now the focal point of negotiations. On the other hand, it provided the USSR with an opportunity, grasped all the more eagerly since it had for so long been on the political defensive in the area, to demonstrate a policy approach radically different from Washington's and to again describe itself as the only genuine defender of the true interests of the Arabs *vis-à-vis* Israel and the supporter of Arab solidarity against the divisive tactics of the US. Furthermore, the establishment of the Tripoli group gave rise to an alignment of Arab states all of whom were primarily oriented towards the USSR—a constellation which had not existed in the Middle East since before the 1967 war. The PLO's tentative moves towards a dialogue with the US were also stopped short, resulting in renewed reliance on the USSR. As a logical extension to its support of the Tripoli group, the USSR exercised its influence to help Algeria and Libya in their attempts to bring about a Syrian-Iraqi reconciliation. Reports of major new Soviet arms supplies late in the year to Syria—as well as to Libya, Algeria Iraq and the PLO—would be consistent with the overall line taken by the USSR since November.

A subsidiary benefit came to Moscow from the fact that South Yemen, having joined the Tripoli group primarily for reasons of ideology and from domestic considerations, thereby put a stop to its incipient move away from the Soviet orbit and into the Saudi sphere of influence. This was of considerable importance to the USSR in the context of its relations with Ethiopia and its general policies in the Horn of Africa.

THE IMPACT OF EGYPT'S POLICY ON IRAN

Another noteworthy development was Iran's decision to play a more active role in Arab affairs than at any previous time, bringing to a peak a trend that had started in the late 1960s. The Shah gave strong personal support to Sādāt's initiatives, disregarding the risk of thereby straining relations with Iraq. He hosted the meeting between President Carter and King Ḥusayn in Tehran, and also held separate talks with Ḥusayn in an endeavour to win Jordanian support for Egypt. Ḥusayn's arrival was reported to have been preceded by a brief visit to Tehran by Israel's Foreign Minister Moshe Dayan—though both sides denied this. The Shah followed up the Tehran talks by a visit to Egypt early in January 1978 when he again voiced his support, not only for Egypt's initiative, but also specifically for the Egyptian stand taken in contacts with Israel. A stop-over in Riyadh on his way home was also part of Iran's efforts to broaden support for Sādāt. The Shah's activities were prompted both by his anxiety for greater stability in the area, and his desire to assert Iran's role as a regional power with a say in any matter affecting the Middle East as a whole. It was also connected with Iran's growing concern with events in the Horn of Africa, where Egypt and Iran share common interests. In January 1978, Iran pledged active support for Somalia and the Eritreans against Ethiopia—a significant extension of Iran's earlier policy of bolstering Oman's strength in its struggle against the Dhufar rebels.

THE SITUATION INSIDE EGYPT

The domestic scene in Egypt did not undergo any noticeable change because of Sādāt's initiative. Some opposition from the legal Leftist party was easily brushed aside, and extra-parliamentary opposition, both from Marxist and Islamic militants was held in check. Much more significant was the broad upsurge of popular expectations that a settlement would have an immediate effect on the average Egyptian's standard of living—expectations that could eventually turn into a liability for the regime.

REACTION INSIDE ISRAEL

By contrast, the November events initiated shifts in Israel's political map, the extent and durability of which cannot be assessed until the new process has had an adequate opportunity to develop. While opinion polls indicated growing popular support for the Prime Minister in the wake of his two meetings with Sādāt, a new kind of opposition began to emerge from among those who had originally welcomed Begin's government. Within the Likud, a section of Begin's own Herut party dissociated itself from his policies at the end of 1977, allying themselves instead with hard-line extra-parliamentary groups such as Gush Emunim. They were joined by a faction within the National Religious Party. The other major group in the Likud, the Liberals—who had originally been less than wholehearted in their support of what they expected Begin's foreign policy to be—now proved his strongest supporters. The major parliamentary opposition, the Labour/Mapam alignment, failed to put forward a clear policy of its own in the immediate aftermath of Sādāt's visit to Jerusalem. Its abstention in the Knesset debate on Begin's peace proposals on 28 December reflected its uncertain stance at the time.

Whether these moves heralded a more far-reaching and more permanent realignment in Israeli politics will not be clear until the contours of the Egyptian-Israeli dialogue become more closely defined.

POLITICAL AND IDEOLOGICAL TRENDS IN THE MIDDLE EAST

It would be wrong, however, to look at 1977 only through the prism of the dramatic events of November and December. Many trends were at work in the area that were unrelated to them. Some were by way of continuing, often in a more marked fashion, currents that had arisen at some point in the past; others were more specific to the period described.

The stability of a considerable number of Middle Eastern regimes was affected by growing economic and social strains, often compounded by a sharply increased public awareness of corruption, profiteering and bureaucratic inefficiency, and by the effects of inflation. This was true of Egypt where trends of this kind, clearly perceptible since the early 1970s, culminated in the January 1977 food riots; of Syria, where the political effects of such phenomena was more of a novelty; of Iran, where it caused the Shah to carry out major changes in the top echelons of government; and of Turkey, where inflation in particular added to other more strictly political difficulties. Algeria and Tunisia were in many ways in a similar situation, and Iraq seemed to be moving in the same direction. Some of the Gulf Principalities displayed similar syndromes, although they were modified by oil wealth (see below). By contrast, Jordan presented a picture of increasing domestic stability, both in the socio-economic and the purely political sphere.

TRADITIONAL AUTHORITY VS POLITICAL PLURALISM

Some Arab regimes found themselves caught between their traditionally authoritarian form of government and the mounting expectations of the politically-conscious sector of the public for greater political pluralism. In 1976, Egypt had moved towards greater pluralism by legalizing three parties, still vaguely held together by common membership in the Arab Socialist Union, which was previously the only legal political organization. In 1977, this experiment did not fare well: the small Leftist party was almost entirely suppressed in the wake of Sādāt's accusation that it had encouraged the January rioters. The Rightist party was, for all intents and purposes, absorbed into the establishment, preserving only vestiges of its separate existence. The Centre party, significantly headed by the Prime Minister since its inception, turned out to be a branch of government rather than a party. A similar process of pluralism carefully controlled from the top was going on in Morocco. In Kuwait, what measure of pluralism that had existed earlier in the 1970s was done away with in 1976 when some key clauses of the constitution were suspended. Baḥrayn had suspended its constitution altogether a year earlier. The Ba'th regimes in Syria and Iraq had attempted to paper over rather than resolve the problem by co-opting political groups outside the ruling party into National Front institutions, but giving them no more than a nominal share in actual political power. In 1977, this looked less convincing than at any time before, and the realities of highly personalized regimes came to be more clearly perceived behind the increasingly transparent cover of the Fronts. In other Arab countries, no attempts were made to disguise personal or single-party rule. Algeria, Tunisia, Sudan and the Arabian Peninsula (except for the places mentioned above) belong in this group.

Hints of potential instability came from some countries with a closely-knit elite as a result of internal jockeying for positions of power. This was the case both in regimes relying on traditional authority (Saudi Arabia and Qatar), and in those deriving their claim to legitimacy from past "revolutionary" takeovers (Iraq, Tunisia and possibly also Syria). Libya stands out in this context in light of the success with which Qadhdhāfī has devised and consolidated a new structure of seemingly "direct democracy" without diminishing the power of the compact establishment he put together at the time of his coup in 1969.

Behind the varying styles of governing, the army remained the mainstay of most Arab regimes and even strengthened its central position. Such was the case in Syria ever since Asad's takeover in 1970. In Egypt, Sādāt's special attention to ensuring army support for his new policy towards Israel in advance was a pointer to the realities underlying his country's political structure. The exception was Iraq, where the party apparatus had, from 1968–74, made the army subservient to its purposes (by a massive infusion into the armed forces of Ba'th loyalists acting as "political commissars") and had subsequently been able to maintain its ascendancy.

In Iran, where the Shah had ended the multi-party system in 1975, the new single political organization, Rastakhiz, was still searching for a meaningful role as a viable link between the Court and Government on the one hand and the wider strata of the population on the other.

In the two parliamentary regimes of the region, Israel and Turkey, the year brought divergent developments. In Israel, the elections in May 1977 carried to power a party which had been in permanent opposition since the establishment of the state. Considering that Israel had never undergone this basic experience of democratic politics, the transition from an old established ruling party to a new one was remarkably smooth and provided proof of both the adaptability and the underlying stability of the country's system of government. In Turkey, the June elections seemed to conform to the pattern of very narrow margins that had become characteristic of many countries in Western Europe, and produced similar results; a precarious coalition government assumed office after protracted negotiations and was brought down in early 1978 by the defection of a handful of parliamentarians from one major party to the other. (In the circumstances following the civil war and the establishment of the Syrian military presence, Lebanon could no longer be counted among the parliamentary regimes in 1977.)

DECLINE OF IDEOLOGY

In Arab countries, domestic stability was clearly not a function of either the traditional or the "revolutionary" type of regime. The former faced the challenge of preserving its authority against the aspirations of new groups brought to the fore by the process of modernization and the accumulation of wealth; the latter had to struggle with the weakening hold over the political public of the ideology which had been the vehicle of its rise to power.

The decline of ideology was characteristic of many of the regimes which had started out with a strong emphasis on ideological beliefs. This was particularly, but not exclusively, true of those regimes where a new team of leaders had taken over from the original coup-makers. In Egypt, Nāsirism had lost much of its momentum as early as the 1960s. But under Sādāt, the escalating process of de-Nāsirization left a void which neither the "Corrective Revolution" of May 1971 nor the platforms of the legal parties were able to fill. In Syria, the tenets of Ba'th ideology had, since 1970, gradually come to be perceived as the outward trappings of Asad's personal power and of the purposes of expediency he used it for. In Iraq and Algeria, similar trends were in evidence. In Sudan, the ideological contours of the regime, blurred from the start, were becoming vaguer still.

Only South Yemen continued as a regime primarily motivated by a Leftist ideology. This was of more than purely local significance: the political thought of the country's leaders had been much influenced by a movement, mainly of the 1960s, called the Arab Nationalists (*al-qawmiyyūn al-'arab*) which projected itself as an all-Arab movement. Some of its fervour persists in South Yemen. The founding father of the *qawmiyyūn* movement, George Habash—now better known as the leader of the Popular Front for the Liberation of Palestine (a military offshoot of the *qawmiyyūn*)—maintains especially close relations with the South Yemeni leadership. These provide a link between the South Yemen regime and like-minded groups in other parts of the Arab world. Elsewhere, radical Leftist ideologies were upheld only by numerically small opposition groups, mostly clandestine ones.

RESURGENCE OF ISLAM

The decline of political ideology went hand in hand with a resurgence of Islam which was almost universal throughout the Arab world. It was felt in Turkey, too; in Iran, by contrast, measures of secularization combined with the revival of pre-Islamic nationalist symbols were more conspicuous in 1977. The re-emergence of fundamentalist Islam—not only as a source of faith and inspiration but as a political force—bears witness to its inner strength which has been virtually unaffected by the assault of almost two centuries of modernization and Westernization. In its most recent phase, however, it was closely connected with the increasing weight of the Arab world on the global scene, with the dependence of the West on Middle Eastern oil, and the oil wealth accruing to its Arab producers. Their self-confidence restored, Islamic societies turned from an apologetic stance to one asserting Islam's uniqueness, often reviving the sense of superiority which had inspired Islam in the days of its first triumphs. Two trends, divergent despite their common roots, can be discerned: conservative Islam, dominant in Saudi Arabia and the Gulf principalities, which the Saudis promote in other parts of the Arab and the non-Arab Islamic world with the full weight of their political and financial resources; and a radical trend, centred in Libya where the establishment has made it its own, and also in marginal but active oppositional groups in other Arab countries. Among the latter, it is the fact that wealth and conspicuous consumption have become characteristic of the centres of conservative Islam which make them protest against it in the name of a purer, more pristine faith.

In Saudi Arabia, the firm imprint of conservative Islam on all aspects of public and social life showed no signs of erosion. Furthermore, Saudi Arabia appointed itself the guardian for the preservation of Islam in the Arabian Peninsula; the charge of "atheism", for instance, was a central motif of its propaganda warfare against Leftist South Yemen. The Saudis also "exported" their own concepts of Islamic life style and legislation to other Arab countries. Their influence in this respect was particularly noticeable in Egypt in 1977, where the more traditional character of Sādāt's regime, as compared with 'Abd al-Nāsir's, had prepared the ground, and where disillusionment with "Arab Socialism" had led to an apparently widespread return to traditional values. Resentment of profiteering and quick enrichment under the policy of "economic openness" as well as, ironically, the conspicuous spending of visitors from strictly traditional but oil-rich areas, with the attendant spread of "permissiveness" strengthened this trend. Saudi influence was most probably at work in assisting the Muslim Brethren in their efforts to re-establish themselves as the main body of Islamic traditionalists in Egypt. Laws dealing with a ban on alcoholic drinks in public places and the restitution of the death penalty for apostasy from Islam were debated in the Legislature.

The radical trend of Islam formed a central strand in Qadhdhāfī's "Third International Theory" (third, that is, in relation to capitalism and socialism), which represents it as the sum total of political, social and economic precepts of universal applicability. Combining religious and nationalist elements, it allots to Libya a unique mission in spreading and defending the faith.

Outside Libya, radical Islam came to the fore in 1977 in Egypt. A subversive group of this type, which had adopted urban guerrilla tactics, was decimated by the internal security services after it kidnapped and later killed a former minister and al-Azhar lecturer. Other such groups apparently exist in Egypt and may be presumed to exist in other Arab countries as well. Their tenets include the restoration of the caliphate and the reintroduction of *sharī'a* (Muslim religious law). They reject contemporary Arab society as "godless" and corrupt, regard established Islam as diluted to the point of having betrayed the true faith, and believe their own value system capable of filling the void created by the decline of political ideology and the "weakness" of conservative Islam. In Egypt, their membership came mainly from students and other well-educated young people, many of them from middle-class families.

The growing strength of Islam led to increased anxiety among the non-Muslim communities of the Middle East: Coptic-Islamic relations underwent a crisis in 1977 which necessitated Sādāt's personal intervention. In Lebanon, the watchfulness of the Syrian army prevented a renewal of the civil war; but Christian, especially Maronite, fears for the future of their communities persisted. The Muslim-Christian enmity underlying Ethiopia's wars in Eritrea and the Ogaden is also relevant in this context. Heightened religious sentiment increased inter-communal tensions within Islam itself: 'Alawī-Sunnī tensions were more strongly evident in Syria than in previous years; Sunnī-Shī'ī relations in Iraq deteriorated into fairly widespread rioting at one point during the year.

REGIONAL GROUPINGS

Taking 1977 as a whole, the gradual evolution of a polycentric rather than monocentric system of relationships in the inter-Arab configuration continued markedly. For 15 years until the 1967 war, Egypt had been the focus of all Arab activities. Since then—partly in the wake of the Arab defeat of that year, partly as a result of the declining appeal of Nāsirism—regional groupings had taken on a life of their own. In 1977, the "Confrontation states" (i.e. those bordering on Israel) formed a grouping of their own. Saudi Arabia came to belong to it as well, partly because of the dependence of the others on Saudi financial aid, particularly for arms procurement, partly because of the special regard in which US policy-makers held Saudi Arabia. This derived from the Saudis' position as the leading oil producer as much as from their resolute anti-Soviet policies in the area. Relations within the group revolved primarily around the strategy and tactics to be adopted by them in the Arab-Israeli conflict.

Other regional groupings were those of the Arab states along the Persian Gulf littoral; the south of the Arabian Peninsula (Oman, South and North Yemen); and the Red Sea area. In all three, Saudi Arabia was the driving force and well on the way to establishing its ascendancy. It was thus the one country with a central role in both the "Confrontation" group and a number of regional groupings. While its standing in the former was greatly affected by the events of November and December, it was remarkable that its regional activities continued much as before. Apart from its role in the "confrontation" cycle, Egypt was the chief promoter of another regional development, the revival, in some measure, of its time-honoured concept of the "Unity of the Nile Valley"; this entailed increased co-ordination of policies with Sudan, accompanied by a considerable amount of joint development planning. Cairo indeed placed even greater emphasis on its relations with Khartoum towards the end of the year, when Sudan was one of the few countries which supported Sādāt's policy. But the principal reasons for the alliance stemmed from circumstances peculiar to the two countries: historical ties, common enmities (Libya, Ethiopia), common political and security interests in the Red Sea area, the common problems of large populations and meagre resources, and potentially complementary economies.

One regional grouping—centred on Damascus and intended to include Jordan and Lebanon—seemed well on the way towards crystallizing early in 1977, but came to grief at the year's end for the reasons described above. Syria, however, may well regard the state of affairs in December as a temporary setback rather than a conclusive failure.

The alignments in the Maghrib, ranging Morocco and Mauritania against Algeria and Libya (with Tunisia rather awkwardly squeezed in by the latter two), developed in a manner entirely independent from the chain of events in the major Mashreq countries, its primary tension emanating from the Western Sahara dispute. Also quite independent were the series of bilateral disputes (Libya-Egypt, Libya-Sudan, Syria-Iraq, Iraq-Kuwait, South Yemen-Oman); each had their own specific background, and most were characterized in 1977 by the increased use of violence.

To some extent, Sādāt's initiative restored a greater measure of monocentrism to the rather diffuse picture sketched above. However, it would not be possible to say at this time whether this was a short-term deviation from, or the reversal of, a trend traceable for at least a decade.

THE IMPACT OF OIL WEALTH ON MIDDLE EAST DEVELOPMENTS

A special place in Middle Eastern developments is occupied by oil production and the wealth accruing from it to the oil-exporting Arab countries and Iran. The worldwide impact of energy issues and oil wealth is dealt with extensively elsewhere in this volume. However, a few remarks should be made here on their impact on the polities and societies of the oil producers and their relation with other Arab countries. These trends did not, of course, originate in 1977, but some became rather more sharply marked in the course of the year.

One conspicuous aspect is the division of the Arab world into rich and poor nations—a division by no means coterminous with existing political alignments. At one end of the scale are the two "under-endowed" but very densely populated countries of the Nile Valley; at the other, the extremely oil-rich but very sparsely populated oil producers of the Arabian Peninsula, foremost Saudi Arabia and Kuwait, followed by Qatar and the UAE. Iraq and Algeria occupy an intermediate position, possessing considerable oil wealth but having to provide for the current and development needs of fairly large populations in relation to their area and oil income.

The life expectancy of each producer's oil reserves (which was subject to widely varying estimates) had a bearing on the urgency, or lack of it, with which it pursued the goal of economic diversification. In this respect, 1977 brought a marked change: development schemes in fields other than the oil industry were slowed down in most oil-producing countries. In particular, the launching of new industrial projects was curtailed, although those already started, as well as work on infrastructure projects, were much less affected. Arms procurement and work on military installations continued as before. Three sets of causes combined to produce the slow-down: a severe lack of skilled and even unskilled local labour, compounded by the unwillingness of the governments concerned to promote or allow a major influx of foreign labour; the limited purchasing power of the local populations; and the uncertainty of developing export markets for products other than oil. One imaginative attempt to overcome the resulting dilemma was devised in 1977 by Kuwait, where the government decided to create a special fund from current oil revenue to be drawn upon in the future, if and when such income begins to dwindle significantly.

THE IMPACT OF MODERNIZATION

Domestically, the tensions inherent in the process of modernization of traditional societies were more pronounced in the oil-producing countries than elsewhere in the Middle East: an especially tradition-bound society, in many cases with a strong tribal background, was being penetrated by particularly advanced and sophisticated technologies. This was especially true of the oil-producers of the Arabian Peninsula (who together supply almost 50% of Middle Eastern oil), considerably less so of Iran, Iraq and the comparatively smaller oil-producers outside the Gulf and Peninsular areas.

The potential tensions were mitigated, or perhaps postponed, by two trends: the employment of foreigners (mostly, but not exclusively, other Arab or non-Arab Muslims) to do the jobs most likely to deflect those engaging in them from the traditional way of life; and by imparting a Western-type education to young people close to the establishment, often the junior members of the ruling families. It was hoped that this group would create a new élite capable of dealing with the managerial, financial and technological complexities facing their countries, yet be so firmly rooted in the established order so as not to present a danger to it.

Nonetheless, new groups (one hesitates to speak of a "new class" at this stage) were emerging who possessed academic, managerial or technological training. The significant expansion of local educational facilities at all levels enabled some of them to acquire these qualifications at home. They joined the traditional merchant community in forming a new urbanized stratum, some members of which challenged the competence of the traditional establishment to run the affairs of state. But the wealth at the disposal of the rulers enabled them to try and "buy off" such groups by granting them financial security and material benefits which, elsewhere, would have been the perquisites of power. This brought into sharper relief the "*rentier* state" character of their polities. Also reached by the outward spread of technology were the armed forces and the agricultural sector. The latter, based on a combination of Bedouin settlement and the introduction of mechanized farming, greatly changed the life style of significant numbers of people lower on the social scale.

The danger perceived as gravest to themselves by the rulers in the Peninsula was the rapid growth of the number of aliens in the population: either they could allow this growth to proceed, or else stabilize or even reduce the number of aliens and thereby slow down economic development. The scope of the problem can be indicated by the fact that in mid-1977 in the UAE and Qatar, aliens constituted between 70 and 80% of the population; in Kuwait—55%; in Saudia Arabia—35%; in Baḥrayn—25–30% (but c. 50% of the labour force). From among the aliens, Palestinians and to a lesser extent Pakistanis were active in all branches of the economy, in the administration and services. Egyptian, Syrian and Jordanian nationals (many of the latter of Palestinian origin) worked mainly in the administration or as doctors, jurists and teachers from the elementary to the university level. Yemenis (estimated at one million in Saudi Arabia alone), Sudanis and Omanis provided mainly unskilled labour. Koreans, Taiwanese, Philippinos, Africans, Indians as well as Pakistanis constituted the main labour force for such infrastructure projects as road building, water works, port installations and power stations. Europeans and Americans, though numerically a smaller group, held key posts as advisers, supervisors or instructors.

During 1977, the authorities in the oil-rich countries adopted a harder line towards these problems than in previous years. Aliens considered politically dangerous or likely to spread social ferment (many of them Palestinians) were deported. Inequalities in political rights, material benefits and social security as between citizens and aliens increased the likelihood of agitation on the part of the latter. A preference emerged for labourers from South and South-East Asia and the

Far East, who mingled less with the locals than did Arab aliens and whose presence was of limited duration, either because they were on contract or because of their own desire to return home after a number of years. By and large, the fear of seeing the indigenous population turn into a minority loomed larger in 1977 than the anxieties caused by slower economic diversification.

THE USE OF OIL WEALTH FOR POLITICAL OBJECTIVES

The impact of oil wealth on the Arab-Israeli conflict is described in two essays in this volume. Apart from the ever-present implied threat of the "oil weapon," special mention must be made of the use of oil money to finance the military procurement programmes of the "Confrontation states" and the establishment of arms industries in Egypt and Syria. The Arab Military Industries Organization, established by an Arab summit decision in 1974, began operating in Egypt in 1977, with funds coming primarily from Saudi Arabia and Kuwait.

The use of oil wealth for granting or withholding financial aid for political objectives was much in evidence, particularly in Saudi Arabia's inter-Arab and anti-Soviet policies. In Egypt, the construction of King Khālid City near Ismāʻīlyya was a conspicuous example. In Syria, Saudi investments and grants decreased during 1977, probably to signal Saudi displeasure at Syria's promotion of its regional dominance. In North Yemen, Saudi money served to tighten the bonds linking the country to Riyadh. Saudi aid was also employed in efforts to detach Somalia and South Yemen from the Soviet orbit—successfully in the first instance (for reasons of a particular nature), unsuccessfully in the second.

Saudi grants to the PLO were intended to make that body conform to Saudi policies. However, payments from Libya and Iraq made with the opposite intent, as well as funds apparently obtained by the most radical PLO elements from Kuwait, Abu Dhabi and others as a form of "protection money" cancelled out the effect of the Saudi grants—an instructive reminder that the political map is not coincidental with that of oil wealth. A new addition in 1977 to the list of oil fund recipients were a number of municipalities in the West Bank and the Gaza Strip. The scheme was probably started at the request of the PLO, but Jordan managed to retain control over the influx of funds by channelling them through Jordanian banks.

The growing dependence of the non oil-producing Arab states on aid from the oil-rich ones gave rise, particularly in Egypt, to resentment characteristic of the needy recipient's feelings towards another's bounty. In some quarters, there seemed to be an incipient "ideologization" of this issue: the slogan of "Arab oil for the Arabs"— originally coined in protest against the dominance of the foreign companies—was coming to mean "Arab oil for *all* the Arabs," implying a claim for equal distribution of all oil wealth throughout the entire Arab world.

SUMMARY

In summary, the year reviewed marked one significant break with the past that touched upon some aspects of the Arab-Israeli conflict, but for the most part there was a continuation of prevailing trends. 1977 also presented possible pointers to the future in the weakening stability of a number of regimes and in the "rich man/poor man" polarization between poverty-ridden and oil-rich areas.

The Middle East and World Affairs

The Continued Quest for Peace: The United States and the Middle East

BERNARD REICH

The Carter Administration's analysis of its role in the Middle East, of the process of negotiation, and of the substance of a settlement evolved pragmatically in statements and "signals" in the course of 1977. Underlying Carter's approach to peace in the Middle East during this period was the view that the time had never been more propitious to work for a settlement,[1] and that to lose this opportunity could be disastrous for the region as well as for the new international political and economic order.[2] More specifically, a just and lasting Middle East settlement was seen to be essential for a more peaceful world and thus for all Americans. As Vice-President Walter Mondale stated on 17 June 1977, "conflict there carries the threat of a global confrontation and runs the risk of nuclear war." It could also have profound economic consequences. The US has a major stake and interest in establishing a lasting peace, which would not only prevent the possible dangerous consequences of war, but would also help to maintain American influence *vis-à-vis* the Soviet Union in the area. Short of war, the conflict tends to encourage instability and radicalization in the region. Genuine peace was thus seen as an essential need of all parties to the conflict.

The need for peace and American interests provide a substantial rationale for US involvement in the Middle East. But this involvement has also assumed a central role in America's foreign policy because of its special relationship with Israel and its rapidly developing links with the Arab states. As Vice-President Mondale said on 17 June 1977: "It is precisely because of our close ties with both Israel and her Arab neighbours that we are uniquely placed to promote the search for peace, to work for an improved understanding of each side's legitimate concerns, and to help them work out what we hope will be a basis for negotiation leading to a final peace in the Middle East."

Recognizing its interests and its capability for a special role, the Administration believed that a new approach was called for. At its base was UN Security Council Resolution 242 (1967). But this was not deemed sufficient, and it was decided "to work with the parties concerned to outline the overall framework for an enduring peace."[3] This approach was to replace Kissinger's step-by-step strategy of limited accords. From the outset there was a realization that a Middle East settlement would come only at the end of a long and complicated negotiating process,[4] with the

[1] See, for example, Cyrus Vance's first press conference as Secretary of State on 31 January 1977 (Department of State Press Release No 32); and Vance's interview with representatives of AP and UPI on 3 February 1977 (DSPR No 37). In a speech in San Francisco on 17 June 1977, Vice-President Mondale noted "both sides want peace."

[2] See, for example, Carter's speech at Notre Dame University, 22 May 1977; and his address to the UNGA, 4 October 1977.

[3] Speech by Vice-President Mondale, 17 June 1977.

[4] Vance has continually cautioned about underestimating the difficulties which the process faced. In an interview with the *New York Times* on 9 February 1977, he noted: "I think it is essential that the necessary groundwork be accomplished before one goes to a Geneva conference. I think to rush into a Geneva conference without thorough and adequate planning would be a mistake" (DSPR No 43, 11 February 1977).

first critical steps to be taken in 1977. Reconvening the Geneva conference, which had first met in December 1973, seemed an appropriate mechanism. The role the US set for itself was to bring about negotiations between the parties and to establish a set of principles (rather than details) that might serve as a basis for a settlement. Carter described this role "as a catalyst to bring about their ability to negotiate successfully with one another."[5] Direct negotiations were obviously necessary, for as Mondale noted in his 17 June speech: "We cannot conceive of genuine peace existing between countries who will not talk to one another. If they are prepared for peace, the first proof is a willingness to negotiate their differences."

A logical consequence of this perspective was that the US could not seek to impose a settlement, a position reiterated many times. However, it viewed the problem as both important and intractable enough for Washington to be more than just the agent bringing the parties together. As a result, American views and suggestions became increasingly an element of the situation. Mondale suggested that the purpose was not to dictate or impose, but "to stimulate fresh thoughts."[6]

Although the Administration thus insisted that it had no intention of imposing a settlement, it began increasingly to formulate its attitudes on some key issues and to suggest that their adoption would facilitate movement towards a settlement. It began to think in terms of persuasion and even leverage in order to secure support for what it thought appropriate to influence progress towards a reconvened Geneva meeting. In an interview with European reporters on 2 May 1977, Carter said: "I would not hesitate if I saw clearly a fair and equitable solution to use the full strength of our own country and its persuasive powers to bring those nations to agreement. I recognize, though, that we cannot impose our will on others, and unless the countries involved agree, there is no way for us to make progress."[7]

By October 1977, the US position had become much more precise. In an interview on 2 October, Zbigniew Brzezinski, the President's National Security adviser, insisted: "The US has a legitimate right to exercise its own leverage, peaceful and constructive, to obtain a settlement. And that's exactly what we will be doing."[8]

In their effort to assist the parties in outlining an overall framework for a lasting peace, President Carter and Secretary of State Cyrus Vance identified three elements as central and indispensable: the definition and assurance of permanent peace; territory and borders; and the Palestinian issue. Over the months, they articulated the official American conception of each of these issues, as discussed below.

ELEMENTS IN THE CARTER FRAMEWORK FOR A MIDDLE EAST SETTLEMENT

1. DEFINING PEACE

As part of Carter's comprehensive approach, peace was defined as being much more than the end of war. It must consist of certain specific elements, most fully expressed bv Carter in Clinton, Massachusetts, in March 1977 as follows:

[5] Carter statement in Clinton, Massachusetts, on 16 March 1977. Quoted in *New York Times*, 29 June 1977.

[6] Speech on 17 June 1977.

[7] Department of State Bulletin (DSB), 30 May 1977, p. 547. See also Vance's press conference of 4 May 1977.

[8] In an interview with the Canadian television network on 2 October 1977, Brzezinski said: "I think the point to bear in mind is that the US is not just an interested bystander, not even just a benevolent mediator." On 3 October 1977, he was also quoted as follows in the *Washington Post*: "The US has a direct interest in the outcome of the Middle Eastern conflict. The US has a direct interest in obtaining a resolution of the conflict. And therefore the US has a legitimate right to exercise its own leverage, peaceful and constructive, to obtain a settlement. And that's exactly what we will be doing."

> . . . The first prerequisite of a lasting peace is the recognition of Israel by her neighbours, Israel's right to exist, Israel's right to exist permanently, Israel's right to exist in peace. That means that over a period of months or years that the borders between Israel and Syria, Israel and Lebanon, Israel and Jordan, Israel and Egypt must be opened up to travel, to tourism, to cultural exchange, to trade, so that no matter who the leaders might be in those countries, the people themselves will have formed a mutual understanding and comprehension and a sense of a common purpose to avoid the repetitious wars and death that have afflicted that region so long.[9]

2. TERRITORY AND BORDERS

A second central element is that of territory (and withdrawal) and borders. The crucial problem is to provide borders that are secure[10] and acceptable to all the parties. They would be permanent and universally recognized. The US does not identify precisely what the future borders separating Israel and the Arab states should be, but the principles involved are clear: substantial Israeli withdrawal from occupied territories and minor adjustments in the pre-1967 lines.[11] But there was also the significant suggestion that defence lines and other factors that would enhance Israel's security might go beyond these borders.[12] In the final analysis, the situation would have to be decided by negotiation and agreement between Israel and the Arabs.[13]

---

[9] *Weekly Compilation of Presidential Documents* (*WCPD*), 21 March 1977, p. 361. In a press conference on 9 March 1977, Carter elaborated his conception of peace: "I think that what Israel would like to have is what we would like to have: a termination of belligerence toward Israel by her neighbours, a recognition of Israel's right to exist, the right to exist in peace, the opening up of borders with free trade, tourist travel, cultural exchange between Israel and her neighbours; in other words, a stabilization in the situation in the Middle East without a constant threat to Israel's existence by her neighbours."

[10] UN Resolution 242 refers to "secure and recognized" borders, while Israel has talked in terms of "defensible" borders. The US has generally relied upon the words of 242. However, in early March 1977, when the then Israeli Prime Minister Rabin visited Washington, Carter talked of "defensible" borders. Carter referred to Vance's recent trip to the Middle East, in which he had tried "to explore some common ground for future permanent peace there, so that Israel might have defensible borders so that the peace commitments would never be violated, and so that there could be a sense of security about this young country in the future" (White House Press Release, WHPR, 7 March 1977). This terminology was not used again. Subsequently, US officials implied that no policy change was intended. Vance told reporters later that day: "There is no change in position by the use of the words 'defensible borders' " (*New York Times*, 8 March 1977). In a press conference on 9 March, Carter elaborated on his views in these words: "The defensible border phrase the secure border phrase, obviously are just semantics . . . The recognized borders have to be mutual" (WHPR, 9 March 1977).

[11] In a press conference on 9 March 1977, Carter noted: "This would involve substantial withdrawal of Israel's present control over territories. Where that withdrawal might end, I don't know. I would guess it would be some minor adjustments in the 1967 borders. But that still remains to be negotiated. I think there might be minor adjustments to the 1967, pre-1967 borders" (WHPR, 9 March 1977). See also Vice-President Mondale's speech of 17 June 1977 in which he noted: ". . . Israel could return to approximately the borders that existed prior to the war of 1967, albeit with minor modifications as negotiated among the parties." By the autumn of 1977, the Department of State was responding to queries on US policy with a letter in which it stated that "major changes in the 1967 lines are not consistent with UN Security Council Resolution 242 . . ." (*Near East Report*, 7 September 1977, p. 149).

[12] In his 9 March 1977 press conference, Carter noted: "Defence lines may or may not conform in the foreseeable future to those legal borders. There may be extensions of Israeli defence capability beyond the permanent and recognized borders." In a speech on 17 June 1977, Vice-President Mondale noted: ". . . there could be separate lines of defence or other measures that could enhance Israel's security."

[13] See, for example, Carter's press conference on 9 March 1977.

3. THE PALESTINIANS

Increasingly the Palestinian question emerged as the most controversial of the elements. The traditional American approach, which focused on refugee and humanitarian aspects of the problem—and, after the June war of 1967, the terrorist dimension—was altered by the Carter Administration. Terrorism had receded into the background, and while refugees were still a concern, the issue was clearly seen in broader and, specifically, political terms.[14]

The earliest statements in 1977 indicated that the Administration saw the need to include provisions for the legitimate interests of the Palestinian people.[15] The idea of a separate Palestinian territorial entity appeared publicly for the first time on 16 March 1977 when Carter said that the solution required some form of homeland for the Palestinians,[16] although its nature and political status would have to be negotiated.[17] The US preferred such a Palestinian entity to be linked with Jordan.[18] To gain the benefits of such a compromise, the Palestinians would be expected to demonstrate their willingness to exist in peace.

Underlying much of Carter's approach was the view that for peace to endure, the Palestinians must have a stake in it.[19] Increasingly, this has meant that they must be involved in the negotiating or peacemaking process. They must be represented at Geneva,[20] though exactly how this would come about was uncertain.[21] One of the options is for the PLO to represent the Palestinians at Geneva.[22] US policy has been much concerned with the role of the PLO, the subject of increasing controversy and disagreement. Underlying this approach is the American commitment in Sinai II: "The US will continue to adhere to its present policy with respect to the Palestine

---

[14] In a press conference in Amman on 6 August 1977, Vance said: "We have always indicated that we think that the problem is a border problem rather than a refugee problem" (DSPR No 373, 8 August 1977).

[15] In an interview with representatives of the Israeli press on 10 February 1977, Vance said: ". . . the question of the legitimate interests of the Palestinian people is, however, a subject which is one of the keys to a peace settlement" (DSPR No 50, 14 February 1977). Similar remarks were made in Vance's first press conference; see note 1 above.

As noted above, in the joint statement with the Soviet Union of 1 October 1977, the US agreed for the first time to the formulation that a solution had to include the means of ensuring "the legitimate *rights* of the Palestinian people." (Emphasis added.)

[16] "There has to be a homeland provided for the Palestinian refugees who have suffered for many, many years" (*WCPD*, 21 March 1977, p. 361).

[17] In a press conference on 12 May 1977, Carter said: "I don't think that there can be any reasonable hope for a settlement . . . without a Homeland for the Palestinians. The exact definition of what that Homeland might be, the degree of independence of the Palestinian entity, its relationship with Jordan or perhaps Syria and others, the geographical boundaries of it, all have to be worked out by the parties involved" (*New York Times*, 13 May 1977).

[18] In an interview on 16 September, Carter noted: "I've never called for an independent Palestinian country. We have used the word 'entity'. And my own preference . . . is that we think, if there is a Palestinian entity established on the West Bank, that it ought to be associated with Jordan, for instance" (*WCPD*, 26 September 1977, p. 1378).

[19] See, for example, Mondale's speech of 17 June 1977.

[20] See, for example, Carter's press conference on 28 July 1977; and his earlier remarks at Dobbins Air Force Base, Georgia, on 8 April 1977 (DSB, 9 May 1977, especially p. 461).

[21] In a press conference on 29 September 1977, Carter noted: "We have no national position on exactly who would represent the Palestinians, or exactly what form the Arab group [at Geneva] would take in which the Palestinians would be represented."

[22] In the US view, PLO representation is only one of the possible alternatives for Geneva. In an interview on 16 September 1977, Carter noted: "We have never called on the PLO to be part of the future negotiations" (*WCPD*, 26 September 1977, p. 137). In his 29 September 1977 press conference, Carter noted: "Obviously they [i.e. the PLO] don't represent a nation. It is a group that represents certainly a substantial part of the Palestinians. I certainly don't think they're the exclusive representatives of the Palestinians. Obviously there are mayors, for instance, and local officials in the West Bank area who represent Palestinians. They may or may not be members of the PLO."

Liberation Organization, whereby it will not recognize or negotiate with the Palestinian Liberation Organization so long as [it] does not recognize Israel's right to exist and does not accept Security Council Resolutions 242 and 338."

Thus, in the view of the Carter Administration, before the PLO can participate fully in the settlement process, it must accept Israel's right to exist and resolutions 242 and 338.[23] "The legitimate rights of the Palestinian people" would, in turn, be included among the elements of the settlement.

THE EVOLUTION OF AMERICAN POLICY

Although President Carter had taken a pro-Israel stand during his election campaign, it was not immediately clear what policy the new Administration would pursue in the Middle East after its installation in January 1977, especially since Dr Henry Kissinger's personal diplomacy had lost its momentum and the President's new National Security adviser had not been prominently identified with Middle East affairs. Although a member of the study group which had produced the controversial Brookings Institution's report, *Towards Peace in the Middle East*, Brzezinski's own role in its work was not prominent.[24] Another member of the group was Prof William Quandt, who became Middle East specialist on the National Security Council staff. It was hardly surprising therefore that the Brookings' report should provide the framework of ideas for the new Administration.

The main proposals of *Towards Peace* were that the US had strong interests in a stable peace in the Middle East, concerned with the well-being of Israel and the Arab states and for the friendship of both; that the best approach to the problem was through a comprehensive settlement; that all parties to a settlement should commit themselves to respect the sovereignty and territorial integrity of the others; that peaceful relations required normal international and regional political and economic relations; that Israel should withdraw by stages to the 1967 borders with agreed modifications; that there should be provision for Palestinian self-determination, subject to Palestinian acceptance of Israel's sovereignty and integrity within agreed boundaries; that, whatever the final status of Jerusalem, it should remain an undivided city; that, while the US should assume a major role in bringing about a settlement, it was unlikely to succeed on its own, and USSR co-operation should be sought to the degree that Moscow was willing to play a constructive role.

In the wake of the 1973 October war, the US emerged as the dominant extra-

---

[23] In a press conference on 28 July 1977, Carter noted that they need "to forego their commitment presently publicly espoused that Israel should be destroyed." See also Vance's press conference on 29 July 1977. In Plains, Georgia, on 8 August Carter said: "If the Palestinians will recognize the applicability of UN Resolution 242, then it would open up a new opportunity for us to start discussions with them and also open up an avenue that they might participate in the Geneva conference" (*WCPD*, 15 August 1977, p. 1213). He also noted that there was a need for "the Palestinians and their leaders [to] recognize Israel's right to exist . . .' See also Vance's remarks to the press in Tā'if, Saudi Arabia, on 9 August 1977 (DSPR No 375, 9 August 1977). Carter reiterated this position in an interview on 16 September 1977 (*WCPD*, 26 September 1977, pp. 1377–8). However, in his press conference on 29 September 1977, Carter restated the pledge to Israel "that we will not negotiate with nor deal directly with the PLO until they adopt UN Resolution 242 as a basis for their involvement, which includes a recognition of the right of Israel to exist." He went on to say: "If the PLO should go ahead and say 'we endorse UN Resolution 242, we don't think it adequately addresses the Palestinian issue because it only refers to refugees and we think we have a further interest than that'—that would suit us okay. We would then begin to meet with and to work with the PLO. If they accept UN 242 and the right of Israel to exist, then we will begin discussions with the leaders of the PLO."

[24] *Towards Peace in the Middle East* (Washington: Brookings Institution, December 1975).

regional power in the Middle East, as well as the main source of economic and military assistance for the peaceful development of the region. Its diplomacy had assisted Israel and the Arabs to achieve three agreements (the Israel-Egypt and Israel-Syria disengagements and Sinai II) which were important steps in moving toward a settlement. These had been produced by Dr Kissinger's intensive shuttles, and had involved extensive American pledges and commitments—for which the parties in the conflict were not prepared to allow any other power or instrumentality to serve as a substitute. However for a variety of reasons, including the American elections and the Lebanese civil war, little progress was achieved in late 1975 and throughout 1976. The Carter victory thus set the stage for a new initiative.

A week prior to his inauguration on 12 January 1977, Carter struck an optimistic note about the situation in the Middle East: "There is a fine opportunity for dramatic improvements there."[25] Both the President and the new Secretary of State, Cyrus Vance, lost little time in assuming an activist policy in the region. Their optimism seemed to be based on Israel's confident military strength, the "moderation of Arab leaders," the receding civil war in Lebanon, and the willingness of all parties to participate in a new round of Geneva talks.[26] By early February, the Administration's interest and concern had become more precise. Vance noted in an interview on 8 February:

> Let me say that we do attach the highest priority to progress in the Middle East and to progress in 1977. There is no issue, insofar as the United States is concerned, which has higher priority; and the fact that President Carter has asked me to undertake this mission [i.e. his visit to the region in February] as the first major diplomatic effort of this country I think is an indication of the importance which this Administration and President Carter attach to the peaceful solution of the Middle East problem.[27]

In mid-February 1977, Vance travelled to six Middle Eastern countries (Israel, Egypt, Lebanon, Jordan, Syria and Saudi Arabia) to lay the ground-work for a new attempt at a settlement. The White House emphasized "the importance the President attaches to making significant progress this year toward a just and lasting peace in the Middle East."[28] At the conclusion of his tour, Vance noted that Arabs and Israelis remained "deeply divided" on how to reach a settlement, and that he didn't want to underestimate the complexity and difficulty of the situation.

As part of the process of establishing a wider area of understanding, a second round of exploratory conversations between Carter and Middle East leaders began in March and continued until the middle of July. The first meeting was with Israel's Prime Minister, Yitzhak Rabin, who came to Washington in March. For Rabin the trip had dimensions beyond those relating to a settlement. He sought to bolster his image at home in anticipation of the forthcoming parliamentary elections and to get positive responses from Carter on a number of specific issues that had emerged in recent months. These included the proposed Israeli sale of *Kfir* jets to Ecuador which the US had prevented; the sale of concussion bombs by the US to Israel pledged by President Ford but halted by Carter; and the possible co-production of

---

[25] *New York Times*, 13 January 1977.

[26] See, for example, Carter's interview on 23 January 1977 (DSB, 14 February 1977, especially p. 125); Vance's first press conference (see note 1 above); Vance's interview with *New York Times* correspondents on 9 February 1977 (DSPR No 43, 11 February 1977); Vance's interview by representatives of the Israeli press on 10 February 1977 (DSPR No 50, 14 February 1977). See also Vance's interview on 8 February with Egyptian and Syrian media representatives (DSB, 14 March 1977, especially pp. 224-6).

[27] DSB, 14 March 1977, p. 226.

[28] Jody Powell, White House spokesman, quoted in *New York Times*, 26 January 1977.

the F-16 jet aircraft by Israel. There was also disagreement over Israeli drilling for oil in the Red Sea.

It was during the Rabin visit that Carter first began to articulate publicly various elements of his concept of an Arab-Israeli settlement and the process by which it might be achieved.

The second leader to arrive in Washington on 3 April was President Sādāt of Egypt. He sought US arms (*TOW* anti-tank missiles and F-5E aircraft) and economic aid. He stressed that the Palestinian question was "the core and crux" of the Arab-Israeli dispute and that "no progress whatsoever can be achieved so long as this problem remains unsolved."[29] Sādāt praised Carter for his comments concerning a Palestinian homeland.

King Ḥusayn of Jordan followed Sādāt in late April, after which Carter met with President Asad of Syria in Geneva on 9 May. Carter appeared pleased with the way the talks had gone and, with Asad at his side, told the press: "There must be a resolution of the Palestine problem and a homeland for the Palestinians."[30] They discussed the question of a Palestinian homeland and Palestinian participation in formal negotiations for a lasting settlement.

Vance met with Israel's Foreign Minister, Yigal Allon, in London on 11 May to brief him on the Carter-Asad talks. At this meeting Israel also sought reassurances about possible US pressures for a settlement, and about its exclusion from a preferred list of countries eligible to receive advanced military technology, weapons and co-production agreements. Israeli fears about the possibility of an American-imposed solution were raised in particular by an article in *Foreign Affairs* written by a former US ambassador to the UN, George W. Ball, entitled: "How to Save Israel in Spite of Herself."[31] Ball's views are known to have been regarded by the Carter Administration as singularly unhelpful. But Vance apparently went a long way towards reassuring Allon.

The negotiating process was interrupted by the elections in Israel in mid-May (see chapter on Israel in this volume). The Carter Administration was dismayed by Menahem Begin's victory, which appeared to slow the timetable for movement toward Geneva and a settlement. Its approach had been based, in part, on an assumption of the Alignment again being prominent in the new government. The ascendancy of Begin's Likud seemed to jeopardize this approach. The Administration sought to put the best face on the Israeli electoral decision; Carter said he hoped ". . . that the election of Mr Begin will not be a step backward toward the achievement of peace."[32] There was one other crucial step in the consultation process before President Carter met Israel's new leadership to discover just how much room for diplomatic manoeuvre still remained: in late May the Saudi Arabian Crown Prince Fahd came to Washington. The positive outcome of his visit was an agreement to make a "major effort toward trying to reconvene the Geneva conference in the second half of 1977." During this visit, as in all efforts of the Administration concerning the search for a settlement, the US deemed the Saudi role crucial for the success of the Carter approach for a number of reasons, including its strong financial position and its ability to exert influence on Egypt and Syria as well as on the lesser Arab states. There was also the important Saudi role in stabilizing oil prices and in ensuring appropriate oil production levels.

---

[29] *New York Times*, 5 April 1977.
[30] *Christian Science Monitor*, 11 May 1977.
[31] *Washington Post*, 22 May 1977. Carter sought to stress the importance of movement towards a settlement in a major speech at Notre Dame University on 22 May 1977.
[32] *Foreign Affairs* (New York: Council on Foreign Relations, April 1977).

Israel's new Prime Minister was given a very warm reception when he arrived in the US in mid-July. Both Begin and Carter went out of their way to allay suspicions of possible fundamental disagreements and to create a climate of optimism. "I believe," said the President, "that we have laid the groundwork now, barring some unforeseen difficulty, that will lead to the Geneva conference in October . . . We see [it] as being very likely."[33] During the visit, Begin outlined a plan for peace which dealt with the various aspects of a settlement. His "plan," which rested firmly on Israel's retention of the whole of the West Bank and of Gaza, was, not surprisingly, rejected out of hand by the Arabs and passed over silently by the Americans.

American diplomacy moved on to a new level in August when the Secretary of State set off on a second Middle East trip to try, in his own words, "to narrow the differences between the parties and move closer to the necessary framework for convening a Geneva conference."[34] Between 1-11 August, Vance visited Egypt, Lebanon, Syria, Jordan, Saudi Arabia and Israel. While the parties remained far apart, they agreed that their foreign ministers would meet with Carter and Vance in September at the time of the UN General Assembly. Meanwhile, the US agreed to "use its influence, offer its advice, volunteer its suggestions and work to bring the parties into fruitful negotiations."[35] Although not meeting with the PLO directly, the US tried through third parties to get the organization to declare its support for UN Resolutions 242 and 338 to recognize Israel's right to exist; but these efforts yielded no results at all (see chapter on the Palestinians in this volume).

US consultations in September and October focused sharply on the issue of Palestinian representation at Geneva as the major obstacle to a meeting. On 12 September, the State Department moved to break the deadlock by setting out the US position:

> . . . the status of the Palestinians must be settled in a comprehensive Arab-Israeli agreement. This issue cannot be ignored if the others are to be solved. Moreover, to be lasting, a peace agreement must be positively supported by all of the parties to the conflict, including the Palestinians. This means that the Palestinians must be involved in the peacemaking process. Their representatives will have to be at Geneva for the Palestinian question to be solved.[36]

The US proposed a formula—first put forward by the previous Israeli government—for a unified Arab delegation at Geneva which would include Egypt, Syria, Jordan, Lebanon and the Palestinians. The question of which Palestinians would participate, and their relationship to the PLO, remained unresolved.

Israel's Cabinet formally agreed on 25 September to a US proposal that Palestinian representatives constitute part of a unified Arab delegation at the opening session of a reconvened Geneva conference. Although this represented a shift in Israel's position, the Foreign Minister, Moshe Dayan, made it clear that this did not alter Israel's view of the PLO. They insisted that Palestinians could participate in the unified Arab mission provided they were part of the Jordanian delegation and not known members of the PLO. No negotiations would take place with this unified Arab delegation. After the opening ceremonial session, the Arab grouping would split up into units representing the various Arab states (Egypt, Syria, Jordan, and possibly Lebanon) for negotiations. There would also be no change in Resolution 242.[37]

---

[33] *Washington Post*, 21 July 1977.
[34] DSPR No 350, 29 July 1977.
[35] *New York Times*, 15 August 1977.
[36] *Ibid*, 13 September 1977.
[37] *New York Times* and *Washington Post*, 26 September 1977.

JOINT US-SOVIET STATEMENT ON THE MIDDLE EAST

Issued in New York and Moscow
1 October 1977

Having exchanged views regarding the unsafe situation which remains in the Middle East, United States Secretary of State Cyrus Vance and member of the Politbureau of the Central Committee of the CPSU, Minister for Foreign Affairs of the USSR, A. A. Gromyko, have the following statement to make on behalf of their countries, which are co-chairmen of the Geneva Peace Conference on the Middle East:

1. Both governments are convinced that vital interests of the peoples of this area as well as the interests of strengthening peace and international security in general urgently dictate the necessity of achieving as soon as possible a just and lasting settlement of the Arab-Israeli conflict. This settlement should be comprehensive, incorporating all parties concerned and all questions.

The United States and the Soviet Union believe that, within the framework of a comprehensive settlement of the Middle East problem, all specific questions of the settlement should be resolved, including such key issues as withdrawal of Israeli armed forces from Territories occupied in the 1967 conflict; the resolution of the Palestinian question including ensuring the legitimate rights of the Palestinian people; termination of the state of war and establishment of normal peaceful relations on the basis of mutual recognition of the principles of sovereignty, territorial integrity, and political independence.

The two governments believe that, in addition to such measures for ensuring the security of the borders between Israel and the neighboring Arab states as the establishment of demilitarized zones and the agreed stationing in them of UN troops or observers, international guarantees of such borders as well as of the observance of the terms of the settlement can also be established, should the contracting parties so desire. The United States and the Soviet Union are ready to participate in these guarantees, subject to their constitutional processes.

2. The United States and the Soviet Union believe that the only right and effective way for achieving a fundamental solution to all aspects of the Middle East problem in its entirety is negotiations within the framework of the Geneva Peace Conference, specially convened for these purposes, with participation in its work of the representatives of all the parties involved in the conflict including those of the Palestinian people, and legal and contractual formalization of the decisions reached at the conference.

In their capacity as co-chairmen of the Geneva Conference, the US and the USSR affirm their intention through joint efforts and in their contacts with the parties concerned to facilitate in every way the resumption of the work of the conference not later than December 1977. The co-chairmen note that there still exist several questions of a procedural and organizational nature which remain to be agreed upon by the participants to the conference.

3. Guided by the goal of achieving a just political settlement in the Middle East and of eliminating the explosive situation in this area of the world, the US and the USSR appeal to all the parties in the conflict to understand the necessity for careful consideration of each other's legitimate rights and interests and to demonstrate mutual readiness to act accordingly.

THE US-SOVIET DECLARATION AND ITS SEQUEL

At this stage of the negotiations, the US found it useful to reinvolve the Soviet Union (as co-chairman of the Geneva conference). After a series of discussions in Washington and New York, a joint US-Soviet statement was issued on 1 October.[38]

The joint statement caused a considerable furore among supporters of Israel and anti-Soviet elements in the US,[39] although the Administration claimed a number of substantial concessions from the Soviet Union. Particular importance was attached to Moscow's endorsement of "normal peace relations" which a White House spokesman interpreted as including open borders and full trade and diplomatic ties between Israel and the Arab states. Although the statement stopped short of calling for formal peace treaties (which had been urged by the US and Israel), Washington's view was that the reference to "legal and contractual formalization" of any Geneva agreement would amount to the same thing. On its side, the US spoke for the first time of the need to satisfy the "legitimate rights of the Palestinian people." No mention was made of Resolutions 242 and 338 because of the Soviets' refusal to refer to them in the joint statement; but Washington explained that the two resolutions still remained the cornerstone of the American approach to a settlement.

Israel and its supporters focused their concern on three factors: the increased involvement of the Soviet Union in the process of securing a settlement; the reference to "the legitimate rights of the Palestinian people"; and the absence of any reference to Resolutions 242 and 338. The Carter Administration found it necessary to defend itself against criticisms that it was moving towards accepting the idea of a separate Palestinian state; that it seemed to be leaning toward an imposed solution (the Ball proposal); and that it was encouraging the impression that it might recognize the PLO—positions all bitterly opposed by Israel.

Carter had clearly not anticipated the extent and strength of the adverse reactions, and quickly set about rectifying the situation through a multi-faceted approach. Meetings were arranged with Israeli and other critics, and public statements issued to help reassure Israel that the Americans' basic position remained unchanged. He sought to reassure a delegation of Jewish members of Congress and supporters of Israel at a gathering in the White House on 6 October by giving them assurances that he had no intention of imposing a settlement or of accepting the right of the PLO to be invited to Geneva. He declared: "I'd rather commit political suicide than hurt Israel."[40] In a speech to the UN General Assembly on 4 October, Carter reiterated the need for a "true peace" based on UN Resolutions 242 and 338. He affirmed that Israel must have "borders that are recognized and secure" and that "the commitment of the US to Israel's security is unquestionable." He also made clear that: "We do not intend to impose from the outside a settlement on the nations of the Middle East." While seeking to reassure Israel, Carter at the same time insisted that "for the Arabs, the legitimate rights of the Palestinians must be recognized."

The immediate crisis in US-Israel's relations was defused at a series of meetings between Carter, Vance and Dayan, which produced an agreed working paper. Although substantive issues remained, the working paper had as its basic purpose

---

[38] For the full text of the US-Soviet statement of 1 October 1977, see p. 29.

[39] An example of this perspective is provided by Congressman John J. Rhodes, Republican Minority Leader of the House of Représentatives, who wrote in the *New York Times* (14 October 1977): "The President succeded in bringing our foremost adversary back into a position of influence in the Middle East and at the same time rousing deep unease about the stability of America's commitment to the only democracy in the Middle East."

[40] *New York Times*, 7 October 1977.

the avoidance of an American-Israeli confrontation and an effort to clear the procedural obstacles on the path to Geneva. Dayan elected to make the terms of the working paper public on 13 October during a parliamentary session in Israel. The paper provided:

1. The Arab parties will be represented by a unified Arab delegation, which will include Palestinian Arabs. After the opening sessions, the conference will split into working groups.
2. The working groups for the negotiations and conclusion of peace treaties will be formed as follows:
   a. Egypt-Israel
   b. Jordan-Israel
   c. Syria-Israel
   d. Lebanon-Israel (All the parties agree that Lebanon may join the conference when it so requests.)
3. The West Bank and Gaza issues will be discussed in a working group to consist of Israel, Jordan, Egypt, and the Palestinian Arabs.
4. The solution of the problem of the Arab refugees and of the Jewish refugees will be discussed in accordance with terms to be agreed upon.
5. The agreed bases for the negotiations at the Geneva peace conference on the Middle East are UN Security Council Resolutions 242 and 338.
6. All the initial terms of reference of the Geneva peace conference remain in force, except as may be agreed by the parties.[41]

The Israeli Cabinet unanimously approved the working paper on 11 October. In part this was to demonstrate Israeli flexibility in co-operating with the Carter Administration. Following this Israeli acceptance, the next problem was to secure support from the Arab states; on 12 October, the US sent the working paper to them for their consideration. Egypt sought an amendment which would name the PLO as one of the participants.[42] Syria's reactions were critical but it refrained from rejecting the proposals outright, as the PLO was quick to do. The basic obstacle remained the form that the Palestinian representation should take at Geneva. The PLO insisted that it was the only legitimate representative of the Palestinian people—a view generally endorsed by the Arab states, but with alternative suggestions emanating from several Arab sources. Despite these alternative proposals—which included representation by the Arab League or by a joint Jordan-Palestinian delegation—the main thrust continued to be how to find the PLO a place in the negotiating process. Israel continued to refuse to deal with the PLO and its spokesmen argued that it could veto the participation of any delegation not represented at the original Geneva conference. The US confirmed Israel's right to do so. Thus the procedural aspects of the conference and the agenda, as well as the details of the substantive positions, remained in discord.

[41] Text as published in *New York Times*, 14 October 1977.
[42] *Washington Post*, 20 October 1977.

ARAB WORLD EXPORTS TO THE US BY COUNTRY, 1966-1976 (US$ million)

	1966	*1968*	*1970*	*1972*	*1973*	*1974*	*1975*	*1976*
Oil Exporting Countries								
Algeria	3	5	11	111	227	1,167	1,448	2,293
Iraq	21	3	3	11	17	1	23	123
Kuwait	29	39	27	52	68	14	126	44
Libya	57	90	42	123	229	1	1,120	2,320
Oman	—	—	—	3	25	23	58	248
Qatar	—	—	—	6	13	86	64	139
Saudi Arabia	96	58	21	205	545	1,786	2,987	5,773
United Arab Emirates	—	—	56	29	71	392	781	1,466
Subtotal A	206	195	169	540	1,195	3,470	6,607	12,406
Non Oil Exporting Countries								
Bahrayn	2	10	9	21	18	65	115	27
Egypt	18	32	24	18	28	75	33	143
Jordan	—	—	—	—	—	—	1	1
Lebanon	9	11	14	22	35	33	35	6
Mauritania	2	—	1	1	1	—	—	—
Morocco	10	11	11	13	14	22	11	17
Somalia	1	1	—	—	—	—	1	1
Sudan	6	7	13	13	10	30	9	27
Syria	5	3	2	3	7	2	7	11
Tunisia	3	3	3	9	35	24	28	60
Yemen Arab Rep.	—	—	—	—	—	1	—	—
Yemen, PDR	1	—	—	3	4	6	1	1
Subtotal B	57	78	77	103	152	258	241	294
Grand Total	**263**	**273**	**246**	**643**	**1,347**	**3,728**	**6,848**	**12,700**
Ratio of Subtotal A to Grand Total (%)	78	71	69	84	89	93	96	98

ARAB WORLD IMPORTS FROM THE US BY COUNTRY, 1966-1976 (US$ million)

	1966	*1968*	*1970*	*1972*	*1973*	*1974*	*1975*	*1976*
Oil Exporting Countries								
Algeria	67	53	62	99	161	315	632	482
Iraq	46	15	22	23	56	285	310	397
Kuwait	89	109	62	111	120	209	366	452
Libya	59	115	104	85	104	139	232	266
Oman	—	—	—	7	9	37	75	57
Qatar	—	—	—	14	19	34	50	74
Saudi Arabia	152	187	141	314	442	835	1,502	2,659
United Arab Emirates	—	—	49	69	121	230	370	404
Subtotal A	413	479	440	722	1,032	2,084	3,537	4,791
Non Oil Exporting Countries								
Bahrayn	12	12	12	27	41	80	90	279
Egypt	189	48	81	76	225	455	683	804
Jordan	48	24	63	65	79	105	195	238
Lebanon	84	82	64	130	162	287	402	49
Mauritania	3	5	4	5	9	11	14	20
Morocco	63	70	89	58	113	184	200	287
Somalia	2	4	3	5	2	2	9	11
Sudan	15	6	7	18	39	64	103	79
Syria	20	6	11	20	21	40	128	300
Tunisia	44	49	49	55	60	87	90	82
Yemen Arab Rep.	—	—	—	2	10	11	8	26
Yemen, PDR	5	3	3	1	3	12	3	4
Subtotal B	485	309	386	462	764	1,338	1,925	2,179
Grand Total	**898**	**788**	**826**	**1,184**	**1,796**	**3,422**	**5,462**	**6,970**
Ratio of Subtotal A to Grand Total (%)	46	61	53	61	57	60	65	69

Source: The Middle East, August 1977.

The Soviet Bloc and the Middle East

DAVID MORISON

Russia, like any other power, has legitimate interests in the Orient; and obviously she has special interests in the Middle East, as well as in all those regions of Asia which adjoin her borders. The Middle East, being that region of the East which lies closest to Russia proper, is still termed by Russians "the Near East."

Of the Comecon and Warsaw Pact countries of Eastern Europe, none has so full a history of Eastern connections and Eastern ventures as the USSR. The USSR's Warsaw Pact allies do now have their own Middle Eastern preoccupations, but these are fundamentally economic rather than political. If they have a foreign policy concern in the Middle East, it is to win and maintain such political friendships as may further their economic interests in the region; they are of course concerned that Soviet foreign policy should not unnecessarily prejudice these friendships and these interests. For example, it was presumably the deterioration in Soviet-Egyptian relations—and not any Czechoslovakian offence—which led Cairo to overcome its scruples about stopping cotton deliveries to both countries in August 1977.[1]

In the same connection, it is significant that Romania has taken advantage of the leeway enjoyed by its own foreign policy to maintain and indeed cultivate a friendship which the USSR had itself broken off. In Cairo, on 13 May 1977, President Ceausescu said that, while "relations between Soviet Union and Egypt primarily concern those two countries", Romanians "very much hoped that relations between the two countries would move from a stage of no confidence to a new phase"; Romania wanted a strengthening and deepening of relations not only between those two countries but "between all the socialist states and all the states of the world." Why indeed, one might ask, should they want anything else?[2]

But Russia's ways are different from Balkan ways; for Russia is a great power, whose favour or disfavour can influence situations (which great powers always consider it their particular duty to do). In the days of the Ottoman Empire, the Tsars felt it to be their duty to protect the Orthodox communities of the Levant. Now that the former territory of that Empire is parcelled into one Jewish and a number of Arab states, the Tsars' own successors have patronized or protected in recent years, for varying periods and with varying success Egypt; Syria; Iraq; Cyprus; monarchist Yemen; republican Yemen; revolutionary South Yemen; the Kurds (against Iraq); the Marxist rebels of Dhufar; and, most recently—in today's new Middle East, when no self-respecting Arab or other country wants to be regarded as protected or patronized by any power, great or small—the Palestinians. Nor should it be forgotten, when comparing the present with the past, that there was something quite protective about the welcome which the Soviet Union accorded to the State of Israel at its birth.

To secure this protection and this patronage—which, more often than not, have yielded it (temporary or more long-lived) local economic and/or military footholds—the Soviet Union has taken advantage of local conflicts as well as anti-Western resentments. Of local conflicts in the Middle East there never seems likely to be a shortage. Therefore, if things had gone on in the same old way, perhaps there would never have been a shortage of Soviet clients. But, fortunately or unfortunately, since 1973 all concerned with the Middle East have had to find for themselves new bearings in a radically altered landscape; and "all" of course includes the Russians. In the Soviet case, in particular, since the great Middle East military and political convulsions of 1973–4 and the resulting world economic disruption, the new international economic significance of the Middle East seems to have impressed itself on the Russians more than anything else. This is evident in the somewhat awed note which is often detectable in even the most bitter of current Soviet complaints about Saudi policy in the region.

One of the most immediate effects of the 1973–4 Middle East upheaval was to deflate the pomposity of Moscow's Arab world propaganda. With the oil embargo, and the subsequent quadrupling of the price of crude oil, the Arab oil states quite took the wind out of the sails of that veteran flagship of Moscow's Arab world propaganda fleet, the windjammer that for so many years had trailed those tattered "Arabs, Be Masters of Your Own Oil!" streamers. It was of course now patently obvious that the Arabs *were* masters of their own oil—and, more than this, that the major Arab oil-producing states were now independent actors on the international stage. Moscow's propaganda was in due course refitted (a) to explain that it was the Arab rulers, and not their peoples, who had now acquired full control of the national wealth, and (b) to denounce the said regimes (having eventually found them to be irredeemably "reactionary") as "imperialist puppets."

Of course, the necessity to recast one particular propaganda charade was in itself just an incident in this kind of game. But behind it lay the long-delayed Moscow recognition that the USSR, no less than the West, now had a new and much altered Middle East to deal with: vastly richer (the surplus wealth of the oil-rich inevitably becoming the standby and resource of poorer sister states); more self-confident (*vis-à-vis*, in particular, the great powers); and, above all, both able and inclined to buy technology and arms in whatever was felt to be the best market. Among the USSR's established Middle East clients, this inclination to "diversify"—to seek additional or alternative foreign providers or associates—was already evident or latent before the stirring events of 1973–4; after that it became an accepted fact and, in the end, unremarkable.

Another effect of the changed Middle East climate after 1973 was that, inevitably, the "closed shop" atmosphere of solidarity and togetherness between the USSR and its Arab protégés, which Khrushchev and his successors had so sedulously fostered, began to evaporate to a point where even Soviet propaganda hardly tried to conjure it back. Certainly the erstwhile protégés still had their requirements of the USSR; but moral patronage, and indeed political "protection" in the conventional sense, were not among them. As regards those Arab states outside the former magic circle, the Soviet leadership could no longer afford to sneer at them, as Khrushchev did in May 1964, during his tour of the UAR: "There is some little ruler sitting there [in Kuwait], an Arab of course, a Muslim. He lives the life of the rich, but he is trading in the wealth of his people. He never had any conscience, and he never will have any."[3] Would such a person, Khrushchev asked, have any real interest in Arab unity? Yet, ten years later, Kuwait's friendship was being assiduously cultivated by Moscow, precisely because it was regarded there as the Arab Gulf state most alive to its wider obligations to Arab and international causes.

What, then, of recent developments in the USSR's attitude to the Arab world's causes, and in particular to the Arab-Israeli conflict? Has there indeed been any development in the Soviet attitude to what most of the world regards as the central political issue in the Middle East?

The Geneva conference on a Middle East peace settlement still remains, in late 1977, a kind of totem pole to which different tribes all pay homage, but with varying degrees of veneration. The Soviet Union itself pays the most fulsome ritual, but fortunately (since otherwise the tedium of its utterances on the subject would be quite unrelieved) it uses its ceremonial pronouncements about the Geneva conference and a comprehensive Middle East peace settlement as a peg on which to hang less well-worn and sometimes even quite novel ideas or observations. Thus Brezhnev, having in a speech on 18 January 1977 pronounced that "it now appears that all the interested sides are inclining towards a renewal of the work" of the Geneva conference, declared in a later speech on 21 March that the USSR, as co-chairman of the conference, was entitled to its own opinion "concerning the main principles and directions of a future peace settlement", and proceeded to detail some of what he felt to be the essential provisions of any eventual peace documents.[4] Though such obeisances and pronouncements may be quickly forgotten, they are nevertheless, one hopes, necessary milestones on the presumably not unending road to peace in the Middle East. So, too, should one regard the US-Soviet statement of 2 October 1977, however variously it has been interpreted. Meanwhile the Arab states differ among themselves about the necessity, urgency, utility, or indeed propriety, of reconvening the Geneva conference; and it is a paradoxical fact that two of the Arab regimes at present most favoured by Moscow, Iraq and Libya, are themselves quite hostile to this cherished object of Middle East policy.

To a large degree, indeed, the Soviet Union "goes it alone" in its approach to Geneva, which is not identical with that of any one of the Arab states—though of course it is near enough to many for a common anti-Israel front to be presented in joint communiques. Moscow's "principled" stand on the question of Palestinian representation at Geneva has enabled the Soviet Union to present itself as a firmer stickler for the Arabs' true rights than many of the Arab states themselves (Egypt, in particular). But, on this question of the Soviet attitude to Geneva, one wonders whether the USSR is most anxious for a settlement or for the chance to preside—jointly, if need be—over its realization, and to have a dominant voice in the post-settlement situation (just as one wonders whether, in the US attitude, the desire for a settlement or concern for peace of mind in Israel and on its behalf are the most potent factors).

Recent developments in Soviet relations with Middle East countries must be considered on a more or less country-by-country basis. But of course it needs to be borne in mind that with the increasingly conciliar character which Arab politics is now assuming—and which, one suspects, is not much to Moscow's liking—Soviet views on joint actions and initiatives undertaken by groups of Arab countries are often not less important than Soviet relations with individual states.

RELATIONS WITH EGYPT

In Egypt, more than in any other of the USSR's close Arab associates, moves towards correcting the one-sidedness of the "client" relationship were already starting even before the new post-1973 situation presented major possibilities for such a correction. At first, Sādāt's declared aim was a "balanced policy." This kind of exercise by any Third World country has always been anathema to Moscow. Later Sadat began to declare, and to repeat frequently, that in fact it was the US that must necessarily be the arbiter of Middle East events, since it "holds 99% of the cards." The USSR's refusal of Egypt's requests for arms and for arms replacements was the complaint to which Sadat gave most prominence in his own public speeches about Soviet-Egyptian relations. The USSR, on its part, sought to present Egypt as having betrayed the Arab cause by its second disengagement agreement with Israel (although the first had apparently met with Soviet approval). What annoyed the Russians as much as anything was that the negotiations which produced the agreement were so conspicuously American in inspiration and organization. Not only had the USSR been edged from its former place in the centre of the stage; it had actually had to withdraw into the wings, grumbling and cultivating the more assiduously those of its Arab friends whose own complaints were, it felt, of a more or less similar nature. (See chapter on Egypt.)

A culminating point in Sādāt's long-drawn-out process of changing horses was Egypt's abrogation, on 14 March 1976, of the Soviet-Egyptian Treaty of 1971. Sādāt contended that this action was forced on him by intolerable Soviet demands—not only had the Russians refused arms supplies, and refused to re-schedule Egypt's loan repayments; they were "now demanding interest on the military loans."[5]

Since this apparently irreversible Egyptian step, Sādāt and his regime have been the target of what must be, in Soviet-Arab relations, a quite unprecedented degree of Soviet public venom. Moscow has daily been telling the Arab world that Sādāt is treacherously playing Israel's game; and to list even the main other Soviet charges against Sādāt's domestic, Arab and international policies would take up half a page. By July 1976, Moscow's Arabic broadcasts were clamouring: "Will the Egyptian people remain silent" at the iniquities of the regime and at the indignities which Egypt's working people and soldiers alike suffered at its hands?[6] When the riots and protest demonstrations broke out in Cairo and elsewhere on 18-19 January 1977, the Soviet media presented this as a mass popular movement clamouring for a reversal of government policy but brutally suppressed by the Egyptian army.[7] What more, Sādāt may well have asked himself in considering possible Soviet reactions to his projected visit to Israel, could Moscow possibly fling at him?

So, within a few years of a war in which Soviet arms had made possible the return of Egyptian lands and the restoration of Egypt's self-respect, the Soviet Union itself had more than lost all the gains of 20 years of cultivating the centre and heart of the Middle East. The Middle East war of 1973 had been Sādāt's war, not Brezhnev's. In the years that followed, Moscow became increasingly concerned lest Sādāt's war should be succeeded by Sādāt's peace. At the end of 1977, this seemed a possibility; with it, the possibility that a Soviet-presided Middle East peace settlement had thereby receded a further step or two.

Syria, Lebanon, Jordan and the Palestinians

Perhaps because it has never felt itself to be dominated by Moscow, Syria has not felt the need for gestures to assert its independence of Soviet influence. Having no formal Treaty of Friendship with the Soviet Union, it has if anything a longer and steadier history of cordial relations with the Russians than Egypt. Moscow has been able to claim Syrian solidarity with its stand against partial and piecemeal disengagement agreements. For a number of years, Moscow has sought to respond to Syria's more committed stance on the Palestine issue by gradually making increasingly serious professions of commitment itself.

It was therefore all the more disturbing for the Soviet leadership when Asad decided that Syria must intervene to end the Lebanese civil war—not on the side of the Palestinians but against them. Nevertheless, the Soviet leaders were measured in their criticisms. "Regrettably", said Brezhnev on 25 October 1976, "Syria has been drawn into the orbit of military activities."[8] On the conference in Riyadh earlier in the month (at which the heads of state of Saudi Arabia, Egypt, Syria, and Lebanon, and PLO Chairman 'Arafāt agreed on the terms of a ceasefire), the Soviet media merely retailed the critical comments made in the Iraqi press. But of course the Russians hated the Saudi role in settling this conflict no less than they hated the US role in Egypt's second disengagement agreement. Thereafter, however, the process of normalization was welcomed in all Soviet statements. Should Moscow have exerted pressure on Syria to prevent the collapse of the Lebanese Leftists and Palestinians whom it had been so vocally championing? And could such pressure have been effective? Moscow obviously decided that the hard-pressed Palestinians would not get more than its continued sympathy—which, after all, has been worth a good deal to them in political terms for some years.

The Palestine "resistance"—the term has become accepted in Soviet usage in recent years—has been elevated to new and higher degrees of Soviet political and ideological approval since the mid-1960s, and more especially since the 1973 war and its aftermath. The demonstrativeness with which Moscow can now afford to applaud or welcome Palestinian representatives and their expressions of gratitude for Soviet support, provides Moscow's propaganda with a useful contrast to the often strained atmosphere of Palestinian encounters and parleys within the Arab fold. Moscow has found that solidarity with the Palestinian cause, as expressed by the PLO, serves as a convenient touchstone of Arab "anti-imperialist" sentiment. The Palestinians in their turn can always assure Moscow that, if they get a state of their own, it will be organized on the best Marxist model.

This bold façade of Soviet-Palestinian solidarity is of fairly recent construction. In 1972, *Pravda* was still condemning the Palestinian organizations for their "desperate" hijacking and other actions; but Yasīr 'Arafāt, on his visit to Moscow that year, "informed the USSR that the ranks of the PLO were being consolidated on progressive lines." Since then, with the rise in the PLO's world public opinion rating, PLO-Moscow solidarity has grown enormously, to the general benefit of both parties. (Also see essay on the PLO.)

The Gulf, Peninsula and Red Sea States

From any run-of-the-mill Moscow broadcast denouncing Saudi policy, one might conclude that Moscow regarded the present Saudi regime as irredeemably "in the American camp." In fact, however, hints of Soviet probes or overtures with a view to better relations with the Kingdom have long been a feature of this "relationship without relations", if it may so be called. On Faysal's death the idea was again mooted; at the time of writing, however, it does not seem to be a high priority on either side. Concerned if not alarmed at the effects of Saudi policy in neighbouring Arab and non-Arab Islamic states (Egypt, Sudan, the Yemens, Somalia), Moscow is on the one hand anxious to make known its adamant hostility to what it sees as a conspiracy to make the Red Sea "an Arab lake", along whose entire coastline Russians would be unwelcome. On the other hand, it views with equal disgust the frequently mooted idea of a Gulf security pact which would similarly inhibit Soviet moves and movements on the other side of the peninsula.

Speaking to a British correspondent in May 1975, the Shah of Iran shrewdly observed: "Kuwait can be the Finland of the area."[9] Moscow has certainly made various efforts in recent years not only to secure Kuwait's goodwill, notably by offers of arms, but also—as when the Kuwaiti Foreign Minister visited Moscow in December 1975—to get Kuwait to subscribe to the Soviet Union's own programme for the Gulf's political and military future, and notably to "the liquidation of foreign war bases" there. There were at that time cordial comments in the Soviet media on opposition in Bahrayn and in the Emirates to reports of US interest in Gulf security projects. But since 1975, there has been a harder tone in Soviet comment on the policies of these once keenly courted states—among which Iran is to be included. In Soviet broadcasts to the area, no theme is perhaps so harped on as the enormous scale of arms supplied to it, and particularly to Iran. Moscow sought to make what capital it could from the Dhufar rebellion by denouncing Iran's repressive role and presenting the Shah's regime as "the gendarme of the region." (See chapters on Iran and the Gulf states.)

Remaining Friends: Iraq and the PDRY

Since the USSR's disagreements with Egypt, its friendship with Iraq has been the more valued; and, since the Yemen Arab Republic (YAR) came in under the Saudi umbrella, the "revolutionary" policies of the People's Democratic Republic of Yemen (PDRY) have earned all the higher Soviet praise.

Of the two, Iraq is regarded by Moscow as a safe "anti-imperialist" bet because of its greater militancy on the Arab-Israeli conflict (although, as has been noted, it does not see eye to eye with the USSR about the Geneva conference). Iraq's multiple oil supply partnerships with Comecon countries, and its now formal Comecon economic links—not to mention the considerable output of the Soviet-aided North Rumayla oilfield—enable the USSR to present Iraq as a very steady associate, despite occasional *Pravda* criticisms of "bourgeois trends" in some echelons of Iraqi society. Principally, perhaps, it is very much in Russia's interest to have a friend at the head of the Gulf who may be relied upon to oppose any Gulf security pacts, except such as are of the most harmless kind from the Soviet point of view. (See chapter on Iraq.)

Since Somalia's defection from its Soviet alliance, the course of PDRY foreign policy has been particularly closely watched by Moscow. Saudi pressure on the PDRY to take Somalia's side against Soviet-protected Ethiopia has been condemned in Soviet comment. (See chapter on PDRY.)

Turkey and Cyprus

Recent years have seen quite a striking increase in Soviet exertions to improve relations with Turkey. The fact that Turkey's actions over Cyprus have not earned it greater Soviet disfavour must be a measure of Moscow's concern to keep on the right side of a strong neighbour which has had notable resentments of its own against the US, especially over the American arms embargo. But Moscow's Turkish/Cypriot diplomatic hand has been a difficult one to play. On Cyprus itself, Moscow falls back on support for UN resolutions. Its own call for an international conference on Cyprus under the aegis of the UN is in line with this "neutral" stand; but of course this is one more Middle East issue—like the Arab-Israeli conflict—over whose solution the USSR feels that it has every right to preside, or to be among those presiding. (See also chapter on Turkey.)

NOTES

1. BBC Summary of World Broadcasts ME/5559/1/A/2 and MF/5663/i.
2. Ibid, ME/5513/A/2.
3. Quoted in Stephen Page, *The USSR and Arabia* (London: Central Asian Research Centre, 1971), p. 81.
4. *Pravda*, 19 January and 22 March 1977. *USSR and Third World*, No 1-2 (1977), p. 16.
5. Cairo Radio, 14 March 1976. *USSR and Third World*, No 1 (1976), p. 35 and No 10 (1971), p. 601. For other expressions of Egyptian restiveness at Soviet ME policy prior to Egypt's expulsion of Soviet experts, see *USSR and Third World*, No 7 (1972), p. 377.
6. *USSR and Third World*, No 2-3 (1976), p. 128.
7. *Ibid*, No 1-2 (1977), pp. 20f.
8. *Pravda*, 26 October 1976.
9. *The Guardian*, London; 4 May 1975.

China and the Middle East

W. A. C. ADIE

THE NEXT REPUBLIC—THERMIDOR OR BRUMAIRE?

The People's Republic of China (PRC) has been too wrapped up in its own affairs in recent years, especially since 1976, to engage in spectacular initiatives, or to make any significant overt changes in the strategic assessments and policies made through the 1960s and 1970s for the present epoch—what the Chinese call the revolutionary line of Chairman Mao in foreign affairs. They were knotted at home in a prolonged power struggle, in which the two major turning points were the deaths of Premier Chou En-lai (January 1976) and of Mao Tse-tung himself (September 1976). Chou's death swung China back towards the "leftist" anarchy and isolation of the Great Proletarian Cultural Revolution that began in 1966, while Mao's death swung it to the right. But these upheavals, culminating in the *coup d'état* of Hua Kuo-feng in October 1976, were only a continuation of the Cultural Revolution which was supposed to have been launched by Mao ten years before to prevent China from developing into a rightist or Soviet-type state-capitalist bureaucratic dictatorship, and which was only officially declared over by the Hua regime. This new regime embodies an uneasy compromise between the men and policies of China's first People's Republic (1949-66) and those of the turbulent time in which Mao and the communist radicals—dubiously distinguished from him in current propaganda as traitors and the "Gang of Four"—struggled to create a second Republic, vaguely inspired by the Paris Commune as well as by historical Chinese models of bureaucratized paternalism—the "legalist" school of statecraft which largely moulded the Imperial or Confucian system.

The compromise was unstable. The men at the top were old, except for Hua (himself originally a radical), and the secret police chief, Wang Tung-hsing, who owed his sudden elevation to the Standing Committee of the Politbureau (the ruling five) for his co-operation in the arrest of Madame Mao and her other supporters, at the time of Hua's coup. There were some forces pulling in the direction of a Yugoslav-type liberalization, with the opening up of trade and other international contacts. But there were others advocating a Stalinist-type regimentation and militarism. Thus, though dissident wall-posters and military leaders demanded more, Hua could only permit oblique de-Maoization through exposure of the "Gang". Though some China-watchers compared this "thaw" with the Thermidor of the French Revolution, when the fall of Robespierre ended its excesses, there was also a nip of Brumaire in the air—the season that brought Napoleon Bonaparte.

As far as the PRC's foreign policy is concerned, ten years of recurrent domestic upheavals have strengthened the military character of the Peking regime and confirmed its established Marxist-Leninist habit of assessing present situations in geo-political and military terms. This is partly a conventional and abstract expression of the strategic plans and tactics it is adopting to *change* a situation as far as it can, with the means presently available to it. This is why it is a mistake to dismiss as mere "rhetoric" or "propaganda" the thumbnail analyses of the world's ills which Chinese leaders regularly intone when welcoming foreign dignitaries, and in speeches at the United Nations, etc. In fact, slight differences in the wording of these ritualized formulations usually signal a substantive modification of tactics.

As everyone is aware, Peking has for years been trying to get across the central idea that it fears attack by the USSR, and therefore wants to mobilize an "international united front" primarily against this menace—but also to a lesser extent against the US, which it portrays as tangled in some kind of love-hate relationship with the USSR to the detriment of everyone else. On this basis, the Middle East is supposed to be the key to the control of Western Europe, the main bone of contention between the two super-powers.[1]

Proceeding from this premise, China should be seeking to minimize Soviet influence in the Middle East; but it has proceeded to do this in a seemingly mysterious way. On the one hand, it has worked hard to build up cultural, economic and politico-diplomatic ties with "conservative" monarchies like Iran and Morocco. (It even opened diplomatic relations with Jordan during the year.) Yet it also publicized its continuing support for revolutionary organizations like the Palestinian groups, who for years were using Chinese weapons to try and overthrow Arab kings and "officialdom", notably in Jordan. There have, of course, been realignments in the Arab world since the Rabat summit in 1974; but the real reason why Peking supplies gunboats to Tunis, for example, *as well as* guns to the Palestinian guerrillas, can only be properly understood in terms of Chinese revolutionary experience—as applied to today's world in the form of Chairman Mao's "line on foreign affairs."

THE "REVOLUTIONARY LINE ON FOREIGN AFFAIRS"

In August 1977, the new leadership legitimized itself by holding the 11th National Congress of the Communist Party of China, which produced a new Central Committee, Constitution and Politbureau. Hua Kuo-feng delivered the Political Report on 12 August.[2] In the section on "The Situation and Our Tasks" he announced a "strategic decision" to "grasp the key link of class struggle", and to bring about "great order throughout the country." Abroad, the international situation was "very good, not just good or fairly good"; facts had shown that "the main trend in the international situation is that countries want independence, nations want liberation and the people want revolution, and this no force can stem." Though the factors for revolution were growing, so obviously were the factors which would inevitably lead to war, mainly because of the global contention and interference of the super-powers. If people of all countries were to close ranks and wage unrelenting struggles, they might be able to put off the outbreak of war or find themselves in a better position when it occurs. Hua stressed that the division of the world into three, as propounded by Mao in 1974 (and explained by Teng Hsiao-ping at the UN General Assembly in April of that year) was of profound significance.

> [It] gives a correct orientation to the present international struggle and clearly defines the main revolutionary forces, the chief enemies, and the middle forces that can be won over and united, enabling the international proletariat to unite with all the forces that can be united with, to form the broadest united front in class struggles against the chief enemies on the world arena. This strategic formulation conforms to the strategic requirements of the contemporary struggles of the international proletariat and the oppressed people and nations of the world, and also of the struggle for the triumph of socialism and communism.

Of course, all this has to be deciphered—the key being the history of the three-cornered struggle between the armies of Mao, Chiang Kai-shek and Imperial Japan as codified in Mao Tse-tung's *Thoughts*, and reiterated in the voluminous writings of Mao and his marshals on "people's war".

Hua also stressed how Mao pointed out at the beginning of 1976 that "in the era in which classes exist, war is an interval between one peace and another. War is a continuation of politics, that is to say, a continuation of peace. Peace itself is politics." In his *Little Red Book*, Mao states that politics is "war without bloodshed."[3] In other words, for Mao and his successors, peace is also war without bloodshed, with the two elements of the dialectic unity war/peace (WARCE) actually existing *concurrently* rather than alternately. Peace is like night-time, simply when and where the struggle is carried on more by covert and/or non-violent means than by conventional, guerrilla or other forms of armed or unarmed "struggle"—all of which at the appropriate conjuncture are inseparably part of revolutionary or people's war.

On the fiftieth anniversary of the Chinese People's Liberation, Army Marshal Yeh Chien-ying (considered by many China-watchers to be the real power behind Hua's regime), affirmed the continuing validity of Mao's concept of people's war, in which "our Party co-ordinates armed struggle directly or indirectly with the struggles of the workers, peasants, youth, women and all other forms of people's struggle throughout the country, and with the struggles in the political, economic, ideological, cultural and all other fields. . . ."

The people's wars of the future would inevitably be fought under modern conditions, and China was equipping itself with modern weapons; but the strategy and tactics would remain the same—"concentrating a superior force to destroy the enemy forces one by one . . . Once the war breaks out . . . we are prepared to make the greatest national sacrifice and make our due contribution to the cause of the liberation of mankind."[4]

The esoteric meaning of the special terminology used in such Chinese expositions as Mao's doctrines on war, revolution and peace has been discussed by the present writer in several previous publications, to which those left unsatisfied by the following brief summary are invited to refer.[5] Here it should suffice to draw attention to what is meant by the tripartite formulae about independence, liberation and revolution in relation to the First, Second and Third Worlds in general, and to indicate their application to the contemporary Middle East situation in particular.

The main point is that these formulae project a scenario on the world stage adapted from the "revolutionary drama" Mao staged in China, which is seen as a sample and scale model of the whole. In fact, an allegory of the doctrines of people's war was promoted by Madame Mao during the Second Republic period in the revolutionary Peking opera *Taking Tiger Mountain by Stratagem.* This explanation rationalized Peking's tactics of accommodation with the US and other developed countries, and of striving for the leadership of the Third World in terms of Trojan Horse trickery or, in party jargon, "united front work." Nixon's visit was explained to the troops in secret circulars along the same lines. Purloined by Taiwan agents and published in English, these "Kunming papers"[6] deserve as much attention as certain other leaked documents have received in our times. Their account of Mao's global strategy, now continued by his successors, has been confirmed by many other overt and leaked documents, as well as empirically by China's actions in the field.

THE STRATEGIC ASSESSMENT AND PLAN

Mao's division of the world into three is a development of his concept of the intermediate zone, or no-man's-land, which originally applied to the situation in guerrilla warfare wherein the insurgent forces control their base areas, the enemy control theirs, with a large contended area in between. These uncommitted forces—the majority—have to be mobilized against the enemy in order to change the balance in favour of the guerrillas who, of course, start out in the minority. In

China, it was the Japanese invasion that enabled the communists to "unite all possible forces"—including, willy-nilly, Generalissimo Chiang himself to a certain extent, and hence many of his looser warlord adherents—against the temporary "chief enemy", Japan, which the communists had done their best to embroil with Chiang, the long-term and real chief enemy.

When Mao first applied this concept to international affairs, the division was between the socialist camp, the intermediate zone and the capitalists. In a subsequent refinement, the intermediate zone was divided further into the first zone (the Third World of former colonies and semi-colonies in Asia, Africa and Latin America), and the second zone (medium and small industrialized powers in Western Europe, Japan, etc). The equivalent of the beleaguered communist bases was China, the "yenan" of the world. The main force of the world revolution, corresponding to the mobilizable Chinese peasants and workers, was the Third World of "proletarian countries"; but as the Sino-Soviet split worsened, it became necessary to stress the community of interest between these ex-colonies and their ex-colonizers in the intermediate zone against "super-power hegemony." So, eventually, the USSR instead of the US became the "chief enemy", and the socialist camp was declared to have disintegrated. The capitalist camp was also presented (with a greater degree of prescription than description) as split between the second zone countries and the US, with leaders of the second zone playing a dual role, like that of the "national-bourgeois" or compradore rulers of Third World countries still linked with the capitalist system headed by America. The description of such leaders as both colluding with this system and contending against it is, of course, another way of expressing Peking's intention to "exploit contradictions" wherever possible, and to isolate a chief enemy, win over the middle-of-the-roaders and destroy the enemy one by one. In their own countries, such leaders represented reaction; but from the *global* point of view they could act as part of the revolutionary forces. The essential point in the scenario is that by adopting this dual role, a "bourgeois" country or leader is going to *facilitate development of the progressive forces* (i.e. pro-Chinese revolutionaries) within a given country.

This is what is meant by the other tripartite formula. "Countries want independence" means that in the first stage, existing trends should be encouraged, by which leaders of the Third World sever their political and economic links with the developed (second zone) countries, or use such links to pressure them into opposing the interests of the super-powers. Chinese propaganda constantly urges the Third and Second Worlds to "safeguard national sovereignty", develop autarky in the national economy and control national resources. That is to say, they are exhorted to expropriate and nationalize industries, plantations etc so as to weaken the international economic order allegedly manipulated by the two super-powers, as well as to undercut the economic and social base of their alleged subordinates—the local "bourgeois" or "revisionist" rulers.[7]

Independence thus means isolation from outside support, which is to facilitate the next stage—a "struggle for national liberation", or Chinese-type revolutionary war, in which violent (preferably armed) struggle is co-ordinated with psychological, economic and many other sorts of warfare.[8] All possible "transitional demands" are exploited and temporary alliances made with "transitional personages" in order to use or recruit their allies and subordinates. "Peoples want revolution" describes the final stage, in which a vanguard ("people") applying Marxism-Leninism—i.e. Mao Tse-tung thought—to local conditions leads the revolutionary "national-democratic liberation war" to victory and proceeds to build socialism and communism.

The starting point for implementing this "great strategic plan" was the daring stratagem of using Nixon himself as a "transitional personage" (literally, stepping-stone person, as explained in the Kunming papers). The real threat from the USSR could thus be exploited by getting at and peeling off Nixon's allies (Tanaka, Marcos etc), as well as influencing public opinion in their countries and the US directly, and using the UN—combining in this way a "united front from below" with the "united front from above", both at the international level and within individual countries. In its original form, this ploy was called "friendly armies' work." Having used the Japanese threat as a basis of agitation to "unite" some of Chiang Kai-shek's troops and sway public opinion, the communists were able to force him into alliance with them against Japan, whereas he had intended to beat them first and handle the Japanese afterwards. Then they were able to persuade certain warlord units on his side (the "friendly armies") to form guerrilla and resistance units in the countryside and cities, from which the invaders had driven Chiang Kai-shek's government troops.

Thus, in the 1970s, the world was supposed to divide between the two colluding/contending super-powers, with Russia replacing America as chief enemy, arousing resistance from the Second World countries (i.e. leaders) who were, in turn, under pressure from those of the Third World. Although Albania and a few other countries were from time to time recognized as truly revolutionary by Peking, the rest of the world was seen as divided into two "families": the bourgeoisie versus proletariat or progressive forces, with the latter becoming increasingly restive in the USSR and other Warsaw Pact states. Already the proletariat was beginning to organize and resist in the capitalist world under the aegis of Maoist ("Marxist-Leninist") parties and guerrilla groups—the equivalent of the agents planted in "friendly armies"; but now using slogans about independence from the super-powers, vigilance against Soviet aggression and the New International Economic Order as the modern equivalent of "resist Japan", "land reform" and other such transitional slogans.

UNITED FRONT WORK IN THE MIDDLE EAST

Since Peking stepped on to the Afro-Asian scene at the Bandung Conference in April 1955, it has operated in the Islamic world outside its borders in much the same way as it did with the Muslim and other ethnic minorities inside them. The handling of "nationalities" and their leaders was another aspect of "united front work", turning enemies into allies, and allies into disciples. At first the emphasis was on the "united front from above", with transitional personages like Egypt's Nāsir and Iraq's Qāsim, the putative common "chief enemy". Imperialism was embodied, above all, in Israel. But from 1965 on, the "united front from below" gained importance, as Peking fostered the Palestinian guerrillas—initially through Syria—and the Dhufar rebels of the Popular Front for the Liberation of Oman and the Arab Gulf (PFLOAG) through Aden. Yāsir 'Arafāt himself stated in Peking (21 March 1970) that Chinese support was a main force propelling the Palestinian revolution. "It is by no means a secret that the first aid which generated the Palestine Liberation Movement (al-Fath) came from Peking."

It was partly through its government-to-government diplomacy and partly through its clandestine links with the guerrillas that China made itself a "force to be reckoned with" in what it saw as key strategic areas—the Gulf, the Red Sea/Horn of Africa area and the Eastern Mediterranean. The combination of both ("walking on two legs") brought it a visit, for example, from the Emperor of Ethiopia and diplomatic and economic relations with Iran. But in recent years the weight has been more on the right foot (diplomacy), than on the left (crypto-diplomacy or united-front-from-below action through guerrillas, student radicals etc).[9]

Politicians and commentators who have not understood the Maoist dialectic have sometimes argued that Peking's support for guerrillas, or "progressive forces" generally, was some kind of *alternative* for normalization of relations; that after the opening of an embassy in a country, Peking would support its government instead of "the people." Both open and secret pronouncements from Peking have made it clear to all except the wilfully blind that although support for insurgents may be withheld or played down for tactical reasons, "national and class struggles" must continue, even though particular governments may establish friendly relations with China. In fact, constantly developing the progressive forces within each country is a most necessary ingredient in exerting pressure on, and building the international united front with, governments and national-bourgeois stepping-stones—which, in turn, facilitates more development of the "progressive forces."

As the then Foreign Minister, Chiao Kuan-hua, stated in a briefing at Tientsin on 20 May 1975, at the time of the establishment of diplomatic relations with Malaysia, China hoped to establish diplomatic and friendly relations with that, or any other, country. It hoped that their leaders would put their countries in order and raise living standards; but it also expected them to remember what happened to Thieu in Vietnam, so that they "know how to behave. If otherwise, they will be targets of revolution. As for our assistance to the local revolutions, it is determined by our national system. We can't change it. If we did, we should be revisionists and not Marxists." Kuala Lumpur's understanding of Peking's position, as stated by a Malaysian diplomat, is that helping revolutionaries is "like their religion."

Referring to overseas Chinese in South East Asia, Chiao also expressed the hope that they would, as local citizens, do propaganda and revolutionary work for China. "Since they are your citizens and they are willing to join the revolution, we cannot interfere. If we do, then we are interfering in your domestic affairs." After visiting Peking, the Prime Minister of Singapore, Lee Kuan Yew, also explained in a carefully-worded answer in Canberra that Peking's "non-interference" applied to the repressive measures taken by incumbent governments against revolutionaries. What Peking was saying to such leaders was, in effect, "they will do their stuff, you go ahead and do yours—try to suppress them, we shall not interfere to stop you." Because, of course, according to Maoist doctrine it is precisely repression that promotes more revolution.

It may be argued that South East Asia is an area of special interest to Peking because of the presence of overseas Chinese communities with mainland relatives and open to the influence of Taiwan, Japan and other counter-revolutionary forces. Also, that under cover of its propaganda against intrusive Soviet influence, including Moscow's campaign for an Asian collective security system and some sort of Asian Helsinki, Peking is trying to encourage "tributary reflex" among its neighbours, which became marked after the fall of Indo-China.[10] When it warns them against letting in the tiger (Russia) through the back door, while driving the wolf (America) away from the front, it is trying to promote what can be called Burmanization of the region (a modern form of the old Imperial tributary system)—in the same way as Russia promotes Finlandization of West Europe: a sort of ratchet-wheel neutralism, creeping Left.

Although the Middle East has few overseas Chinese, ever since Peking's representatives replaced those of Taiwan at the UN and in many capitals, the line taken towards Middle Eastern countries has been the same: to warn against the "tiger", lately with stress on Soviet geo-political aims of controlling such key straits as the Dardanelles, Gibraltar and Bāb al-Mandeb, and the adjacent land areas in southern Europe and the Horn of Africa. During the last months of 1976 and in 1977, Peking media paid special attention to the Gulf and Red Sea areas, and most of the delegations exchanged, trade agreements signed etc, were with such countries as Iran, Kuwait and Bahrayn, as well as with the two Yemens, Egypt, Sudan, Ethiopia and Somalia. In the Maghrib—whereas formerly the emphasis was on "revolutionary" Algeria—relations with Morocco, Tunisia and Malta fitted into the pattern of the broad anti-Soviet front.

Peking media often use non-Chinese sources to put over a current propaganda line in language plainer than their own. For instance, they recently publicized contributions by Eugene Rostow and Edward Luttwak to a new book entitled *Defending America.* Rostow, in an article "The Soviet Threat to Europe through the Middle East", warns that "it is a front on which we could lose not merely a battle . . . but the war itself. For what is at stake in the Middle East . . . is the independence of Europe, and therefore the world balance of power." Luttwak is quoted approvingly as calling for active US efforts to "prevent further Soviet penetration of the Middle East, the Mediterranean basin, and East Africa."[11]

It is against this background that the major moves in Peking's "international united front" work fall into place. At the level of contacts with leading "transitional personages", visits to Peking of Egypt's Vice President Mubārak in April 1976, Pakistan Prime Minister Bhutto in May and President Ratsiraka of Madagascar in June and November 1976 were followed by that of the head of the United Front Work Department of the Central Committee of the Chinese Communist Party, Ulanfu, to Iran and Kuwait with Chi Teng-kuei and a delegation from the National People's Congress (NPC). In December 1976, the Head of State of the Yemen Arab Republic (YAR, North Yemen), Chairman of the Command Council and C-in-C of the armed forces, the late Ibrāhīm Muḥammad al-Hamdī, visited Peking and signed an agreement on economic and technical co-operation (ETCA). In February 1977, the People's Democratic Republic of Yemen (PDRY) sent its Foreign Minister, Muḥammad Sāliḥ Mutī', to Peking. The background to such visits was elucidated by the Peking media's comments on Red Sea affairs generally, and on the Ta'izz conference of heads of state from the YAR, PDRY, Sudan and Somalia;[12] this conference was projected as an opportunity for "uniting" against imperialism, hegemonism and Zionism (i.e. against Europe, USSR/US and Israel).

The major event in this connection was the visit in June 1977 of Sudan's President Ja'far Muḥammad Numayrī and the signing of a Sino-Sudanese ETCA on 9 June. Afro-Arab unity and security of the Red Sea were the main themes of his visit. Sudan's emulation of Egypt in expelling Soviet personnel was heartily applauded by Peking.[13] Vice-President Ismā'īl 'Alī Abucar of Somalia arrived in Peking on 20 June and on 10 July it was reported that Hamza Muhammad Gadaweyne, Chairman of the Security Bureau of the Somali Revolutionary Socialist Party, had met Vice-Premier Chi Teng-kuei in Peking. There is no need to dwell on the background to these contacts—the emergence of a *de facto* alliance between the Moroccan and Saudi monarchies, between Egypt and Western Europe (primarily France) to help Zaïre and other African states perceived to be threatened by indirect Soviet aggression, and the need to retrieve countries already under strong Soviet influence like the PDRY and Somalia. China also supported Zaïre and Somalia, as a logical development of its moves to exploit Egypt's quarrels with the Soviets. Putting into operation an option already explored in 1972, China stepped in with a military agreement in 1976 to enable Egypt to maintain some of its less sophisticated Soviet-made military hardware.

There is reason to believe that after Sadat's first explusion of Soviet advisers, it was mainly action by the Palestinian extremists (Munich massacre etc) that made it impossible for Egypt to conclude arms deals with the West and, in general, for the realignments of 1977 to have emerged earlier. The war and oil price rise of 1973 was, paradoxically, a favourable factor for realignment because the petrodollar balances demonstrated a community of interest between the oil exporters and their major clients, the "Second World", comprising the EEC and Japan. From this developed the concept of triangular co-operation among the Islamic oil-rich as contributors of capital, the developed industrial countries contributing technology (excluding the super-powers, but perhaps including what King Ḥasan called the "creative genius of Israel"), and the less developed (particularly Africa) non-oil countries having their resources developed for the benefit of all.[14]

Revolutionary Palestinians, such as Dr Ḥabash, used to make no secret of the fact that the point of perpetuating the war with Israel as "chief enemy" was, in fact, to destroy the existing Arab governments and to set up a socialist Arabia, in exactly the same way that the Chinese communists used the war against Japan to destroy Chiang Kai-shek and the warlords. They would rebuild the Ottoman empire, just as Mao rebuilt the Manchu empire. The fidā'yyūn were the main force, after the 1967 war, to fulfil the Chinese doctrinal requirement that there must be an armed struggle with which other operations (economic, diplomatic etc) are co-ordinated. They were also a factor not only in rejecting peace negotiations, but also in positively fostering full-scale war on the state-to-state level, the rationale for which was expressed by one sympathizer as follows:

> There is tremendous pressure by the Egyptians on Sadat to go to war against Israel. Another war against Israel would prove the ineffectiveness of the Arab regimes in the eyes of the Arab people. This would later lead to the overthrow of some of these Arab regimes. There is already in Egypt a strong Palestinian-cum-Egyptian student movement . . . This is a growing threat to Sadat, a threat of greater magnitude than Israel.[15]

There is an obvious parallel between this student and worker movement, trying to drive Sadat to self-destruction against Israel, and the 1936 movement in China which forced Chiang Kai-shek to "unite" with the communists against Japan. The difference is, of course, that events in 1973 did not have the intended effect; regionally the Arab regimes were strengthened, and globally the Warsaw Pact gained strength alarmingly in relation to NATO. As a result, Peking now projects another picture of events of the last 12 years, as if there was complete unity between the PLO guerrillas and Arab states: the struggle to recover Palestine is said to be "inseparable from the struggle of the Arab countries to recover their lost territories. *Co-ordinating closely with each other*, the two armed forces pounded the enemy . . ."[16]

Just as in 1972, when Peking began to urge the Third World that it was "not only necessary but compulsory" for them to support the putative struggle of the Second World of middle-sized developed powers against the super-powers, now perhaps the PLO is being urged to support Arab kings and officialdom—its former targets. As the "support" in the first instance was meant to be of a Leninist type, in the sense of driving wedges between the medium and super-powers, as happened with the oil embargo, so perhaps it will be in the latter case. At the moment, however, Peking's emphasis in the PLO's area of operation is to "unite" all possible forces under the slogan of defending national independence and sovereignty.

These were the themes stressed at a ceremony in May 1977, at which China handed over two patrol gunboats, the *Amilcar* and *Gafsa*, to the Tunisian navy.[17] It is worth noting that China has built a drydock and wharf in Malta;[18] but the high spot of its Mediterranean policy, which lies outside the scope of this essay, was its *rapprochement* with Yugoslavia and estrangement from Albania, culminating in

Tito's visit to Peking in September 1977. This policy is a modern form of the "soft underbelly" approach to Europe which originally brought Britain to Gibraltar and Malta.[19]

The same geo-political concept, on a larger scale, is exemplified by the activities of the super-powers and of China in the Indian Ocean region, the underbelly of the Asian heartland in which China and the USSR confront each other. Much Western comment on Indian Ocean affairs has been obsessed with naval matters; but Peking has shown itself to be aware of the dialectic link between naval/military expansion and establishment *on land* of the modern equivalent of a Gibraltar—a territory under Soviet economic, political and ideological influence which affords facilities for transit and calls by warships and military aircraft. Berbera, Aden and the diplomatic infrastructure of their military utility (Soviet aid, arms etc) were prime examples. Though China's direct influence in the Indian Ocean can only be marginal, its successful construction of the Tanzania-Zambia railway and other continuing links with guerrillas as well as governments give it some indirect influence. The normalization of diplomatic relations with India in April 1977 was an important step, but consolidation of the existing ties with Pakistan, Iran and the Gulf states was more immediately relevant to the anti-Soviet united front work. Peking has apparently let the PFLOAG insurgents wither, while courting the Shah, whose troops helped Sultan Qābūs of Oman defeat them, as well as Kuwait which helps to finance the PLO. It should be noted that at the end of 1976, Foreign Minister Huang Hua received a delegation of al-Fath led by Hamdan Abd al-Kader, and at the end of June 1977 another delegation led by Abū Jihād met him and other officials again. As a result, *Agence France-Presse* reported that Peking undertook to increase arms supplies to the PLO.[20] One reason for this would be to minimize dependence on aid from Russia and its proxies, such as Cuba.

Relations with the Gulf states were mainly confined to examples of "united front work" in the cultural and economic spheres, and people-to-people diplomacy or lower-level "mass work" with the usual categories of opinion-leading groups such as journalists, educationists, local government officials and sportsmen. At government level, Peking's Foreign Minister was in Tehran in November 1976, while Kuwait's Foreign Minister, Shaykh Sabāh al-Ahmad al-Jābir, led a delegation to Peking in May 1977. The occasion was used by Peking to call for more unity against "super-power intervention" in the Gulf as well as in the Red Sea area.

At the end of November 1976, Peking held an exhibition in Bahrayn; a long-term trade and payments agreement (to December 1980) and a trade protocol from 1977 were concluded with Egypt on 21 March 1977. In May, letters on trade were signed with Iraq in Baghdad, and in June with Morocco in Rabat. In addition to the ETCAs with Sudan and YAR already mentioned, Peking publicized the activities of its road builders and its geologists in finding chromite in the Ingessana mountains in Sudan. Medical teams were active in Sudan and YAR on the same goodwill-building mission as they fulfil in the national-minority areas of China, as often depicted in Chinese media and drama. A Sinkiang theatre troupe visited Kuwait in preparation for the visit of Ulanfu and his NPC delegation (in the same way that a Yugoslav folk ensemble visited Peking in preparation for Tito's visit). It also went to Baghdad, where China agreed to build a sports hall in November 1976. A radio and television delegation visited Iran; education personnel from Kuwait saw Ulanfu in Peking, and so on. Although Ulanfu, a Mongol, is a Vice-Premier and member of the Political Bureau of the Party, he appears to have taken over the top-level "united front work" which used to be done by Burhan Shahidi (Pao Erh-han), who was purged in the prelude to the Cultural Revolution.

It is hard to evaluate to what extent all this Chinese "united front" role-playing can be likened to the gesticulations of a superfluous conductor, who pretends that he is making a chorus sing what it would sing anyway. The economic side has seen some real Chinese success in spite of the recession caused by 1976 disorders. Under its ETCA, Egypt will import $17m worth of goods from China as part of a $114m deal—$14m more than under the previous year's agreement; Egypt will export $57m.[21]

But, to keep all of this in perspective, we must remember that Taiwan (the "Far Eastern Israel") raised the volume of its two-way trade with the Middle East to $1,210m in the first eight months of 1977. The big gap in the ranks of China's friends in Saudi Arabia—which was visited in July by President Yen Chia-kan of the Republic of China on Taiwan. The two countries have an agricultural co-operation agreement as well as an ETCA, and Taiwan ex-servicemen built a road from Hawiya to Mecca, as their communist cousins built one from San'ā to Hodeida.

NOTES

1. A New China News Agency (NCNA; or, in Chinese, Hsinhua) commentary explained that Africa is the flank of Europe; and that events in Zaïre and Angola were linked with the Red Sea, etc. NCNA, in Foreign Broadcast Information Service (FBIS), 23 May 1977, p. A19. Also see note 11 below.
2. *Peking Review (PR)*, No 35 (26 August 1977).
3. *Quotations from Chairman Mao Tse-tung* (Peking, 1968), p. 59. Also see W. A. C. Adie, "China and the *Détente*', *Lugano Review*, Vol 1 (1975).
4. Yeh in *PR*, No 32 (5 August 1977), pp. 8ff. Also, Su Yu in *PR*, No 34 (19 August 1977), pp. 8–9; see his article "Great Victory for Chairman Mao's Guidelines on War."
5. See "China's Strategic Posture in a Changing World", *Royal United Services Institute and Brassey's Defence Handbook* (London, 1974). *Chinese Strategic Thinking under Mao Tse-tung* (Australian National University Press, 1972). "Peking's Revolutionary Diplomatic Line", *Pacific Community* (Tokyo, April 1973).
6. "Propaganda Outline concerning the International Situation" (Political Dept, Kunming Military Region). Photostat and translation published as a paperback by Institute of International Relations, Taipei. First translation in *Issues and Studies* Vol 8, No 7, (Taipei, April 1972).
7. See, for example, the report on nationalization of oil by Qatar, *PR*, No 9 (25 February 1977), p. 28.
8. For basic documents on "People's War", see Lin Piao in *PR*, No 41 (1960). For the "Algebra of Revolution", see *PR*, No 46 (1960). For Li Tso-peng, see *PR*, Nos 15, 16 (1965), and *PR*, Nos 15, 20, 37–39, 50, 52 (1974).
9. See W. A. C. Adie, "Moscow and Peking in the Middle East: Peking's Revised Line", *Problems of Communism* (Washington, September/October 1972). "Arabs, Oil and Chinese History", *Asian Profile* (Hong Kong, August 1975).
10. See G. Hervouet, "China's Neighbours must Choose between Moscow and Peking", *International Perspectives*, (Ottawa, March/April 1976).
11. *New China News* (Australia), 14 September 1977, p. 13. See also *Al-Saḥāfa* (Sudan), cited in FBIS, 16 May 1977.
12. "Red Sea States Strengthen Unity", *PR*, No 14 (1 April 1977). See also *PR*, No 30 (22 July 1977), p. 25.
13. *PR*, No 24 (10 June 1977). Also, "Well Done the Sudanese People", *PR*, No 22 (27 May 1977), p. 28.
14. *Newsweek*, 16 May 1977.
15. Mehmood Hussein in *Economic and Political Weekly* (Bombay), Vol 8, No 45, pp. 2023–8.
16. *PR*, No 6 (4 February 1977), p. 31.
17. Tunis Home Service in Arabic, 2 May; cited in FBIS, 3 May 1977, p. A17.
18. US Consulate General in Hong Kong, *Summary of Chinese Press (SCP)*, No 6335, p. 45.
19. See Ference A. Váli, *Politics of the Indian Ocean Region* (New York: Free Press, 1976).
20. Agence France Presse, quoted in FBIS, 30 June 1977.
21. *Egyptian Gazette*, 7 April 1977.

The European Community and the Middle East

R. K. RAMAZANI

Major new developments in the relations of the European Community and the Middle East were witnessed during 1977. These developments—political and economic—took place in both bilateral and multilateral contexts. At the bilateral level, they concerned mainly the relations of the European Community with the Mashreq countries, including Egypt, Syria, Jordan and Lebanon. They also involved the relations of the Community with Israel. In comparison with these two sets of relationships, no significant development occurred in the relations of the Community with Iran and Turkey. At the multilateral level, new developments took place in the context of the Euro-Arab dialogue (formally including the European Community and the Arab League) on the one hand, and within the framework of the North-South dialogue (officially known as the Conference on International Economic Co-operation or CIEC) on the other.

EUROPEAN COMMUNITY, MASHREQ AND ISRAEL

The European Community perceived the conclusion of agreements with Egypt, Syria, Jordan and Lebanon (the Mashreq, or the Arab East) in 1977 as: 1) a logical follow-up of its agreements with Tunisia, Morocco and Algeria (the Maghrib, or the Arab West) in 1976,[1] 2) a further development in its "global" Mediterranean policy, and 3) an "important contribution" to its dialogue with the Arab countries. The agreements with the first three countries were signed on 18 January 1977. Although their terms in general resembled one another significantly, each marked a new development against the background of a different kind of past relationship.

The agreement with Egypt was signed in the wake of nearly a decade of slow development in EEC-Egyptian relations. From the inception of the Community until after the Arab-Israeli war of 1967, Egypt had, on the whole, adopted a rather negative attitude toward the EEC—largely because of the latter's emerging good relations with Israel.[2] The Egyptian exploratory talks with the Community that finally began in 1969 led to the 1972 trade agreement between the parties. The experiment, however, proved unsatisfactory in subsequent years partly because of the decline of Egyptian exports to the EEC and the increase in Egyptian trade deficits despite tariff concessions. The 1977 agreement is much broader than the previous one. It covers all areas of economic co-operation except labour, rather than simply trade. Furthermore, the new agreement, unlike its predecessor, is for an unlimited period.[3]

The agreement with Syria is the first "global agreement" between the two parties. Syria, as compared with Egypt, had not concluded a preferential trade agreement with the Community previously because its main exports, oil and cotton, entered the Community market duty-free. The EEC's new Mediterranean policy envisaged technical and financial co-operation. Despite this, the European Commission had no mandate at first to negotiate terms other than those for trade. After September 1976, however, the mandate of the Commission was extended to include financial aid discussions. As a result, the new agreement with Syria was also signed on 18 January 1977.

The agreement with Jordan marked "the start of privileged relationship" with the European Community. As with Syria, it was the first agreement between the two sides, although as early as 1972 Jordan had sought to open negotiations with the Community for a preferential trade agreement. Again, as in the case of Syria, the initial mandate of the Commission did not extend to negotiations with Jordan for financial aid. It was extended only subsequently to cover aid as well as trade. And, as with Egypt and Syria, the Jordanian agreement was also for an unlimited period.[4]

The last Mashreq country to sign an agreement with the EEC in 1977 was Lebanon, although originally it had been the first Arab state in the region to sign an agreement with the Community. As early as 1962, Lebanon had taken the initiative to open negotiations for a preferential trade agreement with the EEC. In fact, however, it only achieved a non-preferential trade and technical co-operation agreement, signed in 1965. This agreement proved unsatisfactory to Lebanon in terms of technical co-operation as well as trade. Although Lebanon finally succeeded in concluding a preferential agreement in 1972, the simultaneous emergence of the Community's global Mediterranean policy introduced a new dimension (economic and technical aid as well as trade) into the subsequent negotiations with Lebanon as it did with the other Arab states. In the Lebanese case, however, the civil war caused some delay in the conclusion of a "global agreement" which was not signed until 3 May 1977.[5]

Generally, the terms of the four EEC agreements with the Mashreq countries concern economic, technical and financial co-operation as well as trade. To consider the latter first, the Arab world takes 13% of the EEC's exports, and is now the Community's main trading partner. Against these facts, it is easier to recognize the significance of the commercial terms of the new agreements. They provide for a 100% tariff cut on non-agricultural exports to the Community from the Mashreq countries as of 1 July 1977, although they maintain ceilings on exports of certain products until the end of that year. On agricultural exports (which are of the greatest concern to the Mashreq countries), however, the Community was not so generous—it granted tariff concessions ranging between 40 and 80%.

The economic, technical and financial co-operation provided for under the agreements will complement the efforts to be made by the Mashreq countries within the framework of their own economic development plans and programmes. Special emphasis is placed on regional co-operation and the implementation of integrated schemes, i.e. those which combine several types of co-operation such as training, investment and trade promotion. Although the agreements are for an unlimited period, they include a financial protocol which runs only until October 1981. Over that period, three types of aid (including European Investment Bank loans, grants and loans on "special terms") will be given to the Mashreq countries. Egypt will receive the bulk of the 300m units of account (UA) total—approximately $333.3m—that is earmarked for the four countries. Egypt's share of UA 170m is followed by Syria's UA 60m, Jordan's UA40m, and Lebanon's UA 30m. EIB loans are normally combined with an interest rate subsidy of 2% financed out of grant aid funds. The "special term" loans are given for a period of 40 years and carry an interest rate of only 1%, with a grace period of 10 years.[6]

Given the extent of the financial needs of the Mashreq countries, the Community admits the inadequacy of its aid to them. Lebanon, in particular, registered its dissatisfaction at the outset. It considered the UA 30m "only as a first step" in meeting the country's enormous reconstruction needs. The Lebanese government estimated total damage during the 19-month civil war at $2.5 billion. The Lebanese negotiators made a strong plea for extra Community aid of UA 100m, in addition to the 30m set aside for technical and financial co-operation under the agreement.[7]

Between January and May 1977, the Community also signed an "additional protocol" and a "financial protocol" with Israel. As early as the summer of 1957—even before the Treaty of Rome had come into effective operation—the Israeli government had sought discussions with the Common Market. Israel first signed only a simple trade agreement with the Community in 1964. Subsequently it sought an "Agreement of Association"; after prolonged negotiations it succeeded in signing a five-year preferential trading agreement with the Community in 1970. The agreement on trade and co-operation signed with Israel in 1975 (which came into operation in 1976) was the first specific embodiment of the Community's new "global Mediterranean policy."[8] The "additional" and "financial" protocols of 8 February 1977, therefore, complemented the basic 1975 agreement. Although the financial amounts for Israel and Lebanon are the same—UA 30m—the types of aid are different. Israel's will be provided only in the form of EIB loans, whereas the Lebanese funds will consist of grants (8m) and "special term" loans (2m), as well as EIB loans (20m).

The Community funds for Egypt, Syria and Jordan also differ from Israel's in terms of the types of aid as well as the amounts involved. The Lebanese, Egyptian, Syrian and Jordanian funds will be a mixture of grants and special term loans as well as EIB loans; the Israeli funds will consist of EIB loans only.

The Community's rhetoric of a "global and balanced" Mediterranean policy did not spare it from both Arab and Israeli complaints. The Arab League protested against the Community's agreement with Israel, and the Israelis used the occasion of the signing ceremony in Brussels to complain that their "agreement was less generous than those the EEC had negotiated with Arab countries."[9]

THE EURO-ARAB DIALOGUE

New developments in the relations of the European Community and the Middle East in 1977 also took place in the context of the Euro-Arab dialogue, and specifically within the framework of discussions between the Arab League and the EEC. The Community authorities claimed repeatedly that the Euro-Arab talks added a "new dimension" to the *already existing* relations of the Community with the Arab states. To be sure, in most instances the Community's relations with the Mashreq states pre-dated the 1973 Arab-Israeli war; but the important fact remains that the nature and scope of these relations changed significantly, primarily as the result of the agreements signed *after* the October war.

Furthermore, the Euro-Arab dialogue was prompted by that war, the Arab oil embargo and the explosion of oil prices. Hence, the Euro-Arab dialogue has done more than simply add a new dimension to the already existing relations of the Community and the Arab states. It has, in fact, transformed them from largely short-term trade relations to long-term economic and technical co-operation as well as expanded trade relations. The Community's new and widened commercial, technical, economic and financial co-operation with the Mediterranean states aims fundamentally at a twofold objective. First, it is to deter the imposition of a new Arab oil embargo. Second, it is to extend European influence in the Mediterranean basin, in part to ensure the safety of oil supplies. The Arab states' bilateral as well as multilateral ties with the EEC aim basically at exerting pressure on Israel and the US through the Community, although these ties are designed to serve their economic, financial and technical interests as well. Finally, granted the immense importance of economic considerations in Israeli policy toward the Community, Israel also seeks to counter Arab political pressure and influence through the extension of its own economic, financial, and technical ties with the EEC.

Within the context of this triangular game of power and influence, the Arab states scored a new gain in 1977. Initial Community support for the Arab states was signalled by the Declaration of 6 November 1973 in the wake of the October war and amidst the Arab oil embargo. The Nine Foreign Ministers recalled "the ties of all kinds which had long linked them to the littoral states of the south and east of the Mediterranean"; but, in fact, the invocation of these ties at that particular time was meant to draw the Community closer to the Arab position on the conflict with Israel. On the basis of this Declaration, the Italian representative told the UN Security Council in December 1973 that the search for a settlement should be guided by the inextricable principles of 1) inadmissability of the acquisition of territory by force; 2) the need for Israel to end the territorial occupation since the 1967 conflict; 3) respect for the sovereignty, territorial integrity and independence of all states in the region, including Israel, and its right to live in peace within secure and recognized boundaries; and 4) recognition of the right of the Palestinian people to the expression of their national identity. Despite the proclamation of these principles and the willingness of the Nine to contribute to an international system of guarantees in any peace settlement, the Community clearly did not consider the Euro-Arab dialogue as the appropriate framework for peace negotiations and settlement in the Middle East.[10]

The dialogue was beset by economic as well as political differences from the outset. Politically, for example, in 1975 at Cairo the two sides were at loggerheads over the participation of the PLO in their plenary session, although the Community finally agreed to it within the context of a larger Arab delegation. The two sides declared jointly that "the Euro-Arab dialogue is the product of a joint political will that emerged at the highest level, with a view to establishing a special relationship between the two groups."[11] Economically, the issue of financing joint projects has proved a major stumbling block throughout the Euro-Arab dialogue. But the single most important difference between the two sides has stemmed from the Community's emphasis on economic co-operation, and conversely the Arab states' desire to establish a broad political framework for their relations with the Community. While this divergency has continued at the official level, unofficially the positions of the two sides have drawn closer together. The first unofficial Euro-Arab conference was held in Florence in April 1977. It placed the Arab-Israeli conflict squarely at the centre of the stage. According to Sir Harold Beeley, former British ambassador in Cairo, on the analysis of the conflict and the measures necessary for its solution "there was almost total agreement" between the two sides.[12] In retrospect, this unprecedented degree of consensus at the unofficial level was somewhat reflected in the most recent official pronouncement on the Arab-Israeli conflict.

On 29 June 1977, the EEC heads of government issued a new statement on the Arab-Israeli conflict during their summit meeting in London. Given the "comprehensive" approach of the Carter Administration on Middle East peace in general and the President's own concept of a "Palestinian homeland" in particular, there is little doubt that the EEC took heart from the increasingly favourable American attitude toward the Arab states in issuing the new statement. Stripped of all the details, it went beyond the 6 November 1973 declaration. It stated that in "the establishment of a just and lasting peace, account must be taken of the legitimate rights of the Palestinians." It also declared that a solution to the conflict will be possible "only if the legitimate right of the Palestinian people to give effective expression to its national identity is translated into fact", meaning—"a homeland for the Palestinian people." While the Arab states were not totally satisfied with the statement, they clearly favoured it. On the other hand, from the

"Israeli point of view, this document is detrimental to what it regards as vital interests. It is far-reaching in that it demands a combination of an Israeli withdrawal from the territories, the setting up of a Palestinian homeland, and Palestinian representation in any new peace negotiations. In this respect, the statement reflects the French pro-Arab line rather than the more balanced attitude of the Netherlands and the Federal Republic of Germany."[13]

A significantly tougher attitude by the Arab governments towards the EEC was announced on 26 October 1977 by Gaher Radwān, the Saudi ambassador to Brussels who headed the Arab League delegation attending the third meeting of the general committee of the Euro-Arab dialogue. While acknowledging that the June 1977 statement by the EEC summit represented "remarkable progress," he added that it was "high time the Nine translated their fine words into deeds." The League's demand was that the EEC should suspend economic and military aid to Israel, and should use its "material means and moral influence" to apply pressure on Israel "to end the illegal and inhuman measures it is taking in the occupied Arab territories."[14] He also pressed for recognition of the PLO as the sole legitimate representative of the Palestinian people. Ambassador Radwān's speech clearly signified a much more determined line by the Arab League in getting the Nine to shift not just towards a more pro-Arab position, but to adopt a clearer anti-Israeli policy. In the absence of a settlement in the Middle East, the Euro-Arab dialogue will predictably become sharper in 1978.

THE NORTH-SOUTH DIALOGUE

New developments in relations between the European Community and the Middle East during 1977 also took place within the context of the North-South dialogue. The upshot of these developments was the formal conclusion of the 18-month Conference on International Economic Co-operation (CIEC) on 3 June 1977. The Arab-Israeli war of October 1973, the Arab oil embargo and the explosion of oil prices lay at the base of the North-South dialogue as well as of the Euro-Arab dialogue. The Arab states effectively linked their oil embargo to the conflict with Israel. In turn, former Secretary of State Henry Kissinger linked peacemaking efforts to the lifting of the embargo, despite his "no linkage" rhetoric.[15] He also aimed at combatting the OPEC oil price policy through US sponsorship of the International Energy Agency (IEA), even while speaking of "interdependence" and "co-operation" with the oil-producing nations. The American-French differences that first surfaced at the Washington conference in February 1974 continued into 1975, with Third World countries taking heart from the trans-Atlantic squabbles. OPEC's successful oil price policy acted as a catalyst for Third World self-assertion. Algeria persuaded other OPEC members that the energy dialogue demanded by the industrialized world must be linked to Third World problems. The hawkish Kissinger-Simon-Enders triumvirate finally accepted the European view that such a linkage was inevitable. The North-South dialogue that ended in early June 1977 had thus begun in December 1975.

Energy, that had been the *raison d'être* for the dialogue, was also the cornerstone of its failure after 18 months of complex and, at times, volatile negotiations. The fundamental reason for the conference's failure to arrive at an agreement on a permanent dialogue on oil price and supply was the determination of most OPEC countries to retain the newly-acquired national control of oil price and production levels. The bid of the non-communist industrialized countries to moderate that control by means of permanent consultations between producers and consumers was, perhaps, a non-starter. Saudi Arabia and Iran, the two largest oil producers in OPEC, were reported to have agreed at the outset to an American proposal to include a commitment to permanent consultations on energy in the conference's final communique; but violent opposition to the proposal from Iraq, Venezuela and to a lesser extent Algeria, produced a deadlock on the energy issue.[16]

The deadlock on energy, however, did not doom the dialogue. Nor did the relative success on other issues usher in a "new economic order." The position of the new US Administration differed significantly, in both style and substance, from that of its predecessor. Secretary of State Cyrus Vance's manifestations of goodwill at the conference echoed the importance President Carter has attached in his foreign policy statements to new American efforts to help the Third World. As contrasted with Kissinger's confrontation tactics, belying his co-operation rhetoric, Secretary Vance's more sympathetic approach to the problems of the Third World had an undeniable appeal. Substantively, too, the Carter Administration's position proved more appealing to Third World leaders than that of the Republicans because it seemed more forthcoming on issues of greatest concern to the developing nations.

The US promised \$375m out of the \$1 bn "special action" aid pledged by the industrialized nations. The EEC shouldered much of this aid pledge with a \$385m contribution. Japan agreed to double the assistance it gives poor countries over the next five years, and Canada offered to write off \$254m in loans made to poor countries in Africa and Asia. The US aid pledge, however, was made contingent on the observance of high standards of efficiency in its utilization. "President Carter will seek from the Congress a substantial increase in the volume of our bilateral and multilateral aid programmes over the coming five years", Secretary Vance declared, "but we will also demand that this aid be more effectively planned, delivered, and administered."[17] The developing countries were not overjoyed by this gesture of the rich nations—\$1 bn represents less than one year's debt servicing for the poorest Third World countries. Nevertheless, they welcomed it without too much complaint.

The rich countries' commitment to a common fund for raw materials did not represent a change in the position of the Common Market countries so much as in that of the US. The Republican Administration had been suspicious of any steps to regulate primary product markets. But the Carter Administration joined the European states in an understanding with the developing countries that the common fund would finance the stabilization of raw material prices through new commodity agreements. Although this kind of arrangement might help assure developing nations of regular export earnings, the Third World nations were disappointed over the failure to earmark any specific amount for the fund. According to some Western estimates, the operation of the fund could eventually reach \$1 bn, but the estimate of the South might reach as high as \$6 bn. Identification of the commodities that will be covered is to be negotiated through the UN Conference on Trade and Development (UNCTAD) in Geneva in November 1977.

Despite strong pressure from the 19 developing nations, no agreement was reached on declaring a general debt moratorium for the Third World. They had insisted on tying this problem to progress in the other key areas of energy, finance and development aid. Their debts total \$200 bn, but they demanded a moratorium on repayments of the very poorest countries, estimated at close to \$40 bn, and rescheduling of debts incurred by others. Furthermore, they demanded a pledge by all the rich countries to increase their aid to seven-tenths of 1% of their wealth as recommended by the UN. The failure to agree on the debt issues, however, was not regarded in a totally negative vein by all concerned. The *Economist*, for example, commented: "The fact that the two sides agreed to disagree was, in itself, a welcome result for the industrial nations."[18]

The good news about the key issue of oil, however, came from outside the conference in 1977. In December 1976, disagreement arose within OPEC when 11 of its members voted in Qatar to increase oil prices by 10% on 1 January 1977 and by a further 5% on 1 July in the same year. Saudi Arabia and the United Arab Emirates—the other two members of OPEC—agreed to increase prices in 1977 by only 5%. The disarray that this unprecedented degree of disagreement created within the ranks of OPEC members—most particularly the Riyadh-Tehran antagonism—was regarded prematurely by certain circles in the industrialized world as the spectre of the collapse of the organization and a source of possible relief from high oil prices.

The really good news for the industrial nations, however, came in the wake of the resolution of differences within OPEC. On 29 June 1977, the organization moved decisively to end six months of acrimony and dissension by announcing that nine of its members would cancel a 5% oil-price increase scheduled for 1 July in an effort to achieve internal unity. Saudi Arabia and the United Arab Emirates agreed later to increase their oil prices by 5% to bring them into line with other OPEC countries, but there was no announcement from Libya. OPEC's new show of unity and self-restraint raised fresh speculation about oil prices in the near future. On the one hand, some energy experts believe that OPEC will have difficulty in raising prices any faster than the general level of inflation during the next few years. This is because of the likelihood of a temporary oil glut as new discoveries in the North Sea and Alaska come on the market. On the other hand, recent studies by the OECD, the CIA and others suggest that by 1985, if present consumption trends continue, world demand could reach 45m barrels a day against a total OPEC output of 35m barrels.[19]

IMPLICATIONS FOR IRAN AND TURKEY

The full implications for Iran and Turkey of the progress made during 1977 in the European Community's relations with the Mashreq countries and with Israel remain to be seen. But, clearly, Tehran and Ankara will watch with close concern the nature and extent of the new commercial, economic and technical relations between the Community, the Mashreq countries and Israel. In December 1973, Iran refused to ask for the renewal of its 1963 agreement with the Community. Instead it subsequently asked for a new agreement that would eliminate all discrimination against Iranian goods and provide free access to Community markets for its future *industrial products.*[20] This would amount to treatment similar to that accorded the Mashreq countries under the Community's Mediterranean policy. Although the Community's interest in Iranian oil and gas supplies undergirds its determination to continue negotiations with Tehran, little progress toward the conclusion of a new agreement was made in 1977.

As an associate member of the EEC, Turkey was concerned with the prospects of the enlargement of the Community if Greece acquired membership before Turkey. Furthermore, it was feared that the candidacy of Portugal and possibly Spain for membership in the Community might adversely affect Turkish interests. This concern was in addition to a multitude of complaints regarding trade, aid and the movement of labour that plague Turkish association with the Community.[21] In contrast, Greek-Community relations seemed promising.[22] Finally, domestic political, economic and social malaise in Turkey, not to mention its continuing differences with Greece over the Cyprus and Aegean issues, detracted from the prospects for Turkish membership in the Community.

DEVELOPMENT OF THE EEC'S TRADE BALANCE WITH THE NON-MEDITERRANEAN MIDDLE EAST (IN MILLIONS UA)

	EEC	*FRG*	*France*	*Italy*	*Neth*	*Bel/Lux*	*UK*	*Ireland*	*Den*
Iraq									
1973	-779	-11	-322	-446	+7	-4	-9	—	+6
1974	-1,756	+50	-818	-856	+13	+10	-155	-1	+1
1975	-915	+698	-542	-1,071	-57	-20	+44	-7	+40
1976	-1,395	+583	-895	-877	-39	-3	-220	+2	+54
Iran									
1973	-965	+60	-88	-255	-364	-74	-163	-20	-61
1974	-4,366	-82	-361	-672	-2,280	-178	-508	-38	-247
1975	-2,335	+485	-501	-431	-998	-158	-529	-38	-165
1976	-3,213	+242	-622	-393	-1,110	-211	-949	-41	-129
Saudi Arabia									
1973	-3,451	-477	-600	-752	-653	-254	-633	-16	-66
1974	-9,536	-1,404	-2,318	-2,329	-229	-927	-2,196	-75	-58
1975	-7,209	-801	-2,148	-1,537	-729	-705	-1,161	-43	-85
1976	-7,766	-474	-2,958	-1,467	-1,031	-967	-804	-26	-39
Kuwait									
1973	-1.525	-41	-282	-234	-369	-89	-477	-16	-17
1974	-2,567	-156	-697	-330	-62	-244	-991	-42	-45
1975	-1,817	-17	-415	-183	-332	-155	-624	-53	-38
1976	-1,354	+95	-146	-23	-445	-55	-734	-24	-22
Bahrayn									
1973	+42	+7	+3	+5	+4	+3	+20	—	—
1974	+40	+8	+2	+9	+4	+2	+29	—	-14
1975	+126	+21	+4	+17	+5	+2	+79	—	-2
1976	+192	+40	+22	+9	+11	+5	+98	+1	+6
Qatar									
1973	-335	-11	-71	-50	-130	-5	-67	—	-1
1974	-737	-58	-203	-157	—	-23	-269	—	27
1975	-510	-59	-149	-79	-41	-4	-173	—	-5
1976	-822	-44	-231	-94	-163	-26	-243	+1	-22
UAE									
1973	-559	-173	-248	-34	-61	+8	-56	—	+5
1974	-1,701	-530	-888	-57	-35	+15	-199	+1	-8
1975	-1,643	-455	-758	-86	-296	-12	-40	+1	+3
1976	-1,559	-360	-818	-85	-382	-64	+157	+6	-13
Oman									
1973	-33	+6	-36	+4	-1	-7	+15	—	-14
1974	-164	+25	-101	-56	+14	-38	+20	—	-28
1975	-60	+60	-51	+17	+5	-34	-25	+1	-33
1976	-70	-5	-39	+6	-35	—	+41	—	-38
North Yemen									
1973	+33	+7	+9	+2	+5	+1	+7	—	+2
1974	+36	+10	+6	+3	+5	+1	+8	—	+3
1975	+57	+13	+13	+6	+6	+2	+15	—	+2
1976	+106	+30	+20	+11	+10	+4	+26	—	+5
South Yemen									
1973	+7	+3	+2	+3	—	-1	+3	-3	—
1974	+11	+5	+3	+2	+5	-1	-4	—	+1
1975	+23	+2	+2	+3	+4	+1	+7	—	+4
1976	+54	+4	+8	+6	+10	+4	+17	—	+5
Total									
1973	-7,565	-630	-1,633	-1,757	-1,562	-422	-1,360	-55	-146
1974	-20,740	-2,132	-5,375	-4,443	-2,565	-1,383	-4,265	-153	-424
1975	-14,183	-53	-4,545	-3,345	-2,432	-1,083	-2,307	-139	-279
1976	-15,827	+101	-5,659	-2,907	-3,174	-1,313	-2,611	-81	-193
Indices									
1973	-100	-100	-100	-100	-100	-100	-100	-100	-100
1974	-274	-337	-329	-252	-164	-328	-347	-278	-280
1975	-187	-8	-278	-191	-156	-256	-170	-253	-191
1976	-209	+16	-347	-161	-223	-311	-192	-147	-132

Source: Marchés tropicaux, 9 September 1977.

NOTES

1. See *Bulletin EC*, 1-1976, pp. 13-16.
2. R. K. Ramazani, *The Middle East and the European Common Market* (Charlottesville: University Press of Virginia, 1964), pp. 85-100.
3. Commission of the European Communities, *Information: EEC-Egypt* 142/77E.
4. *Information: EEC-Syria,* 143/77E; *EEC-Jordan,* 114/77E.
5. *Information: EEC-Lebanon,* 147/77E
6. *Middle East Economic Digest (MEED)*, 25 February 1977, p. 7.
7. Bureau d'Information Européennes, *Fortnightly Economic Information Eruope, Mediterranean Area,* No. 31, 11 July 1977.
8. *Information: Israel and the EEC*, 145/77E.
9. *Events,* 11 March 1977, p. 34.
10. *Bulletin EC*, 5-1976, pp. 6-12.
11. Alan R. Taylor, "Europe and the Arabs: How to Bridge the Gap", *Middle East International (MEI)*, February 1977, pp. 11-12.
12. Sir Harold Beeley, "Extending the Euro-Arab Dialogue", *MEI*, June 1977, pp. 11-12.
13. *Middle East Intelligence Survey*, 1-15 July 1977, p. 53.
14. *The Times*, London; 27 October 1977.
15. R. K. Ramazani, *Beyond the Arab-Israeli Settlement: New Directions for US Policy in the Middle East* (Cambridge, Massachusetts: Institute for Foreign Policy Analysis, 1977).
16. *Washington Post*, 3 June 1977.
17. *Ibid*, 31 May 1977.
18. *Economist*, London; 4 June 1977, p. 97.
19. *New York Times*, 12 July 1977.
20. *Information: The European Community and Iran*, 97/75. For recent developments, see Karl Kaiser, "Iran and the Europe of the Nine: A Relationship of Growing Interdependence," *The World Today*, Vol 32, No 7 (July 1976), pp. 251-9.
21. For details see *MEED*, 15 October 1976, pp. 23-35. See also Gottfried E. Volker, "Turkish Labour Migration to Germany: Impact on Both Economies", *Middle Eastern Studies*, Vol 12, No 1 (January 1976), pp. 45-71. Also Tansu Ciller, "The Economics of Exporting Labour to the EEC: A Turkish Perspective", *Middle Eastern Studies*, Vol 12, No 3 (October 1976), pp. 173-85.
22. For a sympathetic perspective, see John Pesmazoglu, "Greece's Proposed Accession to the EEC", *The World Today*, Vol 32, No 4 (April 1976), pp. 142-51.

The Middle East and the Horn of Africa: International Politics in the Red Sea Area

COLIN LEGUM

The balance of power in the Red Sea area was decisively, perhaps even permanently, changed by the violent conflicts and changing alliance patterns in the Horn of Africa in 1976-7. While it is not possible at the time of writing (December 1977) to gauge the full extent, or even the ultimate direction, of these changes, it seems unlikely that the millenia-old *status quo* on the north-east African shores of the Red Sea can ever be restored.

Seven major questions remained in doubt at the end of 1977. First: can Ethiopia succeed in maintaining any semblance of its former territorial unity? Even more crucially, can it retain any of its three corridors to the Red Sea; or will it become a landlocked country confined to the high mountain plateaux? Second: can the Provisional Military Advisory Council (the Dergue) succeed in establishing its power as a Marxist-Leninist revolutionary regime even with heavy support from the USSR and Cuba? Third: can the Soviet Union succeed either in its major objective, to establish a *Pax Sovietica* over the Horn, or in its alternative of building a new area of influence within Ethiopia itself; or will it finally lose its position both in Somalia and in Ethiopia? Fourth: can Mogadishu succeed in advancing its Greater Somali ideal, or will it come to grief in the Ogaden? Fifth: can the new alliance of anti-Soviet Arab League members achieve their aim of turning the Red Sea into an "Arab lake," which depends on their ability to have the Soviets expelled from the area, and on the emergence of an independent Eritrea? Sixth: will the Western powers develop more effective policies to defend their conflicting interests in the area, i.e. in strengthening the anti-Soviet group of Arab states, without at the same time weakening Israel's security which depends on safe passage for her ships through the Red Sea? Seventh: will the Organization of African Unity (OAU) be able to overcome its internal divisions to enable it to perform, at the very least, a mediating role in the Horn?

With such large questions still in balance, the future of the Red Sea region remains shrouded in dangerous uncertainties. Meanwhile, it is more instructive to concentrate on disentangling the roots of the present violent conflict which has been building up inexorably for several decades at least.

The character of the international crisis in the Horn has been shaped by five major elements: local nationalisms; Arab, and specifically Islamic, interests; inter-African quarrels; USSR ambitions; and Western interests.

THE NATIONALIST FACTOR

Modern Ethiopia inherited two major problems from the long period of Abyssinian imperial expansion. The first was posed by a substantial Muslim minority, and the second by resistance to Amhara domination. Between 30–40% of all Ethiopians are Muslims who have, with varying degrees of intensity, resented the assertively Christian nature of the Ethiopian Kingdom. The Muslims comprise three major distinctive entities: the Eritreans (themselves a minority of possibly 40% among the Tigrinya-speaking inhabitants of their province); the Afars, mainly nomads spread across the Danakil plains, Wollo, the Awash valley as well as Djibouti; and the Somalis, who form a majority in the Ogaden, and at least substantial minorities in Bale, Sidamo and Arussi. These Muslim communities form a wide belt between the Red Sea and the Christian Highlands, thus controlling all the corridors to the sea. During the rule of the late Emperor Haile Selassie, the Eritreans and Somalis—though not the Afars (see below)—created independent-minded nationalist movements which, as a result of the Emperor's repressive policies, developed strong secessionist tendencies.

While not Arabs, but feeling discriminated against *qua* Muslims, these communities came to look to their Middle Eastern neighbours for support. The independence of the Somali Republic in 1960 also produced a new focal point of national loyalty for many Somalis in the Ogaden and Bale provinces of Ethiopia.

Thus two external factors—the Arabs and the Somali Republic—were drawn into the internal nationalist struggles which had increasingly troubled the latter period of Haile Selassie's rule.

The second and related problem of Amhara—or, more specifically, Shoan—domination of the imperial system was deeply resented by the non-Amhara peoples, mainly the Oromos (Gallas). They comprise at least half the population outside the Muslim belt, and were conquered only in the last stage of Amhara expansionism. The Oromos' sense of grievance at their inferior status in the Imperial system was powerfully reinforced by the loss of much of their land to the Shoan élite. Furthermore, the Tigreans—although themselves Amharas—also nursed old grievances over the loss of their former dominant position in the empire to the Shoans.

While Haile Selassie tried to pursue a policy of integrating the numerous national entities into his Imperial system, he nevertheless based his power essentially on Shoan domination. By the time he finally lost his throne in 1974, Ethiopia was already alive with regional and ethnic nationalist rivalries—spearheaded by the violent struggle which had broken out in Eritrea in 1962.

Nevertheless, except for the Eritreans and the Ogaden Somalis, the local nationalist movements were not motivated by any wish to break up the Ethiopian state: their aims were to diminish Amhara—and particularly central Shoan—domination and create a federal system of autonomous provinces. In so far as most of these ethnic or regional nationalisms did not wish to see the country balkanized, it can be said that they shared a sense of Ethiopian patriotism, sharpened by what the Christians especially felt as threats from the Arab world and from Somalia.

These powerful cross-currents of nationalism, both internal and around the periphery of Ethiopia, seriously weakened the power of the state after the Emperor's firm control was removed. His heirs, struggling against these fissiparous internal forces and external aggressions, sought to mobilize a new sense of national purpose by launching a modernizing revolution which rapidly fell into the hands of a Marxist-Leninist group within the Dergue. This development alienated the Addis Ababa regime from its Western friends (notably the US, Ethiopia's traditional supplier of arms), and led them to seek alliances with the Soviet bloc and Cuba.

In fact, however, the Dergue's Marxist revolutionary policy intensified the nationalist conflicts and significantly increased the level of international involvement in the region's affairs.

The process of internationalizing the conflicts in the Horn had, of course, begun much earlier with Arab involvement in Eritrea in the early 1960s, and by Somalia's decision in 1968 to secure Soviet military support for its Greater Somali ambition (see below).

THE ARAB AND ISLAMIC FACTOR

The rise of a Christian Kingdom in a predominantly Muslim part of the world had, over two millenia, produced tensions between Abyssinia/Ethiopia and its northern and western neighbours. The specifically Islamic threat reached its apogee with the narrow defeat of the famous Muslim warrior, Ahmad the Left-Handed in the 15th century; but Ethiopia's rulers—with the single exception of Haile Selassie's short-lived predecessor, Iyassu, during the period of the First World War—always saw Islam as a threat to their Christian polity. This was a major determinant of their suspicious policies towards their own Muslim populations.

Arab interests in the area were of two kinds: religious and geopolitical. Although the religious element was obviously more important during the earlier period of the spread of Islam, it persisted in varying degrees down the centuries and was activated when geopolitical considerations in the Red Sea area assumed new importance for the modern Arab world. Initially, though, there were conflicting interests in the Red Sea between the modern Arab nationalists and the Saudi Arabian traditionalists. The idea of converting the Red Sea into an "Arab lake" was first broached by 'Abd al-Nāsir's former confidant, Muhammad Haykal, as part of a strategy for strangling Israel's shipping. When this proposal was first made in the late 1950s, Nasserism was still seen as hostile to Saudi Arabian interests. It was only after Somalia had granted facilities to the Russian navy in Berbera that the Saudis made it part of their policy to convert the Red Sea into an "Arab sea." Both Ethiopia and Israel (who maintained close diplomatic and military ties until October 1973) saw this move as a threat to their national interests. After Sādāt's break with Moscow, there was a convergence of Arab interests in gaining effective control over the Red Sea. This interest was reflected in two parallel policies: a Saudi-led initiative within the Arab League to persuade Somalia to break with the Soviets; and support for the Eritrean liberation struggle. Since Massawa lies within the province of Eritrea, and Assab within the territory controlled by the Muslim Afars, the secession of these territories would effectively deprive Ethiopia of its two Red Sea ports.

The initiative for the Eritrean Liberation Front's rebellion in 1962 came from the territory's Muslim community. They turned naturally for support to their fellow-Muslims, who also opposed Haile Selassie's pro-Israel policies. Although the Islamic factor was opportunistically exploited to maximize Arab support, religion was never the major factor in the Eritrean struggle—and became decidedly less so after the majority Christian Eritrean community joined in the struggle for independence. Egypt was the first to support the ELF, and was soon followed by Syria, Iraq, South Yemen and Libya, and later also by Saudi Arabia and the other non-radical Arab states. Only the Sudan attempted to maintain a carefully neutral position, not wishing to encourage the secessionist tendencies of its own southern population.

Later, in 1975, when the Dergue severely repressed the Afars (who had rebelled against land nationalization policies), the prestigious Sultān 'Āli Mirreh went into exile in Riyadh, while his son set up the Afar Liberation Front headquarters in Mogadishu. The Dergue's short-sighted conflict with the Afars also weakened Ethiopia's political position in Djibouti, whose population comprises Afars and Issas, the latter a major clan of the Somalis.

Thus the Arab states came to give open support to the forces controlling all of Ethiopia's corridors to the sea.

After independence in July 1977, the new Djibouti Republic joined the Arab League, as the Somalis had done a few years previously, even though neither state is Arab. While the dominant members within the Arab League strongly opposed Somalia's ties with Moscow, they nevertheless gave broad support to its claims to the Ogaden.

Arab strategy in the Horn became more concerted and far more activist after April 1977 once it became clear that the Soviets had committed themselves to a dominant role throughout the area by supplying arms to Ethiopia as well as to Somalia.

THE FACTOR OF INTER-AFRICAN RIVALRIES

Like all regional organizations, the OAU and the Arab League both proved unable to deal effectively with this or any dispute in which their members were sharply divided. The Arab League was split into two camps: on the one side were Saudi Arabia, Egypt, Sudan, Somalia, North Yemen, Iraq, Syria, the Gulf States and the United Arab Emirates—all strongly opposed to the new Ethiopian regime; on the other side were Libya and South Yemen who supported the Dergue. There were also other divisions within the first camp since Saudi Arabia, Egypt and Sudan were prominently engaged in creating an anti-Soviet camp in the Middle East and Africa, while Iraq and Syria (though supporting the Somalis and Eritreans, and therefore very critical of Moscow's shift of policies in the Horn) remained strongly opposed to any sign of anti-Sovietism.

The OAU was no less sharply divided than the Arab League. Although Ethiopia had the open support of only one black African state—Kenya—opinion in the continent was largely hostile to the Somali and Eritrean aim of changing borders by force. The OAU's constitution upholds the borders that existed at the time of independence; these should be changed only through peaceful means, by mediation and arbitration. Neither secession—as proposed by the Eritreans—nor "annexation" of the Ogaden (even under the guise of a national liberation struggle) could hope to command majority support within the OAU. And since neither Ethiopia nor Somalia was willing to compromise on what each regarded as its proper national interest, the OAU was paralysed. Similarly, the Eritreans were totally opposed to any kind of federal deal with Addis Ababa. With their highly successful liberation struggle almost guaranteed of success (unless it can be crushed by massive Soviet military intervention), the chances of successful negotiations seem remote—unless, somehow, a political settlement can be reached covering the entire region.

Kenya's vigorous support of Ethiopia is explained by its own concern over Mogadishu's championing of the right of Somalis living in its Northern Frontier Province to self-determination.

Although Libya and South Yemen had in the past both strongly supported the Eritreans and the Somalis, they moved with the Soviets and Cubans to give support to the Addis Ababa regime in 1976 and 1977. At the same time, Sudan moved sharply away from its former position as mediator between the Eritreans and Ethiopians, and openly supported all the challengers of the Dergue—not only the Eritreans and Somalis, but also the Ethiopian Democratic Union, a broadly-based opposition front.

South Yemen's shift towards the Dergue was related to its close ties with Cuba and the Soviet bloc, and was clearly synchronized with their moves in Ethiopia. Libya's role, however, is much more complex. Although it is now the USSR's biggest military client after Iraq, Col Qadhdhāfī pursues his own idiosyncratic policies. Abandoning his commitment to the Muslim cause in Eritrea was almost certainly dictated by his preoccupation with fighting President Sādāt of Egypt and his close ally, President Numayrī of Sudan—two of the Dergue's leading opponents (see chapter on Libya). Qadhdhāfī's support for Numayrī's opponents—the National Front led by al-Sādiq al-Mahdī—is well-known. After the failure of the National Front's attempted coup in 1976, which was staged from Libya, their activities transferred to Ethiopia. There seems little doubt that Qadhdhāfī—himself a bitter opponent of the Dergue's Marxist-Leninist ideas—found himself in the Ethiopian camp primarily because it offered another opportunity to destabilize Numayrī's regime. Where the reconciliation between al-Mahdī and Numayrī in September 1977 leaves Qadhdhāfī remains uncertain (see chapter on Sudan).

THE SOVIET AND CUBAN FACTOR

Russian interests in the Red Sea area, and particularly in Ethiopia, go back to the time of Peter the Great (see China's Role below). These interests have always been dictated by the Russian navy's need for "blue water ports"—a need made more imperative by the rise of the Soviet Union as a world naval power. The importance of acquiring suitable naval facilities in the Mediterranean, Red Sea and Indian Ocean has been repeatedly stressed in the writings of Admiral of the Fleet, Sergei Gorshkov. The need for Red Sea facilities became much more urgent in the late 1950s and early 1960s in establishing a credible Soviet defence posture after the introduction of US nuclear submarines into that region. Even the minimal deployment of Soviet naval units in the Red Sea and Indian Ocean demanded refuelling and repair facilities in a number of ports; hence the great importance of establishing friendly relations with littoral countries around these seas—more especially after the loss of the Russian naval base at Alexandria.

It is therefore easy to see why Moscow should have responded so eagerly to a request from Somalia in 1967 to help it build up a modern 20,000-strong army. The Somali interest was purely national: if it was to accomplish its "national destiny" of "liberating" the Somalis still living outside their new homeland—it would need safeguards against possible attacks from its three neighbours—Ethiopia, Kenya and the then French-controlled Djibouti. As a *quid pro quo* for helping the Somalis, the Soviets obtained important naval facilities at Berbera. However, it is a most unsatisfactory port, having few natural advantages; besides, the Somalis with their Arab League connections and constantly under pressure from the Saudis—were unreliable allies. There is no doubt that the Somalis always put their pan-Somali nationalist interests above any ideological or other consideration.

Moscow's eyes were always fixed on Ethiopia—a potentially rich country with a dominating position in the continent and with much better ports. So long as Haile Selassie was on the throne and the US had a strong interest in the stability of his regime, there was little hope of the Soviets improving on Somalia. They had previously mishandled the opportunity to acquire facilities offered to them by another Red Sea State—Sudan—when they were expelled by President Numayrī in 1971 after an abortive Leftist coup. However, with Haile Selassie deposed in 1974 and a revolutionary situation developing in the country, the Soviets lost little time in showing their keen interest to help the young military regime. Their extreme anxiousness to engage Ethiopia's alliance was first shown in May 1976 when they reversed their previous stand on the Eritrean question by endorsing the Dergue's peace plan to reach a federal settlement with the ELF and EPLF.

This move upset the Somalis—but not nearly as badly as when they learnt of secret arms negotiations with the Dergue which had begun in Moscow in December 1976. The Soviets and Cubans both began to speak of their "revolutionary duty" to help ensure the success of Ethiopia's "progressive revolutionary forces." Meanwhile, in private, Soviet diplomats developed the following line of argument with the angry Somalis: once the US imperialists were out of Ethiopia, the cause of old divisions in the area would disappear; but to get the Americans out, Moscow had to agree to replace US arms supplies; with Soviet and Somali support, a Marxist-Leninist regime could be consolidated in Ethiopia; this would help ensure a Marxist-Leninist regime in Eritrea; and once the French left Djibouti, nothing would stand in the way of solving the area's "colonial-made" border problems. This was nothing less than a proposal to mastermind the achievement of Marxist states throughout the Horn—and, with the Soviets as the sole supplier of arms to all sides in the region, they would be in a dominant position to help influence the course of events. In this way (as they explained in Mogadishu but, presumably, not in Addis Ababa), pan-Somali aspirations could be met. In short, this was a proposal to establish a *Pax Sovietica* over the Horn of Africa.

The only fault with this imaginative plan was that it had no appeal for the Somalis. They simply did not read the "Ethiopian revolution" in the same way as the Russians: whereas Radio Moscow was drawing parallels between the post-imperial situation in Ethiopia with Russia in 1917, Somalia's President, Siyad Barreh, could only see Col Mengistu Haile Mariam's Dergue as "a pack of murderous fascists," and as "colonialists as bad as any of the old Ethiopian emperors." Siyad Barreh tried to lecture the Russians about Lenin's theory of national-liberation movements which, he said, was the "objective" Marxist analysis of developments in Ethiopia.

President Fidel Castro flew to Aden at the end of February 1977 to try his hand at promoting "revolutionary comradeship." The Somali leaders accepted an invitation from South Yemen to meet Castro in Aden early in March—only to denounce the Cuban leader's ideas for a confederation of Marxist-Leninist states in the Horn. Although the Somalis had themselves initiated the idea of a confederation, they could see no future in negotiating with the Dergue. After this stubborn Somali rejection of Soviet and Cuban proposals for a settlement, Moscow had to face a difficult decision in April 1977 when the US took the initiative to cut off arms supplies to the Dergue: should it abandon the Ethiopian revolution to its fate, or back it and risk losing Somalia as a valued ally? Was a Red Sea state in the hand worth two, or even three, in the wilderness? Moscow elected to back the Ethiopians while, at the same time, renewing its promise of continued military support to the Somalis. Thus, when the war in the Ogaden began to assume major proportions after July, Russian arms were being used by both sides. Instead of a *Pax Sovietica* there was a proxy *Bellum Sovietica*. In November, Somalia renounced its friendship treaty with the Soviets and ordered them to withdraw their 1,600 military advisers and equipment, and to leave Berbera as well.

Soviet policy-makers had a number of options in the Horn. It is not altogether clear why they made the choice they did. The easiest course for them would have been to assist the Somalis, Eritreans and Afars to exploit Ethiopia's weakness, thus producing a number of grateful allies who would be in control of all the Ethiopian ports and, possibly, Djibouti as well—prizes rich enough to satiate even Admiral of the Fleet Gorshkov's appetite for naval facilities. This easy option, however, would have created at least two difficulties for the Soviets: their active help in amputating Ethiopia's coastal provinces would have produced strong anti-Russian reaction over much of Africa; it would have strengthened the anti-Soviet front in the Arab League; and it would have left an embittered, truncated Ethiopia as a potential threat to the area's stability. On the other hand, the more difficult choice of moving up the mountain to Addis Ababa would not only alienate the Somalis and Eritreans (possibly permanently) and strengthen the anti-Soviet group in the Arab League; it also carried the risk that, even with massive Soviet aid, Col Mengistu Haile Mariam's Marxist-Leninist vanguard group might not be able to retain power or be capable of preventing Ethiopia's disintegration. At best it promised a long, hard struggle with a huge military and economic commitment. In calculating all these risks, it seems probable that Soviet strategists felt the Somalis would not actually carry out their threat to break with Moscow because of the "Marxist-Leninist loyalties" of the regime in Mogadishu and, perhaps more important, because they were unlikely to find Western replacements for Russian military aid.

There is always, of course, Moscow's official explanation: that the Soviets had no alternative but to fulfil their "international duty" to assist a "progressive revolutionary movement" in Ethiopia, which was under threat from "reactionaries and colonialists." Since the biggest threat came from Somalia, this explanation seemed to offer a rather harsh verdict on their recent Marxist-Leninist protégé.

Whatever explanation one chooses to believe, there can be no doubt at all about the importance attached by Moscow to Ethiopia. If it were otherwise, they would not have risked losing Somalia's friendship or have committed themselves so heavily in resources and in prestige to what can only be described as a risky gamble. The Russians clearly stand to lose heavily if it fails; but exactly what would they gain if it came off?

They cannot be sure that the Ethiopians (and so the Russian navy) would have access to either Massawa or Assab—and certainly not to Djibouti, whose present leadership is better disposed to Mogadishu than to Addis Ababa. Therefore, unless they can be sure of helping the Ethiopians to overcome the opposition of the Eritreans and Afars, they might end up losing the useful, if unsatisfactory, naval facility they had in Berbera. They could, of course, hope to help spread Ethiopia's revolution (if it were successful) to engulf Somalia and overthrow Siyad Barreh's regime: but this seems somewhat improbable.

The anti-Soviet group in the Arab League have their own views on Moscow's objectives in the Red Sea area; these are discussed below.

THE WESTERN FACTOR

The Western nations have traditionally regarded the Horn of Africa and the wider periphery of the Red Sea as their special "area of influence," and crucial to maintaining the world balance of power. Since the Red Sea littoral states dominate the maritime cross-roads between West and East and, especially, the oil routes for Saudi Arabia and the Gulf producers, it is obviously in the West's interest that the area should not be controlled by any hostile force capable of interrupting oil traffic in times of crisis, or disrupting it altogether in time of war. Yet, despite all these well-worn arguments, the major Western powers resisted all efforts to become involved in any major way in the Horn's unfolding crisis. For the first time since World War II, the Soviet Union was allowed a virtually free hand in an area of "traditional Western influence." The US itself led the initiative to cut off arms supplies to Addis Ababa—having given up hope of influencing the Dergue through military aid—and so reduced its role at a critical period. The French chose this time of crisis to grant independence to Djibouti, retaining only a small military presence—ostensibly to guarantee the republic's sovereignty. Notwithstanding Egyptian, Sudanese and Saudi pressures to sell arms to the Somalis (against Saudi payments) in order to expedite the expulsion of the Soviets, all the Western nations refused to do so. There was a brief moment of havering in July when the US, Britain and France agreed to supply small amounts of "defensive weapons" to Somalia; but even this offer was quickly rescinded when the scale of fighting grew in the Ogaden, and because of strong protests from Kenya.

Both camps in the Horn were comprised of antipathetic elements. On Ethiopia's side, Israel and anti-communist Kenya found themselves in league with the Soviets, Cubans, Libyans and South Yemenis. Despite embarassed denials from the Dergue, Israeli intelligence remained actively at work—with Ethiopian encouragement; and the Israeli navy ran missions to Massawa and Assab. However, the small Israeli military training mission to the Airborne Command and to the *Nebalbal* was finally withdrawn after the shoot-out inside the Dergue between the supporters of Col

Mengistu Haile Mariam and those of Major Sisay Habte in July 1976.

The line-up on the Somali side was similarly contradictory, with Iraq and Syria drawn up alongside Saudi Arabia, Egypt, Sudan and Iran. (The Iraqis—though now the largest recipients of Soviet military aid in the Third World—agreed to supply military spare parts to Somalia after the Russians began to default on deliveries; but because of this prominent Iraqi involvement, the Syrians showed themselves reluctant to pull their military weight in Mogadishu.)

Incongruously—although this was primarily an African quarrel—the black African states stayed clear, with the solitary exception of Kenya. China, too, refused to take sides—except against the Russians (see below).

The Western nations' role, or lack of it, in the Horn was relatively straightforward. Britain, France and Italy were the only European powers who had been prominent in the area in the past. Italy's importance ceased after leaving Somalia in 1960. Britain's role has shrunk steadily since the early 1960s when it decided to withdraw from East of Suez. What remains of its military presence is to be found in the Gulf states and in Kenya, with only a minor role in Sudan. France, pursuing its Gaullist policy of building up influence in the Arab world, was careful to avoid upsetting the Arabs while ready, when necessary, to accommodate their wishes. The US, reflecting the post-Vietnam mood, lived up to President Carter's promise not to get involved in Third World conflicts simply for the sake of opposing the Soviets.

In fact, the major Western priorities East of Suez were to consolidate military facilities in the Gulf, and to develop the Diego Garcia base in the southern Indian Ocean. The presence of American nuclear submarines in the area obviated much of the former need for land-based military and naval facilities. The West could afford to adopt a low profile in the Horn because its interests coincided with those of an influential coalition of Arab and African nations. Although this coalition acted as proxy for the West, it was motivated entirely by its own interests. While relying on this group, the Western powers did not think it expedient to deliver arms to the Somalis—not even through such respectable agents as Saudi Arabia, Iran, Egypt and Sudan.

Western inactivity was justified—or rationalized—largely on the premise that the Russians should be left to dig their own grave in the Horn. A more positive argument was that responsibility for ending the conflict should be left with the OAU and that its initiatives should be encouraged and supported.

But what if the Soviet strategy did *not* fail? Since Western policy-makers ruled out any prospect of success, they felt no need to answer this "hypothetical question." There was also the Israeli fear that the Arabs might succeed in achieving *their* objective of converting the Red Sea into an "Arab lake." The Western answer to this was that only a final settlement in the Middle East could effectively protect the safe passage of shipping through the Red Sea.

The anti-Soviet Arab League group was much less confident than the Western nations about the inevitability of Soviet defeat in the Horn. They were almost obsessively suspicious of Moscow's real aims. Their publicly stated view was that the Soviets were engaged in "recolonizing Africa" and in "building military bases." But through diplomatic channels, they sought to convey the following picture of Soviet objectives: first to get a strong hold over Ethiopia through helping to implant a communist regime there; second, to build on this a base for subversive "Marxist-Leninist" operations against Somalia and Sudan; third, with the help of Libya, to undermine President Sādāt's position in Egypt. For the longer term, they saw the Soviets engaged in pushing their "Marxist-Leninist conspiracies" from Ethiopia into Kenya, and from Sudan through Amin's Uganda into Zaire, to finally achieve an "international revolutionary front" link-up with Angola. In summary, the anti-communist Arab view was that Ethiopia could become a springboard for Russian domination over much of the continent and, of course, of the Red Sea littoral states—including Saudi Arabia. At the very least, they saw Ethiopia providing a revolutionary base to destabilize the whole of north-east Africa—unless the Russians could be stopped. Because of these fears, the anti-Soviet Arab group tried to persuade all the Arab states to adopt a collective policy; but attempts to arrange a summit of all Red Sea states met with little immediate success. (For details see essay on Inter-Arab Relations.)

CHINA'S ROLE

The Chinese chose to play no direct role in the developments in the Horn. They held a position of careful neutrality between Ethiopia and Somalia, and continued their technical aid programmes in both countries. Even when the Dergue embraced Moscow, Peking made no direct criticism. A Somali mission which went to Peking to seek help with replacing spare parts for Soviet military equipment was politely received, but it apparently came away without specific promises.

But if Peking's policy was to avoid direct criticism of Ethiopia's change of direction, its political message to Africa and the Middle East was typified by Radio Peking's commentary on "The Just Voice of the Red Sea countries" (25 February 1977):

> "The Red Sea, together with the Suez Canal, is a vital sea passage leading to the Atlantic, Indian and Pacific oceans and a strategic point linking Asia and Africa with Europe. Through the Suez Canal and the Red Sea, the Soviet Union's Black Sea-Mediterranean Sea Fleet is able to take joint actions with its Indian Ocean-Pacific Ocean Fleet, while the US can link up its Sixth Fleet, stationed in the Mediterranean, with its fleet cruising the Indian Ocean. Therefore, the Red Sea has turned out to be a key link in the global strategy of both super-powers—the Soviet Union and the US. The Soviet revisionists have long regarded the control of the Red Sea as an important link in its contention for world hegemony with the other super-powers. 'Water—this is what Russia needs,' Tsar Peter the First once said bluntly. 'Once Russia enters the Indian Ocean freely, it is able to establish its military and political rule over the whole world.' Today the new Tsars are trying their utmost to convert the old Tsar's dream into reality. A Soviet navy chief asserted that in case war breaks out, the Soviet Union will resort to the means of blockading ports, bases and coasts and occupying islands . . . to cut off the enemy's sea transportation. The Strait of Bāb al-Mandūb at the southern end of the Red Sea is only 20 miles wide. Once the Soviet revisionists bring it under control, they can either threaten, and even cut, the maritime transportation route of their opponents or pose a threat to the Red Sea littoral countries, in particular, blockading the four states which have no other sea ports. Moreover, the Red Sea and its adjacent regions nearby are rich in strategic materials, such as oil, copper, zinc, silver, gold and other precious metals, for which the Soviet social-imperialists cannot hide their greed. In recent years, the Soviet navy has started to infiltrate and expand southward from the East Mediterranean through the Suez Canal and the Red Sea into the Indian Ocean. By hoodwinking and luring, the Soviet Union has step by step grabbed the right to use a number of military installations on the Red Sea coasts. As a countermove, the United States also intensified its actions in the same region. The two super-powers' ever fiercer contention for hegemony in the Red Sea region has aroused great concern and met with violent opposition of the littoral states of the region. People are particularly on guard against the Soviet social imperialists, who talk extravagantly about 'friendship among the world peoples and nations.' President Numayrī has bluntly described Soviet social-

imperialism as an 'international pirate,' which is a vivid summing-up of the Soviet Union's behaviour in the Red Sea region."

On their side, the Soviets saw China playing its usual conspiratorial role. Broadcasting in Arabic, Radio Moscow (26 July 1976) spoke of China's "feverish activity" in the Middle East. "Peking," it added "is dreaming of seizing control of the huge oil resources of the area." It went on to quote a French journalist, Claude Arnaud, as saying: "The Maoists want to set up their control over the gates of the Red Sea. They want to dominate oil extraction and oil routes in the Arabian gulf. This is the strategic objective of the Maoists in the Middle East."

The Middle East in the Global Strategic Context—1977

BRIGADIER KENNETH HUNT

If there was ever an area truly global in its strategic importance, now as before, it is the Middle East. Its energy resources are vital to the economic interests of states throughout the world. The dangers of yet another war there touch the political concerns of many of them closely, and of all indirectly. It is an arena of super-power competition and of East-West military confrontation in the Eastern Mediterranean and the Balkans to the north. Its territory is of geo-strategic importance to both sides. Many strategic threads are thus interwoven, in a seemingly seamless web of issues and problems that stretches from the Eastern Mediterranean to the Persian Gulf and the Arabian Sea.

None of this is new, and 1977 has seen no change in the region itself to be compared with the events in the Lebanon in 1975 and 1976—though this conflict has stubbornly refused to end completely. In the main it was a period of consolidation and manoeuvre, giving the possibility of political movement—or failure to move—in the months ahead. In the Arab-Israeli dispute some expected impetus came from President Carter's new Administration, and in late November President Sādāt's dramatic bid for peace galvanized the area into political action but threw the Arab world into uproar.

If the causes of this dispute, and that between Greece and Turkey, have not yet been altered in their essentials, events on the edge of the region have, with an impact being felt within it. In the Horn of Africa and the Red Sea, Soviet support of Ethiopia has changed the scene. The high political and strategic stakes involved have aroused the concerns of Arab and Western states alike.

From the catalogue of strategic problems, that of energy, intimately linked as it is with the Arabs and Israel, is paramount. Energy in this context largely means oil from the Persian Gulf. Other essays in this volume deal with the economic aspects of oil; here only its impact on strategy is being discussed. Clearly, for both suppliers and consumers, a first requirement is unimpeded access to the Gulf itself, a fact which in the last few years has led to a remarkable flowering of Western interest in that area. Time was—very few years ago—when ensuring security and stability in the Gulf was the province of a small British presence, a self-imposed but thankless task for which disinterest or discouragement was the only reward to be expected. Contrast that position now. A new awareness of vulnerability has led to a surge of interest, to countries vying with each other to sell arms to local powers, or to give them political support. Principal among them is the United States. A heightened degree of American economic dependence on Gulf oil has led to heightened political concern: American arms supplies to Iran, among others, are huge, and American links with Iran now powerful. While President Carter has refused the supply of certain notably advanced weapon systems to Iran, such as AWACS and the F-16 fighter (in pursuance of a well-publicized policy of cutting down arms transfers), the vast bulk of supplies is, and is likely to remain, unaffected. The military impact of these particular decisions is thus not great, particularly as Iran will be hard put to absorb the weapons that are being delivered.

Since freed from its preoccupations with Vietnam, the US Navy has taken a closer interest in the Indian Ocean and Arabian Sea, and in Soviet naval activity there. President Carter's recent initiative, directed at regulating and reducing naval competition in the ocean area, is evidence of his awareness of the political importance that the region now has, as well as his wish for arms control. Iran, of course, is attentive to the presence of Soviet vessels as well. Her new navy, planned to include modern large destroyers and submarines, is being built not merely for the Gulf, but also to extend a maritime presence beyond its exit into the Arabian Sea. The sending of Iranian troops to help the Sultan of Oman to put down the PFLOAG rebellion (financed mainly by communist powers and mounted largely from South Yemen) was not only to serve the aims of regional stability, but to ensure that the other side of the Straits of Hormuz remained in friendly hands. (Jordanian and British military assistance will have had the same aim, linked also to wider interests of good relations with the Gulf rulers.) Iran is thus building up her armed forces with the aid of the West to be able to dissuade external intervention, ensure the flow of oil and, while doing so, become the local arbiter of events.

Iran shares a border and a cool relationship with the Soviet Union, her armed strength obviously having much to do with this. No doubt the Shah has in mind the store that Soviet leaders would set on increased influence in the Gulf, leading perhaps to a permanent military presence there, and even some leverage over oil supplies. Of course, Iran also shares a border with Iraq, disputed in places and the source of past hostilities.

Iraq has a treaty with the Soviet Union, affords military facilities at Umm Qasr to Soviet aircraft and naval vessels, and has recently again been receiving Soviet arms in some quantity. Interestingly enough, Iran herself buys some weapons from the Soviet Union, currently the mobile SAM and air defence guns—whose quality was shown in the October war of 1973—and also modern light armoured vehicles. These purchases, together with periodic economic deals, presumably form part of an Iranian policy of maintaining correct relations with her powerful neighbour, where these also offer advantages. Iran's weight remains, however, firmly on the Western side.

The Soviet Union herself, while cultivating Iraq at the head of the Gulf and South Yemen at the entrance to the Red Sea, is of course heavily involved to the south in the Horn of Africa. Here the potential dividend from her support of Ethiopia—if her efforts are successful—is to become the patron of Marxist states on both sides of the Red Sea and astride its entrance and the oil route via Suez (see the essay on the Red Sea in this volume). While she had influence in Somalia—which proved impossible to reconcile with support of Ethiopia—she had in Berbera a base from which, along with Aden in South Yemen, to maintain surveillance over both the Suez and Indian Ocean tanker and shipping routes, but this is now lost.

This adventurous Soviet policy has given concern not only to the US and other Western powers, but to Saudi Arabia, Egypt and other Arab countries, who look to a Red Sea under Arab, not Soviet, influence. (For Israel the events pose a dilemma: faced with the choice of a Red Sea controlled by the Arabs or by Soviet clients, she has, by her support of Ethiopia, seemed to opt for the latter.) Apart from France, which is carefully attentive to the newly independent Djibouti, the West has clearly been reluctant to become directly involved militarily. It has preferred at this stage to leave the Soviet Union struggling with the area's ethnic, religious and political complexities, happy to see Arab efforts, with Saudi Arabia in the forefront, being directed against Soviet aims (Somalia, though not an Arab country, is a member of the Arab League). An offer to Somalia by the US, followed by Britain, to help with military supplies was made in July 1977, but almost immediately withdrawn.

Saudi Arabia, for long the financial centre of gravity of the Arab world, is now an important political centre too. As such, it is in many ways the centrepiece of Western strategic policy in the Middle East, the chief link between the Gulf and the

Arab-Israeli dispute. For the US in particular, Saudi Arabia is important for three reasons. First, it is the oil producer with the volume of reserves and pattern of economic development which allow it to exploit them slowly, making it the dominant voice in OPEC pricing policy. Second, it is the producer on which the US is most dependent, and with which there are strong commercial links. Third, it is the country with most influence over the Arab confrontation states. American policy, therefore, is attentive to good relations with Saudi Arabia, to serve the twin aims of maintaining the security of oil supplies (with a tolerable price structure) and of achieving a settlement between Israel and the Arabs.

This perfectly understandable stance leads to the apparent paradox of the US supplying arms to Saudi Arabia and other Arab States in the Gulf, in the awareness that there is no guarantee that these will not be used against other American arms going to Israel. Officially, Israel is incensed, rightly counting such weapons as part of the armoury with which she must potentially contend. The saving grace for her is that whatever the US gives the Arabs, she gives Israel more: the balance between them is closely watched. Not least in Congress, where pressure appears to have persuaded Saudi Arabia to reduce the size of her demands for certain anti-tank and air-to-air weapons, and even to drop some demands altogether (for example, buying the F-5 fighter instead of the more advanced F-14 or -15, which was the Saudi intention originally). It is worth remarking here that Congress has a most marked reluctance to allow combat weapons to go to Egypt, despite the *mutual* importance of satisfactory US-Egyptian relations, both to help towards a settlement and to constrain Soviet influence.

In sum, then, the importance to the West of stability in the Gulf and continued access to oil, is reflected 1) in the willingness to help Iran become a strong regional power and to assist the military development of other Gulf states; 2) in Western political support for Iran and Saudi Arabia, most notably by the US; and 3) in the renewed interest shown in the Indian Ocean. (Though outside the scope of this essay, it is also clear that Western policies in Africa generally have a subsidiary aim of preventing the spread of Soviet or communist influence there that might lead to the granting of Soviet military facilities on the Indian Ocean seaboard and elsewhere.)

However, a more immediate threat to the continued flow of oil and to international stability generally is the possibility of another war in the Middle East if there is no progress towards a settlement in 1978. Countries world-wide would be affected by this, but it is the US that is most deeply involved—on the one hand as the effective guarantor of Israel's security and thus the state that can apply most pressure, and on the other as a close associate of Saudi Arabia. The US is perhaps more deeply concerned with the dangers of a break in oil supplies than, say, a decade ago, since American dependence on oil from the Middle East is now so much greater (see essay on Middle East oil in the international economic setting).

No doubt, partly as a result of this dependence, American policy has changed over the years. Once the almost one-sided American support of Israel—against any measurable strategic interests, perhaps, but for political and other reasons as well—handed the Arabs on a plate to the Soviet Union. Such a polarization was neither likely to lead to any settlement, nor desirable as a posture for a US now heavily dependent on oil imports. The policy was therefore gradually changed towards that which had been followed in general by Europeans—a more even-handed stance, with the additional advantage of undercutting the Soviet position sharply, notably in Egypt. By the nature of its history, however, the US is bound to continue to have a special relationship with Israel and to ensure its survival—but not necessarily on Israeli government terms.

Full discussions of the Arab-Israeli dispute and the military balance between the two sides can be found in the essay, "The Arab-Israeli Military Balance in 1977." Specifically with regard to the strategic significance of the dispute, it is necessary to stress that if the West is to maintain its strategic position in the Middle East, it must prevent the Arab confrontation states from once more being thrown into total dependence on the Soviet Union. A military build-up towards another war, eminently possible if negotiations bear no fruit or show no promise, would leave the Arabs with little other option. A renewed Soviet foothold in Egypt might follow—a distinct strategic setback for the West. A new war would also bring the US and the Soviet Union into sharp confrontation again, with political costs and risks that are not measurable. It would almost certainly produce another oil boycott, with resulting global economic and political dislocation and probably unrest, again not easily calculable but profoundly unwelcome. The world-wide strategic importance of avoiding another Arab-Israeli war is crystal clear.

If the two super-powers are embroiled in the Arab-Israeli problem, so are they in the Eastern Mediterranean. Here the US Sixth Fleet faces the Soviet Mediterranean Squadron, each of them supporting national interests and also forming part of the alliance forces of East and West. The Soviet Squadron is essentially an extension of the Black Sea fleet, and it is from that sea that it draws its strength, its base support and its long-range air cover. But Turkey, a member of NATO, sits astride the Black Sea exit and shares a long border with the Soviet Union: the strategic importance of Turkish territory to both sides is plain. Turkey has also afforded important surveillance and communications facilities to the US; among other things, these make it possible to monitor Soviet strategic nuclear activity—a necessary part of the national verification on which strategic arms limitation agreements depend. Though improvements in technology have made unnecessary many of the overseas installations maintained by the US (as in Kagnew in Eritrea), those on Turkish territory remain valuable. The American military facilities on Greek soil are also important to the Western alliance, even if they do not match the value inherent in Turkey's geographical position. For the Soviet Union, not only support of her own naval forces, but the supply of weapons to the Arab confrontation states by sea or by air, must take account of these geographical and political facts.

But, of course, the strategic equation in peacetime is not just a simple one of East versus West, with Greece and Turkey wholly on the Western side and the Soviet Union leading the other. The passage of Soviet ships through the Bosporus and the Dardanelles is regulated by the 1936 Montreux Convention; Soviet overflights of war material to Egypt were permitted in October 1973; and—a complicating feature for NATO and the US—Greek and Turkish forces are arrayed against each other in Cyprus. The quarrels between the Arabs and Israel and between Greece and Turkey give rise to allegiances and enmities that cut across any neat East-West division.

The bitter dispute between Greece and Turkey concerns both the Aegean, where drilling rights and control of the airspace are at issue, and Cyprus. The Turkish invasion of Cyprus in 1974 led in February 1975 to the US Congress, on which there are strong Greek pressures, imposing an arms embargo on Turkey and subsequently, the following July, to the Turkish government closing the 25 US bases in the country. But Greece, too, in her own wave of anti-Americanism, closed her US-occupied bases, and also withdrew (somewhat conditionally as it happened) from the integrated NATO military structure. The situation has been partly restored by the initialling of a US-Greek treaty in early 1976, allowing the continuing American use of four military installations including airfields, a communications station and an electronic surveillance post (in Crete), but disallowing the home-porting of the Sixth Fleet. The US Administration, acutely conscious of the importance of not estranging Turkey, has also worked out a Defence Agreement with that country, involving some $1,000m, which will allow the use of the military installations as well as lift the arms embargo. But this is subject to ratification by the US Congress—a body often less than wise where foreign policy is concerned—which is likely to resist it strongly unless Turkey agrees to make significant concessions over Cyprus. In fact, the Administration seems unlikely to press Congress until such steps are in the offing. But the Turkish view is that concessions on her part in Cyprus—chiefly territorial—depend on constitutional and other counter-concessions by the Greek-Cypriots that would give the Turkish-Cypriot community effective autonomy and security against the Greek-Cypriot majority. The very real problem of reaching such agreement within Cyprus, where feelings and bitterness run high, is compounded by internal political difficulties in Greece and Turkey, notably the latter, where the Demirel government's dependence on a coalition with a slender majority made initiatives over Cyprus hard indeed. The elections of June 1977 solved nothing. If the generally expected clear victory of the party led by Bulent Ecevit, premier at the time of the Cyprus invasion, had ensued, Ecevit might have had the political capital on which to draw for an attempted solution of such a nationally emotive issue. At the turn of the year the replacement of Demirel by a coalition led by Ecevit, plus a Greek government recently reconfirmed in office, gave some promise.

With the American embargo on arms to Turkey still substantially in operation, and anti-American and anti-NATO attitudes still a force to be reckoned with in Greece, the constraints on American (and thus NATO) use of strategically important facilities continue. Only Britain remains in full possession of her Sovereign Base Areas in Cyprus, but these have for the most part been run right down as part of the planned withdrawal of British forces from the Mediterranean.

The Soviet Union has some cause for comfort at this disarray in the Western alliance, and at the problem the US has in pleasing both Greece and Turkey at the same time. She herself has assiduously courted Turkey in order to take advantage of the strains in Turkish-American relations. In March 1977, Turkey and the Soviet Union signed a Treaty of Friendship, when Turkey was given $133m in Soviet credits.

In view of Turkey's parlous economic state, any financial help is most valuable, but improved relations with the Soviet Union are also one way of exerting some pressure on the US. When the Soviet aircraft-carrying cruiser *Kiev* passed through the Bosporus and Dardanelles into the Mediterranean in July 1976, the Soviet Union circumvented the Montreux Convention—which prohibits the passage of aircraft carriers—by labelling it an "anti-submarine cruiser." Turkey's silent acceptance of this was widely interpreted as a gentle message to her allies. But there are limits to how far Turkey can go. Her history and geo-strategic position make her sharply aware of Soviet ambitions, and of the importance of ties with the West for her own political and economic independence. Events have, however, led Turkey to strengthen economic links with Middle Eastern countries, notably Iran, which has granted her a $1.2m credit. Politically, Turkey has supported the Arab position against Israel.

The Eastern Mediterranean, strategically so important to East and West, is then in a disturbed state. The West will work for an outcome which will restore the cohesion of NATO; the Soviet Union for a weakening of ties, in particular between Turkey and the West, so as to improve her own relative position and that of her navy. While the Soviet Mediterranean Squadron is a powerful force—which in war the Sixth Fleet would have to deal with before being able to carry out its own mission of supporting the land battle—it has operating weaknesses. In addition to the problem posed by the choke-point of the Black Sea exit, the Squadron lacks operating bases in the Mediterranean and airfields from which to provide fighter cover. NATO, by contrast, has facilities on the territory of a number of its member-countries, plus those enjoyed by the US in Spain and the UK in Cyprus. Malta is key here through its agreement with Britain.

There is, however, the southern shore of the Mediterranean, where the Soviet Union has recently forged much closer links with Libya (an oil producing country, of course), and where it has long been a supplier of arms to Algeria. The connection with the politics of the Middle East proper is an obvious one; but Soviet support for the Arab position has nonetheless not resulted in her being given military facilities, in Algeria for example, of the kind once enjoyed in Egypt. Furthermore, the political map is now rather more confused. Though Libya has received large consignments of Soviet arms during 1977, she appears to be closely involved in the Soviet supply of weapons to Ethiopia. But Soviet backing for the Marxist government in Addis Ababa is unwelcome to most Arabs, and relations between the volatile and radical Libyan leader Qadhdhafi and the heads of some other Arab countries, notably Egypt and the Sudan, are bad. Soviet policy in courting Libya could have strategic dividends, but it may have a price too—unless, of course, a heightening of Arab-Israeli tension unites all Arabs again and gives more scope for Soviet diplomacy.

The North African seaboard is thus linked with the Red Sea and the Horn of Africa, with the Soviet Union the strategic nexus. But the web that joins so many of the issues from the Mediterranean to the Gulf is still a tangled one, with problems that for the time being often cut across traditional affiliations. Two things, however, remain as clear as they were: the instability inherent in the political divide that still separates the Arabs from Israel, and the vital importance to the world of the flow of Middle Eastern oil. These two facts, linked as they are, provide reason enough for the West urgently to seek a solution that will avert another Arab-Israeli war. But the strategic importance of the region is far from limited to that central problem; it touches the security of Western Europe and political developments in the Arabian Sea and Africa just as surely as it provides the geo-strategic bridge between them.

The Arab-Israel Military Balance in 1977

GEOFFREY KEMP and MICHAEL VLAHOS

The magnitude of the military build-up in the Middle East-Persian Gulf area over the past few years has been unprecedented both in terms of quantity and quality. However, although oil-rich countries such as Iran and Saudi Arabia have joined the ranks of major arms recipients, the most serious military problem during 1977 remained the possibility of a new war breaking out between Israel and her immediate neighbours, especially Egypt and Syria. This essay focuses on the changing nuances of the Arab-Israeli military balance, with special reference to the land-warfare environment.

Since the 1973 October war, the military capabilities of Israel and her major Arab adversaries have improved, but both quantitative and qualitative indices suggest that Israel has made the more significant advances to date. Insofar as it is possible to calculate the military balance and so speculate on the changing military capabilities of both sides, most experts agreed that Israel remained the strongest local military power in the Middle East through 1977. How long this "superiority" will continue, and whether it will be sufficient to deter an Arab coalition (possibly including Jordan and Saudi Arabia) from launching a new war remain uncertain. Before speculating about the emerging strategic environment and alternative military strategies, however, it is necessary to outline some of the elements basic to any calculation of the military balance.

Three factors must enter into an assessment of any military balance between rival coalitions: manpower and weapons levels—the quantitative sum of opposing forces; the technological sophistication of these weapons in the context of their expected mission environments—the qualitative edge; and comparative battle doctrine and force structuring—a crucial measure of expected operational efficiency.

MANPOWER LEVELS AND WEAPONS LEVELS

Despite its small total population, the Israeli Defence Forces (IDF) have kept pace with the Arab order of battle in manpower levels and in force posture. From a total *mobilized* manpower of just under 300,000 in 1973, Israel has recently raised its potential to something over 400,000. However, before mobilization, the Israelis have only 164,000 deployed. Israeli staff planning envisages preparations against a northern and eastern front of Lebanon, Syria, Iraq and Jordan. This combination might field up to 14 divisions—five Syrian, five Iraqi, four Jordanian. With Egypt's ten divisions in the west, the potential combination against Israel could reach 24 divisions. But the increase in Israel's reserves since 1973 has meant that some 11 full-sized divisions can now be fielded, as opposed to the seven rough divisional groupings deployed in 1973.

Without full Jordanian participation, the local Arab manpower ratio after mobilization has deteriorated. Since 1973, mobilizable Israeli manpower has increased by 35-40%, while that of Egypt, Syria and Iraq has remained relatively static. What had been a 2.5:1 ratio against Israel in 1973 is now no more than 1.8:1. With the addition of Jordan to the Arab coalition, the ratio approaches 2:1.

THE ARAB-ISRAEL MILITARY BALANCE

A comparison of the Arab-Israeli inventories in five key weapons systems—tanks, armoured personnel carriers, artillery, combat aircraft and major air-defence systems—shows a shift of the quantitative balance in the four years since 1973. The Israeli arsenal has grown at a consistently higher rate than those of its primary Arab opponents, with the major exception of air-defence systems.

The main battle-tank, the armoured personnel carrier and artillery are the weapons that, in modern battle doctrine, form the core of the "combined arms team" triad. As mutually supporting weapons systems, they are the basis of offensive force structuring, and are still perceived as the key to land battle, in spite of speculation as to the impact of new anti-tank weapons. Table 1 shows the extent to which Israel's relative position in stocks of these three weapons systems has improved. For the first time, the main battle-tank ratio has fallen below the 2:1 factor against Israel. Furthermore, mechanized armoured personnel carriers (APCs) and the artillery arm of the Israeli combined arms triad were neglected until recently. But by 1977, these deficiencies had been greatly improved *vis-à-vis* the Arabs. Israeli armour now possesses both the direct anti-tank support (in the form of APCs) and the indirect fire support (of self-propelled artillery) that it largely lacked in the 1973 war.

In contrast, although Arab inventories have grown, they have not received the self-propelled artillery tubes necessary for highly mobile offensive operations. This deficiency may well restrict their strategic options in event of a new war.

In comparisons of air power, Israeli odds have followed the same significant course of improvement. A 2:1 ratio should ensure Israeli air superiority in war, and leave enough of a combat reserve for her Air Force to engage in high attrition missions such as battlefield support and air defence suppression.

Numbers and ratios can never form an absolute index from which to measure military power. However, among certain "classic" writers on military strategy, success in the offensive was often linked to the attainment of a 3:1 ratio advantage in manpower and weapons levels. Until recently, the Arab "confrontation" states have never faced the prospect of their arsenals falling below this symbolic level necessary for battlefield success. The Israeli General Staff, for its part, felt that it "could live" with such odds. During 1977, however, such key indicators in the Arab arsenal as main battle-tanks and high-performance combat aircraft barely held a 2:1 ratio over Israel. The trend in these weapons ratios means that Israel may very well be able to concentrate its forces in a future war on a chosen sector of the front, and there achieve actual numerical superiority. As long as manpower and weapons level ratios either remain static or develop in favour of Israel, the symbolic perception of the military balance must reinforce the image of Israeli "superiority."

It must be remembered that much of the present Arab situation is due to a condition of "zero growth" in the Egyptian arsenal, caused by deteriorating relations with its main supplier, the Soviet Union. Although Egypt has ordered British *Swingfire* anti-tank guided weapons, and French *Mirage* F1 fighter aircraft, there is as yet no indication that supplies of sophisticated European tanks, APCs, or self-propelled artillery tubes have been negotiated. In any case, replacement of the major Egyptian weapons inventory with Western arms would probably take at least three years.

The maintenance of military forces equal to the largest European establishments has placed a heavy burden on the economies of Israel and her immediate Arab neighbours. During 1977, Israel allocated c. \$4.3 bn toward defence, (c. 35% of GNP); Egypt c. \$4.4 bn (c. 37%). Syria allocated \$1.1 bn, and Iraq \$1.7 bn. The magnitude of these efforts has become possible, in part, because of aid provided to Israel by the US, by the Soviet Union to Iraq and Syria, and by Saudi Arabia to Egypt.

Changes in weapons inventories, 1973-1977: Israel, Egypt, Syria, Iraq[1]

	1973	*1977*
Main Battle-Tanks		
Israel	2000	3000
Egypt	1960	1850
Syria	1600	2500
Iraq	860	1350
Armoured Personnel Carriers		
Israel	1000	4000
Egypt	2000	2500
Syria	1000	1600
Iraq	300	1800
Artillery		
Israel	400 (250 Self Propelled) [SP]	950 (500 SP)
Egypt	1690 (No SP)[2]	1300 (No SP)
Syria	575 ,,	800 ,,
Iraq	300 ,,	700 ,,
High-performance, Operational Combat Aircraft[3]		
Israel	340	620
Egypt	568	543
Syria	290	395
Iraq	218	335
Ratios	*Arabs: Israel*	*Arabs: Israel*
Main battle-tanks	2.21 : 1.00	1.90 : 1.00
Armoured personnel carriers	3.30 : 1.00	1.47 : 1.00
Artillery	6.41 : 1.00	2.90 : 1.00
Fighter-bombers[4]	3.16 : 1.00	2.03 : 1.00

[1] *The Military Balance 1973-1974, 1977-1978* (London: the International Institute for Strategic Studies, 1973, 1977). Jordan, if added, would not appreciably alter the balance in favour of a four-nation Arab coalition. Only in major air defence systems would it be capable, within the next 18 months, of strongly reinforcing Arab superiority in this sphere.

[2] SU-100/122 Assault guns are not considered here to be able to fulfil the role of true self-propelled artillery.

[3] The complete Israeli inventory is included here, as Israeli *Mystère* and *Super Mystère* must be considered the operational equals of the *Hunter* and MiG-17, the latter still deployed in large numbers by Arab air forces.

[4] Egypt, Syria, and Iraq have an enormous proponderance over Israel in terms of anti-aircraft defences. In terms of larger SAMs alone (concentrated at corps and army level), total Arab stocks of SA-2/3/6 number c. 2,000. Jordan is currently in the process of receiving some 532 HAWKs from the US. Israel, in contrast, possesses only some 90 HAWKs for air defence, apart from short-range, divisionally allocated air defence systems such as *Chaparral* and *Redeye*.

TECHNOLOGY AND SYSTEMS EFFICIENCY

Israel has maintained a significant lead in military technology since 1973. Although this lead has widened in some sectors, the gap may narrow after 1978 if the acquisition of sophisticated European systems by Arab states continues. However, in the critical support areas—weapons maintenance, battle efficiency, and operability—Israel is unlikely to lose her longstanding lead for some time to come.

It is possible that Syria will soon receive small numbers of the new Soviet main battle-tank, the T-72. This tank, with its powerful 125mm semi-rifled gun and its improved mobility and suspension systems, might overshadow much of the current Israeli tank inventory. Meanwhile, the standard 105mm gun mounted in Israeli tanks will retain its proven superiority over the 115mm gun of the T-62.

Israel's indigenous main battle-tank—the *Merkava* or *"Chariot"*—entered its pre-production phase in the summer of 1977 and represents a new component in the military balance of the region. Not only will full-scale indigenous production help to free Israel from her present dependence on foreign sources of modern armour, but the *Merkava* embodies special design qualities tailored for the Middle East environment. Armed with the standard Israeli 105mm tank gun, the *Merkava*, at 58 to 62 tons all-up combat weight, is the heaviest of modern main battle-tanks. Its mobility is decidedly secondary to armour which, together with crew protection, have been given paramount consideration in the design. Furthermore, the turret shape and slope of the glacis plate indicate a predominantly hull-down, tank-destroyer role.

As the 1973 October war revealed, the ability of a tank to consistently hit its target tends to overshadow all other considerations in the heat of battle. Tank fire control systems and night/zero-visibility sensors are in some ways more critical to battle performance than the quality of the vehicle they service. In this respect, Israel still holds a decisive edge. The Soviet tanks of the Arab armoured forces lack both optical and laser rangefinders. Israel, in contrast, has equipped her inventory with optical equipment, and is currently in the process of fitting *Hughes* laser rangefinders to her armoured forces. Egypt has contracted for Swedish *ISKRA* 22A laser battle sights. Until these are incorporated into the Arab arsenal, the armour of the states opposing Israel will depend on a graticule in the battle sight for simple stadiametric ranging: a relatively inaccurate system.

In anti-tank guided weapons (ATGW) systems, Israel holds an advantage in possessing the US *TOW* system. Arab armies, with the exception of Jordan, did not acquire missiles of comparable battle efficiency through 1977. The arrival of the French-German *Milan* ATGW in Syria and the British *Swingfire* ATGW in Egypt should return some of the anti-tank "punch" lost to the Arab armies when Israel developed effective *Sagger*-suppression tactics during the 1973 war.

Israel has recently made further improvements in her anti-tank capability by requesting $64m worth of US AH-1G Huey *Cobras* to be employed in an anti-tank role, with eight *TOW* per aircraft. This will give Israel a mobile anti-tank reserve that none of the Arab "inner ring" can presently match. The AH-1Gs will be held, not at divisional or corps level, but by the front HQs. In this fashion, a local Arab breakthrough on the forward edge of the battle area (FEBA) can be dealt with behind the front without redeploying forward units.

In the realm of indirect fire support, Israel seems to have made major improvements in comparison with Iraq, Syria and Egypt. The Arabs are still dependent upon towed artillery and unable yet to acquire either European or new Soviet 122mm self-propelled (SP) guns. Israel continues to request large numbers of medium SP guns from the US. The latest order, for 94 155mm pieces, will bring Israel's SP artillery to over 600 tubes. Also included in the order are an unspecified number of 175mm SP guns, the longest-ranged artillery in the US inventory. The build-up of mobile, long-range artillery in Israel is significant. Not only will it provide counter-battery artillery suppression, but 175mm tubes can also be used very effectively against enemy air-defence sites, which might prove an important factor in the air-defence suppression battle. Finally, Israel has begun development of the proposed *Rigoletto* command-and-control system for mechanized forces, which will provide precise artillery surveying capability and target acquisition ability in a fluid battlefield. In contrast, Arab towed artillery almost predicates a static or ponderously rolling front, and cannot respond to a high degree of battlefield flexibility.

In terms of new technologies in manned aircraft, Israel again held the lead through 1977, though this was primarily by virtue of her squadron of F-15 *Eagles*. In other respects, the US F-4s and the indigenously produced *Kfir* represent an older generation in aircraft design. The *Kfir* is an inspired improvisation of the French *Mirage* airframe and US Pratt and Whitney engines. In contrast, the 180-odd MiG-23 *Floggers* now in the combined inventories of Egypt, Syria and Iraq are a formidable combat aggregate, at the very least the equal of the *Kfir*. Furthermore, the incipient acquisition by Egypt and Iraq of a potential 286 Dassault *Mirage* F1s (214 and 72 respectively) would undermine the current air supremacy of the Israeli Air Force (IAF)—at least on paper. In this context, Israel's request for 200 US F-16s has taken on a certain urgency.

Only in the field of air defence do the Arab states have a clear superiority over Israel. Egypt has c. 700–800 surface-to-air missiles (SAMs) SA-2/3/6; Syria at least as many in 48 batteries; and Iraq nearly 400 SA-6 in 25 batteries. These are now completing the ring around Israel by linking with Jordan. Buttressed and confident of its air defences for the first time in many years, Jordan's newly acquired US *HAWKs* (532), *Redeyes* (270) and *Vulcan* (100) air-defence systems, will, when they are delivered during the next 18 months, allow King Ḥusayn the choice of whether or not to attempt to deny Israel the use of his airspace in the event of war—an option he did not have in 1973.

Nevertheless, Israel has made great improvements in her air defence/air defence suppression capabilities. New techniques in electronic counter-measures (ECM) have reduced the combat effectiveness of the old generation SA-2 and SA-3. Evasive tactics (developed very quickly by the IAF in 1973 against the SA-6) in conjunction with stand-off air-to-surface missiles (ASM) such as the *Maverick* have further reduced the expected lethality of that missile. Egypt has ordered *Crotale* mobile SAMs from France; but until they take their place in the operational inventory, the "inner ring" of Arab states will lack an effective all-weather, low-level SAM system.

The priority combat mission of the IAF remains air superiority, or the defence and control of air space over both Israel and the forward battle areas. So long as the IAF can keep the Arab air forces from the skies—as they have done in all previous wars—the air threats to Israel proper and her land forces are considerably reduced. Aircraft inventories and procurement reflect this paramount doctrine. Mission-specific close-support aircraft such as the Fairchild-Republic A-10 have been rejected in favour of more orders for the *Kfir* and the General Dynamics F-16, which can be considered classic dogfighters. Furthermore, Israel's weakness in medium-altitude SAM coverage can also be attributed to the confidence and reliance placed upon manned aircraft in the air-superiority mission. The Israeli decision to procure four Grumann E-2Cs airborne early-warning aircraft will significantly increase IAF capabilities in the air-to-air theatre. The E-2C can perform tracking, follow over 500 targets simultaneously, and monitor multiple intercepts for c. 30 fighters at a time. There is, so far, no indication that the Arab air forces have placed orders for this type of sophisticated system.

For the immediate future, Israel holds the technological edge at sea. While the navies of Egypt, Syria and Libya are still saddled with the obsolescent SS-N-2 *Styx*, with its evadable beam-riding guidance, Israel is introducing the Mark II version of the successful *Gabriel* ASCM, and is buying the long-range US *Harpoon*. The naval balance could change, however, as Libya and Egypt both receive the Franco-Italian *Otomat* anti-ship cruise missile. In addition, the French Daphne and Agosta type submarines, ordered by Libya and Egypt respectively, will more than match the three Vickers submarines now being received by the Israeli navy.

Israel has always managed to equalize the weapons ratio on the battlefield through the maintenance of peak battle efficiency and operability. This has been true of aircraft sortie rates and turn-around time, as well as with tank repair and recovery. Thus Israel has been able to count on double, or even triple, the operational effectiveness of the opposing Arab arsenals. The Arab maintenance problem has been compounded since 1976 by the lack of spare parts for key equipment inventories in the Egyptian arsenal. Their foremost difficulty has been the increasing depletion of Egypt's MiG-21 fleet. Attempts to persuade India and then Yugoslavia to help have failed. Egyptian hopes now rest with a deal with Rolls Royce to overhaul MiG-21 engines and avionics. Until that time, a third of Egypt's high-performance combat aircraft can be considered out of commission.

Israel's maintenance problem has never been one of operability, but rather of combat resupply in high-intensity conflict. Estimates now place Israeli stocks of ammunition and combat stores between 21 and 28 days for a war at the pace of 1973's. Given the military balance in 1977, that would suffice for a short war, *without* major US aid.

ISRAELI BATTLE DOCTRINE AND FORCE STRUCTURING

Battle doctrine and the tactical structuring of combat units have become a crucial focus for both Arab and Israeli planners. The nature of the "next war" can never be precisely forecast. Nevertheless, unit organization and tactical training for battle must attempt to adapt an army to the climatic conditions of future war. Within this context of doctrinal preparation, a central question facing Israel concerns the *fluidity* of the front of the emerging battlefield. In another war, will Israeli armour be able to create a battle of movement, as it has so often done in the past? Will her tank columns once more be seen encircling the Arab armies from the rear; or will they face the fortified lines of a *hardened* front? For example, the relative narrowness of the Northern/Syrian front would tend to create a very dense battle area in a future war. Massed force levels and high-intensity arms concentrations would "pack the front", and the highly fortified Sa'sa-Aliqin lines in front of Damascus would seem to form an insurmountable obstacle to a war of movement. Elaborate outflanking movements—so often attractive in this sort of static front situation—would be extremely difficult on the broken ground and winding river ravines of Lebanon or Jordan. The terrain in these areas is not conducive to "lightning" strikes.

If Israel were forced to approach a "hard" front and, like Falkenhayn at Verdun, face a "meat grinder" war of attrition, then vastly superior tactics and force structuring would be necessary to maximize its offensive "punch" and hold losses to a minimum. This would require weapons concentration, flexibility of application, and staying power on the battlefield, which in turn would mean enormous supplies of ammunition and a willingness to assume considerable casualties.

In this context, Israel would seem to be restructuring its major combat units to provide its divisions with some of these qualities. The core of rebuilt Israeli battle-power on land will be what is now called in the US army the "heavy division." While the Egyptian, Syrian and Iraqi armies still generally hold to most of the organizational and tactical doctrines of the Soviet divisions of five years ago, the Israeli army has fused its loose arrangements of brigades into a mature organic divisional structure. Each brigade could have a 3:2 mix of armour and mechanized infantry battalions. Each of the 15 manoeuvre battalions would have its own integral anti-tank guided weapon company in mechanized infantry combat vehicles. Four strong divisional artillery battalions would provide completely integrated medium and long-range fire support from over 100 tubes, all self-propelled. The heavy armoured "punch" would be provided by 360 MBTs. In effect, the "heavy division" concept creates a nearly self-sufficient armoured corps, capable of sustained operations on the battlefront.

Israel has the capability of forming six of these "heavy divisions" by pooling the best of its armoured battalions and the bulk of its SP artillery. There are indications that this is being done. Some of the basic restructuring decisions were made early in 1974, with General Israel Tal, then Deputy Chief-of-Staff, presiding over the discussions. Recently, when writing of Israeli defence doctrine in *Maarachot*, Tal underscored the theme of the central importance of armour and the mobile offensive in Israeli battle doctrine.

As Tal constantly reiterates, Arab war objectives in combination with Israel's lack of strategic depth on the northern and eastern fronts, preclude the war option of "flexible defence"—where enemy forces are destroyed at the expense of territorial loss. There is really no alternative to the offensive in Israeli strategy. Unlike the precarious strategic picture before June of 1967, the extended frontiers of today's Israel are not to be made more secure by further expansion. A significant and striking blow against Arab military power would be necessary both to relieve strategic pressure and to create a climate conducive to settlement. One approach to such an objective would be the destruction of at least one Arab army. However, this kind of strategy involves the possibility of a stalemate against a hardened front if the thrust of the offensive fails. Even with new battle doctrines and force restructuring, the Israeli army might find itself unable to achieve breakthrough conditions on the front.

Thus, since *force majeure* operations involve the danger of high attrition, both of weapons and of personnel, alternative war strategies, circumventing the actual battlefront, have been discussed. Among these would be the employment of Israel's superior air power to conduct strategic aerial bombardment in the classic scenario—to raze both the economic infrastructure and the military logistics network of the enemy.

Employed to great effect in Syria in the closing days of the October 1973 war, the use of strategic "reach" nevertheless has its inevitable operational and political constraints. Although targeting options may be selected on an incremental and escalatory scale in order to be of some diplomatic utility, any resort to an all-out "bomber offensive" might be ill-advised. In conjunction with a traditional land campaign, strategic targeting (as in the case of the operations against Syria in 1973) may well provide the impetus needed in a stalemate situation to bring about a cease-fire. As an isolated strategy, however, this approach involves dangerous ramifications. "Terror bombardment" elicits counter-bombardment, perhaps with multitudes of Russian *Scuds*, hastily and ostentatiously supplied. The conflict might well be prolonged and intensified, with the awesome possibility that Israel's presumed nuclear weapons and Arab chemical and biological weapons might be used.

The destruction of an Arab army—preferably the Syrian—offers in contrast both a politically acceptable and emotionally dramatic war objective for Israel, provided the decision can be achieved quickly. For example, the "worse case" now mooted among Israeli officers—a Syrian/Iraqi/Jordanian coalition—offers an insight into current Israeli strategy. With Egypt playing an essentially passive role in the Sinai, the preponderance of Israeli armour and divisional strength could be concentrated either against Jordan or Syria. The temptation to destroy one of the Arab armies in a pre-emptive strike would be difficult to resist.

If, for example, Israel wished to cripple the Syrian army before the Iraqi army could link up on the front, she would have the option of concentrating up to six divisions and most of her armour against a single enemy. In this case, Israel would have numerical superiority in men and equipment over Syria's five divisions.

Pre-emption of this kind implies an immediate offensive on the battlefield to destroy the armies of an Arab coalition. The pre-emptive role of the IAF associated with the 1967 war might well be more limited, and confined at first to key interdiction missions. Close air support would be subsumed by divisional artillery, while the major role of air defence suppression would be undertaken by a combination of long-range corps artillery and Lance SSMs. The primary mission of the IAF would be air superiority, i.e. to keep the skies free of Arab airplanes. The suppression of air-defence systems would be considered later. Only in a SAM-free, or at least low-attrition battle area environment, would Israeli aircraft engage in major close air support missions. Even with air-to-surface missiles such as the *Maverick*, a high performance aircraft such as the F-4 must approach its target in a shallow dive—say, 5,000 to 1,500 feet at a 20 degree angle—to acquire, lock on to, and guide a missile toward its target. That can still be a dangerous mission in a sophisticated SAM environment.

Throughout 1977, against any likely Arab coalition, Israel probably would have been able to mass *superior* forces against one national component of the coalition, as well as having the option to strike first. In contrast, the Arab states surrounding Israel would have found it difficult in 1977—as they will for the next two to five years—to define and implement a war strategy against Israel that might equal their unquestioned political success of 1973. Given Israel's current superiority, an Arab coalition might expect, within the parameters of a conventional/traditional war, to be soundly defeated within five days to a week of the Israeli decision to strike. Only in the circumstance where Arab strategic surprise might *again* be achieved, or in the unlikely instance of an Arab coalition being able to prolong the conflict to three weeks and beyond, would there be a good chance that a combination of casualty rates and battlefield stalemate could rob Israel of the image, if not the substance, of victory.

By the end of 1977, Israel's military strength *vis-à-vis* her immediate Arab neighbours was probably greater than at any time since the aftermath of the June 1967 war. To that extent Israel had reason to feel secure. However, the long-term future does not hold the promise of inevitable Israeli superiority. Eventually the sheer size of the Arab population and its access to advanced technology may lead to a gradual shift in the military balance. In the absence of a peace settlement this trend could, in and of itself, increase mutual suspicions and contribute to the impetus toward a new war, the outcome of which would be uncertain.

The Arab-Israeli Conflict

Major Trends in the Arab-Israeli Conflict

DAN SCHUEFTAN

The dramatic turn of events in the Arab-Israeli conflict, marked by President Anwar Sādāt's visit to Jerusalem in November 1977, was produced in large measure by the constraints inherent in the complex relations among all the parties most directly involved in the Middle East conflict. This conflict bears significantly on Israel's relations with each of her neighbours, but no less on inter-Arab relations and on those within the international system—especially between the super-powers. All the parties directly involved in the conflict have made a practice of exerting pressures on these various levels to advance their sharply divergent aims—the Arabs to secure Israel's complete withdrawal from the territories occupied in 1967, and the restoration of the Palestinians' "legitimate rights" (generally conceived as the establishment of a Palestinian state); Israel to secure the normalization of relations with the Arab states within defensible borders ("full peace" implying acceptance of her legitimacy) and rejection of a Palestinian state; and the two super-powers to expand their influence at the expense of each other in the area.

The strategy of the principal Arab states since the 1973 war has been to cultivate a closer relationship with the Western powers, especially the US, as a means of exerting leverage on Israel, while simultaneously exploiting such relations in order to develop their military and economic strengths. Although events up to October 1977 seemed to vindicate this strategy—especially after the advent of the Carter Administration—the Arabs tended to overlook or minimize some of the constraints on its effectiveness. Among these limitations were: 1) the extent to which the Americans could be expected to exert pressures on Israel to accept a settlement that might possibly endanger her security; 2) Israel's current military superiority, and the Arab awareness of it (coupled with the lessons of 1973); and 3) reluctance or plain refusal on the part of most major Arab states to depend (or renew their dependence) on the USSR in case the US "failed to deliver."

Faced by a less positively favourable American policy, Israel's newly-elected Government employed some of these constraints to its advantage by abandoning the former policy of co-ordinating all substantive and tactical moves with the US before acting on them. By threatening to obstruct the American-sponsored political process through refusing to attend the Geneva conference—even at the risk of a political confrontation with the US—Israel underlined the limits of any settlement proposals worked out between the Americans and the Arabs.

ARAB POLITICAL STRATEGIES

THE "POLITICAL PAUSE" OF 1976

During the last months of 1976 and the beginning of 1977, a transition was beginning to take place in the inter-Arab system from the rivalry that had followed the 1975 Israeli-Egyptian Interim Agreement and the civil war in Lebanon, towards a closing of ranks in anticipation of the expected renewal of an American-sponsored political process. A year earlier, at the beginning of 1976, it seemed as though the Sinai Agreement was the last of the immediate consequences of the 1973 war, rather than the beginning of a new phase of settlements of the same nature. When attempts to achieve a Syrian-Israeli interim settlement similar to that concluded with Egypt failed in late 1975 and early 1976, it became accepted by almost all parties that 1976 would become a year of waiting.

Three major political developments forced this political pause on the Arabs, the first being inter-Arab rivalry over the Sinai Agreement. Egypt had entered into this separate agreement with Israel in September 1975 without making it conditional on the achievement of a similar agreement with Syria—her partner in the October war—nor upon any progress towards advancing the interests of either the PLO or the Jordanian sector. For a while, Egypt thus became almost completely isolated in the inter-Arab arena, caught up in a bitter dispute with Syria: a polarity which had in fact been one of Israel's declared objectives in concluding the agreement. It eased Arab and American pressures for further Israeli withdrawals and temporarily precluded the establishment of a united Arab front which was essential for the renewal of such pressures.

The second development was the civil war in Lebanon which had resulted in the Syrians' armed intervention in 1976; their unexpected alliance with the Maronites against the PLO; inter-Arab rivalries; the dilemma for Soviet policy; and the American role in the crisis: all these developments shifted attention away from the Arab-Israeli conflict and postponed any serious political initiative until after the situation in Lebanon had to some extent stabilized. (For details, see essay on Inter-Arab Relations and chapters on Lebanon and Syria.)

The third development was the American presidential election campaign, which precluded the application of a consistent, credible and resolute US policy. Egypt and Saudi Arabia both appreciated this difficulty, and President Sādāt even stated publicly in 1976, and particularly when election-day came closer, that he would not expect a full-scale American initiative before the newly-elected Administration started its term in office.

The interaction of these three factors was obviously not accidental: towards the end of 1976, the parties directly involved in the Lebanese crisis—Syria with success on its side, the defeated PLO, and the exhausted Christians—came to realize that all the major forces in the Arab world (particularly Saudi Arabia) had concluded that the war in Lebanon had to be terminated. This development became imperative in view of the need to form an effective united Arab front as soon as the new US Administration entered office. Such a front would seek to prevent a protracted phase of "no war, no peace" with all its dangerous implications.

The Riyadh and Cairo summit conferences in October 1976 terminated the crisis in Lebanon and put an end to the Egyptian-Syrian confrontation over the Sinai Agreement. The two conferences also resulted in an Arab alignment in preparation for the renewal of the American-sponsored political process. The Arab states used the period of political stalemate—up to the early months of 1977—for the accumulation of political and strategic assets which could significantly improve their respective bargaining positions.

THE EGYPTIAN INTEREST

For Egypt, more than for other Arab parties, the main objective was the preservation of political momentum towards a settlement before the opportune circumstances established since October 1973 were exhausted. While other Arab states were preparing alternative options in case the US-sponsored political process failed to produce the desired results, Sādāt seemed ready to gamble almost all his political assets on the American counter. However, he had to justify his far-reaching cooperation with the US, to domestic and Arab critics. Thus, it was important for Sādāt to indicate clearly to the US that he could not afford to wait indefinitely for the expected political results, and that unless these were achieved in a reasonable time, there might be a risk of far-reaching change in Egyptian regional and global policy (turning away from "moderation," possibly back to the Soviet Union). Realistically assessing the limits of what he could expect from the US, and eager to appear reasonable in his demands, Sādāt showed particular understanding on two issues: the nature of American pressures on Israel, and the question of US arms supply to Egypt.

Sādāt repeatedly emphasized that Egypt did not expect the US to abandon its special relations with Israel. If his conditions for a settlement were met, he would not mind an even closer relationship to be expressed, for instance, in an Israeli-American defence pact, in which case he would not ask for an equivalent pact with Egypt. Sādāt often dwelt on what he described as Israel's total dependence on the US ("from the loaf of bread to the *Phantom*"), and its key position in the anticipated settlement process ("99% of the cards are in the hands of America"). He was careful to describe the pressures he expected the US to apply on Israel in moderate terms; he spoke of "convincing Israel to accept peace" and of restraining her "arrogance."

Egypt's persistence in following the American option created for it both a strategic and political dilemma. Except for its air force, Egypt's armed forces had on the whole been reconstructed since the 1973 war. However, they had not been modernized, nor had they grown in strength—in contrast to the armed forces of Israel, Syria, Jordan, Saudi Arabia and Libya. This situation adversely affected the Egyptian military option in the event of a political stalemate, thus weakening its political leverage *vis-à-vis* Israel and the US. The erosion in Egypt's comparative military capabilities added to the decline in its inter-Arab status, as well as to reported agitation in the Egyptian armed forces. Egypt let it be understood in the US that it could not afford a long period of stagnation in military power. However, as far as could be judged in 1976 and 1977, Egypt appeared to be satisfied by symbolic acts which implied that the US could become a major military supplier at a later stage. (Also see essay, "The Arab-Israeli Military Balance.")

On the three main issues of conflict with Israel, President Sādāt adhered to his basic positions, although he tried to moderate his language so as to suggest greater flexibility. On the territorial issue, Sādāt insisted on complete and immediate Israeli withdrawal from all territories occupied in 1967, including East Jerusalem. On the Palestinian question, he continued to demand the establishment of an independent, sovereign, PLO-dominated Palestinian state in the West Bank and Gaza Strip, to be linked by a corridor. On the nature of the settlement, he proposed that in return for the fulfilment of his demands by Israel, the state of belligerency (or "an end to the war") could be terminated by a peace agreement. However, during the early period of Carter's Administration, he continued to totally reject the idea of a peace treaty and the establishment of fully-fledged diplomatic (and other peace) relations without a time limit being set.

Sādāt repeatedly emphasized that the "step-by-step" approach had been exhausted with the Sinai Agreement, and that when the political process resumed, a comprehensive settlement should be sought. As a diplomatic framework for such a settlement, Sādāt supported the Geneva mechanism, insisting that Lebanon and the PLO should join the participants originally invited.[1] Unlike the PLO, Lebanon seemed to pose no problem for Israel. Although indicating that Egypt might eventually adopt a more flexible position, Sādāt insisted at this stage that the PLO should participate independently in the Geneva conference on an equal footing with other delegations. Here again, with the conference not yet imminent, Sādāt presumably had no intention of precipitating unnecessary confrontation with other Arab states.

In the Arab world, Sādāt attempted to demonstrate that—contrary to the criticism directed at him following the Sinai Agreement—it was Egypt that could do most to mobilize the US to bring strong pressure on Israel. It was also Egypt that could persuade Washington to adopt a pro-Arab position and isolate Israel in the international arena. In a series of draft resolutions presented at the UN (carefully worded to include a maximum of American political vocabulary relating to the Middle East), Egypt succeeded in fomenting tension between Israel and the US. It also accustomed American public opinion to such minor confrontations. Meanwhile, in the Security Council, the US prevented the adoption of draft resolutions concerning the PLO which were totally unacceptable to Israel. Egypt nevertheless succeeded in November 1976 (after the US elections) to win American support for a resolution in the UN General Assembly deploring some of the major components of Israeli policy in the occupied territories, including a definition of the establishment of settlements there as "an obstacle to peace."

THE INTERESTS OF SAUDI ARABIA

Although Saudi Arabia, Syria and Jordan were all eager for a settlement that would satisfy their different and often contradictory objectives, unlike Egypt, they could afford to wait patiently until gaining what they considered essential. The detailed long-term objectives of Saudi Arabia on the substantive issues of the conflict were difficult to assess. It probably was interested in controlled perpetuation of the conflict in order to maintain the political and economic dependence of Arab states on it. However, having consolidated its leadership in the Arab world and its senior position in the international economic system since the 1973 war, it had no interest in risking these achievements by a violent eruption in the Middle East. Such an eruption, it felt, could be generated by a protracted political stalemate or by Arab disenchantment with the American-sponsored political process. An outbreak of this kind, the Saudis implied, could lead to a massive Soviet come-back in the Middle East; could radicalize Arab regimes in some key states; could isolate Saudi Arabia in the inter-Arab system, and perhaps even threaten the very existence of the Saudi regime. (See essay on Inter-Arab Relations and chapter on Saudi Arabia.)

The Saudis presented themselves as the only Arab political force capable of persuading the US to try and impose terms on Israel acceptable to the Arabs. In this respect, the minimum they could be expected to deliver was pressure on the US to generate an intensive effort towards an overall settlement. Since Saudi policy considerations were made primarily in the context of their inter-Arab and international significance, their specific positions on the major issues of the conflict must be judged within that framework. Saudi Arabia played a major role in working out the common political strategy and objectives of the major Arab states.

SYRIA'S ENHANCED ROLE

Syria's policies and political behaviour from 1976 to November 1977 must be considered against its preoccupation with two issues: 1) the Syrian power bloc and the Eastern Front, which bore directly on the conflict with Israel; and 2) the Lebanese crisis, which did not.

The Syrian power bloc and the Eastern Front were designed to provide Damascus with an effective military option that could be used independently of Egypt. With such a political power base, Syria would also have to be consulted in all major moves in the inter-Arab arena and the Arab-Israeli conflict. Syria established this base by a convergence of interests with Jordan; by establishing a dominant position in Lebanon, asserting its influence over the PLO, and developing an intermediate position between Egypt and Saudi Arabia on the one hand, and Egypt and the

Rejection Front of Arab states on the other. The Eastern Front was based on the prospect of Syrian-Jordanian military co-ordination; on the option of deploying a large expeditionary force from Iraq on Israel's eastern front in time of war, and on using Saudi Arabia—with its military bases and weapons arsenal—as a strategic hinterland, which was closer to Israel's population centres than positions on the Sinai front. The greater length of the Eastern Front (which in effect included Lebanon since 1976) also made possible the effective deployment of very large forces.

The price Syria had paid as Egypt's junior partner was shown by the 1973 cease-fire, as well as the 1975 Interim Agreement—both of which had been decided unilaterally by Cairo. Faced with this history of decision-making that did not serve its interests, Syrian leaders concentrated their political efforts on establishing Damascus as the centre of a political-strategic bloc that could change the balance of power among the Arab states. Such a bloc was designed to become the basis for significantly increasing Syria's bargaining power—in the inter-Arab field, in international relations, and in the conflict with Israel. Syria particularly hoped to exploit this power base *vis-à-vis* the US, the USSR, Egypt and Israel.

Syria did not feel the same urgency as Egypt for a settlement of the conflict with Israel, whose initial proposals for an interim agreement made late in 1975 ("cosmetic modifications" of the Golan line) were obviously unacceptable. The political damage such an accord could have caused Syria would have by far exceeded the insubstantial territorial gains involved. This lack of urgency continued in 1976 and 1977. The crucial issue for Syria was whether it could manoeuvre into a position where the US (and also Israel and Egypt) would consider that its co-operation was indispensable, and that without it no Middle East settlement could endure.

Of course, one major significance of such a development was that Syria expected the US to pay a much higher price for its co-operation than had previously been warranted (1973, 1975). In its strengthened position, Syria could also be expected to concede much less to Israel than might be implied by the balance of forces between them.

Syria's interest in widening its freedom of manoeuvre between the super-powers, the exigencies of the Lebanese crisis, and the need to minimize the danger of an untimely clash with Israel, prompted Damascus to establish working relations with the US, which led to a modest but not insignificant measure of understanding and trust. The American Administration was apparently persuaded that President Asad's regime might, under certain circumstances, play a "constructive, stabilizing and responsible" role in the Middle East. After Washington accepted that Syrian co-operation was necessary for the success of a renewed political initiative, it was also presented with a demonstration of the feasibility of achieving it by its conduct in the civil war in Lebanon. The Lebanese experience certainly improved Syria's bargaining position and helped to lay the foundation for an American-Syrian understanding.

Syria did not engage in intensive or detailed public debate concerning the Israeli and American positions. Nor did it actively participate in the "peace offensive" initiated by Egypt in late 1976. No major change emerged in Syria's position during this period on any of the key issues of the conflict. The Syrians proposed that the Arab side at Geneva either be represented by a single delegation or that the PLO be included in a joint Syrian-Jordanian-Palestinian-Lebanese grouping. This proposal aimed at answering Israel's refusal to accept PLO representation in Geneva, but its main purpose was to give Syria the key position in such a delegation. (Egypt rejected the proposal for that very reason.)

Apparently, Syria's approach to the Middle East settlement continued to be based on the expectation that each gain which Egypt could obtain at the expense of Israel—in exchange for real or tactical moderation, and after satisfying American interests—would eventually be proposed to Syria at much less cost. In this event, Syria expected to be faced with a comfortable choice of options: either to reject the proposal in the name of Arab patriotism and solidarity with the Palestinians (as in the case of the 1975 Interim Agreement); or eventually to accept, on the assumption that rejection in the first instance would further improve the proposal's terms (as in the 1974 Separation of Forces). In pursuing this strategy in 1977, Syria could derive satisfaction from the position it had established in the Eastern Front, its dominance in Lebanon, the working understanding that had evolved between Damascus and Washington, and the greater freedom of manoeuvre it had gained between the super-powers.

THE JORDANIAN INTEREST

Jordan's principal considerations concerning an Arab-Israeli settlement were its position in the West Bank, its struggle with the PLO over this issue and over the question of Palestinian representation on both banks. This obviously reflected the conflict between Jordan and the PLO over the future of the Jordanian entity as well.

Ever since 1974, when Palestinian representation was made the PLO's exclusive responsibility, Jordanian activities have been aimed at demonstrating the political futility of the PLO option, the indispensable role of the Kingdom in any attempt to restore Arab sovereignty to the West Bank, and the nuisance potential of an unco-operative Jordanian position. It was in this context that Jordan's political and military co-ordination with Syria was formulated (including Jordan's support for Syrian moves against the PLO in Lebanon), as well as Jordanian policies concerning the conflict with Israel. (For details, see chapter on Jordan and essay on Inter-Arab Relations.)

Beyond the formal support which Jordanian leaders voiced for Arab positions *vis-à-vis* Israel, and alongside the strategic hazard which Jordan's participation in the Eastern Front presented to Israel, a convergence of interests existed between Jordan and Israel on at least one issue of vital importance: both saw the PLO as an unrelenting enemy, and both shared a common interest in ensuring that any possible Arab sovereignty or political presence in the West Bank must be Jordanian, having as a major objective the suppression of all the PLO elements. Even under the previous Israeli Labour government, let alone under the Likud, there obviously existed a wide gap between Jordan and Israel on the issues of the West Bank and Jerusalem. Nevertheless, a tacit, mutual support manifested itself, *inter alia*, in the continuous encouragement by Israel of pro-Jordanian elements in the West Bank and the Gaza Strip (while PLO supporters were facing difficulties), and in the continuation of the "Open Bridges" policy that helped Jordan maintain her influence in the West Bank.

THE INTERESTS OF THE PLO

Beaten by Syria in Lebanon, and forced to seek help from Egypt, the PLO found its political fortunes in late 1976 and early 1977 at the lowest ebb since 1971. With its last semi-autonomous base in Lebanon now under Syrian control, the PLO lost much of its freedom of manoeuvre in the Arab world, and became increasingly dependent on Syria, Egypt (which it had denounced as "treacherous" after the conclusion of the Sinai Agreement), Saudi Arabia and Jordan.

As a new phase of the political process approached in late 1976, the PLO counted mainly on the commitment of the Arab states not to conclude a final settlement at the expense of the "legitimate rights of the Palestinian people." It relied on an all-Arab consensus and significant international support for the idea that the PLO alone represented the Palestinian people and their rights. The decline in the PLO's fortunes did not altogether disrupt this consensus; nor did it diminish the essential interpretation of the nature of these "legitimate rights"—a PLO-controlled Palestinian state in the West Bank and the Gaza Strip. But the PLO did have to struggle against considerable erosion in Arab and international support on these two issues.

Syria and Egypt, each for reasons of its own, no longer excluded the possibility of giving Jordan a position in the representation of the Palestinians, at the expense of the PLO. Indications that a link between Jordan and a future Palestinian entity in the West Bank could be imposed on the PLO—and not left for the independent Palestinian state to decide, as it wanted—worried the PLO. Although realizing that this trend could result in a Syrian-dominated "Palestinian entity" or a Jordanian-dominated semi-autonomous Palestinian district, the PLO seemed unable to prevent it.

The PLO's outstanding political gains in 1977 were with the US, which became increasingly convinced that the exclusion of the PLO from the political process could frustrate its own efforts. For its part, the PLO indicated that under certain conditions, it might consider co-operating with an American-sponsored initiative.

THE RENEWAL OF POLITICAL INITIATIVES IN 1977

When the Carter Administration took office in mid-January 1977, it found the major Arab states directly involved in the Middle East conflict (Egypt, Saudi Arabia, Syria and Jordan) presenting a united front on all major questions. These included Israeli withdrawal to the 1967 borders; minor, but on the face of it positive, modifications of their position on the nature of a future settlement ("the essence of peace"); and an understanding, fragile and ambiguous, on the Palestine question.

Carter's election had been greeted with reserve and even some suspicion in the Arab world. Egypt, and probably other Arab states, had preferred the Ford-Kissinger team mainly because of its commitment to an energetic renewal of the political process, and also because its already well-defined direction was considered more favourable to the Arabs. However, when Carter's style and Middle East policies became clearer, and when he evinced some urgency with regard to the Arab-Israeli conflict, he soon came to be accepted with greater warmth by Arab leaders and the media they controlled. (See essay on the US and the Middle East.)

The main obstacle to a new political initiative was the Palestinian dimension (see below). This was not primarily a reflection of its inherent importance; rather, it resulted from the fact that the Palestinian issue was the only one that, at that early stage, called for an operative decision on matters of procedure, the implications of which would be of paramount importance to the most sensitive issue of substance. While the Arab states were in basic agreement on territorial demands, and could easily postpone or evade a detailed discussion of the "essence of peace," the Palestinian question could not be glossed over; it raised conflicting interests not only between the Arabs and Israel, but also among the Arab states themselves, between them and the PLO, and between some of them and the US.

The most immediate concern was who would represent the Palestinians in Geneva, and thereafter presumably establish control in the West Bank and Gaza Strip. Some Arab states, particularly Egypt, were aware that the US found itself in a dilemma on this subject, because of its relations with Israel and Jordan, and its total opposition to the PLO. They realized that only by mutually-acceptable tactical flexibility could the Arab states help the US out of its difficulty and thus enable it to confront Israel over the question of a Palestinian state. To meet this complicated consideration, a formula was devised concerning some kind of link between the proposed Palestinian state and Jordan. In December 1976, Sādāt suggested that such a state should be "formally linked" with Jordan (on which Jordan and the PLO should agree). When Sādāt and Ḥusayn met in January 1977, they agreed that "the Palestinian people" (not the PLO) should be given the opportunity of "setting up an independent political entity." This time (unlike a previous attempt in 1974)[2] Sādāt did not shrink from seeking a formula which could not only be interpreted by the King as giving Jordan a position in the West Bank, but could also help the US put pressure on Israel to withdraw from this territory. When Syria and Saudi Arabia both joined in support of a link between the Palestinian entity and Jordan, this position emerged as an accepted and common stand among most Arab states. There was no doubt as to the way King Ḥusayn interpreted the reference to "very close relations" between the "two political entities." As expected, however, the PLO emphasized that the only links it would tolerate were those established according to the free will of a fully independent Palestinian state, after it had acquired complete sovereignty.

Sādāt's formula was basically accepted by the US and thus fulfilled its political function. It was useful to Washington in allowing room for political manoeuvre *vis-à-vis* Egypt, Saudi Arabia, Syria (and even the PLO) on the one hand, and *vis-à-vis* Jordan and Israel on the other. To those supporting the Palestinians' "right of self-determination," the US could point out that the political entity would be independent and have only loose ties with Jordan; it left Jordan room to undermine the Rabat resolutions in an indirect way; Damascus did not have to abandon the option of incorporating the new entity in a Greater Syria; and Israel could be reminded that it had always maintained that the Palestinian question should be solved within a Jordanian framework.

Similar considerations were behind Arab attitudes towards the necessary participation of the PLO at the Geneva conference. In view of the American commitment not to impose PLO participation on Israel, and Israel's acceptance of Palestinian members only within the Jordanian delegation, Sādāt proposed some link between an independent Palestinian delegation and the Jordanians in early 1977 in order to avoid a procedural stalemate. Syria suggested the alternative of an all-Arab delegation, but Egypt opposed this because of Syria's influence on Jordan, Lebanon and the PLO. Jordan opposed the establishment of a link between the Jordanian and Palestinian (PLO-controlled) delegation before Geneva, since, with American pressure, this would help the PLO overcome Israeli opposition to its participation. In fact, Jordan continued to rely heavily on the Israeli resolve to prevent the PLO from becoming the Arab party with which it had to negotiate the future of the West Bank.

Egypt and Syria (and probably also Saudi Arabia) clearly indicated to the PLO that it would have to accept whatever compromise solution could be found by the Arab states and between them and the US for its representation in Geneva. If not, they would not let the PLO's absence in Geneva constitute an obstacle to settlement. Egypt and Saudi Arabia also urged the PLO to moderate its formulations so as to help the US exert pressure on Israel.

THE US INITIATIVES

President Carter's statements met two of the three basic elements in the Arabs' position: the 1967 boundaries and a Palestinian "homeland." This provided a very convenient political basis for the meetings in April and May 1977 between

Carter, Sādāt, Asad and Crown Prince Fahd of Saudi Arabia.

When Sādāt arrived in Washington in early April, he found that a substantial measure of agreement (though by no means complete identity) already existed on all key issues. The Arabs' insistence that, as a pre-condition for negotiations, Israel withdraw to the 1967 lines was practically (though not explicitly and formally) accepted by the Carter Administration, as well as by the mainstream of the US news media. Sādāt's formulas on the Palestinian question and Carter's "homeland" phrase—coupled with the common understanding that the PLO was the dominant factor in the Palestinian arena—left each side enough room for manoeuvre, while also allowing a significant overlap. On the "nature of peace," Sādāt's statements were considered in the US as exceedingly brave for that early stage of discussion. In addition, Sādāt's willingness to work for "normalization" after a settlement was considered almost acceptable as a fair price for the concessions Israel would be required to make. What remained to be discussed during Sādāt's visit were issues of far less significance, such as Carter's definition of "defensible borders" for Israel, which seemed to be rather limited, and the question of whether the normalization of relations with Israel—which Sādāt suggested would take place five years after the Israeli withdrawal—would include the establishment of diplomatic relations.

Jordan, like Israel, was profoundly disturbed by some of the trends of American policy now accelerated under the Carter Administration. King Ḥusayn arrived in Washington towards the end of April, anxious to warn that Carter's support of a Palestinian "homeland" might result in the establishment of a PLO-controlled state in the West Bank, a state that would endanger the very existence of his monarchy. He suggested a Jordanian alternative and reportedly brought up his 1972 plan for a United Arab Kingdom, based on an Amman-centred federation between the two Banks and some measure of autonomy for the West Bank Palestinian section. It was hardly a coincidence that during Ḥusayn's visit, the White House spokesman emphasized America's negative attitude to PLO participation in Geneva under prevailing circumstances, either separately or within the Jordanian delegation, while Carter warned against early over-optimism for ME peace.

President Carter's meeting with Hafiz al-Asad demonstrated both the American recognition of Syria's increasing importance in the inter-Arab arena, and the loss in prestige Carter was prepared to risk in order to secure a chance of Syrian co-operation with his Middle Eastern policy. Asad refused to travel either to Washington or London, where Carter attended a European conference. Instead, he succeeded in having the US President come especially to the symbolic "neutral ground" of Geneva. Asad thus demonstrated his freedom of manoeuvre between Washington and Moscow, but more importantly, showed that Syria could no longer be considered of secondary importance to Egypt in the Arab world, and that her position in the inter-Arab system had been recognized by Washington. Carter's interest was to try and secure the co-operation of this third state in the important Arab triangle (Egypt, Saudi Arabia and Syria) in order to remove a major destabilizing element from the path of the American-sponsored political process. The reported discussions between the two Presidents of possible security arrangements (particularly demilitarization) on the Golan Heights suggest that Carter presented his ideas of meeting Israeli security concerns without a change in sovereignty. In Asad's public statements, however, there was nothing to suggest a departure from familiar Arab positions (totally inadequate in the Israeli view) concerning demilitarized territorial strips astride the border.

The visit to Washington of Crown Prince Fahd of Saudi Arabia came only a few days after the unexpected election results in Israel, and followed a top-level consultation among King Khālid, Sādāt and Asad. Aware that the US considers them as the cornerstone of its Middle East policy, the Saudis made it clear that their co-operation in Middle East politics and in global economic and energy problems depended on Washington's resolve to use its influence on Israel to accept Arab terms for a settlement. Fahd also indicated that the Saudi position in the Arab world that enabled it to exercise a moderating influence on Arab states (and even, to some extent, on the PLO) and secure Arab co-operation with American policies, depended on its ability to generate effective American pressure on Israel. During the visit, Carter made two statements that could indicate that the Saudi message was received. By speaking of a "secure homeland with recognized boundaries" the President came closer than ever before to the concept of a Palestinian state. He also stated a commitment to UN resolutions which—with subsequent State Department clarifications—could have implied that the 1947 UN "partition plan" might one day be resurrected.

The election of the Likud in Israel was considered by Arab decision-makers and the public primarily in terms of its impact on American policy and Western public opinion. Following a deeply-rooted tendency in the Arab world, the option of a compromise settlement worked out directly between Israelis and Arabs was not seriously considered at that time. Arab expectations were that inflexible Israeli positions would facilitate an American drift away from commitments to Israel; that it would thus become easier to isolate Israel from its traditional support in American public opinion and in Congress, as well as in the American Jewish community. Such expectations allayed to a large extent Arab apprehensions about a seemingly more intransigent post-election Israel. The Arab assumption was, so to speak, that an Israel that was unable to bend to international pressures would eventually be broken by them.

The gap between the Israeli and American positions, already noticeable during the March 1977 visit of Prime Minister Rabin to Washington, became formalized during Menahem Begin's talks in July, when Israel publicly abandoned the attempt to co-ordinate her positions with the US. The American decision to focus its sharp criticism on the issue of Israeli settlements in the occupied territories ("an obstacle to peace"), alongside the assertive tenor of Israeli declarations on this subject, encouraged the Arab states to look for a closer identity of views with the US.

The proximity of Arab and American views on some major subjects, as well as the gap between Carter's Administration and the national consensus in Israel (let alone the Begin government) were further demonstrated during the US Secretary of State's second Middle East tour in August 1977. Jordan and Egypt (and reportedly to some limited extent even Saudi Arabia) told Cyrus Vance that they accepted Begin's proposal that the political process should lead, ultimately, to the signing of peace *treaties* (not only a "peace *agreement*" which had been the Egyptian formula since 1971). The US therefore announced significant "progress" and a considerable narrowing of differences between those Arab countries and the Americans over their approach to "the nature of peace" (which in turn was termed "close to the Israeli approach"). A likelier explanation is that by abandoning such previous formulas as "termination of belligerency" and "end of the state of war," and by agreeing to a peace treaty rather than a peace agreement, the Arabs forwarded their political objective by providing the US with a pretext to call on Israel for an equivalent response.

This tendency was further strengthened when the US received indications—reportedly through Saudi Arabia—that if the PLO were encouraged, it might adopt an amended version of Security Council Resolution 242. Carter's subsequent invitation to the PLO to open a dialogue with the US under certain circumstances further widened the gap between the Israeli and American positions. This shift in

American policy helped Egypt and Saudi Arabia (and also Jordan and even Syria) to adopt somewhat more flexible positions on matters of procedure, counting on US backing for the more problematic matters of substance. This strategy expressed itself in the acceptance of the mechanism of foreign ministers' meetings in New York and Washington with President Carter and Secretary Vance. (Sādāt went so far as to accept "working groups" that left an option open for the inclusion of the Israeli as well as Arab foreign ministers, though Syria vetoed the idea.) It also enabled the Administration in September to seek a compromise formula—open to different interpretations in terms of PLO participation—for the reconvening of the Geneva conference.

Thus, when the Middle East foreign ministers went to the US in September 1977 to pursue the political process under the personal sponsorship of President Carter, Saudi Arabia and Egypt not only enjoyed international support for their positions, but also an unprecedented degree of political co-ordination with the US. Syria also enjoyed some measure of understanding with Washington and confidently adopted a wait-and-see approach. Jordan, on the other hand, watched US policy developments with growing concern, paradoxically counting on Israel's uncompromising opposition to the PLO. While the mainstream in the PLO realized that progress was being made in recognizing its indispensable political role, it was also aware of difficulties: the Arab states' determination not to give the PLO veto-power over their decisions; and the Jordanian and Israeli resolve to prevent the organization from establishing itself in the West Bank. The Rejection states (particularly Libya and Iraq) played no significant role in this political process, but with the help of the USSR continued to concentrate on enhancing their military strength, a factor of potential political significance should the settlement moves fail.

THE PALESTINIAN DIMENSION OF THE CONFLICT

Since the 1973 war, and more so since the Separation of Forces agreements in 1974 and the Sinai Agreement in 1975, all the parties have been aware that the Palestinian issue could become a major obstacle to the continuation of the political process. Its saliency was demonstrated by the PLO's improved political position in the wake of the 1973 war, in which paradoxically its role was quite negligible. This led to the formal endorsement of the PLO's status within the inter-Arab framework during 1974–5, and to its wider acceptance in the international community as the representative of the Palestinian Arabs. Thus all parties involved in the Arab-Israeli conflict were obliged to articulate their particular strategies towards the PLO. However, it soon became evident that the formal endorsement of the PLO's status by the Arab states did not endow it with real freedom of action; nor did it decrease the continuing direct and indirect interference by Arab governments in the PLO's fortunes and daily affairs (for instance, through subsidized Palestinian affiliates).

THE ATTITUDES OF ARAB STATES

For different and sometimes contradictory reasons, the major Arab states agreed that the Palestinian dimension of the Arab-Israeli conflict should be settled on the basis of "the realization of the Palestinian people's right to self-determination" in the West Bank and Gaza Strip. However, they interpreted the specific political content of this formula differently. Egypt evidently accepted it as a means of removing the Israeli presence from the territories occupied in 1967 without terminating the conflict, while at the same time being relieved of direct responsibility for "the liberation of Palestine." Syria also probably found it convenient to use the Palestinian issue to strengthen the general Arab commitment not to terminate the conflict with Israel, a commitment which in turn could frustrate Egyptian and other

Arab moves out of step with its own policy.

As the Rabat resolutions had practically been forced on Jordan in 1974,[3] the Kingdom only formally accepted the formula of Palestinian self-determination. Ḥusayn now used these resolutions to demonstrate that recognition of the PLO as the sole representative of the Palestinian people constituted an obstacle to the restoration of the West Bank and Gaza Strip to Arab sovereignty. Thus, Saudi Arabia supported the formula, probably as a means of consolidating its inter-Arab and international position. The Saudis seem to have considered a settlement on this basis and under their sponsorship a reasonable compromise between the different positions of Egypt, Syria and the PLO on the one hand, and the US on the other. (For details, see chapter on Saudi Arabia and essay on Inter-Arab Relations.)

Throughout, Egypt had a clear interest in furthering understanding with Washington on the Palestinian issue, its political standing in the US giving it a good chance of success. Because of his isolation in the Arab world following the Interim Agreement, Sādāt was eager to refute charges of having betrayed "the cause of Palestine," levelled at him in particular by Syria, Libya and the PLO. In the US, Egypt succeeded in presenting its own position on the Palestinian issue as converging with a recognized American interest; namely, to demonstrate to other Arab states that its reliance on US co-operation was the most effective way of regaining "Arab lands" from Israel (as in the 1975 Interim Agreement), as well as in furthering the cause of the Palestinians.

Syria's interest was in demonstrating that a better and more effective alternative was to make its co-operation conditional on American gestures towards the PLO. The outstanding Syrian success came in November 1975 when, with tacit American support, the UN Security Council invited the PLO to join in discussions on the Middle East (subsequently held in January 1976). Syria had insisted on the adoption of this resolution before consenting to renew the UNDOF mandate in the critical period immediately following the Interim Agreement. By virtue of her improved bargaining position in the inter-Arab system, Syria thus demonstrated that she could *force* the US to help legitimize the PLO, whereas Egypt was still trying to *persuade* Washington to move in this same direction, by virtue of the American commitment to the stability of Sādāt's regime.

Little is known about the modality of the Saudis' attempt to mobilize American support for the PLO, but they doubtless argued that US policy in the Middle East would reach deadlock if it failed to find a way of integrating the PLO into the political process. As previously mentioned, the Saudis relied on the argument that they would find it difficult to influence other Arab states (towards consolidating pro-American tendencies) unless they could point to some definite progress on the Palestinian issue. American policy was probably significantly influenced by the Saudis, particularly as they undertook to help moderate the PLO.

THE POSITION OF THE PLO

Since 1974, the PLO had itself been seeking ways to benefit from an American-sponsored political initiative, in spite of deeply-rooted suspicions of American objectives towards itself. While continuing to foster relations with the Soviet Union, some of the mainstream Palestinian leaders understood that blunt and total rejection of an American initiative could be dangerous. Should Israel withdraw from the West Bank in favour of King Ḥusayn, for example, the Palestinians might once again be excluded as a significant political factor when the fate of Palestine was being decided (as had happened in 1947–9).

As the PLO's inter-Arab and international position improved in 1974–5, it made repeated signals to Washington that if an American-sponsored political process could be shown to be benefiting the Palestinian cause, the PLO could in turn facilitate general Arab-American co-operation. As early as June 1974, the Palestine National Council had adopted a multi-phase political programme which in principle allowed the PLO to establish control over the West Bank in the event of Israeli withdrawal (presumably under American pressure). Even in its most strongly-worded condemnations of US policy, the PLO implied that its hostility stemmed from Washington's continued refusal to make it any concessions; that it uncompromisingly rejected past American policy in the Middle East, but could change if US policy changed. Thus, for example, the PLO's denunciation of the 1975 Sinai Agreement was not aimed so much against Israeli withdrawal in exchange for a temporary containment of the conflict, nor against American commitments as such, but against a settlement between Israel and Egypt that totally ignored the Palestinian issue.

THE EVOLUTION OF US POLICY

Since the 1973 war, the US has clearly understood that without a satisfactory approach to the national dimension of the Palestinian issue, its Middle East policy would lead to an early impasse. If its policy were to bolster the role of American-oriented Arab states (particularly Egypt and Saudi Arabia), it would have to convince other regimes (particularly Syria) that it was to their advantage not to reject US initiatives out of hand. A realization of the importance of somehow involving the PLO in the search for a Middle East settlement grew in Washington after that organization was officially endorsed by the Arab states as the sole representative of the Palestinian people at the Rabat summit in October 1974, and after it became more internationally accepted—as reflected by the UN General Assembly's decision to invite 'Arafāt to address it the following month. However, such a policy contained an inherent dilemma: the possibility of alienating two important US partners—Israel and Jordan—who saw the PLO as a grave threat to themselves.

As far as Israel was concerned, the tactical US problem was how not to be too obvious in withdrawing from its written commitments made to Israel as a part of the Sinai Agreement in 1975. In more general terms, the US had to prevent an eventual *rapprochement* with the PLO from reaching a point where Israel could no longer co-operate with American policy. The US tried to overcome this dilemma by a series of calculated steps aimed at establishing the centrality of the Palestinian question and opening a dialogue with the PLO, while trying to reassure Israel that "there was no change" in American policy. Obviously this was only a short-term strategy.

At the same time, the US had to assuage the moderate Jordanian regime's fears that a PLO-controlled state in the West Bank could endanger the very existence of the Hashemite monarchy. The notion of establishing a link between Jordan and a future Palestinian entity on the West Bank was raised in this context by American officials. However, until the autumn of 1977, it seemed to some political observers as if the Carter Administration was giving higher priority to the solution of the Palestinian problem in the West Bank than to Israeli and Jordanian vulnerabilities. As Jordan and Israel had a common interest in frustrating American advances towards the PLO, they appeared to find ways of co-ordinating their political efforts in this direction both in the West Bank and in Washington.

THE ISRAELI ATTITUDE

Israel continued to see the Palestinian question primarily as a product rather than a cause of the conflict with the Arab states, which it sought to solve within an overall Middle East settlement—not within a Palestinian-Israeli context. It consistently refused to recognize the PLO or enter into any negotiations with it, arguing that either step would lend legitimacy to an organization committed to the destruction of Israel. For the same reason, Israel also opposed the establishment of a PLO-controlled—and therefore presumably irridentist—Palestinian entity in the West Bank and the Gaza Strip. Israel thus sought to prevent the US from making the Palestinian issue the core of any attempts to settle the conflict, and from legitimizing—directly or indirectly—the PLO as the body through which "the legitimate interests of the Palestinian people" (a recurrent official American phrase) should be satisfied. Israel strongly criticized American gestures towards the PLO, warning that they could only make a settlement more difficult and increase the risks of a new conflagration.

THE IMPACT OF THE CIVIL WAR IN LEBANON

The Palestinian question receded as a central issue in the Arab-Israeli conflict during the civil war in Lebanon, when enormous political and physical damage was inflicted on the PLO. For a time hopes rose in Egypt, Syria, Saudi Arabia, the US and even in Israel that the chances for an "acceptable" settlement of the Palestinian issue had improved. In Israel, some argued that the PLO's decline would weaken the tendency to integrate it into the Middle East political process. In Jordan, it was hoped that the results of the civil war would bring the Arab states and the US to the realization that exclusive reliance on the PLO was futile. Egypt recognized that 1976 could not become "the year of Palestine," as Sādāt had predicted. Sādāt also realized that a weakened PLO that came to seek Egyptian protection from Syrian domination would be much easier to handle and control than the formerly self-assured and critical organization. Thus, Egypt attempted simultaneously to convince Washington to accept the PLO in the political process, and apply pressure on the PLO to adopt a position (or at least a formula) that would help the US enter into a dialogue with it. By defeating the PLO in the civil war and practically taking over Lebanon (where the organization had its last semi-independent base), Syria undoubtedly strengthened its position in relation to the Palestinian question. It could now afford to take an even tougher stand in negotiating with other Arab states and the US.

DEVELOPMENTS IN 1977

The positions of the various parties to the Arab-Israeli conflict were put to a political test when the new Carter Administration reportedly adopted some recommendations of the Brookings Report (proposing *inter alia* the establishment of some Palestinian entity in the West Bank). It was against this background that Secretary of State Cyrus Vance embarked on a ME tour in February 1977 to assess attitudes towards a new initiative on the Palestinian question.

Reports from Egypt and elsewhere reinforced expectations in the US—also heavily reflected in the Western media—that the PLO was about to modify its position significantly at the Palestine National Council meeting due in Cairo in March 1977; some even expected an amendment of the Palestine National Charter. Although President Carter pursued the issue of Palestinian representation at Geneva with Prime Minister Rabin in early March 1977, Rabin firmly repeated Israel's resolve to resist any form of PLO participation. In a clear attempt to influence the decision of the Palestine National Council (perhaps following an understanding with Egypt, Saudi Arabia and possibly even with some elements in the PLO), Carter made an unprecedented declaration during the critical phase of its meeting in Cairo calling for "a homeland for the Palestine refugees." For the first time he used the terms "Palestinians" and "PLO" interchangeably, a usage which became habitual until October 1977.

Although welcomed by 'Arafāt as "a step in the right direction" (and received with vehement protests in Israel), Carter's statement failed to produce the desired outcome. The Palestine National Council resolutions reaffirmed the commitment to the National Charter (with its declared aim of destroying Israel). However, they left greater scope for interim measures towards the ultimate objective than did the resolutions of the previous Council in June 1974. The Council insisted on the PLO's right to participate at future Geneva talks, and while criticizing the existing diplomatic framework for Geneva (Security Council Resolutions 242 and 338), it did not reject a new version of these resolutions which recognized the national dimension of the Palestinian problem. The explicit reference to a PLO-controlled Palestinian "independent national state" on its "national soil" did not preclude the establishment of such a state in the West Bank and Gaza Strip, as a first stage.

Following the elections in Israel, intensive discussions started in July and August 1977 about reconvening the Geneva conference, with attention focused to an unprecedented degree on the Palestinian issue. This was because Palestinian representation had become the main procedural obstacle which could wreck any chance of having the conference reconvened at all, and so produce an early (pre-Geneva) political stalemate. With this situation apparently in mind and following policy trends perceptible for three years, President Carter announced yet another shift in US policy at the beginning of August, on the eve of Secretary Vance's second visit to Israel. He indicated that if the PLO were to accept Resolution 242, the US would consider this sufficient progress towards its recognition of Israel to justify opening a dialogue between the US and the PLO. Carter went even further by indicating that he understood the inadequacy of the status that Resolution 242 gave to the Palestinian question (referring only to Palestinian "refugees"). This statement was made after Saudi leaders apparently assured Secretary Vance that they could bring about a moderation in the PLO leadership's position if adequate American encouragement was given. However, Carter's statement again failed to produce the intended results. The PLO probably expected a further evolution in the US attitude.

At this stage, Carter did not support an amendment to Resolution 242; nor did he openly attempt to impose such a change upon Israel, which would have violated the written American commitment given on this issue in September 1975. However, the trend was clear. Besides accepting that the Palestinians were not to be considered simply as refugees, Carter had practically exempted the PLO from meeting the second condition implicit in the 1975 Memorandum of Agreement—recognition of Israel's right to exist. And he totally ignored a third condition presented by Secretary Vance during his visit in February 1977 to Jerusalem: that the PLO amend the National Covenant with regard to the destruction of Israel. At this stage (September 1977), the State Department made another official statement, with the approval of the President, to the effect that the Palestinians should be involved in the peace-making process in order to ensure a lasting settlement.

However, during September, the Carter Administration began to realize that its policy was leading towards an imminent breakdown of the political process, since Israel refused to attend the Geneva conference if its political base (Resolutions 242 and 338 and the right to veto additional participants) were to be altered and the PLO invited. The result was a compromise, hammered out by Carter and Dayan in October 1977, which distinguished between Palestinian Arabs and the PLO (see below).

The train of events set in motion by Sādāt's visit to Jerusalem in November 1977, in which he deliberately refrained from mentioning the PLO (and was therefore vehemently denounced by them), forced a reappraisal of the situation on all parties.

ISRAEL'S POLITICAL STRATEGY

The 1975 Agreement was considered in Israel as the end of the first round of accords that followed the 1973 war. Israel hoped to use the subsequent military and political lull to allay the pressures she had been subjected to since 1973, and reinforce her political, economic and military potential in preparation for an eventual political (or perhaps even military) struggle over the consequences of the 1967 war. Israel expected the next confrontation to occur in an adverse environment, after possible political setbacks and an increase in Arab power as a consequence of the threat of a renewed energy crisis and a large-scale military build-up.

ISRAELI STRATEGY IN 1976

In order to assist the US to maintain the political momentum, Israel agreed in early 1976 to consider the possibility of a further "partial" settlement on the basis of "a termination of the state of belligerency" between the Arab states (including Jordan) and Israel. In return, Israel offered far-reaching yet limited territorial concessions: far-reaching if measured by previous partial settlements, but limited compared to what Israel could offer in return for full-fledged peace. However, the Arab states seemed to prefer to wait for an overall settlement after the Lebanese crisis was resolved and the US elections were over.

Israel was prepared at that stage to consider several possibilities for a settlement: overall or "true peace"; a far-reaching interim settlement which would constitute "an end to the state of war"; or a limited small-scale partial agreement aimed at de-escalating the conflict for a further period. However, the Rabin government was convinced that the gap between Israel and the Arabs was still too wide for a real chance to achieve an overall settlement, at least on terms acceptable to Israel. It was convinced that all the parties to the conflict would eventually realize that a new attempt at limited settlements was the only realistic option.

Until the end of 1976, Israeli positions (as formulated after the Interim Agreement of 1975) were not significantly or intensively challenged either by the US or by the Arab states. Towards the end of the year, however, the situation changed. First came indications of Arab recuperation from the consequences of the Lebanese crisis. After the October 1976 Riyadh summit meeting, for instance, Israel became concerned at the possibility of Egyptian-Syrian political and military co-ordination.

Another challenge to Israel was the Egyptian "peace offensive" aimed at the incoming US Administration, at Congress and at American public opinion. Sādāt managed to put Israel in a defensive position, having to explain the difference between Sādāt's meaning and conditions for "peace," and what Israel called a "termination of the conflict." Israel by and large failed to convince American public opinion that although using a new and sophisticated terminology, Arab leaders were simply attempting to sell the same old unacceptable political conditions in a new disguise. Israel pointed out the Arabs' refusal to accept the normal features of peace, such as open borders and diplomatic relations. However, a dominant impression was that, at best, Israel's reservations were of secondary importance and a poor response to the positive movement among Arab leaders towards an acceptance of the reality of Israel. At worst, Israel was suspected of trying to use semantics to avoid paying the full price for Arab willingness to make peace.

When President Carter's policies and style began to unfold after January 1977, Israel was in no doubt about the "moderate" Arab states' influence in persuading him to bring pressure on Israel to accept Arab terms. Thus, it was the US (and not the Arab states) which presented Israel with the crucial challenge. Despite the ritualistic American declarations that the parties to the conflict should themselves negotiate the settlement, and its repeated commitment that a settlement should not and could not be imposed, Israel came to realize that the chances of a settlement she could accept depended on the acceptance of its terms in Washington, or at least on an American abstention from supporting alternative suggestions.

All Israeli policy-makers were keenly aware of the profound American commitment, under any Administration, to political "progress" in the Middle East and to keeping up the "momentum." They were also aware of the association in American political circles between "stalemate" and "deadlock," and the imminent danger of war. Even before the details of Carter's Middle East policy became known, Israel realized that both the President and his Adviser on National Security, Zbigniew Brzezinski, were supporters of the main proposals of the Brookings Report, with its emphasis on a comprehensive settlement, to be implemented in stages. (See essay, "The US and the Middle East.") Israel therefore again formulated her well-known positions concerning an overall settlement, although Israeli spokesmen, and particularly Prime Minister Rabin, repeatedly warned that this might not be a realistic course in prevailing circumstances.

THE ISRAELI CONCEPT OF PEACE

Israel's "maximal" proposals for the "nature of peace" have been very precisely defined: free movement through open borders, diplomatic relations and termination of all expressions of hostility (including economic warfare and propaganda). The Rabin government repeatedly emphasized that in exchange for limited progress towards the final peace objective (such as "termination of belligerency" or "end of the state of war"), Israel could only be expected to make limited territorial concessions.

On the territorial issue, Israel consistently avoided official "map drawing" as to the specific lines she would consider secure and defensible—except in the case of Lebanon where she accepted the international border which was also identical to the 1949 Armistice line. However, Israel always insisted that it would not return to the pre-1967 lines, and that new "defensible" borders should provide the country with the territorial depth required for self-defence. Despite this reluctance to make commitments on specific border changes, various official and unofficial sources have helped to clarify Israeli thinking, at least up to the time of Sādāt's visit to Jerusalem in November 1977.

On the Egyptian front, Israel was prepared to withdraw from most of the Sinai peninsula in exchange for full peace, although retaining special interest in the Rafah gap (between Rafaḥ and al-'Arīsh near the Mediterranean),[4] and in a territorial strip west of the 1967 line (previously the international border between Rafaḥ and Taba, near Eilat on the Red Sea). Israel demanded "control" of Sharm al-Shaykh, which governed the entrance to the Gulf of 'Aqaba (but without insisting on changes in sovereignty or ruling out a long-term lease); and over a defensible territorial link ("not only the road") leading to it from Eilat along the Gulf of 'Aqaba. All these changes were supported by strategic (not historical) considerations. According to a 1968 Cabinet resolution (formally still valid), the Gaza Strip should become part of Israel. There was nevertheless a significant opinion in the Cabinet (publicly supported by Foreign Minister Allon in September 1976) that most of the Strip and all its Arab population might become part of an eventual solution to the Palestinian problem, through some link with the West Bank and Jordan.

The accepted formula on the Syrian border was that Israel would not "descend from the Golan Heights," but neither would it necessarily insist on the 1974 Separation of Forces Line as the final border. This formula implied the possibility that some of the settlements established on the Golan since the 1967 war (many of them now practically on the Separation Line) might find themselves beyond the ultimate border. The justification was once again exclusively strategic—to protect the upper Jordan Valley and safeguard the major water sources of Israel; to maintain an early warning capability (Mount Hermon); and to deter the Syrians from future aggression.

Since Golda Meir's term as Prime Minister, the Israeli Government has been domestically committed to a policy that authorized the Cabinet to negotiate a territorial settlement on the eastern sector, with the proviso that if it involved withdrawal from the West Bank (Judea and Samaria),[5] the issue would have to be "decided by the people" in new elections. Beyond this principle, there were differences in the Cabinet concerning the ultimate fate of the West Bank, differences that became sharper with the approval of the elections in May 1977 (see below). The Defence Minister, Shimon Peres, was identified at that period with the concept of a "functional settlement," namely sharing sovereignty with Jordan, which was close to a proposal first made by the former Minister of Defence, Moshe Dayan. Peres suggested several versions of federal ties between Israel and the West Bank, as well as confederal ties with Jordan, openly rejecting and criticizing the territorial partition concept embodied in the "Allon Plan" (see below). Prime Minister Rabin preferred a division of the territory, and indicated that the ambiguous formulations of the government on this subject were not to his liking. He would have preferred it to come out in clear support of a territorial compromise.

Yigal Allon has been publicly committed since 1967 to a specific plan (bearing his name) which proposes the establishment of defensible borders through the application of Israeli sovereignty over a defence belt along the River Jordan and the Dead Sea, and some smaller border adjustments on the western Israeli limits of the West Bank and in the Jerusalem area. The territories Israel would keep under this plan would be largely those not populated by Arabs, while the populated ridge of the Samarian and Judean hills would revert to Jordanian sovereignty and be linked to Jordan by a corridor in the Jericho area (a contrary view being based, in part, on the strategic importance of the ridge for the defence of the Israeli heartland on the plain to the west). All the country's leaders agreed that Jerusalem must remain undivided and the capital of Israel, with autonomy for religious communities over their holy places.

Despite these differences over the ultimate fate of the West Bank, the Israeli basis for a settlement remained the Allon Plan of 1967, with new Jewish settlements concentrated in the Jordan Valley, the Jerusalem area and the Etzion bloc. An exception to this pattern was the settlement by Gush Imunim (an extreme nationalist religious group) at Kaddum (Elon Morre). This was established at the end of 1975 in the centre of the heavily populated Samarian mountains near Nablus, with the deliberate purpose of disrupting the Allon Plan's option of withdrawal from this area. Although Kaddum was settled in defiance of the Government, it was not removed because of the political difficulty of using force to disperse the settlers. Rabin reportedly intended to remove Kaddum after the elections, but in the event, Begin's government recognized its permanency.

On the Palestinian issue, the Government was united in its total opposition to the establishment of an independent Palestinian state between Israel and Jordan, believing that it would either be PLO-controlled at the outset, or soon become so. It was also united in rejecting the PLO as a partner to any negotiations. On the broader Palestinian issue, however, there were different shades of opinion. Allon was explicit and Rabin implicit in proposing an alternative to the PLO solution to the question of the Palestinian identity which would allow Arab (Jordanian) sovereignty over the Palestinian-populated area of the West Bank. Peres did not accept a territorial compromise that could make such an option workable, and concentrated instead on outright opposition to the PLO and a Palestinian state. A number of less central figures in the government were less unconditional and uncompromising than the majority in rejecting the PLO and the idea of a separate national Palestinian entity. Some Mapam and Independent Liberal coalition members continued to support the "Yariv-Shemtov formula" which proposed that Israel should recognize the PLO providing that it accepted Resolutions 242 and 338, recognized Israel's right to exist, amended the Palestine National Charter, and undertook to stop its terrorist activities.

On the procedural question of reconvening the Geneva conference, Rabin's government—like its predecessor—continued to support Resolutions 242 and 338 (as interpreted by Israel) as the sole basis for negotiations with all its neighbours, including Lebanon. Relying on written American commitments—undertaken in conjunction with the 1975 Interim Agreement—the Israelis uncompromisingly rejected any PLO presence at the conference in whatever form (including in an all-Arab delegation), while accepting the participation of Palestinians in the Jordanian delegation, provided they were not known PLO members. Israel rejected all preconditions to the convening of the conference, particularly the Arab insistence that it undertake to withdraw to the 1967 lines. These positions did not stand the test of operative negotiations with the Arabs, but did represent a considerable consensus in Israel.

THE LABOUR GOVERNMENT'S REACTION TO CARTER'S POLICY

The Labour government was considerably weakened after December 1976 by a domestic political crisis which caused the loss of its parliamentary majority, forced an early general election, and produced an open leadership struggle between Rabin and Peres. At the end of February, with an eye to the impending elections, the Labour Party introduced a significant policy change, explicitly stating that Israel should be prepared to accept "territorial compromise on all three fronts" (including withdrawal from parts of the West Bank) in return for peace.

Between Carter's inauguration in January 1977 and Rabin's visit to Washington in March, Israel was confronted with the first and as yet tentatively-expressed indications of concern in Western public and official circles over its position on the Palestinian question. Persistent reports suggesting that the PLO was ready to moderate its stand—towards accepting Israeli existence, if the latter did not close the door to its participation in Geneva (circulated, *inter alia*, by Knesset members and public figures who had met PLO personalities in Western Europe)—were totally rejected in official quarters, since no such indications had come from the PLO directly.

Rabin's visit to Washington early in March 1977 produced an initial understanding between Israel and the US that the two countries should emphasize areas of agreement and not express their differences publicly. Carter's definition of the "nature of peace" was described as being closer than ever to the Israeli position, and his use of the term "defensible borders" gave rise to some modest hopes of a positive change in the American position on the territorial question. In dramatic contrast, however, was the private meeting between the two leaders, in which it was later revealed that Carter had reacted negatively to Rabin's unconditional rejection of the PLO, even if it were to recognize Israel's legitimacy. He warned that if Israel persisted in this attitude, she would meet with strong criticism in the US. Rabin nevertheless maintained his uncompromising stand.

Israel was surprised and bitterly disappointed when, shortly after Rabin's official visit, Carter chose to commit himself publicly to what it felt to be an outline of the substance of a proposed settlement, including two major elements that sharply contradicted Israeli positions. What caused special concern was that the President committed himself to Israel's withdrawal to the 1967 boundaries (with minor adjustments), indicating that "defensible borders" should consist primarily of security arrangements involving no change in sovereignty or in political boundaries. Rabin immediately responded by saying that only the parties to the conflict should determine the settlement and rejected the 1967 lines as final borders. Shortly afterwards, he publicly rejected any negotiations with the PLO even if it amended the Palestine National Charter.

The second element in Carter's position that shook Israeli hopes for a co-ordinated position with the US was his support for "a homeland for the Palestinian refugees," which was interpreted in Israel as implying the eventual legitimization of a separate Palestinian state in the West Bank and the Gaza Strip. This concern was not allayed by Carter's repeated vague references to the need for a link between a Palestinian entity and Jordan. In fact, Israeli concern increased when Carter spoke of a homeland "for the Palestinians" (and not just "refugees"), and finally by his constant interchange of the terms "Palestinians" and "PLO."

For the first time, an American President had gone public on what amounted to a comprehensive proposal for an overall settlement—and in doing so, taken a stand on critical issues which were diametrically opposed to Israeli positions. Only his statement on the "essence of peace" was considered favourable by Israel. By thus publicly identifying himself with specific proposals—instead of relying on his Secretary of State to float ideas, as was customary—Carter largely relinquished the option of softening, shelving, freezing or withdrawing impracticable proposals without serious damage to his prestige (a tactic which Nixon had used successfully in 1969–70 in relation to the Rogers Plan).

Anxiety in Israel increased in the course of April and May 1977, following Carter's meetings with Presidents Sādāt and Asad. The American response to Arab sensitivities (in particular Carter's special trip to Geneva to spare Asad the political discomfort of Washington or even London) was felt to be out of proportion to the firmness, and sometimes even bluntness, with which Israel was treated.

These developments coincided with other events that would have been accepted in Israel with less suspicion under different circumstances. However, in February, Carter refused to sell Israel a weapon which President Ford had agreed to supply before the elections (thus failing to honour a Presidential commitment); later, the US blocked the sale of Israeli-made *Kfir* aircraft (fitted with American engines) to Ecuador. The Administration also adopted a negative approach to Israel's request to share in the production of F-16 aircraft which the US had promised to supply. These decisions, as well as criticism of the Israeli defence industry in the media (believed to have been inspired by the Pentagon), were interpreted as attempts to cripple Israel's defence capability for the purpose of exerting political pressure. These suspicions culminated in the Administration's attempt to remove Israel from the list of states granted priority in receiving US military supplies and technology.

The gravity with which Rabin's government viewed these trends in US policy was not fully disclosed in Israel. The reason for this restraint was the fear of adverse effects on the Labour Party's election campaign—fears which were later substantiated.

POLICIES OF THE LIKUD GOVERNMENT

Far-reaching changes in Israeli policy were anticipated after the Likud's election victory in May 1977. Both the Likud's platform and the ideology of Begin's party (Herut) within it had focused on the ultimate fate of the West Bank. Ever since 1967, Herut had regarded Judea and Samaria as "liberated territory" where

"Israeli law should be applied." (In these terms, they could not be "annexed" since they constituted an inseparable part of the "homeland.") Immediately after the elections, when still only Prime Minister-designate, Begin introduced this kind of terminology in the US media. Speaking at the new settlement of Kaddum (see above), he promised that there would be many more of its kind. As for the Allon Plan, which discouraged settlements in heavily-populated parts of the West Bank, Begin called it "dead in thoughts and on the map."

The initial impression of Likud's intransigence was softened somewhat by the nomination of Moshe Dayan as Foreign Minister. Dayan had not joined the Likud on the eve of the elections because he did not receive the necessary undertaking—that Israeli law would not be applied in Judea and Samaria as long as contacts in the search for peace continued. In fact, it soon became apparent (from policy declarations in the Knesset as well as statements on less formal occasions) that the Begin government was adopting a policy of continuity in many areas: it adhered to Resolutions 242 and 338 as a basis for Geneva; it refrained from applying Israeli law over Judea and Samaria; it stated that in negotiations aimed at the conclusion of peace treaties, Israel would pose no territorial precondition concerning Judea and Samaria, and would regard all territories, including Jerusalem, as negotiable. Begin even refrained for a while from establishing new settlements, and when he did, chose locations already approved by the former government.

However, the new Government left no doubt that its policies differed radically from those of its predecessor on two major issues—the ultimate fate of the West Bank and its attitude to the US role in peace negotiations. No opportunity was lost to claim that the Israeli voters had put the new government in power on the basis of its deep commitment to oppose foreign domination in the "western part of the land of Israel" (between the River Jordan and the Mediterranean). Begin himself continued to strengthen his public commitment to prevent the division of the territory west of the Jordan River between Israeli and any Arab sovereign rule (Jordanian or Palestinian). In granting permanency to three Israeli settlements in the West Bank in late July, he included Elon Morre as a symbol of this commitment.

For his part, as Foreign Minister, Dayan continued to elaborate concepts he had developed since 1967. His main idea was to create the political, economic and physical infrastructure in the West Bank that would make a "functional" rather than a territorial compromise possible. This formula suggested a solution for the basic Israeli dilemma between her vital defence requirements and historic attachment to Judea and Samaria on the one hand, and her interest in preserving the "Jewishness" of the state on the other. (The Jewish majority would be greatly diminished if more than a million Arabs became Israeli citizens.) This solution would be based upon Israel retaining strategic control of the West Bank—and freedom of access to it—without incorporating the Arab population in the Israeli political system. For this purpose, the Arabs in the West Bank (and presumably the Gaza Strip) would be given the option of retaining their Jordanian citizenship and of participating in the Jordanian political system, while Jordan would be granted an administrative position (but not sovereignty) in these areas.

Such a concept fitted well with the encouragement Israel had given to political ties between Arabs in the West Bank and the Gaza Strip with Jordan since 1967. It was also in accordance with the intention of populating the West Bank, regardless of options for territorial partition; allowing individual Israeli Jews to purchase land in these areas; and treating the West Bank Arabs as a permanent government would have treated them. This idea of functional settlement had been rejected by the Labour Party, in spite of the fact that Peres also supported it. In August 1977, the

Israeli government decided on the principle of gradually raising the level of public services in the administered territories to that prevailing in Israel proper. (See essay on the West Bank and Gaza Strip.) Although government spokesmen presented this decision as a humanitarian act, the Arab countries, foreign public opinion and many observers in Israel itself considered the decision to have been based essentially on the policy of functional division.

The second field where the Likud government introduced a major change concerned the concept of the US role in attempts to reach a settlement. Since the 1967 war, and even more since 1973, previous governments had made a major effort to achieve some policy co-ordination with the US, the American willingness to accept some measure of co-ordination being considered one of the major assets of the 1975 Sinai Agreement. In fact, an American undertaking to this effect was incorporated in the documents signed in September 1975. At the time, Israel hoped that she could subsequently reach an understanding with the US prior to a reconvened Geneva conference, and so arrive at the negotiating table with American-backed positions. To achieve this, Israel was virtually prepared to conduct meaningful negotiations with the US rather than with the Arabs.

The Begin government understood that it could not expect to sustain such co-ordination, though sharply criticized by the Labour opposition for giving it up. Instead, it adopted such slogans as "negotiations with the Arabs in Geneva" (rather than with the US beforehand) "without prior conditions," and "everything is negotiable." This strategy was apparently adopted not because Begin and Dayan were uninterested in co-ordination with the US, nor because they were eager to see Israel isolated in Geneva. The principal reason for the change was that Begin and his government had probably come to the conclusion that Carter's public commitments to the 1967 boundaries (with minor adjustments) and to a Palestinian "homeland" made such co-ordination impossible—for a Labour government, let alone Begin's. The chances of co-ordination became even more remote after President Carter's declaration that all Israeli settlements in the occupied territories were by definition "illegal" and "an obstacle to peace," and by the American invitation to the PLO for a dialogue with the US under certain circumstances.

ON THE BRINK OF US-ISRAELI CONFRONTATION

By evading the substantive issues, and by concentrating on the reconvening of Geneva (which Carter considered so important), Begin's government attempted to postpone, contain and if possible avoid a confrontation with the US Administration. Begin proposed to discuss the differences between Israel and the Arabs at Geneva, and seemed prepared to risk becoming isolated on some issues there as a result of an American-Arab understanding.

During Begin's visit in Washington in July 1977, this approach apparently enjoyed a measure of success, but it soon became obvious that the US did not consider Geneva practicable at that stage for a number of reasons.

1) The concentration on the convening of the Geneva conference raised the issue of Palestinian representation on which the Arabs and Israel held sharply conflicting positions. The subject of PLO participation introduced into the procedural discussions an extremely sensitive substantive issue.
2) Evading matters of substance before Geneva was inconvenient to the Arabs for the same reasons that Israel preferred it. Arab insistence and American concern over the difficulty it might cause to friendly Arab regimes probably prompted Carter to continue to address issues in specific substantive terms, thus demonstrating the wide gap between the US and Israeli positions.

3) The timing, manner and content of some Israeli statements and decisions on the issue of settlements in the West Bank were considered provocative in the US and an embarrassment to the President. This subject, intimately related to the issues of borders and territories, generated intensive public discussion in the US.

After Begin's American visit—throughout August, September and the beginning of October—Israel witnessed with deepening concern, and often with bitter frustration, the erosion of US political support of Israel and the continued shift towards the acceptance of Arab positions. Against the background of President Carter's earlier commitment to a settlement based on the 1967 boundaries and the establishment of a "homeland" for the Palestinians, Israel now faced a concentrated and persistent American effort to force the PLO on it as a major factor in the Middle East settlement. This was a result of substantial Arab progress in persuading Washington that it could not afford to alienate the Arabs, nor risk the consequences of a Middle East stalemate. Israel thus had to answer the US when her positions did not meet minimum Arab requirements for the reconvening of Geneva.

These developments further sharpened Israel's awareness of the fact that the first major problem which it faced in the political process was that of its relations with the US, rather than direct political confrontation with its Arab adversaries. Under these circumstances, the new policy of no prior co-ordination with the US gave Israel some much-needed space of manoeuvre. If the risk of a political confrontation with the US could not be avoided, Israel was capable of obstructing the US sponsored political process by "not playing the game," and—as a last resort, which seriously worried the Arabs—by provoking grave military tension in the area.

Due to the significance and sensitivity of the issue of the PLO, and fearing that coercion on matters termed "procedural" only indicated what it could expect in Geneva on the key substantive issues, Israel signalled that it might stay away from the mooted Geneva conference, rather than resign itself to a settlement on such a basis.

At first, Israel was very careful not to criticize overall US policy publicly. For instance, there was no official reaction to Carter's proposal in August that the PLO start a dialogue with the US on the basis of a conditional acceptance of Resolution 242. It was only on the eve of Dayan's visit to the US in September, and during the visit itself, that Israel clearly indicated that the various positions taken by Washington on the Palestinian issue would have the cumulative effect of bringing about a political reality which Israel perceived as presenting a mortal danger; namely, the embryonic form of a PLO-controlled Palestinian state in the West Bank and the Gaza Strip.

Israel's preparedness to risk a breakdown of the political process was first put to a test in September when it was presented with an American draft which in effect provided for PLO participation in Geneva, and later in October with the publication of the joint Soviet-US statement on the Middle East. (For text of statement, see essay "The US and the Middle East.") Dayan personally went so far as to prepare the American Jewish community for a possible confrontation between Israel and the Carter Administration, if the US persisted in its attempts to force the PLO on Israel. The publication of the joint statement marked the lowest ebb at that stage in Israeli-American relations. Israel considered its content, timing and political context (particularly the American subscription to the Arab term of "the legitimate rights of the Palestinian people" and the vague terminology concerning the "essence of peace") dangerous to herself. Israel indicated that it could not take part in the Geneva conference if this statement by the co-chairmen became part of its political basis.

In fact, the joint US-Soviet statement marked a turning point in US-Israeli relations, for various reasons: Israel's rejection of it; widespread criticism in the Congress and in American public opinion over the reintroduction of the USSR into the political process; and a large-scale mobilization of the American Jewish community in favour of Israel. Realizing the Israeli resolve, the support Israel could mobilize in the US and the fact that without Israeli consent, the US political initiative would abort with potentially grave consequences, Carter agreed to negotiate a compromise with Dayan. However, despite its somewhat improved bargaining position, Israel was well aware that it could not expect the US to accept a formula that would specifically reject a PLO presence in Geneva, and thus preclude the co-operation of Egypt and Saudi Arabia. The result was a Working Paper, a compromise hammered out between Dayan and Carter, focusing on a formula for Palestinian representation that was ambiguous and open-ended enough to serve as a basis for US negotiations with the Arabs, but which could also be interpreted by Israel as blocking the way to PLO participation in Geneva and to a consequent discussion of a Palestinian state.

Although this formula extended Israel's flexibility on the Palestinian issue to the limit, persistent reports suggested that Begin seriously contemplated rejecting it despite Dayan's recommendation. No doubt one important reason for its final acceptance by Israel, however, was that it reconfirmed Resolutions 242 and 338 as "the agreed basis for negotiations" at Geneva (though not the "exclusive basis"). Another reason was the US statement, not incorporated in the Working Paper, that it did not consider the acceptance by Israel of the US-Soviet joint statement a necessary condition for the talks.

Israel rejected the notion of a unified Arab delegation since this was proposed by Syria to ease the incorporation of the PLO (under Syrian influence). Hoping to contain the "erosion" in US positions on this subject, Israel agreed in September to an American proposal (the precise contents of which remained debatable) that a unified delegation would at least take part in the ceremonial opening session. In the Working Paper, Israel also agreed that "the Palestinian Arabs" should participate in a working group where "the West Bank and Gaza issues [were] discussed." This allowed American diplomacy some flexibility, while Israel interpreted it as meaning discussion of Israeli-Arab "common life" in those areas.

Israel was cognizant, however, that the gap between its own positions and those of the US had not diminished, and that the US was committed at top level to positions very close to those of Egypt and Saudi Arabia. These were diametrically opposed on some key issues (notably the territorial question) to the Israeli national consensus—let alone to the positions of the Begin government.

Throughout this period, Israel showed great concern over the means the US might employ if its national interest should dictate a move that Israel rejected. Though the US promised time and again not to use Israel's dependence for economic aid and military supplies as a means of applying pressure, this option was liable to sophisticated manipulation. When bargaining over the Working Paper, for instance, Dayan termed aspects as "brutal"; and the possibility of the US resorting to such a line of action on a wider scale was not discounted.

In the beginning of November 1977, it appeared that a very uncomfortable but not unacceptable balance had been reached in one crucial area for Israeli policy—namely its relations with the US. Israel realized that the outcome of the political process depended to a large measure, though not exclusively, on American policy. The possibility of a political confrontation with the US was at that stage contained, if only temporarily.

Continued American support for the terms of the Working Paper implied that the

US no longer considered applying pressures exclusively on Israel when the paper was not welcomed throughout the Arab world. Though the US continued to seek a compromise on this subject that could be acceptable to the Arabs, Israel's sensitivity seemed to have been taken into greater consideration. Clearly, the Carter Administration had to assess whether or not a persistent policy of high profile pressures on Israel would prove counter-productive. Under the prevailing circumstances, this state of affairs was considered an advance in Israel.

NOTES

1. The terms of the first Geneva conference gave participants the right to veto the invitation of additional parties.
2. In July 1974, before the Rabat conference convened, Sādāt and Ḥusayn had agreed that the PLO would represent the Palestinians "excluding those who live in the Hashemite Kingdom of Jordan." Sādāt was subsequently forced to abandon this formula under Syrian-mobilized pressures. The 1974 Egyptian attempt was more far-reaching in terms of minimizing the role of the PLO.
3. At the Arab summit conference in Rabat in October 1974, the PLO was endorsed as sole representative of the Palestinian people.
4. It is called the Rafaḥ gap because it gives direct access in the midst of impassable terrain to the northern Negev, including Beersheba.
5. Judea and Samaria are the historical Hebrew names for the areas which constitute the West Bank—itself a Jordanian-oriented term.

The United Nations and the Arab-Israeli Conflict

MOSHE GAMMAR

Since 1967, the United Nations (UN) and the General Assembly (GA) have become increasingly pro-Arab due to the numerical strength of the coalition of Arab-Communist-Third World countries. For this reason, Israel has become unwilling to allow the UN more than a nominal role in the Middle East peace-making process. The composition of the GA and other specialized UN agencies and organizations has largely served the Arab states as convenient forums to pass anti-Israeli resolutions which have been mainly of propaganda value, since in the past the US has usually vetoed anti-Israeli moves in the Security Council (SC)—the only UN body with executive powers. However, the political nuisance and isolation inflicted on Israel (and the US) by resolutions passed in the UN cannot be ignored.

UN involvement in the Arab-Israeli conflict occurred on three levels during 1976–7: 1) debates and resolutions on this subject in the GA and other UN agencies and organizations; 2) the activity of the UN Secretary-General (SG), which was largely limited to his Middle East tour in February 1977; and 3) specific activities in the Middle East, including the UN Relief and Works Agency (UNRWA) which operates in 63 refugee camps; and military observers and forces supervising the ceasefire along the Arab-Israeli frontiers. These activities, and especially the latter, have been the most successful and significant part of UN involvement in the conflict (see Table at end of essay).

THE ARAB-ISRAELI CONFLICT AS REFLECTED AT THE UN (AUTUMN 1976)

Unlike previous years, especially 1974 and 1975, the Arab-Israeli conflict was of comparatively low priority in the different UN organizations during the autumn and winter of 1976. This was probably the result of three factors:

1) Inter-Arab rivalry prevented a unified Arab front at the UN. Even after the Riyadh summit conference in October 1976, Egypt and Syria did not co-operate, as was shown by their different draft resolutions submitted for the GA debate on the situation in the Middle East.
2) to suit its "peace offensive," Egypt tried to lower the political temperature in UN debates and resolutions, and to come to prior agreement about them with the US.
3) The weakening of the PLO in general and in the inter-Arab arena in particular (as a result of the civil war in Lebanon), brought a decline in its activity at the UN, as well as in Arab states' activity on its behalf.

On 30 September 1976, after consultation with the parties concerned, the GA Chairman denied the PLO the right of participating in the GA debate, giving it only the right of reply.

On 20 October, Egypt requested the convening of the SC to discuss the situation in the occupied territories in view of the riots in Hebron on 2–4 October, and the alleged desecration of Muslim and Jewish holy scriptures in the Tomb of the Patriarchs.

On 11 November, after four meetings and in order to prevent a US veto, the SC members and Egypt agreed to the reading of a statement by the SC President instead of a Council resolution. The statement deplored Israeli policy in the occupied territories, stating that "any act of profanation of the Holy Places . . . may seriously endanger international peace and security." [1]

At the 19th UNESCO General Conference in Nairobi (which opened on 26 October 1976), two resolutions were adopted: one condemning Israeli practices in the occupied territories, and the other condemning Israel for archaeological excavations in Jerusalem and for failing to preserve the city's cultural heritage. On the other hand, on 8 November, the conference adopted a resolution to allow member-states "to join the regional group of their choice, subject to the consent of the group concerned." [2] This allowed for the readmission of Israel to the European group of UNESCO (from which it had been barred by a general conference resolution in November 1974. This resolution had caused numerous protests by Western states and intellectuals, and had resulted in a sharp decrease in contributions to the organization.)

VOTING IN UNESCO

Resolution	*Yes*	*No*	*Abstentions*
Against Israeli policies in the Occupied Territories	71	5	30
Against Israeli excavations and practices in old Jerusalem	70	25	14
To allow member-states to join a regional group of their choice	70	0	17

During the 1976 GA debate on Middle East issues, a resolution was adopted on 23 November expressing "deep regret that repatriation or compensation of the [1948] refugees" had not been carried out. It called upon Israel "to take immediate steps for the return of the [1967] displaced inhabitants" and to "return the refugees . . . to the camps from which they were removed in the Gaza Strip" (referring to the Israeli housing projects for refugees). [3] On 15 December, the GA adopted the report of the Special Committee to Investigate Israeli Practices Affecting the Human Rights of the Population of the Occupied Territories, and condemned Israeli policies in these territories. [4]

For the first time since it joined the UN, Israel submitted its own draft resolution, calling on Israel, Egypt, Jordan and Syria "to reconvene without delay a peace conference on the Middle East . . . in order to resume negotiations without prior conditions on the establishment of a just and durable peace . . . as called for in SC Resolutions 242 . . . and 338." [5] However, Israel withdrew its draft after five non-aligned states submitted an amendment that the PLO be one of the parties invited to the peace conference, and that GA resolution 3375 of 10 November 1975 be added (which called for the fulfilment of the "inalienable rights" of the Palestinians and for the "invitation of the PLO . . . to participate in all efforts, deliberations and conferences on the Middle East which are held under UN auspices, on an equal footing"). [6]

Syria and Egypt submitted different draft resolutions, both of which were adopted. The Syrian resolution condemned "Israel's continued occupation of Arab territories" and "all measures taken by Israel" in them; affirmed that GA Resolution 3375 and PLO participation were essential to the success of the peace conference; and that peace could not be achieved "without Israel's complete withdrawal" and "the attainment by the Palestinian people of their inalienable rights." It also requested all states to desist from supplying Israel with aid, and the

SC to take "effective measures" to implement "all the relevant resolutions of the SC and the GA."[7]

The Egyptian draft called for the convening of the peace conference "not later than the end of March," and requested the SG to resume contacts with all the parties "for the early convening of the peace conference" and to submit a report back to the SC "not later than 1 March 1977."[8]

VOTING IN THE GENERAL ASSEMBLY

Resolution	*Yes*	*No*	*Abstentions*	*Absent*
A/Res/31/51 on UNRWA and Arab refugees (5 parts)				
A. Assistance to Palestine Refugees	115+	0	2	29
B. Assistance to persons displaced as a result of the June 1967 hostilities		Adopted without Voting		
C. Financing UNRWA		Adopted without Voting		
D. Population and refugees displaced since 1967	118+	2	2	24
E. Palestine refugees in the Gaza Strip	118	2	3+	23
A/Res/31/106 on the Report of the "Palestine Committee" (4 parts)				
A.	129	3+	4	10
B.	134+	0	2	10
C.	100	5+	30	11
D.	97	3	36+	10
A/Res/31/61 The situation in the ME (Syrian Draft)	91	11+	29	15
A/Res/31/62 Peace Conference on the ME (Egyptian Draft)	122	2+	8	14

+ including US.

WALDHEIM'S MIDDLE EAST TOUR

After having met Arab, Israeli, US and Soviet representatives to discuss the reconvening of the Geneva conference according to the GA resolution of 9 December 1976 (see above), Secretary-General Kurt Waldheim decided in mid-December to visit the Middle East in order "to work out a formula" for the reconvening of the conference.[9] He intended to discuss with the Arab and Israeli leaders three issues: 1) the timing of the conference, 2) the agenda, and 3) the participation of the Palestinians, which he regarded as "the principal" and "most urgent" consideration. He expressed concern that without a "breakthrough in the negotiating process" during 1977, the danger of "another military confrontation" was "very real."[10]

Waldheim set off on his tour of the Middle East in February 1977, on the eve of the US Secretary of State's visit, and despite Israel's criticism and rejection of his mission.[11] He visited Cairo (2–4 February); Damascus (4–5 February), where he also met PLO Chairman, Yāsir 'Arafāt; Riyadh (6 February); Beirut (7 February); and Amman (8–9 February).[12] While differing in their attitudes, all the Arab leaders demanded a "speedy" reconvening of the Geneva conference and PLO participation in it.[13]

Waldheim arrived in Jerusalem on 10 February and conveyed to the Israeli leaders his impressions that the Arabs had "changed their attitude favourably" and were ready "to recognize Israel *de facto*."[14] In trying to convince the Israelis to accept PLO participation in the Geneva conference, he stated that the PLO was ready to accept a "mini-state" in the West Bank and the Gaza Strip, quoting

UN OBSERVERS AND FORCES ALONG THE ARAB–ISRAELI FRONTIERS

(Summer 1977)

Name of Force	*Commander*	*Location of HQ*	*Composition*	*Duties*	*Legal Basis and Duration*
United Nations Emergency Force (UNEF)	Maj-Gen Rais Abin (Indonesia)	Ismā'īliyya	Maximum number of soldiers allowed 4,500 Swedish battalion 660 Finnish battalion 665 Ghanayan battalion 665 Indonesian battalion 501 Canadian logistic unit 865 Australian helicopter squadron 43	To man the separation area and the "oil strip" in Sinai, and supervise observance of the ceasefire and of the military clauses of the interim agreement of 1 September 1975	Established according to SC Res 340 and 341 of 25 and 27 October 1973 for a period of 6 months, mandate extended every 6 months during the disengagement agreement, and every year since 24 October 1975
United Nations Disengagement Observation Force (UNDOF)	Maj-Gen Hannes Phillip (Austria)	Damascus	Maximum number of soldiers allowed 1,250 Austrian battalion 500 Iranian battalion 500 Canadian and Polish logistic units 200	To man the separation area in the Golan Heights and to check and supervise the ceasefire and observance of Syrian–Israeli disengagement agreement	Established according to SC Res 350 of 31 May 1974; mandate extended every 6 months
United Nations Truce Supervision Organisation (UNTSO)	Lt-Gen Ensio Silasvuo (Finland), serves as Chief Co-ordinator of UNTSO, UNEF and UNDOF, and as chairman of the military committee at the Geneva Peace Conference	Jerusalem	123 observers detached to UNEF in 7 check-points located at the warning system area and the "oil strip" 84 observers detached to UNDOF in 21 observation posts in the Golan Heights 46 observers in 5 Observation posts along the Lebanese-Israeli border, only on the Lebanese side. 28 men in UNTSO HQ	To man observation and checkpoints and to report on observance of the ceasefire. In Sinai and the Golan Heights, the observers also carry out periodic checks on the observance of the forces limitation agreement	Established according to SC Res 50 of 29 May 1948; to supervise the (first) truce between Israel and the Arab States; after 1949, supervised the implementation of the armistice agreements; after 1967, supervised the ceasefire on the Lebanese, Syrian and Egyptian sectors

'Arafāt that this readiness was "proof that we accept [Israel's] existence."[15] However, this was promptly denied by Muḥammad Ghānim, a PLO spokesman in Damascus.[16] In any event, the Israeli leaders did not share Waldheim's confidence in the Arabs' new flexibility; Rabin repeated the Israeli stand that his Government was ready to convene the Geneva conference "at any time on the basis of the original invitation" (issued on 18 December 1973 to Israel, Egypt, Jordan and Syria).[17]

Waldheim returned to Cairo on 11 February to report on his talks in Israel. Summing up his tour in Geneva on 13 February, Waldheim admitted that the conference could not reconvene by the end of March, adding that it was not "a decisive element" whether the talks began "in four weeks time or later."[18]

On 28 February 1977, Waldheim submitted his report to the SC, stating that for the time being the differences between the two sides concerning PLO participation in the negotiations were too deep to be overcome by "purely procedural means." He added, however, that all the parties concerned recognized that it was of the utmost importance not to hinder the momentum towards peace negotiations.[19]

On 12 March, Egypt called for a SC meeting to discuss Waldheim's report. The debate opened on 25 March, but was adjourned *sine die* four days later without reaching agreement. Egypt had informally circulated a draft resolution urging the resumption of the Geneva conference in order to obtain a settlement which would include the establishment of an "independent national homeland for the Palestinians in Palestine."[20] However, Egypt did not submit its proposal officially because it became clear that it would be opposed by the US and other Western SC members, and thus not receive the nine votes necessary for its adoption.

NOTES

Source references beginning with S/ . . . and A/ . . . are UN documents series so designated.

1. S/12233.
2. *UN Monthly Chronicle*, XIII, xi (December 1977), 5- 6.
3. A/Res/31/51.
4. A/Res/31/106.
5. A/31/L.24.
6. A/31/L.25.
7. A/Res/31/61.
8. A/Res/31/62.
9. First announced in an interview published in *Newsweek*, 20 December 1976.
10. Waldheim in a press conference in Geneva, as quoted by Reuter, 1 February. Similarly, in interviews with *Tishrīn*, 26 January. Egyptian TV, quoted by Middle East News Agency (MENA), 28 January, *Al-Dustūr*, Amman; 31 January. *Al-Usbū al-'Arabī*, Beirut; 9 February 1977.
11. Allon said that while Waldheim would be received in Israel "with all the honour he is due both as an individual and because of his position," Israel had no intention of giving the UN "any role in the peace negotiations," as it considered the US as "the only mediator in the ME conflict." Israeli Broadcasting Authority (IBA) 7 February—Daily Report (DR), 8 February 1977. Tel Aviv press comments were more critical and even hostile, e.g. *Ma'ariv*, 23 and 26 January; *Davar*, 31 January; *Ha'aretz*, 10 and 11 February 1977.
12. Waldheim was accompanied by Under-Secretaries for Special Political Affairs, Roberto Guyer (Argentina) and Brian Urquhart (Britain).
13. For Waldheim's talks, see R Cairo, 3 February—DR, 4 February. MENA, 4 February. *International Herald Tribune* (*IHT*), 4 and 5 February. R Damascus, 6 February. Syrian News Agency (SNA), 7 February—DR, 8 February. R Beirut, 8 February—DR, 9 February. *Al-Usbū al-'Arabī*, 14 February. Agence France Presse, 9 February—DR, 10 February. R Amman, 9 February—DR, 10 February 1977.
14. In interviews with *Jordan Times*, 10 February; *Jerusalem Post* (*JP*), 11 February 1977.
15. *Ibid.* Also *Los Angeles Times* (*LAT*), 8 and 11 February; *IHT*, 11 February; *Washington Post*, 8 February; *New York Times* (*NYT*), 12 February 1977.
16. *LAT*, 11 February 1977.
17. IBA, 10 February—DR, 11 February; *JP* and *Ma'ariv*, 11 February 1977.
18. Reuter, 13 February 1977.
19. S/12290.
20. *NYT*, 29 March 1977.

South Lebanon in the Arab-Israeli Conflict

MOSHE GAMMAR

After the Riyadh summit conference of 16–18 October 1976, which recognized a *Pax Syriana* over Lebanon, South Lebanon remained the only area in the Middle East where hostilities had not entirely ceased.[1] Moreover, South Lebanon was the only issue connected with the Arab-Israeli conflict which still threatened to provoke a new conflagration between Israel and Syria. Three main issues were at dispute between Israel and her Arab adversaries—mainly Syria, but also the PLO and the central Government in Beirut (referred to below as Lebanon).

1) In any military struggle between Syria and Israel, South Lebanon is strategically significant as through this area either side can outflank the main front on the Golan Heights and threaten Damascus, or the Galilee and Haifa respectively. Syria, and consequently Israel, first became aware of the area's importance in 1949 and again in the 1967 war. But it was only after the 1973 war that the issue became active because of Syria's efforts to consolidate its leadership over a bloc composed of Jordan, Lebanon and the PLO. On the strategic level, this effort aimed at establishing a unified Eastern Front from Tyre on South Lebanon's Mediterranean coast to 'Aqaba on the Red Sea. It was from this point of view that Israel examined Syria's growing involvement in the Lebanese civil war in the winter of 1975–6, and found it potentially troublesome. In the spring of 1976, a real possibility seemed to exist of an Israeli pre-emptive military strike following several warnings to Syria not to cross the so-called "Red Line" in Lebanon.[2] It was only in the summer of 1976, after the Syrian-PLO confrontation had become open and Syria's observance of the Red Line established, that tension abated and both sides developed an unstable and uneasy *modus vivendi*.

2) Since 1968, the fidā'iyyūn organizations had built up bases in South Lebanon (especially in the 'Arqūb area, called "Fatḥland" in Israel), consolidated their hold there and used it for operations against Israel. After the civil war in Jordan in 1970–1, the area assumed supreme importance for them, being the only fidā'ī base beyond the effective control of an Arab state and within striking range of Israel. Israel was interested in eliminating the fidā'iyyūn presence in South Lebanon in order to deal a severe blow to the PLO, as well as to secure calm along its northern border. After most fidā'ī forces had moved from the south to the north of Lebanon during the civil war, Israel opposed their return to the area.

3) In order to prevent a Syrian and PLO presence in South Lebanon, and also in the general framework of co-operation with the Christian forces in Lebanon, Israel developed close relations with the Christian villages in the south. As the relationship developed, and despite Syrian and PLO interference, Israel gradually assumed the role of protector of the South Lebanese Christians. In practice, this meant not only growing military assistance, but mainly an increasing commitment to oppose any settlement in South Lebanon which was to the detriment of the Christians, or which threatened to sever relations between them and Israel.

DEVELOPMENT OF THE ISRAELI-MARONITE CHRISTIAN ALLIANCE

In mid-June 1976, Israel initiated what later came to be called "the good fence policy." (For its development, see "The Situation Along Israel's Frontiers," below). At the end of July 1976, Israel's Defence Minister said in a television interview that the country's immediate problem was the future of developments in South Lebanon. "At the moment there is in existence a semi-vacuum," he said, "and we must be very alert to the problem of how and whether it is filled."[3]

In spite of initial denials, Israel supplied Maronite militias in Lebanon with heavy arms, trained their forces in Israel and operated a naval blockade against the PLO. She also assisted Christian villages in South Lebanon against the fidā'iyyūn. Peres hinted at this by saying in mid-August 1976 that the villages were ready and able to defend themselves.[4] During September, the Israeli media began to talk openly of Israeli aid to the Maronites and of the "naval blockade," although these reports were never confirmed officially.

After the first phase of the joint Syrian-Maronite attack in central Lebanon (28–30 September 1976), the Christian militias in South Lebanon launched an attack against PLO units and the Lebanon's Arab Army on 8 October to coincide with the Syrian-Maronite attack of 12–14 October.[5] The Christians succeeded in gaining control over several areas in South Lebanon near the Israeli border. Despite denials by Israeli and Christian spokesmen, Arab and Western as well as Israeli media reported massive Israeli support to the Christians. According to one journalist, "Israel has provided almost everything but troops to aid the Christians."[6]

ISRAELI-SYRIAN CONFRONTATION IN SOUTH LEBANON

After the Riyadh summit, Israel decided to assume a lower profile in her assistance to the Christians, both because of American pressure and in order not to provoke the Cairo summit into rash decisions regarding South Lebanon.

During the second half of November and December 1976—while the fighting continued on a small scale—the issue of South Lebanon was raised in a series of contacts between the US, Israel, Syria and Lebanon. After assuring calm in Beirut, Syria was interested in introducing troops into the area to tighten its control over the whole of the country and over all PLO units. It had a special interest in controlling Tyre and Nabatiyya, both on the Israeli side of the Red Line. However, Israel warned Syria and Lebanon several times, both publicly and through the US, that it would not tolerate the presence of non-Lebanese forces (including the fidā'iyyūn) in the area.

The stalemate over the issue was broken on the night of 23–24 January 1977 when a Syrian unit entered Nabatiyya—interpreted in Israel as a test both for Israel and for the new US Administration. Israel's demand for Syrian withdrawal, accompanied by increased military activity along the Lebanese border, and by Syria's declared determination not to "yield to blackmail"[7] all created a tense atmosphere. This was broken through American efforts on 13 February, when the Syrian unit withdrew from Nabatiyya.

During the second half of February and the beginning of March 1977, the idea of stationing a UN force along the Israeli-Lebanese border was raised by several Lebanese leaders. Israel did not oppose the suggestion, although it preferred the stationing of Lebanese forces in South Lebanon. The issue was raised through Israeli-US-Lebanese-Syrian contacts, and also during Vance's first Middle East tour, but was frustrated by Syrian objections.

The small-scale clashes between Christian and PLO forces in the autumn and winter of 1976–7 changed their character at the end of March 1977 when the Christians launched an attack which culminated in the capture of the Muslim village of al-Tayba on 30 March. The fidā'iyyūn immediately developed a massive Syrian-backed counter-offensive and re-captured al-Tayba on 4 April. As pressure on the Christians increased, Israel put her forces on the alert and publicly warned that she "could not remain indifferent to the fate of friendly Lebanese villages close to her borders."[8] On 10 April, after a brief visit to Damascus, PLO chairman Yāsir 'Arafāt declared a ceasefire which came into force the next day. At the end of April, Peres defined three conditions under which Israel might subsequently intervene in Lebanon: 1) if the Syrian army crossed the Red Line; 2) if the fidā'iyyūn infiltrated into areas close to Israeli settlements; and 3) if any damage was caused to the Christian villages.[9]

ISRAELI MILITARY ASSISTANCE FOR CHRISTIANS

The government change in Israel in June 1977 did not significantly alter Israeli policy concerning South Lebanon. However, it did increase Israel's readiness to declare her commitment publicly, and for the first time officially to confirm military assistance to the Christians in South Lebanon. During his visit to Washington and afterwards, Begin repeatedly stated that Israel would "never let down the Christian minority" or allow it "to be destroyed."[10] He added that "without our help, the Christian minority in South Lebanon would be annihilated."[11] On 8 August, Begin himself confirmed that Israel had been giving military assistance to the Christians in South Lebanon, including the shelling of fidā'ī positions by Israeli artillery.[12] In response, the leaders of the (Maronite) Lebanese Front published a statement on 18 August praising Israel for its assistance to the "besieged residents of the South," and for regarding the Christians as its "natural allies."[13] Meanwhile, the fighting in South Lebanon continued; in early July, Israeli assistance was extended to include Druze villages in the 'Arqūb area which were resisting the fidā'iyyūn.[14]

Later, on 20 July, Lebanon, Syria and the PLO reached an agreement in Shtūrā for the implementation of the 1969 Cairo Agreement. This envisaged a ceasefire in South Lebanon, followed by a withdrawal by both PLO and Christian forces from the battle area near the Israeli border, and the creation there of a demilitarized zone patrolled by Lebanese troops. However, as the fighting continued and no Lebanese force was available, the implementation of the Shtūrā Agreement in South Lebanon was repeatedly delayed.

The situation in the area was the subject of continuing contacts between the US, Israel, Syria and Lebanon. In particular, the issue was discussed during Begin's visit to the US in mid-July and during Vance's second Middle East tour at the beginning of August. Both the implementation of the Shtūrā Agreement and the idea of stationing UN forces were raised, but no agreement was reached.

ISRAELI MILITARY INTERVENTION

In the second half of August, Israel found herself in a new dilemma. No stable settlement was imminent and the Christians, outnumbered and besieged, began to show signs of approaching a breaking-point after a year-long war of attrition.

Israel responded to this situation in a number of ways. As the fighting in South Lebanon escalated during the last week of August and the first week of September, Arab and foreign correspondents in Beirut reported heavy Israeli shelling of villages and positions held by the fidā'iyyūn. Between 12 and 15 September, heavy fighting between the Christians and the fidā'iyyūn developed around the Khardalī bridge (on the Litanī river), and on 17 September the Christians stormed Tall al-Sharīfa, which commands both the Christian-held township of Marj 'Ayūn and the fidā'iyyūn-held township of al-Khiyām. Fierce fidā'ī counter-attacks were repulsed during the next week. Israel assisted the Christians not only by artillery fire and by a naval blockade, but also by deploying an IDF unit in the eastern enclave (which entered no later than 17 September).[15] The fidā'iyyūn responded by carrying out ten *Katyusha* attacks on Israeli towns between 21 and 27 September in which there were no Israeli casualties and only slight damage.

The presence of the Israeli force in South Lebanon, which neither Israel nor the US confirmed at that time, prompted intense diplomatic activity. Through American mediation, a ceasefire agreement was reached on 25 September and was operational within two days. The agreement provided for the fidā'iyyūn to withdraw at least 10 km from the frontier, except in the 'Arqūb area; the IDF troops to pull back across the frontier; and a 1,500-strong Lebanese regular force to control the area vacated by the fidā'iyyūn. The "good fence" was to remain open "in accordance with the wishes of the parties concerned," and the Lebanese-Israeli armistice commission (created in accordance with the 1949 armistice agreement) was to be reactivated.[16]

Israel insisted throughout the negotiations that "the safety of the Christian inhabitants of Southern Lebanon be assured."[17] According to Major Ḥaddād, the commander of the eastern enclave, the agreement had an annex, which included guarantees for the safety of the Christians. He also revealed that he "was given a clear promise" that the IDF "will not abandon the Christian villagers if they are attacked by the fidā'iyyūn."[18]

The IDF unit completed its withdrawal on 27 September, but the situation remained unclear. It was not only that the ceasefire agreement had yet to be fully implemented; but the agreement did not in itself provide a definitive answer to the problem. At best, it provided a breathing-space in which the sides could try to resolve the future of the area.

NOTES

1. For difficulties in defining the parties involved in the Lebanese crisis, see survey on Lebanon. In this chapter, the following terms are used: Maronites for the Lebanese Front; Christians for the Christian militias in South Lebanon; fidā'iyyūn for the Palestinian organization's members.
2. According to Israeli statements, the "Red Line" contained several elements, such as the strength of the Syrian forces, the nature of their deployment and their objectives, and the geographic element. The exact location of the line was not disclosed until 30 September 1977 when the former Israeli Prime Minister, Mr Rabin, revealed in an article in *Yedi'ot Aḥaronot* (Tel Aviv) that it lay between Sidon, Jizzin, and Kafr Mishkī.
3. Quoted by *Ma'ariv*, Tel Aviv; 1 August 1976.
4. Israeli Broadcasting Authority (IBA), 10 August—BBC Summary of World Broadcasts (BBC), 13 August 1976. For reports of Israeli supplies to Maronite militias see, for example, *Time*, New York; 12 August 1976 and 22 August 1977.
5. The Lebanon's Arab Army was formed by Lt (*mulāzim'awal*) Aḥmad al-Khatīb in January 1976, composed of Muslim deserters from the Lebanese army. It occupied South Lebanon and participated in the war on the Palestinian-Muslim side until disintegrating in the autumn of 1976.
6. *International Herald Tribune* (*IHT*), Paris; 22 October 1976.
7. Asad quoted by Associated Press, 10 February 1977.
8. *IHT* and *Ha'aretz*, Tel Aviv; 13 April 1977.
9. *Ha'aretz*, 24 April 1977.
10. During a visit to the Lebanese border—Israel Government Press Office, Daily News Bulletin (GPO/D), 7 August 1977.
11. In a speech in the Knesset summing up his visit to the US—GPO/D, 27 July 1977.
12. *Ma'ariv*, 9 August 1977.
13. Radio of the Phalanges, 18 August 1977.
14. *Ma'ariv*, 7 July 1977.
15. The presence of the IDF unit was confirmed by Israel only after its pullback. Arab sources,

especially Iraqi News Agency (INA), reported the Israeli military presence in South Lebanon as early as the beginning of September, but some of these reports were denied by Israel (e.g. IBA, 3 September—BBC, 5 September). According to a report in *Yedi'ot Aharonot*, the IDF unit entered Lebanon on 17 September; this confirms other Israeli reports that the unit had stayed in the enclave for 11 days. For reports of the naval blockade, see *The Guardian*, London; 22 September 1977.

16. GPO/D, 26 September; Agence France Presse, 27 September—Daily Report (DR), 27 September. For more and somewhat different details, see also Middle East News Agency, IBA, R Cairo, INA, R Beirut, R of the Phalanges and the PLO radio stations, 26 and 27 September. Also, *al-Hawādith*, Beirut; 30 September 1977.
17. GPO/D, 26 September 1977.
18. *Ma'ariv*, 28 September 1977.

The Situation along Israel's Frontiers

MOSHE GAMMAR

Since its establishment, Israel has had no permanently recognized borders with its Arab neighbours. By 1977, there were four kinds of frontiers. In Sinai, the disengagement lines with Egypt were designated by the Interim Agreement signed for three years on 1 September 1975. On the Golan Heights, the lines separating Israel and Syria were established by the Disengagement Agreement of 31 May 1974. In the east, the 1967 ceasefire line divided Israel from Jordan; and in the north, the 1949 armistice line separated Israel and Lebanon, although since the Six-Day war in 1967, Israel claimed this to be only a ceasefire line.

THE EGYPTIAN-ISRAELI FRONTIER

The tranquillity along this frontier, which began with the (first) Disengagement Agreement of 18 January 1974, continued during 1976–7. The Interim Agreement was generally observed and the UNEF mandate, which has to be extended annually, was renewed almost automatically on 22 October 1976.[1]

Between February 1976 and May 1977, however, Egypt submitted 246 complaints to UNEF, referring mostly to overflights. In the same period, Israel submitted 89 complaints mainly in relation to excess forces in the Egyptian Limited Forces' Zone. The US Sinai Support Mission (SSM) reported that during its first year of activity (February 1976-February 1977), it had recorded 28 violations, all of minor significance and mostly committed by Israel.

There were two subjects, however, which produced differences among Israel, Egypt and the US, although all these sides tried to contain them.

1) *Excess Egyptian Forces in the Limited Forces Zone.* Israel made two public complaints on this subject. In August–September 1976, it claimed that Egypt had 18 infantry battalions in the zone (instead of the eight stipulated by the agreement). Egypt explained that due to a reorganization of its army, the battalions were now smaller, but after Israeli insistence, they pulled out some of them. At the same time, differences of opinion arose between Israel and the US over American aerial photos, after which it was decided that these would be interpreted by mixed Israeli-American teams. Between May and July 1977, Israel again complained that Egypt maintained two more battalions than stipulated in the agreement, and had also introduced several ground-to-air SAM-7 missiles into the area. After Begin's and Carter's intervention, the Egyptian Minister of War ordered a pull-out of the excess forces in July 1977.

2) *Oil Drilling Rights in the Suez Gulf.* In September 1976, the Israeli navy prevented AMOCO Company—which had been given a concession by Egypt—from drilling in the Gulf east of the median line. This led to a dispute between Israel and the US since the latter did not recognize Israel's claim to control any of Sinai's territorial waters. Intensive diplomatic activity during September and October failed to produce agreement, and AMOCO was forced to stop drilling in the disputed area. The problem may have been affected by Israel's drilling in the al-Tūr area, which was also in dispute between Israel and the US. After two more incidents involving AMOCO and a Dutch raft, a State

Department spokesman stated on 14 February 1977 that "legally [Israel] as an occupying power does not have the right to exploit natural resources that were not exploited when the occupation began." He added that the drillings were not "helpful to the efforts to get peace negotiations under way." [2]

THE ISRAELI-SYRIAN FRONTIER

The Israeli-Syrian disengagement agreement was strictly observed by both sides during 1976–7, as it has been since June 1974. The only incidents reported were of an UNDOF officer killed and another wounded by a mine in the buffer zone on 20 April 1977, and of an overflight by Syrian MiG-17s on 3 May 1977

After Syria's direct intervention in Lebanon (June 1976), the atmosphere along the Israeli-Syrian frontier became more tranquil and relaxed, as was indicated by two developments. The first was the almost automatic extensions of the UNDOF mandate on 30 November 1976 and 26 May 1977, in strong contrast with the considerable tension and Syrian political demands on previous occasions (especially in November 1975 and May 1976). The second development was the Syrian authorities' agreement in September 1976 to Israel's proposal to allow Druze from the Golan villages to meet their relatives living in Syria. The first meeting took place at an UNDOF post on the border near the village of Majdal Shams on 15 September. Afterwards, this became a bi-weekly and then a weekly procedure. In February 1977, 'Alawis from the village of Ghajar were also allowed to participate.

THE ISRAELI-JORDANIAN FRONTIER

The complete calm and strict observance of the ceasefire which had characterized this frontier since August 1970 continued in 1976–7, with only a few trivial incidents being reported.

The "Open Bridges" policy, initiated by Israel after the 1967 war in order to enable West Bank and later Gaza Strip residents to continue their economic, social and cultural ties with Jordan, [3] continued during 1976–7, with the transit of people and goods growing substantially (see Table). Although the Jordanian authorities were reported to have agreed to reopen a third bridge for transit in June 1977, this decision had not been implemented by the end of September.

For the first time since the 1967 war, Israeli Arabs were allowed to enter Jordan in March 1977, and a number of delegations carried their condolences to Ḥusayn on his wife's death. Among other things, Ḥusayn promised then that he would ask the Saudi authorities to allow Israeli Muslims to go on the pilgrimage to Mecca (Ḥajj), which they had been prevented from doing since 1948.

TRAFFIC OVER THE "OPEN BRIDGES" (1967–76)

June–Dec 1967	*1968*	*1969*	*1970*	*1971*	*1972*	*1973*	*1974*	*1975*	*Jan–June 1976*
Number of people crossing in both directions									
—	243,605	379,000	364,825	440,235	710,032	732,828	863,921	927,451	999,023
Value of goods crossing in both directions (in IL m)									
35.55	72.5	93.9	73.1	94.6	140.2	102.3	191.3	363.0	301.4

THE ISRAELI-LEBANESE FRONTIER

The calm along this frontier, which had begun during the Lebanese civil war due to fidā'iyyūn's preoccupations within Lebanon, was disturbed by only a few minor incidents during 1976–7.

The main development along this frontier was Israel's "good fence" policy, begun in mid-June 1976 after Lebanese residents had asked Israeli border patrols for medical treatment on several occasions. During the summer and autumn of 1976, these services were developed and enlarged, with three clinics opening near the border. In fact, between June 1976 and 1 September 1977, 29,359 Lebanese received medical treatment, of whom 1,150 received hospital care in Israel. From July 1976, Israel also began to provide the Lebanese border villages with water, food and fuel. Subsequently, Israeli merchants began to buy tobacco and other agricultural products from the villages, and Lebanese residents worked in growing numbers in Israel. Paid in Israeli currency, they were allowed to shop in Israel and exchange half of their earnings into Lebanese currency. Between June 1976 and 1 September 1977, the average daily number of Lebanese working in Israel was 855. Israeli cigarette manufacturers bought $447,000 worth of tobacco while Lebanese residents bought goods in Israel valued at IL 1.6m. (For military assistance see above, "South Lebanon in the Arab-Israeli conflict.")

Lebanese residents were also allowed to visit their relatives in Israel. Between January and June 1977, Israeli Maronites were allowed to visit their relatives in South Lebanon, and a bi-weekly bus service was inaugurated. These visits were later stopped because of the security situation and "out of fear that Israeli citizens might be caught under fire." However, the visits of Lebanese continued.

NOTES

1. In the Security Council debate on the UNEF mandate's extension, Egypt tried to introduce two articles. One called upon the SC to report on progress in implementing Resolution 338 every six months. The other declared that if there were no progress in implementing the resolution, the situation in the Middle East might deteriorate. However, under firm Israeli and American opposition, Egypt withdrew its proposals.
2. *New York Times*, 15 February 1977.
3. For details, see *Middle East Record 1967*, (Jerusalem: Israel Universities Press), pp. 284–5; *1968*, pp. 445–6; *1969–70*, pp. 351–2.
4. Israeli Broadcasting Authority, 7 June—BBC Summary of World Broadcasts, 9 June 1977.

A Chronology and Commentary on Political Developments in the Arab-Israel Conflict (October 1976-October 1977)

MOSHE GAMMAR

THE ARAB "PEACE OFFENSIVE"

At the Riyadh summit meeting (16–18 October 1976) and at the Cairo meeting (26–28 October 1976), the leaders of Syria, Saudi Arabia and Egypt decided, in view of the approaching end of the US election year and consequently of the stalemate in the ME political process, to co-ordinate their positions and concentrate once more on the Arab-Israeli conflict. The Arab leaders reportedly agreed to end the Egyptian-Syrian rivalry by a compromise whereby Egypt undertook not to seek further separate agreements nor a separate peace with Israel; Syria would not interfere with Egyptian political activity in mounting a diplomatic and public peace offensive; and Saudi Arabia would apply quiet pressure on the US and help to strengthen Egypt's military capacity by the purchase of arms.

Carter's election in November 1976 caused concern among the Arabs because of the pro-Israeli stand he had taken during the election campaign. The Egyptian media called on Arab rulers to initiate immediate contacts with the President-elect to ensure that, after taking office, he would be more favourable to the Arabs.[1] A week after the elections, Egypt launched its "peace offensive." In a series of interviews and meetings with Western (especially US) media and political figures during the last months of 1976 and the beginning of 1977, Sādāt emphasized Egypt's readiness to sign a "peace agreement" which would be "a document, formally, legally and publicly ending the state of belligerency."[2] He declared that in order "to satsify its feeling of security," Israel could ask for and obtain any guarantees from anyone it wished—even a mutual defence pact between the US and Israel. Egypt would not object provided that such guarantees were given to it as well (Cairo would not ask for a defence treaty). Furthermore, it would not object to the stationing of UN forces or "whatever forces were agreed upon" on the borders and in Sharm al-Shaykh "to guarantee free shipping in the 'Aqaba Gulf." When asked about specific issues, such as the nature of peace or the Arab boycott, Sādāt answered that he was interested in dealing with the "big issues," while "the rest will be solved by themselves."[3] Through the mediation of the Austrian Chancellor, Bruno Kreisky, Sādāt tried to meet Jewish, and even Zionist leaders from the US. In mid-December 1976, a delegation of the US Zionist Organization, headed by its chairman Charlotte Jacobson, visited Cairo and met Sādāt. The visit received considerable publicity in the West, but was not mentioned in the Egyptian media.

The "peace offensive" was accompanied by warnings, especially in statements for internal consumption, that the military option remained in case diplomatic efforts failed; Arab media specifically warned of a possibility of war at the beginning of 1977. The "oil weapon" was mentioned by Saudi leaders on rare occasions, though more frequently by the Saudi press. In January 1977, the Saudi Foreign Minister, Sa'ūd al-Faysal, said: "By limiting the crude oil price rise, we are contributing to the stabilization of the Western economy. In return, we expect Europe and the US to show greater understanding of our arguments on the Palestinian conflict."[4]

The "peace offensive" was largely successful in convincing Western opinion, especially in the US, of Egypt's sincere moderation and interest in peace. The then US Secretary of State, Dr Kissinger, said privately that Sādāt was "obviously a more courageous negotiator" than Prime Minister Rabin.[5] Carter, too, spoke of "the moderation of the Arab leaders" which, together with Israel's longing for peace, "give us hope that real achievements can be achieved in new negotiations between Israel and the Arabs."[6]

THE PLO LINE

As part of the peace offensive, Egypt and to some extent Saudi Arabia as well as circles within the PLO made an effort to present that organization as being ready to moderate its attitudes. During November 1976, PLO and Egyptian sources, especially Farūq al-Qaddūmī, head of the PLO's Political Department, hinted that the PLO might give some kind of recognition to Israel. Expectations were that the forthcoming Central Council (CC) meeting in Damascus, due in mid-December 1976, would decide on the issue. Such feelings were strengthened by the Chairman of the PLO Executive Committee, Yāsir 'Arafāt, who said that "a unified Palestine is my dream—and I have the right to dream," but that "we are prepared to establish an independent regime in any territory that we liberate or from which Israel withdraws."[7] When the CC did not decide on such a move, new expectations arose that the Palestine National Council (PNC), due to meet in Cairo in March 1977, would announce changes in its policy.

The meetings of PLO representatives with prominent figures in the Israeli Council for Israel-Palestine Peace and the Israeli Communist Party (Rakaḥ), also contributed to the moderate image of the PLO. However, these meetings were not official, and PLO spokesmen denied that they had taken place.

On 13 February 1977, the Vienna daily *Arbeiter-Zeitung* published 'Isām Sartāwi's letter of 26 January to Chancellor Kreisky, in which he stated that if a Palestinian state were to be set up in the West Bank, the Gaza sector and the Hamma and 'Awja enclaves, "a state of non-belligerency [could be] established between the new state and Israel." But "a state of peace" required other issues to be settled, the most important of which was Israeli acceptance and implementation of "the rights of the Palestinian refugees to return to their original homes," or the right to compensation for those not wishing to do so.[8] Again, the PLO promptly denied that the letter represented its views.

As the date of the PNC opening (12 March) drew closer, PLO spokesmen emphasized that they regarded the "mini-state" as only a first step towards the PLO's ultimate goal—the "democratic secular state of Palestine." In spite of pressure for moderation, the PNC decided to reject Resolution 242 and all "American capitulationist settlements," and to continue, "without any conciliation or recognition" of Israel, the struggle for "the national rights of our people, in particular the rights to return, self-determination and establishing an independent national state on [our] soil."[9]

ISRAELI RESPONSE TO THE "PEACE OFFENSIVE"

Initially, Israel's official spokesmen dismissed the "peace offensive" as mere propaganda, but found it hard to counteract the image of an "inflexible Israeli attitude" as against "Arab moderation" in the Western, and especially US, public mind and media.

From the end of November 1976 onwards Israel began to challenge the moderate image of Sādāt by initiating proposals of her own. Among these were calls by Allon and Rabin to their Egyptian counterparts, Fahmī and Sādāt, for direct meetings "at any time and in any place"; at the Socialist International Congress in Geneva on 27 November, Rabin suggested that the Geneva conference be turned into a "Helsinki conference of the ME problem." [10] Shimon Peres proposed in January 1977 to establish either a West Bank-Israel federation or a Jordan-West Bank-Israel confederation. [11] For the first time, Israel also submitted a draft resolution at the UN General Assembly during the debate on the situation in the ME (see essay, "The UN and the Arab-Israeli Conflict"). However, Israel's efforts apparently did not succeed in improving its image or in discrediting Sādāt's; Allon's and Rabin's suggestions were rejected by Egypt as "propaganda gimmicks."

ARAB LEADERS CO-ORDINATE THEIR POSITIONS

Shortly before Carter's inauguration on 20 January 1977, the Arab states participating in the political process—Saudi Arabia, Egypt, Syria and Jordan—tried to co-ordinate their tactics and policies. In a series of meetings between Sādāt and Asad (18–21 December 1976), Sādāt and Ḥusayn (13–15 January 1977), and the Foreign Ministers of the "Confrontation" states, the Arabian peninsula oil-producing states and representatives of the PLO (in Riyadh, 9–10 January and in Cairo, 15 January 1977), the four countries reportedly agreed to a united strategy for 1977. This was: 1) to put pressure on the new US administration, mainly through Saudi Arabia; 2) to try to reconvene the Geneva conference during the first half of 1977; 3) to exert pressure on the PLO so that the PNC meeting (due in March 1977) would moderate its attitudes and declare its readiness to establish a Palestinian mini-state in the West bank and the Gaza Strip; and 4) to allow Jordan some status on the Palestinian question. (Since the Rabat 1974 summit resolution, Jordan's only claim to participation in the Geneva conference was through its role as a Confrontation state.)

At the end of December 1976, Sādāt declared that a Palestinian state should have formal links with Jordan. [12] In early January 1977, he added that the relationship had to be agreed upon by Ḥusayn and the PLO. [13] Fahmī said that while it was up to Jordan and the PLO, Egypt would "encourage a link between them." [14]

At the Sādāt-Ḥusayn talks on 13–15 January 1977, both sides referred to the Palestinians as having a right "to set up an independent political entity," and to Jordan only as a Confrontation state. However, Husayn expressed "Jordan's welcome . . . for establishing very close relations with the Palestinian state which will be set up . . . the form of [which] . . . will be decided by the two peoples through their free choice, proceeding from the unity of purpose and fate and the complete identity of interests and feeling." [15] Sādāt said that the Palestinians should have their own delegation at the Geneva conference "but linked by some way or another with the Jordanian delegation." [16] He was thus trying to ease in advance the complications he anticipated over the question of Palestinian representation.

Asad, too, indicated that he would support a Palestinian mini-state linked with Jordan. He said further that if the PLO refused to participate in the Geneva conference, "we will not exert pressure on them"; however, "the movement of the Arab states towards a settlement will not be paralysed." [17]

THE ELECTION CAMPAIGN IN ISRAEL

While the Arab leaders were busy co-ordinating their policy, Israel remained preoccupied with internal affairs. On 20 December 1976, Rabin submitted his (and consequently his government's) resignation and announced the decision to bring forward the elections, due in November 1977, "to the earliest possible date." These were later fixed for 17 May 1977.

The election campaign, preceded by Rabin's resignation as candidate for the Premiership and his subsequent replacement by Shimon Peres in April 1977, had no effect—declared or practical—on Arab and American policies. Israel continued to react to American and Arab moves, rather than to promote new initiatives. However, there was one notable exception. The Labour Party's convention decided on 25 February to change its former position of offering territorial concessions in exchange for peace, to an offer of concessions "on all frontiers" (i.e. including the West Bank). After the former Defence Minister Moshe Dayan (who had been known for his opposition to concessions in the West Bank) threatened to leave the party, Rabin and other party leaders signed a document at the beginning of April 1977 promising him that, in case of a peace agreement involving territorial concessions in the West Bank, the Government would call new elections.

FIRST MOVES OF THE CARTER ADMINISTRATION

The appointment of Professor Zbigniew Brzezinski as National Security Council (NSC) adviser, together with a number of statements by the new Secretary of State, Cyrus Vance, suggested that the Carter Administration's Middle East policy would closely follow the proposals of the Brookings Report. Vance's statement that "it is clear that the legitimate interests of the PLO must be dealt with"[18] was later described as a "slip of the tongue" in which he was referring to the previous formula used by the Ford Administration about the "legitimate rights of the Palestinians." However, Brzezinski went even further than Vance in his statement that a Palestinian state was "inevitable."[19]

The report of the Brookings Institution on the possibility of a ME settlement, published in December 1975, favoured a comprehensive agreement containing seven integrated elements:

1) **Security** All parties to the settlement should commit themselves to respect the sovereignty and territorial integrity of the others, and refrain from the threat or use of force against them.

2) **Stages** Withdrawal to agreed boundaries and the establishment of peaceful relations should be carried out in stages over a period of years, each stage being undertaken only when the agreed provisions of the previous stage have been faithfully implemented.

3) **Peaceful relations** The Arab parties should undertake not only to end such hostile actions against Israel as armed incursions, blockades, boycotts and propaganda attacks, but also give evidence of progress toward the development of normal international and regional political and economic relations.

4) **Boundaries** Israel should undertake to withdraw by agreed stages to the 5 June 1967 lines, with only such modifications as were mutually accepted. Boundaries would probably need to be safeguarded by demilitarized zones supervised by UN forces.

5) **Palestine** There should be provision for Palestinian self-determination, subject to Palestinian acceptance of the sovereignty and integrity of Israel within agreed boundaries. This might take the form either of an independent Palestine state accepting the obligations and commitments of the peace agreements, or of a Palestine entity voluntarily federated with Jordan but exercising extensive political autonomy.

6) **Jerusalem** The report suggested no specific solution for the particularly difficult problem of Jerusalem but recommended that, whatever the solution, it meet the following minimal criteria:

(a) there should be unimpeded access to all holy places, each under the custodianship of its own faith;
(b) there should be no barriers dividing the city;
(c) each national group within the city should, if it so desired, have substantial political autonomy within the area where it predominates.

7) **Guarantees** It would be desirable that the UN Security Council endorse the peace agreements. In addition, there might be a need for unilateral or multilateral guarantees to some or all of the parties, as well as substantial economic aid and military assistance, pending the adoption of agreed arms control measures.[20]

VANCE'S FIRST ME TOUR

The attempt to renew momentum towards a ME settlement began in mid-February 1977 with the US Secretary of State's seven-day visit to a number of capitals to obtain "at first hand" the Arab and the Israeli views on "how it may be possible to move forward to a peace settlement."

Opening his tour in Israel on 15 February, Vance's talks centred on the resumption of the Geneva conference and Israeli attitudes towards the PLO. Vance was told that Israel was prepared for the reconvening of the conference either "in its original format," or for any other framework "between the sovereign states of the area" with the aim of negotiating either "a comprehensive durable peace" or "the end of the state of war." Israel rejected any negotiations with the PLO, even if the organization recognized Israel or accepted Resolutions 242 and 338, but it did not oppose the participation of Palestinians in the Jordanian delegation to Geneva.[21] Vance and his aids apparently obtained the impression that Israel could change its attitude towards the PLO, if it recognized Israel.[22]

Vance told the Israelis that the Carter Administration accepted all the political commitments of its predecessor (as formulated in two published and one unpublished memoranda signed by the US and Israel on 1 September 1975[23] and in December 1973 respectively). These affirmed that Resolutions 242 and 338 were "the sole basis for any negotiations"; that "the composition of the participants of the Geneva conference" had to be determined "only with the consent of all parties concerned"; and that the US had "nothing to discuss with the PLO as a partner in the peacemaking process" as long as it refused to alter "the National Covenant" and did not accept Resolutions 242 and 338 (thus implying that the US attitude could change if the PLO changed its stand).[24]

Vance visited Cairo on 17-18 February after which Sādāt declared that there should be "a declared official relationship" between the Palestinian state and Jordan "even before the Geneva conference starts." This was understood to be a proposal to include the PLO in discussions, while indicating some compromise with the Israeli position; namely, that only Jordan was a valid partner in talks over the future of the West Bank.[25] Vance described this as "a constructive suggestion" which "begins to move" towards the Israeli stand. He said it showed that "more flexibility" existed in Egypt's position than he had thought. Israel's Foreign Minister, called it "a change in the right direction."[26]

Vance held talks in both Beirut and Amman on 18 February. Lebanese leaders said that their country would like to participate in the Geneva conference, but would not join the discussions on Israel's withdrawal since it had no border problems with Israel. Vance promised US support for Lebanon's participation. King Ḥusayn explained that he considered himself bound by the 1974 Rabat resolutions (that "the PLO was the sole legitimate representative of the Palestinian people" and had the right "to establish national authority . . . over any liberated

Palestinian territory.") He rejected a joint Jordanian-Palestinian delegation to Geneva unless the Rabat decisions were first revoked.[27]

In Riyadh on 19 February Saudi leaders asked Vance "to move towards recognition of the PLO in order to break the political logjam."[28] On 20 February, Vance held talks with the Syrian leaders in Damascus, who explained that in their view, there were three components to a settlement: 1) Israeli withdrawal from all the territories occupied in 1967; 2) recognition of the rights of the Palestinians; and 3) an end to the state of war.[29]

Vance's tour was summed up by the *Washington Post* as on the surface providing "little ground for optimism" about a settlement, since the parties delivered "unsurprising recitations of familiar and conflicting positions." However, there appeared to be "a real chance—far less than a probability but greater than a remote prospect—for a settlement," due to the new circumstances in the ME since the 1973 war and to the change in the US role in the area.[30]

RABIN'S VISIT TO WASHINGTON

The first ME leader to hold talks with Carter was Itzhak Rabin, who visited the US from 6–13 March. Carter's speech of welcome, on 7 March, seemed to come very close to Israeli positions. He spoke of his Administration's willingness "to explore some common ground so that Israel might have defensible borders, and so that peace commitments might never be violated. and so that there could be a sense of security about this young country in the future."[31] He defined peace as "the ending of the state of war, open borders, free movement of people and goods, and especially free exchange of ideas."[32] While Rabin was "pleased" with the statement on "defensible borders," it caused "some concern among experienced State Department officials" as well as Arab diplomats in Washington. Jody Powell, the White House Press Secretary hastened to explain that any interpretation of Carter's statement "should avoid a narrow definition of 'defensible borders' in geographic terms" because the President was speaking "in broad terms, reiterating the intent of the UN resolution about the 'secure' borders."[33]

Disclosures made after the elections in Israel revealed that in the private talks between Carter and Rabin, there had been sharp differences in attitude, aggravated by a lack of mutual sympathy between the two leaders. Carter was surprised at Rabin's categorical rejection of any negotiations with the PLO even if it recognized Israel, which stood in contrast to Vance's impression; he called it a "stiff and stubborn" attitude. He made it clear to Rabin that the US commitment not to recognize the PLO as long as the latter did not recognize Israel was still in force; but should the PLO change its attitude, the US would support its participation at Geneva. He emphasized his interest in a speedy reconvening of the Geneva conference, and said the US would not allow "procedural questions to prevent Israel's participation." If the PLO changed its attitude and Israel then decided to boycott the conference, Carter emphasized. "it will be a very serious problem" which "will provoke a very sharp reaction among the American people."

Regarding territorial problems, Rabin emphasized that Israel would not retreat to the 1967 lines, which Carter insisted upon. However, he asked Rabin whether Israel's distinction between "control" and "sovereignty" in the case of Sharm al-Shaykh could apply to other areas as well. Rabin replied that it "might be applicable in some areas," but that he had to consult his Cabinet. Despite Rabin's categorical rejection of the idea of "a third state between Israel and Jordan," Carter insisted upon the necessity of establishing some kind of a Palestinian entity. He also expressed American objection to new Israeli settlements in the occupied territories, saying he hoped that nothing would be done which would oblige the US to express this objection publicly.

In view of these differences, Rabin tried to obtain Carter's agreement not to commit himself to a new policy, or at least not to express it either in his forthcoming talks with Arab leaders or in public, because "any statement of the US . . . is equal to a precondition for the Geneva conference." However, he did not obtain such an assurance.[34]

Although Carter's 9 March statement (see immediately below), was felt by Rabin to be "a disappointing conclusion" to his talks,[35] he did not make public their difficult nature. He preferred to emphasize the "positive" results of his visit: 1) that the US would not enforce a solution; 2) that it was interested in a strong Israel; 3) that the American definition of peace had moved closer to Israel's; 4) that the US attitude towards the PLO had not changed; and 5) that "for the first time, we have heard from an American President support for the need of defensible borders and the possibility of distinguishing between defence lines and political borders."[36]

CARTER ON BORDERS AND A PALESTINIAN "HOMELAND"

At a press conference on 9 March (after Rabin had ended his official visit but was still in the US), Carter made a distinction between "permanent and recognized borders where sovereignty is legal"—the lines of which "I would guess . . . would be some minor adjustments in the 1967 borders"—and "defence lines," which might allow "extensions of Israeli defence capability beyond the permanent and recognized borders."[37]

This statement upset both Israel and the Arab states. Israeli sources expressed "deep disappointment" at its timing as well as over the "1967 borders concept." Rabin said that Israel "appreciates" America's understanding of the ME problem, but that eventually "it is up to the parties to the conflict to make final decisions," and that "when it comes to Israel's defence, Israel will decide what constitutes defensible borders—and not outsiders."[38] Sources in Cairo and Amman, as well as Arab diplomats in the US, expressed concern that Carter had apparently adopted the Allon Plan.[39] Official Arab reaction was more cautious. Sādāt said that "any talk about secure borders must take place within the framework of a comprehensive settlement," which included "the withdrawal of Israeli forces from all occupied Arab lands, respect for territorial integrity and non-acquisition of territories by force."[40]

In an attempt to influence the deliberations of the PNC, then in session in Cairo, Carter told a press conference on 16 March that "there has to be a homeland provided for the Palestinian refugees, who had suffered for many, many years."[41] 'Arafāt welcomed the statement, saying that Carter had "touched the core of the problem."[42] However, the next day a PNC spokesman, Maḥmūd Labadī, said that "even if that is 'Arafāt's opinion, we are not going to say we will not continue the struggle."[43]

Israel, though reacting cautiously, showed concern. Rabin said he "would have been happy if Carter had used a phrase other than 'homeland,'" adding that he would "have nothing against" Carter's statement if the President had meant that "the Palestinian homeland is in Jordan."[44] The Israeli embassy communicated Israel's immediate concern to the State Department, but US officials tried to diminish Carter's commitment; Brezezinski stated that the word "homeland" itself "has no specific connotation. The importance of the statement is in the broader approach it takes." However, on 19 March, Carter told correspondents that "what I said is appropriate. I think some provision has got to be made for the Palestinians in the framework of Jordan or by some other means."[45]

Jordan was also concerned by Carter's statement. Some ministers were reported to suspect that the US intended "to see a Palestinian state set up, not on the West Bank . . . as everyone supposed, but in Jordan itself." This suspicion was strengthened by the reports of CIA payments to Husayn, and created a feeling among Jordanian leaders that a "plot" existed against the Kingdom.[46]

SĀDĀT'S VISIT TO WASHINGTON

Sādāt arrived in Washington for a three-day visit on 3 April 1977, after discussions in West Germany and France. At the welcoming ceremony, Sādāt lauded Carter's remarks about creating a "homeland for the Palestinian refugees," saying that Carter "came very close to the proper remedy." What was needed, he added, was to establish "a political entity, so that the Palestinians can at long last become a community of citizens, not a group of refugees."[47] According to the Egyptian ambassador to Washington, Ashraf Ghurbāl, the two Presidents agreed that "the Palestinians" would have "to be heard directly or by mediators," and that the only remaining question was how to achieve this.[48] However, according to a Lebanese newspaper, Sādāt did not succeed in convincing Carter to establish contacts with the PLO or to convene the Geneva conference with the participation of the PLO "at this stage."[49]

Another issue of disagreement between Carter and Sādāt was that of "defensible borders." Sādāt objected to any arrangement leaving Israeli or foreign defence installations on Arab territory since "sovereignty is indivisible, and there can't be two types of borders." He would agree only to demiltarized zones on both sides of the border on the Egyptian and Syrian fronts "on a reciprocal basis" and to "slight amendments" of the border in the West Bank in order to reunite divided villages—also "on a reciprocal basis."[50] Privately, however, Sādāt went further, and reportedly suggested that if Carter convinced Israel to withdraw, the US could use Sharm al-Shaykh as a naval base.

The third issue of disagreement was the "essence of peace." Here, too, Sādāt toned down his position and, according to US officials, told them that he envisaged a full normalization of relations with Israel within about five years after the Geneva agreement had been signed, and that some interim steps towards normal relations could take place even earlier.[51]

After his visit, Sādāt said in several interviews that five years after the peace agreement there would be a "normalization," but he declined to explain what he meant by this term and continued to reject diplomatic and commercial relations with Israel as well as other aspects of the Israeli-American definition of peace.

ELABORATION OF AMERICAN POLICY

Carter stated on 8 April that "there will have to be a spokesman for the [Palestinian] viewpoint during the [Geneva] conference itself" either "by a surrogate or by them directly."[52] He said on 22 April that he was trying "to learn the attitudes" of the Arab states and Israel, and "to observe and analyse some common ground on which a permanent settlement might be reached." Carter added that he intended "to minimize" his own statements until he had met all the leaders involved, since he had "outlined some of the options" and was "trying to get responses from them before I make further comments."[53]

HUSAYN'S VISIT TO WASHINGTON

King Ḥusayn arrived in Washington on 25 April and in an interview said he was "not optimistic about peace prospects in the ME this year."[54] The two-day talks centred on PLO representation in the Geneva conference, and on Carter's formula for "secure borders" and "a homeland for the Palestinians." Husayn was reported to have objected to a joint Jordanian-PLO delegation and supported Asad's suggestion of a unified Arab delegation.[55] The White House press secretary subsequently reported that the US had not changed its "negative attitude" towards the PLO's participation in the Geneva conference, and that it objected to the inclusion of PLO representatives in the Jordanian delegation.

Husayn stated that Carter had assured him that in speaking of Palestinians, he had in mind only the West Bank and the Gaza Strip, whose status and relationship with Jordan should be defined later. Ḥusayn's 1972 "Federation Plan" seemed to be one of the most probable solutions to this question.[56] Speaking in an interview with *CBS*, Ḥusayn said it was "dangerous to speak about secure borders" in the ME, and emphasized that such borders could be possible only if the Arabs had a "true feeling" that they had got "a just and dignified solution [that] they are ready to live with and to observe."[57]

Carter said after his talks with the King that "it would be a mistake to hope for too much" because the differences between Israel and the Arab states were "very wide and have been lasting for a long period."[58]

"PERSUASIVE POWERS"

Carter announced on 2 May that he would not hesitate "to use the full strength of our own country and its persuasive powers to bring those [ME] nations to agreement" if he saw "a clearly fair and equitable solution." Although the US "cannot impose [its] will on others," it was in the position "of one who can influence countries to modify their positions slightly to accommodate other nations' interests." However, the President emphasized that "unless the countries involved agree, there is no way to make progress."[59]

Two days later, Vance stated that after completing the round of meetings with ME leaders, the US would be "prepared to make suggestions" about what it believed would be a "fair and equitable manner" of dealing with the ME problems, which it would then discuss with the parties concerned "to see how much common ground we can find." Answering a question whether these suggestions did not amount to a comprehensive plan, Vance said that whatever the name, it was "a question that gets into semantics." However, he also stressed that "the ultimate decision . . . must be made by the parties themselves."[60]

On several occasions, Brzezinski told American Jewish leaders that the election of a "weak" Israeli government would invite the US to impose a settlement.

THE ASAD-CARTER TALKS

Unlike other Arab leaders, Asad refused to visit Washington. His meeting with Carter was arranged (during Khaddām's Washington visit on 21–22 April) for 8–9 May in Geneva on "neutral ground"; it would fit between a seven-nation economic summit in London (7–8 May), a four-nation summit in Berlin (9 May) and a NATO Council meeting in London (10 May).

During the two-day talks, Asad reportedly told Carter that a "just peace" had to be based on UN resolutions and include both Israel's withdrawal from all the territories occupied in 1967 and recognition of the "legitimate rights of the Palestinians." He also expressed his belief that the US could and should impose such a settlement upon Israel. Carter answered that the US was preparing an "integrative plan" which could be a basis for the Geneva conference; this would be discussed by Vance during his second ME tour. Asad rejected the idea of "secure borders," but agreed to small demilitarized zones on both sides of the border. He insisted upon PLO participation in the Geneva conference within a unified Arab delegation and suggested (in the name of Syria, Egypt, Jordan, Saudi Arabia and the PLO) the establishment in the West Bank and the Gaza Strip of a Palestinian state linked with Jordan "in the same way some Arab states are linked to each other nowadays." [61]

Summing up the talks, Carter said "there must be a resolution of the Palestine problem and a homeland for the Palestinians . . . some resolution of border disputes and . . . an assurance of permanent and real peace with guarantees for the future security of these countries which all can trust." He added that all the ME leaders he met had agreed to the "general idea" of establishing buffer zones between Israel and her neighbours "manned by international peace forces," and that he agreed with Asad that these buffer zones had to be established on both sides of the border.

A senior US official told correspondents that there was optimism "that really serious negotiations will begin before the end of this year, even if not in the formal Geneva setting." [62]

HARDENING OF ARAB POSITIONS

The Arabs' "peace offensive" had been accompanied throughout by tough demands, such as for an Israeli ban on further Jewish immigration; but the frequency of their hardline statements increased from April 1977. Saudi and Egyptian officials hinted on several occasions that Resolution 242 should be changed to include the Palestinian people's problem; Saudi officials referred to the 1947 borders (established by the General Assembly Resolution 181) as the only legal Israeli borders, which a Syrian spokesman suggested Israel should draw back to. Sādāt said that he was "prepared to give six months"—no more—to Israel to withdraw from the occupied territories, and that he would claim $2,100m compensation from Israel for using the Sinai oilfields. Asad stated that recognition of Israel by Syria could not be a part of any settlement. [63]

ISRAEL'S CONCERN ABOUT AN IMPOSED SETTLEMENT

American statements produced growing concern in Israel, which made several unsuccessful diplomatic overtures after March 1977 to try to convince the US not to take "specific positions" over the terms of a political settlement, but to leave them, as promised, for negotiation between the parties involved. At a Cabinet meeting on 24 April, Allon reported that "the possibility of disagreement between Israel and the US over outstanding issues must not be ruled out." [64]

The cumulative impact of these various American statements and decisions created the impression among Israeli leaders that the US was beginning to exert pressure on Israel in order to force an American settlement in the ME. Among actions regarded as harmful to Israel's defence capabilities were the decision in February not to supply Israel with "concussion bombs" which had been promised by President Ford; the veto on Israel selling *Kfir* jets to Ecuador in March; and the proposal to exclude Israel from the preferred category of states receiving and jointly producing US weapons (put forward in Washington at the beginning of May). Israel's acting Prime Minister, Shimon Peres, declared that the US should offer its good offices to both sides, with a view to "building a bridge of understanding between their positions and smoothing the negotiating procedures," rather than putting forward its own proposals which could lead to confrontation "with either one side or both sides." [65]

THE ALLON-VANCE MEETING; FURTHER STATEMENT BY CARTER

Allon met Vance in London on 12 May to be informed officially of the results of

Carter's talks with Arab leaders. Afterwards, Vance announced that the US would act only as mediator and not initiate any peace plan of its own. He repeated the American commitment not to recognize or enter into direct contacts with the PLO "unless and until it accepts the UN resolutions and recognizes Israel's right to exist as a state." Vance also said that Carter's Administration fully endorsed the "special relationship" between the US and Israel, and that it would supply Israel "with all the arms it required for defence, including advanced technology." [66]

However, Israeli press reports spoke of continuing wide differences of opinion between Israel and the US regarding "defensible borders" and security arrangements, as well as over the problem of the "Palestinian homeland." Vance had also warned Allon that if Israel continued its policy of settlement in the occupied territories, the US would have to oppose it publicly, "which will be a pity." [67]

Carter said in Washington on 12 May that the first American commitment in the ME was "to protect the right of Israel to exist, to exist permanently, and to exist in peace." A part of this commitment was that "Israel had adequate means to protect itself without the military involvement of the US." On the other hand, Carter stated that if the PLO accepted the fact of Israel, Israel should agree to a homeland for the Palestinians. "The exact definition of what that homeland might be, the degree of independence of the Palestinian entity, its relationship with Jordan or perhaps Syria and others, the geographical boundaries of it, all have to be worked out by the parties involved." He added that he believed that "there is a chance that the Palestinians might make moves to recognize the right of Israel to exist, and if so, this would remove one of the major obstacles towards further progress." [68]

FAHD'S VISIT TO WASHINGTON

Prince (Amīr) Fahd of Saudi Arabia arrived in Washington on 24 May for a two-day visit—the first by an Arab leader since the election of the Likud government. His visit was preceded by a meeting between Sādāt, Asad and Saudi leaders in Riyadh on 19 May to co-ordinate their approach to the US.

Before leaving Riyadh, Fahd had said that Saudi Arabia could help to implement the "Carter plan" for energy conservation, but the US would have "to use her weight in order to achieve a just peace for the ME problem"; namely, "Israeli withdrawal from all the territories occupied in 1967" and the return "to the Palestinians [of] their rights in their homeland and to a state of their own." [69]

Carter subsequently denied that Fahd had explicitly linked Saudi oil policy with progress towards a ME settlement and that threats of a Saudi oil embargo had been made. Fahd was given to understand that the US had "some influence in Israel and also the Arab countries," but that it "obviously [has] no control over [them]." [70] However, in an interview, Fahd expressed his belief that the US, "which has a special military, political and economic relationship with Israel," could assist to achieve "a fair peace." [71] Carter said that Fahd had expressed "his strong hope that the Israelis would be reassured about the inclinations of his country towards the protection of their security." [72] This statement was interpreted by Israeli officials as support for Carter's idea about security arrangements beyond Israel's recognized borders. [73]

The main issue in the discussions between Fahd and Carter was the Palestinian question. Both sides were said to have agreed that the Palestinian problem was "still the main obstacle to resuming the Geneva conference," but they reached no agreement about PLO participation in it. [74] However after the talks, Carter said that "the Palestinians should have a secure homeland with recognized borders." [75]

REACTION TO THE ELECTIONS IN ISRAEL

Immediate Arab reaction to the unexpected victory of the Likud was one of surprise and concern about the prospects of a settlement. Arab media unanimously interpreted the victory by Begin (the "Zionist racist terrorist") as a blow to peace efforts, and as increasing the chances of war. Official comments, however, were more restrained. Husayn said he was "concerned" about the election results, but "the positive and courageous stand" of the US was an "encouraging development."[76] Both Sādāt and the Jordanian Information Minister, 'Adnān Abū 'Awda, said that the results did not matter because "there is no difference between the Israeli leaders—all are hawks"; and because the real key to the settlement was in the hands of the US.[77]

While the US and other Western media expressed concern about the influence of the Likud's electoral victory on ME settlement prospects, the Administration's comments were restrained, emphasizing that "the historic friendship between the US and Israel was not dependent on the domestic politics of either nation,"[79] and that the US regarded itself committed to the "political process."[80]

THE WIDENING GAP BETWEEN THE US AND ISRAEL

After an assessment of the new situation, the Administration appeared to have decided to continue its policy and try to put pressure on the Begin government to moderate its attitudes—both in its official statements, and through the American Jewish community and the pro-Israeli lobby in Congress. This was strongly hinted at by Carter who said that the question of whether Begin would be an obstacle to the peace process "can be resolved . . . when he meets with the Congressional leaders and with Jewish Americans . . . I think this might have an effect on him."[81]

On 22 May, Carter stated that he expected "Israel and her neighbours to continue to be bound by UN Resolutions 242 and 338."[82] On 26 May, he repeated that the US was bound by the "premises" of a ME settlement, which had been "spelled out very clearly in UN resolutions . . . voted and supported by our Government." These resolutions included "the right of the Palestinians to have a homeland" and "to be compensated"; Israel's withdrawal from territories occupied in 1967; and "an end of belligerency and a re-establishment of permanent and secure borders."[83] Later on the same day, the State Department specified that the President "had in mind UN Resolutions 242 and 338," the "General Assembly Resolution 181 of November 1947 [which] provided for the recognition of a Jewish and an Arab state in Palestine, and the General Assembly Resolution 194 of December 1948 [which] endorsed the right of Palestinians to return to their homes or choose to be compensated."[84]

In the beginning of June, the President said that "if Israel should disavow those commitments [to UN resolutions made by former Israeli governments], that would be a very profound change," the consequences of which "cannot be accurately predicted."[85]

On 9 June, the US Assistant Secretary of State for Near Eastern and South Asian Affairs, Alfred L. Atherton, stated before the House of Representatives Subcommittee for International Affairs that if no settlement could be achieved, the US would have to reassess its aid to the ME "according to the policy of each country."[86]

On 17 June, Vice-President Mondale said that peace in the ME was essential for Israel. After reviewing Israel's achievements since its establishment, he added that regarding the future, "Israel's three million people" had either the choice to "try by force of arms alone to hold out against the hostility and growing power of the Arab world," or to start "a process of reconciliation" in which "peace protects Israel's security."[87]

The impression that the US and Israel were on a collision course reached a peak when the State Department stated on 27 June (i.e. after Prime Minister Begin had stated that everything, including the West Bank, was negotiable) that peace "requires both sides to make difficult compromises," and that "no territories, including the West Bank," can be "automatically excluded from negotiations." [88] A well-informed American correspondent quoted officials in Washington as having said that "if Begin cannot accept the idea of an Israeli withdrawal from the West Bank, there is no point in his coming next month to see President Carter." [89] Both this report and the statement itself caused embarrassment in Washington and Carter, who apparently had not been told about the latter, imposed a "moratorium" on statements about the ME.

The Carter Administration decided to avoid a public confrontation with Israel after failing to enlist American Jewish support, which instead had consolidated behind Israel. It was also faced with growing criticism from Congressmen and Jewish organizations, as well as mounting tension with Israel—where both the Government and the Opposition joined in criticizing recent American statements. In trying to improve the atmosphere for Begin's planned visit, Carter stated on 1 July that "an overwhelming consideration for us is the preservation of Israel as a free and independent and hopefully peaceful nation." He added that Begin "will be received with the kind of friendship that has always been characteristic of the American people's attitude toward Israel." [90] On 6 July, he assured American Jewish leaders that an overall ME settlement "would have to include diplomatic relations between the countries involved," and that the "Palestinian homeland or entity would have to have formal ties with Jordan." [91]

BEGIN'S FIRST MOVES

In view of the deep concern abroad about his victory and the sharp reaction to his first announcement (that the Allon Plan was dead, and that many settlements would be established in the West Bank), Menahem Begin began a campaign to change his negative image in the US. He gave numerous interviews with Western media and held meetings with US Congressmen and American-Jewish leaders who came to Israel to talk to the new Prime Minister. He also sent his adviser on foreign information, Shmuel Katz, to the US to explain the Likud's attitudes. Both Begin and Katz emphasized their desire for peace and their readiness to discuss any item raised by the Arabs. This campaign, as well as the appointment of Dayan as Foreign Minister and the erection of a coalition government at least partly succeeded in allaying US concern.

The Government programme stated, among other things, that it would honour all the commitments of the previous administration, including the acceptance of Resolutions 242 and 338 as the sole basis for a Geneva conference. It also confirmed that Israeli law would not be applied in the West Bank and the Gaza Strip, as long as negotiations with the Arab states continued.

After taking office, Begin set out to gain the political initiative from the Arab states. On 28 June, he suggested that the Geneva conference be reconvened at any date after 10 October 1977; and on 7 July, he suggested a "political truce" between Israel and the Arab states, to last until the Geneva conference was reconvened.

In mid-July, shortly before Begin's visit to Washington, the Israeli cabinet was reported to have approved a procedural plan for the Geneva conference to be submitted to Carter.

BEGIN'S VISIT TO WASHINGTON; PROCEDURAL PLAN REVEALED

Begin began his official two-day visit to Washington on 19 July, after meeting and receiving the backing of American-Jewish leaders in New York. The talks with Carter were termed "frank but friendly"; however, basic differences between the two leaders were not bridged. The Palestinian issue was discussed "primarily in a procedural context." The issue of Israeli settlements in the occupied territories was raised, and Carter emphasized American opposition to new settlements, but not to an "increase in the population" of existing ones. However, he did not obtain Begin's promise not to establish new settlements—even though he emphasized that he regarded this subject as a matter of mutual confidence. According to Israeli press reports, Begin did express readiness to make border changes in Sinai and the Golan Heights, but objected to any foreign control of the West Bank. Instead, he offered a version of the "Dayan Plan" according to which the residents themselves would manage the civil and administrative aspects of their lives, while Israel would be responsible for West Bank defence and security. However, he did not object to the placing of the West Bank on the agenda of the Geneva conference.

Unlike previous governments, Begin's strategy was to shift the burden of negotiation to contacts with the Arabs rather than with the US. Subsequently he did not try to reach a co-ordinated policy with Washington, and therefore differences did not immediately evolve into a dispute: both leaders "agreed not to agree." After the talks, both expressed optimism, and Carter said that they had "laid the groundwork" for reconvening the Geneva conference in October.[92]

At a press conference at the conclusion of his talks on 20 July, Begin revealed details of his procedural plan for the Geneva conference which he had submitted to Carter. The plan proposed the reconvening of the conference after 10 October on the basis of Resolution 338 (which refers to Resolution 242), with the participation of "delegations of sovereign states" only, and without "prior commitments" demanded or given. He further proposed that the delegations should form sub-commissions to negotiate and conclude bilateral "peace treaties," and that a full session of the conference should then be summoned to sign them. Begin stated that every peace treaty would include an opening article to the effect that "the state of war has been terminated," followed by territorial clauses, a chapter of diplomatic clauses, and finally economic and other clauses concerning specific problems. If the Geneva conference could not reconvene because of Arab insistence on PLO participation, Israel proposed either bilateral mixed committees with US chairmanship similar to the 1949 armistice negotiations in Rhodes, or "proximity talks" as suggested by the US in 1972.[93]

Carter termed the proposal "forward-looking and worthy of consideration."[94] The Arab leaders, however, rejected it categorically, especially since it completely ignored the Palestinian issue, and failed to ensure withdrawal from all the occupied territories. They also rejected the proposed alternatives for the Geneva conference.[95]

VANCE'S SECOND ME VISIT AND CARTER'S ASSESSMENT

The US Secretary of State's second ME visit took him to Alexandria (1–2 August), Beirut (3 August), Damascus (4–5 August), Amman (5–6 August), Tā'if (7–8 August), Jerusalem (9–10 August), and then back to Alexandria, Damascus and Amman (11 August), where he discussed questions of both procedure and substance and put forward American proposals.

With respect to procedure, Sādāt's suggestion that a "working group" of foreign ministers be convened in New York in September during the UN General Assembly (which had been accepted by both the US and Israel) was rejected by Syria. It was agreed, instead, to hold separate talks between the foreign ministers with Secretary Vance in New York.

According to press reports, Vance's substantive proposals included a phased five-year Israeli withdrawal linked to a gradual transition to full diplomatic relations; and an Israeli (or joint Israeli-Jordanian) trusteeship over the West Bank for several years, to be followed by a referendum to determine the area's future. These proposals were said to have been rejected by all the parties. The gap over the Palestinian and territorial issues also remained as wide as ever. However, on the "essence of peace," Egypt, Jordan and Syria were reported to be willing to sign peace treaties with Israel; while Egypt and Jordan were also ready "to consider" diplomatic relations.[96]

Dayan claimed that he had asked Vance to find out if the Arab states had any plans to solve the refugee problem after the peace treaty. Vance got negative answers. When reporting this in Jerusalem, a difference of opinion arose: Vance wanted to postpone dealing with the refugee problem, while Dayan argued that without a solution to it, there could be no final solution for the Arab-Israeli conflict.

After receiving Vance's report, Carter stated on 14 August that he remained determined "to do everything possible to bring about a just and lasting peace in the ME," and that he intended to meet the ME foreign ministers himself, in addition to their scheduled meetings with Vance. In an interview broadcast the same day, Carter said he would continue "to go public with the American position," adding: "I will feel much more secure when we take a strong position that I have the backing of the Congress and the American people." He went on to say that he was hopeful that "a final solution" could be reached, and that "world opinion is very powerful on disputing nations when there is a consensus about what ought to be done." He continued: "There is no single attitude among all Jews in the world or all Israeli citizens . . . [if] Israeli leaders genuinely want a peace settlement, . . . they have to agree that there will be an acceptance of genuine peace on the part of the Arabs, an adjustment of boundaries . . . which are secure for the Israelis and also satisfy the minimum requirements of the Arab neighbours and UN resolutions, and some solution to the question of the enormous numbers of Palestinian refugees who have been forced out of their homes and who want some fair treatment."[97]

On 29 August, Carter said that his Administration was "fervent" in its determination to make progress towards a ME peace "by the end of this year," and to that end "would be aggressive." He added that if there was no progress, "there is going to be a great deal of disillusionment on our part, in the ME and around the world." He said that the Arab leaders had exhibited a "more flexible attitude" than Israel during Vance's trip. Referring to the American media's description of the trip as a failure, Carter insisted that it was "very successful," and that there was still time for progress.[98]

THE BEGINNING OF US-ISRAELI CONFRONTATION

During August and the first half of September, two central issues became a matter of open controversy between the US and Israel: the former's attitude towards the PLO, and the latter's settlements in the West Bank.

Israel had decided to recognize three existing (but hitherto not officially recognized) settlements in the West Bank as "full-fledged settlements" on 26 July. On the same day, the State Department described Israeli settlement in the occupied territory as "illegal" and the decision as "an obstacle to peace." However, on 27 July, Carter said that it was not right to put all the blame on Begin because these and other settlements were "established under the previous government," and because Begin was bound by commitments made during the election campaign in the same way as Carter was bound.[99]

On 28 July, Carter for the first time expressed a US attitude which was interpreted by observers as a positive reference to the PLO. He stated that "the Palestinians" ought to be represented at the Geneva conference, and that the US would enter into discussions with them "at the time they forego their commitment to destroy Israel." [100]

On 8 August, following Vance's report from Ṭā'if that the PLO had conveyed to him its readiness to accept Resolution 242 if it was changed so as to include a recognition of Palestinian national rights, Carter stated that he would accept the Palestinians' recognition of "the applicability of UN Resolution 242" (tantamount to indirect recognition of Israel and its right to exist) as a sufficient condition for their participation in Geneva and for opening discussions with them.[101] This statement gave rise to speculation about an American or French initiative in the Security Council to change the resolution. However, both governments denied such an intention. Expectations of the PLO's qualified acceptance of Resolution 242 also remained unfulfilled; on 28 August, the PLO's Central Committee once again rejected it.

The shift in American attitude caused anxiety both in Jordan and in Israel. Jordan was also worried about a State Department statement that the US "has never recognized *de jure* the occupation of the West Bank by Jordan." Despite official denials by both Israel and Jordan, the press continued to report that Ḥusayn and Dayan had met in London during Dayan's visit (from 21–22 August) and had discussed the American attitude towards the PLO.

When Vance visited Jerusalem on 11 August, a delegation of West Bank personalities submitted a petition to him denying *inter alia* that the PLO was representative of the West Bank population. During August, several other West Bank leaders attacked the PLO and its leadership, a move apparently initiated by Jordan, with Israeli acquiescence. However, because it remained formally bound to the 1974 Rabat summit resolutions, Jordan welcomed the new American attitude. Dayan, on the other hand, termed the shift in attitude as a grave matter. He said on several occasions that if the US held talks with the PLO, it would violate the written American commitment given to Israel in 1975 in return for its withdrawal from Sinai.[102]

Presumably as a counter-move to this shift in Washington's position, Israel announced its decision to raise the standard of services provided by the government in the West Bank and Gaza Strip to that in Israel. Three days later, on 17 August, Israel announced its decision to establish three new settlements in the West Bank. The US again described the establishment of settlements as "illegal" and "obstacles to peace," but tried to play down their importance; it denied that the two countries were on a collision course. The State Department changed the sentence which had originally described the decision about equal services as "an action which could only complicate the peace process" to read: "The Israeli government has emphasized the potential benefit to the population in the occupied territories of the humanitarian aims of this action." [103] Carter stated he did not intend "to go further" than the "open expression of our own concern and the identification of these settlements as being illegal." [104]

On 9 September, the Minister of Agriculture and Chairman of the Joint Government-Jewish Agency Committee for Settlement, Ariel Sharon, said in an interview that "new settlements have been set up in [Judea and Samaria] which have not been reported." [105] Because the widespread criticism evoked by the statement, Sharon hastened to deny charges that new settlements were secretly established, and said he had been misunderstood;[106] the US expressed its satisfaction with the Israeli denial.[107] In view of the forthcoming meetings of the foreign ministers and the fact that Israel refrained from any new activities in this matter, the issue of Israeli settlements in the West Bank receded for the time being, while the more important questions of Palestinian representation in Geneva and the solution of the Palestinian problem remained at the forefront of political activity and public interest.

Israel's longstanding policy of rejecting PLO (or any other independent Palestinian delegation's) participation in Geneva received overwhelming affirmation in a Knesset resolution adopted in September, which stated that the PLO "is not a discussion partner for the State of Israel in any ME peace negotiations."[108] Instead, Israel insisted on the primacy of making peace with "sovereign states." Accordingly, the Government prepared a draft of a peace proposal which was presented by Dayan to Carter at a meeting on 19 September. Little attention was paid to it by the Americans, and after Fahmī's rejection (at his meeting with Carter on 21 September), the draft proposal was abandoned. Begin also rejected Asad's suggestion that the Arab League should represent the Palestinians,[110] provided there were guarantees that the "rights of the Palestinians" would be discussed at the conference.[111]

The US, on the other hand, emphasized the centrality of the Palestinian issue. In an interview published on 9 September, Carter described the PLO's rejection of Resolution 242 as "an obstacle in the way of our efforts to convene a peace conference," and expressed the hope that the organization would "re-examine its position on this matter." Reiterating his views on the requirements of a settlement, the President warned that if "either Israel or the Arabs cling to their very adamant positions of the past and refuse to negotiate freely and aggressively, then there is no hope for a permanent peace." In such a case, he added, "it will be difficult for us to continue to devote that much time and energy to the ME. Dozens of other foreign policy matters require my urgent attention."[112] On 12 September, the US issued a statement declaring that "to be lasting, a peace agreement must be positively supported by all the parties to the conflict, including the Palestinians. This means that the Palestinians must be involved in the peacemaking process. Their representatives will have to be at Geneva for the Palestinian question to be solved."[113] On 18 September, a day before Carter's meeting with Dayan, the American ambassador to the UN, Andrew Young, stated that the PLO should be represented in the Geneva conference, because in its absence no peace treaty could be signed. However, the White House spokesman declined to comment on this.[114]

THE POINT OF US-ISRAELI CONFRONTATION

In the expectation of an approaching confrontation between the United States and Israel, attention became focused on the meetings of the Americans with Dayan rather than with the Arab foreign ministers. The two main issues at Dayan's first meeting with Carter, Mondale and Vance on 19 September were Palestinian representation at Geneva and the Israeli settlements. Carter emphasized that the Palestinians must be represented.[115] According to Israeli press reports, the President suggested that a unified Arab delegation would be the best solution to the problem. Dayan rejected this idea, saying that Israel wanted to negotiate with "sovereign states" and that she had already agreed to the participation of Palestinians in the Jordanian delegation. However, US officials thought that Dayan's answer left the door open for further consideration. Dayan also rejected any negotiations with the PLO as such, but told the Americans that Israel would not reject the participation of PLO sympathizers within the Jordanian delegation, so long as they did not publicly declare their support for the PLO. He expressed Israel's readiness to negotiate with a Palestinian delegation outside the framework of the Geneva conference and on condition that the negotiations were not aimed at establishing a

Palestinian state.[116] On 22 September, Dayan and Vance arrived at a compromise formula, which was approved by the Israeli government on 25 September. The formula, which according to Begin was approved "word for word,"[117] called for a unified Arab delegation in which "Palestinians who are not known members of the 'PLO' may participate . . . as a part of the Jordanian delegation." This unified delegation would take part *only* in the opening ceremony, and then "split up into delegations representing the various states" to conduct bilateral negotiations.[118]

Egypt, Jordan and Syria rejected the proposed formula outright as an "Israeli manoeuvre" to foil the Geneva conference, and emphasized that "there will be no Geneva without the PLO."[119] The US expressed its satisfaction with Israel's acceptance, but emphasized that "some of the conditions set by the Israeli cabinet yesterday do not accurately reflect our views," such as the reference to the PLO. Vance told reporters that "Israel has not gone far enough to help to resolve the continuing procedural stalemate."[120]

During the following week, the US tried to extract further concessions. The Americans were reported to have urged Israel to modify its position and agree to the participation in Geneva of second-rank PLO officials, as well as to an independent Palestinian delegation within the unified Arab delegation. Dayan and other Israeli spokesmen persistently repeated Israel's categorical rejection both of PLO participation in Geneva and of an independent Palestinian delegation—because in both cases it would signify that the creation of an independent Palestinian state was on the agenda. Accordingly, Dayan warned that the implementation of either alternative would destroy the chances for the reconvening of the Geneva conference.

These attempts to pressure Israel prompted a great deal of criticism within the US. On 20 September, Senator Richard Stone, chairman of the sub-committee for the ME and Europe, declared his support for the Israeli draft proposal and accused the Administration of not abiding by its commitments to Israel. On 28 September, two US Senators separately accused the Administration of urging Iran "to threaten to curtail its oil supplies to Israel as a means of putting pressure on Israel to make concessions in the ME negotiations."[121] The State Department's denial of these charges did not diminish criticism of the Administration's policy. In a last effort to break the deadlock, a meeting between Carter and Dayan was arranged for 5 October. But before the meeting took place, an event occurred which brought to a head not only the confrontation between Israel and the US, but also the criticism within the US of the Administration's policy.

THE AMERICAN-SOVIET JOINT COMMUNIQUÉ

On 1 October, Vance and the Soviet Foreign Minister, Andrei Gromyko, issued a joint communiqué which stated that "as soon as possible a just and lasting settlement of the Arab-Israeli conflict" should be achieved. The key issues for such a settlement were "withdrawal of Israeli armed forces from territories occupied in the 1967 conflict; the resolution of the Palestinian question including ensuring the legitimate rights of the Palestinian people; termination of the state of war and establishment of normal peaceful relations on the basis of mutual recognition of the principles of sovereignty, territorial integrity and political independence." This settlement should be achieved through the reconvention of the Geneva conference "not later than December 1977, with the participation in its work of the representatives of all the parties involved in the conflict, including those of the Palestinian people, and legal and contractual formalization of the decisions reached at the conference."[122]

The joint communiqué aroused widespread criticism against the Carter Administration inside the US and in Israel, based on four principles. 1) Failure to mention Resolutions 242 and 338 as the basis for the negotiations, and a peace treaty as their aim. 2) The term "legitimate rights" was interpreted as acceptance both of the PLO as a legitimate negotiating party, and of the idea of a Palestinian state. 3) The American-Soviet statement was interpreted as tending to undo US efforts to restrict Soviet influence in the area by presenting the Russians with an opportunity to regain a prominent position in any future Arab-Israeli negotiations. 4) It implied an imposed solution.

In his address to the UN General Assembly on 4 October, Carter seemed to be trying to mollify both Israel and his American critics. He stated that "true peace—peace embodied in binding treaties—is essential"; that it was crucial for Israel to have "borders that are recognized and secure" as well as "security arrangements"; and that "the commitment of the US to Israel's security is unquestionable." He emphasized that Resolutions 242 and 338 were "the basis for peace," and that there must be "a recognition by all nations in the area—Israel and the Arab countries—[that all the parties] have a right to exist in peace, with early establishment of economic and cultural exchange and normal diplomatic relations." However, the President also held that "the legitimate rights of the Palestinian people must be recognized . . . How these rights are to be defined," he added, "is, of course, for the interested parties to decide in negotiations and not for us to dictate." [123]

THE AMERICANS AND DAYAN AGREE ON A "WORKING PAPER"

At that juncture, the prospects of Dayan's 5 October meeting with Carter and Vance seemed dim indeed. According to Israeli sources, Dayan termed the discussion "brutal." Carter accused Israel of being obstinate and therefore an obstacle to the peace process—"even more than Syria." He urged Israel to agree to the participation of second-rank PLO officials in Geneva, and warned that if Israel continued to be an obstacle, he would address the American public and explain that Israel was hurting American interests. Carter explained that he was well aware that in such a case he would have to face strong opposition in the US, but he would present Israel's supporters with the alternative of supporting either Israeli or American intersts.

Dayan stated in no uncertain terms Israel's objections to, and fears of, a Palestinian state or even an entity. With regard to Carter's promise of a US commitment to Israel's security, Dayan said that Israel would not like to count on the US for defence, even if she could be sure that the US would honour its commitments. But in this regard the American record was poor. Dayan recalled a number of instances in the past when US Presidents had, in Israeli opinion, acted in a way prejudicial to vital Jewish interests. These included Roosevelt's refusal in 1943 to save Jews by bombing German extermination camps; Truman's embargo on arms supplies in 1948; and Johnson's unwillingness to implement Eisenhower's promises of 1957 when Nāsir closed the Tiran straits in 1967.[124] However, at the end of their two-hour discussion, Carter and Dayan arrived at a compromise formula the details of which were then worked out between Vance and Dayan and set forth in what has come to be known as the "Working Paper". Its text was as follows:

1. The Arab parties will be represented by a unified Arab delegation, which will include Palestinian Arabs. After the opening sessions, the conference will split into working groups.

2. The working groups for the negotiation and conclusion of peace treaties will be formed as follows:

a. Egypt-Israel

b. Jordan-Israel
c. Syria-Israel
d. Lebanon-Israel [if and when Lebanon requests to join the conference]

3. The West Bank and Gaza issues will be discussed in a working group to consist of Israel, Jordan, Egypt and the Palestinian Arabs.

4. The solution of the problem of the Arab refugees and of the Jewish refugees will be discussed in accordance with terms to be agreed upon.

5. The agreed basis for the negotiations at the Geneva Peace Conference on the Middle East are UN Security Council Resolutions 242 and 338.

6. All the initial terms of reference of the Geneva Peace Conference remain in force, except as may be agreed by the parties." [125]

In the joint communiqué, announcing this Working Paper, the US and Israel stated that "all understandings and agreements between them on this subject remain in force," and that "acceptance of the joint US-USSR statement of 1 October 1977 by the parties is not a prerequisite for the reconvening and conduct of the Geneva conference." [126] On 12 October, the Israeli government approved the Working Paper as a basis for reconvening the Geneva conference, but made it clear that no further concession would be made. The main achievement of the Paper was to avert a full-scale American-Israeli confrontation. However, the many questions that stood in the way of reconvening the Geneva conference remained unresolved.

The stalemate following the September talks and the US-Israeli Working Paper continued until 9 November 1977, when Sādāt's offer to address the Knesset initiated his visit to Jerusalem (19–21 November) and changed the situation dramatically (see essay on "The Middle East in Perspective").

NOTES

1. *Al-Jumhūriyya*, Cairo; 3 November 1976.
2. Sādāt in an interview with *Time*, New York; 29 November 1976.
3. Middle East News Agency (MENA), 9 November—Daily Report (DR), 10 November 1976. Similarly, MENA, 14 and 17 November 1976.
4. Interview with *Le Monde*, Paris; 21 January—DR, 28 January 1977.
5. *New York Times* (*NYT*), 1 December 1976.
6. *NYT*, 13 January 1977.
7. Interview with *Time*, 29 November 1976.
8. *Die Arbeiter-Zeitung*, Vienna; 13 February 1977.
9. MENA, 20 March—BBC Summary of World Broadcasts (BBC), 22 March 1977.
10. *Ha'aretz* and *Ma'ariv*, Tel Aviv; 28 November 1976.
11. Interview with *Newsweek*, New York; 14 January 1977.
12. Interview with *Washington Post* (*WP*), 29 December 1976.
13. Interview with National Broadcasting Corporation (NBC), quoted by MENA, 3 January—DR, 4 January 1977.
14. R Cairo, 14 January 1977.
15. The joint communiqué as transmitted by R Cairo and R Amman, 15 January—BBC, 17 January 1977.
16. Interview with *The Sunday Telegraph*, London; 16 January 1977.
17. Interview with *Time*, 24 January 1977.
18. At the Senate Foreign Relations Committee hearing on 11 January 1977. Quoted by *NYT*, 12 January 1977.
19. *Ma'ariv*, 4 and 5 February 1977.
20. *Towards Peace in the Middle East: Report by a Study Group* (Washington: The Brookings Institution, 1975), pp. 1– 2.
21. Allon addressing a dinner party in honour of Vance, Israel Government Press Office, *Daily News Bulletin* (GPO/D), 16 February 1977. Similarly, in Allon's replies to two motions for the agenda in the Knesset; *Ma'ariv* and *Jerusalem Post* (*JP*), 16 February 1977.
22. *Ma'ariv*, 3 June 1977.

23. For texts, see *NYT*, 17 and 18 September 1975.
24. Israeli Cabinet communiqué; GPO/D, 20 February 1977. *Ha'aretz*, 17 and 18 February 1977. *The Dept of State Bulletin* (*DSB*), Washington; 21 March 1977, p. 249. *NYT; International Herald Tribune* (*IHT*), Paris; And *Christian Science Monitor* (*CSM*), Boston; 17 February 1977.
25. MENA, R Cairo, 17 February—DR, 18 February 1977. *NYT, Baltimore Sun*, 18 February 1977.
26. *NYT, IHT*, 19 February 1977. Israeli Broadcasting Authority (IBA), 20 February—DR, 28 February 1977.
27. MENA, 19 February 1977. For text of the Rabat decisions, see R Cairo, Voice of the Arabs (VoA), 29 October—BBC, 20 October 1977.
28. *Ma'ariv*, 20 February 1977.
29. R Damascus, 20 February—DR, 21 February 1977.
30. *WP*, 23 February 1977.
31. *NYT, IHT, Ha'aretz*, 8 March; *DSB*, 4 April 1977, pp. 310–11.
32. *Weekly Compilation of Presidential Documents*, 14 March 1977, p. 323.
33. *NYT, IHT*, 8 March 1977.
34. Rabin in an interview with *Ma'ariv*, 15 July; and in an article in *Yedi'ot Aḥaronot*, Tel Aviv; 5 August. Begin in a statement in the Knesset on 27 July, 31 August—*Ma'ariv*, 28 July, 1 September. *Ha'aretz*, 17 March, 23 August. *Ma'ariv*, 3 and 10 June 1977.
35. *Ha'aretz*, 10 March 1977.
36. GPO/D, 13 March 1977.
37. *DSB*, 4 April 1977, p. 306.
38. In a speech before the Congress of Presidents of Major Jewish American Organizations on 9 March—*JP*, 10 March 1977.
39. *CSM*, 10 March; *Ma'ariv*, 11 March 1977.
40. In an interview with American Broadcasting Corporation (ABC) screened on 13 March—*JP*, 14 March 1977.
41. *DSB*, 11 April 1977, p. 385.
42. *The Guardian*, London; 18 March 1977.
43. *Arab Report and Record* (*ARR*) *1977*, London; p. 229.
44. *JP*, 18 March 1977.
45. *JP*, 20 March 1977.
46. *The Times*, London; 3 April; *Ha'aretz*, 22 March 1977.
47. *DSB*, 2 May 1977, pp. 434–6. *IHT, Guardian*, 5 April 1977.
48. Interview with *al-Musawwar*, Cairo; 29 April 1977.
49. *Al-Dustūr*, Paris; 18 April 1977.
50. Sādāt in interviews with Walter Cronkite (CBS) and Barbara Walters (ABC) and in a press conference on 6 April, quoted by MENA, 6 and 7 April—DR, 7 April. R Cairo, 6 April—DR, 12 April 1977. *Al-Dustūr*, 18 April 1977. For Sādāt's alleged remark concerning Sharm al-Shaykh, see *Arabia and the Gulf*, London; 2 May 1977.
51. *NYT*, 9 April 1977.
52. *DSB*, 9 May 1977, p. 461.
53. *DSB*, 16 May 1977, p. 481.
54. Interview with CBS, quoted by *JP*, 25 April 1977.
55. MENA, 27 April 1977. *Ha'aretz*, 26 and 27 April 1977. *Ma'ariv*, 27 April 1977.
56. Husayn in a press conference on 26 April, quoted by MENA, 27 April 1977. *NYT, Ha'aretz*, 27 April 1977.
57. R Amman, 30 April 1977.
58. *Ma'ariv*, 27 April 1977.
59. *DSB*, 30 May 1977, p. 547.
60. *DSB*, 23 May 1977, pp. 516–17.
61. R Damascus, 8–10 May; *al-Nahār*, Beirut; 10 and 13 May; *Ma'ariv*, 9 and 10 May 1977. The quotation from *al-Nahār*, 13 May 1977.
62. R Damascus, 10 May; *NYT, Ma'ariv*, 10 May 1977.
63. Sādāt, in an interview with *Rastakhiz*, as published by MENA, 18 May—DR, 19 May; R Cairo, MENA, 29 May—DR, 31 May 1977. Asad, in an interview with Danish journalists, R Damascus, 14 June—DR, 15 June 1977.
64. *Ha'aretz, Ma'ariv*, 25 April 1977.
65. *JP*, 9 May 1977.
66. *The Guardian*, 13 May 1977.
67. *Ma'ariv*, 16 May, 3 and 10 June 1977.
68. *NYT*, 13 May 1977.
69. MENA, 21 May 1977.
70. United States Information Service (USIS), *News Report*, 26 May 1977.

71. *Newsweek*, 6 June 1977.
72. Carter after the talks, quoted in USIS, *Official Text*, 26 May 1977.
73. *Ma'ariv*, 29 May 1977.
74. Deutsche Presse Agentur (DPA), 25 May 1977.
75. *JP*, 25 May 1977.
76. Interview with *NYT*, 1 June 1977.
77. MENA, 20 May—BBC, 23 May 1977.
79. White House spokesman's statement on 18 May, quoted by *Ha'aretz*, 19 May 1977.
80. State Department statement, quoted by *Ha'aretz*, 19 May 1977.
81. *NYT*, 27 May 1977.
82. *NYT*, 23 May 1977.
83. In a press conference transcribed by *NYT*, 27 May 1977.
84. Official text of the statement.
85. Interview with *US News and World Report*, Washington; 6 June 1977.
86. *Ma'ariv*, 9 June 1977.
87. In his speech before World Affairs Council of Northern California in San Francisco, transcribed by USIS, *Official Text*, 20 June 1977.
88. USIS, *News Report*, 28 June 1977.
89. Quoted by *JP*, *Ha'aretz*, 28 June 1977.
90. *IHT*, 2–3 July 1977.
91. *JP*, 7 July 1977.
92. USIS, *Official Text*, 20, 21, 25 July; GPO/D, 25 July 1977.
93. Official transcript of the press conference.
94. USIS, *News Report*, 20 July. Similarly, USIS, *Official Text*, 13 July 1977.
95. E.g. see interviews of Asad and Husayn with *Newsweek*, 1 August 1977.
96. *NYT, IHT,* 22 August 1977.
97. USIS, *News Report*, 16 August 1977.
98. USIS, *Official Text*, 30 August 1977.
99. USIS. 26 July; USIS, *Official Text*, 28 July 1977.
100. USIS, *Official Text*, 29 July 1977.
101. USIS, *Official Text*, 9 August 1977.
102. E.g. see an interview with *Ma'ariv*, 19 August 1977.
103. USIS, *News Report*, 19 August; *Ma'ariv*, 19 August 1977.
104. USIS, *Official Text*, 24 August 1977.
105. *Ma'ariv*, 9 September 1977.
106. GPO/D, 10 September 1977.
107. *NYT*, 10 September 1977.
108. *JP*, 2 September 1977.
109. Interview broadcast over the IDF Radio, 6 September—DR, 7 September 1977.
110. *JP*, 31 August 1977.
111. Interview with *NYT*, 29 August 1977.
112. *JP, Jewish Chronicle*, London; *al-Nahār*, 9 September 1977.
113. *IHT*. 13 September 1977.
114. USIS, 22 September 1977.
115. USIS, *News Report*, 20 September 1977.
116. *Ma'ariv*, 20, 21 September 1977.
117. IBA, 29 September—BBC, 1 October 1977.
118. GPO/D, 25 September; IBA, 25 September—DR, 26 September 1977.
119. Fahmī as quoted by MENA, 26 September and *WP*, 27 September. For the Jordanian and Syrian reactions, see R Amman and R Damascus, 25 September—BBC, 27 September 1977.
120. *The Times, WP*, 27 September 1977.
121. *NYT*, 29 September 1977.
122. USIS, *Official Text*, 3 October 1977.
123. USIS, *Official Text*, 5 October 1977.
124. *Ma'ariv, Yedi'ot Aharonot*, 21 October 1977.
125. GPO/D, 13 October 1977.
126. USIS, *News Release*, 5 October 1977.

Inter-Arab Affairs

Inter-Arab Relations

DANIEL DISHON

With the assistance of VARDA BEN-ZVI

This survey covers the period from mid-1976 to September 1977. The dramatic change of relations which occurred at the end of 1977 and early 1978 is discussed in the essay, "The Middle East in Perspective."

THE RIYADH CONFERENCE: A WATERSHED

The conference held in Riyadh from 16–18 October 1976 ended one period in inter-Arab relations and ushered in another. This important meeting was attended by Saudi Arabia's King Khālid, the Presidents of Egypt, Syria and Lebanon, the ruler of Kuwait, and the PLO chairman Yāsir 'Arafāt. The pre-Riyadh constellation had clustered around the events generated by the second Sinai Agreement of 1 September 1975. These were characterized: 1) by the increasingly vocal, increasingly strident Syrian-Egyptian dispute for which the Sinai Agreement provided the backdrop, but the roots of which actually went back to the war of October 1973; 2) by the energetic attempt on the part of Syria to carve out for itself an area of exclusive, or at least predominant, influence in Jordan and Lebanon and ascendancy over the PLO (and thus, possibly, over a future Palestinian state); 3) by the inter-Arab reverberations of the civil war in Lebanon and, from June 1976 onwards, of Syria's massive military intervention there; 4) by a vigorous, but eventually unsuccessful, campaign on the part of Iraq and Libya designed to establish a radical bloc of "rejectionist" states by drawing Syria into a combination with themselves, Algeria and the PLO.

All this time, Egypt had been on the defensive and had come to be increasingly isolated in the Arab world. In the Syrian-Egyptian quarrel, Saudi Arabia—its weight in inter-Arab relations steadily on the rise ever since the early 1970s—had at first inclined towards Syria to an almost imperceptible degree, then equally slightly towards Egypt. From the early summer of 1976 onwards, its main endeavour had been to reconcile Syria and Egypt and to re-establish the Syrian-Egyptian-Saudi triangle that had prepared and conducted the 1973 war. It was Saudi urging (seconded by Kuwait) that brought about the Riyadh conference.

Saudi prompting would not of itself have been sufficient, however, had not the overall situation in the Arab world been ripe for realignment. The Syrian army by now held positions commanding the approaches to Beirut, Tripoli and Sidon. The Syrian leadership realized that it had more to gain from completing the occupation of Lebanon with the blessing of the Arab states than against the combined pressures of all of them (with only Jordan loyal to the Syrian line in Lebanon). In a situation in which neither outside Arab states, nor the PLO and their anti-Syrian Lebanese allies, were any longer capable of stopping the completion of the Syrian military moves, the political price Syria would have to pay for Arab sanction would no longer be too onerous. It would be outweighed by the military advantage of not having to fight for the major towns, and by the domestic gains likely to follow a cessation of Syrian armed action against Lebanese Muslims and the PLO. (For the domestic repercussions of Syria's intervention in Lebanon, see survey of Syria.)

Egypt, for her part, realized at this juncture that its approval of Syria's exclusive position in Lebanon could still be traded off for a Syrian undertaking to call off the anti-Egyptian propaganda war. Also, a reconciliation at this point would allow the Egyptians to claim credit later for having saved the PLO from being crushed altogether, and 'Arafāt from being forced out of the PLO leadership by Syria. Saudi Arabia expected—correctly, as it turned out—that its initiative in ending the Lebanese war and the Syrian-Egyptian dispute at one stroke, together with the venue of the conference in Riyadh and King Khālid's chairmanship of it, would enchance its image as arbiter of all-Arab affairs.

Over and above these considerations, all three leaders had become preoccupied with the approach of the US presidential elections, realizing that it would be advantageous if the major Arab states settled their differences in time to present a united front to the incoming Administration. (Explaining the Syrian change of tack at Riyadh, the Damascus daily *Tishrīn* said on 24 October 1976 that since 1977 was likely to turn into a "decisive" year, "a common Arab will" was now needed.)

It was against this background that the Riyadh conference, often called "the restricted summit", convened—and succeeded. (An earlier meeting at Riyadh in June 1976, attended by the Syrian and Egyptian Prime Ministers at a time when the factors listed above did not yet operate, had ended in total failure, leaving the overall situation precisely as it had been.) The provisions worked out in Riyadh for a Lebanese ceasefire and eventual settlement are outside the scope of this essay (see survey of Lebanon). The preamble to the Riyadh declaration stated that the participants were "proceeding from the position of national and historic commitment to the need to strengthen the collective Arab role . . . from a desire to transcend the negative events and effects of the past [a reference mainly to the Egyptian-Syrian quarrel following the second Sinai Agreement], and from the need to go forward in a spirt of reconciliation, peace and reconstruction." A special resolution provided for the end of the propaganda war by laying down that "information campaigns and negative psychological mobilization by all parties should cease", and that information should be "channelled" so as to "raise the spirit of co-operation and fraternity among everyone."

Presidents Anwar Sādāt and Hāfiz al-Asad decided to reinstate their ambassadors in Damascus and Cairo (both had been demonstratively called home at the height of the quarrel in June 1976) and to "clear the atmosphere" between them.[1] To indicate why the atmosphere needed "clearing", it is instructive to recall two statements made only ten days before the Riyadh meeting. On the occasion of the anniversary of the October war, Sādāt had referred to Syria as being led by the "tangled rancorous 'Alawite Ba'th Party"; at the same time a Ba'th Party statement had accused Egypt of "plotting" against Syria to "achieve the new objectives of imperialism and Zionism" and to rob the Arabs of their war gains.[2]

Answering questions put to him by an Egyptian journalist after the Riyadh conference, Asad said that "regardless of any difference that might occur" between himself and Sādāt, neither could "forget that they were partners in the [1973] October war." (This statement must be set against Asad's earlier accusations that during the war there had been US-Egyptian-Israeli collusion designed to produce a Syrian military debacle.)[3] Asad went on to say that he and Sādāt decided that Syrian-Egyptian relations will "remain stronger than any temporary and small differences, which soon disappear . . . The urgent tasks before us [i.e. mainly the co-ordination of Arab policies *vis-à-vis* the US] dictate that these relations remain strong and firm."[4]

Within a week, a full summit convened in Cairo. All Arab League nations took part, a fact worth noting, since some past summits had been boycotted by individual member-states. Algeria, Iraq, Libya, Morocco, Oman and Tunisia were not, however, represented by their heads of state, as the status of a summit conference, usually referred to by Arab media as a "meeting of the kings and presidents", would have required. The summit endorsed the Riyadh resolutions on

26 October. It added a reference to the Arab Solidarity Pact of 15 September 1965, which had banned hostile propaganda and interference in internal affairs between Arab states, undertaking to abide by it "in full and forthwith." Moreover, it went beyond the Riyadh decision by establishing a special all-Arab fund to finance the "Arab security force" in Lebanon, which was made up almost exclusively of Syrian troops (see survey of Lebanon). The day after the conclusion of the summit, the Egyptian War Minister, Gen Muhammad 'Abd al-Ghanī Jamasī, was appointed supreme commander of the Egyptian-Syrian front—a post vacant since 1974. There was, however, hardly any public reference to this function during the remainder of the period reviewed here.

The manner in which the full summit acted almost solely as a "rubber stamp" for Riyadh once more underlined the drive and effectiveness of the Saudi initiative. The two countries clearly defeated by the broad Riyadh and Cairo consensus were Libya and Iraq. Only four months earlier they had made their bid to form a bloc with Syria, conditional on the latter *not* effecting a reconciliation with Egypt. These two let their displeasure be known in no uncertain terms. The Iraqi Foreign Minister, Sa'dūn Ḥammādi, who had represented Pres Aḥmad Ḥasan al-Bakr at the summit, stated afterwards that his country had refused to ratify the Riyadh resolutions. The main reason for Iraq's stand, he explained, was that neither the restricted nor the full summit had provided for the withdrawal of Syrian forces from Lebanon, which Iraq deemed "essential"; Syria's intervention was "not impartial" but directed against one side in the Lebanese war. The Lebanese problem should have been remedied by truly "collective Arab action." [5] Libya, for its part, had also attempted to press for the evacuation of Syrian troops from Lebanon during the summit debates. It later described the Cairo meeting as "a complete failure."

The restricted Riyadh summit and the full summit in Cairo set the basic pattern of inter-Arab relationships for a period of almost a year. This pattern can be characterized as follows:

1) Egypt, Syria and Saudi Arabia came once again to form the core triangle of inter-Arab action, as in 1973. Relations between them and their attitudes towards the rest of the Arab countries determined the *overall* texture of inter-Arab affairs.

2) All outward manifestations of the Syrian-Egyptian quarrel of 1975-6 ceased; but Syria continued to compete with Egypt, in muted tones and semi-concealed ways, for a more active and central inter-Arab role.

3) Syria gained factual recognition of its position as arbiter of Lebanese affairs, but had to contend with pro-PLO pressures exercised by Saudi Arabia, Egypt and Kuwait—the members, alongside Syria, in the ceasefire co-ordination committee set up under the Riyadh resolutions. Egypt no longer disputed Syria's role in Lebanon. Sādāt later said that after Riyadh, "Syrian action was no longer purely Syrian . . . We agreed to the entry of Syrian forces because they became part of the Arab deterrent force." [6] Asad, by contrast, stated in an interview with Radio Cairo on 17 December: "The truth of the matter is that the Arab deterrent force are basically Syrian forces."

4) Egypt gained (or perhaps more correctly regained) recognition as the principal Arab spokesman in addressing the West on the Arab-Israeli conflict—a position that remained virtually unchallenged until the visit to the Middle East of US Secretary of State, Cyrus Vance, in August 1977. It cannot be ruled out that Egypt achieved such status at Riyadh by a promise to Syria to jointly revive the military option against Israel should the "political process" fail to produce the results expected by the Arabs. (Egyptian, Syrian and Saudi references to the possibility of war in the event of renewed political stalemate were frequent in

1977, see below.)

5) Jordan, which before the Riyadh conference had seemed to be moving towards increasing dependence on Syria, gained more room for manoeuvre on the inter-Arab scene, particularly as between Egypt and Syria, and used it skilfully to reassert its position.

6) Saudi Arabia—making use of its political and Islamic leverage and its huge financial resources—fortified its position as a central factor in all-Arab affairs. It successfully promoted itself to the rank of a "confrontation state" (though not bordering on Israel, not directly affected by Security Council Resolution 242, not invited to the Geneva conference in 1973, and not a candidate for participation in its reconvention). Furthermore, having taken the lead in Arab affairs regarding the Persian Gulf in the early 1970s and in Southern Arabian affairs in the mid-seventies, it now extended its activities to the entire Red Sea area as well. The former editor-in-chief of Cairo's *Al-Ahrām*, Muhammad Ḥasanayn Haykal, wrote: "The Arab world is now in what may be termed the Saudi epoch in modern Arab history."[7]

7) The "division of labour" between the three vertices of the "triangle"—as *Syria* perceived it—is indicated in the following comment from the Syrian daily *Al-Thawra* (20 May 1977): "Syria represents a major military power in the Middle East; Egypt a political power, and Saudi Arabia an oil power."

8) Through one or the other of its three member-states, further Arab countries came to be linked to the "triangle": Jordan has already been mentioned; the Lebanese government formed in 1976 came under Syrian tutelage as far as its inter-Arab contacts were concerned; and Sudan had formed close and formal ties with Egypt. Saudi influence was predominant in all the Arab littorals along the Persian Gulf, as well as in the Yemen Arab Republic (North Yemen); during 1977, Saudi Arabia was at work to bring the People's Democratic Republic of Yemen (South Yemen) into the fold of its Peninsular predominance (see also below). Morocco and Tunisia, perhaps mainly because of their local disputes with Algeria and Libya respectively, were also inclined to fall into line with the three central countries over matters of general policy.

9) Three Arab countries—Iraq, Libya and, in the North African context, Algeria—remained outside the constellation described above. During the period under review, each became—or continued to be—the initiator of private vendettas, all of which had an unsettling, if somewhat marginal, effect on the inter-Arab scene. Iraqi and Libyan activities also impinged on the domestic situation of their chief rivals: Syria, Egypt and Sudan (see surveys of these countries). All these disputes were characterized by a rising level of violence. (They will be referred to in greater detail presently.)

10) The PLO, saved from defeat and fragmentation by the Lebanese ceasefire, struggled on to preserve a minimal independent *military* presence and some freedom of action in Syrian-controlled Lebanon, but invested its main efforts in promoting its capacity for *political* manoeuvre by exploiting policy differences between the major Arab states.

A new topic came to preoccupy many of the inter-Arab meetings of 1976 and 1977: that of the Red Sea and its future as an "Arab lake." Growing attention to Red Sea affairs—comparatively speaking an innovation as a subject of inter-Arab dealings—was not a product of the changes brought about at Riyadh, but was primarily triggered by local events (the changes in Ethiopia; the independence of Djibouti) and the orientation of Somalia and Ethiopia towards the major powers. Considerations of the Red Sea's role in the Arab-Israeli conflict were not, however, absent from Arab deliberations on this subject (see essay on the Red Sea).

EGYPTIAN-SYRIAN RELATIONS

The first major step in Egyptian-Syrian relations reflecting the post-Riyadh atmosphere was Asad's visit to Cairo from 18-21 December 1976. In the interval, both sides had spoken of their relations in rather low-key terms. The Egyptian Premier, Mamdūḥ Sālim, said on 11 December, for instance, that "the resumption of Egyptian-Syrian relations at a level that satisfies the two peoples . . . portends good"; and Asad stated on 17 December: "We can say that we have at this stage been able to overcome the difficulties that stood in our way in the previous stage."[8]

The joint statement of 21 December 1976 used less restrained language. Again evoking the October war as the model, Syria and Egypt expressed their "sincere feeling of brotherhood" as well as "the unity of their objectives and comradeship in the struggle to achieve the goals of Arab nation . . . This was totally and magnificently expressed in the October War." The talks between "the two fraternal countries" took place "in an atmosphere of complete understanding." "Throughout history", the statement went on, Syria and Egypt had been "the shield of the Arab nation in confronting foreign schemes aimed at subjugating and dismembering it." The statement went on to outline a common strategy in the Arab-Israeli conflict, stressing Sādāt's and Asad's "determination that the year 1977 shall be a year of movement towards ending occupation and regaining the rights of the Palestinians."

The communiqué reaffirmed Sādāt's leading role in promoting the political approach as applicable to "the current stage of the struggle." At the same time, Syria attempted to ensure that Egypt would not overstep the boundaries of what Syria considered acceptable. Hence, for instance, a reference to maintaining a "firm position" on the 1974 Rabat summit resolutions regarding the PLO; and the appeal to both the US *and* the USSR to "clearly and expeditiously" submit their plans for peace in the Middle East. Hence, also the reference to the military option as implied in the phrase that after ten years of occupation "the Arab nation will use *all its resources* to end the status quo", later reinforced by mention in Syria's party daily *Al-Ba'th* (23 December 1976) of the significance of the Sādāt-Asad meeting for "the liberation struggle, whether by peaceful means or by war." (Similarly, Egyptian Foreign Minister Ismā'īl Fahmī: "We do not rule out . . . resorting to war if the [Israeli] enemy has not learned the lesson." Saudi Foreign Minister Sa'ūd al-Faysal: "If there is no settlement [by] the end of 1977 . . . Israel will succeed in imposing upon us a new military confrontation."[9]

In the field of bilateral relations, the two Presidents agreed to establish a Unified Political Command. The language of the joint declaration on this subject suggests that it was rather less than an operative decision: the command "shall lay down *as soon as possible* the necessary basis for . . . developing the relations of unity between the two countries . . . Joint committees . . . [shall] *study* and establish the bases on which relations of unity . . . can be developed in various fields."

The declaration was further watered down by the Egyptian Foreign Minister who stated that any other Arab state could join the command, since it was "meant to be the nucleus of a union that begins with Egypt and Syria." Only after studying the question of other states joining in would "the constitutional measures be completed."[10] In January 1977, in an address to the Egyptian People's Chamber, he further clarified the issue by saying that the command was "not the birth of a new unity but a declaration of intent." Eventually, "the question will be submitted to referendum so that any unionist step will be an offspring of the popular will."[11] Events soon bore out the notional character of the Command. In February 1977, Syria and Egypt appointed their representatives, but during the period reviewed (i.e. up to November 1977), it was not in fact convened. (Its notional existence should be compared to the more vigorous activities of similar Syrian-Jordanian bodies mentioned below.)

During the first eight months of 1977 there were numerous contacts between the two countries, both at bilateral and multilateral meetings, such as that between King Khālid, Asad and Sādāt in Riyadh on 19 May 1977. Major policy steps, particularly on questions relating to the Arab-Israeli conflict, were generally taken in consultation between the two countries. There was no mutual public criticism (Syrian newspapers, for instance, were on sale in Egypt again from April 1977 after a lengthy ban instituted during the earlier dispute). Yet a note of competition runs through the entire period. Syrian actions often marked off the difference of its policies from Egypt's, at least in detail. It was evident in Syria's continued consolidation of its influence in Lebanon and Jordan and over the PLO—a process which had been so salient a feature of the pre-Riyadh period. It showed in Syria's edging its way into the Egyptian-Sudanese joint command (see below) even though Sudan is not an area of primary interest to Syria. In May, the Syrian Prime Minister, ʻAbd al-Raḥmān Khulayfāwī, said in an interview that Egyptian-Syrian relations "although good, are not as they should be." They should be "more comprehensive."[12]

While agreeing with Egypt in pressing for the speedy resumption of the Geneva conference, Syria differed over some aspects of tactics for its preparation. Already, at the time of the Asad-Sādāt meeting in December 1976, Syria had indicated a preference for the Arabs to be represented at Geneva by a single Arab delegation. At the time, and consistently for the rest of the period under review, Egypt opposed the idea. Syria may have hoped that, through its influence on the Jordanian, Palestinian and, possibly, the Lebanese members of the collective Arab delegation, it would have greater leverage on the conduct of the negotiations than by trying to co-ordinate independent missions. Primarily, however, it was Syria's desire to prevent any possibility of separate Egyptian-Israeli contacts which seems to have motivated Asad—a covert manifestation of the residual distrust towards Egypt, which had been so overt from the end of the October war until the Riyadh conference. It was resentment of this distrust, as well as unwillingness to have Egyptian diplomatic activity supervised or circumscribed, which led to Egyptian objections.

Another point was Syria's rejection of Egypt's exclusive orientation towards the US. Asad pointedly marked the difference by refusing to visit Washington as Sādāt did (4-7 April 1977); instead he chose to meet President Carter in Geneva on 9 May. Equally pointedly, Asad abstained from taking sides in the Soviet-Egyptian quarrel, keeping his own relations with the USSR much as they had been since the early 1970s. He "balanced" his meeting with Carter by a previous visit to Moscow (18-21 April 1977).

The latent differences between Egypt and Syria came out into the open again, more sharply than at any time since Riyadh, during the second Middle East visit of the US Secretary of State. On 2 August 1977, Sādāt—without prior consultation with Syria—suggested that Vance should prepare for the Geneva conference by setting up a "working group" of foreign ministers of all parties concerned, to meet in the US. Two days later, at the conclusion of Vance's visit to Damascus, Asad rejected the idea. Criticizing Sādāt for the first time in ten months, he told correspondents: "When brother Pres Sādāt proposed the formation of this [working] group . . . I do not know whether he has properly considered and assessed the negative aspects of this idea . . . Our brothers in Egypt . . . might see benefits in this working group of which we are not yet aware." Asad hastened to add: "The fact that we have not [previously] discussed this proposal does not mean that there are any differences between Syria and Egypt. Confidence between us is complete."[13] A few days later, Asad rejected the idea in firmer terms: "We shall not agree [to the working group] because we do not find within its terms anything constituting a gain for the Arab cause." He repeated Syria's longstanding preference for "a unified Arab delegation" to go to Geneva. Failing that, Syria, Egypt, Jordan and the PLO should be independently represented, "provided these delegations co-ordinate fully among themselves."[14]

Syria possibly suspected that Egypt might offer, or had already offered, the US greater concessions in moving towards the concept of "contractual peace" than Syria was willing to agree to—and might thus gain advantages for itself. Thus, if the Riyadh conference had revived the 1973 war partnership as the state of affairs to be aspired to between Egypt and Syria, the atmosphere a year later evoked the spectre of a new rift—such as had existed in 1975–6. As the party daily *Al-Ba'th* put it: "The coming phase will be dangerous [for Syria]; it will be a phase for exploding all the peripheral contradictions latent in the Arab area and to *re-explode those that have been patched up*"[15] (emphasis added). In short, if measured by the yardstick of converging or diverging policies towards Israel, Syrian-Egyptian relations seemed to have come full circle at that moment. This impression was reinforced the following month when Syria exploited an Arab League meeting (3–6 September) to propose a radical Arab line at the forthcoming UN General Assembly, including the expulsion of Israel from the UN and sanctions against it. Egypt opposed these proposals, terming them "insistence on the impossible", while Syria retorted by describing Egypt as "a prisoner of the US." Eventually, the immediate need to prepare for the Foreign Ministers' talks in the US later in September, caused the differences to be papered over. They were, however, not settled but merely postponed.

Another aspect of the overall relationship of the two countries was the continued consolidation of Syria's position of predominance in Lebanon, its special ties with Jordan, and its attempts to bend the PLO to its will. This policy line had been characteristic of Syria's inter-Arab stance in the period from the 1973 war to the 1976 Riyadh conference. At the time, it had a distinctly anti-Egyptian slant, aimed at downgrading Egypt's standing in all-Arab affairs and restricting its room of manoeuvre by virtually excluding it from any influence over the course of events in the areas adjacent to Syria. These included the geographical area of Palestine—which Asad had claimed to be "South Syria" in a speech in 1974—and which, in his eyes, the PLO represented politically. Sādāt had indeed interpreted this policy as being directed against Egypt and had—prior to the Riyadh conference—frequently referred to it as "suspect", a misguided Syrian ambition for all-Arab leadership.[16]

If Sādāt had hoped that the Riyadh agreement would put a stop to what he saw as the detrimental effects of this Syrian regional policy, he was disappointed. In Lebanon, the Syrians consolidated their military and political ascendancy to the point of leaving very little room for the intervention of third parties, as between Syria on the one hand and the various Lebanese groupings on the other. (For Syria's relations with these, see survey of Lebanon.) With respect to the PLO, Damascus did not have quite the same measure of success. Syria's attempts in establishing exclusive influence over the main PLO-establishment, particularly al-Fatḥ, were successful only in physical terms (gaining control of the areas around the main camps in Lebanon and, largely, over the supply routes feeding PLO bases). But attempts to block off PLO political leverage on other Arab states, or their political influence with the PLO, proved a failure. Throughout the period under review, the "rejectionist" groups in the PLO were able to appeal to Libya, Iraq and Algeria for support; and al-Fatḥ was able to capitalize on the subtle policy differences between Egypt, Syria and Saudi Arabia as far as the PLO was concerned. The following example relating to three concurrent trends which emerged within a single week in August 1977 may serve as an illustration. (The overall history of individual PLO relations with each of the major Arab states is outside the scope of this essay.)

1) During Vance's Middle East tour in August 1977, a report from Radio Beirut (2 August), most probably Syrian-inspired, spoke of an agreement having been reached by Syria and the PLO according to which "there shall be no links between the [Palestinian] state and Jordan before the Geneva conference . . .; moreover, any links with Jordan later on should be in the form of a confederation between Syria, Palestine and Jordan."

2) At the same time, Egypt (which had proposed the Palestinian-Jordanian link in the first place) ostentatiously convened the recently formed Higher Joint Egyptian-Palestinian Committee (including Yāsir 'Arafāt and Foreign Minister Fahmī), thus indicating that Egypt, rather than Syria, had taken the PLO under its wing. Egyptian spokesmen stressed that the Egyptian policies outlined to Vance had PLO support, and that Egypt was preparing the ground for US-PLO contacts.

3) At the same time, too, King Khālid and Crown Prince Fahd, also implying prior co-ordination with the PLO, made Saudi Arabia appear as the principal agent in taking action to bring the US and the PLO into official and openly-recognized contact.

Syria pursued its Jordanian alliance by successfully developing its policy of "integration", or *takāmul*, (the term used by both sides); yet, as will be presently described, "integration" reached a plateau in 1976 and levelled off in 1977. While Jordan clearly remained more closely tied to Syria than to any other Arab state throughout the period under review, this did not prevent King Ḥusayn from exploiting the "opening" towards Cairo with which the post-Riyadh constellation provided him. An account of Jordanian-Syrian and Jordanian-Egyptian relations will be given in the following sections. Their indirect, but considerable, impact on Syrian-Egyptian relations is important.

SYRIAN-JORDANIAN RELATIONS

Syrian-Jordanian relations had improved, at first almost imperceptibly, then by gradual steps, finally by leaps and bounds, ever since Asad came to power in Syria late in 1970. The new relationship found expression in the fact that in October 1973, Jordanian units joined the Syrian army in fighting the war on the Golan Heights. It entered into high gear in 1975, when the Joint Supreme Leadership Council (made up of King Ḥusayn and President Asad) and the Higher Jordanian-Syrian Joint Committee (headed by the two countries' prime ministers) were established. Slogans such as "one people—one country" or "one country—one people—one army" were used to create an atmosphere of an imminent union more far-reaching in an undefined way than the mere establishment of these two co-ordinating bodies. Meanwhile, a series of practical measures to "integrate" the activities of both states in economic spheres (joint planning and investments in industry and agriculture, mutual trade, joint customs policies), transportation (particularly border traffic), communications and education were put in hand. Over many such problems of a technical and day-to-day nature, the approach seems to have been eminently realistic and practical. Military co-ordination, though mentioned but rarely (for instance by Asad in an interview to Radio Cairo on 17 December 1976), was consistently promoted. (Traditionally, both Jordan and Syria have viewed the western reaches of their common border as an area particularly exposed to the danger of an Israeli military thrust.) It is noteworthy, however, that neither at the height of the use of unionist slogans nor later on, were measures taken which would have implied any erosion of the full and undisputed sovereignty of either country.

Political co-ordination had been close during 1975 and continued to remain so. Up to the Riyadh conference, it had paid off for Syria mainly in the wholehearted political and propaganda support which Jordan, alone in the Arab world, offered for Syria's intervention in Lebanon. During the talks leading to the 1976 Riyadh meeting, Syria had held out for Jordan's participation, but had eventually given way under pressure from the other participants who did not want a Husayn-'Arafāt confrontation to add to the difficult tasks facing the conference. Asad took pains to "compensate" Ḥusayn by stopping over in Jordan for talks with the King, both on his way to Riyadh on 16 October 1976 and on his return three days later.

These frequent high-level contacts continued after the Riyadh conference. The Higher Jordanian-Syrian Joint Committee met in Damascus from 20–22 November 1976 and was mainly devoted to implementing decisions taken at its previous meeting in August 1976. Economic development, both agricultural and industrial, was a major item on the agenda. The concept of an industrial "division of labour" evolved, at least tentatively; the joint communiqué spoke of industrial projects to be "co-ordinated" so as to "avoid duplication." Joint committees were to study the scope of both Syria's and Jordan's investment programmes. The activites of the Jordanian-Syrian Industrial Company (established early in 1976) were to be intensified; the standardization of school curricula was to be expedited; measures to standardize codes of law and court procedure were to be taken in hand. The two Prime Ministers, Syria's 'Abd al-Rahmān Khulayfāwī and Jordan's Mudar Badrān, "expressed their pride in the spirit of true brotherhood which had prevailed during the discussions."[17] Commenting on the meeting on 20 November, the Syrian Prime Minister spoke of the aspirations of the two countries to achieve "one day a form of union or federation."

A meeting of the Joint Supreme Leadership Council (the fourth since its establishment) took place in Amman from 6–8 December 1976 which from Asad's viewpoint, was to be part of his preparation for forthcoming talks in Cairo (postponed until 18 December because of Sādāt's illness, see above). Numerous press reports at the time speculated that the Council would conclude some federal project or similar form of institutionalized "unionist" scheme, the proclamation of which would enable Asad to meet Sādāt from a position of enhanced strength. The joint statement issued on 8 December did not, however, contain such a declaration. It said only that President Asad, King Ḥusayn and their most senior advisers had "made a general review of the co-ordination and integration steps . . . achieved so far . . . on the path of their cherished unity" and were determined "to continue the joint work." It asserted that "the steps . . . accomplished so far make it possible to proceed to a more advanced formula on the level of establishing joint institutions which will embody the common objective, and fulfil the aspirations of our one people in the two fraternal countries." (It was not specified what these institutions would be; but another joint committee was to continue "the general study" of future unionist steps and submit its conclusions "as soon as possible", so that the "relevant decisions will be taken and implemented in accordance with constitutional methods.")[18] With this meeting, the drive for Syrian-Jordanian "integration" seems to have passed its high point—at least temporarily. While Jordan had given unstinting support to Syria over the Lebanese issue as long as the Lebanese war lasted, Ḥusayn was not willing to grant Asad the same measure of support for the purpose of strengthening Syria's position *vis-à-vis* Egypt in the changed circumstances obtaining since the Riyadh conference. On the contrary, the results of that conference had made it possible for Jordan to think of some fence-mending in its relations with Egypt (a line Ḥusayn was promptly to pursue; see below), and the Jordanian leadership did not wish to enter this new stage with the onus of an overly specific commitment to Syria. The phrasing of the joint statement quoted above was thus a compromise, allowing Asad to proceed to Cairo with a reassertion of the special and far-reaching character of Syrian-Jordanian ties, yet not committing Jordan to any specific unionist step.

Beyond the divergent interests of the moment, however, there existed a more basic difference behind the somewhat equivocal phrasing of the above statement. Whatever Asad's precise ideas may have been concerning the long-term future of Syrian-Jordanian relations, Husayn's concept certainly was that Jordan's sovereignty and ultimate freedom of action must not be compromised. The reference to "constitutional methods" was Ḥusayn's cautious, almost veiled, notice to Asad that whatever the future held for them, the King would not let his constitutional prerogatives in his own country be affected.

The issue of a possible federation continued to be mentioned, however. In January, for instance, Ḥusayn told the Jordanian cabinet that "steps towards a federation with sister Syria are continuing at a quick and steady pace." The "federation formula" should be capable of forming the "basis for a larger federation", as well as "harnessing the two countries' resources and potentials so that they may become a common asset for the two sides and for the Arab cause."[19] The following month, Premier Badrān referred to the union of Jordan and Syria: "We are studying every step scientifically, not emotionally."[20]

Although the process of "integration" levelled off towards the end of 1976, this did not mean there was a significant decrease in 1977. Even though slogans of the "one country—one people" type may have been used less frequently, and perhaps less fervently, in 1977 than in 1975 and 1976, the frequency of political consultation at the highest level and the routine work of practical co-ordination continued at the previous pace. In fact, co-operation during this period extended to matters of internal security: the visit to Amman on 13 December 1976 by President Asad's brother Rif'at (who held a leading position in internal affairs in Syria) was interpreted in the Arab press as being concerned with such an issue.

On 5 January 1977, Prime Minister Khulayfāwī met King Ḥusayn in Amman to review the unionist steps envisaged by Asad and Ḥusayn the month before. On 6 February, Husayn and Badrān visited Damascus. In Amman on 16 March, Ḥusayn again received Prime Minister Khulayfāwī, along with Foreign Minister (and Deputy Prime Minister) 'Abd al-Ḥalim Khaddām and Fawzī al-Kayyālī, the latter a representative of the National Progressive Front (the coalition of a number of minor Syrian parties which nominally shared power with the Ba'th). Arab and bilateral relations as well as the two countries' "unionist march" were discussed. Crown Prince Ḥasan headed a Jordanian delegation which visited Damascus from 12-14 April. On 8 May, a senior Jordanian court official met Asad in Geneva to report to him on Ḥusayn's talks with Carter in April, prior to Asad's meeting with the US President. On 18 May, Syrian Foreign Minister Khaddām reported to Jordanian leaders on Asad's meeting with Carter. On 22 June, Ḥusayn made another visit to Damascus.

From 30 June-3 July, the Higher Joint Committee met again in Amman. (The Committee's rules provide for meetings every three months. The interval from November 1976 to June 1977 was the first time that this rule was disregarded.) The Committee reviewed the work of the various sub-committees concerned with integration, and in its concluding statement "expressed its satisfaction with the great strides made by the joint . . . march towards its goal, which springs from the real will of the one people in the two fraternal countries to bypass artifical boundaries and to place their relations on a normal course." No concrete steps of political integration were mentioned, however, and the rest of the statement was devoted to questions of industrial and agricultural co-ordination, mutual trade, customs, transit, transportation, the joint use of electricity, tourism and education.[21] (See also, survey of Jordan.)

In summary, despite the successful promotion of co-ordination in all the *practical* fields listed above, basic views of the future *political* link between the two countries remained divergent. This was brought out strikingly early in August 1977 when Husayn and Asad separately answered an identical question on a federation between Syria, Jordan and the West Bank. Ḥusayn termed the idea "farfetched"; Asad answered: "I am not against anything that reinforces Arab unity."[22]

JORDANIAN-EGYPTIAN RELATIONS

Up to the Riyadh conference in October 1976, Jordanian-Egyptian relations were overshadowed by the Syrian-Egyptian dispute. In accordance with the special Jordanian-Syrian ties which had evolved in 1975 and 1976, Jordan loyally supported Syria's inter-Arab policies, especially *vis-à-vis* Lebanon where Jordan had its own strong interest in seeing the PLO suppressed. Even at the time, though, it was noted that Jordan had not joined Syria in outright condemnation of Egypt's second Sinai Agreement.

When, after the Riyadh reconciliation, Jordanian overtures to Egypt could no longer be interpreted as disloyalty towards Syria, Egyptian-Jordanian relations improved quickly and to a considerable extent. Egypt's interest lay in prying Jordan loose, as far as possible, from its exclusive relationship with Syria—a development Sādāt believed would help him reassert Egypt's own inter-Arab position (in pursuit of the semi-concealed post-Riyadh competition with Syria, which has been referred to above). Sādāt's main leverage was in holding out hope for Jordan to regain—with Egypt's help—its standing in West Bank affairs: namely, that by co-operating with Egypt rather than Syria, Jordan might obtain a better, more direct, and less fettered position there. Reliance on Syria, on the other hand, would result in demands for a tripartite Syrian-Jordanian-Palestinian link which would amount to ultimate supervision from Damascus. One of the first signs of the changing relationship was the decision, in November 1976, to a mutual exchange of ambassadors. (Both embassies had been run by chargés d'affaires for approximately a year.)

In 1977, the highlights of improved bilateral ties were King Husayn's two visits to Egypt, in January and July. During the first visit, from 13-15 January, the new constellation created at Riyadh was explicitly recognized: Ḥusayn "lauded the leading role played by Sādāt in moving the Arab issue", and "welcomed the closer links between fraternal Egypt and Syria" as likely to "solidify cohesion among the Arab confrontration states." Sādāt—accepting what he could no longer change—"welcomed the developing unionist steps between Syria and Jordan."

The joint statement again evoked "the momentum which resulted from the glorious October war" of 1973 (as had the statements issued after the Riyadh and Cairo meetings and the Sādāt-Asad talks). Sādāt and Ḥusayn expressed faith in a "unified Arab strategy" and in "co-ordination of the front-line forces." The main pointer to the give and take which must have proceeded behind closed doors was the phrase referring to the rights of the Palestinians to an "independent political entity." The Egyptians would at this time usually have referred to a "Palestinian state" rather than an entity; Ḥusayn might have preferred the term "political entity" without mention of its being "independent." The term "Palestinian state" appeared lower down in the statement in the context of Jordan's "disposition . . . to establish the *closest* relations with the Palestinian state" to be decided upon "by the two peoples [the Jordanian and the Palestinian] through their free choice" (i.e. not necessarily through the PLO). The PLO was mentioned in the statement only in relation to the Geneva conference.[23] The language chosen indicates both the readiness to compromise for the sake of improved relations, and the constraints circumscribing such a compromise for both sides.

On his return home, Ḥusayn explained that Jordanian-Syrian co-operation and Egyptian-Jordanian co-operation had become "complementary and served a common objective."[24] In another interview, he referred to his meeting with Sādāt as the "crowning of co-ordinated Arab efforts . . . to achieve Arab solidarity . . . to attain an assured victory peacefully or to resort to various possibilities if peace efforts fail."[25]

In the interval between Ḥusayn's January and July visits, with the US Administration launching a new initiative in the Middle East, Sādāt repeatedly referred to the ties which he thought should link the future Palestinian entity to Jordan. There remained some lack of clarity whether, on the question of timing, he sided with the PLO (who demanded a Palestinian state *first*, which would decide on the nature of its links with Jordan only *after* independence), or with Ḥusayn (who envisaged the reverse sequence, e.g. by means of reviving, in June 1977, the 1972 plan for a federation of the East and West Banks (for details, see survey of Jordan).

Ḥusayn's second meeting with Sādāt took place in Alexandria on 9 and 10 July. For the sake of "even-handedness", it had been preceded by a visit to Damascus at the end of June (see above), and by a trip to Riyadh earlier in July (see below). Sādāt again suggested "a clear link" between "the Palestinians and the Jordanians", to be established in advance of a Geneva conference. Ḥusayn, interpreting this as an attempt to pressure him into a reconciliation with the PLO, objected to the proposal. He argued that such ties with the Palestinians, while "inevitable" in themselves, should only be formulated after Israel's withdrawal and after "the Palestinian people practice . . . their right of self-determination" (again implying that this should be done independently of the PLO). No joint statement was issued on this occasion, reflecting the absence of substantive agreement on this point.[26] The Egyptian Foreign Minister, Ismā'īl Fahmī, stated that Ḥusayn and Sādāt had agreed to increase their contacts with the aim of a "further unification of stands."[27] Yet, at the time of Secretary Vance's visit the following month, and with the emergence of the Egyptian-Syrian differences over the proposal for a Foreign Ministers' "working group", Jordan sided with Syria rather than Egypt. With all the increased "elbow room" Jordan had been able to acquire during the last quarter of 1976 and the first half of 1977, its primary obligation, at a juncture of major import, remained to Syria. This remained true until November 1977.

SAUDI RELATIONS WITH JORDAN, SYRIA AND EGYPT

Saudi Arabia kept up a constant stream of high-level contacts with the three confrontation states. (For Saudi activities in other areas of the Arab world, see below.) Among visits to Saudi Arabia were those of Jordanian Prime Minister Mudar Badrān (on 15 December 1976 and again on 14 April 1977); King Ḥusayn (18 December 1976; and again on 6–7 July 1977); Ḥusayn's Chief of the Royal Cabinet 'Abd al-Ḥamīd Sharaf (on 29–30 March, 16 May and 30 July 1977); Syrian Foreign Minister 'Abd al-Halīm Khaddām (13 February, 16 and 30 April and 14 May 1977; on 20 April, Khaddām visited King Khālid in London); Syrian Deputy Defence Minister Nāji Jamīl (27 July 1977); Egyptian Vice-President Husnī Mubārak 17 November 1976); and Egyptian Deputy Premier for Financial and Economic Affairs 'Abd al-Mun'im al-Qaysūnī (24 March 1977).

Saudi visits to Arab capitals included Crown Prince Fahd's trip to Cairo (22 November 1976); Foreign Minister Sa'ud al-Faysal's visits to Cairo (4–5 February

1977, in connection with Saudi financial aid to Egypt); Damascus (1 March 1977); and his tour of Egypt, Jordan and Syria (beginning 7 June 1977) to report to their leaders on Amir Fahd's visit to Europe and the US in May. King Khālid's special adviser, Kamāl Adham, visited Cairo on 29 March, 16 June and 5 August; Damascus on 8 January and 1 March; and Amman on 8 January and 13 August 1977. The August visits were connected with the current Middle East tour of the US Secretary of State.

Furthermore, on two major occasions, Saudi Arabia hosted multilateral Arab meetings. The first, in Riyadh on 9-10 January 1977, was attended by the Foreign Ministers of Egypt, Syria, Jordan, Saudi Arabia, Kuwait, Qatar, the UAE and by a PLO representative. It dealt with the issue of financial assistance by the "supporting" states to the "front-line" states. This meeting, and possibly the follow-up one held less than a week later in Cairo, seem to have resulted in a re-affirmation on the part of the supporting states that the monetary assistance decided upon at the 1974 Rabat summit conference was a continuing obligation and not limited to a single year, as the recipients had feared. As is often the case with discussions of Arab monetary aid, no details or figures were released by the participants.

In the following months, there was occasional guarded criticism of Saudi Arabia on the part of Egypt, Syria and Jordan, hinting at insufficient financial support reaching them from Riyadh, as well as from other oil-producing Arab states. In March, a "responsible Saudi source expressed regret at [such] misrepresentations" which were likely to "benefit only the enemy."[28]

The second Riyadh meeting, on 19 May 1977, was attended by Presidents Asad and Sādāt and King Khālid. Originally initiated to co-ordinate Arab policies in advance of Amir Fahd's visit to Washington later the same month (a visit considered crucial by the leaders of the confrontation states), it was in fact overshadowed by the results of the Israeli election held on 17 May. It was on this occasion that a Radio Riyadh comment (in contrast to the station's traditionally reticent and non-committal line) spoke of Syria, Egypt and Saudi Arabia as the three "most powerful states in the region", adding that Saudi Arabia "enjoys a distinguished political and economic position." Fahd's US visit, the commentator went on, would "decide much of the future of the whole Arab region."[29] According to Egyptian sources, the views expressed at the meeting by the three leaders on US-Arab relations, on ties with USSR and on the Israeli elections, were "identical", and there was "complete understanding."[30]

In view of the general reticence of the three or four really significant spokesmen of the Saudi regime, any attempt to assess basic Saudi trends and objectives on the inter-Arab scene requires an element of speculation. Extreme caution in making public statements has been a deliberate Saudi policy. Its Defence Minister, Amir Sultān Ibn 'Abd al-'Azīz, told an interviewer: "Saudi abstention from entering into vocal public exchanges is one of the main reasons for [our] success at the Riyadh conference."[31] What is clear—from Saudi actions rather than declarations—is that King Khālid and Amir Fahd were, during the period under review, determined to use all of Saudi Arabia's assets—its guardianship of Mecca and Medina and of Islamic traditions; its financial power; its ability to wield the "oil weapon" or refrain from doing so; its influence in the US; its fast-increasing role as an arms arsenal for other Arab countries and as financier of their own arms procurement programmes—in order to propel itself into a position of ultimate arbiter of all-Arab political affairs. Not taking sides in Arab disputes was also an explicit Saudi policy. As Amir Fahd described it: "Saudi Arabia does not believe in the system of [Arab] axes or blocs. It has never taken part in any political axis."[32]

More speculative is the assessment of the place and role of the confrontation states in the Saudi scheme of things. It would probably be correct to say that Riyadh would wish Egypt and Syria to be aligned but not closely allied (so that both would look to Saudi Arabia to keep the alignment intact despite an undercurrent of rivalry); that Egypt should remain preoccupied with (but not endangered by) domestic difficulties and the conflict with Israel, so as to preclude any revival of a forward, activist pan-Arab policy on its part ('Abd al-Nāsir's designs in the Arabian Peninsula are unlikely to be quite forgotten in Riyadh); that Syria should remain engaged in building its own sphere of influence, but should not quite succeed; and that Jordan should have a standing in the West Bank and Gaza, balanced by the presence of that part of the PLO which the Saudis trust, i.e. Al-Fatḥ, to the exclusion of the leftist "rejectionist" groups.

The period from the 1976 Riyadh conference until the autumn of 1977 was one in which these objectives were in the process of being effectively promoted, though their final consummation remained to be achieved.

IRAQI-SYRIAN RELATIONS

Outside the "core triangle", the first set of developments to be reviewed is that of Iraqi-Syrian relations. As already mentioned, Iraq's principal explicit criticism of the October 1976 Cairo summit was that it had sanctioned Syria's military presence in Lebanon. The stress Iraq placed on this particular aspect of the Riyadh and Cairo decisions reflected the consistently anti-Syrian line which Iraq had taken during the Lebanese civil war. With the exception of a short period in the summer of 1976 (when Iraq had hoped to exploit Asad's military and political difficulties in Lebanon to draw him into a bloc with Libya, Algeria, the PLO and itself), Iraq had tried to foil Syria's Lebanese policy at every turn. It had used all forms of propaganda warfare to make Syria's motives in Lebanon appear suspect, and had given political and material support to every Lebanese and PLO group resisting Syria's intervention (including, in 1976, the dispatch of a small contingent of Iraqi army troops to Lebanon).

Iraq's stand on the Lebanese issue was, however, only one of the many facets of its fundamental hostility to Syria. Geo-political and historical arguments of a somewhat speculative character have often been adduced to explain the frequent periods of tension between Baghdad and Damascus. In the present-day context, it would be correct to say that the current Syrian-Iraqi animosity dates back to 1968 when Pres Aḥmad Ḥasan al-Bakr's wing of the Ba'th party came to power in Baghdad. Bakr had been expelled from the Syrian-dominated Ba'th Party in 1966 for being a "rightist." With his ascent to power there came into being two ruling Ba'th parties—in Syria and in Iraq—each claiming to be the "real", "original" and "genuine" one, and each disputing the legitimacy of the other and, by implication, the legitimacy of its authority in the other's country.

Asad's rise to power in Syria in November 1970 further aggravated Iraqi-Syrian relations. Asad's inter-Arab policies from 1971-3—guided by pragmatism and expediency rather than by Ba'thi ideology and doctrine—brought about a Syrian-Egyptian *rapprochement*, as well as improved Syrian relations with Jordan and Saudi Arabia. They thus accentuated the relative isolation on the Arab scene in which Iraq had found itself during most of the early and middle 1970s.

The conclusion of the 1973 war brought further deterioration. Iraqi troops had taken part in the fighting on the Syrian front; but when hostilities ended, Iraq scathingly criticized Syria for accepting the ceasefire and, later, for concluding the Golan Heights disengagement agreement (May 1974), and for participating in the series of political contacts with the US initiated in the aftermath of the war. Iraqi references to Syria's "capitulationist" and "defeatist" attitude and its "collaboration with Imperialism" remained part of the propaganda exchanges in 1976 and 1977; so did Syria's descriptions of the Iraqi regime as "fascist", "oppressive" and "slogan-bound."

Shortly before the Syrian-Iraqi controversies began focusing on Lebanon, tension reached a particular peak in the spring of 1975. Its immediate cause was the question of the distribution of the Euphrates River waters, but its acrimony stemmed from the broader underlying issues referred to above. Iraq asserted that Syria had operated the Tabaqa dam across the upper Euphrates in northern Syria (built between 1968 and 1973 with Soviet aid) so as to deprive Iraq of its share of river water and to prevent the implementation of its agricultural development schemes. Syria denied the Iraqi charges. As the recriminations intensified, Iraq concentrated troops in the border area and Syria followed suit. During the summer of 1975, both sides gradually reduced their concentrations, the crisis atmosphere abated and eventually both armies returned to their usual areas of deployment. The Euphrates waters issue, however, remained unresolved.

At about the same time, in mid-1975, Iraq made one of its periodic attempts to draw Syria into a radical "rejectionist" alliance based on an Iraqi commitment to place troops on the Golan Heights in return for Syria's rejection of Security Council Resolution 242, its refusal to participate in the Geneva conference and, generally, a return to what the Iraqis termed "the path of struggle." A similar attempt had been made in 1972; another was to follow in 1976. But Syria ignored the Iraqi initiative and soon afterwards, in the autumn of 1975, Iraq became the first Arab country to come out in vocal criticism of Syria's role in the Lebanese war.

In April 1976, Iraq added a form of economic warfare to her other anti-Syrian activities: it stopped the transit of oil through the pipeline running across Syria to the Mediterranean, pumping it instead through a new pipeline to the Persian Gulf. Syria lost transit dues estimated at close to $500m annually (a loss all the more keenly felt as Syria's intervention in the Lebanese war was becoming increasingly expensive).

Syria's massive entry into Lebanon in the first week of June 1976 was followed by a renewal of Iraqi troop concentrations on the Syrian borders. Both Pres Bakr and spokesmen for his regime said the troops were "ready to enter Syria" to prepare for "the liberation of Palestine" (as part of the revival, in May and June, of the "rejectionist" bloc scheme; see above). In fact, they were intended to deter Syria from continuing the occupation of Lebanon, or at least to slow it down. When this proved patently unsuccessful, a subtler struggle developed between the two countries with both parading military and civilian defectors, who described the "treasonable activities" of the rival regime. The Syrian defectors spoke of Asad "crushing" the PLO and suppressing the "Lebanese National Movement": the Iraqi defectors of their country's sabotaging Syrian efforts to restore peace in Lebanon. Syria accused the Iraqis of involvement in a series of attacks by a group called the "Black June Organization", which claimed that it was taking revenge against Syria for acts it had committed against Palestinians in Lebanon. "Black June" operations included an attack against the Semiramis Hotel in Damascus (26 September) and against the Syrian embassies in Rome and Islamabad (11 October 1976).

In the new constellation created in October by the Riyadh conference, Egypt, which until then had sided with Iraq in opposing Syria's intervention in Lebanon (though not over any other issue of Arab politics), now resigned itself to the new realities; Libya became more and more engrossed in the quarrels with its neighbours (see below); and Algeria withdrew increasingly into North African affairs, particularly the Western Sahara imbroglio. Iraq thus remained Syria's sole active opponent.

On 26 October (the concluding day of the Cairo summit conference), a transmitter calling itself "The Voice of Arab Syria" began broadcasting a daily programme purporting to present the viewpoint of Syrian leftists opposed to Asad. It called on the Syrian people to overthrow Asad's regime, and on the Lebanese to rise against the "Syrian invaders." Although the station did not disclose its location, it was almost certainly situated in Iraq. It was Radio Baghdad which announced the inception of the transmitter's broadcasts; the station's first comment praised Iraq's stand at the summit conference and denounced that of Syria, and subsequent reports echoed Iraqi views and attitudes. The Iraqi News Agency frequently cited "The Voice of Arab Syria" and quotations from its transmissions became one of Iraq's chief instruments in continuing anti-Syrian propaganda regarding Lebanon. In an effort to curtail other Iraqi propaganda outlets, Syrian troops occupied the offices of pro-Iraqi newspapers in Beirut in December 1976. In the same month, Lebanese sympathizers of the Iraqi Ba'th were arrested by the Syrians. On the other hand, the Iraqi military measures were now called off. After the ceasefire in Lebanon came into force, it became pointless to try and pin down Syrian troops opposite the Iraqi border. During November 1976, Iraqi forces were withdrawn from the border area and Syria followed suit. By the end of the year, most of the Iraqi regulars who had joined the PLO and their Lebanese allies in Lebanon were repatriated as well.

As the situation in Lebanon quietened down late in 1976 and in 1977, Iraq's anti-Syrian propaganda began to stress other themes. Allegations against Syria of following a "capitulationist policy" in the Arab-Israeli conflict and of "betraying the Palestinians" now became central motifs. The UNDOF mandate renewals in November 1976 and May 1977, Asad's meeting with Carter in May 1977, and Secretary of State Vance's visits to Damascus in February and August 1977 were made to serve as special occasions for such charges. The "renegade" character of the Syrian "agent regime" was contrasted with Iraq's "principled", "nationalist" and "progressive" stand. Iraqi media accused Syria of arresting and killing PLO leaders as well as rank and file members, both in Lebanon and in Syria. They pointed to Syria's relations with Jordan as proof of Asad's accommodation with "Arab reactionary forces." Referring to Syrian domestic policies, Iraqi media and spokesmen charged the regime with "arbitrary detention of innocent civilians and members of the armed forces", and with the assassination of many of the detainees.

Syrian propaganda countered by blaming Iraq for "deviating from Arab solidarity", a role which was "in harmony with the Zionist imperialist aims in the Arab area."[33] The principal line of Syrian propaganda, however, dealt with Iraqi internal policies and particularly with the personal role of Saddām Ḥusayn, President Bakr's right-hand man. Ḥusayn (originally Saddam Ḥusayn al-Tikrītī) was referred to by the Syrian media as "the head of the ruling clique in Baghdad", or of "the Tikrītī tribal (or family) regime", a reference to the fact that many prominent figures of the Iraqi Ba'th regime come from the town of Tikrīt. Described as the leader of a "regime of murderers", Husayn was declared responsible for the persecution and, in many cases, the liquidation of Iraqi citizens without trial. Adding an appeal for action to these accusations, a Syrian Ba'th National Command member called on the people of Iraq "to escalate the struggle against fascism" and to rally around the Iraqi "nationalist movement" which was "waging the struggle for a free Iraq."[34] A radio commentary stated that "the killers in Baghdad will be dealt with by the justice of [the Arab] people in Iraq as it has dealt with Nūrī al-Sa'īd, 'Abd al-Karīm Qāsim [assassinated in the Iraqi coups of

1958 and 1963 respectively] and other traitors."[35]

The stoppage of oil transit from Iraq through Syria (which seemed to acquire a permanent character in January 1977, when a second Iraqi pipeline to the Mediterranean was inaugurated which passed entirely through *Turkish* territory) was also exploited by the Syrian media for anti-Iraqi propaganda. By depriving Syria of the transit dues, they argued, Iraq was diminishing Syria's capacity to "carry on the struggle" and was "brandishing against an Arab country" the oil weapon that should be wielded against Israel.[36] In an attempt to apply economic counter-measures, Syria stopped the transit of goods from Syrian ports to Iraq in December 1976.

Propaganda warfare and economic pressures apart, almost every sign of unrest, disaffection or political discontent in either country was attributed by it to subversive activities on the part of the other. Syria blamed Iraqi agents for the attempt on the life of Foreign Minister 'Abd al-Ḥalīm Khaddām (1 December 1976); for the assassination of Muḥammad al-Fādil, President of Damascus University and a prominent Ba'th party functionary (22 February 1977); and for a number of explosions at public buildings in Damascus and near the homes of several leading figures in the regime (July 1977). (For this and other aspects of the internal security situation in Syria, see survey of Syria.) The Syrian government newspaper claimed that Saddām Ḥusayn was heading a special bureau in Baghdad planning and supervising acts of assassination and sabotage in Syria.[37]

Similarly, Iraq accused Syria of responsibility for an explosion which occurred at Baghdad airport on 14 December 1976. More significantly, perhaps, the Iraqi spokesman also blamed Syrian agitators for widespread riots among the Shī'ī population in southern Iraq in February 1977 (see survey of Iraq). The riots had been triggered, so the Iraqi government announced, by the explosion of a bomb placed at the Al-Ḥusayn mosque in Karbalā—the city holy to Shī'īs—by a Syrian agent. Renewed unrest in Iraqi Kurdistan (see survey of Iraq) was also at times blamed by Iraq on Syrian encouragement of Kurdish insurgents.

Both Syria and Iraq denied charges of being engaged in subversive activities on their neighbour's territory. Instead, they pointed to violations of internal security as proof of the existence of widespread *domestic* opposition against the regime existing there. At the time of the changes in the Iraqi RCC (see survey of Iraq), Damascus Radio commented that "the power struggle in Iraq had entered a serious phase" and predicted that Saddām Ḥusayn's next move would be made against Bakr.[38]

By and large, during the period reviewed, it was Iraq which took the initiative, and Syria which was on the defensive in the quarrel (though elsewhere the opposite was usually true). Although each had to pay a price for the maintenance of the dispute, in terms of inter-Arab and domestic political difficulties and economic losses, the price of reconciliation seemed higher in comparison. As President Bakr stated in a speech on the anniversary of his 1968 takeover: "We will not hold out our hand to those [in Syria] who have deviated from . . . the pan-Arab struggle . . ., cheaply conspired against their brothers and massacred our Palestinian and Lebanese brothers just as the Zionists have done."[39]

It is noteworthy that the outside Arab world seemed to share the assessment that, as long as Asad and Bakr were in power, Syrian-Iraqi hostility would persist. While every other inter-Arab dispute elicited frequent and persistent Arab mediation attempts, the complete absence of any Arab effort, in 1976 and 1977, to bring about a Syrian-Iraqi conciliation speaks for itself.

LIBYAN RELATIONS WITH EGYPT AND SUDAN

Like Iraq, Libya found its inter-Arab standing damaged by the Riyadh conference.

Having been cut off from the mainstream of Arab events as long ago as 1973, its isolation now became greater and more manifest. In the immediate pre-Riyadh period, i.e. during the Syrian-Egyptian quarrel of 1975 and 1976, Libya had regarded Syria as at least a potential ally against Egypt and had believed the dispute useful to Libya in its own attempts to challenge Sādāt's leadership. Even in the summer of 1976, when the attempt to draw Syria into a bloc with Iraq, Algeria, the PLO and Libya itself, had failed, Libya still refrained from publicly criticizing Syria. After the Syrian-Egyptian reconciliation of October 1976, however, Libya was left as Egypt's only active Arab adversary in much the same way as Iraq had remained alone in active opposition to Syria.

Furthermore, the Riyadh conference brought into sharper focus the fact that while Syrian-Egyptian differences found expression mainly in political pressures and propaganda warfare, the Libya-Egyptian quarrel assumed the form of subversive activities carried out by each government inside the territory of its neighbour. This was facilitated by the fact of geographical proximity which made across-the-border infiltration possible. But it also reflected different objectives: Syria's anti-Egyptian campaign had been directed against Sādāt's policies and was intended to restrict Egypt's influence in inter-Arab affairs; Libya's actions were meant to undermine Sādāt's power at home and, ultimately, to cause his overthrow (Sādāt retaliated in kind).

Mu'ammar al-Qadhdhāfī's personal vindictive attitude towards Sādāt went back to the latter's rise to power after 'Abd al-Nāsir's death in 1970. An ardent Nāsir disciple, Qadhdhāfī now came to regard himself as Nāsir's potential heir, particularly with regard to the pan-Arab aspect of Nasserist ideology. Concomitantly, he came to dispute Sādāt's claim to be 'Abd al-Nāsir's true successor. Nonetheless, until 1973, Qadhdhāfī hoped to gain the Arab role he believed to be his due by co-operating with Sādāt, expecting that eventually he would be able to make Egypt his springboard to all-Arab leadership. In 1971, Qadhdhāfī was instrumental in establishing the Federation of Arab Republics (of Egypt, Libya and Syria). When the Federation remained void of political content, he began in 1972 to press for a complete merger of Egypt and Libya into a single state. Libyan pressure continued until the eve of the 1973 October war, when Sādāt finally turned down the merger idea.

In preparing for and launching the 1973 war, Egypt as well as Syria completely ignored Libya. Qadhdhāfī for his part criticized the decision to go to war, derided its objectives and described its outcome as totally negative for the Arab cause. From then on, relations between Egypt and Libya deteriorated fast. In 1975, they were further aggravated by a Libyan about-face which was to have strong repercussions in the period under review: Libya, till then strongly anti-Soviet, signed a major arms deal with the USSR—a step which Sādāt interpreted as anti-Egyptian on the part of Libya, as well as on the part of the USSR.

Increasingly, in 1975 and 1976, both Egypt and Libya turned to measures designed to weaken their rival's domestic situation. Libya began to support and encourage discontented groups of a traditional Islamic character within Egypt. For her part, Egypt granted asylum to Libyan political exiles. Most prominent among them was Major 'Umar al-Muḥayshī, a former Libyan RCC member, who had fled the country after an abortive coup in the summer of 1975. Muhayshī was offered Egyptian broadcasting facilities to conduct anti-Qadhdhāfī propaganda and frequently appealed to Libyans to overthrow their regime. According to Libyan sources, Egypt was also exploiting members of the Egyptian work force in Libya for purposes of subversion. (Egyptian labourers, tradesmen and professionals had been brought in by Qadhdhāfī in substantial numbers between 1970 and 1973. By 1975, they had turned into a political liability, but economic realities did not permit him to dispense with them.)

Another factor which in the mid-1970s began to influence Egyptian-Libyan and, eventually, Libyan-Sudanese relations was the steady improvement in Egyptian-Sudanese ties during the period. In part at least, Egypt sought closer ties with Sudan in order to strengthen its position *vis-à-vis* Libya and, conversely, Qadhdhāfī viewed this *rapprochement* as a hostile act on the part of both Sudan and Egypt. In February 1974, Sādāt and the Sudanese President, Ja'far Numayrī, met and agreed on a programme of political co-ordination and economic co-operation. A Joint Higher Ministerial Committee was formed to discuss specific joint projects. It was to meet twice a year, but actually convened only four times in the first three and a half years of its existence. Nevertheless, the alignment soon produced palpable results: Sudan fully supported Egypt's policies in the conflict with Israel and, like Egypt, gradually turned towards the US; joint projects in the fields of agriculture, (irrigation, land reclamation and cultivation), industry, communications and transport, health, education and information were discussed, and some were launched.

Libya, which in July 1971 had given Numayrī valuable assistance in putting down a leftist coup attempt, now began to exploit the precarious domestic situation of the Sudanese regime by offering refuge to Sudanese political expatriates and potential opposition activists. In 1974 and again in 1975, both Numayrī and Sādāt attributed coup attempts in Sudan to Libyan planning and instigation. Another more dangerous attempt occurred in 1976 and forms the immediate background to events during the period under review. In July 1977, Numayrī barely escaped an attempt on his life during a bloody but eventually abortive coup. Egypt sent immediate aid to Khartoum and joined Sudan in blaming Libya for training and equipping the rebels and helping them infiltrate across the border into Sudan. Libya rejected the accusations, claiming that indigenous groups within Sudan had carried out the insurrection alone. (For the nature of opposition to Numayrī, see survey of Sudan.)

On 15 July 1976, in the wake of the coup attempt, Egypt and Sudan signed a joint defence agreement for which, a few days later, they received implicit Saudi blessing. The agreement stipulated that armed aggression against either state or its armed forces would be considered an aggression against both. The two states would "unify" military planning and operations in case of danger. They would set up a Joint Defence Council to meet every six months or when necessitated by circumstances, and a joint staff, to meet at least every three months. The signature was followed by a meeting of the Defence Council (in Cairo, from 7–9 September) and of the two chiefs of staff (in Khartoum, from 6–8 November 1976) when the implementation of the agreement was discussed. (The Defence Council did not meet again during the period reviewed; the chiefs of staff held a second meeting, in Cairo, from 23–26 April 1977.) Immediately after the signing of the defence agreement, Egyptian troops estimated at 10,000 men and including infantry, armour, artillery, and air defence units were concentrated close to the Libyan border. Further reinforcements reached the border area in August and September 1976.

On 8 August, a bomb exploded at a centrally-located government building in Cairo; on 14 August 1976, an explosive charge went off on a train about to leave Alexandria for Cairo. Casualties resulted in both cases. The Egyptian authorities arrested a number of Libyan nationals for both acts, as well as charging Egyptians with having acted under Libyan orders. The Libyans at the same time arrested a number of Egyptians for espionage, subversion and incitement against the regime and for planning acts of sabotage. Egyptian leaders now justified the troop concentrations by pointing out that Libya was setting up training bases for saboteurs close to the border, as well as command posts for directing their forays into Egypt.

Hostile propaganda was stepped up by both sides: a Radio Cairo comment said that "the time has come to put an end to [Qadhdhāfī's] rule"; the Libyan news agency stated that, since Sādāt had "degenerated to the lowest bottom of treason" there was "no justification for his being at the head of the great Egyptian Arab people."[40] Qadhdhāfī accused Egypt of endangering the Sinai front by moving troops into the Western Desert.[41] Sādāt, who had until then referred to Qadhdhāfī as "sick", now called him a "madman." Qadhdhāfī himself did not attack Sādāt personally, but the Libyan media spoke of him as a hashish addict, and named him "the khedive of Egypt", thus evoking associations of feudalism, corruption and subservience to imperialistic overlords.

Qadhdhāfī, while also reinforcing the units holding the Libyan side of the border, apparently hoped at that time to prevent an armed clash. In his Revolution Day speech on 1 September 1976, he announced that relations with Egypt would not be severed, that Libya "will not fight the Egyptian army", and that only those Egyptian workers in Libya who had been enlisted by the Egyptian intelligence service would "pay the price"; the others would continue to live honourably "among their Libyan brothers."[42] Some 30 Egyptians detained in Libya on suspicion of agitation or acts of sabotage were released to mark Revolution Day. Sādāt, however, was not appeased. In interviews and speeches in August and September, he said of Qadhdhāfī: "This time he will not get out from my hands."[43]

In the immediate wake of the Riyadh conference in October, tension abated somewhat. Part of the Egyptian forces were transferred back from the Libyan border to the Suez Canal. Propaganda attacks became less frequent and at the beginning of December 1976, each country allowed the entrance of its neighbour's newspapers, after a ban of two years. The lull was to prove short-lived.

Egypt was now mainly concerned with fostering its new relations with Syria and Jordan, but continued to promote co-ordination with Sudan as well. From 21-23 November 1976 and again from 26-28 May 1977, the Egyptian-Sudanese Joint Higher Ministerial Committee met to review the implementation of previous decisions and to recommend new joint projects. Numayrī visited Cairo from 19-21 May for talks with Sādāt. During this period, Egyptian and Sudanese leaders frequently stressed that the July 1976 defence agreement had added a new dimension to their mutual ties. Egyptian Foreign Minister Fahmī called it a "shining example of wise unionist action", adding that it extended the "strategic depth" of both countries and was "a shield to Sudan against its enemies."[44]

From the beginning of 1977 onwards, Ethiopia came to be numbered as another enemy of Sudan, alongside Libya. Sudan claimed that, with Libyan assistance, camps serving Numayrī's opponents were being set up in Ethiopia close to the Sudanese border. Sudanese opposition elements were now allowed to cross into Sudan from there, in addition to others infiltrating across the Libyan-Sudanese frontier. In January 1977, Egypt declared its support for Sudan against Ethiopia as well as against Libya. (For the effect of developments in Ethiopia on Arab attitudes in the Red Sea area in general, and towards Eritrea in particular, see below.)

Libya's resentment over Egyptian ties with Sudan was further aroused in January 1977 when Egypt and Syria announced that their Unified Political Command (see above) would be extended to embrace Sudan as well. Sādāt, Asad and Numayrī indeed met in Khartoum on 27-28 February 1977 and issued a joint declaration making Sudan a party to the command.[45] The decision underlined the existing political alignments and added to Numayrī's prestige, particularly at home. In practice, however, the enlarged Unified Political Command had not been formed by November 1977. Syria did not take sides in the subsequent stages of the Egyptian-

Libyan and Sudanese-Libyan disputes, and Egypt and Sudan continued to handle their problems bilaterally. Nonetheless, Qadhdhāfī continued to be strongly critical of Sudanese-Egyptian-Syrian co-operation. In a speech in March 1977, he termed it a "dirty alliance against Libya and against the masses in Egypt and Sudan."[46]

The food riots in Egypt in January 1977 (see survey of Egypt) were exploited to the full by Libyan anti-Sādāt propaganda. Sādāt first hinted guardedly that Libya had had a hand in the riots, and the Egyptian media soon made direct accusations to that effect. MENA, for instance, attributed to the Libyan radio "an open admission of a connection between the . . . perpetrators of the [January] subversive operations . . . on the one hand and the Libyan rulers on the other."[47] Libyan media described the measures taken in Egypt after the riots as "anti-democratic and repressive", and began calling Sādāt "a CIA agent." In an open letter to Sādāt, Qadhdhāfī said it would require "a half century of persevering strife to remove the traces" of Sādāt's "aggression on the national cause" and his "high treason"; of the "shame . . . and humiliation" of the 1975 Sinai agreement; "of massing armies" opposite Libyan villages and oases; and of launching a "campaign of starvation and mass killings" against the Egyptian people.[48]

For the first time since the previous autumn, the Egyptian government again announced the arrest of Libyan saboteurs operating in Egypt in March 1977. The Egyptian Attorney-General said that two groups had been assigned the task of carrying out sabotage acts intended to upset the course of the Arab-African summit in Cairo, from 7–9 March. (Qadhdhafī had not attended the summit and had tried to persuade Arab and African leaders to stay away as well.) Egypt reacted by stepping up its preparedness along the border: on 26 and 27 March, the War Minister, Gen Muḥammad 'Abd al-Ghanī Jamasī, inspected the Egyptian forces in the border area "with a view to intensifying their operations."[49] Egyptian troops in the area were reinforced and carried out military manoeuvres. Again, as in July 1976, Egyptian spokesmen explained that this was done to prevent further infiltration of Libyan sabotage groups into Egyptian territory. On 9 April, Libyan crowds demonstrating against Sādāt broke into the Egyptian Relations Office in Benghazi and destroyed it. (Following the establishment of the Federation of Arab Republics in 1971, the Egyptian, Syrian and Libyan embassies and consulates in the three member-states had been renamed Relations Offices.) Libyan reports claimed that the office had become "a den of espionage and terrorism." Its staff and their families were detained and, on 16 April, expelled to Egypt. In retaliation, "citizens of Alexandria" set fire to the Libyan Relations Office there the following day.

At the same time, Libyan sources frequently commented threateningly on the future of the Egyptians working in Libya. (The Libyans at that time put their number at 250,000; the Egyptians at 220,000.) The Libyan media asserted that their expulsion would hurt the Egyptian economy more than Libya's. The stoppage of their remittances would aggravate Egypt's balance of payment problems and their return to Egypt would increase unemployment there. One characteristic comment read: "Sādāt, in his behaviour, intends to oblige us to adopt a decision against them."[50] Beginning late in April, hundreds of Egyptian workers were expelled from Libya, and the issuing of new visas to Egyptian visitors and workers was suspended. However, these measures had little immediate effect on the total number of Egyptians in Libya.

Libya demanded a special session of the Arab League on 28 April to discuss the mounting tension. Egypt opposed the demand; the other Arab states took no stand, and the meeting did not take place. On the same day, *Al-Ahrām* reported that the USSR had addressed a note to a number of (unnamed) Arab capitals, saying in part: "One can clearly see the Egyptian military pressure on Libya as an attempt to stir up an armed clash", and to encourage domestic action against Qadhdhāfī's regime. Fighting actually erupted only in July (see below). It is a moot point whether the Soviet warning caused Sādāt to delay plans already laid for the spring, or whether the warning was ahead of time.

While the above developments took place in the spring and early summer of 1977, Egyptian (and, after a while, also Sudanese) statements placed increasing emphasis on Libyan collusion with the USSR. Rather than stress Libya's own subversive intentions, they now described Tripoli as the main instrument of Soviet schemes, and as the jumping-off ground for the implementation of Soviet plans directed against Arab and African countries. Egypt and Sudan were described as the primary targets against which the USSR had enlisted Libyan as well as Ethiopian support. The community of Egyptian-Sudanese interests in the face of such hostile intent was underlined in official statements as well as in the media of both countries. During his tour of Western Europe and the US in April, Sādāt repeatedly warned of Libya becoming a base for the achievement of Soviet ambitions in Africa and the Mediterranean. The fighting in southern Zaïre in April and May (in which the Egyptian air force rendered some limited assistance to Zaïre) was made an occasion to enlarge on these themes.

In June, an attempt was made at mediating between Egypt and Libya by Bashīr al-Rābiṭī, the Libyan speaker of the nominal parliament of the Federation of Arab Republics. Propaganda warfare was toned down for a few weeks by both sides, and Libya stopped the expulsion of Egyptians. But on 12 June, Qadhdhāfī said that Libya had not asked for mediation and considered it a "rash step." An immediate deterioration followed. Broadcasts from both sides resumed their appeals for the overthrow of the neighbouring regime in terms similar to those used a year before. On 18 July, Egypt accused Libya of support for the extreme Islamic clandestine opposition group, Jamā'at al-Takfīr wal-Hijra (for details, see survey of Egypt).

At the same time, Egypt tried, with a measure of success, to add Chad to the existing anti-Libyan combination of Egypt and Sudan. On 10 July 1977, the Egyptian Vice-President, Ḥusnī Mubārak, accompanied by the chief of staff, Gen Muhammad 'Alī Fahmī, visited Khartoum and, together with Sudanese officials, proceeded to Chad "in the framework of arrangements against Qadhdhāfī's conspiracies" against these countries.[51] The political commentator of Libya's news agency termed Mubārak's mission "a declaration of war" against Libya.[52]

On 19 July, the first major military clash occurred along the Libyan-Egyptian border. The military initiative in the field was Egypt's but, as Egyptian statements show, Sādāt interpreted Libya's actions as intended to goad him into opening hostilities. In speeches shortly after the violence erupted, the President, Prime Minister and War Minister gave their version of the background to Egypt's action. Sādāt said: "During the past three years, Qadhdhāfī has played with fire. This madman is spending his time on subversive activity, sabotage operations and training camps."[53] Prime Minister Mamdūḥ Sālim stated that Egypt had felt threatened by the growing Soviet political and military presence in Libya. Qadhdhāfī was "conspiring in Africa against Eritrea, Somalia, Zaïre, Sudan and Chad", and was stockpiling Soviet arms "in higher quantities than he could absorb."[54] Foreign press reports spoke of sophisticated electronic surveillance systems being built by the Soviets along the Libyan border, enabling both Libya and the USSR to track Egyptian air and naval movements in Egypt itself and in the Mediterranean. The War Minister, Jamasī, elaborated on this theme: "There is a plan to throw a hostile cordon around Egypt and its strategic depth in Sudan. The planners found Libya to the east and Ethiopia to the south to be the best positions for making the cordon, and Zaïre would complete the cordon if it were to be dominated by hostile elements." Jamasī added that the plan was a Soviet one, but Libya's role in it was "consistent with its [own] aims against Egypt."[55]

Against this background armed clashes started in July 1977. According to the Egyptian account, Egyptian forces caught a group of saboteurs on their way into Egypt from a Libyan camp at the Jaghbūb oasis on 12 July. On 16 July, several Egyptian border posts were attacked by Libyan forces. On 19 July, Egyptian posts were again attacked and nine Egyptian soldiers killed. The Libyan version was that Egyptian forces had occupied positions on the Libyan side of the frontier for several months prior to the first major clashes. Some incidents had already occurred in June, when Egyptian forces raided a number of Libyan police posts and kidnapped eight Libyan policemen. The Egyptian authorities had ignored all Libyan attempts to have the men returned. In retaliation, a Libyan unit captured an Egyptian patrol numbering thirteen men on 16 July. On 17 July, the Libyan district commander warned his Egyptian counterpart that he would destroy an Egyptian position set up inside Libyan territory unless it was evacuated within two days. The Egyptians failed to withdraw and, on 19 July, the Libyans destroyed the post.

Fighting on a more massive scale began on 21 July and lasted until 24 July. Egyptian sources first described the operation on 21 July as a pre-emptive attack against a Libyan column moving towards the Egyptian border town of Salūm. Later, however, Egypt's military moves were explained as a retaliatory action for the Libyan attack two days earlier: already, on 19 July, according to Sādāt, "orders were given to repulse [Libyan] aggression." Egyptian forces accordingly entered the Libyan border townlet of Musā'id and engaged the Libyan unit sent to meet them.[56] The fighting at Musā'id remained the principal engagement of ground forces during the four days of fighting. The Egyptian forces left Libyan territory on the following morning. From 22–24 July, most fighting was done by the Egyptian air forces. Libya's Jamāl 'Abd al-Nāsir air base (formerly Al-Adem base), 30 km south of Tobruk, was bombed several times. Tobruk itself was bombed on 23 July. This was the deepest Egyptian air penetration into Libya—a distance of 120 km. Another Libyan air base, at the Kufra oasis in south-east Libya, was also heavily bombed. On 23 and 24 July, Libyan targets near the border were hit from the air. An Egyptian commando force raided a training camp in the Jaghbūb area on 24 July. Some observers, (including the *Financial Times*, 26 July), believed that the main aim of the Egyptian air attacks was to knock out Soviet-built installations along the border.

Fighting stopped on 24 July, following a series of mediation moves, chiefly by Algeria's President, Houari Boumedienne, the Kuwait Foreign Minister, Sabāḥ al-Aḥmad al-Jābir, and the PLO chairman Yāsir 'Arafāt. Sādāt, as well as his War Minister, declared that Egypt's aim had been to "teach Qadhdhāfī a lesson." Military operations were therefore on a limited scale and restricted to military targets only. They rejected the Libyan charge that, at Musā'id and elsewhere, Egyptian fire had been directed against civilians. Sādāt said that while administering a warning to Qadhdhāfī, Egypt was not hostile towards the Libyan people or armed forces. "Egypt does not want [Qadhdhāfī's] aid, money, land or anything else"; nor did it covet Libyan oil. But Sādāt went on: "Let there be no games with the armed forces . . . The lesson taught will be five times harder if even a slight encroachment on our Egyptian western border were to take place [again]. . . . I also warn against any subversive action inside this country. I can blow things up for [Qadhdhāfī] in Libya more and better." Referring indirectly, and somewhat more cautiously, to the Soviet presence in Libya, Sādāt added: "I am saying this so that Libya's brave boy will hear me—we accept neither mercenaries nor major powers in Africa nor, of course, in our Arab world . . . For this reason I warn."[57]

Following the suspension of hostilities, a relative lull set in. Propaganda warfare was again toned down to some extent and on 24 August, prisoners taken in July were exchanged through the mediation of 'Arafāt. An agreement to establish military ceasefire observation posts was concluded by means of direct contacts between the two sides.

Basic attitudes on both sides, however, remained unchanged. The Egyptian position was restated by Premier Sālim in an address to the People's Assembly (parliament). He made the following points:

1) "Egypt denounces any interference in African affairs by any [outside] state or big power.

2) "Egypt does not agree to the presence of a big international power on its border, whatever that power may be.

3) "Egypt will resolutely intervene against any attempt to dominate fraternal Sudan or the sources of the Nile, because this is a matter of life or death to Egypt."

Egypt, Sālim added, did not fear the expulsion of the Egyptian workers from Libya. They could not easily be replaced there. Should they be deported nonetheless, Egypt had worked out a contingency plan for their repatriation.[58]

Libya also reaffirmed some of its basic positions which had led to the build-up of tension prior to the July fighting. For instance, on 25 July, the Libyan newspaper *Al-Jihād* wrote: "Libya will categorically reject any so-called mediation . . . which will be aimed at putting pressure . . . on Libya in order to make it adhere to the capitulationist plans" (*vis-à-vis* the US and Israel). Libya's Prime Minister, 'Abd al-Salām Jallūd, said on 1 August that Egypt, which pretended to have handed out a lesson, had in reality been taught one by Libya. He implied that he saw no chances for a real reconciliation with the existing Egyptian regime, saying that hostile propaganda could stop if Egypt ended it first; but "no solution can be reached unless a *coup* takes place in Egypt . . . [and] unless Egypt's policy returns to the pan-Arab line."[59] The atmosphere, in the autumn of 1977, was thus one of a dispute suspended rather than resolved.

An interesting sidelight was thrown by the Libyan-Egyptian developments on the state of Syrian-Egyptian relations in mid-year. It has already been noted that Syria had not come out in support of Egypt or criticized Libya during the crisis in July. In August, after Egyptian-Syrian relations had just taken a turn for the worse (see above), a delegation of the Libyan Arab Socialist Union visited Damascus for talks with the Syrian Ba'th Party's Foreign Relations Bureau. The visit (which had not been previously announced) was stated to have dealt with "strengthening the current fraternal relations" between the Syrian Ba'th Party and the Libyan Arab Socialist Union.[60]

MAGHRIB AFFAIRS

Algeria's relations with other Arab countries were primarily determined by its dispute with Morocco and Mauritania over the issue of the Western (formerly Spanish) Sahara, and by the attitudes adopted on this question by Arab states not directly involved. (For the division of the Spanish Sahara between Morocco and Mauritania in 1976 and its antecedents, and for the roots of Algerian opposition to it and of its support for the secessionist Polisario, see *Africa Contemporary Record 1974-5*, *1975-6*, and *1976-7*.)

In 1976 and 1977, Algeria continued to support Polisario both by extending diplomatic recognition to the Saharan Arab Democratic Republic (SADR), the independent state proclaimed by Polisario, and by financial and military aid to

Polisario units enabling them to sustain, and at times escalate, their military operations in the Western Sahara. Algeria insisted on the right of self-determination by the inhabitants of the Western Sahara, thus in effect demanding a reopening of the Spanish-Moroccan-Mauritanian negotiations which had led to the division of the territory. Morocco and Mauritania, on the other hand, held that the division was final. In the words of Morocco's Foreign Minister, Aḥmad Laraki (Al-'Irāqī), during a visit to Cairo: "The case of the Sahara is closed completely . . . The Sahara has been annexed . . . for good."[61]

Algeria's main interest in inter-Arab affairs in 1976 and 1977 lay in enlisting other Arab states to support its stand on the Sahara. By and large, these efforts failed. The only country to support Algeria explicitly was Libya, predisposed to do so by an earlier quarrel of its own with Morocco, which had started in 1971. However, Libya stopped short of recognizing SADR. Some Arab countries (notably Egypt, Saudi Arabia and Tunisia) sided with Morocco and Mauritania; but the majority refused to take a stand. Attempts by Algeria to have the Western Sahara question put on the agenda of the Arab League were prevented in 1976 and 1977, mainly by the stonewalling tactics of those unwilling to adopt or declare their attitude.

Algeria repaid Qadhdhāfī for his stand by consistent support (particularly in the Algerian media, less so by official pronouncements) for Libya's line in the latter's quarrels with Egypt and Sudan (see above). Algerian efforts were instrumental in ending the Libyan-Egyptian fighting in July 1977 under circumstances not too unfavourable, politically speaking, to Libya. High-level contacts between Libya and Algeria were maintained from time to time. On 4 May 1977, on the occasion of signing a protocol envisaging economic co-operation, Libya's Premier, 'Abd al-Salām Jallūd, spoke of future "unionist steps" between the two countries; but he failed to elicit any response from Algeria.

Tunisia found itself caught in 1977 between an unfriendly Algeria and a hostile Libya. Relations with the former were strained mainly because Tunisia sided with Morocco over the Sahara; and with the latter because of a dispute over the division of the continental shelf in the Gulf of Gabès. Matters came to a head off Gabès in May 1977, when a Libyan-owned oil rig was anchored in waters claimed by Tunisia. However, Tunisia felt compelled to tread cautiously. A visit to Tunis by the Algerian Foreign Minister, 'Abd al-'Azīz Bouteflika, in February 1977 led to a slight improvement of relations with Algeria; and an agreement, concluded in June 1977 to submit the issue of the continental shelf to arbitration by the International Court of Justice, reduced the strain with Libya.

Because Algeria, as well as its Arab neighbours, were on the whole mainly concerned with the regional issues of North Africa, their impact on general Arab affairs was marginal in 1976 and 1977. That the heads of state of Morocco, Algeria, Tunisia and Libya were all absent from the 1976 Cairo summit is one indication of this fact.

Conversely, the eastern Arab world did not concern itself too much with Maghrib affairs. The exception—ineffectual at that—was a Saudi attempt in 1976 to mediate over the issue of the Western Sahara. Between 11 and 22 November 1976, the Saudi Crown Prince, accompanied by his Foreign Minister, Sa'ūd al-Faysal, held talks with King Ḥasan, President Boumedienne and the Mauritanian President, Mokhtar Ould Daddah. The failure of the talks became evident as soon as they were concluded, when King Ḥasan told an interviewer that Morocco agreed to a dialogue with Algeria on condition that the Moroccan and Mauritanian character of the Western Sahara would not thereby be called into question.[62]

RED SEA AFFAIRS

In 1976 and 1977, Red Sea affairs, which in the past had hardly ever been dealt with as an all-Arab issue, became a central topic at a number of inter-Arab meetings.

A short while after the 1973 war, Muhammad Hasanayn Haykal (then still editor of *Al-Ahrām*) had written of the urgent need for a common Arab Red Sea strategy which would take into account the lessons of the war. However it was only in 1976 that a high level meeting took up the issue. The Sudanese Foreign Minister, Mansūr Khālid, explained the slowness of this process: "For a while the Red Sea was a dormant issue. The Suez Canal was closed, there was no Soviet presence in the area, the sea had lost its strategic value . . . But then the Soviets established air and sea bases in the area, the Suez Canal was reopened, and trade and oil traffic increased through the Red Sea. Ethiopia has now turned towards Russia, and the danger of a Soviet-American confrontation in the area is heightened. The Arab countries bordering the Red Sea do not want . . . to allow any of the super-powers to use the area as part of their strategy. They would like the Red Sea to become a neutral zone."[63]

The first Arab meeting to take up Red Sea affairs was the Jidda conference held from 17-19 July 1976 with the participation of King Khālid and Presidents Sādāt and Numayrī. Its declared purpose was to discuss the security problem posed for Egypt and Sudan by Libyan and Soviet policies (which had caused Egypt and Sudan to conclude the defence agreement of 15 July; see above). It was President Numayrī who later revealed in an interview that the Jidda conference had discussed Red Sea affairs in general with a view to arriving at "a definition of the steps which had to be taken to maintain conformity, co-operation and co-ordination [in that area] in a well defined strategy in the service of the Arab nation." In the same interview, he stated that the Red Sea and the states bordering on it "have long constituted a natural unity."[64] On 31 October, he reiterated that the Jidda meeting had dealt with Red Sea security questions, adding that other Red Sea littorals were expected to join Egypt, Sudan and Saudi Arabia at the appropriate time. He warned of great power conflicts extending to the Red Sea and went on to say that, if Communism made gains in the region "the responsibility devolving on the Red Sea states goes beyond a limited vision."[65]

The next inter-Arab meeting to touch on Red Sea matters was King Khālid's visit to Sudan (31 October-1 November 1976). A joint communiqué stated that King Khālid and President Numayrī "affirmed their eagerness for . . . the security and peace of the Red Sea, and for working to turn it into a lake of peace for all those who live on both sides, and to keep it away from the strategies and conflicts of the super-powers."[66]

The Khartoum meeting of the presidents of Egypt, Syria and Sudan on 27-28 February 1977 (see above) included the following in its joint statement: "The Presidents affirm their desire that the Red Sea be a peace zone . . . to be kept away from international conflicts and pressures endangering the security and stability of the area. They also affirm their desire that the three countries should formulate a unified strategy in this connection and that other states in the area be invited to participate in it."[67] Similar statements were included in joint communiqués issued following frequent visits of leaders of Red Sea countries to the capitals of other littorals, or to Arab states such as the Gulf Emirates, Syria and Tunisia.

While official communiqués continued the use of phrases like "a peace zone" or "neutral region", Arab leaders frequently emphasized the "Arab character" of the Red Sea. For instance, Sādāt (December 1976): "The Red Sea is an Arab lake. This is what we think."[68] Asad (February 1977): "The Red Sea is an Arab sea."[69] Kuwait's Foreign Minister, Shaykh Sabāḥ al-Aḥmad al-Jābir (June 1977) "All the states bordering this sea are Arab states."[70]

Occasionally, a parallel was drawn between the efforts to "preserve the Arabism" of the Persian Gulf (a phrase that had come into frequent use in the late 1960s) and the status of the Red Sea. A joint statement issued on the occasion of the visit of the Sudanese Premier, Rashīd al-Tāhir Bakr, to Qatar argued that it was this similarity which made Red Sea security a "comprehensive, pan-Arab" responsibility."[71]

The principal driving force in making the Red Sea a focus of inter-Arab interest was Saudi Arabia. Its efforts were part of a general drive, dating back to the early 1970s, to rally around Saudi Arabia *first* the Arab countries along the Persian Gulf, *next* the southern part of the Arabian Peninsula, and *finally* the remaining Red Sea littorals. In keeping with its general *modus operandi* in inter-Arab affairs, Saudi leaders preferred to act behind the scenes as far as possible, concealing the broad sweep of their regional policy behind a series of bilateral meetings arranged with each of their neighbours and between other Peninsular or Red Sea states. Saudi predominance along the Arab shore of the Persian Gulf had primarily been established in 1970 and 1971. Saudi influence in North Yemen had been increasing since the end of the civil war there in 1970, and had become an established fact from the time of Lt-Col Ibrāhīm al-Ḥamdī's rise to power in 1974. In 1976, Saudi Arabia began actively to pursue a *rapprochement* with the PDRY (South Yemen), using the promise of economic assistance as the principal means to win the impoverished country over to a more pro-Saudi, less pro-Soviet, line, as well as to a greater readiness for accommodation with Oman.

South Yemen had for years supported insurgents in the southern Omani region of Dhufar in their struggle against the Sultan of Oman. Saudi Arabia did not succeed in persuading South Yemen to cut off its aid to the insurgents entirely, but border tension did abate to some extent during 1976 and 1977. Overall relations improved sufficiently by May 1976 to allow Saudi Arabia and South Yemen to establish diplomatic relations—for the first time since the latter's independence in 1967. By 1977, relations had developed further making it possible for South Yemen's Head of State, Sālim 'Alī Rubay', to visit Riyadh (31 July–2 August 1977).

Saudi Arabia extended its efforts in 1977 to bring North and South Yemen closer together. The two Heads of State met on 15–16 February in Qa'taba (North Yemen) for talks which resulted in some improvement in their relations.

Saudi Arabia's relations with Somalia have been marked by strongly ambivalent hostility. While the Saudis welcomed the non-Arab Somalis to membership of the Arab League, they strongly disapproved of the Mogadishu regime's relations with Moscow, and especially of the naval facilities afforded to the Soviet navy in Berbera. The Saudi policy was to maintain regular contacts with Somalia in an effort to get it to break its Moscow ties and draw closer to the Arab League. The chances of this happening were increased by the USSR's decision in April 1976 to court the Ethiopian military regime. The initiative to shift Somalia's policies towards the Arab world was left to the Sudan. President Numayrı undertook a mission from 15–22 March 1977 to the capitals of Oman, Somalia, South and North Yemen. This initiative led to the Ta'izz conference on 22–23 March. (Although Ethiopia was invited to attend, its regime declined to do so.) Egypt was openly involved in this move, but the Saudis remained discreetly in the background—even though the summit was specifically called to deal with the problems of the Red Sea. The countries represented by their heads of state were North and South Yemen, Sudan and Somalia. While no practical results followed from the meeting, one of its achievements was to bring together two Saudi allies and two countries hitherto hostile to it. The meeting also set a pattern for the future, and constituted an important stage in Saudi strategy for the region. The North Yemen's late Head of

State, Ibrāhīm Ḥamdī, declared that the conference was "not a demonstration against anyone . . . [nor a] plot against anyone", the participants were merely exercising their "legitimate right" to discuss "questions related to joint co-operation, including the protection of our sovereignty over our land and regional waters in the Red Sea area."[72]

According to its final communiqué, the Ta'izz meeting concentrated on aspects of economic and social co-operation. It affirmed that "the leaders agreed on the importance of exploiting the wealth of the Red Sea for the good of the peoples of the countries bordering it." A joint committee would be entrusted with continuing the efforts "to convene an expanded meeting including *all* the countries bordering on the Red Sea." There was also a brief mention of the concept of the Red Sea as a "zone of peace."[73] However, President Barreh of Somalia came away feeling that the conference had been inconclusive. He told an interviewer: "I offered to convene an enlarged conference in order to achieve a unified and comprehensive strategy for the [Red] Sea . . . but . . . in Ta'izz we achieved nothing."[74]

The Sudan's Foreign Minister went directly from Ta'izz to Riyadh to report on the discussions. Crown Prince Fahd explained: "We did not take part in any discussion regarding the security of the Red Sea or other matters, first, because we were not informed of this subject in advance and, second, because we believe that such sensitive subjects must be discussed objectively and scientifically to ascertain the objectives and dimensions of decisions taken on this matter as well as to avoid political complications that might result from them, and to ascertain the political gains that could be achieved from raising such questions. But . . . we are basically interested in the security of the Arab and Islamic world as well as the world as a whole."[75] Saudi Arabia followed up the Ta'izz meeting by sending its Foreign Minister to Somalia (5–6 April) and to Aden and San'ā (9–12 April 1977). Sa'ūd denied that a Red Sea summit had been discussed during the talks there.[76] On the occasion of the Arab League meeting in September 1977, representatives of the four states who had participated at Ta'izz, met separately and again decided to seek an enlarged Red Sea conference at which Saudi Arabia, Egypt and Jordan would participate with them. There was no immediate response to their initiative, however, and no further follow-up in fact took place up to November 1977.

A noticeable change occurred in the Red Sea policies of a number of Arab states during 1976 and 1977 with regard to Eritrea. In the past, non-littoral states—Libya, Iraq and Syria—had been among the main Arab supporters of the Eritrean liberation movement, while Egypt (because of its relations with the OAU), Sudan (because of the situation in its southern border region) and Saudi Arabia (from distaste of the supposedly revolutionary character of the Eritrean groups) had initially had strong reservations. From among the littoral states, only South Yemen had supported the Eritreans. In the wake of the change of regime in Ethiopia, especially after 1974, a policy reversal took place. Libya (pursuing its fight with Sudan which, meanwhile, had come into conflict with Ethiopia), expressed support for the Marxist regime in Addis Ababa, and ceased its earlier support for the Eritreans.

Qadhdhāfī explained Libya's policy change to a conference of Muslim Foreign Ministers in Tripoli on 16 May by saying that Libya had supported the Eritreans as long as "the feudalist reactionary agent", Haile Selassie, had ruled Ethiopia. After the revolution there, things changed. Eritrean demands for independence on religious and ethnic grounds alone were no longer valid.[77] (For rising tension along the Sudanese-Ethiopian border during this period, and for Egyptian expressions of support for Sudan, see above.) Egypt, Sudan, Saudi Arabia, Kuwait and Bahrayn now started coming to the aid of at least one of the three Eritrean groupings. After the Soviet and Cuban intervention on Ethiopia's side, South Yemen ended its support for the Eritreans. When Djibouti became an independent Republic in June 1977, it immediately joined the Arab League. President Sādāt began to speak of the countries forming the Red Sea's western shore as "Egypt, Sudan, Eritrea and Djibouti."[78]

Saudi Arabia's Crown Prince Fahd stated: "The present Ethiopian policy constitutes an open aggression against Arab nationalism. Therefore, we in the Kingdom call for co-ordination and co-operation between the Arab and Muslim states bordering the Red Sea, especially between Sudan, Somalia and the three Eritrean liberation movements. They should unite in order that a strong alignment is established to ward off the danger."[79]

The major Arab states moved much closer to a joint Red Sea policy during 1977 than at any time before. Arab consensus was not, however, complete. South Yemen, though no longer ostracized, was still something of an outsider. The Somalis, too, found much less active Arab support in their campaign in the Ogaden than they had obviously expected as members of the Arab League and as recent recruits to the Egyptian-Sudanese-Saudi anti-Soviet line. Libya had removed itself from the consensus altogether, as it had done over so many other Arab issues. Above all, Saudi Arabia would not let itself be rushed into more decisive action before it considered the time ripe in its own cautious judgement. (For a fuller discussion of the Red Sea conflict see essay on the region in this volume.)

THE ARAB LEAGUE

For most of the period reviewed, the Arab League fulfilled the role to which it had been relegated since the early 1960s: that of taking care of the routine business of Arab co-ordination over matters which did not involve major political decisions. Since 1964, it was the Arab summit conferences which had instead become the forum for major all-Arab decisions—the conclusive testing-ground for the overall state of Arab co-operation or rivalry. Since the late 1960s, and particularly since the utter failure of the Rabat summit in December 1969, it had become the practice to avoid summit meetings at times when there was no fairly broad Arab consensus on major issues, and when the success of the "meeting of Kings and Presidents" could not be considered as reasonably assured in advance. This, in turn, created the impression that any undue delay in convening a summit meeting was evidence of lack of consensus—just as much as an unsuccessful summit meeting would have been. This was particularly true of the period following the 1973 war, when a year without a summit came to be thought of in the Arab world as one of flagging Arab solidarity. The Algiers summit of 1973 had given expression to the broad (though not quite comprehensive) consensus engendered by the war; the Rabat summit of 1974 had centred on the agreement of opinion regarding the PLO (which had been in grave doubt only a few months earlier); the failure to hold a summit in 1975 had reflected the Arab disputes surrounding the second Sinai agreement of that year; the Cairo summit of October 1976 had signalled their termination.

The particular circumstances which made 1977 another year without a summit conference provide an instructive illustration of the dynamics of Arab politics. The 1976 Cairo summit, for all its importance, was soon perceived by many Arab leaders as having left too many questions open. By endorsing the Riyadh resolutions, it had disposed of the major repercussions of the Lebanese war on inter-Arab relations, and had put a stop to the Syrian-Egyptian dispute in its overt form. It had not, however, laid down a clear programme for future action. What remained unsettled were the major aspects of how to present the Arab case to the incoming US Administration; how to deal with the Palestinian issue; and how to create a binding framework for the economic aid to be provided for the "confrontation" states. As early as January 1977, Tunisia's Foreign Minister,

Ḥabīb Shattī, chairman of the routine Arab League meeting then being held, spoke of the need for a new summit conference. It should, he asserted, convene in March in conjunction with the Afro-Arab summit meeting, and should discuss "joint Arab strategy" and the future Palestinian state. However, although the Afro-Arab summit was held in Cairo (from 7-9 March 1977), his suggestion was not acted upon.

In May, North Yemen also came out with an appeal for a summit to decide on the "future Middle Eastern strategy" of the Arab states. On 15 June 1977, Libya formally took up the call, proposing as the main items on the agenda the Palestine question and the occupied territories, Arab economic co-operation and the Western Sahara. However, the venue and date proposed by Libya immediately revealed that its main purpose was to embarrass Egypt: the summit was to be held in Tripoli (where, against the background of the prevailing Egyptian-Libyan tension described above, Sādāt was unlikely to go)—and especially not on 23 July, Egypt's Revolution Day. After some equivocation by a number of Arab states, it became clear that Libya could not muster a majority for its proposal which Egypt proceeded to demolish. The Egyptian Foreign Ministry spokesman said: "The Arab Heads of State are in direct and constant contact with each other on all matters of interest to the Arab nation. It appears that there is nothing new or pressing now that merits the urgent convening of . . . [a] summit conference."[80] As Libyan-Egyptian tension rose to the point of armed hostilities in the following month, *Al-Ahrām* (20 July) recalled the Libyan suggestion, condemning it as an attempt "to plant a time bomb to shatter Arab cohesion and solidarity at this delicate, critical and fateful stage."

In the absence of a summit meeting, and under the pressure of outside events, the Arab League regained, at least for a brief moment, its former role as a forum for genuine inter-Arab discussion and decision-making. The League Council meeting, routinely set for 3 September 1977, found itself faced with the task of preparing Arab policy for the Foreign Ministers' talks with the US Administration and for the UN General Assembly, both scheduled to open later the same month. As noted above, the meeting brought Syrian-Egyptian policy differences into the open again. But the controversy also touched on the question of convening a summit: Syria demanded that a summit be held on October, i.e. at a time when its decisions would still have a bearing on Arab conduct at the UN, and on major developments in the Arab-Israeli conflict which were then thought to be imminent. Egypt was unwilling to let a summit convene at a time when its deliberations were likely to reflect, perhaps even to underline Syrian-Egyptian differences, and when there was no telling which of the two would command a majority at a summit meeting. At Egypt's insistence (and with the support of Saudi Arabia, who backed Egypt on every issue during the September League session) the Council decided to set an Arab Foreign Ministers' meeting for 12 November 1977. This meeting would in turn set a date, agree on a venue and draw up an agenda for the summit. The League's Secretary-General, Maḥmūd Riyād, said that by November the Arab countries would have had time for "intensive contacts to clear the Arab atmosphere."[81] However, a preparatory meeting so late in the year made it almost certain that 1977 would pass without a summit.

A year after the 1976 Cairo summit, its main achievements were thus being called into question. In September 1977, Syria and Egypt were not pulling in the same direction; Saudi Arabia (much against its inclination and basic policy) had been forced to take sides in favour of Egypt; and the year would run out without that reaffirmation of Arab solidarity which a new summit was to have signified.

NOTES

1. Radio Cairo and Radio Damascus, 18 October—monitored by Daily Report, East and North Africa (DR), 19 October; and British Broadcasting Corporation Summary of World Broadcasts, the ME and Africa (BBC), 20, 21 October 1976.
2. R Damascus, 5 October; R Cairo, 6 October—BBC, 7, 8 October 1976.
3. *Newsweek*, 5 January 1976.
4. Middle East News Agency (MENA), 20 October—DR, 20 October 1976.
5. Iraqi News Agency (INA), 25 October—DR, 26 October 1976.
6. *Al-Sayyād*, Beirut; according to MENA, 30 December 1976.
7. *Al-Anwār*, Beirut; in a series published 20-23 May 1977.
8. R Cairo, 11, 17 December—DR, 13, 20 December 1976.
9. MENA, 11 January—DR, 12 January 1977. *Le Monde*, 21 January 1977.
10. R Cairo and R Damascus, 21 December—BBC, 23 December 1976.
11. MENA, 11 January—DR, 12 January 1977.
12. *Al-Akhbār*, Cairo; 9 May—DR, 11 May 1977.
13. R Damascus, 4 August—BBC, 6 August 1977.
14. R Damascus, 9 August—BBC, 11 August 1977.
15. *Al-Ba'th*, Damascus; quoted by Syrian Arab News Agency (SANA), 7 August—BBC, 9 August 1977.
16. See *Al-Siyāsa*, Kuwait; 13 August 1976.
17. R Amman, 22 November—BBC, 24 November 1976.
18. R Amman, 8 December—BBC, 10 December 1976.
19. R Amman, 19 January—BBC, 21 January 1977.
20. *Al-Akhbār*, 23 February 1977.
21. R Amman, 3 July—BBC Weekly, 12 July 1977.
22. *Newsweek*, 1 August 1977.
23. MENA, 14 January; R Amman, 14, 15 January—DR, 17 January 1977. *Al-Ra'y*, Amman; 16 January 1977.
24. R Amman, 20 January—BBC, 22 January 1977.
25. *Akhir Sā'a*, Cairo; 19 January—DR, 25 January 1977.
26. *Jordan Times*, 12 July 1977.
27. MENA, 10 July—DR, 11 July 1977.
28. R Riyadh—DR, 24 March 1977.
29. R Riyadh, 19 May—BBC, 21 May 1977.
30. MENA, R Cairo, 19 May—DR, 20 May 1977.
31. *Al-Hawādith*, Beirut; 3 December 1976.
32. *Al-Siyāsa*, 16 April 1977
33. Statement by the Syrian Ba'th National Command; R Damascus, 7 March—BBC, 9 March 1977.
34. R Damascus, 22 February—BBC, 24 February 1977.
35. R Damascus, 28 March—DR, 30 March 1977.
36. R Damascus, 4 January—DR, 5 January; *Tishrīn*, 5 January; *Al-Ba'th*, 7 June 1977.
37. *Al-Thawra*, Damascus; 22 March 1977.
38. R Damascus, 5 September—BBC, 6 September 1977.
39. INA, 16 July—BBC, 18 July 1977.
40. R Cairo, 5 July; Arab Revolutionary News Agency (ARNA), Libya; 23 July—BBC, 7 July, 26 July 1976.
41. R Tripoli, 24 July—DR, 26 July 1976.
42. R Tripoli, 2 September—DR, 3 September 1976.
43. For instance, *Al-Siyāsa*, 14 August; press conference in Oman—MENA, 15 August; DR, 17 August 1976.
44. MENA, 11 January—DR, 12 January 1977.
45. R Cairo, R Damascus, 28 February—BBC, 2 March 1977.
46. ARNA, 9 March—BBC, 10 March 1977.
47. MENA, 12 February—DR, 14 February 1977.
48. ARNA, 5 February—BBC, 7 February 1977.
49. MENA, 27 March—BBC, 29 March 1977.
50. ARNA, 20 April, 29 April—BBC, 22 April; DR, 2 May. R Tripoli, 27 April—DR, 28 April 1977.
51. *Al-Ahrām*, Cairo; 12 July 1977.
52. R Tripoli, 11 July—DR, 12 July 1977.
53. R Cairo, 22 July—DR, 25 July 1977.
54. R Cairo, 2 August—DR, 3 August 1977.
55. MENA, 2 August—DR, 3 August 1977.
56. Sādāt in a speech at Alexandria University; R Cairo, 26 July—BBC, 28 July 1977.

57. R Cairo, 22 and 26 July—DR, 25 July; BBC, 28 July 1977. R Cairo, 7 August—BBC, 9 August 1977.
58. R Cairo, 2 August—DR, 3 August 1977.
59. ARNA, 2 August—DR, 2 August 1977.
60. SANA, 10 August—DR, 11 August 1977.
61. *Al-Ahrām*, 16 February 1977.
62. *Le Matin*, 22 November 1976.
63. *Events*, 6 May 1977.
64. *Al-Yamāma*, Saudi Arabia; quoted by R Omdurman, 15 October—BBC, 20 October 1976.
65. *Al-Ṣaḥāfa*, Sudan; 2 November 1976.
66. R Riyadh, 1 November—BBC, 3 November 1976.
67. MENA, 28 February—DR, 1 March 1977.
68. Interview to *al-Sayyād*, quoted by MENA, 30 December 1976—DR, 4 January 1977.
69. Press conference after the Khartoum conference; MENA, 28 February—DR, 1 March 1977.
70. MENA, 25 June—DR, 27 June 1977.
71. Qatari News Agency, 16 May—DR, 17 May 1977.
72. R San'ā, 22 March—BBC, 24 March 1977.
73. R San'ā, 23 March—BBC, 25 March 1977.
74. *Al-Jumhūriyya*, Cairo; 12 May 1977.
75. Interview with *al-Siyāsa*, 16 April 1977.
76. *Al-Bilād*, Jidda; quoted by R Riyadh, 20 April—DR, 21 April 1977.
77. ARNA, 16 May—DR, 17 May 1977.
78. Interview with an Iranian correspondent; quoted by MENA, 18 May—DR, 19 May 1977.
79. Interview with *al-Anwār*, 21 May 1977.
80. R Cairo, 19 June—DR, 20 June 1977.
81. MENA, 4 September 1977.

Palestinian Issues

The Palestine Liberation Organization

ISRAEL ALTMAN

Developments in the Palestine Liberation Organization (PLO) from the latter part of 1976 to the middle of 1977 should be seen against the background of the chain of events starting with the Arab-Israeli war in October 1973, and culminating in the ceasefire in the civil war in Lebanon three years later. The major developments during that period were: 1) a consistent improvement in the PLO's international standing contrasting with a decline, from 1975 onwards, in its position in the Arab world; 2) increasing pressures, external and internal, on the PLO to participate in the political process towards a Middle Eastern settlement, leading to some modification of positions which resulted in internal conflict; and 3) the political and military effects wrought by the civil war in Lebanon.

Arab diplomacy following the October 1973 war produced ever-widening recognition of the PLO. This process was highlighted by the Rabat summit conference resolution recognizing the PLO as the "sole legitimate representative of the Palestinian people" (28 October 1974), followed by PLO Executive Committee Chairman Yāsir 'Arafāt's appearance at the UN and the adoption by the General Assembly of Resolution 3236 (22 November 1974), affirming the Palestinian people's right to national independence and self-determination.

However, developments in the political process raised apprehensions within the PLO of a possible ME settlement being arrived at without its active participation, and in which its own aspirations would not be fully taken into account. In order to affirm its position as a partner to any settlement, the PLO found itself faced with the need to modify some of its traditional positions, such as agreeing to Palestinian sovereignty over *part* of Palestine (thereby possibly jeopardizing its claim to the entire area of Palestine). There was also a growing recognition by PLO leaders of the need felt by many Palestinians to reinforce their Palestinian identity, politically and legally, through the actual creation of a Palestinian state.

Lacking a territorial base of its own independent from any host government, the PLO's ideological stand—as the "spearhead" and symbol of pan-Arab commitment to the total liberation of Palestine—had been its major political asset. In the wake of the 1973 war, internal disputes evolved around the question of the legitimacy of deviating from ideological positions which until then were considered to be absolute. Those who opposed any deviation whatsoever formed the Palestinian "Rejection Front" in the autumn of 1974. The PLO leadership (i.e. its central establishment, largely dominated by al-Fath) strove instead to preserve its basic ideological stand, and yet modify certain positions by introducing a distinction between "strategic" and "tactical" goals. "Strategic" goals were those sanctioned by official ideology (embodied in the Palestinian National Covenant); "tactical" goals were dictated by circumstances at a given juncture. The latter were held to be legitimate because they were intended, and perceived, as steps towards the realization of the "strategic" goals.

The second Sinai disengagement agreement in 1975 led the PLO into political conflict with Egypt. In 1976, the PLO's efforts to secure a truly autonomous foothold in Lebanon brought it into military conflict with Syria, formerly its closest ally. The war damaged the PLO's position in the Arab world, and enabled Syria and Jordan to undermine its claim to exclusive representation of the Palestinians. As a result of the war, the PLO's freedom of military movement and action was much more circumscribed by Syria. Yet the hostilities probably improved the organization's ability to handle its combat units more effectively and on a larger scale than before.

The main division inside the PLO—between the Rejection Front and al-Fatḥ—was temporarily bridged during the war, with both sides ranged against the "common enemy": Syria and the pro-Syrian elements in the PLO, chiefly al-Sā'iqa (an organization actually run by Syria).

The PLO's defeats in Lebanon did not diminish international recognition of its role in negotiations for a Middle East settlement. On the contrary, support grew in the US and Western Europe for PLO participation in the negotiating process.

INTERNAL DEVELOPMENTS IN THE PLO

The central issue in internal PLO affairs in 1977 was again the question of its participation in "the political process" towards finding a settlement to the ME conflict, and the modifications it might have to make in its policies to gain a place in that process. This question had been crucial in 1974, but had been pushed into the background in the latter part of 1975 and in 1976 by issues stemming from the PLO's involvement in the Lebanese war.

In the autumn of 1974, four PLO member organizations had formed a coalition to fight what they perceived as the willingness of al-Fatḥ, the largest and leading group in the PLO (as well as of al-Sā'iqa and the Popular Democratic Front for the Liberation of Palestine, PDFLP, led by Nā'if Ḥawātima) to accept in principle a political settlement to the ME conflict and to the Palestinian question. The coalition called itself "The Front of Palestinian Forces Rejecting Capitulationist Settlements [to the conflict]", or more popularly, "the Rejection Front." It consisted of the Popular Front for the Liberation of Palestine (PFLP, led by Dr George Ḥabash), the Popular Front for the Liberation of Palestine-General Command (PFLP-GC, led by Aḥmad Jibrīl), the pro-Iraqi Arab Liberation Front (ALF, then led by Dr 'Abd al-Wahhāb al-Kayyālī), and the Popular Struggle Front (PSF, led by Dr Samīr Ghosha). It was supported most strongly by Libya, Iraq and by some of the other Arab governments whose interest in a rapid political solution to the problem of the territories occupied in June 1967 was not as acute as those which had actually suffered territorial losses.

The Rejection Front argued that under the prevailing global and regional balance of power, a political settlement would of necessity involve territorial and other concessions such as no Palestinian had the right to make. The only legitimate way to regain Palestine, it maintained, was through armed struggle. It demanded organizational changes in the PLO calculated to increase its strength in the Palestinian National Council (PNC) in relation to al-Fath. To avoid taking part in what they described as the PLO leadership's drift towards a political settlement, the Rejectionists suspended their participation in the Executive Committee (EC) in the autumn of 1974. The EC is the PLO's highest executive body and is responsible for carrying out the resolutions and recommendations adopted by the quasi-parliamentary PNC, its highest policy-making institution. The Rejectionists also suspended their participation in the Palestinian Central Council (CC), a smaller forum of PNC members authorized to lay down policies on issues of crucial and immediate importance between regular PNC sessions.

However, the Rejectionist groups did not withdraw from the PNC itself. Anxious to avoid having its authority and power challenged, the Fatḥ-dominated EC continuously delayed reconvening the PNC, despite the repeated and constitutionally well-founded calls by the Rejectionists to do so. [In the PLO Fundamental Statute (*al-niẓām al-asāsī*) of 1964, the PNC's term of office was set at three years. Originally, it was to meet once a year; but following a 1968 amendment, once every six months. The fourth PNC had been formed in 1971 and had last convened in June 1974 (for the 12th PNC session held since its establishment in 1964). The term of office of the fourth PNC had expired in July 1974. Nevertheless, a new (fifth) PNC was neither formed nor convened until March 1977.]

In late 1976 and early 1977, the PLO leadership came under pressure from Arab countries (notably Egypt and Saudi Arabia) to reconvene the PNC in the expectation that its resolutions would be helpful to the "political process." There were also Syrian pressures on the PLO to enlarge the membership of the PNC and to change the balance of power—to Syria's advantage—by adding a large number of delegates who were not members of any one of the PLO's constituent fidā'ī organizations. Syria's intention was to weaken al-Fatḥ's hold on the PNC, so as to prevent a censure of Syria's role in Lebanon during the war; to obtain a tacit legitimization of the Syrian presence there after the war's termination; to ensure the rehabilitation of al-Sā'iqa; and to secure PLO co-operation in implementing the Cairo agreement in Lebanon (see section on the PLO's relations with Syria). It should be noted that the PNC is not an elected body: its delegates are selected by a committee, dominated in fact by the incumbent EC. The selection involves a complicated bargaining process. Hence it was possible for Syria to use its influence to try and change the PNC's size and composition.

When the selection committee completed its work in February 1977, the membership of the fifth PNC was indeed larger than before—289 instead of 187. Nonetheless, al-Fatḥ managed to preserve its dominance.

The newly formed PNC met in Cairo from 12–20 March 1977 for its thirteenth session. Compared to the 12 to 18 preceding months, the session was characterized by the shifts it reflected in PLO alliances and internal conflicts. The open conflict which, during the Lebanese war, had ranged al-Sā'iqa against the rest of the Palestinian organizations (except Aḥmad Jibrīl's faction of the PFLP-GC; see below) had gradually subsided, leaving the Rejection Front again pitted against the PLO leadership. Nevertheless, the March session achieved a degree of understanding between the two sides, most significantly on the issue of the setting up of a Palestinian state in a part of Palestine.

That understanding was facilitated by the Rejection Front's general weakening, following its heavy losses in Lebanon, and the relative decline in the influence that its main backers—Libya and Iraq—had in the region (see essay on inter-Arab relations). The PLO leadership, for its part, was willing to see the PNC session adopt a resolution tough enough to be accepted by the majority of Rejectionist delegates. In exchange, the PLO leadership under Yāsir 'Arafāt was given considerable latitude to negotiate on behalf of the PLO. This was apparent in the PNC's Political Declaration, unopposed by most of the Rejectionist delegates, which avoided an explicit rejection of PLO participation in Geneva. (For text of the Declaration, see Appendix 1).

It is likely that some form of advance agreement had been reached between al-Fath and the Rejection Front leaders on the final PNC political statement. Some reports went so far as to assert that an advance agreement had been reached "on all aspects of the PNC session, as well as on all the important organizational issues in the PLO."[1] They suggested that a political working document, signed by all groups and factions, was to be presented for the PNC's approval. A "secret circular" on the PNC session (ascribed to al-Fath), claimed that the Rejection Front and al-Fath leaders had reached an agreement on the Political Declaration in order to allow the

PLO to emerge from the session with a united Palestinian stand. To make this possible, every faction was asked to put its reservations to any of the Declaration's articles in writing to the PNC chairman so that they would be on record.[2]

Eventually, from among the c. 70 Rejection Front delegates at the PNC (namely, members of the "rejectionist" organizations as well as "independents" affiliated with them), only the 12 PFLP representatives and the one delegate of the pro-Iraqi faction of the PFLP-GC voted against the Political Declaration submitted by the PLO leadership; the others either supported the Declaration or abstained. Voting results were 194 for, 13 against and 82 abstentions.

The PFLP dropped its opposition to the establishment of a Palestinian state in only a part of the territory of Palestine, on the understanding that this would be the first step towards "total liberation." Yet it did not change its positions on two other, no less central, issues. It continued to reject PLO participation in the Geneva conference, arguing that the establishment of a state even in a part of Palestine must be brought about through military rather than political means; and it reaffirmed its opposition to PLO ties with Jordan, or even a dialogue with it in any form. The PFLP voted against the Political Declaration because it contained no clear rejection of PLO participation in Geneva and failed to make any reference to the PLO's hostile position regarding Jordan. Furthermore, it criticized the Declaration for its failure to denounce the contacts PLO officers had held with Israeli and pro-Zionist personalities and groups. (For the internal debate over this issue, see below.) The pro-Iraqi faction of the PFLP-GC criticized the Declaration for the same reasons as did the PFLP, but objected to one additional point: its failure to denounce the Syrian intervention in Lebanon.

The nine ALF delegates voted for the Declaration, along with the seven delegates of Ahmad Jibrīl's faction of the PFLP-GC. Both groups also joined the new EC (formed on 20 March 1977) and the new CC (first convened on 1 May 1977), having boycotted those institutions since the autumn of 1974. The ALF made a point of stressing that its renewed participation in the EC did not reflect a change in its rejectionist attitude; did not contradict its being a member of the Rejection Front; and was, moreover, the "result of consultations held with comrades in the Rejectionist Front who had given their approval."[3] The ALF justified its support of the Political Declaration and its joining the EC and the CC by referring to its "realization of the gravity of the conspiracy menacing the Palestine Revolution" and stressing its "concern for toughening the stands confronting this conspiracy, foiling the imperialist onslaught and thwarting the plans for the capitulationist settlement . . ., all of which would only be achieved through national unity."[4]

An additional ALF consideration was probably that avenues for the pursuit of its political objectives were wider inside the PLO's governing bodies than outside them. The fact that the PNC had not met for three years may have convinced the ALF that participation in that body alone could not give it much of a say in PLO decision-making. A similar consideration seems to have motivated the PFLP's decision to join the new CC though, unlike the ALF, it did not join the new EC.

The Rejectionist organizations' interest in furthering their relations with the main PLO leadership was to some extent related to the situation in Lebanon. Rejectionist groups were at that time engaged intermittently in armed clashes with Syrian, or pro-Syrian Palestinian, forces. In February 1977, for example, the PLO leadership helped prevent a Syrian onslaught on the PFLP, which was believed to be imminent. To this motivation should be added an interest in strengthening the overall authority of the PLO leadership in the face of Syrian pressures.

The co-operation stopped short, however, of significantly increasing Yāsir 'Arafāt's personal authority. A proposal to the effect that 'Arafāt should be authorized to appoint the members of the new EC failed to receive the required two-thirds of PNC votes, due to Rejection Front opposition. The new EC was therefore elected by the PNC, as had been the practice hitherto. (For the EC's composition, see Appendix 2).

In 1977, as in previous years, internal developments in the PLO were determined not only by the evolution of the ME conflict, but also by developments in two other spheres: the PLO's relations with individual Arab states, and the state of inter-Arab affairs. The on-going debate in 1977 within the PLO on the issue of its relations with Syria exemplifies the former; the manifestations of the Syrian-Iraqi dispute in conflicts within the PLO, which had started earlier but continued in 1977, serves as an example of the latter.

During the civil war in Lebanon, al-Sā'iqa (being in effect, a branch of the Syrian Ba'th party) fought alongside the Syrian forces against other Palestinian organizations. Consequently, it was for all intents and purposes disqualified by the PLO as an authentic Palestinian organization. Its leader, Zuhayr Muḥsin (who was also a member of the Syrian Ba'th National Command), was dismissed by the PLO leadership from his post as the head of the PLO Military Department.

Following the end of the war in October 1976, PLO-Sā'iqa tensions gradually subsided, though the continued use of al-Sā'iqa by Syria to promote the latter's objectives in Lebanon led to violent clashes between Fatḥ and Sā'iqa forces in December 1976 in Tripoli, Beirut and southern Lebanon. A reconciliation with al-Sā'iqa was virtually forced on al-Fatḥ by Syria at a CC meeting in Damascus in December 1976, following which Zuhayr Muhsin was reinstated in his PLO post. Al-Sā'iqa's rehabilitation was informally sanctioned by its participation in the March 1977 PNC session.

Yet that development did not terminate the basic dispute between al-Fath and al-Sā'iqa, which forms part of the perennial debate within the PLO concerning its relations with Arab states. Al-Fatḥ has constantly striven to assert the distinctiveness of the Palestinian identity, and to secure maximum independence of Palestinian decision-making and freedom of action, even though some of its leading personalities have acknowledged the existence of special ties with Syria. For instance, Hānī al-Hasan, one of 'Arafāt's associates, was quoted as saying, in July 1977 that Syrian-Palestinian relations were becoming closer "thanks to the historic relationships within the Syrian group of nations, of which Palestine is the southern part."[5]

Al-Sā'iqa, on the other hand, rejected the idea of a distinctive Palestinian nationalism, regarding Palestinian and Syrian interests as identical. In an interview given while the PNC was in session, Zuhayr Muhsin told a Dutch paper: "Between Jordanians, Palestinians, Syrians and Lebanese there are no differences. We are part of one people, the Arab nation . . . Only for political reasons do we subscribe to our Palestinian identity."

Muhsin went on to explain that, in his view, Palestinian nationalism was a matter of expediency: "It is, in fact, a national interest for the Arabs to encourage the existence of the Palestinians *vis-à-vis* Zionism. Yes, the existence of a separate Palestinian identity is being kept up only for tactical reasons. The establishment of a Palestinian state is a new means to continue the struggle against Israel and for Arab unity." Regarding PLO-Syrian relations, Muḥsin's view was that "the Palestinians must work together with Syria in the first place, and only after that with the other Arab states. Only Syria can play an important part in the fight against Israel."[6] Syria's supporters in the PLO also came out in favour of the Syrian position on PLO-Jordanian relations (see below).

In 1977, as in 1976, the Syrian-Iraqi conflict was acted out by proxy by Palestinian organizations in Lebanon. The split that took place in the PFLP-GC was also a reflection of Syrian-Iraqi rivalry. The ideological roots of that split go back to the 12th PNC session in June 1974, and to the question of the PFLP-GC's position on the ten-point political programme adopted by it. The secretary-general of the PFLP-GC, Aḥmad Jibrīl, supported the programme, while the organization's Central Council opposed it. Jibrīl's opponents, led by Abū al-'Abbās, later succeeded in making the organization join the Rejection Front.

Following the Syrian invasion of Lebanon, the internal dispute developed into an open split. Jibrīl's opponents announced his expulsion from the organization, on the ground of his having co-operated with the Syrians.[7] Jibrīl retorted by denouncing Abū al-'Abbās and his supporters as Iraqi Intelligence Service agents.[8] Meanwhile, the two factions, each claiming to be the real PFLP-GC, clashed with each other—first in the refugee camps in the Beirut area, then in southern Lebanon. An attempted reconciliation by PLO leaders late in November 1976 failed to put a stop to the fighting.

On 23 April 1977, an agreement was reached through 'Arafāt's intervention. Ahmad Jibrīl's faction was to retain the name PFLP-GC, whereas their rivals were given the name Palestine Liberation Front (PLF). (This had been the name of Aḥmad Jibrīl's original organization until 1967.) By assigning the two factions two different names, the PLO in effect recognized the existence of two separate organizations. Jibrīl and his group were ousted from the Rejection Front, while Abū al-'Abbās' group was admitted as a member.[9]

The Syrian-Iraqi conflict was also at the roots of the clashes that occurred during the period under review between al-Sā'iqa (sometimes aided by Syrian troops of the Arab Deterrent Force, as well as by Aḥmad Jibrīl's group) and Rejection Front units in southern Lebanon. Because of Israel's objection to the proximity of Syrian soldiers to her borders, Syria made use of pro-Syrian Palestinians to achieve her objectives in these areas. Al-Sā'iqa was also used to establish an indirect Syrian presence inside the refugee camps in Lebanon. For this purpose, al-Sā'iqa's membership was considerably expanded. This led to some tension with al-Fatḥ in December 1976.

THE PLO IN THE ARAB-ISRAELI CONFLICT: POSITIONS, STRATEGIES AND TACTICS

Palestinian operations against Israeli targets were at an ebb during the greater part of the period reviewed. This was caused partly by operational difficulties resulting from the PLO's situation in Lebanon, and partly by its efforts to start a dialogue with the US, which would be facilitated by projecting an image of moderation and respectability. In March 1977, the PNC did admittedly resolve "to continue the armed struggle" and "to escalate the armed struggle in the occupied territory."[10] The change of government in Israel was also followed by increased terrorist activity (mainly the placing of explosives in public places, such as open air markets, shopping centres or bus stations). Yet the main PLO activity during the period was in the political-diplomatic field.

The attitudes on the ME conflict of the dominant elements in al-Fatḥ and the PLO in general (led by Yāsir 'Arafāt) were the outcome of the following principal considerations. On the one hand, it was argued that a serious attempt to reach a political solution to the ME conflict was likely to be made. In this case, the need for participation was increasingly acknowledged, on the premise that once the PLO was recognized as an equal party, it would be able either to play an active role in a settlement which satisfied its aspirations, or torpedo any solution which did not. The advocates of participation in the political process therefore found it advisable for the PLO to project an image of moderation in the conflict to facilitate its widest possible acceptance as an equal party to the settlement. The countervailing argument was that the success of the political process, even the mere reconvening of the

Geneva conference, was far from certain. Ideological concessions made in order to facilitate the PLO's acceptance as an equal party might thus very well prove valueless. Hence the reluctance on the part of the PLO leaders to endorse modifications in their basic stance on crucial issues, such as the recognition of Israel's right to exist.

The PLO's desire to secure a role in the political process, while simultaneously adhering to its established ideological position, resulted in the emergence of the "phased strategy" concept. The PLO would consent to the setting up of a Palestinian state in the West Bank and the Gaza Strip, though not in exchange for recognition of, or for ending the war with, Israel, and only as a first step towards the eventual realization of the ultimate "strategic" goal—the "liberation of Palestine" in its entirety. Similarly, the PLO demanded the right to attend the Geneva conference (or any other international forum dealing with the ME conflict), but not on the basis of Security Council Resolution 242.[11]

The "phased struggle" concept envisaged first, the establishment of a West Bank/Gaza Strip state alongside Israel in pre-1967 boundaries; second, another compression of Israel's size to boundaries laid down in the 1947 Partition Plan; and third, the establishment of a democratic, secular Palestinian state to replace Israel and to extend to the entire area of Palestine.[12]

The adherents of this concept distinguished between tactical or temporary (*marḥalī*) as opposed to strategic or permanent (*dā'im*) solutions to the Palestine problem: "The permanent solution can be realized only through the establishment of a democratic Palestinian state where Muslims, Christians and Jews will live in equality. The permanent peace is [an outcome of] the establishment of that state. This is a long-term goal. The temporary peace rests on the establishment of a Palestinian state on a part of our land."[13]

The assessment that the PLO might gain by taking its place in the political process, as well as the fear that its interests might otherwise be ignored by the Arab states and the great powers, were already reflected in the June 1974 session of the PNC. At that time, the PNC called for the setting up of an "independent fighting national authority on any part of the Palestinian territory to be liberated." The choice of the term "authority" (*sulta*), meaning a temporary or provisional body (the word "state" would have implied permanency), was to convey its purely tactical nature. This was made clear by the rest of the resolution, which stated that after its establishment "the Palestinian national authority will work to unify the confrontation states in order to complete the liberation of all the Palestinian territory . . . All liberating steps will be taken for the purpose of the continuation of the implementation of the PLO's strategy to set up a democratic Palestinian state."

Justification of the "tactical goal" by the PNC had met with strong opposition in 1974. By 1977, however, there already existed a wide acceptance not merely of an "authority", but of a *state* in the West Bank and Gaza. On 14 December 1976, the CC approved a policy favouring the setting up of a Palestinian state under the PLO in the two areas named.[14] In March 1977, the PNC resolved "to continue the struggle to regain the national rights of our people, in particular their rights of return, self-determination and establishing an independent national *state* on their national soil."[15] That decision did not define the territorial extent of the future state, but PLO spokesmen explained that the reference was to the West Bank and Gaza Strip. A territorial and aerial corridor under Palestinian sovereignty was to connect the two areas. An official territorial definition had been avoided to prevent the possible impression that the resolution was tantamount to relinquishing the "strategic" goal, namely the total liberation of Palestine.

The PNC's Political Declaration made no reference to the democratic, secular

Palestinian state to replace Israel. Yet its less publicized (but no less binding) Final Statement read: "The PNC asserts that it adheres to the PLO strategic objective to liberate Palestine . . . so that it will become a home for the Palestinian people where the democratic state of Palestine will be established."[16]

The main argument raised by Rejectionist spokesmen against the West Bank/Gaza state was that its establishment through the political process would necessarily imply recognition of Israel. PLO leaders therefore made every effort to assert that even after a Palestinian state was established on parts of Palestine, the PLO would not recognize Israel, and would use the new state to continue its struggle against her.[17] In March 1977, the PNC itself declared its decision to work for the liberation of all the occupied Arab areas without any conciliation (*sulḥ*) with, or recognition of, Israel.[18] Nevertheless, PLO leaders implied on occasions that the establishment of a Palestinian state on parts of Palestine might be followed by a period of truce between that state and Israel, though not by recognition of the latter.[19]

A document published by a Lebanese daily—described as the PLO's settlement plan submitted to the US—also implied that following the establishment of the Palestinian state, the struggle to realize Palestinian objectives would continue, even though peaceful, rather than military, means would then be employed. The state's armaments might possibly be limited in proportion to its defensive needs, thus excluding ground-to-ground and ground-to-air missile systems. No reference was made in the document to PLO recognition of Israel, but termination of PLO guerrilla warfare was offered in exchange for Israel's recognition of the PLO.[20]

Another development in PLO attitudes was the formal proclamation of its demand to participate in the Geneva conference, though on its own terms. Formerly the PLO had not shown readiness to participate in the conference. Instead, it had sought to transfer the political struggle from Geneva to the UN. In the winter of 1976–77, a shift of emphasis occurred. Rather than reject the idea of PLO participation in the conference, it now rejected Security Council Resolution 242 (and 338) as the basis for its participation. Once these were amended, or replaced, it would insist on its right to participate. Accordingly, in Point 15 of the March 1977 Political Declaration, the PNC "confirms its wish for the PLO's right to participate independently and on equal footing in all the conferences and international forums concerned with the Palestinian issue and the Arab-Zionist conflict, with a view to achieve our inalienable national rights as approved by the UN General Assembly in 1974, namely in Resolution 3236." The same shift was reflected in the PNC's abstention, in 1977, from any negative reference to the Geneva conference—in contrast with its resolutions of June 1974.

The PLO's rejection of 242 was based on the argument that the resolution referred to the problems of the territories occupied in 1967 only, and was irrelevant to the results of the 1948 war, and to the overall problems of the Palestinians which were created at that time. Consequently, Resolution 242 interpreted the issue of the Palestinians as a refugee problem only, rather than as a political one of a people demanding self-determination and statehood. Another argument was that participation at Geneva on the basis of Resolution 242 would signify recognition both of Israel's right to exist and of her pre-1967 boundaries.

Consequently, the PLO demanded that the UN General Assembly Resolution 3236 of 22 November 1974 be made the basis of the Geneva conference instead. Resolution 3236 reaffirmed the "inalienable rights" of the Palestinian people "in Palestine" (i.e. without a reference to a territorial delimitation), listing them as the right to self-determination, national independence and sovereignty, as well as the right of Palestinians "to return to their homes and property from which they have been displaced."

Furthermore, PLO spokesmen made its participation in Geneva conditional on an invitation being addressed to the PLO and signed by both the US and the USSR as co-chairmen of the conference; on PLO attendance from the beginning; on its participation in *all* the conference activities; and on the Palestine question being made a separate item on the agenda.[21] These demands reflected the PLO's suspicion that either an overall or a partial settlement might be reached by other participants at the expense of its own interests.

A possible sequel to the PLO's demand to be invited to Geneva and to establish a West Bank/Gaza state might have been a decision to form a government-in-exile or a provisional government, to represent the organization at Geneva and to prepare for the establishment of the Palestinian state. The PLO was indeed urged to set up such a government by Arab and other countries—in particular by President Sādāt and the Egyptian media.[22] According to Arab press reports, the prolonged discussions held in PLO bodies on this issue late in 1976 and early in 1977 eventually led to a decision in principle to form a provisional government, the remaining question being one of appropriate timing.[23]

Fārūq Qaddūmī was quoted as saying that "we have begun the process of creating a Palestinian entity in exile."[24] But the PNC, which had been widely expected to take the matter up,[25] did not adopt a resolution on this issue. By the end of the period reviewed, no decision to set up a government had been taken. Presumably, the PLO preferred the establishment of a provisional government on even a limited area of "liberated territory", than a government-in-exile. "It is not yet time to establish such a government", said Fārūq Qaddūmī. "We need a land on which to build our economic, political, military and cultural institutions."[26]

Dr 'Isām Sartāwī (member of al-Fatḥ's Revolutionary Council) submitted a statement of PLO positions on the Palestinian problem on 26 January 1977 to the Austrian Chancellor, Bruno Kreisky, in his capacity as chairman of the Socialist International fact-finding mission on the Middle East. The document called for the establishment of a Palestinian state in the West Bank, the Gaza Strip, and the areas of Ḥamma and 'Awja; it asserted that "between the future sovereign state of Palestine and the state of Israel, a non-belligerent status could be established." The document also spoke of a "complete state of peace" between the two states, conditional mainly on Israel's recognition, and implementation, of the right of the Palestinian refugees to return to their homes or to receive compensation.[27]

This document could, on the face of it, have signalled a significant development. It could have been viewed as implying PLO recognition of Israel's right to statehood within frontiers smaller than her pre-1967 lines, yet larger than those of the 1947 Partition Plan. It was, however, emphatically disavowed by senior PLO officials. Fārūq Qaddūmī stated that Sartāwī "absolutely did not submit a document to Kreisky, nor did he speak on behalf of the PLO. He merely submitted a letter containing ideas in his personal capacity."[28] There was no way of knowing what weight to attach to Sartāwī's "personal" ideas.

Prior to the ordinary session of PNC in March 1977, it was expected that the Council would amend the Palestinian National Covenant (drawn up in 1964, amended in 1968). There were several Palestinian statements to that effect[29]—(even though the Covenant itself states that it can only be amended by an extraordinary PNC session).[30] In the event, rather than amend the Covenant, the PNC demonstratively reaffirmed its authority in the Preamble of the Political Declaration (see Appendix 1). Apparently the PLO's position was that the validity of the unamended Covenant had to be preserved until after a Palestinian state had been set up. A document published by a Lebanese daily and said to be the PLO's settlement plan (see above) indeed implied that the PLO's attitude to the Covenant might change after the Palestinians' "elementary rights" had been granted and a Palestinian state established.[31]

A series of 12 meetings on the Palestinian question was held in France in the second half of 1976 and the first quarter of 1977 between PLO members and representatives of the Israel Council for Israeli-Palestinian Peace, through the mediation of French Jewish and Left-wing figures. The PLO team at the meetings—which, according to press reports, were initiated by the PLO—was headed by 'Isām Sartāwī, and consisted only of Fatḥ members. Sartāwī's Israeli counterpart was Professor Mattityahu Peled (a General in the reserves).

The very fact that the meetings were being held produced heated debate within the PLO. Criticism was voiced by pro-Syrian personalities such as Zuhayr Muḥsin, by Fatḥ leaders like Fārūq Qaddūmī, and by Rejectionist spokesmen, all contending that the meetings were not authorized by competent PLO bodies, and were in violation of the principles of the Palestinian National Covenant. The pro-Syrians further criticized the Fatḥ members who conducted the meetings for having taken such an important step without co-ordination with the Arab governments. The PDFLP's denunciation of the meeting was based on the argument that the Israel Council for Israeli-Palestinian Peace was a pro-Zionist group.

Members of the PLO team at the meetings insisted that they had been authorized by Yāsir 'Arafāt. But the head of the PLO Political Department, Fārūq Qaddūmī (a member of the PLO Executive Committee) denied that the EC had authorized the meetings. According to him, they were "a result of individual initiative and have absolutely nothing to do with the PLO or its representatives."[32] It appears likely that if 'Arafāt did indeed give his consent to the meetings, he did so in a personal, non-official capacity.

The main outcome of the meetings was a joint statement issued in Paris on 1 January 1977 and signed by Peled and, according to him, by a PLO representative (probably Sartāwī). In the published statement, the PLO affirmed that its policy was one of "striving for a peaceful solution of the Israeli-Palestinian conflict on the basis of the mutual acceptance of the principles of freedom, sovereignty and security for both peoples."[33] Furthermore, the PLO considered the principles of the manifesto of the Israel Council for Israeli-Palestinian Peace "as an adequate basis for solving the Israeli-Palestinian conflict."[34] (The Council's manifesto of February 1976 upheld the Zionist character of Israel and supported her pre-1967 boundaries.)

Again, as in the case of Sartāwī's letter to Kreisky, the PLO's Political Department denied that any responsible or authorized member of the PLO had signed the Paris statement. Fārūq Qaddūmī stated that the PLO had not permitted any of its members to take part in the meetings, and that reports of a PLO representative having signed an agreement with Peled were groundless.[35] In March, the opponents of the meetings had the upper hand in the PNC's deliberations on the issue. The PNC affirmed the significance of establishing relations and co-ordinating with those "progressive and democratic Jewish forces inside and outside the occupied Homeland" that are struggling against Zionism as a doctrine and in practice."[36] Similarly, the PNC plenary approved the recommendation of its Committee for Affairs of the Occupied Homeland, that "the PNC affirm the importance of supporting progressive and democratic forces that are *hostile to Zionism*."[37] Following the PNC session, the Israeli team discontinued the meetings presumably because, in the light of the PNC resolutions, their continuation would have been interpreted in Israel as readiness on its part to be characterized as anti-Zionist.

An evaluation of the PLO's motives in undertaking these meetings is made difficult by the contradictory attitudes towards them within the PLO itself. It is not unlikely that some PLO personalities sought a channel of communication with leading Israeli figures, and believed that those attending the meetings (who included persons with notable records in the army, in government or in party politics) would be able to provide it. It is also likely that the PLO sought to exploit the meetings to gain legitimacy in the eyes of American Jewry, and to facilitate a dialogue between leading American Jews and its own representatives. The contacts Peled and Sartāwī had with members of the American Jewish community in the US in November and December 1976 would indicate such an intention. At the same time, the meetings may have been intended by the PLO to weaken the Israeli government's position (at home and abroad) rejecting recognition of, and a dialogue with, the PLO. A document published in a Kuwaiti paper and described as a "secret Fath circular", stated that the meetings were indeed held in order "to deepen internal contradictions" in Israel, with the effect of "destroying the Zionist existence from within."[38]

The view that the meetings formed part of the PLO's political warfare against Israel gained validity from reports that the team which supervised the Paris meetings was also in charge of the PLO's counter-immigration campaign to encourage emigration of oriental Jews from Israel back to their Arab countries of origin. This campaign was led by Maḥmūd 'Abbās (code-named Abū Māzin), a member of al-Fatḥ's Central Committee, who specialized in evaluating internal weaknesses of the "Israeli-Zionist society" and in devising ways to increase them.[39] He had worked to persuade Arab governments to offer restoration of citizenship to former Jewish nationals who had emigrated to Israel and were now willing to return. The PNC's Committee for Affairs of the Occupied Homeland had appealed to all Arab governments to co-operate in this scheme.[40] Between 1975 and 1977, most Arab states accepted the arrangement—Jordan, Libya and Lebanon being the exceptions. Saudi Arabia was said to have undertaken to cover the necessary expenses involved.

By mid-1977, however, the quantitative achievement of the campaign was limited: Morocco was the only country to attract more than a few individuals. According to the PLO's own figures of February 1977, no more than 4,500 families (i.e. presumably some 20,000 persons) emigrated there from Israel.[41] Other Arab press accounts published later set that figure at no more than 1,000 persons.[42]

The campaign drew criticism from Palestinian and other Arab commentators. They argued that if large numbers of oriental Jews left Israel, the severity of the internal contradictions between oriental and occidental Jews would diminish; that mass immigration of additional occidental Jews would become possible; that the Jews returning to Arab countries would form a "fifth column [of] agents and spies ready to work for Israel"; that they would exploit the economies of their Arab host countries and "drink their oil"; and finally, that since the Jews were "evil by nature", they would corrupt the countries to which they returned.[43]

Following the PNC's decision to promote contacts with anti-Zionist forces in Israel, the PLO intensified its communications with the Communist Party (Rakah). Members of the PLO and of Rakah had had occasional informal talks in the past, but the first official and public joint meeting took place in Prague on 3-4 May 1977. The PLO delegation was headed by Mājid Abū Sharāra, member of al-Fatḥ's Revolutionary Council; and the Rakah delegation by Emil Tu'ma, member of its Political Bureau.

The Prague meeting drew fire from several directions. Iraq and pro-Iraqi Palestinian groups argued that Rakah was a Zionist party, which formed part of the "racial expansionist Zionist entity's structure.".[44] Pro-Syrian elements in the PLO (in keeping with their negation of independent Palestinian action) criticized the meeting because it had not been sanctioned by the major Arab governments.

Supporters of the meeting (Maḥmūd 'Abbās, Nā'if Ḥawātima and others) defended Rakah as an anti-Zionist party, and maintained that the meeting was approved by the PLO's EC. Along with other Arab observers, they also claimed that it would likely help Rakah in its campaign to win over Arab voters from the Israel Council for Israeli-Palestinian Peace in the imminent Israeli elections.[45] According to the PDFLP's weekly, helping Rakah's election campaign in this way was one of the purposes of the Prague meeting.[46]

The establishment of formal PLO-Rakah contacts should also be seen against the background in 1976 and 1977 of a fundamental change in the PLO's view of Israeli Arabs and their role in the Palestinian struggle against Israel. In the past, the dominant PLO view had been that Arab citizens of Israel could not be relied upon in that struggle, and that efforts should concentrate on enlisting public opinion as well as recruiting individual activists in the territories occupied in June 1967.

The rise of Palestinian nationalism among Israeli Arabs—dramatically demonstrated by the events of the "Day of the Land" (30 March 1976)—gradually changed that view. The new trend was reflected in the recommendations adopted by the PNC in March 1977, which offered guidelines for a campaign designed to involve Israeli Arab citizens in the struggle against Israel. These guidelines referred to PLO support for Israeli Arabs in economic, educational and cultural affairs; envisaged PLO help in preventing the emigration of Arabs from Israel and the sale of Arab land to Jews; provided for a more significant share in the manning of PLO bodies to be granted to Israeli Arabs; and called for greater PLO attention to Israeli Arab affairs.[47]

THE PLO'S RELATIONS WITH ARAB GOVERNMENTS

RELATIONS WITH SYRIA

The end of the Lebanese civil war in October 1976 saved the PLO from military collapse and enabled it to maintain some political freedom of action, even under the conditions of Syrian occupation. Al-Fath's military organization was damaged but not broken, and the PLO retained its hold over the internal affairs of the refugee camps. Yet the end of the war did not put an end to Syria's efforts to bring the PLO under her control. In resisting those efforts, the PLO found succour with Saudi Arabia and, to a lesser extent, with Egypt and Kuwait (the members, alongside Syria, of the quadripartite ceasefire committee established in Lebanon under the Riyadh resolutions).

Eventually, a PLO-Syrian understanding on a *modus vivendi* in Lebanon began to emerge, and was formalized in the Shtūrā Agreement of 25 July 1977 (see below). It resulted from the gradually developing convergence of their points of view on issues related to the Geneva conference and to developments in southern Lebanon—a convergence which, in the summer of 1977, brought the two sides closer together than they had been since the Syrians first turned against the PLO early in 1976.

In the interval, however, PLO-Syrian relations were dominated by tensions created by President Asad's concept of the Palestinian issue in general, and of the role of the PLO in particular. That concept rejected separate Palestinian nationalism and nationhood: the Palestinians should form part of a larger political unit embracing Syria, Lebanon and Jordan as well as Palestine. The struggle for Palestinian territory was thus not viewed by Syria as the exclusive concern of the

Palestinians or specifically of the PLO. The latter should therefore not act independently in the conflict against Israel or over other issues, but should co-ordinate its steps with its Arab allies—first and foremost with Syria.

Syrian pressures on the PLO operated along three lines: to obtain PLO acceptance of a Lebanese solution on Syria's terms; to push through organizational changes in the PLO to increase Syrian influence in it (see above); and to induce the PLO to consent to a dialogue with Jordan.

In Lebanon, Syrian objectives were:

1. Restriction of Palestinian autonomy, which had been based on the PLO's military control of the refugee camps and adjacent areas. For this purpose, the number of armed Palestinians in the camps was to be limited; heavy arms were to be "collected" from the camps; the Arab Deterrent Force (ADF) and later the reconstituted Lebanese armed forces were to be given the right to enter the camps at their discretion.

2. Formation of a Syrian-controlled PLO military presence in southern Lebanon, absorbing Palestinian units and heavy arms formerly at large in the Lebanese cities.

3. Elimination of the pro-Iraqi elements of the Palestinian Rejection Front either by pro-Syrian Palestinian or Syrian forces.

Syria tried to achieve the first two objectives by pressuring the PLO into implementing the 1969 Cairo Agreement and its appendices which, according to her interpretation, regulate the Palestinian presence in Lebanon. (For the various interpretations of the Agreement, see chapter on Lebanon.)

Prior to Syria's intervention in Lebanon, the PLO felt that the 1969 Agreement had become irrelevant. Since its signature, the PLO had grown numerically and increased its military strength; its stature had been enhanced by being recognized by the Arab states as the sole representative of the Palestinians; the authority of the Lebanese government had become shaky; and the PLO had effectively allied itself with local political movements in Lebanon. The PLO thus felt justified in claiming exclusive authority over the refugee camps and over Palestinian activities elsewhere in Lebanon. It insisted that Palestinians must have the right to carry on their struggle against Israel unhindered, with freedom to move and carry arms anywhere in the country, as well as to maintain a military presence and store heavy weapons at any point of their choosing in southern Lebanon.

Under Syrian pressures from January 1976, PLO leaders declared their acceptance of the Cairo Agreement as the basis of a Lebanese settlement but dragged their feet whenever the question of its implementation came up. Following the Syrian offensive of September and October 1976, the Cairo Agreement became—ironically enough—an asset to the PLO. In the face of Syrian pressures and the Maronite attempts to rid Lebanon of the Palestinians altogether, the Cairo Agreement—expressly reaffirmed by the Riyadh and Cairo conferences of October 1976—symbolized the all-Arab legitimization of the Palestinian presence in Lebanon. When Christian-Lebanese spokesmen declared in May 1977 that the Cairo Agreement was null and void because the Palestinians had refused to implement it, and that their presence in Lebanon had therefore become illegal, the PLO asserted emphatically and repeatedly that, according to its own interpretation, it had in fact implemented most clauses of the Agreement. But this clearly contradicted Syria's understanding of the Agreement, according to which PLO military movements outside the refugee camps would have been restricted; its heavy arms handed over to the Syrian-dominated ADF, and its armed presence in the camps sharply reduced. ADF units would also have been entitled to enter the refugee camps.

These disagreements came to a head in February 1977 when Syria brought stronger pressures to bear on the PLO. These included closure of PLO bases and training camps, and harassment of PLO members in Syria; Syrian military concentrations around Beirut refugee camps, accompanied by threats to break into the camps; and closure of the "clandestine" PLO radio station in Lebanon (Voice of Palestine). Syrian military measures in Beirut were rescinded apparently as a result of Saudi intervention, and following a conciliatory message from 'Arafāt to Asad on 15 February 1977. Saudi Arabia, in co-operation with Egypt and Kuwait, rescued the PLO from the application of the Syrian interpretation by creating a majority against it in the quadripartite ceasefire committee. Accordingly, in March 1977, the committee refused to endorse the Syrian interpretation.[48]

Meanwhile, a PLO-Syrian understanding on Lebanon was beginning to evolve against the background of developments in the south, which both considered unfavourable. The transfer of Palestinian forces from northern and central Lebanon to the south (especially to the "Fatahland" area) in late 1976 and early 1977, and the emergence of the Maronite-Israeli alliance (see survey of Lebanon), led to hostilities between the PLO and their Lebanese allies on the one hand, and the forces of the Christian enclaves on the other, with each side trying to enlarge the territory under its control. A successful Christian offensive in March 1977 widened the area accessible from Israel by means of the "Good Fence", and threatened to close the territorial gap separating two of its three enclaves, thereby cutting off some of the besieging PLO forces.

Early in April, the PLO launched a major counter-offensive designed to regain ground lost in March. Syria—likewise opposed to the Christian advance and interested in the transfer of further PLO forces to the south—permitted the passage of large Palestinian reinforcements into the south through Syrian-held areas. Furthermore, Syria supported the counter-offensive through the participation of al-Sā'iqa units, and by letting the PLO use heavy artillery emplacements in the Syrian-held area. The PLO regained the ground it had lost in March, as well as an important town (al-Khiyām) surrendered in February. Syria did not encourage further PLO advances, on the assumption that they would provoke Israeli counter-action. Instead it sought to persuade the PLO that the termination of the Israeli-Maronite alliance and the closure of the "Good Fence" would be made easier by implementing the Cairo Agreement throughout Lebanon. This would lead to the re-establishment of the Lebanese government's authority in the south.

The accelerated preparations for reconvening the Geneva conference also augmented the PLO's interest in reaching an accord with Syria. By ending the dispute with Syria in Lebanon, PLO leaders expected to enhance their prospects of making a mark in the ME conflict. A PLO-Syrian understanding on implementing the Cairo Agreement was now worked out, and formalized on 25 July 1977 in the PLO-Syrian-Lebanese agreement of Shtūrā (for its main provisions, see chapter on Lebanon).

Under the agreement (whose text was kept secret, but which was partially reported in the Lebanese press), the PLO recognized the sovereignty of the Lebanese government over Lebanese territory and its inhabitants in a way which could imply the restoration of Lebanese sovereignty over the refugee camps. The PLO also accepted the principle that only Palestinians who had already been domiciled in Lebanon when the Cairo Agreement was signed in 1969 had a right to reside there now. These two aspects of the Shtūrā agreement—if translated into practice—constituted a setback for the PLO.

On the other hand, the agreement entrusted security within the refugee camps to the PLO's military police force; did not place numerical limits on the number of PLO supporters allowed to carry light arms in the camps, or on the quantities of light arms held there (which had been a controversial issue); and laid down that Lebanese army troops would only enter the camps in co-ordination with the PLO military command. The agreement did not prohibit PLO operations against Israel from southern Lebanon, though it called for the withdrawal of all (or almost all) PLO units to a distance of 15 kms from the Israeli border in the western and central sectors of south Lebanon, and for their concentration in the eastern sector, the 'Arqūb area ("Fatḥland").[49]

A full evaluation of the PLO's gains and losses in Lebanon following the Shtūrā Agreement can only be attempted after its details are fully disclosed and the extent of its implementation becomes known.

In the period between the Riyadh and Cairo conferences and the 13th PNC session (i.e. October 1976 till March 1977), PLO opposition to Syria's line in Lebanon caused the latter to try and bring about changes within the PLO in her favour. In particular, Syria brought pressure to bear for the enlargement of the PNC (hitherto numbering 187 members) by as many as 200 pro-Syrian and pro-Jordanian delegates, who would not belong to any of the PLO's constituent fidā'ī organizations (see above). This step was meant to end, or at least to weaken, al-Fatḥ's dominant position in the PNC. There was even a call by the Syrian government daily for the new PNC to exclude fidā'ī representatives altogether.[50]

The Syrian government also threatened to set up an alternative Palestinian leadership more co-operative towards itself.[51] Addressing the PLO CC convening in Damascus, President Asad presumably wished to convey the desirability of a change in the PLO leadership when he pointed to the importance of the CC's "making a wider and more comprehensive assessment and analysis of what has taken place on the Lebanese scene, in order to draw the conclusions needed and to absorb them in a way which will *ensure that the Palestinian revolution does not slip into any mistakes*."[52] Zuhayr Muḥsin, head of al-Sā'iqa (as usual putting the Syrian line more forcefully than official Syrian spokesmen), explicitly called for the removal of the existing PLO leadership.[53] To back her demands, Syria applied military pressure against the PLO in Beirut in February 1977, and took steps against PLO installations and personnel in Syria, as mentioned above.

Syria listed the major decisions which it expected the PNC's March 1977 session to take. These included acceptance of a Palestinian state on any "liberated" part of Palestine; normalization of PLO-Jordanian relations; the formation of a "strategic PLO-Syrian front"[54] (implying close political co-ordination between the two); re-examination of the Palestinian National Covenant and the PLO's Fundamental Statute (*al-niẓām al-asāsī*); and the exercise of self-criticism (presumably leading to changes in leadership).[55] Syria underlined these expectations by allowing the party organ to quote from an internal party publication, *al-Munāḍil*, the contents of which were not usually made public.

Although the PNC was enlarged, al-Fatḥ succeeded in maintaining its dominant position, and Syria's expectations were expressly met only with regard to the first of the above points. Yet it would be correct to say that, by avoiding any reference in its resolutions and statements to Syria's role in Lebanon and to Jordan's record *vis-à-vis* the PLO, the PNC was in fact displaying some accommodation towards Syria. Had any official reference been made, it could in the circumstances only have been hostile. Even so, one-third of the delegates did not vote for the pro-Syrian PNC chairman candidate, Khālid al-Fāhūm (172 delegates voted for him, 69 against, 21 abstained, and 27 were absent).

RELATIONS WITH SAUDI ARABIA

Lacking an independent territorial base and substantial military and financial resources of its own, the PLO has traditionally sought to use inter-Arab discords to keep its freedom of action from being encroached upon by any single Arab government. Syria's drive to consolidate its influence over the PLO led the latter to seek a counterweight by improving relations with Saudi Arabia. Other considerations on the part of the PLO included Saudi influence in the US, and the fact that Riyadh was its largest single financial backer.

Saudi Arabia's interests were to prevent the PLO from becoming a Syrian satellite; to keep it from drawing too close to the Soviet Union; to foster al-Fatḥ so as to neutralize radical elements within the PLO liable to foment revolutionary agitation in the ME in general, and in Saudi Arabia in particular; and to draw the PLO into the political process and into a dialogue with the US.

As a result, PLO-Saudi ties improved considerably during the period under review, despite substantial ideological opposition within the PLO. The visit by a Fath delegation to Saudi Arabia in January 1977 was a major step in that development. The leading figure in the delegation was Salāh Khalaf (code-named Abū Ayyād), who had been in command of military operations during the Lebanese war. Relative to the overall ideological stance of al-Fatḥ, he was widely considered to represent the "leftist" or radical trend. His participation in the delegation constituted a significant PLO gesture towards Saudi Arabia—a country usually associated in Palestinian ideology with "imperialism and reaction."

Saudi Arabia apparently urged the PLO to demonstrate moderation in the PNC session, and to adopt positive resolutions on PLO relations with Jordan and on the formation of a government-in-exile. It also helped the PLO to withstand Syrian pressure in Lebanon in March 1977 by refusing (along with Egypt and Kuwait) to approve the Syrian-backed interpretation of the Cairo Agreement. Saudi Arabia supported PLO efforts to enhance its political standing in the West Bank through financial aid to West Bank municipalities. Saudi Arabia was also instrumental in the indirect PLO-US contacts held during the period under review, aimed at bringing about American recognition of the PLO.

RELATIONS WITH EGYPT

Like Saudi Arabia, Egypt shared the PLO's interest in blocking Syria's attempts to bring the organization under her control. Following the crisis produced by the conclusion of the second Sinai disengagement agreement of September 1975, PLO-Egyptian relations improved in 1976, mirroring the deterioration of PLO-Syrian relations in Lebanon. As early as January 1976, Egypt demonstrated her support of the PLO's stand in Lebanon by dispatching Palestinian units stationed in Egypt to fight alongside the PLO.[56]

Egypt initiated a move to admit Palestine, represented by the PLO, as a full member of the Arab League in September 1976. (Hitherto, the PLO had the status of "non-voting member.") The Egyptian step was intended, *inter alia*, to consolidate Yāsir 'Arafāt's leadership in the face of Syrian military and political pressures. President Sādāt said at the time that the preservation of 'Arafāt's leadership was a principle of Egyptian policy.[57] In Lebanon, Egypt joined Saudi Arabia and Kuwait in preventing the approval of the Syrian-backed interpretation of the Cairo Agreement (see above). On 18 June 1977, following closer PLO-Egyptian contacts, a Joint Co-ordination Committee was formed (a similar committee being established simultaneously between the PLO and Syria). Nonetheless, this Egyptian support did not eliminate PLO suspicions concerning Cairo's willingness to stand by its public commitments to the PLO; neither did it resolve disagreements on central issues related to the ME conflict.

One such issue was the PLO-Jordanian link. In order to facilitate a rapid reconvening of the Geneva conference and to encourage a US-PLO dialogue, Egypt proposed the establishment of formal PLO-Jordanian ties prior to the conference and, in January 1977, advocated a formal link between Jordan and any future Palestinian state. The PLO regarded the Egyptian proposal as contradicting Egypt's public endorsement of the principle of Palestinian independence. Egypt hinted that the idea was merely an expedient and did not necessarily reflect its genuine attitude on the Palestinian issue. Vice-President Mubārak, for example, was quoted as stating that President Sādāt's intention was to prevent Israel from blocking the Geneva conference on the pretext of opposition to a Palestinian state.[58] Nevertheless, the PLO reacted coolly to the idea. Its spokesmen insisted that only the Palestinian people themselves could decide on their future relations with any Arab state, and would do so only after their sovereignty was finally established.[59]

Another measure Egypt urged on the PLO was to form a Palestinian government-in-exile, an idea she had advocated since 1972. Egypt argued that the creation of such a government would lead to wider international recognition of the PLO; would weaken Israel's argument against its recognition; and would pave the way for the establishment of a Palestinian state.[60] The Egyptian initiative over full PLO membership in the Arab League was presumably connected with this idea. At the time of writing, however, the PLO had neither agreed to formal ties with Jordan prior to the Geneva conference, nor had it formed a government-in-exile.

Another area of disagreement was over the Palestinian National Covenant: Sādāt had reportedly assured the US Secretary of State that the PNC would amend the Covenant; but when the PNC convened, it did nothing of the kind.

RELATIONS WITH JORDAN

Under Syrian pressure—and with Saudi and Egyptian encouragement—the CC meeting on 23 January 1977 instructed the EC to open a dialogue with Jordan. This was followed by a PLO-Jordanian working meeting (22-25 February 1977) in Amman, and by talks between 'Arafāt and King Ḥusayn in Cairo (8 March 1977).

The dialogue met with fierce opposition from Rejectionist organizations and from Nā'if Ḥawātima's PDFLP. On the other hand, pro-Syrian personalities in the PLO tried to justify the talks. Zuhayr Muḥsin, for instance, re-emphasized Jordan's role in the conflict with Israel: "Jordan is a confrontation state in addition to her special and historical responsibility to the West Bank and the Palestinian problem." He thus gave support to Jordan's claim for an active role in resolving the Palestinian question, exceeding the one assigned to her by the 1974 Rabat resolutions. Muhsin went so far as to say that the PLO leadership rather than Jordan had been responsible for the armed conflict in 1970 and 1971[61]—a statement tantamount to heresy when compared with the accepted PLO version of those events. Another way of justifying the dialogue was that it would put the PLO in a better position to play a more direct role in West Bank affairs.[62]

In actual fact, however, the PLO-Jordan meetings did nothing whatsoever to reduce the fundamental conflict of interests between them—being locked in what both considered as a struggle for survival. In King Ḥusayn's view, Jordan was itself a Palestinian state: an independent state in the West Bank was certain to bring an end to his dynasty by drawing the political loyalty of the Palestinian majority in Jordan away from the Hashemites. The PLO, on the other hand, insisted on a completely independent Palestinian state. Furthermore, Article Two of the Palestinian National Covenant was worded in such a way that "Palestine" could be meant to include the East Bank. Many Palestinian nationalists considered the overthrow of the Hashemite monarchy as a primary Palestinian goal.

In the period under discussion, Jordan worked systematically to reassert her claim and her position on the West Bank (see chapter on Jordan). The PLO, for its part, endeavoured to contain Jordan's influence. It tried, for example, to make West Bank municipalities less dependent on Jordan by providing financial aid from other Arab states. Since funds contributed by Saudi Arabia and the Gulf Emirates had to be transferred through Jordan, however, they could not reach the municipalities without Jordanian consent.

Jordan's opening position in the dialogue was to favour the concept of a federation of both banks, as originally outlined in 1972 in King Husayn's "United Arab Kingdom Plan."[63] The PLO's opening position, as laid down in the resolution approving the dialogue, was that PLO-Jordanian relations must be based on the Rabat resolutions. Under their terms, the PLO argued, Jordan was obliged to facilitate the resumption of the PLO's political and military presence in Jordan; to co-operate with the PLO in extending economic support to the population of the occupied territories; and to permit fidā'ī activity against Israel across her borders. Typical of the PLO's rejection of Jordan's renewed "United Arab Kingdom Plan" was Fārūq Qaddūmi's assertion that "there must be an independent Palestinian state with an independent parliament and independent government, as well as its own independent army and independent diplomatic representation."[64]

The meetings resulted in some minor gestures, such as the release of several PLO members from Jordanian jails (February 1977). Reports of Jordanian consent to the resumption of fidā'ī presence in Jordan were denied by PLO leaders;[65] nor were they borne out by subsequent developments. In all substantive respects, the meetings left the situation exactly as it had been before.

RELATIONS WITH IRAQ AND LIBYA

The Syrian-Egyptian *rapprochement* set into motion at the Riyadh conference in October 1976 weakened the relative positions of Iraq and Libya, and consequently their impact on PLO affairs. Both countries continued to offer financial and military support to Palestinian organizations, particularly to those belonging to the Rejection Front. Yet on the whole the ability of those two "rejection" states to influence the PLO had decreased.

Unable to employ her own regular military units in Lebanon after the Riyadh and Cairo conferences, Iraq continued her campaign against Syria there by proxy—mainly by means of the pro-Iraqi faction headed by Abū al-'Abbās (see above). Throughout the first half of 1977, this group was engaged in violent skirmishes with pro-Syrian groups, such as Ahmad Jibrīl's faction and al-Sā'iqa. The PLO leadership, anxious to preserve some measure of unity after the Lebanese civil war, made repeated efforts to bring about a Syrian-Iraqi reconciliation, hoping thereby to end the inter-factional strife within its own ranks as well.

'Arafāt also engaged in mediating in the Egyptian-Libyan dispute. On the other hand, statements made during visits to Libya by the pro-Syrian rejectionist, Aḥmad Jibrīl, seemed to suggest some Palestinian involvement in a renewed Libyan-Syrian *rapprochement*.[66]

THE PLO AND THE USSR

The termination of the PLO-Syrian military confrontation in Lebanon helped to improve PLO-Soviet relations, which had been strained by what the PLO considered as an ambivalent Soviet position on the Syrian-PLO conflict, and by Soviet reluctance to back the PLO all the way. Al-Fath's Salāh Khalaf—who ran the

PLO's military operation in Lebanon during the war—supposedly alleged that it was Moscow which gave the order to Syria to intervene militarily against the Palestinian resistance in Lebanon.[67]

After the war, the PLO sought increased Soviet military aid to re-equip its units. It also tried to enlist Soviet help to secure for the PLO the status of an independent and equal party to the ME settlement by exerting pressure on the US and, through her, on Israel. Marxist and other anti-Saudi elements in the PLO were also interested in closer relations with the USSR as a counterweight to Saudi influence on the organization.

However there were also conflicts of interests between the PLO and the USSR on several issues. The most important of these were Soviet recognition of Israel's right to exist; Soviet support of Resolution 242; the PLO's relations with Saudi Arabia; and Jewish emigration from the USSR to Israel. Another major issue of disagreement was the manner and timing of PLO participation at Geneva. While supporting independent PLO participation and firmly rejecting the idea of a PLO-Jordanian tie, the USSR was understood in late 1976 to have considered postponing full PLO participation until the second stage of the Geneva conference. Thus at first, the PLO would only participate in the work of sub-committees. The Soviet concept was intended to circumvent the procedural difficulties likely to be raised by Israel. Another Soviet proposal was to reconvene the peace conference without the PLO, but to place the question of PLO participation on the agenda at its first session.

A speech by Brezhnev on 21 March 1977, in which he outlined a ME settlement plan without mentioning the PLO by name, was closely followed by the visit of a high-level PLO delegation to Moscow (4-8 April 1977). The composition of the delegation—which included leading members of al-Fatḥ, al-Sā'iqa, the PDFLP, ALF, and PFLP-GC (Jibrīl's faction)—reflected PLO concern over Soviet positions. The marked publicity given to the visit by the Soviet side reflected Moscow's interest in promoting Soviet-PLO relations to a significantly higher level of political co-operation. The visit was highlighted by the first official meeting ever of 'Arafāt with Brezhnev. Moscow stated its commitment to Palestinian people's rights, including the right to establish an "independent Palestinian state" (earlier Soviet references having been only to a "Palestinian state"). Despite the evident desire to play up the importance of the visit, the USSR did not commit itself to supporting PLO participation at Geneva from the start and on an equal footing with the other parties.

The PLO evinced anxiety over intimations of Moscow's intentions to resume diplomatic relations with Israel before the end of 1977 (the declared Soviet position being that a resumption of diplomatic relations was conditional upon Israeli withdrawal to pre-1967 lines). There was also concern over Soviet advocacy of PLO recognition of Israel. Nevertheless, advocates of PLO-Soviet co-operation continued to maintain that the PLO should make efforts to co-ordinate its position with the USSR. Some believed that the USSR was in actual fact committed to the right of the PLO to participate in Geneva on equal footing from the start.[68]

THE PLO AND THE US

The most important development in PLO-US relations in the period under review was the emergence of the Carter Administration's position on the Palestinian problem and the components it identified in a ME settlement. These included a "Homeland" for the Palestinians and a role for the PLO (see essay on "The US and the Middle East").

Until the advent of the Carter Administration, the PLO had usually considered itself to be struggling against the US and its Middle Eastern interests and allies, both in Lebanon and in Israel. Consequently, open animosity and deep mistrust had characterized PLO attitudes to Washington. After January 1977, official US statements met with mixed reactions in the PLO. Whereas Yāsir 'Arafāt stated on several occasions that the US position on the Palestinian issue had changed for the better, other leaders of al-Fatḥ, as well as of the other PLO member organizations, belittled its significance. The latter argued that even if some change had occurred, it could not bridge the fundamental and conflicting interests of the PLO and the US. "In spite of the American recognition of our rights", said Fārūq Qaddūmī, "which in itself is a step forward, we will never change our principled, permanent anti-imperialist position." He added:

> The US has participated on all levels in the creation and sustenance of Israel. Israel is an American strategic need, for the purpose of impeding the Arab liberation movement and of draining off the Arab nation's resources, through wars and conflicts and permanent pre-occupation [with Israel], thus retarding [Arab] economic advancement.[69]

This perception of US policies was doubtlessly influenced by the US making its recognition of the PLO conditional on the latter's recognition of Israel, and on the acceptance of Security Council Resolutions 242 and 338.

Official and unequivocal American recognition of the PLO was indeed a major goal of its leaders. But even before achieving that, direct contact with the US was seen as advantageous to the PLO: for one thing, it would be detrimental to Israel's international standing; for another, the PLO would no longer have to rely on any Arab state as go-between in transmitting its views to the US. Thus, while on the whole maintaining an anti-American posture, the PLO began actively to seek official American recognition late in 1976. To promote this objective, the PLO pursued several courses simultaneously. It attempted to obtain official status for PLO delegations and representatives in the US, and to maintain unofficial contacts with US officials, intended to lead eventually to full recognition. It also sought to improve the PLO's standing in US public opinion, and to project an image of moderation in the Western media generally. Finally, through its meetings with American Jewish leaders, the PLO sought to discredit the US position of non-recognition. In pursuing these tactics, Sabri Jiryīs and 'Isam Sartāwī, two PLO officers, registered their intention to open an information office in Washington with the US Department of Justice on 18 November 1976. They were turned down on the basis of incorrect information found in Jiryīs' visa application. Jiryīs was ordered to leave the US, but tried to return as soon as the Carter Administration took office. However, his visa application was again turned down—this time by Secretary Vance personally on 8 February 1977. Following the initial Jiryīs-Sartāwī setback, Qaddūmī stated that he knew neither who the two men were, nor the purpose of their mission.[70] Most probably, these attempts were approved and encouraged by Yāsir 'Arafāt without consulting the EC[71] (as was apparently also the case with the meetings conducted in Paris by Sartāwī and other PLO officers with members of the Israel Council for Israeli-Palestinian Peace; see above).

The US was reported to have first initiated indirect communication with the PLO in 1975. Contacts became more frequent during the civil war in Lebanon, mainly in connection with the safety of American civilians and diplomats there. On wider ME issues, the US contacted the PLO mainly through Egyptian, Saudi or European intermediaries; but also through direct but informal means. For example, on 24 June 1977 in London, ex-Senator William Scranton met with Bāsil 'Aql, a leading PLO representative in the West. In addition, there was the Cairo meeting between a

PLO officer and three US senators on 11 November 1976; Carter's public greeting of the PLO's UN representative at a UN reception on 3 March 1977; and the meeting between a US congressional delegation and 'Arafāt in Cairo on 12 July 1977.

Nevertheless, throughout the period under review, the US kept its commitment not to recognize the PLO officially as long as it did not recognize Israel's right to exist. Right up to the eve of the PNC session in March 1977, the US had entertained hopes that the PLO would moderate its position on this point. President Carter's statement, in which he employed the term "Homeland" for the Palestinians, was issued while the PNC was in session, and was apparently intended to encourage such moderation. It was received with satisfaction by 'Arafāt, who expressed his personal confidence in President Carter (17 March 1977). However, the statement was criticized by others in the PLO for failing to mention exactly where that "Homeland" should be established.

As described above, the PNC explicitly rejected Resolutions 242 and 338. On 21 March 1977, the State Department declared that the PNC resolutions "did not contribute" to the solution of the ME problem. Up to July 1977, US-PLO relations remained deadlocked—with the PLO unwilling to meet the conditions set by Washington for its official recognition, and with the US unwilling to drop those conditions.

NOTES

1. *Al-Ra'y al-'Āmm*, Kuwait; 14 March 1977.
2. *Al-Siyāsa*, Kuwait; 26 April 1977.
3. Iraqi News Agency (INA), 21 March—British Broadcasting Corporation, Summary of World Broadcasts, the ME and Africa (BBC), 23 March 1977. INA, 1 April—BBC, 2 April 1977.
4. INA, 21 March—BBC, 23 March 1977.
5. *Monday Morning*, Beirut; 17 July 1977.
6. *Trouw*, Amsterdam; 31 March 1977.
7. INA, 7 October—BBC, 9 October 1976. *Al-Nahār*, Beirut; 9 October 1976.
8. *Al-Ba'th*, Damascus; 10 October 1976.
9. INA, 14 May—BBC, 16 May 1977.
10. Points 2 and 3 of the PNC's Political Declaration (see Appendix 1).
11. Point 15 of the Political Declaration (see Appendix 1).
12. Fārūq Qaddūmī (head of the PLO Political Department, and Secretary of al-Fath's Central Committee), *Newsweek*, 7 March 1977.
13. Fārūq Qaddūmī, *Shu'ūn Filastīniyya*, 67 (June 1977), p. 40. Similarly: *al-Mustaqbal*, Paris; 2 July 1977. Nā'if Ḥawātima, *al-Ra'y al-'Āmm*, 19 March 1977.
14. *Al-Ahrām*, Cairo; 18 December 1976.
15. Point 11 of the Political Declaration (see Appendix 1).
16. R Cairo, Voice of Palestine, 21 March—Daily Report (DR), 22 March 1977.
17. Fārūq Qaddūmī in *al-Nahār*, 27 February 1977. R Cairo, Voice of Palestine, 11 May—DR, 11 May 1977. *Al-Mustaqbal*, 2 July 1977. Khālid Fāhūm, *al-Ra'y al-'Āmm*, 27 May 1977, p. 10.
18. Point 9 in the Political Declaration (see Appendix 1).
19. Mahmūd 'Abbās (alias Abū Māzin), *al-Anwār*, Beirut; 5 January 1977. 'Arafāt's interview with the *Washington Post*, 28 May 1977.
20. *Al-Nahār*, 31 July 1977.
21. *Al-Ahrām*, 26 February 1977. Qaddūmī in *Monday Morning*, Beirut; 2 May 1977. Also, *Shu'ūn Filastīniyya*, June 1977, p. 41.
22. *Al-Ahrām*, 8 and 10 December 1976.
23. *Al-Ahrām*, 26 November 1976. Qatar News Agency (*QNA*) 4 January—DR, 4 January 1977 *Al-Siyāsa*, 2 February 1977. *Akhir Sā'a*, Cairo; 2 March and 6 July 1977.
24. Voice of Palestine (Clandestine broadcast from Lebanon), 2 June—BBC, 4 June 1977.
25. See *Ākhir Sā'a*, 16 March 1977.
26. INA, 1 June—BBC, 3 June 1977. Also: Voice of Palestine (Clandestine) 30 December 1976—DR, 3 January 1977.

27. *Arbeiter-Zeitung*, Vienna; 13 February—DR, 14 February 1977.
28. *Al-Ahrām*, 26 February—DR, 1 March 1977.
29. See Nabil Sha'ath, *Washington Post*, 18 November 1977.
30. See Article 29 of the 1964 version of the Covenant, and Article 33 of the 1968 version.
31. *Al-Nahār*, 31 July 1977.
32. *Al-Ahrām*, 26 February 1977.
33. *Ha-Olam ha-Zeh*, Tel Aviv; 5 January 1977.
34. *Ibid.*
35. Saudi News Agency (*SNA*), 2 January—DR, 4 January 1977.
36. Point 14 of the 15-point Political Declaration (see Appendix 1).
37. Point 4 of the Committee's Recommendations, R Cairo, Voice of Palestine, 22 March—BBC, 25 March 1977.
38. Quoted in *al-Siyāsa*, 29 April—DR, 9 May 1977.
39. Maḥmūd 'Abbās expounded the theoretical basis of the counter-immigration campaign and the methods of its implementation in his book *Zionism, Beginning and End*, published by al-Fatḥ and prefaced by 'Arafāt (Abū Mazīn, *al-sahyūniyya, bidāya wa-nihāya*, al-Fatḥ, Maktab al-Ta'bi'a wa-l-Tanẓīm, 1 January 1976).
40. Point 5 of the Committee's Recommendations. R Cairo, Voice of Palestine, 22 March—BBC, 25 March 1977.
41. Qaddūmī in al-Ahrām, 26 February—DR, 1 March 1977.
42. *Al-Hawādith*, Beirut; 22 April 1977. *Al-Sayyād*, Beirut; 26 May 1977.
43. Dr As'ad 'Abd al-Rahmān, "The Return of the Jewish Arabs," *Shu'un Filastīniyya* (July, August, September 1976), pp. 99-109. Similar Palestinian and Syrian criticism in *al-Ba'th*, Damascus; 23 May 1977.
44. R Baghdad, 11 May—DR, 17 May 1977. INA, 12 May—DR, 12 May 1977.
45. *Al-Mustaqbal*, 28 May 1977.
46. *Al-Ḥurriyya*, Beirut; 16 May 1977.
47. Recommendations of the Committee for Affairs of the Occupied Homeland, approved by the PNC, R Cairo, Voice of Palestine, 22 March—BBC, 25 March 1977; and recommendations of the Cultural Committee approved by the PNC, R Cairo, Voice of Palestine, 28 March—BBC, 31 March 1977.
48. *Al-Sayyād*, 7 April 1977. *Al-Nahār*, 25 May 1977.
49. *Al-Usbū al-'Arabī*, Beirut; 25 July, 1 August 1977.
50. *Al-Ba'th*, 24 November 1976.
51. *Al-Hadaf*, Kuwait; 16 December 1976.
52. Syrian Arab News Agency (SANA), 14 December—DR, 14 December 1976. Emphasis added.
53. SANA, 28 January—DR, 28 January 1977.
54. *Al-Talā'i* (organ of al-Sā'iqa), 15 March 1977.
55. Quoted in *al-Ba'th*, 1 February 1977.
56. The 1,000 troops of the 'Ayn Jālūt Brigade of the Palestine Liberation Army.
57. *Al-Ahrām*, 25 September 1976.
58. *Al-Mustaqbal*, 30 April 1977.
59. Khālid al-Ḥasan, quoted by Middle East News Agency (MENA), 2 January—DR, 3 January 1977. Maḥmud 'Abbās in *al-Anwār*, 5 January 1977.
60. Editorials in *al-Ahrām*, 10 October; 8, 10, 11 December 1976.
61. *Al-Ra'y*, Jordan; 31 January 1977. At the time the statement was made, Syria was pressing for changes in the PLO leadership.
62. Khālid al-Fahūm in *al-Akhabār*, Jordan; 23 February 1977. Also see *al-Thawra*, Damascus; 22 January 1977.
63. Statement by Jordanian Prime Minister in *al-Quds*, 23 June 1977.
64. *Al-Ahrām*, 26 February—DR, 1 March 1977.
65. Khālid al-Ḥasan quoted by QNA, 1 February—DR, 3 February 1977. Khālid al-Fāhūm in *al-Waṭan*, Kuwait; 21 April 1977.
66. R Tripoli, Voice of the Arab Homeland, 4 May—DR, 5 May 1977.
67. R Beirut, 26 September—DR, 27 September 1976.
68. See Zuhayr Muḥsin in *al-Usbū' al-'Arabī*, 9 May 1977.
69. *Shu'ūn Filastīniyya*, June 1977.
70. *Le Monde*, Paris; 21-22 November 1976.
71. MENA, 30 November 1976—DR, 1 December 1976.

Appendix 1: The PNC's Political Declaration and the Draft Political Programme presented to the PNC by the Rejection Front*

The 15-point Political Declaration adopted by the PNC, 20 March 1977 (MENA, 20 March 1977—BBC 22 March 1977).

Proceeding from the Palestine National Charter and the previous national council's resolutions; considering the decisions and political gains achieved by the PLO at the Arab and international levels during the period following the 12th session of the PNC; after studying and debating the latest developments in the Palestine issue; and stressing support for the Palestinian national struggle in the Arab and international forums, the PNC affirms the following:

1. The PNC affirms that the Palestine issue is the essence and the root of the Arab-Zionist conflict. Security Council Resolution 242 ignores the Palestinian people and their firm rights. The PNC therefore confirms its rejection of this resolution, and rejects negotiations at the Arab and international levels based on this Resolution.

2. The PNC affirms the stand of the PLO in its determination to continue the armed struggle, and its concomitant forms of political and mass struggle, to achieve our inalienable national rights.

3. The PNC affirms that the struggle, in all its military, political and popular forms, in the occupied territory constitutes the central link in its programme of struggle. On this basis, the PLO will strive to escalate the armed struggle in the occupied territory, to escalate all other concomitant forms of struggle and to give all kinds of moral support to the masses of our people in the occupied territory in

The 14-point draft Political Programme presented to the 13th PNC by the Front of Palestinian Forces Rejecting Capitulationist Settlements, 14 March 1977 (al-Thawrah Mustamirrah, Vol 1, No 9 [March 1977] pp. *8-9).*

1. The PNC affirms the PLO's position rejecting Security Council Resolution 242 and all the other resolutions leading to recognition of the Zionist entity and of its right to exist, and [the PNC also affirms] the PLO's refusal to interact on the basis of those resolutions in any Arab or international conference, including the Geneva conference.

3. The PNC affirms the PLO's complete adherence to the Palestinian National Covenant as the fundamental document guiding our struggle, and to the armed struggle as a fundamental strategy for that struggle, with all the concomitant forms of struggle.

6. The PNC affirms that the PLO regards the struggle in the occupied territory in all its military, political and popular forms as the central link in its [the PLO's] struggles and programmes. On this basis, the PLO strives to escalate the armed struggle in the occupied territory, to escalate all of its concomitant forms of struggle, and to give all kinds of material and moral support to our people in the

* The order of the clauses in the right-hand column has been rearranged so as to allow the reader to compare the stands of the two documents on the same issues. The number of the article as it originally appeared has been given.

order to escalate the struggle and to strengthen their steadfastness to defeat and liquidate the occupation.

4. The PNC affirms the PLO's stand which rejects all types of American capitulationist settlement and all liquidationist projects. The Council affirms the determination of the PLO to abort any settlement achieved at the expense of the firm national rights of our people. The PNC calls upon the Arab nation to shoulder its pan-Arab responsibilities and to pool all its energies to confront these imperialist and Zionist plans.

5. The PNC stresses the importance and necessity of national unity, both political and military, among all the contingents of the Palestine Revolution within the framework of the PLO, because this is one of the basic conditions for victory. For this reason, it is necessary to co-ordinate national unity at all levels and in all spheres on the basis of commitment to all these resolutions, and to draw up programmes which will ensure the implementation of this.

6. The PNC affirms the right of the Palestine Revolution to be present on the soil of fraternal Lebanon within the framework of the Cairo agreement and its appendices, concluded between the PLO and the Lebanese authorities. The Council also affirms adherence to the implementation of the Cairo agreement in letter and in spirit, including the preservation of the position of the Revolution and the security of the camps. The PNC refuses to accept any interpretation of this agreement by one side only. Meanwhile it affirms its eagerness for the maintenance of the sovereignty and security of Lebanon.

occupied land in order to reinforce and strengthen our people's steadfastness in the face of occupation.

2. The PNC affirms the PLO's rejection of the political settlement submitted at the present state of our people's struggle, the more so since the nature of that settlement has become clear: it is an imperialist, Zionist, reactionary settlement, and contradictory to our people's interests and to their inalienable historic rights. The PLO therefore struggles against that settlement and in order to thwart it.

4. The PNC affirms the PLO's awareness of the importance of national unity among all the contingents of the Palestinian Revolution, and of that unity being an essential condition to victory. The PLO therefore struggles for the consolidation of that unity on all levels, on the ground of the National Covenant and this programme, and of adherence thereto.

8. The PNC affirms the right of the Palestinian Revolution to be present on the soil of fraternal Lebanon, and its right to move and operate from it in the direction of the Zionist enemy in the occupied land. The PNC affirms the PLO's rejection of any one-sided interpretation to the Cairo agreement, and the PLO's adherence to all the achievements our masses scored in recent years on all levels.

7. The PNC greets the heroic fraternal Lebanese people and affirms the PLO's eagerness for the maintenance of the territorial integrity of Lebanon, the unity of its people and its security, independence, sovereignty and Arabism. The PNC affirms its pride in the support rendered by this heroic fraternal people to the PLO, which is struggling for our people to regain their national rights to their homeland and their right to return to this homeland. The PNC strongly affirms the need to deepen and consolidate cohesion between all Lebanese nationalist forces and the Palestine Revolution.

9. The PNC affirms the complete cohesion between the Palestinian Revolution and the masses of the Arab people in Lebanon and its nationalist and progressive forces. That cohesion was baptized in blood and in joint struggles in recent years. The PNC also affirms the Revolution's [active] effort to deepen and consolidate that cohesion and to put it in defined organizational, front-like [-*jabhawi*] frameworks.

8. The PNC affirms the need to strengthen the Arab Front participating in the Palestine Revolution, and deepen cohesion with all forces participating in it in all Arab countries, as well as to escalate the joint Arab struggle and to further strengthen the Palestine Revolution in order to contend with the imperialist and Zionist designs.

11. The PNC affirms the complete cohesion of the Palestinian Revolution with the masses of the Arab people under the leadership of the Arab liberation movement in all Arab countries. These masses constitute the real strategic depth of the Revolution. The PLO struggles to advance the forms of struggle common to the different Arab national countries and to the contingents of the Arab liberation movements, and [the PLO struggles also] to arrive at a front-like [-*jabhawiyyah*] form, capable of leading the Arab people's masses in their struggles against all kinds of imperialist, Zionist, and reactionary presence in the Arab region.

9. The PNC has decided to consolidate Arab struggle and solidarity on the basis of struggle against imperialism and Zionism, to work for the liberation of all the occupied Arab areas, and to adhere to the support for the Palestine Revolution in order to regain the constant national rights of the Palestinian Arab people without any conciliation [*sulḥ*] or recognition [of Israel].

5. The PNC affirms the PLO's firm position of refusing to recognize the Zionist entity, to make conciliation with it and to negotiate with it or with any of its limbs or extentions.

10. The PNC affirms the right of the PLO to exercise its struggle responsibilities at the pan-Arab level and through any Arab land, in the interest of liberating the occupied areas.	10. The PNC affirms the Palestinian Revolution's right and liberty to carry out armed struggle against the Zionist entity through any Arab land.
11. The PNC has decided to continue the struggle to regain the national rights of our people, in particular the right of return, self-determination and establishing an independent national state on their national soil.	No parallel clause in this document.
12. The PNC affirms the significance of co-operation and solidarity with socialist, non-aligned, Islamic and African countries, and with all the national liberation movements in the world.	12. The PNC affirms that the Palestinian Revolution led by the PLO is a part of the world front opposing imperialism, and of all the extensions, organs and detachments of that front. The PNC affirms the continuation of the Palestinian revolution's efforts to strengthen the alliance and joint struggle with the members of that front: the socialist states, the national liberation movements, and democratic and labour forces in capitalist countries.
13. The PNC hails the stands and struggles of all the democratic countries and forces against Zionism as one form of racism, as well as against its aggressive practices.	No parallel clause in this document.
14. The PNC affirms the significance of establishing relations and co-ordinating with the progressive and democratic Jewish forces inside and outside the occupied homeland, since these forces are struggling against Zionism as a doctrine and in practice. The PNC calls on all states and forces who love freedom, justice and peace in the world to end all forms of assistance to and co-operation with the racist Zionist regime, and to end contacts with it and its instruments.	14. The PNC affirms the significance of relations and co-ordination with progressive Jewish forces in the world which aim at the demolishing of the racist Zionist regime. The PNC denounces the contacts made with certain Zionists, and [denounces also] the memorandum presented to [Austria's chancellor] Kreisky.

15. Taking into consideration the important achievements in the Arab and international arenas since the conclusion of the PNC's 12th session, the PNC, which has reviewed the political report submitted by the PLO, has decided the following:
   a The Council confirms its wish for the PLO's rights to participate independently and on an equal footing in all the conferences and international forums concerned with the Palestine issue and the Arab-Zionist conflict, with a view to achieving our inalienable national rights as approved by the UN General Assembly in 1974, namely in Resolution 3236.
   b The Council declares that any settlement or agreement affecting the rights of our Palestinian people made in the absence of this people will be completely null and void.

No parallel clause in this document.

No parallel clause in this document.

7. The PNC affirms the PLO's position regarding the Jordanian regime, as this position is expressed in the resolutions of the PNC's past sessions.* [The PNC also affirms] the continuation of the PLO's struggle, through its cohesion with the masses of the Arab people of Jordan and its nationalist forces, for the establishment of a nationalist democratic order in Jordan.

No parallel clause in this document.

8. The PNC affirms the need to develop and advance the organizational form in the PLO, and to consolidate collective leadership, in order to reach a real front-like [-*jabhawi*] form [of organization].**

---

* This is a reference to the fifth point in the 12th PNC's 10-point Political Programme (adopted on 9 June 1974), stating that the PLO "will struggle together with the nationalist [namely: anti-Hashemite] Jordanian forces for the setting up of a national Jordanian-Palestinian front, with the goal of establishing a national democratic government in Jordan, which will unite with the Palestinian entity to be established [in Palestine] as the outcome of the struggle", and to earlier resolutions along that line adopted in each of the PNC sessions starting with the 8th session (28 February-5 March 1971).

** Essentially meaning equal power in PLO institutions (PNC, CC) to its member organizations regardless of their numerical strength.

Appendix 2
The PLO Executive Committee (as at 20 March 1977)

Yāsir ʻArafāt	al-Fatḥ	Chairman. C-in-C of the Palestine Revolution forces
Fārūq al-Qaddūmī	al-Fatḥ	Head of Political Dept
Zuhayr Muḥsin	al-Sāʻiqa	Head of Military Dept
ʻAbd al-Muhsin Abu Maizar	Palestinian National Front —a West Bank group	Head of Pan-Arab and International Relations Dept Official spokesman of the EC; member of the Committee in charge of Dept of the Occupied Homeland*
Yāsir ʻAbd Rabbo	PDFLP	Head of Information and Culture Dept
ʻAbd al-Raḥim Aḥmad	ALF	Head of Dept of Popular Organizations
Talāl Nāji	PFLP-GC, Jibrīl's faction	Head of Higher Education Dept
†Majdī Abu Ramadān	Independent, originally from Gaza. EC member for a short period in late 1967, early 1968	Head of Social Affairs Dept; Head of Central Bureau of Student Affairs, in Egypt
†Dr Aḥmad Sidqi al-Dajāni	Independent. Formerly member of Jordanian parliament. Member of EC for short period in 1968	Chairman of Higher Council of Education and Culture
Muḥammed Zuhdi al-Nashāshībi	al-Sāʻiqa	Head of Secretariat and Administrative Affairs
Wahīd Qamḥāwī	Palestinian National Front	Chairman of the Board of the Palestinian National Fund
Ḥāmid Abū Sittah	Independent	
ʻAbd al-Jawād Sāliḥ	Palestinian National Front	
†Dr Alfred Tūbāsī	Independent, of Christian origin, from Ramallah	
†Ḥabīb Qahwajī	Independent, of Christian origin, from Fasūtah	

*The dept of Affairs of the Occupied Homeland is run by a committee headed by Ḥāmid Abū Sittah, and whose members are Sāliḥ, Tūbāsi, Qahwajī and Abū Maizar.
†Not a member of the former EC.

The West Bank and Gaza Strip

ELIE REKHESS and DAN AVIDAN

POLITICAL DEVELOPMENTS IN THE WEST BANK

Lacking an independent political power base of their own, West Bankers for the last eleven years have had no control over developments affecting the Palestinian issue either in the international or inter-Arab arena. Since the beginning of Israeli rule in the area in 1967, local political activity and opinion have been determined by the relative stature of the three main political forces directly concerned—Israel, Jordan and the PLO. Fluctuations in the relative positions of Jordan and the PLO in the West Bank have been clearly discernible and have corresponded directly with the changes in their relative strength internationally and in the Arab world.

The growing international recognition of the PLO as the sole representative of the Palestinians (which accelerated after the Arab summit conference in Rabat in October 1974) proved to be among the PLO's main assets in its competition with Jordan in 1975-76 for the allegiance of the West Bankers. The West Bank municipal election results of April 1976 clearly reflected this upsurge of PLO influence. In many towns the National blocs—representing radical candidates, PLO supporters, communists and former members of the Arab Nationalist parties—won a decisive victory. In Hebron, for example, Fahd Qawāsimī replaced Shaykh Muhammad 'Alī Ja'barī, a traditional leader known for his favourable views towards Jordan. In Nablus, Bassām Shak'a replaced Hājj Ma'zūz al-Masrī, a wealthy businessman who had close ties with the Hashemite regime. In Ramallah and Tulkarm, mayors Karīm Khalaf and Hilmī Hanūn (both staunch PLO supporters) were re-elected.

However, in the latter half of 1976, when the tide in Lebanon turned against the PLO, its position in the West Bank was considerably weakened. At the same time, Jordan's position in the Arab world was steadily enhanced, as indicated by the close relations established between Jordan and Syria.

JORDANIAN-PLO RIVALRIES

These developments provided Jordan with an opportunity to reassert its position and intensify its efforts to become more deeply involved in West Bank affairs. Having watched the performance of the new mayors, Jordan officially recognized the results of the West Bank municipal elections in late July 1976. Jordan's Minister of Information, 'Adnān Abū 'Awda, chairman of the governmental "Committee for the Occupied Territories' Affairs", congratulated the newly-elected mayors and invited them to Amman to discuss the resumption of financial aid, which Jordan had cut off shortly before the elections. The new mayors soon came to realize that committed though they were to the PLO on an ideological level, they nevertheless depended to a large extent on the financial assistance and co-operation of both the Israeli and Jordanian authorities. In fact, the necessity to cover municipal deficits prompted some local mayors to accept the invitation to visit Amman. The first to arrive was Mayor Fahd Qawāsimī in August 1976, followed late in the year by the mayors of Jericho, Bethlehem, al-Bīra, 'Anabtā, Salfīt and Bīr Zayt.

Mayor Qawāsimī's visit to Jordan occurred just when the Syrian-Palestinian confrontation in Lebanon reached its peak. To fend off PLO criticism of "collaboration" with Jordan, he stressed that the visit had no political significance and was devoted solely to solving economic and social problems. He also maintained that the financial support promised to Hebron did not imply any political or ideological commitment to Jordan. However, Jordanian aid was demonstratively withheld from those municipalities whose mayors declined to visit Amman. Thus, the question of financial assistance clearly served as a means of pressuring West Bank mayors to co-operate with Jordan.

These visits were also significant indicators of the decline in the PLO's influence in the West Bank. In this atmosphere, a number of the mayors not too firmly committed to the PLO—like those of Hebron, Qalqiliya and Jericho—made statements favouring future ties between the West Bank and Jordan on the basis of equality. They agreed that the West Bank should not be under direct Jordanian rule, but did not rule out King Ḥusayn's federation concept. Upon his return from Amman in late October 1976, Mayor Suwaytī of Jericho said that "Jordan is responsible for the West Bank"; the relationship between Jordan and the West Bank should be maintained because of "blood, language, and traditional ties with Jordan."[1] Defending his visit, Mayor Qawāsimī stressed that a distinction had to be made between ties with the Hashemite dynasty and ties with Jordan.

Jordan's pressure on the mayors was only partially successful in that the three most prominent PLO supporters—Karīm Khalaf of Ramallah, Ḥilmī Ḥanūn of Tulkarm and Bassām Shak'a of Nablus—refused to travel to Amman. Khalaf maintained in November that if the Jordanians were ready "to give us money without conditions . . . we will take it. But we cannot give our loyalty to the Jordanian regime, because our loyalty is to the PLO, to our people . . . to our country, Palestine."[2] Failing to persuade all the mayors, Jordan extended its efforts to groups other than municipalities, such as members of the Supreme Muslim Council, the Chambers of Commerce or labour associations; and to prominent pro-Jordanian personalities, such as Anwar al-Khatīb, the former Governor of Jerusalem, and Shaykh Muhammad 'Alī Ja'barī, the former mayor of Hebron.

Ja'barī visited Amman in late 1976 and the beginning of 1977, for the first time since the 1967 war. He declared that the cohesion between the Jordanian and Palestinian peoples was historically inevitable, and that the Rabat summit resolutions could not revoke those of the 1948 Jericho Congress, under which the Palestinians themselves had opted for a merger of the West Bank with Transjordan.[3] These resolutions, he added, could be altered only by the Jordanian Parliament and Government, not by the PLO or by Arab summits. He stressed that it was the people of the West Bank—not the PLO—who should have the final say on the future of the territories, and called for the establishment of a new Palestinian party: "The Party of the Land." This would not necessarily replace the PLO, but would certainly be separate from it.

Even before his trip to Amman, Ja'barī suggested that the time had come to exclude the PLO from the political process which would determine the fate of the West Bank. In October 1976, he stated that as long as there was a body called the PLO, which behaved in the way it did, there would be no solution to the Palestinian question. The PLO, he said, must be courageous and realistic enough to admit that it had failed. "The PLO is incapable of negotiating . . . [It] wrought havoc in Jordan and now it is destroying Lebanon. It would do the same here [in the West Bank] given the chance . . . The [West Bank] people should authorize Jordan to negotiate on its behalf, so that afterwards [the people] will have the opportunity for self-determination."[4]

President Sādāt's statement in late December 1976 on the necessity of establishing formal links between Jordan and a future Palestinian state, and Arab pressures on the PLO to reach some form of reconciliation with Jordan, were signs to West Bankers that Jordan was regaining its position in the Arab world as a party directly involved in determining the political fate of the Palestinians. These external developments encouraged Jordanian efforts to strengthen its influence in the West Bank, and had a marked impact on West Bank political thinking. This was reflected in two ways: by the increasing self-confidence and more explicit expressions of support for Jordan in pro-Hashemite circles; and by the evident uneasiness felt by PLO supporters.

Commenting on Sādāt's statement, the East Jerusalem daily *al-Quds* (known for its favourable views towards Jordan) defined the nature of relations between the Jordanians and the Palestinians as "a geographical, historical, social and economic fusion."[5] It maintained that the concept of a Palestinian state linked with Jordan illustrated the Kingdom's important role in peace negotiations, as it provided an answer to Israel's refusal to accept a third [Palestinian] state between her and Jordan, thus removing an obstacle to Israeli withdrawal from the West Bank. A similar view was expressed in an article published in late January 1977 by Muhammad 'Isā Dūdīn, a relative of Mustafā Dūdīn (for whose role, see below). He, too, argued that reliance on Jordan would provide the only way to terminate the Israeli occupation. "The problem since 1967 is not who will represent us [*man yumaththilunā*], but rather who will liberate us [*man yukhallisunā*] . . . The Rabat resolutions should be amended without delay to confer on the confrontation states responsibility for regaining the occupied territories . . . our fate, future and survival are dependent upon our iron-clad unity with Jordan."[6]

Another Hashemite sympathizer, Mayor Elias Freij of Bethlehem, warmly welcomed Sādāt's proposal. He expressed his belief that, following the establishment of a Palestinian state, "the majority of West Bankers will support a federation with Jordan on a basis of equality. . . . Jordan is our country, the people of Jordan are our people, and setting up such a federation will serve the interest of all."[7] Commenting on the process of reconciliation between Jordan and the PLO, Mayor Freij declared that the PLO had no choice but to "bow" to West Bank pressure for the revival of a reunion with Amman. He concluded that the establishment of close links with Jordan was "imperative."[8]

Pro-PLO leaders, on the other hand, responded uneasily to Sādāt's statement. Refraining from any open criticism of the Egyptian president, and asserting their commitment to the idea of Arab unity, they nevertheless stressed that the first priority was to establish an independent Palestinian state. Only thereafter, explained Bassām Shak'a, the mayor of Nablus, "shall we decide whether it is in our interest to unite with Jordan."[9]

An attempt by pro-PLO mayors to organize a delegation to meet UN Secretary-General Waldheim during his visit to Israel in February 1977 was reportedly frustrated by influential pro-Hashemite figures. Although this may have reflected growing pro-Jordanian influence, other events at the time proved that Jordanian gains remained limited. The city of Nablus, for instance, responded to a PLO appeal to stage a one-day protest strike on 10 February during Waldheim's visit in Israel. Furthermore, 14 local mayors, known for their PLO leanings, published a joint communiqué addressed to Waldheim in which they reasserted their loyalty to the PLO as the sole representative of the Palestinian people.

THE 13TH PALESTINIAN NATIONAL CONGRESS (PNC)

After overcoming numerous difficulties within the PLO and problems in its relations with Arab governments, the PNC convention opened in March 1977 in Cairo. The meeting had a marked effect on the population's attitude toward the

PLO, arousing high expectations in the West Bank and Gaza Strip, and was regarded as a turning point in the PLO's efforts to re-establish its inter-Arab and international standing. Even political personalities favourable to Jordan generally shared the mood of optimism expressed by West Bank PLO supporters. They, too, endorsed the view that the PLO should play a major role in any future Middle East negotiations, but urged the PNC to adopt a more realistic and flexible position to ensure the participation of Palestinians in future Arab peace efforts. The stance of the pro-Jordanians was illustrated by Mayor Freij's call to the PNC to adapt the Palestinian National Covenant to "the realities of 1977."[10]

The local press, while referring to the convention as a "fateful event", took the opportunity to express guarded criticism of the present PLO leadership and to call for enlarged West Bank and Gaza Strip representation in the PNC in order to lend greater substance and validity to its resolutions. Some PLO supporters in the West Bank shared the view that "after the tragedy in Lebanon we began to feel that the PLO no longer had a political line. We now hope that [the PNC] will give rise to new young elements that will clarify the line."[11] This indicated less than complete confidence that the PNC would, in fact, adopt resolutions likely to prove both timely and favourable to the West Bankers themselves.

Mayor Karīm Khalaf of Ramallah, representing a more radical point of view, urged the PNC to reject all US peace proposals, to increase co-operation with the Soviet Union, and to oppose a PLO-Jordanian *rapprochement*. Khalaf's insistence on increased reliance on the USSR reflected his close link to the Soviet-oriented Palestine National Front (PNF) in the West Bank.[12] The PNF sent a detailed memorandum to the PNC convention in which it strongly attacked "pro-American and reactionary Arab policy."[13] It stressed the need to end total Arab reliance on the US. In accordance with the basic guidelines of Soviet Middle East policy, the Front urged the PNC not to rule out the opportunity of PLO participation in Geneva since, in the PNF's view, political efforts carried no less weight than military struggle.

A number of West Bank mayors had been invited to attend the PNC meetings, but were not permitted to do so by the Military Government. However, all 24 West Bank mayors reportedly expressed their full support to the PLO in a memorandum. They conveyed their greetings to the convention, declared that they were rallying behind the PLO and pledged unity with its "loyal revolutionary leadership."[14] PLO sources said another petition sent by 7,000 "nationalist personalities in the occupied homeland"[15] authorized the PNC to adopt any measures that would ensure Israeli withdrawal from all territories occupied in 1967. It supported the establishment of an independent Palestinian state and called for the return of the 1948 refugees.

When the PNC meeting concluded, it was clear that 'Arafāt's leadership of the PLO had been maintained. West Bank support for the PLO was also reaffirmed, as that organization appeared to be overcoming the after-effects of the Lebanese crisis. The final PNC resolutions were enthusiastically welcomed by the West Bank press, radical and moderate alike. *Al-Quds*, for example, said the Palestinian leadership had "proved it is capable of bearing responsibility in these fateful times." It added that "the people of the occupied territories support any positive move that comes from the PNC, despite the fact that they didn't participate in its deliberations for known reasons."[16]

THE QUESTION OF EXTERNAL FUNDS

The PNC's resolutions on the West Bank and the Gaza Strip marked an increased PLO effort to strengthen its ties with the local population, as well as to offset Jordan's attempt to use economic aid as a means of leverage over the mayors. One of the resolutions stressed the importance of providing "comprehensive support for the various national institutions" in the territories, and called for the establishment of a financial fund to support "the people's steadfastness in the occupied homeland."[17] The PLO was thus endeavouring to exploit the fact that since March 1976, Jordan had failed to transfer financial assistance to West Bank municipalities. Although the newly-elected mayors who visited Jordan were promised aid, no funds had actually been transferred. The PLO was apparently anxious to supply direct assistance to the local municipalities from Arab sources not controlled by Ḥusayn and to reduce their dependence on Israeli grants.

In the spring of 1977, the Arab League adopted an aid programme to the West Bank and Gaza Strip municipalities, apparently in response to PLO proposals. Several cities in oil-rich Arab countries were twinned with West Bank and Gaza Strip towns. Following up this initiative, West Bank and Gaza Strip mayors toured Saudi Arabia, the United Arab Emirates, Kuwait, Libya and other Arab countries, where they were reportedly promised large sums of money. PLO patronage over these fund-raising visits was quite apparent: its representatives met the visiting delegations upon their arrival, arranged their schedules, and accompanied them at formal meetings. There were conflicting reports about the amount of money actually raised. Upon their return, the mayors reported that they had collected a total of c. $30m. However, as this money was deposited in banks in Amman and could not be withdrawn without Jordanian approval, Jordan frustrated the PLO plan and preserved its control over funds to the municipalities.

Israel also had every interest in preventing funds going to the municipalities if they in any way enhanced PLO influence in the area. Nevertheless, Defence Minister Ezer Weizman indicated that the new government was not opposed, in principle, to development projects in the West Bank and Gaza Strip being financed with outside aid. Finance Minister Simha Ehrlich further maintained in August that the Treasury had agreed to grant financial incentives to encourage the mobilization of funds from abroad for the improvement of municipal services in the West Bank.

PALESTINIAN ATTITUDES TO PEACE NEGOTIATIONS

The gains made by Jordan and its West Bank supporters in the first half of 1977 proved to be only of a limited and transitory nature and a product of tactical manoeuvres by Egypt, Syria and Saudi Arabia. In the long-run, however, none of these states revealed any readiness substantially to invalidate the Rabat resolutions which had designated the PLO as the sole legitimate representative of the Palestinian people.

Although West Bank support for the PLO had been eroded somewhat in late 1976 and early 1977, it began to gather strength again later in the year, paralleling the PLO's success in improving its position in the Arab world particularly after the PNC convention in March. The new trend in US policy which began to emerge in August and September 1977 also tilted the balance toward the PLO in the West Bank. The US aim—somehow to incorporate the PLO into the peace-making process—made it more difficult for the PLO's opponents to build up support.

The gathering momentum in the diplomatic process towards a Middle East settlement, as signified by the US Secretary of State's visit to the area in August, prompted an increased measure of political activity by both pro-PLO and pro-Jordanian supporters in the West Bank. Nine (pro-PLO) West Bank mayors addressed a memorandum to Secretary Vance which was said to have been delivered via the US Consulate in East Jerusalem. The mayors stated that the Arab Palestinian people were one indivisible unit and that the PLO, under Yāsir 'Arafāt's leadership was their sole legitimate representative. They maintained that any effort to disregard the PLO was pointless as well as a threat to peace; the Arab Palestinian people had the full right to establish their own independent and fully sovereign state; any attempt to impose links with any Arab or non-Arab country before the establishment of an independent Palestinian state would constitute a violation of the Palestinian people's rights. The mayors concluded that once the state had been set up, the people would be in a position to establish links with anyone they chose, in complete freedom and according to their own wishes. It is noteworthy that Mayor Freij of Bethlehem declined to sign the memorandum. At the time of Vance's visit to Israel, he was attending King Ḥusayn's Silver Jubilee ceremonies in Amman.

At a reception given by Foreign Minister Moshe Dayan in Tel Aviv on 11 August, the US Secretary of State briefly conferred with a group of prominent West Bank figures who presented him with two detailed memoranda reflecting a different line of thinking. The pro-PLO mayors had rejected Dayan's invitation to attend the reception. One memorandum was presented by 'Azīz Shiḥāda, a prominent Ramallah lawyer, neither pro-Jordanian, nor a staunch supporter of the PLO. It called for the following:

1) Israelis and Palestinians should mutually recognize the legitimate rights of both peoples to sovereign national statehood in the land which both claim as their homeland.
2) A plebiscite should be held, possibly to be conducted during an interim period—when a "Peace-Promoting Force" acceptable to both Israelis and Palestinians might be needed—to enable the people of the West Bank and the Gaza Strip "to decide freely if they want to join with Jordan" or to set up "their own democratic Palestinian state, which we believe they will. We, the Palestinians, believe that our future lies with the Arab world and particularly with Jordan", but any such link would have to be achieved "by agreement with King Ḥusayn and the Hashemite Kingdom of Jordan", and not offered as a "ready-made solution."[18]
3) A non-aggression pact between Israel and the proposed Palestinian state should be reached as a first step towards closer relations.
4) Negotiated boundaries should be established, open to free passage and free movement of citizens of both states.
5) Shared sovereignty for Jerusalem should be realized through the creation of separate municipalities with a joint central committee.

More pronounced views on a desired linkage to Jordan were presented to Secretary Vance on the same occasion by the former mayor of Hebron, Shaykh Muhammad 'Alī Ja'barī (represented by his son, Burhān), and Mustafā Dūdīn. In his memorandum, Ja'barī stated that "the shortest line for a [Middle East] solution is the line connecting us [in the West Bank] with Amman."[19] He praised the co-operation between the West Bank and Jordan which had existed ever since the Jericho Congress in 1948, stressing his conviction that most Palestinians support a "Jordanian solution" which would ensure the security of Israelis and prevent communist infiltration to the area. Mustafā Dūdīn, a Hebronite who formerly served in several Jordanian cabinets, similarly suggested to Secretary Vance that the least complicated solution to the Middle East conflict would be an immediate return of the West Bank to Jordan.

During Vance's visit to Israel, a delegation of West Bank mayors and dignitaries were in Amman to participate in King Ḥusayn Silver Jubilee ceremonies. These included among others the mayors of Bethlehem, Bayt Sāḥūr, Bīr Zayt and Silwād. The mayors of Nablus, Tulkarm, Ramallah and Hebron had rejected Ḥusayn's invitation, reportedly on instructions from the PLO.

One of the prominent participants in Ḥusayn's celebrations was Ḥusayn al-Shuyūkhī, a Hebron lawyer residing in Ramallah. Upon his return to the West Bank in mid-August, Shuyūkhī initiated an overt anti-PLO campaign. While accepting in principle that the PLO was the sole representative of the Palestinians, he distinguished between the organization as such and its leadership, headed by Yāsir 'Arafāt, which he described as dictatorial, totalitarian and corrupt. Shuyūkhī blamed 'Arafāt for making a fortune at the expense of the Palestinians and and for failing to safeguard Palestinian interests. In spite of these views, Shuyūkhī denied any contact with the United Front of the Palestinian Forces (*jabhat al-quwwāt al-filastiniyya al-muttahida*) which distributed leaflets in the West Bank in late August depicting 'Arafāt as proclaiming himself "divine."[20] The leaflets blamed 'Arafāt for making a fortune at the expense of the Palestinians and challenged him to prove that he belonged to the Arab Palestinian people.

Shuyūkhī also challenged the PLO claim to be the sole representative of the Palestinians in the West Bank and Gaza Strip, maintaining that all Palestinians, and particularly the majority residing in the territories, should be given the right to participate in determining their fate. "We are not a flock of sheep, whose fate should be determined by a man ['Arafāt] who does not even own a house in the West Bank and who has no brother in this area so that he can feel what we feel."[21] Shuyūkhī further maintained that under the present circumstances, Palestinian interests could best be advanced "by leaving it to the Arab states to act for a peaceful solution . . . I am against any Palestinian going to Geneva. Those who sit around the negotiating table should be those who participated in the war [against Israel]. An independent Palestinian delegation at Geneva would absolve the Arab states of all their responsibilities and commitments towards the Palestinian people."[22] In fact, Shuyūkhī was implicitly preparing the ground for Jordan to reassume responsibility toward the Palestinians (in particular those of the West Bank) and represent their interests at a future Geneva conference. It later became apparent that Shuyūkhī's initiative was actually backed by Jordan.

Shuyūkhī claimed that his views were widely shared by many West Bankers. However the only prominent figure to publicly support some of his ideas, though denying any formal link, was Mustafā Dūdīn, a member of the group that conferred in mid-August with Secretary Vance in Tel-Aviv. Dūdīn explicitly stated that the PLO had no rights whatsoever to represent the interests of the Palestinians in the territories. He reiterated his call for the return of the West Bank to Jordan, and disclosed in late September that a West Bank delegation was being organized for the purpose of travelling to the Arab countries to demand that responsibility for a settlement in the West Bank be restored to Jordan. However, such anti-PLO campaigns initiated in August and September 1977 failed to attract widespread public support in the West Bank, and Shuyūkhī's claim to represent a large faction of the local population remained unsubstantiated.

This failure should be interpreted in terms of the political atmosphere which prevailed in the area in late 1977. Secretary Vance's visit to the Middle East in August—followed by President Carter's meetings with the Israeli and Arab Foreign Ministers in the US in September and October—all marked the intensification of American efforts to accelerate the peace-making process and reconvene the Geneva conference. It became increasingly apparent that American policy supported the incorporation of the PLO, in one way or another, in any future peace negotiations. As lawyer 'Azīz Shihāda stated on 17 September, at a time when the PLO enjoyed international recognition as the sole representative of the Palestinians, "the West Bank could not espouse an anti-PLO stance."[23]

One of the issues raised within the framework of American diplomatic efforts in late 1977 was the question of a West Bank and Gaza Strip delegation to participate at Geneva. Israeli and American proposals that a non-PLO delegation of mayors and dignitaries should represent the Palestinians as part of a unified Arab delegation, or within the framework of a Jordanian-Palestinian delegation, aroused general criticism in the West Bank and further illustrated pro-PLO attitudes there at that time.

The local mayors adopted a unified stand, rejecting the notion of a separate West Bank and Gaza Strip delegation. They reiterated their oft-repeated argument that they were not authorized to negotiate political issues. As the mayor of Nablus remarked: "We did not receive a mandate from the people to negotiate the creation of a Palestinian state; the elections were held for the municipal councils only. We are not here as a substitute for the PLO, and we do not represent the whole of the Palestinian people."[24] In late September, the West Bank mayors addressed a memorandum to both Geneva co-chairmen, US Secretary of State Cyrus Vance and Soviet Foreign Minister Andrei Gromyko. They asserted that the PLO under 'Arafāt's leadership was the sole legitimate representative of the Palestinian people, and that any efforts to solve the issue without its participation would be fruitless.

Ḥilmī Ḥanūn, the mayor of Tulkarm, expressed a slightly different viewpoint. He said that if the PLO agreed to the inclusion of some mayors in the PLO delegation, "we would have no objection." Hanūn added that going to Geneva on the basis of UN Resolution 242 was totally unacceptable to the West Bankers as it "narrows the scope of the problem . . . We are a nation, we have the right to live as such . . . Treating us as refugees means that we shall continue to live in the area under Israeli occupation."[25]

Other West Bank voices, mainly from pro-Jordanian circles, argued that insistence upon an exclusive PLO presence in Geneva could lead to the reconvening of the peace conference with no Palestinian representation at all. In this case, they feared, Israel could possibly reach a peace agreement with the Arab states ignoring the Palestinian question altogether. To prevent this from happening, they insisted that the Palestinians should ensure their representation in Geneva—whatever the political framework proposed.

RELATIONS BETWEEN THE MILITARY GOVERNMENT AND THE LOCAL POPULATION

The municipal elections held in the West Bank in April 1976 substantially changed the relationship between Military Government authorities and the newly elected mayors. Many of the latter—PLO supporters known for their militant attitude towards the Israeli Administration—soon found themselves confronted with a difficult dilemma. They realized that in order to function efficiently and implement their election campaign promises, they had to come to terms with the Military Government. At the same time, having portrayed themselves as part of a new and militant municipal leadership, and being ideologically committed to the PLO, they had an interest in arousing unrest directed against the authorities in response to PLO appeals. The mayors' involvement in the organization of disorders in the West Bank in the summer of 1976 clearly indicated that during the period immediately following the elections, they opted for confrontation rather than search for a *modus vivendi* with the Military Government.

UNREST DUE TO THE IMPLEMENTATION OF VAT

The decision of the Israeli authorities in late June 1976 to apply Value Added Tax (VAT) to the West Bank and Gaza Strip—introduced shortly before in Israel—gave rise to disturbances and clashes between military forces and demonstrators in July and August. The local press strongly opposed the implementation of VAT, claiming that Israel not only intended to impoverish the West Bank by drawing off local capital from the area, but also to reinforce the *de facto* annexation of the territories. The mayors' efforts to mount a sustained protest was supported (mainly by means of radio appeals) by the PLO which depicted it as a show of PLO solidarity. Jordan also saw an opportunity to exploit signs of opposition to the Israeli occupation as a means of promoting its own nationalist posture in the eyes of the local population.

The disturbances revealed another important aspect of the pattern of political behaviour in the West Bank; namely, the divergence of interest between the new mayors and the leaders of the Chambers of Commerce. The latter displayed a relatively moderate attitude and demanded an end to the August 1976 strike, which paralysed business activity in the West Bank for three weeks. Obviously they were motivated by economic considerations and acted under pressure from major businessmen in the West Bank. On the other hand, the new mayors (most of whom did not belong to the business community) could afford to call for continued agitation and so fortify their "nationalist image."

A period of relative quiet followed the Defence Ministry's decision to postpone the implementation of VAT until early December 1976. At the end of this interim period, however, disturbances broke out again. Commercial and school strikes were organized in almost all West Bank towns. Road blocks were set up, tyres burnt and rocks hurled. In Qalandiya, a 15-year old boy was wounded when shots were fired by security forces dispersing demonstrators. In the wake of the riot attempts, curfews were imposed in Nablus, Ramallah and Qalqiliya. Once again, the unrest was promoted by the more radical among the newly-elected mayors; namely, Bassām Shak'a of Nablus and Karīm Khalaf of Ramallah. However, following a compromise reached between the Military Government and the West Bank Chambers of Commerce, the local population as well as the mayors resigned themselves to the implementation of the tax. According to the compromise, all but 1,500 to 2,000 prominent businessmen earning over IL 500,000 a year were exempted from the bookkeeping work involved in VAT payments.

In contrast to the stormy events in the latter part of 1976, a period of relative quiet descended over the West Bank in 1977. Civil protest on a rather limited scale was occasionally organized, but soon subsided. Such was the case until mid-March 1977 when the PNC convention in Cairo became the occasion for student demonstrations in support of the PLO. Trade and school strikes were also held in most West Bank towns in late March 1977 to mark the first anniversary of "The Day of the Land."

As in previous years, the Jewish settlements' issue continued to stir up resentment in the West Bank. In April 1977, disturbances broke out in Nablus following attempts by Rabbi Meir Kahana to lay the cornerstone for a new settlement near the town. A month later, two inhabitants of Qabatiyya were killed by IDF soldiers during demonstrations against alleged attempts by Gush Emunim to settle at a nearby location. However, after the Israeli general elections in May 1977 until the end of October, there were no large-scale manifestations of civil unrest in the West Bank (see below).

STRICTER CONTROLS BY THE MILITARY AUTHORITIES

A major reason for the relative calm which prevailed in the West Bank during 1977 seemed to be the more resolute policy adopted by Military Government authorities in dealing with the local municipal leadership. The stricter Israeli policy was apparently a direct reaction to the militant stand taken by some of the more radical mayors in the latter part of 1976 and was possibly calculated to weaken their positions (especially in Nablus and Ramallah). One of the new preventive measures taken by the Military Government was the permanent stationing of military forces inside West Bank towns (rather than being on call outside).

While the mayors persisted in their running confrontation, they nevertheless came to realize that their ability to organize future disorders had been severely hampered by the new policy adopted by the Military Government. Moreover, their experience clearly showed that to continue to foment disturbance would have little effect on that Government's determination to carry out its policies. The local population was coming to feel the accumulative impact of the upheavals. This was reflected in an editorial in *Al-Quds* (14 December 1976) which welcomed the Nablus municipality's efforts to restore normal life. It stressed that "destroying part of our country's economy and educational life does not harm the occupation as it does our cause . . . We must conduct ourselves with a clear mind, open to the events and the developments of the future without indulging in emotionalism."

Another reason for this relative quiet derived from the severe setback the PLO suffered in Lebanon and, more generally, as a result of the Lebanese civil war. Some PLO circles had hoped that precisely because of the developments in Lebanon, disturbances in the West Bank would continue and even intensify, so as to demonstrate Palestinian support for the PLO. A senior PLO official interviewed in Beirut in March 1977 confirmed that the PLO was encouraging West Bank dissent, hoping to keep it visible and voluble. "With the situation in Lebanon what it is, it makes sense to keep the protests and demonstrations going along in the West Bank."[26] In reality, though, the impact of the Lebanese crisis had the opposite effect.

Another factor contributing to the maintenance of quiet in the West Bank, particularly in the latter part of 1977, was the rise to power in Israel of the Likud. The new government's hawkish image apparently aroused apprehensions in some West Bank mayors and led them to decrease their involvement in organizing civil unrest. The willingness of local teachers and other educators to co-operate with the authorities also helped in preventing student demonstrations.

In spite of a notable decline in the level of civil disturbance in the West Bank in 1977, the Military Government's relations with some of the newly elected mayors was still characterized by substantial friction. The Military Government apparently tried to restrict the authority of the mayors to the performance of purely administrative municipal duties. Furthermore they were deprived of some prerogatives enjoyed by their predecessors, such as being consulted on appointments to local education departments. They were instructed not to interfere in family reunions or the granting of amnesties for political prisoners, and to discontinue visits to the prisons on religious occasions. Duties traditionally exercised by some of the mayors were assigned to others. For example, the mayor of Hebron was reportedly excluded from discussions over prayer arrangements in the Tomb of the Patriarchs. Instead, local religious dignitaries and ex-mayor Shaykh Ja'barī—who had been considered the local spokesman on this issue during his term of office—were consulted by the authorities. The Military Government also tried to strengthen public and municipal bodies, such as the Chambers of Commerce and the local education departments, in an effort to further weaken the influence of the mayors.

The Military Government's stricter policy elicited a sharp reaction in the East Jerusalem press. *Al-Quds* commented in March 1977 on the "iron-fist image of the Military Government." It added that there were reports from several municipalities about worsening relations between the mayors and some senior functionaries in the Military Government. "These functionaries have behaved in an unbecoming and irresponsible manner towards the municipalities in an effort to demonstrate the muscles of authority for no reason."[27]

The deterioration in relations between the authorities and the municipalities took various forms. For example, the Military Government delayed loans and grants to the municipalities; the West Bank mayors complained that "political" clauses were inserted into the loan contracts between the two sides. Such clauses stipulated that the Hebrew version of the contract was the binding one and that, in case of dispute, action would be brought in an Israeli court. Since the politically-minded mayors refused to accept such clauses, the process of transferring loans became more protracted. The departure of several pro-PLO mayors for a fund-raising mission in Arab states in the latter part of 1977 was also delayed on the grounds that the relevant municipal development plans had yet to be approved.

Another legal dispute with political overtones arose over the mayors' refusal to deduct increased income tax rates from municipal salaries in accordance with the recent reform of the Israeli internal revenue system. The Military Government countered by subtracting these sums from regular payments transferred to the municipalities while the mayors, in turn, refused to accept the cheques for smaller sums.

POLICY OF THE LIKUD GOVERNMENT

The election of the Likud government in May 1977 aroused expectations of a more forceful Israeli policy in the West Bank and Gaza Strip. However the new administration did not introduce any immediate changes in Israel's basic policy guidelines, as formulated in 1967.

In his capacity as the newly-appointed Minister of Defence, Ezer Weizman maintained that, as Israel did not intend to withdraw from the West Bank and the Gaza Strip, it should seek ways to coexist peacefully with the Arab population in the territories and try to minimize points of friction. This, he explained, meant allowing the local population greater latitude in handling their own civil affairs according to their religious and cultural traditions and their customary social principles.

In line with previous policies, he stressed the importance of tranquillity for economic prosperity. Weizman repeated on several occasions that peaceful coexistence between Israel and the populations of the West Bank and Gaza Strip could be achieved by assisting the local inhabitants to raise their standard of living.[28] Central to this policy was the mid-August Cabinet decision to raise the standard of public services (health, transportation, welfare) in the West Bank and Gaza Strip to that enjoyed in Israel. Most West Bank leaders viewed this decision as "one more step towards annexation" and labelled it as a "veiled move" aimed at integrating the territories with Israel. Mayor Qawāsimī of Hebron said that if the decision was aimed only at improving living conditions, it was welcome; but if the aim was to annex the territories to Israel, "we emphatically reject it."[29] However, by late October 1977, there were still no indications that the government had taken any practical steps to implement its decision.

POLITICAL DEVELOPMENTS IN THE GAZA STRIP

The pattern of relationships between the Military Government and the local population in the Gaza Strip, economic growth and general tranquillity which characterized the area 1976–77 all had their origins in the events of the previous decade.

In the period between 1967-71, the Palestinian organizations in the Gaza Strip succeeded in establishing numerous strongholds mainly in the densely-populated refugee camps, from where they carried out frequent sabotage operations either against Israeli forces or against targets in the local population. The organizations achieved a dominant basis of influence over the local inhabitants and were able to hamper the Military Government's efforts to normalize the situation. In that atmosphere, the local leadership proved reluctant to co-operate with the Israeli authorities. This attitude was exemplified by the behaviour of Rāghib al-'Alamī, the then mayor of Gaza, who refused to maintain a working relationship with the Military Government. During these four years of militant confrontation between the urban pro-PLO/pro-Egyptian leadership and the Military Government, a number of prominent figures were banished to Sinai for limited periods. But leaders with pro-Jordanian leanings or with a more co-operative attitude towards the authorities also failed to achieve any real positions of influence.

The beginning of 1971 marked a change in Israeli policy toward the Gaza Strip. After the removal of Mayor 'Alamī in early January, a sustained military campaign was launched against the PLO; their forces were almost entirely eliminated in the Gaza Strip, and their influence declined significantly. An integral part of the campaign was substantially to diminish the numbers of Palestinian forces in the highly-populated refugee camps, which had previously been their haven. Roads were built and electricity installed; refugees whose houses were demolished in this operation were offered alternative and better housing outside the camps. Subsequently, over the last three years, c. 3,000 refugee families have been resettled. This rehousing programme together with extensive employment opportunities in Israel contributed to a substantially higher standard of living of the entire Gaza population.[30] These developments, along with the general decline of the PLO's standing in the Arab world after its expulsion from Jordan in 1971, paved the way for a new relationship in the Strip between the Military Government and local leaders. Although there were occasional demonstrations over such issues as the imposition of the Value Added Tax (VAT), or over the condition of Arabs in Israeli prisons, these were of a limited nature. In general, the local population was reluctant to endanger its recently acquired economic prosperity by engaging in hostile activity. The result has been a prolonged period of relative calm.

Unlike the West Bank, where municipal elections were held in spring 1976, the municipal leadership in the Strip underwent no major changes. The Gaza mayoralty of Hājj Rashshād al-Shawā retained its influential position as a central political factor both in domestic politics and *vis-à-vis* the Military Government.

PRO-HASHEMITE VS PRO-PLO/PRO-EGYPTIAN ELEMENTS

Gaza politics continued to be dominated by historical and sociological divisions between a pro-Hashemite group and pro-PLO/pro-Egyptian elements. The latter drew most of their support from the more radical younger generation whose leaders were from the educated élite—mainly liberal professional men who, during the period of Egyptian rule, occupied key posts in the local administration. These included Dr Ḥaydar 'Abd al-Shāfī, a former member of the PLO Supreme Council in Gaza, and Ibrāhīm Abū Sitta, formerly a member both of the PLO Executive Committee and of the Egyptian-appointed Executive Council of Gaza. The pro-Hashemites came mainly from the older established generation, often defined as traditional or conservative. Many of them belonged to the business and commercial élite who benefited from the economic ties that developed between Jordan and Gaza after the June 1967 war. This group remained under the uncontested leadership of Mayor Rashshād al-Shawā, a wealthy citrus grower and prominent businessman, whose family has long-standing ties with the regime in Jordan. Shawā was appointed mayor of Gaza in September 1971, resigned in September 1972, but was reappointed in October 1975 and is still in office. Mainly through the services of the al-Shawā family, Jordan granted the Gaza Strip population economic and commercial concessions, such as permits for Gaza lorries to export agricultural produce to Jordan and other Arab countries via "open bridges" across the Jordan river.

With all political organizations banned, the rival Gaza groups channelled much of their activity into two local philanthropic societies. The Red Crescent Society, headed by Dr Ḥaydar 'Abd al-Shāfī and Ibrāhīm Abū Sitta, was identified as a PLO stronghold in Gaza, mainly involved in financing medical institutions and raising external Arab capital for economic investment in the area. Jordanian interests were represented by the Benevolent Society for the Welfare of the Gaza Strip Inhabitants. Directed by 'Abd al-Karīm al-Shawā, a relative of the Gaza mayor, this society functioned as a kind of consular agency for Amman. It granted one-month permits to Gazans who wished to travel to Arab countries via Jordan, and eleven-month permits to university students in Arab countries. It also approved shipments of citrus from Gaza to Jordan and verified Israel-issued certificates.

The pro-PLO/pro-Egyptian group frequently found ways of giving expression to its political orientation. Thus, at the end of 1976, when Egypt agreed to unfreeze the bank deposits of Gaza citrus growers (blocked in Cairo since 1967), Shaykh Furaykh al-Musaddar thanked President Sādāt and declared that all Gaza Strip residents would remain faithful to Egypt under his leadership. A Gaza delegation, whose members included Dr Ḥaydar 'Abd al-Shāfī, Ibrāhīm Abū Sitta and Mahmūd Nijm, visited Egypt in January 1977 and was received by Sādāt and his Foreign Minister. The PLO's local representative, Jamāl Surānī (member of a well-known Gaza family) assumed the leadership of the delegation, which declared its support for Egypt, stressed Sādāt's role as leader of the Arab nations, and praised Egypt's contribution to the peacemaking process in the Middle East. It also reaffirmed its full support for the PLO under 'Arafāt's leadership and emphasized the need to co-ordinate the efforts of Egypt, Syria and the Palestinians in restoring Arab solidarity—pointedly omitting any mention of Jordan.

These pro-Egyptian manifestations were reflected in Cairo's renewed interest and greater involvement in Gaza. In March 1976, President Sādāt announced the reinstatement of the Gaza Strip Executive Council[31] with Ibrāhīm Abū Sitta named as Director for Civil Affairs. In January 1977, Sādāt appointed Vice-President Husnī Mubārak to be in charge of Gaza Strip affairs, and instructed all Egyptian government agencies to respond immediately to applications from Gaza Strip residents, paying special regard to their education and labour needs. Egyptian consular delegations in Europe were also instructed to facilitate the provision of refugee *laissez-passez* documents to Gaza Strip residents. Later in the year, Egypt agreed to increase the quota of Gaza students to Egyptian universities and to pay pensions to Gazans previously employed by the Egyptian government.

One possible explanation for Egypt's greater attention to the Gaza Strip was that it wished to strengthen its base in the area at the expense of pro-Jordanian groups. Also, by strengthening its position in Gaza, Egypt could hope to extend its influence over the PLO and counter similar efforts by Syria.

While stressing their allegiance to Cairo, members of the pro-PLO/pro-Egyptian group repeatedly expressed support for the PLO as the sole legitimate representative of the Palestinian people. In March 1977, for example, shortly before the PNC convention in Cairo, Zuhayr al-Rayis, a known PLO sympathizer, declared that all Palestinians everywhere were united under the PLO leadership. He expressed support for 'Arafāt and rejected any attempt to change the PLO's status as the sole representative of the Palestinians until the goal of a Palestinian state had been achieved. Only then would it be possible to discuss the question of federative or unitary links with other Arab states. In October 1977, a group of 20 Gaza dignitaries sent a memorandum to the UN Secretary-General and the Arab League

Secretary-General reaffirming the PLO as the sole legitimate representative of the Palestinians, and demanding PLO participation in all discussions on the Palestinian problem. They added that the Gaza Strip was an indivisible part of Palestinian territory and its inhabitants inseparable from the Palestinian people. The memorandum was signed mainly by staunch PLO supporters such as Dr Ḥaydar 'Abd al-Shāfī, Ibrāhīm Abū Sitta and Fa'iz Abū Rahma, but also by Mayor Rashshād al-Shawā.

THE ROLE OF GAZA'S MAYOR

Mayor Shawā, although basically pro-Jordanian, found it necessary throughout 1977 to express his commitment to the PLO, the strength of this commitment varying according to the relative positions of Jordan and the PLO in the inter-Arab and international arenas. At the beginning of 1977, following the PLO's defeat in Lebanon, Shawā often challenged its leaders by demanding larger representation for Palestinians in the PNC—from "wherever they are."

In the spring of 1977, Shawā embarked on a fund-raising mission to Abū Dhabī and Saudi Arabia. On his return, he announced that Abū Dhabī had responded with a $2m grant for Gaza's municipal services; Riyadh, named by the Arab League as twin city to Gaza, had promised to examine a $100m request for a five-year project. Shawā conceded that he had met with PLO officials in Damascus, and that the organization had assigned a special envoy to accompany him to Abū Dhabī. It was noteworthy, however, that during his fund-raising tour, Shawā stopped over in Amman where he conferred with Prime Minister Badrān, and where he also deposited the money reportedly collected in Abū Dhabī.

Shawā visited Jordan again in August at the head of a large delegation to participate in King Ḥusayn's Jubilee ceremonies. (In February, after Queen 'Aliā's death, he had led a similar delegation to offer condolences to the King.) In Amman, Shawā reiterated his support for the PLO, but went on to praise the Jordanian regime for its efforts to "liberate the occupied territories."[32] He expressed Gaza's gratitude for Jordan's help to them to "face Israeli pressure." Progress towards terminating Israeli occupation, Shawā concluded, was conditional upon closer co-operation between Jordan and the PLO.

However, in October 1977, Shawā came out uncompromisingly in favour of PLO participation at Geneva. In response to Israeli and American proposals that the Palestinians should be represented at Geneva by a West Bank and Gaza Strip delegation, Shawā declared in October that "the PLO is our sole representative; the invitation to Geneva must come through the PLO; I cannot imagine that a reasonable Palestinian will go to Geneva without the nomination or the overt agreement of the PLO."[33]

Despite Shawā's periodic declarations of support for the PLO, his close ties with the Hashemite regime exposed him to vehement criticism from pro-PLO circles in Gaza, and particularly from the radical East Jerusalem paper, *al-Fajr*. Throughout 1976 and early 1977, he was attacked for having accepted the Military Government's appointment as mayor in 1975; for mishandling city affairs; for raising municipal taxes; and for implementing Military Government projects, allegedly intended to impose Israeli-controlled home rule in the Gaza Strip. However, the basic reason for such criticisms was Shawā's pro-Jordanian position.

In an attempt to counteract these accusations, Shawā urgently demanded municipal elections in February 1977. He explained that "we want to pursue the same course as the West Bank municipalities which held elections [in April 1976]. This is in order to co-ordinate the citizens in the West Bank and Gaza. . . . We do not want the people to say that we are an appointed municipal council."[34]

PLO broadcasts strongly attacked Shawā's proposal to hold elections, and coupled their criticism with an attack on his favourable stand toward Jordan. One PLO radio commentary read: "He [Shawā] . . . wants to hold elections that will guarantee his re-election as mayor by using bribes and favouritism and buying the conscience of some hesitant weak persons . . . imagining in advance his victory with the backing of the Zionist occupiers who usually supervise the ballot boxes . . . [he] placed himself at the disposal of the Zionist aggressive forces and drove away the nationalists and revolutionists, handing them over to the enemy."[35] The commentary added that Shawā's "political inclinations" tended towards a "well-known Arab side [i.e. Jordan], that opposes any kind of national sovereignty and independence for our Palestinian people . . . and this is contrary to all he utters about his alleged support of the PLO."

While not totally rejecting Shawā's proposal for holding elections, the Military Government replied that the issue involved complicated legislative arrangements and required a longer period of study, especially as elections had not been held in Gaza since 1946. Israeli sources suggested that because of the election results in the West Bank in 1976, the Military Government was anxious to avoid the possibility of a PLO candidate becoming mayor. In late March, Shawā withdrew his threat to resign. Manoeuvring with careful calculation between verbal commitments to the PLO and close and friendly ties with Jordan, Shawā succeeded in preserving his position as the most prominent and influential leader in the Gaza Strip.

NOTES

1. Israel Broadcasting Authority, 30 October—Daily Report (DR), 3 November 1976.
2. *The Guardian*, London; 16 November 1976.
3. The Jericho Congress had prepared the ground for Jordan's annexation of the West Bank in 1948.
4. *Yediot Aharonot*, Tel Aviv; 14 October 1976.
5. *Al-Quds*, East Jerusalem; 10 January 1977.
6. *Al-Anbā'*, Jerusalem; 25 January 1977.
7. *Al-Quds*, 24 January 1977.
8. *Jerusalem Post*, 26 January 1977.
9. *The Guardian*, 4 January 1977.
10. *Al-Sha'b*, East Jerusalem; 9 March 1977.
11. *Ibid.*
12. The PNF was established in the West Bank and in the Gaza Strip in late 1973 by members of the Jordanian Communist Party, ex-members of the Arab Nationalist Party and by supporters of the Palestinian organizations. The PNF regarded itself as an integral part of the PLO. It was recognized in 1974 by the PLO as its representative in the West Bank.
13. *Al-Ittihād*, Haifa; 18 March 1977.
14. Voice of Palestine, Radio Cairo, 14 March—British Broadcasting Corporation, Summary of World Broadcasts: the ME and Africa (BBC), 17 March 1977.
15. *Ibid.*
16. *Al-Quds*, 21 March 1977.
17. Voice of Palestine, Radio Cairo, 22 March—BBC, 25 March 1977.
18. *Jerusalem Post*, 12 August 1977.
19. *Ha'aretz*, Tel Aviv; 12 August 1977.
20. Israel Television, 24 August—BBC, 26 August 1977.
21. *Al-Anbā'*, 2 September 1977.
22. *Ibid.*
23. *Jerusalem Post*, 18 September 1977.
24. Quoted in A Sinai and A Pollack (eds.), *The Hashemite Kingdom of Jordan and the West Bank* (New York, 1977), p. 251.
25. *Ma'ariv*, Tel Aviv; 12 October 1977.
26. *The New York Times*, 23 March 1977.
27. *Al-Quds*, 19 March 1977.
28. Disposable *per capita* private income increased in the West Bank on the average, at constant prices, from IL 831 in 1967 to IL 1,365 in 1975. The planned investment by the

Military Government in building and road construction in the West Bank and the Gaza Strip in 1976–77 totalled IL 60m. Projects under construction included, *inter alia*, the extension of the Shifa Hospital in Gaza and the Rafidiya Hospital in Nablus, at a total investment of c. IL 45m. Government Press Office, *The Administered Territories —Background Data*, June 1977.

29. Israel Broadcasting Authority, 15 August—BBC, 17 August 1977.
30. Disposable *per capita* private income increased on the average, at constant prices, from IL 553 in 1967 to 1,158 in 1975. The percentage of families possessing TV sets rose from 3% in 1967 to 34% in 1976. *The Administered Territories*, *op cit.*
31. This body was originally set up by Egypt in 1962. It consisted of 13 members, five of whom were Palestinians, and the remainder Egyptians. All were appointed by the Egyptian Minister of War and were in charge of government departments.
32. *Al-Dustūr*, Amman; 12 August 1977.
33. *Al-Quds*, 3 October 1977.
34. *Al-Dustūr*, 17 February—DR, 18 February 1977.
35. Voice of Palestine, Radio Cairo, 15 February—DR, 17 February 1977. The broadcast was probably referring to an incident which occurred in November 1971 when Ziyyād al-Ḥusaynī, a leading commander of the PFLP in the Gaza Strip, committed suicide at Shawā's residence in Gaza, after hiding there for some weeks.

Middle East Economic Issues

Major Trends in Middle East Economic Development

ELIYAHU KANOVSKY

The purpose of this survey is to describe and analyse economic developments in Egypt, Syria, Jordan and Saudi Arabia—those Arab countries which are of major importance in the Middle East within the context of the Arab-Israeli conflict. The war in Lebanon since mid-1975, which has abated since the massive Syrian intervention in 1976, has brought in its wake the destruction of much of its economy. However, aside from its political implications, the war in Lebanon has had an important impact on the economy of Syria, and to some extent, on Jordan. This essay is primarily concerned with the period since the Yom Kippur war of October 1973, but in economics, as in other disciplines, current developments can be understood only in the context of longer-term trends. However, unlike political developments, there is a considerable time lag, especially in underdeveloped countries, with respect to the availability of data. Even in late 1977, data for 1975 are often noted as provisional, and only limited data are available for 1976. Furthermore, with respect to Egypt and Syria in particular, there are serious doubts with respect to the reliability of even "final" data. There is little point in making broad generalizations regarding Egypt, Syria, Jordan and Saudi Arabia. While they have characteristics common to all underdeveloped countries, their differences in terms of economic policies and performance are great—even leaving aside the special features of Saudi Arabia. These differences and the main factors accounting for them, are analysed here.

EGYPT: A DECADE OF ECONOMIC STAGNATION

The basic and possibly most important fact about the Egyptian economy is that it has failed to show any real growth on a per capita basis over an extended period. According to official estimates, the Gross Domestic Product (GDP) at factor cost increased by an annual average rate of 4.2% between 1963-4 and 1974. However, an analysis of the underlying data clearly indicates that official figures tend to exaggerate the economy's growth rate. It appears doubtful that real economic growth exceeded the rate of population increase, i.e. almost 2.5% per annum during this period.[1] It is not unlikely that during the decade from 1964-74 there was even an absolute per capita decline in production.

The failure of the economy to grow over such a long period has dire implications. It implies first of all an aggravation of the problem of unemployment, overt or disguised. An official report stated that the unemployment rate was 10.4% in 1974, but that "the level of real unemployment is higher than the figures show."[2] Economic stagnation usually also entails a deterioration in average living standards. Official data indicate that average per capita private consumption, in real terms, was 7.4% *lower* in 1974 than in 1963-4.[3] To the extent that the gap between the official price index and real market prices has widened, the decline in living standards has been even greater. There are widespread reports of a relatively small proportion of Egyptians accumulating considerable wealth and maintaining consumption levels rivalling those of the *nouveau riche* in other countries. This would imply an even greater decline in living standards for the bulk of the population than that indicated by the national average.[4]

Long-term economic stagnation has other adverse effects as well. When aggregate demand rises, as has been the case especially since the 1973 war (in terms of civilian or military public consumption, investment demand and, to some extent, private consumption), the result is either inflationary pressures, or an increase in the import surplus, or a combination of both. If there had been significant increases in real per capita production, inflationary pressures and balance of payments problems would have been less severe.

AGRICULTURE

Egypt's economic problems and their underlying causes become more readily apparent when we examine the primary sectors, agriculture and industry. Despite official policies since the 1950s—which put the greatest emphasis on industrial development, including the transfer of resources from agriculture to industry—the farm sector has remained dominant. Agriculture in 1974 accounted for one-third of GDP and employed 47% of the labour force.[5] Farm exports accounted for 51% of total commodity exports in 1974–75 (two-year average) and, indirectly, mainly through the provision of raw materials for the textile industry, for a substantial part of non-farm exports. The performance of agriculture also affects other sectors such as trade, finance and transportation. Thus it is no exaggeration to state that the performance of the farm sector is of major importance to the Egyptian economy of the 1970s. In the early 1960s there were high hopes and projections about the contribution that the Aswan High Dam, various land reclamation projects (mainly related to the utilization of waters from the High Dam) and the Land Reform Programme would make to significantly improving production, providing a surplus for food exports and expanding Egypt's traditional export crop, cotton.

The first stage of the Aswan High Dam was completed in 1964 and many large-scale reclamation projects were executed during the first half of the 1960s. However in terms of agricultural production, the results proved to be most disappointing. According to official Egyptian estimates, the average annual growth rate of agriculture in 1964–74 was 2.2% (cf 3.6% pa in 1954–64). The decline is most significant. In the earlier decade, agricultural production per capita was increasing by 1.4% pa; in the latter decade it was declining annually by 0.2%. Estimates of the US Department of Agriculture are even lower, showing that the index of agricultural production increased by an annual average rate of 2.7% in 1954–64, slightly exceeding the population growth rate, and then declined sharply to 1.2% pa, far below the population growth rate. In effect, agricultural production per capita in 1974 was over 11% lower than in 1964.[6]

Only a brief mention can be made here of some of the major factors which have adversely affected Egypt's primary sector since 1964. One thing should be clear: it is *not* that Egyptian agriculture has reached any so-called saturation point. Studies indicate that, given existing land and water resources, there is considerable potential for expansion of production, assuming that modern techniques are applied, and that the authorities adopt and implement policies which would favour such developments.[7]

Agriculture—unlike industry—continues to be largely private, but since the early 1960s the State has imposed severe controls. It fixes prices for the major crops, to be delivered to official agencies. The prices, especially in recent years, have been very far below international levels. In 1974, for example, prices paid to farmers for cotton were *one-fifth* of those obtained by the State for cotton exports. Industry, in turn, was provided with this raw material at a very low cost. The price paid for rice (a major export) was even less than one-fifth of the international price.[8] Part of the rice crop is used to provide the urban population with low-cost staple food, but the effect of these policies is to impose a heavy tax on agricultural production, with all its disincentive effects. Furthermore, since 1964 there has been a sharp drop in investment in agriculture, *both* absolutely and relatively. Since the State accounts for c. 90% of gross fixed investment in the economy, the decline in agricultural investment has been a matter of deliberate policy. Even within the limits of investment in the farm sector, the distribution has been far from optimal. Very little is allocated to extension services, such as instructing farmers in the utilization of modern techniques.[9]

The Aswan High Dam was designed to provide major benefits to agriculture in terms of flood control, perennial irrigation, as well as increased water supplies. However, many of the so-called side effects have been most adverse. The loss of alluvium (silt), which had previously flowed to the Nile Delta, has reduced soil fertility, requiring the use of fertilizer to compensate for this loss. "The area affected by waterlogging and salinity has been increasing at an alarming rate over the past ten years since the High Dam came into operation (1965)."[10] This, in turn, requires major investments in drainage systems and improved water management. Another major "side effect" of the High Dam has been an alarming increase in the spread of bilharzia, a debilitating disease.[11] According to some estimates the disease affects c. 70% of men in rural areas. Others put the annual economic costs at c. $400m. If accurate, this would be equivalent to c. 12–13% of the value added in agriculture in 1974.[12] An Egyptian-American team of farm experts which studied Egyptian agriculture towards the end of 1975 noted: "Poor nutrition is widespread (in the rural areas) causing anemia, retarded growth, high death rates, and low school attendance among children. . . . The health of the people is further adversely affected by some serious endemic diseases, overcrowded houses, and lack of sanitation."[13] The rural population is over one-half of the total population. Despite the poverty conditions and high rates of unemployment in the cities, one can well understand the continued rural-urban trend.

INDUSTRY

Since the early 1960s all of the larger and most of the medium-sized industries (in Egyptian terms) are State-owned. By and large, public sector enterprises have been favoured by the government; industry, generally, has also been heavily favoured in allocations made from the public purse, and in many other respects. Since the 1960s, industry (defined to include manufacturing, mining and crude oil production) has accounted for c. 22% of GDP, with no tendency towards any relative increase. The share of total investment allocated to the industrial sector (c. 90% of which is from the treasury) has consistently been far higher than its share of GDP. Nonetheless, official data indicate that value added in industrial production increased by an annual average rate of 3.2% between 1963–4 and 1974.[14] Here, too, there is reason to believe that the official data tend to overstate the growth rates.[15] Most probably, the growth of industrial production in the 1963–4 to 1974 period did not exceed the population increase. The growth rate of industrial production was far lower than in the previous two or three decades.

There is little doubt that the nationalization of most of the industrial sector, and the so-called employment drive since the early 1960s, had very adverse effects on this sector. The employment drive meant, in effect, that various enterprises were compelled to hire people in numbers far exceeding their requirements—and not necessarily on the basis of qualifications. An analysis published in the *Arab Economist* of December 1975 indicated that the factors inhibiting growth were mismanagement of industrial enterprises, particularly the larger ones which are State-owned; government bureaucracy in the decision-making process affecting investment, production, employment, etc; the establishment of "unsuitable" industries; a wage and salary structure which inhibits initiative and incentives; foreign trade restrictions; bottlenecks arising from shortages of foreign exchange, and the inability to import equipment, spare parts, and raw materials.[16] A more recent official report notes shortages of raw materials, inadequate maintenance and insufficient technical know-how.[17]

Little official data are available for economic performance in 1975, and even less for 1976. Provisional estimates for agricultural production indicate a rise of 2.0% in 1975.[18] Thus, per capita output continued to decline. It would appear that large-scale foreign aid permitted much greater imports of industrial equipment, spare parts, raw materials etc for industry, which in turn enabled a sizeable increase in industrial production. The official estimates are that it increased by almost 12%, but here too there may be an element of exaggeration.[19] According to a statement by the Minister of Industry, industrial production increased by 11% in 1976 (of which 70% was from the public sector and 30% from the private sector).[20] It would seem that the reference is to gross production, in current prices. In view of continued inflation, it would appear that real growth was far smaller.

It would seem that there was a more substantial increase in GDP in 1975, in part bolstered by the reopening of the Suez Canal in June 1975 and reconstruction in the Canal area. However, a recent statement by the Deputy Prime Minister indicates that 1976 was again a poor year for the economy, with a growth rate of 4%.[21] If the past history of overstatement of economic performance is a guide, 1976 was again a year of stagnation, at least in per capita terms.

FUTURE PROSPECTS

Many official statements point to four possible "bright spots" on Egypt's economic horizon: petroleum, the Suez Canal, tourism, and remittances from Egyptians working abroad, mainly in oil-rich Arab countries. Egypt was the first country in the Middle East to initiate commercial production of petroleum (1909). However, the development of this resource was neglected for many decades. Small-scale development took place during the 1950s, and more intensive exploration since the mid-1960s, with the aid of Western oil companies. In early 1967, the projection was that by 1970 crude oil production would reach 30m tons pa, based on already discovered fields.[22] In reality, it reached a peak of 17m tons in 1971 (excluding 3-4m tons from the Sinai oilfields taken over by Israel in 1967). In 1972 there was a sharp decline to 10.7m tons. The decline continued in 1973 and 1974 (in part because of the Arab-Israeli war), with production in 1974 down to 7.5m tons. In 1975 production rose to 11.6m tons, a small part of which was due to the return of the Sinai oilfields by Israel towards the end of 1975. In 1976 production rose to 16.4m tons.[23] About one-half of the *increment* was from the Sinai fields (c. 2.7m tons).[24] In other words, oil production in 1976 was still significantly below the peak reached in 1971, if one adds the Sinai oilfields.

Since 1973, Egypt has actively sought out Western oil companies for intensified exploration and, indeed, many exploration and production-sharing agreements have been concluded. There is every prospect that oil production will continue to rise, but whether the current optimism is warranted, only time will tell. Official projections are that by 1980 oil production will reach 50m tons, leaving the country with a surplus for export of $1.1 bn.[25] It would appear that c. 30m tons is based on development of existing oilfields; the balance on hopes of new discoveries. A CIA estimate (April 1977) states that "Egyptian oil output could reach 700,000 b/d in 1980 and 1m b/d by 1985." This is equivalent to c. 35m tons in 1980 and 50m in 1985.[26] In the context of Middle Eastern oil, Egyptian reserves are of minor consequence, but a large increase in oil production would certainly ease Egypt's economic plight, though it would be far from "solving" the country's fundamental economic problems.

When the Suez Canal was reopened in June 1975, the official projections were that revenues from transit dues would reach $500m in the first year (rates were set at approximately double those prevailing in 1966). In fact, revenues reached only $215m. For 1976 the projections were for $551m; actual revenues were $385m. Since the Canal is unable to accommodate larger oil tankers, most of its income is derived from dry cargo ships, in sharp contrast with the situation before 1967 when oil tankers provided c. three-fourths of transit dues. Work was begun in 1976 on a project to widen and deepen the Canal to accommodate 150,000-ton loaded tankers, and 270,000-ton tankers in ballast (on the return trip to the Persian Gulf). Cost estimates of this project have steadily risen from $900m (at the end of 1976) to $1,200m (in mid-1977). Furthermore, it appears that the expected date of completion is now 1980, rather than 1978. However, the longer-term plans to widen and deepen the Canal to accommodate 250–300,000-ton supertankers appear to be in doubt.[27] Official projections are that Suez Canal revenues will reach $769m in 1980, i.e. twice those actually received in 1976. However, though continued growth can be anticipated, the official projections are probably over-optimistic.

After five or six years of delay in initiating the project, the Suez-Mediterranean oil pipeline (from Suez to Alexandria) was finally completed in early 1977, at a cost of c. $500m. It is designed to provide an alternative to the route around Africa for supertankers which cannot transit the Canal. However, its profitability is open to question since the number of clients who have committed themselves to use the pipeline (i.e. the percentage of capacity utilized) is still small.[28] The completion of the project to widen and deepen the Suez Canal by 1980, may make it more competitive with, rather than complementary to, the oil pipeline.

Following the Six-Day war of June 1967, there was a sharp drop in the number of tourists coming to Egypt. After the ceasefire along the Suez Canal in 1970 there was an upturn, and in 1972 numbers again reached the pre-1967 level of c. 500,000. Since 1974, the government has put far greater emphasis on this sector and the number of tourists, and income from tourism, have been rising steadily. An estimated 800,000 visited Egypt in 1975. Income from tourism was $185m in 1975, rising to c. $350m in 1976.[29] There is little doubt that Egypt has the potential for a major expansion of this sector, and it is one area (aside from petroleum) which has succeeded in attracting foreign investment.

The rapid growth of the oil-rich Arab countries, their severe labour shortages and high wage rates have attracted many Egyptians to work abroad. Furthermore, the Egyptian government has been encouraging this emigration both to reduce unemployment levels and to increase its foreign earnings from remittances by migrant workers. With rare exceptions, Egyptians working abroad are considered as temporary residents rather than permanent immigrants. Remittances are estimated to have reached $320m in 1975 and $445m in 1976. The probability is that these will increase, though the rate of growth is likely to decline. The November 1976 census indicated that the resident population of Egypt was 36.7m and that 1.4m Egyptians were abroad.[30] One can assume that about one-half of those abroad were working (primarily in the Arab oil countries), and that the others were their dependants. However, while Egypt has a surplus of unskilled labour and of many categories of university graduates, it suffers from severe shortages of skilled labour and some professional skills, and emigration in these categories compounds the difficulties faced in increasing domestic production. It would also appear that the emigration of many teachers (attracted by far higher salaries in the Arab oil countries) has aggravated the shortage of educational personnel, especially in rural areas.[31]

BALANCE OF PAYMENTS

The symptom—not the fundamental cause—of Egypt's economic ills is the vast increase in the balance of payments deficits. However, the lack of foreign exchange also tends to inhibit the growth of production since the importation of machinery and equipment, spare parts and raw materials is curtailed. Egypt has suffered from serious balance of payments difficulties since 1963, but these problems have become far more acute since 1973. Between 1967 and 1969 the average annual deficit (exports of goods and services minus imports, in millions of dollars) was 283; between 1970 and 1972, it had risen to 471; in 1973, 564; in 1974, 1,363; and in 1975 it rose very sharply to 2,474m.[32] However, these figures are incomplete for two reasons: 1) imports within the context of economic aid are excluded, at least in part;[33] 2) imports of military equipment are excluded.

There are many factors accounting for the sharp deterioration in Egypt's balance of payments. *Measured in current dollars*, commodity exports rose from $817m in 1970 to $1,672m in 1974, and then dropped slightly to $1,567m in 1975. However, the increase was wholly due to rising international prices. Measured in constant (dollar) prices, Egypt's exports in 1974 and 1975 were c. 30% lower than in 1970–2, and even 20% below the level reached in 1965. On the other hand, commodity imports rose from $1,084m in 1970 to $2,914m in 1974 and $3,941m in 1975. The precipitous increase in imports was due *both* to higher international prices and a major real increase in imports. The real decline in commodity exports is basically due to the stagnation (in per capita terms) in industry, and especially in agriculture. While in earlier years, agricultural exports (mainly cotton and rice) exceeded agricultural imports, there has been a sharp deterioration in recent years. Agricultural exports declined from c. $900m in 1974 to $750m in 1975; agricultural imports rose from $310m in 1973 to $1,050m in 1974 and c. $1,500m in 1975. Projections were that they would reach $2,000m in 1976.[34] The resumption of large-scale US aid to Egypt since 1974 has financed some of these imports. Other than oil, industrial exports have been minor, mainly textiles. Between 1974 and 1976 there was a tendency towards a slight decline in these exports, reaching E£ 206m in 1976, possibly the equivalent of c. $300m.[35]

Preliminary estimates for 1976 indicate that commodity exports rose slightly (c. 3%), with the sharp decline in other exports compensated for by increased oil exports. As a result of stringency in foreign exchange (partly due to a cutback in Arab aid), imports were curtailed, except for agricultural goods. On the other hand, the export of services (invisibles) increased very sharply since 1973, mainly in remittances from Egyptians abroad, tourism, and Suez Canal dues (since mid-1975). The import of services increased less rapidly. However, as noted earlier, the import surplus (exports of goods and services minus imports) rose sharply until 1975. The continued rise in service exports and the curtailment of imports in 1976 sharply reduced the import surplus to $1,518m, bringing it back to a level 11% higher than in 1974. The restrictions on imports in 1976 apparently had an adverse effect on industrial production as well as on investment (the curtailment of imports of machinery, raw materials, spare parts, etc). The official forecast is that imports will expand greatly in 1977, and that the import surplus will again rise sharply.[36]

FOREIGN DEBT

In addition to financing a much larger import surplus, the Egyptians were faced with a rapidly rising foreign debt—a consequence of balance of payments deficits in earlier years, as well as payments on account of imports of military equipment, mainly from the Soviet Union. As noted earlier, these imports are not included in the official figures, though payments, in the form of commodity exports, apparently are included. According to one source, Egypt's total foreign debt at the beginning of 1977 was the equivalent of $12.2 bn, including $4.2 bn to Soviet bloc countries, c. $1 bn to the Arab oil countries, and the balance to international organizations (mainly the World Bank and the International Monetary Fund), and to various other countries and banks. Other sources put the debt to the Soviet Union on account of military equipment at c. $8 bn, far higher than the above source which estimated the debt (both civilian and military) to the Soviet bloc at $4.2 bn.[37] The latter estimate indicated a total foreign debt of c. $15 bn. Even if GNP is calculated by the highly-overvalued official exchange rate, the foreign debt was equivalent to one and one-quarter times the GNP. At the official parallel exchange rate, the foreign debt was equivalent to twice the GNP.

What is more relevant is the current burden of principal and interest payments, as measured by its ratio to total exports (goods and services). Even based on this slender evidence, there is little doubt that Egypt has been finding it increasingly difficult to make payments; and private foreign suppliers, as well as foreign governments, have been called upon from time to time to "reschedule" debt payments. In addition, Cairo was resorting to short-term loans from foreign banks, at interest rates ranging up to 19%—a reflection of the risk element involved in lending to Egypt.[38] It appears that the servicing of the foreign debt (payments on account of principal and interest) in 1975 and 1976 approximated total exports of goods and services, in effect leaving Egypt dependent on foreign aid to finance all, or almost all, of its imports. In October 1977, Egypt unilaterally suspended its debt repayments to the Soviet Union for ten years.

Grants and concessional loans (long-term loans at low interest rates) from the richer Arab states, the US and other Western countries have been rising sharply. Grants from Arab countries (Egypt receives about one-half of total Arab aid) rose from an average annual level of $280m between 1968 and 1972, to $635m in 1973, and almost $1 bn in 1974 and in 1975.[39] This is aside from unreported amounts in military aid—direct payment to suppliers of military equipment sent to Egypt. It would appear that Arab grants to Egypt were reduced in 1976 to $635m. At a meeting of Arab foreign ministers in January 1977, it was decided that Arab grants to Egypt in 1977 and in 1978 would again be reduced to $570m. It is estimated that total Arab economic aid to Egypt (including loans) was c. $2 bn in 1975 and $1.5 bn in 1976.[40] On the other hand, aid from the US, the World Bank, the IMF, and from a number of other countries has been increasing.

A meeting was held in Paris in the spring of 1977, under the aegis of the World Bank, with representatives of 13 Western and Arab countries and various international organizations. From Egypt's analysis of its need for foreign aid, it appears that the anticipated deficits, in terms of both payments on account of foreign debt plus the projected import surplus in 1977, would require aid of $5.4 bn, plus continued aid of $2.8 bn pa in 1978–80. This is aside from the annual Arab grant. US aid in 1976 was close to $1 bn, and will probably be $1.25 bn in 1977. Arab aid will consist in part in postponement of $1.5 bn in debts (a higher figure than mentioned in earlier reports), plus new loans and guarantees of loans of c. $2 bn. Loans from international organizations and from other countries would bring the total aid package to over $5 bn.[41]

CONCLUSIONS

Large-scale foreign aid will certainly ease the short-run problems faced by Egypt.

To the extent that it permits Cairo to import the necessary machinery and equipment for investment, raw materials and spare parts this will aid in stimulating production. However, it does not "solve" the country's fundamental economic problems. Certainly, large and growing military expenditures—over and above the importation of military equipment—have seriously aggravated Egypt's economic problems. No precise figures are available, but a recent statement by the Deputy Prime Minister noted that "defence costs us 20%-25% of our GNP. We have simply got to divert most of that money to productive use."[42] However, the more basic problems besetting the Egyptian economy are the result of harmful public policies. The anticipated increase in Suez Canal revenues, oil production and exports, tourism, and possibly remittances, even if less than the optimistic official projections, will certainly aid the economy. However, fundamental changes are dependent on significant improvements in the basic sectors—agriculture and industry. There is little evidence that such changes are taking place.

The introduction of "Arab socialism" in the early 1960s proved to be very detrimental. Professor Hansen noted that "the nationalization [of industrial enterprises] . . . had detrimental effects . . . on labour productivity . . . an indicator of growing inefficiency. . . . It is . . . also clear that equalization [of incomes] has not gone very far. There are still big capitalists in urban real estate . . . moreover, the ruling class, the establishment, appears to live a very comfortable life, far removed from that of the toiling masses."[43]

Even prior to the 1973 war, and to a greater extent since the war, Egyptian official policies indicate a greater emphasis on the private sector, an attempt to attract foreign private investment (the so-called "open door policy"), and other measures designed to restructure the economy. The Planning Minister stated at the end of 1975 that "Egypt's economic troubles began 20 years ago; the country's major problem now is that production is inadequate for consumption, saving, and investment."[44] The reference is apparently to the steady increase in nationalization and governmental controls which began after the Suez-Sinai war of 1956, and even more so since the early 1960s. In mid-1976, a special minister charged with restructuring Egypt's economy and government noted various errors committed since the 1960s, and concluded that "ideological prescriptions are a waste of time. It is a question of improving the men at the centre."[45] The various attempts to attract foreign and even local private investment to industry have met with very little success. The only areas of foreign private investment have been in petroleum, some hotels, banks and real estate; there has been very little in manufacturing. Local private investors also appear to have concentrated on real estate, mainly luxury housing for the rich.[46] One new development in October 1977 was the agreement with Ford International to build a new motor assembly plant.

What are the prospects for fundamental changes which would bring about long-term improvement in production, investment and efficiency, and over the longer run, reduce Egypt's balance of payments deficits? One long-time student of Egyptian economic affairs stated that "an immense expansion of the bureaucracy has been the most conspicuous feature of Arab socialism in Egypt. With bureaucracy has come inefficiency in investment, production and trade decisions . . . There are . . . signs that Egypt is turning her back to socialism, but governmental ownership and control of the economy remain a basic fact of her economy. The greatest obstacle to reform in Egypt is that, with the passage of time, vested interests in the conservation of the system have grown up and become strong. And when the groups that have vested interests in the existing system also constitute the ruling class, fundamental changes may well-nigh be impossible to achieve. This is precisely the situation in Egypt."[47]

SYRIA: AN ECONOMY IN CRISIS

Syria has a relative abundance of natural resources, certainly in per capita terms—including cultivable land, water, and certain mineral deposits, as well as petroleum. Over a period of c. 15 to 20 years, until 1957, the economy was expanding rapidly. Despite a high rate of population growth (estimated at 3.3% pa), the per capita growth rate of the economy was c. 5-6% pa during this period. The leading sector was agriculture which, despite periodic droughts, expanded rapidly, with cotton introduced on a larger scale in the mid-1940s. During this period private enterprise was dominant, and the government confined itself to infrastructural investments, including a marked expansion of the educational system. Light industry, mainly textiles, food processing and construction materials, also showed rapid growth. Investment (largely private) was steadily increasing, giving reasonable assurance of continued economic growth. Military expenditures during this period were quite small, absorbing 4-6% of GNP, and an even smaller share of available resources (GNP plus the import surplus). Between 1950 and 1957, commodity exports were rising by c. 15% pa, while imports were increasing by 4-5% pa.

A sharp break in Syria's economic development began in 1958. This was due in part to the union with Egypt, and the introduction of a land reform programme which was very poorly administered. The large-scale nationalization of industry and of other sectors since 1963 was an additional blow to the economy. There was a large exodus of the skilled, managerial and professional classes, as well as a flight of capital. The official economic development plans favoured industry, but the loss of skilled labour (in its broadest context) and the appointment of inefficient administrators to manage public sector enterprises proved to be serious deterrents to economic growth. Between 1957 and 1969, per capita net domestic product was stagnant. Unemployment (both overt and disguised) increased; real living standards did not improve, and may even have deteriorated. Military expenditure (over and above arms imports from the Soviet Union) absorbed an increasing share of GNP and of resources. Exports increased very slowly and, discounting international price changes, were no higher in 1968 than in 1957. This was mainly due to the poor performance of agriculture which, on a per capita basis, showed an almost steady decline.

The 1967 Arab-Israeli war had but a minor direct economic impact on Syria. However, it was followed by a sharp growth in military expenditures. Measured in current prices, they absorbed 11% of GDP in 1970-2 (10% of available resources), excluding arms imports from the Soviet Union. Some improvement in the rate of economic growth probably occurred after 1967. This was due to some modification of public policies, including greater incentives to the private sector and far higher levels of investment, mainly in the public sector. However, the rapid growth of military expenditure absorbed most of the increased resources, and it appears that living standards continued to stagnate. There is also some evidence of rising unemployment rates between 1970 and 1973. Despite higher taxes, oil transit dues (from the Iraqi pipeline as well as Tapline from Saudi Arabia), and increased economic aid from the oil-rich Arab countries budgetary deficits were rising. The government thus had to resort increasingly to borrowing from the banking system to finance the deficits, with all its inflationary implications.

A year of severe drought was experienced in 1973, and agricultural production declined by 30%. The war of October 1973 had an additional adverse effect on the economy. There was extensive damage to the civilian economy, officially estimated at $1,200m. Net domestic product declined by at least 12%, about one-half a result of the drought. Inflation, which had become severe towards the end of 1972, continued to plague the economy. However, there was a sharp rise in foreign aid to Syria from the rich Arab states as well as from a number of Western and Eastern European countries, in addition to massive arms shipments from the Soviet Union. The increment in foreign *economic* aid greatly exceeded war damages to the civilian economy.

1974 was a very good year for the Syrian economy. Weather conditions were favourable, and agricultural production rose to the 1972 level. Crude oil production and exports had been initiated in 1968 (the oilfields had been discovered in the later 1950s), and newly-developed phosphate mines added to production and exports. More important, Syria benefited greatly from the far higher oil and phosphate export prices. It would appear that net domestic product increased by c. 18%. Living standards, which had declined very sharply in 1973, regained their 1972 level. However, there was evidence of a widening of income differentials within the country (similar to developments in Egypt since the early 1970s). Syria also benefited from a sharp increase in oil transit dues, mainly from the Iraqi oil pipeline. Despite very favourable international terms of trade (export prices rose far more sharply than import prices), the import surplus (exports of goods and services minus imports) rose very steeply. However, this was more than offset by increased foreign aid.

1975 was also a very good year for the Syrian economy, though the rate of growth was far lower than in 1974.[48] Weather conditions were good, though less favourable than in 1974; there was a small decline in farm production. Production was also adversely affected by the dispute between Syria and Iraq over the division of the waters of the Euphrates. But the decline in agricultural production was more than offset by continued growth in crude oil production and refining, and an expansion of electric power. However, the major source of growth was the continued rise in government expenditures, both current and for development. There is evidence that the shortage of skilled and professional manpower was continuing to be a very serious constraint, inhibiting both investment and increases in current production. The inefficiency of the dominant public sector restricted economic growth, despite the abundance of foreign economic aid. Inflationary pressures continued as a result of deficit financing—a consequence, in large measure, of far higher military expenditure (over and above the far higher level of Soviet military shipments). Exports (goods and services) increased by 15%, but this was wholly due to an increase in crude oil exports. In fact, Syria's traditional exports fell. Imports (goods and services) rose sharply (34%), and the import surplus (exports of goods and services minus imports) rose from $293m in 1974 to $613m in 1975. However, foreign aid (mainly from the oil-rich Arab countries) continued to rise, more than offsetting the deficit, and Syria's international reserves continued to climb, reaching $735m by the end of 1975.[49]

CURRENT ECONOMIC PERFORMANCE

Data for 1976 are only partially available. However, an analysis of economic developments in previous years helps to put the events of 1976 into proper focus. 1974 and, to a lesser extent, 1975 were years of rapid growth for the Syrian economy. The crucial question is whether these years were the beginning of a new trend, in marked contrast with the stagnation of 1957–67 and the slow growth of 1967–72. Or did 1974–5 presage the beginning of a period of rapid growth similar to what had prevailed in the 15 or 20 years before 1957? All the indications are that 1974–5 were exceptional years in which, for the most part, the Syrian economy benefited from developments exogenous to the economy. These include: 1) Far higher international prices for crude petroleum, especially in 1973 and 1974.

Though Syria is a minor oil producer in Middle Eastern terms (8.75m tons in 1975), a large part of the increase in industrial production since the early 1970s (crude oil is included in the data on industrial production) is due to the increased volume of production and higher prices. 2) Due to the geographic position of Syria, it was able to exact high transit dues from the Iraqi pipeline. In addition, the 1973 agreement with Iraq permitted Syria to use Iraqi oil for its own refineries at very low prices. In 1973-5, Syria exported almost all of its own crude petroleum, utilizing Iraqi crude for its refineries. 3) Phosphate production, which began in the early 1970s, benefited from large international price increases since 1973. 4) There was a large increase in foreign aid since 1973, mainly from the Arab countries. This was of major importance both in terms of financing a far higher level of investment in the public sector, as well as the much larger import surplus.

All this would seem to indicate that, in most respects, Syria had not solved its more basic problems in any fundamental manner. Its main sector, agriculture, continued to stagnate. Although the Euphrates Dam project might bring about major growth in agricultural production (as envisaged by Syrian planners), there is no evidence at this point to substantiate such optimism. International comparisons are always hazardous, but the Aswan Dam in Egypt has failed to bring about any increase in the rate of growth of farm production. Reports published in the spring of 1977 note that, of the 240,000 hectares (a hectare is equal to 2.471 acres) in the Euphrates basin, only a small pilot project has been developed. More important, "Syria faces unexpectedly high gypsum content in the soil of the basin—which makes conventional irrigation methods unworkable. The result is that the per hectare cost has jumped from $3,000 three years ago to a minimum of $5,000 now."[50] Syria's main problems stem mainly from poor macroeconomic management; from a dearth of skilled, professional and managerial personnel; from a large and inefficient public sector; and from its policy of allocating a higher and higher share of its resources to military expenditures. The apparent improvement in the Syrian economy in 1974-5 was due mainly to the exogenous factors noted above.

EFFECTS OF THE LEBANON CONFLICT

Events in 1976 have had, in the main, a serious adverse impact on the Syrian economy. During the latter half of 1975, Syria was becoming increasingly involved in the Lebanese war, but Syria's problems became far more acute in 1976. Syria took a dominant role in the hostilities. The original budget for 1976 had called for a 10% increase in military expenditures to c. $1,000m (excluding arms imports). Actual expenditures in 1976 were undoubtedly far higher. According to news reports, of the $90m pledged by Arab countries to help defray the cost of the Syrian "peacekeeping forces" in Lebanon, only $60m had been paid, and it appeared doubtful that the balance would be forthcoming.[51]

The 1973 oil transit agreement between Iraq and Syria expired at the end of 1975. During this period Iraq was building an oil pipeline from its northern oilfields to southern terminals in the Persian Gulf, which was completed at the end of 1975. Furthermore, the Iraqi-Turkish pipeline was also in the process of construction, scheduled for completion at the end of 1976. The Iraqis demanded a new agreement with Syria, calling for lower transit dues as well as full payment for Iraqi oil purchased by Syria for its domestic refineries. Negotiations broke down and in April 1976, Iraq stopped oil transit through Syria, causing an estimated loss of c. $300m pa to Syria.

According to official reports, grants to Syria from the Arab oil countries declined sharply in 1976 to $402m (cf a peak of $654m in 1975).[52] Though not clear, it would appear that this includes Arab payments in support of Syrian forces in Lebanon.[53] The decline in aid to Syria was reportedly related to inter-Arab political developments, but from the cutback in Arab grants to Egypt in 1976, it would also appear to be related to the financial position (real or perceived) of the Arab oil states.

For many years an estimated 100,000 Syrians migrated annually to Lebanon as seasonal labourers, mainly doing unskilled work in agriculture and construction. The effect was to reduce Syrian unemployment, as well as to bring in foreign currency which aided the Syrian balance of payments. The war sharply curtailed this migration and, in addition, many other Syrians who had been long-time residents of Lebanon fled home. A large number of Lebanese and Palestinians (residing in Lebanon), generally the poorer classes, also fled to Syria as the fighting intensified. In a speech made in July 1976, President Asad stated that 500,000 Syrian residents in Lebanon had returned to Syria, as well as an estimated 500,000 Lebanese and 150,000 Palestinians. If these figures are reasonably accurate, they would indicate an influx of refugees equivalent to 15% of the Syrian population. In addition to all the political and social complications, this constitutes a severe strain on the Syrian economy, especially since the reasonable presumption is that the large majority of wealthier Lebanese who left the country sought refuge elsewhere.

For many years Beirut had constituted a main port of entry for imports destined for Iraq, Saudi Arabia, Jordan and other countries in the area. Syria had benefited from transit dues. The closure of Beirut port during the war created a severe problem of congestion in Syrian ports, as well as the loss of transit fees. Lebanon had also been an important trading partner of Syria. While alternative markets are available they are generally more expensive, at least in terms of transportation costs.

CONCLUSIONS

It would appear that while in earlier years Syria had benefited from favourable changes in its international terms of trade, this was no longer so in 1976. Crude oil prices were quite stable following the precipitous increases in 1973 and 1974; and phosphate prices, which had risen sharply in 1974 and 1975, fell in 1976. These developments added to the strains on Syria's economy.

No official data are yet available on national product in 1976. It would appear that if the national product did rise, the increase was, at best, modest. However balance of payments figures do indicate a sharp deterioration. Measured in current dollars, exports (goods and services) increased by 4.9%. In real terms this probably meant a decline. On the other hand, imports rose sharply, by 35.2%. The result was that the import surplus which had doubled in 1975, doubled again in 1976, to reach $1,227m. The sharp rise in the import surplus, plus the curtailment of Arab aid, has apparently caused a critical situation. Syria's international reserves declined from $735m at the end of 1975 to $361m at the end of 1976.[54] It appears that the situation was becoming more critical in 1977. According to one report, "the foreign exchange shortage is said to be so severe, in fact, that state organizations, as well as private enterprises, are going to the black market to purchase hard currency for needed imports."[55]

One visible sign of the budgetary and balance of payments problems faced is the continued delay in finalizing the five-year Development Plan which was to have been initiated in January 1976. More important, the rising military expenditures, over and above Arab and Soviet aid, must necessarily restrict allocations either to investment or the level of consumption, or both. The *announced* military budget for 1977 of c. $1 bn does not include Arab aid or Soviet military equipment. If past history is a guide, the announced budget does not include *all* Syrian military expenditures and, in any case, it is usually exceeded. Other sources state that the military budget for 1977 is the equivalent of $1.5 bn. Syria will thus be expending from 14–21% of its GNP (from its own resources) in 1977. This will mean a cutback in the investment budget, with all its implications for current and future economic growth.[56] The Syrian economy would certainly benefit from a combination of favourable factors, such as good weather for agriculture, higher oil and phosphate prices, and increased foreign aid. But to achieve high rates of economic growth over the longer term would require a major reallocation of resources towards peaceful development, and a restructuring of the economy towards greater incentives for production and efficiency, and penalties for those enterprises which do not meet these standards. The public sector enterprises, in many cases, incur heavy losses, and absorb rather than contribute to the expansion of resources.[57] However there is little evidence that such changes are soon to take place.[58]

JORDAN: UNDERLYING STRENGTH OF ITS ECONOMY

The economy of Jordan has been prospering since the end of the civil war in 1971 and the abolition of the Syrian closure of its borders in 1972. This may be surprising, but it is no more than a continuation of the underlying trends which were apparent before the Six-Day war in 1967. During the period between the early 1950s and May 1967, the Kingdom of Jordan had shown unusually rapid growth, with GNP per capita rising by an annual average of 5–7%, approximating the high growth rates of the Israeli economy during this period—though from a much lower base. Few of the underdeveloped economies (other than those with an abundance of petroleum and a small population) have been able to achieve such high growth rates over a period of 10 to 15 years. By 1966, the Jordanian GNP per capita exceeded that of all other Arab countries, with the exception of Lebanon and the three richest Arab oil states. Foreign aid, mainly US government grants, amounted to c. $100m in 1966, in addition to military aid. Though small in absolute terms, it was large in relation to the size of the economy; this enabled the Kingdom to invest in development projects without restricting the rapid growth of civilian consumption—both public and private. The authorities, by and large, adopted pragmatic economic policies, stimulating a rapid expansion of the economy, and putting great emphasis on the development of human resources.

RELATIONS BETWEEN EAST AND WEST BANKS

For various reasons, possibly political as well as economic, the government of Jordan laid heavy emphasis on the development of the East Bank, including irrigation projects (the East Ghor Canal); manufacturing (oil refinery, textile, paper, cement and many other smaller plants); phosphates; electric power; the expansion and modernization of ‘Aqaba port; air and land transportation; the development of the capital city of Amman, and its industrial suburb, Zarqā’. The result was a rapid migration of both native residents and refugees from the West Bank to the East Bank, where employment opportunities were growing and wage rates were *far* higher. (A smaller number of Palestinians—mainly from the West Bank—were attracted by the much higher salaries in the oil-rich Gulf states.) Though the old city of Jerusalem was the focus of the tourist industry, the government laid greater stress on the development of tourist sites in the East Bank. Before the Six-Day war, an estimated 80% of industrial production and 65% of agricultural production in Jordan was from the East Bank, and development plans indicated that the disparity was destined to increase. Other sectors—trade, finance, transportation, public and personal services—were tied, in the main, to the progress of the primary economic sectors. The only important exception was the tourist industry which, at the time, was still mainly on the West Bank. The East Bank's share of the Kingdom's population rose from c. 38% in 1949 to 60% in May 1967—the result of large-scale internal migration. As a consequence, over 40% of the East Bank's population in May 1967 was Palestinian, and the proportion was steadily increasing. Amman's population was about two-thirds Palestinian at that time. The available evidence indicates that c. 60% of the East Bank's population is now of Palestinian origin, and that Palestinians occupy central positions in the Kingdom's economy.

The Six-Day war proved to be a temporary and relatively minor setback for the East Bank economy. This was due in part to the resumption of trade relations between the East and West Banks within a few months after the war. 1967 also happened to be a year of exceptional crops, and damages to the civilian economy during the war were minor. However, the main factor was that in 1967 the East Bank economy was far more advanced, and whatever dependence it may have had in earlier years on the West Bank was steadily diminishing. As a consequence, industrial production, construction and most of the economic sectors were in a sharp uptrend during the first half of 1968. This continued until mid-1970, despite internal problems with the fidā'iyyūn groups, and some border "incidents" with Israel, including the destruction of part of the East Ghor Canal project and the disruption of agriculture in that region. Military expenditure rose sharply as a result of Jordan's internal and external problems, but foreign aid rose even more sharply. The 250,000 refugees from the West Bank and the Gaza Strip who fled to the East Bank were not a significant *economic* problem; in fact, it was estimated that the rapid growth of the economy in 1969 lowered the unemployment rate below that which prevailed before the Six-Day war.

ECONOMIC GROWTH SINCE 1970

The internal struggle in the Kingdom culminated in full-scale civil war, beginning in the summer of 1970. Many economic sectors were at a virtual standstill for many months. The civil war ended in the summer of 1971 with the complete elimination of the fidū'iyyūn. However, this was followed by an economic war waged by other Arab countries, primarily Syria, which closed its borders both with respect to bilateral trade and, more important, to transit. Even before the closure of the Suez Canal in June 1967, most of Jordanian imports came from Western countries via Beirut, and thence via Syria to Jordan. The importance of this route was enhanced by the closure of the Suez Canal. The Syrian embargo (including the overflying of Jordanian aircraft) caused economic havoc in Jordan. The embargo was lifted, in stages, during 1972, but was not abolished completely until December of that year. The Iraqi and Egyptian embargoes on trade with Jordan were short-lived, and caused minor damage to the economy. However, Libya and Kuwait cut off their grants to Jordan. Saudi Arabia compensated, in part, by increasing its aid, and the US increased its grants and loans to make up most of the remaining deficit.

Following the sharp decline in GDP in 1970 (both as a result of the civil war and severe drought), there was a small increase (c. 4%) in 1971, and a substantial increase (c. 8%) in 1972, despite the severity of the Syrian embargo in those two years. 1973 was again a year of severe drought, and to a minor extent the Yom Kippur war had a temporary adverse effect on the economy during the last quarter of the year.

Towards the end of 1972, the Jordanian government announced a new three-year Development Plan (1973–5). 1973 was adversely affected by the drought and the war, but even so there was an uptrend in most economic sectors, including industrial production, construction and even tourism during the first nine months.

The uptrend was much sharper in 1974 and 1975. The provisional estimates for the 1973–5 Plan indicate that most of the targets were either achieved or were close to achievement, including investment in irrigation projects, the establishment of new industries or the expansion of existing ones, particularly phosphates; various tourist projects; roads, airports, rail connections, and the expansion of capacity at 'Aqaba; electric power, and others. GNP expanded by an annual average rate of c. 7%, close to the target of 8%.

Measured in current dollars, exports of goods and services in 1975 were almost five times their 1966 level, and almost four times their 1972 level (the base year of the 1973–5 plan). There were both favourable and some unfavourable exogenous factors. 1975 was a year of drought, which adversely affects the comparison with 1972. On the other hand, the price of phosphates in the world market (Jordan's main commodity export) was 5.2 times higher in 1975 than in 1972. However, even discounting international price changes, total commodity exports in 1975 were 32% higher than in 1972, despite the drought and its effects on farm production. Exports were also more diversified, reflecting developments in the economy as a whole. Of far greater importance, quantitatively, than commodity exports, is that of services (invisibles). This was also the case before the Six-Day war. In 1975 commodity exports were $153m; service exports, $426m. The latter consist mainly of tourism, remittances from Jordanians abroad, income from investments abroad (mainly interest received from foreign banks where Jordan's international reserves are held), and smaller amounts from other sources such as oil transit dues, transit of goods to other countries, etc.

On the other hand, imports have also risen rapidly, due both to far higher international prices as well as a real increase. Commodity imports rose from $237m in 1972 to $649m in 1975. In real terms, the increase was 38%. Including services, imports rose from $333m in 1973 to $952m in 1975. The rising volume of imports reflects far higher levels of investment (in equipment and machinery); expanded production (of raw materials); and far higher levels of consumption. The last is especially evident from the increase in non-food imports, and especially consumer durable goods, which rose from $16.5m in 1972 to $43.3m in 1975. In part this reflects higher international prices, but mainly represents the rapid increase in real living standards in Jordan.

Though exports (of goods and services, measured in current dollars) were four times their 1972 level in 1975, and imports were less than 2.9 times their 1972 level, the import surplus increased sharply, from $188m in 1972 to $373m in 1975. However, grants from the rich Arab countries and from the US increased even more rapidly. (It should be noted that imports of military equipment are usually not recorded either in the balance of payments or in official government figures with respect to foreign aid.) In the years 1972–4, annual grants received by Jordan very closely approximated the annual import surplus. Fundamentally, they enabled the government to be liberal with respect to imports, and to make little or no attempt to restrict consumption. In 1975 foreign grants rose very sharply, reaching $435m, exceeding the import surplus of $373m. All this was aside from concessional loans from foreign governments which rose from $20.7m in 1972 to $57.5m in 1975. The result was a sharp rise in Jordan's international reserves, from $272m at the end of 1972 to $492m at the end of 1975.[59]

Towards the end of 1975, Jordan announced a most ambitious five-year Development Plan for the years 1976–80. It aims at a growth rate of GNP averaging 12% pa, far in excess of what had been achieved before 1967—and far higher than that achieved in other countries (other than the oil-rich states with small populations). In relation both to past history and to the size of the Jordanian economy, the scope of investment envisaged in the Plan is most ambitious. Aid from the rich Arab states (Kuwait resumed its aid after October 1973), from the US and various Western European countries is assured. The main constraint to achieving these goals is not financial—it is the level of skills of the labour force, including that of the economic and political leadership.

The booming conditions in the oil-rich countries also create a serious problem for Jordan's development. Officials estimated that c. 300,000 Jordanians were abroad in 1976, of which about one-half were employed; the others, their dependants. The total labour force in the East Bank was only c. 400-450,000. But it is not only a problem of numbers. Those attracted by the oil-rich countries are primarily the skilled and professional groups, who are also very much needed at home. Jordan puts no restrictions on emigration; this compels Jordanian employers to offer salaries which do not fall too far below those in the oil-producing countries. This has raised labour costs in Jordan and added to inflationary pressures. The government has taken various measures to stem the tide, including a ban on advertisements for labour from foreign employers. In addition, it has expanded programmes for vocational training within the country. According to Labour Ministry officials, the gap between salaries offered in Jordan and those in the oil states has narrowed, and the tide of emigration has been stemmed, though certainly not stopped. A more interesting phenomenon is that during the last few years Jordan has been attracting workers from Syria and Egypt, as well as from Pakistan. Most of these are manual labourers, mainly unskilled. According to estimates published in mid-1977, there were c. 60,000 foreign workers in Jordan, including c. 20,000 Syrians, many of whom had previously worked in Lebanon prior to the civil war. It was reported that in March 1977, Egyptians were arriving at a monthly rate of 10,000. Apparently the government was preparing to take measures to impose much stronger restrictions on this influx.[60]

Incomplete data are available for 1976, the first year of the 1976-80 plan, but it appears that two exogenous factors adversely affected the economy. The price of phosphates (determined in international markets) fell sharply—45% below the high level prevailing in 1975, though still about three times the price in 1970-2. Thus, though the volume of phosphate exports expanded significantly, from 1.1m tons in 1975 to 1.65m in 1976, receipts were only $62m (cf $63.5m in 1975). The second factor was another poor agricultural year. In the 1973-6 period, only 1974 was a year of favourable weather—the others were years of drought, though 1976 was somewhat better than 1975. However, other economic sectors showed significant advances in 1976. Industrial production increased 27.4%. The influx from Lebanon, as a result of the civil war, included many of the wealthier classes; this in turn added further stimulus to the economy. Construction, in particular, increased dramatically. The government made attempts to attract many of the international firms which fled Lebanon, and had some success. Remittances from nationals abroad again increased rapidly, including investment in Jordan by its citizens working abroad. They rose from $161m in 1975 to c. $360m in 1976. It is estimated that an additional $240m was remitted by Jordanians abroad, which was not exchanged through the banking system. Income from tourism rose from c. $108m in 1975 to $190m in 1976. The number of construction permits issued for Amman and Zarqā', which had reached an all-time high in 1975, increased again by over 50% in 1976. This is an indicator of future growth. Gross fixed investment (in current prices) increased by 44% which, even after discounting a rate of inflation of c. 15%, would indicate a real increase of c. 25%. GDP (at factor cost) in real terms, increased by c. 5%, and GNP by 23%.[61]

Fuller details on the balance of payments are unavailable at this time.

Commodity exports increased by 41% and commodity imports by 31% (both measured in current prices). Given the initial wide gap, this meant an increase in the trade deficit. However, the export of services (remittances, tourism, etc) increased so sharply that the import surplus declined from $373m in 1975 to $298m in 1976. It appears that grants from Arab countries to Jordan were sharply curtained—from $214m in 1975 to $58m in 1976. US grants increased, but not sufficiently to offset the cutback in Arab aid. Total grants received declined from $435m in 1975 to $381m in 1976. Nonetheless, grants still exceeded the import surplus. Concessional loans also declined somewhat, from $58m in 1975 to $54m in 1976. As usual, no data are available on grants in the category of military aid.[62]

CONCLUSIONS

Much has been written of the economic impact of the influx of refugees from Lebanon on the Jordanian economy. There is no doubt that it added to aggregate demand—and, to some extent, to the speculative fever in real estate prices and construction. However, the strong uptrend in the Jordanian economy antedates the Lebanese war which began in 1975, and the return of some of the Lebanese to their country since the latter half of 1976 seems to have had only a minor effect on Jordan's economy—except for a reduction of stability in real estate prices in Amman, and possibly some reduction in overall inflationary pressures.

All the available evidence indicates that, despite the drought and sharp decline in phosphate prices in 1976, the new 1976-80 Development Plan has made a good start. That GDP advanced despite the drought—which could not have happened before 1967—is a clear indication of the changing structure of the economy and its underlying strength. There is room for doubt regarding the ability of Jordan to achieve the most ambitious aims of the new Development Plan in full; but barring internal or regional upheavals, there is every reason to project that most of the goals will be achieved. Jordan has been transformed within the last decade from a labour-surplus to a labour-deficit economy, *both* because of emigration and rapid economic growth. This is not a new trend.

The steady decline in unemployment rates had begun in the 1950s, and continued in the 1960s, other than in years of severe external or internal disturbances. The continued economic advance will inevitably mean more labour shortages which, in turn, should help reduce the rate of emigration, and attract immigrants from other countries.

The pragmatic economic policies of the Jordanian government, encouraging and stimulating private as well as public enterprise, the avoidance of show-piece projects, the selection of enterprises within the technological and skill capacities of the labour force, and the continued upgrading of the level of education and skills, have proved to be a most successful combination for economic development. Once the exogenous disturbances (wars, embargoes, etc) were removed, the underlying strength of the economy again became apparent. This was the case in 1968-9, and even more so since 1972.[63]

SAUDI ARABIA: THE OIL GIANT

Saudi Arabian oil production in 1976 was second only to that of the Soviet Union, and its potential was by far the largest of any country—over one-quarter of the world's known reserves. Despite constantly rising production, newly-discovered deposits have steadily raised this total. Saudi Arabia accounted for 15% of world petroleum output in 1976, but since it consumes only a tiny fraction of this, its exports are by far the largest in the world. Its share of OPEC production has been rising steadily—reaching 28% in 1976, and possibly c. 30% during the first half of

1977. Between 1960 and 1970, oil prices were stable; but the result of increasing production was to increase oil revenues from $334m in 1960 to $1,214m in 1970. Oil production (including the Saudi share of the Neutral Zone) rose by an annual average rate of 11%, while world oil production (and consumption) was rising by only 7-8% pa.

Oil dominated the economy in terms of exports, state budgets and the GNP as a whole. The latter was rising by c. 10% pa. The non-oil sectors were woefully under-developed—even by Middle Eastern standards—until the early 1960s when a more determined attempt was begun by the government to develop the non-oil economy. Agriculture was supported, in part, to encourage settlement of the nomads. However, the growth rate of agricultural production was no more than c. 3% pa, approximating the growth rate of the population. Much stress was laid on the development of manufacturing—mainly light industry—in addition to the construction of oil refineries. Electric power was extended to the towns and cities. The urban areas grew especially rapidly. Transportation and communications were allocated the largest budgets, and educational facilities, on all levels, expanded rapidly.

OIL PRODUCTION

Between 1970 and 1973, there was a sharp acceleration in oil production, which rose by 26% pa.[64] The OPEC cartel began to become more powerful and successfully imposed higher oil prices. Following a decade of price stability (during the 1960s), the Tehran agreement between OPEC and the major Western oil companies raised the price of oil by 21%, as of February 1971. During a number of subsequent agreements between February 1971 and June 1973, *before* the Yom Kippur war, additional price increases totalling 61% were imposed. Shortly after the outbreak of war in October 1973, an additional price increase of 77% was announced. Towards the end of 1973 an additional price rise of 128% was agreed, as of 1 January 1974.[65] As a result of both higher production and higher prices, Saudi oil revenues increased from $1,214m in 1970 to $4,340m in 1973. It is noteworthy that despite the cutback in oil production during the last quarter of 1973 (the oil embargo), Saudi output for the year as a whole increased by 26%, the same high rate of growth as in each of the previous two years. It further expanded its production by 12.7% in 1974. In fact, its output increased even during the first quarter of 1974 (10% above the level of the last quarter of 1973) even though the Arab oil embargo was still officially in force.

Saudi Arabia's expanded production made the oil glut more pronounced and, as industrial nations' recession deepened in 1975, the Saudis were compelled to curtail production by 16.3%. Meanwhile, the sharply higher oil prices increased Saudi revenues from $4,340m in 1973 to $22,574m in 1974, and $25,676m in 1975. The higher revenues in 1975, despite lower production and exports, were due to the 10% increase in oil prices set by OPEC as of 1 October 1975, and to an increase in royalty and tax rates related to the partial nationalization of Aramco, the major American oil company operating in the country.[66] The absorption of such vast financial resources was beyond the immediate capacity of the Saudi economy, due to an overall lack of educated and skilled manpower and of managerial personnel, and an inadequate infrastructure.

GDP in 1974-5 was estimated at $38 bn, of which crude oil and natural gas production accounted for almost $30 bn (78% of GDP). Petroleum refining—the only manufacturing of significance—provided an additional $1.6 bn (4% of GDP). About 8% of crude oil production was refined in the country. Other manufacturing amounted to $263m; agriculture, $393m; construction, $1,345m; transportation and communications, $1,115m; electricity, gas and water, $90m. The balance was accounted for by public, business and personal services.[67]

FIVE-YEAR DEVELOPMENT PLAN

Saudi Arabia announced an ambitious and very expensive five-year Development Plan in mid-1975, with public expenditure estimated at $142 bn. These estimates were based on prices prevailing locally in 1974–5. The plan envisaged an overall average annual growth rate (in real terms) of 10.2%, including a 9.7% growth rate in the oil sector; 13.4% in the non-oil private sector; and 12.9% in the government sector. Agricultural production was planned to increase by 4% pa; manufacturing by 14%. The bulk of the required investment was to be financed by oil revenues supplemented by earnings from State investments abroad. About 60% of anticipated expenditure was allocated to construction of highways, airports, ports, water desalination plants, gas, electricity, schools, housing, hospitals, military bases, industrial plants and irrigation projects. Planned military expenditure—including arms purchases and the construction of bases, etc—was set at $22 bn, more than 16% of the total expenditure.[68]

However, the planners had very seriously underestimated the non-financial constraints, already mentioned, on carrying out this ambitious plan. Severe bottlenecks in the ports were only one aspect of these problems. Foreign labour was hired in increasing numbers, with projects invariably assigned to foreign firms. The constraints were of such magnitude that inflationary pressures became increasingly pronounced. Officially, the consumer price index rose by 16.5% in 1973; 21.4% in 1974; and 34.6% in 1975—unofficial estimates were much higher. In 1976 the consumer price index rose by 31.5%, but unofficial estimates in early 1977 put the rate of inflation at, minimally, 40%.[69] Such increases were inevitable given the rapid expansion of the money supply (including quasi-money) which increased by an annual average rate of 40% in 1972–4, and 79% in 1975. The 1976 rate of growth approximated that of 1975, with all its consequences for further inflation.[70] No construction price index is available, but it appears that these costs have risen at an even more rapid rate. According to one study, *on the basis of prices prevailing in mid-1976*, the implementation of all the projects as well as other expenditures envisaged in the Development Plan would cost $283 bn—double the original amount.[71]

These unanticipated problems led the authorities to undertake a number of measures. Great efforts went into clearing up port congestion, which was not significantly reduced until early 1977. Many of the projects were "stretched out", either by design or because of practical constraints. In the euphoria of the oil revenue deluge in 1974 and 1975, it would appear that the authorities, at least implicitly, dismissed the possibility of future financial constraints. More recently, especially since the latter half of 1976, they have become more selective in their choice of projects; many of the earlier ones have been either cancelled or postponed indefinitely; others were subjected to a more cost-conscious scrutiny. Inflated tenders from foreign contractors were turned down. No less important, the authorities appear to have removed any restraints on expanding oil production. They appear to be convinced that in order to execute the Development Plan—even on a reduced scale—the financial requirements will be far greater than anticipated. Meantime, to counteract internal unrest arising from inflation, subsidies were introduced for essential commodities. These subsidies rose from $372m in 1974–5 to almost $2 bn in 1975–6. They were scheduled to rise even further in 1976–7.[72] In the new budget for 1977–8, $2.6 bn was included for wage and salary increases for government employees.[73] While such measures may have been politically and socially unavoidable, their almost inevitable effect will be to further increase inflationary pressures.

The large influx of foreigners and the accelerated rural-urban trend created severe housing shortages in the cities and towns. To cope with this problem, the government ordered "a massive programme" to construct 59,000 housing units at a cost of c. 62.4 bn riyals ($17.7 bn), for which purpose an appropriation of 9 bn riyals ($2.5 bn) was made in the 1976–7 budget. This was in addition to subsidized loans to the private sector to encourage housing construction.[74]

MILITARY EXPENDITURE

Military expenditures have increased rapidly in recent years. According to American estimates, they averaged $220m pa between 1967 and 1971. In 1972, they rose abruptly to $687m; in 1973 to $988m; and in 1974 to $1,450m. The imports of arms rose from $52m in 1972, to $69m in 1973, and then to $393m in 1974.[75] According to the official budget (under the heading Defence and Aviation) the appropriations were: 1973–4, $1,523m; 1974–5, $2,490m; 1975–6, $6,721m; and 1976–7, $9,039m.[76] Bearing in mind that the original five-year Plan had allocated a total of $22 bn to the armed forces for the whole period, it seems apparent (from the appropriation of $15.7 bn during the first two years of the plan) that military expenditures will greatly exceed original estimates. This is apparently due to a number of factors, including the rising cost of "sophisticated" armaments sold by the US and other Western arms suppliers; the changed perception of the Saudi leaders of their "defence requirements"; rising domestic construction costs, especially for building military bases; and the necessity to raise salaries of military personnel, at least to keep abreast of inflation. It is also possible that payments by Saudi Arabia to arms suppliers for shipments direct to other Arab countries (mainly Egypt and Jordan) are included in these budgets. However, these expenditures probably account for only a fraction of total Saudi military spending.

ECONOMIC AID

Following the Six-Day war in 1967, Saudi Arabia (together with Kuwait and Libya) initiated a programme of economic aid to other Arab countries, mainly Egypt and Jordan and, to a lesser extent, Syria. Between 1968 and 1972, Saudi aid was approximately $150m annually, of which about one-half was in the form of grants, and the balance given as concessional loans (long-term loans at low interest rates).[77] Aid was not increased during this period, even though Saudi oil revenues rose from $926m in 1968 to $2,745m in 1972, and its international reserves from $662m to $2,500m. According to official reports, grants to Arab countries were: 1973, $498m; 1974, $1,015m; and 1975, $1,588m.[78] There were also direct loans to Arab countries, as well as to international organizations such as the IMF and the World Bank (which pooled contributions from other major oil exporters and the wealthier industrial nations for aid to the poorer countries. Bilateral loans amounted to $97m in 1973–4, $211m in 1974–5, and $577m in 1975–6. These would appear to be concessional loans; however, the c. $600m lent in 1974–5, and again in 1975–6, to international organizations may have been at rates of interest closer to those prevailing in the commercial markets.[79] According to the official budget, total foreign aid was set at $1,320m in 1975–6, to be reduced to $841m in 1976–7.[80] However, as a result of the intense political pressures arising from the acute balance of payments problems of Egypt, it may very well be that actual aid exceeded this amount. No data are yet available with respect to Saudi grants to the Arab countries in 1976; but reports from Egypt, Syria, and Jordan (noted earlier) suggest that *grants* from the Arab donors were substantially reduced in 1976; and this most probably also includes Saudi Arabia, as well as the two other major Arab donors, Kuwait and Abū Dhabī. However, it is possible that loans, commercial and possibly concessional, were increased.

POPULATION AND IMMIGRATION

Mention was made earlier of the manpower constraints on Saudi economic development. Population figures for the country have always been of dubious quality. According to official statistics, the 1974 census showed a population of 7m, of whom 27% were Bedouins; 2.7m resided in cities of 30,000 or more. The official data do not indicate the number of foreigners in the country at that time, but a sample survey taken in 1973 of "workers in the establishments of the private sector" indicated that 54% were immigrants. Foreigners in the category of professional and technical workers made up 75% of the total.[81] However, such figures must be viewed with caution. An American economist noted in 1975 that "based on conversations with various [Saudi] officials, our estimate [of the population] in 1974 is 3.75-4m . . ."[82] Another report in 1975 quoted a "government expert" as the source for an estimated population of c. 4m, including over 1m foreign workers. The official figure for foreign workers at that time was 400,000.[83] Why the government should wish to exaggerate the size of the Saudi population and understate the number of foreigners is not made clear. What is clear though, is that the small native population and its low level of education and skills severely restrict the execution of the ambitious development plans.

Data in the new Development Plan indicate that the labour force was c. 1.6m in 1974-5, of whom 20% were foreigners. By the end of the plan period (1979-80), the projections were that the labour force would increase to 2,334,000, of whom 813,000 (25%) would be foreigners.[84] Yet over 1m Yemenis—mostly unskilled—were unofficially estimated to be in the country in 1976.[85] In addition, there were large numbers of Arabs from other countries, as well as Indians, Pakistanis, Europeans and Americans. The Westerners are most often the key managerial and professional personnel; but despite high salaries, there were increasing difficulties in recruiting and keeping this high-level manpower as cultural and social problems proved to be a serious deterrent.[86] There are also internal difficulties in absorbing such a large foreign population. There were reports in 1976 estimating that the large influx into Saudi Arabia since 1974 had brought about a situation where the number of foreigners approximated the number of citizens, and that this was causing alarm in the National Security Council. This may induce the Council to press for a slowdown in the development plans.[87] In these respects, the Saudis were facing problems similar to those experienced by Kuwait and other oil-rich Arab countries.

CURRENT ECONOMIC PERFORMANCE

All of the above-mentioned problems do not imply that Saudi economic development has ceased. What they do imply is that: 1) the pace of economic development will be slower than anticipated, and far costlier. 2) The prospects for developing agriculture and industry on a significant scale, and thereby reducing imports or developing non-oil exports are poor, for the foreseeable future. 3) Saudi Arabia will continue to be overwhelmingly dependent on oil revenues, supplemented by income accruing from its foreign investments.

Whether the adoption of such an ambitious Development Plan was in the best interest of the country is beside the point. Unofficially, there has been a scaling down of the plan's scope, a stretching out of the time span, and some re-ordering of priorities in favour of fewer industrial projects (other than those related to the oil sector) and of greater emphasis on investment in infrastructure. It would appear that the Saudi government is, at least officially, still committed to the plan, though a statement by the Minister of Industry in April 1977 indicated clearly that he accepted that industrialization would take time. "We have no illusion of achieving in a short space of time what took centuries in the West."[88]

The export surplus (exports of goods and services minus imports) rose sharply from $152m in 1970 to $2,702m in 1973, and then skyrocketed to $24,022m in 1974, as a result of the steep rise in oil prices. Exports (goods and services) rose from $8,295m in 1973 to $32,647m in 1974, while imports (goods and services) increased from $5,593m to $8,625m. Imports were clearly unable to increase at anywhere near the same pace as exports within such a short period. Even after deducting Saudi grants to other countries, the surplus rose from $2,204m in 1973 to $23,007m in 1974. In 1975, as a result of the decline in oil exports, total exports (goods and services) were $30,907m. However, imports continued to rise rapidly from $8,625m in 1974 to $12,900m. The surplus declined from $24,022m in 1974 to $18,007m in 1975. After deducting grants to other Arab countries, the decline was from $23,007m to $16,419m.[89] Officially, Saudi international reserves rose from $3,877m in 1973 to $23,319m in 1975 (end of year figures). Possibly of greater relevance are (net) foreign assets of the central bank which rose from $5,082m at the end of 1973 to $39,322m at the end of 1975. It would appear that much or most of the foreign assets, over and above those defined as international reserves, were also highly liquid. Certainly such sums are formidable.

However, the perception of the Saudi leadership appears to be different. It is that the gap between income and expenditure—as reflected in government budgets and in the balance of payments—appears to be narrowing; that the rate of growth of expenditure and imports is far higher than the prospective growth of income and exports. In interviews in May 1977, both the Minister of Finance and Economy and the Governor of the Central Bank, stated: "We don't have a surplus, we have a temporary liquidity." Saudi Arabia, in their view, is a vast country, woefully underdeveloped—"This is a developing country and needs every cent . . . Actual expenses are still less than revenues. But we are talking about the day the two curves meet"—i.e. when revenues rise at a slower pace than expenditures. They noted that bills were coming due for vast capital projects, and that the cost of imported technology and services was rising. "The costs of development are very high. Oil production is increasing, but we believe that the absorption capacity is going up even faster." They believe that by 1980 there will be no surplus, and that the accumulated reserves might be exhausted by 1990, even after allowances are made for increased oil production and higher prices. In the words of the Minister of Planning: "To assume that Saudi Arabia is a rich country is a fallacy." This, the minister stated, explained the Saudi policy of keeping the financial surplus in highly liquid assets, mainly in the US. To back up their contention that the gap between revenues and expenditures was narrowing, they noted that in the fiscal year ending June 1976, the government spent $22 bn, while its revenues were $28.8 bn. In the fiscal year ending June 1977, they anticipated that the surplus would narrow, with revenues rising to $31 bn, and expenditures to £27 bn.[90]

Whether the perception of the Saudi ministers is accurate or not only the future will tell. But it does explain many of the actions of the Saudi government, including the curtailment of foreign aid, at least in terms of outright grants; the curb on government expenditure since mid-1976; and, in the view of this writer, the decision of the Saudis to expand rapidly both current oil production as well as productive capacity in order to forestall the eventuality foreseen by the ministers—budgetary deficits after 1980. In 1976, the Saudis sharply expanded oil production, by 21.6%, taking full advantage of the end of the recession in the US and in many other Western countries, and the consequent rising demand for oil. World oil production in 1976 rose by c. 7.6%, and in the other OPEC countries at about the same rate.[91]

At the December 1976 meeting of OPEC, Saudi Arabia, joined by the United

Arab Emirates (UAE), split with the other 11 members who decided on a price increase of 10% as of 1 January 1977, to be followed by an additional increase of 5% as of 1 July 1977. Saudi Arabia and the UAE decided on only a 5% increase, as of 1 January. What is more, Saudi Arabia raised its price for the heavier grades of crude oil—which are more difficult to market—by only 3% to 3.6%. While the Saudis spoke of "political" motivations for their relative oil price moderation, it appears that economic considerations were paramount.[92] During the first half of 1977, Saudi Arabia made every attempt to raise its oil production rapidly, but various exogenous factors (bad weather and a fire at its main oil port terminal) hampered any significant rise in output. At the meetings of OPEC in mid-1977, Saudi Arabia and the UAE finally agreed to raise their prices by 5% (over and above their previous 5% increase in January), and the others agreed not to implement their planned additional increase of 5% as of July 1977. However, the Saudi policy of increasing output as rapidly as possible—given the technical and market constraints—seems to be continuing. In May 1977, Aramco announced plans to increase productivity capacity by almost 50%, from c. 11m b/d to 16m b/d by 1982.[93]

CONCLUSIONS

Saudi Arabia's vast oil reserves, sufficient to last for c. 60 years at the 1976 rate of production, and the high probability that there is much oil yet to be discovered, put it into a separate category from most other Arab countries. Since petroleum is its only known source of income, its concern is both with the short and the long run. In the longer run, raising the real price of oil (i.e. above the rate of inflation in the West) can only be counter-productive in that it adds further stimulus to the West's efforts to develop and implement new technology, and to undertake measures designed both to conserve energy and to find alternative sources. Such efforts certainly are long-term. In the short-term, the Saudi perception of its financial needs, and the concern that expenditures are rising rapidly, constitute a strong inducement to increase oil exports. While many in the West are concerned that the petroleum supply will fall short of demand at the existing price by the mid-1980s, and therefore that prices will rise sharply, there appears to be concern among some of the Arab oil producers that conservation measures and the development of alternative sources of energy might create downward pressures on oil prices, at least in real terms (in constant dollars).[94]

As for the shorter run—until around 1980—many studies indicate that demand for OPEC oil will be approximately constant, mainly as a result of rising production in Mexico, the North Sea and Alaska. Even the pessimistic CIA report of April 1977 does not project serious problems until the early or mid-1980s. This, of course, presupposes knowledge as to the extent of new discoveries in the next few years, as well as other assumptions regarding energy demand. However, even this report projects only a slight rise in demand for OPEC oil rising from 31m b/d in 1976 to 32m b/d in 1977, and then remaining constant in 1978 and 1979.[95] Given Saudi perceptions of financial needs, it seems likely that it will continue to expand output, and acquire a growing share of the OPEC oil market.

NOTES

1. The official national accounts both in current and constant prices are from the National Bank of Egypt (NBE), *Economic Bulletin (EB)*, Vol 29, No 1, (1976), pp. 123-4, and earlier issues. The population data and price indices are from International Monetary Fund (IMF) *International Financial Statistics (IFS)*, May 1977, pp. 154-5. The implicit

price deflator derived from a comparison of the current and constant price series of GDP is 3.0% pa. However, the other official price indices show a higher rate of inflation. The wholesale price index rose by an annual average rate of 4.7% during the 1963-4/1974 period, and the consumer price index by 5.4% pa. Furthermore, there are both unofficial reports and some official statements noting that the price indices seriously understate the extent of inflation. See, for example, Economist Intelligence Unit (EIU), *Quarterly Economic Review (QER)*, No 1 (1976), p. 4. Thus, by all accounts, the real growth rate of the economy is undoubtedly overstated. One can also examine the official GDP constant price series in terms of its sectoral components. If one excludes "other services" which mainly reflect the fictitious increase in "production" arising from the rapid expansion of government bureaucracy, the growth rate of GDP is reduced from 4.2% to 2.9%. As will be noted later, there are also indications that the official figures on agricultural and industrial production—about 50% of GDP—are overstated.

2. NBE, *EB*, Vol 27, No 4 (1974), p. 296.
3. Data for private consumption in current prices were corrected by the official consumer price index, and then calculated on a per capita basis. They show that per capita private consumption was E£ 63.07 in 1963–4 and E£ 58.41 in 1974, measured in 1970 prices. The official exchange rate of the Egyptian pound (E£), was $2.300 in 1963–4 and $2.5556 in 1974. In recent years, especially, the gap between the official exchange rate and its "real" value has become very wide, as indicated by the official "parallel" exchange rate which has been fluctuating at a rate over 40% lower than the official rate. The black market rate is even lower. See IMF, *IFS*, May 1977, pp. 152-5.
4. See, for example, *New York Times (NYT)*, 10 February 1976.
5. NBE, *EB*, Vol 29, No 1 (1976), pp. 123, 130.
6. The Egyptian data are in terms of value-added in GDP. See NBE, *EB*, Vol 29, No 1 (1976), p. 124, and earlier issues. US Dept of Agriculture, *Indices of Agricultural Production in Africa and the Near East 1956-75* (Washington DC, 1976), pp. 22-23; and earlier issues. Since the Egyptian data, until 1973, are in terms of fiscal years, the terminal years are averages of the relevant fiscal years.
7. See, for example, M. Clawson, H. H. Landsberg, and L. T. Alexander, *The Agricultural Potential of the Middle East* (New York: American Elsevier, 1971), pp. 2-4.
8. US Dept of Agriculture, *The Agricultural Situation in Africa and West Asia*, 1976, p. 9.
9. For an analysis of Egyptian agriculture, see US Dept of Agriculture, co-operating with the US Agency for International Development and the Egyptian Ministry of Agriculture, *Egypt: Major Constraints to Increasing Agricultural Productivity* (Washington, 1976).
10. *Ibid*, p. 34.
11. NBE, *EB*, Vol 28, No 2 (1975), p. 139.
12. *The Economist*, 24 July 1976. *Middle East International (MEI)*, London; February 1977, p. 29. *The Environment*, November 1974, pp. 18-26.
13. US Dept of Agriculture, et. al., *Egypt: Major Constraints to Increasing Agricultural Productivity* (Washington, 1976), p. 48.
14. NBE, *EB*, Vol 29, No 1 (1976), p. 124, and earlier issues.
15. A study of Egyptian industry indicates that manufacturing output increased by 12.6% between 1963-4 and 1969-70. See R. Mabro and S. Radwan, *The Industrialization of Egypt 1939-1973* (Oxford University Press, 1976), p. 87. The official data on value added in industry indicate a growth of 20.0% during this period. See NBE, *EB*, Vol 29, No 1 (1976), p. 124, and earlier issues. The official data do not provide an index of industrial production, and though industry includes mining and crude oil production, the bulk of industrial production is concentrated in manufacturing. It appears likely that the official figures are exaggerated.
16. *The Arab Economist*, December 1975, pp. 17-18.
17. *Middle East Economic Digest (MEED)*, 1 April 1977, p. 18.
18. US Dept of Agriculture, *Indices of Agricultural Production in Africa and Near East*, 1976, p. 23.
19. The current price series for industrial production shows an increase of 17.8% and, in constant prices, 11.9%. This would imply a price deflator of 5.3%. The official wholesale price index shows a rise of 7.5% in 1975. See IMF, *IFS*, May 1977, p. 153. In view of the widespread reports of a very large gap between the official price indices and the real extent of inflation, there is room for scepticism, though the changes in the wholesale price index need not be identical with those of industrial prices.
20. *MEED*, 15 July 1977, p. 17.
21. *Events*, 25 March 1977, p. 37.
22. EIU, *QER*, March 1967, p. 16.
23. EIU, *QER—Egypt*, No 2 (1977), p. 12.
24. *MEED*, 24 June 1977, p. 16.

25. *The Middle East*, June 1977, p. 111.
26. Central Intelligence Agency (CIA), *The International Energy Situation: Outlook to 1985*, April 1977, p. 11.
27. *MEED*, 13 August 1976, p. 14; 4 February 1977, p. 17; 14 June 1977, p. 22. EIU, *QER—Egypt*, No 1 (1977), p. 11; No 2 (1977), p. 16.
28. *MEED*, 25 March 1977, p. 16; 1 July 1977, p. 19. EIU, *QER—Egypt*, No 2 (1977), p. 13.
29. *MEED*, 15 July 1977, p. 17. EIU, *QER—Egypt*, No 1 (1977), p. 17.
30. *MEED*, 1 April 1977, p. 17.
31. *NYT*, 26 December 1976.
32. IMF, *IFS*, May 1977, pp. 154-5.
33. See NBE, *EB*, Vol 28, No 4 (1975), pp. 458-60.
34. US Dept of Agriculture, *The Agricultural Situation in Africa and West Asia*, August 1976, p. 9. *The Financial Times (FT)*, 28 June 1976.
35. *MEED*, 15 July 1977, p. 17. At the official exchange rate, these exports were equivalent to $527m. However, most of these were within the context of bilateral trade agreements, and those sold on other markets were probably at rates approximating the parallel market exchange rate. In 1976, the official exchange rate was E£ = $2.5556; the official parallel rate fluctuated at around E£ = $1.44. At the latter rate, industrial exports were equivalent to $297m.
36. EIU, *QER—Egypt*, No 2 (1977), p. 4.
37. EIU, *QER—Egypt*, No 2 (1977), p. 7. *The Middle East*, January 1977, p. 54.
38. *FT*, 28 June 1976.
39. IMF, *IFS*, May 1977, p. 155.
40. *MEED*, 21 January 1977, p. 19; 4 March 1977, p. 13.
41. *Mideast Markets (MM)*, 23 May 1977, p. 8.
42. *MM*, 28 March 1977, p. 16.
43. B. Hansen, "Arab Socialism in Egypt", *World Development*, April 1975, pp. 201-11.
44. *The Middle East*, January 1976, p. 15.
45. *MEED*, 25 June 1976, p. 11.
46. *FT*, 24 November 1976.
47. B. Hansen, "Middle East Development Prospects in 1973", in A. S. Becker, B. Hansen, and M. H. Kerr, *The Economics and Politics of the Middle East* (New York: Elsevier, 1975), pp. 24-25.
48. Officially, net domestic product in constant prices increased by 22.7% in 1975 (cf an increase of 18.5% in 1974). The latter is probably exaggerated, but the reported advance in 1975 appears to be *greatly* exaggerated. Most of the increase in 1974 was in agriculture and industry. In 1975, agriculture plus industry increased by 2.0%, according to official figures. Industry is defined to include manufacturing, mining, crude oil production and electricity. Most of the increase was in "government" which includes public administration and the military forces, and other services. Excluding "government", net domestic product increased by 18.2% in 1974 and by 14.6% in 1975. See Central Bank of Syria, *Quarterly Bulletin*, Vol 13, Nos 3-4 (1975), p. 42. It also appears probable that the gap between real and official rates of inflation has widened, and that there is an under-correction of the current price series in the national accounts.
49. *Ibid*, pp. 59-61. IMF, *IFS*, June 1977, pp. 335, 348.
50. *MM*, 11 April 1977, p. 4.
51. *NYT*, 28 March 1977.
52. IMF, *IFS*, June 1977, p. 335.
53. Other reports indicate that Arab aid to Syria in 1976 was $300m. See *MM*, 11 April 1977, p. 4.
54. IMF, *IFS*, June 1977, pp. 335, 348, 349.
55. *MM*, 11 April 1977, p. 4.
56. EIU, *QER—Syria, Lebanon, Cyprus*, No 2 (1977), p. 8. *MEED*, 4 March 1977, p. 13. *MM*, 11 April 1977, p. 4.
57. *Ibid*.
58. In the section of this chapter relating to the Syrian economy, I have briefly summarized the main trends and problems, based on my study. For sources, see E. Kanovsky, *The Economic Development of Syria* (University Publishing Projects, jointly with the Horowitz Institute, Tel Aviv University, 1977). The sources presented in this chapter refer only to those which have become available since completion of the above study.
59. Central Bank of Jordan, *Monthly Statistical Bulletin* (*MSB*), June 1976. Tables 23, 26, 36. IMF, *IFS*, June 1977, pp. 218-21.
60. *MEED*, 3 June 1977, p. 29.
61. IMF, *IFS*, June 1977, pp. 218-22. *FT*, 25 May 1977. *MEED*, 10 June 1977, p. 28. The only available price index is the consumer price index which showed a rise of 15% in 1976. No

investment price index is available, but it is probable that it did not differ too markedly from the changes in the consumer price index. The unusually wide gap between the growth of GDP and GNP is due largely to the very large increase in remittances.

62. EIU, *QER—Saudi Arabia, Jordan,* No 2 (1977), pp. 16–17. IMF, *IFS*, August 1977, pp. 208–11. *MEED*, 8 July 1977, pp. 10, 44, 45. Central Bank of Jordan, *Monthly Statistical Bulletin*, April 1977, Table 36.
63. In the section of this chapter relating to the Jordanian economy, I have briefly summarized the main trends and problems, based on my study. For sources, see E. Kanovsky, *The Economic Development of Jordan* (University Publishing Projects, jointly with the Horowitz Institute, Tel Aviv University, 1976). The sources presented in this chapter refer only to those which have become available since completion of the above study.
64. EIU, *Annual Supplement—Saudi Arabia, Jordan* (1976), p. 9. *QER—Saudi Arabia, Jordan*, No 3 (1976), p. 4. *Oil in the Middle East—Annual Supplement 1976*, pp. 2-3. The British Petroleum Company, *BP Statistical Review of the World Oil Industry 1975*, pp. 18-19.
65. Saudi Arabian Monetary Agency (SAMA), *Annual Report 1975*, p. 21.
66. SAMA, *Annual Report 1976*, p. 17. *BP Statistical Review of the World Oil Industry 1975*, p. 18.
67. SAMA, *Annual Report 1976*, pp. 144-5.
68. *Ibid*, pp. 48–49 US-Saudi Arabian Joint Commission on Economic Co-operation, *Summary of Saudi Arabian Five-Year Development Plan*, October 1976, pp. 21, 53.
69. IMF, *IFS*, June 1977, p. 312. *MEED*, 24 June 1977, p. 32. EIU, *QER—Saudi Arabia, Jordan*, No 1 (1977), p. 10.
70. IMF, *IFS*, June 1977, pp. 312-3. At this writing, data on the money supply are available only until November 1976.
71. T. H. Morañ, "Why Oil Prices Go Up", *Foreign Policy*, No 25 (Winter 1976-7), p. 64.
72. SAMA, *Annual Report 1976*, pp. 4, 119.
73. *MEED*, 24 June 1977, p. 32.
74. SAMA, *Annual Report 1976*, p. 4.
75. US Arms Control and Disarmament Agency, *World Military Expenditures and Arms Transfers 1965-74* (Washington DC, 1976), pp. 44, 68.
76. It is not clear from the official figures how high actual expenditures had been. See SAMA, *Annual Report 1976*, p. 121.
77. SAMA, *Annual Report 1391/92*, p. 35; *Annual Report 1390/91*, p. 34.
78. IMF, *IFS*, June 1977, pp. 312-13, 385.
79. SAMA, *Annual Report 1976*, p. 11.
80. *Ibid*, p. 119.
81. Kingdom of Saudi Arabia, Central Bureau of Statistics, *The Statistical Indicator 1976*, Tables 2-1, 2-2, 2-3, 10-1, 10-2.
82. R. Kanuerhase, *The Saudi Arabian Economy* (New York: Preager, 1975), p. 13.
83. *MEED*, 18 April 1975, p. 39.
84. SAMA, *Statistical Summary, First Issue, 1975-76*, p. 29.
85. *MEED*, 18 June 1976, p. 5.
86. See, for example, *MEED*, 18 June 1976, pp. 3-5.
87. *MEED*, 16 July 1976, p. 29.
88. EIU, *QER—Saudi Arabia, Jordan*, No 2 (1977), p. 9.
89. IMF, *IFS*, pp. 312, 313, 385. Private transfers have been included as an import of services.
90. *The Washington Post*, 23 May 1977, p. A14. *International Herald Tribune*, 31 May 1977, p. 2; 30 April 1977.
91. *Petroleum Economist*, January 1977, p. 5.
92. *Washington Post*, 18, 30 December 1976. *Daily Telegraph*, 18 December 1976. *Wall Street Journal*, 10 January 1977. For a fuller discussion of Saudi Arabian motivations, see E. Kanovsky, *Saudi Arabia's Moderation in Oil Pricing—Political or Economic?* (Shiloah Centre, Tel Aviv University, 1977).
93. *Newsweek*, 23 May 1977.
94. See, for example, *Business Week*, 30 May 1977, p. 25.
95. CIA, *The International Energy Situation: Outlook to 1985*, April 1977, p. 14.

Middle East Oil in the International Economic Setting

DANKWART A. RUSTOW

The oil exporting countries of the Middle East and North Africa maintained their predominant position within the international petroleum market throughout 1976 and 1977. Disagreements over price within OPEC (the Organization of Petroleum Exporting Countries) were aired for the first time in public and led to a temporary breakdown of the common price structure during the first half of 1977. Yet neither the organization's long-range cohesion nor its control of world oil prices seemed to have been seriously impaired by this interlude of dual price structure.

All oil exporting countries continued to increase their imports (of goods and particularly of services) as they worked to transform their oil wealth into economic and social development for the longer term. Still, most of them have continued to show surpluses in their balance of trade and of payments. Hence their foreign financial reserves continued to accumulate, notably in Saudi Arabia. On the diplomatic scene, their newly acquired economic and financial power was increasingly recognized, in particular at the UN and at such meetings as the Conference on International Economic Co-operation (or "North-South dialogue").

THE RISE OF MIDDLE EAST OIL

Developments of 1976 and 1977 further consolidated the structure imposed on the world oil market since the autumn of 1973. In the quarter century before 1973, oil had replaced coal as the leading energy source for the industrial world; yet among large industrial powers, only in the US and in the USSR is there substantial indigenous production. (In 1976, the Soviet Union overtook the US as the leading producer, with Saudi Arabia continuing in third place.) Western Europe and Japan have instead relied heavily or exclusively on oil imports. The shift from coal to oil thus meant a growing reliance on imported energy. The volume of petroleum in international trade nearly tripled in each of the decades preceding 1973, from 3.7m barrels a day (b/d) in 1950 to 9m b/d in 1960, to 25.6m b/d in 1970, and to as much as 34.2m b/d in 1973. This expansion in volume was accompanied by a shift to the Middle East and North Africa as the major producing areas. In 1950, Venezuela produced nearly the same amount of oil as the four countries then in production around the Persian Gulf (Iran, Iraq, Saudi Arabia, and Kuwait). Yet by 1973, Venezuelan production had only doubled, whereas that in the Middle East had increased fourteenfold. In 1976, the Middle East and North Africa accounted for 42% of world oil production, 70% of world exports, and 66% of proven reserves (the last figure including a small amount for West Africa).

As production shifted, so did patterns of leadership among the oil producing countries. After World War II, Venezuela was the first country to introduce the so-called principle of "fifty-fifty" profit-sharing between governments and producing companies. In 1960, OPEC was founded on Venezuela's initiative (the other initial members being the four Persian Gulf countries mentioned earlier). But in OPEC's first major contest with the international oil companies in 1970–1, Libya took the initiative in raising tax rates and prices, and Iran in having the governments of the Gulf negotiate jointly with the score of companies active in producing oil in the region. In the crisis of 1973, and increasingly since, the leading partner in OPEC has been Saudi Arabia.

The 50:50 division of profits, established in the Middle East in 1951-4, had shifted by 1965 to 65:35 in favour of governments, and by 1972 to 83:17. Until 1971, steady or falling prices in a vastly expanding market had enabled the companies to meet the higher payments to governments while increasing their own net income from petroleum production. By 1972, still higher payments were beginning to eat into the companies' earnings. Meanwhile, the opening up of the US as a major market for Middle East oil (as a result of the decline of domestic production since 1970 and the lifting of the 14-year old import quotas in the spring of 1973), led to an unprecedented 15% rise in OPEC production, with nearly half of that increase coming from Saudi Arabia.

The companies' inability to absorb further financial demands, and the emergence of Saudi Arabia and the US as the leading exporter and importer respectively, were the three developments that set the stage for the crisis of autumn 1973: the embargo proclaimed by all Arab exporting countries against the US and certain other importers; the cuts in production (amounting to 25% between September and November 1973) enforced by all of them except Iraq; and the two rounds of price increases unilaterally imposed by all 13 OPEC members, Arab and non-Arab alike. As a result, government revenue from each barrel of Saudi Arabian light petroleum (OPEC's "marker crude") rose from \$1.77 to \$3.05, and to as much as \$9.37 by mid-1974; and total oil revenues of Middle Eastern and North African governments from \$10.8 bn in 1972 to \$17.6 bn in 1973 and \$75.7 bn in 1974.[1]

OPEC AND THE OIL COMPANIES

OPEC has maintained its ascendancy in the world market, but not through the time-honoured cartel tactic of limiting total production and allotting shares to its members; several proposals along these lines have been discarded since the early 1960s. The restrictions imposed by Arab governments in the autumn of 1973 have remained the only instance of *co-ordinated* production cuts, and here the immediate motivation was political: pressure on the US and through the US on Israel. Several individual OPEC members have periodically set production ceilings, either to prevent a lowering of the cumulative yield over the entire lifetime of a field, or to prevent too rapid or early an accumulation of foreign exchange. But only in Venezuela and in Kuwait, and occasionally in Libya, have those ceilings seriously cut into production. On the other hand, there have always been other countries willing (and, except in 1973, able) to make up for the deficiency.

The market for petroleum, which OPEC now controls, differs from that of many other mineral raw materials through its strong vertical integration. In the quarter century after World War II, seven major companies dominated all phases of petroleum operations, from exploration and production through transportation and refining to sales to the ultimate consumer: Exxon, BP, Shell, Gulf, Texaco, Standard of California, and Mobil. Thus more than half of world production outside the Soviet bloc, and more than three-quarters of non-communist trade in petroleum, has consistently been in the hands of these companies. The crisis of 1973 marked a notable shift of control from companies to governments within an unchanged vertically-integrated structure.

The key elements of control are the periodic meetings at which OPEC governments set an agreed price for "marker crude." The earlier more intricate system (of "posted prices", royalties, income taxes, government and company equity shares in production, and company buy-back prices) was greatly simplified in 1975. Since then, the floor and ceiling for the prices that international companies can charge for OPEC oil have been determined by a fixed level of government revenue per barrel and government official sales prices. Prices for OPEC crudes other than the "marker crude" are expected to be set by individual governments with due allowance for differentials of gravity, sulphur content, and distance from markets. But since tanker rates and demand for crudes of various types tend to fluctuate, the system does not work with complete precision.

There has been no challenge to the right asserted by OPEC countries since October 1973 to set prices and, if they choose, production levels—two privileges earlier claimed and zealously defended by the companies. Compared to this loss of control over price and volume, official "nationalization" of former production concessions has usually been of far less importance; indeed, in many countries it amounted to no more than a bookkeeping transaction that further increased the government's revenue from the average barrel of exported petroleum. Of all the Middle Eastern oil countries, only Iraq has completely severed its connection with the international oil companies, taking charge of its own production and marketing. A lack of established marketing outlets, along with a desire for a larger market share, presumably explain why Iraq is persistently reported to be offering slight discounts below the officially established OPEC price levels.

Elsewhere in the Middle East and North Africa, the multinational companies (despite the total or partial official nationalization of their local affiliates) continue to be in charge of production and contractual bulk purchasing of most of the oil. The companies benefit from the arrangement first of all by having access (in preference to any competitors) to large quantities of crude oil, and secondly by the 3 to 5% spread between the set level of government revenue and the government official sales price. After deduction of the physical production cost, this represents a *de facto* discount in their favour.

It should be noted, however, that the National Iranian Oil Company is handling an increasing share of the production and marketing of Iranian oil (currently c. 20%), and that it has entered a variety of partnership arrangements with international companies in overseas ventures, such as the North Sea, in order to gain additional experience. There has been much discussion, both in the Middle East and among outside observers, of the possibility of a progressive shift by oil exporting countries from the production and export of crude oil to various "downstream" operations such as refining, shipping, overseas marketing, or the establishment of a petrochemical industry. In the underpopulated Arab oil countries, at least, such projects will have to compete—not only for funds, but especially for scarce trained manpower—with a wide variety of infrastructure development projects, so that in most of them this remains a remote rather than an immediate prospect.

OPEC PRICES AND THE OUTSIDE WORLD

OPEC countries produce half the world's oil, and c. 90% of the portion that enters foreign trade. But non-OPEC exporters, whether among developing or industrial countries (Oman, Malaysia, Mexico; Canada, Norway, the Soviet Union) all imitated the fivefold price rise of 1973–4, and have since adjusted their prices upward in line with OPEC's. Within limits set by government price controls, even American domestic oil producers have followed suit. Fuels competing with oil, though not geared directly to OPEC's price, have responded to the same upward pull: the price of coal more than doubled in 1973–5, and that of uranium rose even more steeply. These increases were caused by a series of labour disputes in the US coal industry (which accounts for a quarter of world output) and by cartellization among uranium producers—both encouraged by the certainty that a quintupled oil price gave coal and uranium customers little choice but to foot the bill. This ability of OPEC to act as price leader not only for the world's petroleum, but even for the entire energy market, has greatly enhanced the economic strength of the organization. It also puts into question the widely held hope that alternative fuels, developed over a decade or more, will eventually set a ceiling to OPEC price increases. The obvious possibility is that by the time such new fuels come to the market, they will have risen near enough to the OPEC price so as not to offer effective competition.

Nor has elasticity of demand—that is, consumer resistance to steeply rising prices—yet acted as a brake on OPEC. World oil consumption, which had risen rapidly throughout the 1950s, 1960s, and early 1970s, declined by 1.2% in 1974 and 1% in 1975—only to rise again by 6% in 1976, setting record levels in 1976 and 1977. It is generally agreed among experts that these figures reflect a combination of the impact of the price rise of 1973–4 and of the global recession of 1973–5.

Before 1973, every 1% increase in the world's gross product was accompanied by a proportionate or slightly larger increase in its energy consumption. Since 1973, this "GNP/energy coefficient" is estimated to have delined from 1.0 to 0.9. Before 1973 there was, as we saw, a rapid shift from other energy sources, notably coal, into oil. (Between 1966 and 1973, the proportion of petroleum in global energy consumption rose from 38% to 45%.) Since 1973, the share of oil in total energy has remained constant (1973, 45.1%; 1976, 44.8%). And since it is likely to take a decade or more to develop major new alternatives, no sharp decline in the share of oil is likely in the near future.

In short, the world has started economizing with its energy and has stopped shifting from other energy sources toward oil. Yet a stable ratio of oil in the energy total combined with *any* positive GNP/energy coefficient means that oil consumption will rise (though not as fast as before) in times of prosperity, and go down only in times of depression—which is precisely the effect that has obtained since 1973.

OPEC's own market has reflected not only these global economic conditions, but some rather significant shifts in petroleum geography. First, consumer countries have preferred to rely on non-OPEC sources that are beginning to flow into the market. North Sea oil became available in large quantities in 1975; the Soviets saw in high-priced oil a convenient source of much needed hard currency and stepped up their exports to the West; and the first oil was produced in Alaska in 1977. Second, in the US (outside Alaska), production of oil has declined steadily since 1970, and natural gas since 1972. Hence in 1974–5, as oil consumption declined during the recession, oil imports continued at a virtually unchanged rate—as natural gas was replaced by oil, and domestic oil by imports. Then in 1976 and 1977, oil imports rose far more sharply than did overall consumption from 6.0m b/d in 1975 to 8.8m b/d in the first half of 1977. While a certain amount of this additional oil was from such sources as Mexico and Norway, OPEC supplied as much as 84% of US imports in 1977; conversely, the rise in US imports since 1975 was equivalent to c. 10% of OPEC's production in that earlier year. From 1977 to about 1981, it is likely that US imports will level off as additional oil becomes available from Alaska, only to rise once again when Alaskan oil has been absorbed by rising consumption and declining oil and gas production in the "lower 48 states." Even the energy savings proposed by President Carter in April 1977 would, at best, bring imports in 1985 back down to their 1973–5 level of c. 6m b/d.

These contradictory trends of a reduced GNP/energy coefficient, global recovery from the 1972–5 depression, diversification of oil supplies in the international market, and steeply rising US requirements have meant that demand for OPEC oil since 1973 has oscillated more sharply than global consumption. Thus, whereas world oil consumption dropped by 5% in 1974–5, rose by 8% in 1975–6 and by a further 3% early in 1977, the corresponding figures for OPEC were −12%, +12% and +3%.

Even so, further rises in OPEC price levels in 1975 partly compensated for the temporary decline in demand. Thus the total value of OPEC countries' exports (including a very minor amount of non-oil exports) dropped from $119 bn in 1974 to $110 bn in 1975, to rise once again to $129 bn in 1976 and to $140 bn in 1977 (projected from the first quarter).[2]

Prospects were that demand for OPEC oil would fluctuate only slightly between 1977 and 1981 or 1982, reflecting changes in the global business cycle, as oil from the North Sea, Alaska and Mexico make up for the decline in US production and any added demand corresponding to economic growth. A renewed sharp increase in demand for OPEC oil was foreseen by many observers for the early or mid-1980s—the exact date depending on whether the world made a rapid or halting recovery from the recession of the 1970s, and whether leading countries, foremost the US, succeeded in adopting effective programmes of conservation and production of energy alternatives.[3] A sharp increase in demand for imported oil suggested, in turn, the possibility of a set of price rises comparable to those of 1973-4. Presumably such considerations were reflected in the statement of Saudi Arabia's Petroleum Minister, Shaykh Aḥmad Zakī al-Yamānī (following the adjournment of the Conference on International Economic Co-operation in 1977) that indexing of the price of oil was not opportune for the next few years and would be made unnecessary by market developments after that.

DIVISIONS IN OPEC AND THE DUAL PRICE STRUCTURE OF 1977

Ever since mid-1974 there have been recurrent reports of behind-the-scenes disagreements at the OPEC ministerial meetings (usually held twice a year), with Saudi Arabia favouring smaller price increases or none, and others—notably Iran and Algeria—pressing for sizable increases. The price increases of the mid-1974 to mid-1976 period, averaging at a cumulative rate of 8.3% a year, reflect the resulting compromises. More specifically, a 7.5% increase in the winter of 1974-5 was followed by a 9.2% increase in October 1975, an average increase of 7% in January 1977 (of which more below), and a further average increase of 3% in July 1977. During the world's slow recovery from recession, these rises were thus kept deliberately below the prevailing rate of inflation: the IMF calculates that world consumer prices rose by 15% in 1974, 13.3% in 1975, and 11.2% both in 1976 and early 1977. (Prices of imports by OPEC countries presumably rose much more sharply, although no reliable calculations are available.)

The reported differences in pricing preferences of OPEC members reflect both economic and ideological factors. Saudi Arabia—with an oil revenue *per capita* of over $4,000 per annum, limited resources of population, agriculture and industry, and rapidly accumulating the world's largest foreign exchange reserves abroad—has a tangible stake in preserving the health of the world economy on which the value of her foreign assets depends. By contrast, Algeria has been running a negative balance of payments on the basis of oil production that is virtually at maximum capacity; hence it stands to lose financially in the long run if the price of oil rises less rapidly than the combined rate of inflation and of nominal returns on investment. Iran, with ample population and non-oil resources, also is interested in maximum short-term returns and, moreover, counts on its ample reserves of natural gas to sustain the economy once her oil runs out. Venezuela and Indonesia, reluctant to invest large sums in exploring entirely new tracts, but with limited present reserves, also have good reason for favouring rising prices.

Economically, the OPEC members thus naturally divide into those with *per capita* incomes from oil below $1,000 (Venezuela, Iraq, Iran, Algeria, Nigeria, Indonesia, Gabon, and Ecuador), and those with oil incomes *per capita* above $4,000 (Libya, Saudi Arabia, Kuwait, Qatar, and United Arab Emirates). Kuwait and Libya, however, have more commonly sided with the first group, preferring to limit their incomes by cutting production rather than by slowing down price increases. Their foreign exchange accumulations are much smaller in absolute terms than those of Saudi Arabia, so that their effect on the total world economy is not as palpable. Moreover, the more "radical" orientation of their foreign policy implies a relative lack of concern about the general health of the international capitalist economy.

These latent differences surfaced for the first time at the OPEC ministerial meeting in Qatar in December 1976. Eleven of the thirteen members insisted on a 10% price increase for January 1977, and a further 5% increase for July 1977. But Saudi Arabia, joined by the United Arab Emirates, refused to go beyond an immediate increase of 5%. The result was the first breakdown of OPEC's common price structure. Yet it is important to keep in mind first, that the dispute was not between those who wanted to raise or lower the price, but between those who wanted to raise it by different amounts; second, that no general pattern of competitive price cutting ensued; and third, that the dual price structure persisted for only six months. The overall result seemed to confirm both the basic cohesion of the OPEC cartel (for which there is, after all, a collective reward of c. $100 bn a year), and the dominant position of Saudi Arabia within it.

Not surprisingly, OPEC members such as Algeria, Iran, and Indonesia that have been eager for maximum short-term returns, have already been producing at (or near) full capacity, whereas those favouring lower short-term returns have not. For example, whereas Algeria was producing virtually at full capacity in late 1976, Iran could have expanded production by 15%, and Saudi Arabia by as much as 35%. Saudi Arabia's spare capacity of c. 3m b/d was indeed larger than the total production of any other single OPEC member except Iran. This meant that if the common price broke down and Saudi Arabia and the Emirates went to capacity production, they could take away c. 20% of the business of the other 11 members, converting any 10% price increase into a net loss of c. 10%.

The actual effects of the dual price structure were not as drastic as that. A 35% increase in production, such as Saudi Arabia is theoretically capable of, must be phased in gradually. The international companies which handle distribution cannot shift their sources of supply at will—first, because crude oils of various gravities or sulphur contents are not freely interchangeable at the refinery; second, because the companies can ill afford to break binding contracts or even customary supply relations; and third, because the experience of the embargo and cutbacks of 1973 makes a shift to Arab sources seem particularly risky. The Saudis themselves limited the impact of the dual price structure, since they made their additional oil available only to major companies, rather than on the spot market—and the major companies, in addition to having the widest estabished distribution networks, have similarly wide networks of supply and thus are the companies most keenly interested in preserving what they regard as "global market stability."

Still, the financial effects of OPEC's temporary dual price structure on individual member countries were clear-cut. Comparing production figures for the first half of 1977 with those of the second half of 1976, we see that the OPEC total declined by 5%—a natural result of the widespread stockpiling in anticipation of the January 1977 price rises. Libya and Nigeria went against this trend, increasing their production by 4% and 5% respectively, despite their 10% price rises. The reason for this was an exceptionally cold winter in the US which, combined with an acute natural gas shortage and environmental regulations, created an exceptional demand for their low sulphur oil. Indonesia, which had voted with the majority but then implemented only a 6% increase, saw production rise by as much as 10%. But in the Persian Gulf, where total production went down by 7%, Saudi Arabia and Abū

Dhabī (largest of the Emirates) registered gains of 2% and 3%, whereas the other Gulf producers experienced heavy losses: Iran 12%, Iraq 13%, Qatar 16% and Kuwait as much as 19%. This in turn meant that, whereas Saudi revenues increased by about 7% over the previous six months, Iran's went down by 3% and Kuwait's as much as 11%.

At the OPEC meeting in mid-1977 in Stockholm, the Saudi and Emirate delegates agreed to join the others at the price level of 10% above 1976; in return, the other 11 dropped their insistence on a further 5% increase for the remainder of the year. Yamānī referred to the experience as an important lesson for producing and consuming countries. Presumably the lesson to other producers was that they could ill afford to set a price above that sanctioned by the Saudis; and to consumers, that Saudi Arabia was in full earnest in trying to persuade its OPEC partners to slow down oil price increases—as it had been assuring high American officials for two years. Perhaps there was a further intended lesson, already announced by Yamāmī in December, that he expected the US to show its "appreciation" for such Saudi moderation by bringing Israel closer to an agreed solution to the conflict between itself and the Arabs.[4]

EXPORT SURPLUSES AND INVESTMENTS

The vast surpluses that OPEC countries began to amass in 1974 are still growing, though at a slower rate. Merchandise imports, which in 1974 amounted to a little more than one-quarter of the value of exports, have doubled since then. This reflects the vast needs for economic development, including "infrastructure" facilities, as well as for heavy arms purchases by some countries (notably Iran and Saudi Arabia). Net imports of services also loom large and for most countries seem to be on the increase. These reflect both heavy shipping charges due to port congestion and the acute need for foreign expertise. Thus in 1975, the ratio between imports of services to goods was c. 1:4 in Algeria, 1:3 in Iran and Iraq, 1:2 in Libya, and as high as 1:1 in Saudi Arabia.

The 13 OPEC countries together spent less than half of their export earnings in 1974, but nearly three-quarters in 1976. Yet this cumulative figure hides considerable disparities. Algeria has shown a current account deficit since 1975, and Iran since 1976. By contrast, Saudi Arabia's surplus (on its current account of goods, services and transfers) was as high as $23 bn in 1974, and still stood at nearly $14 bn both in 1975 and in 1976, a rate that seemed to be holding up in 1977. This meant that the holdings of foreign currency reserves by the government and the Saudi Monetary Authority have mounted extremely rapidly: at $14.3 bn in 1974, they exceeded those of the US; at $35.4 bn in 1975, they surpassed those of West Germany to become the largest in the world; at $45.8 bn in 1976, they exceeded those of West Germany and the US combined.[5] At the end of 1976, Saudi income from this cumulative surplus was conservatively estimated at $3.8 bn a year, or more than their total oil earnings in 1972.

The uses to which OPEC countries have put their growing surpluses, as estimated by the Bank of England, are shown in Table 2. There was a heavy concentration in the Eurocurrency market in 1974, probably a holding action while making longer-range plans. Since 1975, there has been a shift toward dollar investments and holdings of US government securities, reflecting both the major investors' distrust of the economic and political climate in many Western European countries, and the increasingly close relations between Riyadh and Washington. A growing proportion of the total annual surplus (21% in 1974, 29% in 1976) has gone (a) into foreign aid, and (b) into direct investments outside the US and the UK—two categories which the Bank of England unfortunately does not attempt to separate. These figures therefore included the highly publicized direct investments by Iran in Krupp,

Table 1—Oil Exporting Countries of the Middle East and North Africa: Production and Trade, 1975-1977

	Population	Petroleum								Foreign Trade					
	(m)	Production (m barrels per day[2])			Capacity (m b/d)	Prices[1] (US$/barrel)				Exports (US$ bn)			Imports (US$ bn)		Exports US$ *per capita*
	mid-1976	*1975*	*1976*	*Jan-June 1977*	*mid-1977*	*1 Jan 1975*	*1 Oct 1975*	*1 Jan 1977*	*1 Aug 1977*	*1975*	*1976*	*1977*	*1975*	*1976*	*1976*
Algeria	17.3	.98	1.08	1.09	1.1		13.10	14.30	14.45	4.4	5.2	2.8	5.9	5.3	300
Iran	33.9	5.39	5.92	5.64	6.8	10.67	11.62	12.81	12.81	20.1	23.4	12.0	10.3	12.9	690
Iraq	11.5	2.26	2.28	2.21	3.1	10.48	11.45	12.67	12.65	8.3	8.8	5.0	4.2	3.5	770
Kuwait[3]	1.0	2.09	2.18	1.81	3.3	10.37	11.30	12.37	12.37	8.6	9.8	4.5	2.4	3.3	9,800
Libya	2.4	1.48	1.93	2.08	2.5	11.43	12.49	13.92	14.20	6.0	8.4	5.1	3.6	4.7	3,500
Oman		0.34	0.37	0.35		11.07	11.63	12.77	12.77	1.4	1.6	0.8	0.7	0.7	
Qatar	0.1	0.44	0.49	0.41	0.65	11.77	11.17	11.84		1.8	2.2	1.0	0.4	0.8	22,000
Saudi Arabia[3]	9.2	7.22	8.76	9.35	11.8	10.46	11.51	12.09	12.70	27.7	36.1	20.2	6.9	11.8	3,900
United Arab Emirates[4]	0.7	1.70	1.95	2.02	2.4	10.87	11.92	12.50	13.26	6.9	8.5	4.7	2.7	3.4	12,000
Total countries		**21.89**	**24.94**	**24.97**	**32.1**					**85.4**	**104.0**	**56.2**	**37.0**	**45.9**	
for comparison:															
13 OPEC Countries[5]		27.44	30.92	31.07	39.2					109.8	128.7	70.7	54.5	67.7	
United States[6]		10.01	9.73	9.63						107.6	115.0	61.1	103.4	129.6	
World		55.2	59.6	61.3						795.1	903.5		815.6	924.4	

[1] Government official sales prices for the most prevalent variety of crude. Prices changed on the dates given, except in Libya, where the figures given are average prices between that date and the next.
[2] 1m b/d of crude petroleum is approximately 49.8m tons per year (based on world average gravity).
[3] Including one-half of Neutral Zone.
[4] The oil producing Emirates are Abū Dhabī, Dubai, and Sharjah.
[5] OPEC members are 8 of the 9 above (except Oman), Ecuador, Gabon, Indonesia, Nigeria, and Venezuela.
[6] Production figures include natural gas liquids.

Sources: BP Statistical Review of the World Oil Industry 1976 (production 1975-76). *The Petroleum Economist* (production 1976: September 1977, p. 375; prices 1/7/77: August 1977, p. 331). *Petroleum Intelligence Weekly*, 17 October 1977 (capacity). Parra, Ramos & Parra, *International Crude Oil and Product Prices*, April 1977, pp. 2f. (prices 1975-77). International Monetary Fund (IMF), *International Financial Statistics* (IFS), September 1977, p. 30f. (foreign trade).

Table 2: OPEC Prices, Revenues, and Deployment of Surpluses, 1974-77

	1974	*1975*	*1976*	*1977 (First quarter)*
	US Dollars per Barrel			
1) Petroleum Price	9.47	10.30	11.51	12.09
	(Billions of US Dollars)			
2) Government Oil Revenues	89.8	96.8	113.2	31.9
3) Exports	118.8	109.8	128.7	35.1
4) Imports	33.3	54.5	67.7	
5) Balance of Trade	85.5	55.3	61.0	
6) Balance of Payments Surplus	57.0	35.7	35.3	9.6
of which:				
a) US treasury and banks	9.5	3.1	4.8	2.3
b) Dollar investments	2.1	6.9	6.7	1.2
c) Eurocurrencies	15.0	4.3	6.4	2.0
d) UK treasury and banks	5.3	-0.3	-2.4	0.1
e) Sterling investments	0.7	0.3	0.5	0.1
f) Other currencies	9.0	5.0	7.0	1.5
g) Foreign aid, other investments etc	11.9	12.4	10.3	2.3
h) Contributions to international organizations	3.5	4.0	2.0	0.1

1) Government revenue (1974) and sales price (1975-77) for the "marker crude"; the 1974 and 1975 figures are annual averages. Note that in January 1977, the marker crude increased only 5% as against 10% for most other OPEC crudes.
2) These reflect payments as made, which lag behind oil exported; see note 2 to text.
3) The difference between lines 2 and 3 consists of non-oil exports, production cost and company revenue for oil, and late payments (cf line 2).
5) line 3 minus line 4.
6) This is the current account balance of goods, services and private transfers. The breakdown given in the source has been simplified; they include the following entries in the original:
a) US treasury bonds, notes, and bills; and US bank deposits.
b) Includes "holdings of equity, property etc."
c) Foreign currency deposits and foreign currency borrowing in the UK (i.e., only the London part of the Eurocurrency market)
d) UK government stocks and treasury bills, and sterling deposits in the UK; the minus signs indicate net reduction of holdings.
e) Includes "holdings of equity, property etc."
f) Bank deposits outside the US and the UK.
g) "Special bilateral facilities", including "loans to developing countries"; as well as "other investments", including "holdings of equity, property etc."

Sources: Rustow and Mugno, *OPEC: Success and Prospects* (New York, 1976), p. 135 (line 1, 1974). Parra, Ramos & Parra, *op. cit.* (line 1, 1975-77). IMF, *IFS*, September 1977, pp. 30f (lines 3-4). Bank of England, *Quarterly Bulletin*, December 1976 and June 1977 (lines 2, 6 and 6a-h).

Kuwait in Daimler-Benz, and Libya in Fiat, as well as Kuwaiti expenditures on economic development in other Arab countries, and sizable annual subsidies by Saudi Arabia (that have done much to strengthen the "moderate front" in inter-Arab politics and reverse the advance of Soviet influence in north-east Africa). The oil countries' contributions to international organizations reached a peak in 1975, and have since declined.

There has been recurrent speculation that the rapidly growing foreign exchange needs of the oil countries, and the beginning of a negative balance on current account in such countries as Algeria and Iran, would threaten the common OPEC price structure and lure member-countries into a progressive price war for market gains at each other's expense. Against this it must be considered that, in terms of increased earnings, such gains would of course be illusory; and that the countries with dwindling or negative current accounts have already resorted to several other obvious alternatives (such as borrowing on the international capital market while their credit is good, and pressing for *higher* rather than lower prices within OPEC councils). Above all, it must be realized that the large surplus production capacity of Saudi Arabia works as a price guarantee in both directions. If successive downward turns of a spiralling price war should push everyone toward capacity production, the Algerians would lose money on the very first round, as would the Iranians once the price dropped by c. 15%—whereas the Saudis could make up for declining unit earnings by increased production until the price had dropped by one-third or more.[6]

Indications toward the end of 1977 were that OPEC should not be seriously threatened for the next several years, either by competition from outside or by fatal internal dissension. The experience of the dual price system early in 1977 indicated that the cartel's existence was so much in the interest of all members that price unity would be reconstituted even after a temporary lapse. For the next several years, however, the inflow of new oil from the North Sea, Alaska, Mexico, and other sources will probably meet much of the increasing demand and thus slow down or arrest any momentum toward increases in OPEC's real (or even nominal) price. By the 1980s, demand for OPEC oil may be expected to increase once again—how fast and how sharply depending on the ability and willingness of the US and other importing countries to curtail their consumption of energy and to stimulate its domestic production. A sharp rise in demand, in turn, could be expected to lead to even sharper rises in price.

All this implies a continuing major role for Middle Eastern oil producing countries in economic, financial and political councils, both of the region and of the world at large. The preponderance of Saudi Arabia within OPEC also makes it likely that the organization, in pursuing its future pricing policy, will keep in mind the global business cycle and the effect of the oil price on the health of the world's industrial economy.

NOTES

1. For the factors leading to OPEC's rise, see D. A. Rustow and J. F. Mugno, *OPEC: Success and Prospects* (New York, 1976). The appendix contains detailed statistical information up to and including 1975.
2. See Table 2, line 3. Export data are for the period of the actual movement of goods; those for government oil revenues (Table 2, line 2) for the period of payment, which by virtue of prevailing terms usually lags two months. Thus, if a $7.5 bn payment due to Saudi Arabia for oil exported in 1974 but made in 1975 is credited to 1974 (cf. Rustow and Mugno, p. 131, line 1) the revenue figures, too, show a decline from 1974 to 1975.
3. See Organization for Economic Co-operation and Development, *World Energy Outlook* (Paris, 1977); United States Central Intelligence Agency, *The International Energy Situation: Outlook to 1985* (Washington, 1977); Caroll Wilson et al., *Energy: Global Prospects 1985 to 2000* (New York, 1977); Dankwart A. Rustow, "US-Saudi Relations and the Oil Crises of the 1980s", *Foreign Affairs*, Vol 55, No 3, pp. 494-516.
4. For Yamānī's remarks at a press conference following the Qatar meeting, see *Keesing's Contemporary Archives*, 1977, p. 28320.
5. See International Monetary Fund, *International Financial Statistics*, September 1977, p. 377. For further details on the surpluses of the under-populated Arab countries, see *IMF Survey*, 24 November 1975 and 24 October 1977.
6. For a fuller discussion see Rustow and Mugno, *OPEC*, p. 101, and Rustow, "US-Saudi Relations", p. 503-5.

Middle East Oil Developments

BENJAMIN SHWADRAN

The Middle East oil crisis lost most of its urgency in 1977, and the general impression was that the consuming countries were adjusting to the new realities without serious consequences to their economic and financial structures. Through the Organization of Petroleum Exporting Countries (OPEC), the Middle East oil producers have pursued a policy of increasing prices and of gaining full control over the oil industry, both by 100% takeovers of concessionary companies and by the expansion of oil and natural gas industries through joint-venture undertakings. They also strove to acquire marketing outlets for the ever greater quantities of oil produced, while holding the companies to taking fixed quantities. Moreover, they tried to persuade non-concessionary companies to participate in prohibitively expensive joint-ventures to further develop oil and natural gas production, refining, pipeline construction, and the petrochemical and oil transportation industries. At the same time, practically all the producing countries proceeded rapidly to implement their huge economic development plans. During the period under review (January 1976 to August 1977), these ambitious plans ran into trouble because of desperate manpower shortages and technical-physical limitations. It often became necessary to adopt more realistic targets. (The policies of OPEC and of the Western nations are discussed in the essay, "Middle East Oil in the International Context.")

A continuing major issue in the energy crisis was the ultimate extent of energy resources (especially oil) in the world. While estimates differed considerably, most were pessimistic, especially those originating in the US. A general conclusion was that the West, especially, would become increasingly dependent on the oil resources of the Middle East, primarily those of Saudi Arabia. The implications were not only economic, but also heavily political, and were reflected in the policies of the consuming countries towards the Middle East.

However, the American oil companies and the Middle East oil producers, each for different reasons, refused to endorse the pessimistic energy forecasts. The companies maintained that there were great potential energy resources in the US waiting to be discovered. They argued that the best method to stimulate exploration would be to remove all controls and allow oil prices to rise freely in order to achieve two objectives: 1) raise the necessary risk capital for the search of oil and natural gas, and thus substantially increase America's energy resources; and, 2) greatly reduce oil consumption. Both would prevent, or at least lower in great measure, US dependence on Middle East oil. The Middle East oil producers realized that an optimistic view about the abundance of future energy supplies would reduce the importance of their own resources and of their international political significance. Yet some of them were also concerned that the major consumers' anxieties about future supplies would leave them with no choice but to explore and activate all available alternate energy sources.

The much enhanced economic power of the Middle Eastern oil producers has been one of the major consequences of the oil crisis, and must be given full weight in considering the implications of future energy policies. The current and accumulating surpluses of the major oil producers are a major factor in the free world's balance-of-payments problems—total surpluses of oil producing countries being almost equal to total balance-of-payments deficits of developed and developing oil consuming countries. Regardless of the actual magnitude of the surpluses of the oil producing countries, or of any methods devised for recycling them, the unmistakable fact is that Middle East oil producing countries have become another major financial, investment and business centre of the West. They are not only the greatest new market for industrial exports, but also for the most advanced technologies. Therefore, the Western nations are no longer just interested in Middle East oil, or in getting back the petrodollars, but in acquiring highly profitable contracts and joint-venture enterprises, as well as in reciprocal investments by the oil producers in their economies.

These developments have seriously affected the policies of both the major Middle East oil producers and the industrialized nations, the latter fearing a gradually-emerging double dependence on the former—for oil and money. New questions have been raised. For example, would the great oil producers ever use the money weapon against their major customers and, if so, when? One reply was given by the outstanding Saudi Arabian spokesman, Petroleum Minister Ahmad Zakī al-Yamānī, 22 August 1975. He declared that "money power" would not be as successful as the oil weapon unless there were changes in the international monetary system and unless Arab financial institutions were established to give them greater influence in the international business world. "And just as the oil weapon was ineffective in 1967 because it was not ready for use, so the money weapon will be ineffective if we use it prematurely." Since then, however, many of the prerequisites listed by Yamānī have been realized.

The complicated relationship between the oil consuming and oil producing countries, and the relationships among the consuming countries themselves continue to have a strong impact on negotiations for a solution to the Middle East political crisis. Almost every move in that direction by any of the parties involved is heavily determined by its repercussions on the oil issue.

ORGANIZATION OF PETROLEUM EXPORTING COUNTRIES

The last increase in the price of oil before the OPEC decision at Doha in December 1976 was made on 1 October 1975, even though that year was a difficult one for producers. The Middle East oil production rate had dropped by more than 10% compared with 1974, and the negative percentages of some countries—among them the major producers—were much higher: Iran −12.2%, Kuwait −19.2% and Saudi Arabia −16.8%. The only major producer to show an increase was Iraq, with 19.9%.

Two factors operated in bringing about the October 1975 increase. Although the posted price of oil set by OPEC for 1 January 1974 remained constant until October 1975, other changes had greatly augmented the producers' revenue. The 25% participation share of the producing countries in the concessionary companies, which became operative as of 1 January 1973, was raised to 60% during 1974. Quite apart from the posted price figure, OPEC decided at the end of 1974 to raise royalties from 12.5% to 20%, and governments' share in profits from 55% to 85%. Moreover, the price charged to companies for oil bought back from governments was raised from 93% of posted price to 94.85%. These changes substantially increased the governments' oil revenue. The pattern of unilateral price increases, which began in October 1973, also continued during 1974. The second factor was the rapidly expanding economic development programmes, with resultant inflationary pressures; this led many producers in the region to demand higher prices in 1975.

When OPEC met in Libreville (Gabon) in June 1975, it decided on a price increase in principle, but postponed implementation until its next meeting. However, the pattern of division among OPEC members became apparent. Iran demanded a 35% increase, claiming that such a percentage was necessary to compensate for the inflation rate increase which oil producers had to pay for their imports. Saudi Arabia advocated a reduction in prices, or at least a freeze, to enable consumers to increase their demand for oil. The meeting which opened in Vienna on 24 September was a stormy one, and when Saudi's chief delegate Yamānī left the conference, OPEC was thrown into a crisis. But a compromise was worked out, Yamānī returned, and a 10% increase was unanimously decided upon.

In order to fully appreciate the difficulties and tensions prevailing in OPEC, it is necessary to establish the underlying determinants of the policies of its different members. The Middle East oil producing countries may be divided into three economic categories and into different political orientations. The first group consists of countries or principalities of the Persian Gulf which depend heavily, if not exclusively, on their oil income. They are relatively small oil producers, and would always follow majority decisions of OPEC; they are the passive members. The second group consists of relatively major oil producers (Iran, Iraq and Algeria), with large populations and massive development projects. They need oil revenues to finance ambitious development programmes, and are ready to sell all the oil they can, provided the price is very high. The third group consists of countries with small populations, enormous oil resources and high production records—Saudi Arabia, Kuwait and the United Arab Emirates. They would want to see oil revenues flow over a long period but not at too high a price, as they do not need the money for current operations. They are convinced that very high prices would ultimately deprive them of their oil wealth, causing the quick activation of alternatives for oil.

In addition to these economic factors, there are political determinants. Except for Iran, the other producers in the second category belong to the radical grouping in the Middle East; they are not concerned with the Western economic system and would not mind if high oil prices aggravated the general Western economic recession. On the contrary, it would increase their own economic importance and their political power. They would thus always find themselves in the grouping which demanded the highest prices. On the other extreme, the third category is closely identified with the Western economic and political system, perhaps less for ideological than for practical reasons. The future of their present regimes is not only closely related to, but totally dependent upon, the Western system. They would therefore wish to limit oil prices to a level which would not endanger or even weaken the Western economic structure.

THE POLICIES OF IRAN

Iran is practically a political and economic category by itself, whose economic needs seem on the surface to have outweighed political considerations. Of all the major Middle East oil producing countries, Iran has the most ambitious and most active economic development programme. It has the greatest population in the area, and more than anything else needs the financial resources which can be obtained only by higher oil prices. It is determined to achieve economic independence in the shortest possible time, and is not concerned with the risk of activating oil alternatives since by the time this could happen, Iran believes it will no longer need to rely on oil for revenue purposes. Whatever oil was left could be utilized for such industries as petrochemicals. In fact, it might take advantage of the energy alternatives itself. Moreover, Iran's economic power and military strength, which are being built up simultaneously, would assure its political and security position.

THE POLICIES AND ROLE OF SAUDI ARABIA

In this welter of conflicting interests in the Middle East oil struggle, Saudi Arabia plays a unique role, which involves economic, political and power-ambition objectives. As the greatest oil power in the Middle East (if not in the world) in terms of production, reserves and revenue, it has tried to play the role of regional superpower. Nevertheless, politically and militarily, it is vulnerable. Saudi's present system dictates a close alignment with the West, especially the US, for its survival. It is surrounded by radical countries which stand ready to help sweep it into the revolutionary camp. While high oil prices might for a time increase Saudi Arabia's "money power", lower oil prices would in fact give it the best hope of maintaining—and even increasing—its economic power and security, and of playing the leading role in the Middle East.

For long-term economic reasons, Saudi Arabia must see itself threatened by the development of alternative energy sources. The best way to avert these alternatives is obviously to avoid too high oil prices. Therefore, both for economic and political reasons, Saudi Arabia, more than any other major oil producer in the area, must depend on Western oil markets and on the Western economic system. As Saudi's Petroleum Minister said at the Doha OPEC conference on 14 January 1977: "If any other exporting country seeks to increase the price of oil, then it is motivated by purely personal interests. In the case of Iran, for example, once its production began to decrease, its interests dictated an increase in price. The essential aim was to obtain as much money as possible and industrialize itself. What would it matter if the world finds alternatives for oil then? But for us, the Arabs, who possess gigantic quantities of proven oil reserves, we will be the ones to lose heavily if the world finds new sources of energy for its factories. We would become economically weak, and worst of all, politically weak as well. If we reached such a position then we, the Arabs, would be finished politically—most definitely we would be. The Palestinian cause? That would fade away as a result. The Palestine cause is alive in the world because of oil. If it had not been for oil then the world would not give a thought to Palestine. It is painful to realize that such elementary facts regarding oil policy continued to be ignored or unknown to the Arab public."

As the greatest producer in OPEC, Saudi Arabia does not need the support of the smaller producers to maintain the cartel. As Yamānī explained to an energy symposium in Bonn on 14 October 1975, the general rule in cartels was that the strongest member has to carry weaker members on its shoulders. "It will eventually tire of its burden and refuse to bear it any longer, and therefore any cartel will come to an end and collapse. However, this is not the case with OPEC. In most cartels, the strongest member seeks to sell as much of its goods as possible, but Saudi Arabia's interest lies in selling less of its oil."

However, this statement was contradicted by the position taken practically from the beginning by Saudi Arabia when OPEC attempted production programming. The ninth OPEC conference meeting in Tripoli (Libya) in July 1965 had not actually proposed any curtailment of output, but had formulated limited percentage increases for 1966 over 1965, on an experimental basis. Nevertheless, in February 1966, the Saudi Arabian Petroleum Minister declared that OPEC's crude oil production controls were unacceptable to his country. Saudi Arabia's actual increase in production for the year was 18%, double that originally agreed upon. In August 1976, Yamānī summarized production control efforts. "Since 1964 some members of OPEC have wanted to impose what they call production programming. Saudi Arabia opposed that, and we will continue to oppose it." In fact, OPEC rates of production have been determined not by any agreed policy or system, but by market demand levels.

With pressures for price increases building up during the first half of 1976, one of the major issues within OPEC was that the same members who were demanding high increases were actually selling their oil below the agreed posted prices. This issue was raised by Iraq at OPEC's one-day session in Geneva on 24 April 1976. It accused other OPEC members of undercutting the price by offering special credit terms and by lowering premiums charged on higher quality oil. Saudi Arabia replied that Iraq itself was one of the main price cutters. No action was taken except to ask the Economic Commission to study the question.

At the approach of the OPEC meeting scheduled for the end of May in Bali (Indonesia), various members began to advance their demands. Libya stated on 22 May that it would ask for a substantial oil increase, while Saudi Arabia announced that it would seek "to prevent undercutting of oil prices by OPEC members rather than insist upon higher oil prices." Iraq attacked Saudi Arabia for demanding a price freeze. It claimed that Saudi policy "played into the hands of the imperialist monopolies and enabled them to export their inflation." Iraq demanded a 15% price increase.

THE BALI CONFERENCE

When the Bali conference opened on 27 May, Iran joined the group demanding a 15% increase. The Saudi representative said at the opening: "We will oppose any increase in price; we have a strong position on that." He added that the freeze of prices would be extended to the end of the year. The conference bowed to Saudi Arabia and decided not to increase prices. The close alignment between Saudi Arabia and the United Arab Emirates (UAE) was already obvious at Bali. Mana Said al-Otaiba, the UAE Minister of Petroleum and Mineral Resources, listed the reasons for price freezing: 1) to help the emerging world economic recovery take hold before the next oil rise; 2) to allow for a period of relaxation to assist progress of the North-South Dialogue; and 3) "to ensure the long-term retention of their oil markets by the OPEC producers and discourage the development of substitutes by the consumers." As a proponent of the basic interests as classified above, Kuwait supported Saudi Arabia in keeping prices frozen. A victorious Yamānī told newsmen: "Nobody can increase prices without Saudi Arabia." In fact, the Saudi success in carrying the day probably resulted from its reported warning to the other members that they could increase oil prices at their discretion, but in such a case, Saudi Arabia would establish its own pricing scheme.

However, the radicals in OPEC were not about to relent. About ten days after Bali, the Libyan Oil Minister challenged Saudi Arabia over its refusal to increase the price of crude oil. "We are ready to dissolve OPEC if Saudi Arabia keeps working against the interests of the oil nations. There is a good chance for an OPEC without Saudi Arabia. We won't tolerate the way Saudi Arabia froze OPEC prices with the help of some countries like Abū Dhabī, Kuwait and Algeria." Other OPEC members attempted to convene a special meeting to reconsider the price issue. While Indonesia's Minister of Mines said in June that another meeting was possible, Yamānī replied: "I don't see why we should go to a special meeting." The price freeze, he stated, would stay in effect until the end of the year.

In late August and early September, Indonesia's Mines' Minister toured the OPEC member-countries with the aim of convening a special meeting before Doha. His conclusion was that it was "considered most unlikely that any such conference will be convened since the idea—whatever support it may have within the OPEC membership as a whole—is still inflexibly opposed by Saudi Arabia." About a week later, Yamānī again explained the reasons for his country's position: "Saudi Arabia's views are based on the clear economic interests of OPEC, which is to say that oil prices should not be raised in a way which would reduce demand for oil, and as a consequence weaken OPEC's position. In fact, demand for oil did fall to a point where OPEC members began to compete with each other. Some countries such as Iraq lowered their oil prices substantially and entered into competition with other exporting countries, which resulted in a weakening of OPEC's position on the international plane."

THE DOHA CONFERENCE

As the time for the Doha conference approached, the lines began to form. On 20 October, the Shah stated that Iran would ask for a minimum 15% price increase. On 9 November, the UAE announced it would not endorse any increase of more than 10%. Six days later, the British Prime Minister, James Callaghan, warned that the price rises hinted at would bring economic instability into world affairs. With an eye to Saudi Arabia, he added: "Fortunately a number of statesmen in the OPEC countries recognize the interdependence of both economic and political factors." The US was reported to have made great efforts with the producing countries, through local ambassadors, not to increase prices. The Kuwaiti Minister of Finance felt that the consumers were already reconciled to an increase, and their campaign was simply to reduce it from 25% to 15%. However, Iraq reported that it would press for 25%. Late in November, Iran was said to be aiming for a 12% increase, while Saudi Arabia was inclined to accept 8%, but not more than 10%.

Early in December it was reported that the OPEC Economic Commission (a body whose recommendations have a poor record of plenary acceptance) proposed a 26% increase, which it claimed was the inflation rate for OPEC countries since October 1975. Shortly before the conference was due to open in Doha, however, Yamānī came out in favour of a continued oil price freeze for another six months. He maintained that recent developments had shown that the world economic recovery was not as strong as was first thought.

When the Doha conference opened in January 1977, the extremists lined up behind Iraq and demanded a 25% hike in prices; Iran, Libya and Algeria asked for more than 10%, while Saudi Arabia stood by a price freeze. The key technical issue on which the increase would be justified was the inflation rate of the products purchased from the industrialized countries. No clear-cut answer to this question was possible, because of conflicting estimates. A study by the Petroleum Industry Research Foundation of New York gave the inflation rate since October 1975 as 2.7%. On a longer-term basis, the same study calculated that from the first quarter of 1974 to the third quarter of 1976, the composite price index of OPEC imports rose by 25.8%, and that the price of crude oil over the same period rose by 18%. Therefore, a 7.8% increase in oil prices might be justified. These figures were rejected by some OPEC members as being f.o.b. values, while c.i.f. figures amounted to 40%. The Iraqi Oil Minister claimed that since 1974, the price of goods imported by his country had risen by 81%. International Monetary Fund figures showed an inflation rise of only 4%, while OECD f.o.b. export prices had risen by 2% to 3% in the previous 15 months.

Saudi Arabia resorted to the same tactics at Doha as at Vienna. Yamānī left the meeting for consultations with his government, and the conference marked time. The threat was the same as in Bali: Saudi Arabia would adopt its own price structure unless its demand for a six-month price freeze was accepted. In an effort to compromise, Saudi Arabia and the UAE eventually offered a 5% increase in prices. However, in a reversal of policy, Yamānī threatened that the Saudis would lift their 8.5m barrels daily (b/d) production ceiling and permit full production capacity of 11.8m b/d in 1977, ultimately expanding this to c. 14.5m b/d should market conditions be favourable. However, this time the eleven other members were not willing to bow to the Saudis. The result was the two-tier price structure.

SAUDI POLICY AFTER THE DOHA CONFERENCE

This challenge to Saudi leadership produced a series of contradictory explanations by its spokesmen. On 23 August 1976, the Minister of Planning, Hishām Nazīr, outlined in *Newsweek* a number of reasons for an oil conservation policy. He said the Saudis would resist any pressure to increase their oil production beyond present levels. Asked if this wouldn't cause serious problems for oil consumers in the rest of the world, he replied: "This is true, but there must be more conservation everywhere." Yet, four months later, Saudi Arabia was ready to increase production to c. 14.5m b/d.

The Saudi Petroleum Minister listed on 17 December 1976 the reasons for his country's action: "We expect the West to appreciate what we did, and especially the US, and that appreciation has to be shown on two different fronts: 1) the North-South Dialogue in Paris; and 2) the Arab-Israeli conflict." He warned that "if there is no progress, that would be one of the reasons to modify our decision." When pressed further, he explained: "The political part is the North-South Dialogue and the Arab-Israeli conflict. The economic part is the world economy. And we weigh things together." Asked how much the political part weighed in this decision, Yamānī replied: "Well, I should say this time it is mostly, if not completely, economic." However, King Khālid appeared to take a different stand. According to *Agence France Press* (28 January 1977), in reply to a question as to whether Saudi Arabia would use its petrodollars to oppose the accession to power of communist parties in Italy and France, the King said: "Oil is an economic and commercial problem which should not be brought into political questions."

Yamānī outlined his attitude to OPEC in an interview with *Business Week* in the middle of November 1976: "In the past OPEC used to get together to decide on the price of Saudi crude and we accepted that. Now they want to decide a price for our crude which is much higher than what we think is reasonable for the world economy, and, therefore, we refused. So they are deciding for their own crude, and we are deciding for our own crude." He recalled that in 1975 Saudi production went down from 8.5m b/d to 5.6m because it stuck to OPEC decisions, while in Iraq production went up by c. 30%. He added that it would be "normal" to raise production levels to whatever the international market requested. Asked if this wouldn't mean the collapse of the whole structure of the world prices, he replied: "There is no structure of the prices. If they did not accept the price of the marker crude, there is no agreement." Yamānī also questioned OPEC's power to set oil prices. "Did you know that OPEC is not empowered to set oil prices, and that the law establishing it does not mention this subject at all? OPEC as an organization was set up to meet the problem of artificially depressed prices created by the major companies, as well as to co-ordinate between the member-countries. The subject of setting and increasing prices was not mentioned at all. By adopting our present position, we are restoring matters to their original state. The question of prices is a matter of sovereignty; so this is our oil and it is our right to set the price at which we sell it."

However, the other members of OPEC, bitter and resentful of Saudi Arabia's moves, were not ready to surrender. Iran's chief delegate, Finance Minister Jamshid Amuzegar, emphasized his country's determination to proceed not only with the 10% increase as of 1 January 1977, but also with the additional increase of 5% as of 1 July 1977. Referring indirectly to Saudi Arabia's determination to increase production, Amuzegar said that "if any country wants to increase its production of oil without needing the money, if they deliberately want to hurt their colleagues, you can ask them about it." The Iranian press was less diplomatic. On 20 December, the official newspaper *Rastakhiz* wrote: "The Third World and all the anti-colonialist elements of the world express their hatred towards Yamānī for selling the interests of his nation to the imperialists." On the same day an editorial in *Kayhan* denounced Yamānī as a "stooge of capitalist circles, and a traitor not only to his own king and country, but also the Arab world and the Third World as a whole." Libya's Minister of Oil felt that Saudi opposition to the wishes of the majority of OPEC would lead to the creation of a new international organization for oil producing countries. A Kuwait newspaper actually reported that the Soviet Union might become a member of the new organization.

Iraq's Oil Minister, Tayih Abdel-Karim, speaking at Doha on 18 December 1976, considered the OPEC conference a "great success in view of the external pressures and internal manoeuverings that characterized the meeting." He accused Saudi Arabia of wanting to impose on OPEC a freeze in oil prices as a guarantee for the implementation of plans for a Middle East settlement. But he declared that "the world liberation forces and Arab public opinion are well aware that this stand is no more than a means of neutralizing the Arab oil weapon, as well as being a threat to weaken OPEC by breaking the price structure." As to the Saudi threat to increase oil production, Abdel-Karim said he believed they would not be able to maintain an isolated stand on prices and production. "Oil and energy are not issues in the Arab world, and Arab public opinion will not allow any one Arab oil producing country to undermine the,price structure and violate OPEC solidarity." The Algerian Oil Minister said on 18 December that OPEC could absorb the 5% difference "unless Saudi Arabia raises production. That would be an act of direct aggression against OPEC."

Reaction in the West to Saudi Arabia's action was more favourable. President Gerald Ford praised Saudi Arabia and the UAE for exercising international responsibility and concern for the adverse impact of an oil price increase on the world economy. He described the other eleven OPEC members as taking a course of action "which can only be termed irresponsible." Frank Zarb, Federal Energy Administrator, declared that even a 5% increase would not be helpful to the world economy; the Saudis assisted by the UAE recognized the economic consequences of the situation, pursued a course of moderation and insisted on it. William Simon, US Secretary of the Treasury, described Saudi Arabia as "a true friend of the West in general and of the US in particular." However, the US Administration emphatically denied that it had made any commitments to the Saudis as a *quid pro quo*. On 18 December, President-elect Carter described the decision of the two OPEC members as "responsible"; but he, too, denied any link between this decision and efforts toward a solution of the Middle East problem. "I do not believe that the oil price decision should be a factor in the ultimate political decision concerning the Middle East." The European Economic Community Commission, in a statement issued in Brussels, declared that the increase in the price of crude oil represented a considerable burden for the world economy, "notably for the member-states of the Community."

The Saudi threat to increase production seemed at first to have worked. During the first half of January 1977, production dropped sharply in Iran and in Kuwait, although at least part of this was due to the unloading of heavy purchases made during the last quarter of 1976 in anticipation of the price rise expected at the Doha conference. Nevertheless, the threat was taken seriously and efforts were made to heal the breach. As the current president of OPEC, Qatar was the first to try its hand. However, the anticipated rush for cheaper Saudi oil was not realized. In spite of all the rosy predictions of economic recovery and prosperity both in Europe and the US, demand for oil did not increase. A real glut accumulated: instead of a sellers' market, a buyers' market operated.

As the months passed, Saudi Arabia became more willing to accept a compromise which would be both practical and face-saving for all concerned. In exchange for the other eleven members giving up their decision to implement the additional 5% rise in July, Saudi Arabia and the UAE would increase their prices to 10%. In this way OPEC unity would be restored. Negotiations continued for months, until this compromise was quietly accepted by the OPEC conference which opened in Stockholm on 12 July 1977. Thus ended a stirring chapter in OPEC's history. However, while the compromise patched up the current difficulty, the basic conflicting interests and ideological differences were not resolved.

SURPLUSES AND RECYCLING

Two of the consequences of the high oil prices have been the issue of surpluses which have accumulated in the hands of the producers, and the attempts of recycling them to the consuming countries in the form of purchases (goods and services), investments and loans. There is no unanimity among financial experts either as to the extent of the surpluses or about the effectiveness of their recycling. The first figures for surpluses following the great price hikes were of necessity somewhat exaggerated, and the assessment of the producing countries' capacity to absorb the enormous additional revnues could hardly have been made accurately. But certain norms have now been established, and discernible investment patterns have emerged.

According to the US Treasury, the combined OPEC surpluses in 1974 amounted to $60 bn, dropped to $41 bn in 1975, and were estimated to have gone up to $45 bn in 1976. The same source calculated the cumulative surplus of 1973-6 as between $135-$145 bn. On the other hand, Morgan Guaranty Trust Company of New York estimated that the $65 bn peak of 1974 fell to $32 bn in 1975, rose to $38 bn in 1976, but would decline again in 1977.

Nor were the figures of oil revenues firmly established. The Morgan Company's evaluations were $102 bn in 1974, $97 bn in 1975 and c. $112 bn in 1976. The estimate for 1977 was $128 bn. The Bank of England figures were $90.5 bn in 1974, $93.3 bn in 1975, and $112.2 bn in 1976.

There was a clear relationship between OPEC surpluses and the balance-of-payments deficits of the Western world. The deficit of OECD countries during the period 1974-6 was estimated at $65 bn, and that of developing countries at $79 bn, making a total of $144 bn. The OPEC surpluses for the same period were $138 bn.

The US Treasury reported that OPEC investments in America rose spectacularly from c. $1 bn at the end of 1972 to over $32 bn in March 1977. A total of $13.8 bn went into Treasury securities, nearly $9 bn into bank deposits, and over $8 bn into federal and corporate bonds and US corporate stocks.

OPEC countries have also made heavy investments in the Eurocurrency market with an estimated $22.5 bn in 1974, $8 bn in 1975 and $10.5 bn in 1976. Britain received $7.5 bn in OPEC investments in 1974. In 1975, this fell to $250m, and rose to just under $1 bn in 1976. The US Treasury also recorded that the communist countries were the recipients of $4 bn.

The instability of those investments was reflected in what happened to sterling balances. Investments in the UK by oil producers rose to $6 bn in 1974; fell $300m in the first quarter of 1976, and by a further $1.1 bn in the second quarter. This movement was also reflected by the proportion of oil revenue paid in sterling, which amounted to only 3% in the second quarter of 1976.

WESTERN ATTITUDES TO OPEC POLICIES

By the end of 1976, a number of economists and financial experts had reassessed the results of high oil prices on the Western economies. (Their conclusions were summarized in *Business Week*, 20 December 1976.) In the three years since OPEC raised the price of crude oil from $2.75 to almost $12 a barrel, the consuming nations paid OPEC an additional $225 bn for its oil. They lost $600 bn in output. To finance the balance-of-payments deficits, the less developed countries amassed $170 bn in external debts and some may face the prospect of moratorium or default.

According to one specialist at the Brookings Institution in Washington, the US paid more than $60 bn in GNP because of high oil prices; this was estimated to have cost more than 2m jobs in 1976 alone. He ascribed the losses to the price hike which had triggered a decline in real disposable income, leading in turn to a cut in consumption and investment spending. "To the degree that the industrial world will continue to react to OPEC-induced inflation, the 13 Oil Ministers have become the macro-managers of the world, superseding policymakers in even the strongest industrial nations. . . . The basic problem is that OPEC has both reduced the productivity of the world's existing industrial capital and has added energy efficiency to the problems of scientists and engineers, who are seeking new labour-saving inventions that would increase productivity and growth."

A US National Security Council financial expert wrote: "What we have is a situation which is unmanageable in structural terms. The international economy simply cannot take collective balance-of-payments deficits of $40–60 bn a year indefinitely without a massive redistribution of that surplus to the developing countries and the weaker industrial nations, such as Britain and Italy. Just who will continue to lend to the weaker countries on that scale?"

By the end of 1976, the outlook for solving the problems created by the high oil prices was very gloomy indeed. On top of this, OPEC added 10% more to the burden of the consumers between 1 January and 1 July 1977. *Business Week* (10 January 1977) calculated that the new increase would cost the US alone $75 bn in GNP, 3m jobs, and $70 bn in disposable income in 1977. The non-OPEC world as a whole stood to lose c. $220 bn in GNP.

PIPELINES

During the period under review the Middle East saw a severe, if not revolutionary, change in the use of trans-national oil pipelines. Because of the curtailment of consumption during 1974–5, the price of oil tanker transportation fell drastically, causing the worst ever crisis in the tanker industry. This drop in the tanker rate had far-reaching consequences on the trans-national pipelines in the region.

Iraq had only one outlet for her northern oilfields, through Syria and Lebanon. As a result, Iraq suffered not only from exorbitant demands for transit fees and loading tolls, but also from frequent interruptions and sabotage. Iraq's experience with Syria after the nationalization of the Iraq Petroleum Company was so bad that she decided to find alternatives for the line. After a long and bitter struggle between Iraq, Syria and Lebanon, agreements were signed early in 1973 covering both transit fees and loading tolls, as well as supplies of crude oil at stated prices. Since the price of oil went up and the price of tanker transit went down, Iraq sought to modify both. Syria, on the other hand, asked for a substantial rise in transit fees and resisted a price increase. Iraq, meanwhile, began building a domestic pipeline from Kirkūk in the north to Fao in the south. The line was "strategic" in that it could transit the oil in either direction—north to south or south to north. When it was officially inaugurated in December 1975, the Iraqi vice-chairman of the RCC complained that his country had lost $700m over the past three years as a result of the crude oil supplies and transit agreements reached with Syria and Lebanon in 1973, and stood to lose another $500m in 1976 if the agreements remained operative. (Also see chapter on Iraq.)

Negotiations with Syria-Lebanon broke down completely. Iraq notified those of its customers who normally lifted their oil from the Mediterranean ports, that they were to transfer to Basrah. The flow of Iraqi oil through Syria-Lebanon thus came to a halt. Syria stood to lose c. $138m annually. The two refineries at Ḥoms in Syria and at Tripoli in Lebanon were deprived of Iraqi oil, and had to find other sources of supply.

The idea of building an alternative pipeline to the Mediterranean by way of Turkey was discussed as early as 1968, after the Iraq Petroleum Company pipeline was sabotaged. In 1973, an agreement was signed with Turkey to build a pipeline from the Kirkūk oilfields to the port of Dortyol in the Iskenderun bay. The annual capacity of the line was to be 25–35m tons, with 40% of the flow going to Turkey for home consumption and the balance for export. Sections of the pipeline were to be built and operated by each country: 373 km in Iraq and 632 km in Turkey. The latter was to receive 35 cents per barrel transit fee. The agreement covered a period of 20 years. After some delays, the building of the line began in earnest in 1976 and was officially inaugurated on 3 January 1977. A dispute over the price Turkey was to pay for the oil held up deliveries, which were scheduled to begin in April 1977.

Tapline (Trans-Arabian Pipeline)—running from Saudi Arabia to the Mediterranean through Jordan, Syria and Lebanon and owned by the partners of Aramco—experienced the same difficulties as the Iraqi pipeline. Tapline stopped pumping Saudi oil for export at Sidon on 9 February 1975, claiming losses of $100m annually. This cut off supplies for the refineries in Jordan and Lebanon, and meant the loss of transit fees to the three countries through which the pipeline passed. Under Saudi pressure, Tapline agreed to supply small quantities of oil for the refineries on an *ad hoc* basis. Saudi Arabia refused to purchase the line from the Aramco partners.

The Sumed (Suez Mediterranean) pipeline—an alternative to the Suez Canal and in competition with the Israeli Eilat-Ashkelon pipeline built after the closure of the Canal in 1967—was finally inaugurated in December 1976. The length of the line was 210 miles from Ain Sukhna in the Suez bay to Alexandria. For security reasons it was laid 64 km away from the Canal. Its flowthrough capacity is 40m tons annually, to be increased to 120m tons through a parallel line and pumping stations. Opinion in Egypt was sharply divided whether it was advisable, after the opening and widening of the Suez Canal, to invest additional resources in the pipeline which would be competing with it.

One of the greatest natural gas projects ever undertaken was concluded at the end of 1975 between Iran, the USSR, West Germany, Austria and France. It provided for the delivery of up to 13.4 bn cubic meters of natural gas annually. A 3,800-mile gas pipeline was to be built from Kangan on the Persian Gulf to Astara on the USSR border, and from there through the Ukraine and Czechoslovakia to West Germany, Austria and France. It was described as the big international "switch deal." Iran was to supply the gas to the USSR; the latter was to receive c. 2 bn cubic meters for its own use and deliver 11.4 bn cubic meters to the European countries: Germany 5.5 bn, France 3.66 bn and Austria 1.84 bn. The contract was for 25 years. The cost of constructing the line from the gasfields to the USSR border was estimated at c. $3 bn. The price for the gas at the time was estimated at c. $1 per 1,000 cubic feet to the Soviet border, and c. 65 cents surcharge by Moscow as transit fee, putting the full price for the European countries at the German border at c.

$1.65 per 1,000 cu ft. Payment by the European countries to Iran was to be 80% in the form of equipment and 20% in hard currency.

Czechoslovakia joined the three other European countries in November 1976. It signed an agreement with Iran for a 3.6 bn cubic meters of natural gas annually. The supply to the USSR was to be increased accordingly.

INTERNATIONAL ENERGY AGENCY (IEA)

The major Western oil consumers (excluding only France) formed the International Energy Agency in 1974 in response to the energy crisis triggered off by the oil price hike. However, OPEC members saw it as an attempt by the consuming countries to undermine their own organization. Among the original proposals advocated by the US to the IEA was a uniform floor price for oil to guarantee a safe return on investments for oil alternatives. Although the European members initially refused to agree to such a measure, by the end of January 1976, the IEA did adopt a resolution to put a floor price of $7 a barrel on all imported oil as part of a long-term energy programme. Its implementation requires unanimous approval by all IEA members however.

During 1976, the IEA adopted other measures such as the automatic sharing of energy sources in case of a 7% cut of supplies in an emergency situation; this was to take place two weeks after the outbreak of any new crisis. The Agency claimed in October 1976 that as a result of its efforts, member-countries had reduced their energy consumption in 1975 by 4.8% compared to 1973 levels. Compared with the expected increase of the average 1968–73 growth rate, the drop in consumption amounted to 14.3%—a cutback which probably had more to do with higher oil prices than with IEA initiatives. Indeed, the Agency's complaint that there was no substantial reduction in US consumption seems to confirm this view.

EURO-ARAB DIALOGUE

The European Economic Community (EEC) decided early in 1974 to open a dialogue with Arab League countries for a bilateral programme of assistance in development and investments in return for orderly supplies of oil at stabilized prices. France clearly indicated that this move was in opposition to the US efforts to organize the consuming countries into the IEA. The US strongly opposed the proposed dialogue. In a letter to the German Chancellor, Willy Brandt, President Richard Nixon criticized the Community's decision as an anti-American move. There was also a sharp difference of opinion among Community members themselves. However by July 1974, both the US objections and the internal Community differences were overcome.

From the very beginning, serious differences of opinion emerged between Community members and Arab League representatives as to the nature and scope of the dialogue and over representation. The Community wished to limit the scope to economic issues; the topics to energy; and representation to sovereign members of the League. The Arab League representatives insisted that political and economic issues were inseparable; that the main purpose was to establish relations between the Community and the Arab League based on assisting the Arab countries in their development, and that the Palestine Liberation Organization should be represented as a full League member.

Preliminary meetings were held in Paris, Cairo, Rome and Abū Dhabī, but all failed to solve these basic differences. The fourth round of the dialogue, held in Luxembourg in May 1976, was called the General Committee of the Euro-Arab Dialogue. No tangible results were achieved. The Europeans conceded that political issues should be included; the Arab League secretary-general concentrated on practical and concrete matters; and the chairman of the Arab League delegation devoted his presentation exclusively to the Palestinian question. The final communiqué declared: "The General Committee established the organizational framework of the Dialogue so as to provide an institutional structure for the relations between the European Communities and the Arab world." Not a word was said about oil.

The outcome of the second session of the General Committee, held in Tunis from 10-12 February 1977, was rather unique. The Arabs pressed the Europeans for investment in poor Arab countries, while the Europeans maintained that the rich Arab oil producing countries should finance the needs of their fellow Arabs. The Europeans offered to provide technical advice and assistance. The final communiqué elaborated on the Palestinian issue, with a guarded presentation of the positions of both sides, the Europeans "undertaking to consider" the proposal to establish a committee for political consultation. In spite of such diplomatic language, the basic differences between the Arabs and Europeans persisted (see essay on the Middle East and the European Community).

Oil Statistics

ANNUAL CRUDE OIL PRODUCING OF MAJOR ARAB OIL PRODUCING COUNTRIES
(MILLION BARRELS)

	1972	*1973*	*1974*	*1975*	*1976*
Saudi Arabia	2,202	2,774	3,096	2,583	3,140
Iraq	523	718	681	821	835
Kuwait	1,202	1,103	930	761	787
UAE of which:					
Abū Dhabī	384	476	516	512	583
Dubay	55	80	88	93	115
Sharjah				14	15
Qatar	177	208	189	160	178
Oman	103	107	106	124	134
Total for Major Arab Producing Countries in Asia	*4,646*	*5.466*	*5,606*	*5,068*	*5,787*
Libya	805	796	551	551	700
Algeria	384	392	373	345	384
Total for Major Arab Producing Countries in Africa	*1,189*	*1,188*	*924*	*896*	*1,084*
Grand Total for Major Arab Producing Countries	**5,835**	**6,654**	**6,530**	**5,964**	**6,871**
World Total	18,575	21,134	21,175	20,117	21,737
% of Arab to World Total	31.4	31.5	30.8	29.7	31.6

Source: Petroleum Economist.

OIL PRODUCTION AND PRODUCTION CAPACITY OF ME MEMBERS OF OPEC, 1976
(MILLION B/D)

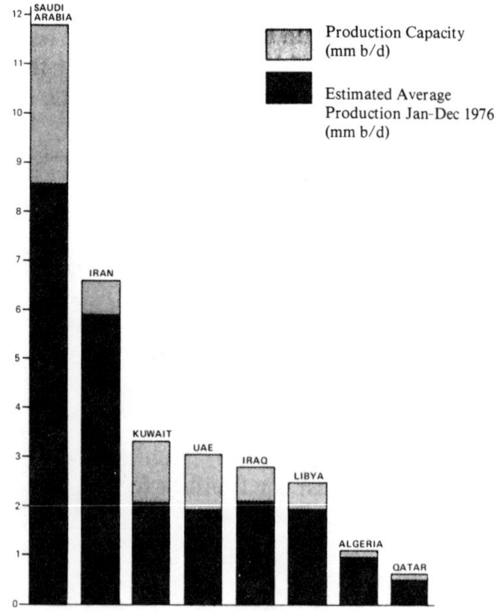

Source: *The Middle East*, February 1977.

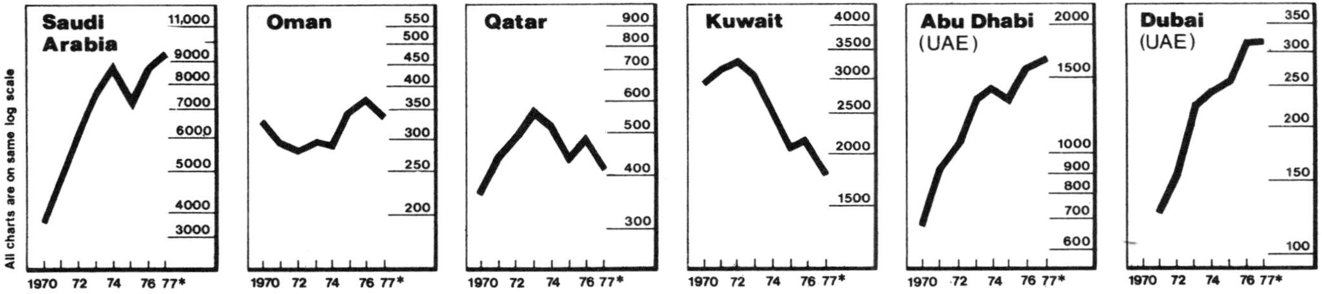

*Jan–Sept 1977.

OIL AND GAS RESERVES

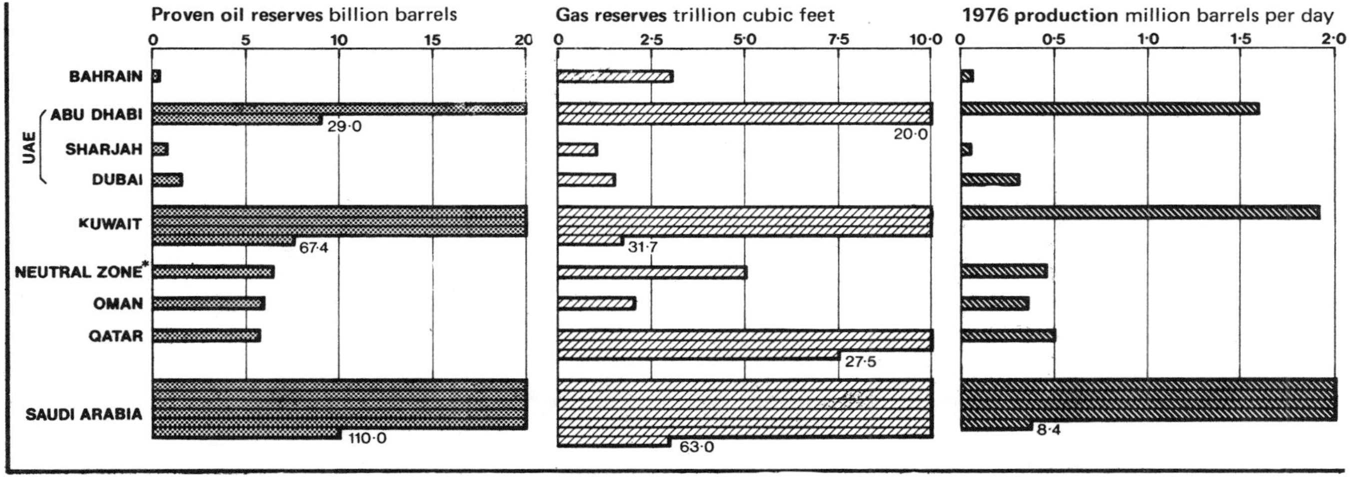

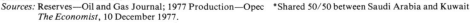

Sources: Reserves—Oil and Gas Journal; 1977 Production—Opec *Shared 50/50 between Saudi Arabia and Kuwait
The Economist, 10 December 1977.

OIL STATISTICS

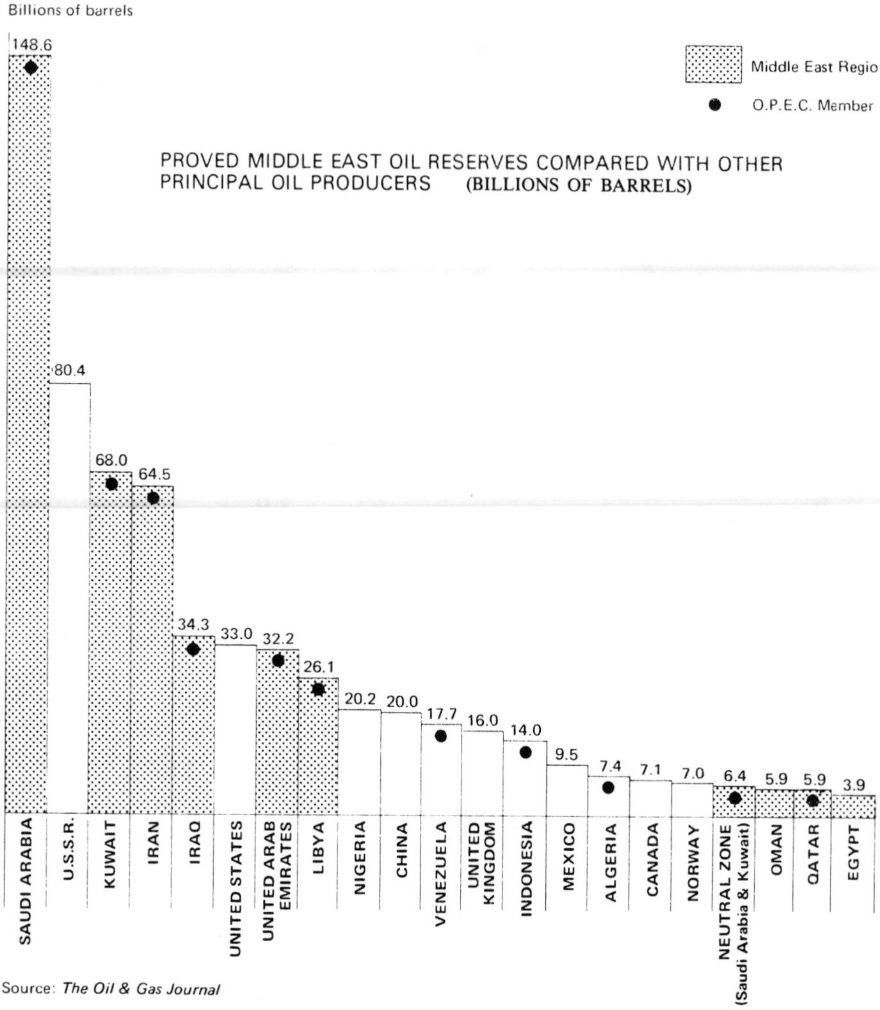

Source: *The Oil & Gas Journal*

REFINERY PROJECTS (THOUSAND B/D)

	Present capacity	*Planned additions*
Saudi Arabia	603	890
Abū Dhabī	15	120
Dubay	nil	200
Kuwait	685	nil
S. Yemen	170	nil
N. Yemen	nil	nil
Qatar	9	45
Oman	nil	less than 10
Total	**1,482**	**1,265**

Source: The Economist, 10 December 1977.

OIL STATISTICS

ESTIMATED GOVERNMENT OIL REVENUES OF MAJOR ARAB OIL PRODUCING COUNTRIES
(MILLION US$)

	1972	*1973*	*1974*	*1975*	*1976*
Saudi Arabia	3,107	4,340	22,600	25,700	33,500
Kuwait	1,657	1,900	7,000	7,500	8,500
Iraq	575	1,840	5,700	7,500	8,500
UAE	551	900	5,500	6,000	7,000
Libya	1,598	2,300	6,000	5,100	7,500
Algeria	700	900	3.700	3,400	4,500
Qatar	255	410	1,600	1,700	2,000
Total	**8,443**	**12,590**	**52,100**	**56,900**	**71,500**

Source: Petroleum Economist.

TOTAL ARAB OIL EXPORTS TO MAJOR INDUSTRIAL COUNTRIES, 1976.
(3.9 BILLION BARRELS)

1. Percentages by country

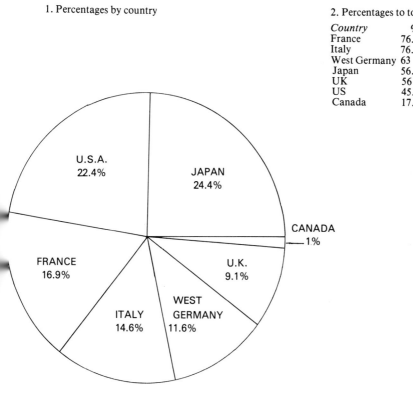

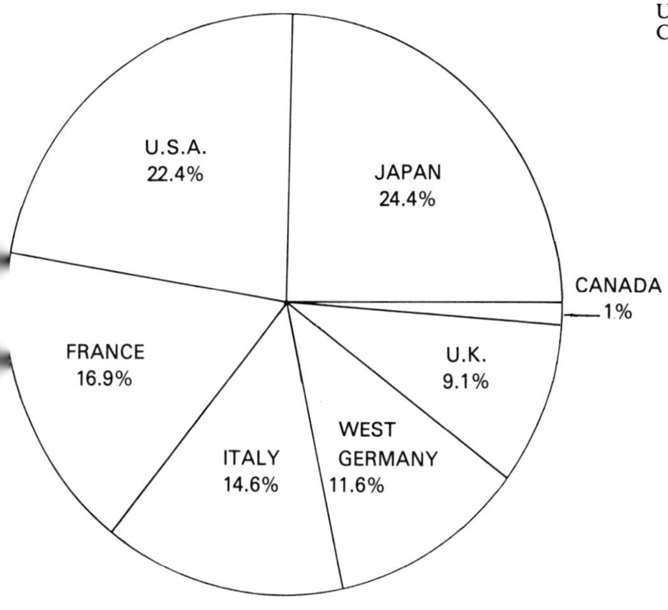

2. Percentages to total oil imports.

Country	*%*
France	76.3
Italy	76.3
West Germany	63
Japan	56.8
UK	56
US	45.3
Canada	17.6

OIL PRODUCTION, REVENUE AND USE, 1976

	Saudi Arabia	*Oman*	*Qatar*	*Kuwait*	*Abū Dhabī (UAE)*		*Dubay (UAE)*
Production* ('000 b/d)	9,300	342.8	415.9	1,865	1,670		316.9
Capacity ('000 b/d)	11,840	350	650	3,340	2,050		340
Oil:							
revenues ($m)	37,800	1,300	3,600	7,357	4,800		1,500
as % of GDP	57†	62.9	na	70‡	• ⟶	65.9	⟵ •
as % of exports	99.9	99.7	96.7	91.3	• ⟶	96.8	⟵ •
Refinery capacity (b/d)	703,000	—	7,400	609,000	15,000		—
Domestic consumption (b/d)	160,000	24,000	5,700	30,000	12,500		na

*Jan-Sept 1977 †1974-75 ‡1975-76

Sources: Mainly Oil and Energy Trends; Petroleum Intelligence Weekly; central Bank reviews; Petroleum ministry statistics. *The Economist*, 10 December 1977.

EEC TRADE WITH 10 MAJOR ARAB PARTNERS 1976*
(AS % OF TRADE WITH ALL ARAB STATES)

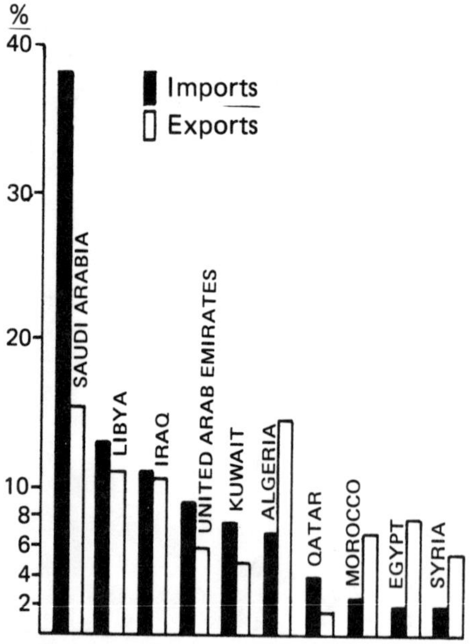

*based on figures for January—November

(These 10 countries provide 96% of EEC imports from the Arab world and absorbs 86% of EEC exports to it)

Source: The Middle East, July 1977.

Part II

Country-by-Country Review

MIDDLE EAST COUNTRIES

BASIC DATA

Country	Capital	Most important natural resources	Area 1000 Km^2	Population in million 1975	GNP per capita US$ 1974
Bahrayn	Manamah	Crude Oil	0.6	0.25	2,250
Egypt	Cairo	Cotton, Crude Oil, Cereals, Rice, Fruits, Vegetables, Iron	1,000	37.23	280
Iraq	Baghdad	Crude Oil, Dates, Cement	435	11.12	1,160
Israel	Jerusalem	Citrus Fruits, Potash	20.7	3.46	3,790
Jordan	Amman	Phosphates, Vegetables, Fruits	98	2.70	430
Kuwait	Kuwait	Crude Oil	24	1.00	11,640
Lebanon	Beirut	Fruits, Citrus Fruits, Vegetables, Forests	10.4	3.20	1,080
Libya	Tripoli	Crude Oil, Vegetables, Fruits	1,760	2.44	3,360
Oman	Muscat	Crude Oil	212	1.50	1,660
Qatar	Doha	Crude Oil	20	0.90	5,830
Saudi Arabia	Riyad	Crude Oil	2,400	8.97	2,080
Somalia	Mogadishu	Livestock, Hides, Bananas, Cereals	637	3.17	90
Sudan	Khartoum	Cotton, Gum, Cereals	2,500	17.76	230
Syria	Damascus	Cotton, Crude Oil, Vegetables, Fruits, Livestock	185	7.35	560
United Arab Emirates	Abu Dhabi	Crude Oil	83	0.65	13,500
Yemen (North)	San'ā	Coffee, Cotton, Maize, Fish	195	6.67	180
Yemen (South)	Aden	Coffee, Fish	288	1.69	230

CURRENCIES

Country	Currency Unit	Approximate Equivalent in other currencies*				
		US Dollar	Pound Sterling	Deutsche Mark	Swiss Franc	French Franc
Bahrayn	Bahrayni Dinar = 1000 Fils	2.53	1.47	5.77	6.10	12.28
Egypt	Egyptian Pound = 1000 Milliemes	2.56	1.49	5.93	6.23	12.50
Iraq	Iraqi Dinar = 1000 Fils	3.45	1.97	7.87	8.32	16.75
Israel	Israeli Pound = 100 Agorot	0.06	0.03	0.12	0.11	0·28†
Jordan	Jordan Dinar = 1000 Fils	3.04	1.80	6.94	7.34	14.78
Kuwait	Kuwaiti Dinar = 1000 Fils	3.49	2.03	7.97	8.42	16.98
Lebanon	Lebanese Pound = 100 Piastres	0.32	0.19	0.72	0.77	1.55
Libya	Libyan Dinar = 1000 Dirhams	3.45	1.96	7.87	8.32	16.75
Oman	Omani Riyal = 1000 Baiza	2.89	1.68	6.60	6.98	14.07
Qatar	Qatar Riyal = 100 Dirhams	0.25	0.15	0.58	0.61	1.23
Saudi Arabia	Saudi Riyal = 100 Halalas	0.28	0.16	0.65	0.68	1.38
Sudan	Sudanese Pound = 1000 Milliemes	2.87	1.67	6.55	6.93	13.95
Syria	Syrian Pound = 100 Piastres	0.25	0.15	0.58	0.61	1.24
United Arab Emirates	Dirham = 100 Fils	0.26	0.15	0.59	0.62	1.25
Yemen (North)	Riyal = 100 Fils	0.22	0.13	0.50	0.53	1.07
Yemen (South)	Yemen Dinar = 1000 Fils	2.93	1.70	6.68	7.07	14.23

*As in London on 11/7/1977. † As in London on 13/4/78.

Arab Republic of Egypt

(Jumhūriyyat Misr al-'Arabiyya)

SHIMON SHAMIR and RAN SEGEV

President Anwar Sādāt's historic decision to address the Knesset in Jerusalem in November 1977 took the world by surprise; but, in fact, his initiative in engaging in direct talks with Israel was the logical culmination of policies adopted by him since the October 1973 war. They reflected both the national interest of Egypt, whose people had borne the brunt of the economic cost of being in the forefront of the struggle for "the Arab cause," and the Egyptian army's growing awareness of the severe risks of engaging in another major war with Israel. Having expelled the Russian military personnel, and having come to rely heavily on the United States as a more effective ally in the diplomatic struggle with Israel, the road to success for Sādāt lay either through impressing the Americans of the moderation and serious desire of Egypt to engage in direct peace talks or, alternatively, to affect the Israelis directly and reach an agreement with them. Either way, nothing could have been more convincing in Western eyes than the Egyptian President standing on the rostrum of the Israeli parliament in Jerusalem. The view taken by the Arab world was bound to be different—but Sādāt realized that what mattered at the end of the day was whether his bold move brought credible gains for the Arab cause. There were obvious risks in Sādāt making the journey to Jerusalem, but there were perhaps greater risks in his not doing so.

During 1977, the Sādāt regime had to cope with mounting social pressures at home due to economic difficulties, growing criticism from Leftist and Nāsirite circles, pressures from Islamic radicalism, a resurgence of Muslim-Coptic friction, and the attempts of pre-revolutionary parties to return to political life. The violent eruption of the "food riots" of 18–19 January 1977 were followed in July by the kidnapping and assassination of a former Minister of Religious Affairs by an Islamic terrorist groups. These two acts of violence led to tighter internal security measures. On the other hand, the limited multiparty system was allowed to continue—a sign of the essential stability of the Sādāt regime.

In foreign affairs, the search for a settlement of the conflict with Israel remained Egypt's main concern and overshadowed all other issues. Egypt's efforts up to October 1977 focused on facilitating the reconvening of the Geneva conference—mainly through collaboration with the US. This political objective was the main element in the continuing Egyptian-American *rapprochement*, the others being economic, technical and military.

At the same time, relations with the Soviet Union continued to deteriorate, with Moscow viewing Sādāt's growing involvement with Washington and other Western capitals with strong disfavour. On more specific questions, Soviet-Egyptian relations were troubled by the problem of unsettled debts; by Russia's refusal to supply spare parts to the Egyptian military; by Soviet support to anti-Egyptian forces in the region; and by its alleged support to subversive movements within Egypt itself.

Egypt's position in Arab affairs in 1977 was interlinked with all these considerations. Egypt sought to increase Saudi support for its policies and its economy; it tried, not very successfully, to maintain a reasonable level of co-operation with

Syria despite policy differences and mutual distrust; it escalated its struggle against the Libyan regime, strengthened its bonds with the Sudan and improved its relations with Jordan. Egypt's relations with the PLO remained ambiguous.

POLITICAL AFFAIRS

PRESIDENT SĀDĀT'S ROLE

The internal position and prestige of President Anwar al-Sādāt declined significantly in 1977 from the high point reached during the post-war euphoria of October 1973, but did not sink to the low ebb of the preceding "no war—no peace" period. Most of Sādāt's troubles resulted from unfulfilled expectations of the post-war period. The "open door" policy did not bring any perceivable relief in the economic hardships suffered by the great majority of Egyptians—inflation, low wages, unemployment, supply shortages and poor public services. On the contrary, the various austerity measures taken to alleviate these difficulties only increased the burden on the public, intensifying discontent. The liberalization of the economy, prescribed by the "open door" policy, increased social tensions by allowing the conspicuous enrichment of a class of entrepreneurs and middlemen, and by permitting the ostentatious display of wealth by privileged Egyptians and foreign visitors. This exposed Sādāt to the accusation that he had abandoned the Revolution's commitments to the underprivileged classes and had struck up an alliance with the Egyptian bourgeoisie. The eruption of these frustrations in the January food riots inflicted a heavy blow on Sādāt's position and prestige.

Mounting social pressures, together with the decline of the Nāsirist vision and the substitution of a policy of pragmatism, contributed to the emergence of radical opposition groups which, during 1977, increasingly challenged Sādāt's leadership and policies. He came under crossfire from the Egyptian Left—which raised the banner of Nāsirism—and from radical Islam, which denounced the regime as an "infidel" system. The two movements thrived on the support of anti-Sādāt propaganda launched from abroad: the former receiving the blessing of the Communist world in its criticism of Sādāt's US-orientation and economic policies; and the latter backed by Qadhdhāfī's fierce attacks on the programmes and personality of Sādāt. Both movements sharply attacked Sādāt's commitment to diplomacy as the best means of settling the Arab-Israeli conflict, thus increasing his vulnerability to political pressures from within and without.

The political liberalization measures, which had allowed the emergence of three political parties and had enhanced Sādāt's popularity in Egypt, underwent a partial reversal in 1977. Faced with the challenge of growing protest movements and increased terrorism, Sādāt imposed a series of emergency decrees which gave the state almost unlimited power to deal not only with subversive groups and saboteurs, but also with strikers, demonstrators and critics. His Prime Minister, Mamdūh Sālim launched a rigorous campaign to impose law and order. The return to these measures robbed Sādāt of one of his most precious advantages over his predecessor Jamāl 'Abd al-Nāsir in the public eye.

Unlike Nāsir, Sādāt did not try to base his leadership on personal charisma, but on the traditional authority of a family head. In his public appearances, Sādāt posed as a benevolent patriarch, stressing his deep commitment to the welfare of his people and expecting in return respect and obedience. He consistently addressed delegates of the People's Assembly, high-ranking officials and commanders of the armed forces as "his sons," commending and reprimanding them in paternal fashion. In his personal memoirs, serialized in the new magazine *October*, he explained that "leaders are fathers, as well as teachers of their people." [1] He named Kemal Ataturk, "the father of the Turks," as the leader who had inspired him most.[2] In a television interview on the occasion of the anniversary of the Corrective Revolution,[3] the President said: "In my capacity as the head of the family, I say that I will never make any of my sons suffer what I did. I must carry out reforms and let my sons do better, because all [Egyptians] are my sons and I am responsible for them."[4]

Sādāt put great emphasis on autochthonous Egyptian values. "For 7,000 years," he said, "this people have been raised on such values as love, family spirit and loyalty."[5] The values of rural Egypt were particularly stressed. "I am a *fellah*" (peasant) was a recurring theme in many of Sādāt's public addresses, an approach which evidently had some appeal for the Egyptian masses.

THE PROCESS OF DE-NĀSIRIZATION

The process of de-Nāsirization continued in 1977, thus further crystallizing the separate identity of Sādāt's regime. The shortcomings and failures of the Revolution were increasingly attributed to Nāsir's mistakes. His policies were blamed both for the past over-dependence on the Soviet Union and for the "senseless polarization" of the Arab world. The 1967 defeat was also attributed to Nāsir's personal errors. In an address to the nation, Sādāt declared: "I am saying it for the first time today: from 5 June 1967, Nāsir was indeed a shattered man." In addition, Nāsir's regime was associated with "excessive measures, arrests, detention, dismissals and destitution."[6]

Sādāt suggested the following historical perspective for the record of the Revolution: "The fifties were years of achievements; the sixties were years of successive defeats; and the seventies witnessed the beginning of decisive resolutions and complete victories."[7] The Commission for Rewriting the History of the Revolution (established by Sādāt in October 1975 under the chairmanship of Vice-President Ḥusnī Mubārak) continued its work in 1977. Among the main topics it examined were the causes of the 1967 defeat and the origins of the 23 July 1952 Revolution.

Sādāt's 15 May Corrective Revolution continued to be presented as a major breakthrough in Egypt's political evolution and the basis of the present regime's legitimacy. In a speech to the Third Army, Sādāt declared: "From 15 May onward, we began carrying out the battle of liberation and the battle of construction simultaneously—the battle of building the Egyptian [person] through freedom, democracy and security; and the battle of building the Egyptian's honour, security and dignity."[8]

Sādāt contrasted his programme implicitly and explicitly with that of his predecessor. Thus, in a speech to the Second Army in Ismā'īliyya, he said: "Our socialism is a democratic socialism. It is combined with democracy and does not crush the individual for the sake of the group, as was advocated in the past. . . . For the first time in many years, even since before the 23 July Revolution, we have started building democracy and total freedom. We have started building a sound democracy. Our socialism is aimed at achieving the dignity of the citizen, not at crushing him; at achieving his self-respect not his humiliation; at achieving prosperity for him, not his impoverishment."[9]

The trial of functionaries accused of political repression during the Nāsir era continued. On 23 December 1976, Lt-Gen Muḥammad Sādiq, the former Deputy Prime Minister and War Minister who was Director of Military Intelligence in the 1967 war, was given one year imprisonment and a three-year suspended sentence after being found responsible for torturing officers during investigations into the causes of Egypt's defeat in the Six-Day war. Eleven officers and soldiers—most of them members of the Military Intelligence or guards in the military prisons—were found guilty of similar charges and given sentences ranging from one to ten years.[10] On 15 June 1977, the Cairo Criminal Court sentenced the former Egyptian War Minister, Shams al-Dīn Badrān, and Lieut Muhammad Safwat al-Rubi to imprisonment with hard labour for a total of 30 years on charges of torturing villagers in the Kamshīsh affair, as well as Muslim Brethren, Infantry school officers and detainees in military prison. 13 others were sentenced to shorter periods on similar charges. The verdict on Shams Badrān—and some others living abroad—was issued in their absence.[11]

However, the authorities tried to ensure that the de-Nāsirization measures did not get out of hand and spill over to Sādāt's own regime. The President warned that overdoing the defamation of Nāsir was "inconsistent with the values of our society and the nation's conscience."[12] Sādāt often qualified his criticism of the Nāsirite era by pointing out some of its achievements as well as aspects of continuity from Nāsir's regime to his own. Sādāt demonstrated leniency towards Nāsir's associates by the early release from prison of some of those convicted of belonging to "centres of power." Two former Ministers who had participated in the abortive conspiracy of May 1971, Sha'rāwī Jum'a (Interior) and Diyā' al-Dīn Da'ūd (Labour and Social Affairs), were released from prison on 2 January 1977 "on orders from President Sādāt." Jum'a had originally been sentenced to death and Da'ūd to ten years hard labour.[13]

SĀDĀT RE-ELECTED AS PRESIDENT

Sādāt had originally been elected for a six-year term, which was due to expire on 15 October 1976. In spite of previous indications that he would not seek another term, he explained that his position had changed because of the need to deal with crucial economic problems and carry out the "administrative revolution."[14] On 25 August 1976, Sādāt was unanimously nominated by the People's Assembly as the only candidate for the Presidency. The Assembly's deliberations were accompanied by mass rallies and marches, organized mainly by the Arab Socialist Union (ASU) and labour syndicates, which expressed support for Sādāt's nomination.[15]

In Sādāt's acceptance speech, he outlined the main points of his programme. 1) The complete liberation of all Arab lands, and the establishment of a lasting peace based on justice and the rights of the Palestinian people. 2) The crystallization of the nature of Egypt's socialism. 3) Political stability and social harmony. 4) A policy of economic, political and conceptual "openness." 5) Unifying the ranks of the Arab nations, but not according to "phony slogans" (such as the call for political unification between states). 6) The development of the armed forces to prepare them for "restoring the rights" (of the Arabs to their occupied land).[16]

The referendum was conducted on 16 September 1976; on the following day it was announced that 9,145,683 voters out of a total electorate of 9,564,482 had supported Sādāt's election for the Presidency. Only 5,605 voted against.[17] Two days later Sādāt addressed the nation: "When the result of the referendum on my first constitutional term of Presidency appeared six years ago, it showed a great percentage of support—90%. . . . Now the result of your free vote has reached 99.93% in favour. . . . The number of those who said "no" dropped from 900,000 to 6,527 [sic]. . . . This almost unanimous free expression has many meanings. . . . These meanings are national unity and the concept of one family joined by love and not split by rancour." The President added that he regarded the result as an expression of confidence in his policies.[18]

After taking the oath as President on 16 October 1976, Sādāt promptly issued a Republican decree reappointing Air Force Lt-Gen Ḥusnī Mubārak as Vice-President. Mubārak served as Acting-President in Sādāt's absence from the country.[19]

POLITICAL CONTROL

While the problem of constitutional legitimacy was thus smoothly solved, that of political control presented increasing difficulties, the gravest being the proliferation of militant opposition groups. These difficulties were in part the direct consequence of Sādāt's liberalization measures. Political parties which had been banned for more than 20 years and which were clearly outside the area of political consensus on which Sādāt's regime is based, asserted their existence and demanded legitimacy. Criticism in the press became bolder and, as reflected in Sādāt's angry reactions, often transgressed what the authorities considered a responsible exercise of the freedom of speech. Sādāt's policies were increasingly challenged in the People's Assembly, and on at least one occasion a sharp exchange between the President and dissenting delegates erupted in front of television cameras.[20] There were also difficulties with the Judiciary which was showing a greater tendency towards independence. Thus, the acquittal of a large number of suspects arrested for participation in the food riots prompted Sādāt to refer cases of Communists accused of similar offences to military courts.

To ensure his political control, Sādāt relied first of all on his Prime Minister Mamdūḥ Sālim who, in the 3 February Cabinet reshuffle, was given back the Ministry of Interior which operates most of the internal security systems. (Sālim himself had risen from the ranks of the police.)

The military was always the most formidable power base of the regime, but the tendency had been to keep it as separate as possible from internal politics. The War Minister, Gen 'Abd al-Ghanī al-Jamasī, a respected professional soldier, embodied the apolitical posture of the Armed Forces. However, in 1977, Sādāt had to turn to the military for support on a number of occasions, calling it in, for instance, to suppress the food riots after the failure of the regular police to restore order. As mentioned above, the cases of Communists accused of sabotage and conspiracy against the regime were also increasingly turned over to military courts, and Sādāt took the same course with the trial of members of radical Islamic terrorist groups (see below).

The President also made extensive use of the mass media. In his capacity as President of the ASU (which has a controlling share in the ownership of the Press), he made changes in the staff of the major newspapers to fit the needs of the regime. Frequent appearances on state radio and television were also designed to strengthen the bonds between public and leader.

With all the sharp criticism of state bureaucracy—sometimes voiced by the President himself—it necessarily remained the main instrument for implementing policies and one of the main pillars of the regime.

Sādāt could employ the government-sponsored Egypt's Arab Socialist Platform (later Party) led by Prime Minister Sālim and Sādāt's brother-in-law, Maḥmūd Abū al-Wāfiya.[21] The Party controlled the overwhelming majority of the People's Assembly (see below), which for most of 1977 operated under the presidency of another of Sādāt's relatives—Sayyid Mar'ī. Sādāt also made use of the various associations of peasants, workers, professionals and other social sectors—which were all directly or indirectly government-controlled—to mobilize and demonstrate support for his policies. Despite his dependence on all these institutions, Sādāt remained Egypt's unchallenged ruler. He tended to leave the day-to-day management of the country's affairs to key officials, but retained in his own hands decision-making powers on all crucial issues.

Mrs Jihān Sādāt assisted the President as a public figure in her own right, although this aroused considerable resentment among the conservative public. In October 1976, she was elected by acclamation as chairlady of the Local Council in al-Minufiya.[22]

Towards the end of his seventh year in office, Sādāt's problems seemed to be growing, with no solutions on the horizon. In an analysis of the President's position at the end of September 1977, a foreign correspondent quoted a diplomat in Cairo: "It's been two years since Sādāt has had a policy success. He needs something or the situation will continue to deteriorate. When you have the appearance of a political vacuum, you get people moving to protect their own interests first and you risk chaos." [23]

THE JANUARY 1977 FOOD RIOTS

The riots that occurred in Egyptian cities on 18 and 19 January were the most serious anti-government protests since the 1952 Revolution—in terms of mass participation, life and property losses, means used to restore order, and the purport of the challenge to the regime.

The disturbances came as a reaction to the austerity measures announced by the Deputy Prime Minister for Financial and Economic Affairs, Dr 'Abd al-Mun'īm al-Qaysūnī in the People's Assembly on 17 January. In presenting his 1977 budget proposals, Qaysūnī spoke of the need to reduce the budget deficit and curb inflation, and announced a series of cutbacks including a drastic reduction in subsidies on food and other vital commodities. This economic programme was designed to meet the demands of the International Monetary Fund, the US government, private American banks and the Arab oil-producing countries—all of whom repeatedly advocated such action as a prerequisite for advancing further loans to Egypt. [24]

The measures announced by the government would have amounted to an increase of up to 50% in the prices of such commodities as butane gas, petrol and flour. Purchases in excess of the rationed quantities of sugar, rice, tea, cooking oil and the like would also have become more costly. The actual size of the price increases was not considerable, but for low-income families—who constitute the great majority of Egyptians and spend most of their income on basic commodities—they would have meant a very substantial additional burden.

Thousands of demonstrating workers, mainly from the "Misr Helwan" plant, started moving from the Helwan industrial area to Cairo on 18 January. They were joined in the city by other demonstrators, many of them students from Ein Shams University, shouting such slogans as "We want food," "Down with Sādāt's palaces," "Jihān, Jihān, the people are hungry," and also "Nāsir, Nāsir." [25] Similar demonstrations were initiated in Alexandria by workers of the naval shipyard, who were soon joined by students and others in the city. The riots spread widely, to Dumyat and Zagazig in the Delta, to the Suez Canal cities and to several towns of the Upper Nile valley as far as Minya and Aswan. The disturbances escalated further on the second day of the riots on 19 January.

The rioters, many of them youths, attacked public buildings and facilities such as police stations and Ministry offices, burnt buses and street cars and tore down traffic lights and road signs. They smashed what they regarded as symbols of luxurious living: night clubs, cinemas, smart cafes, expensive shops and big limousines. Buildings of the Centre and Rightist newspapers, *al-Ahrām* and *al-Akhbār*, were also damaged.

The immediate police reaction, to try and disperse the rioters by using large quantities of teargas, met with only limited success. In a number of places, actual shooting battles occurred between demonstrators and the police. On 19 January, the Central Security Force (a crack police unit) was brought in, and finally the army went into action. At 4.00 p.m. a curfew was imposed and orders given to shoot anyone found outdoors. Tanks and armoured cars were deployed to guard Sādāt's home and public buildings. The President, who had returned from his Aswan winter residence, assumed personal command in Cairo. By the morning of 20 January, order had been restored and the curfew was lifted two days later.[26]

The number of persons killed in the disturbances was put at 79 and those injured at 800. Damage to public and private property was initially estimated at E£ 200m. The police arrested 1,250 suspected rioters, including 200 members of "clandestine subversive organizations."[27]

This was not the first case of violent anti-government protest in recent years. Shortages and high prices had caused food riots in Cairo two years before, on 1 January 1975. In 1975–6, there were various reports of workers' strikes leading to clashes with police (at the textile mills in Mehalla al-Kubra in March 1975; in Dumyat in March 1976; and within the Suez Canal Authority in May 1976). Isolated clashes with local authorities and police were also reported from rural areas (such as Qana in July 1976). Student demonstrations and sit-ins in Cairo and Alexandria were reported almost monthly. On 18–19 September 1976, Cairo bus drivers, protesting against high prices and delays in bonus payments, paralysed public transportation in the city. A number of violent clashes with the police erupted and many arrests were made.[28] A particularly violent clash with security forces took place in Bayla on 1–2 January 1977, when demonstrators protested against inflationary prices and inadequate public services. The distrubances spread to a number of other localities.[29]

However, the January 1977 riots were the first to take the form of a nation-wide political protest against the regime itself. This was also the first time that the authorities needed the massive intervention of the military to regain control. No longer sporadic or local outbursts, the riots imposed a substantial constraint on Sādāt's "open door" and de-Nāsirization policies.

THE GOVERNMENT'S RESPONSE TO THE RIOTS

The authorities were quick to reconsider their economic programme in the light of this violent public reaction. On 19 January, Egypt's Arab Socialist Party (the government-supported Centre Party) issued a statement reporting that Prime Minister Sālim (the Chairman of the Party) had asked the President to suspend the new economic measures, and that Sādāt had responded favourably to this request. The Party's position on the new measures was clearly stated: "The parliamentary body of Egypt's Arab Socialist Party announces its disapproval of commodity price increases that would harm the popular classes."[30] On the following day, the People's Assembly Planning and Budget Committee decided on the "cancellation of the decisions on increasing the prices of supply commodities and all public commodities affecting the masses." This was coupled with a decision on "increasing custom duties and duties on imported luxury commodities."[31]

At the end of a five-hour meeting on 26 January, the Government announced its resolution to explore ways of reducing public spending "without harming the people's needs, investments or the improvement of services; to increase wages in the public and private sectors retroactively from 1 January; to improve the supply of basic commodities; to accelerate the completion of housing units for low-income families; and to improve transportation and communication services."[32]

On 20 January, the Government began to appeal to the IMF, the US, the European Community and the Arab oil-producing countries for urgent and extensive financial aid. In fact, there was a marked tendency to utilize the disturbances as leverage on Egypt's creditors. Ominous statements by spokesmen and analysts appeared in the media. As one of Sādāt's representatives to the Saudi government explained to a foreign correspondent: "There will be a sea of money or a sea of blood."[33] Egyptian and Saudi sources in Cairo disclosed at the end of February 1977 that Saudi Arabia, Kuwait, Qatar and the United Arab Emirates had decided to grant Egypt $1 bn in immediate aid, and another $1 bn in deposits in Egyptian banks in order to finance development projects.

From the first statement issued by the Ministry of Interior on 18 January, it became clear that the Government chose to attribute the riots to subversive opposition groups. Contrary to the observations of foreign correspondents, who had noticed a great diversity among those participating in the disturbances—including supporters of militant Islamic groups (particularly among those who stormed the "high life" establishments)[34]—the internal security authorities focused exclusively on the Communists and Left-wing Nāsirites. The 18 January statement spoke of "Marxist rabble-rousers" among the workers and of "Marxist students"; it blamed the riots on "Communist elements who were operating within an organized Communist framework, supported by certain elements who call themselves Nāsirites."[35]

The Public Prosecutor Ibrāhīm al-Qalyūbī was more specific. He disclosed on 26 January that the investigations had established the existence of four secret Communist organizations involved in the food riots: the Egyptian Communist Party, the Communist Labour Party, the Revolutionary Current and the 8th of January Organization. He claimed that the aim of these organizations was "to change the basic principles of the existing regime, to overthrow the current economic and social systems and subsequently to seize power."[36]

Other announcements by the authorities spoke of a conspiracy by the members of these organizations "to burn down Cairo." Some were alleged to be linked to the Palestinian Popular Front for the Liberation of Palestine led by George Habash; others to the South Yemenite National Liberation Front. The authorities reported the discovery of leaflets inciting workers and students to rebel against the regime and listing the slogans which were actually used in the riots. A total of 105 members of the legal Leftist National Progressive Unionist Rally (NPUR) were among those arrested,[37] and it was reported that the Public Prosecutor's Office would demand the removal of Parliamentary immunity enjoyed by those who were delegates in the People's Assembly.[38] The authorities also arrested a number of well-known journalists and editors, including Yūsuf Sabrī of *Rūz al-Yūsuf*, Muhammad Salmawi of *al-Ahrām*, and Ḥusayn 'Abd al-Rāziq of *al-Akhbār*.[39]

In his address to the nation on 3 February, Sādāt said: "It is an indisputable fact that it [the January riots] was a criminal plan which was designed to be imposed on the Egyptian people. . . . Those who wanted this subversion had several aims. They wanted to weaken our negotiating strength when we go to meet the Jews in Geneva. . . . The plan was also aimed at striking at Egypt's position in the Arab world. . . . A third target for this plan was of course the 'open door' policy which Moscow is angry about. . . . I promise my people that such things will not happen again."[40]

In the same speech, Sādāt presented an 11-point decree, acting on the powers vested in the President under Article 74 of the Constitution which provides that "in case of a threat to national unity, or the security of the homeland, or the ability of the state's institutions to perform their constitutional duties, the President of the Republic shall take immediate measures to deal with this danger." The new decree stipulated that imprisonment with hard labour, up to a life sentence, could be imposed for committing, organizing or instigating the following acts: participation in clandestine, hostile or paramilitary groups; sabotaging public, co-operative or private property; participating in a gathering which incites the masses to interfere with the proper functioning of the constitutional authorities, or public and private establishments; participating in a workers' strike which could jeopardize the national economy; and participating in a sit-in which could jeopardize public security. The decree also demanded a property statement from every citizen within three months, and exempted from taxes farmers who owned three feddans or less, or earned E£ 500 a year or less.

As Article 74 of the Constitution also stipulates that a referendum should be held within 60 days of the adoption of measures under its provisions, a referendum was called for the following week. In the campaign which preceded it, trade unions, professional associations and other organizations declared their support for the President and for the measures he took to prevent a recurrence of disturbances. However, the Left and several independent personalities, including the former RCC member Kamāl al-Dīn Ḥusayn, criticized the new decree as unconstitutional.[41] (This led to Husayn's expulsion from the People's Assembly on 14 February.) The result of the referendum, announced on 11 February, showed that 9,166,179 or 99.42% of all the valid votes cast were in favour of the decree, and only 54,138 against.[42]

THE POST-RIOT TRIALS

In the months subsequent to the riots, the Public Prosecutor's office dealt with suspects arrested during and following the disturbance. Many were released, including the journalists from *al-Ahrām, Rūz al-Yūsuf* and other of their colleagues in March.[43] The release of Dr 'Ismat Zayd al-Dīn, the nuclear physicist arrested in Alexandria, was personally announced by the President to the Alexandria University Council.[44]

Bills of indictment were presented against groups of suspects in different localities. Defendants accused of subversion, rioting, sabotage and looting were referred to the Supreme State Security Court; those under 18 years of age to Juvenile Courts; and those found in possession of looted property to the Criminal Courts.[45] The verdicts in the cases of the first group tried by the Supreme State Security Court were announced on 14 June. One was found guilty and sentenced to six months imprisonment, while 43 were declared innocent. On 29 June, the Supreme State Security Court in Matariya, Qubba Gardens, Zaytūn, Jabāliyya and Wayli sentenced 13 defendants to five to ten years hard labour, and acquitted 44. On 9 July, the Alexandria Court sentenced 29 defendants to hard labour and acquitted 148.[46] The regime was thus enabled to deal with the challenge presented by the riots with a combination of firmness and flexibility.

While Sādāt succeeded in imposing his authority, the methods he used, particularly in attributing all the disturbances to a Communist conspiracy, considerably eroded the credibility he had achieved with such difficulty in 1973. More important, the main causes of the riots had not been solved, nor were they likely to disappear.[47] The Egyptian economy still suffered from heavy indebtedness, and in August there was again talk of reducing the subsidies. Social divisions remained as wide as ever, and agitation against the regime among workers, students and others continued.

THE PRESIDENT AND THE LEFT

Sādāt's initial position towards the Marxists (who had dissolved their Communist organizations in 1965 in order to join the institutions of the regime) was quite favourable. He sought to incorporate them into a broad national front which would serve as the base for the regime, and accordingly included two Marxists in his second Cabinet. However, basic differences in interests and goals soon emerged. The rift with the Soviet Union in 1972 and the move towards the US in 1973 led to inevitable tension between Sādāt and the predominantly Soviet-oriented Egyptian

Communists. The growing dependence on conservative oil-producing Arab countries also necessitated a complementary anti-Communist posture. Above all, Sādāt's "open door" policy established a trend which was precisely the opposite of what the Marxists had hoped to achieve by their collaboration with the regime: it strengthened links with capitalist economies, broadened the scope for private enterprise in Egypt, and froze or even ignored the socialist legislation adopted under Nāsir.

Working through *ad hoc* committees, Sādāt eliminated quasi-Marxist interpretations of the regime's programme and gradually played down socialism. Addressing the Higher Council for Universities, Sādāt asked: "What kind of socialism is this under which people . . . are incapable of producing their own food, when they are an agricultural people. . . . I urge [a policy of] 'open door.' Anyone in this country who wants to increase production and jobs, let him come to me."[48] In 1977, Sādāt began to offer a substitute concept: "We advocate a democratic socialism . . . a democracy based on the fact that all producers and the state sit together and decide what is best for us."[49] However, Sādāt's democratic socialism was a somewhat eclectic improvization, lumping together the preservation of state control and some other elements of Nāsirist Arab Socialism with certain liberal concepts and ideas of the welfare state. Sādāt promised that all the features of this system "would be completely crystallized by the end of the parliamentary session this year [1977]."[50]

Realizing that the gap between this and "scientific socialism" was too wide to be bridged, some Marxists resorted to clandestine activities, particularly among students and urban workers. Egyptian Marxists abroad also initiated a vigorous campaign against Sādāt's policies. In August 1975, the self-dissolved Egyptian Communist Party (ECP) announced its re-establishment in Beirut. The ECP manifesto presented a line conspicuously analogous to Moscow's, criticizing Sādāt's US orientation, the Sinai Agreement, "open door" and "suppression of Socialism."[51] A Marxist magazine began appearing in Paris in 1977 under the name *al-Yasār al-'Arabī* (*The Arab Left*), which described Sādāt's policies as part of "an American-Zionist-Reactionary master plan."[52]

Nevertheless, the main figures in Egyptian Marxism continued to work through legitimate channels. When three political parties were authorized in 1976, the Marxists joined the Leftist National Progressive Unionist Rally (NPUR) and occupied key positions in it. Khālid Muḥyī al-Dīn, the Marxist veteran of the original "Free Officers" junta, became its leader. The NPUR's platform called, among other things, for defending what the masses had achieved through the 23 July Revolution; safeguarding the peasants' and workers' 50% share in state institutions; guaranteeing employment to graduates of institutes of higher learning; giving high priority to the liberation of the occupied territories in Sinai; continuing to subsidize basic commodities; and implementing development schemes which would achieve balanced economic progress.[53]

A major Marxist strategy was the attempt to rally around all the opponents of Sādāt's de-Nāsirization policy. Disregarding their own bitter experience under Nāsir, they focused on the relatively more Leftist orientation of the old regime and tried to mobilize the forces of Nāsirism, which have a far wider constituency in Egypt than Marxism *per se*. On the issue of de-Nāsirization, the Marxists had the advantage of being able to talk not merely as a radical opposition group but as the upholders of the "genuine" programme of the 23 July Revolution, and could thus expect both legitimacy and popularity. The Marxists sought to utilize Sādāt's vulnerability on this question, not even shying away from public confrontations with him.

In one such open clash in the People's Assembly, Aḥmad Kamāl—who had emerged in 1977 as the leading Leftist spokesman in the Assembly—interrupted Sādāt's speech at the point when he was discussing Nāsirism, to shout at him: "There is a difference between what is now being applied and what we believe is in accordance with the programme which the immortal leader Jamāl 'Abd al-Nāsir had drawn up and in which your Excellency participated!" Invited by Sādāt to point out these differences, he listed the "open door" policy which had become "a consumers' openness"; the multi-party system which was "a threat to the concept of the alliance [of the working forces of the people]"; yielding to the pressure of (conservative) Arab states; replacing the Eastern (Soviet) influence with that of the Western world; losing the achievements of the October war to Kissinger's manoeuvres; and using the government-controlled media for launching a campaign against the 23 July Revolution.[54]

Sādāt's reaction to Leftist criticism became increasingly more outspoken in 1977. Under Nāsir, he explained, the Marxists "occupied leading positions in the centres of influence, in the information media, the press, culture, in the state posts, everywhere. They began to proliferate because 'Abd al-Nāsir was exhausted [after the 1967 defeat]." Although the Marxists collaborated with the Nāsirite "centres of power," they were spared by the Corrective Revolution and have "exploited this to the maximum—so that they would be able to jump to power."[55] Today, he added, they try "to exploit the name of 'Abd al-Nāsir in an attempt to revive the detention camps, custodianships, coercion and the socialism of poverty for everyone."[56] Sādāt concentrated on exposing the fallacy of this Marxist identification with Nāsirism. Repeated themes in his speeches were: "They say they are Nāsirists, but they are Communists." "They don the garb of 'Abd al-Nāsir." "They are the society for exploiting the name of 'Abd al-Nāsir."[57]

Although Sādāt had accepted the differentiation between the Communists and the "legitimate Left," and between the "pro-Soviet Leftists" and the "Egyptian Leftists" in principle, this distinction became blurred in 1977. In his 3 February speech, he accused the whole Left in the People's Assembly—the holders of "the two seats [won by the NPUR] and the three [independents] who do not want to admit that they belong to the Left"—of resorting to the Communist method of exploiting the hardships of the people to incite them against the government. On 26 June, he went further—calling the leaders of the NPUR "agents of the Soviet Union."[58]

It is difficult to tell whether the Leftists were indeed engaged in a grand design aimed at undermining Sādāt's regime, or whether they served as a natural scapegoat for its troubles. There was probably more than a grain of truth in both interpretations; in any event, Sādāt's accusations followed a consistent pattern. The Marxists were blamed for the January 1975 disturbances, for various confrontations with the authorities such as the November 1976 students' demonstration,[59] and of course for the January 1977 riots. There was consistency too in the treatment of Marxists by the internal security services. Mass arrests and the "shattering" of conspiracies took place even before Janary 1977—particularly in March–April 1976. As mentioned above, the food riots were followed by mass arrests among Leftists, including 105 NPUR members and a number of journalists. Considerable pressure was also applied on the Leftist publications. At the end of February, the editor of the Marxist monthly *al-Talī'a*, Lutfi al-Khūli, saw no other option but to resign. In April, Sādāt accepted the resignation of 'Abd al-Raḥmān al-Sharqāwī and reshuffled the editorial staff of the Leftist weekly *Rūz al-Yūsuf*.[60] In the same month, it was reported that leading Leftist figures, including Khālid Muhyī al-Dīn, Kamāl al-Dīn Rif'at, Ismā'īl Sabrī 'Abdallah, and Muhammad

'Awda, were prohibited from leaving the country without special authorization from the General Intelligence.[61] On 28 July, the Prime Minister declared: "Marxist Communists are still at work underground. We should get to them face to face before they rise to the surface and achieve their objective."[62]

Two months later, at the end of September, the State Security Department broke up a "subversive" organization whose 34 members (including doctors, chemists, students, workers and officials) belonged to the ECP and the Egyptian Communist Workers' Party. A security spokesman disclosed that leaflets seized from the organization had called for the regime's overthrow; Sādāt decided to try those apprehended before a military tribunal.[63]

The Leftists' response was a combination of self-defence and counter-offensive. Speaking at an international press conference in Cairo, Khālid Muḥyī al-Dīn rejected the charge that the NPUR and Communist elements were responsible for the January riots. He insisted that the masses' reaction to the Government's economic decisions was "a popular movement stemming from social differences in Egypt which have increased during the past two years."[64] To a foreign correspondent he explained that "if President Sādāt does not take a lesson from the events of 18 and 19 January it will be very bad for the future of Egypt. The real meaning of the troubles is that the present government policy has failed." He pointed out that his Party now had 160,000 member, only a small percentage of whom were Communists: "most are Nāsirists rather than Marxists."[65] Before its editor resigned, the Marxist *al-Talī'a* went one step further and charged that the Government was making the Left the scapegoat for its mistakes.[66]

A case of Leftist criticism which produced a particularly sharp backlash took place during a public symposium organized in Rome by the Institute for International Co-operation, which belongs to the Italian Socialist Party. Sādāt's policies were attacked in that symposium by the three participating Egyptians: Khālid Muhyī al-Dīn; former *Talī'a* editor, Lutfī al-Khūli; and the Leftist journalist, Muhammad Sayyid Aḥmad (*al-Ahrām*). The Minister of State for Local Government and Popular Organization, Ḥāmid Maḥmūd, described their criticism as "ideological and ethical sabotage." Muhyī al-Dīn claimed that the speeches were misquoted in Egypt.[67]

Articles written by Leftists in the Egyptian press showed clearly that they had been walking a tightrope. On the one hand, they reflected the awareness that the deteriorating economic and social conditions provided them with a growing body of potential supporters which could be used as leverage on the Government. On the other hand, they recognized their weakness *vis-à-vis* the state security apparatus—a fact which motivated them to seek some acceptance by the authorities.[68]

THE CHALLENGE OF RADICAL ISLAM

Ever since the consolidation of power in Nāsir's hands early in 1954, the 23 July Revolution and the forces of radical Islam were sworn enemies. The latter detested and contested the secular foundations of Nāsir's all-embracing *qawmiyya* (nationalism) and *ishtirākiyya* (socialism), and were in turn systematically persecuted by the Nāsirite internal security police. Sādāt's rise to power promised to change this relationship. His traditional outlook, his collaboration with conservative Arab-Islamic regimes and his anti-Communist posture—in addition to the fact that he had eliminated the Nāsirite "centres of power" (the Muslim Brethren's main oppressors)—offered a basis for *rapprochement*. But this was only partly achieved. It so happened that Sādāt's coming to power coincided with a wave of Islamic radicalization throughout the Arab world.[69] Stepping into the vacuum created by the decline of Nāsirism and nourished by the social and economic crises in Egypt, radical Islam manifested itself in a number of militant trends whose extremism ruled out any compromise with Sādāt's temporal regime.

THE ABDUCTION OF AL-DHAHABI

On 3 July 1977, the Ministry of Interior reported that nine persons had that morning abducted Dr Muḥammad Ḥusayn al-Dhahabi, former Minister of Religious Affairs, from his home. Some of the kidnappers were captured, but those in the car with al-Dhahabi managed to escape. An Islamic group called *al-Takfīr wal-Hijra* announced that it had taken this action in retaliation for Dhahabi's attitude to their movement; they demanded, as a condition for his freedom, the release of the (60) members of their group held by the authorities and the payment of a ransom of E£200,000.[70] Two days were spent negotiating between the authorities and emissaries of *al-Takfīr wal-Hijra*, but the ex-minister's body was found on the morning of 6 July. In fact, he had been killed two days before when the ultimatum set by the kidnappers expired. The alleged murderer was caught.[71]

On the following days, members of the group planted bombs in cinemas, parks and other public sites, and booby-trapped places where police search parties were expected. It was learnt that they had plans to kidnap a number of blacklisted public figures. All these acts, their spokesman explained, were part of the war they had declared against Sādāt's regime.[72]

The *al-Takfīr wal-Hijra* group was not unknown to the Egyptian public. Reports of its existence had been published as early as 1973, but arrests started only in 1975. On 23 November 1976, the authorities announced that they had frustrated a campaign of assassination and terrorism by arresting 14 members of this group. More arrests were made on 19 December 1976 and in March 1977.[73] Following Dhahabi's kidnapping, the security forces engaged in large-scale operations aimed at rounding up all *al-Takfīr wal-Hijra* members. By 16 July, 600 suspects had been arrested, including a number of military personnel. The arrest of the group's leader, Shukrī Ahmad Mustafā, was announced on 8 July; his long-wanted deputy, Aḥmad Tāriq Abū 'Alīm, was finally apprehended on 11 August.[74]

According to information subsequently released, *al-Takfīr wal-Hijra* had originally been connected with the clandestine Islamic Liberation Party which operates in many Muslim countries. (The attack on the Military Technical College on 18 April 1974, led by Sāliḥ 'Abdallah Sariya, was attributed at the time to that party.) The groups leader, Shukrī Aḥmad Mustafā, had once been a member of the Muslim Brethren but had left because in his opinion it was not sufficiently faithful to Islamic goals.

Al-Takfīr wal-Hijra is a fundamentalist movement rejecting Westernization and all modern innovations, as well as the institutions of established Islam. Two central elements in its doctrine are the denunciation of the present social and political order as "an infidel system" (hence *Takfīr* or infidelization), and the call for disengagement from that heretic society (hence *Hijra* or emigration).[75] The movement has a distinct messianic character, its leader having been declared a *Mahdī*. His followers believe that he will eventually lead a great campaign to conquer the world and establish true Islam in it. The followers of the movement commit themselves to absolute obedience: desertion is punishable by death. The organization provided military training and had stockpiles of arms and ammunition. Members were obliged to sever all their previous social and economic ties and join a commune. Many were high school and university students, teachers and engineers, as well as workers, peasants and a considerable number of women. According to the Egyptian authorities, the organization received financial support from Libya.[76]

Following the arrest of *al-Takfīr wal-Hijra* members, two other extremist Islamic organizations were discovered. The one called itself *Jund Allah* (God's Soldiers) and engaged in terrorist activities, mainly in the Alexandria area; 104 members of this group were arrested.[77] The other called itself *Jamā 'at al-Jihād* (The Holy War Society). It, too, operated in Alexandria; 80 of its members were detained.[78]

On personal orders from the President, the defendants in the *al-Takfīr wal-Hijra* case were tried before a military tribunal on 23 August. The 54 accused (three still at large) were charged with kidnapping and murder. The defendants, who repeatedly interrupted the proceedings by shouting Islamic slogans, pleaded not guilty. The trial of 198 others was scheduled for 4 October.[79] The organization's leader, Shukrī Aḥmad Mustafā, was sentenced on 31 October to six months imprisonment and prohibited from attending the trial because of his threat to kill the head of the Military Prosecution.

The wave of Islamic terrorism led Sādāt to propose further emergency legislation to deal more firmly with terrorist groups.

THE MUSLIM BRETHREN

The Muslim Brethren's attitude towards these developments was somewhat ambiguous. On the one hand, they denounced the actions of the terrorist groups, but on the other, described their members as victims of the prevailing system. While they evidently shared the sentiment which motivated the more radical Islamic groups, they did not want to compromise their own semi-legitimate status enjoyed under Sādāt. It was due to Sādāt's policies that many Brethren who had been persecuted in the Nāsir period were rehabilitated. For instance, in January 1976, the former Secretary-General of the Brethren, 'Abd al-Hakīm 'Ābdīn, was allowed to return after 22 years of exile in Saudi Arabia. On 9 February 1977, Sādāt repealed a 25-year prison sentence and granted amnesty to Sa'īd Ramadān who, since leaving Egypt in 1954, was the Brethren's outstanding spokesman in Europe.[80]

Although the Muslim brotherhood was not formally re-established and its followers remained divided into many factions, it managed to publish a number of organs regularly, of which the monthly *al-Da'wa* was the most popular. The Brethren were politically active on university campuses and in various professional and labour circles, and met with little interference from the authorities. On 14 September, a religious service marking the beginning of 'Īd al-Fitr developed into a demonstration of strength by the Muslim Brethren, with 5,000 supporters congregating without any previous publicity of the event.[81]

The re-emergence of the Brethren was in line with the regime's general tendency to strengthen Islam in the state and public life. There was a gradual increase in the activities of Islamic institutions and associations, in the teaching of Islamic subjects in state schools, in religious broadcasting and in the media. The rulings of Muslim *'ulamā'* were also given more publicity.

ISLAMIC LAW

The most significant development took place in the field of legislation where there was a growing tendency to introduce new bills based on the *sharī'a* (Islamic Law). In December 1975, the Minister of Justice formed a "Supreme Committee for Introducing Legislation according to the Islamic Law." The Committee drafted three *sharī'a*-based bills: prohibiting the drinking, possessing, producing or selling of alcoholic drinks; punishing robbery by the amputation of limbs; and slander by flogging.[82] (The serving of alcoholic drinks in public places was forbidden by law on 1 August 1976.) Other bills proposed in the People's Assembly and its committees included execution by stoning for adultery, discouraging women's employment outside the home, and co-ordinating the banking system with the Islamic law on usury.[83]

One of the most controversial issues was a draft law proposed by the President himself calling for the death penalty for apostasy. It stipulated that the evidence of two adult Muslims would be sufficient to condemn an apostate if he failed to return to Islam within 30 days.[84]

Sādāt's Islamic policy apparently had considerable appeal for the predominantly conservative Egyptian society. Unlike the destructive actions of the militant Islamic groups which—as many observers pointed out—deeply alarmed not only the Westernized but also the traditional sections of society, Sādāt's policies focused on concrete measures of Islamization. Whether these measures were ever intended to be fully implemented remained an open question and thus threatened to become one more unfulfilled expectation.

COPTIC-MUSLIM TENSION

The wave of Muslim militancy aroused anxieties among Egypt's Coptic minority, which had felt a growing sense of concern ever since Nāsir ousted Gen Najīb in 1954. Copts complained that despite the regime's proclamations of equality, they were under-represented in public life. They contested the official 1976 census which established their numbers at 2.3m, claiming that on the basis of church registers, they had twice as many members.

Violent incidents between Muslims and Copts reappeared in Egyptian life during 1977. Severe clashes occurred during the month of Ramadān when Muslim fanatics stoned churches in al-Faiyum and Asyut. There were also attempts to plant bombs and damage community property.[85]

The Copts were particularly alarmed by the attempt to introduce a bill imposing capital punishment for Muslim apostates (see above). This could have had serious implications for Copts, in light of the common practice among them to convert temporarily to Islam—in order to dodge the Coptic marriage and personal status legal restrictions—and then return to Christianity. The Coptic Patriarch Shinuda III declared a five-day fast in protest against the bill—an unprecedented gesture. The Patriarch and 44 Bishops, who constitute the Synod, were cloistered in St Mark's Cathedral in Cairo to start their fast on 5 September.[86] To calm the anxieties of the Copts, the Prime Minister was sent in person to discuss the matter with Patriarch Shinuda. According to Church sources, the Prime Minister promised that the Government would not permit the proposed law to proceed to the People's Assembly for debate.[87]

On 21 September, President Sādāt received two separate delegations: from the Islamic Research Council, headed by the Shaykh of al-Azhar, and the Coptic Holy Synod, headed by Patriarch Shinuda. He called upon the religious leaders to guard against what he described as "conspiracies concocted by the enemies of Egypt and the Arab homeland to foment sectarian strife."[88] Another call for national unity was issued by the President in his 28 September speech to the People's Assembly, in which he disclosed recent cases of Muslim-Coptic clashes, attributing them to foreign subversive elements.[89]

THE MULTIPARTY SYSTEM

During the Nāsirite period, after all political parties were abolished at the beginning of 1953, the multiparty system became identified with decadence and corruption. Sādāt's 1971 Corrective Revolution aroused expectations that "guided democracy" would be abandoned; but during his first years in office, the President argued that Egypt was not yet ready for a multiparty system. Nevertheless, increasing public pressure and the dynamics of Sādāt's policies of liberalization and openness led in this direction. The August 1974 "ASU Development Programme" legitimized debate among Right, Centre and Left within the framework of the ASU and the confines of the national consensus. This was followed in October 1975 by a promise that these different trends within the ASU would be constituted as "platforms" (*manābir*). More than 40 groups declared their intention to establish platforms, but in March 1976, only three were authorized. The Centrist Egypt's Arab Socialist Platform, led by Mamdūḥ Sālim and Maḥmūd Abū al-Wāfiya (Sādāt's brother-in-law), was fully endorsed by the Government and the bureaucracy. The Rightist Liberal Socialist Platform, headed by Mustafā Kāmil Murād (a veteran of the "Free Officers"), stood for free enterprise, while the Leftist National Progressive Unionist Rally (NPUR), headed by Khālid Muḥyī al-Dīn, represented the Marxist and amorphous Nāsirist trend. The three platforms—now often referred to as "Organizations" (*tanzīmāt*)—competed in the October 1976 elections for the People's Assembly (see below). Attempts by a number of lawyers, university lecturers and even members of the armed forces to form other political groupings were thwarted by the authorities.

A further step towards party pluralism was taken by Sādāt in his speech at the opening session of the People's Assembly on 11 November 1976, when he declared: "In view of the success of the election experiment and continuing the march toward true democracy . . . I have adopted a decision . . . that the three political Platforms should be transformed into parties as of today . . . The hand of the ASU must definitely and finally be lifted from these parties. Each party will be absolutely free in running its activities, within the limits of the law and the Constitution." [90] A draft law regulating the operation of these parties was finally approved by the People's Assembly on 20 June 1977.

The first Article of the new law proclaimed that "Egyptians have the right to establish political parties and every Egyptian has the right to belong to any political party in accordance with the provisions of this law." However, the fourth Article stipulated six conditions for the establishment of a new party, which precluded any class, sectarian or factional basis for a new party; prohibited parties which were an extension of organizations abroad; and disqualified paramilitary organizations. A Committee consisting of the Secretary of the ASU Central Committee, three ministers and three former heads of Justice departments (or their deputies) was authorized to deal with applications for the establishment of new parties (Article 8). The law specified that the founders of a new party should include at least 20 members of the People's Assembly (Article 28). Article 30 confirmed the legality of the three existing parties. [91]

PROLIFERATION OF PARTIES

The expectation that more political parties would emerge after the promulgation of the new law was confirmed in October, when 22 independent members of the People's Assembly announced their intention to form a fourth party. [92] Inevitably, this reform also encouraged trends outside the boundaries of political legitimacy (as defined by the regime) to aspire for party status. A number of the old parties which had existed in the monarchy period explored possibilities of re-establishing themselves. [93] The group with the greatest potential strength and presenting the most serious challenge to Sādāt's authority was the former Wafd, which had been the leading nationalist party in Egyptian politics before 1952.

The resurgent Wafdist forces were led by the former party secretary, Fu'ād Sarrāj al-Dīn, who re-emerged in public life after a long period of silence. He started mobilizing support from members of the People's Assembly and published a book entitled "Why the New Party." [94] On 23 August, he was allowed to deliver a speech before the Egyptian Bar Association commemorating the death of the last leader of the Wafd Party, Mustafā al-Nahhās. Sarrāj al-Dīn strongly criticized the existing regime and announced his intention to request permission to establish a Democratic Wafd Party.[95]

The revival of the Wafd was bitterly resented by many elements in Egyptian society, particularly the Leftists for whom Sarrāj al-Dīn is a symbol of the old "feudal" and "reactionary" Egypt. Yet the Wafdists seemed to have an extensive constituency, partly based on opponents of the 1952 Revolution, on sections of the provincial middle classes and on elements of the Coptic minority. The few occasions on which they were allowed to make a public appearance turned into impressive pro-Wafdist mass demonstrations.

Unlike the existing Rightist and Leftist parties, the pro-Wafdist represented a force which challenged the very foundations of Sādāt's regime. Understandably, official spokesmen began showing displeasure with the increasing boldness of the Wafdists, and pressure was applied on People's Assembly delegates and leaders of the Bar Association who were co-operating with Sarrāj al-Dīn. The media was also encouraged to denounce the movement; Marxist and Muslim Brotherhood journalists responded by launching fierce attacks on the Wafd.[96]

The authorization of parties thus opened a Pandora's box, unleashing forces which could fragment Egypt's political structure through the proliferation of opposition groups. The main threat to the regime came from three political camps which had previously remained unorganized and ineffective: the Marxists and Nāsirists, the Muslim Brethren and the Wafdists. Given the opportunity to instutionalize their existence, these forces looked as if they could easily develop into a formidable challenge to the regime. Sādāt sought to curb this development in 1977 both by activating his security and political control systems, and by trying to play the opposition forces off against each other.

THE PEOPLE'S ASSEMBLY

Elections for the People's Assembly were held in two rounds: the first on 28 October, and the second on 4 November 1976 in those constituencies where no candidate had obtained the required number of votes. With more than 1,500 candidates contesting 350 Assembly seats, the elections were hailed as "the first free democratic elections since the 1952 Revolution."[97] The candidates were divided among the three competing political "platforms" or "organizations," but many also ran as independents. The election campaign aroused lively debate over such issues as the right of industrial workers to strike and future relations with Israel. In rural districts, the campaign revolved more around questions of family, religion, agriculture and electrification. In a number of constituencies there were clashes among supporters of rival candidates, and between them and the police. Four people were reported killed and 55 wounded.[98]

The results in 171 constituencies were announced on 6 November: Egypt's Arab Socialist Organization won 280 seats; the Liberal Socialist Organization, 12; the NPUR, 2; and Independents, 48.[99]

Continuing the trend that had started a year before, the new Assembly expressed some criticism of Sādāt himself and of government policies, particularly on such issues as the structure of the budget, economic policies and the shortcomings of the bureaucracy.[100] However, there were cases of pressure being brought on Assembly delegates as well. On 29 March, the People's Assembly deprived Abu al-'Izz al-Harīri of his parliamentary immunity following charges of instigating demonstrations during the January food riots.[101] Another delegate, Kamāl al-Dīn Ḥusayn, was expelled from the Assembly for having proclaimed as unconstitutional the internal security measures decreed by Sādāt (see above).

THE ARAB SOCIALIST UNION (ASU)

Created in 1962 as a mass organization, the ASU embodied Nāsir's concept of guided democracy and the Nāsirite slogan of "the alliance of the working forces of the people" (peasants, workers, the intelligentsia, the military and "national capitalists"). The ASU was a direct continuation of two similar mass organizations which had existed in the past: the Liberation Rally and the National Union. Like its forerunners, it has met with sharp criticism over its level of performance as well as with scepticism over its effectiveness as a channel for political participation. For a number of years, Sādāt showed a tendency to downgrade the ASU's importance and a desire to dismantle its vast bureaucracy; his apparent aim was to turn it into a supreme body to supervise the activities of the emerging new political parties.

In his 11 November 1976 speech, in which he proclaimed the authorization of political parties, Sādāt said: "The hands of the Socialist Union must definitely and finally be removed from these parties." He went on to define three areas of activity which would alone remain for the ASU: the auxiliary organizations—particularly those of women and youth; partnership in the ownership of newspapers; and operation of the expanded Central Committee.[102]

The decrees providing for the formation of the ASU's Youth and Women's Organizations were issued in September 1975; in March 1976, elections were held for the various bodies to run them. The former consisted of boys and girls under the age of 18, and the latter women over 18. These sectors of Egyptian society were considered unprepared for full-fledged party activities, and thus in need of the sponsorship of the ASU.[103]

Although the ASU retains a controlling position over the press, its Secretary-General was instructed to work out arrangements to enable the three authorized parties to have their own publications (instead of taking over the three major Egyptian dailies, or being allocated space in each newspaper in proportion to the party's size).[104] Egypt's Arab Socialist Party started publishing its weekly *Misr* on 28 June. The Liberal Socialist Party's weekly *al-Aḥrār* was scheduled to appear on 11 November 1977 and that of the NPUR, *al-Taqaddum*, in mid-February 1978.[105]

According to the 20 June 1977 Political Parties Law, the expanded ASU's Central Committee consists of all members of the People's Assembly plus up to 120 other members, including the chairmen and representatives of professional unions, the General Federation of Workers, the General Worker's Union, the Co-operatives' Federation, the Federation of the Chambers of Commerce and Industry; heads and representatives of the Federations of Writers and Students; and members of the Higher Council of the Press. According to established ASU principles, half of the Committee members must come from among the workers and peasants. The President of the Republic, who is also the Chairman of the ASU, serves *ex-officio* as the Central Committee's Chairman. The ASU's Secretary-General serves automatically as the Secretary of the Central Committee.[106] The new Central Committee convened on 3 July 1977 and re-elected the former ASU Secretary-General, Mustafā Khalīl, to this post; he thus also became Secretary of the Central Committee.

Also in accordance with the Political Parties Law, the Central Committee issued regulations to transfer ASU assets to the parties, dismantle abolished ASU bodies and dismiss all full-time ASU functionaries.[107]

THE GOVERNMENT

A new Government was sworn in on 10 November 1976. It was again headed by Mamdūḥ Sālim and included 32 ministers, five of them serving as Deputy Prime Ministers. The Government was reshuffled after the January food riots, and new

THE EGYPTIAN GOVERNMENTS — NOVEMBER 1976–OCTOBER 1977

Portfolio	*10 November 1976*	*3 February 1977*	*26 October 1977*
Prime Minister	Mamdūh Sālim	Mamdūḥ Sālim	Mamdūḥ Sālim
Deputy Prime Ministers			
Financial and Economic Affairs	ʻAbd al-Munʻīm al-Qaysūnī	ʻAbd al-Munʻīm al-Qaysūnī	ʻAbd al-Munʻīm al-Qaysūnī
Social Development and Services	Muḥammad Ḥāfiz Ghānim	Muhammad Ḥāfiz Ghānim	Muḥammad Ḥāfiz Ghānim
Foreign Minister	Ismāʻīl Fahmī	Ismāʻīl Fahmī	Ismāʻīl Fahmī
Minister of War and War Production	Gen Muḥammad ʻAbd al-Ghanī al-Jamasī	Gen Muḥammad ʻAbd al-Ghanī al-Jamasī	Gen Muḥammad ʻAbd al-Ghanī al-Jamasī
Production Minister for Electricity and Energy	Sultān Aḥmad	Sultān Aḥmad	Sultān Aṃad
Financial and Economic Affairs			
Economy and Economic Affairs Co-operation	Ḥāmid ʻAbd al-Latīf Sā'iḥ	Ḥāmid ʻAbd al-Latīf Sā'iḥ	Ḥāmid ʻAbd al-Latīf Sā'iḥ
Finance	Maḥmūd Salāḥ al-Dīn Ḥāmid	Maḥmūd Salāḥ al-Dīn Ḥāmid	Maḥmūd Salāḥ al-Dīn Ḥāmid
Trade and Supply	Zakariyā Tawfīq ʻAbd al-Fattāḥ	Zakariyā Tawfīq ʻAbd al-Fattāḥ	Zakariyā Tawfīq ʻAbd al-Fattāḥ
Planning	Muḥammad Maḥmūd al-Imām	Muḥammad Maḥmūd al-Imām	ʻAbd al-Munʻīm al-Qaysūnī
Production			
Industry and Mineral Resources	ʻĪsa Shāhīn	ʻĪsa Shāhīn }	
Oil	Aḥmad ʻIzz al-Dīn Hilāl	Aḥmad ʻIzz al-Dīn Hilāl }	Aḥmad ʻIzz al-Dīn Hilāl
Agriculture and Irrigation	ʻAbd al-ʻAzīm Abū al-ʻAtā	Ibrāhīm Maḥmūd Shukrī (Agriculture) ʻAbd al-ʻAzīm Abū al-ʻAtā (Irrigation)	Ibrāhīm Maḥmūd Shukrī ʻAbd al-ʻAzīm Abū al-ʻAtā[1]
Minister of State for War Production	Jamāl al-Dīn Sidqī	Jamāl al-Dīn Sidqī	[abolished]
Transport, Communications and Maritime Transport	ʻAbd al-Fattāḥ ʻAbdallah	ʻAbd al-Fattāḥ ʻAbdallah	ʻAbd al-Sattār Mujāhid
Tourism and Aviation	Ibrāhīm Najīb	Muḥib Ramzī Stīnū	Muḥib Ramzī Stīnū
Minister of State for Agriculture and Industrial Co-operatives, Water Resources, and Sudanese Affairs	ʻAbd al-ʻAzīz Ḥusayn	ʻAbd al-ʻAzīz Ḥusayn	[abolished] Muḥammad Ḥāfiz Ghānim[2]
Social Development and Services			
Interior	Maj-Gen Sayyid Husayn Fahmī	Mamdūḥ Sālim	Gen Muḥammad Nabawī Ismāʻīl
Education	Mustafā Kamāl Ḥilmī	Mustafā Kamāl Ḥilmī	Mustafā Kamāl Ḥilmī[3]
Health	Ibrāhīm Badrān	Ibrāhīm Badrān	Ibrāhīm Badrān
Justice	Samīḥ Talʻat	Samīḥ Talʻat	Samīḥ Talʻat

Training	‘Abd al-Laṭīf Bultiyya	‘Abd al-Laṭīf Bultiyya	Sa‘d Muḥammad Aḥmad
Social Affairs	‘Ā’isha Rātib	Amāl ‘Uthmān	Amāl ‘Uthmān
Information and Culture	Jamāl al-Dīn al-‘Utayfī	‘Abd al-Mun‘īm Maḥmūd al-Sāwī	‘Abd al-Mun‘īm Maḥmūd al-Sāwī
Waqf, Minister of State For al-Azhar Affairs	Shaykh Muḥammad Mutawalī al-Sha‘rāwī	Shaykh Muḥammad Mutawalī al-Sha‘rāwī	Shaykh Muḥammad Mutawalī al-Sha‘rāwī
Housing and Reconstruction	Ḥasan Muḥammad Ḥasan	Ḥasan Muḥammad Ḥasan	Ḥasb Allah Muḥammad al-Kafrāwī
Ministers of State			
People's Assembly Affairs	Fu'ād Muḥyī al-Dīn	Fu'ād Muḥyī al-Dīn	Fu'ād Muḥyī al-Dīn
Cabinet Affairs, Follow-up and Control	Albert Barsūm Salāma	Albert Barsūm Salāma	‘Isā Shāhīn[4]
Local Government, Youth, Popular and Political Organizations	Muḥammad Ḥāmid Maḥmūd	Muḥammad Ḥāmid Maḥmūd	Muḥammad Ḥāmid Maḥmūd
Scientific Research and Atomic Energy	‘Abd al-Ma‘būd al-Jubaylī	‘Abd al-Ma‘būd al-Jubaylī	(abolished)
Foreign Relations	Muḥammad Riyād	Muḥammad Riyād	Muḥammad Riyād
Administrative Development	‘Alī ‘Abd al-Majīd ‘Abduh	‘Alī ‘Abd al-Majīd ‘Abduh	‘Alī ‘Abd al-Majīd ‘Abduh
Minister of State			Butrus Ghālī
Minister of State			Na‘īm Tālib
Minister of State			‘Alī Sulamī

[1] Responsible for Irrigation and Land Reclamation
[2] Responsible for Sudanese Affairs only
[3] Responsible for Education and Scientific Research
[4] Responsible for Follow-up and Control

ministers sworn in on 3 February 1977. Another reshuffle took place on 26 October (see Table). The appointment of Mamdūḥ Sālim to head the November 1976 government was presented by the President as reflecting progress toward "a sound democratic rule" since his party, Egypt's Arab Socialist Party, had won the majority of seats in the People's Assembly.[108] Mamdūḥ Sālim had also served as Prime Minister in the two previous Governments, formed on 16 April 1975 and 19 March 1976.

The main task of this Government was to deal with the severe economic crisis. Even before its formation, Sādāt stressed that the next phase in implementing economic policy demanded a greater effort towards an "open door" economy and the solution of the bureaucratic and administrative problems which had frustrated development.[109] The major portfolio changes showed a wish to form an effective team to deal with the economic crisis. The veteran economist, 'Abd al al-Mun'īm al-Qaysūnī, was appointed to the newly-created post of Deputy Prime Minister for Financial and Economic Affairs. The portfolio of Economy and Economic Co-operation and that of Finance were given to two of his close associates. Another significant change was the replacement of the Minister of Housing and Reconstruction, 'Uthmān Aḥmad 'Uthmān (the founder of the biggest construction company in Egypt), following allegations of a conflict of interests. The Cabinet ministries were grouped into five categories in order to facilitate co-ordination.

The main changes in the government reshuffle of February 1977, were the replacement of the Ministers of Interior, Information and Culture, Social Affairs, and Tourism and Aviation—some of these as a result of the January riots. The most significant change was the dismissal of the Interior Minister, Sayyid Ḥusayn Fahmī, who had served in that post since April 1975. He had been criticized for the failure of the security organizations to anticipate and control the demonstrations in January. His portfolio was assumed by the Prime Minister, who had been Interior Minister from May 1971 until his appointment as Prime Minister in April 1975. The dismissal of the Minister of Information and Culture, Dr Jamāl al-Dīn al-'Uṭayfī, was attributed to his liberal views and closeness to the Marxists, to whom he had opened the television medium. Two Deputy Ministers of the Interior were also appointed: Muḥammad Nabawī Ishmā'īl and Kamāl Ḥamid Khayrallāh.

The October 1977 reshuffle brought seven new Ministers into the Government, three of them as Ministers of State. Most of the changes took place in economic portfolios and were seen to reflect on intention to accelerate both the "administrative revolution" and economic development. The Interior portfolio was given to one of the formerly-appointed Deputy Ministers, Muḥammad Nabawī Ismā'īl. Another important appointment was that of Butrus Ghāli as Minister of State. Of Coptic origin, Ghāli was a well-known journalist and editor of *al-Siyāsa al-Duwaliyya*, in which he stood for a policy of giving greater priority to solving Egypt's domestic problems and reducing its involvement in the Arab-Israeli conflict.

One of the main characteristics of all these Governments was the preference they gave to technocrats and bureaucrats in filling ministerial posts, thus continuing the trend that had begun in the 1960s.

ARMED FORCES

Total armed forces number 345,000. Defence expenditure during 1977–8 amounted to £E1.72 bn ($4.37 bn). Military service is compulsory for three years. The Army numbers 300,000, including an Air Defence Command, and consists of two armoured divisions (each with one armoured and two mechanized brigades); three mechanized infantry divisions; five infantry divisions (each with two infantry brigades); one Republican Guard Brigade (division); three independent armoured brigades; seven independent infantry brigades; two airmobile brigades; one parachute brigade; six commando groups; six artillery and two heavy mortar brigades; one anti-tank guided weapon brigade; and two surface-to-surface missile regiments (up to 24 *Scud*). It is equipped with 1,100 T-54/-55, 750 T-62 medium, and 80 PT-76 light tanks; 2,500 OT-62/-64, BTR-40/-50/-60/-152, *Walid* armoured personnel carriers; 200 BMP-76PB armoured fighting vehicles; 1,300 76mm, 100mm, 122mm, 130mm, 152mm and 180mm, 40 203mm guns and howitzers; about 200 SU-100 and ISU-152 self-propelled guns; 300 120mm, 160mm, 240mm mortars; 300 140mm, 240mm rocket launchers; 30 *FROG*-3/-7, 24 *Scud, Samlet* surface-to-surface missiles; 900 57mm, 85mm and 100mm anti-tank guns; 900 82mm, 107mm recoilless rifles; 1,000 *Sagger, Snapper, Swatter* anti-tank guided weapons; 350 ZSU-23-4, ZSU-57-2 anti-aircraft guns; SA-6/-7/-9 surface-to-air missiles; six Fournier RF-4 aircraft (there is a shortage of spares for Soviet equipment). (*Beeswing* anti-tank guided weapons on order.)

The Air Defence Command numbers 75,000 and has 108 combat aircraft; nine interceptor squadrons with 108 MiG-21MF interceptors; 360 SA-2, 200 SA-3, 75 SA-6 surface-to-air missiles; 2,500 20mm, 23mm, 37mm, 40mm, 57mm, 85mm and 100mm anti-aircraft guns; missile radars include *Fan Song, Low Blow, Flat Face, Straight Flush* and *Long Track*; gun radars *Fire Can, Fire Wheel* and *Whiff*; early warning radars *Knife Rest* and *Spoon Rest* (there is a shortage of spares for Soviet equipment). (*Crotale* surface-to-air missiles are on order.) There are about 500,000 reserves.

The 20,000-strong Navy is equipped with 12 submarines (six W- and six R-class, ex-Soviet); five destroyers (four *Skory*, one ex-British Z-class); three escorts (ex-British); 12 SO-1 submarine chasers (ex-Soviet); 12 guided-missile fast patrol boats (six *Osa*, six *Komar*) with *Styx* surface-to-surface missiles (six building); 30 motor torpedo boats (six *Shershen*, 20 P-6, four P-4); three large patrol craft; 14 ex-Soviet mine counter-measures (six T-43, four *Yurka*, two T-301, two K8); 16 landing craft (nine *Vydra*, four SMB-1, three *Polnocny*); three SRN-6 hovercraft and ten *Sea King* helicopters. (Two submarines, 30 *Otomat* surface-to-surface missiles are on order.) Reserves number about 15,000.

The Air Force numbers 25,000 and has about 365 combat aircraft (there is a shortage of spares for Soviet equipment). 25 Tu-16D/G medium bombers (some with *Kelt* air-to-surface missiles); five Il-28 light bombers; three fighter-bomber regiments with 80 MiG-21, 90 MiG-17; four ground-attack fighter/strike regiments, three with 60 Su-7, one with 38 *Mirage* IIIE, also some 25 Su-20, 18 MiG-27 *Flogger* D; 24 MiG-23 *Flogger* B interceptors; four C-130, two EC-130H, 30 Il-14, 19 An-12, one *Falcon*, one *Boeing* 707 transports; 12 Mi-4, 32 Mi-6, 70 Mi-8, six *Sea King*, 30 *Commando* and 42 *Gazelle* helicopters; 150 MiG-15/-21/-23, Su-7, L-29 and 40 *Gomhouria* trainers. (There are 44 *Mirage* F-1 on order.) There are about 50,000 paramilitary forces which include 6,000 National Guard, 6,000 Frontier Corps, 30,000 Defence and Security and 7,000 Coast Guard.

FOREIGN AFFAIRS

EGYPT'S GLOBAL POLITICS

Egypt's pro-American orientation, adopted after the 1973 war, reflected the Sādāt regime's decisive—though not necessarily irreversible—move away from the USSR. Nāsir's original decision to align Egypt with Moscow had been governed by a number of considerations. The USSR was trying to establish its presence as a major factor in the Middle East and was thus prepared to give Egypt unprecedently extensive political, military and economic support. It fit in with the role Egypt was playing in the Afro-Asian world, the strong anti-imperialist thrust in its national ideology and policies, and accorded with its historical experience which was free of hatred and suspicion towards the Russians. Even though there were basic differences between Communism and the "Arab socialism" introduced by Nāsir's regime, there was also some ideological similarity, particularly with regard to the role of the state in the economy.

Nevertheless, Egypt never completely severed relations with the US. It continued to seek—and obtain—substantial American economic aid; and the traditional attachment to Western culture and values was sustained, especially among the Egyptian élite, the majority of whom totally rejected Communism.

For Egypt, the ideal situation was to pursue a policy of "positive neutralism"—designed to enable it to receive aid from both the US and the USSR simultaneously. However, in the latter half of the 1960s, the US was no longer willing to support Egypt without some degree of political co-operation; it reduced its aid significantly, which for all practical purposes left Egypt in the Soviet sphere of influence.

Sādāt's dramatic decision to move towards the US after the 1973 war was based on a number of considerations: his assessment that only the US could impose a settlement on Israel satisfactory to Egyptian interests; his realization of Egypt's growing dependence on the Arab oil-producing countries, especially Saudi Arabia, with its economic ties to the West and its hostility towards the Soviet Union; and his recognition of the Soviet Union's failure to bring about the modernization of Egypt's economy, in contrast to the opportunities offered by American technology and resources to achieve this aim. There was also an element of resentment and suspicion, aroused by the massive Soviet presence in Egypt, which was increased by Moscow's involvement in the abortive Communist coup in Sudan. Finally, certain elements among politically-minded Egyptians had a strong sense of disillusionment with Nāsirism and with ideology in general; there was a decline in the anti-imperialist fervour which had created the political climate for the pro-Soviet orientation.

Such considerations, and particularly the USSR's unwillingness to supply Egypt with certain types of sophisticated weapons, led to Sādāt's decision in 1972 to expel the Soviet military personnel. However, he was careful to avoid a complete break with Moscow in order to keep his options open, especially the military one.

RELATIONS WITH THE SOVIET UNION

The Arab-Israeli Conflict In its diplomatic contacts with the USSR throughout 1977, Egypt had to contend with Moscow's insistence that it be included in the diplomatic efforts to reconvene the Geneva conference, of which it was a co-chairman; and with Russian castigations of the close co-ordination between Cairo and Washington in the Middle East "political process." Sādāt made it clear on several occasions that even if the Geneva conference were reconvened, the USSR could not expect to play a major role. In one of many interviews on this subject, he explained: "The Soviet Union has little in its hands; this is the opportunity of those who hold 99% of the solution in their hands (i.e. the US)." [111]

Payments of Debts Egypt's default in meeting its indebtedness to the USSR—estimated at between $4–8 bn—occupied a central place in relations between the two countries (see essay, "Major Trends in Middle East Economic Development"). The Deputy Prime Minister for Financial and Economic Affairs, 'Abd al-Mun'im al-Qaysūnī, put the figure at $3.7 bn.[112] But he said the dispute was only over the military debt, since an understanding had already been reached about rescheduling the greater part of non-military repayments.[113] Sādāt, however, presented a different picture. In a speech to the ASU Central Committee on 28 September 1977, alluding to the rescheduling of this debt, he declared: "So far, the Soviet Union has not said either 'yes' or 'no'. By its conduct, the Soviet Union appears to be inclined towards the word 'no' even if it has not actually said this."[114] Earlier, in August, when Sādāt had halted cotton shipments to the USSR and Czechoslovakia (made as partial repayments), he said: "It is possible that we will continue our trade in agreed goods because we are obliged to repay our civil debts. All we want is a moratorium period to reschedule our debts. Yet, we are committed to repay the debts annually. We will not evade our commitments because they are commitments of honour."[115] As for the military debts—"which constitute more than half"—Sādāt implied that payments would be deferred, citing the "recognized international principle that the settlement of military debts following any war shall be deferred until after the reconstruction of the state which incurred these debts."

Arms Supply Before, during and for a short time after the 1973 war, the Soviet Union supplied weapons in large quantities to Egypt and replaced a great part of its losses in the war. This supply reportedly stopped after the new orientation in Egypt's policy became clear. However, according to senior Israeli intelligence sources, the USSR continued to supply some weapons, ammunition and spare parts via third parties. Moreover, despite the supposed suspension of Soviet arms supplies, there was very little change in the pattern of Egyptian air and ground exercises; fuel and ammunition were still used at rates comparable to those before the 1973 war.[116] Nonetheless, Egyptian sources insisted that there was no renewal of arms supply directly from the USSR, except for the delivery of 50 replaced MiG engines.

Following the June 1977 meeting between Fahmī and Gromyko, Sādāt said that it had become clear that the USSR was continuing its embargo policy. Referring to the previously-signed contracts which Egypt claimed had not been honoured, he quoted the Soviet side as saying: "There are no old contracts. . . . We will not sell you replacements for the arms you lost in October as we have sold to Syria. No, do not ask for this again from us."[117] Sādāt also accused Moscow of barring other countries equipped with Soviet arms (such as India and Eastern European countries) from delivering arms to Egypt and, in particular, of blocking an arms deal with Czechoslovakia.

Regional Issues The resentment and suspicion aroused by the USSR's involvement in the two abortive coups in Sudan (in 1971 and 1976) was greatly exacerbated by the Soviet arms build-up in Libya. Egypt regarded this as an offensive move—less to strengthen Libya's defence capability than to establish a base for conducting an aggressive policy against itself.

Tension over Soviet support to Libya reached a peak at the end of April 1977 when the USSR delivered a strong message to several Arab capitals accusing Egypt of having "escalated the tension in its relations with Libya" by "stationing [its] forces on the Libyan border." The message went on to say: "Great responsibility rests on the Egyptian government, regardless of the objectives it is seeking, whether that of controlling the Libyan oil resources or diverting the attention of its people from the various problems of Egypt. If the Egyptian leadership drives the situation towards a clash with Libya, and if it continues in its efforts to attack the existing regime in Libya, it must realize that all the responsibility for the results which are difficult to anticipate, rests upon Egypt."[118] Egypt interpreted the message as a veiled threat that the USSR would intervene on Libya's behalf.

Apprehension over Soviet policy in Libya was compounded by Moscow's general African policy, particularly its support of Ethiopia and its supposed involvement in Zaire. According to Egypt, these countries figured in a master plan conceived by the Soviet Union for creating a "hostile zone" around Egypt and Sudan (see below).

A further indication of Egypt's bitterness towards the USSR was Sādāt's allegation of Soviet complicity in the food riots of January 1977, which he saw as an attempt to undermine his regime by utilizing communist elements within Egypt (see above).

Egyptian-Soviet Negotiations Despite mutual denunciations and propaganda warfare, both countries tried to avoid a total severance of relations. The USSR wished to recoup at least part of its investments in Egypt as well as keep the door open for a possible realignment, while Egypt wanted to retain a "Soviet option" to reduce its dependence on the West and maximize its bargaining position.

Two meetings were held between the Soviet and Egyptian Foreign Ministers in which attempts were made to resolve these disputes: the first from 3–4 November 1976 in Sofia, and the second during Fahmī's visit to Moscow from 8–11 June 1977. The joint communiqué issued after the June meeting stated only that during the conversations "Andrei Gromyko and Ismā'īl Fahmī comprehensively discussed . . . Soviet-Egyptian relations and considered concrete measures aimed at overcoming the existing difficulties in the relations between the two states."[119] Referring to that meeting, Sādāt said: "There was no progress whatsoever on the two main points of disagreement between me and the Soviets: the question of the replacement of spare parts and the arms lost during the October war, which they did for Syria; and the rescheduling of debt payments."[120]

According to Sādāt's speech to the ASU Central Committee, the USSR made any meeting between him and Brezhnev conditional on his readiness to sign a political agreement or renew the Friendship and Co-operation Treaty of May 1971, abrogated in March 1976. The President said that he had firmly rejected these conditions.[121]

RELATIONS WITH THE US

The Arab-Israeli Conflict President Sādāt repeatedly stressed that only the US could impose a settlement on Israel. "As we all know," he said, "Israel's lifeblood comes from the US. If the artery carrying this were cut, not only would the arms supply stop, but there would not be a loaf of bread in Israel. The Israelis admit this in their press and statements."[122]

There were two sides to the thrust of Sādāt's strategy in mobilizing US support. One side was the search for an agreement on the principles for a political solution which, once determined, he expected to be imposed on Israel. In the general framework of this effort, Sādāt not only accepted the special relationship between the US and Israel, but was also ready to accept its formalization in a defence pact between the two states. Such a pact was seen as a substitute for Israel's demand for secure borders. This view was expressed on several occasions; for instance, Sādāt told a visiting US Congressional delegation: "If you [the US] make a security pact with them [Israel], I have no objections at all."[123]

The other side of Sādāt's strategy was the veiled threat that if the US failed to exert pressure on Israel, its interests in the Middle East would be jeopardized. "The US," he said, "has interests in this area. Previous Administrations have disregarded these American interests and backed Israel on the basis that it was the one protecting US interests in the area. After the October war, they discovered that the US has interests other than those of Israel. Therefore, this is the core of the operation."[124]

Economic Aid Expectations of a heavy influx of American capital to resuscitate the flagging Egyptian economy remained high in 1977. This was to be achieved through direct investment and through American encouragement to other investment sources, such as the IMF and the International Bank. It was expected that the combination of US capital and technology would repair Egypt's infrastructure and promote rapid industrialization. In meeting with a group of US professors, Sādāt said that he was particularly hopeful that Egypt, having just begun to mechanize its agriculture, would benefit from America's "magnificent new technology."[125]

Arms Supply Sādāt also expected that the US (with other Western powers) would replace the USSR as Egypt's arms supplier, and that Egypt would benefit from their advanced weapons' technology. This policy, called "the diversification of weapons," was described by Sādāt as a "more serious decision than the 1972 decision expelling the Soviet experts and the 6 October decision. Why? Because this decision brought us into the technology which the Soviet Union refused to give us. The early warning system (given to Egypt by the US), now operating in Sinai, is of the best type of technology. The station which the Russians gave, and then took away after the battle, was based on the technology of 20 years ago."[126] (For details, see below.)

Relations with the Carter Administration The Egyptians were at first apprehensive that the new Carter Administration might slow down the tempo of the political process towards a settlement, especially since Secretary of State Henry Kissinger, who had gained Sādāt's personal trust, was replaced. They also had misgivings about the direction of US policy in view of President Carter's pro-Israeli campaign statements. Nevertheless, Sādāt emphasized his determination to continue to co-operate with the US, saying "There is no room for emotion in politics. Politics are interests. We act where our interests lie. So what has taken place in the US is quite normal. We must deal with the person the American people have deemed fit and chosen."[127] (Egyptian-US diplomatic relations are discussed more fully in the "Chronology and Commentary of Political Developments in the Arab-Israeli Conflict," and in the essay on US Policy in the Middle East.)

US Secretary of State Cyrus Vance's visit to Egypt (17–18 February 1977) was followed by Sādāt's visit to Washington (3–6 April 1977), during which he reportedly took up with Carter the principal issues of dispute with Israel: borders, the nature of peace and the Palestine question. He also discussed Southern Lebanon and Africa.[128] Vance paid a second visit to the Middle East (1–10 August 1977).

As a result of these various high-level diplomatic contacts, some progress was made in all three spheres of Egyptian interests.

First, a considerable level of co-ordination was established on the issues of the Arab-Israeli conflict. Although agreement was not reached on all the procedural problems hindering the convening of the Geneva conference, the talks showed that on the basic substantial issues, the gap between the American and Egyptian positions was narrower than that between the Americans and the Israelis (for details, see below: Egypt and the Arab-Israeli Conflict).

In the sphere of economic aid, the Deputy Minister for Economic Affairs, Jamāl 'Abd al-Nāzir, said in reviewing the results of the "open door" policy in July 1977 that in the three years following the 1973 war, the US gave considerably more aid than the USSR had done in the past seven years. He put the amount of US aid at $2,400m (cf the USSR's $145m), of which $905m was given in kind; $750m allocated to industrial and agricultural projects; another $250m as a grant; and the rest in agricultural surplus products credits.[129] It was estimated that US aid in 1977 would reach c. $1 bn of which $750m would be given directly in the form of loans and grants-in-aid, the rest as surplus agricultural products.[130]

Sādāt chose not to make arms supply a major issue in his talks with Carter. Explaining this decision in an interview with an Iranian newspaper, he said: "If we are able to achieve peace this year, I will not insist on receiving the quantity of arms I asked them to sell me, and I really did not make this subject constitute a problem."[131] Nevertheless, Egypt was not left entirely empty-handed. In his testimony before a Congressional subcommittee on 15 September 1977, Assistant Secretary of State Alfred Atherton stated: "Given American interest in supporting Egypt's co-operation in our search for a genuine peace in the Middle East, we clearly have a major interest in helping meet its legitimate defence needs." The Administration proposed to sell 14 C-130 aircraft, at an approximate value of $184.4m. This was in addition to the six C-130 aircraft that had been sold to Egypt in early 1976. Atherton went on to say that the proposed sale of remotely piloted vehicles (RPVs) was valued at c. $66.5m.[132]

RELATIONS WITH AFRO-ASIAN STATES

The end of the policy of "positive neutralism" also marked a falling off of Egypt's intense activity and leadership role among the Afro-Asian nations. Egypt realized that the Third World non-aligned movement could be of little help in accomplishing its major foreign policy goals; in addition, the pro-American stand adopted by Egypt since 1973 made it more difficult to continue to play a major role in the Afro-Asian grouping because so many of its constituent states took a strong anti-American line.

Egypt's political activity in the Third World in 1976–7 was devoted mainly to promoting the all-Arab cause in Africa and to maintaining its own specific interests. Egypt continued to act as mediator between the Arab world and Africa, while trying to prevent any reversal of the Arab success after the 1973 war when most African states severed diplomatic relations with Israel. Mindful of the widespread frustration felt by Africans because of the rise in the cost of oil imports, Egypt took the initiative in convening the Afro-Arab summit in Cairo on 7 March 1977. At the conference, Egypt's regional policy in Africa was described by General Jamasī as aiming to defend its vital security interests against the USSR's design in the region—"to throw a hostile cordon around Egypt and its strategic depth in Sudan." Jamasī added: "The planners [i.e. Soviet Union] found Libya to the east and Ethiopia to the south to be the best positions to make a cordon, and Zaire would complete the cordon if it were to be dominated by hostile elements. It is on this basis that Egypt decided to assist Zaire in order to break one of the links of this cordon and prevent it from being completed."[133]

Egyptian involvement in Africa was clearly directed against the Soviet Union's protégés. In the Red Sea, Egypt supported Sudan and Somalia against Ethiopia. And in the case of Zaire, she gave direct military support against the invaders from Angola. The Egyptian expeditionary force included 55 pilots and a number of technicians who stayed on in Zaire in May 1977.[134]

Egypt's relations with most Asian states continued to be good, although there was less warmth in ties with India than during the heyday of friendship between Nāsir and Nehru. Egyptian sources claimed that the Soviet Union had forced India to refuse to give Egypt spare part replacements for Soviet weapons. As of 1976, Egypt was getting a limited quantity of spare parts and other items from China. Japan's assistance was mainly economic and technological, especially for projects connected with the development of the Suez Canal.

EGYPT AND THE ARAB WORLD

BETWEEN EGYPTIANISM AND ARABISM

Sādāt has generally tended to lay more stress on "Egyptianism" than on pan-Arabism, both on the ideological and political planes. This trend found expression in September 1971 when the country's name was changed from the United Arab Republic (*al-Jumhūriyya al-'Arabiyya al-muttaḥida*) to the Arab Republic of Egypt (*Jumhūriyyat Misr al-'Arabiyya*). In the *October Paper* (the principal ideological document of Sādāt's regime published in April 1974) and on numerous other occasions, Sādāt emphasized Egypt's distinctive features and autochthonous values (see above: Sādāt's Position). Thus, in his speech on 16 July 1977 commemorating the 25th anniversary of the Egyptian revolution, he opened with a review of Egypt's unique place in history. "The cradle of the first civilization in the world emerged from this soil 7,500 years ago" (i.e. antedating the Arabic language and the advent of Islam).[135] Emphasis was also given to Egypt's own distinctive personality and to glorifying the characteristics of the Egyptian farmer and soldier, particularly after the 1973 war.

Nonetheless, Sādāt still remained loyal to the vision of Arab unity, albeit in a different form. In his efforts to achieve Arab political unity, 'Abd al-Nāsir had not hesitated to use subversion and propaganda warfare to overthrow Arab regimes who opposed him. Sādāt, on the other hand, stressed the need for pragmatic co-operation and recognized the legitimacy of various Arab regimes. This difference was pointed up in Sādāt's speech to the leaders of the Students' Federation early in 1977:

> Before 1970, the year 'Abd al-Nāsir died, had there been any hope of any Arab unity? We had our guns trained on the entire Arab nation. . . . [on the other hand,] I created Arab unity. What is Arab unity? A political slogan? No, Arab unity means that in time of crisis we all stand together and use all the weapons we have. This happened in the October war. For the first time in centuries, the Arabs adopted a historic stand in support of the military battle and completely cut off the oil flow to the West.[136]

According to Sādāt, this pragmatic co-operation should occur particularly in the economic sphere, with Arab states increasing their aid to Egypt.

The tension between Egypt's particularism and its allegiance to the all-Arab cause was visible in both the inter-Arab and domestic spheres. Egypt's pursuit of its own interests was exemplified in its readiness to sign bilateral agreements with Israel (e.g. the 1975 Second Sinai Agreement), which was vehemently condemned by other Arab states. At the same time, it was loyal to the all-Arab cause in refusing to sign a separate agreement with Israel and in its insistence upon the participation of the PLO in a reconvened Geneva conference. (For Egypt's position in the conflict, see below.)

In the domestic sphere, Sādāt posited Egypt's economic rehabilitation as the central theme of his policy. The Egyptian media stressed that the country's difficulties were due to its over-extended commitment to the Arab cause. Egyptian leaders demanded that the Arab world recognize the pivotal role being played by Egypt in this cause, and therefore make a concerted effort to provide the country with massive economic aid. During 1977, disappointment continued to be voiced about the level of Arab aid received; this was accompanied by calls for a greater concentration of the national effort on Egypt's domestic problems. Following the food riots of January 1977, Mustafā Amīn, a Right-wing journalist, wrote: '

> We believe that Egypt should call for an immediate Arab meeting and that the Arab countries should be frankly told that Egypt has shouldered the burden of the Arab cause for 30 years and, as a result, has suffered hunger, become impoverished and made sacrifices. Thus, from now on, we will devote every piaster to Egypt and the Egyptian people. This will continue for 10 years, after which we will resume the task that we can't carry out while we are hungry.[137]

EGYPT'S INTER-ARAB STATUS

The decline of Egyptian hegemony in the Arab world that had begun in the latter part of Nāsir's time, accelerated under Sādāt's regime. Nāsirism was the only political movement in the Arab world that actually began to realize the vision of Arab unity by forming unified political entities (such as the union with Syria in 1958–61). In its campaign to consolidate a unified Arab bloc under the leadership of Cairo, Nāsir had relied on Egypt's large population, its industrial and technological potential, and its revolutionary appeal. However, in the late 1960s and during the 1970s, Egypt's increasing difficulties—as an underdeveloped country and a "Confrontation state"—made it dependent upon the oil-producing Arab states, particularly Saudi Arabia. In the mid-1970s, Syria enhanced its position as a regional power in the Mashreq, establishing its hegemony in Lebanon and cementing its ties with Jordan, without Egypt being able effectively to counter Syria's influence in that area. (See chapter on Syria and essay on Inter-Arab Affairs.)

The Riyadh conference of October 1976 indicated that the three leading centres of power at play in the inter-Arab arena at that time were Egypt, Syria and Saudi Arabia. The first two relied mainly on military power, while Saudi Arabia had economic and political leverage.

Egypt's dilemma is that, in order to enjoy the resources of the Arab world, it is obliged to preserve a pivotal position in the promotion of Arab causes. Egypt therefore finds itself caught in a vicious circle—the greater its commitment to the Arab cause, the greater its dependence on the wealthy Arab states. Egypt's pivotal position thus stems from its commitment to the Arab cause, but this commitment imposes a measure of dependence on others.

Egypt's inter-Arab standing in 1977—as expressed in inter-Arab forums—can be summed up as follows: Egypt was one of the three leading Arab states—with Saudi Arabia in a predominant position; Egypt maintained close relations with the Saudis and a relationship of co-operation with Syria tinged with suspicion and competition; its relationship with Libya was one of active and bitter hostility; and its co-operation with the Sudan—a development of particular significance—had implications for the entire southern area of the Red Sea.

RELATIONS WITH SAUDI ARABIA

Egypt's relations with Saudi Arabia have steadily improved under Sādāt. Whereas Nāsir condemned the Saudi regime as "reactionary," Sādāt recognized its legitimacy and as a result, antagonism between the two states disappeared altogether. Certain aspects of Sādāt's regime and personality, particularly the stress laid on Islam, have contributed to this *rapprochement*, as has the change in Egypt's global orientation and its anti-Soviet policy.

One of Sādāt's motives in improving relations with Saudi Arabia was his assumption that the Saudis were capable of using the "oil weapon" for political purposes. This assumption was verified in the October war, and ever since Egypt has sought to utilize Saudi power to influence US policy. While political observers spoke of a "Cairo-Riyadh axis," Egyptian spokesmen preferred to describe it as part of a general policy of inter-Arab co-operation (in contrast to the "axis" that Syria sought to forge with Jordan). In 1977, political co-ordination with Saudi Arabia was mainly pursued with respect to Sādāt's political strategy in the Arab-Israeli conflict. Ongoing contacts between the two states were highlighted by Sādāt's two visits to Saudi Arabia—in October 1976 (the Riyadh summit) and in May 1977, when a "mini-summit" of the leaders of Egypt, Syria and Saudi Arabia was held.

Saudi financial support became much more urgent after the January 1977 food riots. In March, Deputy Prime Minister Qaysūnī went to Riyadh to discuss Egypt's economic plight with the four Arab member-states of the Gulf Organization for the Development of Egypt. The meeting produced a promise of $1,500m for 1977. Qaysūnī noted that this allocation was "earmarked for solving the problem of Egypt's balance of payments, which is considered Egypt's top current problem."[138]

Saudi aid for military expenses was also of the highest importance. According to Sādāt, Saudi Arabia has "committed itself to the development of our armed forces over the next five years because the Soviet Union had refused to make up any losses."[139]

EGYPT'S RELATIONS WITH SYRIA

Co-operation between Egypt and Syria, which was at its closest at the outbreak of the October 1973 war, diminished considerably in the next two years; following the second Sinai Agreement of September 1975, a clear-cut rift and "cold war" developed between the two countries. Damascus accused Egypt of having waged the October war and initiated the subsequent political moves solely for its own particular interest and without any consideration for its Syrian ally. Egypt maintained that its political moves were the best means available for achieving all-Arab goals and severely condemned Syria for its obstructionism. The propaganda war culminated during 1976, with Syria accusing Egypt of betraying the Arab world by signing a separate agreement with Israel, and with Egypt exploiting the resentment felt by most Arab states at Syria's interference in Lebanon to enlist a broad Arab coalition against it. The Riyadh summit (17–18 October 1976) put an end to this "cold war" (see essay on Inter-Arab Affairs). While initiating a period of renewed co-ordination between the two countries, this was not devoid of the mutual suspicions that had accrued since the 1973 war.

One of the main motives for the renewed co-operation agreed at Riyadh was the recognition in late 1976 by both Sādāt and Asad of the importance of formulating a unified Arab stand to present to the new US Administration. Egyptian sources stressed that Syria had endorsed Egypt's political strategy: "Both Egypt and Syria were now talking the same language. . . . They both believed that the US had a major role to play in mediating to bring about a Middle East settlement."[140] Nevertheless, Syria displayed considerably less optimism than Egypt and continued to emphasize the necessity of preparing for a renewal of the military option.

This joint strategy together with alternatives to the political option were discussed by Asad and Sādāt in Cairo from 18–21 December 1976. The main difference between them centred on the question of Palestinian representation in Geneva. Egypt opposed the Syrian idea of a united Arab delegation, which would include PLO representatives. Although at the end of the talks, the Egyptian Foreign Minister announced that both leaders had agreed that the PLO should participate in the Geneva conference as an independent delegation, implying that Syria had gone along with the Egyptian position, Syria nonetheless continued to call for a unified delegation.[141]

It was announced that the two Presidents would discuss joint military strategy during the coming phase, taking into consideration that "the only alternative to the failure of a peaceful settlement . . . would be the use of force to regain what has been taken by force."[142] Accordingly, the two leaders decided to establish a Unified Political Command, which Fahmī said was intended to "bolster bilateral relations as well as co-ordination and integration." Another decision was to set up joint committees to prepare guidelines for future co-operation in all spheres.[143]

The two Presidents issued decrees on 4 February 1977 naming themselves, their deputies, their Prime Ministers, Foreign Ministers and War Ministers as members of the 10-man Joint Political Command. On 27–28 February, Sādāt and Asad again met in Cairo and then went to Khartoum for a meeting with President Numayrī, where it was decided that Sudan would join the Unified Political Command (see below). However, the establishment of the Command did not bring about any real change in Egypt-Syrian relations; no substantial steps were taken to activate it, and co-operation remained based on pragmatic political considerations coloured by mutual distrust.

In inter-Arab politics, Egypt has shown concern and suspicion since 1973 at Syria's efforts to assert itself as a "regional power" by establishing its hegemony in Lebanon, by its increased control over the PLO and by strengthening its ties with Jordan. At the Riyadh summit, Egypt was left with little choice but to acknowledge Syria's hegemony in Lebanon. Cairo played only a marginal role in the reorganization of the Lebanese state following the 1975–6 civil war—in striking contrast to its influence on Lebanese affairs in the late 1960s. After the Riyadh summit, Egypt concentrated on Jordan and the PLO in trying to contain Syrian efforts to expand its sphere of influence. To Jordan, Egypt stressed its ability to influence the character of the Palestinian representation at Geneva, and the future relationship between Jordan and the Palestinians.

Another cause of Egyptian concern in 1977 was the Americans' upgrading of Syria's role in the Arab-Israeli conflict—from that of Egypt's "junior partner" to independent status. This was exemplified by Egypt dropping its proposal for a working group of Arab and Israeli Foreign Ministers, made to the US Secretary of State in August 1977, after strong Syrian opposition (see "Chronology and Commentary on Middle East Developments").

EGYPTIAN-LIBYAN RELATIONS

The tension in Egyptian-Libyan relations since the early 1970s increased after the October 1973 war and reached its peak in the summer of 1977 when border incidents developed into open military conflict. Four major factors account for these hostile relations. 1) Cultural differences: Libya is still largely organized along tribal lines and according to traditional Islamic-Arab values; it has so far achieved only a relatively low level of modernization. Egyptian society, on the other hand, is led by a comparatively large Westernized urban élite. 2) Difference in strategic location: as a "Confrontation state," Egypt is exposed to constraints not applicable to Libya; hence Egypt's sensitivity to Libyan criticisms. 3) The wide gap in resources: while sparsely-populated Libya enjoys rich oil resources, over-populated Egypt has relatively few natural resources and its people endure considerable economic hardship. 4) The common border: this makes it easier for each party to exert pressure on the other through subversion, and by concentrating their forces along the border.

The personal clash between Sādāt and Qadhdhāfī also played a central role in the widening gulf between the two neighbours. Whereas Qadhdhāfī is impulsive and doctrinaire, Sādāt is a pragmatic and rather conservative statesman who regards the young Libyan leader as unstable, reckless and irresponsible. Sādāt's allegations against Qadhdhāfī became increasingly sharp, with accusations of treachery and blind fanaticism, and repeatedly references to him as a disturbed person and "a spoiled child." [114]

Such personal tension and rivalry not only stemmed from differences of character, temperament and style, but were above all due to ideological differences. Driven by a messianic vision, Qadhdhāfī regarded himself as Nāsir's successor in the Arab world. He believed in the idea of immediate Arab unity, fundamental Islamic "dynamism" and radical "revolutionism." Aspects of Qadhdhāfī's ideology have taken hold in various opposition circles in Egypt itself—ranging from the neo-Nāsirites on the Left to the Muslim fundamentalists on the Right. Sādāt, on the other hand, rejected immediate Arab unity as unrealistic, and emphasized the value of pragmatic co-operation between Arab states. Adhering to practical considerations in foreign policy, Sādāt tended to uphold the *status quo*; Qadhdhāfī, like Nāsir, was intent on destroying it.

Egyptian officials and the media began to level serious allegations against Libya in January 1977, claiming that it was organizing subversive activities in Egypt in order to spread terror and demoralize the population. Thus in March 1977, Egypt reported the arrest of 20 people said to have been sent by Libya to carry out acts of sabotage.[145] Sādāt also accused Libya (though mainly the USSR) of having incited and organized the food riots of January and of having supported extremist Islamic subversive groups in Egypt. Although these accusations were clearly exaggerated, they nevertheless reflected a genuine conviction of the Egyptian regime that Libya was providing substantial support to opposition groups in the country in an effort to overthrow Sādāt. (Also see chapter on Libya.)

The basic disagreement between the two countries over the Arab-Israeli conflict was a major element in their rivalry. Libya categorically rejected Egypt's political and military strategy in the conflict (see below). In turn, Qadhdhāfī's plan of concentrating Arab forces in Syria to launch an all-out attack on Israel was ridiculed by the Egyptian Premier in his address to the People's Assembly on 2 August 1977. He claimed that when he had asked Qadhdhāfī how long this operation would take, he answered "ten years." "I asked him, if you had part of your territory occupied, would you wait ten years before you liberated it?" [146] On the political plane, Qadhdhāfī presented Egypt's policies towards Israel as a violation of its commitment to the Arab cause. In an effort to isolate Sādāt, Libya tried to broaden the "Rejection Front" coalition opposing Egypt in the Arab world.

Following the October war and Egypt's rift with the USSR, Qadhdhāfī began to strengthen his ties with Moscow. After Iraq and Syria, Libya became the biggest client for Soviet arms and military personnel. Egypt was concerned that this massive Soviet assistance to Libya would change the military balance between the two countries and give Qadhdhāfī the self-confidence to continue challenging the Sādāt regime. In addition to attacking Libya for promoting terrorist activities in Egypt and Sudan, the Egyptian media began to stress the danger of Libya being transformed into an aggressive Soviet base to be used against both countries. When Egypt began to deploy more of its forces along its Western front against this threat, the USSR addressed a sharply-worded message to Cairo (see above).

Large-scale military clashes occurred along the Egyptian-Libyan border between 21 and 24 July 1977. On 2 August, Gen Jamasī told the People's Assembly that they were the culmination of an escalating process dating back to 1974 when "acts of sabotage began in the Western Desert" and then extended into Egypt itself and into Cairo. "As a result of this, in August 1976, the Western Desert was transformed into a military area, and the border guard forces were reinforced by a small part of the armed forces." [147] He added that the Egyptian forces had been dispersed in isolated posts along the 300-km border. On 16 July 1977, one of these posts was attacked. Egypt considered it as "a warning that the Libyan side had begun its premeditated military provocation." Therefore, when on 19 July a Libyan armoured force—consisting of c. 75 armoured vehicles and tanks—opened fire on several Egyptian posts, "the Egyptian armed forces had no choice but to intervene." Some 20 Libyan armoured vehicles were destroyed. "From that day on, orders were given to repulse the aggression of the Libyan regime and not just to exchange fire on the border." [148] (For details of the clashes and the consequent mediation effort, see essay on Inter-Arab Affairs and chapter on Libya.)

RELATIONS WITH SUDAN AND EGYPT'S INVOLVEMENT IN THE RED SEA AREA

Egypt's relations with Sudan have improved steadily since 1973, with mutual co-operation increasing substantially, especially after both countries began to regard Libya as having a direct interest in destroying their regimes. An agreement for the political and economic "integration" (*takāmul*) of Egypt and Sudan was signed in February 1974; the Integration Committee, composed of ministers and senior officials, has since held frequent meetings. Economic co-operation increased in the sphere of joint development projects, mainly to exploit the Nile waters, in agricultural development, transport and industrial investment. Diplomatic co-operation became particularly close with Numayrī almost automatically supporting Sādāt's policies—the only Arab leader who publicly endorsed the second Sinai Agreement (September 1975). Both promoted closer ties with Saudi Arabia and developed a joint front against Libya. In a particularly stern warning to Tripoli in July 1977, Cairo said that "Egypt will consider aggression against Sudan from Libya . . . as an aggression against the Arab Republic of Egypt." [149] Internationally, too, their policies have moved away from their previous pro-Soviet orientation and towards the US. Sudan joined the Egyptian-Syrian Unified Political Leadership on 28 February 1977, although this trilateral framework has remained skeletal.

The main sphere of integration which increased in 1977 was military. Practical co-operation began after the abortive coup in Sudan in July 1976, when Sudanese troops stationed in the Canal zone were flown home to assist Numayrī suppressing the coup. On 15 July 1976, the two countries signed a 25-year joint defence agreement in which both parties undertook to regard aggression aimed against the other as directed against itself. The agreement also provided for the establishment of a Joint Defence Council and a Joint Staff Command. The joint defence agreement was ratified in Cairo on 15 January 1977. (Also see chapter on Sudan.)

The Chiefs of Staff of the two countries met from 7–8 November 1976 in Khartoum, and from 20–23 April 1977 in Cairo. A major item on the agenda of the April meeting was the security of the Red Sea and its transformation into an Arab-controlled zone—a policy also designed to prevent Soviet penetration into the area. Sādāt emphasized Egypt's particular interest in the Red Sea because of its importance in the conflict with Israel—either for a naval blockade in the event of war, or as a bargaining point in the political process. He sought to show that any Israeli demand for a presence at Sharm al-Shaykh to ensure freedom of Israeli navigation could be dismissed if the Arabs controlled the Red Sea. Describing the naval blockade of the October war, Sādāt said "it was neither near Sharm al-Shaykh nor near the straits, nor even near Bāb al-Mandūb," [150] thus implying that Arab control in the Red Sea was based on the long Egyptian-Sudanese coast. However, it was Saudi Arabia and Sudan, not Egypt, who played a leading role in the Arab effort to turn the Red Sea into an "Arab lake." (See essay, "The Middle East and the Horn of Africa.")

Egyptian support for Zaire against an invasion from Angolan territory and its opposition to the Ethiopian military regime were both described in Cairo as measures designed to help the security of Sudan as well as being vital to Egyptian interests. Thus, Gen Jamasī explained that:

> Egypt and Sudan are currently being subjected to some conspiracies by foreign states which are exploiting certain African states to create a kind of hostile zone round them. . . . Angola's aggression against Shaba in Zaire constituted a serious threat to Zaire as a state which shares geographic borders with Sudan. He who controls it—controls Sudan, and consequently control the Nile waters and Egypt.[151]

EGYPT AND THE ARAB-ISRAELI CONFLICT

BASIC CONSIDERATIONS

On the ideological level, Sādāt shares the Arab world's categorical rejection of the moral and historical justification for Israel's existence. Zionism is seen as one of the three historical invasions to which the Arab world has been subjected—"the confrontation with the Mongols . . . with the Crusaders . . . and the Zionism invasion"[152] —in which it has been Egypt's role to defend the "great Arab homeland." At the same time, the awareness of Israel's military superiority and of its international legitimacy, along with the commitment of the US to its existence, has led Egypt to acknowledge the unfeasibility of destroying Israel by force. Sādāt said in response to criticism of this stand:

> America entered the war against me for ten days for the sake of Israel, while I was still on the land of Egypt and had not arrived at the Israeli borders. Why? Because America is Israel's protector. The Soviet Union, as you know, clearly and frankly tells you: 'Do not harm the borders of Israel'. . . . The two are guaranteeing Israel. In the entire world and at the UN, 130 countries are guaranteeing Israel."[153]

Accordingly, at the present stage, Egypt adheres to a policy of limited goals which are primarily those adopted by Nāsir after the 1967 war:

1) Total withdrawal of Israeli forces from the territories occupied in 1967, except for minor changes in the West Bank (for further details, see below).
2) the realization of the "legitimate rights of the Palestinians," the Palestinian problem being defined as the core of the Arab-Israeli conflict. Egypt's current concept of the implementation of this target is to establish a Palestinian state in the West Bank and the Gaza Strip, possibly with a corridor between them (see below).

Egypt has developed an interest in reducing its involvement in the conflict due to three main constraints: economic, inter-Arab dependency and the threat of massive destruction.

Economic Constraints There was a growing awareness among Egypt's intelligentsia, expressed in the media and in official statements, of the high price being paid for Egypt's active involvement in the Arab-Israeli conflict. Thus Sādāt explained his desire to conclude a peace agreement with Israel, saying: "If we were able to achieve peace this year . . . military expenses would definitely drop . . . I truly need all the funds I can get to rebuild my country. Until this moment, our average military expenditure is very high, and we cannot afford to weaken our armed forces as long as we are confronting Israel."[154] Similarly, in his speech to the People's Assembly on 15 March, Gen Jamasī spoke of the "heavy burden that Egypt has shouldered over the past 28 years." He pointed out that "the support of the other Arab countries did not reach the required level."[155]

Inter-Arab Constraints Egypt's deep involvement in the conflict created a situation of growing dependency on other Arab states. In order to maintain its military strength to confront Israel, Egypt needed considerable financial aid. It also needed co-operation for its political strategy—especially as Egypt's role as the major Confrontation state exposed it to strong criticism from some other Arab states.

Military Constraints Gen Jamasī stressed in his speech of 15 March 1977 that Israel was not only rapidly strengthening its conventional forces, but also that there was a growing possibility of its introducing nuclear weapons into the area.[156] Egypt's strategists were acutely conscious of the country's special vulnerability to such highly destructive weapons.

Egypt continued to stress its readiness to negotiate a political settlement based on Resolution 242. Sādāt emphasized this in a significant statement to the ASU Central Committee on 16 July 1977:

> It must be clear that we are ready to sign an agreement [*ittifaqiyya*] providing for a lasting and just peace [*salām*]. Here I say that the political and legal meaning of this is that we are ready to end the state of war, politically and legally. This also means that for the first time in its history, Israel's legal existence within its borders will be recognized. The real challenge is to exploit this positive atmosphere to move towards real peace. This will ultimately lead to one clear result; namely, that if Israel adheres to the principles of international law, it will become one of the Middle East states which will live in peace. This is the price of peace and this is the real challenge. I say this so that our position is clear and so that the East and the West will hear us.[157]

In using the term "real peace" for the first time, Sādāt indicated a willingness to go beyond the ending of a state of belligerency. (For indications of what Egypt had in mind, see below.)

Until October 1977, however, Egypt continued to reject any final reconciliation with Israel. Sādāt expressed his refusal to end the conflict once and for all, and at the same time reaffirmed Egypt's open-ended commitment to the Palestinian cause. That the establishment of a Palestinian state on the West Bank and Gaza Strip was not necessarily the final solution of the Palestinian problem, was clearly indicated by Sādāt in his opening address to the PNC in March 1977 when he reaffirmed that only the Palestinians themselves could define their goals:

> The Palestinian people make their own decisions with respect to their destiny and matters concerning them, and no other factor may act as guardian or impose its opinions on them. We in Egypt insist that the will of the Palestinians continue to be free and independent of any restrictions and interference.[158]

On a number of occasions, Egyptian spokesmen implied that, even from their point of view, Egypt's demands were not final. On the territorial issue, Fahmī indicated that if Israel did not fulfil Egypt's demands of a return to the 1967 borders, and of a corridor between the two parts of the Palestinian state, Egypt would demand the "return to the partition resolution of 1947."[159] He also demanded that Israel "cease its efforts to increase Jewish immigration." With regard to open borders with the Arab states after a peace agreement was concluded, Fahmī said this "would become a natural and decided thing," once Israel "realized the demands of the Palestinians for the establishment of a secular state in which Jews and Palestinians live in a single democratic state." [160]

Sādāt's strategy was based on co-ordination with the US, which was seen as the only power that could bring about Israeli withdrawal (see above).

Egypt remained ideologically and politically committed to the "Arab cause," particularly with regard to the Palestinian issue. Sādāt frequently asserted that "the Palestinian matter is the core of the issue, and not Sinai and not the Golan. There are effects that have come after the Palestine issue and as a result of it. . . . Egypt by its very nature cannot be isolationist. Egypt cannot ignore its historical responsibility. Even when the Palestinians attacked us on the second Sinai Agreement . . . I told 'Arafāt that even if you attack us, Egypt will not deny its responsibility and will not leave the issue." [161] Moreover, this commitment, together with Egypt's relations with the Arab world, ruled out the possibility of Egypt signing an agreement with Israel which would constitute a formal separate settlement.

In the event of diplomatic efforts failing, Egypt kept its military option open. Sādāt stressed: "A peaceful solution to the Middle East problem is carried on at the same time with the possibility of a military solution. We began to carry on a peaceful solution after the fighting ended [in the October 1973 war]. I believe that the campaign is open and increasing, whether it is carried out politically or militarily. . . . Political activity would not reduce the importance of military action . . . the diplomatic campaign is not separated from the military one. This is one campaign—one day it takes a diplomatic form, and the next, a military form." [162]

DIPLOMATIC MOVES

Towards the end of 1976, Sādāt stressed the urgent need to "convene the Geneva conference to decide the framework for an overall settlement." [163] Following the Riyadh and Cario meetings in October 1976 (discussed above), Egypt stepped up its efforts to reconvene the Geneva conference, efforts sometimes referred to as the "peace offensive." Until October 1977, these were channelled along two lines—inter-Arab and the US. In the Arab world, the main focus was on Syria, which seemed more ready to co-operate with Egypt after December 1976 (see above). The question of Palestinian participation was the main obstacle to the convening of the Geneva conference, and Egypt tried to solve this problem through contacts with Jordan (in January 1977), and meetings with PLO leaders in the spring of 1977, before and after the PNC conference in Cairo in March 1977.

Egypt tried to remove these obstacles by establishing common ground with the US on the principles of a possible political settlement. Contacts were held with Secretary of State Cyrus Vance on his first tour to the Middle East in February 1977; in April 1977, Sādāt visited the US and met President Carter. Again, in August, Vance returned to Egypt on his second tour of the Middle East, and in September, Egypt's Foreign Minister held talks with President Carter, Vance and other high-level officials. (For details, see "Chronology and Commentary on Middle East Political Development.")

During September and October 1977, Sādāt expected that the obstacles in the way of a reconvened Geneva conference would be removed through US-Egyptian co-operation. However, following Fahmī's resumption of contacts with the US in mid-September, he found that Egypt no longer occupied the central place in Middle East negotiations, and that other major parties—Israel, Syria and the USSR—were moving to more influential roles. Attention became focused on the Israeli-US Working Paper (for details, see the survey of the Arab-Israeli conflict). Egypt neither rejected nor expressed unequivocal acceptance of the paper, but sought amendments and clarification.[164] As late as 18 October, Sādāt still expressed optimism, saying that it was not so important whether the Geneva conference was convened or not; what was important was that "we have the initiative and as long as the initiative is in our hands, the whole problem can be solved."[165]

THE SUBSTANTIVE ISSUES:
In its political contacts, Egypt presented its position on three substantial issues: Israeli withdrawal to the 4 June 1967 borders; the nature of peace; and the establishment of a Palestinian state.

The Withdrawal of Israeli Forces to the 4 June 1967 borders This demand was a basic component of Egypt's position. Sādāt said it was also grounded in Resolution 242 which articulated the principle of the inadmissibility of the acquisition of territory by war. He declared that "Israel must end its occupation of the Arab territories it seized in 1967. Peace [*salām*] is inconceivable while there is still occupation . . . withdrawal from the occupied territories is an integral part of the process of replacing war with peace. This applied to all the occupied territories—Sinai, the Gaza Strip, the West Bank and the Golan Heights."[166] In an interview given to *al-Usbū' al-'Arabī*, Sādāt made it clear that Egypt was firm on this point, and that this was the first subject discussed in his meetings with Carter in which he had firmly rejected Israel's demand for "secure borders" in the sense of new border demarcations; these he regarded as a pretext for expansionism.

On the possibility of an Israeli military presence beyond the 1967 borders—which had been mooted earlier by the Americans—Ashraf Ghurbāl, Egypt's Ambassador to the US, said that in the contacts between the two Presidents, "We made it clear to the Americans that the Arabs would not agree to the presence of Israeli forces in territories beyond the legal border of 1967."[167] Ghurbal added that the two sides had reached an understanding concerning the subject of minor changes in the 1967 borders in the West Bank: "Carter is talking about returning to the 1967 borders with minor changes . . .[which] relate to humanitarian considerations, such as not dividing villages in the West Bank and putting them on this or the other side of the border. . . . [The] US made it clear that except for these minor changes, she is in favour of complete withdrawal to the 1967 borders."[168]

The rejection of any Israeli territorial gains also applied to Jerusalem. In an interview with British Independent Television, Sādāt emphasized the rejection by the Arab and Muslim world of Israeli sovereignty over the Arab part of Jerusalem. He suggested that "the whole of Jerusalem, the Arab part and the Israeli part," be internationalized.[169]

Sādāt proposed a number of elements which would fulfil Israel's demand for secure borders, bolster the stability of the agreement and secure both sides against military aggression. Firstly, the borders could be guaranteed by international bodies or by the US; such guarantees should be given reciprocally. Secondly, Sādāt suggested demilitarized zones and UN forces along the borders, and other similar measures. In an interview with the US Congress delegation visiting Egypt in November 1976, he said: "From my side and the Egyptian front, I say I'm ready for UN forces, or whatever forces agreed upon, to be stationed on the frontiers between Egypt and Israel . . . to give the feeling of security to the Israelis."[170]

As for the problem of securing freedom of navigation for Israel's port in Eilat, Sādāt categorically rejected an Israeli presence in any form in Sharm al-Shaykh; but he declared his acceptance of the principle of freedom of navigation and his readiness to guarantee it by UN forces. "Either they [the Israelis] take our word that navigation is free through 'Aqaba Gulf . . . or if they are not ready, I am ready to accept any UN contingent in Sharm al-Shaykh to guarantee this." [171]

The Nature of Peace In an interview given to the London *Sunday Times* Sādāt distinguished between a peace agreement and a peace treaty, "A peace agreement simply means we are going to end the state of war. . . . After signing a peace treaty, [Israeli Prime Minister] Rabin would ask me to exchange ambassadors, but I cannot do that. . . . I am ready to end the state of belligerence." Sādāt rejected the Israeli and American view of a peace agreement that provided for the normalization of relations with Israel, arguing that "after four wars and so much bitterness no one could do this . . . because it ignores the whole psychological dimension of the problem. . . . Let us first approach the problem with an agreement of non-belligerency; 90% of a peace settlement could be established that way." [172] The journalist Mūsā Sabrī, a confidant of Sādāt, said that the nature of peace was one of the main subjects discussed in the talks between Sādāt and Carter, and that "this has been a point of basic difference." [173]

However, there were signs that Egypt was moving away from its insistence upon an agreement that would only confirm the "end of belligerency" and was taking a more positive attitude towards an agreement, or possibly even a treaty, that allowed for the normalization of relations. "Responsible Egyptian sources" said that in his talk with Carter, Sādāt had intimated that once a peace agreement had been reached, "the Arab boycott of Israel would end and Israeli ships would be able to go through the Suez Canal." [174] At the end of July, Sādāt spoke of the normalization that could take place after a certain period of time had elapsed, following the signing of a "peace agreement." He said:

> After 29 years of violence, hatred and bitterness, and after four wars, to come in one minute and say: open borders, diplomatic relations, economic exchange and things like that . . . we cannot ignore the psychological element, which represents 70% of the problem. That is why I have said, yes, this would be possible five years after peace is established.

In the same interview, Sādāt said that during this five-year period, "each one of us should try to convince his people; this requires some time. But let us not say that we must begin by initiating air flights or this and that, because this is what the old Israeli arrogance has been trying to impose on us." [175] In his address to the ASU of 16 July, Sādāt stated that the positive attitude that would exist after the ending of the state of war would provide a "real challenge . . . to move towards real peace."

The Palestinian State Egypt maintained that it was the Palestinians themselves who should define the term "Palestinian rights." However, in a number of statements, he stressed two definite commitments with regard to the Palestine issue as a whole: firstly, that "the Palestine question is the core of the problem"; secondly, that "a Palestinian state must be established on the West Bank and the Gaza Strip."

Towards the end of 1976, Sādāt said in an interview that "a certain relationship between the Palestinians and Jordan should be declared to take place whenever the Palestinian state is created." [176] Later, at the end of Vance's first visit to Egypt, Sādāt stressed that this relationship should assume an official character, and that it should be established before the creation of a Palestinian state, and even before the Geneva conference. [177] He evidently hoped that by stressing this link, the problem of Palestinian representation could be resolved and thus pave the way for the reconvening of the Geneva conference (see below).

PROCEDURAL ISSUES BLOCKING THE GENEVA CONFERENCE

Sādāt came to the conclusion that the "step-by-step" process towards a political settlement was no longer viable, and that Egypt should achieve a comprehensive settlement within the framework of a reconvened Geneva conference. He believed, however, that careful preparations were necessary in order to ensure its success. One feature of the preparations was that the co-chairmen of the conference—the US and the USSR—should reach an understanding in advance about the principles of a settlement, which would be set down in a working paper that would be binding at Geneva.[178] Accordingly, on his visit to the US in April 1977, Sādāt suggested the establishment of "a working group at the US Department of State" to be headed by Vance, who "would hold contacts with all the parties concerned, including the Soviet Union."[179]

Another feature of the preparations was to be the establishment of a "working group" composed of the Foreign Ministers of all the countries concerned, that would have contacts in September 1977 during the UN General Assembly. Sādāt first made this proposal at the beginning of Vance's second visit to the Middle East on 1–2 August. But when Syria strongly objected, Egypt dropped the proposal.

Egypt advocated that the Geneva conference should be convened with five separate Arab delegations at the foreign ministery level—Egypt, Syria, Jordan, Lebanon and the Palestinians.[180] However, when it became clear in the summer that the US was supporting the Syrian proposal of a united Arab delegation, Egypt seemed ready to follow suit.

Egypt's stand on Palestinian participation in the Geneva conference has fluctuated over the past few years. A joint communiqué issued after the meeting between Sādāt and Ḥusayn in Alexandria in July 1974 declared that "The PLO was the legitimate representative of the Palestinians, except the Palestinians residing in the Hashemite Kingdom of Jordan," thus substantially undercutting the PLO's claim to be the sole legitimate representative of all the Palestinians.[181] Egypt reversed its position on the eve of the Rabat summit (October 1974), and then endorsed the Rabat resolution which made the PLO the sole legitimate representative of the Palestinian people and excluded Jordan from any claim to represent them.

In 1977, this demand for PLO participation became the main obstacle to the reconvening of the Geneva conference. Egypt's adherence to PLO's participation (which was somewhat less firm than Syria's) was based on the following reasons: 1) Egypt still regarded itself as bound by the Rabat resolutions; 2) if Egypt agreed to go to Geneva without the PLO, it would be exposed to strong Arab criticism; and 3) PLO participation would relieve Egypt from direct involvement in the debate on the Palestinian issue, and from the need to make concessions on this most sensitive problem. Furthermore, in the first half of 1977, Egypt was evidently encouraged to take this position by the favourable statements made by President Carter on this issue.

The Egyptian effort to find a way to overcome this obstacle was three-pronged, being directed toward the US, Jordan and the PLO. On his visit to Washington (April 1977), Sādāt called the US to open a dialogue with Palestinians.[182] Explaining this demand, Egypt's Ambassador, Ashraf Ghurbāl, said that it was based on the US role as a mediator between Israel and the Arabs. He rejected the American precondition for starting a dialogue, namely that the PLO should recognize the state of Israel, asserting that "Israel has not recognized the right of the Palestinians to a homeland."[183]

A number of alternatives were examined in talks between Egypt and Jordan, the most notable being to incorporate PLO representatives in the Jordanian delegation. This idea was discussed in the Sādāt-Ḥusayn talks at Aswan on 13–15 January 1977.

Though the idea was rejected by Ḥusayn, Sādāt declared that the Palestinian delegation should be "linked by some way or another with the Jordanian delegation." [184] Later, in the summer of 1977, in an interview with French television, he repeated this idea. [185]

A number of meetings were held between Sādāt and PLO representatives in which he tried to induce some moderation in the PLO's declared stand in order to facilitate its participation in Geneva. Sādāt hinted at this need in his speech at the opening session of the PNC (19 March 1977): "Your supreme duty at this stage is not to act with all the means at your disposal [i.e. voicing maximalist demands] in order to restore the Palestinian land today and not tomorrow, because any delay in achieving this goal means a perpetuation of the occupation." [186]

EGYPT AND THE MILITARY OPTION

The maintaining of a military option constituted a vital element in Sādāt's strategy for the Arab-Israeli conflict and served a dual purpose: to break a political deadlock, as in the 1973 war; and to exert pressure in the international arena to actively promote a settlement.

Egyptian spokesmen stressed on a number of occasions that Egypt would resort to war if it failed to achieve its goals by political means. Sādāt asserted that: "Peace and war are two options we always face, and the decision is always in our hands. When the destiny of a nation is in danger, we must retain the freedom to choose and to cope with the circumstances and the possibilities according to the dictates of our overriding national interest, and to our loyalty to the great Arab homeland and our principles." [187] He pointed out in an American television interview that Israel's military superiority—achieved through its special relationship with the US—would not prevent him from going to war. "We are capable of confronting the Israelis. . . . Let me remind you that there was such a gap [in military strengths] during the October war. The current gap is much narrower than the one during the October war." [188]

Sādāt also stressed that the reopening of the Suez Canal and the resettlement of the Canal cities would not prevent him from using the military option. He observed that the Canal had been reopened shortly before the Sinai Agreement when it was still within range of Israeli artillery. But he was convinced that the Egyptian army could defend it. He also warned Israel against attacking the Canal cities, saying that he would "consider any attack against any of the Canal cities as aggression against the depth of the Republic; [Egypt would] retaliate by attacking the depth of Israel." [189]

In a speech before the People's Assembly on 15 March 1977, Gen Jamasī reaffirmed Egypt's preparedness to resort to war in the event of a political deadlock. He observed that the scope of such a war would be widened and would require military co-ordination with Syria and with the Red Sea littoral states. Egyptian spokesmen stressed several times that by taking control of the Red Sea area, the Arabs could isolate Israel. Analyzing the importance of the military alliance with Syria, Jamasī said: We all realize that among the reasons for the October 1973 victory was the historic cohesion between brothers-in-arms in Syria and Egypt. . . . From the military point of view, it represented the peak of successful strategic action." [190]

ECONOMIC AFFAIRS (0.391 Egyptian pounds = US$1; £E 0.73 = £1 sterling)

For a comprehensive account of recent economic developments in Egypt and performance in 1976–7, see essay entitled "Major Trends in Middle East Economic Development."

BALANCE OF PAYMENTS (million SDRs)*

	1973	*1974*	*1975*
A. Goods, Services and Unrequited transfers:	65	-272	-1,151
Merchandise: exports fob	839	1,390	1,291
Merchandise: imports fob	-1,199	-2,423	-3,246
Trade balance	*-360*	*-1,033*	*-1,955*
Services: credit	353	589	888
Services: debit	-466	-689	-970
Total goods and services	*-473*	*-1,133*	*-2,037*
Private unrequited transfers, net	5	35	74
Government unrequited transfers, net	533	826	812
B. Long-Term Capital, net	-52	-130	260
C. Short-Term Capital, net	85	277	-454
D. Exceptional Financing	—	—	225
Total, A through D	**98**	**-125**	**-1,120**
E. Monetary Changes	-98	125	1,120

*Exchange rates, Dollars per SDR:
1973 = 1.206; 1974 = 1.224; 1975 = 1.17
Source: IMF, *Balance of Payments Yearbook*, December 1976.

MAIN TRADE PARTNERS (million Dollars)

	1974	*1975*	*1976*
EXPORTS TO:			
Italy	67	99	343
Czechoslovakia	99	113	113
United Kingdom	56	33	109
United States	11	15	100
France	37	31	85
East Germany	61	80	80
Greece	14	9	64
Romania	38	63	63
Japan	152	5	62
China	34	56	56
West Germany	55	27	53
Netherlands	16	28	53
Poland	42	52	52
USSR	42	52	52
Belgium	26	5	41
Total (including others)	**1,516**	**1,576**	**2,286**
IMPORTS FROM:			
United States	389	581	891
West Germany	145	342	642
France	352	346	366
Japan	25	189	362
United Kingdom	65	203	342
Italy	90	230	322
USSR	207	232	232
Australia	213	190	171
East Germany	61	109	109
Netherlands	57	90	99
Romania	120	95	95
Lebanon	81	94	94
Switzerland	52	87	84
Greece	27	35	80
Yugoslavia	34	51	80
Total (including others)	**2,352**	**3,534**	**4,984**

Source: IMF, *Direction of Trade*, 1970–76.

STATE BUDGET (£E million)

	1974	*1975*	*1976*
Receipts—Total	**1,180**	**1,543**	**1,754.7**
Central Government revenue	780	1,060	1,071.2
Local Government revenue	65	88	83.1
Public economic sector	335	395	600.4
Current Expenditure	**1,269**	**1,713**	**1,791.2**
Central Government current expenditure	779	889	755.3
Local Government current expenditure	61	88	370.0
Public Authorities' deficits	402	86	112.2
Public Organizations' deficits	15	8	—
Subsidies	12	642	553.7
Current Account surplus or deficit	-89	-170	-36.5
Investment expenditure	565	757	1,252.2
Overall Deficit	**-654**	**-927**	**1,288.2**
Total Financing	654	927	1,288.2
External borrowing (net)	11	316.8	668.2
Domestic borrowing (net)	643	610.2	620.5
Social insurance and pension funds	245	275.5	321.8
Savings certificates	43	30.0	42.0
Postal savings	18	13.7	16.1
Public economic sector	23	166.0	115.6
Banking system	314	125.0	125.0

Source: Central Bank of Egypt, *Economic Review.*

OUTPUT BY SELECTED SECTORS (£E million, 1975 prices)

	1976 Estimated	*1978* Projections	*1980* Projections	*Average annual increase 1976–80*
Agriculture	2,116	2,247	2,384	3
Industry	3,449	4,103	5,145	12
Oil	581	747	989	15
Power	100	145	200	17
Construction	416	589	780	15
Suez	146	230	304	15
Other	3,201	3,914	4,736	11
Total output	**10,009**	**11,975**	**14,538**	9

ECONOMIC STRUCTURE (1974)

	Gross domestic product £E million*	*%*	*Employment 000*	*%*
Agriculture	1,225	34	4,212	47
Services	792	22	1,853	21
Manufacturing	688	19	1,118	12
Trade and Finance	361	9	883	10
Transport and Communications	167	5	405	4
Construction	135	4	315	3
Real Estate	127	3	139	2
Other	149	4	114	1
Total	**3,644**	**100**	**9,039**	**100**

*At current factor cost prices

ARAB REPUBLIC OF EGYPT

MEDIUM TERM ECONOMIC TARGETS (£E million, 1975 prices)

	1976 Estimated	*1980 Target*	*Average annual growth rate*
Total consumption	5,498	8,382	8.8
Total investment	1,086	1,930	15.4
Exports	1,269	2,800	22.0
Imports	1,696	3,158	16.8
GDP at market prices	5,498	8,382	11.0
Gross Domestic Savings (GDS)	659	1,572	23.0
GDS as per cent of GDP	12.0	18.8	—

SELECTED DEVELOPMENT PROJECTS

Project	*Site*	*Investment £E million*	*Start-up date*
Integrated steel plant	Alexandria	800	n.a.
Phosphate mining	Western Desert	362	1982
Special steels	Khatatba	100	n.a.
Aluminium smelting	Naga Hamadi	88	n.a.
Wire rods	Samalout	79	1981
Heavy truck and bus assembly	Helwan	52	1980
Sugar plant and refinery	Baliana	50	1979
Passenger cars	Helwan	48	1980
Sponge iron	Helwan	34	n.a.
Sheet glass	Cairo	20	1978
Tractors	n.a.	20	1979
Foundry (iron pipes)	Cairo	16	n.a.
Soda ash/ caustic soda	Alexandria	14	1980

Note: The projects listed above are officially described as tentative and should therefore be regarded as no more than an indication of some of the proposals under 'active consideration' by the authorities.
Source: (of four preceding tables): Grindlays Bank Group, *Egypt*, June 1977.

NOTES

1. *October*, Cairo; 22 May 1977.
2. *Ibid*, 15 May 1977.
3. The official term for the 1–15 May 1971 operation which destroyed the Nāsirite "centres of power" which had allegedly conspired against Sādāt.
4. Middle East News Agency (MENA), 14 May 1977.
5. *Ibid.*
6. R Cairo, 3 February 1977.
7. "Memoirs," *October*, 24 July 1977.
8. R Cairo, 6 June 1977.
9. *Ibid*, 5 June 1977.
10. *Al-Ahrām*, Cairo; 24 December 1976.
11. *Ibid*, 16 June 1977.
12. MENA, 3 June 1977.
13. Iraqi News Agency (INA), 2 January 1977.
14. MENA, 14 May 1977.
15. MENA, 24 and 25 August 1976.
16. MENA. 26 August 1976.
17. MENA, 17 September 1976.
18. R Cairo, 19 September 1976.
19. MENA, 15 June, 1 July 1977.
20. MENA, 16 July 1977.
21. Al-Wāfiya resigned in January 1977 after the food riots and was replaced by Dr Fu'ād Muḥyī al-Dīn. However, he returned to his post in October.

22. *Al-Ahrām*, 15 October 1976.
23. Thomas Lippman from Cairo, *Washington Post (WP)*, 29 September 1977.
24. *New York Times (NYT)*, 20 January 1977.
25. David Hirst from Cairo, *The Guardian*, London; 19 and 20 January 1977.
26. *Ibid*, 20–23 January 1977. Thomas Lippman from Cairo, *WP*, 20 January 1977.
27. MENA, 20 and 28 January 1977.
28. R Cairo, 21 September 1976. Thomas Lippman from Cairo, *WP*, 21 September 1976.
29. *Al-Ahrām*, 3 January 1977.
30. *Ibid*, 20 January 1977.
31. R Cairo, 20 January 1977.
32. *Al-Ahrām*, 27 January 1977.
33. *The Guardian*, 26 January 1977.
34. *The Economist*, London; 29 January 1977.
35. R Cairo, 18 January 1977.
36. *Al-Ahrām*, 26 January 1977.
37. MENA, 28 January 1977.
38. INA, 2 February 1977.
39. R Cairo, 21 January 1977.
40. *Ibid*, 3 February 1977.
41. *Al-Akhbār*, Cairo; 5 February 1977.
42. *Al-Ahrām*, 12 February 1977.
43. *Al-Akhbār*, 8 March 1977.
44. *Al-Ahrām*, 4 May 1977.
45. MENA, 19 and 20 February, 1 June 1977. R Cairo, 12 and 26 April, 2 May 1977.
46. R Cairo, 29 June; MENA, 28 July 1977.
47. *The Economist*, 29 January 1977.
48. MENA, 30 January 1977.
49. Speech to workers' leaders in Cairo: R Cairo, 29 January 1977.
50. Speech to transport workers in al-Matariya: R Cairo, 18 June 1977.
51. *Al-Hurriyya al-Safīr*, Beirut: 3 and 11 August 1975.
52. *Al-Yasār al-'Arabī*, Paris; September 1977, p. 3.
53. *Al-Ahrām*, 8 September 1976.
54. R Cairo, 16 July 1977.
55. Address to the nation: R Cairo, 3 February 1977.
56. Speech in Ismā'īliyya: R Cairo, 5 June 1977.
57. Speeches on 3 February and 5 June 1977.
58. Speech in Alexandria: MENA, 26 June 1977. Prime Minister Sālim had consistently argued that NPUR was controlled by the Communists: see *al-Ahrām*, 31 January 1977.
59. As described in Sādāt's speech to the Higher Council for Universities: MENA, 30 January 1977.
60. *Rūz al-Yūsuf*, Cairo; 14 and 21 March 1977. MENA, 21 April 1977.
61. *Rūz al-Yūsuf*, March 1977.
62. MENA, 28 July 1977.
63. MENA, 30 September, 1 and 2 October 1977. According to *Le Monde* (4 October), the arrested Leftists were affiliated with the NPUR.
64. INA, 31 January 1977.
65. Robert Fisk from Cairo: *The Times*, London; 27 January 1977.
66. "The masses of January—between the Government and the Left"; *al-Talī'a*, Cairo; February 1977.
67. *Al-Jumhūriyya*, Cairo; 8 May 1977. MENA, 9 May 1977.
68. See, for example, 'Abd al-Sattār Tawīla, "Sādāt and the Communists," *Rūz al-Yūsuf*, 14 February 1977.
69. See Bernard Lewis, "The Return of Islam," *Commentary*, January 1976.
70. R Cairo, 3 July 1977.
71. R Cairo and MENA, 4, 5, 6 July 1977.
72. United Press International (UPI), Cairo; 7 and 16 July 1977.
73. MENA, 23 November 1976. *Al-Ahrām*, 20 December 1976. *Akhbār al-Yawm*, Cairo; 19 March 1977.
74. MENA, 6, 8, 9, 12 July, 11 August; *The Times*, 16 July 1977.
75. See article by Dr Lutfī 'Abd al-'Azīm in *al-Ahrām*, 14 July 1977.
76. MENA, 21 July 1977.
77. MENA, 26 July; *October*, 28 August 1977.
78. *Al-Ahrām*, 30 and 31 August 1977.
79. MENA, 6 and 7 July, 23 August, 3 and 28 September, 31 October 1977.
80. Saudi News Agency (SNA), 9 February 1977.

81. *The Times*, 15 September 1977.
82. *Al-Jumhūriyya*, 1 January 1977.
83. *Al-Akhbār*, 1 September 1977.
84. *Al-Ahrām*, 15 July; *The Times*, 16 July 1977.
85. Associated Press (AP) from Cairo, 10 September 1977. Sādāt's speech at the People's Assembly: R Cairo, 28 September 1977.
86. *Events*, Beirut; 23 September 1977.
87. Don Schanche from Cairo, *WP*, 15 September 1977.
88. R Cairo, 22 September 1977.
89. R Cairo, 28 September 1977.
90. R Cairo, 11 November 1977.
91. Text in *al-Ahrām*, 21 June 1977.
92. *Al-Ahrām*, 21 June, 11 October; *October*, 16 October 1977.
93. *Rūz al-Yūsuf*, 21 February 1977.
94. *Ibid*, 16 May 1977.
95. *Le Monde*, Paris; 25 and 31 August. *Akhbār al-Yawm*, 27 August. *Arabia and the Gulf*, London; 5 September 1977.
96. *Rūz al-Yūsuf*, 5 September; *al-Ahrām*, 16 September; *al-Jumhūriyya*, 16 September; citing *al-Da'wa*.
97. Irene Beeson from Cairo: *The Guardian*, 1 November 1976.
98. Thomas Lippman from Cairo: *International Herald Tribune (IHT)*, Paris; 26 October 1976.
99. MENA, 6 November 1976.
100. R Cairo, 16 July 1977.
101. INA, 29 March; *al-Ahrām*, 22 February 1977.
102. R Cairo, 11 November 1976.
103. *Al-Akhbār*, 21 July 1977.
104. MENA, 13 November 1976. R Cairo, 10 January 1977.
105. *Al-Ahrām*, 29 June, 7 October; *al-Akhbār*, 14 October 1977.
106. *Al-Ahrām*, 21 June 1977.
107. R Cairo, 29 June, 16 July; MENA 3 July; *al-Akhbār*, 21 and 29 July 1977.
108. R Cairo, 10 November—Daily Report (DR), 11 November 1976.
109. *Ibid.*
110. *The Military Balance 1977–78* (London: International Institute for Strategic Studies).
111. *Al-Usbū' al-'Arabī*, Beirut; 4 July 1977.
112. MENA, 12 May—BBC, 14 May 1977.
113. *Al-Ahrām*, 29 May 1977.
114. R Cairo, 28 September—DR, 29 September 1977.
115. MENA, 15 August—DR, 16 August 1977.
116. *NYT*, 3 February; *IHT*, 4 February 1977.
117. R Cairo, 16 July —DR, 18 July 1977.
118. MENA, 27 April—BBC, 29 April 1977.
119. Tass, 11 June—DR, 13 June 1977.
120. *Al-Usbū' al-'Arabī*, 4 July 1977.
121. R Cairo, 16 July—DR, 18 July 1977.
122. *Al-Usbū' al-'Arabī*, 4 July 1977.
123. MENA, 9 November—DR, 10 November 1976.
124. *Al-Usbū' al-'Arabī*, 4 July 1977.
125. MENA, 14 July—DR, 15 July 1977.
126. *Al-Usbū' al-'Arabī*, 4 July 1977.
127. R Cairo, 10 November—DR, 11 November 1976.
128. *Al-Usbū' al-'Arabī*, 4 July 1977.
129. *Al-Ahrām*, 19 July 1977.
130. *Al-Musawwar*, Cairo; 29 April 1977.
131. Sādāt interview with Iranian newspaper *Rastakhiz*, quoted by MENA, 18 May—DR, 19 May 1977.
132. US Information Service, Official Text, 16 September 1977.
133. MENA, 2 August—DR, 3 August 1977.
134. *IHT*, 25 May 1977.
135. R Cairo, 16 July—DR, 18 July 1977.
136. MENA, 1 February—DR, 2 February 1977.
137. *Akhbār al-Yawm*, 22 January 1977.
138. MENA, 23 March—BBC, 25 March 1977.
139. R Cairo, 14 August—DR, 15 August 1977.
140. R Cairo, 4 December—BBC, 6 December 1976.

141. R Cairo, 21 December—DR, 22 December 1976.
142. *Al-Ahrām*, 18 December 1976.
143. *Ibid*, 23 December 1976.
144. See R Cairo, 7 August—DR, 8 August 1977.
145. *Al-Ahrām*, 27 March 1977.
146. R Cairo, 2 August—DR, 3 August 1977.
147. *Ibid.*
148. *Ibid.*
149. MENA, 26 July—BBC, 28 July 1977.
150. *Al-Usbū' al-'Arabī*, 4 July 1977.
151. MENA, 25 May—DR, 26 May 1977.
152. "The October Paper," *al-Ahrām*, 1 May 1974.
153. MENA, 1 February—DR, 2 February 1977.
154. MENA, 18 May 1977. Interview given to *Rastakhiz.*
155. *Al-Ahrām*, 16 March 1977.
156. *Ibid.*
157. R Cairo, 16 July—DR, 18 July 1977.
158. MENA, 12 March 1976.
159. R Cairo, 14 January 1977.
160. MENA, 19 April—DR, 19 April 1977.
161. MENA, 20 April 1977.
162. *Ibid.*
163. Sādāt interview with *Time*, New York; 29 November 1976.
164. *NYT*, 20 October 1977.
165. R Cairo, 19 October 1977.
166. *Al-Ahrām*, 18 July 1977.
167. R Cairo, 19 May 1977.
168. *Ibid.*
169. Quoted by MENA, 21 February—DR, 22 February 1977.
170. MENA, 9 November—DR, 10 November 1976.
171. *Ibid.*
172. *The Sunday Times*, London; 28 November 1976.
173. *Al-Akhbār*, 10 April 1977.
174. MENA, 9 April—DR, 11 April 1977.
175. Interview to CBS, quoted by MENA, 31 July—DR, 1 August 1977.
176. *WP*, 30 December 1976.
177. R Cairo, 17 February—DR, 18 February 1977.
178. R Cairo, 26 December 1976.
179. Interview to CBS Television, quoted by MENA, 31 July—DR, 1 August 1977.
180. Sādāt's interview to *WP*, 30 December 1977.
181. R Cairo, 18 July—BBC, 20 July 1974.
182. MENA, 9 April—DR, 11 April 1977.
183. R Cairo, 19 May 1977.
184. Sādāt's interview with *The Sunday Telegraph*, London; 16 January 1977.
185. Quoted by MENA, 24 July—DR, 26 July 1977.
186. MENA, 12 March 1977.
187. MENA, 20 April 1977.
188. Quoted by MENA, 31 July 1977.
189. R Cairo, 5 June—DR, 7 June 1977.
190. *Al-Ahrām*, 16 March 1977.

The Gulf States

ARYEH SHMUELEVITZ

GENERAL ISSUES AND DEVELOPMENT

The British decision in 1968 to withdraw from the Persian Gulf region was the catalyst which caused the pattern of traditional disputes to change into a system of close co-operation among the littoral states of the Gulf. After a period of concessions and reconciliation, efforts gradually turned to negotiations on all aspects of regional co-operation. Although not all disagreements were resolved—especially over border claims—and the actual extent of effective co-operation was disappointing, considerable achievements were made: a *rapprochement* between Iran and Iraq in 1975; border agreements between Saudi Arabia and the UAE (1974) and between UAE and Oman; political arrangements among Saudi Arabia, the other Arab Gulf states (except Oman) and South Yemen to end the Dhufar rebellion; the establishment of diplomatic relations between Iraq and Oman; and an agreement between Iraq and Saudi Arabia to divide the Neutral Zone.

Progress in regional co-operation included the following. 1) Transportation: building roads to connect the Gulf states; relieving port congestion; proposals to merge air and shipping companies. 2) Communications: radio, television and telephone links. 3) Information and propaganda. 4) Financial aid to Arab and Afro-Asian states. 5) Industrial consultation. Such questions as a common market or common currency were only discussed in principle, while security problems proved too controversial for any real progress to be made. Iran did not participate in most of these activities, being clearly set apart from the Arab littoral states.

In 1977, the Gulf littoral states were mainly engaged in three areas of common activity: 1) defence problems of the Gulf and internal security; 2) continuing discussions on economic, technical and cultural co-operation; and 3) co-ordination of financial aid and political support to countries in the Arab and Third Worlds.

GULF DEFENCE AND INTERNAL SECURITY

The idea of a defence alliance between the Gulf littoral states was first raised in 1968, following the British decision to withdraw from the region. However, the matter was not officially pursued until 1976—after the *rapprochement* between Iran and Iraq, and the agreement between Arab Gulf states and the People's Democratic Republic of Yemen (PDRY) to end the Dhufar rebellion and evacuate foreign military units and advisers from that area. With the help of Oman, a Kuwaiti initiative resulted in a Gulf Foreign Ministers' conference in Muscat on 25–26 November 1976. Five working papers on defence were submitted by Iran, Iraq, Kuwait, Oman and the UAE respectively. The views put forward showed wide differences of approach—from a comprehensive mutual defence alliance suggested by Iran, to a complete rejection of the need for any such alliance by the UAE. Between these two extremes were various proposals for loose co-operation in such matters as the exchange of security information and non-aggression agreements. The conference was considered a great failure, differences obviously being too deep to allow for real co-operation. It seemed impossible to remove or even allay suspicions, especially between the Gulf states and Iran, as well as between Iraq and Kuwait, Iraq and Saudi Arabia, and Iraq and Oman. Summing up the mood of the conference, its chairman, the Omani Minister of State for Foreign Affairs, said that there was "a situation, or better an atmosphere" which did not make joint defence co-operation possible at present.[1]

However, some co-ordination in defence affairs was agreed among the Arab littoral states. According to the Baḥrayni Chief of Staff in February 1977, military co-ordination at Gulf and Arab levels had become a focal point.[2] This was confirmed by the UAE Defence Minister in May 1977 who stressed that co-ordination in the field of armaments and training (so that the Gulf armies could become a single army capable of defending any country) was important and a duty in view of the limited manpower resources of states such as the UAE and Kuwait.[3] There were also reports of Kuwaiti initiatives for a defence pact among Arab Gulf states, which would be followed by negotiations with Iran. Two developments in the Gulf area in 1976–7 perhaps served as catalysts to bring about this co-operation. First, arrangements for bilateral co-operation among Arab Gulf states in matters concerning internal security, such as those reached by Saudi Arabia with Baḥrayn, Kuwait, UAE and Qatar. Second, the negotiations begun in mid-1977 for co-ordination in the defence of the Red Sea and Persian Gulf regions as an inter-Arab question, with Saudi Arabia serving as the main link. This was discussed by the Presidents of Sudan and Somalia and the Egyptian Naval Commander.

Co-operation among all Gulf states was again raised in September 1977 following the reported suggestion that the US might move to defend the Gulf to secure the Western world's oil supplies from the region. The Arab Gulf states reacted strongly against this idea. For instance, Kuwait's Acting Foreign Minister, 'Abd al-'Azīz Ḥusayn, insisted that the Gulf states had the faith and determination to deal with Gulf security by co-operating among themselves.[4] However, little progress was made in removing the obstacles to such co-operation, nor did the Arab Gulf states lose their suspicions of Iranian military ambitions. Neither was any real change concerning the presence of the Americans in Baḥrayn or the Soviets in Umm Qasr in Iraq.

ECONOMIC, TECHNICAL AND CULTURAL CO-OPERATION

The trend among the Arab Gulf states to increase and intensify economic, technical and cultural co-operation continued in 1977, with meetings and conferences to discuss these questions becoming a regular feature. In February 1977 alone, four conferences were held: the Gulf Health Ministers met in Doha, Qatar; the Agriculture Ministers in Abu Dhabi; the Information Ministers in Riyadh; and the Arabian Gulf Organization for Industrial Consulting (AGOIC) in Doha. At a second meeting, the Ministers of Health discussed proposals to improve health services in the Gulf, for instance, by establishing a regional pharmaceutical industry, as well as centres for hygiene instruction, for an anti-malaria campaign and for medical research. They also proposed to establish a permanent conference secretariat in Riyadh.

The Ministers of Agriculture discussed ways to exchange information on cultivation, fishing and husbandry. They also decided to set up a desert plant research centre, a cattle vaccine plant and an organic fertilizer complex, all as joint ventures.

The Information Ministers made considerable advances in co-operation by approving a draft agreement on the Gulf television system proposed by Saudi Arabia, as well as its memorandum on co-ordination between Gulf tele-communications and television networks. Among other decisions were the setting up of a radio and television regional training centre in Qatar; acceptance of a UAE memorandum on the Gulf States' information co-ordination centre in Abu Dhabi; and agreement about the level of participation in joint information projects. They also decided on the senior personnel and publications of the Gulf News Agency, which opened in October 1977 at Manamah, capital of Baḥrayn. The Information Ministers also asked a committee of experts to report on future television transmission in the Gulf region; on a special satellite to exchange news and television programmes; and on an oil information centre.

AGOIC was formed in February 1976 with its headquarters in Doha (Qatar). Its tasks were to submit plans for joint industrial projects, make recommendations on regional co-ordination, develop technical co-operation, and carry out feasibility studies. In February 1977, the Executive Council approved the AGOIC's financial and administrative regulations, its 1977 budget ($1.27m), and the senior personnel of the general secretariat. (The Secretary-General comes from Saudi Arabia and his deputy from Iraq.)

The organization started to function in April 1977, encouraged by the decision of Saudi Arabia and Oman to support its work. But it also faced many difficulties, especially over duplication in industrial projects. This led Saudi Arabia, Kuwait and the UAE to call for a conference of the Ministers of Planning and Industry in September to co-ordinate industrial planning by formulating a joint policy, and to avoid further duplication as had occurred in major industries like oil refining, iron and steel and fertilizer.

This question was also taken up at the first conference of the Arab Ministers of Economy and Trade held in Baghdad in October. A key working paper proposed a common market of the Arab Gulf states. Although possibilities of strengthening and consolidating economic and commercial co-operation were discussed, the only operational decision taken was to convene the conference annually.

The idea of a common currency was first discussed in 1976, but no progress was made on this issue either. Kuwait, Baḥrayn, the UAE and Qatar wanted a single Gulf currency to be instituted within months. But it soon became clear that it could not be implemented until a common economic policy was tackled first. However, the United Arab Shipping Company (UASC)—a joint venture of Baḥrayn, Kuwait, Iraq, Qatar, Saudi Arabia and the UAE—was launched in July 1976 with headquarters in Kuwait. It began operating in April 1977 after the Kuwait Shipping Company agreed to participate in the venture. This success opened the way for discussions on the merger of air companies in the area. Gulf Air—jointly owned by Baḥrayn, Qatar, Oman and the UAE—opened negotiations in April for a merger with Kuwait Airways Corporation. The activities of the Gulf International Bank also increased.

CO-ORDINATION OF FINANCIAL AND POLITICAL AID

The Gulf Arab oil-producing states extended their co-operation in providing financial aid to countries in Asia, Africa and Latin America during 1976 and 1977. The Gulf Authority for Egyptian Development was established in August 1976, with an initial capital of $2,000m to finance Egypt's 1976–80 Five-Year Development Plan. The Authority transferred the second loan of $650m to Egypt in August 1977.

The oil-producing principalities joined Saudi Arabia in the campaign against Soviet and Cuban influence by extending financial and economic aid to PDRY and Somalia. An agreement was signed between Kuwait and the PDRY providing for an annual supply of 1m tons of Kuwaiti crude oil to the Aden refinery. The Arab Gulf states' aims were to stop PDRY support for the rebellion in Dhufar, and strengthen Somalia in its war with Ethiopia. They also hoped to persuade both to co-operate with the anti-Soviet Red Sea littoral states in defending the Red Sea region.

GULF EXPORTS (million US dollars)

	1972	*1973*	*1974*	*1975*	*1976*
Baḥrayn	326	450	1,170	1,107	1,346
Kuwait	2,573	3,447	9,857	8,644	9,820
Oman	231	330	1,135	1,445	1,575
Qatar	398	626	2,012	1,804	2,192
UAE	1,157	1,936	6,412	6,879	8,542

GULF IMPORTS (million US dollars)

	1972	*1973*	*1974*	*1975*	*1976*
Baḥrayn	376	511	1,127	1,198	1,664
Kuwait	797	1,052	1,552	2,390	3,317
Oman	161	169	711	668	667
Qatar	139	195	271	413	817
UAE	482	821	1,705	2,669	3,351

Source: IMF, *Direction of Trade.*

NOTES

1. R. Kuwait, 26 November—British Broadcasting Corporation, Summary of World Broadcasts; the ME and Africa (BBC), 27 November 1976.
2. *Akhbār al-Khalīj*, 14 February 1977.
3. *Al-Majlis al-Mussawara*, Kuwait; 14 May 1977.
4. 'Abd al-'Azīz Ḥusayn in an interview with the Middle East News Agency (MENA), 16 September 1977.

Bahrayn

When Baḥrayn attained independence at the end of 1971 following the British withdrawal from the Gulf area, the ruling Khalīfa family seemed prepared to share the administration of government with other prominent families whose members already held important key posts. A constitutional monarchy was established, with a National Assembly and a government, in which fewer than 50% belonged to the royal family. However, the ruling family soon faced growing opposition and pressure both from the National Assembly and subversive activities—especially from the Front for the Liberation of the Occupied Arabian Gulf. The Government's pro-Saudi and pro-US policy, as well as its inability to solve economic problems, were much criticized. Under this pressure, the Ruler decided in August 1975 to dissolve the National Assembly, suspend the Constitution and take over legislative as well as executive power.

During 1976–7, there was no plan to resume parliamentary life in Baḥrayn; expectations for reconvening of the National Assembly did not materialize. The Government continued to suppress opposition activities, while trying to gain prestige by tackling three major issues: social security, aliens and diversification of the economy.

POLITICAL AFFAIRS

OPPOSITION ACTIVITIES

The dissolution of the National Assembly in August 1975 had been accompanied by the detention of people suspected of subversive or other oppositional activities. According to Amnesty International, at least some of those detained were still in prison awaiting trial in 1976–7. Amnesty also claimed that in November 1976, after the murder of Abdalla Madani, owner and editor of the weekly *al-Mawāqif*, 250 people were detained and 50 tortured: several died as a result of torture, and others were sent to hospital.

According to official reports, all the detainees belonged to the Popular Front for the Liberation of Oman and the Arab Gulf (PFLOAG), "an illegal communist organization." Only five were brought to trial charged with the murder of Madani; three were found guilty and sentenced to death. Their executions were the first in Baḥrayn since 1954 and were intended as a deterrent against increased subversion. The other two accused were acquitted, but remained in prison charged with possessing arms and belonging to the illegal PFLOAG. The authorities insisted that the murder was political; the accused denied this, claiming that it was carried out under the influence of alcohol. The Minister of the Interior did not deny Amnesty International's accusations. He only claimed that those detained belonged to an illegal organization whose aim was to destroy the social and political system in the Gulf region and to spread subversive principles. He added that PFLOAG had been able to infiltrate youth clubs and other organizations, and that the government had closed two of these clubs.[1]

Another member of the PFLOAG was sentenced in April 1977 to ten years imprisonment for an attempted bomb attack on a police station and for threatening a local newspaper publisher. The suspect was already in police custody following the dissolution of the National Assembly; a quantity of home-made explosives was found in his house during a police raid.

ARMED FORCES
The Army numbers 2,300 and consists of one infantry battalion and one armoured car squadron. It is equipped with eight *Saladin* armoured cars; eight *Ferret* scout cars; six 81mm mortars and six 120mm recoilless rifles. There are nine patrol launches and two *Scout* helicopters which are manned by police.[2]

SOCIAL AFFAIRS
SOCIAL LEGISLATION
The government passed a number of laws in the social and labour fields in the second half of 1976. A social insurance law covered industrial accidents, sickness, unemployment and death, and also maternity and family allowances. The insurance scheme, compulsory and contributory, was administered by an independent office supervised by the Ministry of Labour and Social Affairs.

A social security law, which came into force on 1 October, introduced a pension system for workers instead of granting a lump sum on retirement. The scheme was initially implemented in companies with more than 1,000 workers, but will eventually be comprehensive and cover men and women, Baḥraynis and aliens.

EMPLOYMENT
A third law had two main aims: to improve the quality of the labour force and give priority to Baḥrayni workers. It provided for the establishment of training offices, manned by qualified staff, in every company employing more than 200 workers in order to upgrade skills. The law, which came into force on 1 January 1977, also tightened controls by requiring employers to notify the Ministry of Labour and Social Affairs of any vacancy which they proved could not be filled by Baḥraynis. This law was an important part of the attempt to solve two of the country's most critical problems—the severe shortage of skilled manpower and the urgent need to prevent aliens becoming a majority. In the past, there was a 3:2 ratio of Baḥraynis to non-Baḥraynis in the labour force; but during the economic boom of 1974–6, the ratio tilted in favour of the aliens and came closer to 1:1.

FOREIGN RELATIONS
Baḥrayn generally follows Saudi foreign policy at Arab League meetings as well as in international forums. It does not have diplomatic relations with the USSR, and remains somewhat suspicious of Iran, although the latter has entirely given up its demand to annex the country. However, Baḥrayn tried to maintain good relations with Tehran while at the same time increasing co-operation with Saudi Arabia as well as other Gulf littoral states.

RELATIONS WITH SAUDI ARABIA
Apart from economic aid and co-operation (see below), the most important development in relations with Saudi Arabia was the building of a major airbase in Baḥrayn—at an old RAF airstrip south of the Awali-Zallaq road—to be used by the Saudis. Due to become operational by the end of 1977, this was the first Saudi military base outside the country, and was considered a natural extension of the Saudi air defence system, as well as a contribution to the collective security of the Arab Gulf and to the defence of Baḥrayn. No protests were heard against the airbase, even from Iran, which would be explained by the fact that the Iranians were also maintaining a military presence in Oman, ostensibly to preserve Gulf stability and security. The construction of the Saudi airbase coincided with the American relinquishment of naval facilities at Jufair base.

TERMINATION OF NAVAL AGREEMENT WITH US

On 30 June 1977, the US Navy's Middle East force—comprising a three-ship fleet and headquarters—handed over its Jufair naval and airbase to the Baḥrayni Government at the termination of the six-year lease agreement. The fleet continued to operate in the area, but without the home port in Jufair. It also maintained a lower profile in the island, as required under two new agreements. The first provided facilities to the fleet when it called periodically at Baḥrayni ports; the other permitted the US to maintain in Baḥrayn—probably in the US installations in Jufair—the Defence Department School and an administrative office. The new arrangement probably added some difficulties to the operations of the fleet, but basically nothing was changed. But for Baḥrayn, "facilities without a military base" caused much relief, because the former agreement "constituted a balloon that could exploded by anyone wanting to make senseless accusations."[3] However, in October 1977, there were rumours that the official information was not true and that the old agreement remained in force.

ECONOMIC AFFAIRS (0.396 Baḥrayni dinars = US$1; 0.731 BD = £1 sterling)

DEVELOPING SERVICE INDUSTRIES

The Government came to the conclusion that huge industrial complexes could not be built, and that the need to diversify economic resources necessitated by the gradual fall in oil production could more suitably be based on service industries. The aim was to turn Baḥrayn into a service centre for the Gulf littoral states and for international companies. Several additional factors contributed to this decision. First, the great boom in industrialization in the Gulf states and the need for foreign consultants and managers with their headquarters in Baḥrayn. Second, the decline of Beirut as a financial centre in the Middle East. Third, the natural advantage of Baḥrayn's location in the centre of the Gulf, with good communications and transport facilities. (The basis for these had been established much earlier when Baḥrayn was the centre of British administration in the Gulf.) Fourth, the growing co-operation among Arab Gulf littoral states, which had already shown the practical advantages of turning Baḥrayn into a centre for service industries. For example, the drydock—financed by OAPEC member-states for the repair and overhaul of ships in the Gulf—was built in Baḥrayn and started operating in October 1977. Fifth, Baḥrayn is more convenient for the personnel of foreign firms than other Gulf states because it is relatively liberal in the observance of Islamic laws and traditions.

During 1976–7, Baḥrayn already began implementing its new economic policy by slowing down the pace of growth in public expenditure, and concentrating on small service projects. Many licences were granted by the Government to banks to join the tax-free offshore banking scheme introduced in mid-1975, their number reaching 67 in 1977. The Gulf Air headquarters was also in the process of enlargement. A new Baḥrayn-British venture, Arabian Exhibition Management, was established in May 1977 with the aim of making Baḥrayn the major industrial exhibition centre for the region. Foreign firms also began to establish their headquarters there: Reuters inaugurated its Financial News Service Monitor in Baḥrayn in February 1977—the first centre in the Middle East to be connected to the world-wide retrieval system for financial information.

Before Baḥrayn could hope to become an attractive service centre, however, the Government needed to solve three problems: the shortage of housing and hotel accommodation, the high cost of living, and competition from other Gulf principalities. New housing projects were started in 1976–7, and contracts awarded to build hotels. In July 1977, the Government also established a central housing authority to ensure better control over all housing projects and reduce high prices.

Manamah was considered one of the world's four most expensive cities. Food prices were already being subsidized by the Government; but high salaries, also an important factor, were not so easily controlled. A survey by the Union Bank of Switzerland disclosed that a typical manager's secretary (with shorthand, typing and one foreign language) earned 50% more than her counterpart in New York and nearly four times more than one in London.[4]

All efforts to reduce the rivalry of other Gulf principalities—also interested in diversifying their economy by establishing service industries—have so far failed; but the need for co-ordination was raised at almost every regional meeting. The main rivals are the principalities comprising the UAE, especially Dubay, which is trying to build a drydock; in October 1977, it also started to operate a regional exhibition centre (the Middle East Construction Exhibition 77) sponsored by its Chamber of Commerce. Baḥrayn decided to try to outstrip its competitors by developing specialization with quality services.

SAUDI FINANCIAL AID AND CO-OPERATION

Like Oman, Baḥrayn has to rely on foreign financial aid to carry out its development projects. The main financial contributors have been the Gulf Arab oil-producing countries, especially Saudi Arabia, which has increased its assistance. The Arab oil-producing states of the Gulf agreed to support the budget to the sum of $100m a year, while the development funds of Kuwait, Saudi Arabia and Abu Dhabi were committed to electricity projects up to 1980.

Saudi aid and co-operation included the financing and building of a sports city ($138m) and the construction of a low-income housing project ($10m). The Saudis decided to finance the entire cost of the Baḥrayn-Saudi causeway to be started in 1978—an important contribution to Baḥrayn's hope of establishing a service centre on the island. It also offered Baḥrayn the annual income of the Abu Sa'fah oilfield on its border (c. $100m); and a joint cement works at Hufuf (Saudi Arabia 75%, Baḥrayn 25%) with a capacity of 1.8m tons of cement a year and 6,000 tons of clinker.

GOVERNMENT FINANCE (million Baḥrayni dinars)

	1973	*Actuals 1974*	*1975*	*Expected Actuals 1976*	*Budget Estimates 1977*
Revenues and grants	**45.1**	**123.7**	**135.0**	**191.5**	**224.6**
Oil revenues	29.4	103.4	110.9	156.4	149.6
Non-oil revenues	15.7	18.1	24.1	34.5	45.0
Grants	—	2.2	—	0.6	30.0
Expenditures	**42.1**	**77.9**	**121.8**	**202.2**	**249.5**
Current expenditures	34.5	44.4	67.6	88.0	111.0
Capital expenditures	7.6	33.5	54.2	114.2	138.5
Surplus or deficit (-)	3.0	45.8	13.2	-10.7	-24.9
Net extrabudgetary operations[1]	-5.4	-9.3	23.4	4.3	—
Financing (surplus-)	**2.4**	**-36.5**	**-36.6**	**6.4**	**24.9**

[1] *Residual item reflecting mainly transactions through the Government's Reserve Fund Account. Data: Ministry of Finance and National Economy.*

PETROLEUM SECTOR

	1973	1974	1975	1976
		(million barrels)		
Production				
Crude oil from onshore field	24.9	24.6	22.3	21.3
Refined oil products	86.4	87.9	76.4	77.5
Share of Abu Sa'fah offshore oil	19.7	22.9	10.7	19.6
Revenue		(million Baḥrayni dinars)		
Total oil receipts	29.4	103.4	110.9	156.4
Abu Sa'fah oil receipts	11.7	40.0	37.8	68.3

Source: IMF Survey.

EXPORTS OF PETROLEUM PRODUCTS (thousand US barrels)

	1972	1973	1974	1975
Naphtha	5,835	7,501	10,098	5,709
Gasoline	7,099	8,342	9,366	8,996
Kerosine	982	1,441	2,320	2,841
Jet Fuel	14,100	10,378	7,674	7,230
Diesel	14,264	19,166	18,310	18,723
Fuel	29,724	32,549	37,152	26,730
Lube-Dist	592	880	662	632
Asphalt	229	279	276	423
Sulphur	—	—	—	168
L.P.G.	—	—	—	99
L.A.R.	3,631	2,422	—	—

Source: Baḥrayn Ministry of Finance and National Economy, *Statistical Abstract.*

BALANCE OF PAYMENTS (million US dollars)

	1973	1974	1975	1976
Non-oil exports and re-exports	149.5	181.4	212.5	345.6
Imports	-323.8	-445.3	-589.2	-980.6
Services, transfers and nonmonetary capital (net)	*49.8*	*82.0*	*176.3*	*232.3*
Monetary movements (net (increase in assets -)	*23.3*	*-111.8*	*-125.3*	*-53.6*

Source: IMF Survey.

FOREIGN TRADE BY CLASSIFICATION (thousand Baḥrayni dinars)

	Exports		Imports	
	1974	1975	1974	1975
Food and Live Animals	7,874	4,878	24,854	24,695
Beverages and Tobacco	1,512	1,972	4,583	5,965
Crude Materials, Inedible (except fuels)	369	292	2,776	2,976
Mineral Fuels, Lubricants and related materials	476	368	4,174	4,222
Animal and Vegetable Oils and Fats	21	7	276	485
Manufactured Goods classified chiefly by material	1,173	1,191	48,084	57,017
Chemicals	39,741	47,021	14,778	18,521
Machinery and Transport Equipment	8,733	13,091	52,548	85,973
Miscellaneous Manufactured Articles	11,743	15,058	23,473	32,957
Commodities and Transactions not classified according to kind	80	74	330	90
Total	**71,722**	**83,952**	**175,876**	**232,900**

Source: Baḥrayn Ministry of Finance and National Economy, *Statistical Abstract.*

EXPORTS, BY DESTINATION (million US dollars)

	1972	*1973*	*1974*	*1975*	*1976*
Japan	23.5	67.8	368.8	169.9	234.3
Saudi Arabia	20.1	37.4	61.6	80.3	167.5
Singapore	25.3	28.6	83.0	74.0	119.4
US	20.0	18.1	129.3	251.7	119.0
Australia	32.8	41.0	162.4	101.6	106.6
United Arab Emirates	4.5	11.2	36.9	59.4	84.5
Philippines	0.2	1.3	43.1	40.8	49.6
UK	19.6	35.6	56.6	40.8	30.3
Others	55.3	68.4	228.7	288.8	337.0
Total	**201.3**	**309.4**	**1,170.4**	**1,107.3**	**1,248.2**
EEC	24.6	41.1	77.7	52.2	54.2

Source: IMF, *Direction of Trade.*

IMPORTS, BY SOURCE (million US dollars)

	1972	*1973*	*1974*	*1975*	*1976*
Saudi Arabia	134.6	196.2	687.2	621.8	703.2
UK	53.8	60.1	65.1	108.2	172.8
US	29.2	43.9	80.3	91.8	145.1
Japan	28.8	37.6	65.3	69.2	135.8
West Germany	8.0	12.8	20.9	29.0	62.8
South Korea	—	0.7	1.4	2.2	48.0
Australia	16.7	32.8	23.5	22.6	45.3
China (PRC)	—	18.8	28.4	36.5	38.4
Others	52.3	106.5	159.6	141.6	312.6
Total	**323.4**	**509.4**	**1,131.7**	**1,188.9**	**1,664.0**
EEC	82.6	101.0	133.7	217.4	328.2

Source: IMF, *Direction of Trade.*

NOTES

1. *Al-Mawāqif*, Manamah; 21 March 1976.
2. *The Military Balance 1977–78* (London: International Institute for Strategic Studies).
3. *Akhbār al-Khalīj*, 29 June 1977.
4. *Financial Times*, London; 14 December 1976.

Kuwait

Kuwait became independent in June 1961, and in the following year established a semi-constitutional monarchy with the ruling family—al-Sabāḥ—holding all key posts in the government, administration and army. Since then the National Assembly has gradually gained more influence, although the executive was nominated by the Ruler and was responsible to him. (Various key posts were given to loyal personalities, who were not members of the Royal family.) Huge oil revenues enabled Kuwait to develop industry and agriculture, public services and social welfare. They also attracted large numbers of expatriates (mainly Palestinians, Jordanians, Egyptians, Indians, Pakistanis and Iranians); who, according to the 1976 census, comprised c. 52% of the population. Pressures began to build up against the Government in recent years, both from the National Assembly and the expatriates. These intensified when the once-exemplary social services began to deteriorate. Housing was especially acute, but education and health services also declined, mainly due to the lack of skilled manpower and the rapid rise in population.

POLITICAL AFFAIRS

DISSOLUTION OF THE NATIONAL ASSEMBLY

The Prime Minister, Crown Prince Shaykh Jābir Aḥmad Jābir al-Sabāḥ, submitted his Government's resignation to the Ruler on 29 August 1976, on the grounds that its task had been made impossible by the almost wholly unco-operative attitude of the National Assembly. The Ruler accepted the Prime Minister's resignation, but at once asked him to form a new Government and issued a decree suspending several articles of the constitution. The changes affected the National Assembly; relations between the Assembly and the Ruler; limitations on introducing changes in the constitution; and restrictions on the enlargement of the Government. Although the National Assembly was dissolved, its members are to be remunerated until the end of their terms in 1979, and work continued on the new parliament building. The Ruler ordered a special committee to be set up to examine the constitution; any proposed changes were to be put to a referendum within four years.

Such measures indicated that the suspension of constitutional rule would only be temporary.

The ruling family thus gained direct control over the Government while they tried to solve the major economic and social problems which in their opinion endangered the monarchical system. The Assembly's powers were temporarily vested in the Head of State and the Council of Ministers, which was divided into six legislative committees: Political and Security; Information and Guidance; Public Utilities; Legislation; Education, Social and Health; and Economic Affairs.

The Ruler also announced a number of curbs on the press which had previously enjoyed a large measure of freedom. A special decree was issued introducing changes in the law on all published material. This restored the Government's power (previously revoked by the Assembly in 1972) to suspend the publication of a newspaper by an administrative order for a period of up to three months, or to prevent its publication by a court injunction: 1) if it was proved to be serving the interests of a foreign country, or a foreign agency, or to be receiving foreign financial aid without official permission; or 2) when its policy was against the national interest. The

Prime Minister spoke of "those who do not believe in the national interest," accusing them of distorting the freedom granted under the constitution and creating chaos designed to destroy values, beliefs and genuine Arab ethics. He added that press freedom had resulted in some papers becoming tools in the service of elements alien to Kuwait. The Deputy Prime Minister and Minister of Information advised newspaper editors to refrain from speculating on internal political affairs and controversies in inter-Arab relations. Shortly after these warnings, several dailies and weeklies well-known for their Leftist ideas (e.g. *Hadaf, Talīʻa, Risāla*) were closed for three months, and articles or announcements financed by other Arab states cancelled.

Several factors contributed to this interruption of the democratic process. First was the growing power of the National Assembly. The 1975 elections had brought a greater number of young and educated men into the Assembly which gradually refused to act merely as a rubber-stamp. About one-third of the Assembly members were known to have independent views—a majority of them Leftist, while others belonged to wealthy, well-established and Rightist rivals of the ruling family. Pragmatism dictated that Left and Right co-operate as an opposition group. Under its influence, and sometimes even pressure, the Assembly frequently took an independent line on foreign and domestic issues. For example, the Assembly adopted pro-Palestinian and anti-Syrian resolutions during the crisis in Lebanon, thus endangering the traditional neutral policy of Kuwait in inter-Arab conflicts. The Assembly also adopted a firm stand on oil affairs, forcing the Government to limit oil production to preserve resources; it also resisted Government agreements with the oil companies in order to secure better terms. Many draft bills opposed by the Assembly were intentionally delayed. By mid-1976, Assembly debates had degenerated into strong personal attacks on Ministers, including even members of the Royal Family who were not usually criticized in Parliament.

Second, the Left increased its strength and influence. According to the Government, it had succeeded in penetrating socio-cultural clubs and trade unions, even seizing control of some of them.[1] The Leftist elements came mainly from foreign nationals, especially the Palestinians (and to a lesser extent from Lebanese, Syrians, Iraqis and Egyptians) and formed a majority in various federations and unions (see below). Gaining this control, they became even more active, distributing anti-Government leaflets, holding demonstrations, sharpening press criticism of the regime, and extending their influence to the National Assembly through Leftist members.

Third, there were some terrorist incidents—attributed to Leftist expatriates—including arson and placing explosives in public institutes. Drastic measures were threatened by the Minister of Interior and Defence, including deportations of "dangerous elements." Between 1975 to mid-1976, 10,700 people, almost all Arabs, were deported.[2]

Fourth, tension had grown within the large community of foreign nationals, especially after the outbreak of the civil war in Lebanon. This sharpened awareness of the fact that Kuwaitis had become a minority in their own country: the 1976 census showed that they comprised only 47.5% of the population (c. 501,230 out of 1,055,000).[3] The Kuwaitis saw this development as a threat to their national identity—mainly from the largest of the foreign communities, the Palestinians, who held influential positions in business and education and had put strong pressures on the Government to condemn Syrian intervention in Lebanon.

Fifth, agitation mounted in the foreign community—as well as among Kuwaitis—due to the showdown in industrial development because of manpower shortages, the limited domestic market and the country's marginal export potential (other than for oil). Above all, it resulted from the deterioration in education and health services, and especially housing. Aliens, who are not allowed to own property in Kuwait, were hardest hit. One of the first acts of the new Government was to announce a massive programme to provide homes for all Kuwaitis by 1980. It allocated $4,820m for housing in the 1976/7–1980/1 Five-Year Plan.

POLICIES OF THE NEW GOVERNMENT

A new Government was formed on 6 September 1976. In fact, it was the same Government which had resigned on 29 August, with the addition of three new Ministers in charge of Planning, Waqfs (which was again separated from the Ministry of Justice), and Legal and Administrative Affairs. The appointment of a member of the ruling family to the last portfolio indicated a determination by the new Government to give higher priority to legislative and administrative reforms. Indeed, it soon began to promulgate laws previously blocked by the National Assembly. These were concerned with preventing any further deterioration in internal security, and with promoting more widespread support for the Government by allocating funds to solve urgent local social and economic problems.

Among the measures approved were a new Social Insurance Act to cover accidents at work, sickness, disability, old age and death; a decree to bring Kuwait's legislation into line with Islamic law—the *Sharī'a*; a special law enabling Kuwaiti citizenship to be granted to non-Kuwaitis in the defence and police forces and the national guard; and special permission granted to Kuwaiti citizens to set up an independent oil company. Another decree established a constitutionally inviolate "Fund for Future Generations"—a decision taken because of the enormous difficulties of industrialization. It was launched with capital of $2,931m, to be replenished each year by 10% of the state's general reserve, with the aim of accumulating capital for the post-oil era.

These more liberal social measures were accompanied by greater press restrictions and stiffer penalties for offenders against the Press and Publication Law. A number of newspapers were suspended, although one court tried to defend press freedom in April 1977 by ruling that constructive criticism was permissible. Another decree provided for heavier punishments, including the death penalty for murder, kidnapping and rape. Sex offenders, hoaxers and rumour-mongers also faced stiffer penalties, and it was reported that the Government was proposing to introduce whipping as a deterrent to combat the rising crime rate. Furthermore, sabotage-warning systems were bought especially for guarding oil installations, and a British police expert was invited to "investigate" all aspects of national security.

Promises to amend the constitution and restore parliamentary activity had not materialized by the end of 1977. Instead, it was explained that the Assembly would reconvene only after a period of four years; also that amendments to the constitution and the electoral law would take a long time, since the constitution contained many "imported" articles which had proved unsuitable for Kuwait. Nevertheless, the nomination of the committee to revise the constitution was postponed several times—finally until 1978. In the meantime, people and associations were asked to express their views on the country's constitutional experience to the Ruler directly together with their suggestions for revision.

OPPOSITION ACTIVITIES

The Government's new measures produced strong criticism, especially from the Left; a storm of protest followed the dissolution of the National Assembly. This decision and other amendments to the constitution were condemned as illegal by such bodies as the General Federation of Kuwaiti Workers; the Writers', Lawyers',

Journalists' and Teachers' Unions; the Istiqlāl Club and the General Federation of Kuwaiti Students. Leaflets were distributed attacking the new measures.

The Government reacted by dismissing the boards and executives of these organizations, claiming that by involving themselves in political activities they had deviated from their societies' official aims and regulations. A number of people, mainly those involved in distributing leaflets, were arrested. The Government appointed new directors to these organizations in an effort to create a new non-Leftist leadership. However, in most cases the members refused to co-operate with the new leaders, whereupon the Government suspended their activities and sometimes even closed them down altogether. This happend with Kuwait's largest cultural and social society—Istiqlāl (independence) Club—which was dissolved on 28 July, and its assets liquidated.

However, towards the end of 1977, anti-regime activities seemed to be dying out, with only some newspapers continuing to criticize the Government. This trend was particularly evident after the Appeal Court's decision in April 1977 in favour of constructive press criticism.

DEFENCE AND SECURITY

1976 DEFENCE DEVELOPMENT PLAN

After about three years of discussion, the Government, the Supreme Defence Council and the National Assembly (until its dissolution) finally approved a new seven-year Defence Development Plan in 1976 at a cost of c. $3,000m. This provided for: (a) compulsory military service; (b) building of new military camps, a naval base, and new military colleges and technical schools; and (c) purchase of the most modern and sophisticated weapons and equipment from various sources, either West or East, according to a new policy of diversification of arms supply.

The main reason for this "major overhaul" of Kuwait's armed forces was the military aggrandizement of its neighbours, especially those in the north and the south. Iraq had several times engaged in aggressive activities, most recently in September 1976, as had Saudi Arabia in mid-1977 off the coast of the Partitioned Zone (see below). The decision to diversify sources of arms supplies was taken mainly to avoid any possibility of future political or economic pressure, and to have scope in choosing the most suitable modern weapons. Speculation that diversification was aimed at channelling more modern equipment to other armies, such as those confronting Israel, was strongly denied. Kuwait insisted that the weapons were mainly for its own defensive purposes, to preclude any military threat to its independence.

ARMS SUPPLY AGREEMENT WITH THE USSR

The most significant arms supply agreement was with the USSR, concluded in August 1976 and approved by the Kuwaiti government in November. This included the purchase of $400m worth of air-to-air and ground-to-air missiles, advanced artillery and tanks, and anti-personnel weapons. However, it soon became clear that the Kuwaitis were not ready to allow Soviet experts and instructors to train their army either inside Kuwait or in the USSR. The Soviets, on the other hand, insisted on a package deal including their own advisers and experts. Negotiations continued through exchanges of military delegations. Finally, in mid-1977, it was agreed to implement only that part of the agreement concerning the purchase of ground-to-air missiles, *SAM* 7. The Kuwaiti personnel were to be trained by Egyptian military experts both in Egypt and in Kuwait. Other parts of the agreement were postponed indefinitely, although the Kuwaitis claimed that they would be implemented in the near future. However, in the beginning of August, the Kuwaiti

Minister of the Interior and Defence denied that an arms deal had been signed with Moscow, and stated that Kuwait had no intention of signing such a deal "for the time being."[4]

The difficulties put in the way of these negotiations were undoubtedly caused by Kuwait's neighbours, especially Saudi Arabia, who have no relations with the USSR. They were anxious to exclude Soviet experts from the Gulf area, particularly at a time when they were doing their utmost to have them removed from the southern part of Arabia—the PDRY. The Kuwaitis were themselves involved in these efforts. They recognized the risks of Marxist indoctrination accompanying military training and the undesirability of letting Soviets into their military installations.

WESTERN ARMS SUPPLIES

The Kuwaitis did not neglect their traditional arms supplier—Britain—while buying more from France and the US. They were contracted to receive about four *Mirage* F1s from France every month (until they achieved squadron strength) and four *Skyhawk* bombers from the US; also *Hawk* anti-aircraft, *Sidewinder* air-to-air missiles, and troop carriers. Britain was to supply 150 *Chieftain* tanks. Negotiations also continued with the UK and France on further supplies of tanks, heavy artillery, military aircraft, missile ships and launchers for the new naval force.

DEVELOPING A NAVY

The need for a naval force became particularly urgent in view of the naval activities in the Gulf by Iran, Iraq and Saudi Arabia. Iraq had succeeded in capturing the islands of Warbah and Būbiyān which belonged to Kuwait, while Saudi Arabia occupied two Kuwaiti islands—Umm Maradim and Gharu—off the coast of the Partitioned Zone. In March 1977, the Government signed an agreement with a Japanese firm to build the first phase of the naval base, which was to be continued by Yugoslav and Pakistani experts. The latter also undertook to assist the Kuwaitis in building a naval force once the base was completed.

ARMED FORCES

Total armed forces number 10,000. Defence expenditure in 1976 was 592.2m dinars ($2.06 bn). Military service is compulsory for 18 months. The 8,500-strong Army consists of one armoured brigade and two infantry brigades and is equipped with 12 *Chieftain*, 50 Vickers, 50 *Centurion* medium tanks; 90 *Saladin* armoured cars and 20 *Ferret* scout cars; 130 *Saracen* armoured personnel carriers; ten 25-pounder guns; 20 AMX 155mm howitzers and SS-11, *HOT, TOW* and *Vigilant* anti-tank guided weapons. The Navy numbers 500 (Coastguard) and is equipped with 12 inshore patrol boats; 16 patrol launches and three landing craft. The Air Force numbers 1,000, excluding expatriate personnel, and is equipped with 49 combat aircraft; two fighter-bomber squadrons (forming) with four A-4M; one ground-attack fighter squadron with four *Hunter* FGA57 and five T67; one interceptor squadron with ten *Lightning* F53, two T55 and 12 *Mirage* F-1CK; one counter-insurgency squadron with 12 BAC-167 *Strikemaster* Mark 83 and one helicopter squadron with six AB-204B, four AB-205, two *Whirlwind*, 24 *Gazelle* and 12 *Puma*; two DC-9, two DHC-4, one *Argosy* and two *Hercules* transports; six *Jet Provost* T51 trainers (in store) and 50 *Improved HAWK* surface-to-air missiles. (Eight *Mirage* F-1BK/CK interceptors, 26 A-4KU and six TA-4KU ground-attack fighters are on order.)[5]

FOREIGN AFFAIRS

The main task of the Kuwaiti Foreign Ministry since independence in 1961, was, and still is, to secure the independent existence of this small but very rich state, and to help guarantee its future financial prosperity. The following principles were therefore adopted. 1) Maximum co-operation between the Gulf littoral states to maintain peace, stability and prosperity in the area. Kuwait was very active in promoting this co-operation despite difficulties and traditional disputes (see above). 2) Strict neutrality in inter-Arab affairs, and qualified non-alignment in international relations. Kuwait is the only Gulf principality which maintains relations with both Western and Eastern blocs. 3) Extending financial aid mainly in the form of investments, to countries all over the Middle East, Africa, Asia, Latin America and, lately, even Eastern Europe.

Aid and investments are made through six financial bodies: (a) Kuwait Investment Company (KIC), 50% state-owned; (b) Kuwait Foreign Trading, Contracting and Investment Company (KFTCIC), 80% state-owned; (c) Kuwait International Investment Company (KIIC), privately owned; (d) Kuwait Fund for Arab Economic Development (KFAED), state-owned; active not only in the Arab but also the Third World; (e) Kuwait Real Estate Investment Consortium (KREIC), owned by private sector in co-operation with the government; (f) Kuwait International Finance Company (KIFCO), state-owned. A great many countries were given financial aid through these bodies in 1976–7.

The most important step in Kuwait's investment policy in 1977 was the agreement of March with Romania to establish a joint petrochemical complex on the Black Sea at a cost of $1,250m (49% by Kuwait). This will be fed with Kuwaiti crude oil—the first industrial investment in a communist state.

Kuwait's major preoccupation in 1977 was over developments affecting its own position in the Gulf, particularly its deteriorating relations with Saudi Arabia and its *rapprochement* with Iraq. Prior to the reconciliation with Iraq in July, the Kuwaitis strengthened their relations with Iran in order to minimize the possibility of an open attack against themselves.

RELATIONS WITH SAUDI ARABIA

Relations with Saudi Arabia became tense after the Kuwaitis had voted for the 10% increase in oil prices at the Doha OPEC conference, in opposition to the Saudi proposal for a 5% increase. (See essays on Middle East oil.) This tension was further aggravated by a number of other factors, such as Kuwait's opposition to the Egyptian-Saudi policy concerning a US-sponsored settlement of the conflict with Israel; by the fact that no agreement based on an equal share of profits between Saudi Arabia and Kuwait could be reached on the price of crude of the Japanese Arabian Oil Company (AOC) which operates an offshore oilfield in the Partitioned Zone; by strengthened relations between Kuwait and Iran; and, above all, by the Kuwaiti arms deal with the USSR.

The Saudis reacted in mid-1977 by seizing the two disputed Kuwaiti islands off the Partitioned Zone. Only in September, three months after the OPEC compromise on oil prices, did negotiations reopen on OAC crude prices leading to a settlement. However, the question of the islands occupied by Saudi Arabia remained unresolved.

RELATIONS WITH IRAQ

The Iraqis had taken the opportunity of the dissolution of the Kuwaiti Assembly in September 1976 to attack the regime and renew their demands for annexation; they even sent troops to invade a small area in northern Kuwait. Although Iraq was ready to come to terms in mid-1977, it insisted on holding the occupied Kuwaiti islands, Warbah and Būbiyān, at the mouth of the Shatt al-'Arab overlooking the approach to their naval base and port of Umm Qasr.

The Kuwaitis responded by sending their Minister of the Interior and Defence to Baghdad for talks from 27 June to 5 July 1977. These were described by Kuwaiti officials as the most significant approach to Iraq in the past decade. It was agreed that both sides would withdraw their border forces by distances of up to 15 km, and ease border formalities, a committee would be established comprising senior officials of the two Interior Ministries to follow up and solve routine border problems; and a ministerial committee would be formed to meet alternatively in Baghdad and Kuwait at frequent intervals to continue negotiations on border problems and develop bilateral relations.[6]

The troops were soon withdrawn from the disputed area and the border between the two countries were reopened. However, the question of the continued occupation by Iraq of the Kuwaiti islands of Warbah and Būbiyān was not solved. Reports that the Kuwaitis had agreed to a long-term lease of the islands to the Iraqis—thus formalizing the presence of Iraqi troops—were angrily denied.

Kuwait was also involved in other developments in the Gulf, especially in efforts to increase co-operation in political, financial, cultural and security fields (for details, see above).

INTER-ARAB RELATIONS

In inter-Arab relations, Kuwait tried hard to maintain its neutrality and preserve its position as an acceptable mediator. But because of internal pressure from the large Palestinian community and fear of anti-government activities, Kuwait sided with the Palestinians in Lebanon (although it refrained from attacking the Syrians); it also supported the Palestinian position concerning the US proposals for a settlement of the Middle East conflict. (See also essay on Inter-Arab Relations.)

RELATIONS WITH EAST AND WEST

The major issue for Kuwait on the international scene was the development of closer relations with the Soviet Union and other East European countries, which culminated in the (eventually abortive) arms deal with the Russians and the joint petrochemical venture with the Romanians. During 1977, cultural, scientific and health links and exchanges were expanded with the USSR, but no developments were reported concerning financial co-operation first requested by Moscow in 1976. Kuwait deposited only $30m in the Soviet Foreign Trade Bank.

The West continued to be the main source of imports to Kuwait and the main purchaser of exports. Leading suppliers were the US, Japan, West Germany and Britain. Western firms still predominate in international contracts, although Kuwait warned that because of inflationary pressures, it would approach firms in advanced Asian countries. In fact, a major change was the appearance of South Korean firms in the Gulf (including Kuwait) who promised to implement entire projects and provide the total labour force needed from Korea. They were principally successful in competing for infrastructure projects, such as roads, bridges and ports.

ECONOMIC AFFAIRS (0.281 Kuwaiti dinars = US$1; 0.520 KD = £1 sterling)

By 1977, it became evident that Kuwait had been largely successful in replacing Beirut as the banking and financial centre—the Zurich—of the Middle East. Two major factors contributed to this success. First, the fact that Kuwait can ensure a wide range of financial activities indefinitely because, at a production rate of 2m b/d, its large oil reserves will last from 60 to 100 years. Second, Kuwait was involved in financial aid and investments all over the world worth $20-22,000m (c. $16,000m from the state and $4-6,000m from private sources).

However, the country's financial situation was unstable because of a high rate of inflation—officially set at 15–20% per annum. This led the Minister of Finance to warn that unless people moderated their consumption (mainly imports), the Government would either have to raise taxes or the prices of essential services.

Kuwait's plans for extensive economic diversification, particularly in industry, ran into difficulties because of shortages in manpower, especially skilled manpower; the small domestic market; and poor prospects for exporting industrial products. Therefore, after the boom years of 1974–6, Kuwait faced a slowdown in industrial diversification. Attention turned to increasing investments and activities in infrastructure, with special emphasis on the social services (see above). The fact that industrialization cannot easily replace oil when resources are depleted was a further impetus to the Kuwaiti campaign to become a highly developed financial centre with banking, insurance, stock market and investment facilities. Only in this way can Kuwait hope to build for a future without oil.

GOVERNMENT EXPENDITURE (millions of Kuwaiti dinars)

	1973–74	*1974–75*	*1975–76**	*1976–77*
Defence, Security and Justice	71.0	75.3	143.0	149.7
Education	52.3	59.6	103.2	106.4
Health	23.8	28.1	50.2	59.7
Information	7.4	8.1	16.5	15.5
Social and Labour Affairs	7.7	8.2	17.2	18.6
Electricity and Water	14.1	15.6	27.7	30.4
Public Works	13.6	14.0	23.4	28.0
Communications	7.2	8.6	15.6	17.1
Customs and Ports	8.5	9.5	17.8	19.4
Finance	1.6	1.7	1.8	2.4
Oil	—	—	1.5	2.5
Housing and Govt. Property	3.3	4.1	5.9	13.7
Amiri Court and Other	20.8	20.8	32.2	40.3
Unclassified and Transfer Expenditures	207.1	567.9	284.2	425.3
Land Purchase Expenditure	25.1	135.0	89.2	80.0
Development Expenditure, of which:				
Public Works	30.4	49.7	96.5	140.1
Electricity and Water	31.3	43.5	91.3	99.1
Communications	5.6	4.9	12.7	15.5
Other	5.9	30.6	2.7	9.4
Total	**536.7**	**1,085.2**	**1,032.6**	**1,272.0**

*Fiscal year of 15 months.
Source: Central Bank of Kuwait, *Quarterly Statistical Bulletin.*

IMPORTS, BY SOURCE (millions of US dollars)

	1972	*1973*	*1974*	*1975*	*1976*
Japan	128	186	265	387	776
US	104	147	219	430	501
West Germany	66	82	173	273	370
UK	81	107	127	244	282
France	34	28	61	79	216
South Korea	6	10	18	31	196
Italy	37	44	62	108	186
Taiwan	12	27	29	41	107
Others	329	412	602	795	1,014
Total	**797**	**1,043**	**1,556**	**2,388**	**3,648**
EEC	258	313	520	808	1,197

Source: IMF, *Direction of Trade.*

EXPORTS, BY DESTINATION (millions of US dollars)

	1972	*1973*	*1974*	*1975*	*1976*
Japan	500	717	2,815	2,342	1,946
UK	401	474	1,705	714	892
Netherlands	348	363	395	839	703
Taiwan	88	101	365	444	625
South Korea	85	106	316	424	564
France	356	436	1,043	523	380
Saudi Arabia	30	63	72	126	272
Philippines	23	63	177	242	254
Others	1,075	1,467	4,073	3,532	2,620
Total	**2,906**	**3,790**	**10,961**	**9,186**	**8,256**
EEC	1,647	1,720	4,328	2,796	2,511

Source: IMF, *Direction of Trade.*

INDUSTRIAL PRODUCTION[1]

	1969	*1970*	*1971*	*1972*	*1973*	*1974*	*1975*	*197*
Brackish Water (mn gallon)	5,587	5,755	5,507	5,397	6,495	7,286	8,329	9,05
Potable Water (mn gallon)	5,866	6,635	7,674	8,584	9,191	10,031	11,601	14,38
Electric Energy (mn kwh)	2,012	2,213	2,636	3,295	3,668	4,092	4,653	5,20
Fertilizers (metric ton)	293,333	233,492	253,409	606,000	699,000	651,000	652,350	520,00
Sand-Lime Bricks (m^3)	97,225	87,882	196,446	230,451	148,383	166,121	170,477	213,55
Flour Milling (ton)	82,755	84,307	95,504	96,480	98,297	110,390	110,294	127,50
Chlorine (ton)	—	670	653	733	2,557	4,199	6,107	4,30
Caustic Soda (ton)	—	2,488	2,449	2,955	5,207	7,878	10,186	8,55
Salt (ton)	—	1,708	1,844	1,835	2,166	2,165	3,219	6,40
Hydrochloric Acid (gallon)	—	160,709	131,339	139,856	193,928	269,469	197,254	219,14
Sodium Hypochlorite (gallon)	—	166,270	94,368	105,646	393,900	1,939,400	2,907,520	1,327,92
Hydrogen (m^3)	—	12,854	14,805	15,576	17,723	28,895	24,108	19,49

[1] Other than crude petroleum and refined products.
Source: Central Bank of Kuwait, *Quarterly Statistical Bulletin.*

NOTES

1. Political parties are forbidden in Kuwait.
2. *Baghdad Observer*, 6 August 1976.
3. *Kuwait Times*, 24 January 1977.
4. *Al-Anbā'*, 9 August 1977.
5. *The Military Balance 1977-78* (London: International Institute of Strategic Studies).
6. R Baghdad, 3 July 1977.

Oman

Oman became independent at the end of 1971, 18 months after Sultan Sa'īd ibn Taymūr had been deposed by his son Qābūs with the approval of the royal family and Britain. Qābūs continued his father's autocratic regime, but with some important modifications. He started to establish a modern administrative system and embarked on development projects, making use of growing oil revenues which by then had become a major factor in the national budget. However, a large part of the budget was used to suppress the rebellion in the province of Dhufar which had started in the mid-1960s and was supported by the People's Democratic Republic of Yemen (PDRY), with the aid of the People's Republic of China, and later the USSR and Cuba. Oman was assisted by British army personnel (even after independence), a Jordanian contingent and an Iranian expeditionary force of c. 3–5,000 persons including air force and air defence units, which entered the war in 1973. The rebellion was gradually brought under control, and in March 1976, an agreement was reached through the mediation of Saudi Arabia and other Arab Gulf states which provided for an ending of the rebellion, suspension of all aid to the rebels, and evacuation of all foreign military units. Although a member of the Arab League since 1971, Oman had continued to encounter hostility from the PDRY as well as Libya, Syria, Iraq and Algeria. However, relations began to improve after the March agreement, especially with Iraq.

During the period under review the Omani Government was mainly occupied with the liquidation of the remnants of the rebellion in Dhufar, while at the same time improving relations with its Arab neighbours and implementing its development plan with the help of Saudi Arabia and Kuwait.

DEFENCE AND SECURITY

END OF DHUFAR REBELLION, BUT NO RECONCILIATION

In the second half of 1976 and the beginning of 1977, the Omani Government claimed that military action against the rebels in Dhufar Province and along the border with the PDRY had ended; that the Popular Front for the Liberation of Oman (PFLO) was crushed, and that remnants of its military units had retreated to their bases in South Yemen. Members and leaders of the PFLO (among them the commander of military and ideological training and a member of the Dhufar Central Committee) surrendered after returning to Oman from the PDRY. On the other hand, the PFLO leaders in Aden claimed that military activities were still going on in Dhufar, and the Voice of the Oman Revolution continued to broadcast from Aden—issuing communiqués describing PFLO raids. Evidence that the agreement had not brought all resistance to an end was supplied by the continuing Marxist military presence in Oman and periodic announcements of the surrender of armed PFLO units crossing over from the PDRY.

At the end of 1976, the Omani Government still refused to ask Iran to withdraw its troops in accordance with the March 1976 agreement. Saudi Arabia and other Arab Gulf states involved in the mediation were primarily interested in removing the Iranians from the Arabian Peninsula. Tehran declared its readiness to withdraw its expeditionary force the moment it was asked to do so by the Sultan of Oman. But he insisted that before such an approach could be made, the PDRY would first have to reaffirm its good intentions, expel the Cuban military advisers, stop sending infiltrators into Dhufar, and recognize Oman as a friendly neighbouring state.

At the beginning of 1977, Saudi Arabia, Kuwait and other Gulf and Arab Red Sea littoral states increased pressure on both Oman and the PDRY to move to a full reconciliation, as this was becoming an important factor in the negotiations to establish close co-operation among the Red Sea littoral states (see essay on Inter-Arab Relations). The Omani Government agreed to the evacuation of the Iranian expeditionary force from Dhufar and the British from the RAF base on the island of Masirah. The Iranians started to pull out in the second half of January 1977, leaving a residual force in Oman to operate radar installations and anti-aircraft units. The Iranians also continued to operate "Midway," their principal logistics depot and airbase in Dhufar, and to fly across Omani airspace. The Omani Armed Forces, still developing their air defence system after receiving the first batch of *Rapier* missiles from Britain, asked the Iranians to continue their aid in this field. An official Iranian spokesman said that its military support for Oman would continue, and that the army units leaving Oman would return to Dhufar in the shortest possible time if needed.

THE AIRBASE ON MASIRAH

In March 1977, the British handed over their Masirah Island airbase and their station near Salalah to the Omani Government, leaving behind c. 200 technical advisers with the task of gradually transferring the command of the Omani Armed Forces to the Omanis themselves.

Reports that Oman was going to allow the US to set up an airbase on Masirah Island—which caused alarm in the PDRY—were categorically denied by the Sultan, who said that if the US or any other friendly state asked for transit rights or refuelling facilities on Masirah, Oman would grant them, but it would not allow the establishment of any permanent foreign military installations. He added that the island would become a training centre for the Omani air force.

The idea of establishing a US base would have aroused strong reaction in the US as well as in the Arab world, and would have caused considerable political embarrassment. However, it was expected that in due course the Sultan would allow the island to be used for US reconnaissance flights over oil tanker routes—as it was in the time of the British. There were also suggestions that Oman had tried to interest Iran and Saudi Arabia in using Masirah as a military base (the latter is already establishing an airbase in the neighbouring state of Baḥrayn).

ARMED FORCES

Total armed forces number 13,000, excluding expatriate personnel. Defence expenditure in 1977 was 158m Omani riyals ($457m). Military service is voluntary. The Army numbers 11,800 and consists of two brigade headquarters; eight infantry battalions; one Royal Guard regiment; one artillery regiment; one signals regiment; one armoured car squadron; one parachute squadron and one engineer squadron. It is equipped with 36 *Saladin* armoured cars; 24 75mm pack howitzers; 25-pounder, 36 105mm and three 5.5-in guns; 120mm mortars and ten *TOW* anti-tank guided weapons. The 450-strong Navy consists of three patrol vessels (one Royal Yacht, two ex-Dutch mine counter-measures); one training ship (ex-1,500-ton logistic ship); four fast patrol boats and four small landing craft. (Two minesweepers, three fast patrol boats and one logistic support ship are on order.) The Air Force numbers 750 and has 36 combat aircraft; one ground-attack fighter/reconnaissance squadron with 16 *Hunter*; one ground-attack fighter squadron with 12 *Jaguar*; one counter-insurgency/training squadron with eight BAC-167; one tactical transport squadron with 15 *Skyvan*; two transport squadrons, one with three BAC-111 and two *Viscount* and one with seven BN *Defender* and one *Falcon*; one helicopter squadron with 20 AB-205, three AB-206, one AB-212 and five AB-214 helicopters and one surface-to-air missile squadron with 28 *Rapier* surface-to-air missiles. Paramilitary forces consist of 3,000 in the tribal Home Guard (Firqats).

ARAB RELATIONS

The continuing small-scale activities of the Dhufar rebels became less important in 1977 than the need to reconcile PDRY and Oman. Although President Numayrī of Sudan announced in March that, as a result of his mediation, PDRY would establish diplomatic relations with Oman, this was denied from Aden. In fact, the PDRY reaffirmed its support for the PFLO in a joint communiqué published in March following an official visit of Cuba's Prime Minister, Fidel Castro, to South Yemen. Cuba also declared its support for the PFLO in its "struggle for total national liberation and liquidation of foreign and Anglo-Iranian bases."

Nevertheless, attempts to create a peaceful atmosphere in the area were pursued during various official visits of the Sultan of Oman and his Minister of State for Foreign Affairs to other Gulf principalities, Saudi Arabia, Sudan, Egypt and Jordan; and at various regional conferences, such as the Red Sea leaders' conference held in Ta'izz in March 1977. Omani concessions to pave the way for reconciliation helped it in consolidating relations with Arab states such as Sudan, Syria, Morocco and Iraq. But, above all, they helped Oman to draw more financial aid from those interested in peace and stability in the area, such as Saudi Arabia and Kuwait.

ECONOMIC AFFAIRS (0.345 Omani riyals = US$1; 0.639 OR = £1 sterling)

1976 FINANCIAL CRISIS

Oman faced a serious financial crisis in 1976, mainly due to its growing balance of payments deficit. One reason was that c. 70% of national revenues were allocated to military expenditure, not only because of the war in Dhufar, but also because rapid modernization of the Omani army was necessary for it to replace the foreign expeditionary forces. Rapid economic development was also accompanied by a great deal of extravagance, waste and inefficiency, and there was profligate spending by the Sultan who, like his father, remained to a large extent isolated from the people and government activities. Finally, the drop in oil revenues helped to worsen the crisis (production from several new oilfields found in south Oman starting only in 1977).

The immediate measures taken in 1976 were: (a) to concentrate on completing projects already under construction; (b) to stop all work on new projects and on planning new projects, and (c) to adopt a new economic policy, which was the basis for the new Five-Year Development Plan 1976–80.

FIVE-YEAR DEVELOPMENT PLAN (1976–80)

The new policy proposed a gradual cut in government expenditure, consolidation of the national debt and, above all, diversification of economic resources. The Government realized that although oil would continue to provide a sound basis for the national economy for some time, it should not be relied on solely. Therefore, the Five-Year Plan included projects to develop raw materials (coal, copper); agriculture (to achieve self-sufficiency in food by early 1980); fisheries (to become an exporter from 1978) and, above all, infrastructure.

Under the Plan, growth of more than 50% in private consumption was expected, with government consumption remaining stable. Output in manufacturing, electricity and water, and house ownership would double, while that of agriculture, fisheries and internal trade would rise by over 50%. The Plan provided for public sector investment of $2,710m and private sector of c. $1,220m. Major government investment would be: petroleum and mining ($446m), civil works and construction ($437m), electricity and water ($123m), ports ($121m), agriculture and fisheries ($118m), and manufacturing ($116m). Major private sector investment would be: petroleum and mining ($481m), housing and construction ($420m), and manufacturing ($211m).

FOREIGN AID

In the first year of the new Plan, Oman faced difficulties because it was still suffering from a lack of money, of skilled manpower and of basic infrastructure. But the first problem was at least partially solved during 1977 by richer neighbours in the Gulf—Saudi Arabia, Kuwait and the UAE—providing financial aid. Four Saudi loans totalling $97m were provided in July 1977 to finance the construction of 135 km of road and 16 administrative and social centres in Dhufar. This decision revived speculations first raised in 1975 of another Saudi interest: to construct through or near Dhufar an alternative outlet for its oil to the Indian Ocean coast terminal.

The Saudis also granted $100m for a copper mining project to be carried out by Oman Mining Co, a joint venture of the Omani Government (51%) and a US firm (49%). The Saudis also gave $250m to help the Omani Government pay for the purchase of an air defence system from Britain. The Saudis were reported to be willing to give Oman up to $1,000m by the end of 1977, on condition that they agree to map out the border between them in a special committee comprised of delegates from both sides. The Saudis nominated their delegates, but by August 1977, the Omanis had nominated only their Chairman, the Minister of the Interior.

Kuwait's aid included participation in the construction of a cement factory (40%); a loan of $45m from Kuwaiti funds for a gas pipeline; two loans totalling $47m from the Kuwait Fund for Arab Economic Development (KFAED) to help finance the development of natural gas projects; a 39% share in a new housing bank to help finance housing projects; and participation in several agricultural projects. Kuwait was also discussing plans for a $250m joint petrochemical and joint refinery venture.

The UAE provided Oman with a loan of $15m from the Abu Dhabi Fund for Arab Economic Development (AFAED) for the gas pipeline project, and a $31m grant to finance the building of a 132 km road, which would link Ibrī and Nizwā. The UAE was already building a road linking the town of al-Ayn (not far from the border between Abu Dhabi and Oman) and the town of Sohār on the Omani coast.

BUDGET ACCOUNTS AND PUBLIC DEBT (millions of Omani riyals)

	1974	*1975*	*1976*
EXPENDITURE			
Interest on Public Debt	3.3	6.0	6.3
Other Current Expenditure	66.0	75.0	114.0
Gross Capital Formation	127.0	157.0	203.0
Other Capital Expenditure	51.0	16.0	—
National Security and Defence	118.0	241.0	274.5
Total:	**365.3**	**495.0**	**597.8**
RECEIPTS			
Oil Revenue	291.5	373.1	470.0
Other Receipts	11.7	14.6	25.0
Aid	8.3	71.6	18.0
Total:	**311.5**	**459.3**	**513.0**
Balance (+) or (-)	-53.8	-35.7	-84.8

Source: UN, *Statistical Yearbook.*

ENERGY PRODUCTION AND CONSUMPTION (in million tonnes of Coal equivalent)

	Production Total	*Consumption Total*
1972	20.66	0.13
1973	21.51	0.15
1974	21.27	0.23
1975	25.01	0.26

Source: UN, *Statistical Yearbook.*

IMPORTS, BY SOURCE (million US$)

	1972	*1973*	*1974*	*1975*	*1976*
UK	47.5	59.8	110.6	131.2	139.8
United Arab Emirates	—	—	—	120.7	125.7
Japan	7.7	13.8	49.2	53.0	87.7
West Germany	5.6	8.7	43.3	68.0	45.7
US	7.3	10.2	40.5	64.6	44.0
India	3.9	5.8	18.8	27.5	33.6
Netherlands	5.7	6.9	19.5	35.6	22.3
France	82.9	12.8	19.5	20.8	20.8
Others	25.3	44.6	156.6	148.0	147.7
Total	**185.9**	**162.6**	**458.0**	**669.4**	**667.3**
EEC	153.3	101.5	227.5	275.6	243.2

Source: IMF, *Direction of Trade.*

EXPORTS, BY DESTINATION (million US$)

	1972	*1973*	*1974*	*1975*	*1976*
Japan	97.5	116.2	400.9	527.0	680.9
US	6.7	6.1	33.1	127.2	248.0
France	34.3	56.1	135.8	96.8	100.6
Canada	4.9	32.0	132.5	54.0	93.6
UK	8.3	10.4	60.9	93.5	19.9
West Germany	—	—	6.4	7.9	18.7
Singapore	19.2	20.1	9.6	83.3	16.4
Italy	—	—	91.9	6.8	14.0
Others	60.2	85.0	262.2	448.5	379.6
Total	**231.1**	**325.9**	**1,133.3**	**1,445.0**	**1,571.7**
EEC	60.9	96.1	352.7	493.2	153.3

Source: IMF, *Direction of Trade.*

Qatar

Qatar achieved independence from the British colonial power at the end of 1971. Its autocratic regime was left in the hands of the ruling Thāni family—related to the ruling Saudi family—whose members continued to occupy most of the key government posts.

During 1976-7, Qatar became an international centre because its Oil Minister was elected president of OPEC. However, internally it was mainly occupied with the question of the Crown Princeship, with its oil and gas industries and the problem of diversifying the economy.

POLITICAL AFFAIRS

THE QUESTION OF THE CROWN PRINCESHIP

The Ruler issued a decree on 31 May 1977 appointing his eldest son, Maj-Gen Shaykh Ḥamad bin Khalīfa al-Thāni (a Sandhurst Military Academy graduate and Commander-in-Chief of the armed forces) as Crown Prince and Minister of Defence in the newly established Ministry of Defence. He continued to retain his post as C-in-C, thus securing the backing of the army in case of any attempt to remove him or prevent his succession. The appointment settled a long and tortuous dispute that had existed since the present Ruler seized power in February 1972, and had brought the government to a virtual standstill. It was a compromise, putting an end to the struggle for succession mainly between Shaykh Suḥaym (the younger brother of the Ruler, and Minister for Foreign Affairs) and Shaykh 'Abd al-'Aziz (the younger son of the Ruler and the Minister of Finance and Oil).

The reasons for the 5-year old dispute were the absence of any clear tradition marking out a definite line of succession; and the complicated dynastic history of the ruling family, considered to be one of the biggest in the Gulf. On the death of the present Ruler's father, Shaykh Ḥamad bin 'Abdalla, Shaykh Khalīfa was too young to rule so his uncle, Shaykh 'Ali bin 'Abdalla, assumed power, appointing Shaykh Khalīfa as Crown Prince. However, when Shaykh 'Ali abdicated in 1960, he was succeeded by his son Aḥmad and not by Khalīfa. Twelve years later, in 1972, Shaykh Khalīfa, then Prime Minister, managed with the help of his brother Suḥaym and the backing of the Saudis, to seize power, promising his brother the Premiership and the Crown Princeship. This promise never materialized because Shaykh Khalīfa instead promoted his young son, Shaykh 'Abd al-'Azīz, whose qualifications included his success in managing the Ministry of Finance and Oil and his knowledge of English. Shaykh Suḥaym remained Minister for Foreign Affairs, but since 1972 demonstrated his discontent by repeated absences from his office at the Ministry and from Cabinet meetings. Furthermore, during the last months of 1976 and the beginning of 1977, he tightened his connections with the Saudis so as to secure their support in the increasingly acute struggle.

In the end, the quarrel between the Minister of Finance and Oil and the Saudis at the Doha OPEC meeting led to a solution, because it put Shaykh 'Abd al-'Azīz out of the running for the Crown Princeship (see below). At that point the eldest son and Commander-in-Chief, Shaykh Ḥamad entered the scene with the backing of the army Chief of Staff, Ḥamad al-'Atiyya, a member of one of the most powerful families in Qatar and Shaykh Ḥamad's maternal uncle. The Saudis did not oppose Shaykh Ḥamad's candidacy, especially as Shaykh Suḥaym agreed to Ḥamad's succession, on condition that he have the powerful position of Prime Minister, which was now promised to him by the Ruler. However, no reorganization in the Government had taken place by October 1977, and the Ruler continued to hold the post of Prime Minister. This was the second time that promises made to Shaykh Suḥaym were not carried out.

ARMED FORCES

Total armed forces number 4,200, with all services forming part of the Army. The Army numbers 3,500 and consists of two armoured car regiments, one Guards infantry battalion and one mobile regiment. It is equipped with 30 *Saladin* armoured cars; ten *Ferrett* scout cars; eight *Saracen* armoured personnel carriers; four 25-pounder guns and 81mm mortars. The 400-strong Navy is equipped with six patrol craft and five coastal patrol craft. The Air Force numbers 300 and is equipped with four *Hunter* ground-attack fighters; one *Islander* transport; two *Whirlwind*, four *Commando* and two *Gazelle* helicopters and *Tigercat* surface-to-air missiles. (Three *Lynx* helicopters are on order.)

SOCIAL AFFAIRS

The authorities continued their liberal policy of allowing foreign workers to come to Qatar, despite the fact that they now make up c. 81% of the work force.

In June 1977, Qatar celebrated the graduation of the first group of students from the teacher-training college, and the establishment of a university in Doha. Qatar has particularly close educational ties with Jordan, stemming from a cultural agreement signed in 1972.

ECONOMIC AFFAIRS (3.951 Qatar riyals = US$1; 7.309 QR = £1 sterling)

OIL NATIONALIZATION AND THE GAS DISASTER

Qatar became the centre for OPEC activities in 1977 following the election of its Minister of Finance and Oil, Shaykh 'Abd al-'Azīz bin Khalīfa al-Thāni, as chairman of the Council of Ministers of OPEC and president of OPEC for 1977. On the eve of the election, Qatar concluded agreements to take over the remaining 40% interests held by foreign companies (BP, CFP, Shell, Exxon, Mobil and Partex) in the Qatar Petroleum Co, and the remaining 40% interest held by the Royal Dutch/Shell group in the Shell Co of Qatar. This gave the Qatar Government full control and ownership of every aspect of oil production. The Qatari minister's election as OPEC chairman was seen as the culmination of the nationalization policy.

A major economic development was the discovery of a massive 80 bn cubic foot natural gas field off the north-west coast. Considered one of the biggest gas fields in the world, with production capacity of 1,700 cu ft a day for 100 years, it opens a new major source of revenue for Qatar as an exporter of liquefied natural gas (LNG), a fuel which is growing in world demand. Qatar has already developed natural gas liquefaction plants which utilize nearly all the associate gas from Qatari oilfields for the fertilizer plant, the cement factory, the refinery, power stations, and for export—mainly to Japan.

However, Qatar suffered a major blow in April 1977 when fire destroyed almost the entire natural gas plant. This not only set back the gas industry but also the whole development plan because most of the industrial plants were to be fed by gas. While the fire revealed the vulnerability of a small state like Qatar to accidents in the economic field, its difficult role as chairman of a divided OPEC showed its vulnerability in the international political arena.

In spite of the close relations between Qatar and Saudi Arabia—based partly on the fact that the Qataris are Wahhabis like the Saudis, and that the ruling families are related—the Qataris voted with the majority at the OPEC conference in Doha (December 1976) in favour of a higher oil price increase, in oppositon to Saudi policy. (See essays on Middle East oil.) The Saudis were seriously offended and relations between the two countries deteriorated rapidly. The Saudis began to support Baḥrayn in its dispute with Qatar over the islands of Huwar, and even hinted that just as they had supported the present ruler in seizing power in February 1972, they could now use their influence to reinstate his deposed uncle.

All Qatar's efforts to appease the Saudis were unsuccessful. Relations only began to improve in mid-1977, following the compromise reached over an oil price increase and the fact that the Ruler's younger son and Minister of Finance and Oil—the man responsible for the Qatari stand at the OPEC conference—was not nominated as Crown Prince. But relations have not yet become as close as before. The Saudis were thus involved, however indirectly, in the appointment of the Crown Prince, perhaps the most important event in Qatar in 1977.

DIVERSIFYING THE ECONOMY

Following the four-fold increase in oil prices at the end of 1973, Qatar, like other Gulf states, started to diversify its economy by large-scale industrialization. But the difficulties inherent in this process soon became clear: the lack of manpower, the danger in allowing large numbers of foreign labourers into a tiny country with a small population, and the problem of marketing the products of these industries. The result was a slowdown in implementing the development projects and in preparing new industrial projects intended to serve Qatar and the Gulf as a whole, such as a cement factory, and a liquefied gas plant. Special attention was paid to infrastructure and local skilled manpower in order to make industrial products cheaper and more competitive in foreign markets.

1977 BUDGET

The development budget for 1977 was increased by 44%, reaching c. $1,600m (cf $1,110m in 1976). The most important allocations were for education $227m, electricity $228m, housing $163m, and health $99m.

The industrial projects included in the 1977 development budget were an iron and steel plant already under construction ($82m); a petrochemical plant ($92m); a gas liquefaction plant ($73m); and expansion of a chemical fertilizer plant ($62m).

GOVERNMENT FINANCE (million Qatar riyals per fiscal year)[1]

	1973	*1974*	*1975*	*1976*[2]	*Budget 1977*
Revenue	**1,720**	**7,319**	**7,135**	**8,811**	**8,948**
Oil	1,616	7,053	6,623	8,262	8,138
Other	104	266	511	549	810
Expenditure	**1,352**	**2,464**	**4,432**	**5,894**	**7,319**
Foreign grants	370	522	892	306	431
Other	982	1,942	3,540	5,588	6,888
Net lending and equity participation	**183**	**999**	**1,767**	**2,134**	**3,721**
Surplus or deficit (—)	**185**	**3,856**	**936**	**782**	**-2,092**

[1] The Qatari fiscal year is identical with the Islamic calendar (Hijri) year which is 11–12 days shorter than the Gregorian calendar year. The fiscal years 1973–77 are the Hijri years 1393–97, which end, respectively, on the Gregorian calendar days 24 January, 1974, 12 January, 1975, 2 January, 1976, 21 December, 1976, and 10 December 1977 (tentative date).

[2] Provisional figures.

Data: Ministry of Finance and Petroleum.

CRUDE OIL PRODUCTION ('000 barrels)

	Daily Average	*Total*	*Index*[2] *(1970 = 100)*
1970	362.4	132,261	100.0
1971	360.7	157,206	118.8
1972	482.4	176,543	131.2
1973	570.3	208,160	152.4
1974	518.4	189,216	140.5
1975	437.6	159,724	121.3
1976[1]	499.3	182,256	137.8
1977 (Jan–June)[1]	417.8	74,248	115.3

Source: OPEC, *Annual Statistical Bulletin.*
[1] Production figures extrapolated from index.
[2] Index source: IMF, *International Financial Statistics.*

EXPORTS, BY DESTINATION (millions US$)

	1972	*1973*	*1974*	*1975*	*1976*
UK	57.5	68.1	353.9	314.9	415.5
France	35.4	74.5	240.0	188.1	296.5
Virgin Islands	—	—	165.6	296.6	254.6
Netherlands	96.4	153.3	6.8	63.9	225.2
Thailand	34.9	61.2	170.6	85.1	145.6
Italy	45.4	69.7	189.1	117.1	131.3
Sweden	11.8	—	47.8	65.9	130.6
US	2.8	23.7	80.6	57.0	120.3
Others	110.0	172.0	269.7	244.0	269.8
Total	**394.2**	622.5	**1,524.1**	**1,422.6**	**1,989.4**
EEC	280.0	233.4	329.3	257.1	301.4

Source: IMF, *Direction of Trade.*

IMPORTS, BY SOURCE (millions US$)

	1972	*1973*	*1974*	*1975*	*1976*
Japan	17.4	21.6	48.4	134.5	252.1
UK	36.6	53.4	37.9	134.2	171.3
US	14.4	19.9	27.7	55.3	84.6
West Germany	7.3	10.5	16.7	51.7	74.5
United Arab Emirates	2.6	4.5	7.0	6.3	71.2
Netherlands	2.8	4.2	8.3	18.0	45.8
France	11.5	9.6	7.1	16.5	35.0
Switzerland	0.2	2.7	3.0	12.6	31.2
Others	45.6	68.0	114.8	148.3	207.7
Total	**138.4**	**194.4**	**270.9**	**577.4**	**973.4**
EEC*	60.9	80.9	102.6	236.9	340.0

Source: IMF, *Direction of Trade.*
*EEC totals derived from: Statistical Office of the European Communities, *Monthly External Trade Bulletin.*

BALANCE OF PAYMENTS (million US $)

	1973	*1974*	*1975*	*1976*[1]
Oil exports, fob	598	1,955	1,763	2,131
Other exports, fob	18	37	51	72
Imports, cif	–195	–271	–458	–817
Services and private transfers	–140	–53	–227	–348
Current account balance	**280**	**1,667**	**1,130**	**1,039**
Capital and official transfers[2]	–283	–613	–527	–720
Overall balance	**–3**	**1,054**	**603**	**318**

[1] Preliminary figures.
[2] Includes errors and omissions. Capital and official transfers are on a fiscal-year basis (see footnote 1 of the table on Government Finance); other items are on a calendar-year basis.
Source: IMF Survey, 15 August 1977.

United Arab Emirates

When the United Arab Emirates (UAE) was finally established at the end of 1971, on the eve of the British withdrawal from the Gulf region, it consisted of the following principalities which formerly belonged to the Trucial States: Abu Dhabi, Dubay, Sharjah (also called Shariqah), Ras al-Khaymah (which joined the federation only in February 1972), Fujayrah, Ajman and Umm al-Qaywayn.

The federal regime was based on a provisional constitution effective for five years which, while preserving the autonomy of each principality, provided for the following federal bodies: 1) a Supreme Council of Rulers, in which Abu Dhabi and Dubay had the right of veto; 2) a Federal Government; 3) a Federal National Council with advisory powers, consisting of 40 members nominated by the respective Rulers and approved by the President (Abu Dhabi and Dubay, 8 each; Sharjah and Ras al-Khaymah, 6 each; Fujayrah, Ajman and Umm al-Qaywayn, 4 each); and a Supreme Federal Court. The principalities were proportionally represented in all federal governing and administrative bodies according to population.

	Area sq. miles	*1975 Population census*
Abu Dhabi	26,000	235,662
Dubay	1,500	206,861
Sharjah	1,000	88,188
Ras al-Khaymah	650	57,282
Fujayrah	450	26,498
Ajman	100	21,566
Umm al-Qaywayn	300	16,879
Total	30,000	*655,937[1]

The Presidency was entrusted to the Ruler of the most powerful and richest principality, Abu Dhabi: Shaykh Zāyid was and still is an ardent supporter of the federation. The Vice-Presidency was given to the Ruler of the second richest and most powerful principality, Dubay: Shaykh Rāshid was and still is in favour of a very loose-knit federation.

The five-year history of the federation has been dominated by the struggle between the federalists and autonomists, with Abu Dhabi leading the former and Dubay the latter.

FEDERAL AFFAIRS

CONSTITUTIONAL DEVELOPMENTS

At the end of 1975, the federalists increased their pressure, and were successful in 1976 in establishing a federal army (in which the various local armies were incorporated), as well as in unifying police and border army units into a federal police force and a border guard. This pressure reached its peak in the last four months of 1976 and the beginning of 1977 when a decision had to be made on the continuation of the federation, and the re-election of its governmental bodies. The federalists used this opportunity to extract more concessions from the autonomists in favour of unification.

The main problem was over the provisional Constitution, whose five-year term expired at the beginning of December 1976. The federalists, led by President Zāyid, demanded a permanent Constitution, as it had become quite clear to them that the federation was a *fait accompli*. But the autonomists had widespread support for their proposal that the provisional Constitution be extended for another five years.

Other no less important issues were: 1) the principalities' contributions to the federal budget. Until 1976, Abu Dhabi had paid 98% of the budget and Sharjah, Fujayrah and Ajman the rest. Dubay, the second richest principality, as well as Ras al-Khaymah and Umm al-Qaywayn refused to contribute, claiming that to do so would diminish their autonomous status by strengthening the central government and giving it the opportunity to interfere in their own financial affairs. They also claimed that the federal bureaucracy was wasteful. 2) The demand for federal control over immigration, especially illegal immigration, more effectively to prevent the infiltration of immigrants not only to the UAE, but also between the principalities. 3) The need to establish federal machinery to settle disputes between federation members, especially border issues. When such a dispute occurred between Dubay and Sharjah over several metres on the border—where the Charles de Gaulle shopping centre was to be built—the federal authorities, including the President, could not bring the sides to a compromise. The President also claimed that there was no place for border disputes between federation member-states. 4) The demand to incorporate the information, security and intelligence services into federal bodies. 5) The demand to establish a government in which competence, rather than the representation of Emirate interests, would be the criterion for the choice of ministers.

The main pressure came from the President, Shaykh Zāyid, who refused to put forward his candidacy for re-election until these five issues were resolved—in favour of greater federalism. He knew he was the only candidate acceptable to all sides, including the autonomists themselves, and to the federation's neighbours—Saudi Arabia, Kuwait and Iran. Because of his generosity, he was also generally popular.[2] Although there were some fears that his aim was to increase Abu Dhabi's influence, and perhaps extend its control under the guise of federalism, the majority saw in it a wish to push forward the federation concept, which they favoured.

The result was a compromise, reached after several meetings of the Supreme Council of Rulers in October-November 1976. Shaykh Zāyid agreed to the extension of the provisional Constitution (with some modifications) for another five years, and to give up the idea of federal machinery to overcome disputes between the principalities. In return it was agreed: 1) to amend article 142 of the provisional Constitution in order to place the unified army under the control of the central Government (and a central budget), and forbid individual Rulers to buy arms or raise troops. 2) To establish a public security office attached to the President's office in which the intelligence services of the principalities would be merged. A special law was approved to this end. 3) To bring under the supreme control of the President, through the federal agencies, matters relating to immigration and residence permits, as well as border control. The immigration problem had to be dealt with urgently as the number of aliens in the UAE had reached c. 75% of the population. 4) To put all information media under the control of the federal Ministry of Information. 5) Each principality would contribute 20% of its revenues to the federal budget. This would bring about more involvement in federal affairs by the principalities which had previously refused to pay, and so reduce the burden on Abu Dhabi. 6) To reshuffle the Government, reducing the number of ministers from 29 to 23 and appointing more technocrats.

The President issued a decree on 28 November 1976 extending the provisional Constitution for a further five years, as of 2 December 1976. On the following day, the Supreme Council of Rulers unanimously elected Shaykh Zāyid b. Sultān al-Nihayān as President of the UAE, and Shaykh Rāshid b. Sa'īd al-Maktūm as Vice-President for second five-year terms. Abu Dhabi, through Shaykh Zāyid, at once set about promoting federalism by strengthening the UAE's governing and administrative bodies.

FEDERAL NATIONAL COUNCIL

The Federal National Council was dissolved on 2 December 1976, and replaced by the President according to the previously agreed system of proportional representation. The most important change was the appointment of a "commoner" to the key post of Speaker: Tiryam 'Umrān Tiryam, former UAE ambassador to Egypt and widely known for his Western ideas. Under the new leadership, the Assembly showed itself determined to tackle urgent problems with great resolution.

One of its successes was in pressuring the government to raise the salaries of civil servants and other state employees by up to 150% (at the lowest-paid level) by warning of growing unrest among employees, as well as of corruption. Following this success, the Assembly prepared a new proposal for a 150% increase in salaries over the next two years, because even with the mid-1977 raise, employees were barely keeping abreast of the cost of living. The Assembly also proposed steps to raise the cost of living allowances, payable to cover rent and fuel, until the further increase was approved by the Supreme Council and carried out in 1978. This development not only strengthened the advisory power of the Assembly, but also created a kind of alliance between the Assembly and state employees (a majority of whom are federally-oriented Arab residents).

THE NEW GOVERNMENT, JANUARY 1977

The new Government, formed early in January 1977, reflected the agreed proportional balance for the various principalities: eight from Abu Dhabi, five from Dubay, four from Ras al-Khaymah, three from Sharjah, and one each from Fujayrah, Ajman and Umm al-Qaymayn. However, it also included a number of capable technocrats such as the Minister of Planning, Sa'īd al-Ghubāsh, formerly UAE ambassador to Washington. Nevertheless, key Government posts were still held by members of the important ruling families. The Abu Dahbi ruling family set an important example, however, by the decision of the Crown Prince, Shaykh Khalīfa bin Zāyid, to hand his post as Deputy Premier to another member of the family and concentrate instead on his duties as Deputy Supreme Commander of the Federal Armed Forces and Head of Abu Dhabi's Executive Council. Yet widespread criticism continued about the frequent absences of ministers from cabinet meetings and their offices, often because of duties and business in their own principalities.

The priorities set by the federalists for the new Government for 1977 were: (a) strengthening the federal institutions. Abu Dhabi was the first to attach its Departments of Education, Health and Information, with their budgets, to the respective federal ministries. (b) A new population policy to tackle the problems of immigration and residency. (c) Above all, the introduction of federal economic development planning. The new Minister of Planning faced a very complicated task: to draw up a joint development plan for the principalities, which until then had implemented their own economic and social projects without planning or consultation; this often led to competition and duplication, such as in the number of newly-built modern international airports.

DEFENCE AND SECURITY

During 1976 and the beginning of 1977, the federal authorities merged all the defence forces of the UAE under the operational command of a Chief of Staff, the Jordanian Maj-Gen (*liwā*) 'Awwād Khālidī—a compromise choice prompted by the principalities' fear that Abu Dhabi might seize control of the army. The armed forces incorporated the Trucial Oman Scouts—the British-trained federal corp—which comprised c. 3,500 men; the National Guard of Sharjah, c. 250 men; the Motorized Force of Ras al-Khaymah, c. 300 men; the Defence Army of Dubay, c. 1,500 men; and the Defence Army of Abu Dhabi, c. 24,000 men. This 30,000-strong federal army was divided into three commands based on Abu Dhabi (the west region), Dubay (the central region) and Ras al-Khaymah (the northern region). With the reorganization, the new federal command was able to send a contingent of 700 troops to join the Arab Deterrent Force in Lebanon, and to prepare a development plan for the 1977 fiscal year.

Indeed, the largest single allocation in the 1977 budget was for the Ministry of Defence—$658m. Besides regular expenses, this budget had to cover the gradual re-equipment of the Federal Defence Forces with modern weapons. The Chief of Staff declared that arms supplies would be bought from more than one foreign source and without middlemen. The first approach was to France, which resulted in an agreement, signed on 29 April 1977, providing for the supply of military equipment and armaments including *Mirage* aircraft (which were already in use in the former Abu Dhabi Air Force with Pakistani pilots), *Puma* and *Gazelle* helicopters and tanks, and the entire accompanying technical expertise. The agreement was concluded by the Deputy Commander-in-Chief of the Armed Forces, the Abu Dhabi Crown Prince Shaykh Khalīfa bin Zāyid, who became more active after he left his position as Deputy Premier at the beginning of January. Abu Dhabi in fact remained the principal paymaster of the federal army and its new arms purchases.

ARMED FORCES

According to another source, the armed forces total only 26,100.[3] The Union Defence Force and the UAE armed forces (Abu Dhabi, Dubay, Ras Al-Khaymah and Sharjah) were formally merged in May 1976. Defence expenditure in 1977–8 was 392.3m dirhams ($100.6m). Military service is voluntary. The Army numbers 23,500 and consists of one Royal Guard brigade; three armoured car battalions; seven infantry battalions; three artillery battalions and three air defence battalions. It is equipped with 80 *Scorpion* light tanks; 125 *Saladin*, six *Shorland*, Panhard armoured cars; 60 *Ferret* scout cars; Panhard M-3 and 30 *Saracen* armoured personnel carriers; 22 25-pounder, 105mm guns; 16 AMX 155mm self-propelled howitzers; 81mm mortars; 120mm recoilless rifles; *Vigilant* anti-tank guided weapons and *Rapier* surface-to-air missiles. 700 men are deployed with the Arab Peacekeeping Force in the Lebanon. The 800-strong Navy is equipped with six large, nine small patrol craft and 14 coastal patrol craft (police). The Air Force numbers 1,800 and has 38 combat aircraft; two squadrons with 24 *Mirage* V, eight *Hunter* ground-attack fighters; one squadron with six MB-326 counter-insurgency. Transports include two C-130H, one G-222, four *Islander,* three DHC-4 and one Cessna 182. Helicopters include eight AB-205, six AB-206, three AB-212, ten *Alouette* III and five *Puma.* (Two G-222 and four DHC-5D transports on order.)

SOCIAL AFFAIRS

THE PROBLEM OF ALIENS

The biggest single problem of the UAE remains immigration. In every principality there is an imbalance between nationals and immigrants, but it is especially felt in the two richest states, Abu Dhabi and Dubay, because their large development plans have necessitated increasing numbers of skilled and unskilled labour. The nationals themselves have little stimulus to work because they have easy access to comfortable incomes, if not to wealth. No one knows the exact balance between nationals and immigrants. Various estimates suggest that aliens comprise between 66% and 75% of the 656,000 population; in Abu Dhabi probably even more. In the latter principality, the balance between males and females is typical of a country of immigration: 73% males against 27% females in 1975.[4] Immigrants from India, Pakistan, Baluchistan and Afghanistan come to work in construction, the public service and commerce. There are also Omanis, Pakistanis and Arabs in the Armed Forces; Palestinians, Egyptians, Iraqis and Yemenis in the administration; and Iranians in commerce.

The principalities faced a considerable dilemma: on the one hand, they were in great need of the foreign labour force, otherwise no development could be carried out and no modern administration, army or trade established. On the other hand, with such an overwhelming majority, the aliens (especially the illegal immigrants) were a constant threat to stability and internal security. Admittedly, the foreign workforce was passive on the whole; nevertheless, their salaries were low, living conditions very poor; they did not enjoy family life, political rights or social security. This situation had already caused a number of strikes and demonstrations for better pay and conditions. In October 1976, for example, a strike in Dubay developed into a riot. The police intervened, arrested all the Indians and Pakistanis and were ready to deport them. But the company asked that the majority be allowed to remain since it was in great need of their labour; consequently, the police deported only the ringleaders.

The Government initiated a campaign against illegal immigrants, attempting to prevent their entrance or to detain and deport those inside the country. This campaign ended at times in tragedy, as happened in September 1976 in Fujayrah when two ships with more than 1,000 Pakistanis were intercepted: several people were killed, others ran away or were caught and later deported to Pakistan. Another group was caught in February 1977 in Sharjah; after serving prison terms and paying fines for illegal infiltration, the immigrants were deported.

The most important steps taken by the federal Government to control immigration were the rules and regulations issued in July 1977, as well as the strengthening of the Border Guard by special naval and motorized units. The new regulations required that all foreign workers be registered; companies were given 45 days, from the beginning of August, to report to the authorities on the number and conditions of their foreign workers. This registration aimed not only at tightening control over the foreigners, but also at helping decide their legal status, guaranteeing their rights, and obtaining exact data on manpower in the country for planning purposes. The regulations also stipulated that work permits for foreigners would be valid only for four years, with the possibility of a one-year extension. Any foreign worker found inciting people to cease work or to strike, or found assaulting his employer, or intentionally damaging tools, would be deported. The general reaction among the foreign workers to the regulations was not known. However, the Ministry of Social Affairs and Labour was attacked by armed groups who entered the Inspection Department (where documentation concerning residency and work permits for aliens was kept); they caused considerable damage and took sealed work permits. It was the first time that such an aggressive act had occurred in the UAE (gangs of permit forgers may have been responsible).

The situation became more serious when a group of Palestinians were involved in the attempt on the life of the Syrian Foreign Minister, 'Abd al-Ḥalīm Khaddām, at the Abu Dhabi airport in October 1977 which resulted in the death of the UAE Minister of State for Foreign Affairs, Sa'īf bin Sa'īd al-Ghubāsh. The Palestinians' freedom to carry arms suddenly caused alarm. A group of people who reacted by holding a demonstration in Ras al-Khaymah demanding the deportation of the Palestinians were shot at by Palestinians and several died. This made the federal Government all the more determined to establish full control over foreigners. But again Dubay took a different attitude by declaring the Jabal 'Ali area—a huge industrial complex—a free zone where Arab and Asian workers would need no visa or work contract. Dubay had been the centre of labour unrest since mid-1976; therefore the decision was a great surprise, especially as no measures were proposed to control these foreign workers.

FOREIGN AFFAIRS

The federal Government—instructed by the President—succeeded in gradually improving relations with the Gulf littoral states, especially the two Gulf powers: Saudi Arabia and Iran. Moreover, by distributing considerable aid to many countries in the Arab and Third Worlds (money provided mainly by Abu Dhabi), the UAE gained prestige and many friends among the Afro-Asian states, and strengthened its ties with Arab countries. The policy of extending financial aid continued in 1977. The UAE's involvement in all Gulf activities towards more co-operation, standardization and the establishment of unified institutes, companies and communication increased; and co-operation with Saudi Arabia and Iran grew stronger.

Various border agreements had previously been reached in principle by the UAE with its neighbours. These included treaties with Saudi Arabia in 1974 on the questions of Buraimi (a fertile oasis) and the corridor to the sea between Abu Dhabi and Qatar; and the arrangement with Oman over the Buraimi oasis. However, no delineation was actually carried out until 1977. In July, the President issued a decree establishing a special committee headed by the federal Foreign Minister to study and delineate land and sea borders with Oman, Saudi Arabia, Qatar and Iran. There is no doubt that border demarcations would contribute much to the federal identity of the UAE, and to the solution of border problems within the state. It was characteristic of Shaykh Zāyid's foreign policy to attempt to solve problems by compromise in order to maintain good relations with everyone.

RELATIONS WITH SAUDI ARABIA

Co-operation with Saudi Arabia expanded to several new fields in 1976–7. Co-operation in security was agreed in October 1976 during the visit of the Saudi Minister of the Interior, Prince Nawwāf ibn 'Abd al-'Azīz, to the UAE.

The UAE joined Saudi Arabia in December 1976 in the campaign against an oil price increase of more than 5%, and voted with it in the Doha OPEC conference. Afterwards, it promised to increase oil production by 1m b/d as Saudi Arabia had done to enforce the policy. However, the threat was not carried out, and the UAE Minister of Oil and Mineral Resources, al-'Utayba, denied that the UAE had undertaken to increase production, adding that there was no intention to raise output or to harm the economies of other OPEC members (see essays on Middle East oil). Both countries continued to co-operate in this sphere, agreeing to a rise of 10% over the whole year (1977)—a compromise reached on the eve of the OPEC conference in July. Other fields of co-operation were within the general Gulf framework, with the UAE always on the same side as the Saudis.

RELATIONS WITH IRAN

Iran and the UAE institutionalized their co-operation by signing an agreement in December 1976 to implement economic projects in capital investments, agriculture and industry, and co-operation in UAE development projects. One was to establish a Joint Investment Bank, with an initial capital of $100m. Later, in April 1977, four memoranda were signed to pave the way for major joint ventures between the private sectors in the two countries in agriculture, tourism and department stores. The first was a joint venture between Iran Air and an UAE interest to construct a 1,000-room luxury hotel in Esfahan; the second established a chain of department stores in Iran, Baḥrayn and Dubay; while a third memorandum concerned a joint venture in cattle and livestock breeding in Khuzistan. Basically, the agreements allowed a level of economic activity which could increase Iranian influence in internal UAE affairs and strengthen the status of Iranian immigrants.

Co-operation with Iran did not prevent the UAE from taking an anti-Iranian stand over oil prices, and from opposing the Iranian demand for a defence alliance among the Gulf littoral states. The presence of Iranian army units and administration in the islands of Abu Musa and the Greater and Lesser Tumb has caused some trouble, especially over the division of revenues from oil production around the islands. This did not affect relations in 1977, however, and one of the principalities directly involved—Ras al-Khaymah—stated that it was actually in the UAE's interest to co-operate with Iran.

RELATIONS WITH THE WEST

Diplomatic relations have been extended to West Europe, North America and Japan. From their inception, UAE investment companies have preferred the West European market to all others, including Arab countries. They also preferred to trade and obtain arms from the Western industrial powers. The UAE still has no relations with the Soviet bloc.

ECONOMIC AFFAIRS (3.898 UAE dirhams = US$1; 7.214 Dh = £1 sterling)

THE PRINCIPALITIES

Internally, each principality was mainly concerned with financial and economic questions. There was a general trend to try to guarantee future economic development (when oil reserves decline) by industrialization. But oil exploration continued in 1977, with new fields found in Sharjah and Ras al-Khaymah; this increased Sharjah's chances of joining the oil-producing club in 1978.

In Abu Dhabi, where only about 60% of development projects were completed in recent years, there were serious second thoughts about the pace of economic diversification. Several factors contributed to the delays: corruption in the department of the Crown Prince—the Head of the Abu Dhabi Executive Council; various ministries' intervening to change projects in mid-stream; shortage of manpower; inadequate feasibility studies; and lack of co-operation between the principalities in imposing customs and duties on products to protect local industries. The new Three-Year Plan (1977–9) tried to tackle these problems by slowing down the ambitious development programme, and by concentrating mainly on small projects, infrastructure, help to the private sector, and investment in feasibility studies, especially for the major industrial project in Ruways.

As a result of the corruption scandal and the decision to attach the Departments of Education, Health and Information to the federal government, there was a reshuffle in the Executive Council of Abu Dhabi in January 1977. The 1977 budget reflected the new economic policy: the biggest allocations went to housing, services, public buildings and transport.

In Dubay, industrial development was intensified in 1977, especially in the prestigious huge industrial complex in Jabal 'Ali. Dubay became the biggest Middle Eastern borrower of Eurodollars (c. $500m) for an aluminium smelter project and a gas processing complex. It continued its drydock project in co-operation with a Greek firm (and in competition with Baḥrayn, see above).

The other small principalities continued to look for subventions to stretch their limited resources, which came mainly from Abu Dhabi, while intensifying oil exploration, onshore and offshore. They were mainly engaged in establishing service industries in transportation, tourism and repairs, in addition to a few heavy industries, such as the cement plant in Ras al-Khaymah. Co-ordination between the principalities remained poor in 1977; the main reasons, perhaps, were considerations of prestige and the lack of federal planning power.

THE 1977 BUDGET

The federal budget for 1977 was finally approved in mid-June at a record of $3,333m (cf $1,040m in 1976).[5] The increase was due mainly to the inclusion of Abu Dhabi's Departments of Health, Education and Information in the federal budget (see above). Therefore the actual increase was c. $560m, which was largely to ensure the completion of projects still under way.

Although there were hopes that all the principalities would contribute to the budget in accordance with the understanding reached in November 1976, Dubay, Ras al-Khaymah and Umm al-Qaywayn still continued to refuse. The whole question was discussed again in the second of two unprecedented meetings of the Supreme Council of Rulers in June, in which Shaykh Zāyid suggested that each principality should contribute at least 50% of its revenues to the 1977 budget. Again, Sharjah, Fujayrah and Ajman agreed and the other three led by Dubay refused. In fact, 50% of the revenues of the three small principalities which agreed would cover only 2% of the federal budget. The issue was politically important to rich oil-producing Dubay, whose attitude was strongly criticized as its considerable oil revenues were mainly used to carry out huge industrial projects which many observers felt would become "white elephants." Dubay was still refusing to contribute to federal funds by the end of 1977.

DEVELOPMENT PROJECTS

Deterioration of the internal economy, its low absorptive capacity and the slow rate of project implementation made it necessary for the new Government to cut development expenditure (see above). According to a report by the Minister of Planning submitted to the UAE Council of Ministers (August 1977), out of a total of 8,282m dirhams (Dh) earmarked for development projects until the end of 1976, only 11.5% had been spent. During the first half of 1977, no new projects were started, and only 30% (Dh 365m) was spent from the federal budget's annual development allocation.

As a result, the Ministry of Planning is considering the revision of the Three-Year Investment Plan 1977–9 in order to reduce the projected investment (fixed at Dh 4,876m). It also intends to declare this a transitional plan under which all projects must be completed before new ones are introduced in 1980.

OIL

With the export of more than 711m barrels of oil, the UAE's oil revenues amounted to $8,400m in 1976, and are expected to exceed $9,250m in 1977.

Abu Dhabi supplied 82% of UAE's total oil production (cf 16% by Dubay and 2% by Sharjah). Exploration and development also continued at a high level, particularly offshore, where *Compagnie Française des Pétroles* was working on behalf of the Abu Dhabi National Oil Company (ADNOC). Abu Dhabi production rose by 14% in 1976, but only by 8% in the first half of 1977 (cf the corresponding period in 1976); overall output levels continued to be subject to a "ceiling." Production in Dubay rose by 24% in 1976, with the same level of output maintained during the first half of 1977. Sharjah's oil output has remained constant.

TRADE BALANCE

In 1976, the UAE had a trade surplus of Dh 21,540m (cf a surplus of 18,086m in 1975). Total exports amounted to Dh 35,141m (93% from oil exports)—an increase of 23% over 1975. Imports rose by 25% and amounted to Dh 13,601m in 1976. (For the sources of imports, see table below.)

INTERNATIONAL RESERVES

According to IMF estimates, the UAE's international reserves exceeded $1,600m in June 1977 (cf $2,000m at the end of 1976). However, these official reserves exclude UAE's long-term investments abroad made through various Investment Boards (for which no figures have ever been disclosed).

BANKING

Recent developments in the banking sector reflected the general failure of the federal authorities to introduce an economic policy which would reconcile the contradictory interests of the member Emirates of the UAE. In April 1977, a dispute erupted between Abu Dhabi and Dubay over the latter's decision to allow a breach of the two-year moratorium on new banks. In fact the UAE is the most "over-banked" centre in the world, with 56 banks operating more than 300 branches (i.e. one branch per 2,000 persons).

In spite of the existence of the Currency Board, most oil revenues are channelled through the commercial banks. The Board has not yet succeeded in obtaining the full status of a Central Bank, which would enable it to act as a last-resort lender for the commercial banks, and to become the official agency through which the government channels its huge reserves. The IMF is now preparing a draft law for a Central Bank, which may be approved by the Supreme Council of Rulers by the end of 1977. The Central Bank would be given new powers to control credit and the money supply—urgent measures in view of the deterioration of the internal economy, which has faced an annual inflation rate of between 25% and 40% during the last three years.

FEDERAL BUDGET (Dh million)

	1976	*1977*
REVENUE		
Emirates' contributions	4,079	13,000
Income from Ministries	72	150
of which:		
Finance and Industry	(8)	(66)
Communications	(24)	(32)
Agriculture and Fisheries	(13)	(15)
Interior	(8)	(8)
Total Revenue	**4,151**	**13,150**

EXPENDITURE	*1976*	*1977*
Defence	—	2,565
Education and Youth	457	1,241
Health	267	904
Interior	343	620
Communications	53	397
Electricity and Water	256	289
Public Works and Housing	268	292
Labour and Social Affairs	85	169
Special Expenditure*	—	4,243
Total Expenditure (including others)	**2,778**	**11,235**

*These include federal assistance to autonomous agencies, pensions, end-of-service benefits and foreign grants.

Source: Middle East Economic Survey, Beirut/Nicosia; 22 August 1977. *Middle East & North Africa 1976–77* (London: Europa Publications).

INVESTMENT PLAN 1977–9 (Dh million)

1. Projects to be implemented by the Ministry of Public Works and Housing:	
Council of Ministers	14.0
Federal National Council	46.0
Ministry of Planning	13.3
Controller's Office	12.3
Ministry of Finance and Industry	25.2
Ministry of Foreign Affairs	10.0
Ministry of Interior	211.6
Ministry of Education and Youth	1,156.5
Ministry of Health	856.1
Ministry of Communications	999.5
Ministry of Public Works and Housing	577.5
Total (including others)	**4,195.0**
2. Projects to be implemented directly by the various Ministries	681.5
General Total	**4,876.5**

Source: Middle East Economic Survey, 5 September 1977.

UAE IMPORTS (ABU DHABI AND DUBAY) c.i.f.

	1975	*1976*		*change*
	Dh million		*% of total*	*75/76*
BY PRODUCT				
Machinery and transport equipment	4,388	5,734	42	+31
Manufactures	3,886	4,554	34	+17
Food, drink and tobacco	1,173	1,449	11	+24
Raw materials (incl. fuel)	929	1,237	9	+33
Chemicals	405	475	3	+17
Other	129	152	1	+18
Total	**10,910**	**13,601**	**100**	**+25**
BY COUNTRY				
Japan	1,736	2,369	17	+36
United Kingdom	1,890	2,293	17	+21
United States	1,645	1,825	13	+11
Germany	752	1,016	8	+35
France	535	530	4	-1
Netherlands	262	387	3	+47
Italy	355	386	3	+9
Saudi Arabia	79	383	3	+384
Other	3,656	4,412	32	+21
Total	**10,910**	**13,601**	**100**	**+25**

Source: Abu Dhabi Statistical Office and Customs Department.

UAE CRUDE OIL PRODUCTION (million barrels)

	1971	*1972*	*1973*	*1974*	*1975*	*1976*	*1977 1st half*
Abu Dhabi	341	384	476	516	512	583	307
Dubay	46	56	80	88	93	115	57
Sharjah	—	—	—	8*	13*	13*	6*
Total UAE	**387**	**440**	**556**	**612***	**618***	**711***	**370***

*estimated
Source: Petroleum Economist.

UAE TRADE BALANCE (Dh million)

	1971	*1972*	*1973*	*1974*	*1975*	*1976*
Oil exports	3,411	4,377	7,459	27,525	26,838	32,645
Non-oil exports and re-exports	579	768	1,149	1,696	1,799	2,496
Total exports	3,990	5,145	8,608	29,221	28,637	35,141
Imports	1,469	2,113	3,279	6,750	10,571	13,150
Trade balance	**2,521**	**3,032**	**5,329**	**22,471**	**18,086**	**21,991**

Source: UAE Currency Board Bulletins.

ABU DHABI REVENUES AND EXPENDITURE (Dh million)

	1973	*1974*	*1975*	*1976*
REVENUE:				
Oil receipts	3,043	13,703	14,390	18,954
Other	179	428	625	689
Total	**3,222**	**14,131**	**15,015**	**19,643**
EXPENDITURE:				
Recurrent	2,513	4,677	6,506	9,509
Development	524	1,010	2,250	3,057
Capital payments	354	1,236	2,701	2,129
Total	**3,391**	**6,923**	**11,457**	**14,695**
Balance	-169	+7,208	+3,558	+4,948

Source: Finance Department, Government of Abu Dhabi.
Also, *Grindlays Bank Group*, August 1977.

NOTES

1. Grindlay Bank Group, August 1977. Census total includes an estimate for nationals abroad.
2. He gave many grants from Abu Dhabi revenues to the small principalities and to other states in and outside the Gulf area.
3. *The Military Balance 1977–78* (London: International Institute for Strategic Studies).
4. *Financial Times*, 11 February 1977. *Middle East Economic Digest (MEED),* Special Report, UAE, London; July 1977. *MEED*, 5 August 1977.
5. *Emirates News*, 18, 19 June; 20 July 1977.

Iran

YAIR HIRSCHFELD and ARYEH SHMUELEVITZ

Iran's political system passed through an important stage of development in the period under review (October 1976 to September 1977), during which the authority of the Shah and his government was conspicuously challenged. In the past, the political regime and the Shah's rule have been based on an active coalition between government agencies and the army which, under the Shah's guidance and control, were responsible for planning and implementing policy. The Shah also enjoyed the support of a silent coalition of the lower urban and rural classes and the upper-middle and upper classes, whose loyalty was maintained through a combination of concessions and repression. However, at the beginning of 1977, it became apparent that economic and social difficulties were undermining the political system by diminishing popular support for the Shah's regime.

The Shah's reaction to this challenge may be divided into three stages. From November 1976 to April 1977, he and his government acted along orthodox lines. However, it became increasingly difficult to maintain a policy of concessions and repression because of deepening economic problems and the new US Administration's stand on human rights. The promise of "popular participation" was shown to have little substance.[1] In the second stage, from April to August 1977, the Shah evinced greater readiness to permit criticism and admit failures. It ended with the fall of Prime Minister Amir 'Abbas Hoveyda, after 13 years in office.

The third stage, which began with the nomination of Jamshid Amuzegar as the new Prime Minister on 7 August, witnessed an attempt to adapt existing political patterns of behaviour to economic and social challenges. A new active coalition between government agencies, the army, the private sector and intellectuals was allowed to participate in defining and executing policy, although strictly under the Shah's direction and within the limitations of the existing system. However, traditional policies towards the lower urban and rural classes seemed likely to continue.

In general, the Shah demonstrated considerable capacity for carrying out flexible policies during 1977, thereby enhancing the stability of his regime, at least for the time being.

POLITICAL AFFAIRS

THE LEGACY OF 1976: SOCIAL AND ECONOMIC POLICY FAILURES

In a long interview granted to Iran's daily newspaper *Kayhan* on 28 October 1976, the Shah said that if the Government continued to increase its involvement in the economic affairs of the state, "all Iranians will perish." He announced that the policy of accelerating economic growth at all costs would end, and belt-tightening begin. His interview was a clear admission of government policy failures; an acknowledgement of the existence of grave problems; and a promise to concentrate more on removing economic and social grievances. It is against this background of economic and social problems that Government policies and their consequences in 1976–77 can best be understood.

INFLATION AND HOUSING

In 1975, the Shah had prescribed a severe price-control system to cope with inflation; but this proved a costly failure. The supply of vital commodities such as eggs, chicken, meat, bread, onions and sugar was severely curtailed or, at times, blocked completely. A black market developed where prices were up to ten times the official rate, as with cement. In order to maintain its price control policy, the Government was compelled to intervene increasingly in the economy—going into the retail trade and interfering in private firms, for example, by preventing the formation of cartels. The Government found itself involved in price-fixing of consumer goods, including even such articles as wedding dresses. Special courts had to be set up to prosecute price control offenders. Early in January 1977, the Minister of Commerce, Manuchehr Taslimi, admitted that these courts could not cope with the situation: out of the 1,500 cases of overcharging filed daily, only 300 could be dealt with. This made the whole price system ineffectual.[2]

Similarly ineffective was the rent freeze introduced in 1974: the law had loopholes and the courts did not possess sufficient power to deal with violators. Consequently, people in cities had to pay 60 to 70% of their income on rent; land and construction costs went up, and because higher-income housing was so attractive a field for private builders, low-cost housing was neglected. A government scheme introduced in February 1976 to induce private contractors to construct cheap flats was quietly dropped because of contractors' opposition and the government's failure to supply the cheap cement it had promised. Total expenditure for construction in the private and public sectors actually decreased by 17% from 1975 to 1976. The housing situation was exacerbated by municipal restrictions which prevented building beyond the city area (see below).

Thus, price controls and the housing policy produced inflation—unofficially estimated at between 20 and 30% in 1976. Moreover, despite the higher oil revenues and the government's social welfare policy, the income-expense ratio of the lower-middle class has steadily worsened over the last 27 years. Statistics published by *Ayandegan* show that since 1950 average lower-middle salaries rose 18 times, while expenses increased 45 times. Many salary-earners, and particularly lower and lower-middle graded civil servants, appear to spend several times more than they earn, which led to questions being raised about the possible source of such extra funds.

BUREAUCRACY

The government failed to live up to its many promises to eliminate, or even ease, the difficulties of every Iranian citizen in dealing with state bureaucracy. Over 30 procedures were sometimes necessary to obtain the simplest of official permits. There were also complaints about the negative attitude of government clerks towards citizens, and of contradictory rules enforced by different government agencies.

Bureaucracy and government inefficiency often prevented the poorest sections, in particular, from receiving social benefits. Muhammed Reza Neqabat, director of the National Social Security Fund, admitted that it took many months before applicants received what was due to them.[3] Others failed to apply for benefits at all.

PORT CONGESTION

During the latter part of 1975, ships were forced to wait up to 250 days for unloading because of the limited capacity of Iran's ports. This caused an enormous increase in costs, as well as significant delays in government projects.

INDUSTRIAL CAPACITY

Iranian industry was reported to be working at about only 60% of capacity in May

1977. (Textile industry 61%, brick kilns 46%, cement 96%, sugar 90%, cars 51%, tractors 32%.) The main reasons quoted for this were power blackouts; inadequate transport facilities; shortage of building materials, particularly cement; bureaucratic difficulties; low labour productivity; lack of, or excessively high costs for, skilled workers and managers; and government measures which reportedly discouraged private investment in industry. In this context, the Share Participation Law (the fourth principle of the White Revolution which provides for the compulsory sale of 49% of industrial shares to workers) has been repeatedly quoted. In several cases the government forced factory owners to sell shares below their actual value. Moreover, the Ministry of Labour and Social Affairs ordered industrial enterprises to pay bonuses to workers during 1975 and 1976—even where losses were sustained. As these bonuses are in general equivalent to 100 days' pay they imposed a heavy burden on industrial entrepreneurs.

AGRICULTURAL SHORTCOMINGS

Approximatey 50-55% of Iran's population live in rural areas, including about 55,000 villages. However, only 35% of Iran's work force is employed in agriculture, and less than 15% of GNP is earned by the rural sector. The situation is aggravated by an annual exodus of 250,000 farmers to Tehran or provincial cities, even though wage rates for agricultural labour have risen at a rate of 35% annually since 1975. Nevertheless, a typical daily wage of $4.30 (Rls 300) in one of the more prosperous farming areas, compares unfavourably with $14.20 (Rls 1.000) for semi-skilled labour in towns.

This situation seriously affected agricultural production and basic food costs. Consumption of food is reckoned to be growing at the rate of 12.5% annually, while agricultural production has remained stagnant throughout the last 25 years.[4]

	1951-52	*1974-75*
Wheat	2,924,000 tons	2,886,000 tons
Barley	809,000 tons	751,000 tons
Rice	709,000 tons	826,000 tons
Potatoes	98,000 tons	354,000 tons
Onions	?	136,000 tons

This situation was further aggravated by the great quantity of agricultural produce wasted by bad storage, inefficient transport and probably also by passive resistance of peasants opposed to government agencies which force them to sell at low prices. The value of agricultural produce wasted annually has been estimated at $1,000m.[5]

The failure of the government's agricultural policies has been blamed on the relative neglect of the primary sector, the negative effect of price controls on production, and the failure to maintain large-scale co-operatives. The existing 118 co-operatives have taken up 12% of the arable land, but supply only 6% of the produce marketed. The main reasons for this failure were apparently the farmers' opposition to giving up independent work and inefficient bureaucratic administration.

UNFAVOURABLE BALANCES OF TRADE AND PAYMENT

If oil exports are excluded, statistics for March 1976-March 1977 show a most unfavourable balance of trade. Non-military imports during 1976-7 reached $14,100m, as compared with a mere $625m in exports (the official but inexact figure for arms imports was $3,500m).

It is true that 60% of imports consist of investment goods (machinery and parts

24%, steel products 17%, vehicles and parts 12%, and electric machinery 7%), and form part of Iran's industrialization efforts. Nevertheless, Iran's imports of consumer goods (minus capital goods and arms) still account for $3,800m—six times as much as exports.

Two other factors adversely affect the balance of payments. First, the cost in foreign currency of Iranians going abroad greatly exceeds earnings from foreign tourists. Second, Iranian money is exported illegally on a large scale. Estimates indicate that during 1976 and the first half of 1977, at least $2,000m was transferred to Western Europe and the US. The flight of money is, of course, a direct reaction to official economic policies, and probably also reflects a general feeling of economic as well as social and political anxiety.

POLITICAL IMPLICATIONS OF SOCIAL AND ECONOMIC POLICY FAILURES

Economic policy failures in 1975-6 started to erode public support for the Shah's regime which, since the beginning of the White Revolution in 1963, had been based on an active coalition of government agencies and the army and a silent coalition of the lower rural and urban classes, and the urban upper-middle and upper classes. Opposition to the regime was recruited from former big landowners, the *'ulama*, bazaar merchants and the Left-wing intelligentsia.

The Shah had originally gained the support of all government agencies and civil servants by making them responsible for implementing his ambitious industrialization and modernization programmes. Army support was ensured by the Shah's close personal surveillance of army officers; the provision of sophisticated weapons; a system of rapid advancement within the military hierarchy and in some cases also within the government, and a highly comfortable way of life for middle and higher-ranking officers.

The Shah had gained the support of the poorer rural masses by carrying out land reform, which had eliminated or at least decreased their dependence on landowners, and turned many of them into smallholders themselves. The poorer urban classes were won over by free education and social security benefits. Industrial workers among them enjoyed, in addition, the benefits of the profit-sharing system and a general increase of industrial wages. The upper-middle and upper classes—particularly industrialists, bankers and big merchants—profited from government loans and from the general economic boom resulting from the oil bonanza.

However, the failure of social and economic policies during 1975 and 1976 threatened to alienate many of these social groups previously loyal to the Shah's regime. Inflation and expensive housing upset the poorer urban classes; price controls upset the farmers, shopkeepers and industrialists: while government bureaucracy (and corruption) upset everybody. Rationalization (necessarily accompanied by dismissals) and a severe campaign against corruption jeopardized the loyalty and co-operation of civil servants. Profit-sharing and the rent freeze alienated property owners, industrialists and other capitalist groups.

This growing mood of dissatisfaction and anxiety seriously curtailed the Shah's ability for political manoeuvre and for decisive action to face the country's serious problems.

THE ROLE OF THE RULING PARTY

The Shah's wish to bolster his power base by establishing a loyal and disciplined mass movement had led to the foundation of the *Rastakhiz* (Resurrection) Party on 1 March 1975. In launching the movement, the Shah had called upon every Iranian "who believes in the constitution, the monarchy and the principles of the Sixth Behman [White] Revolution" to join the new party. At the same time all other political parties were banned.[6]

From March 1975 until October 1976, the *Rastakhiz* Party built up a mass movement, enrolling over 5m members. (Out of Iran's 35m population, only c. 7.5m were eligible for party membership. Ineligible were those below the age of 18, the armed forces, citizens living outside Iran, nomadic tribes, seasonal migrants, prisoners and the mentally ill.) These restrictions on party membership were aimed at preventing a politicization of the army, as well as infiltration of the party by hostile elements.

Prior to the party congress on 28–29 October 1976, the constitution required all *Rastakhiz* members to vote for delegates who, in turn, would choose from among their number the party's new Secretary-General (in succession to the former Prime Minister), the Political Bureau, and other political functionaries. The democratic nature of this process led party members to expect that they would have an active role in political decision-making. For instance, discussions on the relationship between the *Rastakhiz* Party, the *Majlis* and the Government produced demands for party control over personal nominations as a means of exerting influence over political affairs. This was more than the Shah was prepared to concede, and pressures for these changes were suppressed. With regard to democratic discussion within the party, the Shah stated: "Everything is freely subjected to discussion in the party. He [the party member] can easily bring up a subject and receive his answer to the subjects raised from higher officials."[7]

During 1975 and early 1976, the Shah had explained that the party's main aim was to create democracy through increased popular participation; however, at the end of October 1976, he stated: "The purpose of the party is to provide social, political and even philosophical education for our people . . . and to create the right mentality. The traditionally individualistic mentality of the Iranians should be gradually tamed. We must turn to community work and community mentality."[8]

The party congress proceeded according to the Shah's wishes. Jamshid Amuzegar, Minister of Interior Affairs and the country's chief oil negotiator, was elected Secretary-General by the 5,200 delegates; the party's constitution and articles of association were approved; and the party was committed to expanding its organization and to educating Iranians in its philosophy.

The Shah's success in organizing a disciplined congress and in getting the endorsement of his candidate, ensured that the ruling party would serve as a pliant instrument in his hands. Amuzegar's considerable ability as an organizer and administrator promised to turn the party into an effective working organization; and his high personal prestige made it easier for the Shah to control the government. On the other hand, the discipline enforced upon the party alienated many members and further eroded the Shah's popular support at a time when he badly needed it to tackle Iran's serious problems.

THE ROLE OF THE SHAH: NOVEMBER 1976 TO APRIL 1977

GOVERNMENT CHANGES

In his speech from the throne inaugurating the 24th session of the *Majlis* and the 7th session of the Senate on 6 October 1976, the Shah called for an improvement in Iran's educational system and its adaptation to the country's economic needs. He demanded improvements in the road system and a great increase in the country's port capacity. He also denounced an "almost runaway increase in wages and salaries in the private sector," and promised to "curb severely illegal profiteering and swindles" which he blamed for the housing shortage and excessively high rents.

The need to implement this programme with vigour appears to have been the main reason for government changes early in November. The Education Minister, Hushang Sharifi, was replaced by Manuchehr Ganji, a former Secretary-General of the Iranian Committee of Human Rights, and Dean of the Faculty of Law at Tehran University. The Minister for Transport and Roads, Javad Shahrestani, was replaced by Ibrahim Farahbakhshiyan, a former Governor-General of Luristan province. The new Minister of Labour and Social Affairs was Manuchehr 'Azmun, formerly deputy-director of National Iranian Television, chief of Pars News Agency, Under-Secretary in the Ministry of Interior Affairs and assistant to the Prime Minister. He replaced Qasem Mo'ini, who moved to the Ministry of Internal Affairs. 'Azmun was charged by the Shah both with creating a more productive work force (by increasing labour discipline and productivity) and with ensuring that workers received their entitled social security benefits. The new Minister of Justice, Gholam Reza Kiyanpur, was charged with promoting judicial reform (see below) speeding up the court system by simplifying procedures and improving administration, thus enabling the quick and severe punishment of criminals and violators of the existing rent-freeze and price-control regulations.

The former Minister of Co-operatives and Rural Affairs, Reza Sadeqiani, left the government, and the Ministry itself was dissolved. Most of its departments were merged with the Ministry of Agriculture; though its marketing operations were transferred to the Ministry of Commerce, and its industrial activities to the Ministry of Industry and Mines. These changes were intended to achieve a greater degree of rationalization within the existing bureaucracy. (For political implications, see below.)

Jamshid Amuzegar left his post as Minister of Interior Affairs, but remained in the cabinet, as a Minister of State. He also kept his responsibilities as Iran's chief negotiator in oil affairs. Amuzegar was replaced as Minister of Interior Affairs by Qasem Mo'ini, formerly Minister of Labour and Social Affairs. Finally, Karim Pasha Bahadori, formerly the chief of Empress Farah's Special Bureau, was appointed Minister of Information and Tourism. (For a table showing the government changes announced on 4 November 1976 and subsequently, see below.)

Further minor changes were made in the Government by Hoveyda at the end of February. Difficulties in Iran's electrical power supply and delayed work on the power system led to the Minister of Energy, Iraj Vahidi, being replaced by Parviz Hekmat, formerly Under-Secretary for Technical Affairs in the Plan and Budget Organization. At the same time, the Minister for Science and Higher Education, 'Abdul-Hoseyn Sami'i, was replaced by Qasem Mo'tamedi, a former Chancellor of Esfahan University.

"WAR ON WASTE" AND THE IMPERIAL COMMISSION FOR EFFICIENT RESOURCE APPLICATION

On 7 November 1976, three days after presenting 'Abbas Hoveyda's new government, the Shah decreed a "War against Waste" and announced an Imperial Commission for Efficient Resource Application. Its secretary was 'Ali Mussavi-Nasl, formerly Deputy-Minister of Roads and Transport, planning director of National Iranian Steel Company and professor at Aryamehr University. However, the Commission came under the Shah's personal supervision and was attached to his Special Bureau, headed by Nasratollah Mo'iniyan. The director of the Imperial Inspectorate, General Fardust, and the director of the Special Army Inspectorate, General Firuzmand, were named as members of the Commission, and each ministry was asked to appoint two representatives. *Rastakhiz* also appointed two farmers, two workers, and two representatives of owners of medical insurance cards, rural co-operatives and consumer co-operatives respectively. Finally the Iranian Chamber of Commerce, Industry and Mines, as well as the mass media, were also each asked to appoint two members.

The Commission's mandate was to devise and implement plans for eliminating waste and raising productivity in both state-owned and private industry; to eliminate waste in the transport, storage, purchasing and marketing of food products; to deal with congestion and delays at ports; to eliminate power failures; to evaluate causes for delays in implementing some development projects; and to improve the operations of rural and consumer co-operatives. The Commission was also required to implement the Ramsar Education Conference's proposals to reform the education system. Eight committees were established: on energy, insurance, industry, rural and consumer co-operatives, ports, national development and education. The eighth committee was to co-ordinate the Commission's work.

These moves by the Shah offered substantial political advantages. First, the creation of the Imperial Commission legalized and at the same time institutionalized public criticism of various social and economic shortcomings (see above). Second, by placing the Commission under his personal supervision, the Shah created a sense of great urgency, while at the same time increasing his personal control over all executive affairs. Third, the appointment of representatives from every layer of society—not just from the government—created the impression of popular participation in dealing with the country's most serious problems (although the representatives of the rural and consumer co-operatives, as well as the Iranian Workers' Organization, were chosen by *Rastakhiz* and not by the organizations themselves). Fourth, the involvement of high officials from every ministry in the Commission's work made it a more effective instrument for day-to-day control of all government activities. Fifth, its authority to investigate deficiencies in the public and private sectors, opened the way to government control of, and involvement in, the management affairs of private companies.

At the end of May 1977, the Commission announced that 1,468 projects to reduce industrial wastage and 1,283 projects to increase productivity had been devised while hundreds of other projects had been rejected because of deficient planning. The work of the Commission was fulsomely praised by the Shah, who announced that it would become a permanent institution.

1977-8 BUDGET ALLOCATIONS

The first indication of the government's preparedness to undertake sacrifices in order to carry out effective measures to ease social and economic grievances was given in the budget for the fiscal year 21 March 1977–20 March 1978, announced in mid-February. (A delay of six weeks was due to last minute cuts resulting from the drop in oil income, see below.)

The budget's outstanding features were a dramatic increase of 50% in allocations for economic development, an increase of 36% for social programmes, and a slight cut in defence and administrative expenditures. (See table at end of this chapter.)

Four clear political trends were distinguishable from the economic and social budget allocations of 1977-8:

1) Increasing attention was given to infrastructure and the removal of bottlenecks. A substantial increase of 32% was granted to education; however, as in the previous year, this will be used for *quantitative* expansion. The following increase of Iran's school population is envisaged:

	1976-7	*1977-8*
Pre-School Age	290,000	430,000
Primary School	4,800,000	5,300,000
Guidance Level School	1,400,000	1,600,000
Secondary School	850,000	930,000

Vocational and Teachers' Training	349,000	421,150
Higher Education	150,000	170,000

The transport vote, which rose by c. 50%, gave special priority to the construction of 6,700 km of feeder roads—the key to developing hitherto untouched rural areas—and a far smaller plan for highway construction (307 km).

Similar emphasis was placed on rural electrification, although more than a third of the 70% increase in the electricity allocation ($1,400m) went to long-term nuclear programmes (see also below).

2) Government involvement in industrialization continued, with investment exceeding $1,600m—a 30% increase over the previous year. Almost half ($760m) will go to the steel and metals industry; c. 13% ($240m) to chemicals and petrochemicals; c. 8% ($130m) to paper and cellulose; and c. 6% ($100m) to transport, including tractors, railways and shipbuilding.

3) While the government plans to continue its agricultural policy, large farming units have proved unsuccessful (see above) and their establishment will be slowed down. Only five additional farm co-operatives will be added to the existing 95. The allocation of $110m or 3% of the total budget to rural development seems remarkably small, considering that 50% of the total population lives in rural areas.

4) Contrary to earlier declarations, the government will build more houses, in particular for teachers, police and gendarmerie, radio and television employees, customs officials, workers in state-owned mines and industries, as well as for earthquake and flood victims. The $1,280m provided for housing is 56% higher than in the previous year. Only a small fraction of this amount—$28.5m or 2.2% of the total housing vote—will be distributed in the form of housing credits. A similar significant increase was provided to expand health and social welfare facilities.

A striking twenty-fold increase was allotted to industrial credits (from $100m to $2,000m) to be channelled to the private sector. In comparison, the $213m allocated to agricultural credits seems relatively small. The marked increase of government allocations for the private sector, particularly industry but also agriculture, reflects a genuine wish to encourage private initiative and prepare the ground for a future lessening of government involvement in economic affairs. At the same time, however, one cannot escape the impression that the enormous increase of loans available to the private industrial sector reflects and promotes political goals as well.[9]

The government took another step at the end of February 1977 to improve Iran's industrial capacity: a revision of the profit-sharing law. Hitherto, workers were supposed to receive 20% of net profits regardless of the work they performed, whereas the new regulations called for bonuses to be calculated on the basis of individual productivity. They were thus meant to encourage workers to stay with one employer, increase production and discipline: the government was clearly submitting to pressure from the private industrial sector.

POLITICAL CONTROL AND INTERNAL SECURITY

The government's moves to deal with social and economic grievances were paralleled by action to control the country's most potentially powerful pressure groups: the commercial and industrial entrepreneurs, workers, farmers and the intelligentsia.

Early in 1977, two bills were prepared to give legality to measures that might be required to assert greater control over private enterprise. The first bill, approved on

15 February, empowered the government to take complete control of production in the private sector in the case of a national emergency. It authorized the government to replace private employees by its own officials, who would thereafter be paid by the enterprises they took charge of. A second bill, approved at the end of May, provided for arbitration councils to deal with economic crimes, to be headed by Ministry of Justice officials.

In February 1977, the government tried to tighten its control over the Iranian Workers' Organization (which comprises all legal unions) by appointing Hoseyn Qorban-Nasab as its new president. He was told by the Shah that the organization would be held responsible for maintaining industrial discipline and for promoting skill and efficiency. Another element of government control was provided by the Prime Minister himself serving as chairman of the organization's decision-making body, the High Labour Council.

The labour law was also amended to empower the government, in an emergency, to invoke disciplinary clauses against harmful labour activities. The new Minister of Labour, Manuchehr 'Azmun, announced that the "Ministry of Labour" had simultaneously become a "Ministry of Employers." It strongly encouraged the employment of foreign labour, which was seen by some as a means of weakening Iranian workers' economic leverage. Similarly, the redistribution of the functions of the Ministry of Co-operatives and Rural Affairs (see above) had the effect of diluting the power of the co-operatives and increasing their dependence on government bureaucracy.

Stricter measures against the intelligentsia and even tighter censorship were taken at the end of 1976. These new steps were designed to prevent the publication of undesirable literature and the performance of locally-produced films, even if their criticisms were allegorical. Even the loyal and self-disciplined Iranian press was obliged to submit headlines to the censor.[10] The government also acted more vigorously against the outlawed opposition, especially the Confederation of Iranian Students Abroad (CISA) and the Tudeh communists.

The CISA is an organization of Iranian Marxist and non-Marxist radical student groups in Western Europe and North America. Their congresses in the US and Europe were organized in co-operation with the National Front—the former political movement of Muhammad Mosaddeq which united traditional Right-wing opposition forces. The CISA also staged demonstrations and hunger strikes in San Francisco, Houston, Chicago, New York, Bonn, Rome and Paris.

The Tudeh communists (the Moscow-oriented Communist Party of Iran) continued to operate from East Germany, conducting an international propaganda campaign against the Shah's regime through clandestine radio stations and Marxist periodicals. However, one of their stations, the Iran Courier (believed to broadcast from Bulgaria), was closed down on 30 November 1976. Among the recent successes of Tudeh's secretary-general, Iraj Eskandary, in mobilizing international communist support were the promises of co-operation from the Italian Communist Party and from the Cuban regime.

Besides periodic armed clashes with Iran's security forces, a series of terrorist acts and assassination attempts were carried out by the CISA and the Islamic-Marxists—an Iran-based organization of militant Leftist intellectuals who are also ardent Muslims. On 27 August 1976, three American employees of Rockwell International were killed in Tehran. At the beginning of November, the Iranian cultural attaché at Iran's embassy in Paris was shot. In May 1977, the Jewish Agency building in Tehran was attacked; two of the attackers were shot and two policemen seriously wounded.

Although this clandestine opposition violence was somewhat more frequent than in previous years, and although it succeeded in catching the headlines of the world press, it appeared not to constitute any real challenge to the Iranian government, having little popular support inside the country itself. Nevertheless, the Iranian security forces intensified their activities. During October 1976, they killed nine and captured four members of the outlawed opposition in armed clashes. In November, they killed another three and uncovered a "terrorist network" under the leadership of Behram Aram, who was accused of having masterminded the assassination of the three Rockwell International employees. In December, they killed nine and arrested eleven in armed clashes. Zara Agha, a woman convicted of responsibility for a bomb explosion at Sulaymaniyya police station, was executed by firing squad on 21 December.

Iran's treatment of prisoners came under severe criticism from Amnesty International and from other international pressure groups, especially after the Carter Administration announced its new policy on human rights. At first the Iranian government simply denounced these criticisms as "plots." Moreover, a great effort was made to explain to Western public opinion the illegal and terrorist tendencies of the outlawed opposition. However, as in the past, the Shah personally decreed that a substantial number of political prisoners be freed. A new policy was also initiated in February 1977 of publishing the names of those released. The following table gives an idea of the numbers involved between March 1976 and March 1977.

Date of Order for Discharge	*Numbers of Prisoners*
21 March 1976	305
23 April 1976	179
30 June 1976	862
24 October 1976	451
26 October 1976	1,146
7 December 1976	282
2 February 1977	317
28 February 1977	1,165
17 March 1977	653
26 March 1977	91
Total	**5,451**

THE GROWTH OF OPPOSITION AND THE GOVERNMENT'S RESPONSE

POLICY ON HUMAN RIGHTS

Despite official statements that the government would not submit to international pressure on the human rights issue, there were signs early in 1977 of greater susceptibility to American policy. On 1 February, Iranian newspapers reported that the Shah had personally instructed Savak (the intelligence agency) and prison authorities to refrain from torture. In April, a political trial of 11 members of the so-called "revolutionary wing of the Tudeh Communist Party" and the Confederation of Iranian Students Abroad was held in public—the first time in several years. In May, two days before the US Secretary of State arrived in Tehran to attend the CENTO conference, an appeal was heard and the sentences reduced.

A Red Cross delegation was permitted to visit 20 Iranian prisons holding 3,087 prisoners between mid-April and early June. At the end of June, the leader of the mission, Alexander Hay, handed the Shah a copy of the official Red Cross report. It was understood that the prison authorities intended to implement proposals to improve conditions, and that the same delegation would inspect the prisons later in 1977. Also in June 1977, prisons were opened to visits by newsmen from the Belgian paper *Le Soir* and the BBC.

A proposed amendment to the military prosecution law was discussed in the

Majlis in July. This provided new guarantees for political dissidents' rights: those arrested would be brought to trial within 24 hours and either charged or released. Civilian prisoners would be given the right to choose their own lawyers and to inspect prosecution dossiers. All military trials would be held in public, unless the prosecutor considered this a danger to public order, the national interest or morality.

NEW OPPOSITIONAL ACTIVITY

The increasing social discontent (discussed above) led to new kinds of oppositional activity: the writing and distribution of mimeographed copies of signed letters of complaint, as well as declarations and pamphlets addressed to the Shah or his Special Bureau, to the Prime Minister and to the Secretary-General of the *Rastakhiz* party. At first these letters only criticized government policies. When it became apparent that neither the government nor SaVak was acting against the signatories, however, increasing demands for reform and for a greater degree of freedom were put forward, in many cases by well-established people who belonged to "loyal" sections of Iranian society. Some had been members of different National Front organizations, but were subsequently integrated into the existing political system.

Hundreds of letters were reported to have been distributed: one of 200 pages was written in February 1977 by Haj Seyyid Javadi, former co-editor of *Kayhan*. He denounced the dependence of the legislative and judicial branches of government on the executive, and accused government offices of responsibility for the country's economic problems. In May, a former senator and historian, Ibrahim Khajenuri, wrote to *Rastakhiz*'s Secretary-General, Jamshid Amuzegar, questioning the party's right to exist in its present form. He argued that "parties established by order are merely for show rather than based on faith and belief." Khajenuri added that most Iranians remained aloof from the party and did not believe in its usefulness. He charged that party activists worked either to "ensure personal gains" or "ward off imagined harm." Finally, Khajenuri demanded the establishment of a genuine opposition party, as well as an open, sincere and frank public discussion of Iran's political system.

At the end of May, 54 lawyers sent a telegram to the Director of the Shah's Special Bureau, Nasratollah Mo'iniyan, to protest against the proposed reforms by the Ministry of Justice to increase government control over the Judiciary (see above). In June, 40 members of the unofficial writers' union wrote to the Prime Minister, calling for freedom of expression and an end to censorship. They asked for permission to found an *avant-garde* newspaper and for official recognition of their union. The signatories included the country's best-known historian, the former ambassador to India, Fereydun Adamiyat, as well as the prominent writer, Dr Sa'edi, who had already been imprisoned several times.

Also in June, 10,000 copies were circulated of a two-page letter to the Shah signed by Dr Shahpur Bakhtyar, Dr Karim Sanjabi and Daryush Foruhar. All three were former members of the National Front, "dissidents" who had been close to the Pan-Iranists—a party of strong nationalist tendencies which was curbed after 1970 when it opposed the Shah's renunciation of Iranian sovereignty over Baḥrayn. The letter called on the Shah to "end despotic government; observe the principles of the Constitution and the Universal Declaration of Human Rights; forego a one-party system; allow freedom of the press and of association; release political prisoners; permit exiles to return; and establish a government based on majority representation."

On 12 July, after meeting publicly in a Tehran hotel, 64 lawyers signed a declaration which called for the Judiciary and Parliament to be freed from the "grip of executive power in Iran;" for properly held elections; for the delegation of decision-making from the Shah to the Iranian nation; and for strict obedience to the letter and the spirit of the Iranian Constitution. The declaration specifically called for the abolition of all "extra-constitutional courts"—which referred to military tribunals, as well as to the special courts set up in connection with the price control system.

Most of the signatories of these letters appeared to belong to the wealthier classes, and it seems probable that some of them acted as proxies for Iranian industrial and business circles. Remarkably, from April through August 1977, when loyal sections of the population engaged in oppositional activities, the outlawed opposition groups refrained from any terrorist action.

GOVERNMENT RESPONSE TO NEW OPPOSITION

The development of opposition from within the established political system posed a new challenge to the Shah and his government—particularly at a time when economic difficulties were continuing to exacerbate grievances, and when US pressures reduced the Shah's options. He responded to this challenge by cautiously defusing the accumulating pressures.

The Shah's first noteworthy move was to reinforce his image as a benign and fatherly ruler to his people, and as a leader who wanted to take personal charge of their problems. At the beginning of May 1977, accompanied by the Empress, he toured Khorāsān province in north-east Iran, talking and listening to farmers. On occasion, he told farmers that their demands and expectations were not justified, or explained shortcomings. He also issued orders on the spot aimed at making quick improvements where these were possible. Similar visits were made in June by the Prime Minister to Kashan, and by Empress Farah to Gilan. Characteristic of these tours were the religious piety demonstrated by the Shah and the Empress, as well as their traditional donations to religious funds. Instructions were reportedly given for an effective follow-up to these provincial tours, with the Imperial Inspectorate ordered to check what improvements had been made in each area.

Another official step was to initiate public discussion and encourage open criticism. At the end of May, the *Rastakhiz* newspaper published Senator Khajenuri's letter in full (see above), together with a reply by the Secretary-General, Jamshid Amuzegar. The public was invited to join in the debate, which continued in the columns of the *Rastakhiz* newspaper throughout May and June.

This encouragement of public discussion had two aims. First, to legitimize criticism, direct it into party channels, and even possibly revive popular participation in *Rastakhiz* activities. Second, to enable party spokesmen to propagate official answers to complaints and criticism. Thus it was argued that the reintroduction of a multi-party system would throw Iran back to the period between 1941 and 1953 when the country was weak, both internally and externally. In contrast, the policy of "national unity" within the one-party system contributed to building up a strong Iran. The country's economic and social difficulties, so the argument went, were a by-product of Iran's rapid economic growth, which had worked (and was still working) in favour of the nation as a whole, and also in the interest of each section of the population.

The public discussion took a new turn in mid-June when the Empress openly condemned censorship, saying that neither Rembrandt nor Iran's national poet, Hafez, could have created their works had they been subject to censorship. A few weeks later, the Prime Minister joined the Empress in calling for freedom of expression. Shortly afterwards, the Imperial Commission for Efficient Resource Application (see above) published a highly critical report about inefficiencies in different branches of government. Another move encouraging criticism was the announcement in early July that film censorship had been greatly relaxed.

This promise of more freedom from mid-July led the newspapers to adopt a highly critical tone in reporting government activities and in condemning restrictive measures—while always careful to pledge loyalty to "*Rastakhiz* ideology." Their criticisms also stopped short of demanding popular participation in decision-making.

FAILURE OF ECONOMIC POLICIES

During the summer of 1977, it became plain that the government's measures to overcome the nation's social and economic difficulties had failed. Statistics published by Iran's Central Bank showed that the overall rate of inflation from 21 March to 21 August 1977 was 16.6%. Unofficial estimates claimed that the actual cost of living over the five-month period was up by 20%. Central Bank statistics showed that food prices had increased by 36.6% and clothing by 35%; but unofficial estimates put the increases at 50% and 40% respectively.[11] The increase in housing costs was even worse—55% between March and August 1977 (see Inflation and Housing above).

Another dramatic development was the increasing shortage of electric power supplies, a problem which assumed critical proportions by June/July 1977 due to contractual difficulties, inadequate water levels and a gross underestimate of demand. Power failures particularly disrupted industries in the south and in the Tehran area. In mid-June, the Ministry of Energy announced measures to conserve power by scheduling rotating black-outs, at first once a week and later several hours daily. Offices and shops had to turn lights off after 8 p.m. The situation grew worse during July when 100 factories were ordered to close down for ten days. Subsequently, over 180 factories in the Tehran area were shut for all of August and September. Factories forced into inactivity included some in the food-processing industry—which created scarcities in chickens, eggs, butter, cheese and other items. Apart from state-owned industries, 900 privately-owned factories sustained heavy losses.

THE SHAH'S NEW ROLE

THE FALL OF PRIME MINISTER HOVEYDA

The cumulative effect of open criticism and increasing economic difficulties made the government's position increasingly untenable. On 6 August 1977, acting on the personal order of the Shah, Prime Minister 'Abbas Hoveyda announced his own resignation and that of his cabinet. Continuously in office since January 1965, Hoveyda had been Prime Minister longer than any other Iranian politician in this century, and his tenure had been associated with the stability of Iran's political system. Not surprisingly, therefore, his resignation was seen as a watershed in Iran's modern history.

Thirteen members of Hoveyda's cabinet who were also dismissed included the head of the powerful Plan and Budget Organization, 'Abdul Majid Majidi, and the Ministers of Agriculture; Industry and Mines; Energy; Commerce; Transport and Roads; Housing and Town Planning; Labour and Social Affairs; Science and Higher Education; and Information and Tourism. Three Ministers of State, who had worked as personal assistants of Hoveyda, also left with him.

Hoveyda's fall was a clear admission that the basic assumptions which had guided the government's economic policies during the period of the fifth Five-Year Plan (1973-8) had been unrealistic. It signalled the end of the drive for unlimited economic growth at any cost, created the feeling that public criticism had finally been effective, and encouraged hopes for a removal of existing social and economic grievances.

However, a remarkable feature of Iran's modern political system was the Shah's continued loyalty towards his dismissed Prime Minister and at least four former ministers. Hoveyda was appointed Minister of Court, while Majidi was appointed secretary-general to the Empress Farah Foundation, and continued as a leader in the *Rastakhiz* Party. The Minister of Industry and Mines, Farrokh Najmabadi, was appointed managing director of Iran's National Steel and Copper Industries. Qasem Mo'tamedi, Minister of Science and Higher Education, became chancellor of Tehran University; and Minister of Labour and Social Affairs, Reza 'Azmun, was appointed Governor-General of Fars province. However, the former ministers of Agriculture, Energy, Commerce, Transport and Roads, Housing and Town-Planning were not re-employed—indicating particular Royal displeasure with their performance.

THE NEW GOVERNMENT UNDER JAMSHID AMUZEGAR

The composition of Amuzegar's new cabinet, formed on 7 August 1977, revealed six main tendencies.

1. *Continuation of Iran's Foreign and Security Policies* This tendency was reflected by the continuance in office of the Foreign Minister, 'Abbas 'Ali Khal'atbari; the Minister of War, Reza 'Azimi; the Minister of State and director of Savak, Ne'matollah Nasiri; the Minister of State and director of Iran's Atomic Energy Organization, Akbar E'temad.

2. *Continuation of Social, Education and Justice Policies* This tendency was shown by the renomination of Shoja ed-din Sheykh-ul-Islamzadeh as Minister of Health and Social Affairs; of Manuchehr Ganji as Minister of Education and Sciences (for an administrative aspect of this move see also below); and of Gholam Reza Kiyanpur as Minister of Justice.

3. *Co-operation with Leaders of Former Economic Policies* The powerful Minister of Economy and Financial Affairs, Hushang Ansari, remained in office; as did Safi Asfiya, as Minister of State for Economic Affairs.

4. *Broadening of Amuzegar's Personal Power Base* Six of the new ministers were formerly close associates of Amuzegar, while the new director of the Plan and Budget Organization, Muhammad Yeganeh, was a close personal friend (who had been Minister of State in the former government and was in charge of Iran's Foreign Aid Programme). Other former associates of Amuzegar were the Minister of Interior, Asadollah Nasr Isfahani (formerly Governor-General of Fars); the Minister of Information and Tourism, Daryush Homayun (editor and co-proprietor of the daily *Ayandegan* and, since November 1976, Deputy Secretary-General of the *Rastakhiz* party); the Minister of Transport and Roads, Morteza Salehi (a former Governor-General of Khuzistan); the Minister of State for Parliamentary Affairs, Mahmud Kashefi (formerly Parliamentary Under-Secretary in the Ministry of Finance in 1972, and General-Secretary of the Employment and Administrative Affairs Organization in 1974); the Minister of State for Executive Affairs, Manuchehr Agah (formerly Economic Under-Secretary in the Ministry of Finance and Parliamentary Under-Secretary in the Ministry of Interior); and the Minister of State, 'Ali Farshchi (who had held senior posts in the Ministry of Finance and Ministry of Interior Affairs as well as serving with Amuzegar in *Rastakhiz*).

5. *Increased Efficiency in Economic Affairs* Amuzegar appointed four of the country's most successful administrators to key economic ministries. Muhammad Reza Amin, the former managing-director of the National Iranian Steel Company, was put in charge of the Ministry of Industry and Mines. Taqi Tavakkoli, the former director of the National Iranian Copper Company, headed

the Ministry of Energy. Firuz Towfiq, formerly head of the Iranian Statistics Centre, was appointed Minister of Housing and Town Planning; and Ahmad 'Ali Ahmadi, former Under-Secretary in the Ministry of Agriculture, was appointed Minister of Agriculture.

6. *Improving Relations with Industrialists, Business and Workers* The nomination of Kazem Khosrowshahi—a private businessman, leading industrialist and influential member of the Chamber of Commerce, Industries and Mines—as Minister of Commerce suggested that the new government was seeking to improve relations with Iran's private sector. On the other hand the return of Amir Qasem Mo'ini to the Ministry of Labour and Social Affairs, in place of Manuchehr 'Azmun, was clearly intended to improve relations with the workers' organization.

(For the composition of the new Iranian Government, see Table overleaf.)

THE NEW GOVERNMENT PROGRAMME

Amuzegar presented his new cabinet to the *Majlis* on 18 August and at the same time announced the main objectives of his Government's programme. 1) Elimination of bottlenecks to maintain balanced economic and social growth, with emphasis on public investment in infrastructure (power, water, communications, education and health). 2) Greater encouragement for the private sector, particularly to promote industrial production. 3) A radical campaign against inflation, but not at the expense of economic growth. 4) Promotion of the agricultural sector through incentives and protection for farmers. 5) Top priority to low-cost housing, through incentives to the private sector, and through direct government intervention where necessary. 6) In education, particular emphasis on vocational training, combatting illiteracy, and improving educational facilities. 7) In social services, particular attention to free health care. 8) Strong emphasis on rationalizing government departments and reducing public expenditure. (A start was made by merging the Ministry of Science and Higher Education with the Ministry of Education.)[12] In matters of defence and foreign affairs, Amuzegar's government announced a continuation of existing policies.

NEW PRINCIPLES OF THE WHITE REVOLUTION

The Shah declared two new principles of the White Revolution on 17 August 1977. The "18th Principle" established controls over land prices: the government was ordered to take action to ensure that the relative rise in the price of land each year would not exceed the maximum annual level of inflation. This could involve the use of state land for housing construction, or direct control measures to prevent land speculation and reduce investments in real estate. The "19th Principle" aimed at ensuring strict financial integrity in public life. The edict directed all ministers, governors-general, senior judges, ambassadors, directors-general of government departments, directors, managers of state corporations and important mayors to declare all their private assets, and those of their immediate families. The decree also ordered that "company shares or bank shares of similar holdings" owned by such officials be converted to government bonds or put in trust in banks during their term of office.

PUBLIC REACTIONS TO THE NEW GOVERNMENT

The fall of the Hoveyda government prompted a change in political behaviour by several political groups. The Chamber of Commerce, Industries and Mines, as well as the Iranian Workers' Organization—bodies hitherto largely concerned with implementing government policy—were transformed into real pressure groups.

This was particularly striking with the Chamber of Commerce, Industries and Mines, which organized a public campaign for the abolition of the price-control system. Representatives of the Chamber—particularly its president, Senator Taher

The Government

	20 July–4 November 1976	4 November 1976–6 July 1977	7 July 1977
Prime Minister	Amir 'Abbas Hoveyda	Amir 'Abbas Hoveyda	Jamshid Amuzegar
Minister of Court			'Abbas Hoveyda
Other Ministers			
Foreign Affairs	'Abbas 'Ali Khal 'atbari	'Abbas 'Ali Khal'atbari	'Abbas 'Ali Khal'atbari
War	Reza 'Azimi	Reza 'Azimi	Reza 'Azimi
Interior Affairs	Jamshid Amuzegar	Qasem Mo'ini	Asadollah Nasr Isfahani
Economic and Financial Affairs	Hushang Ansari	Hushang Ansari	Hushang Ansari
Industry and Mines	Farrokh Najmabadi	Farrokh Najmabadi	Muhammad Reza Amin
Housing and Town Planning	Homayun J'abar Ansari	Homayun J'abar Ansari	Firuz Towfiq
Commerce	Manuchehr Taslimi	Manuchehr Taslimi	Kazem Khosrowshahi
Transport and Roads	Javad Shahrestani	Ibrahim Farahbakhshiyan	Morteza Salehi
Energy	Iraj Vahidi	Iraj Vahidi[1]	Taqi Tavakkoli
Agriculture	Mansur Ruhani	Mansur Ruhani	Ahmad 'Ali Ahmadi
Co-operative and Rural Affairs[2]	Reza Sadegiani		
Labour and Social Affairs	Qasem Mo'ini	Manuchehr 'Azmun	Amir Qasem Mo'ini
Post, Telegraph and Telephone	Karim Mo'tamedi	Karim Mo'tamedi	Karim Mo'tamedi
Justice	Sadeq Ahmadi	Gholam Reza Kiyanpur	Gholam Reza Kiyanpur
Health and Social Affairs	Shoja ed-din Sheykh-al-Islamzadeh	Shoja ed-din Sheykh-al-Islamzadeh	Shoja ed-din Sheykh-al-Islamzadeh
Education[3]	Ahmad Hushang Sharifi	Manuchehr Ganji	Manuchehr Ganji
Science and Higher Education	'Abul-Hoseyn Sami'i	'Abdul-Hoseyn Sami'i[4]	
Culture and Arts	Mehrdad Pahlbod	Mehrdad Pahlbod	Mehrdad Pahlbod
Information and Tourism	Gholamreza Kiyanpur	Karim Pasha Bahadori	Daryush Homayun
Ministers of State			
Director of the Plan and Budget Organization	'Abdul Majid Majidi	'Abdul Majid Majidi	Muhammad Yeganeh
Economic Affairs	Safi Asfiya	Safi Asfiya	Safi Asfiya
Director of Savak	Ne'matollah Nasiri	Ne'matollah Nasiri	Ne'matollah Nasiri
Director of the Iranian Atomic Energy Organization		Akbar E'temad	Akbar E'temad
Women's Affairs	Mrs Mahnaz Afkhami	Mrs Mahnaz Afkhami	Mrs Mahnaz Afkhami
Parliamentary Assistant to Prime Minister	Ziya ed-din Shadman	Ziya ed-din Shadman	Mahmud Kashefi
Assistant to the Prime Minister and Director of National Mobilization and Civil Defence			Qasem Khaza'i
Assistant to the Prime Minister and Director of Public Endowments			'Ali Farshchi
Minister of State	Fereydun Mahdavi	Fereydum Mahdavi	Manuchehr Agah (Executive Affairs)
Minister of State	Hadi Hedayati	Hadi Hedayati	Sadeq Kazemi (Assistant to the Prime Minister)

[1] Replaced by Parviz Hekmat on 22 February 1977.

[2] The Ministry of Co-operatives and Rural Affairs was dissolved early in November 1976. Its agricultural affairs were delegated to the Ministry of Agriculture; its commercial affairs to the Ministry of Commerce; and its industrial affairs to the Ministry of Industries and Mines.

[3] The Ministry of Education was merged with that of Sciences and Higher Education on 7 August to become the Ministry of Education and Sciences under Manuchehr Ganji.

Ziya'i—publicly demanded measures to enforce labour discipline. Claims were also presented for government repayment of losses sustained by the private sector due to power shortages. In September, further demands were put forward for increased subsidies for exports, and for diplomatic pressure by the Foreign Ministry to secure a reduction of protective customs tariffs in countries offering potential markets.

In August 1977, the president of the Iranian Workers' Organization, Hoseyn Qorban-Nasab, strongly opposed a new scheme which would provide measures to enforce labour discipline (see above). He also argued against the proposal for making the payment of bonuses to workers dependent on a firm's net profits, claiming that this would simply encourage industrialists to declare net losses. Another of Qorban-Nasab's demands was for a change in the share-participation law in order to involve all workers in the management of industrial enterprises according to the number of their shares.

On the other hand, farmers and co-operatives did not come out with any clear-cut demands. While several *Majlis* deputies spoke about the need to improve Iran's agriculture, their main concerns were to supply cheap food and reduce food imports; little was said about improving the farmers' economic condition.

Another significant development was the revival of the *Majlis* as an institution for public discussion: newspapers began to provide wide coverage of its debates.

DEVELOPMENT OF THE AMUZEGAR GOVERNMENT'S ATTITUDES

TOWARDS POPULAR PARTICIPATION

Hopes that the liberal image of the new government would be substantiated by growing popular involvement in government were disappointed. In an interview in September 1977, the Shah not only opposed the establishment of a multi-party system, but even hinted that he would not tolerate any opposition to the *Rastakhiz* Party. Anybody, he said, who did not identify with *Rastakhiz* was "either suffering from mental unbalance or wished Iran to be brought under foreign domination."[13] Nevertheless, at the same time (August/September 1977), a pattern of at least limited popular participation in government decision-making was developing. The Shah indicated that if public criticism led to the formulation of *specific* policies, either he or the government would consider implementing them. One example of this was the change in the government's attitude towards construction permits beyond city limits (see above). When, after the formation of the Amuzegar government, the Tehran municipality ordered illegally constructed houses to be destroyed, public criticism mounted. The *Rastakhiz* Party identified itself with this criticism, and the Shah intervened personally. Thereafter, the government itself prepared a master plan to regulate housing construction beyond the borders of 80 Iranian cities. This official response created the feeling that if criticism was channelled through *Rastakhiz*, there was a chance of bringing about change.

TOWARDS PRIVATE ENTERPRISE

The Amuzegar government adopted a distinctly changed attitude towards the private sector. Previous governments had impeded private enterprise by becoming increasingly involved in economic and labour affairs (see above). For example, they forced industrialists to sell 49% of their shares to workers and pay them substantial bonuses. Although the new government expressly committed itself to the continuation of share-participation for workers, it changed its attitude in all other matters in favour of private enterprise. The Shah stated explicitly in September that one of the government's main aims would be to decrease state intervention in economic affairs and increase incentives to the private sector.[14]

Steps to liberalize the price-control system were taken early in September when the government introduced a new scheme regulating rents and house prices. The scheme granted home-owners important tax reductions if they sold or rented houses at fixed prices. This was clearly a move away from direct government controls (such as the rent freeze) towards influencing the private sector by incentives and encouragement—the new general line of government thinking.

The government also abandoned its former policy of interfering in labour relations in favour of workers against industrialists. It announced that wages would be curbed, and hinted that any labour unrest might induce the government to cut projects and so create unemployment. The Shah declared that labour shortages would be overcome by the dispatch of regular army units "wherever and whenever needed"—a statement clearly intended to apply political and economic pressure on workers.[15]

TOWARDS WORKERS AND THE POORER URBAN CLASS

Amuzegar's government committed itself to continue the previous policy of guaranteeing the material well-being of workers and the poorer urban-dwellers. Reference has already been made to the new policy to provide more low-cost housing, control of land prices, inducements to landlords to sell or rent at reasonable prices, and permission to build beyond the city limits. The government also passed a law enabling municipal authorities to rent houses which had been kept empty for over three months.

On the other hand, the measures outlined above to enforce labour discipline, show that the government was not prepared to allow the workers to assert their economic power.

TOWARDS THE INTELLIGENTSIA

Amuzegar's government appeared to be opting for the support of Iran's intellectuals through its efforts to create a more liberal image. The choice of Daryush Homayun as Minister for Information and Tourism was interpreted as a positive gesture towards Iran's intellectuals. Homayun himself emphasized this by declaring that his major aim was to improve the political climate through providing far more information to the mass media and the public in general.

NUCLEAR PROGRAMME

Iran's ambitious nuclear plans were first announced in 1974. In March 1975, a contract was signed for the purchase of eight 1,200 megawatt nuclear reactors from the US. Another contract for two 900 megawatt reactors was signed with FRAMATOME of France; now under construction the south near Ahvāz, they are due to become operational in 1982–3. A third contract was concluded in 1976 with Kraftwerk-Union of West Germany for two 1,200 megawatt reactors to be built in Halileh village near Būshehr on the Persian Gulf. The German reactors are due for completion in 1980–1. By 1994, the total nuclear programme should encompass 20 nuclear reactors with a total capacity of 23,000 megawatts.

In the next stage of its nuclear programme, Iran endeavoured to ensure a supply of enriched and reprocessed uranium. It therefore bought shares in two French enrichment centres, EURODIF and COREDIF, as well as in the German branch of Babcock & Wilcox. The country has also begun prospecting for uranium at a cost of $300m over ten years. Australian, West German and French companies have been engaged to make aerial surveys for radioactive material over 640,000 sq km. Iran has also embarked on joint ventures for uranium exploration and production with Niger, Zambia and Gabon. Contracts have been signed with French and other unnamed sources for the delivery of c. 30,000 tons of uranium until 1994.[16]

The implementation of the ambitious nuclear programme was seen by the Iranian leadership as vitally important for economic development and the strengthening of Iran's regional power role. However, American pressures to enforce non-proliferation rules more rigorously threatened to torpedo the programme.

There were fears that President Carter might go even further than the Ford Administration which, in October 1976, ordered the suspension of negotiations for the supply of the eight reactors previously contracted. However, in August 1977, negotiations resumed with the US for the delivery of these reactors.

The Shah saw Carter's declared intention to introduce strict regulations to prevent nuclear non-proliferation as a threat to supplies of nuclear fuel from any Western power.[17] In fact, Iran adheres to the Nuclear Non-Proliferation Treaty, and as early as 1974 demanded that the Indian Ocean region be declared a nuclear-free zone. However, it indicated that it would not comply with any new stringent US restrictions which might impede the use of nuclear technology for peaceful purposes. Akbar E'temad, the director of Iran's Atomic Energy Organization, declared in April 1977 (after the Carter Administration announced its intention to halt the development of plutonium as a fuel in nuclear power reactors) that "US nuclear curbs will not affect Iran."[18] To emphasize its stand, Iran negotiated the supply of another two nuclear reactors from Germany, and two from France (in mid-October 1977). Moreover, it also negotiated with the Austrian Government for the reprocessing of nuclear waste, although similar negotiations with West Germany were stopped by the Shah because of public criticism in that country.

At the end of May 1977, Akbar E'temad visited China; and in July, the Soviet Union, where he was reported to have inspected nuclear installations and initiated talks on Irano-Soviet atomic co-operation.

DEFENCE AND SECURITY

The following table shows US arms ordered before March 1976, and due to be supplied in 1977.

US Arms Due for Supply in 1977[20]

To Imperial Ground Forces		*To Imperial Air Force*		*To Imperial Navy*	
Helicopters		Aircraft		Ships	
AH-IJ	34	F-14	42	MKIII'55 Partol Boats	7
214 A/C	120	F-4E	31		
		F-5F	28	Helicopters	
Artillery and Missiles		RF-4E	12	RH 53-D	3
M109 (155mm-SP)	127	SAM			
M110	28	I-Hawk Batteries	27		
TOW (Anti-Tank Missiles)	12,667+	Missiles	1,150		

The biggest item still under discussion was a surveillance system to cover all Iran's borders. Known as IBEX, the system, prepared in 1974, includes 11 ground monitoring posts, six airborne units and several mobile ground units. A contract was signed on 17 February 1975 with Rockwell International. However, the programme was held up after questions were raised about its effectiveness both in the US and Iran. These anxieties were increased in the US after an Iranian reconnaissance *Phantom* with sophisticated instruments on board was shot down over the border between Oman and PDRY in November 1976.

At the end of April 1977, the US was reported to have approved the sale of five surveillance planes, an integral part of the Airborne Warning and Control System (AWACS).[19] At the same time it was announced that President Carter was favourably considering a proposal to supply over 100 F-16s to Iran (see above). However, he was said to have opposed the sale of 250 F-18 Ls because the aircraft fell under the category of "advanced technology." The contract for AWACS was also not finalized by late 1977.

ARMED FORCES

Total armed forces number 342,000. Defence expenditure in 1977–8 was Rls 562.48 bn ($7.9 bn). Military service is compulsory for two years. The Army numbers 220,000 with the following formations: three armoured divisions; four infantry divisions; four independent brigades (two infantry, one airborne, one special force); one surface-to-air missile battalion with *HAWK*, and Army Aviation Command. Equipment consists of 760 *Chieftain*, 400 M-47/-48 and 460 M-60A1 medium tanks; 260 *Scorpion* light tanks; *Fox* and *Ferret* scout cars; about 2,000 M-113, BTR-40/-50/-60/-152 armoured personnel carriers; 650 guns and howitzers, including 75mm, 330 105mm, 130mm, 100 155mm, 175mm self-propelled and 203mm towed and self-propelled; 64 BM-21 rocket launchers; 106mm recoilless rifles; *ENTAC*, SS-11, SS-12, *Dragon*, *TOW* anti-tank guided weapons; 650 23mm, 35mm, 40mm, 57mm, 85mm towed, ZSU-23-4, ZSU-57-2 self-propelled anti-aircraft guns; *HAWK* surface-to-air missiles. (1,220 *Chieftain* medium, 110 *Scorpion* light tanks, BMP mechanized infantry combat vehicles, ASU-85 self-propelled anti-tank, ZSU-23-4 self-propelled anti-aircraft guns, *Rapier*, *Improved HAWK*, SA-7/-9 surface-to-air missiles on order.) Aircraft include 45 Cessna 185, ten O-2A, six Cessna 310, three F-27 and five *Shrike Commander*; 120 AH-1J, 100 Bell 214A, 20 *Huskie*, 52 AB-205A and 40 CH-47C helicopters. (193 Bell 214A and 82 AH-1J on order.) 1,000 men were deployed in Oman. 388 men are with the UN Disengagement Observation Force in Syria. Reserves number 300,000.

The 22,000 strong Navy is equipped with three destroyers (one with *Seacat*, all with *Standard* surface-to-air missiles); four frigates with Mark 2 *Seakiller* surface-to-surface missiles and *Seacat* surface-to-air missiles; four corvettes (ex-US patrol frigates); 20 patrol boats (nine under 100 tons); five minesweepers (three coastal, two inshore); two landing ships and two landing craft; two logistic support ships; eight SRN-6 and six *Wellington* BH-7 hovercraft. (Three *Tang*-class submarines, four *Spruance*-class destroyers, 12 guided-missile fast patrol boats with *Exocet* surface-to-surface missiles and two landing craft on order.) Naval air formations consist of one maritime reconnaissance squadron with six P-3F *Orion*; one anti-submarine warfare squadron with six S-65A and one transport squadron with six *Shrike Commander* and four F-27. Helicopters include five AB-205A, 14 AB-206A, six AB-212, 20 SH-3D and three RH-53D. There are three Marine battalions. (Three P-3C maritime reconnaissance aircraft and three RH-53D helicopters are on order.)

The Air Force numbers 100,000 and is equipped with 341 combat aircraft. Formations consist of ten fighter-bomber squadrons with 32 F-4D, 141 F-4E with *Sidewinder* and *Sparrow* air-to-air missiles and *Maverick* air-to-surface missiles; ten ground-attack fighter squadrons with 12 F-5A and 100 F-5E; two fighter squadrons with 40 F-14A *Tomcat*; one reconnaissance squadron with 16 RF-4E; one tanker squadron with ten Boeing 707-320L; four medium transport squadrons with 57 C-130E/H and five Boeing 747; four light transport squadrons with 23 F-27, three *Aero Commander* 690 and four *Falcon* 20; ten *Huskie*, six AB-205, four AB-206A, five AB-212, five Bell 214C, two CH-47C and 16 *Super Frelon* helicopters. Trainers include nine T-33, 18 F-5B/F and 30 *Bonanza* F33A/C. There are five surface-to-air missile squadrons with *Rapier* and 25 *Tigercat*. (69 F-5E/F, 40 F-14, 160 F-16 fighters; four Boeing 747, two F-27 transports; one Boeing 707-320C tanker; 19 F-33A/C *Bonanza* trainers; 50 CH-47, two AS-61A, 38 Bell 214C helicopters; *Blindfire* surface-to-air missiles radar and *Phoenix*, *Sparrow* and *Sidewinder* air-to-air missiles on order.) Paramilitary forces consist of 70,000 Gendarmerie with light aircraft and helicopters and 40 patrol boats.[21]

FOREIGN AFFAIRS

Iran's foreign policy has traditionally contained two major elements: national and regional security commitments with a strongly Western orientation; and a firm position on higher oil prices. For Iran, as for other major Middle East oil-producing countries, oil has acquired a national symbolic importance beyond purely economic considerations. By taking a strong position on oil-pricing within OPEC, the Shah has been able to present himself as a truly national, independent and progressive ruler. However, these policies came under challenge at the end of 1976 when strong forces in Washington began to question the provision of unlimited support for the Shah's defence programmes, and when the Administration began to take a tough line against Iran's support for higher oil prices. Moreover, the Iranian government was further concerned by the Soviet military build-up in the Indian Ocean and by activities in Iraq, the PDRY and Pakistan. Additional problems were the failure of Iran's attempts to establish a system of collective security in the Persian Gulf, and its dispute with Saudi Arabia over OPEC's pricing policy. The cumulative effect of these difficulties was serious enough to force Iran to seek ways of improving the situation and to re-examine some of the premises of its established policy.

From mid-October 1976, Iran worked for improved relations with Moscow, whose response was favourable; relations remained friendly until late 1977. Tehran also tried to improve relations with its Persian Gulf neighbours by withdrawing most of its troops from Oman in January 1977, and by ostentatiously cutting its military budget for 1977–8. Its initiative for collective security in the Gulf faded away. Instead, Iran endeavoured to improve bilateral relations with individual Gulf states, on the basis of equality. In the rift with Saudi Arabia over the oil price, a compromise was found which enabled both states to keep face.

Parallel with these efforts, Iran worked to strengthen existing friendships with other Northern Tier states, India and the Arab world. Its adherence to the CENTO defence pact was emphasized; and economic co-operation between Iran, Turkey and Pakistan was enhanced within the framework of Regional Co-operation for Development (RCD), as well as through bilateral relations. In June 1977, an important step was taken towards stabilizing Iran's north-eastern frontier by the ratification of a treaty with Afghanistan on the use of the Helmand river waters. Relations with India and Egypt remained very friendly, and in Africa, Iran succeeded in gaining a new ally—Somalia.

Finally, the Iranians sought to establish friendly and confidential relations with the Carter Administration. From April 1977, they started making far-reaching concessions over human rights, and since July, moderated their oil policy—expecting in return support for their nuclear programme and continuation of arms transfers.

In general Iran's foreign policy-makers appear to have succeeded in strengthening the country's security as well as its regional power position in 1976–7, mainly by adopting more moderate policies.

RELATIONS WITH THE US

The policy pursued by the Nixon and Ford Administrations of transferring practically unlimited supplies of weapons to Iran came under review by Congress in the middle of 1976, and subsequently by the Carter Administration. The first important move indicating a change of attitude occurred in June 1976, when the Senate passed amendments to the Foreign Assistance Act of 1961 and the Foreign Military Sales Act, which sought to limit security assistance to "any country, the government of which engages in a consistent pattern of gross violations of internationally recognized human rights."[22] Although Iran was not directly mentioned, media coverage of the treatment of political prisoners there made it apparent that the Senate intended to scrutinize closely future arms supplies to Tehran.

This impression was substantiated when, during and immediately after Secretary of State Kissinger's visit to Iran early in August 1976, a number of influential US senators, particularly Edward Kennedy and Hubert Humphrey, began to criticize US arms supplies to Iran. They argued that the unlimited supply of weapons increased tension and instability in the Persian Gulf area; that Iran was unable to absorb such huge quantities of sophisticated weapons; that Iran's proximity to the Soviet Union and its engagement in regional struggles increased the risk of the Russians obtaining information about highly secret US military equipment; that the large number of US citizens employed by the Iranian government (estimated at 25,000) could become hostages; and finally that the country's considerable armoury might tempt it to embark on adventurous policies, or transfer arms to other regional powers, which might not be compatible with US interests in the area.

The new US Administration also applied considerable pressure to dissuade Tehran from supporting a substantial increase in the oil price at the December OPEC conference at Doha. (For details, see essay "Middle East Oil Development".) Government circles feared that Carter's morally-orientated foreign and activist energy policies could lead, even unintentionally, to the US limiting its support for Iran, or possibly to a split developing between the two countries.[23] In immediate practical terms, this could jeopardize Iran's nuclear and defence programmes.

CHANGING RELATIONS WITH THE USSR

Iran's troubled relations with Moscow underwent sharp changes during the latter part of 1976. Iran had reacted uneasily to reports of a secret $4,000m arms agreement signed between the Soviet Union and Iraq on 17 August 1976. The deal reportedly included MiG-25s and MiG-23s, troop-carrying helicopters and T-62 tanks—supposedly in return for the Soviet right to use Iraqi bases. There were reports at the same time of increased Soviet activity in the PDRY, and even in Pakistan. Iranian anxiety was further augmented by reports that the Soviet naval build-up in the Indian Ocean had given it a 2:1 lead over the Americans. (For a different perspective see essay, "The Military Balance in the Middle East.") Their concern intensified between July and November 1976 over signs of increasing Moscow antagonism towards Tehran. When the Prime Minister, 'Abbas Hoveyda, visited Moscow in July 1976, he was given a cool reception. Soviet journals accused Iran of heightening tensions and mistrust in the region.

On its side, Tehran suspected that the Soviets had at least a passive hand in the assassination of three American employees of Rockwell International at the end of August (see above). Their killing was seen as an indirect protest against the installation of sophisticated intelligence systems on the Iran-Soviet border. Tehran similarly suspected that Moscow had encouraged Libya and the PDRY in their forceful attack on Iran at the 5th Summit Conference of Non-Aligned Countries at Colombo in August 1976, when Qadhdhāfī had accused Iran of acting as a "proxy of imperialism" in its fight against non-aligned countries and demanded steps to "prevent the infiltration of imperialism into our ranks."[24] An anti-Iranian broadcasting station set up in Libya was also thought in Tehran to have been sponsored by the Soviets.

Faced with these increasing signs of Soviet hostility, the Iranian government deliberately set about improving relations. The defection of a Soviet pilot in a two-seater AN-2 offered Iran an opportunity in mid-October to show goodwill—the pilot and plane were returned to Soviet authorities. Also in October, a $550m arms deal was concluded with the USSR involving the sale of tank-transporters, armoured personnel carriers and SAM-7 missiles.[25]

From the end of October, both sides strove for improved relations. Although Soviet policy towards Iran has always been a matter of speculation, it seems very probable that the sudden switch in policy came as a result of the Soviet desire to exploit growing differences between Tehran and Washington. A major step to improve relations was made when the *Iran Courier*, a clandestine radio station broadcasting hostile propaganda and supposedly directed from Moscow, was closed on 30 November 1976.

A protocol on joint Iranian-Soviet industrial projects signed on 2 December 1976, provided for significant extension of economic co-operation. The Soviets undertook to expand the steel works and construct a thermal power station in Esfahan; to set up a heavy industry complex in Khorāsān (Iran's north-eastern province bordering the USSR); to construct eight silos with a capacity of 3m tons; to link Iran's railway with the Soviet Central-Asian system; to electrify the Tabriz-Jolfa railway, and to create a fish-breeding centre on the Caspian.

Shortly afterwards, on 15 December 1976, Iran and the Soviet Union signed a technical agreement providing for mutual co-operation in the fields of science and higher education, agriculture, forestry and environment protection.

FOREIGN POLICY CHANGES IN 1977

IMPROVING RELATIONS WITH THE US

The Shah and his Government made a number of important adjustments in their policy in order to restore relations with the US and gain the confidence of the Carter Administration. The first major move was the Shah's commitment to improving Iran's human rights record, and to creating a more liberal political climate (see above). The second was to cut the military budget for 1976–7, and to withdraw from Oman: decisions designed to counter US Congress criticisms of Iran's "extravagance and adventurism," as well as to achieve regional political goals. Similarly, the third change—moderating its oil policy—was not only motivated by a wish to improve relations with Washington: there were also immediate economic considerations involved, as well as fence-mending with Saudi Arabia. This shift in oil policy is probably only temporary—the Shah's political, psychological, economic and social stake in oil is too high to permit any meaningful long-term concessions in this field.

These policy adjustments were accompanied by a propaganda campaign to explain Iranian policies to the US and Western Europe, which focused on Iran's vital importance to Western interests. Friendly personal relations were established with the new US Secretary of State, Cyrus Vance, when he visited Tehran in May 1977 to attend the CENTO Ministerial Council. In July, the Shah sent the Empress to Washington to meet the President and his wife. This was followed by the Shah's own visit to Washington in November which, while tarnished by an angry demonstration by Iranian students in exile, at least succeeded in arresting the deteriorating relations between the the two nations.

RELATIONS WITH THE SOVIET BLOC

The improvement of relations with Moscow, which began in the latter part of 1976, was confirmed by the arrival of a new Russian ambassador, M. Vinogradov, in February 1977. In March, the Iranian press gave prominence to several articles from the *Novosty News Agency* which praised existing Soviet-Iranian ties and called good neighbourliness a "policy of peace." In mid-May, the Soviet Trade and Industrial Organization signed a memorandum with the Iranian Chambers of Commerce, Industries and Mines, providing for increased co-operation with Iran's private sector. Talks were held in Tehran in June on extending railway and road links between the two countries; parallel talks took place on expanding Iranian transit trade to Western Europe via the Soviet Union. These transit facilities could help ease Iran's problems of port and road congestion (see above). In July, when Iran's electrical system broke down, the Soviets agreed to supply additional power. At the same time, Akbar E'temad, head of the Iranian Atomic Energy Organization, visited the Soviet Union and negotiated a nuclear technology co-operation agreement. (Also see Nuclear programme, above.)

A barter agreement for the sale of 1m tons of Iranian crude oil to the Soviet Union was signed at the beginning of August 1977, in exchange for military supplies. This is the first known instance of oil being imported into the USSR.

These increasingly friendly relations were further demonstrated when the Shah and the Empress paid a state visit to Poland and Czechoslovakia in August 1977.

SECURITY IN THE PERSIAN GULF

Iranian fears of overt and subversive Arab activities against the Shah's rule are of longstanding, and were especially strong between 1958–67.[26] Tehran's response was to gain military control over the entrance to the Gulf, occupying three strategically important islands near the Straits of Hormuz in November 1971. It also secured a northern outlet to the Gulf by enforcing its control over the left bank of the Shatt al-'Arab in April 1969. During the late 1960s and early 1970s, Iran considerably extended its military presence on its own side of the Gulf coast. The Iranians also pursued an unwritten security doctrine whereby all sections of their armed forces had at least to equal the combined military capacity of all the Arab states in the Persian Gulf. To prevent any possible external threat to Gulf security, they intervened militarily in Dhufar (Oman), as well as in Pakistani Baluchistan. Their diplomacy, too, was directed towards maintaining supremacy in the Gulf by exploiting tensions between the Arab Gulf states.

These policies secured for Iran a substantial role as a regional power, which enabled it to help buttress "pro-Western" regimes in the area. However, its activist policy created strong resentments among all the Arab states in the Gulf, and nourished their suspicions of Iranian expansionist ambitions. Amir Taheri, the editor of *Kayhan*, pointed out in 1975 that Iran's Gulf policy was at least partially responsible for Iraq's increasing *rapprochement* with Moscow during the early 1970s.[27] This Arab resentment also impeded the development of close Irano-Arab co-operation in the Gulf.

A conference on Persian Gulf security held in November 1976 in Muscat (Oman) was attended by all Foreign Ministers of the Persian Gulf littoral states. The fact that the conference was held at all was regarded as a victory; nevertheless, it apparently failed to achieve any tangible results, except to encourage both radical and conservative Arab regimes to increase their opposition to an Iranian-initiated collective security system.

However, at the beginning of 1977, the Shah formally announced that he would abandon attempts to promote such a security system.[28] He said that existing disagreements among the Arab Gulf states made the time unpropitious to promote a regional collective agreement. Instead, he would concentrate on improving bilateral relations.

In January 1977, Iran announced the withdrawal of almost all of its 3,200 forces from Oman. By the end of January, only air defence units remained at the Midway airbase, 100 km north of Salalah.

In mid-February, a 2% cut in Iran's defence spending was announced. A substantial part of the $2,260m saving was accounted for by delaying construction of several air bases and Chah Bahar naval base (in the extreme south-east on the Indian Ocean); and by cancelling the planned purchase of several destroyers for the Iranian navy.

A reported offer by Sultan Qābūs of Oman in June that Iran take over the military base at Masīrah island was not taken up.

RELATIONS WITH IRAQ

The longstanding border hostility between Iraq and Iran was settled in March 1975 when the Shatt al-'Arab line was changed in favour of Iran from the eastern shoreline to the thalweg-line; the Iranians, for their part, renounced military and political support for the Kurds. In spite of traditional mistrust, when Iraq's Foreign Minister, Sa'dūn Hammādī, visited Iran from 11-14 January 1977, he was given a very friendly welcome. In July, six bilateral agreements were signed covering trade and cultural relations; co-operation in tourism, agriculture and fishing; railway systems linkages; and co-ordination of activities of common interest between the Interior Ministries.

The Iranian press was careful to point out that the Government had no contact whatosever with the Kurdish leader, Mulla Mustafā Barzānī, who had gone to the US.

RELATIONS WITH SAUDI ARABIA

The OPEC conference held at Doha in December 1976 ended in an open struggle between Iran and Saudi Arabia over the price of oil. (For details, see essays on Oil in the Middle East Context and Inter-Arab Affairs.) Although Iran's position was supported by ten other OPEC members, the Saudi stand challenged the leading role Iran had held within the organization ever since OPEC's successful negotiations in Tehran in February 1971. After Doha, the Shah could no longer claim that Iran's mediating role between OPEC's moderate and more militant members enabled him to dictate the organization's line of action. As late as mid-July 1976, the Shah had argued that "whatever side Iran leans towards [in OPEC] will be the winning side."[29] Domestically, the Saudi policy seriously threatened to curb Iran's oil income at a time when increasing economic and social difficulties were diminishing the Shah's political support (see above). On the international level, Saudi moderation made Iran appear as the leader of the extremist camp within OPEC—an image which threatened to impede Iran's already problematic relations with Washington. Finally, on the regional level, the Iranians were aware that any open rift with Saudi Arabia over the oil price could affect the political stability and security of the whole Gulf region. This disagreement and the Shah's personal sense of having been misled by the Saudis made for troubled relations.[30]

In reaction to the Saudis' policies, the Iranian press led a personal campaign against the Saudi Oil Minister, Aḥmad Zakī al-Yamānī, accusing him of being a "stooge of capitalist circles," of "scheming to wreck OPEC's achievements" and hinting that he profited personally from the two-tier price system offered to oil companies. Similarly, in mid-January, the Shah sent his War Minister, Reza 'Azimi, as his "personal emissary" to King Khālid. However, from about mid-February 1977 onwards, this policy was replaced by distinct moves for reconciliation. Attacks on Yamānī ceased and past misunderstandings were attributed to Western "intrigue," which had a "vested interest" in pulling Iran and Saudi Arabia apart.

In mid-April, the Shah sent as his personal envoy, his step-brother, Prince

Gholamreza, to King Khālid. Soon afterwards it became known that a compromise on the ending of the two-tier price system had been reached. (See essay on Middle East Oil Developments.) The Saudis also reportedly agreed to grant Iran a loan of $3,000m. Although Iran definitely needed the loan, the fact that it could have been obtained elsewhere, underlined a political motive, and established Saudi Arabia and Iran as economic partners on an equal standing. This new friendship was demonstratively shown at the OPEC conference in Stockholm in the beginning of July 1977, when Iran's chief negotiator in oil affairs, Jamshid Amuzegar, stressed that Iran's oil policy was identical with the Saudis'.

RELATIONS WITH UAE AND OTHER PERSIAN GULF STATES

The UAE Foreign Minister, al-Ghubāsh, headed a 14-man delegation to Tehran at the end of May 1977 to discuss bilateral relations. It was agreed to establish a Ministerial Commission for Economic and Technical Co-operation, and to set up an Iranian-UAE bank with a capital of $100m to deal mainly with UAE investments in Iran. A number of joint ventures were proposed in agriculture and industry as well as measures introduced for increased Iranian exports to the UAE.

Relations with Kuwait similarly improved when Kuwait's Under-Secretary of Foreign Affairs, Shaykh Rashid 'Abd al-'Aziz al-Rashid, visited Tehran in February, followed by the Foreign Minister, Sabah al-Aḥmad al-Jabir al-Sabah, in May. Although bilateral relations were discussed, it is believed that Iran was mediating between Kuwait and Iraq in their dispute over the islands of Warbah and Būbīyān.

Relations with Qatar, Baḥrayn and Oman remained cordial throughout 1976–7.

RELATIONS WITH OTHER ASIAN AND AFRICAN STATES

ACTIVITIES WITHIN CENTO

The 24th CENTO Ministerial Council, convened in Tehran on 14 May 1977, was used by Turkey and Iran to obtain assurances of continued US commitment. At the end of the conference, the Turkish Foreign Minister emphasized CENTO was "making great efforts to fulfil its task as an extension of the NATO alliance's requirements in the East."[31] The Iranian press pointed out that CENTO was not only taking measures as a defence alliance against overt (Soviet) aggression, but was mainly preparing to cope with subversion, with the provision of illicit funds for rebellion and insurrection, and with foreign soldiers dispatched to intervene in local wars, as in the case of Cubans in Africa and South Yemen.

All CENTO forces, including those from the US and UK, participated in manoeuvres near Reza'iya in the extreme north-west corner of Iran near the Turkish border, from 3–10 August 1977.

REGIONAL CO-OPERATION FOR DEVELOPMENT (RCD)

RCD was founded in July 1964 in Ankara by the Presidents of Turkey and Pakistan and the Shah of Iran, in order to extend existing military co-operation (within CENTO) to the economic field.

At the annual meeting of the RCD Ministerial Council in İzmir in 1976, the decision was taken to strengthen regional co-operation by introducing a common market between the three member-countries and a Bank for Regional Development, which would finance joint development projects, especially the extension of road and railway communications. In March 1977, the final version of the İzmir treaty was signed in Tehran. Practical steps were taken for co-operation in cultural affairs, industry and communication; custom tariffs were reduced, and border formalities simplified—all initial steps in implementing the "common market."

Another high-level meeting was held at the end of May 1977 in Meshhed, in north-eastern Iran, when additional steps were taken to increase regional co-operation.

RELATIONS WITH PAKISTAN

In the past, the Shah had looked upon a relatively stable and pro-Western Pakistan as an important guarantee for Iran's security. During the Indo-Pakistani war in December 1971, he openly supported Pakistan; afterwards he warned that Iran would not stand by and watch the dismemberment of the country, but would regard a future attack on Pakistan as an attack upon itself.

These close ties began to weaken when Iran engaged in moves to develop a parallel relationship with India (see below). The former Pakistani Prime Minister, Zulfiqar 'Ali Bhutto, reacted by strengthening relations with the Soviet Union and Libya in 1976 and early in 1977, a move which was strongly resented in Tehran. Nevertheless, an Iranian-Pakistani Joint Governmental Commission signed an Economic Co-operation Protocol on 24 May 1977, according to which Iran will invest in 14 projects in Pakistan including textile, cement and fertilizer factories and stock-breeding. A month later, on 21 June 1977, Prime Minister Bhutto paid a visit to Tehran, clearly aimed at re-establishing the former friendly relationship.

The military coup in Pakistan of 5 July was welcomed by the Iranian press. Pakistan's new Minister of Foreign Affairs, Agha Shahi, paid a visit to Tehran in mid-July 1977 to be reassured of Iran's continued support.

RELATIONS WITH AFGHANISTAN

Relations with Afghanistan have been cool but correct since Muhammad Daud Khan made himself ruler in July 1973 and embarked on a pro-Soviet policy. During 1977, however, a distinct improvement of relations took place.

The instrument of ratification of the Helmand River Treaty was exchanged in Tehran on 5 June 1977. Although the treaty (regulating the joint use of the Helmand river waters) was signed in 1973, ratification had been held back by Muhammad Daud Khan. The agreement, welcomed in Tehran as an important move towards stabilizing Irano-Afghani relations, specifies the amount of water each side is to obtain in different seasons of the year; provides for the establishment of joint bodies to ensure the smooth operation of the agreement; and provides machinery to resolve disputes.

Two days after the exchange of instruments of ratification, the Irano-Afghani Ministerial Commission announced that Iran would assist Afghanistan in joint industrial and agricultural undertakings, in establishing the Afghanistan Development Bank, and in extending the country's road and railway network.

RELATIONS WITH INDIA

Iran has sought India's friendship since mid-1972, hoping thereby to increase stability in the Indian Ocean region and draw India away from the Soviet Union. This policy was pursued in 1976–7 through a number of measures including economic co-operation. Projects included the joint construction of a refinery in Madras; the supply of cheap Iranian oil to India; the joint production of iron ore and aluminium in India; the joint management of an Irano-Indian navigation company, and a scheme to employ Indians in Iran. In the summer of 1976, Iran opened a transit route via Pakistan for Irano-Indian trade.

India's new Prime Minister, Morarji Desai, met the Shah during a stopover in Tehran on 7 June 1977. In September, Iran's Minister of Economic and Financial

Affairs visited New Delhi and conferred with his Indian counterpart on measures to improve economic co-operation.

RELATIONS WITH EGYPT AND OTHER ARAB STATES

Throughout the 1970s, Iran has sought the friendship of Egypt and other Arab states in order to isolate Iraq and prevent Arab intervention in Persian Gulf affairs. Continued Irano-Egyptian friendship was demonstrated during 1977 by visits of Egypt's Prime Minister Sālim and Vice-President Mubārak to Tehran. Economic co-operation continued throughout the year, and included Iranian investments in the Port Said free zone, the construction of a joint spinning factory, the continuation of activities of the Egypt-Iranian Bank and a joint navigation company. The precise extent of Iran's financial aid to Egypt during 1976 and 1977 is not known, but it appears to have been considerably less than the $1,000m or more given in 1974 and 1975.

Friendly relations were maintained with Jordan, Morocco, Tunisia and Syria. An important new step was made in establishing ties with Somalia in May 1977, when Iran's Minister for Foreign Affairs, Khal'atbari, visited Mogadishu for the first time.

ECONOMIC AFFAIRS (69.5 Iranian riyals = US $1; 129 Rls = £1 sterling)

The new Prime Minister, Jamshid Amuzegar, in presenting his programme in August 1977, urged austerity and hard work. He said that Iran could not afford to squander its oil resources, and Iranians would have to give up their expensive personal habits to save the oil wealth. The aim of the new economic policy was mainly to reduce reliance on oil exports as a source of foreign currency, and therefore make the country self-sufficient in basic products and services.

The new economic policy reflected the acute necessity to find ways to overcome such difficulties as the high rate of inflation (officially 10%, but unofficially admitted to be 30% a year); shortages of power for industry, of skilled manpower and of building materials over the last two years; and a delay of six to twelve months in the completion of most major development projects. In fact, these difficulties were mainly the result of the 1974 decision to revise the fifth Five-Year Plan, and to double government expenditure.

AGRICULTURE

During 1976–7, there was an increase in the production of major agricultural produce. On the basis of the preliminary figures from the Ministry of Agriculture and Natural Resources, the goals set in the fifth Development Plan were achieved. With the high priority given to agriculture, the government extended easy credit facilities to this sector, and various projects were undertaken to increase production. These financial contributions coupled with favourable weather conditions were the major factors contributing to the increase in agricultural production.

INDUSTRY

The manufacturing sector continued its rapid growth; the overall production index of the selected manufacturing industries showed a 16% increase. The highest rates of growth were achieved by the paint industry (56%), tyre industry (37%), electric tools (27%) and automobile industries (27%).

OIL

Iran succeeded in gradually increasing its oil exports during 1977, from 5.6m b/d to about 6m towards the end of the year—in spite of raising its oil prices by 10%, twice the Saudi rate. In order to maintain this level of production for at least ten years, the National Iranian Oil Company (NIOC) is expected to invest more than $7,000m in oil industry expansion, covering pipeline networks, building terminals, drilling, exploration and development of existing wells. In the framework of this plan, it was decided recently to invest more than $2,500m to increase production by secondary recovery.

TRADE BALANCE

In 1976, the trade balance surplus was $7,544m (cf $7,710m in 1975 and $13,439m in 1974). While income from exports increased by 13% (cf their stagnation in 1975), imports increased by a relatively moderate rate of 25% (cf an increase of 90% in 1975 over 1974). Japan was the most important market for Iranian exports in 1976 (20% of total exports), followed by West Germany (9%), UK (8%) and the Netherlands and US (each 7%). On the other hand, West Germany was the main supplier country (18% of total imports), followed by the US and Japan (each 16%) and the UK (8%).

BALANCE OF PAYMENTS

The balance of payments in 1975 had a small surplus of $110m (cf a surplus of $7,926m in 1974). The reduction resulted from huge increases in imports and considerable long-term government investments in foreign assets abroad.

Iran's international reserves were estimated to be more than $11,000m in June 1977 (cf $8,800m at the end of 1976 and $8,900m at the end of 1975).

BUDGET

In 1976–7, total governmental budget expenditure was estimated at Rls 1,964 bn, an increase of 9% over the previous budget. About 30% of this expenditure was allocated to investment, the same percentage as in 1975–6. The projected deficit was estimated at Rls 45 bn (cf a balanced budget in 1974–5).

As for the 1977–8 budget, expected expenditure was Rls 2,311 bn, an increase of about 18% over 1976–7, of which 38% was allocated to investment. The forecast budget deficit is estimated at Rls 122 bn, about three times the deficit in 1976–7.

DEVELOPMENT PLANS

The Sixth Development Plan for 1978–83 is under preparation. The Ministry of Economic Affairs estimated that for the first four years of the Fifth Five-Year Plan (1973–8), the annual growth rate was 25.4%, and that total investment expenditure for all five years would reach Rls 5,394 bn, about 24% above the estimated total.

(Economic section by Moshe Efrat)

INTERNATIONAL LIQUIDITIES (million Dollars)

	1974	*1975*	*1976*	*1977*
		(end of the year)		*(August)*
Gold	160	153	152	152
SDRs	55	65	75	77
Reserves with IMF	517	1,122	1,160	1,155
Currency	7,652	7,556	7,447	10,177
Total	**8,384**	**8,896**	**8,834**	**11,561**

Source: Société Générale de Banque (Brussels), November 1977.

IRANIAN BUDGETS (billion Riyals)

	1976-77	*1977-78*
A. REVENUE		
Taxes, of which:	313.6	420.9
Company tax	(119.5)	(129.6)
Income tax	(33.7)	(53.1)
Wealth tax	(9.0)	(15.3)
Import tax	(118.5)	(177.7)
Sales tax	(32.9)	(45.2)
Oil and Gas, of which:	1,408.9	1,372.8
Oil sales to major companies	(1,203.8)	(1,046.7)
Direct oil sales	(129.3)	(267.7)
Oil sales to other companies	(70.4)	(53.2)
Gas sales	(5.4)	(5.2)
Other Revenue Sources	97.1	124.8
Loans and Interest on Loans	93.5	270.3
Total Revenue (including others)	**1,918.7**	**2,188.6**
B. EXPENDITURE		
Public Affairs	211.9	200.8
Defence	568.5	561.1
Social Affairs, of which:	399.2	544.0
Education	(174.7)	(230.9)
Health, Medicine and Nutrition	(62.4)	(77.4)
Welfare	(59.5)	(84.7)
Urban Development	(16.6)	(27.9)
Housing	(57.3)	(89.4)
Rural Development	(7.8)	(8.0)
Economic Affairs, of which:	581.0	874.7
Agriculture and Water	(163.8)	(130.8)
Electricity	(131.3)	(212.4)
Industry	(88.3)	(115.7)
Oil and Gas	(53.2)	(143.4)
Mines	(16.2)	(18.0)
Commerce and Tourism	(21.5)	(84.6)
Transport and Telecommunications	(106.7)	(168.8)
Total Expenditure (including others)	**1,964.4**	**2,311.2**

Sources: Middle East Economic Survey, Beirut-Nicosia; 14 March 1977. Bank Markazi (Tehran), *Annual Report and Balance Sheet, Year 2534. Middle East Economic Digest* (various issues).

BALANCE OF PAYMENTS (million Dollars)

	1973	*1974*	*1975*
A. Goods, Services and Transfers	-20	11,897	4,739
Exports of Merchandise (fob)	5,143	21,007	20,074
Imports of Merchandise (fob)	-3,985	-7,258	-12,466
Exports of Services	534	1,023	1,836
Imports of Services	-1,707	-2,842	-4,687
Private Unrequited Transfers, net	-1	-4	-4
Government Unrequited Transfers, net	-4	-30	-15
B. Long-term Capital, nie	640	-4,400	-2,712
C. Short-term Capital, nie	13	44	-668
D. Errors and Omissions	-567	-515	-1,248
Overall Balance	**66**	**7,026**	**110**
Monetary Movements	-66	-7,026	-110

Sources: IMF, *International Financial Statistics*, September 1977; IMF, *Balance of Payments Yearbook*, May 1977.

FOREIGN TRADE (million dollars)

	Exports		*Imports*	*Balance*
	Oil	*Total*		
1972-73	4,394	4,850	2,591	+2,259
1973-74	9,659	10,764	3,623	+7,141
1974-75	20,618	21,201	6,646	+14,555
1975-76	19,654	20,242	11,673	+8,569
1976-77	23,547	24,198	12,905	+11,293
1976–77 (1st qtr)	5,529	5,698	3,296	+2,402
1977–78 (1st qtr)	5,726	5,870	3,485	+2,385

NATIONAL INCOME AND PRODUCT (at current prices, billion Riyals)

	1972	*1973*	*1974*
Agriculture	234.4	303.3	333.9
Oil	531.0	1,388.0	1,311.7
Manufacturing and Mining	231.9	312.7	383.6
Construction	78.9	136.4	276.5
Water and Power	21.6	25.7	29.6
Transport and Communication	77.9	96.2	133.1
Banking, Insurance and Brokerage	85.9	137.2	202.0
Trade	116.1	158.7	198.0
Ownership of Dwellings	141.7	168.2	235.0
Services	233.9	357.9	463.7
Gross Domestic Product (at factor cost)	**1,753.3**	**3,084.3**	**3,567.1**
Net factor income from abroad	-5.9	18.3	10.8
Net indirect taxes	77.3	48.3	59.1
Gross National Product	**1,824.7**	**3,150.9**	**3,637.0**
Less: Depreciation of fixed capital	*91.0*	*122.1*	*162.0*
Net indirect taxes	*77.3*	*48.3*	*59.1*
Net National Income	**1,656.4**	**2,980.5**	**3,415.9**

Source: Bank Markazi, *Annual Report and Balance Sheet, Year 2534.*

GROSS NATIONAL PRODUCT AND GROSS DOMESTIC PRODUCT AT 1972 PRICES (billion riyals)

	1967	*1972*	*1977*	*Average annual rate of growth during the Fourth Plan period (%)*	*Average annual rate of growth during the Fifth Plan period (%)*
Consumption expenditure	540	898	2,168	10.7	19.3
Private sector	(442)	(645)	(1,322)	(7.9)	(15.4)
Public sector	(98)	(253)	(846)	(20.8)	(27.3)
Gross Domestic fixed capital formation	151	287	1,052	13.7	29.7
Private sector	(77)	(141)	(319)	(12.9)	(17.7)
Public sector	(74)	(146)	(734)	(14.6)	(38.1)
Balance of payments, current account	-5	-20	465		
Gross National Product at market price	686	1,165	3,686	11.2	25.9
Population (millions)	26.5	31.0	35.9	3.0	2.9
Per Capita GNP (riyals)	25,894	37,522	102,665	7.7	22.3
Per Capita GNP (US dollars)	384	556	1,521	7.7	22.3

DISTRIBUTION OF GOVERNMENT CREDITS DURING THE FIFTH PLAN (billion riyals)

	Current credits for maintenance of the operational status quo	*Development credits*			*Grand total*
		Fixed	*Non-Fixed*	*Total*	
	(1)	*(2)*	*(3)*	*(4) = (2 + 3)*	*(5) = (1 + 4)*
General Affairs (Total)	**402.90**	**380.56**	**49.86**	**430.42**	**833.32**
Headship of State	10.20	—	—	—	10.20
The Legislature	5.10	—	—	—	5.10
Administration of General Affairs	30.50	0.70	4.20	4.90	35.40
Administration of Judicial, Registration and Endowment Affairs	28.90	1.96	3.30	5.26	34.16
Provincial Administration	9.40	0.40	1.80	2.20	11.60
Internal Order and Security	221.20	0.60	7.90	8.50	229.70
Foreign Relations	21.80	—	—	—	21.80
Financial Administration	36.30	1.00	5.40	6.40	42.70
Statistics and General Technical Services	19.40	30.00	5.40	35.40	54.80
Information and Mass Communications	16.20	26.90	19.36	46.26	62.46
Government Buildings and Installations	0.60	319.00	0.50	319.50	320.10
Manpower Administration	3.30	—	2.00	2.00	5.30
Defence Affairs (Total)	**1,968,70**	—	—	—	**1,968.70**
Military Defence	1,967.40	—	—	—	1,967.40
Civil Defence	1.30	—	—	—	1.30
Social Affairs (Total)	**369.12**	**556.07**	**384.89**	**940.96**	**1,310.08**
Education	216.80	128.87	205.57	334.44	551.24
Culture and Arts	11.10	9.60	11.00	20.60	31.70
Public Health, Medical Service and Nutrition	76.63	42.50	117.61	160.11	236.74
Social Security and Welfare	50.44	9.00	21.56	30.56	81.00
Youth Affairs	6.15	15.00	11.60	26.60	32.75
Urban Development	1.40	45.00	3.60	48.60	50.00
Rural Development	4.60	60.00	1.80	61.80	66.40
Housing	—	230.00	—	230.00	230.00
Environmental	2.00	6.10	5.75	11.85	13.85
Multi-purpose Regional Development	—	10.00	6.40	16.40	16.40
Economic Affairs (Total)	**131.85**	**1,911.47**	**85.93**	**1,997.40**	**2,129.25**
Agricultural and Natural Resources	72.70	236.85	59.89	296.74	369.44
Water Resources	3.50	159.24	2.00	161.24	164.74
Electricity	2.07	240.00	7.83	247.83	249.90
Industry	11.00	352.14	4.95	357.09	368.09
Oil	—	333.00	—	333.00	333.00
Gas	—	51.00	—	51.00	51.00
Mining and Quarrying	2.00	62.00	1.36	63.36	65.36
Transport and Communications	25.60	400.00	—	400.00	425.60
Postal Services and Telecommunications	11.90	66.30	6.70	73.00	84.90
Tourism	1.08	10.84	1.58	12.42	13.50
Commerce	2.00	0.10	1.62	1.72	3.72
Grand Totals	**2,872.57**	**2,848.10**	**520.68**	**3,368.78**	**6,241.35**

Source (of three preceding tables): *Iran's Fifth Development Plan 1973–78 (Revised)*, May 1975.

PROJECTED OVERALL GOVERNMENT FINANCES DURING THE FIFTH PLAN (1973–78)

	billion riyals	*billion dollars*
RECEIPTS		
Oil and gas	6,628.5	98.2
Direct taxes	547.0	8.1
Indirect taxes	668.0	9.9
Other receipts[1]	253.0	3.7
Foreign loans	150.0	2.2
Banking credits (net)		
Sale of Government bonds (net)	50.0	0.7
Total receipts	**8,296.5**	**122.8**
PAYMENTS FROM GENERAL REVENUE		
Current expenditures	3,393.3	50.2
General affairs	(452.9)	(6.7)
Defence affairs	(1,963.7)	(29.1)
Social affairs	(754.0)	(11.1)
Economic affairs	(217.8)	(3.2)
Fixed capital formation	2,848.1	42.2
Repayment of principal of foreign loans	405.0	6.0
Other payments	905.0	13.4
Investment abroad	745.1	11.0
Total payments	**8,296.5**	**122.8**

[1] Includes 135 billion Riyals (2 billion dollars) revenue from public sector Investment in and loans to other countries.

MAIN TRADING PARTNERS (million Dollars)

EXPORTS TO:	*1974*	*1975*	*1976*
Japan	4,331	4,526	4,049
Federal Germany	1,126	1,334	1,807
United Kingdom	1,093	1,412	1,709
Netherlands	2,727	1,458	1,565
United States	2,133	1,398	1,483
France	651	1,150	1,309
Virgin Islands	768	807	1,163
Italy	1,022	1,036	1,155
Spain	237	315	842
Canada	623	744	677
India	550	461	553
Belgium	302	434	432
Norway	143	167	292
Sweden	117	266	243
USSR	193	210	115
Total (including other countries)	**18,865**	**18,056**	**20,431**
Imports from:			
Federal Germany	991	1,824	2,304
United States	974	2,051	2,133
Japan	847	1,662	2,098
United Kingdom	450	877	992
Italy	180	338	686
France	217	415	630
Switzerland	105	213	434
Spain	34	76	125
Belgium	146	251	421
India	95	322	394
Australia	65	162	173
Korea	31	69	146
Sweden	71	137	149
Romania	48	150	142
USSR	212	231	126
Total (including other countries)	**5,426**	**10,346**	**12,887**

Source: IMF, *Direction of Trade, 1970–76.*

IMPORTS STRUCTURE IN 1976-77 (9 months)

	% of total
Machinery, plant, electrical equipment	31.8
Common metals	20.2
Transport equipment	12.7
Agricultural products and foodstuffs	10.8
Textiles	5.6
Chemical products	5.5
Others	13.4
	100.0

NOTES

1. The term "popular participation" is used here in the sense explained by Robert Dahl in "Political Man," *Modern Political Analysis* (Englewood Cliffs, New Jersey, 1970). It indicates a variety of political activities inlcuding the mere gaining of information; participation in elections; membership in political parties and in various economic, social and political pressure groups; agitation for a çhange of policies; and, finally, active participation in the definition and execution of policies.
2. *Kayhan International*, Tehran; 5 January 1977.
3. *Ibid.*
4. Statistics Centre of Iran.
5. *Rastakhiz*, Tehran; 29 May 1976.
6. *Ettela'at*, Tehran; 2 March 1975.
7. *Ibid*, 18 July 1976.
8. *Rastakhiz*, 26 October 1976.
9. For a theoretical treatise on distributive policies in Third World countries with similar social and political structures see: S. N. Eisenstadt, *Traditional Patrimonialism and Modern Neopatrimonialism* (Beverley Hills: Sage, Series No 90-003, 1973), pp. 13-30.
10. *The Guardian*, London; 30 December 1976.
11. *Iran Economic Service* (*IES*), Tehran; 13 September 1977.
12. *Kayhan*, Tehran; 19 August 1977.
13. *Ibid*, 12 September 1977.
14. *Ibid.*
15. *Ibid.*
16. *Kayhan International*, 16 April. *International Herald Tribune*, Paris; 27 April 1977.
17. *Newsweek*, New York; 24 January 1977.
18. *Kayhan International*, 16 April 1977.
19. *The New York Times*, 27 April 1977.
20. Prepared by the Senate Foreign Relations Committee's Subcommittee on Foreign Military Assistance and released in August 1976. Quoted from A. J. Cottrell and J. E. Dougherty, *Iran's Quest for Security: US Arms Transfers and the Nuclear Option* (Cambridge, Massachusetts: Foreign Policy Report, May 1977), pp. 14-15.
21. *The Military Balance 1977-1978* (London: International Institute for Strategic Studies).
22. US Congress Senate, HT 13 680 *An Act to Amend the Foreign Assistance Act of 1961 and the Military Sales Act. 94th Congress, 2nd session 14 June 1976* (Washington DC: Government Printing Office, 1976), pp. 100–1. Quoted in Cottrell and Dougherty, p. 51.
23. See also, Z. Brzezinski, "Recognizing the Crisis" in *Foreign Policy,* 17/1974–75, pp. 63–74.
24. R Belgrade 18 August—Daily Report (DR), 18 August 1976.
25. *Financial Times*, London; 25 July 1977.
26. For a description of radical Arab policy against Iran see, R. K. Ramazani, *The Persian Gulf: Iran's Role* (Charlottesville: University Press of Virginia, 1973), pp. 33-68.
27. A. Taheri, "Policies of Iran in the Persian Gulf Region" in A. Amirie (ed), *The Persian Gulf and the Indian Ocean in International Politics* (Tehran: Institute for International Political and Economic Studies, 1975), p. 267.
28. Interviews with the Shah in *Newsweek*, 24 January 1977 and *Al-Siyasa*, Kuwait; 2 February 1977.
29. *Ettela'at*, 18 July 1976.
30. *Newsweek*, 24 January 1977.
31. R Ankara, 18 May—British Broadcasting Corporation, Summary of World Broadcasts: the ME and Africa (BBC), 17 May 1977.

Iraq

(Al-Jumhūriyya al-'Irāqiyya)

URIEL DANN and OFRA BENGIO

The twelve months from September 1976 to August 1977 brought no upheavals in Iraq on either the domestic or the foreign scene. The second Ba'th regime, which took power in 1968, continued in the latter part of 1976 and in 1977 on a plateau of relative ease which it had reached after the turbulence of its first five years. On this plateau the regime has found it much less difficult to take measures to deal with internal challenges to the present leadership and to handle Iraq's sensitive foreign relations.

The second Ba'th regime has remained true to the principles of its programme as set out in the political report to the Eighth Regional Congress of January 1974. Iraq has continued to be dominated by two men: Field-Marshal (*muhīb*) Aḥmad Ḥasan al-Bakr, secretary-general of the Regional (i.e. Iraqi) Command of the Arab Socialist Resurrection (Ba'th) Party and chairman of the Revolutionary Command Council (RCC); and by Saddām Ḥusayn, Bakr's younger kinsman and his deputy in both these offices. Since the RCC is formally the sovereign body of the Republic, Bakr is *ex officio* Head of State. He is also chief of the executive authority (i.e. Prime Minister), Minister of Defence, and Commander-in-Chief of the armed forces. Bakr and Ḥusayn exercise their power through the Ba'th Party, both ideologically and organizationally. The RCC comprises only Ba'th members.

The security forces are co-ordinated by the Directorate of General Intelligence, which is subordinate to Ḥusayn. The army has less political influence than at any time in independent Iraq's history, though it remains important as a potential centre of subversion and insurrection. The regime's security precautions are based on a system of rewards and punishments. Party surveillance is institutionalized through morale officers and Party commissars, with their own chain of command leading to Saddām Ḥusayn; purges are conducted, but no longer with denunciatory publicity. The professional status and pride of the officer corps are nurtured with excellent service conditions, supplies of sophisticated military weapons, and much official flattery. (Ḥusayn is himself a civilian, having trained as a lawyer; but he wears a full general's uniform.) The lower officer ranks have for some time been recruited from Party cadres. The Party militia—the People's Army—has developed into a formidable instrument; it is a well-equipped rival and, if necessary, a counterweight to the army on the home front.

The Ba'th pursued its ideological programme as expressed in the slogan "[all-Arab] Unity, Freedom [from Western imperialism] and Socialism." That "socialism" in the main means "étatism" was confirmed by the RCC decision on 29 March 1977 that henceforth the term "socialist sector" replace "public sector" in all official statements. The party's political role was to maintain a semblance of pluralism in the Progressive Patriotic and Nationalist Front (PPNF), which includes the Iraqi Communist Party, several Kurdish parties and Nasserite splinters—all under strict Ba'th guidance. Non-Ba'thi constituents have a few representatives in the Council of Ministers, which is not a policy-making body. The PPNF derives its ideological basis from the National Action Charter of 1971 which elaborates the Ba'thi character of Iraqi polity as laid down in the Provisional Constitution of 1970. The Kurdish problem, the bane of every regime since the 1958 revolution, became less pressing with the collapse of Kurdish armed resistance which followed the Iraqi-Iranian agreement of 6 March 1975. At the same time, the establishment of a Kurdish "Autonomous Region of the North"—comprising the governorates of Dihōk, Sulaymāniyya and Arbīl—seemed to provide a basis for more ordered development under strict control from Baghdad.

The regime's foreign relations also achieved equilibrium in 1976–7. For years after its accession, the regime's record was one of almost unrelieved gloom; both the Ba'th ideology of revolutionary radicalism and the inclinations of its leaders gave the regime a reputation in the region for subversion and aggression, and of generally being a bad neighbour. As their sense of security grew, Bakr and Ḥusayn switched, with some measure of success, to a foreign policy of goodwill. The exception was Ba'thi Syria with which relations grew even worse (see essay on "Inter-Arab Relations" and chapter on Syria). Towards Israel, Iraq maintained a reputation of unbounded hostility, though not of unlimited risk-taking. Outside the Arab world, relations with the Soviet Union continued to be friendly and co-operative. Diplomatic relations with the US were not renewed, though economic contacts developed rapidly.

The home front provided a darker picture. A series of riots at Najaf and Karbalā showed that the Ba'th regime had been no more successful than its predecessor in reconciling the Shī'ī masses to the modernizing and centralizing state. In the north, the quiet of the first year after the Kurdish collapse gave way to signs of new unrest. And within the party élite, Bakr and Ḥusayn had to cope with signs of dissent at a level not experienced for three years.

POLITICAL AFFAIRS

The membership of the Regional Command was increased by eight to an unprecedented 21 (plus five candidate members), following elections on 10 January 1977 at an extraordinary session of the Eighth Regional Party Congress (see Table I).[1]

Table I:
The Ba'th [Iraqi] Regional Command as of January 1977, and Subsequent Changes

Aḥmad Ḥasan al-Bakr	Secretary-General
Saddām Ḥusayn	Deputy Secretary-General
'Izzat Ibrāhīm (al-Dūrī)	
Taha Yāsīn Ramadān (al-Jazrāwī)	
Na'īm Ḥamīd Ḥaddād	
Tāyih 'Abd al-Karīm	
Muḥammad Maḥjūb	
'Izzat Mustafa	Expelled from Regional Command on 23 March 1977; replaced by Burhān al-Dīn Mustafa ('Abd al-Raḥmān).
'Adnān Ḥusayn (al-Ḥamdānī)	
Ghānim 'Abd al-Jalīl	
Tāhir Tawfīq (al-'Ānī)	
'Abd al-Fattāḥ Muḥammad Amīn (al-Yāsin)	
Ḥasan 'Alī (al-'Āmirī)	
Sa'dūn Shākir	Members since January 1977
Ja'far Qāsim Ḥammūdī	Members since January 1977
'Abdallah Fāḍil	Members since January 1977
Tāriq 'Azīz	Members since January 1977
'Adnān Khayrallah (Talfāḥ)	Members since January 1977
Ḥikmat Ibrāhim (al-'Azzāwī)	Members since January 1977
Muḥammad 'Āyish	Members since January 1977
Fulayyiḥ Ḥasan al-Jāsim	Since January 1977. Expelled from Regional Command on 23 March 1977; replaced by Muḥī 'Abd al-Ḥusayn.

A fortnight later, on 23 January, the Council of Ministers was also augmented to an unprecedented 40 members when Bakr appointed every single member of the Regional Command, except Saddām Ḥusayn, to be a minister. A dozen remained without portfolios as Ministers of State (see Table II). Membership of the RCC declined for a time to five, with the expulsion of 'Izzat Mustafā on 23 March. (He was also expelled from the Regional Command together with Fulayyiḥ Ḥasan al-Jāsim. Two candidate members were promoted in their places.) For six months, the only five RCC members were Bakr (chairman), Ḥusayn (vice-chairman), Taha al-Jazrāwī, 'Izzat Ibrāhīm al-Dūrī and Sa'dūn Ghaydān. On 22 June, Muḥī 'Abd al-Ḥusayn was appointed secretary-general of the RCC, with Hishām Ibrāhīm as chief of the President's Office.

But many of these appointments were short-lived. Just eight months later, on 4 September 1977, Bakr dismissed 11 of the Ministers of State. On the same day, by an amendment to the Provisional Constitution of 1970, every member of the Regional Command was appointed to the RCC as well, thereby increasing RCC membership to 22—the new constitutional maximum. (For the composition of the RCC as from 4 September 1977, see Table III.)

It is not yet possible to evaluate the real significance of the enlargement of the Council of Ministers with members of the Regional Command, and of the subsequent transfer of these members to the much more important RCC: what is clear, though, is that those who were upgraded were hand-picked Party members loyal to Bakr and Ḥusayn. But the rapid and sweeping nature of the changes must inevitably cast some doubt on the regime's stability—or, at least, on the confidence of its two leaders.

The health of both gave some cause for concern. Bakr, now 65, has been ailing since the early 1970s when he was reported to be suffering from a serious heart condition. There can be no doubt that his general health is poor. Ḥusayn was virtually out of public circulation throughout April and May. Rumour had it that he had been wounded in an attempt on his life; more probably, he suffered from recurrent spinal trouble caused by a bullet wound he received when taking part in the Ba'th assault on General Qassem in October 1959. By mid-summer, Ḥusayn had returned to his duties. It was only natural that, during his long absence, reports should circulate about disquietude in upper Party echelons, about demands to restrict Ḥusayn's powers, and attempts to remove him altogether. Neither positive confirmation or denial was forthcoming by the end of the period under review.

There was little conventional political life in Iraq in 1976–7. The Iraqi Communist Party which (unlike the Kurdish Democratic Party) is a genuine continuation of its early organization, kept a low profile. Its daily, *Tarīq al-Sha'b*, appeared regularly. As a partner in the PPNF, the ICP indulged in occasional "constructive criticism" whenever "socialist" or "anti-imperialist" measures did not seem to go far enough. Nothing noteworthy is known of its organizational activities.

The project of a National Council, a pseudo-parliamentary legislature mooted by the regime between 1971 and 1974, was not again resurrected.

THE SHĪ'Ī TROUBLES

In the first week of February 1977, serious disturbances racked the provinces of Najaf and Karbalā—the centre of the Shī'ī in Iraq. According to the hostile reporting of Radio Damascus, these were triggered off by political executions at Abū Ghurayb prison in Baghdad on 1 February. But it has never taken much provocation to explode the latent resentment of the Shī'ī masses against the centralizing and modernist Sunnī authorities of Baghdad—particularly during the 'Āshūrā festival commemorating the martyrdom of the Imām Ḥusayn bin 'Alī in

Table II
The Council of Ministers as of 23 January 1977, and Subsequent Changes

Portfolio	*Name of Minister*	*Remarks*
Chief of the Executive Authority and Minister of Defence	Field Marshal Aḥmad Ḥasan al-Bakr	President of the Republic, RCC Chairman, Secretary-General of the Ba‘th Regional Command. Commander-in-Chief of the armed forces
Interior	‘Izzat Ibrāhīm (al-Dūrī)+	
Oil	Tāyih ‘Abd al-Karīm+	
Communications	Sa‘dūn Ghaydān+	Ba‘thi
Foreign Affairs	Sa‘dūn Ḥammādī+	Ba‘thi
Public Works and Housing	Taha Yāsīn Ramadān (al-Jazrāwī)	Commander-in-Chief of the People's Army, Acting Minister of Municipal and Rural Affairs on 23 March, in place of ‘Izzat Mustafā
Transport	‘Abd al-Sattār Tāhir Sharif	Kurd. Secretary-General of the Kurdish Revolutionary party. Replaced by ‘Azīz Rashīd ‘Aqrāwī on 22 June 1977.
Information	Tāriq ‘Azīz+	Editor of *al-Thawra*, the Ba‘th organ.
Finance	Fawzī ‘Abdallah (al-Qaysī)+	Ba‘thi
Agriculture and Agrarian Reform	Ḥasan Fahmī Jum‘a+	Communist. Replaced by the Ba‘thi Latīf Nasīf al-Jāsim on 5 April 1977.
Industry and Minerals	Nājiḥ Muḥammad Khalīl	
Health	Riyāḍ Ibrāhīm Ḥusayn +	Ba‘thi
Justice	Mundhir Ibrāhīm (al-Shāwī)+	Ba‘thi
Labour and Social Affairs	Bakr Maḥmūd Rasūl (Bābakr al-Phishdārī)	Kurd. Chairman of the Legislative Council of the Autonomous Area in the North, October 1974–February 1977. (In February, Aḥmad ‘Abd al-Qādir al-Naqshbandī succeeded as Chairman of the Legislative Council)
Internal Trade	Ḥasan ‘Alī (al-‘Āmirī)+	
Foreign Trade	Ḥasan ‘Alī (al-‘Āmirī)+	In acting capacity. Appointed Minister of Trade on 23 March 1977, after the merger of the Internal and Foreign Trade ministries,
Planning	‘Adnān Ḥusayn (al-Ḥamdānī)+	
Youth	Burhān al-Dīn Mustafā (‘Abd al-Raḥmān)	On 5 April 1977, he was relieved and appointed Minister of State for Kurdish Affairs. Karīm Maḥmūd Ḥusayn (al-Mullā), member of the Baghdad Ba‘th Branch Command, was appointed Youth Minister.

Higher Education and Scientific Research	Muḥammad Sādiq al-Mashshāt	
Education	Muḥammad Mahjūb+	
Waqfs	Aḥmad ‘Abd al-Sattār al-Jawārī+	Ba‘thī
Irrigation	Makram Jamāl (al-Tālabānī)+	Kurd. Central Committee member of Iraqi Communist Party.
Municipal and Rural Affairs	‘Izzat Mustafā	Relieved on 23 March 1977. Replaced by Taha Yāsīn Ramadān (al-Jazrāwī) in an acting capacity until the abolishment of the ministery on 11 May 1977
Minister of State for Foreign Afairs	Ḥāmid ‘Alwān (al-Jubūrī)	Head of the Office of the Deputy Chairman of the RCC from 10 May 1976 until 23 January 1977, when he was replaced by Ghānim ‘Abd al-Jalīl
Minister of State	Ghānim ‘Abd al-Jalīl + *	Appointed Head of the Office of the Deputy Chairman of the RCC on 23 January 1977
Minister of State for Kurdish Affairs	Fulayyiḥ Ḥasan al-Jāsim+	Relieved on 23 March 1977. Replaced by Burhān al-Dīn Mustafā on 5 April 1977
Minister of State	‘Ubaydallah Mustafā al-Barzānī+	Kurd. Mullā Mustafā Barxāni’s eldest son; in open conflict with his father since 1971.
Minister of State	‘Aẓīz Rashīd ‘Aqrāwī	Kurd. Until April 1974, played an active part in the Kurdish Nationalist movement headed by Mullā Mustafā Barzānī and member of the KDP Politburo. In April 1974, he was appointed Minister of State and has been since co-operating with the regime. On 22 June 1977, he replaced ‘Abd al-Sattār Tāhir Sharīf as Minister of Transport
Minister of State	‘Abdallah Ismā‘īl Aḥmad+	Kurd
Minister of State	‘Āmir ‘Abdallah +	Central Committee member of the Iraqi Communist Party
Minister of State	Na‘īm Hamīd Ḥaddād + *	Secretary of the Progressive Patriotic Nationalist Front
Minister of State	Tāhir Tawfīq (al-‘Ānī)	
Minister of State	‘Abd al-Fattāḥ Muḥammad Amīn (al-Yāsīn)*	
Minister of State	Sa‘dūn Shākir*	
Minister of State	Ja‘far Qāsim Ḥammūdī*	
Minister of State	‘Abdallah Fādil*	
Minister of State	Lt. Col. ‘Adnān Khayrallah (Talfaḥ)*	Saddām Ḥusayn’s brother-in-law
Minister of State	Hikmat Ibrāhīm (al-‘Azzāwī)+*	
Minister of State	Muḥammad ‘Āyish	Chairman of the General Federation of the Trade Unions since 1968
Minister of State	Muḥī ‘Abd al-Ḥusayn	Since 24 March 1977

\+ In the Council formed in May 1976.
* Relieved from the Council on 4 September 1977.
At the beginning of 1977 non-Iraqi sources reported on a government decision to abolish family names of officials in high posts indicating geographical or ethnic origins. Previous family names are retained in the table in brackets. (The decision was probably made to counteract clannishness.)

the seventh century. The disturbances culminated on 5-6 February when tens of thousands gathered in and about the mosques and shrines of Najaf and Karbalā, and along the pilgrims' route between the two cities, shouting abuse at the regime and the state. On 7 February, a Syrian army sergeant, Muḥammad 'Alī Na'na, was arrested while trying to place a bag of explosives in the courtyard of the Imām al-Ḥusayn mosque in Karbalā. Thereafter the commotion died down.

The reaction of the Iraqi authorities was restrained. Troops were brought in from outside the area to impose a curfew and control, rather than attack, the demonstrators. Nevertheless, about a dozen people were killed in scuffles and by executions without trial, and hundreds were detained. On 23 February, the RCC constituted a special court—headed by one of its members, Dr 'Izzat Mustafā—to try those arrested, but with injunctions to leniency. The regime predictably made the most of Na'na, who was presented as an agent of Syrian intelligence and "confessed" on Baghdad television. Equally predictably, Damascus claimed that Na'na, a deserter from the Syrian army, was an Iraqi agent. Either version is credible.

In an epilogue to the affair, the RCC deprived Dr 'Izzat Mustafā and his colleague on the special court, Fulayyiḥ Ḥasan al-Jāsim, of their various public appointments on 23 March. The former was expelled from the RCC, the Council of Ministers (where he had served as Minister of Municipal Affairs) and the Regional Ba'th Command; the latter from the Council of Ministers (where he had served as Minister of State for the Autonomous or Kurdish Region) and the Regional Command. The reason given was their "neglect of duty" and their "lack of faith in the principles of the revolution." Reliable sources suggest that the two disgraced leaders—and particularly 'Izzat Mustafā—had incurred Bakr's and Ḥusayn's anger by protesting against the executions which had anticipated the decisions of their own court. But there can be no doubt that Party members of such prominence ('Izzat Mustafā had been on the RCC since 1969) would not have been disgraced without graver cause than a temporary controversy over Shī'ī troublemakers.

The main Ba'th partners in the PPNF, the Communists and the legal Kurdish parties, gave the regime their support throughout the affair. However, anti-regime propaganda was subsequently distributed by two underground organizations: the Iraqi National Grouping (*al-tajammu' al-watanī al-'irāqī*) and the Islamic National Front (*al-jabha al-wataniyya al-Islāmiyya*). Little is known about either; they might well be covers for Syrian operations.

DEFENCE AND SECURITY

A $1 bn military agreement with the USSR, concluded in May 1976 during Premier Kosygin's visit to Baghdad, has placed Iraq at the top of the list of Third World countries receiving Soviet military aid. The 1976 agreement, double that of the previous deal made in 1974, provides for large numbers of MiG-21 and 23 jets, surface-to-air missile equipment, radar, T-62 tanks, BTR and BMP armoured vehicles, and coastal artillery (probably 130mm). It is expected that the latest deal also provides Iraq air force with its first MiG-25s. Previous Soviet deliveries already included MiG-23s and 21s, T-62 medium and PT-76 light tanks, and *Scud* missiles.[2] Soviet naval and air forces enjoy land and shore facilities in Qurna and Umm Qasr in southern Iraq, and at Khirriya near Mosul. (Details of a new French military deal are given under Foreign Relations, below.)

The Bakr University for Military Studies was inaugurated in Baghdad in December 1976. Stubborn rumours persisted about the officer corps, whose loyalty to Bakr was not questioned; but there were doubts abroad about Ḥusayn. In his public appearances, Bakr has always emphasized the importance of the army for the Ba'th regime, whereas Ḥusayn has been more inclined to stress its subordination to

Table III
The Revolutionary Command Council as of 4 September 1977

Aḥmad Ḥasan al-Bakr	Chairman since 1968
Saddām Ḥusayn	Vice-Chairman since 1969
Taha Yāsin Ramadān	Member since 1969
'Izzat Ibrāhīm (al-Dūrī)	Member since 1969
Sa'dūn Ghaydān	Member since 1968. The only RCC member who is not a member in the Regional Command
Na'īm Ḥamīd Ḥaddād	Members appointed 4 September 1977
Ṭāyih 'Abd al-Karīm	
Muḥammad Maḥjūb	
'Adnān Ḥusayn (al-Ḥamdānī)	
Ghānim 'Abd al-Jalīl	
Ṭāhir Tawfīq (al-'Ānīl)	
'Abd al-Fattāḥ Muḥammad Amīn (al-Yāsin)	
Ḥasan 'Alī (al-'Amırı)	
Sa'dūn Shākir	
Ja'far Qāsim Ḥammūdī	
'Abdallah Fāḍil	
Ṭāriq 'Azīz	
'Adnān Khayrallah (Talfāḥ)	
Ḥikmat Ibrāhīm (al-'Azzāwī)	
Muḥammad 'Āyish	
Burhān al-Dīn Mustafā ('Abd al-Ḥusayn)	
Muḥī 'Abd al-Ḥusayn	Member since 4 September 1977; RCC Secretary since 22 June 1977

the Party.

In national and purely Ba'thi affairs, the People's Army was given considerable importance by the regime. A widely publicized exercise in the Diyāla region in June seems to have been a full-fledged field manoeuvre in a strategic setting—like others held in 1975 and 1976.

The Party youth organization, *al-Futuwwa*, was extended. (Ever since the 1930s, whenever the climate was favourable, Iraqi nationalist politicians have promoted *futuwwa* youth battalions, named after supposedly knightly communities in medieval Iraq.) A peculiar attribute of *al-Futuwwa* was the cult of Bakr, venerated as the "Father-Leader."

ARMED FORCES

Total armed forces number 188,000. Defence expenditure in 1977-8 was ID 491.5m ($1.66 bn). Military service is compulsory for two years. The Army numbers 160,000 and formations consist of four armoured divisions (each with two armoured, one mechanized brigade); two mechanized divisions; four infantry divisions (each with one mechanized, two motorized brigades); one independent armoured brigade; one Republican Guard mechanized brigade; two independent infantry brigades and one special forces brigade. Equipment consists of 1,350 T-62, T-54/-55, 50 T-34, AMX-30 medium, 100 PT-76 light tanks; c. 1,800 armoured fighting vehicles including BTR-40/-50/-60/-152, OT-62, 100 BMP: 700 75mm, 85mm, 100mm, 122mm, 130mm, and 152mm guns/howitzers; 50 SU-100, 40 ISU-122 self-propelled guns; 120mm, 160mm mortars; BM-21 rocket launchers; *Sagger,* SS-11 anti-tank guided weapons; 20 *FROG*-7, *Scud*-B surface-to-surface missiles; 800 23mm, 37mm, 57mm, 85mm and 100mm anti-aircraft guns; ZSU-23-4, ZSU-57-2; SA-7 surface-to-air missiles. (T-62 medium tanks and *Scud* surface-to-surface missiles on order.) Reserves number 250,000.

The 3,000-strong Navy is equipped with three SO-1 submarine chasers; ten Osa-class guided-missile fast patrol boats with Styx surface-to-surface missiles; 12 P-6 torpedo boats; four patrol boats (under 100 tons) and two minesweepers.

The Air Force numbers 25,000 (10,000 air defence personnel) and is equipped with about 369 combat aircraft. Formations consist of one bomber squadron with four Tu-16; one light bomber squadron with ten Il-28; 12 ground-attack fighter/interceptor squadrons: four with 90 MiG-23B, three with 60 SU-7B, three with 30 MiG-17 and two with 20 *Hunter* FB59/FR10; five interceptor squadrons with 115 MiG-21, 20 MiG-19; one counter-insurgency squadron with 20 *Jet Provost* T52; two transport squadrons with 12 An-2, six An-12, ten An-24, two Tu-124, 13 Il-14, two *Heron* and two *Islander*, seven helicopter squadrons with four Mi-1, 35 Mi-4, 16 Mi-6, 30 Mi-8, 40 *Alouette* III and ten *Super Frelon*. Trainers include 30 MiG-15/-21/-23UTI, Su-70, *Hunter* T69, Yak-11 and L-29. Also SA-2, SA-3 and 25 SA-6 surface to air missiles. (L-39 trainers, 20 *Alouette* III helicopters on order.) Paramilitary forces consist of 4,800 security troops and 50,000 in the People's Army.[3]

THE KURDISH PROBLEM

The perennial Kurdish problem produced no major crisis in the period under review. However, an accumulation of incidents suggests that the issue of the Kurdish community remains a potential and recognized threat to the regime.

Efforts were made to maintain and promote the autonomous region as envisaged in the law of 11 March 1974. It is symptomatic of the ambiguity of the territory's situation that although it was officially designated "the Autonomous Region of Kurdistan" in 1974, its identity has since been blurred by the description "the Autonomous Region of the North." By 1977, it was almost invariably referred to simply as "the Autonomous Region", without even an oblique reference to the Kurds. The chairman of the Regional Executive Council, Hāshim Ḥasan ʻAqrāwī, doubled as the secretary-general of the legal Kurdish Democratic Party (KDP), whereas the chairman of the Legislative Council, Aḥmad ʻAbd al-Qādir (al-Naqshbandī), was chairman of the Baʻth Party Command, Northern Branch.

The authorities of the region were reasonably active in fields of culture and development, and always appeared to show utmost deference to the central government and the Baʻth regime. Kurdish was reaffirmed as the official language of all departments "that have no connection with the central authorities", but it is difficult to assess the practical significance of such decrees. The Kurdish university of Sulaymāniyya, opened in 1968, was functioning with c. 2,500 students. The Kurdistan development budget for 1977 was given as ID 211.5m, with the stated objective of "equalling the development of other provinces of the country, and eliminating past backwardness." (The central development budget for 1977 was ID 2,357m.)

However, the stress of economic development in Kurdistan was on light industry, by its nature tied to urban centres. It thus fulfilled a socio-political as well as an economic purpose: industrialization speeds urbanization, which in turn dissolves tribal affinities which have always been the backbone of Kurdish ethnocentricity—if not necessarily of organized nationalism.

The authorities also permitted the return of a reported 40,000 Kurdish refugees from exile in the south of Iraq. Yet this was only a fraction of the number deported there after the débacle of March 1975. Moreover, the returnees were apparently deliberately resettled in northern towns. Under strong prompting from the Iranian authorities, the government was also active in arranging for the return of Kurdish refugees from Iran. The majority of these had already returned in late 1975 and the first half of 1976, when they were moved by the government to the south of Iraq.

In Baghdad, the responsibility for co-ordinating the affairs of the Autonomous Region devolved on the Minister of State appointed for this purpose, who was directly accountable to Bakr, as chairman of the Council of Ministers. Until March 1977, this post was held by Fulayyiḥ Ḥasan al-Jāsim (see above), and after his dismissal, by Burhān al-Dīn Mustafā. The Kurdish Vice-President of the Republic, Taha Muḥī al-Dīn Ma'rūf, continued to perform ceremonial functions in the capital and abroad, but his office was devoid of any political function.

Apart from the KDP, the legal political parties purporting to represent Kurdish nationalism were the Kurdistan Revolutionary Party (whose secretary was 'Abd al-Sattār Tāhir Sharīf), and the Kurdish Progressive Party. The only reported activities of either were loyal addresses to Bakr and the institutions he headed.

Nevertheless, the Kurdish scene had its darker side. In an admission of astonishing frankness, the Minister of Youth and Sports, Karīm Maḥmūd al-Mullā, told the Viennese *Arbeiter-Zeitung* (30 April 1977) that "individual Kurdish groups in northern Iraq are still fighting." He added that the Syrian-supported Kurdish national forces active from 1961 to 1975—the "radical peshmarga"—were involved in an increasingly hopeless struggle.

This confirms the impression gained from an unimpeachable source outside Iraq that the deathly silence which reigned in Iraqi Kurdistan after the collapse of March 1975 came to an end in the early summer of 1976. However, contrary to the Iraqi minister's assertion quoted above, the frequency and extent of violence has since grown rather than lessened. Acts of sabotage and assassination were reported throughout the north, the targets being development projects or "Kurdish quislings." Such incidents were by no means confined entirely to the Autonomous Region or even to Iraq; in March 1977 the Beirut office and residence of the Lebanese KDP secretary was damaged in an attack. Iraqi statements made it clear that organized bands were at work.

Baghdad allegations of Syrian guidance are undoubtedly true, at least to the extent that the Kurdish resistance has been based in Damascus since 1975, with Barzānī's former aide and rival, Jalāl Tālabānī, at its head. Tālabānī's organization is called the Patriotic Union of Kurdistan. Other Kurdish bodies claiming to sustain the struggle against the Iraqi government are the KDP—Provisional Leadership (from among Mullā Mustafā Barzānī's followers), and the KDP—Preparatory Committee, headed by Maḥmūd 'Uthmān.

The Iraqi regime has reacted with predictable harshness. In a single trial that received publicity in April 1977, a "special court" sentenced ten defendants to death; the sentences were carried out. It may be safely assumed that much else has gone unreported. More generally, it seems that scores of Kurdish villages in the border zone opposite Iran and Turkey have been demolished by the authorities and their population deported, in order to facilitate control. Work on strategic roads continued.

Nevertheless, it is easy to get an exaggerated impression from Kurdish exiles' propaganda and the shrill reactions from Baghdad. Kurdistan has never been easy to rule, and the paralysis of exhaustion and despair in the region could not have been expected to last. Even so, there is little reason to doubt that the government still retains firm control of Iraqi Kurdistan.

FOREIGN RELATIONS

Iraq's foreign policy has shown no signs of change in any of its fundamentals. In Arab as in international affairs, existing trends tended to persist, both as a deliberate policy of the Ba'th regime, and because of the dynamics of inter-Arab relations.

In the Arab world, the regime continued to combine—not without success—a "radical" attitude emanating from Ba'th principles and practice, with Arab solidarity. It encouraged the absorption of Arab nationals in Iraq by granting such favourable conditions as social insurance, seniority rights and offers of employment, but only small numbers were involved. At the non-governmental level, the chief agent of the regime was the "National" (*qāwmī*) Command of the Ba'th Party, distinct from the infintely more consequential Regional Command, and separate, of course, from the rival "National Command" of the party at Damascus. The secretary-general of the Iraqi-based National Command remained Michel 'Aflaq, father-founder of the Ba'th movement and, since 1966, in exile from Syria. At 67, 'Aflaq played no more than a ceremonial role. In practice his place on the National Command was assumed by the assistant secretary-general, the Syrian-born Shiblī al-'Aysamī. Typical of the field of activity assigned to the National Command were publicized contacts with leftist groups from Lebanon (see also below), and Iraqi participation at the second Conference of Socialist and Progressive Parties held in Malta in June 1977.

At the governmental level, the chief executives of Iraq's inter-Arab policies were Ḥusayn himself and the Interior Minister, 'Izzat Ibrāhīm. The Foreign Minister, Dr Sa'dūn Ḥammādī, played a relatively minor role.

RELATIONS WITH THE ARAB LEAGUE

Dr Ḥammādī's proposal in May 1977 to revise the Arab League Charter "in order to strengthen joint Arab action" and to institutionalize summit meetings may be attributed to the wish to paper over cracks in Iraqi relations with the dominant majority of the League. There was throughout 1977 an antagonism, undramatized but continuous, between Iraq and the bloc in the Arab League represented by Egypt, Saudi Arabia and Sudan over such central issues as the Arab-Israeli conflict and Lebanon. (The quarrel with Syria, though connected to both, was *sui generis*.) Iraq was not invited to take part in the Riyadh "restricted summit" of October 1976 which arranged for the Lebanese ceasefire and settled the terms of the Syrian presence there (the Arab Deterrent Force).

However, Iraq did attend the Cairo summit which on 26 October 1976 endorsed the Riyadh resolutions by a majority vote. (For details of both conferences, see essay on "Inter-Arab Relations" in this volume.) Iraq's attitude was hostile throughout and in token of her disapproval she was represented at Cairo by her Foreign Minister and not, like most participants, by the Head of State or, in her case, his virtual deputy. The Iraqi argument, summed up in Dr Ḥammādī's words, was that "the resolutions did not provide for the withdrawal of the Syrian forces from Lebanon—the heart of the matter." The Iraqi media repeated this criticism in less restrained form. (For the relations between Iraq and Syria, and the Iraqi position in the Lebanese conflict, see also below.)

RELATIONS WITH EGYPT

Relations with Egypt were pointedly polite. This may surprise at first glance, considering the relative position of each country on most questions of operational concern: relations with the US and the Soviet Union, Lebanon, the Arab-Israeli conflict and the PLO. The explanation lies partly in the unwillingness of either regime to stir up unnecessary enmities; in the main it was the Iraqi realization that attacking Egypt meant aid and comfort to Syria. Beyond the run of meetings and agreements in matters of friendly coexistence, including Iraqi economic assistance to Egypt, the Iraqi offer to mediate in the Libyan-Egyptian confrontation of July 1977, although not acted upon, deserves mention.

RELATIONS WITH SAUDI ARABIA

Iraqi-Saudi relations were more complex, due to the extreme ideological divergence between the regimes, past tensions, and continuing rivalries in the Persian Gulf area. (On respective oil policies, see essay on "Middle East Oil in its Regional Setting".) On the other hand, as in the case of Iraqi-Egyptian relations, neither regime was interested in a confrontation. The result was a noticeable tendency of both governments to skirt risky issues. In May 1977, an Iraqi delegation led by Interior Minister 'Izzat Ibrāhīm and including the Foreign Minister, visited Riyadh as well as the Gulf capitals. In August, the RCC established an "Arab Gulf Office", headed by the Minister of State and member of the Ba'th Regional Command, Ḥasan 'Alī, who was to be responsible to Saddām Ḥusayn in person. This step may yet affect relations with Saudi Arabia; so far its implications are not clear.

RELATIONS WITH THE GULF STATES AND NORTH AND SOUTH YEMEN

Relations with the various Persian Gulf states, as well as the People's Democratic Republic of Yemen (South Yemen) and the Yemen Arab Republic (North Yemen) were emphasized by the exchange of high-level delegations. While it was natural to stress the cordiality of relations with the PDRY, the conservative regimes of the Gulf region presented difficulties. This applied particularly to Oman in view of past Iraqi support of the Dhufar rebels. However, on their May 1977 tour, the Interior and Foreign Ministers overcame any awkwardness by dwelling on the need for general Arab solidarity and the prospects of developing bilateral relations in trade and economic co-operation. They consistently deprecated the idea of a "Gulf security pact." The really significant themes like Iraqi subversion and Persian Gulf strategy, including the position of Iran, were avoided. Within these limitations the tour was a success, culminating in an audience granted to the Iraqis by Sultān Qabūs bin Sa'īd in Muscat.

Kuwait was a special case. The year under review started under the impact of the coup of 29 August 1976, when the Kuwaiti regime dissolved parliament and suspended key clauses of the constitution (see chapter on the Gulf states). Iraq was infuriated and denounced the measures as reactionary. However as the weeks passed, it became clear that the Iraqi regime would not resort to overt action, and the 'Izzat Ibrāhīm mission in May 1977 further defused the situation. A spectacular *détente* was achieved during the visit to Baghdad of the Kuwaiti Minister of the Interior and Defence, Sa'd al-'Abdallah al-Sabāḥ from 27 June to 3 July 1977, when the following arrangements were concluded. 1) The establishment of a ministerial committee to solve the border problem between the two countries and to develop co-operation in general. (Iraq had for long made specific territorial demands on Kuwait, particularly for the cession of the islands of Būbiyan and Warbah.) 2) Another ministerial committee to supervise daily contacts along the borders. 3) A mutual withdrawal of troops from the border, to a distance of one to two kilometres. The agreement was duly implemented, and relations between Iraq and Kuwait were thereby put on a seemingly firmer footing than any that had been known for many years. However, the basic incompatibilities between the two states had not been resolved; no territorial readjustment had been negotiated, and there was no reason to believe that Iraqi subversion in Kuwait would end.

RELATIONS WITH JORDAN

On the western side of the Fertile Crescent, relations with Amman mirrored the Ba'thi split personality: hostility towards a conservative regime, yet the wish for a favourable image. The tone of the Iraqi media was often unfriendly, though official contacts over mainly economic issues were maintained, with moderate results. In August 1977, an agreement between the two countries allocated to Iraq a free zone in 'Aqaba port for ten years.

RELATIONS WITH SYRIA AND LEBANON, AND THE PALESTINE CONFLICT

Relations with Damascus remained unrelievedly bad, though two qualifications are necessary: diplomatic relations were maintained (even though a senior Syrian member of the Baghdad embassy was expelled early in September 1977); and no open hostilities occurred between the armed forces. (There was at least one clash, with a number killed, in Lebanon between the Iraqi-directed Arab Liberation Front and the Syrian al-Sā'iqa.) But the war of words raged at all levels. The recurrent reproach was of "sham-Ba'th", applied equally by both sides. One touch worth singling out was the juxtaposition, at Damascus, of the "Tikrītī tribal regime" (a reference to the local origins of Bakr and Ḥusayn and their reliance on family appointments) with "the capital of the Omayyads, the bastion of Arabism." This harking back to a glorious past when Damascus was the centre of an Arab empire had no parallel in Iraqi propaganda.

Mutual charges of sabotage and indiscriminate terror were kept up and seemed to be substantiated in many cases, though certainly not in all. Another cause of trouble was the new Mediterranean pipeline through Turkey (see below), which the Syrian government saw as a deliberate attempt to injure her own vital economic interests. There were occasional rumours of mediation from outside, at least one of them said to be under Soviet auspices; nothing tangible transpired.

The position of the Iraqi regime in the Lebanese and Arab-Israeli conflicts was influenced by the position taken by Syria over these issues—especially in the case of Lebanon. With the implementation, however faulty, of the Riyadh resolutions of October 1976, Iraqi influence in Lebanon inevitably suffered a decline. For the rest of the period under review, Iraq kept up correct diplomatic relations at ambassadorial level with President Sarkīs' government. At the same time, the Iraqi government made public its view that no settlement of the fundamental issues was possible until the "Syrian intervention" was liquidated. The regime continued to oppose the Arab Deterrent Force, both in the Arab League Political Council and through the media. On the Lebanese domestic scene, Iraq supported the Nationalist Movement together with the Rejection Front among the PLO. After his father's death, Walīd Junblāt was handsomely acknowledged as leader of the Progressive Socialist Party, and was received by Bakr in Baghdad. There is some evidence that the regime tried its hand at armed subversion in Lebanon, but to little effect, both because of geographical separation and the Syrian grip on the situation. Compared to earlier stages of the civil war, the Iraqi profile in Lebanon was low.

Iraq continued is unflinching support of the Rejection Front. Whatever sophisticated formulae Iraqi functionaries adopted in addressing world opinion, the gist of its attitude to the Arab-Israeli conflict remained unchanged: Israel had no right to exist; "political solutions" were impossible. An Israeli withdrawal to the 1967 line was acceptable, but only as an agreed first stage. A Palestinian government-in-exile could be set up only if its territorial base could be expected to be established at once. Otherwise it was a snare to lull the Arab nation into acceptance of Israel. These were the fundamentals of the issue; not even the Palestinians themselves had the right to abandon them. The regime permitted no deviation from this stance: it compelled its partners in the PPNF, the Communists and the Kurds, fully to conform.

This yardstick of totality was also applied in operational politics: Iraq condemned the Prague talks of May 1977 between PLO representatives and the Israeli Rakaḥ (i.e. Communist) Party, although the latter was anti-Zionist by definition. It was enough that Rakaḥ was legal in Israel to make it part of the "Zionist entity"—a perfectly logical stand to take, given the Iraqi premises. It goes without saying that Syria was continuously flayed for her alleged readiness to compromise on Palestine; Egypt and Saudi Arabia, on the other hand, were not generally singled out for censure in this context.

The Iraqi-directed Arab Liberation Front was involved in one of the few armed clashes (near Ashdot Ya'kov in the Jordan Valley, in August 1977) between Israeli and PLO forces.

Iraq suffered a prestige loss when Yossef Navi, an Israeli who had broadcast anti-Israel propaganda from Baghdad for a year, returned to Israel in July 1977. Navi had responded with his family when the Iraqi regime had called on Iraqi-born Israelis to return to the land of their birth in 1976.

RELATIONS WITH IRAN AND TURKEY

In the non-Arab world, Iraqi relations with Iran, her closest neighbour, followed the line set out in the Algiers and Tehran agreements of 1975. This point was made by leaders on both sides, and it conforms to reality. In particular, Iran refrained from interfering in Iraqi Kurdistan; and Iraq, in Iranian Khuzistan ("Arabistan") and Baluchistan. The five committees of the joint Iraqi-Iranian co-operation commission envisaged by the Tehran agreement were reported operational. They became conspicuously active when the RCC member and Minister of the Interior, 'Izzat Ibrāhīm, visited Tehran in July 1977 and was received in audience by the Shah.

The outstanding event in Iraq's relations with Turkey was the inauguration of the Kirkūk-Yumurtalik (Adana) pipeline on 4 January 1977 after 18 months of construction. The pipeline, which skirts Syrian territory, can convey 35m tons of crude oil annually from both the Rumayla and Kirkūk fields to the Turkish Mediterranean terminal. However, in August 1977, the pipeline was reported out of commission for technical reasons. It is significant that one of Saddām Ḥusayn's rare visits abroad was to Ankara, in February 1977. One possible reason for the visit was disagreement over oil prices.

RELATIONS WITH AFRICA

The regime stressed its support for the Eritrean Liberation Front and Somalia in their conflicts with Ethiopia. In this context, Iraqi spokesmen expressed their conviction that the Red Sea was by right, and ought to become, an "Arab lake." (The Iraqi position did not differ in this respect from that of most other Arab states.)

RELATIONS WITH THE USSR AND EAST EUROPE

Iraq remained tied to the Soviet Union by bonds of "deep understanding and developing friendship" in the spirit of the 1972 Treaty of Friendship. Moscow was commended for its practical support of the Arab cause except on two issues: Soviet acceptance of Israel's right to exist; and its military support for Ethiopia.

In the quarrel with Syria, the Soviet Union showed a clear bias towards Iraq for reasons connected with the politics of Damascus no less than those of Baghdad. Co-operation extended to many fields of economy and culture. The agreement signed in May 1976 during Premier Kosygin's visit was expected to triple Soviet economic assistance in the next six years. Firm commitments in 1976—mostly for power and irrigation projects—are conservatively estimated at $150m. Soviet specialists are also working on a comprehensive land and water use programme. This will include $1 bn in contracts signed in December 1976 for four major irrigation and power projects—the Haditha and Habbaniyah dams on the Euphrates River and two canals linking irrigation areas in western and northern Iraq. Additional projects under negotiation include the $1 bn Hindia and Fallujah dams. Priority was given to raising output at the Soviet-developed Rumayla oilfield to the 800,000 b/d rate originally scheduled for the end of 1975. Water injection equipment ordered in August 1976 under the new economic agreement is intended to raise output substantially by 1978. Work continued at other fields as part of Moscow's 20-year oil development plan for Iraq.

The first meeting of the Joint Commission of Iraq and the Council for Mutual Economic Co-operation (CEMA), established in 1975, ended in November with the establishment of working groups to recommend suitable projects for multilateral co-operation. Areas under study include petroleum, agriculture and light industry. While some observers feel that the CEMA connection will only provide integrated planning for Iraqi projects, in fact the administrative framework to disburse multilateral aid funds has been created through Baghdad's association with CEMA. About 2,900 Soviet technicians were estimated to be in Iraq in 1976.

Romania signed a new economic agreement in May 1976 that gave priority to petroleum development, land reclamation, agriculture and inland fisheries. Czechoslovakia agreed to continue to expand the Basrah refinery, which was completed in 1974 with Czech credits. East Germany will participate in constructing a railroad between Baghdad and the Syrian border. Bulgaria will complete food processing and livestock projects in 1977. Hungary has expanded oil exploration under a 1969 credit, and agreed to construct several housing projects.

At the end of January and the beginning of February 1977, Ḥusayn visited Moscow at the head of a strong delegation. The Iraqi armed forces continued to receive their hardware overwhelmingly from Soviet sources (see Defence and Armed Forces, above).

Nevertheless, Iraq could not be regarded as a satellite of the Soviet Union. By any rational standard based on the assumptions of the regime, her co-operation was in her own national interest and did not go beyond that. Moscow evidently had no decisive say in the shaping of Iraqi foreign or domestic policies and came in for criticism when her viewpoints diverged from those of Baghdad, as they did in connection with the Palestine problem or Ethiopia.

The regime maintained correct, though not close, relations with China.

RELATIONS WITH THE WEST

France was again assured of the friendship felt toward her in the hearts of the Iraqi people since 1967 when it cut off its arms sales to Israel during the Six-Day War. The entente found practical expression in a contract for the sale of 72 Mirage fighters to Iraq. The project centring on the building of the French Osiris reactor at Tawītha, to the south of Baghdad, made progress. On its completion in three to five years, the project could turn Iraq into the first Arab country capable of producing nuclear weapons. At the end of June 1977, Prime Minister Raymond Barre paid a two-day "working visit" to Baghdad, at the head of a high-powered delegation.

Diplomatic relations with the United States were not renewed, after having been broken off in 1967 at the time of the Six-Day War. The Iraqi governement continued to assert that American assistance to Israel was the obstacle to an exchange of ambassadors. No doubt the special relationship between the US and

Saudi Arabia was also important in this respect. On the other hand, there was a growing section for American affairs, staffed by Americans, in the Belgian embassy in Baghdad. Although statistics for the period under review are not available, it is known that the recent steep upward trend in trade between the two countries has continued. The Iraqi media adopted an unfriendly and occasionally hostile attitude to the US but, with the exception of the Communist press, it was rarely abusive.

ECONOMIC AFFAIRS ($1 = 0.30 Iraqi dinars; £1 = 0.524 ID)
Iraq maintained its rapid economic expansion in 1977 in spite of the serious negative impact of the cessation of oil exports through the Iraqi-Syrian pipeline in 1976, and the bottlenecks encountered in implementing development projects.

OIL

In September 1977, Iraq began to export oil through the new 980-km Kirkūk-Dortyol pipeline, which has the capacity to transit 25m tons of oil annually from north Iraq to the Turkish Mediterranean port. In fact, this new pipeline is only one component of Iraq's master-plan to release it from dependence on Syria for oil transport from the Kirkūk fields. In the spring of 1976, the "strategic pipeline" had already begun to carry c. 50m tons a year from Kirkūk to the Basrah area on the Persian Gulf. These two new pipelines now enable Iraq to export 75m tons annually from the Kirkūk oilfields (cf 55m tons in the past through Syrian territory to the Mediterranean). Thus Iraq has not only succeeded in freeing itself from dependence on Syria in exporting oil (stopped by Baghdad in April 1976 due to a dispute with Syria over transit fees), but also in strengthening its economic and political position *vis-à-vis* Syria. For besides demanding exaggerated transit fees for oil shipments, Damascus had also unilaterally reduced Iraq's share of the vital waters of the Euphrates river. One possible result of these developments was the new attitude of Syria's Oil Minister, who declared, "Let us separate politics from economics." He also proposed a negotiated arrangement with Iraq over mutual economic problems.

Iraq also implemented other parts of its strategic oil policy, which aims at exporting 200m tons of oil in 1980. Among these were the expansion of port facilities on the Persian Gulf; development of the rich oilfields of North Rumayla and the new fields of Bugurgan-Abu Ghurayb in the south.

Despite the closure of the pipeline through Syria, Iraq succeeded in increasing its oil exports to 120m tons in 1977 (cf 109m in 1976) due to the new pipelines and to increased production in the southern oilfields.

INDUSTRY

Because Iraq's main irrigation projects, though now completed, were well behind schedule, investments in this sector have not yet contributed to any important change in agricultural production. On the other hand, according to the Minister of Industry and Minerals, investment in industry over the past five years was 3.5 times greater than during the previous 20 years. Nevertheless, returns were among the lowest of all developing countries, to the extent that the industrial establishments were running at a deficit of over ID 125m a year, and operating 30% below production capacity. The main difficulties were caused by the shortage of skilled manpower and management inefficiency.

However, a large number of industrial plants were completed in 1977, among them an urea plant at Khor al-Zuhair, a paper mill at Basrah, a tyre factory at Diwāniyya (satisfying one-third of the local consumption), and seven new cement plants (increasing production from 2.7m to 7m tons a year), which will help overcome the delay in executing development projects due to shortages of construction material.

TRADE BALANCE

Iraq had a $5,000m surplus in its 1976 balance of trade (cf $3,500m in 1975). While export revenue (98% from oil) rose by 14%, import payments declined by 22%—mainly due to a government decision to pursue a more cautious import policy because of the difficulty in absorbing huge investments. France was the leading market for Iraqi exports (17%), followed by Italy (15%) and Brazil (13%). The leading suppliers of imports were West Germany (18%), Japan (15%), France (8%) and the UK (6%).

BALANCE OF PAYMENTS

Iraq's balance of payments showed a deficit of $395m in 1975 due to special loans arranged to overcome uncertainties in oil revenues due to overseas marketing difficulties. Foreign exchange reserves increased to $4,400m at the end of 1976, reflecting a surplus in the balance of payments. (cf $2,727m in reserves at the end of 1975, and $3,273m at the end of 1974.)

PUBLIC FINANCE

The national budgets (excluding the Autonomous Governmental Agencies and the public economic sector) amounted to ID 4,010m in 1977 (cf c. 3,000m in 1976). While the ordinary budget increased by 12% in 1977 to ID 1,653m, allocations for development investments rose by 55% to ID 2,357m. One significant feature was the increasing importance of oil revenues in financing development investments (rising to 93% of the total in 1977 from 83% in 1976), and the decreasing importance of foreign loans (from 13.5% in 1976 to 3.5% in 1977).

DEVELOPMENT PLAN

The government decided in June 1977 to redraft certain parts in its $49,000m Five-Year Plan (1976-80). The plan originally gave priority to agriculture and industry (each sector receiving one-third of total investment), and aimed to achieve an annual growth rate of 16.8% for the whole economy: 30% a year for industry, 15.5% for the oil sector, and 7.1% for agriculture.

(Economic Section by Moshe Efrat)

BALANCE OF PAYMENTS (in million Dollars)

	1973	*1974*	*1975*
A. Goods, services and transfers	801	2,219	1,424
Exports of merchandise (fob)	2,204	6,680	7,459
Imports of merchandise (fob)	-850	-2,754	-4,423
Exports of services	256	554	510
Imports of services	-800	-2,027	-1,666
Private unrequited transfers (net)	1	2	2
Government unrequited transfers (net)	-11	-237	-458
B. Long-term capital, nie	98	-430	-385
C. Short-term capital, nie	18	42	-1,135
D. Errors and omissions	-253	-142	-299
Overall balance	**664**	**1,688**	**-395**
Monetary movements	-664	-1,688	395

Sources: IMF, *International Financial Statistics* and *Balance of Payments Yearbook.*

1977 BUDGET (in million Iraqi dinars)

1. **Revenue**	
A. Ordinary Revenue:	
Taxes on income and resources	43.3
Taxes on commodities	180.8
Profits of public economic establishments	1,373.9
Transferred revenue	19.1
Services	5.0
Total Ordinary Revenues (including others)	1,652.9
B. Revenues Allocated for Development Plan	2,357.1
C. Revenues of Autonomous Government Agencies:	
Oil refining and gas industry	43.8
Fertilizer industry	9.4
Iraqi posts	24.0
Oil products and gas distribution	39.4
Total Revenues of Autonomous Government Agencies (including others)	1,988.3
Total State Revenue	**5,998.3**
2. **Expenditure**	
A. Ordinary Expenditure, by Ministry:	
Office of the President	2.8
Foreign Affairs	9.1
Finance	576.8
Interior	182.2
Labour and Social Affairs	5.0
Health	44.6
Defence	491.5
Education	49.3
Public Works and Housing	15.9
Agriculture and Agrarian Reform	25.9
Oil	6.5
Total (including others)	1,652.9
B. Allocations for Economic Development Plan	2,357.1
C. Expenditure of Autonomous Government Agencies	2,328.9
Total State Expenditure	**6,338.9**

Source: Middle East Economic Survey.

IRAQ'S MAIN TRADING PARTNERS (in million dollars)

	1974	*1975*	*1976*
Exports to:			
France	1,128.9	982.6	1,448.9
Italy	1,060.0	1,512.2	1,231.1
Brazil	632.2	832.2	1,054.2
Turkey	297.7	458.4	585.8
Japan	183.4	359.4	526.6
United Kingdom	226.2	204.6	446.5
Yugoslavia	182.5	352.4	407.2
Spain	248.6	445.6	352.9
India	244.8	240.4	288.5
Austria	309.0	228.1	219.6
Netherlands	25.9	164.5	176.9
Portugal	125.9	216.3	152.6
Federal Germany	277.2	116.3	140.5
Canada	37.3	131.2	135.7
United States	2.0	20.7	111.8
Total (including other countries)	**5,839.0**	**7,293.9**	**8,296.3**

	1974	*1975*	*1976*
Imports from:			
Federal Germany	190.7	754.2	599.3
Japan	269.7	764.6	494.2
France	174.7	263.3	262.4
United Kingdom	126.2	238.2	203.3
United States	188.2	370.3	163.2
Italy	79.4	164.4	132.1
USSR	108.4	103.1	119.6
Netherlands	38.2	61.0	83.4
China	50.4	68.1	83.3
Belgium	53.0	99.3	74.7
Czechoslovakia	56.7	60.9	74.0
Sweden	53.7	91.9	73.9
Yugoslavia	13.5	15.3	56.5
Denmark	16.0	39.1	55.2
India	56.3	71.2	55.2
Total (including other countries)	**2,364.4**	**4,202.9**	**3,277.8**

Source: IMF, *Direction of Trade, 1970-76.*

NOTES

1. The Congress was originally convened in January 1974. The elections to the Regional Command were held at the suggestion of Secretary-General Bakr.
2. *Communist Aid to the Less Developed Countries of the Free World, 1976* (Washington: CIA, August 1977).
3. *The Military Balance 1977-78* (London: International Institute for Strategic Studies).

Israel

(Medinat Yisrael)

MISHA LOUVISH

Israel reached a watershed in both its internal and external affairs in 1977. The Labour Party, which had dominated every government since independence in 1948, finally lost its ascendancy in the May 1977 elections to the Likud alliance, headed by Menahem Begin, leader of its bitterest historic rival, the Herut movement, who formed a new Coalition government. Even before the new government took power, there were ominous signals from Washington that the Carter Administration was intending to adopt a more "even-handed policy" in the Middle East: while it would remain faithful to its commitments to the Jewish State, it intended to balance this commitment with the obligations involved in retaining the new goodwill of Egypt, as well as the older established relations with Saudi Arabia and Jordan, and it also showed a strong interest in winning Syrian friendship. Thus the prospects were of changes in the quality of Israel-American relations. This new dimension was further sharpened by the historic decision of Egypt's President Anwar al-Sādāt to open direct negotiations with Israel by his dramatic journey to Jerusalem in November 1977. For the first time after almost 30 years of Israel seeking an opportunity for direct negotiations with its Arab neighbours, the door was thus finally opened by Egypt. This compelled Israelis to address themselves seriously to the concrete issues involved in negotiations for a peace settlement.

Although Israel was militarily stronger in 1977 than it has ever been, its economic crisis was extremely acute and produced serious domestic discontents. This was partly reflected in the worrying emigration of Israelis to live and work, at least temporarily, in the United States and other countries. However, the rate of immigration increased slightly over the previous year. In October 1977, the new Government announced a radical change in the country's economy by abolishing all currency controls and offering greater freedom to private enterprise in keeping with the Likud's election platform.

POLITICAL AFFAIRS

BACKGROUND TO THE ELECTIONS

As 1976 drew to a close, the parties were manoeuvring for position in preparation for the elections to the Ninth Knesset, due on 1 November 1977. Despite the fillip to Prime Minister Yitzhak Rabin's prestige as a result of the Entebbe rescue operation on 3 July, it was generally felt that his Government, installed in June 1974 after the resignation of Mrs Golda Meir, had failed to fulfil expectations. Rabin, untried in politics and without the charisma of the founders' generation, had not succeeded in establishing his authority in the ruling Labour Party, which was still under the shadow of tensions between its constituent factions. In particular, there were strained relations between him and Defence Minister Shimon Peres, who made no secret of his intention to contest the leadership.

Left-wing elements in Mapam, the United Workers' Party, were pressing to end its alliance (known as the Alignment) with Labour. The growing influence of younger and more strongly nationalist elements in the National Religious Party (Labour's coalition partner, with brief intervals, since Israel's establishment) threatened the stability of the "historic alliance." The Independent Liberals, the junior partner in the coalition, were also restive, particularly over the failure to improve Government efficiency.

The Likud ("Union") which at its first appearance in 1973 had succeeded in winning 39 seats in the 120-member Knesset to the Labour-Mapam Alignment's 51, was expected to narrow the gap still further. A new element was also introduced into the political equation by the establishment of the Democratic Movement for Change (DMC), headed by Professor Yigael Yadin, a former chief of staff of the Israel Defence Forces (1949–52) and a noted archaeologist. It was generally expected, however, that the Alignment would still emerge from the elections as the largest party, and would be able to retain power by forming a coalition with the DMC.

The political picture was radically transformed in mid-December, when the orthodox Torah Front (Agudat Israel and its labour wing) moved a note of no-confidence in the Government over an alleged violation of the Jewish Sabbath at a ceremony to receive the first three F-15 planes from the United States. The National Religious Party (NRP) violated coalition discipline by abstaining, and Rabin used his statutory powers to expel the three NRP ministers from the Cabinet on 19 December. Although the no-confidence motion was defeated, the Likud promptly tabled another. Having lost his majority, Rabin tendered his resignation (which by law involves the entire Cabinet) to President Ephraim Katzir on the following day. It was generally believed that Rabin's move against the NRP had not merely been motivated by a desire to uphold constitutional principle, but was a political initiative designed to precipitate a contest for the Labour leadership and catch the DMC unprepared.

It was obvious that no possible coalition could command a majority in the House, and that the elections would have to be brought forward. Nevertheless, President Katzir went through the motions required to set up a new government: after consulting representatives of all the parties in the Knesset, he called upon Rabin to make the attempt on 4 January. Meanwhile, however, six private members' bills to dissolve the Knesset had been presented by various parties. On 5 January, the election date of 17 May was agreed upon, with 12 April as the last day for submitting lists of candidates (the length of time being partly due to various legal provisions).

The local authority elections, normally held simultaneously with those for the Knesset, were postponed to a date between May and November 1978. The Histadrut, the General Federation of Labour, decided to hold its elections—usually scheduled about a month before the parliamentary polls—on 21 June.

Wishing to achieve freedom of action, the two Independent Liberal ministers had handed in their resignations a few hours before Rabin's; but the High Court of Justice ruled that, since 48 hours had to pass before a minister's resignation took effect, they had to remain members of the Cabinet until a new one was formed. It also ruled, however, that the expulsion of the NRP ministers took effect on the same day as their dismissal.

After the High Court's rulings, the vacant ministries were reallocated as follows: Religious Affairs to Justice Minister Hayim Zadok; Social Welfare to Labour Minister Moshe Bar'am; Interior to Police Minister Shlomo Hillel; and Housing to Shlomo Rosen, Minister of Absorption.

PARTIES IN THE EIGHTH KNESSET

The following parties were represented in the Eighth Knesset:

The Alignment Israel Labour Party—United Workers' Party (*Hama'arakh Mifleget Ha'avoda Hayisre'elit—Mifleget Hapo'alim Hame'uhedet*) with 49 seats,

THE RABIN CABINET

(Installed on 4 June 1974; left office on 20 June 1977)

Prime Minister	Yitzhak Rabin	Alignment—Labour	
Deputy Prime Minister and Foreign Affairs	Yigal Allon	Alignment—Labour	
Agriculture and Communications	Aharon Uzan	Alignment—Labour	
Commerce and Industry	Hayim Barlev	Alignment—Labour	
Defence	Shimon Peres	Alignment—Labour	
Education and Culture	Aharon Yadlin	Alignment—Labour	
Health	Victor Shemtov	Alignment—Mapam	
Housing	Avraham Ofer	Alignment—Labour	Died 2 January 1977
	Shlomo Rosen	Alignment—Mapam	From 17 January 1977[2]
Immigrant Absorption	Shlomo Rosen	Alignment—Mapam	
Information	Aharon Yariv	Alignment—Labour	Resigned 4 February 1975—ministry abolished
Interior	Yosef Burg	NRP	31 October 1974–19 December 1976[2]
	Shlomo Hillel	Alignment—Labour	From 17 January 1977[2]
Justice	Hayim Zadok	Alignment—Labour	
Labour	Moshe Bar'am	Alignment—Labour	
Police	Shlomo Hillel	Alignment—Labour	
Religious Affairs	Yitzhak Raphael	NRP	31 October 1974–19 December 1976[1]
	Hayim Zadok	Alignment—Labour	From 17 January 1972[2]
Social Welfare	Michael Chazani	NRP	From 31 October 1974; died 2 July 1975
	Yosef Burg	NRP	30 July–4 November 1975
	Zevulun Hammer	NRP	4 November 1975–19 December 1976
	Moshe Bar'am	Alignment—Labour	From 17 January 1977[2]
Tourism	Moshe Kol	Independent Liberal	
Transport	Gad Yaakobi	Alignment—Labour	
Without Portfolio	Israel Galili	Alignment—Labour	
	Gideon Hausner	Independent Liberal	
Deputy Ministers:			
Agriculture	Jabber Muadi	Progress and Development	
Communications	Eli Moyal	Alignment—Labour	

[1] The NRP did not support the Rabin Cabinet at first; its three ministers were co-opted on 31 October 1974. They were expelled from the Cabinet on 19 December 1976—see text.

[2] For reallocation of vacant ministries on 17 January 1977, see text.

following the resignation of two. The **Israel Labour Party** (43 seats) was founded in 1968 by a merger between 1) Mapai (*Mifleget Po'alei Eretz Yisrael* or Israel Workers' Party), led by Mrs Golda Meir; the dominant party in the pre-State Jewish community since 1930, as well as in independent Israel. 2) Rafi (*Reshimat Po'alei Yisrael* or Israel Workers' List), founded in 1965 by David Ben-Gurion, now led by Moshe Dayan and Shimon Peres. 3) *Ahdut Ha'avoda* (Unity of Labour) originating from a split in Mapai in 1944; led by Israel Galili and Yigal Allon. The three wings nominated their representatives in agreed proportions (Mapai 57%, the two others $21\frac{1}{2}$% each) for places in the party's governing bodies, as well as the Cabinet and other posts; but there was a strong movement towards breaking down such divisions and barriers. In particular, the cohesion of the old Mapai group had been weakened by the death of its most powerful figure, Pinhas Sapir; the weakness of his successor, Yehoshua Rabinowitz; the rise of younger leaders who lacked emotional attachment to the old framework; and Prime Minister Rabin's failure to establish his authority over the party.

Allied with Labour was **Mapam** (*Mifleget Hapo'alim Hame'uhedet* or United Workers' Party) with six seats. Founded in 1949 as an alliance of Left-wing parties, including *Ahdut Ha'avoda*, which seceded in 1954. Since then, Mapam's backbone has been the *Hashomer Hatza'ir* kibbutz movement. Its veteran leaders were Meir Yaari, now in semi-retirement, and Yaakov Hazan. Labour and Mapam submitted joint lists of candidates to the Knesset, local authorities and Histadrut, but Mapam reserved freedom of action on certain matters.

The Likud (Union), with 39 seats. Formed shortly before the 1973 elections on the initiative of General (Reserves) Ariel Sharon, by a merger between 1) the Herut Movement (*Tenuat Haherut*), led by Menahem Begin; 2) the Liberal Party (*Hamiflaga Haliberalit*), led by Simha Ehrlich—these two were already united as the Herut-Liberal bloc; 3) the State or National List (*Reshima Mamlachtit*), formed in 1969 by supporters of Rafi who refused to join the Labour Party; 4) the Free Centre (*Hamerkaz Ha'atzma'ī*), which joined with the State List and the Complete Land of Israel Movement (*Tenuat Eretz Yisrael Hashelema*). The Free Centre split in January 1976, when two of its four members formed the Independent Centre (*Hamerkaz Hahofshi*), which joined with the State List and the Complete Land of Israel Movement to form the National Labour Movement (*Tenuat Ha'avoda Haleumit*, commonly known as *La'am*—"For the People"), led by Yigal Hurvitz. The Free Centre seceded from the Likud in October 1976. Gen Sharon also left and formed his own list, *Shlomzion* ("Peace of Zion"), when his demands for the abolition of sectionalism in the Likud and its amalgamation into a single party on a basis of individual membership were rejected.

The National Religious Party (*Hamiflaga Hadatit Haleumit*) with ten seats and three ministers. The three main factions within the Party were headed, respectively, by Interior Minister, Yosef Burg; Religious Affairs Minister, Yitzhak Raphael; and Social Welfare Minister, Zevulun Hammer.

Agudat Israel, the non-Zionist orthodox religious party, and **Po'alei Agudat Israel**, its labour counterpart, had contested the 1973 elections together as the Torah Religious Front, but stood separately in 1977.

The Independent Liberal Party (*Hamiflaga Haliberalit Ha'atzma'it* or ILP), with four seats and two ministers; the junior partner in the Alignment's coalition government. It was led by Moshe Kol, who announced that he would not stand for re-election.

The New Communist List (*Hareshima·Hakommunistit Hahadasha* known as Rakah), led by Meir Wilner and Taufīq Tūbī. Joined with a group of the Black Panthers (formed by city slum activists in 1971) and some Arab municipal leaders to form the Democratic Front for Peace and Equality (*Hehazit Hademokratit Leshalom Uleshivyon* known as **Hadash**).

The Citizens' Rights Movement (*Hatenua Lizekhuyot Ha'ezrah* or CRM), founded by Shulamit Aloni; won three seats in 1973, and joined up briefly with Arie Eliav, who had left the Labour Party. But the new group broke up, leaving the CRM with two members. Eliav formed the Independent Socialist Faction (*Hasi'a Hasotzialistit Ha'atzma'it*).

Moked (Focus), with one member, Meir Pa'il. Combined with the Independent Socialist Faction, Uri Avneri's *Meri* (Radical) group, and other Left-wing socialist and pacifist elements to form **Shelli**, an acronym of *Mahaneh Shalom Leyisrael, Shivyon Leyisrael* (Camp of Peace and Equality for Israel).

NEW LISTS CONTESTING THE ELECTIONS

The Democratic Movement for Change (*Hatenua Hademokratit Leshinui*), founded in December 1976 by a merger between Professor Yigael Yadin's Democratic Movement, the Shinui (Change) Movement, founded after the Yom Kippur War by Professor Amnon Rubinstein, and other groups. There were discussions about the possibility of the Free Centre, the ILP and the CRM joining the DMC to form a large centre party; but only the first was ready to accept Yadin's conditions: that its Knesset members give up their seats and all membership be on an individual basis—no factions would be recognized. The Free Centre dissolved and joined the DMC on 19 January 1977. Twelve days later, a group of Labour Party members, most of them in managerial positions (headed by Meir Amit, manager of Koor, the Histadrut industrial combine) also joined DMC.

OTHER LISTS

- Arab Reform Movement
- Beit Yisrael (House of Israel—Yemenites)
- Coexistence with Justice (Arab list)
- Flatto-Sharon, submitted by Samuel Flatto-Sharon, independent (see below)
- *Kach* (Thus) led by Rabbi Meir Kahana, of the Jewish Defence League
- New Generation (*Dor Hadash*); non-party list of native-born Israelis
- Women's Party
- Workers' Front for Equality (*Hazit Po'alim Leshivyon* or *Hofesh*), headed by Shalom Cohen, formerly of the Black Panthers; and Yehoshua Peretz, former secretary of the Ashdod port workers
- Zionist Panthers, breakaway from Black Panther Movement
- Zionist and Social Renewal, led by Mordecai Ben-Porat, who resigned from the Labour Party

(For Hadash and Shelli, see New Communist List and Moked, above.)

POLITICAL SCANDALS

As 1977 opened, the press was full of reports of charges of bribery and tax offences against Asher Yadlin, a prominent member of the Labour Party and Chairman of Kupat Holim, the medical insurance fund of the Histadrut, the General Federation of Labour. Yadlin had been nominated on 5 September 1976 as Governor of the Bank of Israel; but a few days later, it was revealed that the police were investigating various allegations against him. On 24 October, after waiting in the hope that Yadlin would be cleared, the Cabinet withdrew the nomination and appointed Arnon Gafny, Director-General of the Ministry of Finance, to the post. Yadlin was charged on 21 December with bribery and other offences involving IL 280,000 (c. $32,000).

Another scandal, which broke towards the end of 1976, ended in tragedy. A correspondent of the weekly *Ha'olam Hazeh*, who had also been involved in raising the charges against Yadlin, made a statement to the police in November concerning suspicions of misconduct against Housing Minister Avraham Ofer (Labour) when he was head of Shikun Ovdim (the Histadrut housing corporation) before joining the Government. Although the allegations were widely publicized, Ofer's Cabinet colleagues refrained from giving him direct information about the progress of the investigation in order to avoid any suspicion of political interference with the work of the police. On 3 January 1977, Ofer committed suicide, leaving a note protesting his innocence of all the charges against him, but declaring that he did not have the strength "to bear any more." He was reported to have been particularly depressed by the lack of support from his political associates and the prospect of a long-drawn-out ordeal in the news media.

When Yadlin came to trial, he pleaded guilty to some of the charges, including IL 124,000 in bribes, and evasion of IL 10,200 in land taxes by making a false declaration. He claimed that he had handed over IL 80,000 of the bribe money to the Labour Party, adding that he had raised "millions" for the party's election campaign. The judge, however, did not accept this statement and sentenced him to five years' imprisonment and fines totalling IL 250,000. Labour Party leaders categorically denied Yadlin's allegations.

In mid-March, less than three weeks after his re-election as Labour candidate for the leadership (see below), Prime Minister Rabin was himself involved in a scandal when an Israeli correspondent in Washington discovered that Mrs Lea Rabin had a dollar account in a Washington bank. According to Israeli law, this should have been closed when Rabin left the US in 1973 at the end of his term as Israeli Ambassador. Although the account had been operated by his wife, Rabin publicly accepted his share of "formal and moral responsibility." As there was over $21,000 in the account, the Attorney-General, Aharon Barak, was forced to prosecute. Rabin withdrew as head of the Labour Party's Knesset list on 7 April and was given an administrative fine of IL 5,000; ten days later, Mrs Rabin was fined IL 250,000 in the District Court.

A week later, it was reported that the Treasury was investigating foreign-currency accounts held by former Foreign Minister Abba Eban in the US. Eban declared that the accounts were connected with his literary work, and that he had been given an official permit to operate them in 1967. Although no copy of the permit could be found in the Treasury archives, several witnesses testified that they had seen it. Eban was ultimately cleared, but only after the elections.

THE ELECTION CAMPAIGN

The resignation of the Government precipitated a leadership struggle within the Labour Party. Abba Eban, who had been the first to announce his candidacy against Rabin, withdrew in favour of Peres, despite their differing views on foreign policy. Peres was also backed by some of the younger leaders who had previously supported Rabin. It was agreed that the leadership issue would be decided by a vote at the forthcoming national conference instead of by the Central Committee, as was customary. About two-thirds of the 250,000 registered members voted in the elections to the Convention on 1 February.

The conference opened on 22 February in the presence of delegates from 17 overseas socialist parties. On the following day, Rabin was elected by a narrow majority: 1,455 votes to 1,404 for Peres. The Convention also adopted a large number of policy resolutions, most of them prepared in advance by the Standing Committee. The most important debate was over the party's policy for peace and security: the Likud's "not-an-inch" approach was rejected as not leading to peace," but a return to the lines of the 4 June 1967 was also ruled out, in the interest of "defensible borders." The final resolution declared: "Israel will persevere in her efforts for permanent peace with Egypt, Jordan and Syria within defensible borders, prepared for territorial compromise with each of them—and with Lebanon within the present borders. Israel will not return to the borders of 4 June 1967, which constituted a temptation to aggression. The peace agreement with Jordan will be based on the existence of two independent states: Israel, with its capital in united Jerusalem, and an Arab state to the east of Israel. Israel rejects the establishment of an additional separate Palestinian state west of the Jordan. The separate identity of the Palestinian and Jordanian Arabs can find expression in the neighbouring Jordanian-Palestinian state, in peace and good-neighbourliness with Israel."

The conference favoured "continuation and consolidation of rural and urban settlement in the Jerusalem area, the Golan, the Jordan Valley, the Rafah area and the Ophira [Sharm al-Shaykh] area . . . within the framework of the Government of Israel's policy to ensure defensible peace boundaries." Former Defence Minister Moshe Dayan objected to expressions in the policy resolutions which implied that the West Bank was Jordanian territory, and advocated the maintenance of the *status quo* without annexation. He proposed the deletion of the passages specifying the areas for settlement, and those expressing readiness for a territorial compromise with each of Israel's neighbours. His proposals were defeated.

In opposition to the Standing Committee's proposal, the conference also resolved that party representatives who had already served two terms in the Knesset and other elected bodies should not be nominated for a third term without the approval of at least 60% of the party's Central Council. One-third of the Knesset and other lists were to be reserved for members of the Oriental communities, 20% for women and 15% for young people. A new Central Committee of over 800 was elected—c. 200 directly by the branches, and the rest nominated by an appointments committee to represent various sections of the party.

There had been considerable opposition within Mapam to continuing in the Alignment. Its conference, which was held on 19 January, formulated a number of conditions, notably that Labour should state its readiness for a territorial compromise on all fronts, including Judea and Samaria, and that its nominee for the Premiership should be a person who supported this policy; but even this compromise was opposed by two-fifths of the delegates. Meeting a few days after the Labour Party conference, the Mapam Central Committee resolved that its conditions had been met, and decided by an 80% vote to continue the Alignment.

As the Knesset elections approached, unrest grew among the hawkish members of the Labour Party. Mordecai Ben-Porat, a close associate of Peres and Moshe Dayan resigned from the party and formed an independent list "For Zionist and Social Renewal." Dayan met the Likud leader, Menahem Begin, to discuss the possibility of running on the Likud list; but no agreement was reached, reportedly because of Begin's unwillingness to accept that there should be no annexation of Judea and Samaria so long as peace discussions were proceeding. There was talk of the formation of a "Front of Land of Israel Loyalists" to include Dayan and Ariel Sharon. Dayan asked the Labour Party for an assurance that the nation would be consulted (by a referendum or new elections) before the cession of any territory in Judea and Samaria. As the party platform had already been approved by the conference, it could not now be altered; but five Labour ministers and a score of other party leaders signed a letter stating that they would insist on such a pledge being included in the coalition agreement when the next government was formed. Prime Minister Rabin wrote that he had no objection to this undertaking. Dayan accordingly announced that he was ready to have his name put on the Labour list of candidates.

After Rabin withdrew from the Labour nomination (see above), Shimon Peres was elected by an overwhelming majority in the Central Committee to head the list, with only eight members opposing and 18 abstaining. The vote was preceded by Peres' agreement that Yigal Allon would be number two on the list and would receive the Defence portfolio, if he wished it, in the next government. Despite Mapam's strong objections to Peres as a reputed hawk, it decided, after lengthy debate, to continue its association with Labour in the Alignment. As no resignations were possible until the formation of a new government after the election, Rabin announced that he was taking a vacation and, though retaining ultimate responsibility, he asked Peres to preside at Cabinet meetings, thus making him *de facto* Prime Minister.

Of the 17 Labour members of the Knesset who had served two or more terms, seven (including the Speaker, Israel Yeshayahu, and Israel Galili, Minister without Portfolio) failed to obtain the necessary 60% of the votes at the secret ballot in the Central Committee. Twenty of the first 50 names on the list, regarded as having a fair prospect of being elected, were nominated by the party regions; the other 30 were nominated by an appointments committee, which also decided on the order. First in the list were Peres, Allon and Eban; Dayan was seventh, and Rabin, by his own request, was given 17th place, the same as in the 1973 elections.

On 1 March, the Council of the Likud approved its election platform on foreign affairs. It declared that a Likud government would participate in the Geneva Peace Conference and would invite the neighbouring Arab states, "directly or through the agency of a friendly state . . . to conduct direct negotiations for the signature of peace treaties between them without prior conditions." In the negotiations with Syria and Egypt, a Likud government would "strive for an agreement, taking into consideration the interests and needs of the parties" (a formula which left the way open for territorial concessions). In regard to the "West Bank," the previous formula of "no renewed partition of the Land of Israel" was replaced by a declaration that: "Judea and Samaria will not be handed over to any foreign rule; between the sea and the Jordan there shall be only Israeli sovereignty." The platform rejected any possibility of negotiations with "the organization known as the PLO" under any circumstances.

The Likud's economic platform, adopted at a subsequent meeting, called for the reduction of government involvement in economic activity, particularly by the sale of government-owned enterprises, and the replacement of government loans to industry by the raising of money on the capital market. Each of the Likud's sections chose its leading candidates by secret ballot in separate central councils.

Although the DMC had been in existence only a few weeks, public opinion polls indicated that it might expect to win c. 20 seats—which would be an unprecedented achievement for a new party. In order to set an example of democratic procedures, its governing bodies and list of parliamentary candidates were elected directly by the single transferable vote system. Over 33,000 members registered for these elections, and 151 submitted their candidatures for the Knesset. 77% of the membership voted on 18 February, each being asked to place 30 candidates in order of preference. The party council was chosen by a similar method. The results aroused some surprise and controversy. The DMC's opponents suggested that organized groups had manipulated the voting—pointing out that the first ten names in the list included three former leaders of the Free Centre; that two Druzes (little more than 1% of the population) were in 12th and 13th places; and that women, former members of the Shinui Movement, and the poorer neighbourhoods were under-represented. The DMC retorted that their example had induced other parties to adopt more democratic methods of choosing their parliamentary nominees.

The main plank in the DMC's election platform was reform of the electoral system on similar lines to those proposed in the bill backed by Labour and the Likud in the 8th Knesset. On peace policy, the DMC declared that Israel's defence border should be "the River Jordan, including areas west of it essential for Israel's defence. In order to retain its Jewish and democratic nature," the proposals continued, "Israel must be ready for territorial compromise while safeguarding its security needs." Security considerations would be "the guiding principle in determining settlement priorities." The platform also opposed the establishment of "a separate sovereign Palestinian state west of the River Jordan" and any withdrawal in the east which was not part of a full peace agreement. The economic planks of the platform, which were similar in some respects to those of the Likud, called for more opportunity for individual initiative and less government interference. DMC representatives would be given freedom of action on questions relating to religion and the State.

Strong opposition developed in the NRP against Yitzhak Raphael, former Minister of Religious Affairs, who headed one of its factions. While Knesset candidates were nominated by the factions, the final list was decided upon by the Executive Council, which ousted Raphael in favour of two of his younger lieutenants. Rabbi Hayim Druckman (not belonging to any faction but closely associated with the Gush Emunim religious activists' movement) was put in second place, by common consent; this reinforced the influence of the younger, more hawkish circles in the party.

The veteran leader of the Independent Liberal Party, Tourism Minister Moshe Kol, announced that he would not run again and was replaced at the head of the list by Gideon Hausner. A surprise was the failure of Yehuda Sha'ari, chairman of the ILP Knesset group, to secure renomination near the top of the list. Shortly before the election, Hillel Seidel, one of the ILP's Knesset members, joined the Likud and organized a section within its framework called *Ahdut* (Unity).

Public meetings played only a small part in the election campaign, the principal media of propaganda being press advertisements, television and radio. Time was allocated in proportion to the parties' Knesset strengths—an arrangement announced as unfair by the DMC. The party campaigns were largely financed by statutory allocations from the Treasury—also in proportion to Knesset representation.

The Likud mounted a vigorous and effective campaign under the direction of General (Reserves) Ezer Weizman, a former Chief of Operations of the Israel Defence Forces, who had joined Herut on leaving the army in 1969. The Likud's two main watchwords were "Force No 1" and "Change the Government"—claiming that after 29 years of Labour domination, it was time for a change, and that the Likud was the only viable political alternative.

Concentrating on domestic affairs, it portrayed Labour as riddled with corruption, utilizing to the full the impression made by the conviction of Asher Yadlin and the other scandals which had touched the Alignment. It condemned the Government's economic record, especially the inflation rate (38% in 1976), and the series of injurious labour disputes which reached a climax during the election campaign (see below). In foreign affairs, the Likud presented itself as a party of peace, underplaying its opposition to any withdrawal from Judea and Samaria. In the later stages of the campaign, a special effort was made to build up the image of its leader, Menahem Begin, as a sympathetic personality and a statesman of world stature. The Likud campaign was upset on 23 March when Begin was admitted to hospital after a heart attack. Although not released until 13 April, when his doctors said he had made a complete recovery, Begin's absence had no apparent effect on the election result.

The early stages of Labour's campaign (conducted by Yosef Sarid, one of the party's younger Knesset members) were hampered by uncertainty arising from the leadership struggle. After the Convention, Labour sought to present itself as an example of democracy in action; it played up the unexpected results of the DMC's internal elections, and the fact that its leading candidates lived in the most prosperous parts of Tel Aviv and Jerusalem—in contrast to the Alignment's broadly-based list which included 14 candidates from the Oriental communities and eight women in the first 50. With the main slogan, "We Are the Address," Labour admitted responsibility for past shortcomings, but claimed credit for achievements and asked for renewed confidence in its capacity to provide a reinvigorated leadership. It portrayed the Likud as a "one-man show," and its leader as an erratic driver who had failed the test at eight general elections. Prominence was also given to a statement by the Liberal leader, Simha Ehrlich, in which he suggested that unemployment might be a necessary condition for solving the country's economic problems. In reply to charges of corruption, the Alignment claimed credit for the complete freedom of action given to the Attorney-General and the police in investigating all such allegations without political interference; it retaliated to Likud's attacks by publicizing Herut's role in the affairs of the Tel Hai Fund, which had accumulated liabilities of c. IL 40m to finance aid for the *Irgun Zevai Le'umi* (IZL) fighters and their families. The Alignment forecast the possibility of a political deadlock and national chaos if Likud gained in strength. It argued that the Likud's policy of compulsory arbitration in labour disputes could lead to the use of the army as a strike-breaking force and to violent clashes between police and workers.

The NRP's campaign centred on its achievements in producing a generation of pioneering religious youth, its devotion to national ideals and its support for the integrity of the Land of Israel. It appealed to broader circles of the electorate on the lines of "You don't have to be religious to vote NRP," and—in contrast to past years—presented itself as a positive alternative to the Labour-dominated regime, rather than a potential partner.

The DMC presented Professor Yadin as the most suitable candidate for Prime Minister, backed by a capable and experienced team, with a comprehensive programme of social and political reform. Its main barbs were aimed at the Alignment, although it also attacked the Likud as an old-style party, and hinted at the possibility of a Labour-Likud deal after the elections.

The Left-wing Hadash (Democratic Front for Peace and Equality), appealing mainly to Arab votes, and Shelli (Peace and Equality for Israel) warned of the danger of a Right-wing victory and the ascendency of Right-wing elements in the Alignment. Both called for efforts to achieve agreement with the Palestinian Arabs on the establishment of a Palestinian state side by side with Israel, and both expressed readiness to withdraw to the June 1967 lines as part of a peace settlement. Hadash came out for recognition of the PLO as the representative of the Palestinian people, and praised the Soviet Union as a bulwark of world and regional peace; Shelli stressed the compatibility of its policy with essential Zionist aims, and called for the inclusion of military and political guarantees for Israel's security in any peace settlement.

Before the Government crisis in November 1976, public opinion polls indicated that the DMC could obtain as many as 22 seats in the next Knesset, and that General "Arik" Sharon's Shlomzion list could win nine, with losses of 14 seats for the Alignment and 11 for the Likud. Subsequent polls indicated a slight decline for the DMC and a steady drop for Sharon, with the Alignment retaining a lead over the Likud on the whole. However, there were wide divergencies between the results of polls held at about the same time, as well as a very high proportion of people—about 40%—refusing to answer or expressing no opinion (see Table).

PUBLIC OPINION POLLS
(During 1977 Election Campaign)

	Dec 76[1] %	*Dec 76*[2] *seats*	*Jan 77*[1] %	*Jan 77*[2] *seats*	*Mar 77*[3] %	*Mar 77*[3] %
Alignment	19	33	21.8	35	32	35
Likud	13.9	36	19.2	35	23	24
DMC	10	18	11.2	19	23	11
NRP	2.4	9	5.0	9		
Agudat Israel and PAI	0.5	5	1.3	5	7	7
Shlomzion	5.6	7	1.8	6	2.5	1
Others	2.6	11[4]	1.4	11[4]	7.5[5]	5.5[5]
No opinion	31.8	27%	26.5	28%	15	17
Not answering	13.3	9%	11.8	11%	—	—

[1] Public Opinion Research Institute—Jewish population only; *Ha'aretz*, February 1977.
[2] Research and Report, Jerusalem—Jewish population only; *Yediot Aharonot*, 28 January 1977.
[3] Herbert (Hanoch) Smith—not including those refusing to answer; *Ma'ariv*, 22 April 1977.
[4] Including 4 Rakah (Communists—supported mainly by Arabs) and 3 Arabs associated with the Alignment, assuming no change in the Arab sector.
[5] Including 3% Democratic Front for Peace and Equality (Rakah—see note 2) and 2.5% Arab lists in March; 3.5% and 1% respectively in April.

A survey of public satisfaction with the Government's handling of national affairs showed a striking contrast between general approval of its record on foreign affairs and defence, and pronounced disapproval on economic and social affairs. While 53% thought that the Government was successful or generally successful in handling foreign affairs and defence in March—rising to 63% in April—almost 75% thought it was not so successful or not at all successful in dealing with economic affairs. Furthermore, c. 60% held an unfavourable opinion of its performance in the social sphere (see Table).

After Rabin's retirement from the contest, Peres was left with little more than a month to impress himself on the electorate as a potential Prime Minister, during which time his credit as a successful Minister of Defence was damaged by the publication, on 26 April, of the State Comptroller's annual report. This pointed out instances of inefficiency and waste in the maintenance of army supplies and in other aspects of the Israel Defence Force's administration (although army spokesmen claimed that by giving the facts out of context the findings created a wrong impression). Then, on 11 May, less than a week before the elections, 54 paratroopers and airmen were killed in a helicopter crash during a training exercise—the worst single disaster in Israel's military history. While no one directly blamed the Defence Minister or the army command for the incident, the Likud published full-page advertisements asking "What Else Has to Happen?" hinting that Peres had been too busy with party politics to look after the armed forces. In a television confrontation between the Likud and Alignment leaders, postponed because of the crash on 15 May, Begin was confident and incisive, while Peres was subdued and unimpressive.

POLL ON GOVERNMENT'S HANDLING OF PUBLIC AFFAIRS (%)

	Successful	*Generally successful*	*Not so successful*	*Not successful*	*No opinion or other answers*
Economic Affairs:					
March	6.5	9.0	30.0	43.0	11.5
April	7.0	10.0	27.0	45.0	11.0
Social Problems:					
March	6.0	14.0	31.0	33.0	16.0
April	9.0	17.0	30.0	30.0	13.0
Foreign Affairs and Defence:					
March	23.0	30.0	19.0	11.5	17.0
April	39.0	24.0	15.0	9.0	12.0

Based on survey by Herbert (Hanoch) Smith, *Ma'ariv*, 25 April 1977.

Uncertainty among the electorate persisted until a few days before the elections; but dissatisfaction with the Government's performance in internal affairs and the concerted opposition hammering on the theme of corruption in high places appeared, in the final stages of the campaign, to have swayed the balance heavily against the Alignment.

An unusual candidate was Samuel Flatto-Sharon, a Jewish financier who had lived in France from 1939 to 1971, when he emigrated to Israel and acquired citizenship. On 26 December 1976, he was arrested at the request of the French authorities, who wanted him extradited on charges of large-scale fraud and tax evasion. Nevertheless, he was released on bail, at a record IL 10m. Because of the failure of the French to extradite the PLO leader Abu Daoud (see below), there was widespread agitation against handing over an Israeli citizen to France. A petition against his extradition was signed by 30,000 people, including 62 members of the Knesset, the protest being supported by both coalition and opposition leaders in a Knesset debate on 8 February. Flatto-Sharon presented a one-man list in the elections and conducted a lavish press campaign, with the assistance of paid vote-getters. His watchword was "The Solitary Man in the Knesset" and he undertook, if elected, to use his financial resources and business contacts in the service of the people of Israel.

ANALYSIS OF THE ELECTION RESULTS

At first glance, the Alignment's election losses appeared to be exactly balanced by the Likud's gains and the seats won by the DMC (see Table), but most of Shlomzion's votes were presumably gained at the Likud's expense, and part of the DMC's undoubtedly came from former supporters of the Independent Liberals and the Citizens' Rights Movement. Clearly, the major net result was the achievement by Likud of undisputed first place and a percentage of the popular vote approaching that gained by Labour in the past. The Labour Alignment, together with allied Arab lists, now had exactly half the number of seats they held in 1969, and commanded little more than a quarter of the places in the House. The results were a disappointment for the DMC, less because of the number of seats won, but because the Alignment's heavy defeat dashed its hope of supporting whichever of the two major parties agreed to its programme of social and political reform. The Democratic Front's gain of one seat was less than expected, but it now represented a majority of the Arab votes. The united Zionist Left, represented by Shelli, won a smaller percentage of votes than its constituent parts had done in 1973. The most crushing defeat was suffered by the Independent Liberals, who had held a modest but influential place throughout Israel's political history, and had participated in almost all previous Cabinets.

ELECTIONS TO NINTH KNESSET, 17 MAY 1977, AND EIGHTH KNESSET, 31 DECEMBER 1973

	Popular Vote					Knesset Seats		
	1977 Total	*%*	*1973 Total*	*%*	*Net gain or loss (%)*	*1977*	*1973*	*Net gain or loss*
Eligible voters	2,236,293		2,037,478					
Votes cast (%)	1,771,726	79.2	1,601,098	78.6				
Invalid Ballots (%)	23,906	1.3	34,243	2.1				
Quota for Knesset seat[1]	14,173		12,451					
Likud	583,075	33.4	473,309	30.2	+3.2	43	39	+4
Alignment	430,023	24.6	621,183	39.6	-15	32[2]	51[3]	-19
Democratic Movement for Change	202,265	11.6	—	—		15	—	+15
National Religious Party	160,787	9.2	130,349	8.3	+0.9	12	10	+2
Agudat Israel	58,652	3.4	}60,012	3.8[4]	+1.0	4	}5	—
Po'alei Agudat Israel	23,956	1.4				1		
Democratic Front for Peace and Equality	79,733	4.6	53,353	3.4[5]	+1.2	5	4	+1
Flatto-Sharon	35,049	2.0[6]	—	—		1	—	+1
Shlomzion	33,947	1.9	—	—		2	—	+2
Shelli	27,281	1.6	32,616	2.1[7]	-0.5	2	1	+1
United Arab List	24,185	1.4	39,012	2.5[8]	-1.1	1	3	-2
Citizens' Rights Movement	20,621	1.2	35,023	2.2	-1.0	1	3	-2
Independent Liberals	21,277	1.2	56,560	3.6	-2.4	1	4	-3
Zionist and Social Renewal	14,516	0.8						
Beit Yisrael (Yemenites)	9,505	0.5	3,195	0.2	+0.3			
Arab Reform Movement	5,695	0.3	—	—				
Women's Party	5,674	0.3	—	—				
Kach (Meir Kahane)	4,396	0.25	12,811	0.8	-0.55			
Workers' Front	2,498	0.14	13,312	0.9	-0.8			
New Generation	1,802	0.1	—	—				
Zionist Panthers	1,798	0.1	5,945	0.4	-0.3			
Coexistence with Justice (Arab)	1,085	0.06						
Other Lists (in 1973)			40,624	2.8				

[1] Only lists receiving at least 1% of the valid votes cast—i.e. 17,478 in 1977—are entitled to share in the allocation of seats. The quota for one Knesset seat is one hundred-and-twentieth of the total valid votes cast for the lists qualifying.
[2] Moshe Dayan withdrew from the party after the elections.
[3] Arie Eliav and Mordecai Ben-Porat withdrew from the party before the 1977 elections.
[4] In 1973, Agudat Israel and Po'alei Agudat Israel formed one list: the Torah Religious Front.
[5] In 1973, Rakah—New Communist List.
[6] Received enough votes for two seats, but only one candidate on list.
[7] In 1973, Moked (Focus) and Meri (Radicals).
[8] In 1973, Progress and Development (Arab) and Bedouins' List.
[9] Hillel Seidel joined the Likud before the elections.

A closer analysis of the voting showed that the Likud and the religious parties gained especially among the communities of Oriental origin (see Table). The Alignment lost votes mainly to the DMC in European areas, and directly to the Likud among the Oriental communities. An analysis of the voting pattern in prosperous and poor districts in the three main cities revealed that almost all the DMC's support came from the former, and that the Likud gained a clear majority in the poorer districts (see Table).

THE VOTE IN THE CITIES BY ETHNIC COMPOSITION
(in percentages of total valid vote)

Type of City	*Likud*	*Alignment*	*Religious*	*DMC*	*Change from 1973* *Likud*	*Alignment*	*Religious*
Oriental	42	20	27	3	+11	−17	+6
Oriental majority	39	24	17	6	+7	−17	+3
European majority	37	26	13	12	+3	−16	+2
European	32	24	15	17	−1	−16	+2
Jerusalem	40	16	23	12	−1	−12	+3
Tel Aviv	40	25	11	13	+2	−14	+2
Haifa	29	28	9	20	−2	−17	+2

From "The Knesset Elections—An Analysis of the Upset" by Hanoch Smith, published by the American Jewish Committee.

THE VOTE IN THE THREE BIG CITIES BY ECONOMIC-ETHNIC DIVISION
(in percentages of total valid votes)

City	*Likud*	*Alignment*	*Religious*	*DMC*	*Gain or Loss* *Likud*	*Alignment*	*Religious*
		Rich Districts (EUROPEAN)					
Tel Aviv	32	27	9	20	−4	−14	+2
Haifa	26	27	7	27	−7	−16	+1
Jerusalem	29	19	19	22	−5	−13	+5
		Middle Districts (MIXED)					
Tel Aviv	45	26	11	6	+9	−16	+2
Haifa	31	30	11	12	+4	−18	+1
Jerusalem	39	20	15	15	−1	−14	+4
		Poor Districts (ORIENTAL)					
Tel Aviv	53	17	16	3	+6	−11	+11
Haifa	41	19	17	2	+6	−13	+3
Jerusalem	52	16	16	7	+4	−12	+2

Source as above.

Most commentators believed that the election results were not merely due to the events and actions of the immediate past, but to deep-lying social developments. "The upset in the elections," wrote Professor Louis Guttman, Scientific Director of the Israel Institute of Applied Social Research, "is not a passing phenomenon. The change is the result of a process that may have started as far back as 1970, and perhaps even earlier."[1] Dr Dan Horowitz, Senior Lecturer in Political Science at the Hebrew University of Jerusalem, noted that proportionately more members of the Oriental communities, native-born Israelis and young people supported the Herut Movement and its successors since the early 1960s than the electorate as a whole. In his view, reduced immigration and the large number of children in Oriental families meant a continual increase in the proportion of the Israel-born and Oriental communities on the electoral roll. At the same time, the number of older voters, most of European origin who tended to support the Alignment, was diminishing. Horowitz added that immigrants from Muslim countries, not accustomed to the European idea of class structure being the root cause of social deprivation, blamed the political establishment whenever they had cause for complaint: as the Labour movement had been in power since independence, the Right was almost the sole beneficiary of the social protest vote. Moreover, Herut's "hawkish" attitudes were readily accepted by those who had lived, or whose parents had lived, under Arab rule. At the same time, the gradual depoliticization of the governmental and other public bureaucracies had weakened the hold of the apparatus of the ruling party over the newcomers.[2]

KNESSET ELECTION RESULTS, 1949 TO 1977

	Labour[1]	*Non-Socialist*[2]	*Religious*	*Left*[3]	*Other*[4]
1st — 1949	67	26	16	4	7
2nd— 1951	65	35	15	5	—
3rd— 1955	64	33	17	6	—
4th— 1959	68	31	18	3	—
5th— 1961	63	34	18	5	—
6th— 1965	67	31	17	4	1
7th— 1969	60	36	18	4	2
8th— 1973	54	43	15	5	3
9th— 1977	33	46	17	7	17

[1] Including Arab associated or affiliated lists.
[2] Including Herut, Liberals, Independent Liberals, State List (from 1969) and Shlomzion (1977), alone or in combination.
[3] Including Communists, Moked (1973) and Shelli (1977).
[4] Including Sephardim, Yemenite, WIZO and Fighters (1949), Ha'olam Hazeh (1965 and 1969), Citizens' Rights Movement (1973 and 1977), DMC and Flatto-Sharon (1977).

THE HISTADRUT ELECTIONS

Still reeling under the shock of the parliamentary disaster, the Labour Alignment had to plunge immediately into the campaign for the election of delegates to the 13th Convention of the Histadrut (the General Federation of Labour), which would determine the composition of its governing bodies for the next four years. Here the Alignment still held a decisive overall majority, the preservation of which was now more vitally important than ever before.

In view of the crucial significance of the contest, doubts were expressed as to the suitability of Yeruham Meshel, the incumbent Secretary-General, to head the Alignment's list, and suggestions were made that some of the political leaders who now had time on their hands should be transferred to the labour front. However, as there was no time to organize support for another candidate, Meshel was renominated on 19 May. A total of 11 lists were submitted for the Histadrut elections, representing all the major political parties except the religious ones, which have their own labour federations.

The Alignment's list included leaders of some of the larger workers' committees, but no prominent political figures. The Likud list was headed by David Levy, a young father of ten from the new immigrants' town of Beit Shean, who had come from Morocco during the period of mass immigration. The DMC did not make the obvious choice of Meir Amit as its candidate for Secretary-General, as he stood to win a Cabinet post if the DMC joined a coalition. Its list was headed instead by Yigael Yadin, which left the options open. The CRM, which had not stood for the Histadrut elections in 1973, joined forces with the Independent Liberals. *Ha'oved Hadati* (Religious Workers)—whose leader, Rabbi Menahem Cohen, was a Labour member of the Knesset—was closely allied with the Alignment.

In the campaign, the Likud called on the electors to complete its parliamentary victory by giving it control of the Histadrut. It fiercely denounced the Alignment leaders as not being genuine representatives of the workers; referred to them as "Yadlin's associates" (see above); and hinted at corruption in the Histadrut's affairs. Aroused by the Knesset defeat, the Alignment mobilized all its forces, including prominent political leaders. The awakening was particularly marked in the kibbutzim, which sent out their members to erect Alignment signboards and canvass in urban areas, especially the neighbouring new immigrant towns. The Alignment's propaganda stressed the need for a strong Histadrut, under Labour leadership, as a counterweight to a Likud-dominated government. It also warned against the dangers of unemployment, an issue already given prominence by the Liberal leader, Simha Ehrlich, as well as by the Likud's invitation to Professor Milton Friedman to advise on economic policy (see below). A mass march of Alignment supporters, headed by Mrs Golda Meir and other top leaders, was held in Tel Aviv.

Of the 1,354,794 members, 69% voted, the total number of valid votes being 917,126. The results were a surprise to both sides (see Table). Not only did the Alignment's share of the total drop much less than expected—leaving it with firm control of the Federation—but it gained almost 60,000 more votes than it had done on 17 May (whereas in 1973, it had received c. 150,000 more votes for the Knesset than for the Histadrut). Though failing to achieve its declared objective, the Likud considerably improved its strength. The major sufferers, as in the Knesset elections, were the smaller parties, whose main strength was outside the Histadrut. The Alignment also maintained its majority in Na'amat (*Nashim Ovdot Umitnadvot* or Women Workers and Volunteers, formerly *Mo'etzet Hapo'alot*, Working Women's Council) and in almost all the local labour councils, which held elections simultaneously. In Jerusalem, the Alignment received 44% of the votes and the DMC 10%, necessitating a coalition between the two in order to elect the Alignment candidate as secretary.

ELECTIONS TO THE 13TH CONVENTION OF THE HISTADRUT THE GENERAL FEDERATION OF LABOUR, 1973 AND 1977
(with 1977 Knesset votes for main parties)

	1977			*1973*		*1977*
	Votes	*Delegates*	*%*	*Votes*	*%*	*Knesset*
Alignment	507,236	841	55.31	447,541	58.35	430,023
Likud	258,466	428	28.18	174,038	22.69	583,075
DMC	73,594	122	8.02	—	—	202,265
Hadash	27,781	46	3.03	18,240[1]	2.38	79,733
Religious Workers	16,491	27	1.80	32,782	4.27	—
ILP and CRM	11,685	19	1.27	45,811	5.97	41,898
Shelli	10,162	16	1.11	21,118[2]	2.75	27,281
Others	11,711	—	1.28	27,470	3.61	—

[1] In 1973, Rakah (New Communist List).

[2] In 1973, Moked (Focus), Meri (Radicals) and Left Union.

One reason given for the result was the shock felt by voters who had turned their backs on Labour in the Knesset elections, but had not expected or wanted the Alignment to be so severely defeated, and now took advantage of a "second chance" to return to the fold. On the other hand, a survey conducted by the Israel Institute of Applied Social Research immediately after the Knesset elections indicated that if they were held again, the result would be almost the same.[3] Another reason for the change between 17 May and 21 June was that, while the voters had been dissatisfied with the Government, they wanted an independent leadership in the Histadrut that would protect their interests against any actions by the new Administration that might affect them.

THE NEW GOVERNMENT

The election results dictated the composition of the new Government within fairly narrow limits. Theoretically, Peres could have formed a coalition with the support of the DMC, the NRP, the ILP and the CRM (32 + 15 + 12 + 1 + 1 = 61), but this was not possible in practice because of the Alignment's crushing defeat and the NRP's swing to the Right. Begin, together with Shlomzion (whose two members joined Herut on 29 May), the NRP and Flatto-Sharon, could command 58 votes, but needed the support of either Agudat Israel or the DMC for a majority. The Alignment firmly rejected invitations to join a government of national unity.

Rabin announced on 23 May that he was resuming his duties as Prime Minister next day in order to sum up the achievements of his term at a series of Cabinet meetings, and hand over in orderly fashion to the next government. However, Peres remained responsible at party and parliamentary levels.

Begin was admitted to hospital on 23 May and remained there for almost a week. Nevertheless, talks began between Likud and DMC delegations, interrupted only when Begin startled the country by offering Moshe Dayan the post of Foreign Minister. Although the appointment had been previously approved by the Likud executive, it aroused fierce public controversy. As Ezer Weizman of Herut was slated for the Defence portfolio, the Liberals had expected to receive the post, in addition to Finance (their nominee being Arye Louis Dulzin, treasurer of the Jewish Agency). The DMC also claimed it, in the hope of exercising a restraining influence on foreign policy.

Labour spokesmen denounced Dayan's readiness to serve under Begin so soon after the elections, in which he had stood on the Labour list, as "political prostitution," and demanded his resignation from the Knesset. Dayan retorted: "The question facing me was whether Begin being with me was better for Israel or not, and not how many days after the election this happened. Begin said I would be the best Foreign Minister he could name for his Government, given the items now on the agenda." He added that Begin had assured him that Israel would be prepared to go to Geneva on the basis of Security Council Resolutions 242 and 338 without preconditions; that the Arabs would be free to make proposals on any subject, including Judea and Samaria; and that Israeli law would not be extended to the West Bank (i.e. the area would not be formally annexed) while negotiations were going on. War widows and parents bereaved in the Yom Kippur War opposed Dayan's return to the Government (from which he had, in effect, resigned in April 1974 after the publication of the Agranat Report on the war), and almost a thousand demonstrators gathered to protest outside the Herut headquarters.

The ferment among the Liberals died down, however, after the Likud Executive reaffirmed the right of the Prime Minister-elect to nominate candidates for the portfolios to be held by the Likud, but added that he would submit the nominations to the Executive for approval. The DMC returned to the negotiations after being assured that the composition of the Cabinet was still open for discussion. Meanwhile, the Likud started negotiations with the NRP and Agudat Israel, which submitted several conditions concerned mainly with religious affairs. On the publication of the offical election results, President Katzir held statutory consultations with representatives of the parties, and on 7 June entrusted Begin with the task of forming a Government.

The negotiations with the NRP and Agudat Israel were rapidly concluded, but the latter had to secure the approval of the Council of Sages, composed of recognized authorities on rabbinical law, whose rulings are binding on them in all matters. The Council authorized the Aguda to join a coalition with the Likud, but not to accept full responsibility by taking up a Cabinet portfolio. The talks with the DMC raised many problems—especially concerning foreign policy and settlement in the administered areas, but also in connection with Cabinet posts to be given to DMC nominees, and the reorganization of the Government. Begin was anxious to form his Government as quickly as possible so that he could go to Washington to meet

President Carter, and concluded negotiations with the NRP and Agudat Israel on 12 June.

The coalition agreement between the three parties envisaged a number of social reforms, including a five-day week, a basic minimum wage, a national pension system, a national health insurance scheme, and provision of apartments for rental. A coalition committee was to draft a bill, subject to the consent of all three parties, to change the electoral system to one combining elements of regional and proportional representation. Of the 43 clauses in the agreement, however, 35 were concerned with religious principles or observances, such as restrictions on the publication and distribution of pornographic material; the amendment of the Anatomy and Pathology Law 1953 to provide that no autopsy be performed without the family's consent in writing; stricter implementation of the Sabbath work laws; the amendment of the recently passed Termination of Pregnancy Law (see below) to prohibit abortions on the grounds of difficult family or social conditions; more assistance for the State religious education system and the independent educational system of Agudat Israel; and extension of the powers of rabbinical courts. A particularly controversial clause provided that any girl would be exempt from army service—without further investigation, as customary hitherto—on submitting a duly attested declaration that service would be incompatible with her religious mode of life. Another dealt with the definition of a Jew for the purposes of admission to Israel under the Law of the Return and for official registration. The Prime Minister undertook to make every effort to secure a parliamentary majority for a private members' bill providing that only conversions in accordance with the *halacha* (Jewish rabbinical law) would be recognized for these purposes.

Begin presented his 13-member Cabinet to the Knesset on 20 June. The Police portfolio was incorporated into Interior; Tourism was combined with Commerce and Industry; a new Ministry of Energy and Infrastructure was established; Labour was merged with Social Welfare in a Ministry of Social Betterment; and Communications with Transport. Each of the sections of the Likud, as well as the NRP, elected its nominees for the posts allotted to it. For the first time, an NRP nominee was appointed Minister of Education and Culture. The Ministries of Labour and Social Betterment, Justice, and Transport and Communications were left open for nominees of the DMC in case it decided to join the coalition later; in the interim, they were managed by Yoram Eridor, M. K. (Likud—Herut), Deputy Minister in the Prime Minister's Office.

One of the first clauses in the new Government's basic policy guidelines, presented to the Knesset for approval together with the list of ministers, declared: "The Jewish people has an eternal, historic right to the Land of Israel, the inalienable heritage of its forefathers." The Government would "plan, establish and encourage urban and rural settlement on the soil of the homeland." It would "place the aspiration for peace at the forefront of its concerns," and would be ready to take part in the Geneva conference when invited to do so by the US and the Soviet Union "on the basis of Security Council Resolutions 242 and 338." The Government would not invoke its authority (under a law passed in June 1967) to apply Israeli law and jurisdiction to any part of the Land of Israel "so long as negotiations are being conducted on a peace treaty between Israel and her neighbours." The guidelines also promised to provide "equality of rights for all citizens and residents, without distinction of religion, race, nation, sex or ethnic group"; to encourage Jewish immigration, and institute economic, social and educational reforms.

In presenting his new Government to the Knesset, Begin asked for a year's grace to rectify "longstanding distortions in the economic, social and political fields." As leader of the largest opposition party, Peres declared that Begin had paid an extremely high price in "extremely vital areas of national interest" in order to acquire his coalition partners. He had given in to the numerous demands of the religious parties and, to gain support for his "all-or-nothing" foreign policy, he had handed over control of economic affairs to the Liberals in the Likud, who, he said, intended to tamper with the public economy and the pioneering settlement movement. Nevertheless, the Knesset gave the Government a vote of confidence by 63 to 53.

Talks with the DMC resumed after the installation of the new Government, but were suspended during the Prime Minister's visit to the US in July. Among the concessions mooted by Likud representatives were the following: DMC members would have freedom of expression on the question of territorial concessions; if DMC ministers objected to proposals for settlement in the Israel-administered territories, the final decision would be taken by the Knesset Foreign Affairs and Security Committee; DMC members would enjoy freedom of conscience on religious affairs. There was a strong feeling within the DMC in favour of joining the Government on the grounds that it could help to counter extremist trends inside the Likud, and that it had appealed for electoral support in order to influence the social and economic structure, and not to remain in opposition. However, the negotiations broke down in August over the question of electoral reform. As a compromise between proportional representation and single-member constituencies the DMC proposed that 80 members be elected in 16 five-member constituencies and 40 by countrywide proportional representation (as in the Labour proposal supported by the Likud in the 8th Knesset). The NRP feared that this system would endanger its parliamentary representation; it was willing to agree to the bulk of the members being elected in six multi-member constituencies, provided that surplus votes in the constituencies were added to the countrywide party totals in computing the final results. Begin hinted at the possibility of compromising on 10 constituencies, but the DMC insisted on its original proposal. Neither would it let the matter be decided by a committee representing the four coalition parties, since the Likud's agreement with the NRP effectively gave the latter the power of veto.

Begin was again admitted to hospital on 30 September suffering from exhaustion, and did not return to work for nearly three weeks. Finally on 21 October, a few days before the Cabinet vacancies were due to be filled, the DMC accepted the terms offered and joined the Government. Professor Yadin explained that he had become convinced that Israel faced "the toughest test since 1948" over the proposal to reconvene the Geneva conference (see below), and that the time had come to strengthen the Government. He had also been impressed by the Government's flexibility in negotiations with the Americans. However, his deputy, Prof Amnon Rubinstein, argued that joining the Government would be a betrayal of the movement's basic principles and its promises to the electors. Nevertheless, the DMC Council approved the proposal by 68 votes to 45, and its representatives were co-opted to the Cabinet on 24 October. In order to maintain a balance, Begin appointed two additional ministers—one Herut and one Liberal—on 10 January 1978.

The new Government made few changes in major civil service posts, apart from the Prime Minister's Office and the Ministry of Agriculture. The Director-General of the Prime Minister's office, Amos Eranne, was replaced by Dr Eliahu Ben-Elisar; and the Secretary to the Cabinet, Gershon Avner, by Arieh Naor—both members of Herut. Shmuel Katz, a former member of the IZL high command and founder-member of Herut, was appointed as the Prime Minister's adviser on overseas information. Amihai Paglin, former IZL chief of operations, was appointed as Begin's adviser on counter-terrorism. Prof Shlomo Avineri, who had

THE BEGIN CABINET
(installed on 20 June 1977)

Prime Minister	Menahem Begin	Likud—Herut
Deputy Prime Minister	Yigael Yadin	DMC*
Agriculture	Ariel Sharon	Likud—Herut
Construction	Gideon Pat	Likud—Liberal
Defence	Ezer Weizman	Likud—Herut
Education and Culture	Zevulun Hammer	NRP
Energy and Infrastructure	Yitzhak Moday	Likud—Liberal
Finance	Simha Ehrlich	Likud—Liberal
Foreign Affairs	Moshe Dayan	Independent
Health	Eliezer Shostak	Likud—La'am
Immigrant Absorption	David Levi	Likud—Herut
Industry, Commerce and Tourism	Yigal Hurvitz	Likud—La'am
Interior and Police	Yosef Burg	NRP
Justice	Shmuel Tamir	DMC*
Religious Affairs	Aharon Abu-Hatzeira	NRP
Labour and Social Betterment	Israel Katz	DMC*
Transport and Communications	Meir Amit	DMC*
Deputy Ministers		
The PM's Office	Yoram Eridor	Likud—Herut
Defence	Mordecai Zippori	Likud—Herut
Finance	Yehezkel Flomin	Likud—Liberal
Industry, Commerce and Tourism	Yitzhak Peretz	Likud—La'am

*Took office on 24 October (see text)

been appointed Director-General of the Foreign Ministry by Yigal Allon, resigned and was succeeded by a career diplomat, Ephraim Evron. The Director-General of the Ministry of Agriculture was replaced by the former Deputy Director-General, who had contested the elections as a candidate for Agriculture Minister Sharon's Shlomzion Party. Sharon also replaced the Director of the Israel Lands Authority and the Mekorot Water Corporation. The Minister of Education and Culture appointed three personal advisers, all prominent members of his NRP. All the heads of the Israeli missions abroad, and the senior staff of the Finance Ministry, as well as of most other ministries, kept their posts.

The fact that several members of the new Government owned their own businesses (Sharon owned a farm) raised problems of a kind new in Israel; a committee consisting of a judge, a banker and a jurist was appointed to consider the problem. It recommended that, in order to avoid possible conflicts of interest, a minister owning a business must sell it to a stranger or a relative who had been actively involved in it for at least a year (but not to his wife); or lease it for a fixed sum to a non-relative. The recommendations were adopted by the Government on 23 October.

POST-ELECTION DEVELOPMENTS

Meir Zarmi resigned as Secretary of the Labour Party after the elections, and Shimon Peres was elected Chairman of the Party at the beginning of June 1977.

Yitzhak Shamir (Likud—Herut), a former leader of *Lohamei Herut Yisrael* (Fighters for Israel's Freedom), was elected Speaker of the Knesset on 13 June, with 61 votes to 30 for former Police Minister, Shlomo Hillel.

One of the new Government's first decisions was to admit 66 Vietnamese refugees to Israel; they had been rescued on 10 June by the Israeli freighter *Yuval* from a small fishing boat off the coast of Vietnam.

Two proposals raised by Prime Minister Begin after his visit to the US in July met with considerable public criticism, and were ultimately dropped. One was to combine Holocaust Memorial Day (held during the season of the Warsaw Ghetto uprising) and the Memorial Day for the war dead (held on the eve of Independence Day) with the fast of the 9th of Av, which commemorates the destruction of the Temple. This was widely criticized as liable to obscure the memory of the Holocaust by combining it with a religious observance. A proposal to hold a military parade on Israel's 30th Independence Day was adopted by the Cabinet against the objections of Defence Minister Ezer Weizman and others, mainly on the grounds of cost. The proposal was later abandoned in favour of a symbolic march of survivors of the underground organizations of the War of Independence period.

ELECTORAL REFORM

At the beginning of the year, a new effort was made to complete the committee stage of a private member's bill for electoral reform, sponsored by the Labour Party, which had been given a preliminary reading in 1974. Preparation of the bill by the Knesset's Law and Constitution Committee for its first reading had been held up owing to obstruction by Dr Zerah Wahrhaftig (NRP), the Chairman of the committee, and disagreement between Labour and the Liberal section of the Likud over the terms of the bill. On 1 February, agreement was reached between Labour, the Liberals, the La'am section of the Likud, and the CRM, that 80 members should be elected in 16 five-member constituencies and the other 40 by countrywide proportional representation. The Herut section of the Likud, after having opposed reform for many years, decided at its convention on 5 January to "seriously consider changing the electoral system" and also approved the bill in mid-March. Despite this solid majority support, prolonged filibusters in committee by representatives of Mapam, the NRP and Agudat Israel prevented further progress.

ISRAELI SETTLEMENT POLICY

Israel established 77 new settlements between June 1967 and September 1977 in the areas under military government: 26 on the Golan Heights; 21 in the lower Jordan Valley and the eastern slopes of Samaria; seven in the Etzion bloc, north of Hebron; three in western Samaria; 17 in the Rafah area (north-eastern Sinai) and the southern tip of the Gaza Strip; and three on the east Sinai coast. Most of the settlements were established close to the ceasefire lines laid down after the Six-Day war in June 1967, in areas which the Government hoped to keep under Israeli control in any peace agreement. It was intended to integrate the Rafah area settlements with the Southern Project, planned in co-operation with the Land Settlement Departments of the Zionist Organization, which provided for the establishment of 100 settlements, with a population of 150,000, in 15 years in an area of over 1m dunams (250,000 acres) in the Negev, stretching from the south-eastern tip of the Gaza Strip to Beersheba. The Gush Emunim religious activist movement—supported by the Complete Land of Israel (*Eretz Yisrael Hashlema*) movement and most of the Likud and the National Religious Party—called for Jewish settlement all over Judea and Samaria (the West Bank) and made repeated unauthorized attempts to establish settlements close to Arab population centres there.

Prime Minister Rabin declared on 6 January 1977 that the settlements established since 1967 beyond the "Green Line" (the former armistice lines) enhanced the country's security and provided a firm basis for Israel's demand for peace with defensible borders. He added that the Government's settlement priorities called for the strengthening of the "confrontation lines" along the Golan Heights and the

Jordan, and at Ophira (Sharm al-Shaykh), bolstering Jerusalem and the Hebron hills, and creating a buffer zone (in the Rafah area) south of the Gaza Strip. Transport Minister Gad Yaakobi told the Cabinet on 2 January 1977 that planning had started on a deep-water port for the Rafah area (presumably at the new town of Yamit).

During the first half of 1977, only one new settlement was established in the West Bank: near Masha, in western Samaria, just across the Green Line c. 10 km from Kafr Qasim. When there were delays in carrying out a Government decision to establish the settlement, Gush Emunim collected signatures from 64 out of the 120 members of the Knesset in support of their claim to settle in the area. On 27 February, a Gush Emunim group tried to squat on the site, but left when troops arrived and ordered them off. The settlement was ultimately established, with government permission on 1 May.

The Rabin Government was criticized by Left-wing circles for its failure to carry out its announced decision to remove the Gush Emunim group from the grounds of the army camp of Kaddum. The group—which called its settlement *Elon Morre* ("Plain of Moren"—Genesis 12:6)—had been permitted to stay on the grounds temporarily after its unauthorized attempt to settle at nearby Sebastiya (Biblical Samaria).

Two days after the elections, Likud leader Menahem Begin made some far-reaching statements at the installation of a scroll of the Scriptures in the synagogue at Kaddum. "In a few weeks or months there will be many Elon Morres; there will be no need for a Kaddum," he declared. He rebuked a foreign correspondent for calling the area "occupied territory." "Since May 1977, I hope you will start using the term 'liberated territories'," he said. "A Jew has every right to settle in these liberated territories in the Jewish land." In reply to a query whether the new Government would "annex" the territories, he declared: "We don't use the word annexation; you annex foreign land, not your own country." In an interview broadcast in the US by ABC on 22 May 1977, he declared that Judea and Samaria were "an integral part of our sovereignty."

Israel radio reported on 1 July that a Likud committee had presented to the Cabinet Settlement Committee a plan for the establishment of five new towns in Judea and Samaria, as well as 43 new settlements in that area, the Golan Heights, the Gaza Strip and Sinai, and a network of east-west roads through the West Bank. No serious consideration was given to the plan. However, on 26 July, the Committee did grant official recognition to the Gush Emunim settlements at Kaddum, 'Ofra and Ma'ala Adomin. 'Ofra, north of Jerusalem on the road to Ramallah, had been set up officially as a work camp; Ma'ala Adomin, east of Jerusalem, had been officially established as an industrial area with residential accommodation. Government circles welcomed President Carter's statement on 28 July minimizing the importance of the decision.

On 17 August, the Joint (Government and Zionist Organization) Settlement Committee decided to establish three new settlements in the areas under military government, at Yatir on the former armistice line, south of Hebron; at Mevo Horon B, in the former no-man's-land near Latrun; and at Tzur-Natan B, just across the armistice line east of Kfar Sava. The US Ambassador called on the Prime Minister on 19 August with a message from President Carter expressing disapproval of the establishment of the settlements, but Government sources pointed out that they were all close to the pre-1967 borders and would therefore be within the "minor adjustments" which even the US envisaged in a final agreement with the Arabs. On 21 August, the Cabinet expressed its regret at the American criticism, saying: "Israel does not and cannot accept the assertion that settlement by Jews in the Land of Israel is illegal. The Government of Israel reiterates that settlement does not, and shall not, constitute an obstacle to negotiations for peace treaties.''

Agriculture Minister Ariel Sharon, in a television interview on 2 September, outlined a 20-year plan for settling 2m people in a new belt of settlements running from the Golan Heights along the Jordan to Ophira (Sharm al-Shaykh) at the southern tip of Sinai. There would also be a shorter strip on the western slopes of Samaria, and the Jerusalem corridor would be widened and connected up with the settlements in the Jordan Valley. Sharon pointed out that all these areas were sparsely populated. ''Israel's main objective,'' he said, ''should be to double its Jewish population to 6–8m'' over the next 20–30 years. ''If we want a strong, independent state, we must give up settling just on the coastal strip and move elsewhere''; otherwise Israel would consist of a mass of concrete from Ashkelon to Nahariya—all within the range of Arab guns—and have to rely on friendly powers for protection.

Gush Emunim expected the new Government to give full backing for its plans to expand its settlements; when this support was not forthcoming, they made preparations early in September to set up 12 new settlements in the heart of the area. The Government asked it to exercise restraint in view of the negotiations with the US, but some of its groups refused to wait any longer. On 28 September, after consultations with Gush Emunim representatives, Begin proposed that the groups be allowed to settle in army camps. To regularize the status of the settlers, it was suggested that they be called up for reserve duty; but this proposal was objected to by Defence Minister Ezer Weizman, as well as by the Opposition parties, who denounced it as bringing political issues into the Army. The idea was dropped. Instead, it was decided that they would have the status of civilian employees working for the armed forces. One group, which set out to settle near Jericho, was stopped by the Army on the Defence Minister's orders, which were confirmed by the Prime Minister; others were allowed to encamp on the grounds of existing settlements and army or border police camps. Six settlements were established by Gush Emunim groups in this way; Beit Ḥomotayim (Dotan) near Sanur, between Tulkarm and Jenin; Maḥaneh Shomron, near Sebaste, north-west of Nablus; Nabi Sālih, north-west of Ramallah; Beit-El, north of Ramallah, Upper Beit Horon, on the Ramallah-Latrun road; and Giv'on (Biblical Gibeon), north of Jerusalem. In mid-November, the Treasury requested the Knesset Finance Committee to authorize IL 81m from budget reserves to reimburse Gush Emunim for their past outlays and their expenditures up to the beginning of the new financial year.

Plans for the development of Yamit in the Sinai were announced on 30 September during a visit by the Prime Minister and the Housing Minister. The population was to be increased from c. 1,000 to 30,000 in the next two years, and a master plan for a population of 100,000 was to be prepared. Ceremonies were held to dedicate the town's first residential quarter, a field school for nature study, and a *yeshiva* combining Talmud study with military training. The name of the area was to be changed from the Rafah Approaches (*Pitḥat Rafiaḥ*) to *Ḥevel Yamit*—the Yamit Region. Begin also visited the new settlement of Ne'ot Sinai, 2 km east of El-'Arish, where he was greeted by the Mayor. Representatives of the nearby kibbutz of Kerem Shalom, affiliated to Mapam, and of ten other kibbutzim in the Negev, demonstrated against the visit which, they declared, would hinder the quest for peace.

In an interview with *The Jerusalem Post* (12 September), the Foreign Minister advocated a ''functional'' division of authority in the West Bank. ''There are now two clear, undisputed states—Israel and Jordan—and an undefined area between them,'' he said. ''For that area, there could be all kinds of arrangements with Jordan, or with Israel and Jordan combined. . . . There are three things we want on the West Bank. We want to be able to have new settlements, but only where we can buy the land. . . . We also want to be free to travel all over the area without the need for visas or permits . . . and we want the right to maintain military bases.''

At the UN General Assembly debate, Dayan said on 10 October that if the Arabs had proposed partitioning the West Bank and the Gaza Strip between them and Israel, ''we would have discussed and examined their proposals.'' Israel's aims in the areas occupied since 1967 were to have her security protected; to be guaranteed freedom of navigation in all international waterways; to protect the main sources of Israel's water supplies, such as the headwaters of the Jordan River, and to achieve equal rights and full coexistence between Israel and the Palestinians in the Gaza Strip, Judea and Samaria. On the settlements in the areas, Dayan said: ''Let me make one point clear. The settlements will not decide the final borders between Israel and her neighbours. The border will be decided upon in negotiations between Israel and her neighbours.''

THE ISRAELI ARABS

ELECTION RESULTS

The results of the Knesset elections in the Arab sector showed gains for the Democratic Front for Peace and Equality (DFPE), which was established by the New Communist List with the co-operation of some local council heads and a section of the Jewish Black Panther Movement (see Elections, above). The DFPE won 49% of the Arab and Druze votes (cf 37% for the NCL in 1973), but the effects of the increase were reduced by a lower poll in this sector—73% (cf 77% in 1973). Thus the DFPE, in fact, won only five seats—one more than in the 8th Knesset. The party was particularly strong in the towns (71%) and urban areas (50%) cf 51% and 44% respectively in 1973. 90% of its total Knesset strength came from the Arab sector (cf 92% in 1973).

The percentage of votes that went directly to the Alignment fell from 13% to 11%, part of the loss apparently going to the Democratic Movement for Change which received 4%. The biggest loser was the United Arab List which won only one seat, having obtained 16% of the votes (cf 26% and three seats for the corresponding Arab lists in 1973).

KNESSET ELECTION RESULTS, 1977 and 1973

	1977		1973	
Votes cast	145,266		133,058	
Percentages	73%		77%	
	Votes	%	**Votes**	%
DFPE	71,718	49	49,326	37[1]
United Arab List	23,582	16	35,699	26[2]
Alignment	16,327	11	17,065	13
National Religious Party	6,628	5	9,027	7
Arab Reform Movement	5,346	4	—	—
Democratic Movement for Change	5,181	4	—	—
Others	16,484	11	21,941	16

[1] New Communist List
[2] Progress and Development (2 seats) and Bedouin List (one seat)

However, in the elections to the Histadrut convention, the Alignment kept its strength among the Arab workers, with 60% of the votes, while the DFPE, with 32%, made only slight gains. These results compare with 59% and 29% respectively in the previous elections. The Likud received 7%, about the same as in 1973.

LAND POLICY AND ILLEGAL BUILDING

There was some unrest among the Israeli Arabs over Government land policy and actions to combat illegal building, especially in Galilee and the Negev. Memorial meetings, held on 30 March 1977 in Israeli-Arab centres in memory of six Arabs killed in the 1976 anti-expropriation riots, passed off peacefully in most localities, despite persistent calls from PLO and other Arab radio stations for violent protests. However, troops took action in the villages of Jatt and Bāqa al-Gharbiyya when youngsters blocked the main road, and soldiers were accused of brutality and provocation. The Cabinet rejected a proposal by Mapam and Independent Liberal ministers to appoint a committee of enquiry, but Police Minister Shlomo Hillel said that all specific complaints against individuals would be investigated.

The Minister of Agriculture in the new Government, Ariel Sharon, devoted considerable attention to the problems associated with the Negev Bedouin, such as their movements northward with their flocks in search of pasture, their claims to ownership of extensive grazing areas, and building without permits. On 23 August 1977, he said that Bedouin had set up c. 800 encampments, with a total population of 10,000, in the coastal area between Ashkelon and Hadera.

At a meeting with Negev Bedouin shaykhs on 28 September, Sharon said that there was a "covenant of blood" between him and the Bedouin (some of their tribes had co-operated with the Jews before Israel's independence); but he warned them that the Government would not tolerate the illegal construction that had spread in the area and would carry out demolition orders issued in the past. He said the Government had given the Bedouin generous aid: it had invested IL 100m in the development of seven settlement areas (and planned to spend another IL 400m) where Bedouin could buy land at 1% of the usual price. The Government had also built them schools and clinics and leased them 400,000 dunams (100,000 acres) at "symbolic prices" for field crops and grazing. On 16 October, agreement was reached between a government committee and Bedouin representatives that the demolition of nine illegally built houses would be held up, and the Bedouin promised to halt unlicensed building.

A riot broke out on 8 November 1977 in the Galilee Arab village of Majd al-Kurum on the Acre-Safad road over the execution of a court order for the demolition of an illegally built house. Villagers who tried to interfere were dispersed with tear-gas by a police force numbering over 180; but others set up roadblocks and stoned passing traffic. When soldiers escorting an ambulance to hospital were attacked, they fired in the air. Three police officers also opened fire and one Arab was killed—according to a police investigating committee, by a ricocheting bullet. Thirty were detained, and four villagers hospitalized; 22 policemen and two civilian workers were injured. There were also allegations of police brutality in the pursuit of rioters who fled into the village.

The matter was raised in the Knesset on 17 November by representatives of the Likud, the Alignment, the DMC, the DMPE and Shelli, who called for an official inquiry. The Ministry of the Interior was blamed for not providing adequate land for building in the Arab areas. The Interior Minister replied that all Arab localities had received additional allocations of land for building in the Arab areas; Majd al-Kurum's land reserves, he said, had been increased by 30%. He added that over 3,000 structures had been erected in the north without permits, but it had been decided to take legal action against only 167.

ISRAELI ARABS AND PILGRIMAGE TO MECCA

A delegation of Israeli Arabs, who went to Amman in February 1977 on an official visit of condolence to King Ḥusayn on the death of his wife, reported that the

Jordanian Government might try to persuade Saudi Arabia to allow them to go to Mecca for the annual *hajj* (pilgrimage). On 13 November, an official spokesman in Amman announced that the Saudi authorities had agreed to allow Israeli Muslims, defined as "Muslims of Arab lands occupied since 1948," to enter Saudi Arabia for the *hajj* with Jordanian travel documents. The spokesman added that Jordan would be willing to supply such documents, but the concession had come too late for the 1977 pilgrimage.

BIR'AM AND IKRIT

There was growing support after the elections for a proposal to allow the former residents of the Christian Arab villages of Bir'am and Ikrit in northern Galilee to return to their homes. They had been evacuated on security grounds during the fighting in 1948 and 1949 and resettled in other Christian Arab villages in the north. The previous government had rejected demands for their return, under pressure from the neighbouring Jewish villages, on the grounds of security risks in a border area and the establishment of a precedent. The Labour Party Central Council resolved towards the end of July 1977, by 142 votes to 58, to reaffirm its opposition to the villagers' return. The new Cabinet appointed a committee to consider the question again, but it had not reported by the end of 1977.

AREAS UNDER MILITARY GOVERNMENT

PROGRESS IN THE WEST BANK AND THE GAZA STRIP

A survey, published in August 1977 by the Israel Defence Forces spokesman and the Office for the Co-ordination of the Administered Territories in the Ministry of Defence, gave the following figures for the developments in the West Bank and the Gaza Strip:

		Judea and Samaria	**Gaza Strip**
Population:	1968 (end)	584,100	357,800
	1976 (end)	689,700	444,400
	Increase	18%	24%
Birth-rate per thousand:	1968	44.3	43.0
	1975	44.9	50.7
Gross National Product (IL million):	1968	344	131
	1976	4,554	2,074
Private expenditure per capita (IL):	1968	611	373
	1976	5,942	3,678
	1976 at 1968 prices	1,114	734
Percentage of families owning:			
Radios	1967	58	50
	1976	83	89
Electric refrigerators	1967	5	3
	1976	30	29
Television sets	1967	2	3
	1976	30	34
Number of motor vehicles:	1967	2,974	2,423
	1976	14,256	10,713

A report issued by the Gaza Military Government in mid-August 1977 showed that health services had been constantly improving during the past ten years. The budget had grown from a little over IL 2m in 1967–8 to over IL 91m in 1977–8—an almost ten-fold increase in real terms. Fifty more doctors and almost 600 other additional personnel were employed in the health services, which now included a school for practical nurses and a score of new clinics, as well as over 200 new hospital beds—an increase of almost 25%.

On his retirement in September 1977 from the post of Military Commander in the Gaza Strip after nearly four years' service, Brigadier David Maimon ascribed the relative quiet in the area to good relations between the Military Government and the local population; to "the suppression of terrorism" which had been rife in 1971 and 1972; and to a dramatic improvement in economic conditions. "In the past four years, we have come to know the people of Gaza, their culture, their way of life, their sensitivities," he told the *Jerusalem Post*. "This has paved the way for mutual understanding and enabled us to live together in peace." Maimon also stressed the importance of the Jewish settlements in the Rafah area, south of the Strip. "The solution to Gaza's security lies in these new settlements," he said. "Until we began to settle there, the area was dominated by gun-smugglers and terrorists. Today it forms the border between the desert and agriculture."

"EQUALIZATION OF SERVICES"

The Cabinet announced a policy of "equalization of services" for inhabitants of the areas under military government on 14 August. The decision aroused criticism in Israel and abroad, but according to the Cabinet Secretary Arye Naor, it was "humanitarian, not political." The object was to provide the population with the same standard of governmental services—health, welfare, etc.—as the citizens of Israel proper. However, Naor also noted that the coalition parties were committed to the total integration of the areas into Israel "when the time is ripe; it was wrong to use the term 'annexation' since you cannot annex what belongs to you." Steps announced to implement the decision included prevention of the exploitation of local Arabs by Jewish farmers in the Rafah area; a medical health scheme for the inhabitants of the West Bank and the Gaza Strip; and an offer of credit to bus companies in the areas to buy new vehicles. It was reported that the improved services would be financed by money raised in Arab countries and by more efficient tax collection. Yossi Sarid, M.K. (Alignment-Labour), declared that the decision "smells of annexation." Several West Bank leaders rejected it; Fahd Qawāsimī, Mayor of Hebron, said that it signalled "outright annexation" of the areas. (Also see essay, "The West Bank and Gaza Strip.")

DEFENCE AND SECURITY

THE ARMED FORCES*

Total armed forces number 164,000 (123,000 conscripts); mobilization to 400,000 in 72 hours. Military service is 36 months for men and 24 months for women (Jews and Druzes only: Muslims and Christians may volunteer). Annual training for reservists thereafter up to age 54 for men and 25 for women. Defence expenditure in 1977–8 was IL 40.2 bn ($4.27 bn). The Army numbers 138,000 (120,000 conscripts, male and female), with 375,000 on mobilization; in 20 armoured brigades, nine mechanized brigades, nine infantry brigades and five parachute brigades. 11 brigades (five armoured, four infantry, two parachute) normally kept near full strength; six (one armoured, four mechanical, one parachute) between 50% and full strength; the rest at cadre strength. Equipment consists of 3,000 medium tanks, including 1,000 *Centurion*, 650 M-48, 810 M-60, 400 T-54/-55, 150 T-62, *Chariot*;

*Data provided by *The Military Balance 1977–78* (London: International Institute for Strategic Studies).

65 PT-76 light tanks; c. 3,600 armoured fighting vehciles, including AML-60, 15 AML-90, RBY *Ramta* armoured cars; c. 4,000 M-2/-3/-113, BRDM, BTR-40/-50P (OT-62)-60P/-152 armoured personnel carriers; 500 105mm, L-354, M-109 and 155mm, 60 175mm, some 203mm self-propelled howitzers; 450 120mm, 122mm, 130mm and 155mm guns/howitzers; *Lance*, *Ze'ev* (*Wolf*) surface-to-surface missiles; 122mm, 135mm, 240mm rocket launchers; 900 81mm, 120mm and 160mm mortars (some self-propelled); 106mm recoilless rifles; *TOW, Cobra, Dragon*, SS-11, *Sagger* anti-tank guided weapons; about 900 *Vulcan/Chaparral* 20mm missile/gun systems and 30mm and 40mm anti-aircraft guns; *Redeye* surface-to-air missiles. (125 M-60 medium tanks, 700 M-113 armoured personnel carriers, 94 155mm howitzers, 175mm gun, *TOW, Lance* on order.)

The Navy numbers 5,000 (1,000 conscripts), 6,000 on mobilization, and has one Type 206 submarine (two building); six *Reshef*-class fast patrol boats, guided-missile with *Gabriel* surface-to-surface missiles; 12 *Saar*-class fast patrol boats, guided-missile with *Gabriel* surface-to-surface missiles, c. 40 small patrol boats (under 100 tons);12 landing craft (three under 100 tons); three *Westwind* 1124N maritime reconnaissance aircraft; Naval commando: 300. (Seven *Reshef*-class fast patrol boats, guided-missile and *Harpool* surface-to-surface missiles on order.)

The Air Force has 21,000 (2,000 conscripts, air defence only), 25,000 on mobilization and 549 combat aircraft (in addition, there are combat aircraft in reserve, including 25 *Mystère* IVA); 12 fighter, ground-attack/interceptor squadrons: one with five F-15, six with 165 F-4E, three with 30 *Mirage* IIICJ/BJ, two with 100 *Kfir/Kfir* C2. Six fighter, ground-attack squadrons with 235 A-4E/H/M/N *Skyhawk*; one reconnaissance squadron with 12 RF-4E, 2EV-1; transports include 10 Boeing 707, 24 C-130E/H, 12 C-97, 20 *Noratlas*, 10 C-47, 2 KC-130H, 14 *Arava*, 15 Do-28, 10 *Islander*. Ten Do-27, 25 Cessna U206, two *Turbo-Porter* light aircraft; trainers include 24 TA-4H, 80 *Magister, Mystère* IV, *Super Mystère*, 20 *Queen Air*, 20 *Super Cub*. Helicopters include 12 *Super Frelon*, 28 CH-53G, 6 AH-1G, 40 AB-205A, 25 AB-206, 30 UH-1D, 15 S-65, 30 *Alouette* II/III. 15 surface-to-air missile batteries with 90 *Hawk*. (20 F/TF-15A interceptors, 35 F-4 fighters, ground-attack, 4 E-2C airborne early warning aircraft, *Sidewinder* air-to-air missiles on order.) Reserves (all services) number 460,000; paramilitary forces include 4,500 Border Guards and 5,000 *Nahal* Militia.

AIR CRASH

On 11 May, an Israel Air Force Sikorsky CH-53 helicopter, taking part in a combined forces exercise, crashed 3 km north of Jericho; 54 soldiers—44 paratroops and 10 airmen—were killed; there were no survivors. Judge Dov Lenin, who acted as military coroner, found that the pilot had been flying too low and that the aircraft had been overloaded. On his recommendation, the commander of the helicopter unit was tried for negligence and failure to ensure observance of flight safety regulations before a military court, which ordered him to be reprimanded. This tragedy was used in the elections by the Likud to attack the Alignment (see above).

A large call-up exercise, the third since the Yom Kippur War, was held on 19 June 1977. Thousands of men were summoned, mainly by the transmission of call-up codes by radio and television.

LEGAL AFFAIRS

THE BENSION AFFAIR

Yehoshua Bension, former manager of the Israel-British Bank, was released from prison on 8 September after serving two years of a 12-year prison sentence for embezzling $39m from the bank's funds. The sentence was remitted by the

President on grounds of ill-health, on the recommendation of Prime Minister Begin as acting Minister of Justice. The Prime Minister's office explained that Benison's release had been based on medical opinion; Professor Ezra Sohar had described Bension as "a very sick man, whose life expectancy is brief even under the best conditions," adding that he could not receive adequate treatment under prison conditions. The opinion had been endorsed by Bension's own physician, Professor Moshe Rachmilevich.

The release provoked angry controversy, with Opposition spokesmen suggesting that Bension had been released because he was a supporter of Gush Emunim and the Complete Land of Israel Movement. Former Police Minister Shlomo Hillel, M.K. (Alignment-Labour) said that Begin's action amounted to "the politicization of the institution of pardon." Not only had the Supreme Court rejected Bension's appeal for release on medical grounds, but the official committee dealing with such appeals had also rejected it on numerous occasions, as had a Health Ministry committee of three doctors in a recent report. Justice Yoel Sussman, President of the Supreme Court, took the unprecedented step, after consulting some of his colleagues, of writing to the Prime Minister protesting against the exercise of the Presidential prerogative to by-pass normal legal processes. Opposition members brought up the question in the Law and Constitution Committee of the Knesset; when a majority decided not to discuss the matter there, it was brought up in the plenum. Begin vigorously denied that he had been guided by anything other than purely humanitarian motives.

SOCIAL AFFAIRS

PROBLEMS OF CRIME

The existence of "organized crime" in Israel was raised at a press conference by Ehud Olmert, M.K. (Likud—La'am) on 5 August 1977, as well as in a series of articles in the *Ha'aretz* daily at about the same time. Olmert alleged that there were criminals who specialized in murder, arson, extortion, robbery, dissemination of drugs, sale of stolen property, smuggling, forgery and violent loan collections. He added that there was a trend for underworld figures to take over legitimate enterprises, but that the police did not have evidence which would stand up in court to convict the top men. Olmert also alleged that Maj-Gen (Reserves) Rehav'am Ze'evi had threatened him 18 months previously, after Olmert had charged that a "high-ranking officer" was protecting leading figures in the criminal underworld. Ze'evi denied the allegation and sued Olmert for libel. While Commissioner Haim Tavori, Inspector-General of Police, admitted only that there was "organization by individuals to commit crimes," Interior and Police Minister Yosef Burg admitted on 7 August that there was organized crime in Israel, and a police committee, headed by Assistant-Commander Michael Bochner, was appointed to investigate the situation.

In its report, published on 4 September, the Bochner committee said that there was no "super-organization" like the "syndicate" in the US which dominated many gangs and enjoyed a monopoly over a particular type of offence; but there were groups that had specialized in particular crimes on a basis of mutal aid and internal discipline. The report stated, however, that there was no criminal in Israel who enjoyed immunity from the law: "We have not discovered any organized penetration of the police, the courts, or governmental and published agencies," it declared. Among the social causes of crime mentioned by the report were the loss of public confidence in the integrity of persons in key positions as a result of recent scandals; legal restrictions on the use of foreign currency; customs regulations; lenient sentences; long delays in sentencing arrested criminals, and terrorizing of witnesses. Police morale was low, owing to poor pay and inconvenient hours, and there was a shortage of patrolmen and investigators. The Interior Minister announced immediate measures to improve the situation, including the strengthening of police intelligence and the transfer of 400 men from desk jobs to operational duties, at a cost of Il 140m. A committee, headed by Erwin Shimron, a prominent lawyer, was appointed to make comprehensive long-term recommendations.

Another shock to the reputation of the police came in the last week of August, when 18 Tel Aviv policemen were arrested on suspicion of stealing property from places where they were investigating burglaries.

POPULATION

Israel's total population at the beginning of 1977 was 3,575,400 of whom 3,020,400 were Jews, 429,100 Muslims, 82,000 Christians, 43,900 Druzes and others. At the end of 1977, this figure was estimated to have risen to 3,665,000: 3,076,000 Jews and 574,000 others. Almost all the growth was due to natural increase: Jewish immigration for 1977 was estimated at 25,000, but emigration was believed to be about 15,000.

Over half of the Jewish population—52.1%—was born in Israel; 21.5% in Asia and Africa; and 26.4% in Europe and America. Classifying the Israel-born according to the father's birthplace, 11% were born in Israel of Israel-born fathers; 46.2% were of Asian or African origin, and 42.8% of European or American origin. The largest group—428,000—originated in Morocco and Tangiers; 346,000 in Poland; 290,000 in Romania; 259,000 in Iraq; 248,000 in the Soviet Union; 162,000 in Yemen, and 75,000 in America and Oceania.

There were 914,000 families in Israel in 1976 (not counting Bedouin and inmates of institutions). The average Jewish family consisted of 3.5 persons, 13% numbering six persons or more; non-Jewish families averaged 6.4 persons each, 57.3% numbering six or over.

One sign of the rise in the standard of living was the doubling of the number of private cars since 1970, reaching 292,400 and covering 30% of the families. 57% of the families had telephones. The percentage of families living in overcrowded conditions, with three or more persons per room, had dropped from 10.2% in 1967 to 3.6% in 1976. The average income per family was IL 44,000 (c. $5,500). The average family had 1.5 breadwinners, over one-third having two or more members working.

TERMINATION OF PREGNANCY LAW

The termination of Pregnancy Law, which was passed on 31 January 1977 after prolonged and sometimes acrimonious debate, permitted legal abortion after approval by a committee consisting of a gynaecologist, another physician and a social worker, provided that the mother was below marriageable age or over 40; the infant was bound to be born physically or mentally handicapped; the birth would injure the mother's physical or emotional health; or the continuation of pregnancy could lead to a serious social or family hardship. It was estimated that 60,000 illegal abortions were performed annually in Israel. However, the law was bitterly opposed by the religious parties on the grounds that Jewish rabbinical law permits abortion only when the mother's life is in danger. There was also objection from wider circles to the last provision of social or family hardship, and some physicians argued that more attention should be paid to the dissemination of information on methods of birth control rather than on facilitating abortion.

RELIGIOUS AFFAIRS

CLASH OVER SABBATH OBSERVANCE

Clashes over the question of Sabbath observance in the mainly orthodox town of Bnei Braq, near Tel Aviv, led to considerable tension in July 1977. The town council, 10 of whose 15 members belong to religious parties, decided to close a section of Hashomer Street (a thoroughfare with a non-religious neighbourhood on one side and a newly-built religious quarter on the other) to Sabbath traffic. The Ministry of Transport ruled that the council's decision was *ultra vires*. There were violent clashes between religious and non-religious residents, reinforced by supporters from outside, and between demonstrators and police. At the beginning of July, a man was killed when his car crashed into a chain stretched across the road by the council to prevent Sabbath traffic, and a public committee was set up to consider the question.

The matter was taken up at the national level by Interior Minister Yosef Burg (NRP) and Rabbi Shlomo Lorincz, M.K. (Agudat Israel). Agudat Israel supporters hinted they might press their leaders to withdraw from the Government coaltion over the affair, and Prime Minister Begin promised to seek a solution. Moshe Shahal, M.K., Chairman of the Alignment's Knesset group, accused the Government of surrendering to the demands of extreme religious circles, while Religious Affairs Minister, Aharon Abuhatzera (NRP), declared that a small group of anti-religious agitators who did not like the country's new leadership was trying to foment fears of religious coercion. The public committee recommended that two blocks of the street be closed to through-traffic on Sabbaths and religious holidays, and by the end of the month quiet was restored.

RELEASE OF ARCHBISHOP CAPUCCI

The Catholic Archbishop of Jerusalem, Hilarion Capucci, who was sentenced on 9 December 1974 to 12 years' imprisonment for transporting arms and explosives for Palestinian terrorists, and whose release had been demanded on several occasions by Palestinian hijackers, was set free on 7 November 1977 in response to a request for clemency from Pope Paul VI. The previous Government was reported to have decided towards the end of 1976 to liberate Capucci, but had shelved the matter in view of the forthcoming elections. An earlier letter from the Vatican was returned because it was addressed to President Katzir, *Tel Aviv*; the latest appeal sidestepped the issue of Jerusalem by not mentioning the President's address and was delivered by hand by a Papal representative. In his reply to the Pope, President Katzir said he was relying on the former's assurance that the release of Capucci would not be detrimental to Israel's security. Capucci flew to Rome, and later went to South America.

RABBINICAL ELECTIONS

The five-year terms of the Chief Rabbis (Sephardi and Ashkenazi) and the Chief Rabbinate Council expired on 15 October 1977, but were extended by up to nine months by a law passed in the Knesset four days later. Rabbi Shalom Mashash, Chief Rabbi of Morocco, and Rabbi Bezalel Zolti were elected Sephardi and Ashkenazi Chief Rabbis of Jerusalem respectively on 13 November after prolonged and repeated delays; the former office had been vacant for seven years and the latter 17 years since the deaths of the incumbents.

FOREIGN RELATIONS

Israel's foreign relations during 1977 were dominated by the question of progress towards peace with her Arab neighbours and the reconvening of the Geneva conference. During most of the year, these matters were handled mainly in discussions with the US, but President Sādāt's historic visit to Jerusalem in November made it possible, for the first time since the armistice talks in 1949, to discuss the issue directly with the leading Arab state.

RELATIONS WITH US

There were early signs that President Carter might change US policy towards Israel. First, there was the American ban on the sale of the Israel-made *Kfir* jet aircraft to Ecuador, and soon after the announcement of delay in approving the sale of US-made CU 72 cluster bombs to Israel, which had been promised by the Ford Administration. Prime Minister Rabin urged the Cabinet, however, to keep a sense of proportion over what he called "these non-central issues" at that early stage of the Carter Administration's term.

At the end of a visit to Israel on 15–17 February 1977 (the first stage in a tour of six Middle East countries), US Secretary of State Cyrus Vance said that he now had "a much clearer understanding" of Israel's position with respect to a settlement, and pledged "full consultations" with the leaders of Israel and the other countries involved. A Cabinet communiqué issued on 22 February stated that Vance had reiterated America's commitment to a strong and secure Israel as a *sine qua non* for peace talks; expressed Washington's desire for close mutual trust and "intimate consultation" with Jerusalem, emphasized the "special relationship" between the two countries; described America's role as a "catalyst" in negotiations between the parties, not as a formulator of its own peace plans; called for meticulous preparation in advance for the resumption of the Geneva peace conference in the second half of the year; restated the Administration's commitment to the political obligations undertaken at the time of the Sinai II agreement in 1975; and refused to consider the participation of the PLO at Geneva unless it recognized Israel's right to exist and changed the Palestine National Convenant accordingly.

Vance's visit was followed by one to Washington by the Prime Minister. On his arrival on 5 March, Rabin pledged that Israel would take part in any "meaningful framework of negotiations" that would advance peace with the Arabs. In spite of his aim to arrive at a common understanding with the Carter Administration on the political issues involved in reaching a Middle East settlement, differences of view surfaced at a news conference. On the day after his talks with Rabin, President Carter indicated that his Administration favoured Israel's withdrawal from the occupied territories, with only "some minor adjustments" in the 1967 border; he also mentioned the concept of a "homeland for the Palestinian refugees." Rabin told correspondents that a tough struggle lay ahead between Jerusalem and Washington over these two questions. However, he felt there had been a meaningful change in the American concept of a peace settlement (which included free trade, tourist travel and cultural exchange), and that the President recognized Israel's defence needs. In a report to the Cabinet on 20 March, Rabin implicitly rejected Carter's distinction between security borders and political borders. *The Jerusalem Post* pointed out that this was the first time an American President had advocated a "homeland" for the Palestinians; previous US policy had only favoured due consideration for their "legitimate interests."

There was continuing concern about repeated statements by Carter and Vance which were seen as foreshadowing an American attempt to "impose" a Middle East solution. While welcoming Vance's statement on 4 May that the US would soon make "suggestions on all the core issues" of the conflict, acting Prime Minister Shimon Peres said that experience had shown that whenever the US presented its own proposals, it entered into confrontation with either or both of the parties in the conflict. "An imposed solution by the US can only be upon Israel," he said, "because the US cannot impose a solution on the Arab countries."

The Foreign Minister, Yigal Allon, told the Cabinet on 8 May that he had expressed concern to Washington about the proposal to exclude Israel from the list of favoured nations for the purpose of arms supplies and joint weapons production. Peres said that the "special pattern of relations" between Israel and the US in these spheres was vital to Israel's security. Noting massive US arms sales to Arab countries, especially to Saudi Arabia, *The Jerusalem Post* commented that without an assurance that this special relationship would persist, "the very notion of even-handedness, upon which the US diplomatic effort must be based, is dangerously undermined."[3] Israel's exclusion from the "favoured" club could only serve to arouse "grave questions. . . . The new Administration has already reneged on pledges by its predecessor to provide Israel with FLIR nightseeing systems and concussion bombs. Negotiations for the purchase of F-16 fighter planes and of additional helicopters have been characterized by tardiness. The proposed sale of Israel's own *Kfir* fighter aircraft to Ecuador has been vetoed and an Israeli request for the diversion of funds earmarked for the sale of US tanks to local production has been turned down." Now, the paper speculated, there might be a return to the "reassessment" phase in American policy (previously experienced in mid-1975 after the failure of negotiations for the Sinai II agreement). However a few days later, on 12 May, Carter assured a Senate delegation that Israel would still be included among the nations entitled to preferential treatment over arms supplies and co-operation. This assurance was repeated when Allon met Vance in London; Allon told the Cabinet on 15 May that Israel could be "thoroughly satisfied" with Carter's renewed statement of firm commitment to Israel's deterrent strength.

This more satisfactory trend appeared to change after the results of the Knesset elections on 17 May. The transition Prime Minister, Mr Rabin, warned on 29 May that the formulation of "a specific American plan to solve the problems of the region" would make the Arab positions more extreme.

On 29 May, Allon publicly criticized the White House spokesman's reference to UN General Assembly resolutions of November 1947 and December 1948, stressing that only Security Council Resolutions 242 and 338 could constitute a basis for negotiations. At his last Cabinet meeting on 5 June, Rabin said that Carter's statements on the need for a "homeland" for the Palestinians were "a serious retreat" from past American policy and "could easily be interpreted as consent to establish a new state for the Palestinians." While arguing that the Government's readiness for territorial compromise had enabled Israel to obtain sympathy on the questions of defensible borders and the Palestinians, he added: "A grave argument might have developed between us even if the present Government had stayed on after the elections."

Statements by the Likud leader, Menahem Begin, in the first flush of enthusiasm after his election victory, indicated a hard line over the future of Judea and Samaria (also see essay on the West Bank and Gaza Strip). Begin sent Shmuel Katz, a veteran supporter of South African origin, to explain his outlook to American public opinion; (Katz was later appointed as the Prime Minister's adviser on overseas information). The impression made by Begin's statements was mitigated by the effect of the first contacts between such spokesmen of the new regime and representative Americans. Begin himself established cordial relations with the new US Ambassador, Samuel Lewis. Senator Richard Stone, Chairman of the Senate sub-committee on the Middle East and South Asia, said after meeting Begin in early June: "We had a wonderful talk; I am very happy." He felt that the new Israeli Government "will give us the chance for the kind of negotiations for peace that

President Carter seeks.'' In the discussions with the DMC about joining the coalition, however, the Likud refused to express its readiness for ''territorial compromise'' or even for ''compromise,'' or to accept Resolutions 242 and 338, although it was prepared to declare that Israel would be ready to attend a Geneva conference ''summoned'' on the basis of the resolutions.

Presenting his Cabinet to the Knesset on 20 June, Begin reiterated the eternal, historic and unchallengeable right of the Jewish people to the Land of Israel, but did not specifically define his policy on the future of Judea, Samaria and the Gaza Strip. He said he hoped that he could tell President Carter that a national consensus of well over 110 Knesset members (i.e. with the exception of Shelli and the Communists) rejected withdrawal to the 1967 borders and the establishment of a Palestinian state in Judea, Samaria and Gaza. Moshe Dayan appealed to all the Zionist parties to form a united front on the basis of what they had in common, and not to squabble with each other until the Arabs, the US or someone else presented concrete proposals. ''The new Government differs from its predecessors on one issue: its objection to partition of the West Bank,'' he said. ''If the Arabs ever propose partition, we could disagree among ourselves and even divide over it. But there is no point in doing so now, when they reject all our proposals and insist on total withdrawal.'' Government circles were encouraged by Carter's cordial message to Begin on his accession as Prime Minister, particularly his reference to the ''special relationship'' between the two countries and the principle of ''partnership'' in solving the Middle East conflict.

Begin told the Zionist General Council on 23 June that Israel had a good chance to win in its struggle against the establishment of a Palestinian state and a return to the 1967 borders, ''which would endanger Israel's very existence.'' But he added: ''The words 'not negotiable' are not in our dictionary. Everything is negotiable. The negotiations, however, must be free . . . without any externally devised formula for a settlement.''

The US State Department's policy statement of 27 June, which declared that ''no territories, including the West Bank, are automatically excluded from the items to be negotiated,'' was described by Rabin as ''an unprecedented act of discourtesy'' and a contradiction of what Carter had told him during their talks in March.

At a meeting of the Foreign Affairs and Defence Committee, Foreign Minister Moshe Dayan gave details of the proposals Begin was to submit to President Carter. Press reports indicated that he would resist handing over the West Bank and the Gaza Strip to foreign rule or to withdraw Israeli forces from any part of them, but he would be ready to make a substantial withdrawal in Sinai and adjust the present lines on the Golan Heights without withdrawing entirely from that area. While Israel would be prepared to attend a new Geneva conference, Begin proposed separate negotiations in mixed commissions with Egypt, Syria, Jordan and—if that country so desired—Lebanon; but he would not agree to a Palestinian delegation at Geneva. (For details of Begin's US visit see ''Chronology and Commentary on Political Developments in the Arab-Israeli Conflict'' and ''The US and the Middle East.'')

In his talks with Jewish leaders after the meeting with Carter, Begin laid stress on the personal rapport which he claimed had been established between himself and the President. Despite previous apprehensions, there had been no confrontation. After his first talk with Carter, he had ''slept like a child'' for the first time in many nights. Both leaders had agreed that disagreements ''are not going to be the cause of any rift at any time between the US and Israel.''

In a briefing of Israeli correspondents in Washington, a ''senior Israeli official'' contrasted Begin's policy with that of the previous Government which, by trying to get American agreement to Israel's positions, had only invited pressure for concessions. However, in a radio interview on 23 July, Rabin criticized Begin in turn for failing to challenge the US position. He said: "The confrontation which failed to materialize during the Washington talks is certain to occur at the Geneva conference; with the US position unchanged, Israel will be completely isolated." Rabin added that Carter's public statements on the principles of a peace agreement were the worst made on the subject by an American President in ten years. In a parliamentary debate on 27 July, Shimon Peres warned against "groundless optimism": by avoiding substantive political issues in favour of short-term agreements with the US on procedure, Begin had waived American support and might well have set a snare for the future of Israel-US relations. Begin replied that he had neither concealed differences with the US nor generated euphoria, but he declared, "The whole world is now talking about our rights in the Land of Israel and about our peace initiative." He appealed to the Alignment not to deny consensus with the coalition Government over the rejection of a PLO delegation at Geneva, the establishment of a Palestinian state and a pullback to the 1967 borders.

During the US Secretary of State's second visit on 9–10 August, Begin compared the PLO's National Covenant with Hitler's *Mein Kampf*, and declared that Israel would not negotiate with the PLO even if it accepted Resolution 242. He declared that the "confrontation" some people expected had not materialized, and that there had been a "breakthrough in the peacemaking process." Vance replied, however, that there had been "no narrowing of gaps."

Begin announced on 6 September that the Foreign Minister would carry to Washington the draft of a peace treaty with Egypt, which would also apply to Syria, Jordan and Lebanon. The first article read: "The state of war is hereby terminated"; other articles provided for diplomatic, consular and economic relations, and the solution of the problem of refugees (including Jewish refugees from Arab countries). President Carter would also be informed of the principles on which the borders should be drawn, but would be asked not to communicate these to the Arabs. On his way to attend the UN General Assembly, Dayan stopped in Brussels on 15 September to meet NATO leaders, making a surprise unexplained return to Israel two days later for consultations with Begin.

In Dayan's talks with Carter and Vance, the Americans proposed that in order to get over the difficulty of Palestinian representation at the Geneva conference, a united Arab delegation might include Palestinians. This idea was first opposed by the Israelis, but on 25 September the Cabinet issued a statement agreeing that a united delegation should take part in the ceremonial opening session and that Palestinian Arabs, who were not known as members of the PLO, could participate as part of the Jordanian delegation. Nevertheless, negotiations should be conducted separately with each of the delegations representing the Arab states. American sources denied that the Cabinet statement was an accurate reflection of the US proposals, but Begin declared on 29 September that it was "word for word" identical with the proposals agreed upon between Carter and Dayan.

The US State Department dropped a bombshell on 1 October, by releasing the text of a joint statement, agreed on by Cyrus Vance of the US and Andrei Gromyko of the USSR, co-chairmen of the Geneva conference. This was regarded in Israel as indicating a serious shift in American policy which would complicate the situation by bringing the Soviet Union back into the picture. While American Jewry was girding itself for a massive protest against the US-USSR statement, Carter, Vance and Dayan agreed during a marathon session on a Working Paper for the resumption of the Geneva conference. (For text of joint statement, see essay, "The US and the Middle East." For reactions to the joint statement and details of the Working

Paper, see essay "A Chronology and Commentary on Political Developments in the Arab-Israeli Conflict.") The Cabinet unanimously approved the Working Paper on 11 October and a Knesset motion to debate it was defeated by 41–28 on the 13th.

During the following weeks, while the US was discussing the Working Paper with Arab countries, Begin was reported to have told Carter in a personal message that any effort to widen the role of the united Arab delegation at Geneva would be seen in Israel as a retreat from the agreed principles of the paper. On 6 November, Dayan turned down a reported proposal by President Sādāt to set up a preliminary working group to prepare an agenda for Geneva. Begin told reporters that Israel rejected a proposal by Zbigniew Brzezinski, President Carter's Adviser on National Security, that the West Bank be politically attached to Jordan as an autonomous area and demilitarized, with Israel maintaining a "non-offensive" military presence there for a temporary period. He reiterated that Israel would not allow the West Bank to be placed under "foreign rule." The Cabinet agreed on 13 November to consider Sādāt's suggestion that the Palestinians be represented at Geneva by an Arab professor teaching in America.

A few days previously, however, Sādāt had initiated a rapid series of moves that completely transformed the situation and opened up a new phase in the quest for Mid-East peace. For the first time since 1949, direct negotiations were envisaged between Israel and an Arab country for a solution of the conflict.

RELATIONS WITH EGYPT

At a meeting on 30 December 1976, the then Foreign Minister, Yigal Allon, criticized Sādāt's demand for Israel's withdrawal to the 1967 borders as "hard-line and unrealistic."[4] But on 2 January 1977, he described Sādāt's call for the linkage of any Palestinian state created in the West Bank with Jordan as "a step in the right direction."

The situation with Egypt on the lines demarcated in the 1975 disengagement agreement was on the whole satisfactory during 1977. Israel occasionaly complained to the UN Emergency Force about Egypt stationing more than the permitted number of troops and missile stations in the limited-forces area, but infractions were generally quickly rectified. Egypt showed goodwill by returning a number of bodies of Israeli soldiers killed in the 1973 war. (See also essay "The Situation along Israel's Frontiers.")

The dramatic transformation in Israeli-Egyptian relations came like a thunderbolt from the blue when President Sādāt declared at the opening session of the Egyptian People's Assembly on 9 November 1977 that he was ready to go to Jerusalem to meet the Israelis in their own parliament. Only "minutes" after the statement was made, according to *The Jerusalem Post*, a "top aide" of Israel's Prime Minister, recalling that Begin had offered to meet Arab leaders "any place at any time," said that Sādāt would be "more than welcome." On the following day, Begin asked Melvin Price (head of a delegation from the US Congress Armed Services Committee which was about to go on to Cairo from Jerusalem) to tell Sādāt that, if he decided to come to Jerusalem, he would be received with all honour.

On 11 November, Begin broadcast an appeal to the Egyptian people, declaring: "It will be a pleasure to welcome and receive your President with the traditional hospitality you and we have inherited from our common Father, Abraham. And I, for my part, will, of course, be ready to come to your capital, Cairo, for the same purpose: no more wars—a real peace and for ever." He concluded: "It is in this spirit of a common belief in God, in Divine Providence, in right and justice, in all the great human values which were handed down to us by the Prophet Muḥammad and by our Prophets . . . that I say to you with all my heart: *Shalom*. It means *Sulh*. And, vice versa, *Sulh* means *Shalom*." (Begin was presumably thinking of the distinction between the Arabic *salam*—"peace" and *sulh*—"reconciliation.")

On the following day, addressing a French delegation representing a fund to aid the Israel Defence Forces, Begin formalized the invitation: "In the name of the Government of Israel, I hereby officially invite Egyptian President Sādāt to come to Jerusalem to conduct talks on a permanent peace between Israel and Egypt." However, he was informed through the American embassy in Tel Aviv that Sādāt expected a written and official invitation. This was delivered to US Ambassador Samuel Lewis for transmission through the US Ambassador in Cairo, after the Prime Minister had made a statement in the Knesset on 15 November in reply to motions for the agenda welcoming the proposed visit on behalf of six coalition and opposition parties. Begin also thanked President Carter, through diplomatic channels, for his assistance in preparing the way for the Sādāt visit.

On the same day, the Knesset heard a reply from Defence Minister Ezer Weizman to a parliamentary question on an interview given by the Chief of Staff, Gen Mordecai Gur, three days earlier but published only on 15 November in *Yediot Aharonot*. "It should be clear to President Sādāt," Gur had said, "that if he is planning a further deception on the lines of the Yom Kippur War, his intentions are clear to us; we know that the Egyptian army is in the thick of preparations to start a war against Israel towards 1978, despite Sādāt's declaration of his readiness to come to Jerusalem." Gur said that, like all other Israelis, he would be delighted if the Egyptian President really came to Jerusalem to make peace, but "the authoritative information that is flowing to us points in the opposite direction." He asserted that the Egyptians were conducting intensive exercises and had built gigantic fortifications on the east bank of the Suez Canal, which could absorb five divisions in a few hours; the forces prepared to fight Libya could also be transferred against Israel in no time. In the Knesset, Weizman expressed his regret at the Chief of Staff's statements, which were "made without my prior knowledge and without approval." He said he hoped they "will not have a harmful effect on the present process towards peace between ourselves and our neighbours." On the following day, Weizman summoned Gur and formally reprimanded him.

On 17 November, Sādāt accepted Begin's invitation. It was agreed he would arrive on Saturday, 19 November, after the end of the Jewish Sabbath, for a two-day visit. On 18 November, 60 Egyptian officials, most of them security men headed by Hassan Kāmil, chief of Chancery for President Sādāt, arrived at Ben-Gurion airport to prepare for the visit. Within 48 hours, a modern communications centre, with 60 teleprinters and over 250 telephones connected directly to Cairo, was set up at the Jerusalem Theatre. Facilities were also installed at the airport and the King David Hotel, where the main Egyptian delegation was to be housed.

Sādāt arrived on schedule on 19 November and was welcomed by President Katzir, the Prime Minister and the entire Cabinet. He singled out for special attention former Prime Minister Golda Meir, Agriculture Minister Ariel Sharon (who had led the Israeli force that crossed the Suez Canal in October 1973), Defence Minister Moshe Dayan, and Chief of Staff Mordecai Gur. All stood to attention for the historic moment when the Egyptian and Israel national anthems were played on Israeli soil. Crowds waving Egyptian and Israeli flags lined the road and cheered the convoy's approach to Jerusalem. The two leaders held their first talk the same evening.

On 20 November, President Sādāt attended prayers at the al-Aqsā mosque and visited the Church of the Holy Sepulchre, accompanied by Jerusalem's Mayor Teddy Kollek. In response to a request from the President of the Supreme Muslim Council in Jerusalem, Shaykh Ḥilmī Muhtasib, Sādāt offered to repair the al-Aqsā mosque, damaged by fire in 1969, a joint statement on the offer being issued by Mayor Kollek and Muḥammad Ḥasan al-Tohāmī, the Egyptian Deputy Prime Minister. Sādāt also toured Yad Vashem, the memorial centre to the holocaust of European Jewry, where he wrote in the visitors' book: "May God guide our steps for peace. Let us end all suffering for mankind." At a working lunch, Begin was accompanied by Deputy Prime Minister Yadin and Foreign Minister Dayan, and Sādāt by Egyptian Acting Foreign Minister Butrus Ghālī and Labour Minister Muḥammad Sayyīd Aḥmad. In the afternoon, President Sādāt went to the Knesset, where he laid a wreath at the foot of the monument to the fallen soldiers of the Israel Defence Forces.

Sādāt addressed the Knesset in Arabic, the rules having been amended earlier to make this possible. He opened with a passionate call for peace, but added: "The Arab nation, in its drive for permanent peace based on justice, does not proceed from a position of weakness or hesitation." He warned that he had not come to Jerusalem for a separate agreement between Egypt and Israel, for a partial peace merely terminating the state of belligerency, or for a further disengagement agreement; none of these would be "the radical solution that would steer us to permanent peace." He admitted that the Arabs used to reject Israel. "We refused to meet with you anywhere, yes," he said. "We used to brand you as 'so-called Israel'; yes . . . yet today I tell you, and I declare it to the whole world, that we accept living with you in permanent peace based on justice. . . . As we really and truly seek peace, we really and truly welcome you to live among us in peace and security."

However, Sādāt added: "Peace cannot be worth its name unless it is built on justice—and not on the occupation of the land of others. . . . You have to give up, once and for all, the dreams of conquest. . . . Our land does not yield itself to bargaining, it is not even open to argument." Peace meant that "Israel lives within her borders, secure against any aggression. To such logic, I say yes. . . . We accept all the international guarantees . . . you want from the two super-powers or from either of them, or from the Big Five, or from some of them." He explained that "Peace for Israel" would mean that "Israel live within her borders with her Arab neighbours in safety and security, within the framework of all the guarantees she accepts and which are offered to the other party."

In reply to the question of how "permanent peace based on justice" could be achieved, Sādāt declared: "There are Arab territories which Israel has occupied, and are still occupied, by armed forces. We insist on complete withdrawal from these territories, including Arab Jerusalem." He was emphatic that the "Palestine cause was the crux of the entire problem," but significantly made no reference to the PLO throughout his speech. Sādāt proposed that a peace agreement in Geneva would be based on:

1. "Ending the Israeli occupation of the Arab territories occupied in 1967.
2. "Achievement of the fundamental rights of the Palestinian people and their right to self-determination, including their right to establish their own state.
3. "The rights of all states in the area to live in peace, within their . . . secure boundaries. . . .
4. "Commitment of all states in the region to administer relations among them in accordance with the objectives and principles of the UN Charter. . . .
5. "Ending the state of belligerency in the region."

In his extempore reply, Prime Minister Begin paid tribute to Sādāt's courage and recalled that Israel's leaders had always wanted peace and offered friendship and co-operation to the Arabs. "We seek a real full peace, with complete reconciliation between the Jewish people and the Arab people. . . . In this very area, we shall all live together for ever and ever—the great Arab people in its states, its countries, and the Jewish people in its country, the Land of Israel. . . . Let us negotiate . . . as free men for a peace treaty." Israel had not invited President Sādāt in order to drive a wedge between the Arab nations. "We wish for peace with all our neighbours, with Egypt, with Jordan, with Syria and with Lebanon." Begin invited the President of Syria and King Ḥusayn of Jordan to follow in Sādāt's footsteps; he also asked "genuine spokesmen of the Arabs of the Land of Israel to come and hold talks with us about our common future, to ensure human liberties, social justice, peace and mutual respect." He was ready, if invited, to go to Damascus, Amman or Beirut, to negotiate there.

Begin went on to stress the eternal bond between the Jews and their homeland, and their right to reconstitute their national home in it, as recognized by the Balfour Declaration, the League of Nations Mandate and the Weizmann-Faysal agreement of 1919. He explained that President Sādāt had been aware, even before coming to Jerusalem, that "we have a different position from his on the permanent borders. . . . I call upon the President of Egypt and all our neighbours: do not say that on any subject whatsoever there will be no negotiations. . . . Everything can be negotiated. No party should say the contrary. No side shall present prior conditions. . . . We shall conduct these negotiations as equals. No victors and no vanquished. . . . Let us start the negotiations. Let us continue with them, resolutely, until we succeed, in good time, in signing a treaty for peace between us."

Shimon Peres, Chairman of the Labour Party and the only other speaker, said: "Peace must be based on a reciprocal compromise, in contrast to war, which is built on a unilateral victory. We shall support a true and honourable compromise. We shall not demand of any of the parties a compromise in . . . its true capacity for self-defence. . . . We are prepared for [territorial] compromises with each of the Arab states . . . so long as they do not affect security. . . . Between ourselves and Egypt, there is no cause whatsoever for the existence of any dispute. . . . The hostility between us has been a prolonged mistake; a settlement between us is within reach." Nor was there any reason for conflict between Israel and Jordan. The Israelis were also prepared for negotiations for a permanent peace with the Syrians, and a peace treaty could be reached quickly with Lebanon. "We are aware of the existence of the Palestinian identity," Peres continued. "Every people can decide on its own identity and this does not need the confirmation of any other people. But an expression of the Palestinian identity must be found without endangering the security of Israel."

In the evening after the historic Knesset session, a working dinner was held, with 15 from each side. Afterwards, the two leaders met alone. Begin told *Yediot Aharonot* that Sādāt had told him that the Yom Kippur War "was and shall be the last war."

On Monday, 21 November, Sādāt had private meetings with Begin and Defence Minister Ezer Weizman, and then went on to the Knesset to meet separately with party representatives: first, the Coalition parties; next, the Democratic Front for Peace and Equality (Communist) and Shelli (Camp for Peace and Equality); and, finally, the Labour Alignment. Sādāt told the Coalition factions that "the October war should be the last war. . . . If we agree on these two principles—security and no war again—whatever happens can be solved by peaceful negotiations." The Israelis, however, would have to take "very hard decisions." In talking to the Alignment representatives, he congratulated Peres on his "very constructive speech" in the Knesset, and said he was "very deeply touched" by Mrs Golda Meir having returned especially from America to meet him, "because the peace process that we started together after the October 1973 war was started by Mrs Meir, when we concluded the first disengagement agreement.'' He agreed with the Israelis about security—''but not expansion, or through boundary compromise.'' He also said he was deeply moved by the welcome he had been given by the Israeli children. Mrs Meir presented him with a gift, ''from a grandmother to a grandfather,'' for the President's grandchild, who had been born the day before.

At a joint press conference, Begin read out an agreed statement: ''In response to the sincere and courageous move by President Sādāt, believing in the need to continue the dialogue along the lines proposed by both sides during their exchanges and the presentation of their positions in their historic meeting in Jerusalem, and in order to enhance the prospect of a fruitful consummation of this significant meeting, the Government of Israel, expressing the will of the people of Israel, propose that this hopeful step be further pursued through dialogue between the two countries concerned, thereby paving the way towards successful negotiations leading to the signing of peace treaties in Geneva with all the neighbouring Arab states.''

Sādāt added that the Israeli Prime Minister ''has got the full right to come and address our Parliament there in Cairo.'' But ''for certain reasons that we discussed together,'' they had to postpone such a visit. Begin said that the key word was ''continuation: we agreed that we are going to continue our dialogue, and ultimately out of it will come peace.'' During the President's visit, he said, ''A momentous agreement was achieved already, namely: no more war, no more bloodshed, no more threats.'' Both leaders replied affirmatively to a question: ''Are you now both convinced of the sincerity of the desire for peace of each of you?'' One of the main motives behind the visit to Israel, Sādāt said, was ''to give the peace process new momentum and to get rid of the psychological barrier that, in my idea, was more than 70% of the whole conflict, and the other 30% is the substance.''

In reply to a question whether his statement that solutions must not be sought through war cancelled his previous stand (that if he could not get back the territories by diplomatic means, he would get them back by force), Sādāt said: ''My people now are 100% behind me. They don't want any war. . . . But mark this. I said also in the Knesset, and I differed with Premier Begin about it—he considered it as a condition—I said that the issue of the withdrawal from the occupied territories should not be even on the table, except for the details of it, not as a principle.'' In reply to a question about territorial withdrawal, Sādāt said: ''Our land is sacred.'' Begin, after explaining the importance of security to Israel, commented that he could respect President Sādāt's statement—''and because I respect it, I can say now: Our land is sacred.'' Summing up the meeting, Begin said: ''This visit is a real success for both countries and for the cause of peace.'' Sādāt concluded: ''Let us hope, all of us, that we can keep up the momentum in Geneva; and may God guide the steps of Premier Begin and the Knesset, because there is great need for hard and drastic decisions. . . . All my deep gratitude to the Israeli people, whose welcome I can never forget.''

In the afternoon, the two leaders were received by President Katzir. Before his departure for the airport, Sādāt received a delegation of Arabs, including Anwar al-Khaṭīb and Nihad Jarallah of Jerusalem, Hikmat Masrī and Na'im 'Abd al-Ḥadi of Nablus, Elias Freij, Mayor of Bethlehem, Mustafā Dūdīn of Hebron, Ibrāhīm Abū Sitta of Gaza, and Sulaymān Azaya, Major of Dayr al-Balaḥ in the Gaza Strip.

RELATIONS WITH LEBANON AND SYRIA

The ''Good Fence'' policy of humanitarian aid to the inhabitants of southern Lebanon continued in 1976–7. Field clinics were set up for the Lebanese along the frontier at Metulla, Dovev and Ḥanita, where 30,576 persons—about two-thirds of them Christians—received medical aid in the 16 months from 1 June 1976 to 1 October 1977; c. 1,300 were sent for treatment to Israeli hospitals. The villagers were also able to purchase essential supplies in Israel; Israeli instructors offered agricultural assistance and counselling, and Lebanese were invited to Israel for study tours in agricultural areas. Almost 300 tons of Lebanese tobacco, valued at $447,000, were purchased from Lebanese growers by Israeli buyers, and 676 Lebanese workers were employed in Israel at the beginning of October. A mobile postal unit, operating along the "Fence," accepted mail for dispatch via the Israeli postal service, and Lebanese were enabled to visit their relatives in Israel. (Also see essay, "The Situation along Israel's Frontiers.")

Francis Rizq, political adviser to Major Sa'ad Ḥaddād, commander of the mainly Christian forces in south Lebanon, told the press on 18 April 1977: "The people of Lebanon have entered into a fraternal alliance with Israel, from which they will not deviate and for which they are ready to pay with their blood." He read out a letter from Ḥaddād, which said: "Our former enemy, Israel, is today the only and the last support we have." Rizq visited Israel frequently and appeared on Israel television.

A close watch was kept on the situation in southern Lebanon to prevent reinforcements from reaching Palestinian Arab irregulars and Syrian forces from approaching the frontier. There appeared to be tacit agreement among Israel, Lebanon and Syria on prior notice of moves which might otherwise lead to misunderstanding. However, towards the end of January 1977, Israel complained, via the US, of the deployment of Syrian forces near Nabatiyya (close to the nearest point to Israel on the Litani river, which was regarded as Israel's "red line" in the area) as "a unilateral step on which there was no agreement." The Lebanese authorities claimed, however, that the troops had been sent solely to collect heavy arms from the warring sides. The Israeli Defence Minister said that the Syrians were well aware "that if they bring tanks and guns closer to our border, they will heighten the tension in the Middle East to a very dangerous point." At a Cabinet meeting on 30 January, it was stated that Israel was keeping a low profile and trying to solve the problem patiently by diplomatic means. Foreign Minister Yigal Allon said on 31 January 1977 that, while Israel was "firmly opposed" to the presence of Syrian forces in South Lebanon, she would welcome the presence of "genuine Lebanese army units there to keep the peace." On 13 February, when the Syrians started moving their forces northward from Nabatiyya, Prime Minister Rabin suggested that they wanted to test the mettle of the new US Administration and the credibility of the Israeli policy of keeping southern Lebanon free of foreign forces.

In April, tension rose again. On 4 April, Israeli artillery fired several rounds at Palestinian forces in the area, after shells had fallen in Misgav Am, c. 2 km from the border. *The Jerusalem Post* (8 April) commented: "It is no secret that [Israel] has been helping the pacific-minded residents of South Lebanon, both Christians and Muslims, to help themselves against the terrorists. But official Israeli policy has consistently been to reject the advice of those reckless armchair warriors who would long ago have involved the country physically in the battles of Lebanon." On 13 April it was reported that Israel had told the US that she would no longer remain indifferent to the deployment of Palestinian irregulars along the border or to attacks on Christian enclaves in the area. The situation quietened down, so far as Israel was concerned, for the next three months. Towards the end of May, Syria agreed to extend the mandate of the UN Disengagement Observation Force (established in 1974); this was approved by the Security Council on 24 May.

There were signs that the new Begin Government was prepared to adopt a stronger stand over South Lebanon. The Prime Minister told the Knesset on 28 July that, while Israel had no territorial designs on any part of Lebanon, she could not agree to watch the terrorists wipe out the isolated Christians, and so she had helped them. On 9 August, he was more specific. Admitting for the first time Israeli military operations in support of the Lebanese Christians, Begin said: "We help them militarily. It shouldn't be a secret. When a barrage is opened on Christian villages, we aim our fire at the source of the hostile fire."

In mid-September, as the struggle between the Christians and the Palestinians intensified, there were indications of greater Israeli involvement. Israeli troops were apparently sent into southern Lebanon on 16 September to protect the women and children in Christian villages while their men were away fighting. Four days later, Begin declared that Israel was ready "to discuss, without delay, a general ceasefire in Lebanon." Israel was reported to have warned Beirut and Damascus that any movement south by Syrian troops would be regarded with the utmost gravity. During the next few days, Katyusha rocket shells, fired from across the border, fell in Nahariya, Safad and Kiryat Shmona, injuring several persons; an Israeli soldier was killed and three others injured in a clash between a patrol and Palestinians on the border near Har Dov. The ceasefire went into force on 26 September and the Defence Minister warned that Israel would not allow the situation in southern Lebanon to deteriorate again.

In October there were several breaches of the ceasefire from PLO mortar positions, and Israeli gunners fired back. On the whole, however, the situation was quiet until 6–8 November, when 18 Katyusha rockets fired from Lebanon landed in Nahariya, killing three persons and injuring five. On 9 November, Israeli planes and artillery strafed PLO bases north and south of Tyre. The Israeli Chief of Staff said that the decision to use the air force and artillery was intended "to explain to the PLO and to all the other organizations—including the Syrians—that their policy is dangerous." He denied that Arab civilians had been hit; Begin said that he was sorry if there had been any civilian casualties.

On 28 November, Syria agreed to a further renewal of UNDOF's mandate.

RELATIONS WITH WESTERN EUROPE

While Western European countries remained mainly friendly towards Israel, particular resentment was felt at the European Economic Community's statement on Middle East policy (issued in London on 29 June) supporting the Palestinian people's "legitimate right to a homeland" and rejecting "territorial conquests by force." Moshe Dayan told the British ambassador in Tel Aviv, the current chairman of the group of EEC ambassadors serving in Israel, that the Community should not have issued such a declaration without first learning the new Government's policy. At the Cabinet meeting on 3 July, Dayan said that the declaration represented a further erosion in the EEC's attitude to Israel and would hamper the peace-making process.

Contact was maintained with the European organizations such as the European Parliament, where Knesset delegations participated as observers. Among the European representatives who visited Israel were delegates from the European Parliament, headed by its president, and from the scientific committee of the Western European Union. There were also a number of official visits from European statesmen, such as German Foreign Minister Dietrich Genscher, former German Chancellor Willy Brandt, Netherlands Prime Minister Joop den Uyl, Austrian Chancellor Bruno Kreisky, and Danish Prime Minister Anker Jurgenson. Moshe Dayan visited the German Federal Republic in November, and Begin made a state visit to Britain in December 1977.

On 8 February 1977, Israel signed an additional protocol to the 1975 agreement with the European Economic Community, providing for co-operation in such fields as industry, technology, science and environmental problems, as well as a financial protocol for investment aid from the European Bank. The Foreign Minister expressed his satisfaction with the additional protocol, but described the financial protocol as limited and unsatisfactory. (Also see essay, "The European Community and the Middle East.")

Israel's chilly relations with France deteriorated further in January 1977 because of the hasty release of Maḥmūd Dā'ūd 'Awda, known as Abu Daoud, a leading member of al-Fatḥ, whom Israeli intelligence believed had helped plan most of the Black September operations, including the murder of Israeli athletes at the Munich Olympics in 1972. Abu Daoud had been arrested in Paris by French counter-espionage agents at the request of the German Federal Republic. Although Israel and West Germany asked that he be held pending extradition proceedings, he was released by a Paris court on 11 January and flown to Algeria. The Foreign Minister described the French action as "an ugly surrender to threats by terrorist organizations," violating the extradition treaty between France and Israel, and disregarding the EEC's anti-terrorism pact. Mordecai Gazit, the Israeli Ambassador to France, was recalled for consultations and an official protest note was handed to the French ambassador in Israel. The affair also affected public attitudes to the French request for the extradition of the Jewish financier Samuel Flatto-Sharon (see above: Election Campaign). Ambassador Gazit returned to his post on 4 February, and the French Foreign Minister's visit to Israel at the end of April indicated some progress towards normalization.

However, there was still widespread dissatisfaction with France's leading role in persuading the European Community to adopt policies regarded as unfavourable to Israel's positions in the Middle East conflict. At the beginning of August, Israel protested against the French decision that the anti-boycott law would not apply to Arab-imposed restrictions on trade with Israel; in the Knesset, representatives of the Labour Alignment, the NRP and the DMC called for a Jewish boycott of French commodities and services. The Foreign Minister advised a cautious reaction however.

Portugal and Israel agreed in May 1977 to establish diplomatic relations. The Israeli Consulate-General in Lisbon became an embassy on 13 May, but the opening of a Portuguese embassy in Israel was delayed.

RELATIONS WITH THE SOVIET BLOC

There was no change in the attitude of the Soviet bloc countries towards Israel in 1977, with the exception of Romania (see essay, "The Soviet Bloc and the Middle East"). A few Israeli scientists were permitted to participate in international conferences in the USSR, and Hebrew books, carefully vetted to exclude political material, were exhibited in an Israeli pavilion at the first International Book Fair in Moscow in September.

Prime Minister Begin paid a five-day visit (25–30 August) to Romania, the only East European country with which Israel still retains diplomatic relations. Although he had friendly talks with President Ceausescu, Prime Minister Manescu urged total Israeli withdrawal to the 1967 borders, participation of the PLO at Geneva and the creation of a Palestinian state. He also expressed Romanian concern about the establishment and legal status given to new Israeli settlements in the West Bank, as well as to the extension of Israeli public services legislation to the West Bank and Gaza. Begin strongly rejected these criticisms. Begin spent the Jewish Sabbath with the Romanian Jewish community, which he described as "the most moving day in my life since the day Israel declared its independence." On his return, he said that the visit had been "important, interesting and very moving."

RELATIONS WITH LATIN AMERICA

Israel continued to maintain friendly diplomatic relations with all the Latin America and Caribbean states, except for Cuba and Guyana. It has resident envoys in 18 countries and non-resident envoys in seven. There were numerous exchange visits between Israel and Latin American groups and leaders, including the foreign ministers of Costa Rica and Guatemala, and ministers from Costa Rica and Mexico. Technical and economic co-operation continued in a wide variety of fields. President Katzir's cordial state visit to Mexico in November-December 1977 eliminated the last vestiges of the tension which had arisen from Mexican support for the anti-Zionist resolutions at the UN in 1975.

RELATIONS WITH ASIA AND OCEANIA

Israel is represented by ambassadors in eight Asian countries, as well as by a consul-general in Hong Kong and a consul in Bombay. There are resident ambassadors in New Zealand and Australia, the latter also acting as non-resident ambassador in Fiji, Tonga and Samoa. There was some improvement in relations with most Asian countries, despite strong Arab diplomatic initiatives.

For the first time, a senior Japanese minister, Deputy Defence Minister Koichi Hamada, paid an official visit to Israel; there was also a visit by parliamentary delegations. Progress in technical and scientific co-operation was made with Burma and Nepal, including the planning of two industrial projects with the former and an agricultural project with the latter. Several official visitors came from South Korea and Thailand. The change of government in India also aroused hopes of closer relations. A parliamentary delegation from Australia was led by several ministers, and the New Zealand Minister of Justice made his first visit on this level.

RELATIONS WITH AFRICA

Israel's formal diplomatic relations in Africa were confined to South Africa, Malawi, Swaziland and Lesotho (the latter through a non-resident ambassador), but economic ties and informal diplomatic links were maintained with a number of black African countries through reperesentatives serving as interest officers for Israel in the embassies of third countries. Despite the diplomatic rupture between black Africa and Israel occasioned by the October 1973 war, many close friendships persisted. For example Prime Minister Yitzhak Rabin flew to Geneva on 4 February for a three-hour conference with President Felix Houphouet-Boigny of the Ivory Coast. A joint communiqué issued after the talks stressed the importance of Resolutions 242 and 338 and declared that "dialogue is the best method for achieving peace in the region." Rabin noted that the communiqué was in line with "what Israel considers to be the correct objective and basis for a Middle East solution." An Ivory Coast source said, however, that further contacts were needed before diplomatic ties could be renewed. This was the second meeting between an Israel Premier and an African Head of State since the Yom Kippur War: the first was between Rabin and President Leopold Senghor of Senegal in 1976.

Relations with South Africa were not much discussed in Israel during 1977, but the extent of co-operation between the two countries was widely publicized in Africa. Government spokesmen repeatedly denied reports of military links between Jerusalem and Pretoria; a "top official" stated categorically in March that there were no Israeli officials helping or training the South African army to fight its black citizens.[5] It was emphasized that Israel's commercial ties with South Africa accounted for less than one-third of the latter's overseas trade. In mid-May, Foreign Minister Yigal Allon and several Knesset members turned down invitations to attend the independence celebrations of Transkei when it appeared that they would be the only foreign government representatives present. A "highly-placed source" said: "We shall have to be more careful in the future to tone down the salience of the relationship."[6]

ISRAEL AND WORLD JEWRY

IMMIGRATION

The number of Jews coming to settle in Israel in 1977 was 21,500, of whom 12,500 were registered as immigrants and 9,000 (mainly from Western countries) as potential immigrants. This figure was 9% more than the 1976 total. Two-fifths of the newcomers—8,400—came from the USSR (cf 7,000 in 1976). There was also an increase of c. 30% in the number of immigrants from North America, to over 4,000; 3,000 came from Latin America (2,000 of them—25% more than in 1976—from Argentina).

The upward trend in immigration from the USSR was apparent in the last quarter of 1977, and was ascribed to the effect of the Belgrade Conference on Human Rights. The percentage of "drop-outs"—i.e. Jews leaving the Soviet Union but opting, on arrival at the transit station in Vienna, to go to some country other than Israel—rose to 60% in April, but fell gradually to 45% in November. Most of the "drop-outs" came from the large cities: the percentage from Odessa, for example, reached 98%. According to a survey presented to the Jewish Agency Executive on 15 April, a total of 135,900 Jews left the USSR between November 1968 and March 1977, of whom 19,000 dropped out on the way. During this period, 329,000 requests for emigrants' visas were submitted, leaving 194,000 still waiting for permission to leave. There were wide differences between various regions in the Soviet Union; for example, 82% of the applications from Lithuanian Jews were granted, and 41% of the community left; so did 52% of the Jews of Soviet Georgia. On the other hand, less than 2% of the Jews in Russian Soviet Federated Socialist Republic, where the great majority lived, were allowed to leave. There were frequent manifestations of solidarity with those Soviet Jews who were not allowed to leave the country.

ZIONIST AND JEWISH AGENCY INSTITUTIONS

The Zionist General Council pledged support for the new Government in its efforts to achieve peace on 22 June 1977. It expressed deep concern at the plight of Syrian Jewry, and called on world opinion to support basic human rights for the Jews of Syria. It approved a budget of IL 415m for the World Zionist Organization.

The Jewish Agency Assembly, meeting on 26–30 June, held workshops dealing with immigration and absorption, settlement on the land, communal activities in development towns and education. Considerable attention was devoted to aid in the solution of Israel's domestic social problems. The question of merging the Jewish Agency's Immigration and Absorption Department with the Ministry of Immigrant Absorption, as recommended in 1976 by the Horev Committee, was referred for discussion to the joint Agency-Government co-ordination board. The Assembly placed on record its "unequivocal solidarity with Israel in its continuing struggle for genuine peace and security," and called for recognition of the rights of Jews from Arab countries to compensation for confiscated property. It approved a budget totalling $457m for 1977–8.

PREPARATIONS FOR ZIONIST CONGRESS

Preparations for the 29th World Zionist Congress, to be held in Jerusalem on 20 February 1978, included a membership drive in 27 countries. Over 1m Jews outside Israel registered—10% more than at the previous drive in 1971, including 893,000 from the US. Elections were held in 19 countries; in others, agreement was reached between the parties on the allocation of Congress seats. A considerable drop was expected in the representation of the Zionist Labour Movement, because of Labour losses in the parliamentary elections in Israel, and the effect on Jewish communities abroad of the change in Israeli leadership. (190 out of the 620 delegates to the Congress are appointed by the Zionist parties in proportion to their strengths in the Knesset.) World Jewish organizations affiliated to the Zionist Organization were to receive 15 delegates each to the Congress, five members in the Zionist General Council, and one member of the Executive in Israel and one in the US in an advisory capacity. These included World Maccabi (the Jewish sports organization), the World Sephardi Organization, the World Union of Progressive Judaism and the World Council of Conservative Synagogues.

Among the Jewish bodies that held their conferences in Israel during the year were the Women's International Zionist Organization, the World Union of Jewish Journalists and the World Congress of Jewish Community Centres. 2,000 Jewish sportsmen from abroad—including 353 from the US, 149 from France, 146 from SA, 140 from Brazil, 122 from Britain, and 103 from Argentina—as well as 450 from Israel, took part in the 10th Maccabiah games, which opened at the Ramat Gan stadium on 12 July 1977. Numerous young Jews from Europe and North America—50% more than in 1976—took part in the annual summer projects of the World Zionist Organization's Youth and Pioneering department, which revolved around the theme of "Ten Years of Reunited Jerusalem." There were also delegations from bodies working for the support of Israel, such as the State of Israel Bond Drive, Keren Hayesod, the United Israel Appeal, and Hadassah (the Women Zionist Organization in the US).

GOVERNMENT RELATIONS WITH AMERICAN JEWRY

Menahem Begin established close personal relations with American Jewry. Rabbi Alexander Schindler, chairman of the Conference of Presidents of Major Jewish Organizations in the US, paid frequent visits to Israel and was closely consulted and briefed on matters of foreign policy and Israel's relations with America. During Begin's visit to the US in July 1977, he made a point of paying his respects to religious leaders like Rabbi Schneerson, head of the Lubavitch Hasidim, and Rabbi Joseph Soloveitchik of Boston.

There was some concern among Jews abroad about concessions to the religious parties in Israel by the new Government. Four American rabbis (Rabbi Stanley Rabinowitz and Wolfe Kelman, representing the Conservative Jews; Ely Pilchik and Joseph Glaser, of the Reform movement) met the Prime Minister and the Chief Rabbis in Israel in mid-August to discuss the proposal to change the Law of Return to recognize only orthodox conversions to Judaism. Together with two local Conservative and two Reform rabbis, they met Begin, Interior Minister Yosef Burg and Religious Affairs Minister Aharon Abuhatzera on 22 August. After the meeting, they reported that Begin remained committed to working for a change in the law according to the Coalition agreement, and had suggested that they try to reach a compromise over the question with the Orthodox rabbinate in the US.

ECONOMIC AFFAIRS (15.995 Israeli pounds = US $1; 30.875 IL = £1 sterling)

Economic developments during the first part of 1977 were seriously affected by the Government's lack of a parliamentary majority and the impending elections which (as has generally been the case in Israel) stimulated widespread wage claims, especially in the public sector. The new Government at first appeared to be pursuing a cautious policy of continuity, but in October introduced a radically new economic policy.

THE 1977–8 BUDGET

The then Finance Minister, Yehoshua Rabinowitz, presented the 1977–8 budget in the Knesset on 24 January 1977: estimates totalled IL 122.5 bn—12% more in real terms than in the previous year, mainly because of a 35% increase in debt services. The Government, however, no longer had a majority and the Opposition, which now included the NRP, refused to support it. They were only prepared to agree to a severely truncated interim budget of IL 31.8 bn for the first four months of the financial year.

LABOUR UNREST

Early in January 1977, Arnon Gafny, the Governor of the Bank of Israel, called for an agreement between the Government, the Histadrut and the employers to freeze wages, profits and prices for six months in order to prevent wage inflation that would destroy the economic achievements of 1976. He pointed out that industrial workers had won wage rises of 40–45% during the past year, and warned against the effects of similar increases for civil servants. The Government and the Histadrut agreed to establish a joint voluntary arbitration board, but few groups had recourse to its services.

A spate of labour disputes broke out early in 1977, especially in the public sector. At the beginning of February, c. 70,000 workers were involved in strikes, go-slows or threats of industrial action; they included postal employees, government psychologists, bank staffs, marine officers, air traffic controllers, engineers, university teachers and customs officers. In mid-February, the Government and the Histadrut agreed to a moratorium on increases in wages, taxes, prices and dividends until the end of June, but the employers' associations refused to co-operate and various groups of workers in the public services increased their pressure. There were also repeated interruptions of the operation of El Al Israel Airlines and Ben-Gurion Airport, which continued until the middle of the year. Towards the end of February, the Government gave way on a wide front, and increases were granted to engineers, technicians and various classes of professionals in public employ. The increases were estimated to total IL 2 bn, half of which (after deducting taxation and savings) would go to consumption, thus driving inflation up to 30% for the fiscal year, instead of 25% as previously estimated. The Finance Minister later admitted that the increases were a breach of Government wages policy, but said they must be viewed against the background of the circumstances prevailing in a democratic society at election time. In view of the increases, the NRP refused to support legislation to enforce the wages, prices and taxation freeze, and it had to be dropped.

There was strong pressure from industrial workers for wage increases to offset the gains of the public sector, and the Histadrut decided to demand "compensation"—a 4–5% increase retroactive to 1 January. The employers' associations condemned the demand as a breach of the two-year collective labour contracts concluded with the Histadrut in 1976, but ultimately they gave in. The shock waves of labour unrest also generated two lengthy disputes which seriously damaged the shipping industry: one of dockers in March, which held up citrus exports and caused grave losses to growers; the other of marine officers in April.

ALIGNMENT GOVERNMENT'S ACHIEVEMENTS

Reviewing the outgoing Government's achievements during its term of office, Finance Minister Yehoshua Rabinowitz said on 12 June that the balance of payments deficit—over $4 bn in 1973—had been reduced by $780m in 1976. This was mainly due to a halt in the rise of imports and an 18% increase in exports.

Private consumption had continued to rise, but the rate of increase in the last quarter of 1976 had been 3% below the level reached before the Yom Kippur War. 70% of the price increases in 1974, 55% in 1975 and 70% in 1976 were the combined result of foreign price rises and government measures to shift economic activity from manufacture for the domestic market to export. The foreign debt, however, had risen to $9.3 bn by the end of 1976, and GNP had increased very slowly.

LIKUD GOVERNMENT'S POLICIES

The Nobel prizewinner Milton Friedman, of the University of Chicago, was invited to advise the new Government on its economic policy. Yehezkel Flomin, one of the Likud's spokesmen on economic affairs, said that Friedman had been chosen because his views were close to one of the Likud's central planks: the elimination, as far as possible, of government intervention.

The Governor of the Bank of Israel, Arnon Gafny, said at the end of May 1977 that his advice to the next government was to cut the budget deficit by IL 4–6 bn a year by freezing social services, reducing subsidies on the prices of staple commodities, postponing expansion projects, raising interest on government loans, preventing wage increases, and transferring labour from public services to export industries. He predicted that if these policies were implemented, inflation would not exceed 25% in 1977 and 20% in 1978.

The new Finance Minister, Simha Ehrlich, said that economic surgery should first affect the affluent and not injure the economically disadvantaged. He would try to ensure full employment: "Heaven forbid that a Jew should remain unemployed," he said. Addressing the Manufacturers' Association on 29 June, the Prime Minister called for a programme of "social justice without socialism," and invited the Histadrut and the employers to join the Government in negotiating a "social contract" to achieve economic stability and combat inflation. However, this proposal was opposed by the new Minister of Industry, Commerce and Tourism, Yigal Hurvitz, who said it would hurt investments by freezing profits, and by Avraham Shavit, President of the Manufacturers' Association, who called instead for a "long economic leap forward."

To give the new Government time to reconsider fiscal policy, the Finance Minister introduced a two-month interim budget, which was passed on 12 July; but only five days later, he announced a series of drastic measures to reduce inflationary pressure and prevent a fall in foreign-currency balances. These included cuts of over IL 1 bn in subsidies, involving 25% increases in the prices of subsidized commodities and services; cuts of IL 1.4 bn in defence estimates, and IL 900m from other State expenditures. Low-income groups were to be compensated for the price increases. Replying to Histadrut protests at his failure to consult its leaders, as had been customary in the past, Ehrlich said that secrecy had been necessary to prevent hoarding and a run on the shops. The Histadrut called for a one-hour stoppage of work in protest against the Government's measures, but response was limited. On 31 July, the Cabinet approved a budget of IL 124 bn for the entire financial year 1977–8, comprising the two interim budgets, which was passed by the Knesset. It was based on the budget originally submitted by the previous Government, with some modifications, and assumed price inflation of 27% during the fiscal year.

However, it became clear in the autumn that further measures would have to be taken. By the end of August, the currency in circulation had increased by IL 6.5 bn—IL 1 bn more than had been foreseen for the entire fiscal year; in September another IL 4 bn had to be printed. An 8.8% cost-of-living allowance on wages up to IL 7,000 per month was paid from October. On 23 October, the

Cabinet adopted a scheme for the gradual reduction of subsidies on staple commodities and public transport; prices were set to rise immediately by up to 10%. It soon transpired, however, that the Government had been preparing drastic measures designed to introduce a new economic era.

NEW ECONOMIC POLICY

A radically new economic policy, based on the free convertibility of the Israel pound and the abolition of controls on current foreign currency transactions, was announced by the Finance Minister on 28 October after the adoption of the plan at a special Cabinet meeting. Every Israeli was to be permitted to hold unlimited amounts of foreign currency in local bank accounts, as well as to keep up to $3,000 in cash and another $3,000 in foreign banks. The 15% defence duty on imports and the incentives granted to exporters were abolished. Value Added Tax was increased from 8% to 12%, and purchase taxes were eliminated or reduced. Imports, equivalent to the expected effective devaluation, were levied on stocks. The total volume of bank credits, except export credits, was to be practically frozen for three months, and government departments were required to absorb domestic cost increases resulting from devaluation in the current budget. Subsidies on basic foodstuffs and public transport were reduced, involving price increases of 15%, and electric power costs went up 25% following the fuel price rise previously announced. The flat-rate foreign travel tax was abolished and replaced by VAT at the 12% rate; but it soon became clear that this could not be enforced as travel tickets could easily be purchased by foreign-currency remittances under the new conditions, and the imposition was withdrawn a few days later. Overall, the domestic price level was expected to rise by c. 10% by the end of December, and total inflation for the year to reach 38–40%—the same as in 1976. To compensate lower-income groups, welfare payments, pensions and children's allowances were immediately raised by 12%.

Ehrlich said that the plan would usher in a new era of economic growth, and that GNP would rise by c. 5% in 1978 after several years of stagnation. Israel would now "join the club" of Western nations and could become an important financial centre. The reform would stabilize the economy; stimulate exports and local manufacture to replace imports; attract foreign investment; eliminate longstanding economic distortions and bureaucratic hindrances to economic activity; reduce the temptation to violate the law, and provide an incentive for the repatriation of illicit foreign currency balances. The Government, he said, was aware of the risk and uncertainty involved in the reforms, but was convinced that they were necessary for the sake of economic recovery.

When the banks reopened on Monday, 31 October, they sold dollars freely to the public for IL 15.50 and bought them for IL 15.15—compared with the previous rate of IL 10.35 per dollar. There was no rush on foreign currency however. On the contrary, in the first week of the new regime, the public sold $65m to the banks and invested IL 2.7 bn in government bonds and saving schemes.

Protests against the new policy came from works committees and labour councils in various parts of the country, and the Histadrut decided to put up a concerted fight against it. Secretary-General Yeruham Meshel described the new policy as "a declaration of class war by a Government that concerned itself only with the problems of moneyed classes." Gideon Ben-Yisrael, who organized the protest campaign, said that if the policy was implemented, "We shall find one Israel of people who are well off, and another whose income will not stretch till the end of the month." Demonstrations and one-day or half-day strikes were held all over the country. The Histadrut estimated that about half a million people took part; but some groups, such as bank employees, refused to stop work, and Likud spokesmen alleged that some workers had been coerced into striking.

Finance Minister Ehrlich told the Knesset on 31 October that real wages would not decline under the new economic policy. Demonstrations would make no difference, he said, and whatever the Government could do to make things easier for the public, it would do without strikes and demonstrations. Speaking as an Alignment member of the Knesset, Meshel said: "If you have decided on a free economy, we shall not agree to keep only wages under control." The Histadrut would no longer agree to sign wage agreements for two years, and it would insist on immediate compensation for the price increases caused by the policy.

Begin declared on 2 November: "This Government, which was formed on the basis of the people's will, will not be frightened by threats from without or within. The Bolshevik-like tones heard these days will quickly disappear." At a Cabinet meeting on 6 November, he said that the country was engaged in a struggle for its economic future and for democracy. He accused the Alignment, through its majority in the Histadrut, of trying to bring down the Government by extra-parliamentary means. Ehrlich said that the Government would compensate the bottom 30% of wage-earners for price increases resulting from the new policy.

The new economic policy dominated the Histadrut's quadrennial Convention, on 7–9 November—the stormiest in the federation's history. There were noisy scenes at the preparatory session when the Alignment majority rejected a Likud proposal to send greetings to the Prime Minister on the grounds that this had not been the practice at previous conventions. Begin rejected the invitation to attend the official opening as he claimed that some of the delegates had shouted, "Begin go home." When addressing the formal opening session, President Katzir said it was natural for the Histadrut to seek to prevent an excessive share of the economic burden from falling on the workers: there were then noisy protests from Likud delegates who objected to the President making "political remarks." Nevertheless, he continued by urging the Histadrut "to conduct this struggle with understanding, restraint and a genuine desire for co-operation among all parties." Likud delegates denounced the Histadrut's demonstrations against the Government's new economic policy, and the proceedings were punctuated by vociferous interruptions. At one point police had to be called in to separate quarrelling Likud and Alignment delegates. The Absorption Minister, David Levy, who had headed the Likud list at the Histadrut elections and had voted against the new economic policy in the Cabinet, made a conciliatory speech and offered co-operation to "my friend Meshel." When re-elected Secretary-General, Meshel was given a standing ovation and promised to serve all members without distinction of party.

ECONOMIC PERFORMANCE 1977

The main features of the economy during the year, according to preliminary estimates, were stability in GNP and private consumption per capita; a fall in investments; a reduction of defence expenditure; a moderate rise in civilian government expenditure; an increase in exports, and a reduction in the adverse balance of payments. The GNP, at fixed prices, rose by c. 1%, continuing the slow-down which started after increases of c. 11% in 1971 and 1972. Total resources at the disposal of the economy, at fixed prices, dropped by c. 1%; the slight rise in GNP was counteracted by the fall in imports. Public expenditure, at fixed prices, fell by 10% (8% in 1976), owing to the drop in defence outlays (see Tables).

Exports increased by 11–12% at fixed prices, after a rise of 15–16% in 1976. Commodity exports in dollars, at current prices, rose by 25%: a 40% increase in diamond exports, 19% in other industrial goods, 8% in citrus and 21% in other agricultural products. Imports of goods and services fell by c. 3% (similar to 1976), mainly owing to a drop of c. 25% in defence imports. The deficit on current account was reduced from $3,268m in 1976 to $2,695m in 1977—a drop of $572m during the year, and of 33% since 1975. Foreign currency reserves increased from $1,000m at the end of 1976 to $1,380m at the end of 1977.

Industrial output and agricultural output each rose by 6%. Over 1m tourists visited Israel, a 25% increase over 1976. Private consumption dropped by over 1%, mainly owing to the continuing fall in the purchase of durable goods. The consumer price index rose by over 42% (cf 38% in 1976). In November alone, as a result of the new economic policy introduced at the end of October, there was a rise of 12%.

Largely owing to back pay, due to retroactive increases granted in the early months of the year, the average wage in July–September rose to IL 4,209 (c. $400), 48% higher in nominal terms, and 11.7% higher in real value than in the corresponding period of 1976. The table below shows the increase in various branches of the economy.

RESOURCES AND USE OF RESOURCES, 1970 and 1975–77 (preliminary estimates in IL millions)

	At 1970 prices				At current prices
	1970	**1975**	**1976**	**1977**	**1977**
Expenditure on private consumption	11,316	15,282	15,910	16,177	84,492
Government expenditure	6,728	11,044	10,184	9,218	54,949
Gross domestic capital formation	5,373	8,225	7,043	6,293	34,393
Export of goods and services (including subsidies on exports)	5,083	7,989	9,219	10,273	59,019
Total Resources	**28,500**	**42,540**	**42,356**	**41,961**	**232,853**
Less import of goods and services (including net taxes on exports)	9,697	15,426	14,960	14,582	94,830
GROSS DOMESTIC PRODUCT (at market prices)	**18,803**	**27,114**	**27,396**	**27,379**	**138,023**
Less net factor payments to abroad	313	764	814	658	4,202
GROSS NATIONAL PRODUCT (at market prices)	**18,490**	**26,350**	**26,582**	**26,721**	**133,821**

USE OF RESOURCES 1975–77 (preliminary estimates)

	Percentage change from previous year			Percentage of total		
	1975	**1976**	**1977**	**1975**	**1976**	**1977**
Expenditure on private consumption	0	4	1.5	35.9	37.6	38.6
Government expenditure	10.5	-8	-9.5	26.0	24.0	21.9
of which:						
Civilian	6.5	5	3	6.3	6.6	6.8
For defence	12	-12	-14	19.7	17.4	15.1
Gross domestic capital formation	-2	-14.5	-10.5	19.3	16.6	15.0
Export of goods and services	2.5	15.5	11.5	18.8	21.8	24.5
Total use of resources	2.5	-.5	-1	100.0	100.0	100.0

AVERAGE GROSS WAGES PER MONTH, JULY–SEPTEMBER 1977, WITH INCREASE OVER JULY–SEPTEMBER 1976

	In Israel Pounds	*% Increas*
Public Services	3,958	53
Industry	4,417	43
Construction	3,570	32
Finance and Business Services	5,369	52
Transportation	6,037	50
Personal Services	2,795	43
Commerce and Hotel Services	3,811	42
Agriculture	2,827	39

IMPORTS, CLASSIFIED BY ECONOMIC USE ($ millions)

	1973	*1974*	*1975*	*1976*
Consumer Goods:				
Food	118.6	144.8	159.8	141.1
Transport Vehicles	40.0	60.6	37.1	47.0
Other (Durable and Non-durable)	127.8	153.0	126.4	129.3
Production Inputs (Raw Materials):				
Diamonds	488.0	443.0	469.2	670.3
Fuel	211.0	596.4	637.9	681.2
Spare Parts	225.2	299.9	341.8	276.2
Other	1,118.8	1,808.4	1,740.0	1,557.8
Investment Goods:				
Machines and Equipment	350.4	426.9	543.0	493.3
Ships and Aircraft	224.8	150.5	42.7	53.3
Other Transport Vehicles	107.0	126.8	66.9	73.1
Goods n.e.s.	0.1	5.0	7.8	9.8
Total (gross)	**3,012.3**	**4,215.3**	**4,172.6**	**4,132.4**

Source: State of Israel, Central Bureau of Statistics, *Foreign Trade Statistics Monthly* (August 1977).

EXPORTS, CLASSIFIED BY PRODUCT GROUP ($ millions)

	1973	*1974*	*1975*	*1976*
Citrus Fruit	108.6	121.6	176.4	171.9
Fresh Fruit and Vegetables	27.9	23.7	34.5	46.7
Other Agricultural	35.2	47.6	66.7	107.5
Mining and Quarrying	48.1	90.2	84.4	60.8
Foodstuff Industry	105.5	128.7	125.7	154.2
Textile, Clothing and Leather	154.8	167.2	161.9	195.8
Rubber and Plastic	29.3	36.3	44.7	53.6
Chemicals	79.7	218.4	185.7	219.8
Polished Diamonds (gross)	617.1	641.1	604.7	799.7
Other Industrial	252.7	350.9	420.0	606.5
Total Exports (gross)	**1,458.9**	**1,825.7**	**1,940.7**	**2,415.2**

Source: State of Israel, Central Bureau of Statistics, *Foreign Trade Statistics Monthly* (August 1977).

IMPORTS, BY SOURCE ($ millions)

	1973	*1974*	*197*	*1976*
United States	549.5	754.2	998.9	892.3
Countries not specified	278.2	762.2	693.4	730.8
United Kingdom	478.8	543.4	577.9	638.0
West Germany	511.9	687.4	435.9	417.6
Netherlands	166.2	223.3	181.6	242.0
Italy	151.6	224.5	206.1	171.7
Switzerland	86.4	125.9	125.8	156.1
France	129.7	154.0	154.7	150.9
Other	1,887.8	1,978.4	2,623.1	2,325.7
Total	**4,240.1**	**5,453.3**	**5,997.4**	**5,725.1**

Source: IMF, *Direction of Trade, 1970–76* (August 1977).

EXPORTS, BY DESTINATION ($ millions)

	1973	1974	1975	1976
United States	267.0	305.6	307.5	436.5
West Germany	136.5	134.8	160.5	201.1
United Kingdom	138.8	157.0	171.5	185.9
Netherlands	97.8	135.9	129.3	165.7
Countries not specified	35.6	44.6	31.3	140.1
Hong Kong	96.9	118.6	113.2	140.0
France	66.7	91.1	112.1	136.8
Iran	36.8	63.1	120.0	125.8
Other	582.9	854.9	795.7	876.6
Total	**1,459.0**	**1,905.6**	**1,941.1**	**2,408.5**

Source: IMF, *Direction of Trade, 1970–76* (August 1977).

INDEX OF PRICES AND PRODUCTION (1973 = 100)

	1973	1974	1975	1976	1977 *
Share Prices	100.0	94.0	108.7	133.7	184.4
Wholesale Prices	100.0	151.6	213.3	279.1	359.2
Consumer Prices	100.0	139.8	194.7	255.7	321.6
Wages: Daily Earnings	100.0	137.2	193.4	255.3	366.7
Industrial Production	100.0	104.2	106.8	111.5	118.8
Industrial Employment	100.0	102.9	103.7	106.2	107.3

*January–June only

Source: Data derived from IMF, *International Financial Statistics* (December 1977).

NOTES

1. *The Jerusalem Post*, 26 August 1977.
2. *Davar*, Tel Aviv; 12 September 1977.
3. *The Jerusalem Post*, 9 May 1977.
4. *Washington Post*, 30 December 1976.
5. *Jerusalem Post*, 23 March 1977.
6. *Ibid*, 15 May 1977.

Jordan

(Al-Mamlaka al-Urdunniyya al-Hāshimiyya)

ASHER SUSSER

Celebrations commemorating the Silver Jubilee of King Ḥusayn (Hussein)[1] reached their peak in Amman on 11 August 1977—a fitting symbol of the political stability and economic growth that have characterized Jordan since the final eviction of the PLO forces in July 1971. The removal of the PLO units has also deprived the local opposition of the power base on which they had come to rely from 1968–70. Since then, the opposition forces have remained ineffectual. It is therefore hardly surprising that Ḥusayn should reject any renewed PLO political or military presence in Jordan under any circumstances whatsoever.

Only one serious incident with armed Palestinians occurred in the period under review (September 1976–August 1977): this came on 17 November 1976 when four Palestinians of the Iraqi-based "Black June" group attacked the Amman Intercontinental Hotel. It was later stormed by Jordanian Special Forces (paratroopers) who killed three of the group; the fourth man was captured and hanged a month later—evidence of the Jordanian Government's tough attitude to such activities. However, this attack by a breakaway group from al-Fath proved to be an isolated incident by men from outside Jordan, and not by PLO sympathizers from inside.

The mainstay of Ḥusayn's regime—his army and internal security forces—remained loyal, though there were reports of an abortive coup attempt by some army officers in May 1977. No major changes took place within the ruling élite itself. Ḥusayn remained the chief decision-maker. As in the past, there were differences of opinion, as between Ḥusayn and his younger brother, Crown Prince Ḥasan; but there was no indication that Ḥusayn's authority was ever in contention. Ḥasan dealt primarily with formulating and implementing economic policy.

The death of Queen 'Aliā in a helicopter crash on 9 February 1977 may have been a severe personal blow to Ḥusayn, but it had no political significance. Rumours of foul play seem to have been unfounded.

POLITICAL AFFAIRS

THE BADRĀN GOVERNMENT

Zayd al-Rifā'ī, who had been Prime Minister since May 1973, was replaced by Mudar Badrān on 13 July 1976. The replacement of Rifā'ī—a staunch supporter of the close relationship with Syria—was evidence of Ḥusayn's cautious policy towards Damascus (see below). The change may also have been prompted by criticism of Rifā'ī's enthusiasm for closer ties with Damascus by members of the inner circle such as Crown Prince Ḥasan. Another perhaps more pressing reason was the need to appoint a government capable of concentrating on domestic affairs: problems of inflation and the standard of public services were beginning to arouse public discontent.

Badrān formed a new cabinet on 27 November, replacing most of Rifā'ī's ministers. Ḥusayn's directives to the new cabinet indicated that he expected it to concentrate on the country's economic affairs.

Unprecedented prosperity came to Jordan following the completion of the Three-Year Development Plan (1973–75) and the beginning of the new Five-Year Plan (1976–80). (See Jordanian section of essay, "Major Trends in ME Economic

Development.") Yet this prosperity also produced dissatisfaction since wages were lagging behind the inflation rate of c. 20% a year, while astronomic rises in land prices, construction costs and rents seriously affected the middle-class. The Governor of the Central Bank, Muḥammad Sa'īd al-Nābulsī, maintained during 1977 that anti-inflationary measures taken by the bank had stabilized the money supply since mid-1976. He claimed in August 1977, that the rate of inflation was c. 14%. But other sources maintained in mid-1977 that inflation was still running at 20% due to the heavy inflow of both state and private funds over the past two years. However, there had been a fall in property values, and the government was planning housing projects for labourers and other lower-paid salaried workers. Even so, the problems of rising prices and the necessity to improve public utilities remained the central domestic issues preoccupying the Badrān Government.

Measures taken to tackle rising prices included price controls and the subsidizing of basic commodities such as sugar, meat, bread and fuel. Some foodstuffs were imported to combat shortages; meat and grain storage facilities were also being expanded to control prices. The expansion of 'Aqaba's port capacity was also expected to reduce freight costs and therefore prices. Badrān instructed the Ministry of Supply in July 1977 to tighten price controls on food and to punish merchants who violated them. With a few exceptions, exports of fruit and vegetables were to be banned, unless the market was saturated.

The Government made a special effort to ease the lot of the armed forces and of civil servants. Army salaries were increased by 6–20% and new cost-of-living and field service allowances were approved for the armed forces as of 1 December 1976. At the beginning of 1977, a new pay scale was also approved for 18,000 civil servants. The first of a planned chain of special supermarkets for the exclusive use of the 30,000 civil servants was opened in Amman in April, with prices slashed by as much as 50%. In April, Ḥusayn asked the Government to begin work on a social security scheme to guarantee the "working individual and the good citizen" welfare and social security, and to allow the workers' families to have a "decent livelihood."[2]

After the Government was formed, the Premier adopted a new style intended to promote the impression of greater democratization. This move was probably designed to defuse internal discontent which, though not of proportions that posed any danger to the regime, nevertheless gave cause for concern. To underscore the new approach, extraordinary cabinet meetings were held in all the provincial capitals (Irbid, Ma'ān, Kerak and Salt) on 3 and 23 August, 4 November 1976 and 30 March 1977, in which local government and municipal officials were invited to participate. Ḥusayn himself held a meeting in Amman with the heads and members of municipal councils on 13 April 1977. These moves were all part of what Badrān called "an objective dialogue with the citizens."[3] Ḥusayn added: "We in Jordan are proud of the direct and simple democracy characterizing the relationship between citizens and officials."[4]

In some ways, this style of government was a substitute for parliament, dissolved in November 1974 after the Rabat summit resolutions, which had recognized the PLO as the sole legitimate representative of the Palestinians. The elected lower house, the Council of Deputies, could not continue to function without infringing upon the PLO's exclusive representative status, since half of its 60 members represented the West Bank. The appointed Senate did continue to function, but only in the symbolic role of representing the Jordanian parliament, particularly in contacts with other parliaments. The Jordanian constitution vests legislative authority entirely in the hands of the Government when parliament is dissolved. The fact that in this respect no constitutional changes were required after 1974, and that the political system continued to function much the same as before, only emphasized

THE BADRĀN CABINETS

Portfolio	13 July 1976	27 November 1976
Prime Minister, Foreign and Defence Minister	Mudar Badrān	Mudar Badrān
Development and Reconstruction, Minister of State for Foreign Affairs	Ḥasan Ibrāhīm P) [1]	Ḥasan Ibrāhīm P) [1]
Information[2]	'Adnān Abū 'Awda P)	'Adnān Abū 'Awda P)
Culture (and Youth) [2]		Sharīf Fawwāz Sharaf
Education	Dhuqān al-Hindāwī[1]	'Abd al-Salām al-Majālī
Minister of State for Premiership Affairs	Marwān al-Qāsim	'Abd al-Salām al-Majālī
Finance	Sālim Masā'ida[1]	Muhammad al-Dabbās
Tourism and Antiquities	Ghālib Barakāt P) [1]	Ghālib Barakāt P) [1]
Public Works	Aḥmad al-Shūbakī[1]	Sa'īd Bīnū
Agriculture	Salāḥ Jum'a[1]	Salāḥ Jum'a[1]
Supplies	Salāḥ Jum'a[1]	Marwān al-Qāsim
Awqāf, Islamic Affairs and Holy Places	Kāmil al-Sharīf	Kāmil al-Sharīf
Transport	Maḥmūd al-Ḥawāmida[1]	'Alī al-Suḥaymāt
Interior	Sulaymān 'Arār	Sulaymān 'Arār
Justice	Aḥmad 'Abd al-Karīm al-Tarāwina	Aḥmad 'Abd al-Karīm al-Tarāwina
Health	Muḥammad al-Bashīr[3]	Muḥammad al-Bashīr[3]
Communications	'Abd al-Rā'ūf al-Rawābida	'Abd al-Rā'ūf al-Rawābida
Trade and Industry	Rajā'ī al-Mu'ashshar[1]	Najm al-Dīn al-Dajānī P)
Labour	'Isām al-'Ajlūnī[1]	'Isām al-'Ajlūnī[1]
Municipal and Rural Affairs	Marwān al-Ḥamīd[1]	Ibrahīm Ayyūb

P) Of Palestinian Origin.

[1] Served in last Rifā'ī Cabinet.

[2] Until the formation of the 27 November cabinet, there was one ministry for Information and Culture. This was now separated into two ministries through the establishment of a new ministry for Culture and Youth.

[3] Killed in the helicopter crash with Queen 'Aliā on 9 February 1977. No replacement was made by September 1977.

the lack of importance of parliament in the country's power structure. Ḥusayn had decided against renewing parliamentary activity by holding elections on the East Bank alone as such a step would have signified Jordan's final detachment from the West Bank. *Al-Dustūr* explained that Ḥusayn had thereby "avoided transient decisions and momentary emotions in order to achieve a vision for the future which sees the inevitability of Jordanian-Palestinian harmony in some sort of unity."[5] However the regime evidently felt it necessary to provide some semblance of democracy, but without really disseminating power in any substantial way.

Political parties in Jordan remain illegal, as they have been since 1957. Government control of the media was not noticeably relaxed either. At a meeting with representatives of the press on 4 September 1976, Badrān stressed the importance of "co-operation between the press and the state" in dealing with public issues "within a positive context." He also emphasized the "danger of superficial treatment not based on accurate information." The duty of the press was "to enlighten the public by presenting the facts", he said, and not by raising "certain specific points which might lead to mere agitation without serving the issue in question and without highlighting the best solutions."[6]

The Government retained its right to censor and suspend newspapers—a right exercised on a number of occasions during 1977. Thus, for example, the daily *al-Rā'y* was suspended for three days in August for publishing a report that the Military Retirement Law was being amended to make the period of pensionable service 20 instead of 16 years. The suspension reflected both the Government's attitude to the press, and its sensitivity to any report that might arouse discontent in the army.

DEFENCE AND SECURITY

A number of new appointments were made during 1976, in senior posts in the Jordanian army and Public Security (police). In January, Ḥusayn appointed Lt-Gen (*farīq*) Zayd Bin Shākir (Ḥusayn's cousin) as Commander-in-Chief of the Armed Forces instead of Ḥābis al-Majālī, who had held this post since 1970. Maj-Gen (*liwā'*) Muḥammad Idrīs (a Circassian) replaced Bin Shākir as Chief of Staff, and was promoted to the rank of Lt-Gen. In October, Maj-Gen Sāliḥ al-Kurdī, a former commander of the Air Force, was reappointed to this post replacing Brig (*'amīd*) 'Abūd Sālim. In November, Maj-Gen Ghāzī 'Arbiyāt was appointed Director of Public Security instead of Lt-Gen Anwar Muḥammad, and Brig Khālid al-Tarāwina replaced Maj-Gen Qāsim al-Nāsir as Director of Civil Defence. These appointments reflected more continuity than change, with the senior officer corps originating from the same sectors of the East Bank population that have provided the Jordanian army with its high ranking officers since its establishment.

Reports of an abortive coup planned by army officers began to circulate in late May 1977. Rumour suggested an assassination attempt on Ḥusayn during the Independence Day military parade on 25 May. It was impossible to verify precisely what had happened from available sources, or if such a coup had in fact been planned. Lt-Gen Bin Shākir dismissed these reports as unfounded.

According to official Jordanian sources, 180 men, detained in a military prison in Zarqā for desertion, had staged a break-out on 26 May after their request for release under the Independence Day amnesty had been turned down. Five detainees were killed and fourteen wounded in the escape attempt. By mid-June all but nine had been rounded up. It remained unclear whether the break-out was related to an abortive coup. In any event, there did not appear to be widespread unrest in the army, or other indications of any substantial weakening in the basic loyalty of the armed forces to the regime.

Since the October 1973 war, the Jordanian armed forces have been undergoing a process of modernization aimed at strengthening its air arm by acquiring Northrop F-5 combat aircraft and an anti-aircraft missile defence system; increasing the mobility of its ground forces by converting infantry divisions into mechanized divisions equipped with anti-tank weapons; and developing the artillery.

Jordanian arms were supplied exclusively by the West, mainly the US, depending primarily on Saudi Arabia for finance. At the beginning of September 1976, the Jordanian government announced that it would purchase 14 batteries of Hawk surface-to-air missiles and 100 complementary Vulcan anti-aircraft guns at a cost of $540m to be financed by Saudi Arabia. In May 1977, Lt-Gen Bin Shākir said that the delivery of the Hawk anti-aircraft missile system would begin in August. This followed prolonged and difficult negotiations with the US. Following Congressional opposition to the sale in late 1975, an agreement was reached between the Ford Administration and Congress whereby the missile system was to be supplied provided it was installed in fixed positions in the Amman and Zarqā area, and at air bases and radar stations. Jordan did not publicly accept these restrictions, but sources in Washington maintained that Jordan had in fact agreed to them.

ARMED FORCES

Total armed forces number 67,810. Defence expenditure in 1977 was JD 67m ($200.6m). Military service is compulsory for 24 months. The army numbers 61,000 and formations consist of two armoured divisions; two mechanized divisions; two infantry divisions; four special forces battalions, and two anti-aircraft brigades. Equipment consists of 320 M-47/-48/-60, 200 *Centurion* medium tanks; 140 *Ferret* scout cars; 600 M-113, 120 *Saracen* armoured personnel carriers; 110 25-pounder, 90 105mm, 155mm, 203mm howitzers; 35 M-52 105mm, 20 M-44 155mm self-propelled howitzers; 16 155mm guns; 81mm, 107mm, 120mm mortars; 106mm and 120mm recoilless rifles; *TOW, Dragon* anti-tank guided weapons; 200 M-42 40mm self-propelled anti-aircraft guns; *Redeye* surface-to-air missiles. (100 *Vulcan* 20mm anti-aircraft guns and *Improved HAWK* surface-to-air missiles are on order.) An engineer detachment is deployed in Oman. The Navy numbers 160 and is equipped with ten small patrol craft. The Air Force numbers 6,650 and is equipped with 78 combat aircraft. Formations consist of three ground-attack fighter squadrons with 60 F-5A/E; one interceptor squadron with 18 F-104A; four C-130B, one *Falcon* 20, four CASA 212A *Aviocar*, two *Dove* transports; 18 *Alouette* III helicopters; four F-5B, one *Hunter*, two F-104B, ten T-37 and 12 *Bulldog* trainers. (There are four S-76 helicopters on order.) Reserves number 30,000. The 10,000 strong paramilitary forces consist of 3,000 Mobile Police and 7,000 Civil Militia.[7]

JORDAN, THE PALESTINIANS AND THE MIDDLE EAST CONFLICT

Though Jordan formally accepted the Rabat Arab summit resolutions of October 1974 (which recognized the PLO as the sole legitimate representative of the Palestinians), Ḥusayn did not for a moment abandon his rivalry with the PLO for predominance in the determination of the political fate of the Palestinians. A significant development in this rivalry was the increasing official recognition by the Arab states of Jordan's special relationship with the West Bank and the Palestinian problem—the Rabat resolutions notwithstanding.

The PLO had emerged from the Lebanese civil war with its capacity for independent political action substantially weakened following its military defeat at the hands of the Syrians and the assumption of Syrian control over its last autonomous base of operations (see chapter on Lebanon). On the other hand, Jordan's special relationship with the Palestinian problem was specifically acknowledged in the framework of Arab policy—as outlined by the Riyadh and Cairo conferences in October 1976. It was therefore not surprising that Ḥusayn regarded the Cairo summit as "the most successful of the conferences in which the Arab leaders have met."[8] He evidently regarded its outcome as providing him with a new opportunity to reassert Jordan's position in the West Bank, at the expense of the PLO.

Sādāt's statement published in the *Washington Post* on 30 December 1976 calling for a future Palestinian state to be formally linked with Jordan, was naturally welcomed by Amman as a reflection of "the aspirations of the Palestinian people concerning their future interests, prospects and stability." Jordan's Minister of Information, 'Adnān Abū 'Awda, praised Sādāt's "realistic and objective evaluation of the expected peace settlement."[9] This Jordanian-Egyptian *rapprochement* was strengthened by a joint statement issued on 15 January 1977 following talks between Ḥusayn and Sādāt in Aswan. Ḥusayn welcomed the establishment of the "strongest ties" (*awthaq al-'alaqāt*) between Jordan and the Palestinian state, their form to be determined "by the two [Jordanian and Palestinian] peoples through free choice proceeding from the unity of objective and destiny and complete identity of interest and feelings."[10]

Following his talks with the US Secretary of State on 17 February, Sādāt announced that "an official and declared link should take place between this Palestinian state and Jordan, even before Geneva starts." He added that Jordan and the PLO should enter negotiations on the exact form of this link.[11] However, Ḥusayn was reported to have told Vance during their talks in February that he was reluctant to establish a link with the PLO, and that Sādāt's proposal would not be acceptable unless the Rabat resolutions were revised by the Arab states. While Sādāt was thus seeking a formula to enable PLO participation in the Geneva conference, Ḥusayn clearly had no intention of helping to pave the way for the PLO's entry to Geneva without substantial changes in the status accorded to the organization at Rabat.

Ḥusayn's talks with Sādāt in Alexandria in July did not resolve these differences. Although they could agree that a clear link should be established between Jordan and a future Palestinian entity, they continued to differ on the status of the PLO in this regard, and on the timing of such a link. Egypt's Foreign Minister Fahmī claimed after talks on 10 July that Sādāt and Ḥusayn had concurred that Jordan and the Palestinians should come to an agreement on their ties before the Geneva conference. However in a television interview in Egypt on the previous day, Ḥusayn indicated that this was not really the case. He said he believed that "strong, special and distinctive relations should be established in the future," but that this should come "after the liberation of the land."[12] In Ḥusayn's view this meant a connection with the Palestinian people but not with the PLO (see below).

The idea of a link between Jordan and a future Palestinian state was also endorsed by President Asad of Syria. However, this view came within the framework of Asad's broader vision of "Greater Syria", which would create a federated unity between Syria, Lebanon, Jordan and a future Palestinian state under Syrian hegemony—an idea which Ḥusayn also proved reluctant to go along with. Nevertheless, the Syrian effort to gain greater control of the PLO, and Jordan's general policy of striving to minimize its role in any future settlement, brought to the fore the mutual interests of Ḥusayn and Asad in undermining the existing PLO leadership.

Against the background of the Lebanese civil war, Ḥusayn found it opportune to step up his criticism of the PLO. He claimed that the time had come for the Palestinian leaders "to rise to the level of events",[13] and to "be truly representative of the Palestinian people in their aspirations and adequate to the task."[14]

Jordan supported Syria's efforts of late 1976 and early 1977 to increase the membership of the Palestinian National Council (PNC) which both claimed was necessary to make the PNC representative of all Palestinian communities. (See essay on the Palestine Liberation Organization.) Although this effort to weaken the present PLO leadership was unsuccessful, it did not end either Jordanian or indirect Syrian criticism of 'Arafāt's leadership. During a visit to Jordan in June, the Commander of the Palestine Liberation Army (PLA),[15] Misbaḥ Budayrī, blamed the PLO for the Jordanian civil war of September 1970 and for the war in Lebanon, and called for changes in the PLO's leadership.

In late 1976 and early 1977, with Syria still seeking to increase its control over the PLO and with Sādāt advocating ties between Jordan and the PLO, the PLO came under increasing pressures from Egypt, Syria and Saudi Arabia to enter into a "dialogue" with Jordan to improve relations between them. The PLO Central Council decided on 23 January 1977 to enter into such a dialogue. A PLO delegation arrived for talks in Amman on 22 February.

However, mutual distrust kept the two sides poles apart. The meeting between Yāsir 'Arafāt and King Ḥusayn in Cairo on 8 March, during the Afro-Arab conference, was the last official contact between Jordan and the PLO during the period under review, but there was clearly no chance for meaningful reconciliation. The PLO insisted that reconciliation should be based on the Rabat resolutions and on Ḥusayn's agreement to a PLO political and military presence in Jordan. This "presence" was rejected outright by Ḥusayn even before the February talks began. The PLO just as emphatically rejected Ḥusayn's federation plan of March 1972, which Jordan had proposed as the basis for negotiation. Each party was, in fact, seeking precisely the same objective: political control over the largest Palestinian concentration on the East and West Banks of the Jordan. This control was of crucial importance to each for long-term political survival.

Egypt's advocacy of formal ties between Jordan and a future Palestinian state encouraged Ḥusayn to revive the federation plan as the basis for future East Bank-West Bank relations. Ḥusayn had never really abandoned the plan. Even after the Rabat summit, his statements on Jordan's future relations with the Palestinians were usually couched in terms that did not exclude it. However, in the first half of 1977, Ḥusayn's stand was made more explicit. On 21 June, Premier Badrān revealed that during the talks between Jordan and the PLO in February, Jordan had presented the PLO delegation with the Jordanian federation plan of 15 March 1972, which he outlined: 1) the East and West Banks would each have a local government, parliament and governor; 2) there would be a federal government, probably in Amman, responsible for foreign affairs, defence, finance, economy, education and planning. Ḥusayn's main aim behind the federation plan was to provide a measure of autonomy to the Palestinian "region" of the federal kingdom, thus at least giving some satisfaction to Palestinian aspirations for national self-assertion, but without providing the West Bank with a PLO-led independent power base which could at a later stage endanger Hashemite rule on the East Bank.

On the day after Badrān's statement, Ḥusayn visited Damascus, and in July he went to Saudi Arabia, Egypt, Kuwait, Baḥrayn, Qatar and the UAE in an apparent effort to try and gain support for his plan. Although the PLO was alone in openly criticizing the revival of the federation plan, there was no indication that it had been accepted by the other Arab states—a fact which underscored the limits of the gains made by Jordan in early 1977. Jordan was again recognized by the other Arab states as a major element in determining the future of the Palestinians. But although this result was achieved largely by the tactical manoeuvres of Egypt and Syria, neither was ready to go so far as to undermine the PLO's status in order to restore to Ḥusayn the position he had held before the Rabat decisions.

On the contrary, with Saudi Arabia, they continued to insist on the PLO's right to participate in the diplomatic process; at the same time, the US was also showing increasing interest in PLO involvement in the Geneva conference negotiations. The outcome of these diplomatic moves would clearly determine whether the PLO or Jordan would be the primary negotiator over the Palestinians' future in the West Bank. Ḥusayn began to show concern at the new tilt in US policy. He made several statements hinting that excess pressure on Israel might be counter-productive, as Israel "might launch a surprise attack to avoid the pressure."[16] He maintained that the US could wield considerable influence on Israel, but warned that Israel's "capacity to make serious moves that might lead to unexpected results in the area should not be under-rated."[17]

A central theme in Jordan's policy on the Palestinian question was to repudiate the idea that the PLO had the exclusive right to speak for the Palestinian people as a whole on the issue of self-determination. While Jordan supported Palestinian involvement in the peace-making process, it sought to minimize the PLO's role in this process—and, in effect, to neutralize the PLO in determining the future of the West Bank and Gaza. Ḥusayn repeatedly asserted that the Palestinians in the West Bank and Gaza had not been given a say in determining their political future or in the choice of their leadership; the PLO, he said, "must not be forced upon the Palestinians."[18]

Although Jordan accepted PLO participation in the Geneva conference—and at times expressed support for independent PLO participation—Ḥusayn's preference was to incorporate the PLO into a "single delegation representing the whole body of Arab belligerents, within which majority rule would be observed."[19] He suggested that Palestinians who did not belong to the PLO should also be represented at Geneva. Following his talks with the US Secretary of State in August, Ḥusayn said that the procedural question of Palestinian representation could be avoided if the substantive issues were decided in advance, thus indicating his unwillingness to press the issue of PLO participation.

While Ḥusayn did not conceal his disapproval of the Rabat resolutions, he still wished to be the primary negotiator over the future of the West Bank; but he was reluctant to accept this role without a clear-cut mandate from the Arab states, without which he knew his efforts would be pointless. In talks with Sādāt in January 1977, Ḥusayn agreed that Jordan would participate in the Geneva conference in its capacity as a "confrontation state"—not as the representative of the Palestinians. A way was thus found for Jordan to participate in Geneva, despite the Rabat conference's recognition of the PLO as the sole arbiter of the future of the West Bank. This status would enable Jordan to exert influence on the negotiating process without openly violating the Rabat resolutions.

Throughout 1977, and more emphatically after the Likud election victory in Israel in May, Ḥusayn consistently advocated cautious and careful preparations for the Geneva conference. He called on the Arab states to "arrive at an understanding on what is acceptable and reasonable so that we can secure positive results."[20] The Jordanian position was that Geneva was not an end in itself and if convened prematurely, it could lead to failure and increase the chances of war. Ḥusayn claimed that the military balance lay in Israel's favour. Such statements might well have reflected a genuine fear of a future war, but they were also intended to serve two other purposes. 1) To warn the other Arab states not to make too far-reaching demands upon Israel, particularly in respect to the PLO and an independent

Palestinian state, which Jordan did not regard as favourable to itself, but also believed that Israel would not accept. To press either of these demands would therefore produce deadlock and lead to war. 2) To present Israel as strong enough to make substantive territorial concessions, and encourage US pressure on Israel in this direction.

Jordan accepted UN Security Council resolutions 242 and 338 as the basis for any settlement, including the question of the Palestinians' national rights. Within this framework, Jordan demanded total Israeli withdrawal from all the territories occupied in 1967; a solution to the refugee problem either by repatriation or compensation; the right of Palestinians to self-determination; and mutual guarantees for peace.

On territorial issues, Jordan rejected both the Allon Plan and the functional concept of the Begin government (which spoke of a division of government authority between Jordan and Israel but did not favour the territorial division of the West Bank). The furthest Ḥusayn was prepared to go on this point was to agree to the possibility of reciprocal border rectifications. Ḥusayn also maintained that if Israel agreed in advance to the concept of total withdrawal, Jordan would not oppose withdrawal in stages. Jordan was prepared to discuss demilitarized zones, but doubted whether this was really practical. However on the nature of peace, Ḥusayn was more forthcoming than any of the other Arab leaders, expressing the opinion that open borders, free trade and normal relations were a reasonable *quid pro quo* for full Israeli withdrawal.[21] Israel's Foreign Minister, Moshe Dayan, said after the US Secretary of State's visit to the Middle East in August, that only one Arab state was prepared to include diplomatic relations with Israel in a peace treaty,[22] an apparent reference to Jordan.

On the issue of self-determination, Ḥusayn accepted that the Palestinians had the right to establish "a national and political entity", but he refrained from giving his support to a fully independent Palestinian state which he saw as a direct threat to Jordan, particularly if headed by the PLO. According to him, Palestinian self-determination should be achieved by a referendum on the West Bank and the Gaza Strip—possibly under international supervision and "free from fear and pressure." Ḥusayn claimed that "everything is in doubt on the West Bank including the PLO leadership." As the people of the West Bank and Gaza had "not been heard from",[23] the Palestinian people had "to consider and decide who will represent and lead them, and what kind of relations they will have with specific countries."[24] However, future ties with Jordan were to be finally determined by a referendum of both the Jordanians and Palestinians. Ḥusayn saw a PLO-run West Bank state as a possibly dangerous destabilizing factor; this, he said, was "all the more reason to . . . trust in the Palestinian people, not organizations."[25] He stressed that the Palestinians and Jordanians were one people, and that it seemed "simply impossible that there should be no legal, constitutional connection" between the East and West Banks, which "are one country."[26]

Ḥusayn clearly operated on the belief that if he could neutralize the PLO, the West Bank and Gaza populations would accept an arrangement based on his own federation plan. Two major factors provided Jordan with reasonable opportunities for manoeuvre in the West Bank. The first was that Amman has remained an influence in determing the West Bank's political fate despite its defeat in 1967. This was certainly the case before the Rabat resolutions, but thereafter as well—though in a somewhat altered form. Secondly, Jordan preserved its legal and day-to-day economic ties with the area, which provided it with considerable leverage.

The PLO has been and continues to be popular in the West Bank. There can be no doubt about the sense of identification of many West Bankers with what they genuinely regard as the standard-bearers of Palestinian nationalism. Yet the overt expression of this identification and the political realism attached to it tends to fluctuate according to the population's expectations of whether the PLO or Jordan can make most tangible political gains in the Arab and international arenas and, thereafter, in the West Bank itself. A fundamental characteristic of West Bank politics is the influence of external factors on the political behaviour and attitudes of the local population. Lacking an independent power base of their own, West Bankers have repeatedly been compelled to acquiesce in developments in the inter-Arab and international arenas over which they have little influence. Thus, while PLO popularity remained high in the West Bank until early 1976—as reflected in the results of the municipal elections of April that year—Syria's confrontation with the PLO in Lebanon served as yet another turning point.

Encouraged by the changing fortunes of the PLO, and well aware of the impact this could have on the West Bank, Jordan recognized the newly elected mayors in July 1976, and invited them to Amman to discuss the resumption of economic aid which had been stopped shortly before the West Bank municipal elections. Not all the mayors accepted the invitation; even those who did so in late 1976 did not produce statements of loyalty to Jordan. But by the very fact of their presence, they were consciously giving their assistance to Jordan's political aims. The visits, firmly opposed by the PLO and its supporters in the West Bank, reflected a weakening of the PLO's influence in the area, as at least some of the mayors were obviously prepared to make moves that the PLO did not approve.

More salient examples of the changing atmosphere came at the end of 1976 and the beginning of 1977. Sādāt's statement at the end of December 1976 on the necessity to establish formal ties between Jordan and a future Palestinian state, was followed by the joint communiqué issued by Ḥusayn and Sādat in mid-January, in which Ḥusayn welcomed the "establishment of the strongest ties" with such a state. West Bankers were left with the impression that Jordan had re-established itself for the first time since Rabat as a central party to efforts to reach a settlement of the Middle East crisis. Jordanian media hastened to explain to the West Bank population that Jordan's comeback was not a "seasonal" matter, and that Jordan's role "was always primary and would remain so."[27]

The changing situation left a marked imprint on the West Bank, where Jordan's supporters "came out of the cold" where they had been since Rabat, while the PLO's staunch supporters were suddenly thrown off balance. One of Amman's supporters, Hebron's ex-mayor Muḥammad 'Alī Ja'barī, found it opportune to produce a series of pro-Jordanian statements during his visit to Jordan in late 1976 and early 1977. Upon his return to the West Bank on 15 January 1977, he maintained that the resolutions of the 1948 Jericho conference[28] were the true basis for Palestinian-Jordanian relations, and that it was the West Bankers themselves who should have the first say in determining their own fate. He thus fully endorsed Ḥusayn's West Bank policy, undermining the Rabat resolutions and the PLO.

Ḥusayn's attempts to use funds as a means of leverage over the West Bank mayors aroused the PLO and its supporters on the West Bank to advocate the collection of funds in Saudi Arabia and the Gulf in an attempt to find an alternative source of finance not controlled by Ḥusayn. As it happened, Jordan did not actually produce any substantial aid. Mayors from the West Bank and Gaza did make fund-raising tours between late March and May 1977 of the richer Arab states, reportedly accompanied by PLO emissaries. However, their trips apparently had the prior approval of Amman, and most of the funds they collected were deposited in Amman, where they could be withdrawn by the mayors only with Jordanian approval.

The crucial area of competition between the PLO and Jordan remained in the Arab and international arenas. Here the PLO began to show signs of increasing success, particularly in the latter part of 1977, which made an impact on the relative standing of Jordan and the PLO in the West Bank. Following the convening of the PNC in March 1977, the PLO leadership appeared to be regaining its confidence after surviving the Syrian attempts to undermine its authority. This factor, as well as the emerging trend of US policy in August and September to accept the incorporation of a PLO element in the Geneva conference, appeared, once again, to be reducing Ḥusayn's position in the West Bank. These swings and roundabouts reflect the gains and failures of Ḥusayn and the PLO in their external rivalry for predominance in determining the fate of the Palestinians.

During his visit to Israel in August, Cyrus Vance received memoranda from West Bank mayors expressing their support for the PLO, as well as from other West Bankers representing views more acceptable to Jordan. The pro-PLO memorandum was not signed by all the mayors (the mayor of Bethlehem, for one, was reported to have declined to do so). On the other hand, only a few of the mayors of the larger West Bank towns joined the delegation that went to Jordan to congratulate Ḥusayn on the occasion of his Silver Jubilee celebrated on 11 August. The delegation expressed its appreciation "for the fraternal and historic ties linking the people of the occupied West Bank with Jordan." [29] Ḥusayn told them that he had no other goal than to be "one of you and with you", and repeated his concept of the Palestinians' right to self-determination "without any outside influences." [30]

Shortly afterwards, in late August, one of the members of the West Bank delegation, Ḥusayn al-Shuyūkhī of Ramallah, started a campaign in the West Bank against the PLO by denying its right to represent the Palestinians in the East and West Banks of the Jordan. There were various indications that Shuyūkhī's effort (followed in September by pro-Jordanian statements by the former Jordanian Minister of Labour and Social Affairs, Mustafā Dūdīn) was inspired by Jordan. But it failed to make any serious impact in the West Bank, where the PLO appeared to be regaining ground at Jordan's expense for the reasons given above.

JORDAN'S RELATIONS WITH THE ARAB STATES

THE JORDANIAN-SYRIAN RELATIONSHIP

Though Jordanian-Syrian relations had already begun to improve on the eve of the October 1973 war, it was in early 1975 that the two countries entered into a new phase of political, economic and military co-operation. In June 1975, the Higher Jordanian-Syrian Joint Committee was formed, headed by the respective Premiers, and in August that year the Joint Supreme Jordanian-Syrian Leadership Council, headed by Ḥusayn and Asad, was established. (Also see essay on Inter-Arab Relations.)

However, from the outset, Jordan showed considerable caution in developing its relations with Syria. Steps taken towards "integration" (*takāmul*) have been limited and gradual. Jordan avoided any action that could infringe either upon its sovereignty or its capacity for independent decision-making. Jordan's main motive in entering on a special relationship with Syria seems to have been to bolster its position in the Arab arena, and make political gains at the expense of the PLO.

Special ties between Jordan and Syria continued to develop during 1975 and 1976, but began to slacken somewhat from early in 1977. Frequent reports of an imminent federation between the two countries have been replaced by those of the weakening of ties and of differences between Ḥusayn and Asad over their future relations. Asked in August 1977 what he thought of the Syrian idea of a federation between Syria, Jordan and the West Bank, Ḥusayn replied that it struck him "as farfetched." [31]

During 1975 and 1976, political co-ordination had focused on Jordan's and Syria's disapproval of the second Sinai agreement, and Jordan's support for Syria's involvement against the PLO in Lebanon. But Ḥusayn had reason to be disappointed with the Syrian attitude to the PLO as it emerged in the aftermath of the Lebanese civil war, and the renewal of diplomatic momentum for a Middle East settlement during 1977 which tended to expose differences rather than favour closer co-operation. Jordan's relative moderation toward Israel was fundamentally different from the Syrian attitude. The two countries also had different perceptions of the PLO's role in any future settlement. Jordanian policy was in essence to neutralize the PLO, while the Syrians sought to impose their control over it: they were prepared to undermine the PLO's present leadership in co-operation with Jordan, but were evidently not prepared to totally abandon their support for the organization and what it stood for. There were also various indications that Saudi Arabia (as well as some leaders in Jordan, such as Crown Prince Ḥasan) had had reservations about the Amman-Damascus axis for some time, and these may also have contributed to the slowing down of the process of *rapprochement*.

Frequent high-level consultations, including meetings between Ḥusayn and Asad, continued during 1977; but there were fewer such meetings within the official framework of the Joint Leadership Council and the Higher Joint Committee. Since its foundation in August 1975, the Joint Leadership Council had met at more or less half yearly intervals (December 1975, May 1976, December 1976); but by September 1977, it had not convened again. Similarly, the Higher Joint Committee—which was supposed to meet at regular three-monthly intervals, and had in fact more or less done so during 1975 and 1976—did not meet between November 1976 and the end of June 1977.

The joint statement issued by Asad and Ḥusayn on 8 December 1976 (following the meeting in Amman of the Joint Leadership Council) declared that "the co-ordination and integration steps which have been accomplished so far make it possible to proceed to a more advanced formula on the level of establishing joint institutions which will embody the common objective and fulfil the aspirations of our people in the two countries." A senior level joint committee was entrusted to study the "various aspects on which the unitary structure will be based" and submit the results of its studies to the Joint Leadership Council "as soon as possible."[32] Syrian Premier Khulayfāwī met with Ḥusayn and Premier Badrān in January and March 1977 in Amman to discuss progress toward federation and the "development of the unionist march between them."[33] However, since then no further progress was apparently made, and the level of "integration" between the two countries remained much as it had been in 1976, limited primarily to economic co-ordination and co-operation. Advances were made in other spheres, such as the partial unification of school curricula and textbooks, though by late 1977 this had not gone beyond the elementary level.

In the military sphere, steps were taken in 1975–76 to make wartime co-operation easier. However as far as is known, these did not include the establishment of a joint military command. A primary motivation of the Syrian regime in its relationship with Jordan was to enhance military co-ordination between the Syrian and Jordanian armies as part of its effort to establish a powerful north-eastern front to face Israel. Jordan's 70,000 strong army—reputed for its efficiency—was probably the most important asset Ḥusayn had in his deliberations with Syria.

RELATIONS WITH EGYPT

After the signing of the second Sinai agreement between Egypt and Israel in September 1975, Jordan's relations with Egypt deteriorated seriously. Jordan supported Syria's criticism of Egypt, though on a lower key; while Egypt attacked Jordan for supporting Syria's involvement in Lebanon. Egypt and Jordan continued their propaganda exchanges until the Riyadh and Cairo conferences of October 1976 where Syria and Egypt sorted out their differences, thus also paving the way for an improvement in Jordan's relations with Egypt. Immediately after the Cairo summit, both Ḥusayn and Badrān were full of praise for Sādāt's contribution to its success.

Sādāt's advocacy of formal links between Jordan and a future Palestinian state was a source of encouragement for Jordan. However, his idea that these ties be manifested in an agreement between Jordan and the PLO before Geneva, was not accepted (see above). Though Ḥusayn had recognized Sādāt's leadership role in the search for a Middle East settlement, his continued insistence on the convening of Geneva in 1977 with PLO participation, and suggestion of a joint Jordanian-PLO delegation displeased Ḥusayn. On the eve of his visit to the US, Ḥusayn said that those telling the Arabs that peace could be established in 1977 "were playing with fire." He regretted that Arab leaders were following each other to the US, without taking the trouble to consult one another and define a common position.[34]

RELATIONS WITH SAUDI ARABIA

The Saudi contingent, which had been stationed in Jordan since 1967, was withdrawn in November 1976. However, this step did not appear to have any political significance.

A central theme in Jordanian-Saudi relations in 1976–77 was the question of reduced Saudi economic aid to Jordan (see essay on "Inter-Arab Affairs"). Though Jordan did not accuse Saudi Arabia of failing in its commitments, both Ḥusayn and Badrān made strenuous appeals for more financial support. During 1977, there were reports that Saudi Arabia was holding back aid promised to Jordan for political reasons, such as Saudi disapproval of Jordan's close ties with Syria, and displeasure with Ḥusayn's reluctance to seek a reconciliation with the PLO. Other reasons given were the evident prosperity in Jordan, which had apparently made her usual backers less ready to give financial support; as well as the Saudi's own difficulties in financing their ambitious development projects.

Frequent contacts were maintained in 1976–77 between senior Jordanian and Saudi officials, including visits by Ḥusayn to King Khālid while both were in Britain in late February and early March 1977. Ḥusayn again held talks with Khālid in Saudi Arabia in July. Though political developments in the area probably featured prominently, delayed Saudi aid was reported to have been high on the agenda in the July meeting. According to this report, Khālid and Fahd had listened sympathetically to Ḥusayn's financial troubles and had promised to clear the promised funds. Even though relations with Syria had cooled, this did not apparently succeed in bringing "any substantial warmth back into the Saudi-Jordanian relationship."[35]

RELATIONS WITH OTHER ARAB STATES

Jordan's relations with Kuwait and the Gulf states have remained favourable. They continued to focus on economic aid to Jordan in return for Jordanian military assistance. This either took the form of Jordanian military and police training missions in the Gulf, or Gulf army and police officer training in Jordan. Senior Jordanian officials travelled frequently to the Gulf; Ḥusayn himself visited the UAE and Qatar in December 1976, Oman at the end of January, and Kuwait, Baḥrayn, Qatar and the UAE in July. Gulf rulers also visited Jordan: the Baḥrayni Crown Prince and ruler of Rās al-Khayma in January, and Sultan Qābūs in May.

Jordan also provided military assistance to North Yemen. Jordan and the People's Democratic Republic of Yemen (South Yemen) agreed to establish full diplomatic relations in March 1977.

Iraqi media were occasionally hostile to Jordan, but Amman did not follow Syria into an open rift with Iraq. The two countries continued to develop their trade relations, with Jordan providing Iraq with import facilities at Aqaba, thereby easing the problem of congestion in Iraq's own ports.

Jordan claimed that the four men who attacked the Intercontinental hotel in Amman on 17 November 1976 had been trained in Iraq "with the knowledge and under the supervision of the Iraqi authorities."[36] Nevertheless, this incident was not allowed to develop into an open clash with Iraq.

JORDAN'S RELATIONS WITH THE MAJOR POWERS

RELATIONS WITH THE US

The US and Jordan have maintained their friendly relationship, which Jordan considers of vital importance to the continued survival of the Hashemite regime. Ḥusayn displayed considerable sensitivity to his public image in America and to American policy on the Palestinian question. As in the past, the US continued to serve as a primary supplier of economic aid to Amman, as well as being almost the sole source for its military hardware. The overseas military and economic aid programme presented to Congress for the US fiscal year beginning on 1 October 1977 included $131.5m and $93m respectively for Jordan in grants and loans.

The *Washington Post* published an article on 18 February 1977—the day Cyrus Vance arrived in Amman—revealing that Ḥusayn had been on the payroll of the CIA since 1957. Ḥusayn did not deny that Jordan had received funds from the CIA, for security and intelligence purposes, but he indignantly rejected the insinuation that these payments had been for his personal benefit and a form of bribery. Ḥusayn maintained that as far as he was concerned the CIA was part of the US government, and whenever there was an identity of interests he would "continue to advocate fruitful co-operation."[37] US officials tried to minimize the impact of the disclosure; both President Carter and Secretary Vance said they did not think such payments were improper. Vance said such funds were a form of US assistance to friendly governments, and not secret payments to individuals. The *Washington Post* article asserted that Carter had ordered the payments stopped, but Ḥusayn said he had not been informed of this. Later reports indicated that Jordan may continue to receive funds for intelligence assistance, but possibly not directly from the CIA.

Shortly before leaving Jordan at the end of his February visit, Vance sought to calm Jordanian concern by declaring that he had "reaffirmed the close and harmonious relationship" between the two countries, and had "reaffirmed unequivocally the US commitment to Jordan's economic progress and to our co-operation in the pursuit of peace."[38] Ḥusayn nevertheless remained suspicious that pro-Israeli circles in the US were trying to undermine "the credibility and integrity of those who are able and willing to contribute to the forces of peace", asserting that it was "hardly coincidental" that the *Washington Post* article was published on the day Vance arrived in Amman.[39]

Against this background, the statements and clarifications by President Carter and his adviser, Zbigniew Brzezinski, in March and April 1977 on the necessity for a homeland for the Palestinians only made the Jordanians all the more anxious. Carter and Brzezinski did not exclude the possibility that the homeland could be within a Jordanian framework. Noting the large number of Palestinians in Jordan, Carter said on 8 April that some relationship or confederation between Jordan and the Palestinians could be possible. These statements on a possible Jordanian connection were most probably intended to placate both Jordan and Israel, but in Amman they aroused fears that Carter might have accepted the idea that the East Bank should become a Palestinian state, or part of a Palestinian state on the East and West Banks and in the Gaza Strip, thus rendering the Hashemite regime redundant. Ḥusayn and Jordanian government officials began to suspect that the revelations on CIA payments were not unconnected with the statements on the Palestinian homeland, and feared that they had been published to undermine the Hashemite regime to pave the way for a Palestinian homeland on the East Bank.

When Ḥusayn visited the US at the end of April and beginning of May 1977, he sought reassurance that US support had not changed; and American officials were anxious to dispel his fears. Carter welcomed Ḥusayn on 25 April as a key leader in the peace effort and as a "staunch friend and permanent ally of the United States."[40] Ḥusayn was reportedly reassured that the US would remain firm in its support for Jordan. He said in July that his impression was that Carter did not seek the establishment of a Palestinian Homeland in Jordan, but in the West Bank and the Gaza Strip. Nevertheless, Ḥusayn's concern with US policy on the Palestinian question was apparently again aroused following the more evident tilt in US policy in favour of the PLO, as it emerged during and after Secretary Vance's August trip to the Middle East.

The Israeli Foreign Minister, Moshe Dayan, and Ḥusayn were rumoured to have met in Britain at the end of August. Dayan's statements at the end of August and in September, to the effect that Ḥusayn was disturbed by the course US policy was taking, were probably based on reliable information.

AGREEMENT WITH EEC

Jordan has had elaborate economic ties with numerous Western European countries for many years, particularly with Britain and West Germany, which it continued to further during 1976–7. An agreement was signed in Brussels on 18 January 1977, between Jordan and the EEC. This included a financial protocol under which Jordan would receive 40m European units of account (c. $50m) in loans and grants for investment in development projects. The agreement also provided for tariff reductions on Jordanian products marketed in the EEC countries. (See also the essay, "The European Community and the Middle East.")

RELATIONS WITH THE SOVIET UNION

Since 1975, Jordan's improved relations with the Soviet Union have found expression in more frequent official contacts and exchanges of delegations. Ḥusayn himself visited Moscow for the first time since 1967 between 17–28 June 1976. Since the Rabat resolutions of October 1974, the USSR's representative to the Geneva conference, Vladimir Vinogradov, has visited Jordan three times—in March and December 1975 and March 1976. In February 1977, the head of the USSR Foreign Ministry's Near Eastern Department, Mikhail Sytenko, held talks with Jordanian leaders in Amman. Against the background of Soviet interest in reconvening the Geneva conference, these frequent consultations apparently centred on Jordan's role at Geneva, as a means of overcoming the expected difficulties in incorporating the PLO in the political process. In April 1977, shortly before and during his visit to the US, Ḥusayn said that the USSR could play an important role in the Middle East peace process which should not be ignored. Ḥusayn evidently hoped that such involvement would be to Jordan's benefit in terms of potential Soviet leverage over the PLO; or, that by advocating Soviet involvement, he could improve his bargaining position with the US.

Since Ḥusayn's 1976 visit, economic and technical co-operation agreements have been signed between the two countries. Soviet delegations visited Jordan in November and December 1976 to discuss co-operation in the fields of electricity supply, oil exploration and technical and vocational training. During 1976–7, Jordanian ministerial and Senate delegations visited the USSR, and a Soviet military delegation visited Jordan between 30 May and 6 June 1977.

Jordan's relations have also improved with Eastern European countries. Jordan signed economic agreements with Hungary, East Germany and Bulgaria.

RELATIONS WITH THE PEOPLE'S REPUBLIC OF CHINA

The Jordanian Foreign Ministry announced on 14 April 1977 that Jordan and China had agreed to establish diplomatic relations and exchange ambassadors. Jordan and Taiwan immediately severed diplomatic relations, although Jordanian officials did not expect trade between the two countries to be affected. The agreement with China was reached after prolonged talks between Jordan's ambassador to the US, 'Abdallah Salāḥ, and officials at the Chinese liaison office in Washington.

ECONOMIC AFFAIRS ($1 = 0.326 Jordanian dinars; £1 = 0.64JD)

For a comprehensive account of Jordan's economic development and performance in 1976–7, see Jordanian section of essay, "Major Trends in Middle East Economic Development."

CENTRAL GOVERNMENT EXPENDITURE (in thousands of Jordanian dinars)

	1974	*1975*	*1976*
1. General Administration	1,055	1,041	1,219
Recurring	1,055	1,041	1,219
Capital	—	—	—
2. Defence	44,500	55,342	55,560
Recurring	44,500	55,342	55,560
Capital	—	—	—
3. Internal Order and Security	8,115	8,630	11,689
Recurring	7,915	8,319	11,407
Capital	200	311	262
4. International Affairs	1,554	2,382	2,407
Recurring	1,488	2,054	2,297
Capital	66	328	110
5. Finance Administration	38,794	58,130	54,298
Recurring	24,250	37,112	34,424
Capital	14,544	21,018	19,874
6. Economic Development Services	31,989	50,473	45,576
Recurring	4,208	5,219	6,982
Capital	27,781	45,254	38,594
7. Social Services	19,379	23,334	29,132
Recurring	16,800	20,618	24,234
Capital	2,579	2,716	4,898
8. Culture and Information Services	2,973	4,328	5,766
Recurring	2,341	3,361	4,385
Capital	632	967	1,381
9. Communications and Transport	3,144	5,773	17,296
Recurring	2,282	3,189	4,025
Capital	862	2,584	13,271
Total	**151,503**	**209,433**	**222,923**
Recurring	104,839	136,255	144,533
Capital	46,664	73,178	78,390

Source: Central Bank of Jordan, *Monthly Statistical Bulletin*, July 1977.

BALANCE OF PAYMENTS (in million Jordanian dinars)

	1974		1975		1976	
	Credit	*Debit*	*Credit*	*Debit*	*Credit*	*Debit*
A. Goods and Services	114.36	198.16	185.84	304.17	332.34	431.55
Merchandise	49.75	155.68	48.88	232.94	68.71	338.74
Services, net	22.13	—	65.73	—	170.82	—
B. Transfer payments	86.85	0.11	140.36	0.56	127.85	1.35
C. Capital and Monetary Gold	4.14	—	—	6.63	—	31.31
Net Errors and Ommissions	—	7.08	—	14.84	1.51	—

Source: Central Bank of Jordan, *Monthly Statistical Bulletin*, June 1977.

JORDAN'S MAIN TRADING PARTNERS (in millions of Dinars)

	1974	*1975*	*1976*
Exports to			
Egypt	1.260	0.918	1.187
Iraq	1.616	2.404	2.327
Syria	2.875	3.580	6.392
Kuwait	2.776	2.395	3.282
Lebanon	4.001	2.018	1.660
Saudi Arabia	5.539	4.761	7.468
EEC	0.063	1.978	2.520
Czechoslovakia	0.708	1.920	1.521
Yugoslavia	1.202	0.504	0.189
India	6.576	1.973	1.712
Japan	3.790	1.909	1.915
Total (including others)	**8.541**	**10.929**	**12.205**
Imports from			
United States	17.583	24.176	31.047
West Germany	14.513	24.937	51.885
United Kingdom	12.037	21.876	23.720
Japan	7.379	17.106	21.512
India	2.968	4.339	13.239
Saudi Arabia	3.693	22.914	34.489
Italy	5.869	11.124	19.534
Egypt	7.109	6.231	9.575
France	3.719	7.592	10.535
Romania	2.885	8.835	9.465
Syria	5.807	6.312	7.450
Total (including others)	**156.507**	**234.013**	**339.539**

Source: Central Bank of Jordan, *Monthly Statistical Bulletin*, various issues.

NOTES

1. On 11 August 1952, the Jordanian Parliament passed a resolution declaring Ḥusayn's mentally unstable father, Tallāl, unfit to rule, and proclaimed Ḥusayn as King. Because he was under age at the time, a Council of Regents ruled until he officially assumed full regal powers on 2 May 1953 upon reaching the age of 18, according to the Muslim calendar.
2. *Jordan Times*, 7 April 1977.
3. *Ibid*, 5 November 1976.
4. R Amman, 13 April—Daily Report (DR), 14 April 1977.
5. *Al-Dustūr*, Amman; quoted by R Amman, 10 April—DR, 12 April 1977.
6. R Amman, 5 September—DR, 7 September 1976.
7. *The Military Balance 1977-78* (London: International Institute for Strategic Studies).
8. R Amman, 28 October—DR, 29 October 1976.
9. Middle East News Agency (MENA), 2 January—DR, 3 January. *Jordan Times*, 3 January 1977.
10. *Al-Rā'y*, 16 January 1977
11. *International Herald Tribune*, Paris; 18 February 1977.

12. R Amman, 10 July—British Broadcasting Corporation, Summary of World Broadcasts, the ME and Africa (BBC), 12 July 1977.
13. R Amman, 11 October—DR, 12 October 1976.
14. *Kayhan International*, Tehran; 17 November 1976.
15. The PLA had a unit stationed in Jordan and maintained favourable relations with Jordan and Syria. Both countries used the PLA as a means to undermine the present leadership of the PLO.
16. *Al-Akhbār*, 13 August 1977.
17. *Al-Rā'y*, 17 August 1977.
18. *Die Zeit*, Hamburg; 11 February 1977.
19. *Le Monde*, Paris; 21 April 1977.
20. MENA, 21 June—DR, 22 June 1977.
21. *Newsweek*, New York; 1 August 1977.
22. *Ma'ariv*, Tel Aviv; 19 August 1977.
23. *Newsweek*, 1 August 1977.
24. *France-Soir*, Paris; 5 February 1977.
25. *Newsweek*, 1 August 1977.
26. *Die Zeit*, 11 February 1977. *Newsweek*, 1 August 1977.
27. R Amman, 6 January 1977.
28. At this conference, in December 1948, the groundwork was laid for the annexation of the West Bank to Jordan.
29. R Amman, 11 August—DR, 12 August 1977.
30. *Al-Rā'y*, 12 August 1977.
31. *Newsweek*, 1 August 1977.
32. R Amman, 8 December—BBC, 10 December 1976.
33. R Amman, 16, 17 March—DR, 17 March 1977.
34. *Le Monde*, 21 April 1977.
35. *Events*, Beirut; 29 July 1977.
36. R Amman, 17 November—BBC, 19 November 1976.
37. *Newsweek*, 7 March 1977.
38. *New York Times*, 20 February 1977.
39. *Newsweek*, 7 March 1977.
40. *Jordan Times*, 26 April 1977.

Lebanon

(Al-Jumhūriyya al-Lubnāniyya)

ITAMAR RABINOVICH and HANNA ZAMIR

Unlike the Lebanese civil war of 1958, that of 1975–76 resulted in a far-reaching transformation of the Lebanese political system. It established a Syrian hegemony over Lebanon; led to the virtual disappearance of the Lebanese state (at least temporarily); destroyed the mechanisms, arrangements and conventions which had previously regulated inter-communal relations; and damaged, possibly permanently, the country's economic and administrative infrastructure. These consequences were apparent when the inter-Arab conferences of Riyadh and Cairo finally succeeded in ending the worst of the fighting in October 1976. However, the damaging internecine conflict continued into 1977, though in a more muted form. What remains painfully unclear is the shape of the future Lebanese state, or whether it will regain full independence within its former boundaries.

THE LEBANESE POLITICAL SYSTEM

The Lebanese political system, the product of long historic development, was in many respects unique and paradoxical. It was based on a genuine attempt to build a pluralistic polity that would accommodate the needs of an extremely heterogeneous society. It maintained a Christian bias despite the disappearance of the Christian numerical majority of the 1920s. Its institutions of constitutional democracy functioned reasonably well despite the fact that a sizeable part of the population remained outside their operations and played no significant part in the political process. The attachment of the Lebanese system to political and economic liberalism, and its explicit recognition of the lingering sway held by confessional loyalties left it out of step with developments in the surrounding Arab world. The deficiencies of this sytem were widely known in Lebanon; but it was equally well known that it was possibly the only system that could hold Lebanon together and preserve it as an independent entity. Despite ritualistic criticisms, the major Lebanese political forces supported the *status quo*—and so did the regional balance of forces.

The Lebanese political system survived, and in a sense emerged strengthened from, the civil war of 1958. Fu'ād Shihāb (1958–64) was instrumental in steering Lebanon out of that crisis; but he failed in his efforts to reform and modernize the country's institutions. Shihāb's failure produced a fundamental national dilemma towards the mid-1960s: while the Lebanese entity appeared to be more stable than in previous years, its inherent flaws were equally evident; yet it was certain that any attempt at fundamental reform or even substantial revision were doomed to failure since they were bound to upset the delicate balance on which the whole system rested. Furthermore, it was realized that pressures on the fragile system were likely to increase under the impact of modernization and social mobilization (which inevitably weakened the position of the society's conservative elements and strengthened the extra-parliamentary opposition). These assumptions were current in the academic literature of the period, and were also accepted by some of the participants in the political process.

However, in the years which followed the Shihāb presidency, attention focused not on the country's fundamental dilemma, but on pressing immediate problems. Some of these derived from the way power was transferred to the new president,

Charles Helou. Shihāb had left the presidency rather reluctantly, and with his entourage sought to perpetuate his influence through a weak successor. Because of the president's cardinal political role, the entire Lebanese system was seriously affected by the weak new incumbent. Unlike the Shihāb period, there was no stable parliamentary majority; the relationship between President, Prime Minister and Parliament was far from satisfactory. If internal forces made changes difficult to undertake, the impact of external forces brooked less delay: the inter-Arab rivalries of 1964–67, the rising tension in the Arab-Israeli conflict and, finally, the Six-Day war in 1967—these forced the government to make a number of difficult decisions harmful to political stability.

LEBANON AND THE PALESTINIAN QUESTION: DECEMBER 1968–MAY 1973

New and ominous pressures began to develop at the end of 1968, when the growing presence and activity of the Palestinian organizations in and from Lebanon's territory became a major catalyst. The period began in December 1968 when, in retaliation for attacks on El-Al aircraft, Israel raided Beirut airport, thus demonstrating to the Lebanese public the price they would have to pay for allowing virtual freedom of action to the Palestinians. The period ended in May 1973, when the Lebanese army made a final abortive effort to establish control over the Palestinian organizations.

Until 1968, the Palestinians were mainly seen as constituting a refugee problem. There was no question of incorporating them into the Lebanese system, both because of the general Arab line and because of the Christians' reluctance to upset further the state's demographic balance. However, the authorities became worried by the beginnings of an autonomous Palestinian build-up within Lebanon, and by the serious risk of Israeli retaliation against Palestinian attacks across the border. Indeed, developments after late 1968 produced a number of grave consequences for Lebanon's political stability: 1) erosion of the state's authority and the notion of Lebanese sovereignty; 2) exacerbation of Christian-Muslim tension; 3) strengthening the Left and weakening the parliamentary system; 4) aggravation of "the problem of the south"—a mostly Shī'ī inhabited area increasingly aware of its underprivileged position.

Lebanon enjoyed a brief period of relief after September 1970, when the Palestinian organizations were weakened by their conflict with King Ḥusayn in Jordan. Sulaymān Faranjiyya, the newly-elected president, was seen as a strong and conservative leader. But by 1972, Lebanon had taken on a new importance for the Palestinians as the only free base still available to them.

The Lebanese political élite, though acutely aware of these developments, felt itself powerless to take any effective action. The Palestinians were unlikely to make any concessions voluntarily, and any attempt to force them to curb their activities was bound to arouse not only them, but also Lebanese Muslims, and probably Syria and other outside forces as well. Even if the Lebanese army was able to subdue the Palestinians, the price would be too costly. This view was reinforced by the army's abortive attempt to restrain the Palestinians in the spring of 1973. But a more fundamental conflict—with forces challenging Lebanon's very existence—was forced on the Lebanese élite in April 1975 by a clash between the Phalanges and a Palestinian group. However, the causes of the civil war must also be sought in other developments in the early 1970s.

MAJOR FACTORS IN THE CRISIS OF 1975–76

With the Palestinian issue as a catalyst, the following political processes were intensified.

1. THE IMPACT ON LEBANON OF BROADER DEVELOPMENTS IN THE ARAB WORLD

The events of 1973-74—the October war, the oil boycott, the accumulation of financial resources—generated a feeling of increased collective power in the Arab world. The Islamic conservative bloc, centred on Saudi Arabia, grew in importance, and there was a marked increase in Arab and Islamic solidarity. One consequence was to increase Muslim unwillingness to accept Christian hegemony in Lebanon. This trend was underlined by a further shift in the population balance towards a larger Muslim majority, as well as by changes in Western attitudes to the region. Whereas previously it was always assumed that the US and, to a lesser extent, France would not tolerate a serious challenge to Lebanon's Christian character, it had already become apparent before 1975 that they were seeking influence in other parts of the Arab world, and would be increasingly reluctant to intervene on behalf of Lebanon's Christians.

2. SOCIAL DEVELOPMENTS IN LEBANON

The inadequacies of social and economic policies and the wide gap between social classes were well-known characteristics of the Lebanese system; but their political significance became magnified by the combined impact of recent developments. The dividing lines between rich and poor, and between Christian and Muslim, overlap to a great extent; feelings of economic and sectarian deprivation have nourished each other. The phenomenal growth of Beirut exacerbated these problems by concentrating a great number of discontented people at the political centre, while reducing the relative importance of the Christian strongholds in Mount Lebanon and the North. Accelerated inflation, due to the rise in oil prices, aggravated social tensions. Increased activity by the radical Left provided the disaffected elements with organizational bases, an ideological framework—and weapons.

3. THE RISE OF SYRIAN INFLUENCE

Lebanon's position in the Arab world was crucially affected by two major developments in 1970: the decline of Egypt's regional position as a political centre for Muslim and Arab nationalists in Lebanon, especially after Nāsir's death; and the crystallization of a comparatively stable regime in Syria whose foreign policy sought to capitalize on Egypt's decline by building influence in its own immediate environment. Syria possessed several excellent means of applying pressure on Lebanon: through some of the Palestinian organizations, the Shī'ī community, and the Lebanese Ba'th party; through almost half a million seasonal Syrian workers residing in Lebanon; through the capacity to cut Lebanon off from its economic hinterland; and, as a final resort, by the threat of direct or indirect military intervention. The influence which Syria acquired in Lebanon was far greater than Egypt's ever was. Syria is closer to Lebanon; its interests in it are more vital; and it rejects, at least implicitly, the legitimacy of a Lebanese entity. For instance, Syria refused to set up an embassy in Lebanon, arguing that it would be preposterous for one part of Greater Syria to have diplomatic relations with another part.

4. THE MOBILIZATION OF THE SHĪ'Ī COMMUNITY

Shī'i feelings of deprivation had found only scant political expression in earlier years, due to the weakness of their traditional leadership. But a dynamic religious leader, Imām Mūsā al-Sadr, emerged in the early 1970s and formed a close working alliance with the Syrian president. Thus a new and effective element seeking to alter the *status quo* entered the Lebanese political scene.

5. MALFUNCTIONING OF THE SYSTEM

The proper functioning of the complex and delicate mechanisms of the Lebanese polity depended to a great extent on the leadership qualities and political wisdom of its leaders. Since the mid-1960s, under Presidents Helou and Faranjiyya, the system has not operated smoothly. The established Christian and Muslim leaders largely failed to read "the writing on the wall", and continued their traditional pattern of bickering for traditional goals without recognizing the qualitative change in the gravity of the problems they faced. Thus in the spring of 1975, jockeying for the Presidency and Prime Ministership continued in spite of the growing crisis.

MAIN PHASES OF THE 1975–6 CRISIS

The history of the civil war in Lebanon can be divided into four distinct phases, as follows.

1. *The Spring and Early Summer of 1975.* The crisis began with a clash in April 1975 between the Phalanges and radical Palestinian elements. Its first phase was primarily a struggle between the Phalangist militia and Palestinian groups.

2. *The Summer of 1975 to January 1976.* The crisis developed into a broader civil war between the Christian militias and Muslim, Leftist and Palestinian groups. The militias sought to preserve the *status quo*; their opponents, to transform to varying degrees the political system.

3. *January 1976–March 1976.* Realizing their inability to re-establish the traditional system, the Christians modified their strategy and sought to set up a Christian state based on Mount Lebanon, the northern littoral and access to the port of Beirut. In January 1976, they were on the verge of achieving their goal, which prompted Syria to intervene overtly in the war. Syria tipped the balance against the Christians, and became the dominant factor in Lebanon. It tried to use its newly-won position to impose moderate reforms, granting the Muslims more representation and a greater share of power in the government.

4. *March 1976–October 1976.* During this period a dramatic about-face took place in Syria's policy. The Syrian reforms were accepted by the Christians who realized they could not, under the circumstances, hope for a better arrangement. But Syria's traditional allies in Lebanon rejected the reforms. For reasons explained below, Syria decided to uphold its plan—even at the price of shifting its support to the Christians and actually intervening and fighting against its former allies. But Syria's direct military intervention in May and June failed and, until the end of September, Syria limited its role to indirect support of the Christians and pressures on the rival camp. Syria's candidate, Ilyās Sarkīs, was sworn in as President of a practically non-existent state on 23 September, but on the whole, a political and military stalemate set in during the summer. Syria finally launched a second military offensive early in October. It proved successful, but Syria chose to stop short of a complete military victory and instead to use her new military achievements at the Riyadh conference.

THE BELLIGERENTS

The Lebanese civil war has usually been seen as a conflict between a Right-wing Christian camp and a Left-wing Muslim-Palestinian one. Such a view is erroneous and misleading in that it fails to convey the complexity and diversity of the rival groups and the internecine conflicts within the major communities. In fact, the "Left-wing Muslim" camp included Christian elements, as well as moderate Muslim leaders who did not subscribe to leftist ideology. The "Right-wing Christian" camp was more coherent, but it too was far from homogeneous. Though mainly Christian, its leaders regarded themselves primarily as defenders of the

Lebanese system. It is therefore more appropriate to speak of a "pro *status quo* camp" and an "anti *status quo* coalition." The situation was further confounded following Syria's massive intervention in the summer of 1976, when a third camp—composed of pro-Syrian elements from both sides—began to crystallize. This three-pronged division acquired operative importance only after the Riyadh and Cairo conferences. For the period of the full-fledged civil war, only the major groups and personalities in the two original coalitions of 1975 need be considered.

The Pro Status Quo Camp

Traditionally, the Catholic groups among the Lebanese Christian communities were most closely identified with the Lebanese entity. The Greek Orthodox community favoured the ideas of Arab nationalism, and resented the political supremacy of the Maronite Catholics. While the crisis of 1975–76 brought the Christian communities closer together, the major share of military and political activity remained in Maronite hands. During the crisis, five major orientations crystallized in the Maronite community which in part reflected earlier attitudes and in part were reactions to the crisis situation: 1) parties with a Christian Maronite bias, and their militias; 2) the Maronite ecclesiastical establishment; 3) confessional Maronite groups; 4) moderate political leaders advocating concessions and compromise; and 5) the Christian leadership of the army.

1. PARTIES WITH A CHRISTIAN-MARONITE BIAS AND THEIR MILITIAS

These were the major forces operating among the Maronites. They included the Phalanges led by Pierre Jumayyil, the National Liberals led by Camille Chamoun, and the private militia of Sulaymān Faranjiyya, who acted both as a nominal president and as the Maronite leader of North Lebanon. Despite differences of personality and policy, these three groups and their leaders functioned in comparative harmony.

A. *The Phalanges* On the Christian side, the Phalangist movement played a major role in developments which led to the crisis, and in its conduct. Since the 1930s, the movement had sought to protect the Lebanese entity against its various challengers. During that period it underwent a number of changes, turning from a militant youth movement into a civilian party. The Phalanges adopted a more moderate outlook on social and political issues, and supported moderate reforms that might have reduced tensions between Christians and Muslims, and lessened other social conflicts in Lebanon. But at no stage were the Phalanges willing to surrender Christian supremacy in the Lebanese state; nor did they fully relinquish the proclivities of a militant movement.

After the failure of the Lebanese army to curb the Palestinian organizations in the spring of 1973, the Phalanges began to store arms and prepare for a clash which soon appeared inevitable. Still, the party's moves were not dissociated from the immediate context of Lebanese domestic politics; they were also motivated by Jumayyil's Presidential ambitions as well as by the desire to play the leading role in government coalitions. The Phalangists, who acted as defenders of the traditional way of life in Beirut's Christian neighbourhoods, clashed violently with armed Palestinians in April 1975—thus triggering off the civil war. As the fighting expanded, mainly between a primarily Christian camp and a Muslim, Leftist and Palestinian coalition, the Phalangist militia bore the main burden of the fighting on the Christian side. They increased their membership, established training camps, and procured arms, including heavy weapons, Jumayyil's two sons—Bashīr and Amīn—served as their father's chief aides.

The Phalanges refused to regard the crisis as a Christian-Muslim conflict. In their view, it was a struggle between Christian and Muslim Lebanese on the one side and the extreme Left and the Palestinians on the other. During the late summer of 1975, the Phalanges' leadership appeared to have reached the conclusion that it was no longer possible to preserve Christian hegemony over all of Lebanon, and so shifted its strategy towards achieving a partition. The Christian sector (or state) was to be based on Mount Lebanon, the northern littoral and eastern Beirut. After the shift in Syria's position in the spring of 1976, the Phalanges played an important role in co-ordinating the efforts of the Christian forces with those of Syria. As a rule, the party supported Damascus' policy in Lebanon.

B. *The National Liberals* The National Liberals, headed by Camille Chamoun, were the second mainstay of the Christian camp. President during the 1958 civil war, Chamoun remained politically active. During the Shihāb period, he was boycotted by the political establishment of the day which felt that his conduct, before and during the civil war, had been unacceptable. Chamoun's arch-enemy was Kamāl Junblāt. Although their rivalry was ideological, its bitterness was heightened by their struggle for influence in the electoral area of the Shūf. Chamoun began a gradual political comeback after 1964, and acquired renewed support in primarily Maronite, but also in other Christian—and even Shī'ī—circles. While the Phalanges drew most of their support from the middle and lower classes, Chamoun's party represented the Christian establishment. Unlike the Phalanges, which advocated moderate reforms, the National Liberals retained a distinct conservative colouring.

Chamoun was in opposition during Charles Helou's presidency (1964–70). In 1968, together with Pierre Jumayyil and Raymond Eddé, he founded a "Tripartite bloc" to bolster the position of the Maronites against the pressures of Muslims, the Left and the Palestinians, and to co-ordinate the Maronite electoral campaigns. Despite Maronite gains in the 1968 elections, Chamoun had to satisfy himself with indirect representation in the government. But he and his party played a more central role under the administration of President Faranjiyya, who was elected in 1970. Chamoun returned to the cabinet in June 1975 when, after the outbreak of the crisis, Rashīd Karāmī formed his "communal balance government." As Minister of the Interior, Chamoun was Faranjiyya's right-hand man: appropriately, he established his headquarters at the Ba'abdā presidential palace. Chamoun also played an important role—as leader of his party and its militia—in the 1975–76 crisis. Like Jumayyil, he was aided by his two sons—Dori and Dany.

C. *President Faranjiyya* When elected President in 1970, Faranjiyya was regarded as a strong personality and a staunch defender of Lebanon's Christian character. His personality and image, together with comfortable domestic and external circumstances, enabled him to conduct a successful policy during his first two years in office. Its aim was to restabilize the institutions of government, restrain the Palestinian organizations, and restore public order. The weakening of his government coalition and the resurgence of Palestinian activity towards the end of 1972 began to change that favourable situation. After a serious political crisis in the spring of 1973, the President began to lose control. The latter part of Faranjiyya's term of office was marked by an accelerating deterioration in relations between the Lebanese system and the Palestinian organizations, and by the malfunctioning of the system itself. These developments culminated in the outbreak of the civil war in April 1975.

Faranjiyya nevertheless continued to display a resolute attitude; he remained attached to his conception of a Christian Lebanon, and showed a readiness to resort to unorthodox solutions. Like other Christian leaders during the crisis, Faranjiyya functioned in a dual capacity: as President (where his ability was very limited due to the system's collapse), and as leader of his own "Zughartā Liberation Army." This militia had been formed in 1969 and was led by the President's son, Tony, who had also served in parliament and the cabinet.

In early 1976, there were many among his rivals who accused President Faranjiyya of being responsible for the crisis and demanded his resignation. He refused, and the attempt by Lieut Khatīb's dissident army to depose him (see below) was aborted by Syrian troops. Faranjiyya remained in office until the end of his term in September 1976.

2. THE MARONITE ECCLESIASTICAL ESTABLISHMENT

The Maronite church's activity during the civil war was seriously affected by the dichotomy between the position of the Patriarch, Butrus Khuraysh, and that of Father Sharbal Qasīs, head of the Maronite Monastic Order and of the Lebanese Association of Monastries. In previous periods, Maronite Patriarchs played a cardinal role, openly or behind the scenes, in Lebanese politics. Khuraysh failed to achieve such political prominence; but when revealed, his opinions appeared moderate. These views brought him close to the moderate Maronite leader, Raymond Eddé. Qasīs, in contrast, believed in a purely "Lebanese Lebanon" and objected to its having "an Arab face." He spoke openly of the need to limit the number of Palestinians in the country. During the crisis, it was Qasīs rather than the Patriarch who represented the Church in such forums as "The Maronite Summit" and the "Lebanese Front." Qasīs supported the various Christian militias with money and arms. His rivals accused him of subverting the Patriarch's position and the unity of the Church, but Qasīs claimed total loyalty to the Patriarch.

3. CONFESSIONAL MARONITE GROUPS AND FORUMS

A number of Maronite groups emerged during the crisis, as follows.

A. *The Maronite League* An extremist organization led by Shākir Abū Sulaymān, an active supporter of Father Sharbal Qasīs. All members had to be Maronite, and they took part in active combat alongside other Christian militias.

B. *Guardians of the Cedar* An extremist Maronite militia which surfaced in July 1975, based on the Ashrafiyya quarter in Beirut. The Guardians' leaders voiced the most far-reaching denunciations of efforts to "Arabize Lebanon" and of the Palestinians' role in the country. Operationally, they co-operated with the other Christian militias.

C. *The Maronite Summit, the Kafūr Front and the Lebanese Front* The major Maronite leaders and militant clergymen met at the "Maronite Summit" at the time of—possibly in response to—the meeting of the "Muslim Summit" at the end of December 1975 (see below). The Maronite Summit was held at the presidential palace in order to draw up a common strategy. Faranjiyya himself did not participate, but his rivals accused him of doing so and of being a partisan rather than an all-Lebanese president. In the spring of 1976, the senior Maronite leaders met again at the "Kafūr Summit." In September 1976, the same leaders officially created "the Lebanese Front" and announced a formula for the joint command of all their militias.

4. MODERATE CHRISTIAN LEADERS

Other Maronite leaders, who did not share the positions of the three senior Maronite politicians, were not as well organized, and did not possess an independent power base. These leaders advocated considerable concessions to the Muslims in the redistribution of political power in Lebanon, and were opposed to the notion of partition which surfaced late in 1975.

Until the spring of 1976, the most prominent spokesman for this school of thought was Raymond Eddé, son of the former President Emīl Eddé and leader of the National bloc party. Eddé had been a strong opponent of the Shihāb administration. In 1968 he joined the Tripartite bloc, but had gradually drawn away from his two partners due to personal and ideological differences. The gap between them grew under Faranjiyya, and Eddé allied himself with such Muslim leaders as Rashīd Karāmī and Kamāl Junblāt. After the outbreak of the civil war, Eddé voiced moderate opinions and refrained from taking part in the fighting. He was particularly opposed to the idea of partition. After Syria's entry into Lebanon, Eddé emerged as an adamant critic of its presence and policy. In the summer of 1976 he formed the Front for National Unity, which initially attracted some moderate Muslim leaders, but failed to establish itself.

In the spring of 1976, Eddé was replaced by Ilyās Sarkīs as the prominent leader of the moderate Maronites. Sarkīs had been Shihāb's right-hand man, Governor of Lebanon's Central Bank and the Shihābī bloc's unsuccessful Presidential candidate in 1970. Following six years of marginal political existence, Sarkīs appeared in April 1976 as a candidate for the presidency. He was openly supported by Syria and easily defeated Raymond Eddé. The two shared a belief in the need for reforms and Christian concessions; but unlike Eddé, Sarkīs was willing to accept a Syrian hegemony in Lebanon and was, in fact, a willing Syrian collaborator.

5. THE CHRISTIAN LEADERSHIP OF THE ARMY

The Lebanese army was traditionally conceived as the ultimate guarantor of the Lebanese system. Led by Fu'ād Shihāb, the army refused to take part in the 1958 fighting, thus enabling Shihāb to appear as undisputed national arbiter. Between 1958-75, Christian supremacy in the army was eroded, though not obliterated. In 1975 the army's commander, General Ḥannā Sa'īd, and other Christian officers were among the tacit supporters of the *status quo*. Their strategy was to keep the army out of the fighting so as to be able to intervene effectively at a later stage. But the disintegration of the army completely aborted this strategy.

The Anti Status Quo Coalition (The Muslim-Leftist-Palestinian Camp)

This camp was a loose, heterogenous coalition composed of a large number of groups and individuals. The major share of its fighting was undertaken by the Palestinian organizations and by Muslim and Leftist militias. Among the Palestinians, the Rejectionists played a clear-cut role in the struggle (see essay, "The Palestine Liberation Organization"). The PLO's leadership refrained from any official intervention in the war until January 1976, though groups subordinate to it participated in the fighting, as did Palestinian groups under Syrian authority.

Part of the Muslim leadership was politically active in the crisis, but in the absence of fighting units it took no direct part in the war. In January 1976, the Muslim-Leftist-Palestinian camp was reinforced by Lieut Khatīb's Lebanon's Arab Army, composed of Muslim officers and soldiers who had seceded from Lebanon's disintegrating army. The LAA withered during the fighting, and by the end of 1976 was reduced to a small force in South Lebanon.

Within this broad coalition, the following categories can be distinguished: 1) older Leftist and opposition parties; 2) organizations and militias that were formed on the eve of and during the crisis; 3) traditional *Zu'amā* and the Sunnī community's establishment; 4) the militant leadership of the Shī'ī community; and 5) Palestinian organizations, which were in turn subdivided into Rejectionist organizations, the PLO establishment and pro-Syrian groups.

This loose coalition began to disintegrate following divergent reactions to Syria's massive intervention in Lebanon. At one point, serious differences of opinion seemed to develop between the PLO and Kamāl Junblāt. During the summer of 1976, a number of groups and individuals drifted away from the Left to form a central bloc which sought an accommodation with Syria.

1. OLDER LEFTIST AND OPPOSITION PARTIES

These included Kamāl Junblāt's Progressive Socialist Party, the two Ba'th parties, the Communists, the Najjāda and the Syrian nationalists.

A. *Kamāl Junblāt and his party* The cardinal role in this group, and indeed much beyond it, was played by Kamāl Junblāt and his Progressive Socialist Party (PSP). Despite the existence of a party organization and party ideology, Junblāt's influence derived from other sources: support by the bulk of the Druze community; his power position as a Za'īm in the Shūf area; his personality and standing as a Leftist leader in Lebanese and regional terms; and his international contacts.

Junblāt had been a major figure in Lebanese politics since the early 1950s. His dynamic personality and frequent changes of position tended to disguise a fundamental consistency of purpose which underlay his career until his assassination in March 1977. His main goals can be defined as a fundamental reform of Lebanon's political institutions, the promotion of his own influence, and the advancement of the Left's position in the country. In 1969 he founded the National Front as a framework for Leftist and Palestinian organizations in Lebanon. As Minister of the Interior in 1970, he legalized the formerly prohibited opposition parties. The process which drew him closer to radical and Palestinian groups—and away from the Maronite leadership—continued during the first half of the 1970s.

Junblāt's plan of reform was formulated in a document which the National Front published in the summer of 1975. His major demands were: (a) abolition of the confessional system; (b) amendment of the constitution that would alter relations between the branches of government; (c) amendment of the electoral law; (d) reorganization of the army; (e) amendment of the citizenship law. These demands served as a platform of the Lebanese Left during the civil war. But they were strongly rejected by the Christian leadership, which viewed them as tantamount to a transformation of the Lebanese system. They also suspected that the plan of reform was in reality meant to pave the way for Junblāt's candidacy for the Presidency.

Syria's effort to impose its own plan in February 1976 led to a conflict with Junblāt who opposed the proposed Syrian reforms as too moderate, resented the perpetuation of the confessional system, and apparently also realized the full significance of Syrian hegemony in Lebanon. The conflict grew in intensity as Junblāt demanded more fundamental reforms and escalated the fighting in an effort to force the Syrians' hand.

Junblāt and the PSP had a small militia which participated in the fighting, particularly in Mount Lebanon. But Junblāt's military contribution was marginal, and the main brunt of the fighting in his camp was borne by the Palestinian organizations and the Muslim militias.

B. *The Communist Party* The Communist Party has existed in Lebanon since the late 1920s, the country's communal structure and the existence of an intelligentsia providing it with a permanent basis. Its control of some trade unions broadened this base. But the party never succeeded in extending beyond these defined limits, and its standing was affected by a split into pro-Soviet and pro-Chinese factions. In the late 1960s, the party changed its political strategy: it decided to become a Lebanese "mass party" and to pursue a "popular front" policy. It drew closer to, and co-operated with, Palestinian and Nasserite organizations, the two Ba'th parties and Junblāt's PSP. In recent years, the party has made important inroads into the Shī'ī community. It also formed a militia, the Popular Guard, which fought in the civil war.

C. *The Ba'th Party* The Lebanese Ba'th split into pro-Syrian and pro-Iraqi parties headed by 'Isām Qansū and 'Abd al-Majīd al-Rāfi't respectively. Each party was supported by its patron and, as a rule, reflected the point of view either of Damascus or Baghdad. Until January 1976, both parties supported the same side in the civil war; but controversial decisions over the conduct of the war generated bickering within each. Following Syria's overt intervention, the pro-Syrian Ba'th, having failed to mediate between Syria and Junblāt, drew away from the Lebanese Left. The pro-Iraqi Ba'th, by contrast, increased its activity, directing it primarily against Syria.

D. *The Communist Labour Organization* This organization is a radical Leftist group, led by Muhsin Ibrāhīm, which seceded from the Arab Nationalist Movement in 1968. Although Muḥsin Ibrāhīm claimed that his organization had no militia of its own, it did take an active part in the fighting.

E. *The Najjāda* The Najjāda, a primarily Muslim-Sunnī party, was founded in the 1930s as a semi-military organization. It never reached the size or political eminence of its original counterpart, the Phalanges. A persistent critic of the Lebanese system, the Najjāda leader, 'Adnān al-Ḥakīm, stood for the presidency in the Chamber of Deputies (CD) in 1970 and received one vote—his own. The Najjāda has a rather conservative social orientation and did not participate actively in the fighting. Following Syria's intervention, it moved to the centre.

F. *The Syrian Social Nationalist Party* The SSNP (or PPS in the French acronym) was founded in the early 1930s by Antūn Sa'āda who preached the formation of a Greater Syria, to embody the notion of a Syrian-territorial-secular nationalism. The party was then inimical to both Arab and Lebanese nationalism, its structure and ideology influenced by the Fascist movements of the 1930s. The party has since undergone a number of transformations. In the early 1970s it turned Leftward, renewing its opposition to the *status quo* in Lebanon and establishing contact with other opposition groups. It divided into two major factions: one led by In'ām Ra'd and the other by George 'Abd al-Masīḥ.

With the outbreak of the civil war, the party played a limited role in the fighting on the anti-establishment side. This activity tied in well with the party's new orientation, suited the historic rivalry with the Phalanges and, in part, reflected an identification with the Syrian regime of Ḥāfiz al-Asad, who appeared to some party members as a leader capable of implementing the Greater Syrian vision. Following Syria's intervention in the war, the party faction led by In'ām Ra'd endorsed its policy, while George 'Abd al-Masīḥ and his followers continued to support the Lebanese Left.

2. GROUPS AND MILITIAS ORGANIZED ON THE EVE OF AND DURING THE CRISIS

Most of the fighting by Lebanese (as distinct from Palestinian) groups in the civil war was waged by a series of organizations which were formed during the early 1970s and became the major organs of extra-parliamentary opposition. Except for one organization—the Movement of October 24th—all these groups defined themselves as Nasserite. In the context of the post-Nasser era, this meant identification with the fundamental principles of the original Nasserite movement (Arab unity, social progress and a strengthening of the Arab world's position *vis-à-vis* the West).

They were supported by those forces which viewed themselves as upholders of the Nasserite legacy—primarily Libya. The major Nasserite organizations were as follows.

A. *The Independent Nasserites* headed by Ibrāhīm Qulīlāt This group was composed mainly of strong younger armed Muslims who tended to view and present themselves as a progressive social movement which supported the Palestinians and were strongly opposed to the idea of partitioning Lebanon. The organization's militia, *al-Murābitūn*, was a major fighting force on the anti-establishment side, primarily active in Beirut, where it fought against the Phalanges. According to Qulīlāt, the *Murābitūn* began their activity in secret in the early 1970s. His organization stood in opposition to Syria's volte-face in 1976.

B. *The Nasserite Organization—Union of the Toiling People's Forces* This was the only Nasserite organization to be represented in parliament. One of its two leaders, Najjāḥ Wākīm, was elected to the CD in 1972. Of all the Nasserite groups, his was the closest to Syria. The organization's militia, *Firqat al-Nasr* (Victory's Division) participated in the fighting in the Beirut area. But in the confusion brought about by Syria's change of policy, it ceased to fight, giving Syria full political but no military support. Its second senior leader, Kamāl Shātīlā, tried in vain to mediate between the Syrians and Kamāl Junblāt.

C. *The Nasserite Organization—The Correctionist Movement* This group, headed by 'Isām 'Arab, seceded from the Union of the Toiling People's Forces due to personal quarrels. Its militia, *Quwwāt Nāsir* (the Forces of Nasser), participated in the fighting.

D. *The Popular Nasserite Organization* This was a local group in Saida of limited military and political significance. It was headed by Mustafā Sa'd son of Ma'rūf Sa'd, a CD member who had been killed in the Saida incidents on the eve of the civil war.

E. *The Movement of October 24th* This was a local organization which crystallized in Tripoli during the 1969 clashes between the Lebanese authorities and the Palestinians. Its membership was drawn mostly from the strong armed Sunnī youth of Tripoli. It adopted a Leftist ideology, supported Palestinian demands, and voiced strong criticism of the Lebanese political system. It participated in the fighting between Tripoli's Muslims and Zughartā's Christians, and later opposed Syria's growing involvement in Lebanon.

3. TRADITIONALL ZU'AMĀ AND THE RELIGIOUS ESTABLISHMENT OF THE SUNNĪ COMMUNITY

The Lebanese civil war presented the traditional political leaders of the Sunnī community with a difficult dilemma. These leaders—headed by Sā'ib Salām and Rashīd Karāmī—had come to recognize the community of interests they shared with the Christian establishment (although friction between them and the Maronite leaders had increased in the late 1960s and early 1970s). The Sunnī leaders aspired for greater authority and had to take into account the pressures of more radical elements inside the Sunnī community. Nevertheless, they regarded the demands raised by the National Front as far-fetched, fearing that they would precipitate a grave crisis. The actual outbreak of the crisis aggravated their dilemma. The polarization of Christian-Muslim relations and the distinct confessional nature of the crisis increased the pressure on leaders like Karāmī and Salām to place themselves squarely in the Muslim-Leftist-Palestinian camp. Yet this course of events also underscored their feeling that the radical leaders of that camp were growing in strength at their own expense.

The traditional leaders took no part in the fighting and tried to exercise their influence to promote a compromise settlement. As a matter of fact, they did not possess any militias or other semi-military forces, though Salām had once announced the formation of a (conservative) Muslim militia designed to protect West Beirut. The social groups, which in earlier years had provided the armed supporters of the traditional leaders, were now under the influence of the new militias. Karāmī continued to serve as a nominal Prime Minister throughout the crisis.

The Sunnī religious leadership chose a position between those of the traditional and radical leaders. The Mufti, Ḥasan Khālid, endorsed the reform plan presented by the National Front. He saw no point in withdrawing the demands of the Muslim communities merely because they were also raised by the Leftists. The Mufti's most notable political act was to convene an "Islamic Summit" at his residence in December 1975. The meeting was attended by Muslim religious dignitaries (the Shī'ī Imām and Druze Shaykh), moderate Sunnī political leaders (Salām, Yāfī and Karāmī) and Yāsir 'Arafāt. Resolutions were adopted against the partition of Lebanon and the army's involvement in the fighting. In his 20 July 1976 speech, President Asad of Syria mentioned that the participants of that summit had called him on the telephone to ask for Syria's intervention in the civil war.

The traditional Zu'amā drifted gradually in 1976 towards the middle of the road, as Syria changed its policy and the radicals became entrenched in their positions.

4. THE MILITANT SHĪ'Ī LEADERSHIP

The gradual build-up of the militant leadership of the Shī'ī community under Imām Mūsā al-Sadr, in association with Syria's policy and in co-operation with other opposition elements, had contributed to the weakening of the Lebanese political system in the early 1970s (see above). In 1974, Sadr formed the "Movement of the Dispossessed" to combat injustice and the confessional system in Lebanon. In the summer of 1975 the military arm of the movement, called "The Battalions of Lebanese Resistance" or "Hope", began to play a marginal role in the fighting, although Sadr and his associates denied that the organization, as such, was involved. In contrast to his limited military role, Sadr remained politically active and visited a number of Arab states as a mediator.

Feeling threatened by the Imām's activity, the traditional political leadership of the Shī'ī community opted for a different policy. These leaders—primarily Kāmil al-As'ad but also Sabrī Ḥamāda, 'Ādil 'Usayrān and Kazīm al-Khalīl—tried to bring about a compromise and settlement. Even so, they were unable to regain the ground lost to Sadr. When Syria increased its involvement in Lebanon and as its dispute with Junblāt grew in acrimony, Sadr was one of those who tried to mediate. When these efforts failed, he chose to support Syria's policy, but took no part in the fighting.

5. THE PALESTINIAN ORGANIZATIONS

Among the Palestinian organizations, three major attitudes toward the civil war could be distinguished, as follows.

A. *The PLO Establishment* The leadership of the Fatḥ and to some extent the Democratic Front strove to keep out of the fighting in Lebanon until January 1976. The PLO was engaged in a political campaign which had already resulted in a number of achievements in the autumn of 1975, and its leaders were expecting additional gains at the Security Council in January 1976. Overt intervention by the PLO in the Lebanese civil war could affect these achievements, as well as its more basic goals in Lebanon. From the PLO's point of view the situation which obtained until the outbreak of the civil war was the most convenient it could hope for. It saw Lebanon as its last autonomous base in the Arab world. The Lebanese government was too weak to curtail the PLO's freedom of political and military activity while the country's pro-Western position limited Israel's ability to act against the Palestinians in Lebanon.

However, as the power of Muslims and Leftists increased during the crisis, the PLO leaders began to seek to improve their own position in Lebanon, beyond the terms established by the Cairo Agreement of 1969.

Until the end of 1975, the PLO's formal and well-publicized policy was to refrain from taking part in the fighting. It emphasized that it was not a party to the conflict, and even proposed to mediate between the warring camps. The Palestinian leaders were anxious to prevent the Lebanese army or external powers from intervening in the war. Actually, though, groups belonging to the PLO participated in the fighting in various parts of the country. The PLO leadership made a number of efforts to mediate between the Syrians and Kamāl Junblāt. Two separate agreements concluded in Damascus between Syria and the PLO were also interpreted as an attempt by some of the Palestinian groups to reach a separate agreement with Syria without the Lebanese Left. But these agreements were not implemented, and the PLO remained in active conflict with Syria until October 1976.

B. *The Rejectionist Organizations* These viewed the Lebanese civil war as a conspiracy designed to liquidate them. Consequently they played an active role in the fighting alongside the Leftist organizations, whom they considered their only firm and reliable allies. This policy was also in line with their broader interpretation of the Middle East conflict, according to which social revolution in the Arab world was a pre-condition for success in the struggle against Israel. Without such a revolution, there could be no complete mobilization of all Arab resources for that struggle.

C. *Al-Sā'iqa* This pro-Syrian organization reflected Syria's policy toward the crisis.

THE EVOLUTION OF SYRIAN POLICY, APRIL 1975 OCTOBER 1976

Until January 1976, Syria's policy in the Lebanese civil war was to promote its traditional clients, but at the same time to prevent either a deterioration or overt Syrian participation, and thus avoid a showdown with the US and Israel. At that time, when the Christians were on the verge of partitioning the country, Syria finally decided to dispatch Palestinian units of its regular army to Lebanon. This unopposed measure gave Syria predominance in Lebanon, from which it sought to impose a solution. A successful bid would have stabilized the situation (in comparative terms) under Syrian hegemony, and would have served another Syrian policy aim: to demonstrate (primarily to the US) that Syria even more than Egypt could implement regional policies and be a stabilizing factor. (For the broader context of Syria's policy in Lebanon, see the chapter on Syria.)

These aims were defeated by a combination of local and regional factors which, for a variety of reasons, refused to accept the Syrian settlement.

1. Part of the Leftist and Muslim militias who regarded it as far too moderate.
2. The PLO which came to regard Syrian hegemony in Lebanon as a serious threat to its own autonomy in its last independent base.

3. Syria's rivals in the Arab world—Egypt, Iraq, Libya—which opposed any aggrandizement of Syria's position and objected to its policy in Lebanon.

The result was a resumption of the fighting in the spring of 1976, with the Christians already in an inferior position, and Syria extremely reluctant to intervene on their behalf. Such action would have been a reversal of policy, run contrary to the image which the Ba'th regime sought to project, and raised the very sensitive issue of sectarian politics. But in the event, these considerations were overruled by others:

1. Failure to intervene would have meant defeat of the original purposes of the Syrian invasion.
2. A Christian defeat would have led to the establishment of a radical state on Syria's borders, possibly under the influence of the rival Iraqi Ba'th regime. This could affect both Syria's domestic politics and its foreign policy.
3. Failure to impose its authority would have led to a loss of influence over the PLO and the Palestinian issue which greatly concerned the Syrian regime.

Syria thus decided to intervene, and found itself supporting the Christians and actually fighting some of its former allies. In time, actual operational failures, coupled with Arab and domestic criticism of this policy, led the Syrian government to terminate its active participation in the fighting. However, this half-hearted intervention was sufficient to put the Christians on the offensive, though not sufficient to enable them to decide the issue.

As mentioned above, Syria terminated the stalemate which prevailed in the summer of 1976 by launching a successful second military offensive in October. But Damascus did not pursue its initial easy success, rather choosing to use it as a bargaining asset at the Riyadh conference. Several considerations explain this decision:

1. Syria's policy in Lebanon did not seek to rely exclusively on the Christians and diminish their opponents. It was preferable for Syria to be an arbiter between weakened Lebanese factions.
2. The direction of Syrian policy in Lebanon encountered strong criticism in Syria itself. A violent suppression of Muslim and Leftist elements was likely to increase this criticism.
3. Saudi Arabia exercised pressure on the Syrian government to change its policy in Lebanon. The Saudis were also dissatisfied with the direction of that policy, and were urging the need to mend fences in the Arab world, in anticipation of the American presidential elections (see survey of Inter-Arab Relations).
4. There was a good prospect of Syria achieving much of what it wanted in a political settlement.

THE RIYADH AND CAIRO SUMMIT CONFERENCES AND THEIR AFTERMATH

Two Arab summit conferences were convened in October 1976 to deal with the Lebanese crisis: a preparatory conference attended by six states in Riyadh (16–18 October 1976); and a plenary Arab summit conference held in Cairo (25–26 October). (For the conferences themselves, see essay on Inter-Arab Relations.)

The consequences for Lebanon of these conferences were threefold. First the full-fledged, violent fighting ceased, although the underlying problems which had led to the war remained unresolved and were even exacerbated. The struggle was diverted into other, less violent, channels. Second, Syria's hegemony in Lebanon was institutionalized and legitimized by an Arab consensus. The presence of the Syrian army in Lebanon was accepted under the title of "Arab Deterrent Force" (ADF). Third, the institutions, instruments and procedures established by the two summit conferences provided the framework within which the Lebanese conflict could be contained.[1]

1. THE TRANSITION FROM FIGHTING TO CEASEFIRE

At the Riyadh conference, a ceasefire was decided upon and an optimistic timetable set for the withdrawal of armed persons and the collection of heavy weapons from the belligerents. In order to impose and supervise the ceasefire, the conference decided to turn the Inter-Arab Peace Force in Lebanon into a 30,000-man ADF composed mainly of Syrian forces, but nominally under the supreme command of the Lebanese president. Fighting ended within a month—except in the South (see below), as the ADF was deployed over most of Lebanese territory. The ceasefire held up well except for sporadic and limited incidents.

The task of collecting the belligerents' heavy weapons encountered much graver problems. While both sides agreed in principle to the transfer, each insisted that the other should be the first to proceed. However, in January 1977 (a month later than the time originally set), the ADF headquarters announced the completion of the collection of heavy weapons, and the departure of all regular Palestinian forces which had arrived in Lebanon during the fighting. In fact, this announcement was misleading: the parties had handed in only a small proportion of their heavy weapons and hid the rest—the Syrian press itself admitted as much; nor did all the regular Palestinian units leave the country.

2. SYRIAN DOMINATION OF THE ARAB DETERRENT FORCE

Syria's dominant military presence in Lebanon had been given a stamp of approval by the Riyadh and Cairo conferences. There were at the time over 22,000 Syrian soldiers in Lebanon—as against c. 5,000 soldiers from Libya, Sudan, Saudi Arabia and the Persian Gulf states, dispatched after the Arab Foreign Ministers' decision in June 1976 to send an Arab Peace Force to Lebanon. During November and December 1976, Syria sent fresh troops into Lebanon, which were joined by token units from Saudi Arabia, Sudan and the Persian Gulf states. At the same time, Libya recalled its contingent. In January 1977, the ADF numbered 30,000 soldiers—27,000 of them Syrian. Damascus was given a further bonus when the Cairo summit decided to establish a fund to finance the maintenance of the force for six months, with a possible extension.

Only a few voices in Lebanon were raised in protest against the institutionalization of the Syrian military presence. The most forceful opponent of this development was the Maronite politician Raymond Eddé, who stated publicly that the Syrian army, itself a participant in the war, could not function as peacekeeper. He also accused Syria of aiming to dominate Lebanon, politically and militarily. Kamāl Junblāt, Eddé's political ally, was not as vehement in his protest. At the time, there were manifestations of Syrian-Christian tension, as well as rumours of Syrian-Leftist and Syrian-Palestinian *rapprochement*. Yet by and large, the Christian leadership did not come out against the Syrian military presence. What they, and particularly Camille Chamoun, did take exception to was Syria's entry into areas held by themselves, especially East Beirut. Moderate Muslim leaders, headed by Rashīd Karāmī, were sympathetic to the presence of an inter-Arab force in Lebanon; but they thought it should be under the authority of the cabinet rather than the president. Ilyās Sarkīs himself stated that the inter-Arab force was acting temporarily in lieu of the Lebanese army, which had disintegrated during the fighting. He added: "The decision to end the mission of the inter-Arab force will be historic, since it would mean that we will have regained our power."[2]

The original mandate of the ADF expired in March 1977, but was extended twice—in March and September 1977—at the request of President Sarkīs, who explained that the task of re-establishing the Lebanese army had encountered serious difficulties.

3. THE ISSUE OF THE PALESTINIAN PRESENCE IN LEBANON

The prominence given to this issue in the discussions and resolutions of the Riyadh conference reflected the tacit awareness that the Palestinian presence in Lebanon was one of the underlying problems which had precipitated the civil war. The PLO, once again recognized as representing the "Palestinian resistance", stressed its respect for Lebanon's sovereignty and undertook not to intervene in its domestic affairs. "The legitimate authority in Lebanon"—as represented by President Sarkīs—undertook, in turn, to respect the PLO's presence and activity in Lebanon's territory within the framework of the 1969 Cairo Agreement and its appendices. To guarantee the application of the Cairo Agreement, the Riyadh conference adopted two resolutions. First, to form a committee composed of the representatives of Saudi Arabia, Egypt, Syria and Kuwait to co-ordinate with the Lebanese president the implementation of the Cairo Agreement and its appendices within 45 days after the formation of the ADF. Second, to delegate the actual enforcement of the agreement to that force. (For the efforts to implement the Cairo Agreement, see below.)

THE RESTORATION OF STATE AUTHORITY AND GOVERNMENT ADMINISTRATION

During the last two months of 1976 and throughout 1977, various efforts were made to restore the authority of the central Lebanese government, to reconstitute the institutions of the state and its administration, and to normalize the daily life of the people. Of cardinal importance was the formation of a new cabinet which, together with the other institutions of the Sarkīs Administration, was seen by Syria as an instrument for exercising and maintaining its influence in Lebanon.

1. FORMATION OF A NEW CABINET

Rashīd Karāmī's cabinet had been in office since June 1975, but did not function at all throughout the civil war. As was customary, Karāmī handed in his resignation when the new president began his term of office (September 1976); but Sarkīs preferred to postpone the formation of a new cabinet until order had been restored. Karāmī thus remained in office until December 1976, when Sarkīs charged Salīm al-Ḥuss, his confidant and economic adviser, with the task of forming the new cabinet. Ḥuss chose a team of technocrats (see Table 1). None of them belonged to traditional political families, and only one had any significant political experience.

The new government won a vote of confidence on 24 December and was granted emergency powers for a period of six months, which allowed it to rule by decree without parliamentary approval in certain areas. In June 1977, these powers were extended by the Chamber of Deputies for another five months. The Ḥuss government performed smoothly. It met regularly, adopted resolutions and enacted decrees to implement them. But its critics charged that, in reality, it was nothing more than a rubber stamp for the policy of Sarkīs and Syria. In support of this criticism, they pointed to the reorganization of the Lebanese army, and to the imposition of press censorship.

2. THE REORGANIZATION OF THE ARMY

A reorganized Lebanese army was to be one of the cornerstones of the reconstituted Lebanese state. But two major difficulties stood in the way. First, there was the extent to which the authority of the army had disintegrated. Second, there were the conflicting interests of Syria and the various Lebanese factions, each seeking to staff key army posts with their own supporters.

The bulk of the Lebanese army—officers and soldiers alike—had simply deserted

Table 1
The Lebanese Cabinet (formed on 9 December 1976)

Portfolio	Name	Community	Profession
PM; Economy and Trade; Industry and Oil; Information	Salīm al-Ḥuss	Sunnī	Banker
Deputy PM; Defence; Foreign Affairs	Fu'ād Butrus	Greek Orthodox	Politician[1]
Interior, Housing and Co-operatives	Salāḥ Salmān	Druze	Physician
Public Health; Hydroelectric Resources	Ibrahīm Shī'ītū	Shī'ī	Physician Ex-deputy[2]
Tourism; Public Works and Transport	Amīn al-Bizrī	Sunnī	Engineer
Planning	Michel Dawmit	Maronite	Businessman
Labour and Social Affairs; Education; Agriculture	As'ad Rizq	Greek Catholic	Surgeon
Justice; Finance; Post, Telephone and Telegraph	Farīd Rafa'īl	Maronite	Banker

[1] Butrus had served several times as CD and cabinet member; he was a member of the Shihābī bloc (*nahj*). In 1968, with the decline of the Shihābī bloc, he failed to be re-elected.
[2] Shi'ītū was elected to the CD in 1968, in South Lebanon and was considered a pro-Shihābī.

to their homes and did not participate in the war. The remainder had broken up into a number of armies, as follows.

1) The GHQ army consisted of a small number of officers and soldiers, mostly Christians, who remained under the authority of the army's commander, Brig-Gen (*'amīd*) Ḥannā Sa'īd. They did not take an active part in the fighting, though Sa'īd's sympathies were clearly on the side of the Christians.

2) Lebanon's Arab Army, a breakaway element of the Lebanese army, headed by Lieut (*mulāzim awal*) Ahmad al-Khatīb. Since January 1976, it had fought on the side of the Leftists and the Palestinians, and had taken an anti-Syrian position.

3) The Vanguards of Lebanon's Arab Army was a small pro-Syrian force headed by Lt-Col (*muqaddam*) Fahīm al-Ḥājj. It was organized in May 1976 in preparation for Syria's massive invasion of Lebanon.

4) Lebanon's Army, commanded by Major (*rā'id*) Fu'ād Mālik, fought on the Christian side and was particularly close to Chamoun's National Liberals.

In January 1977, Syria and President Sarkīs began the reorganizing process. Syrian units took over the barracks in West Beirut that were held by Khatīb's men. Khatīb himself was taken to Damascus and placed under house arrest. In February, the government issued a decree ordering all army officers to tender their resignations within three months, which the government was authorized to accept or reject. (The date was later extended to the end of 1977.) In March, the army's commander, Ḥannā Sa'īd—who was known to be close to Chamoun—was replaced by the pro-Syrian Brig-Gen Victor Khurī. Later, the head of the army's *Deuxième Bureau*, Brig-Gen Jūll Bustānī, was replaced by another pro-Syrian officer, Major Jūnī 'Abdu. Sa'īd's removal brought about a protest strike in Beirut's Christian areas.

The reconstitution of the Lebanese army was closely linked to other issues, such as the implementation of the Cairo Agreement and the settlement of the problem of the South. One proposed solution envisaged the dispatching of the Lebanese army to police South Lebanon, but by the end of September 1977, very few units had been established. The one significant force formed by that time was the Biqāʻ Command, consisting of c. 3,000 soldiers, led by Brig Khūrī's brother and stationed in the Biqāʻ and North Lebanon. Most of the members of this force were formerly in the pro-Syrian Vanguards of Lebanon's Arab Army.

3. IMPOSITION OF PRESS CENSORSHIP

The first measure passed by the Ḥuss government in January 1977—and clearly influenced by Syria—was a decree imposing censorship of the press and radio. In December 1976, Syrian soldiers had already taken control of those papers supporting the Leftists, Iraq or Libya, as well as pro-Christian newspapers which had protested against Syria's infringement of Lebanon's traditional press freedom. After the censorship decree, the Syrian soldiers evacuated the editorial offices they had occupied.

Several prominent Lebanese publishers, editors and journalists reacted to this censorship by leaving the country. Ghassan Tuwaynī moved to Paris, where in addition to the Beirut edition of *al-Nahār*, he published an uncensored version of the same newspaper, and an English language bulletin. The pro-Iraqi *al-Dustūr* also reopened in Paris. Other newspapers moved to London.

4. ECONOMIC RECONSTRUCTION

The civil war devastated Lebanon's economy. Although statistics are scarce and mostly unreliable, Ḥuss confirmed the figure of $12 bn worth of war damage (see table). Reconstruction proceeded very slowly, with Lebanon having to rely on pledges of Arab financial aid: but only small sums were transferred during 1977. Saudi Arabia granted only LL 55m and Kuwait LL 30m. But the Saudis—and probably others—made it clear that they were waiting for signs of a return to stability. Speaking of the situation in South Lebanon, the Saudi ambassador in Beirut suggested that his government was using the promise of aid as a means of exerting pressure on Lebanon.

THE CONTINUED POLITICAL STRUGGLE

Although the two chief coalition protagonists of the civil war terminated their violent conflict after the Riyadh and Cairo conferences, the gap between their respective positions was not bridged, and their struggle continued along political channels throughout 1977. They disagreed over such issues as Lebanon's political future, the Palestinian presence, and the problem of the South.

The pro *status quo* coalition called itself "The Lebanese Front", while the anti *status quo* groups continued to use the name "National Movement." A third and intermediate force has been termed "the Central Camp."

1. THE LEBANESE FRONT

The Phalanges, the National Liberals and their militias formed the central core of this Front. Relations between them were usually harmonious, except when Camille Chamoun and his National Liberals took hard-line positions, and Pierre Jumayyil and the Phalanges sought to play a moderating role. The Front regarded the Palestinian presence as the main obstacle to restoring sovereignty and normal life. In their view a political dialogue could not be seriously undertaken until the Cairo Agreement was strictly implemented.

The Front's leaders met in January 1977 in Sayyidat al-Bir Monastery, near Barumānā, to discuss a new formula for religious, social and economic coexistence among the Lebanese communities. The communiqué published at the end of the conference came to serve as the Front's unofficial platform. It included a decision to act "to safeguard and preserve Lebanon and to be committed to its honour and dignity, in order to defend the rights of this homeland and its people by all internal and external means to be decided upon." The communiqué added that one of the Front's aims was to "liberate all the occupied Lebanese territory and to try to distribute the Palestinians residing in Lebanon among the member-states of the Arab League, each according to its absorption capacity."[3] The Front also announced that the conference had passed several secret resolutions which could not yet be made public.

The language of the communiqué indicated that what the Front had in mind was a wide-embracing autonomy, in which each cultural community could look after its own affairs, especially those pertaining to freedom and culture, education, economy, security and social justice. Each could also regulate its cultural and spiritual ties with the outside world, according to its own choice. Moreover, the national economy should be established "on modern and just bases."[4] The conference's political discussions ranged widely too—from decentralization and cantonization, to a loose federation of two virtually autonomous states (*wilāyā*).[5]

2. THE NATIONAL MOVEMENT

The power of the anti-establishment coalition—the Palestinian organizations, the Muslim militias and the Left headed by Kamāl Junblāt—had been weakened by the war and the clashes with Syria. The militias had virtually disintegrated, and the Lebanese Left suffered a critical blow with Junblāt's assassination. But there were signs that Junblāt, too, had moderated his position before his death, and that he and his allies were trying to come to terms with Syria. Nevertheless, critics of Syria's policy in Lebanon (mainly Raymond Eddé, who was by that time living in Paris) pointed the finger at Syria, which they claimed had a clear interest in removing Junblāt from the scene. In an ironic twist, Junblāt—who had been a revolutionary and innovative leader—was succeeded as head of the Druze community, the Social Progressive Party and the Lebanese Left (in the traditional Lebanese way) by his son, Walīd. His assumption of power had a moderating effect on the National Movement, particularly on its attitude to Syria.

In July 1977, the National Movement published its views in "A Political Programme for a Settlement of the Lebanese Crisis." Typical of the divided state in which the Lebanese Left found itself in 1977 and of the circumstances under which it had to operate, two versions of the programme appeared. The more moderate one was published by the pro-Leftist *al-Safīr* (which appears in Lebanon and is thus subject to censorship); the much more radical version by the Iraqi News Agency.[6]

The authors of the programme expressed their "constant willingness to accept a political compromise, putting an end to the fighting." While claiming that this willingness was unconditional, a number of qualifications were nevertheless set, which in the past had been unacceptable to the rival camp and, in part, to Syria. Thus, no explicit demand was presented for the abolition of confessionalism. Instead, the platform called for a consolidation of Lebanon's Arabism, or the restoration of Lebanon's political and administrative unity. Such unity was also to include a "rebuilt, patriotic and balanced army." The platform also called for an improvement of Lebanese-Palestinian relations, including "a recognition of the Palestinian Resistance's right to operate and act on the Lebanese scene," and opposed a "diminishing of the Palestinian presence in Lebanon." The more radical version of the programme included a denunciation of the "Lebanese Right", which it accused of seeking to "partition Lebanon in collusion with Israel, and of exercising pressure on the Arab [Syrian] forces in order to induce them to liquidate the Palestinian existence and perpetuate itself as the sole spokesman for the Lebanese."

3. THE CENTRAL CAMP

The Central Camp remained a loose collection of moderate and pro-Syrian parties, personalities and forces in 1977. It included such Sunnī *zu'ama* (traditional leaders) as Rashīd Karāmī, who coalesced to form an Islamic Alignment; religious leaders of the Muslim communities; Nasserites of the Kamāl Shātila faction; and the pro-Syrian Ba'th which had seceded from the National Front in 1976. These diverse elements were united in their support for a national dialogue, for President Sarkīs and for Syria's policy in Lebanon. Indeed, the Central Camp was to be the core of a "Broad National Front" which Syria wished to see established as the local political base for its own policies and those of Sarkīs.

However, Syria and the President's attention had to be diverted to more immediate issues, such as the problem of the South and relations with the Palestinian organizations. There were also disagreements over whether such a Front should be extended to include Left and Right-wing elements. Consequently, the "Broad Front" remained a theoretical objective. Politicians who adhered to the Central Camp limited themselves to frequent visits to Damascus, to regular meetings with Sarkīs, and to making pronouncements on such topical issues as the problem of the South, the Cairo Agreement and Lebanon's political future.

The National Front was formally established on 13 September 1977 after a visit to Damascus by Walīd Junblāt. It embraced only the Progressive Socialist Party (PSP) and the Lebanese branch of the Ba'th Socialist Party. The Front came in for strong criticism from the Communists and the Nasserites, who described it as a "sell-out" to the Syrians.

RELATIONS WITH SYRIA

During 1977, Syria continued to implement the Lebanese policy which it had formulated at the time of the Riyadh conference. This policy had two objectives. In the first place, Syria sought to avoid the use of force and to discourage manifestations of open opposition to its policies in Lebanon and in the Arab world. Secondly, it sought to consolidate, institutionalize and perpetuate its influence in Lebanon by relying on the presence of its troops; by direct occupation of eastern and northern Lebanon; by ensuring the co-operation of President Sarkīs and by gradually expanding central administration; and by encouraging co-operation among other local political forces. Although this policy was never made explicit, statements by Syrian spokesmen reflected Syria's assumption of responsibility for Lebanon's affairs and its legitimate authority for their conduct. Thus, Radio Damascus announced that "Syria acts with those loyal to Lebanon and will not hesitate to take measures in order to decide the situation and ensure the progress of peace and security."[7]

The Sarkīs Administration seemed to accept its dependence on Syria. Sarkīs himself and a number of his senior officials paid frequent visits to Damascus. Less frequent, but equally significant, were the Syrian functionaries' visits to Beirut to co-ordinate policies. Such efforts were officially approved in a joint statement issued in Damascus by Presidents Sarkīs and Asad which "confirmed the importance of co-ordination between the two countries in everything related to their interests"; and "entrusted their assistants to formulate a joint working plan, inspired by the need for co-ordination between the two countries."[8]

By and large, the Lebanese government did not disavow Syria's policy on any major issue, such as the problem of the South and relations with the Palestinian organizations. One notable exception was Col Aḥmad al-Ḥājj, the ADF nominal commander who was replaced in April 1977 by Col Sāmī al-Khatīb, probably because of his opposition to Syrian policy. The Kuwaiti press reported that Ḥājj was relieved of his command after having formally asked Sarkīs to terminate the mandate of the ADF, since it was "proven that it was incapable of exercising control over all of Lebanon's territory, particularly in the South."[9]

Khatīb's appointment as nominal commander of the ADF was a revealing instance of Syria's *modus operandi* in Lebanon. Like Sarkīs, Khatīb had been a mainstay of the Shihāb regime, serving as one of the key figures at the *Deuxième Bureau*. When the Faranjiyya Administration was trying to purge the government apparatus of the remnants of Shihābī influence in 1973, Khatīb and several other officers proved their loyalty by fleeing to Syria.

There were other indications of the importance Syria attached to the security forces as a vital local instrument of control in Lebanon. In April 1977, a Syrian military delegation visited Lebanon to discuss the reorganization of the Lebanese army, and in July a course was held in Syria for Lebanese police officers.

SYRIA AND THE LEBANESE POLITICAL FORCES

Although Syrian efforts to expand the Central Camp into a Broad National Front failed, Damascus had some success in either liquidating or moderating Leftist opposition. Syrian forces stationed in Lebanon eliminated two centres of resistance: Lieut Ahmad al-Khatīb's Lebanon's Arab Army and the pro-Iraqi faction of the Ba'th, centred in Tripoli. Walīd Junblāt, Kamāl's son and successor, sought and apparently achieved a *rapprochement* with Syria after visits to Damascus in May and July 1977. Raymond Eddé remained a vehement critic of Syrian policy, but became less effective after his move to Paris.

Syria's policy towards the Palestinian organizations was ambivalent. At the Riyadh conference, Syria had renounced its aim of bringing 'Arafāt and the PLO leadership to their knees, regarding the PLO instead as the representative of the Palestinians. When the PLO was under strong attack by the Christian militias, Syria came to its assistance. At the same time, Damascus acted to subordinate the Palestinian organizations in Lebanon to its authority. The ADF, while refraining from entering the refugee camps, took commanding positions around them. Particular care was taken to restrain the Rejectionist Front, and force was used against its members (either by the ADF or by the pro-Syrian Palestinian organizations). The effectiveness of these measures was shown by the small number of incidents involving Palestinians during the latter part of 1977.

On the opposite side of the Lebanese political spectrum, Camille Chamoun occasionally criticized Syrian policy; but Pierre Jumayyil supported it consistently, and was always successful in bringing Chamoun back into line. Thus, although Chamoun had at first opposed the admission of Syrian troops into Christian areas and the appointment of a new supreme commander of the Lebanese Army, he ended up accepting both. He well understood that Syria would not hesitate to use force, and that there was no prospect of any external help to counter it. Maronite leaders, like other Lebanese personalities, were frequent visitors to Damascus, although Chamoun less so than Jumayyil.

RELATIONS WITH THE PALESTINIANS

During the civil war, the Lebanese Front realized that although the National Front was its nominal opponent, the Palestinian organizations in fact comprised the major opposition fighting force. While Syria co-operated with the Lebanese Front in 1976 in trying to curb the Palestinian organizations, it was very far from sharing the view that the Palestinians, or at least a large part of them, should be evacuated from Lebanon. In the first half of 1977, Lebanese Front leaders continued to call for such an evacuation and included this point in their January 1977 programme (see above). But it was only in August that the Lebanese Front made a formal demand for the Palestinians' evacuation, and their redistribution among the member-states of the Arab Leauge. However, these were not the real terms in which the Palestinian issue was discussed or treated in Lebanon.

At the Riyadh and Cairo conferences, it was decided that the Palestinian presence and activities in Lebanon should be regulated by the application of the Cairo Agreement within 45 days. But the Four-State Committee was unable to reach an interpretation acceptable to the various parties. The Committee's work was hindered by the fact that there was no single authoritative version of the Cairo Agreement, and that several of its stipulations were vague (see Table 2). Finally, in April 1977, the Lebanese government decided to implement the agreement according to its own interpretation, which Syria broadly endorsed. However, the Lebanese government was pressured to give way on a number of points which Damascus considered were unacceptable to the Palestinians. Syria also wanted the supervision of the agreement (and consequently of the Palestinian organizations) to be entrusted to the ADF. In May 1977, the extended mandate of the Four-State Committee expired without an authoritative interpretation of the Cairo Agreement having been reached.

In the spring of 1977, both the Lebanese and the Palestinians announced their intentions to abide by the Cairo Agreement, though little was actually done to implement it. The Lebanese Front tried to exploit this situation and announced that the agreement was null and void. Their announcement generated strong denunciations from Palestinian leaders; but this, too, had little real effect.

In an attempt to achieve a *modus vivendi* with the Palestinian organizations, Syria initiated the Shtūrā conference in July which formulated a three-phased solution to the problem. The first two phases, which dealt with the problem of controlling the camps and heavy weapons, were to be completed by the end of August. As it turned out, the intensification of the fighting in the South in July completely overshadowed these aspects (see Table 3). South Lebanon was considered in the third and best-known phase of the Shtūrā agreement (for details, see below).

THE PROBLEM OF THE SOUTH

South Lebanon can be seen as a microcosm of the fundamental processes taking place in the country in 1977. It presented the Riyadh settlement with its most dangerous, complicated and consistent challenge. When the ceasefire brought about by the Riyadh and Cario conferences went into effect, South Lebanon existed in a political and military vacuum. During the conflict and until the summer of 1976, there was practically no fighting in the South; as a result, it began to attract refugees from other, less fortunate, areas. Palestinians left the region to participate in the fighting elsewhere; Lieut Khatīb's Lebanon's Arab Army occupied the positions previously held by the Lebanese army, but remained passive.

It was only in the summer of 1976 that clashes began between units of Khatīb's army and local embryonic Christian militias. The fighting spread in the aftermath of the fall of Tall al-Za'tar, in August 1976, when Palestinian units began to withdraw to the South. The local Christian militias were commanded by officers of the Lebanese army, who made a point of emphasizing their affiliation with the proper authorities of the Lebanese army. Politically, they were linked with the Lebanese Front in the North. It was only after the change of government in Israel in May 1977

Table 2
Major Provisions of the Cairo and Malkert Agreements and their Interpretations[1]

	The Cairo Agreement[2]	*The Malkert Agreement*[3]	*The Lebanese Interpretation*	*Palestinian Organization's Interpretation*	*The Syrian Interpretation*[4]
Lebanon's Sovereignty	Acceptance that the civil and military Lebanese authorities will continue to exercise effective responsibility to the full in all regions of Lebanon and under all circumstances. Control by the Palestine Armed Struggle Command of the actions of all members of its organizations and to prevent any interference in Lebanese affairs.	Both parties eagerly agree to serve the Palestinian cause and to continue its struggle, and to preserve the independence of Lebanon and its sovereignty and stability, and in the light of contracted agreements and Arab decisions.	It is a requisite of state sovereignty that the constitutional authority—legislative, executive and judicial—should exercise total jurisdiction over the whole of the territory, and over the residents of that territory as well as the state's nationals, and over moveable or fixed property whether located on land, in the air space or in territorial waters. There is a basic need for the Palestinians not to interfere directly or indirectly in the internal affairs of Lebanon. This includes not aligning themselves with any Lebanese party or group against another.	The Palestinians respect and do not violate the sovereignty of Lebanon; however, the application of the understanding of the concept of sovereignty does not conflict with but binds a sovereign state to observe agreements and treaties signed with other states and official bodies. The PLO respects both the internal and external security of Lebanon, and considers itself bound to any arrangements that do not conflict with the Cairo Agreement and its supplements. Being a member of the League of Arab States, the PLO reserves the right to organize its internal affairs, its rights, its immunities and the diplomatic privileges which it and its agencies enjoy.	The formulation of a special procedure for defining relations between the Lebanese authorities and the Palestinians.
Presence, Numbers, Membership	The right of Palestinians presently living in Lebanon to work, reside and move freely. A census of the complement of The Palestine Armed Struggle Command through its leadership. Permission for Palestinian residents in Lebanon to join the Palestinian revolution through armed struggle within the limits imposed by Lebanese security and sovereignty. Organization of the entry, exit and movement of Palestine Armed Struggle elements.	Movement [*in the camps*] will be allowed without arms and in civilian dress. *Movement in the [frontier] areas* will be allowed by arrangement with local Lebanese commanders and according to agreement. The Palestinian side pledges to deport all foreigners with the exception of those engaged in non-combatant work of a civilian or humane nature (including doctors, nurses, translators and interpreters). By the term foreigners is meant non-Arab commandos.	Right to work, residence and movement of Palestinians currently resident in Lebanon. A person is entitled to the above rights if he was in Lebanon on 3 November 1969; if he holds a card issued by UNRWA and has his name entered in its registers on the said date; and if he is subject to the valid laws and regulations of Lebanon pertaining to refugees. A commando is a Palestinian affiliated to any one of the organizations recognized by the Chairman of the PLO [Executive Committee] and is the holder of a membership card issued by his organization. Persons who are not Palestinians shall not join commando organizations based on Lebanese territory. This prohibition does not apply to non-combatant personnel who are engaged in humanitarian or civilian activities, such as doctors, nurses, male nurses, translators, etc, provided advance approval has been obtained from the Lebanese authorities.	Rights of residence, movement and work for Palestinians currently resident in Lebanon. A Palestinian who is registered in the records of the Directorate-General of the Palestinian Refugees, of the Directorate-General of Public Security and of UNRWA, and is lawfully resident on Lebanese territory, shall be deemed as possessing the said rights. A commando is an Arab militant who believes in the principles of the Palestine National Charter and acts within the framework of the PLO to achieve its objectives. This definition does not apply to non-Arab foreigners, but covers those who are engaged in humanitarian and civilian non-combatant activities, such as doctors, male nurses, technicians, translators, etc. The Chairman of the PLO [Executive Committee] will control the proper issue of [membership] cards.	

Refugee Camps	The presence of command centres for Palestine Armed Struggle Command inside the camps to co-operate with the local authorities and guarantee good relations. These centres will handle arrangements for the carrying and regulation of arms within the camps, taking into account both Lebanese security and the interests of the Palestinian revolution. The establishment of local committees from Palestinians living in the camps to look after the interests of the Palestinians there, in co-operation with the local authorities and within the context of Lebanese sovereignty.	*Presence in the camps of personnel* 1) No commando presence; 2) Formation of permanent Palestine Armed Struggle Command units; 3) Confirmation of militia presence for the guarding and internal protection of the camps. By militia is understood Palestinians residing in the camps who are not members of the resistance force and who practice normal civilian duties; 4) Establishment of a guardpost for Lebanese internal security forces at a location to be agreed upon close to each camp.	On the initiative of the Chairman of the PLO [Executive Committee], Palestine Armed Struggle Command (PASC) a centre will be established in each camp under the command of an officer. Its membership will be representative of the camp population at an average rate of two persons for every thousand of the lawful residents of the camp. Its men shall carry light individual arms only. The duties of the centre are: 1) in the field of internal security—to assist the Lebanese security forces in enforcing Lebanese laws and regulations within the camp when required to do so; 2) in the field of local defence—to establish local defence of the camp against any attack launched by the foreign enemy pending the arrival of the Lebanese regular forces, which will undertake the defence of the camp in co-operation with the militia. The militia's numbers shall be representative of the number of inhabitants of the camp at a rate of three per thousand. The militia's arms shall consist of light weapons.	Internal and external security measures and the control of arms in Palestinian camps are the responsibility of the PLO.	Application of the Lebanese interpretation to the Cairo Agreement with regard to the refugee camps in Beirut and the [various] areas, except the South. Charging Syria with the responsibility for defending the camps, a task that Syria will carry out through the ADF. Assertion of the Lebanese authorities—and the ADF—to enter the camps which are part of Lebanon's territory, subject to the sovereignty of the state. The ADF will protect against Israeli attacks; the ratio of 7/1000 to be cancelled and domestic protection of the camps to be left in Palestinian hands.*
Weapons		*Presence in the camps of arms* 1) The militia will be permitted to carry light arms individually; 2) No medium or heavy weapons will be permitted within the camps (e.g. mortars, rocket launchers, artillery, anti-tank weapons, etc.).	All medium and heavy arms must be removed completely from the refugee camps. All official members of the various guerrilla groups must be taken out of these camps. Only seven out of every 1,000 residents of the camps will be allowed to carry arms inside the camps, and only on condition that these seven are not affiliated to any guerilla group.	The paragraph concerning arms and ammunition requires a more accurate interpretation to be agreed upon by both parties.	Heavy weapons to be collected from the camps and transferred to the South under Syrian supervision. Limitation of the quantity of heavy weapons inside the camps, collection of weapons exceeding this limit and their placing under Palestinian supervision.*
Activities	It was agreed to faciliate operations by Palestinian commandos.	All [commando] operations from Lebanese territory are suspended. Departure from Lebanon for the purpose of commando operations is forbidden. [Military] training is forbidden in the camps, but allowed at the training base at Nabī Sabbat.	No military presence or deployment shall be permitted for commandos or military or armed elements outside the agreed border positions. PASC centres in the camps and training centres are excluded. One centre will be allocated for military training at the agreed location of Nabī Sabbat. All military training outside this centre is prohibited.	Locations provided for in the schedule of permitted movement shall be altered at the request of the Palestinian party as may be necessary for external security (in the face of the enemy).	

	The Cairo Agreement[2]	The Malkert Agreement[3]	The Lebanese Interpretation	Palestinian Organization's Interpretation	The Syrian Interpretation[4]
Activities			Commando operations are covert military operations carried out by a commando against the Israeli enemy inside the occupied territory. All operations out of Lebanese territory will be frozen in accordance with the decisions of the Joint Arab Defence Council. Vehicles belonging to the various Palestinian organizations cannot circulate on Lebanese territory unless they are registered with the Lebanese authorities and adhere to the rules and regulations of the Lebanese traffic department.	The Chairman of the PLO [Executive Committee] will organize all matters relevant [to the Palestinian struggle] in such manners as not to conflict with the requirements of Lebanese security and sovereignty.	
Jurisdiction		Lebanese laws will be implemented on the basis of Lebanese sovereignty and offenders will be referred to the responsible courts. Contraventions in military sectors will be submitted to local liaison committees; contraventions inside the camps will be the charge of the internal security forces in co-operation with the Palestine Armed Struggle Command; contraventions outside the camps shall be subject to Lebanese law.	The Lebanese Internal Security Forces, in co-operation with members of the PASC will be authorized to enter the camps and arrest any person who has committed criminal offences, even inside the camps. Any sentences issued by the Lebanese judicial authorities against residents of the camps will be carried out to the letter. If Palestinians commit violations outside the camps, the Lebanese authorities will deal with them in accordance with Lebanese law. Members of the various guerilla organizations have no authority whatever to arrest any Lebanese or non-Lebanese on Lebanese territory.	[Commando activity] is the chief subject related to the security of the Palestinian Revolution and its affiliates; the Chairman of the PLO [Executive Committee] is bound to implement the Cairo agreement and its annexes, and to assist the Lebanese Security Forces to prosecute any persons found violating the security and sovereignty of Lebanon.	
Sources	*Nahār*, 20 April 1970; *Al-Usbū' al-'Arabī*, 15 December 1970; *'Amal*, 16 December 1976; *Arabia and the Gulf*, 16 June 1977.		*Sayyād*, 28 April 1977; *The Middle East*, June 1977; *Qabas* (Kuwait), 25 July 1977.	*Arabia and the Gulf*, 6 June 1977.	**Anwar*, 20 May: *Sharq*, 7 June; *Ḥawādith*, 17 June 1977.

(1) For provisions dealing with the South, see Table 4.
(2) The Cairo Agreement, signed on 3 November 1969, followed the first of the major clashes between the Lebanese authorities and the Palestinian organizations, with a view to regulating the relations between the two sides.
(3) The Malkert Agreement, signed on 25 May 1973, followed the second round of major clashes and was designed to implement the Cairo Agreement in the light of the developments which obtained at that time.
(4) No single authoritative version of the Syrian interpretation of the Cairo Agreement has been published. Fragments of one version were published by *al-Anwār*. A later publication in *al-Ḥawādith* seems to include the additions made by Syria to the Lebanese interpretation; these were made during the visit by Syria's FM Khaddām to Beirut in June.

Table 3
The Main Provisions of the Shtūrā Agreement[1]

SOVEREIGNTY
The Lebanese authorities—executive, legislative and judicial—will exercise complete power over all Lebanese territory and its inhabitants through the Internal Security forces.

It will be forbidden to interfere in any internal Lebanese affairs or, for example, to spread propaganda—party political or ideological—which promotes activities restricting freedom, truth and investigation.

The Arab Deterrent Force will be entrusted with the supervision of the implementation of the measures stated in this plan and will curb infringements and carry out searches in places which are not allowed by the bases of the execution of the Cairo Agreement.

PALESTINIAN PRESENCE AND MEMBERSHIP
The right of residence in Lebanon is restricted to those Palestinians who were present in Lebanon on 3 November 1969, which will be established by means of official records and documentation.

Lebanese rules and regulations will be implemented for all those not resident in Lebanon before 3 November 1969 with the assistance of the Arab Deterrent Force.

Non-Arab foreigners are refused membership of the organizations and participation in field operations, and permission is only granted to those doctors, nurses and translators who have obtained prior permission from the Lebanese authorities. Those who do not conform to this will be expelled.

All Lebanese belonging to any of the resistance organizations will be dismissed.

The number of armed men from the [Palestine] Armed Struggle Command and the militia will be restricted to the agreed figure.

REFUGEE CAMPS
The external defence of the camps will be guaranteed by the Arab Deterrent Force conforming to arrangements after joint consultation with the PLO.

A local committee will be formed from the camps' inhabitants in each camp to oversee these interests and conduct relations with the Lebanese.

Good relations with the Lebanese authorities will be guaranteed by the establishment of a [Palestine] Armed Struggle Command police post in each camp under the command of an officer, which will be charged with co-operation with the Internal Security forces in the implementation of rules and regulations inside the camp.

The Arab Deterrent Force will intervene for security reasons whenever it is impossible for the Internal Security forces and members of the [Palestine] Armed Struggle Command present in the camp to intervene; it will also be responsible for taking over locations not provided for in the bases of the Cairo Agreement.

WEAPONS
Heavy arms will be surrendered to the assembly areas. Weapons held by members of the [Palestine] Armed Struggle Command and the militia will be restricted to light arms.

It will be forbidden to import arms and ammunition in any quantity except to make up a demonstrable deficit or to replace losses incurred during military operations with the enemy.

The purchase, storage and transportation of arms and ammunition outside the border zone will be forbidden with the exception of arms belonging to the [Palestine] Armed Struggle Command and the militia bases in the camps.

ACTIVITIES
There will be only one training camp located at Nabī Sabbat, and no military training will be permitted.

The base will be used for training in the use of permitted weaponry only, and the Arab Deterrent Force may supervise and ensure this.

No resistance personnel will be permitted to travel outside the border positions wearing military or camouflage dress or bearing weapons.

Source: Arabia and the Gulf, 19, 26 September 1977.

[1] For provisions dealing with the South, see below.

that the connection between Israel and the Christian militias in South Lebanon was formally admitted; but such links appear to have existed from the start. They were part of Israel's "good fence" policy, which combined humanitarian elements with an effort to prevent the Palestinians, or any other hostile elements, from returning to the immediate vicinity of the Israeli border.

The Riyadh and Cairo conferences created a new situation throughout Lebanon, but particularly in the South where the major elements were as follows.

1. With the expected restoration of government authority, the South could, in theory, be brought under the control of the Sarkīs Administration and its armed forces.
2. The Palestinians, who did not accept Syrian efforts to exercise control over them and to confiscate their heavy weapons, regarded South Lebanon as an area where some freedom of action and an arsenal of heavy arms could be maintained.
3. Syria regarded South Lebanon with mixed feelings. Like the Palestinians, it wanted to close the "good fence" and terminate Israeli influence. It also realized the crucial importance of controlling this area as a means of exerting military and political leverage on Israel. The Syrians further recognized that developments in the South were bound to affect their overall position in Lebanon. Nor were the Syrians unaware of the danger of a military deterioration along the southern border with Israel.
4. From the Israeli viewpoint, several objectives seemed important: to maintain the "good fence" and contact with the population in South Lebanon; to prevent the establishment of either Palestinian or Syrian units along the border; and to prevent a return to the pre-1975 situation there.

The vacuum in South Lebanon was created by the conflicting interests of the major parties in the area. Since the Lebanese army had not been sufficiently rebuilt by 1977, the Lebanese state could not impose its authority. Syria was willing to police the area with its own forces, but Israel refused to permit Syrian troops so close to its border. As a result, the local Christian militias and Palestinian units fought it out between themselves supported by Israel and Syria respectively. The US played an important mediating role, seeking to prevent both a clash between Syria and Israel, and a resumption of hostilities in the Lebanese conflict. Other parties—the Sarkīs Administration, the Lebanese Front and the Shī'ī leadership—played marginal roles in the issue. The importance of the problem was summed up by *al-Nahār*: "The Lebanese war which began in the South [the fishermen incidents in Saida in February-March 1975 were considered to be a prelude to the civil war] will come to an end in the South, or the peace which has been coming to Lebanon will come to an end in the South."[10]

FIGHTING IN THE SOUTH

Fighting in the South continued with varying degrees of intensity throughout 1977. The Christians were organized in three enclaves which were connected to Israel through the "good fence" system. These were the eastern enclave (the Marj'ayūn-Qulay'ā region); the central enclave (the 'Ain Ibil-Rumaysh region); and the western enclave (based on the single Christian village of 'Almā al-Sha'b).

According to their commander, Maj (*Rā'id*) Sa'ad Ḥaddād, the militias were under the authority of the Lebanese army, and were not purely Christian, but included Shī'ī, Sunnī and Druze fighters from the area. Their opponents—"the Joint Forces" of the Palestinians and the Left—were in reality an almost purely Palestinian force. Without any interference from Syria (and possibly with Syrian connivance), the Palestinians managed to transfer sizeable forces to the South.

These forces dominated the western section of the Lebanese-Israeli border area, which remained comparatively calm during the fighting. In the eastern sector, they were based in the Khiyām and Tayba area, and in the central sector at Bint Jubayl and 'Aytarūn area.

Fighting in the South took one of three forms. There were Palestinian attacks on the Christian enclaves, and there were Christian offensives seeking either to create territorial contiguity between their enclaves, or to remove Palestinian positions which caused them particular trouble. But most of the time there was stalemate, with both sides occasionally shelling each other's positions.

Two major outbursts of fighting occurred in the South in 1977—in late March and early April, and again in the late summer. The fighting in March began when the Christian militia leaders attempted to establish a direct territorial link between the Christian enclaves which surrounded Qulay'a and Rumaysh. Following initial Christian successes, the Palestinians and the Syrians reacted strongly. The Palestinians regarded the militias' success as a direct threat to their own positions, as well as a first step towards the creation of a buffer zone along the Lebanese-Israeli border. They believed that such a zone could seriously curtail Palestinian activities against Israel in the future.

Syria, in turn, was anxious to prevent an extension of Israeli influence in the South, and consequently provided the Palestinians with indirect assistance. The resulting counter-offensive succeeded in the recapture of Tayba and Khiyām, and threatened to bring about a total collapse of the Christian militias. Such a development was also undesirable to the Syrians, who realized that a complete Palestinian victory could lead to a deterioration in the South, as well as to direct Israeli intervention. Together with Sarkīs, Syria therefore exercised a restraining influence on the Palestinians and was instrumental in achieving the ceasefire which ended this period of fighting.

The fighting had a devastating effect on the South. About 200,000 people or a third of the population left the area as refugees. Several southern CD members and other public leaders organized a "Front for the Protection of the South" which sought a political solution to the problem; but their efforts were largely ineffectual.

The second round of fighting took place in the late summer and should be seen in terms of the various efforts which preceded it to settle the problem.

THE NABATIYYA AFFAIR

One such settlement effort had already taken place in the period January-February 1977. Late in January, as the military situation was getting out of hand, a battalion-sized Syrian unit, formally part of the ADF, entered the town of Nabitiyya. Israel objected strongly to Syria's crossing of the loosely defined "red line." But the Syrian position was that the ADF was Lebanon's army; that the South was Lebanese territory; and that Israel had no right to intervene in the affairs of Lebanon. In order to diffuse the situation, the US initiated a settlement providing for a phased Syrian withdrawal, which was completed by mid-February.

PROPOSAL TO STATION A UN FORCE

The continuation of the fighting in the South and the failure of Syria's efforts to station its own troops in South Lebanon prompted several Lebanese leaders, primarily Camille Chamoun, to propose at the end of February that UN peacekeeping forces be called in. The idea itself was not new—it had been raised several times, especially by Raymond Eddé, in the late 1960s and early 1970s. Several alternatives were raised in February (and later during the summer), such as increasing the number of UN observers along the Lebanese-Israeli border from 40 to 400, or reconstituting the ADF under a UN mandate. This idea met with opposition by various Arab states, particularly Syria. The Syrians realized that those Lebanese politicians who promoted the idea were not merely seeking a solution to the problem of the South, but were also trying to introduce an independent element that would provide them with a measure of autonomy from Damascus.

PROPOSAL TO DISPATCH LEBANESE ARMY UNITS

In March, when the futility of the proposals to garrison the border area with UN observers became apparent, the idea was raised to dispatch Lebanese army units to the South. This proposal was warmly welcomed by Syria; but Israel objected on the grounds that since the Lebanese army had yet to be restored, the proposal was really a thinly-veiled attempt to bring Syrian troops into the area. In April and May, the possibility of using units of the Vanguards of Lebanon's Arab Army for this purpose was considered. But nothing came of it, and Sarkīs himself stated that "obstacles hinder the dispatching of a Lebanese force as long as the reorganization of the army has not been completed."[11]

EFFORTS TO REGULATE THE PALESTINIAN ORGANIZATIONS

The failure of all these attempts to devise a solution to the problem of the South shifted the efforts of the various parties towards an attempt to regulate the status and activity of the Palestinian organizations. Implicit in these efforts was the assumption that once this was achieved, the South and, indeed all of Lebanon's more fundamental problems, could be attended to in a calmer atmosphere. Prime Minister Ḥuss expressed this feeling when he stated that "a settlement of the situation in the South depends on the application of the Cairo Agreement, a political detente and the restoration of the army."[12] But the Cairo Agreement and its various appendices, as well as the 1973 Malkert Agreement, were complicated and vague and open to conflicting interpretations (see Table 4).

THE SHTŪRĀ AGREEMENT

Fighting on a large scale resumed in South Lebanon in July 1977, the initiative being taken by the Christian militias from a variety of motives. Their commanders were concerned by the increasing concentration of Palestinians in the area, as well as by the accumulative effect of the protracted war on the morale of the Christian population. They were also presumably trying to force Israel's hand, assuming that the Likud government was likely to back up statements made by the new Prime Minister with a more firm commitment to the Lebanese Christians.

At the same time (following intensive preparatory negotiations between Syrian, Lebanese and Palestinian representatives), a conference opened in the Lebanese town of Shtūrā. The participants were Syria (represented by C-o-C Ḥikmat Shihābī); Lebanon (represented by the commander of the army, Victor Khūrī); the Palestinians (represented by Salāh Kalaf), and the ADF (represented by its nominal commander Sāmī al-Khatīb). The conference sought a formula to implement the Cairo Agreement throughout Lebanon, including the South; it ended with the signing of Shtūrā (see Table 3). Since three of the four participants were Syrian or pro-Syrian, it is hardly surprising that the agreement closely reflected Syria's point of view. Its most important stipulations were that the Palestinians would withdraw to a distance of 15 km from the Israeli border; that the Lebanese army would enter this area; that the southern littoral would be defended at this stage by the ADF; that a committee based in Saida and composed of representatives of the four parties—Syria, Lebanon, the Palestinian Organizations and the ADF—would

Table 4

Articles dealing with the South in the Cairo and Malkert Agreements and their Interpretations

THE CAIRO AGREEMENT

Study of the distribution of suitable concentration points in the border regions are to be agreed upon with the Lebanese High Command.

It was agreed to facilitate operations by [Palestinian] commandos through: 1) Assisting commando access to the border and the specification of access points and observation posts in the border region; 2) Ensuring the use of the main road to the 'Arqūb region.[1]

THE MALKERT AGREEMENT

Western sector of border regions: Presence and concentration outside the camps is forbidden. . . .

Central sector of border regions: Presence will be permitted outside Lebanese villages in certain areas by agreement with the local Lebanese sector commander. Resistance forces are not permitted east and south of the line running al-Kusair/al-Ghandouriya/Deir Kifa/al-Shihabia/al-Salasel/al-Saltania/Tabnin/Haris/Kafra/Sadikin/Qana. This prohibition applies to all these points inclusively. Concentration of resistance forces at a guardpost south of Hadatha is permitted. The number allowed is between five and ten men in civilian clothes, with all military appearance to be avoided. They will be supplied by animal transport. At all these places the total number permitted must not exceed 250.

Eastern sector of border regions: Three bases will be permitted in the southern 'Arqūb at Abu Kamha, al-Kharbiya (al-Shahid Salah base) and Rashaya al-Fakhar (Jabal al-Shahr). Each base will contain no more than 30 to 35 men each. Supply for these bases will be by motor-transport. Elements at these bases will be forbidden to proceed in the direction of Marj'ayūn unless they have a permit. The carrying of arms in Marj'ayūn is forbidden. . . . In the northern 'Arqūb and at Rashaya al-Wadi, presence is permitted at a distance from the villages, but not west of the Masnaa-Hasbaya road. . . . At Baalbeck no commando presence is permitted except at the Nabī Sabbat training base.

Note: Medium and light arms are permitted in these sectors; commando presence inside Lebanese villages is not allowed; all units which have been reinforced in Lebanon from abroad will be adjusted.[2]

THE LEBANESE INTERPRETATION

In the western sector: The presence and positioning of commandos in this sector is not allowed.

In the central sector: Permanent concentrations in this sector are not allowed, but transit posts may be set up in places approved by the Military Command provided the following rules are observed: no proximity to inhabited villages: no proximity to military positions; abstention from concentration east and west of a line drawn through al-Kassir, al-Ghanduria, Deir Kifa al-Shahbiya. Bir al-Salasil, al-Sultaniya, Tibnin, Harris, Kafra, Saddiqin and Kana; a commando detachment may be stationed to the south of Hadata village, provided the size of its personnel is no larger than ten, and supplies will be transported by animals; the total personnel of all transit points in this sector does not exceed 250.

In the eastern sector: Positioning is allowed in the 'Arqūb only in the area lying to the east of a line drawn through al-Wazzani, al-Hasbani river valley and the Hasbani-Masnaa road. Positioning to the west of this line is prohibited. Positioning will conform to the following points. 1) Positioning will be at least one kilometre from villages. 2) The number of posts south of the 'Arqūb will be three; namely, Abu Kamha al-Gharbiya, the martyr Salah base and Jebel al-Shihar near Rashaya al-Fukar, provided the number in each post is no more than 30 to 35 at most. Supplies will be transported to these posts by civilian motor vehicles. 3) Positioning will be prohibited in the course of the Hasbani river.

In general the numbers in the 'Arqūb area shall be commensurate with the capacity of the territory; otherwise the size of concentrations will constitute a danger to the security of Lebanon.

In order to enable guerrillas to put up immediate self-defence in locations of concentration on the borders against any aggression by the enemy, the following medium weapons may be retained. In the central sector and all transit points: nine 60mm mortars; six 81mm mortars; three 120mm mortars; six Strelas. In the eastern sector ('Arqūb), each platoon consisting of approximately 100 men may retain the following weapons: three 60mm mortars, two 81mm mortars, and throughout the whole sector, eight 120mm mortars and 12 Strelas (SAM-7s).[3]

THE PALESTINIAN INTERPRETATION

Nabatiyya is the permanent military headquarters of the commando forces leadership in the South. Movement along the central sector of the Tyre road is permissible according to the agreements.

Table 4 continued

The Cairo Agreement and its supplements provide for the creation of a Joint Military Control by the authorities of the PLO and Lebanon in order to facilitate and organize [frontier] passage and control trespassing. Explicit reference to this point is imperative at this stage.[4]

THE SYRIAN INTERPRETATION

The heavy weapons collected from the refugee camps are to be transferred to the South under Syrian supervision.

The Lebanese interpretation of the Cairo Agreement is to be applied except for the South.

The movements of the Palestinians in the South are to be facilitated in co-ordination with the Lebanese authority when that authority is extended to the South. (The Lebanese interpretation was modified under Syrian pressure—*Anwār*, 20 May 1977.)[5]

[1] *Arabia and the Gulf*, 16 May 1977.
[2] *Ibid.*
[3] *The Middle East*, June 1977; *Arabia and the Gulf*, 13 June 1977.
[4] *Arabia and the Gulf*, 6 June 1977.
[5] *Al-Ḥawādith*, 17 June 1977.

supervise the implementation of the agreement; and that the Palestinians were to remain—with some restrictions—along the border in the 'Arqūb area.[13]

The implementation of Shtūrā met with the usual difficulties that have obstructed all previous agreements with regard to South Lebanon. The Christian militias announced that "fighting in South Lebanon would come to an end only after the departure of the Palestinians".[14] Palestinian spokesmen issued conflicting statements. It was announced that there was a "willingness to evacuate the [Palestinian] forces from the South, as soon as regular Lebanese forces arrived to fill the vacuum."[15] At the same time, it was stated that "the presence of the organizations in the South is a guarantee for the Arabism of the area, and for the perpetuation of the Palestinian cause."[16] Israel took a negative attitude to the Shtūrā agreement for two reasons: it was opposed to the institutionalization of the Palestinian presence, even along a limited section of the border; and it was convinced that ultimately the Shtūrā agreement sought to extend Syria's predominance into South Lebanon and to close the "good fence."

Fighting broke out again on a large scale in September 1977. This time, in order to provide the Christian militias with support against powerful Palestinian counter-attacks, Israeli forces crossed the Lebanese border. This phase ended with a cease-fire on 25 September 1977, following intensive American mediation efforts.

ECONOMIC AFFAIRS ($1 = 3 Lebanese lira; £1 = 5.6 LL)

1977 was a year of economic transition, from the collapse which characterized the 19 months of civil war, to gradual normalization—but notably without reconstruction. Estimates of the speed with which Lebanon could make its economic come-back seem to have been over-optimistic, mainly because of the uncertain political climate, which was directly reflected by the business community's reluctance to make long-term commitments or investments.

One of the most difficult problems for the Lebanese government was how to reconcile urgent relief and reconstruction with long-term development planning. The challenge was made even more difficult due to the lack of finance—linked as it is to the political aims of donor countries, mainly the Arab oil exporting states.

Because of Lebanon's limited resources, the burden of the reconstruction was particularly heavy to bear. There were various estimates of the civil war losses, but none based on serious analysis. While the Beirut Chamber of Commerce and Industry, with its conservative approach, put the figure at LL 7,500m (private sector 80% and public sector 20%), official declarations declared losses of LL 20,000m.

FOREIGN ECONOMIC AID

During 1977, Lebanon was promised more than $150m of grants, two-thirds from Western countries (mainly the EEC), and the remainder from Saudi Arabia, Kuwait and Abū Dhabī. However, these grants fell far short of the financial aid required for relief purposes and urgent public works. Despite promises of substantially more aid, mainly from the Arab oil exporting countries in the Persian Gulf, foreign assistance to finance reconstruction remains a major uncertainty.

PRICES AND WAGES

A major problem in 1977 was how to ease the burden of inflation, running at an annual rate of 80%-90% during the civil war period. The government took two main counter-inflationary measures: it limited pay increases to between 15% and 35%, and fixed a maximum legal profit margin on basic foodstuffs and consumer items for wholesalers, distributors and retailers.

TRADE BALANCE

The trade deficit in 1975 amounted to $934m (cf $984m in 1974 and $644m in 1973). In 1975, exports and imports decreased by 13% from the previous year. Saudi Arabia was the most important market for Lebanese exports (taking 33%) followed by Libya (10%), Egypt and Syria (each above 5%). The US remained the most important supplier of imports (19%), followed by Italy (10%), France, West Germany and UK (each 8%).

According to preliminary estimates, total exports during the first half of 1977 amounted to more than $200m (cf $183m in 1976 and $516m in 1974).

BUDGETS AND DEVELOPMENT PLAN

Current budget expenditure for 1977 was LL 1,654m—a nominal decrease of 5% compared with 1976. In addition, the government approved LL 400m for reconstruction and development projects.

The government also approved the priorities for the Five-Year Development Plan as proposed by the Reconstruction and Development Council, which was established in January 1977. No details concerning the extent of investments, sources of finance and official targets have yet been disclosed.

(Economic Section by Moshe Efrat)

CIVIL WAR LOSSES (in million Lebanese liras)

Private Sector Losses	
1. Commerce, of which	3,000
Contents of port warehouses	(1,900)
Stocks and equipment	(600)
Buildings, furnishings, etc.	(500)
2. Industry, of which	1,500
Plant and equipment	(1,000)
Stocks and inventory	(500)
3. Agriculture	300
4. Tourism, of which	180
Hotels (Beirut)	(125)
Restaurants (Beirut)	(25)
Other (outside Beirut)	(30)
5. Road vehicles	90
6. Housing	1,000
7. Private schools	50
8. Universities	30
9. Private hospitals and clinics	10
10. Miscellaneous	15
Total Private Losses	**6,175**
Public Sector Losses	**1,335**
Total Losses	**7,510**

Source: Beirut Chamber of Commerce and Industry (estimate); *MEED*, 30 September 1977.

1978 BUDGET EXPENDITURE (in million Lebanese liras)

Presidency	2.1
Chamber of Deputies	7.0
Prime Minister's Office	59.2
Justice	19.9
Foreign Affairs	44.0
Interior	145.3
Finance	43.1
Defence	490.5
Education	367.1
Public Health	65.9
Labour and Social Affairs	89.3
Public Works and Transport	398.7
Agriculture	44.6
Hydraulic and Electrical Resources	27.3
Total (including others)	**2,083.0**

Source: Al-Nahār, reprinted in *MEED*, 14 October 1977.

LEBANON'S MAIN TRADING PARTNERS (in million US dollars)

	1973	*1974*	*1975*
Exports to:			
Saudi Arabia	100.0	396.1	396.1
Libya	45.9	91.6	124.1
Egypt	9.1	73.8	72.2
Syria	29.7	87.5	61.1
Greece	2.4	66.2	53.6
Kuwait	40.4	50.8	46.8
Iraq	19.2	41.9	44.2
UAE	14.4	33.1	43.1
Iran	5.4	12.4	39.3
Jordan	19.6	23.4	26.0
Turkey	6.2	27.8	25.2
Qatar	9.5	15.5	23.3
France	62.0	132.6	19.8
United States	27.6	29.6	32.8
United Kingdom	56.8	61.2	17.6
Total (including others)	**608.4**	**1,455.4**	**1,206.8**
Imports from:			
United States	146.8	315.5	405.3
Italy	112.5	252.0	204.4
France	137.1	242.3	179.5
Federal Germany	143.0	228.8	178.0
United Kingdom	100.8	156.6	173.0
Japan	48.8	103.4	92.4
Romania	24.6	83.0	85.0
Turkey	21.5	120.7	73.1
Switzerland	54.5	49.8	57.8
Belgium	0.3	63.6	55.2
Saudi Arabia	26.6	55.2	49.7
Iraq	46.2	52.3	47.0
Netherlands	26.2	61.6	43.2
Spain	20.9	48.2	38.7
Australia	5.9	11.0	31.3
Total (including others)	**1,252.5**	**2,438.9**	**2,141.6**

Source: IMF, Direction of Trade, 1970–1976.

NOTES

1. For the text of the Riyadh Arab summit's decisions, see *'Ukkāz*, Saudi Arabia; 19 October 1976. For the text of the Cairo Arab summit's decisions, see *al-Nahār*, Beirut; 27 October 1976.
2. Radio Beirut, 21 November—Daily Report (DR) 22 November 1976.
3. R Beirut, 23 January—BBC, 25 January 1977.
4. Ibid.
5. *Al-Dustūr*, Paris; 11 July 1977.
6. Iraqi News Agency (INA), 7 July. *Al-Safīr*, 8 July 1977.
7. R Damascus, 18 April 1977.
8. Syrian Arab News Agency, 2 February—BBC, 4 February 1977.
9. *Al-Kabas*, Kuwait; 14 April 1977.
10. *Al-Nahār*, 12 November 1976.
11. Middle East News Agency (MENA), 5 May 1977.
12. R Beirut, 10 July 1977.
13. *Al-Usbū' al-'Arabī*, Beirut; 1 August 1977. The text was not officially published.
14. United Press International, 10 August 1977.
15. MENA, 17 August 1977.
16. R Cairo, Voice of Palestine, 17 August 1977.

Libya

(Al-Jamāhīriyya al-'Arabiyya al-Libiyya al-Sha'biyya al-Ishtirakiyya)

GIDEON GERA

Libyan politics were dominated by two main developments during 1976–7: the establishment of "People's Power," a system of direct democracy; and the serious deterioration of relations with Egypt, which culminated in the "Four-Day War" of July 1977 and was reflected in Libya's overall foreign policy. Both evolved against a background of increasing oil revenues, which permitted the country to continue its ambitious $25,000m Five-Year Economic and Social Transformation Plan.

"People's Power" is a form of participatory democracy, with a network from local to national level of Basic Congresses, People's Committees and a General People's Congress. Although formally charged with decision-making, in practice these institutions mainly approve and implement decisions taken at the centre. Although the supreme executive institutions were renamed, from Revolutionary Command Council (RCC) to General Secretariat, and from Cabinet to General People's Committee, there were no basic changes in the Libyan regime: the country was still ruled by a military group, firmly led by its chief, Mu'ammar al-Qadhdhāfī, and assisted by a central bureaucracy. Opposition, inspired and directed mainly by 'Umar al-Muḥayshī, a former RCC member residing in Cairo, remained largely ineffectual.

Relations with Egypt, strained since the abortive merger between the two countries in 1973, were marked by public hostility and rancour between the two Heads of State and by acts of open subversion on both sides. Hostility grew in 1977 to the point where Sādāt decided on a military operation in July. In the brief fighting which ensued, the Egyptians failed to achieve a clear-cut success, and the war only served to strengthen Qadhdhāfī's determination to work for the downfall of Sādāt and his policies. Libya took the lead in organizing an anti-Sādāt front in the Arab world after the Egyptian leader's visit to Israel in November 1977 (see essay "The Middle East in International Perspective"). This conflict with Cairo brought a coincidence of interests between Tripoli and Moscow; co-operation grew closer, especially in the supply of Russian arms.

Libya's activist "revolutionary" role, backed by its immense oil wealth, gave it a standing in the Arab and wider world disproportionate to its actual importance and size, having just over 2.55m people.

As far as can be judged, the Qadhdhāfī regime seems, after eight years of power, to be fairly strongly established and to be engaged in serious long-term economic and social development. The main threat at present comes from Egyptian hostility and its encouragement of Libyan opposition.

POLITICAL AFFAIRS

"PEOPLE'S POWER" (SULTAT AL-SHA'B)

The idea of direct popular rule (*sultat al-sha'b*) was repeatedly expressed by Qadhdhāfī since his advent to power in September 1969. His aversion to political "middlemen" as well as to entrenched bureaucratic structures and procedures—an aversion probably stemming from his Bedouin origin—contributed to his diappointment with the Nasserite model of the single party, the Arab Socialist

Union (ASU or *al-ittiḥād al-ishtirākī al-'arabī*), which was tried out in Libya, mainly from 1971 to 1973. Under that system, the ASU functionaries seemed to form an additional layer of bureaucracy, which Qadhdhāfī perceived as an obstacle to his objectives. This disappointment led him to declare the "Popular Revolution" of April 1973, in which all laws were to be re-examined; culture cleansed of negative foreign influences and society of "sick" elements; the administration purged of superfluous bureaucrats; and popular committees formed to run the daily affairs of the people. Thereafter Qadhdhāfī gradually elaborated his political thought into a new doctrine and new institutions. Minor revisions have been made to the proposals for government reorganization since they were first announced by Qadhdhāfī on 28 April 1975 until, by the end of 1976, the overall framework of the ASU (which was to include all adult Arab inhabitants of sound mind) was implicitly discarded.

"People's Power" is a form of direct democracy. All the inhabitants of a village, town or quarter of a city constitute a Basic People's Congress (BPC or *al-mu'tamar al-sha'bī al-asāsī*). Each BPC elects a leadership committee of ten, including a secretary and two assistants. All the leadership committees within a municipal area (*mudīriyya*)—approximately the size of a county—constitute the People's Congress of that municipality; this in turn elects a leadership committee of five and secretaries. Members of BPCs are also organized corporatively in trade and professional unions, and may belong to federations (such as those comprising students and women). Only members of BPCs (that is, inhabitants registered on BPC rolls) may enrol in unions, whose functions are strictly non-political.

Members of BPCs also elect People's Committees (PComs or *lajna sha'biyya*), usually from among qualified personnel and their leadership committees. PComs run local (municipal) government and elect their own chairmen. They also exist in government administrations (except in technical and security-sensitive bodies), in public utilities and corporations and at the two universities. All BPC secretaries and their assistants, the chairmen of unions and federations and of various PComs—together with Cabinet ministers and the Revolutionary Command Council (RCC)—constitute the General People's Congress (GPC or *al-mu'tamar al-sha'bī al-'āmm*).

The attempted coup by RCC member and Minister of Planning, 'Umar al-Muḥayshī, in August 1975, and subsequent government and army purges led Qadhdhāfī to accelerate preparations for the first GPC, which met in Tripoli from 12–19 January 1976. The Congress approved RCC policy and adopted the new Five-Year Economic and Social Transformation Plan (see below) as well as the budget. On 1 September 1976, the seventh anniversary of his coming to power, Qadhdhāfī heralded the beginning of "a new phase in the Libyan Revolution" and the final establishment of "People's Power," under which the head of state and cabinet would be nominated by the GPC. These new institutional arrangements were to be put before the GPC's second session, scheduled for November 1976.

THE SECOND GENERAL PEOPLE'S CONGRESS, NOVEMBER 1976

In preparing for the second GPC session, Qadhdhāfī attended a BPC meeting at the village of Tā'urghā on 3 October 1976, where he exhorted all Libyans to join BPCs and participate in forging their country's destiny. Later, on 23 October, he reorganized the high command of the armed forces, assuming for himself the newly-created post of Supreme Commander. The Chief of Staff, Abū Bakr Yūnis Jābir, was appointed as the new Commander-in-Chief, while the Assistant Chief of Staff, Mustafā al-Kharūbī, took his place. These promotions, evidence of the continuing control of the armed forces by Qadhdhāfī's close RCC associates, released him from routine duties. Also on 23 October, the cabinet was reorganized (for a

LIBYAN CABINETS[1] 1975-1977

	12 July 1975	23 October 1976 (Change/Additions)		3 March 1977 (Changes)	
Prime Minister	'Abd al-Salām Aḥmad Jallūd*				
Ministers[2]				*Chairman, GPC*	'Abd al-'Ātī al-'Ubaydī
Interior	Khawaylidī al-Ḥamīdī*				
Foreign Affairs	'Abd al-Mun'im al-Hūnī*	*Minister of State for Foreign Affairs*	'Alī 'Abd al-Salām al-Traykī+	*Foreign Affairs*	Yūnis Abū al-Kāsim+
Planning and Scientific Research	'Umar 'Abdallah al-Muḥayshī*[3]	*Planning*	Mūsā Aḥmad Abū Fraywa+		
Justice	Muḥammad 'Alī al-Jaddī				
Health	Muftāḥ al-Ustā 'Umar				
Labour and Civil Service	'Abd al-'Ātī al-'Ubaydī				Muḥammad al-Tāhir al-Maḥjūb+
Petroleum	'Izz al-Dīn al-Mabrūk				
Agriculture and Agrarian Reform	Muḥammad 'Alī al-Tabbū				
Housing	Muḥammad Aḥmad al-Manqūsh				
Communications	Nūrī al-Faytūrī 'Umar al-Madanī				
Economy	Abū Bakr 'Alī al-Sharīf				
Industry and Mineral Wealth	Jādallā 'Azūz al-Talḥī			*Trade*†	
Treasury	Muḥammad al-Zarūq Rajab				
Education	Muḥammad Aḥmad al-Sharīf				
Social Affairs and Social Security	Muḥammad 'Abd al-Salām al-Faytūrī				
Municipalities	Muftāḥ Muḥammad Ku'ayba		Abū Zayd 'Umar Dūrda+		
Maritime Transport	Mansūr Muḥammad Badr				
Electricity	Jum'a Sālim al-Arbash				
		Youth	Muftāḥ Muḥammad Ku'ayba		
		Dam and Water Resources	'Umar Sulaymān Ḥamūda+		

	12 July 1975	23 October 1976 (Change/Additions)		3 March 1977 (Changes)
Ministers of State				
Minister of State	Muhammad Abū al-Kāsim al-Zuway			*Information and Culture*†
RCC Affairs	Taha al-Sharīf Bin 'Āmir			*Liaison*†
Nutrition and Marine Wealth	'Amrū Aḥmad al-Muqasabi			
Agriculture Development	'Abd al-Majīd al-Qa'ūd			*Land Reclamation and Development*†
		Cabinet Affairs	Milād 'Abd al-Salām Shumayla+	*GPC Affairs*†

* Member of the RRC.
\+ New Appointment.
† Appelation of Ministry changed as of February 1977.
1 As of 3 March 1977, the General People's Committee (GCP).
2 As of 3 March 1977, Ministers became Secretaries.
3 Escaped from Libya on 9 August 1975 after attempted coup.

SCHEME OF "PEOPLE'S POWER" (QADHDHĀFĪ'S DIRECT DEMOCRACY)

(AS ADOPTED IN LIBYA SINCE MARCH 1977)

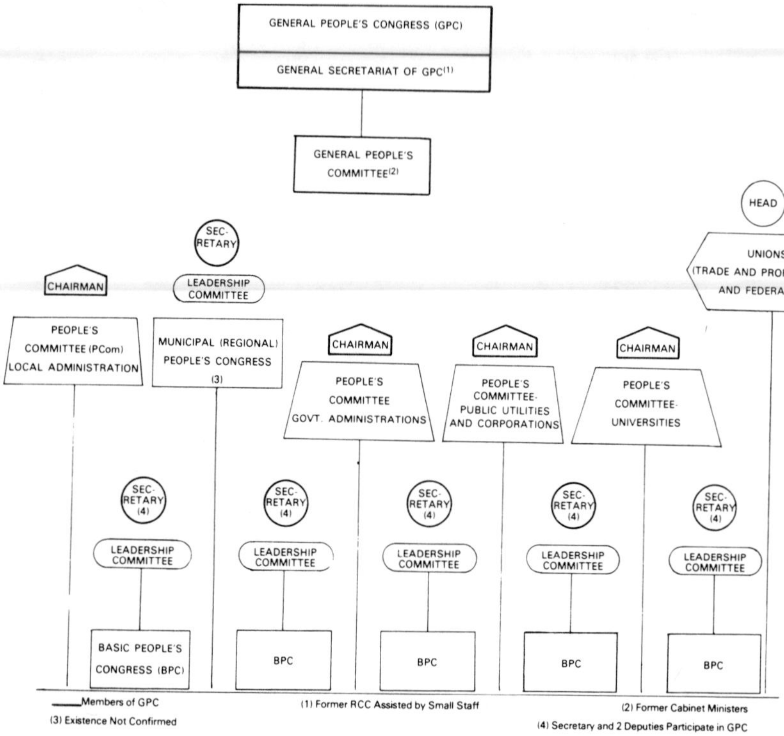

complete list, see Table). Five new ministers were appointed and two new portfolios created: Cabinet Affairs and Dams and Water Resources. A geology professor from Tripoli University was chosen for the latter post, but all the other appointees were senior civil servants, thus reaffirming the technocratic character of the Libyan cabinet. However, two appointments had political significance. First, a new Minister of Planning finally replaced Muhayshī (more than a year after his escape). Second a new Minister of State for Foreign Affairs confirmed the final disgrace of the former minister, RCC member 'Abd al-Mun'im al-Huni, who had been living in self-imposed exile in Cairo since early 1976. Although sympathizing with Muḥayshī, al-Huni had not completely severed all ties with the regime.

The GPC sessions, held from 13 to 24 November, were tightly controlled by Qadhdhāfī through the public address system. From his table on the rostrum, he could cut off speakers when he chose and recognize others. He also decided the duration of sessions and the agenda: the GPC did not deal at all with defence and security matters, and only briefly with foreign affairs.

In his opening speech, Qadhdhāfī described "People's Power" as Libya's "true democracy" which was without precedent in history, except in classical Athens. However, participants were reminded that they were not deputies and could neither change nor add to BPC resolutions; if the PCom leadership was inefficient, it should be replaced. On 22 November 1976, the draft of a new constitutional declaration was submitted to the Congress: popular direct democracy was to be the basis of the Libyan political system, with BPCs, PComs, Unions and the GPC as its main institutions.[1] A General Secretariat (GS) was to replace the Cabinet; the Qurān was to be the "legislation of society," while the name of the State was to be changed to reflect the new order. The functions of the chairman of the GPC were also spelled out. This draft was to be discussed by BPCs all over the country.

However, most of the GPC's proceedings were devoted to local affairs, debated after reports by ministers and the presentation of both the regular ("administrative") and development ("transformation") budgets. The discussion revealed the increasing propensity of PComs to demand more money to improve conditions in their localities and exceed their budgets. Repeated intervention was required by the Prime Minister, 'Abd al-Salām Jallūd who warned that future development would be threatened by present increases in local government allocations. Jallūd said that "municipalities had a feeling that the revenues of the country were unlimited. That was why . . . [they] did not bother to exert any effort to increase their own revenues." He added: "Non-oil revenues did not grow as required because a large number of citizens evaded paying certain obligations."[2] This minor confrontation between the representatives of "People's Power" and the Cabinet required Qadhdhāfī's intervention. The budgets were finally approved, however, with small increases to local projects.

A number of GPC resolutions on development reflected other domestic problems: unequal growth of various regions, and urban growth in spite of insufficient water supplies and other economic factors conducive to development. Little progress had been made in regrouping the scattered populations of isolated areas (mainly in the southern desert) to more promising sites; and the decline of date palms, once a major source of income, caused concern.

THE SABHĀ GPC AND THE ESTABLISHING OF "PEOPLE'S POWER"[2]

Qadhdhāfī inaugurated the countrywide discussion of the draft on "People's Power" on 29 November 1976. He reminded Libyans that "People's Power" did not mean anarchy, since the people would rule through their congresses, committees and unions. The GPC chairman would not be a President or Chief of State, but simply an administrator. There would be "no Constitutional Declaration or man-made constitution, but . . . only laws based on the Qurān." (However, Qadhdhāfī rejected the idea of declaring a new caliphate, because the incumbent or his heirs could become dictators.) The RCC would also be abolished under the new system, otherwise "there would be no meaning or necessity" for the institutions. But, he assured his audience: "Individually, members of the RCC are . . . at the disposal of the Libyan people, who are free to place them in any position . . . and benefit from their services." [3]

In fact, this last sentence became the keynote of the special session of the GPC, which took place at Sabhā between 28 February and 3 March 1977. Although 1,000 km from Tripoli, Sabhā was chosen for the occasion because it had "entered history as the cradle of the Revolution"—an allusion to Qadhdhāfī's initial political activities there as a high school student between 1957-61.[4] This was part of a growing personality cult of Qadhdhāfī, who was referred to in many BPC discussions as an "indispensable" leader of the people, and was given other new laudatory titles by the Libyan news media.

After an introductory address by Jallūd, the 970 members of the GPC discussed the draft declaration submitted to them in November 1976. In his interventions, Qadhdhāfī elaborated on various aspects of the declaration explaining, for instance, why the neologism *Jamāhīriyya* (i.e. "public" or polity of the masses) should replace *Jumhūriyya* (republic); this indicated a new era of the masses, just as the term "republic" had indicated the end of monarchies in an earlier age.

The basic resolutions having obviously been decided upon in advance, the Congress was able to issue a four-point "Declaration on the Establishment of People's Power" on 2 March 1977.[5] This was based on the December 1969 Constitutional Declaration; the 15 April 1973 speech by Qadhdhāfī proclaiming "popular revolution;" the *Green Book*;[6] and the GPC's own previous resolutions. The Declaration proclaimed "the end of any form of conventional institution of government—authoritarian, family, tribal, factional, class, parliamentary, partisan and coalition of parties."[7] The four points were as follows.

(1) The official name of Libya was to be "The Arab Libyan People's Socialist Public" (*al-jamāhīriyya al-'arabiyya al-libiyya al-sha'biyya al-ishtirākiyya*).

(2) The Qurān was to be the code of society.

(3) Direct "People's Power" was to be established based on BPCs, unions and the GPC. The functions of these institutions were to be defined by law.

(4) Since the country's defence was the duty of all citizens, general military training was to be established.

The GPC elected "the revolutionary intellectual and master leader, Mu'ammar al-Qadhdhāfī, as the Secretary-General of the GPC."[8] The General Secretariat also included the other four remaining RCC members: former Prime Minister Jallūd; the Commander-in-Chief and the Chief of Staff, Abū Bakr Yūnis and Kharūbī; and the former Minister of the Interior, Khuwaylidī al-Ḥamīdī.[9] The Cabinet was replaced by a General People's Committee (GPcom or *al-lajna al-sha'biyya al-'āmma*), consisting of a chairman and 25 secretaries. The membership of the GPcom was identical with the former Cabinet, except for minor organizational changes. Because the Minister of Interior was now in the General Secretariat, and the Minister of Labour and Civil Service was appointed as GPcom chairman, two senior civil servants were appointed as secretaries to replace them. One other secretary changed his title.[10]

On 8 March 1977, Qadhdhāfī publicly thanked the "genuine leaders of the Great Revolution"—the four remaining RCC members—and "those Free Unionist Officers" still at the head of their units. He jibed at others who quit ("dogs barking late at night") and proclaimed his duty "to stay with the masses . . . in order to realize further achievements."[11]

The consensus of most observers on the significance of "People's Power" was summed up in the phrase: "The rules stay, only the names have changed."[12] In practical terms, the alternations in political institutions simply meant a continuation of the military regime which came to power in 1969. The new institutions did reflect deep-rooted tribal traditions: the elders of the community met and voiced opinions, but final decisions rested with the chief, who then acted with the authority of the council of elders. The system of People's Congresses was obviously useful to Qadhdhāfī in maintaining his authority while, at the same time, the BPCs gave the people an outlet for their grievances. The congresses also seemed to provide an impetus to local affairs by their influence on local government. This impetus and the rather limited power of the PComs were both clearly reflected in the November 1976 GPC debate, during which many unfulfilled expectations about agrarian, educational and health development were voiced.[13] The new system produced no change in centralized government bureaucracy, which was expanding rapidly and apparently remained unaffected by repeated campaigns for greater efficiency. It should be stressed again that sensitive government departments such as the armed forces and security services were excepted from the system of "People's Power."

OPPOSITION ACTIVITY

Like the traditional tribal system, "People's Power" allowed no place whatsoever for dissenting voices. Already, in its January 1976 session, the GPC resolved that political activity could take place only within the BPCs and the GPC; it limited unions and federations to non-political tasks. Any deviation would be "relentlessly crushed." Any individual or group electing to follow a course other than "the way of perfect democracy," as approved by the people, would lose his right of legal recourse, and thus become outcast and outlawed.[14]

Nevertheless, political opposition, though unorganized, continued to make itself felt. In January and April 1976, there was student unrest at the Universities of Benghazi and Tripoli. There were also reports of dissatisfaction among wealthy and old-established urban families, whose importance in the country had declined since 1969 and whose way of life hardly accorded with the Islamic puritanism of the regime. In general, however, political apathy was the rule.

Against this background, the increased harshness of measures against the small opposition was noticeable, probably reflecting the regime's reaction to Egyptian attempts at subversion. In November 1976, ten government employees, teachers and students were sentenced to life imprisonment for membership in an illegal party.[15] In December 1976, a court trying Muḥayshī (*in absentia*) and his group condemned 22 officers to death. These sentences were carried out in April 1977. At the same time, an alleged Egyptian saboteur and three or four accomplices were executed. Significantly, these were the first executions carried out by the regime since coming to power in 1969 (death sentences on prominent monarchists having either been commuted or pronounced on absentees). Muḥayshī was by the RCC stripped of his Libyan citizenship on 14 February 1977 on the grounds of treason and his disclosure of strictly classified state secrets. The decree emphasized Muḥayshī's "foreign" origin by mentioning his "tribal" affiliation: al-Sharkasī (of Turkish-Caucasian ancestry). Unsurprisingly, Muḥayshī's Libyan Patriotic Grouping (*al-tajammū' al-waṭanī al-lībī*) stepped up its activities from Cairo. Even with strong Egyptian backing, however, his efforts did not seem to represent a serious threat to Libyan security.

In fact, the continuing stability of Qadhdhāfī's regime seemed firmly based on tight military and police control; on the prosperity most Libyans were enjoying; on the close link of the leadership with the Islamic-Arabic culture deeply rooted in Libyan society; and on the growing importance of their country in world affairs which seemed to please many Libyans. Furthermore, the popular support Qadhdhāfī apparently enjoyed (being the man who rid the country of foreign military bases, ousted the Italians, successfully and profitably challenged the oil companies, and significantly improved the common lot) seemed to have grown—even amongst those who disliked his theories—since he stood up to Sādāt in July 1977.

ARMED FORCES

Total armed forces number 29,200. Defence expenditure in 1976 was 67.9m Libyan dinars ($229m). Military service is voluntary. The Army numbers 22,000 and formations consist of one armoured brigade; two mechanized infantry brigades; one National Guard brigade; one special forces brigade; three artillery and two anti-aircraft artillery battalions. Equipment consists of 200 T-62, 1,000 T-54/-55 medium tanks; 100 *Saladin*, 75 EE-9 *Cascavel* armoured cars; 100 *Ferret* scout cars; 220 BTR-40/-50/-60, 110 OT-62/-64, 60 *Saracen*, 250 M-113A1, BMP armoured personnel carriers; 75 105mm, 70 122mm, 155mm howitzers; 300 *Vigilant, Sagger* anti-tank guided weapons; *Scud* surface-to-surface missiles; 120 23mm, L40/70, 57mm anti-aircraft guns; six AB-47, five AB-206, four Alouette III helicopters; some Cessna 0-1 light aircraft. (400 *Cascavel/Urutu* armoured fighting vehicles on order.) The 2,700-strong Navy is equipped with one frigate (with *Seacat* surface-to-air missiles); two corvettes (three more building); three guided-missile fast patrol boats with SS-12M surface-to-surface missiles; 11 patrol craft (ten large, one coastal) and one logistic support ship. (Ten guided-missile fast patrol boats, 80 *Otomat* surface-to-surface missiles and one tank landing ship on order.) The Air Force numbers 4,500, including expatriate personnel. It is equipped with 162 combat aircraft of which some may be in storage. Formations consist of one bomber squadron with 12 Tu-22; four interceptor squadrons, two with 30 *Mirage* IIIE and two with 30 MiG-23 *Flogger E*; four ground-attack fighter squadrons with 50 *Mirage* V; two counter-insurgency squadrons with 30 *Galeb*; one reconnaissance squadron with ten *Mirage* IIIER; two transport squadrons with eight C-130E, nine C-47, two *Falcon*, one *Jetstar*; ten *Mirage* IIIB, two *Mystere* 20, five MiG-23U, 12 *Magister* and three T-33 trainers; four helicopter squadrons with 13 *Alouette* II/III, three AB-47, nine *Super Frelon*, eight CH-47C and 12 Mi-8; three surface-to-air missile regiments with 60 *Crotale* and eight batteries with 60 SA-2, SA-3 and SA-6 surface-to-air missiles. (38 *Mirage* F-1 and 16 CH-47C helicopters on order.)[16]

FOREIGN AFFAIRS

The resolution on foreign affairs adopted by the GPC during its November 1976 session was largely a re-endorsement of the main elements of Qadhdhāfī's foreign policy: continued striving for Arab unity; a call to reconvene the institutions of the Federation of Arab Republics; support of the Palestinians and rejection of any negotiated settlement of the Arab-Israeli conflict; strengthening of ties with Muslim countries and Africa (which should receive more Libyan investments); spreading Islam; and support of "liberation movements" throughout the world. One new departure, however, was the call to reinforce friendship with the USSR.

Since 1970, Libyan foreign policy has reflected both the "revolutionary" idealism of its leaders and a calculated determination to advance the country's political, strategic and economic interests. Some of Libya's foreign ventures—couched in purely idealistic terms—have served national objectives as well. Thus, Islamic activities in Africa, both missionary and cultural, tended to be concentrated in countries where Libya had political and economic stakes, such as those on its southern border.[17] The main incentive to pursue a more realistic policy may well have been Qadhdhāfī's failure to realize one of his main aspirations: to establish at least a nucleus of Arab unity.

The abortive union between Libya and Egypt in 1973 stimulated the former to extend its relations with the outside world. From 1969 to 1976, Libya increased the number of its diplomatic missions from 28 to 93, while foreign representations in Tripoli rose from 35 to 80. During that period, Libya concluded 311 co-operation agreements of various kinds, including 76 with Arab countries, 28 with Islamic states, 107 with African states and 49 with the Eastern bloc. It also established 18 joint banks (a favourite instrument of Libyan foreign policy) mainly with other African countries. 370 Islamic missionaries were sent abroad, again mostly to Africa, where a number of cultural centres were also established.[18]

RELATIONS WITH EGYPT

The hostilities between Egypt and Libya in July 1977 were the culmination of a continuous deterioration in the two countries' relations since 1973. A main cause of this conflict appears to have been the growing incompatibility between their leaders, Sādāt and Qadhdhāfī, which led to all differences between the two countries being personalized. The Federation of Arab Republics (FAR), established in 1971 between Egypt, Syria and Libya, failed to satisfy Qadhdhāfī's urge for Arab unity; since 1972 he sought to bring about an immediate merger between his country and Egypt. He also implicitly claimed to be 'Abd al-Nāsir's heir and to be the moral and ideological leader of any federation. Sādāt ridiculed this pretension, quietly excluded the Libyans from preparations for the 1973 war, and torpedoed the projected merger. The record of Libyan-Egyptian relations since 1974 was one of mutual vilification and increasingly violent subversion. Qadhdhāfī came close to openly admitting his role in instigating violence in Egypt (and later in the Sudan) when, responding to a question about his involvement in the resistance against Sādāt and Numayrī, he said: "No one can prove that we were involved in *putsch* attempts and revolts. We feel responsible for the revolution in the entire Arab world, and for this revolution we do accept responsibility." [19]

When Sādāt gave asylum to the former RCC member, Muḥayshī, in February 1976 and allowed him to use the Egyptian mass media to "expose" Qadhdhāfī and his regime, a series of retaliatory acts of sabotage occurred in Egypt; this led Sādāt to deploy a considerable force along the Libyan border in the summer of 1976. Although claiming that only the BPCs' reluctance had prevented him from severing relations with Egypt, Qadhdhāfī in fact reacted cautiously. He withdrew his forward troops and supplied "starving" Egyptian forces with fresh water and food. Subsequent negotiations to patch up the quarrel were foiled by Egypt's refusal to extradite Muḥayshī, but tension abated somewhat.

The food riots in Egypt in January 1977 (which Sādāt blamed on outside influences) once again heightened tensions between the two countries. Reacting to statements by Sādāt, Qadhdhāfī published an open message to his rival on 5 February 1977, listing some of their political differences: "You have said . . . you can end the differences between Egypt and Libya in half a minute if Mu'ammar lives up to his word . . . How could we in half a minute end the Palestine case, the agreement of shame and humiliation concerning usurped Sinai, the shame of kilometer 101, your amassing your army to face Libyan villages and oases, your unholy alliance . . . against the Libyan Arab Republic and, lastly, the campaign of starvation and mass killings you are launching against the Egyptian people . . . Our dispute needs a half century of strife.''[20]

Increased propaganda by Muḥayshī's Libyan Patriotic Grouping probably inspired a counter-movement—the Progressive Revolutionary Front of Egypt. Broadcasting from Tripoli, it admitted its part in the January riots and denounced Sādāt as ''the people's butcher.''[21] Egyptian ridicule of the establishment of the ''polity of the masses'' (*Jamāhīriyya*) prompted another attack by Qadhdhāfī on Sādāt and his ''unholy'' alliance with Numayrī. The execution of an alleged Egyptian saboteur at Benghazi on 7 April 1977 caused a new round of violence, against Egyptian institutions in Libya and vice versa. In his May Day speech, Qadhdhāfī denounced the continued Egyptian military build-up on his border. An attempt to relieve the tension through a meeting of the Egyptian Prime Minister and the Libyan Chairman of the GPcom was vetoed by Qadhdhāfī in mid-June 1977.

About the same time, the quarrel was carried into various inter-Arab and international forums. Egypt (together with Sudan and Iran) refused to participate in the Eighth Conference of Islamic Foreign Ministers, held in Tripoli on 16–22 May 1977. At the annual OAU conference at the end of June 1977, Egypt and Sudan encouraged Chad to complain publicly about Libyan occupation of parts of its northern provinces since 1973. A visit to Chad in mid-July by the Egyptian Vice-President, together with rumours of Egyptian military aid to that country created a feeling of encirclement in Libya.

Meanwhile, tension built up along the Libyan-Egyptian frontier, with Egyptian patrols apparently penetrating into Libya to prevent infiltration of ''saboteurs.'' Cairo was clearly nervous about possible Libyan support of radical Muslim groups such as *al-Takfīr wal-Hijra.*[22] The Egyptians captured five Libyans on 12 July 1977 (''saboteurs'' according to Cairo, ''policemen'' according to Tripoli); four days later, the Libyans retaliated by taking 13 Egyptians prisoner. On 17 July, the Egyptian commander received an ultimatum to withdraw his troops from Libyan soil within 48 hours. When this order went unheeded, the Libyans—who had meanwhile moved up at least part of their 9th Armoured Brigade—shelled and attacked Egyptian positions, killing nine soldiers and capturing 33. Sādāt responded by authorizing an operation which would teach Qadhdhāfī ''an unforgettable lesson.''[23]

On the morning of 21 July, an Egyptian force attacked Libyan armour west of Musā'id (a few kilometers west of the frontier), occupying that village and partly destroying it. Considering this ''a direct aggression on the *Jamāhīriyya,*''[24] the Libyans countered by shelling the Sollum area, which they continued to do throughout the fighting. During the next three days, the Egyptians repeatedly bombed 'Abd al-Nāsir airbase, and despite their withdrawal from Musā'id, the Libyans announced further raids on Libyan settlements on 22 July. On 23 July (when Cairo finally admitted bombing Kufra airfield in the far south of Libya), it stepped up its attacks on airfields and radar stations which served the Libyan missile air defence system. The Libyans threatened that: ''If the unjustified aggression did not stop, the *Jamāhīriyya* forces would retaliate strongly in the depth of Egypt''—a clear hint at ground-to-ground missiles.[25] Jallūd said on 2 August 1977 that had Nāsir airbase been destroyed, two or three Egyptian bases would have suffered the same fate. In the main action on 24 July, the last day of the fighting, the Egyptians carried out a helicopter-borne commando raid on the oasis of Jaghbūb, where a ''saboteur'' camp was supposedly destroyed. But by nightfall, Sādāt ordered his troops to cease firing and thus the Four-Day War ended.

That same day, Libya had called up reserves, and on 25 July broadcast a call for Arab and Muslim volunteers to reinforce the small Libyan army. In addition, the

Libyans had launched a vigorous psychological offensive. Popular support was mobilized by appealing to patriotic and religious sentiment (the Libyan forces were called "The Army of God"), and demonstrations were organized acclaiming Qadhdhāfī. Sādāt's "treasonable" ties with the US were condemned, as was his "ingratitude" (Nāsir airbase having been used by Egypt as a flying school from 1970 to 1974). Prominence was given to the reported reluctance of Sādāt's army to fight Libya, and captured Egyptian officers were invited to make television statements embarrassing to Sādāt.

Qadhdhāfī was quick to realize that in a struggle between adversaries so unequal, his most effective weapons were not military. He encouraged the mediation of PLO Chairman 'Arafāt (22 July) and of Algeria's Boumedienne (24 July), who finally convinced Sādāt to agree to a ceasefire. Egyptians forces withdrew from Libya on 24 July. Four days after prisoners were exchanged on 24 August, a high-level meeting took place at Sollum between a Libyan minister and his Egyptian counterpart in the presence of 'Arafāt. Both sides agreed to end their hostile propaganda campaigns—an undertaking which did not endure for very long.

Altogether, the Egyptian operation may be assessed a failure. Libyan military losses were not heavy, although they probably exceeded the admitted total of 27 killed, 22 wounded, two aircraft and three to nine tanks destroyed. (The equipment could easily be replaced out of existing stocks.) The Egyptians, on the other hand, suffered embarrassing losses; the Libyan Popular Resistance forces (mainly Cyrenaican Bedouin) had also been actively engaged.

More important strategically, Qadhdhāfī's defiance enhanced his prestige, and his popular support had probably never been greater. No officer moved against the regime during the fighting as Muḥayshī might have promised his Cairo sponsors. His veteran companion, Commander-in-Chief Yūnis, was promoted to Brigadier-General (higher than Qadhdhāfī's formal rank), and one of the "retired" RCC members, Mukhtār al-Qirwī "reappeared" in public during the September celebrations. The war also produced a palpable fillip to Libyan national pride. Furthermore, the strategic value of Libya's immense geographical depth was proved again, and its possession of strategic deterrent weapons justified. Qadhdhāfī's often criticized policy of making Libya into a military power which his Arab opponents could not ignore was vindicated. Finally, Sādāt was put on the political defensive. His ties with the US (which was alleged by Jallūd to have "participated" in the combat, at least by giving intelligence) were described by Qadhdhāfī as part of an American-Israeli conspiracy against all Arabs, which Libya was compelled to resist. Sādāt's initiation of hostilities, he added, made him "an historical criminal who must be punished."[26]

Qadhdhāfī's obdurate attitude towards Sādāt continued, as expressed, for instance, in his September 1977 insistence on France stopping the supply of weapons to Egypt. (The French had excellent and most profitable relations with Libya.) Similarly, his offer of 7 October 1977 to put Libyan forces at Egypt's disposal "to liberate Sinai" was clearly intended to embarrass Sādat. This build-up of hostility marked Qadhdhāfī out as one of the natural leaders of the Arab front against Sādāt following his peace initiative with Israel in November 1977.

There seemed to be only one major constraint on Libya's anti-Egyptian policy—its continuing dependence on the c. 250,000 Egyptians active in the whole range of its economy, from unskilled labour to professional personnel (see below). A total and sudden exodus would cause fearful damage to Libya's economy and undermine the Transformation Plan. During 1977, an attempt was nevertheless made to get rid of the Egyptians. No more entry visas were issued in May, and in June a majority of BPCs voted to terminate Egyptians' employment. However, the idea of recruiting replacements in Eastern Europe (in addition to Turkey and Tunisia) proved to be impractical, as Jallūd discovered during a tour undertaken for that purpose in May 1977. Therefore, despite the departure of thousands of Egyptians in July and August, it seemed unlikely that Libya would be in a position to expel all their fellow-countrymen.

The tension between Libya and Egypt abated briefly at the end of October 1977 when each country permitted the reopening of the other's main Consulate, at Benghazi and Alexandria. At the beginning of November 1977, the Libyans resumed issuing entry permits to all Egyptians in possession of employment contracts in Libya. However, Sādāt's visit to Israel later in the month led the regime to sever relations with him and his government. Thus the basic differences and animosity between Egypt and Libya showed signs of worsening even further—giving new point to Jallūd's statement of 2 August 1977 that the Libyans expected no solution unless there was a coup in Egypt or a total change in its policies.[28] (For relations with Sudan, see chapter on Sudan.)

INTER-ARAB AFFAIRS

The worsening relationship with Egypt has been a major preoccupation of Libyan foreign policy since 1975, overshadowing many other considerations. Libya's relations with other Arab countries were shaped by its uncompromising radical position on the Arab-Israeli conflict, combined with its animosity to Sādāt. The main elements of Libya's inter-Arab policy were to reject all Egyptian moves and initiatives concerning a political settlement of the Arab-Israeli conflict; to cast suspicion on Egyptian alliances (especially with Sudan, which severed relations with Libya in July 1976 after accusing it of sponsoring an attempted coup); to align itself with Iraq and the "rejectionist" Palestinian organizations; and to continue attempts to orchestrate Arab policies on the Palestinian question (by implication isolating Sādāt).

Syria's reconciliation with Egypt in October 1976 led to a distinct coolness in Libyan relations with Damascus. The Libyan contingent was withdrawn from the Arab Peacekeeping Force in Lebanon in October 1976, and in the following month Syria was condemned by the GPC. In February 1977, many Syrians working in Libya were suddenly laid off and sent home.

Although relations with Saudi Arabia were ambivalent, Riyadh was almost never explicitly attacked in Libyan propaganda. For their part, the Saudis attended the Islamic Foreign Ministers' Conference in Tripoli in May 1977, which was boycotted by Egypt and the Sudan. They also participated with Libya in establishing an Arab-Latin American Bank in July 1977.

RELATIONS WITH THE PALESTINIANS

Despite his support of the most extreme tendency among the Palestinians, and his close relations with and support of the Popular Front for the Liberation of Palestine (PFLP), the Popular Democratic Front for the Liberation of Palestine, and the PFLP-General Command, Qadhdhāfī took care not to alienate 'Arafāt and the PLO establishment who in turn were repeatedly useful to him. He even defended 'Arafāt's favouring a Palestinian "mini-state" in the belief that this "could finally bring about the destruction of Israel."[29] Qadhdhāfī repeated his rejection of the proposed Geneva conference, describing it as "a humiliation" of the Arabs.[30] Libya ardently supported (and continues to support) the Palestinian and Muslim cause in the Lebanese civil war. However, support of the Palestinians did not prevent Libya from re-establishing diplomatic relations in late 1976 with Jordan (these having been severed during the "black" September of 1970).

Because of his support of radical Palestinians and "liberation movements" everywhere, Qadhdhāfī was repeatedly accused—especially by Sādāt—of being a mainspring of terrorist activity. However, since the autumn of 1976, Libyan leaders have taken pains to emphasize their opposition to airplane hijackings and other forms of terror. Qadhdhāfī even revealed that he told the PFLP "that hijackings only bring discredit to their cause."[31] The main reason for this new line appeared to have been economic: "To achieve emancipation from foreign economic dependence, close co-operation with friendly developed countries is needed in order to build a strong economic base. Therefore Libya is projecting a new image—of a responsible neighbour in the world community."[32]

However, Qadhdhāfī did not change his definitions: to struggle for national liberation was not terrorism. "To me terrorism has a specific meaning . . . the illegal use of the power of the stronger against the weaker, the oppressed, who cannot defend himself."[33] "The new terror is the Imperialist threat against our countries . . . the Zionist invasion is an expression of international terror."[34] Despite this ideological stance, it seemed that in practice Qadhdhāfī adopted a more cautious position, continuing to deny any involvement with international terrorism.[35]

RELATIONS WITH THE MAGHRIB

Libyan relations with her western neighbour Tunisia have been clouded since January 1974 by the blockage of unification efforts between the two countries by the Tunisian Prime Minister. In March 1976, Tunisia's former Foreign Minister, Muḥammad Masmoudi (the architect of the stillborn 1974 agreement who subsequently became closely associated with Qadhdhāfī) was briefly detained in Cairo during investigations into a Libyan plot to kidnap Muḥayshī. Soon afterwards, the Tunisians announced the arrest of some Libyans who allegedly intended to kidnap or kill their Prime Minister. Retaliating, the Libyans captured some Tunisian soldiers. In August 1976, the two countries decided to refer their main dispute—the demarcation of territorial waters on the continental shelf—to the International Court of Justice (the issue has not yet been resolved).

After an exchange of prisoners in April 1977, relations seemed to have improved, but tension rose again—this time over Tunisian naval interference with an Italian oil rig drilling for Libya on a major off-shore site, which Tripoli claimed to be 45 km east of the demarcation agreed upon in 1967. "Libya has oil and Tunisia has not, but this does not justify Tunisian oil exploration inside the Libyan continental shelf," Qadhdhāfī remarked on 2 June 1977.[36] However, Libya accepted mediation by the Secretary-General of the Arab League, who persuaded both countries to agree to arbitration on 12 June 1977. In August, Libya agreed to unlock a 1974 loan to Tunisia for agricultural development. The two countries signed a document on 23 September 1977 containing detailed measures to boost mutual economic relations including trade, tourism, communications, the establishment of joint corporations and the utilization by Tunisia of Libyan oil by-products.

Over the years, Qadhdhāfī has maintained close relations with Algeria, both regimes sharing similar political attitudes towards the Third World, the Arab-Israeli conflict, oil and other questions. Since the end of 1975, both countries have co-operated in supporting the Polisario movement in the former Spanish Sahara against Morocco and Mauritania. Algeria's President Boumedienne was also instrumental in arranging the ceasefire between Egypt and Libya in July 1977. However, during the autumn of 1977, Qadhdhāfī seemed to be aiming towards *rapprochement* with Morocco, probably because of his isolation in the Arab East, thus possibly putting a strain on relations with Algeria. He also launched a proposal for a North African federation, in which the former Spanish Sahara would figure (as a political "entity whose form remains to be defined"), together with Mauritania, Morocco, Algeria and Tunisia.

ISLAMIC POLICY—THE PHILIPPINES AND ERITREA

Libya's activist policy in support of Islamic causes all over the world was exemplified by its hosting of the Eighth Conference of Islamic Foreign Ministers in Tripoli on 16–21 May 1977. The conference served to highlight two problem areas of Libya's Islamic policies: the Philippines and Eritrea. The truce agreement between the Manila Government and the Muslim Moro Liberation Front, achieved under Libyan auspices in December 1976, broke down and fighting resumed. Since 1970, Libyans had also supported the Eritrean Liberation Front in its struggle against the Ethiopian regime. But this policy began to change in 1976. "Islam is not confined to Eritrea alone," Qadhdhāfī told the Islamic conference. "The proportion of Muslims in Eritrea is not a major one . . . The Eritreans say 'We are Arabs and want to be independent.' This does not concern us."[38] In shifting its support to the military regime in Ethiopia, Libya appeared to be abandoning the ELF, but still maintained connections with it (see essay on developments in the Horn of Africa).

RELATIONS WITH CHAD, MALTA AND ITALY

Two other economically and strategically inspired Libyan foreign initiatives developed in Chad and Malta. Libya extended its border southward into a part of Chad supposedly rich in iron and uranium, thus augmenting the iron ore of southern Libya which is to be used by the steel complex at Misrātah on the Mediterranean. Libya has never admitted the truth of Chadi complaints about annexation (made publicly at the 1977 OAU summit in Gabon), but included the disputed region in unofficial maps of its territory.[39]

Libya has now become a major investor in Malta, which is of particular economic significance to the island. Tripoli's main interest lies in pre-empting the possible use of Malta as a base for Western military operations against itself—an ever-present threat in the minds of Libyans. The British naval base is not due to be finally relinquished until 1979.

The $415m share in Fiat bought in November 1976 gives Libya a 9.6% ownership, as well as an economic (and potentially political) role in Italy. Two senior Libyan officials now serve on Fiat's board of directors.

Again, there are historical undertones to this northward effort: Qadhdhāfī alludes to the Arab origin of many Sicilians. He has also attempted to revive the Arab heritage of Malta, insisting that Arabic be a compulsory high school subject.

RELATIONS WITH THE SOVIET BLOC

Relations between the USSR and Libya began to improve in 1974, following Qadhdhāfī's break with Egypt, and growing Soviet disappointment with Sādāt's pro-American orientation. During a visit to Moscow in May 1974, Prime Minister Jallūd persuaded the Soviets to implement the 1972 agreements on economic co-operation and to conclude an arms deal with Libya (comprising tanks, aircraft and various missiles). The ensuing amelioration of relations led to Kosygin's visit to Libya in May 1975, during which an additional arms deal was agreed upon (this time including *Scud* ground-to-ground missiles) together with the supply of a 10-megawatt nuclear facility for peaceful atomic energy. This set the stage for Qadhdhāfī's visit to Moscow from 6–9 December 1976. Shortly before, on 24 November, a significant new term was included in the GPC resolution to strengthen Libyan friendship with the USSR: "The Congress stresses the importance of the strategic dimension of this friendship, serving interests common to the Soviet Union and the Arab nation."[40]

Qadhdhāfī received princely treatment in Moscow. The Soviets publicly stressed not only their strong support of Libya's aspirations, but also the equality of the two countries in their mutually beneficial relationship. The joint communique issued on 9 December 1976 defined this relationship as "sincere friendship and comprehensive co-operation" in political, economical, cultural, technical, scientific and "other" fields. Earlier, at a Kremlin dinner, Qadhdhāfī said that "this friendship is not ephemeral but . . . strategic."[41] On the bilateral level, the communiqué expressed satisfaction at the co-operation developing between the two countries and called for its expansion. During the visit, a protocol was signed on economic, cultural and technical co-operation, and an agreement reached on maritime transport. Besides expressing their support of the PLO and the "liberation" of "all Arab territory," both sides concurred that Arab relations with the USSR and "the Socialist family" should be strengthened, and "decided to curb attempts to damage Arab-Soviet friendship."[42] This statement appears to have been aimed at Sādāt and implied Soviet support for Libya's attitude.

Since that visit, a steady stream of Soviet delegations has been to Libya, often as prominent guests at the various Libyan celebrations. In June 1977, at a meeting of the Intergovernmental Commission supervising the execution of agreements between the two countries, a protocol was signed to implement peaceful use of atomic energy, probably meaning the 10-megawatt nuclear facility promised by Kosygin in 1975.

The Libyans received public Soviet support during the hostilities with Egypt in July 1977 and afterwards. (The Egyptians alleged that Soviet naval helicopters had jammed their radar, thus actively aiding the Libyans during the fighting.) In fact, since Qadhdhāfī's advent to power, Libyan relations with the USSR have been decisively influenced, for better or worse, by Egypt. Since 1974, Libya has considered the USSR as a supplier of development assistance and of military supplies for which hard currency is paid—for unlike most other Arab states, Libya was not indebted to the Soviets. But the paradoxical relationship between Moscow and Tripoli was based, more than anything else perhaps, on their joint struggle against a common enemy—Sādāt's Egypt.

Libya also developed its relations with other Eastern European countries, whose corporations were especially important in developing infrastructure. As far as could be judged at the end of 1977, however, the increasing scope of Libyan relations with the Soviet bloc was essentially a "marriage of convenience." Qadhdhāfī was far from relinquishing his own brand of ideology, the "Third International Theory," which explicitly rejects communism.

RELATIONS WITH CUBA

The sensation of the Non-Aligned Conference in Algiers in 1973 had been the conflict between Qadhdhāfī and Cuba's Fidel Castro. The Libyan leader had challenged Castro's claim to being "non-aligned" and baited him with expounding Moscow's line on the Third World. All this was forgotton in 1977. In March, Castro attended part of the GPC Sabhā session, and in May the Cuban Vice-President paid an official visit to Libya. The two countries also adopted a similar policy in supporting the Ethiopian military regime.

Reports by the Egyptian press that Cuban military personnel had arrived in Libya in July 1977 were not confirmed by other sources.

RELATIONS WITH THE UNITED STATES

Relations with Washington have been troubled ever since the overthrow of pro-

Western King Idrīs in 1969, and the withdrawal of the Americans from the air base near Tripoli (Wheelus Field) on 11 June 1970. Unease was perpetuated by continued friction with foreign (mainly American) oil companies, especially after nationalization began in 1973, and by the Americans' Middle Eastern policies, in particular towards the Arab-Israeli conflict. Libyan hopes at the beginning of 1977 that the Carter Administration would reconsider American policy were disappointed, and Sādāt's growing co-operation with the US only reinforced Libyan antagonism. Moreover, Western capitalism was condemned equally with Eastern communism in Qadhdhāfī's "Third International Theory." The US responded to this criticism by reducing the level of its diplomatic representation in Libya, and by preventing the delivery of some military transport aircraft purchased by the Libyans before 1970.

The Libyans saw further proof of US hostility towards them when their country was listed fourth in a report of potential enemies (presented by the outgoing Secretary of Defence to Congress in January 1977) because of its "irresponsible support for international terrorism."[43] While the Libyan press assailed this statement, Qadhdhāfī tried to get the Carter Administration to reconsider its policy and release the promised aircraft. A member of Qadhdhāfī's staff went twice to the US, but to no avail. In his speech on the anniversary of the US evacuation of Wheelus Field (11 June 1977), Qadhdhāfī publicly invited President Carter to change "unjust US policy towards us" as Libya wanted to "normalize" relations, raise diplomatic representations to ambassadorial level and get its aircraft (which Qadhdhāfī proposed could be transformed into civil planes, if that would ease the delivery problems for the Americans).[44]

Continuing disillusion with the Carter Administration and its Middle Eastern policies was expressed by Qadhdhāfī in his speech on 7 October 1977—"Vengeance Day," the anniversary of the departure of the last Italian "colonialists" from Libya: "The US is waging a war against nationalists in which Washington replaces Rome, both ancient Rome of the days of Carthage and that of the Italian-Libyan war . . . Washington today is the ancient imperialist Rome. It carries the banners of war against Arab nationalism, against the East . . . He who allies himself with the US now becomes an enemy of the Arab nation . . . a real enemy, even if he carries the Ka'aba over his head."[45]

Despite this chronic strain in political relations and apart from the nationalization of the oil companies, commercial contacts have continued undisturbed. In particular, American agricultural technology has contributed significantly to Libyan development.

ECONOMIC AFFAIRS (0.296 Libyan dinars = US $1; 0.5246 LD = £1 sterling)
According to Libyan statistics, the overall growth of the economy in 1976 was estimated at 18.2% (cf an average planned growth of c. 11%). Per capita income increased from $4,620 in 1975 to $5,190 in 1976. However, the regime had to cope with increasing local demands voiced by the BPCs for more money. The "revolution of rising expectations" also found expression in the November 1976 GPC.

OIL

The first three months of 1977 marked the 41st consecutive quarter (since 1966) in which the value of oil exports exceeded 99% of Libya's total export sales. Ever since Libya first began to export crude petroleum in the early 1960s, its economy has become increasingly dependent on that single resource. However, from 1969 to 1976, Libya successfully adopted an oil policy by which: 1) production was reduced, leading to a slower depletion rate of what is, after all, a finite natural resource; and 2) the price was raised *five-fold*, leading to annual revenues from sales almost tripling between 1970 and 1976, even though production had been cut back to only 56% of the 1970 level.

In 1976, annual oil income surpassed its 1974 level, after dropping in 1975 (see tables, below). This was due to the first significant increase in Libyan oil exports since 1970. Oil liftings from existing wells were augmented; off-shore exploration was said to have yielded good results; and preparations were well advanced for the construction of a 400-km pipeline to bring oil from new fields in western Libya to the sea. The country's oil liftings were expected to surpass 800m barrels in 1977 (cf c. 675m barrels in 1976).

DEVELOPMENT PLANS

While Libya's short-term economic future continues to be oil-dependent, the government has adopted a longer-term policy of importing growing amounts of capital goods in an effort to accelerate economic development and become self-sufficient. The 1976-80 Transformation Plan for Economic and Social Development allocates LD 1,226m (c. $4,141m) or 17% of its LD 7,170m (c. $24,219m) total to agriculture; 15% or LD 1,090m (c. $3,682m) to industry and mineral wealth; LD 1,005m (c. $3,395m) to communications and maritime transport; another 17% or LD 1,191m (c. $4,023m) to the energy sector; and LD 794m (c. $2,682m) for housing. Total investments planned amounted to $25,600m, of which $5,170m was allocated for 1977. Since only 70% of the planned investments was made in 1976, however, one may doubt whether these targets will be attained. In the first half of 1977, actual expenditure amounted to 36% of the annual allocation.

Another target of the five-year plan is to raise GDP from LD 1,557m (c. $5,259m) in 1975 to LD 3,440m (c. $11,620m) by 1980, at a compound annual rate of 16%.

Libya's development plans are understandably ambitious, As recently as 15 years ago, the country was pastoral and pre-industrial, with a chronic balance of trade deficit and a dearth of workers who were skilled or even literate. Since then, the oil windfall has eliminated the trade deficit and allowed Libyan officials to allocate massive sums of money in the effort to modernize both the economy and society. Even though expenditure on health and education multiplied each year since 1969-70, the majority of skilled workers, managers, doctors and other professionals in higher education and the health sciences are non-Libyans.

Foreign manpower accounted for a third of the total labour force in 1975; by 1980, this may rise to 40%. Because most of the foreign employees are still Egyptians (up to 80% in mid-1977), aggravated relations between Cairo and Tripoli could cause a considerable slowdown in development projects. In fact, the Libyan hope for a better life through overall development has been frustrated by one basic problem: the persistent shortage of manpower.

Whereas progress towards "Libyanization" in education and health is necessarily slow, the process is much more rapid in other sectors of the economy where the state has decided to take over, such as foreign banks, the export-import trade and some oil companies.

FOREIGN TRADE

Libya's imports came from more than 79 countries in 1975; it sent exports to 34 states. More than 99.99% of the value of Libyan exports came from oil. Groundnuts, edible oils and animal skins and hides sent to various countries bordering on the Mediterranean comprised the rest of Libya's exports. Imports, however, were more diverse, covering all ten SITC (Standard International Trade Classification) groupings. Overall, in 1975, Italy was the largest source of Libyan imports, followed by West Germany, France, Japan and Great Britain. Italy was also the largest supplier in six of the ten SITC classes. The exceptions were Argentinian beef, American beverages and tobacco, Tunisian animal and vegetable oils and fats, and, lastly, British chemicals.

Libya's chief imports were manufactured goods (combined classification), followed by machinery and transport equipment, and food and live animals.

For the fourteenth consecutive year, Libya enjoyed a balance of trade surplus in 1976. Exports exceeded imports by LD 1,211m (c. $4,090m), more than doubling the 1975 surplus of LD 553m (c. $1,868m).

Libya's international reserves were $3,716m, of which $3,609m was foreign exchange at the end of June 1977.

At the end of 1976, the Central Bank of Libya held LD 1,064m (c. $3,594m) in foreign assets, with only LD 0.8m (c. $2.7m) of foreign liabilities.

INFLATION

At the end of June 1976, inflation, as measured by the consumer price index, stood at 3.9% for the preceding 12 months.

(Economic Section by Ira E. Hoffman)

FIVE-YEAR ECONOMIC AND SOCIAL TRANSFORMATION PLAN
(Allocations by Sector, in thousands of Libyan dinars)

Development Sector	*Total allocations 1976–80+*	*Allocations 1976++*	*Allocations 1977†*
Agriculture and agrarian reform	412,269	111,086	104,110
Internal agricultural development	857,760	165,840	176,050
Dams and water resources	86,040	—	15,714
Nutrition and maritime wealth	49,161	8,836	14,030
Industry and mineral wealth	1,149,418	142,495	190,693
Oil and gas exploration	670,000	90,000	95,000
Electricity	683,195	116,585	152,750
Education	491,655	111,990	120,850
Information and culture	99,163	19,800	21,155
Manpower	56,002	7,349	11,565
Public health	197,655	35,330	45,060
Social affairs and social security	13,157	9,527	4,250
Youth and sports	52,220	—	9,500
Housing	794,236	150,000	185,000
Security services	35,000	10,000	11,000
Municipalities	564,108	109,850	125,000
Transport and communications	659,854	87,585	121,595
Maritime transport	373,500	70,850	73,250
Trade and marketing	36,730	6,280	4,760
Planning and scientific research	13,045	7,635	3,640
Reserves for projects	230,027	32,012	35,028
Total	**7,525,000**	**1,285,000**	**1,520,000**

+As amended in December 1976.
++As approved on 18 January 1976.
†As approved on 28 December 1976.
Source: MEED, 18 February 1977.

BALANCE OF TRADE (millions of Libyan dinars)

	1972	1973	1974	1975	1976
Exports	797.7	1,032.4	2,110.8	1,805.3	2,487.1
Annual rate of growth (1972=100)	100	129	265	226	312
Imports (fob)	n.a.	544.0	956.0	1,252.0	1,276.0
Annual rate of growth (1973=100)	—	100	176	230	235
Balance of trade	**n.a.**	**488.4**	**1,154.8**	**553.3**	**1,211.1**

Source: IMF, *International Financial Statistics.*

BALANCE OF PAYMENTS (millions of US$)

	1972	1973	1974	1975
Goods, services and transfers	238	66	1,832	-480
Exports of merchandise, fob	2,942	4,019	8,267	6,753
Imports of merchandise, fob	-1,291	-2,011	-3,746	-4,473
Exports of services	225	216	434	372
Imports of services	-1,484	-1,957	-2,918	-2,896
Private unrequited transfers, net	-52	-44	-137	-72
Government unrequited transfers, net	-102	-156	-69	-164
Long-term capital, nie	-43	-510	-422	-1,241
Direct investment	-4	-148	-241	-416
Other government	-40	-364	-179	-817
Other	1	1	-2	-7
Short-term capital, nie	243	409	374	386
Deposit money banks	-5	-56	-31	102
Other	249	465	405	284
Errors and omissions	-25	-1,023	-59	-216
Total	**+413**	**-1,059**	**+1,725**	**-1,550**

EMPLOYMENT IN HEALTH AND EDUCATION SECTORS, 1974

	Total	Non-Libyans	Libyans
Physicians	2,100	1,972	128
Dentists	136	125	11
Chemists and pharmacists	218	175	43
Nursing staff	7,927	2,863	5,064
Technicians and assistants	1.267	735	532
Secondary school teachers	2,170	1,225	945

Source: Libyan Arab Republic, *Statistical Abstract of Libya, 1974.*

VOLUME OF PETROLEUM EXPORTS (1970 = 100)

1970	1971	1972	1973	1974	1975	1976	1977 (first ¼)
100	82.1	65.7	65.8	45.1	43.3	57.2	60.0

EXPORT PRICES OF CRUDE PETROLEUM (1970 = 100)

100	123	130	186	554	500	533	595

Source: IMF, *International Financial Statistics.*

VOLUME OF OIL EXPORTS, BY DESTINATION (thousands of barrels)

	1972	%	*1973*	%	*1974*	%	*1975*	%	*1976*	%
US	63,762	8.0	74,910	9.4	479	0.1	116,795	22.4	181,559	26.
West Germany	173,963	21.9	181,452	22.9	120,424	22.1	103,965	19.9	136,019	20.
Italy	164,517	20.7	206,579	26.0	183,535	33.7	107,362	20.6	128,755	19.
France	79,218	10.0	44,252	5.6	32,416	6.0	19,606	3.8	35,684	5.
Spain	21,092	2.7	11,996	1.5	20,017	3.7	32,228	6.2	34,730	5.
Netherlands	49,234	6.2	31,427	4.0	4,908	0.9	10,537	2.0	16,387	2.
UK	106,784	13.5	90,935	11.5	66,770	12.3	18,441	3.5	16,280	2.
Trinidad	61,136	7.7	35,354	4.5	13,826	2.5	33,373	6.4	11,552	1.
Norway	1,710	0.2	1,409	0.2	649	0.1	2,841	0.5	4,255	0.
Switzerland	12,341	1.6	11,865	1.5	7,640	1.4	2,378	0.5	2,751	0.
Belgium	9,352	1.2	19,896	2.5	10,824	2.0	1,942	0.4	1,624	0.
Denmark	678	0.1	1,272	0.2	1,646	0.3	835	0.2	148	—
USSR	13,999	1.8	12,906	1.6	—	—	—	—	—	—
Others	34,714	4.4	69,434	8.7	80,838	14.9	80,678	15.4	104,746	15.
Total	**793,310**		**793,687**		**543,972**		**522,346**		**675,859**	

Source: Central Bank of Libya, *Economic Bulletin.*

VALUE OF OIL EXPORTS, BY DESTINATION (millions of US$, at current prices)

	1972	*1973*	*1974*	*1975*	*1976*
US	184.7	324.9	7.1	1,364.7	2,258.4
West Germany	505.6	791.4	1,575.1	1,212.4	1,687.5
Italy	477.9	898.5	2,401.9	1,255.1	1,603.5
France	230.9	193.5	427.6	231.5	445.0
Spain	62.3	51.8	263.7	377.7	428.2
Netherlands	143.2	138.2	64.1	121.9	201.5
UK	311.7	397.4	876.6	213.2	201.5
Others	392.1	660.2	1,511.1	1,316.0	1,569.9
Total	**2,308.9**	**3,455.9**	**7,127.2**	**6,092.5**	**8,395.5**

Source: IMF, *International Financial Statistics.*

EXPENDITURE ON LIBYAN OIL[1] (1970=100)

		1970	*1971*	*1972*	*1973*	*1974*	*1975*	*1976*
Price index		**100**	**123**	**130**	**186**	**554**	**500**	**533**
US	**Q**	100	160	185	218	1	340	528
	E	100	196	241	405	8	1,698	2,814
West Germany	**Q**	100	82	79	82	54	47	62
	E	100	100	102	153	302	235	328
Italy	**Q**	100	77	54	67	60	35	42
	E	100	95	70	125	332	175	224
France	**Q**	100	79	48	27	20	12	21
	E	100	97	62	50	108	59	114
Spain	**Q**	100	78	37	20	34	55	59
	E	100	95	48	38	188	274	315
UK	**Q**	100	91	60	51	37	10	9
	E	100	111	78	95	207	52	49
Others	**Q**	100	74	76	76	50	55	59
	E	100	91	99	142	276	275	312
Total	**Q**	100	82	66	66	45	43	56
	E	100	101	85	122	250	216	298

[1] Expenditure Index $= \frac{\text{Price Index} \times \text{Quantity Index}}{100}$

Sources: Price index derived from IMF, *International Financial Statistics;* quantity index derived from Central Bank of Libya, *Economic Bulletin.*

IMPORTS, BY COUNTRY OF ORIGIN, 1974 AND 1975

	Value in LD (000)		Percent	
	1975	*1974*	*1975*	*1974*
Italy	271,893	202,990	25.9	24.8
W. Germany	127,262	93,871	12.1	11.5
France	92,694	84,672	8.8	10.4
Japan	86,821	57,127	8.3	7.0
UK	57,653	40,636	5.5	5.0
Greece	44,921	28,881	4.3	3.5
US	41,903	31,729	4.0	3.9
Argentina	29,411	8,335	2.8	1.0
Romania	29,033	18,680	2.8	2.3
Spain	26,214	23,207	2.5	2.8
Lebanon	25,824	29,844	2.5	3.6
Holland	21,500	18,096	2.1	2.2
China P.R.	21,182	18,096	2.0	2.2
Yugoslavia	15,432	17,471	1.5	2.1
Other Countries	156,993	144,290	14.9	17.7
Total	**1,048,736**	**817,843**	**100.0**	**100.0**

Source: Libyan Arab Republic Ministry of Planning, Census and Statistics Dept., *Report on External Trade Statistics for the Calendar Year 1975* (Tripoli, December 1976).

NOTES

1. Libya's "Constitutional Declaration" was promulgated by the RCC on 11 December 1969.
2. R Tripoli, 16 November—Summary of World Broadcasts: The Middle East and Africa (BBC), 18 November 1976.
3. Arab Revolutionary News Agency (ARNA), 29 December—BBC, 31 December 1976.
4. ARNA, 21 February—BBC, 23 February 1977.
5. The declaration was an improved version of the draft presented to the November 1976 session of the GPC.
6. *The Green Book* is a statement by Qadhdhāfī of his ideology, the first part of which appeared early in 1976. English edition: Mu'ammar al-Qadhāfī, *The Green Book*, Part I: "The Authority of the People" (London: Brian and O'Keefe, 1976).
7. ARNA, 3 March—BBC, 4 March 1977.
8. *Ibid*. Qadhdhāfī is assisted by a small staff, consisting mainly of trusted ASU veterans.
9. The RCC originally had 12 members. One died in an accident in 1972; three ceased to participate actively during the following years; and three others were involved in the Muḥayshī affair.
10. See Table.
11. R Tripoli, 8 March—BBC, 11 March 1977. "Free Unionist Officers" was the name of the group of officers headed by Qadhdhāfī who overthrew the Libyan monarchy on 1 September 1969.
12. *The Guardian*, London; 25 May 1977. See also, *The Swiss Review of World Affairs*, April 1977.
13. See the *Washington Post*, 22 November 1976.
14. *Al-Fajr al-Jadīd*, Tripoli; 19 January 1976. Paragraph 5 of the resolutions.
15. Political parties were prohibited in Libya in 1952. After the 1969 coup, party activities were still considered treasonable, and were formally outlawed in 1972.
16. *The Military Balance 1977-78* (London: International Institute of Strategic Studies).
17. This (as with many other of Qadhdhāfī's deeds) accorded with Sanūsī proceedings in Saharan and sub-Saharan regions since the 1860s.
18. ARNA, 22 November—BBC, 24 November 1976.
19. Interview on Cologne television, 28 September—Daily Report (DR), 30 September 1976.
20. ARNA, 5 February—BBC, 7 February 1977.
21. R Tripoli, 12 February—BBC, 15 February 1977.
22. Literally, "infidelization and emigration." For details, see survey of Egypt.
23. R Cairo, 22 July—BBC, 24 July 1977.
24. R Tripoli, 21 July—BBC, 23 July 1977.
25. R Tripoli, 23 July—BBC, 25 July 1977.
26. R Tripoli, 1 September 1977.
27. R Tripoli, 7 October—BBC, 11 October 1977.
28. ARNA, 2 August—DR, 2 August 1977.

29. *La Stampa*, Milan; 21 November—DR, 29 November 1976.
30. R Tripoli, 11 June 1977.
31. *Newsweek*, New York; 20 September 1976.
32. Interview of Acting Minister of Planning, in *The Middle East*, London; October 1976.
33. Cologne television, 28 September 1976—DR, 30 September 1976.
34. R Tripoli, 11 June 1977.
35. Libya claimed to have stopped supporting the IRA militarily, limiting itself to moral and political aid. In July 1977, Tripoli established diplomatic relations with Dublin.
36. R Tripoli, 2 June—DR, 3 June 1977.
37. *Le Monde*, Paris; 23 September—DR, 26 September 1977.
38. ARNA, 16 May—BBC, 18 May 1977.
39. For maps showing the disputed region, see *The Middle East*, October 1976.
40. *Al-Jihād*, Tripoli; 25 November 1976.
41. ARNA, 7 December 1976.
42. Tass and ARNA, 9 December 1977.
43. *International Herald Tribune*, Paris; 29-30 January 1977.
44. ARNA, 12 June—DR, 12 June 1977.
45. R Tripoli, 7 October—BBC, 10 October 1977. The Ka'aba is the sacrosanct stone in Mecca which is the focus of Islamic ritual and the object of Muslim pilgrimage.

The People's Democratic Republic of Yemen

(Jumhūriyyat Al-Yaman Al-Sha'biyya Al-Dīmuqrātiyya)

HAIM SHAKED and TAMAR YEGNES

The establishment of diplomatic relations between the People's Democratic Republic of Yemen (PDRY or South Yemen) and Saudi Arabia in March 1976 had important implications for both domestic and foreign policy. On the domestic front, the move produced bitter political rivalry between the two factions at the top echelon of the Unified Political Organization—The National Front (UPONF). The first faction, headed by the veteran politician, ideologue and UPONF Central Committee Secretary-General, 'Abd al-Fattāḥ Ismā'īl al-Jawfī, demanded continuation of the party's uncompromising pro-Marxist foreign policy orientation, which was opposed to any kind of co-operation with the political and economic systems of the West. The second faction—headed by the Chairman of the Presidential Council and the UPONF Central Committee Assistant Secretary-General, Sālim 'Alī Rubay'—supported a more flexible foreign policy which would not link the PDRY solely with the Eastern bloc, and thus possibly draw the country out of its total isolation, at least within the Arabian Peninsula. The *rapprochement* with Saudi Arabia fitted into this concept, all the more so since an improved relationship with the Saudis could alleviate some of the grave economic problems besetting this poor South Arabian state.

This struggle within the party's top leadership over the regime's inter-Arab (and hence international) orientation was also connected with a political power struggle within the party itself, sharpening ideological differences about the nature and means of attaining the "Southern Yemeni revolution." 'Abd al-Fattāḥ Ismā'īl and his supporters appeared to be apprehensive that any contact with "reactionary" Saudi Arabia might damage the PDRY's status and image as a Leftist radical state struggling to establish "scientific socialism" and promote "mass mobilization" with single-minded determination.

In foreign affairs, the new diplomatic links brought into clearer focus the Saudi Arabian-Soviet struggle for influence in the Arab world. The Saudi interest was clear-cut: by drawing the PDRY to its side it stood to neutralize—if not paralyse—a dangerous centre of Leftist, radical opposition and subversion, which challenged the traditional tribal system of the Arabian Peninsula. On a more concrete level, the Saudis felt that by reducing the PDRY's influence, they might end the conflict in the Dhufar area of the Sultanate of Oman. Despite its reduced military strength, the Dhufari Front continued to be a focus of ferment (and therefore danger) involving also a non-Peninsular power—Iran—in matters regarded by the Saudis as purely "local." (See chapters on Oman, Iran and Saudi Arabia.) By bringing the PDRY into their orbit, the Saudis also hoped to reduce the support it provided to Leftist elements in North Yemen—a constant threat to the improving relations between Riyadh and San'ā. Another Saudi interest was to integrate the PDRY into that group of states which wished to establish Arab hegemony over the Red Sea and extrude the Russians from the area—and especially from the strategic Bāb al-Mandūb straits.

The Soviets, on the other hand, were understandably apprehensive about losing their position at the southern entrance to the Red Sea. These fears were increased by the radical change in their relations with North Yemen, Sudan and Somalia since 1975. (See essays, "The Soviet Bloc and the Middle East" and "The Middle East and the Horn of Africa.") The intensive struggle between the USSR and Saudi Arabia for the PDRY's allegiance remained undecided at the end of 1977—due partly to the unresolved internal power struggle in South Yemen.

POLITICAL AFFAIRS

POWER STRUGGLE WITHIN THE UPONF

A power struggle within the National Front (NF), which has ruled South Yemen since its independence in 1967, reached its climax when the radical Leftists removed President Qaḥṭān al-Sha'bī on 22 June 1969 and established a three-member Presidential Council under the chairmanship of Sālim 'Alī Rubay'. His position of influence was rivalled by only one of the other Council members, 'Abd al-Fattāḥ Ismā'īl al-Jawfī. The third member was the Prime Minister and Defence Minister, 'Alī Nāsir Muḥammad Ḥusnī. The radicals' seizure of power was the beginning of a protracted and complicated process of imposing absolute party control over the civilian as well as the military sectors. This process was still continuing during 1976–7.

The military sector consisted of the PDRY Armed Forces; that is, the regular army, the General Security Units and the Popular Militia. The Supreme Commander of the regular army was Sālim 'Alī Rubay'. The General Security Units, controlled by the Ministry of the Interior, usually performed only police duties. The Popular Militia, which came under the direct control of the NF, was composed mainly of workers, peasants and students who were regarded by the NF as more "revolutionary-minded" than those in the General Security Units. The Militia was active in suppressing tribal rebels and in fighting against infiltrators who crossed the North Yemeni-South Yemeni border. They also participated in road construction and in agricultural projects. After independence, and particularly since June 1969, both the regular army and the General Security Units were rigorously purged and reorganized. Officers who belonged to the 'Awāliq tribes (concentrated mainly in the Fourth and Fifth Governorates), who were regarded as "reactionary and traditional-minded," and suspected of supporting subversive activity, were purged, exiled or executed. They were replaced by officers mainly from the Dathīna area in the Third Governorate.[1] In mid-1970, it was reported that "Revolutionary Military Commands" were being formed in the army, with soldiers put through intensive Marxist indoctrination courses. Arab sources reported at the time that the continuous purges being carried out from top to bottom, and the replacing of "reactionary" elements by those loyal to the regime made a military coup in South Yemen extremely unlikely.[2]

In praising Soviet bloc assistance for the South Yemeni Armed Forces at the beginning of September 1977, the Prime Minister and Defence Minister 'Alī Nāsir Muḥammad Ḥusnī said that the army had now been "cleansed of reactionary elements and those of a feudal origin." He added that South Yemen had reorganized its military forces in such a way as "to preclude the possibility of military coups. . . . South Yemen has overcome the danger of military coups."[3]

Also since 1969, there has occurred a virtual takeover of the state by the NF, accompanied by serious conflicts inside and outside the ruling party, a central issue being the desirable pace at which social change should be implemented. While the less radical elements favoured a gradual advance, the more extremists supported intensive and immediate "mass mobilization." Another divisive issue was whether to adopt the Soviet or the Chinese model to achieve social and economic revolution, and whether or not to support an uncompromising communist line. These controversies were interwoven with older political quarrels stemming both from traditional tribal feuds and personal disputes.

The most important rivalry was that between the factions of 'Abd al-Fattāḥ Ismā'īl and Sālim 'Alī Rubay' which intensified since the end of 1975. In October 1975, the ruling NF party had merged with two smaller political organizations: the People's Vanguard, which had connections with the Ba'th Party; and the People's Democratic Union, South Yemen's Communist party. The union was named "The Unified Political Organization, the NF" (UPONF or *al-tanẓīm al-siyāsī al-muwaḥḥad, al-jabha al-qawmiyya*). Controlled by the NF, it set up a new Central Committee composed of 79 members (61 regular and 18 candidates). Fifty-three members of the Central Committee belonged to the NF, while the other two parties had 13 members each. The Central Committee elected 'Abd al-Fattāḥ Ismā'īl as its Secretary-General and Rubay' as his assistant. The Committee also reaffirmed the NF's ideological principles, which had been formulated before and after independence in the "National Charter" of June 1965 and elaborated upon at subsequent party conferences.

The merger of the three political bodies—which led to a union of extreme Leftist elements and the NF—added to the already tense relations between the PDRY on the one hand, and North Yemen and Oman, who were backed by Saudi Arabia on the other. While the Saudis were alarmed by this turn of events, the Soviet Union welcomed the merger and promised to continue economic and military aid.

At first, observers regarded the formation of the new organization as a victory for the faction led by 'Abd al-Fattāḥ Ismā'īl. However, during December 1975 and January 1976, Rubay' and his followers—who were active in the tribal hinterland, particularly in the Fifth and Sixth Governorates (*Ḥadramawt*)—succeeded in reshuffling the Central Committee and in changing the composition of the Government in their favour. This move was aimed not only at strengthening Rubay''s position in the UPONF, but was also meant to satisfy the Ḥadrāmī claim for a more equitable representation in the party and the Government.[4]

The implications of the strengthened position of the Rubay' faction went beyond the limits of South Yemen's domestic politics. Rubay' was said to favour a *rapprochement* with Saudi Arabia and to advocate the flexible and gradual implementation of revolutionary principles, while his rival 'Abd al-Fattāḥ Ismā'īl supported a more rigid and orthodox Marxist line, both internally and externally. Such internal ideological conflicts and jockeying for key posts failed to establish the dominance of either faction in the months following January 1976. Outwardly, at least, the leadership continued to act as a homogeneous group striving to attain the declared goals of the South Yemeni revolution.

THE ROLE AND IDEOLOGY OF THE UPONF

The evolution of the regime was summed up by 'Abd al-Fattāḥ Ismā'īl in an interview with Cuban television towards the end of 1976:

> "The experience of the revolution in our country has gone through three main phases. The first was the phase of the armed popular revolution against British colonialism which occupied our country for 129 years. The second phase of the revolution began in our country in the post-independence era, considered by us extremely important, for the armed revolution in our country did not only aim to evict the colonists, but also had [other] far-reaching goals and implications. We were involved during the second phase, after independence, in a heroic resistance and in a political, ideological and class struggle so that the national in-

dependence of our country would not be transformed into a bridge for the new colonialism. The struggle was against Rightist and reactionary forces. . . . It was against the remnants of the new colonists who were attempting to stand in the path of the developing revolution, while at the same time were trying to place our country in the lap of the new colonialism. In fact we were able, through bitter struggle waged by the progressive tide, to win on 22 June 1969 [i.e. the date of the deposition of President Qaḥṭān al-Sha'bī]. The progressive tide was able, as a result, to eliminate the Rightist forces and the reservists of the new colonialism, and to acquire the reins of leadership at the level of our party and at the level of governmental authority in our country.

"The third phase was the phase of implementing the slogans; slogans of the national democratic revolution. . . . We were, in fact, able to realize many revolutionary economic, social, educational and military changes, beginning with the establishment of a national democratic authority that expressed the spiritual and material interests of the majority of the people, with the nationalization of foreign monopolistic companies [mainly between mid-1969 and mid-1970], and with the implementation, through the struggle of peasants as represented by their initiatives and uprisings led by our organization, of the Agrarian Reform Law [enacted in March 1968]—and ending with the adoption of numerous social measures at the level of the family, the elimination of illiteracy and the preparation of cadres." [5]

Turning to the ideology of the UPONF he said:

"The basic aims and principles founded by the revolution . . . depend primarily and foremost on the clearly specified ideological position of the experience of the revolution in our country. We have chosen the revolutionary thought, the scientific socialistic thought, and the ideology of the working class as an intellectual position to be used as a guide in our struggle, in analysing our situation and in continually changing this situation. We have chosen . . . a clearly-defined class position, asserting that the class forces, to whom the interests of the revolution belong, are the revolutionary workers, peasants, intellectuals and the various other social forces. We also asserted the growing role of the working class in occupying a developed leadership position, considering that the working class is the historically prepared class to lead the revolutionary process in our country. . . . We also specified within our internal system the bases upon which our organization and party rest, which are basically represented by democratic centralism and collective leadership, by criticism and self-criticism, and by many other party and revolutionary standards."

PEOPLE'S COUNCILS

One of the first steps taken by the regime in 1976, following the achievement of a measure of balance between the rival factions, was the establishment of local People's Councils. On 27 December 1976, the UPONF Central Committee concluded a session with the following announcement on the subject of local councils:

"To confirm what is enshrined in the Constitution[6] and the basic documents of the Unified Political Organization on the setting up of national democratic state organs, we want work to be continued to accomplish this goal and work on the establishment of these organs to be completed. Since the establishment of Local People's Councils in the Fifth Governorate has been completed with great success, thus demonstrating the ability of the Unified Political Organization to hold free, general and direct elections by secret ballot in electoral constituencies, we are greatly encouraged to extend this to all governorates so as to give a more progressive shape to the institutions of the national democratic organs in this phase of the national democratic revolution.

"Our political authority is embodied in the strong alliance of workers, peasants, soldiers and *petit bourgeois* revolutionary intellectuals. This force exercises political authority and gives it expression in a conscious and organized manner through the local People's Councils, elected by them and emanating from their ranks, directly expressing their will [subject] to their supervision and obliged to present to them progress reports on their work. . . .

"In this regard, the Central Committee resolves as follows:

1) That general elections should be held in all the governorates of the Republic for the establishment of local People's Councils at governorate level in the second half of 1977, with the exception of the People's Council in the Fifth Governorate, which will continue to function as a lawfully constituted council until a new election of the local People's Council.

2) That the Presidential Council be charged with the task of taking all measures for the preparation and holding of the elections."

The Central Committee further resolved that by August 1977, the Cabinet should present to the UPONF Central Committee a draft law on local elections "in the light of the operational experience gained in the Fifth Governorate," as well as a schedule for holding the elections. The Cabinet would submit the draft to the Supreme People's Council.[7] The organization committees of the UPONF in the governorates should take full responsibility for the elections. The elections should be held in the tenth year of national independence (i.e. 1977), as part of the general plan for the tenth independence anniversary.[8]

Rubay' issued a decree on 2 June 1977, concerning the eventual setting up of the People's Councils in the governorates, provinces and districts. According to the decree, the councils would be composed as follows: at governorate level, 31 to 41 members; at provincial level, 21 to 25 members; at district level, 11 to 19 members.[9]

The elections for representatives to the local People's Councils in the First, Second, Third, Fourth and Sixth Governorates were held in mid-November 1977, when women voted for the first time.[10]

GROWING ASCENDANCY OF RUBAY'

Towards mid-April 1977, it was reported in Kuwait that 'Abd al-Fattāḥ Ismā'īl had been "expelled" from the PDRY, and was visiting Cuba as a result of "severe disputes" between him on the one hand, and Rubay' and the Prime Minister and Defence Minister, 'Alī Nāsir Muḥammad Ḥusnī on the other.[11] It should be noted that between 14 and 21 April 1977, 'Abd al-Fattāḥ had led a PDRY party and governmental delegation to Czechoslovakia and Hungary, where several agreements were signed. He returned to Aden on 21 April. No official South Yemeni source alluded to the trip to Cuba, let alone to 'Abd al-Fattāḥ Ismā'īl being in exile.

The Lebanese newspaper *al-Sayyād* reported in mid-September that Rubay''s wing had won the struggle against 'Abd al-Fattāḥ's wing. The paper commented that the majority in the UPONF leadership now supported Rubay''s policy of *rapprochement* with Saudi Arabia, and opposed "a Soviet plan to establish a federation composed of Ethiopia, Somalia and PDRY."[12] On 2 September, the Health Minister, 'Abd al-'Azīz al-Dāli', was dismissed by Rubay' and transferred to the Foreign Ministry. No explanation for this dismissal was given, but it was probably connected with the internal power struggle.

BAN ON QĀT

One issue which exemplified the revolutionary zeal of the regime and its break with tradition was the ban imposed on 2 January 1977 on the consumption, sale and purchase of the favourite narcotic chewing leaf, the *qāt*. The legal ban followed a campaign by the PDRY Government against the use of *qāt* which is reported to have caused a loss of c. 7m working hours during 1976. Towards the end of January 1977, eight *qāt* growers, accused of demonstrating in Dāli' (Second Governorate) in protest against the ban, were sentenced to death. Two others were jailed for ten years. In March, Rubay' commuted the death sentences to various terms of imprisonment.

OPPOSITION TO THE REGIME

Since independence, opposition within the regime emanated mainly from NF members in Aden or in local party cells in the hinterland. Between 1967 and 1975, several abortive coups were reportedly initiated by NF members attempting to exploit local power centres in order to seize power. However, throughout 1976 and the first eight months of 1977, information on opposition activities only came to light following the attempted assassination in Cairo on 6 August 1976 of Muḥammad 'Alī Haytham, who had served as Prime Minister from June 1969 until he was dismissed in August 1971. Expelled shortly afterwards, he was suspected of having connections with opponents to the regime inside the PDRY. The Egyptian press alleged that the Second Secretary in the PDRY embassy in Cairo, 'Alī Sayf Muḥsin, was directly involved and was connected with a Palestinian PFLP member named Salāḥ Muḥammad al-'Amrī, as well as with the Director of the Yemen Airline Company, Sāliḥ 'Isā, who took part in the assassination attempt. (The latter two were arrested in Cairo.) However, the PDRY's Foreign Ministry denied any connection with the incident.

On 23 August 1976, an aircraft on an internal flight in Egypt was taken over by hijackers who demanded the freeing of 'Amrī and 'Isā. The hijackers were captured, and in November 1976, an Egyptian military court sentenced the Palestinian Salāḥ Muḥammad al-'Amrī to death and Sāliḥ 'Isā to life imprisonment with hard labour. 'Amrī was executed in Cairo on 19 April 1977.[13]

After recovering from his wounds, Haytham put the blame for the attempt on the "Communist regime" in Aden. He declared that the PDRY regime had provided the Soviets with an air and naval base as part of an "overall strategy" to turn the Indian Ocean into an international conflict area.[14] According to Haytham, c. 1,500 opponents to the regime had been executed since 1972 and c. 250,000 had been expelled.

Another source of opposition to the regime were the various clandestine organizations, concentrated around the expelled leaders of FLOSY and SAL,[15] around ex-Sultans and—following the widescale purges in the military during 1969–70—also around dismissed army officers. These opposition circles were originally backed financially and militarily by Saudi Arabia and North Yemen, as well as by tribes inside South Yemen which had been incited to revolt and launch guerrilla activities against the NF regime in all the governorates of the hinterland and inside Aden itself. However, following the agreement for a formal union between the two Yemens, signed in October 1972 (which was not, however, implemented), the subversive activities of these opposition groups greatly diminished. This was due to the withdrawal of assistance; to counter-attacks by the South Yemeni regular army and Militia units against rebel tribes; and to lack of coordination and internal rivalries among the opposition groups. They thus came to constitute no more than a nuisance to the NF regime, especially after the improvement of the PDRY's relations with Saudi Arabia. Reports of underground guerrilla activities also became less frequent. In February 1976, following a relative period of calm through the preceding half year, "mercenaries" were reported to be trying to infiltrate the PDRY through the Third Governorate (bordering on North Yemen). Since then, however, no subversive activities have been reported.

THE GOVERNMENT (Formed on 31 December 1975)

Prime Minister and Defence	'Alī Nāsir Muḥammad Ḥusnī
Foreign Affairs	Muḥammad Ṣāliḥ Mutī'
Interior	Qāsim Ṣāliḥ Musiḥ
Industry and Acting Minister of Planning	'Abd al-'Azīz 'Abd al-Wālī Nāshir
Local Administration	'Alī Sālim al-Bayd
Culture and Tourism and Acting Minister of Information	'Alī 'Abd al-Razzāq Bādhīb
Minister of State for Cabinet Affairs	Nāsir Nāsir 'Alī
Minister of State for Security	Muḥammad Sa'īd 'Abdallah
Agriculture	Muḥammad Sulaymān Nāsir
Communications	Ḥaydar Abū Bākir al-'Attās
Education	Sa'īd 'Abd al-Khayr al-Nubār
Finance	Fādil Muḥsin 'Abdallah
Health	'Abd al-'Azīz al-Dālī'[1]
Justice	'Abdallah Aḥmad Ghānim
Labour and Civil Service	'Alī As'ad Muthannā
Trade and Supply	Maḥmūd Sa'īd Madhī
Housing	Nāsir Muḥammad Yāsīn
Acting Minister of State for Presidential Affairs	'Alī Sālim Lawār[2]

[1] Dismissed in September 1977.
[2] Appointed in late December 1976.

ARMED FORCES

Total armed forces number 21,300. Defence expenditure in 1977 was 15.3m South Yemeni dinars ($43.7m). Military service is compulsory, but the term of conscription is unknown. The 19,000-strong Army consists of ten infantry brigades, each of three battalions; two armoured battalions; one artillery brigade; one signals unit, and one training battalion. Equipment consists of 200 T-34, T-54 medium tanks; ten *Saladin* armoured cars; ten *Ferret* scout cars; 25-pounder, 105mm pack, 122mm, 130mm howitzers; mortars; 122mm recoilless rifles; 23mm self-propelled, 37mm, 57mm, 85mm anti-aircraft guns; SA-7 surface-to-air missiles. 500 men are deployed in the Arab Peace-keeping Force in the Lebanon. The Navy, which is subordinate to the Army, numbers 300 and is equipped with two submarine chasers (ex-Soviet SO-1 class); two motor torpedo boats (ex-Soviet P-6 class); three minesweepers (ex-British *Ham*-class); six small patrol craft, and two landing craft (ex-Soviet *Polnocny*-class). The Air Force numbers 2,000 and is equipped with 33 combat aircraft (some believed to be in storage). Formations consist of one bomber squadron with six Il-28; one fighter squadron with 12 MiG-21; one fighter-bomber squadron with 15 MiG-17; one transport squadron with four Il-14, three An-24, some C-47; one helicopter squadron with eight Mi-8, Mi-4 and three MiG-15UTI trainers. Paramilitary forces consist of the Popular Militia and the 1,500 Public Security Force.[16]

FOREIGN AFFAIRS

RELATIONS WITH SAUDI ARABIA

The establishment of diplomatic relations with Saudi Arabia on 10 March 1976 ended nine years of continuous tension between the two neighbouring states, which had deteriorated several times into border hostilities, albeit on a limited scale. There were several motives for South Yemen's decision to seek a *rapprochement* with the Saudis: its ever-growing financial deficit and severe economic problems, together with a hope that Saudi Arabia would alleviate these difficulties; a desire of certain elements within the UPONF to end the PDRY's political isolation in the Arabian Peninsula; the almost total collapse of the insurgent Popular Front for the Liberation of Oman (PFLO) in Dhufar, due to severe defeats throughout 1975 resulting from a strengthened Iranian military presence there. All this made NF leaders reassess their policy of assisting the PFLO, thereby removing a major stumbling block for co-operation with Saudi Arabia. Another possible reason was that an improvement of relations with the Saudis would bring an end to subversive activities of those opposition groups operating from Saudi Arabia, and possibly also from North Yemen. (For relations between South and North Yemen, see survey on North Yemen. For Saudi policy towards PDRY, see survey on Saudi Arabia.)

At the beginning of 1976, several Arab sources reported that "suitable circumstances" had been created for the setting up of diplomatic relations between the two countries. A joint Saudi-South Yemeni statement on 10 March 1976 spoke of the "desire to create an atmosphere of mutual understanding" and a "concern to establish normal relations" in order to bring "progress, prosperity and peace for themselves and security and stability for the Arabian Peninsula, so that they may devote their efforts to opposing the Zionist aggression and to preventing foreign interference which do harm to the safety and security of the region." The joint statement also referred to co-operation in the economic and cultural fields.[17] This normalization of relations was immediately welcomed by North Yemen and the Sultanate of Oman. In fact, throughout 1976–7, fierce internal political rivalry between Rubay''s pro-Saudi wing and 'Abd al-Fattāh Ismā'īl's pro-Soviet wing reflected a struggle between those two countries to secure their positions in South Yemen and thereby their influence in the Red Sea area.

Another feature of Saudi-South Yemeni relations was the special effort made by the former to offer financial assistance. For instance, the Saudis were reported to have given $400m to the PDRY at the beginning of 1976[18] (see Economic Affairs, below). In September 1976, officials of the Saudi Oil and Mineral Resources Ministry and the Finance and Economy Ministry were reported to be studying the possibility of building a 2,000-km pipeline linking the eastern part of the Kingdom with a point on the South Yemen shore to transport crude oil from Saudi Arabia and Kuwait.[19] However, no further reports appeared on the implementation of this project. An agreement for refining Saudi oil in Aden was signed in May 1977 (see below). In June 1977, the Saudi Development Fund signed a long-term loan agreement of SR 70m to finance an electric power project in the PDRY, which was ratified by Rubay' in August 1977.[20]

Saudi Arabia's Foreign Minister, Sa'ūd al-Faysal, arrived in Aden for a three-day visit on 9 April 1977 during which he inspected a number of projects. A joint communiqué issued at the end of his stay spoke of the "determination to strengthen and cement the relations of co-operation . . . developing the relations between the two countries in all fields."[21]

In turn, Rubay' arrived in Saudi Arabia on 31 July 1977 for a three-day official visit—the first by a South Yemeni Head of State. A joint communiqué issued on 2 August spoke of a "design to consolidate their bilateral relations within the framework of Arab and Islamic glorious legacy"; it expressed "their satisfaction with the high level of their relations" and "affirmed the importance of making the Red Sea a zone of peace and stability, and of keeping it out of any conflict and clear of international ambitions."[22]

RELATIONS WITH OMAN

At the end of 1975, there were reports of South Yemen restricting its assistance to the PFLO and of a possible improvement of relations with the Sultanate of Oman. The shooting down of an Iranian Phantom F-4 by PDRY forces on 24 November 1976 gave rise to foreign and Arab comments that the presence of Iranian military forces in Oman was the real obstacle blocking moves towards the normalization of relations. The incident led to heightened tensions, with Oman accusing PDRY of trying to sabotage the Gulf foreign ministers conference—also attended by Iran—which was scheduled for 25 and 26 November. However, Saudi Arabia's mediation, which led to the return of the Iranian aircraft and pilot in late December 1976, prevented a further deterioration in relations.

The Under-Secretary of the Omani Foreign Ministry said that "Oman will fully co-operate with the efforts being made [by Saudi Arabia] to improve relations with the PDRY." He added: "There are signs indicating that the PDRY authorities have now begun to realize the importance of achieving stability in the Gulf area . . . Saudi Arabia has been trying to bring about a reconciliation" between PDRY and Oman.[23] In January 1977, the PDRY Minister of Culture and Tourism and Acting Minister of Information, 'Alī 'Abd al-Razzāq Bādhīb, said that "the forces of world imperialism, under the leadership of the US, and the forces of reaction, led by Iran which regards itself as the vigilant police force working in the interests of imperialism and colonialism, were attempting to obstruct the progressive transformations that were going on in Democratic [South] Yemen . . . Iranian military presence in Oman did not only constitute a danger to the Arab Gulf area, but also constituted a serious threat to all the other neighbouring Arab countries."[24]

At the Red Sea Conference held in Ta'izz (North Yemen) on 23 March 1977—attended by the leaders of Sudan, Somalia, North Yemen and South Yemen—President Ja'far al-Numayrī announced that the PDRY and Oman had decided to end the dispute between them over South Yemen's support for the Dhufar rebellion.[25] Several days later, reconciliation between the two states was reported to have been achieved after mediation efforts by the Presidents of Sudan and the UAE. (Sudan's President Numayrī visited Oman between 15 and 17 March 1977, and South Yemen from 20 to 23 March. UAE President, Shaykh Zāyid b. Sultān, visited South Yemen from 17 to 19 March 1977.) A senior South Yemen official was also scheduled to visit Oman to discuss the normalization of relations.[26] However, at the beginning of April 1977, South Yemen claimed that reports of normalization were completely unfounded. Adeni sources said that the continuous "Iranian military presence and the continued presence of foreign military bases on Arab territory in Oman" were the cause of tense relations.[27]

Nevertheless, in April 1977, there were reports of serious disputes between the UPONF and the PFLO.[28] Several senior PFLO officials were reportedly arrested in Aden and so prevented from meeting President Castro during his visit in March 1977. The reason for the dispute was said to be Aden's refusal to allow PFLO guerrillas (stationed in the Sixth Governorate, bordering on Oman) to cross the border to launch operations there since the PDRY wished to avoid any further confrontation with Omani forces. The PFLO regarded the prohibition to cross the border as part of "a co-ordinated plan between Aden and Riyadh on ending the crisis" between Oman and South Yemen.

At the beginning of June 1977, the Kuwaiti press reported that the PDRY Foreign Minister had made a secret visit to Oman for talks aimed at ending the conflict. In the same month, 'Abd al-Fattāḥ Ismā'īl, speaking on the occasion of the 12th anniversary of insurgency in Dhufar, completely denied any mediation between PDRY and Oman; he said that South Yemen continued to adhere to its position in support of the PFLO and added: "The starting point of any political settlement in Oman is the complete withdrawal of the Iranian forces, the liquidation of the military bases, and freedom for the Omanis to determine their own destiny." [29] A secret meeting between the foreign ministers of Oman and South Yemen was reportedly held in Riyadh on 25 June 1977 under the auspices of the Saudi Foreign Minister. The meeting was considered a step forward in the mediation efforts being undertaken by Saudi Arabia, but did not resolve the dispute. [30]

RELATIONS WITH OTHER ARAB STATES

The improvement of relations with Saudi Arabia was accompanied by a gradual improvement of South Yemeni relations with other Arab countries. In October 1976, the Kuwaiti-based Arab Fund for Economic and Social Development (AFESD) granted an $8.8m loan for the completion of a fisheries project at Mukallā. Another AFESD loan of $9.3m was announed in January 1977 for the same project. Kuwait's offer of assistance for Aden's refinery project was announced in the first half of 1977. In May, following the nationalization of BP, an agreement was signed to refine Kuwaiti crude oil in Aden (see below).

Several delegates were sent to Arab countries in 1976–7 to discuss economic affairs and explain the difficulties facing South Yemen due to the rising oil prices. In January 1977, the South Yemeni Minister of Finance signed an agreement in Vienna with the OPEC Special Fund for a loan of $4.4m, of which $2.4m was to come from Abū Dhabī. [31]

In March 1977, Jordan and South Yemen agreed to establish diplomatic relations at ambassadorial level. [32] In the same month, an economic, technical and cultural agreement was signed with Sudan.

Although the PDRY was thus busy improving relations with the more traditional and conservative Arab states, her ties with Iraq and Libya remained close.

RELATIONS WITH THE PLO AND URBAN GUERRILLA GROUPS

The *rapprochement* with Saudi Arabia and an apparent change in the direction of moderation did not affect the PDRY's vigorous support of the militant Palestinian organizations and international terrorist activities. The radical Palestinian organizations—the PFLP in particular—had organizational and ideological links with the UPONF leadership. On several occasions captured members of international terrorist organizations mainly the Japanese Red Army as well as the Baader-Meinhoff group, revealed during interrogation that they had been trained in a camp in South Yemen by Palestinian PFLP members. [33]

The PDRY position was stated clearly by 'Abd al-Fattāḥ Ismā'īl: "We speak primarily about our close link with the movement of the Arab revolution with all its democratic and progressive forces . . . The Lebanese incidents do not mean the liquidation of the Lebanese progressive nationalist movement, nor do they mean the liquidation of the Palestinian resistance; they mean the liquidation of the Arab liberation movement in its entirety. For this reason we say that our stand is a firm principled one with the nationalist and progressive movement in Lebanon and with the Palestine Resistance, because their defeat is a defeat for us and their victory is a victory for us." [34]

The PLO leader, Yāsir 'Arafāt, visited Aden on 18 February 1977 where he met the pro-Saudi group of Rubay', Prime Minister Ḥusnī and Foreign Minister Mutī' for discussions on the "regional and international situation in the light of the political activities presently being undertaken in the Middle East." [35]

In May 1977, South Yemen—together with Libya, Iraq and Somalia—were accused by the US State Department of providing various forms of assistance to terrorists. [36] However, this statement was dismissed on 12 May by a PDRY Foreign Ministry source as "just one of many false allegations; the backing and support extended to the just struggle of the Palestinian and other peoples did not constitute an act of terrorism, as imperialist, Zionist and racist circles chose to interpret it . . . PDRY will continue to stress its denunciation and disapproval of international terrorism in every shape and form and will continue to adhere to the principles it believed in, backing the just struggle of peoples and supporting the heroic struggle being waged by national liberation movements to free their people from the injustice and persecution perpetuated by imperialist and racist regimes." [37]

The PFLP Secretary-General, George Ḥabash, arrived in Aden on 21 September, to discuss "developments affecting the Palestine cause and the dangers threatening it, particularly in Southern Lebanon, as well as issues relating to the Red Sea and the Horn of Africa." [38]

RELATIONS WITH THE SOVIET UNION AND CUBA

While the PDRY's relations with conservative and Western oriented states were developing, her existing ties with the Soviet block remained unchanged, despite some disagreements reported. In September 1976, 'Abd al-Fattāḥ Ismā'īl said in an interview with Cuban television: "Our foreign policy rests upon the principle of solidarity among nations and peaceful coexistence between states with differing social systems." He added: "We all realize that imperialist, Zionist, colonialist and neo-colonialist forces, and all reactionary forces associated with them have always persisted in resisting the people, to prevent their political liberation and economic independence." [39]

The Soviets continued to support the PDRY, and especially encouraged the pro-Soviet, anti-Saudi faction headed by 'Abd al-Fattāḥ Ismā'īl. Foreign Minister Mutī' visited the Soviet Union from 10 to 12 May 1977, where he was received by Brezhnev and Gromyko. A joint communiqué broadcast on 13 May said that both sides had expressed their determination to continue to deepen their friendly relations. Both sides supported the "anti-imperialist struggle" waged by the peoples of the Arabian Peninsula and the Gulf for political and ecônomic independence, and both sides expressed concern at the attempts made by "reactionary forces" to create tension in the Red Sea area, which should be "a zone of peace, in view of the fact that the Red Sea is considered to be a channel for the passage of major world maritime lines." [40]

Soviet economic assistance was mainly in the fields of agriculture, fishing, construction, electricity, oil and minerals. It was reported in September 1977 that the Soviets were to participate in several projects, including oil prospecting in the north-east of the country, by supplying equipment and providing experts. They would also take part in an irrigation project in the Ḥadramawt region. [41]

The Egyptian *Ākhir Sā'a* reported at the beginning of March 1977 that Cuban military experts had arrived in Aden to train the South Yemeni armed forces in the use of Soviet equipment. [42] A similar report published the following month added that the Cuban experts had come to replace the Soviets and East German advisers. [43] (The Adeni Intelligence Service was reported to include a considerable number of East Germans; South Yemen agents had also been trained in East

Berlin.) The Cuban Communist Party and the UPONF signed an inter-party agreement in April 1977, providing for an exchange of party experts and the training of cadres.[44] Rubay' visited Cuba in the last week of September 1977.[45]

INVOLVEMENT IN THE HORN OF AFRICA

The visit of Fidel Castro in Aden from 10 to 12 March 1977 was closely related to the particular Soviet-Cuban move to achieve Somali-Ethiopian co-operation, and to the more general attempt to develop closer relations between the "Marxist-Leninist" regimes in the Horn of Africa and the communist world.

The PDRY, which had in the past supported the Somali Republic and especially the Eritrean liberation movement against the Ethiopian government, changed its position after the emergence of a professing Marxist-Leninist regime in Addis Ababa. It began to adopt a similar position to that of the Soviets and Cubans in support of the Ethiopians, but without completely abandoning the Eritreans. (See essay, "The Middle East and the Horn of Africa.") In August 1977, *al-Ahrām* commented on this dual relationship: "The attention of observers has been drawn to the large-scale moves that have been carried out by the PDRY, supporting the Ethiopian government in its pressure on the Popular Front for the Liberation of Eritrea. . . . It has been learned that the visit which was made by PDRY Interior Minister and Central Committee member Qāsim Sālih Muslih to Addis Ababa from 7 to 9 August [1977], which was not announced in Aden, was aimed at supporting the Soviet position and strengthening PDRY relations with all the members of the Ethiopian military leadership council. . . . The visit also aimed at co-ordinating the role which could be played jointly by the PDRY and Ethiopia *vis-à-vis* the deteriorating situation in Ogaden. . . . It is known that the PDRY's military, political and moral support for Ethiopia continues and that the number of their military experts in Ethiopia has reached 180."[46]

RELATIONS WITH THE US

The UPONF faction which supported a *rapprochement* with Saudi Arabia also favoured a restoration of relations with the US. (Although Washington had recognized South Yemen's independence in 1967 and raised the status of the US Consulate-General in Aden to that of an embassy, there had never been an exchange of ambassadors. South Yemen broke off relations with the US in October 1969, prohibited US citizens from entering the country, and ordered the expulsion of the US *chargé d'affaires*.) There were several reports in 1977 of contacts between South Yemen and US representatives: in March, a Kuwaiti paper reported "official" contacts between the two countries and the imminent establishment of diplomatic relations.[47] Later, in September, moves in this direction were said to have definitely begun.[48]

ECONOMIC AFFAIRS (0.345 Yemeni dinars = US$1; 0.62 YD = £1 sterling)

Independence in 1967 brought with it severe economic and administrative problems which affected all sectors of the economy and administration. The departure of the British army which had provided local employment to many Adenis, the sharp cut in British financial aid and the closure of the Suez Canal—all in 1967—caused economic stagnation, budgetary deficits, a sharp rise in prices, decreased income and unemployment. These problems were accentuated by the nationalization of foreign firms, mainly engaged in banking and insurance, which took place at the end of 1969 and in 1971; by the severe drought at the end of 1968 and early 1970; by the confiscation of lands without compensation; and by the shortage of skilled and unskilled labour following large-scale emigration, which was estimated in

November 1976 by Rubay' himself to have reached 1m.[49] The reopening of the Suez Canal in mid-1975 brought some improvement, but did not make a decisive contribution towards remedying Aden's unemployment problem.

These severe and continuing economic problems were undoubtedly a main motive for Rubay''s faction in seeking Saudi and Saudi-backed financial assistance. Following the establishment of diplomatic relations between the PDRY and Saudi Arabia in March 1976, it was reported that Saudi Arabia and Kuwait offered "unlimited" help to bolster the South Yemeni economy, especially by developing an oil refinery complex based on the British Petroleum (BP) refinery in Aden.[50] Built in 1954, this had not been affected by the nationalization of major foreign firms in 1969. However, even after the reopening of the Suez Canal, the refinery was still operating at only one-fifth of its total capacity of 7.9m tonnes a year. At the beginning of 1977, it was reported that negotiations for the transfer of the refinery's ownership from BP to the PDRY government had been going on for some time, and that the PDRY was negotiating with Kuwait, Iraq, Iran, Saudi Arabia, Qatar and the United Arab Emirates to become partners in its joint ownership. Such an agreement would be "the first of its kind in the region," as well as the first project in the PDRY in which Iran was expected to be involved.[51]

The PDRY Industry Minister and Acting Minister of Planning, 'Abd al-'Azīz 'Abd al-Wālī Nāshir and the Director of BP signed an agreement in Aden on 4 April 1977 which provided for a new corporation, the National Aden Refineries Company, to take over the refinery. BP would continue to provide most of the managerial and training staff as well as technical assistance.[52]

At the end of April, the PDRY Industry Minister said: "The Government of the revolution had met with great understanding on the part of its Arab brothers and friends with regard to the importance of ensuring the continuation, development and promotion of the Aden refinery's operations through the conclusion of contracts to import crude oil from the Kingdom of Saudi Arabia and the friendly USSR. In actual fact, Soviet crude [oil] was already arriving in Aden and crude from Saudi Arabia would be arriving soon." He added that economic delegations from Kuwait, the United Arab Emirates and Libya were expected to arrive "to participate in the supply of crude oil to the Aden refinery and to assist in boosting its production."[53]

In the following months, it was reported by Gulf sources that the Soviet Union had indeed sent large quantities of crude oil to Aden. After being refined, the oil was supplied to the Soviet fleet deployed in the Red Sea and the Indian Ocean. In May, Saudi Arabia and the PDRY signed an agreement for 1m tons of Saudi oil to be refined annually in Aden. A similar agreement to refine 200,000 tons annually was signed with Kuwait.[54]

At the beginning of August 1977, the PDRY joined the Arab Common Market. As of 1 January 1978, PDRY's imports from member-states would be exempt from 50% of the customs duty. This would increase by 10% annually until imports were totally exempt from duty.[55]

According to the World Bank, South Yemen's GNP at market prices was $200m in 1974 (cf $170m in 1973). However, because of the rate of inflation, the real rate of growth was at a low level and probably did not exceed the annual rate of population increase (2.5–3%). Since economic activity is mainly concentrated around Aden and its various shipping services, the reopening of the Suez Canal considerably ameliorated the country's economic expansion.

In 1977, the PDRY received more than $50m in foreign loans—$35m from Saudi Arabia—to finance an electricity scheme and a housing project; more than $7m were loaned by the IDA for an education project. In addition, Aden received financial support in grants from the Saudis, although no details were disclosed as to the amounts involved.

The improvement of economic activity during 1977 permitted an increase of international reserves to c. $100m (cf $82m in 1976 and $55m in 1975).

In 1976, the trade deficit amounted to $34m (cf a surplus of $111m in 1975). This was due to a steep reactivation of the economy, reflected in a 50% increase in imports, to $254m (cf the 35% decrease in imports in 1975). During the same period, exports remained constant at $288m. (For the PDRY's main trading partners, see table below.)

In 1974–5, current budget expenditure amounted to more than 29.3m dinars (YD), an increase of 25% over 1973–4. 44% of the budget was allocated to Defence and Security, 16% to Education and National Guidance, and 6% to Health. Due to the stagnation of the sources of revenue financing this budget, the deficit increased from YD 10m in 1973–4 to 15.5m in 1974–5.

In 1976–7, the government increased its efforts to implement Development Budget investment, amounting to YD 17.2m, of which 27% was allocated to public works, 24% to agriculture and 17% to fishery development. In fact, this budget is part of the Five-Year Development Plan (1974–9) which aims at an investment of YD 75.3m. Almost all investments will be implemented through the public sector (99.5%), while 55% of the long-term programme will be financed from foreign aid.

CURRENT BUDGET (million Yemeni Dinars)

	1972–73	*1973–74*	*1974–75*
1. Revenue			
Taxes on personal income	1.078	1.028	0.939
Taxes on corporate income	1.388	1.273	2.008
Other taxes	0.132	0.130	0.130
Excise duties	1.269	1.588	2.410
Import duties	4.406	4.408	3.632
Stamp duties	0.378	0.410	0.370
Other indirect taxes	0.387	0.476	0.423
Non-tax revenue	2.100	4.232	3.899
Total (including others)	**12.046**	**13.545**	**13,811**
2. Expenditure			
General Administration	1.886	2.493	3.664
Defence and Security	9.798	10.200	13.000
Public Works and Communications	1.041	1.297	1.304
Finance and Economy	1.154	1.570	1.553
Health	0.996	1.274	1.671
Education and National Guidance	2.711	3.923	4.735
Agriculture	0.417	0.591	0.758
Total (including others)	**21.681**	**23.524**	**29.354**

Source: Central Statistical Office Bulletin.

BALANCE OF PAYMENTS (million SDRs)*

	1972	*1973*	*1974*
A. Goods, Services and Unrequited Transfers	-26.1	-42.9	-82.7
Merchandise, exports fob	98.1	89.7	194.8
Merchandise, imports fob	-134.6	-146.0	-301.5
Trade balance	*-36.5*	*-56.3*	*-106.7*
Services: credit	22.5	22.8	43.8
Services: debit	-37.1	-37.4	-54.7
Total goods and services	*-51.1*	*-70.9*	*-117.6*

Private unrequited transfers, net	25.0	27.6	34.2
Government unrequited transfers	—	0.4	0.7
B. Long-term capital	11.6	21.5	43.5
C. Short-term capital	14.2	22.7	19.0
D. Allocation of SDRs	3.1	—	—
Total (A through D)	**2.8**	**1.3**	**-20.2**
E. Monetary changes	-2.8	-1.3	20.2

*Exchange rates, US Dollars per SDR:
1972 = 1.085; 1973 = 1.192; 1974 = 1.202
Source: IMF, *Balance of Payments Yearbook*, March 1977.

MAIN TRADE PARTNERS (million Dollars)

	1974	*1975*	*1976*
1. Exports to:			
Canada	109	193	204
Japan	13	7	25
Angola	12	12	12
Yemen Arab Republic	9	15	11
Australia	31	26	9
China	5	5	5
Italy	0.5	0.5	3
Total (including others)	**230**	**282**	**288**
2. Imports from:			
Kuwait	119	41	52
Japan	16	23	42
United Kingdom	15	20	24
Italy	4	5	13
France	5	3	12
India	23	9	9
West Germany	9	2	8
Total (including others)	**268**	**171**	**254**

Source: IMF, *Direction of Trade 1970–76.*

FIVE-YEAR DEVELOPMENT PLAN 1974/75–1978/79 (million Yemeni Dinars)

	Total	*from which*	
	1974/75–1978/79	*1976/77*	*1977/78*
1. Capital investment by Ministry:			
Economy and Industry	3.878	0.582	0.297
Agriculture	20.797	4.083	2.453
Public Works	16.285	4.652	3.678
Communications	3.103	0.785	0.439
Education	6.060	1.320	1.530
Social Services	8.092	1.566	1.719
2. Capital investment by public corporations:			
Fish wealth	9.447	2.916	2.733
Electric power	5.298	0.726	0.706
Water	1.519	0.444	0.224
Petroleum and minerals	0.879	0.168	0.200
Total	**75.358**	**17.242**	**13,979**

Source: Aden Ministry of Planning.

NOTES

1. Shortly after independence in 1967, the NF divided the country into six administrative governorates, thus abolishing the more numerous traditional divisions of sultanates.
2. *Al-Ahrām*, Cairo; 5 December 1970.
3. Reuter, 1 September 1977.
4. Rubay', whose main power was in the backward hinterland, has encouraged poor peasants since 1971 to seize the property of wealthy owners, and to establish agricultural or fishing

co-operatives. At the same time, he worked for the establishment of local People's Councils, which later became the party cells in the governorates.

5. Interview with Cuban television on 9 September 1976, as published in the Adeni weekly, *al-Thawrī* of 11 September 1976.
6. The Constitution was proclaimed at the end of 1970. See *Middle East Record 1969–70* (Jerusalem: Israel Universities Press, 1977), pp. 1057–9.
7. The Supreme People's Council, highest organ of state power, was established in 1971.
8. R Aden, 28 December—BBC Summary of World Broadcasts (BBC), 31 December 1977.
9. R Aden, 2 June—Daily Report (DR), 3 June 1977.
10. R Aden, 16 November—BBC, 18 November 1977.
11. *Al-Yaqza*, Kuwait; 11 April 1977.
12. *Al-Sayyād*, Beirut; 15 September 1977.
13. Middle East News Agency (MENA), 19 April—BBC, 21 April 1977.
14. R Tehran, 19 August—BBC, 28 August 1976.
15. The Front for the Liberation of Occupied South Yemen (FLOSY) and the South Arabian League (SAL), both active in South Yemen before independence, became the main subversive opposition organizations to the NF. Their leaders were either expelled or had fled, mainly to North Yemen and Saudi Arabia, from where they frequently stirred up tribes against the central authorities in Aden. FLOSY's former leader, 'Abdallah Asnaj, is the Foreign Minister of North Yemen.
16. *The Military Balance 1977–78* (London: International Institute for Strategic Studies).
17. R Riyadh, 10 March—BBC, 11 March; R Aden, 10 March—BBC, 12 March 1976.
18. *Al-Siyāsa*, Kuwait; 13 March 1976. *Financial Times (FT)*, London; 25 March 1976.
19. R Riyadh, 8 September 1976.
20. R Riyadh, 15 June—DR, 16 June 1977. R Aden, 12 August—DR, 15 August 1977.
21. R Aden, 12 April—DR, 13 April 1977.
22. R Aden, 2 August—BBC, 4 August 1977.
23. R Riyadh, 28 December—DR, 29 December 1976.
24. R Aden, 17 January—DR, 18 January 1977.
25. Reuter, 23 March 1977.
26. *Al-Ra'y*, Amman; 27 March 1977.
27. R Aden, 5 April—DR, 7 April 1977.
28. *Al-Yaqza*, 11 April 1977. *Arabia and the Gulf*, London; 25 April and 9 May 1977. Reports based on information from Aden.
29. R Aden, 9 June—BBC, 11 June 1977.
30. *Al-Siyāsa*, 26 June 1977.
31. *Emirates News*, 26 January 1977.
32. R Amman, 12 March—DR, 14 March 1977.
33. The incidents of the hijacking of a Lufthansa plane in February 1972; the abortive hijacking attempt of a KLM plane in March 1974; the hijacking of a plane on an international flight in Egypt in August 1976, and other international terrorist activities were all linked with support provided to them by South Yemen.
34. R Aden, 14 October—BBC, 19 October 1976.
35. Reuter, 18 February 1977.
36. *The Times*, London; 8 May 1977.
37. R Aden, 12 May—DR, 13 May 1977.
38. R Aden, 21 September—BBC, 23 September 1977.
39. *Al-Thawrī*, Aden; 11 September 1976.
40. Tass, 13 May 1977.
41. *Middle East Economic Digest (MEED)*, London; 23 September 1977.
42. *Akhir Sā'a*, Cairo; 2 March 1977.
43. *Al-Ḥawādith*, Beirut; 23 April 1977.
44. Agence France Presse (AFP), 15 April—DR, 15 April 1977.
45. R Aden, 23 September—DR, 27 September 1977.
46. *Al-Ahrām*, 26 August 1977.
47. *Al-Yaqza*, 7 March 1977.
48. *October*, Egypt; 11 September—DR, 12 September 1977.
49. R Aden, 7 November—BBC, 9 November 1976.
50. *MEED*, 3 December 1976.
51. *Al-Siyāsa*, 9 February 1977.
52. R Aden, 4 April—DR, 5 April 1977.
53. R Aden, 30 April—BBC, 2 May 1977.
54. *MEED*, 9 May 1977. *Al-Watan*, Kuwait; 6 June 1977. *Al-Wathba*, Abū Dhabī; 25 June 1977.
55. R Aden, 2 August—BBC, 4 August 1977.

The Saudi Arabian Kingdom

(Al-Mamlaka al-'Arabiyya al-Sa'ūdiyya)

HAIM SHAKED and TAMAR YEGNES

Saudi domestic affairs were characterized by two main features in 1976 and 1977. First, there were continuous reports about conflicts and rivalries over political influence and the succession to the throne between the Jilwā and Sudayrī branches of the Royal Family. King Khālid's sickness, which kept him in hospital in London from February to the end of April 1977, encouraged persistent rumours of intensified rivalries within the Royal Court. The Saudi leadership either ignored or denied these reports, and maintained outward signs of close co-operation in administering state affairs. The second main feature was the continuing frantic pace of economic and social development. Momentum was provided not only by the enormous increase in oil revenues, but also by a greater sense of urgency about the importance of building a strong modern army at the same time as creating a self-reliant economy. This new urgency was nourished by anxieties about the period still available either before alternative sources of energy are developed, or before Saudi Arabia's enormous oil resources become exhausted.

The speed of development was limited by two constraints: Saudi Arabia's meagre human resources; and fears that the modern Western or Westernized education required for even gradual development might inflict serious damage on traditional values, and so pose a threat to traditional structures. These potential dangers were increased by the need to train a new military élite capable of handling sophisticated weaponry, and by the rapid growth of an ambitious urban *nouveau riche* sector. The growing importance of non-Saudi manpower—and ideas—posed additional problems.

Saudi Arabia's status rose considerably in 1976–77 in the Arabian Peninsula, in inter-Arab affairs and in the West, especially the US. Its influence was strengthened both in the Persian Gulf arena—where a special effort was made to consolidate relations with Iran and the Gulf states—and on the Arabian and African coasts of the Red Sea. (See essays on Inter-Arab Relations, and the Middle East and the Red Sea.) On the larger Middle Eastern scene, Saudi Arabia succeeded to some extent in strengthening its status as a cornerstone in the triangle it formed with Syria and Egypt. Through a combination of mediation, subtle pressure and promises of financial aid, the Saudis not only sponsored the settlement of local rivalries in Lebanon and Oman, but also persuaded North Yemen to weaken its Soviet ties.

In the international sphere, Saudi Arabia continued its traditional Western and anti-Soviet orientation. Although it attempted to diversify its technological and military dependence, the US remained by far the main supplier of armaments and technology. Riyadh assumed major importance to the US for a variety of reasons, ranging from its control of enormous oil and petrodollar resources to its relatively moderate stance in the Arab-Israeli conflict, and its ability to exert influence over other Arab states and strengthen anti-Soviet attitudes. Saudi Arabia's position in Middle Eastern and international affairs thus came more and more to resemble an upside down pyramid, with a relatively narrow base and a towering apex.

POLITICAL AFFAIRS

INTERNAL POLITICAL STRUGGLE

The smooth transfer of authority to King Khālid after King Faysal's assassination in March 1975 did not eliminate the rivalries connected with the next succession within the extended Royal Family. That Family includes several thousand princes, descendants of the legendary founder of the Saudi Arabian Kingdom, 'Abd al-'Aziz b. Sa'ūd. They belong mainly to two branches, each related to one of 'Abd al-'Azīz b. Sa'ūd's wives. One branch, which stemmed from a wife of the powerful Jilwā family of the north-eastern Shamar tribe, included the late King Faysal; King Khālid; the Second Deputy Prime Minister and Head of the National Guard, Prince 'Abdallah b. 'Abd al-'Azīz; and Prince Muḥammad—the eldest and most prestigious living son of King 'Abd al-'Azīz b. Sa'ūd. The second branch, stemming from a wife of the influential Sudayrī tribe, was represented by prominent figures in government and administrative posts. The best known of these are the "Sudayrı Seven"—seven full brothers who held the most influential portfolios in the Cabinet. Well known as supporters of socio-economic modernization and development, they were regarded as a challenge to the King and his Jilwā brothers. Their most prominent member is the Crown Prince and First Deputy Prime Minister, Fahd b. 'Abd al-'Azīz.

A shrewd, decisive and able administrator, Prince Fahd had played a major role under the late King Faysal, and continued to do so under King Khālid. In May 1975, he was entrusted with considerable authority over domestic and foreign affairs. The King, being ill and a weaker personality than his predecessor, essentially functioned as Head of State (*dawla*). As such, he discharged the duties of a traditional leader involved in ceremonial routine, the judicial process, and the cultivation of traditional royal connections with tribal chiefs. Prince Fahd enjoyed the support and co-operation of his full brothers: Sultān (Minister of Defence and Aviation, and Inspector-General of the Army); Turkī (Sultān's Deputy and Head of Military Intelligence); Nā'if (Minister of the Interior, also responsible for internal security); Aḥmad (Nā'if's Deputy), and Salmān (the Governor of Riyadh province). The Cabinet was composed mainly of princes and technocrats loyal to Fahd, such as Prince Mut'ib b. 'Abd al-'Azīz (Housing and Public Works); Prince Mājid b. 'Abd al-'Azīz (Municipalities and Rural Affairs); and Dr Ghāzī 'Abd al-Rahmān al-Qusaybī (Industry and Power).

The leading Princes' continuous attempts to create their own power centres have intensified over the last five years and have been especially evident in the expansion and modernization of the Saudi military forces. This development should be seen not only in terms of the Saudi wish to build a strong army in support of its foreign policy, but also against the background of domestic power struggles. Thus, while Sultān's first priority was to strengthen the air force, Fahd—as Interior Minister in Faysal's cabinet, and more recently through his brother Nā'if—concentrated on maintaining the loyalty of the internal security units. 'Abdallah, for his part, has concentrated since 1975 on consolidating his position as head of the National Guard—c. 20,000 men organized to provide security for the royal establishment and to act as a counterweight to the 45,000-strong regular army.

However, rivalry within the Court did not prevent the Royal Family from acting as one body in relation to other parts of Saudi polity and society. Nevertheless, it had to take cognizance of influential personages and groups such as the *'ulamā* (religious scholars and dignitaries) and tribal chiefs, whose conservative attitudes put them at odds with the young, mostly western-educated Saudis. The latter—whether princes or commoners, Saudi or non-Saudis—were the new technocrats, high-ranking bureaucrats and international businessmen, who shared the aim of utilizing oil revenues to promote rapid development.

Since coming to power, the 65-year old King's heart condition has caused increasing concern because of sensitive political implications. Virtually no accurate information about King Khālid's health was made available. On 11 February 1977, the King arrived in London where he was reported to have undergone two successful operations on his left thigh. About the same time, a cabinet meeting approved a suggestion by Fahd, Sultān and Nā'if to raise the salaries of all military ranks.[1] The new monthly pay for a private soldier (*jundī*) more than doubled from SR 840 ($240) to SR 1850 ($520); that for a General (*farīq awwal*) went up to SR 13,350 ($3,800) a month from SR 11,005 ($3,140). All senior officers were also granted an annual housing allowance equal to three months' salary.

While King Khālid was in London, it was reported in Arab media that he was planning to abdicate in Fahd's favour, and that Fahd wanted his own position clarified "within the next five weeks," before his scheduled visit to the US.[2] Before Fahd left for Washington on 20 May 1977, he categorically denied the above report in an illuminating interview. "The purpose of such reports which are published and disseminated by certain international quarters is, in my opinion, to spread some sort of confusion. But these people do not know the nature of the regime in this country and its method of succession. They believe that it is easy to arouse our instincts and desires without considering the fact that for us a position is a duty rather than an honour. Unfortunately, some Arabic newspapers have published such reports despite their advance knowledge that this will not happen. They know the international economic and political reputation the Kingdom enjoys. Nevertheless, some quarters think that such reports will cause a political disturbance . . . King Khālid enjoys the confidence of his kinsfolk, people and country. He is the man who has lived through the era of the visionary founder of the Kingdom, King 'Abd al-'Azīz, of King Sa'ūd and of King Faysal. With his vast experience, he is the best informed on the affairs of government, and during his office as Head of State he has been able to enhance Saudi Arabia's political power both in the region and in the world. King Khālid is good-natured. I wish I did not have to speak about him for my testimony of him is biased. But he is a man of history and only God knows how much he exhausts himself for the sake of his religion and country. I strongly deny what has been reported and I would say that those who spread such news are playing a game of which the people of the area are well aware."[3]

On King Khālid's return to Riyadh from London on 30 April, he toured various provinces for several weeks, renewing tribal allegiances. Shortly afterwards, in May, the salaries of civil servants were doubled.[4]

Prince 'Abdallah's visit to several Arab and European countries in late June was connected in some Arab quarters with the Jilwā-Sudayrī rivalry. One interpretation was that the old Jilwā Prince Muḥammad and the Head of the National Guard, 'Abdallah, feared that King Khālid's ill-health would be utilized by Fahd and the other Sudayrīs to push Prince 'Abdallah aside from the royal succession[5] and thereby monopolize political power. Prince Fahd's supporters were identified with those favouring rapid development, and Prince 'Abdallah's with the conservative faction more concerned with traditional values.[6] According to some sources Khālid had expressed his wish to relinquish power in mid-June, "but had been persuaded to delay his decision until the Princes of the Royal Family agreed on a smooth succession to the throne."[7] Fahd had stipulated that 'Abdallah should give up his post of Head of the National Guard in favour of Fahd's full brother Salmān, the Governor of Riyadh. Thus the Sudayrī branch would gain full control of all the armed and security forces. However, this report was strongly denied by the Saudi ambassador to London.[8]

There was renewed speculation in July about an open rift in the Royal Family having been prevented by King Hasan of Morocco, who mediated between Fahd on the one side and 'Abdallah and Muhammad on the other. The struggle for succession was said to be continuing "behind a well-maintained façade of secrecy," with Fahd working to reduce the effectiveness of the National Guard, or even integrate it into the armed forces proper, since it represented "the only major [armed] force in Saudi Arabia outside his control." Fahd was said "to have presented an overall plan to restrict the purchase of heavy armaments to the regular forces. At the same time, the complement of the National Guard would be curtailed and its equipment limited to light weapons." Evidently, the role Fahd had in mind for the National Guard was "much closer to that of a police force than the autonomous paramilitary formation it is at present." In the long run, he wished to prevent it from becoming a force aligned behind Prince 'Abdallah.[9]

During the second half of 1977, there were hints that Fahd was making an effort to gain the allegiance of another important branch within the Royal Family—that

THE GOVERNMENT
(Appointed in October 1975)

Portfolio	Incumbent
Prime Minister	King Khālid b. 'Abd al-'Azīz
First Deputy PM	Crown Prince Fahd b. 'Abd al-'Azīz
Second Deputy PM and Head of National Guard	'Abdallah b. 'Abd al-'Azīz
Defence and Aviation, and Inspector General of the Armed Forces	Sultān b. 'Abd al-'Azīz
Foreign Affairs	Sa'ūd al-Faysal
Interior	Nā'if b. 'Abd al-'Azīz
Oil and Mineral Wealth	Aḥmad Zakī al-Yamānī
Finance and National Economy	Muḥammad Abā al-Khayl
Information	Muḥammad 'Abduh al-Yamānī
Housing and Public Works	Mut'ib b. 'Abd al-'Azīz
Municipal and Rural Affairs	Mājid b. 'Abd al-Azīz
Planning	Hishām Muḥyī al-Dīn Nāzir
Commerce	Sulaymān 'Abd al-'Azīz al-Sulaym
Agriculture and Water	'Abd al-Raḥmān Āl al-Shaykh
Industry and Power	Ghāzī 'Abd al-Raḥmān al-Qusaybī
Communications	Shaykh Ḥusayn Ibrāhīm Mansūrī*
Labour and Social Affairs	Shaykh Ibrāhīm al-'Anqarī
Posts, Telegraphs and Telecommunications	'Alawī Darwīsh Kayyāl
Education	'Abd al-'Azīz al-Khawaytir
High Education and Supreme Head of Universities	Ḥasan 'Abdallah Āl al-Shaykh
Justice	Muḥammad Ibrāhīm Āl al-Shaykh
Health	Ḥusayn al-Jaza'irī
Pilgrimage and Waqfs	'Abd al-Wahhāb 'Abd al-Wāsi'
Minister of State	Muḥammad 'Abd al-Latīf al-Mulḥim
Minister of State	'Abdallah Muḥammad al-'Umrān
Minister of State	Shaykh Muḥammad Ibrāhīm Mas'ūd

*Appointed in August 1976

of the late King Faysal's sons (some of whom were full brothers, sons of one of Faysal's wives, 'Iffāt). This branch consisted of princes holding high-level civil and military posts. Fahd certainly succeeded in winning the allegiance of the young educated Foreign Minister, Prince Sa'ūd al-Faysal. On the other hand, another son, Prince Muḥammad al-Faysal, resigned as Head of the Water Desalination Authority—a highly sensitive post—on 7 July 1977. A few days later, the Deputy Interior Minister, Prince Aḥmad b. 'Abd al-'Azīz, and the young Chief of Youth Welfare, Prince Faysal b. Fahd—both Sudayrīs—were promoted to ministerial rank. On 6 September 1977, the youngest son of the late King Faysal, Turkī al-Faysal, was appointed Head of the General Intelligence Service with the rank of Minister, replacing 'Umar Maḥmūd Shams who retired.

THE ESTABLISHMENT'S ATTITUDE TOWARDS DEVELOPMENT

While the present Saudi rulers have gained a reputation of outpacing the late King Faysal in the promotion of economic development and business, their basic attitudes differ very little. For well over a decade, Saudi rulers have had two major fears. First, they have been anxious that development and modernization might release social forces which would undermine the traditional basis of the country's ruling institution. Second, they have been apprehensive that an alternative source of energy to oil would be developed before Saudi Arabia had a self-contained and diversified economy based on industry and skilled manpower. Generally speaking, the late King Faysal was troubled more by the first than by the second fear. During the last years of his reign and since his assassination, however, the second has become predominant. This fear was quite clearly expressed in September 1977 by the Oil and Mineral Wealth Minister, Aḥmad Zakī al-Yamānī: "We want to transform what we are producing into something that will bring us income in the future when our oil resources are exhausted. If we acquire technology, it would be easy for us to produce more oil than the industrial states require."[10]

Another complementary facet of Saudi development was the large number of commercial, economic and other agreements signed with foreign companies throughout 1976 and 1977. These huge, but not always successful, efforts were primarily designed to develop infrastructure and industry, expand communications, construct roads and build electricity plants. Considerable effort also went into the development of agriculture and water resources, the settlement of Bedouin, and mineral exploration. There was a considerable investment both in training local cadres and in importing thousands of skilled and unskilled workers. In addition to the half million Yemenis (many of whom arrived following the end of the civil war in Yemen in 1970), almost 400,000 Syrians, Egyptians, Pakistanis, South Koreans, Palestinians, Sudanese, Americans, Europeans and Japanese were working in the Kingdom. It has been calculated that the ambitious $142 bn second Five-Year Development Plan for 1975-80, announced in May 1975 (for details see table at end of chapter), would require 730,600 workers in order to fulfil its targets.[11] The 1977-78 Saudi budget of $18.5 bn allocated 67% for development.[12]

This scale of modernization and immigration[13]—the latter traditionally regarded in conservative Muslim countries as a source of dangerous foreign ideas and habits—provoked tensions of various kinds: feelings of xenophobia, and anxious controversy between those who favoured the concept of rapid development based on huge-scale projects, and those who preferred a gradual, even slow, process of selective development. In the absence of channels for public debate, these issues were mainly reported in the foreign press, although there were also some veiled references to them in Saudi newspapers. In letters to the editor, as well as in other columns and commentaries, there was criticism of rapid development, and particularly of the need to import labour because of its impact on the traditional Muslim (Wahhābī) way of life and values.

However, Prince Fahd was forthright in arguing the case for a rapid pace of development: "The process of economic and social development in any country is no easy matter, and there are bound to be problems. The [Saudi] government . . . is facing, and will go on facing, many difficulties on the road to development, but that does not mean any weakening in resolve to continue on the path. The cancellation of one or two projects [probably referring to the electricity and sewage projects cancelled in 1976] does not mean that we have turned our backs on the [Five-Year] development plan. On the contrary, all the economic measures taken over the past two years were designed with the disturbed international economic situation in view, so that we could keep to our development plan targets in spite of fluctuations in the international situation. Our development plan aims to raise the standard of life of our Saudi people in all fields—education, health, social affairs, and production, in the spirit of the Islamic faith."[14]

PROJECTED CONSULTATIVE COUNCIL

Shortly after King Faysal's assassination, and probably in order to satisfy the wishes of young and modern-educated circles inside and outside the Royal Court, Fahd declared that a Consultative Council (*majlis shūrā*) would be established in the future. This was to be composed of tribal chiefs, religious leaders, professionals, businessmen and civilian and military members of the younger, educated generation. However, no further information was forthcoming about proposals to set up such a Council. Meanwhile, contributions to letters-to-the-editor columns continued to complain about inefficient administration and lack of or damaged facilities. No published letters openly opposed or questioned the nature of the regime itself—not even after the press was reorganized in mid-1976 and ostensibly permitted to publish "positive, constructive criticism."[15] This reorganization still left all the mass media under strict official control and censorship.

When asked in April 1977 about popular participation in government, Fahd answered: "We are part of the world by which we are influenced and which we influence. Our creed has its own system and norm of conduct with which we are happy. I am for participation and we have declared our desire to strengthen the provincial councils and the Consultative Council . . . We believe that there must be popular participation within the proposed idea, namely, the Consultative Council and the provincial councils. Of course, these councils will include selected men in the country, men of opinion and expertise. I believe that any political, social or economic plan put before these selected men will be thoroughly studied and examined, especially when [the members of] these councils are giving their opinions purely in the public interest, and not for individual interests. We are in the course of achieving this and I hope that studies to implement it will not take long . . . The delay in achieving this is not because we do not want it but because we are a country that is advancing rapidly . . . Nevertheless, this participation does exist at present. The government's doors are wide open to public opinion. The people come daily to His Majesty's Council and the Royal Court and demand frankly what they think is necessary for this country . . . We are in the course of establishing a Consultative Council, but we want a council that we will not have to reconsider in the future. We want a council that will be careful in selecting its members and carrying out its functions. I sincerely believe that participation in opinions is better than one man's opinion."[16]

CLANDESTINE OPPOSITION

Since the abortive attempts by Saudi underground groups to topple the regime in 1969–70, any sign of internal subversion has been swiftly and fiercely suppressed. The improvement of Saudi relations with Egypt following the cessation of the Yemen civil war in 1970—and since 1971 also with Syria—led to a sharp decline of open hostility by either state against Saudi Arabia. The restoration of diplomatic relations with South Yemen in 1976 also reduced anti-Saudi criticism from that quarter.

Accusations—mostly emanating from extremist Palestinian organizations—that the Saudi regime was a "capitalist tool" of the US were published throughout 1976 and 1977 in Lebanese Leftist newspapers. The large fires which broke out twice—on 11 May 1977 and 4 June 1977—at the huge Abaqīq oilfield, and which caused damage estimated at more than $100m, reportedly resulted from a ruptured pipeline and not from sabotage, as several sources claimed.[17]

During the period under review, there was no real external threat to the Saudi regime, and internal opposition was inactive. (Also see essay on Inter-Arab Relations.)

ARMED FORCES

Total armed forces number 61,500. Defence expenditure in 1977–8 was 26.69 bn Saudi riyals ($7.53 bn). Military service is voluntary. The Army numbers 45,000 and consists of one mechanized division; one armoured brigade; two infantry battalions; one parachute battalion; one Royal Guard battalion; three artillery battalions; six anti-aircraft artillery battalions and ten surface-to-air missile batteries with *HAWK*. Equipment consists of 400 AMX-30, 75 M-47/-60 medium, 60 M-41, 150 *Scorpion* and AMX-13 light tanks; 200 AML-60/-90, some *Staghound* and *Greyhound* armoured cars; *Ferret* scout cars; M-113, Panhard M-3 and *Commando* armoured personnel carriers; 105mm guns; 75mm recoilless rifles; SS-11, *Dragon*, *Vigilant* and *Harpon* anti-tank guided weapons; anti-aircraft guns; *Rapier* and *HAWK* surface-to-air missiles. (200 M-60 medium and 100 *Scorpion* light tanks; 250 AMX-10P armoured fighting vehicles; 250 armoured personnel carriers; guns/howitzers; AMX-30SA self-propelled anti-aircraft guns; *Shahine* (*Crotale*) and six batteries *Improved HAWK* surface-to-air missiles are on order.) 700 men are deployed in the Lebanon to the Arab Peacekeeping Force. The 1500-strong Navy is equipped with one guided-missile fast patrol boat; three fast patrol boats (*Jaguar*-class) and one large patrol craft (ex-US coastguard cutter). (Six guided-missile fast patrol boats, four mine counter-measures, four landing craft and *Harpoon* surface-to-surface missiles are on order.)

The Air Force numbers 15,000 and is equipped with 137 combat aircraft. Formations consist of two fighter-bomber squadrons with 70 F-5E; two counter-insurgency/training squadrons with 30 BAC-167; two interceptor squadrons with 37 *Lightning* F52/F53; two transport squadrons with 39 C-130E/H; two helicopter squadrons with 16 AB-206 and 24 AB-205. Other aircraft include four KC-13C tankers, one Boeing 707, two *Falcon* 20 and two *Jetstar* transports; 12 *Alouette* III and one AB-204 helicopters. Trainers include 20 F-5B, seven *Lightning* T54/55 and six *Cessna* T-41A. (20 F-5F fighter-bombers, 11 BAC-167 counter-insurgency aircraft; *Maverick* air-to-surface missiles and *Sidewinder* air-to-air missiles are on order.) Paramilitary Forces: 35,000 National Guard in regular and semi-regular battalions, and 6,500 Frontier Force and Coastguard with 50 small patrol boats and eight SRN-6 hovercraft.[18]

FOREIGN AFFAIRS

INTER-ARAB RELATIONS

The first eight months of 1977 saw a direct continuation of the process in which Saudi Arabia gradually asserted its seniority within the Arab world. This process began in the early 1970s and was intensified after the October 1973 war. Saudi Arabia's skilful manipulation of the "oil weapon" and its unprecedented oil income—together with internal changes in some Arab states and regional realignments—all contributed to enhancing Riyadh's role.

King Faysal's successors largely pursued his policies on major issues in the Arab world. What differed after his assassination was a more activist involvement in inter-Arab affairs and in OPEC. Khālid and Fahd adopted a two-pronged approach to inter-Arab relations. 1) They carefully avoided any clear-cut public identification with any single Arab country, bloc or camp. In this respect, they were highly successful in maintaining a delicate balance in their relations both with the so-called "progressive-revolutionary" states such as Syria, and with the "reactionary" states such as the Persian Gulf Principalities. 2) They sought by this non-alignment to establish a solid claim to neutrality in Arab affairs, which they used to promote their relations as mediators or arbitrators in inter-Arab conflicts. While their stated objectives were to contribute towards maintaining Arab fraternity and regional stability, in actual fact they utilized their mediating role to sponsor settlements which conformed with their current interests.

Saudi Arabia's greater acceptance by the "progressive" Arab states did not eliminate all its problems. The lack of homogeneity among the "progressives" presented the Saudis with a new but severe problem—that of alignment with any one of the rival states. Indeed, from the early summer of 1976 onward, and more specifically after the Riyadh conference of October 1976 (see chapter on Inter-Arab Relations), the Saudis' main endeavour was to reconcile, or at least moderate, the tension in Syrian-Egyptian relations. The severest test for this policy came over Sādāt's decision to visit Israel in November 1977. Riyadh's careful and belated criticism of the Egyptian initiative was enough to reassure the Syrians, Iraqis and Palestinians, but was not in any way calculated to deter Sādāt.

In a statement in April 1977 about the Saudi-Egyptian-Sudanese-Syrian alignment, Fahd declared: "Saudi Arabia does not believe in the system of axes or blocs. It has never taken part in any political axis or similar system . . . Our policy is one of mutual respect and of preserving one another's political entity. Therefore, Saudi Arabia is not party to [any] axis . . . What there is, in fact, is mutual co-ordination between all the Arab countries and ourselves in the interest of the welfare and stability of our nation."[19]

While Saudi assistance to Egypt continued, there was apparently a wide gap between Egyptian expectations and Saudi performance: this gave rise to criticism by the Egyptians of Riyadh's "miserly" behaviour. Rejecting this complaint, Fahd said: "The Arab oil states gave their support in the past, and will spare no effort in the future, limited only by their capabilities and the obligations they have to their own people and their development. They feel that this support is a natural and sacred obligation, dictated by the Arab's united destiny and the hopes and aspirations of the Arab world."[20] On 16 July 1977, President Sādāt disclosed that a year before the Saudis had committed themselves to finance the entire cost of the Egyptian armed forces over the next five years.[21]

A Syrian criticism of Saudi Arabia was that "those who fought in October 1973 have been affected by the rise of oil prices, whereas those who did not fight are in the process of amassing unimaginable fortunes."[22] This argument, too, was rejected in March 1977 by Saudi officials who promised to continue financial assistance to the confrontation states. However, there were reports of an 80% reduction in Saudi financial aid to Syria, and of a Saudi refusal to renew the Saudi-Syrian economic agreement signed in April 1972. Some reports attributed this Saudi action to Syria's alleged ambition to create a confederation of Jordan, Syria, Lebanon, and a future Palestinian state which might—in conjunction with Soviet and Leftist elements—endanger Saudi Arabia's northern border.[23] In July, probably after this anxiety was reduced by new developments in inter-Arab affairs, Saudi Arabia announced its readiness to renew its economic and commercial agreement with Syria for another year.[24]

Saudi Arabia's attitude towards Jordan was directly affected by fluctuations in Jordan's relations with Syria: the Saudis appeared not to favour too close relations between Damascus and Amman. The appointment of Ibrāhīm al-Sultān as the new Saudi ambassador to Jordan in April 1977, and the visit by King Ḥusayn to Riyadh on 6 July appeared to reflect some relaxation in the tension which had built up earlier in the year.

Saudi relations with Lebanon were characterized by a consistent attempt to maintain links with the opposing sides in the Lebanese crisis. In its efforts to maintain a balanced policy towards the main Lebanese factions, Riyadh sent financial assistance to the Palestinian refugees (c. $10m in 1976). But there were indications that these allocations were channelled to the PLO via al-Fatḥ, which was considered the most conservative of the Palestinian organizations. A PLO representative in Saudi Arabia, Abū-Hishām, said on 11 October that since the beginning of 1977 the Saudi government had supplied the organization with $29m raised by Saudi "popular committees." On the other hand, the Saudis also reportedly provided the Christians with significant assistance.[25]

Saudi participation in the Arab Deterrent Force towards the end of 1976 increased its ability to influence the rival parties in Lebanon more directly. The Saudis approved their membership in the Four-State Committee and advocated the implementation of the Cairo agreement of November 1969. They regarded the renewal of hostilities, especially in South Lebanon, as a severe threat to regional stability, which might be exploited by Israel. In an effort to prevent a new eruption of the Lebanese crisis during 1977, the Saudis strove to achieve two objectives: a united Arab attitude, and a reduction of friction between the Christians, Palestinians and Syrians. It was announced on 11 October that Riyadh had deposited $9m with the Arab League towards the cost of the Arab Deterrent Force.

The Saudi aim within the Arabian Peninsula was to maintain a position of political and military dominance—a policy facilitated by its economic supremacy in the area. A salient feature of 1976–7 was the Saudis' extensive diplomatic contacts with Kuwait, Qatar, Baḥrayn, Oman, the United Arab Emirates, and North Yemen.[26] These contacts led to a greater level of co-operation in the fields of industry, commerce, information, communications, road construction, education and security.

Saudi policy in the Peninsula—as elsewhere in the region—was determined by its apprehension of revolutionary, Leftist-oriented elements (mainly in North and South Yemen but also in Kuwait and Baḥrayn) which publicly and clandestinely opposed the "reactionary" tribal structure of the rich oil-producing countries. The Saudis concentrated their efforts on maintaining the *status quo* in the Peninsula, which meant eliminating or at least containing local rifts, and guarding against upheavals in the Persian Gulf and Red Sea areas. (See essay on The Middle East, the Red Sea and Africa.)

The Saudi Minister of Interior, Prince Nā'if b. 'Abd al-'Azīz (who is in charge of internal security), was active in inter-Peninsula security co-operation and proposed a conference of the Gulf states in April 1977. In June 1977—following reports that Saudi Arabia had taken control of two Kuwaiti islands—an official Kuwaiti source dismissed the idea as "fabricated and baseless."[27] On 17 August, the Kuwaiti Minister of Interior and Defence, Shaykh Sa'd 'Abdallah Sālim al-Sabāḥ, met Fahd to "define the continental shelf in the Partition Zone" shared by the two countries.[28]

While Saudi Arabia maintained this relatively high level of activity with the Persian Gulf states, its main efforts in 1976–7 focused on southern and south-eastern neighbours. Here the Saudis concentrated on reducing tension between North and South Yemen (see chapter on North Yemen), and on providing political and financial assistance to the Omani rulers to crush the rebel movement in the Dhufar region (see chapter on South Yemen). In August 1977, Beirut sources reported that Riyadh had agreed to contribute $50m for the Omani air defence system.[29]

Saudi relations with Iran continued to develop along contradictory lines. On the one hand, there was deeply-embedded, albeit undeclared, competition arising from mutual fear. This rivalry was evidenced by the huge increase in arms flowing to both countries and also by their different oil policies (see essay on Oil in its Middle East Context). On the other hand, routine relations were conducted on a friendly basis. Both countries shared a common interest in preventing political up-heavals which might upset either their domestic traditional political structure, or the balance within the Peninsula and in the Gulf region. This mutual interest, buttressed by the common fear of Leftist communist movements, had taken the form of an unwritten agreement during King Faysal's reign regarding "areas of influence." The Saudis were apparently allowed a relatively free hand within the Peninsula, while Iran was allowed preponderance in Persian Gulf waters.

Saudi Arabia's dual attitude to Iran was exemplified by the Dhufar rebellion. While the Saudis supported Iran's military intervention on the side of the Omani rulers, they were at the same time worried that Iran's military presence in Oman could upset the delicate Iranian-Saudi Arabian balance; hence the Saudi interest in wanting the Iranians to leave after the rebellion was crushed.

The Iranians and Saudis shared a common concern for the security of their oil-fields and an assured safe exit for their oil. This led to attempts in 1977 to con-solidate the defence of the Gulf states through a joint defence agreement, but by late 1977 nothing had come of these moves.[30]

Saudi Arabia was reported to be building an airbase in Baḥrayn, the Kingdom's first military base abroad. Gulf diplomatic sources suggested that it was "only a natural extension of the Saudi air defence system since Baḥrayn falls within Saudi Arabia's strategic airspace." The establishment of the base was seen both as a con-tribution to the collective security of the Gulf and as defence assistance to Baḥrayn. Iranians were not expected to object to this extension of Saudi air power—"first, since it is being presented as an element in activating Gulf security; and second, because Iran still maintains a military presence of her own . . . in Oman."[31]

Sources in Beirut reported in August that Saudi Arabia was negotiating with Oman to lease a route across the Dhufar region for an oil pipeline. It was also said to be ready to establish a military pact with Kuwait, the United Arab Emirates and Qatar for joint defence of petroleum wells in the Gulf.

Saudi policy in the Red Sea area was conducted on several levels simultaneously. On the inter-Arab level, the presentation of the Red Sea as an "Arab lake" demonstrated Riyadh's active involvement in fighting for the Arab cause. As an extension of this idea, the Saudis proclaimed the importance of protecting the Arab world from Israeli threats in the area. Although the Saudis had sponsored the idea of a united front of the Arabian Peninsula coastal states at the First Conference of Red Sea Countries held in July 1972 in Jidda, they did not play an open role in convening the Ta'izz quadripartite conference in March 1977. The sponsors were North and South Yemen, Somalia and, especially, Sudan. (See essays, "Inter-Arab Affairs" and "The Middle East, the Red Sea and Africa.")

On the opposite shore of the Red Sea—in the Horn of Africa—it was the anti-revolutionary, anti-communist, anti-Soviet and Arab Muslim factors that motivated the Saudis into playing an active role in support of the Eritreans, and Somalia and Sudan against Ethiopia. When Cuba's President Fidel Castro visited East Africa in April 1977, Saudi Arabia was alarmed at his reported suggestion that Somalia, Ethiopia and South Yemen should unite in a Soviet-oriented federation. Commenting on events in the Red Sea in May 1977, Fahd said: "The moves appearing in Ethiopia . . . indicate a far-reaching threat to the states in the whole area. The present Ethiopian policy is flagrantly hostile to Arab nationality. Therefore, we in Saudi Arabia call for co-ordination and co-operation among the Arab and Islamic states of the Red Sea, particularly among Sudan, Somalia, and the three Eritrean liberation fronts, who must merge and create a strong alliance against the expected danger to save the area from becoming involved in a dreadful conflict."[32]

In March 1977, the Saudi-Sudanese ministerial co-ordination and follow-up committee held its first meeting. In July, three loan agreements totalling SR 90m were signed.[33] In August, the Saudis were reported to be involved in mediation between Sudan's President Numayrī and the exiled opposition leader, Sādiq al-Mahdī. Having made it absolutely clear—particularly during and after the July 1976 abortive coup—that they supported the stability of the Numayrī regime, the Saudis were interested in any move to end the breach between Numayrī and al-Mahdī's Islamic-oriented supporters. (See chapter on Sudan.)

Uncompromising anti-communist attitudes prompted Saudi leaders to undermine Soviet efforts to build up influence in the Red Sea through South Yemen, or through its newly-acquired ties with Ethiopia.[34] This unequivocal Saudi Arabian attitude was undoubtedly welcomed by the Americans and the French—the latter being concerned with maintaining its influence in the area after the independence of Djibouti. At the end of August 1977, Riyadh announced its readiness to assist Djibouti with long-term economic aid.[35]

INTERNATIONAL RELATIONS

Saudi Arabia's attitude towards the international system has been determined by two factors: its self-image as guardian of the Islamic spirit and community against hostile political, social and economic forces; and its strong interest in perpetuating a conservative traditional system of government. There has been a continuity of this policy ever since it began to crystallize two decades ago under the late King Faysal.

Basically this attitude did not distinguish between the different systems of the "West" and the "East": both were seen as potential threats to the traditional world of Islam and its norms. The Saudi preference for the "West" over the "East"—in relation to financial, economic, military, and political co-operation—was more a question of necessity than a moral choice. The "East" represented communism or social upheaval, and atheism—regarded as far more dangerous enemies than the forces and ideas of the "West." Furthermore, it was commonly accepted that only the "West" could supply the technology required for the modernization of Saudi society. But any Western influence beyond the limited scope of technology (transfer and supply of industrial and military hardware) was treated with great suspicion. This choice—which explains the Saudis' "pro-Western" orientation, and their special relationship with the US—has become more evident since the October 1973 war. The relationship has acquired a new dimension because the West, and mainly the US, has come to regard Saudi Arabia as the main bastion of pro-Western and moderate attitudes in the area.

Saudi relations with the West have been strongly influenced by a number of factors. First, mutual economic dependence based on the Saudis' importance to the West as a major supplier of oil and an investor of vast sums of petro-dollars on the one hand, and on Western technological and military aid and trade on the other. (Western attitudes to Saudi Arabia are discussed in the essays, "Middle East Oil in the International Economic Setting," "The US and the Middle East," and "The European Community and the Middle East.")

Second, relations have been influenced by the Saudis' attempt to diversify their sources of technological and military aid away from the US, in an endeavour to protect themselves from possible American pressures. Of all Middle Eastern states, Saudi expenditure on defence is second only to Iran's, with arms purchases worth $7,500m in 1976. The Saudis indicated on a number of occasions in 1976 that they were preparing to shift their investments from the US to Western Europe or Japan. However this had not occurred by the end of 1977.

Third, the Saudis' anti-communist and pro-Western stance has been closely connected with their apprehension of the rise of radical Leftist elements in the Middle East and the immediate vicinity. Thus, for the Saudis, the elimination, or at least the containment, of Soviet influence has become a cornerstone of their Peninsular and regional policy, as described above.

Fourth, the marked enhancement since the early 1970s, and particularly since the October 1973 war, of the Saudis' status in the Arab world has led them to assume a dual role: representing the Arab cause to the West, and defending certain Western economic and military interests in the Middle East—though not where these conflict with Saudi support for the cause of the Palestinians and of the "confrontation states."

RELATIONS WITH THE UNITED STATES

In September 1976, arms sales to Saudi Arabia, (including *Sidewinder* air-to-air missiles) valued at $700m were announced by the Pentagon. However, on 24 September, the US Senate Foreign Relations Committee announced its opposition to the projected sale to Saudi Arabia of 650 *Maverick* air-to-ground missiles at a cost of $300m. Two days later, the Saudis were reported to have threatened to impose a new oil embargo on the US if Congress enacted legislation aimed at interfering with the Arab boycott of Israel.[36] On 27 September, this report was denied both by the State Department and the Saudi Information Office in Washington.[37] Simultaneously, US Secretary of State Henry Kissinger was reported to have appealed to the Foreign Relations Committee to reconsider its decision, expressing concern over the effect of that decision on US-Saudi relations. On 28 September 1976, the Committee's opposition to the sale of *Maverick* missiles was withdrawn, and an effort to block the deal in the House of Representatives apparently collapsed after a warning by the State Department that failure to supply the missiles might jeopardize US-Arab relations.[38]

In February 1977, shortly before the new US Secretary of State, Cyrus Vance, was due to arrive in Riyadh to begin a new round of diplomacy, President Carter sent a message to King Khālid with "new US views on the Middle East question and its peaceful solution." The Saudi newspaper *'Ukkāz* wrote: "The US political leadership desires to give its Secretary of State new ground for negotiations with us regarding our fateful question, which is connected not only with us but with the destiny of the whole Arab nation . . . It is certain that . . . Saudi Arabia will be committed in these negotiations to its policy . . . [which] is not spontaneous, but reflects the continued concept of its practical views regarding a peaceful solution."[39] Cyrus Vance arrived in Riyadh on 20 February and met Prince Fahd and Foreign Minister Sa'ūd al-Faysal. After the meeting, the latter said that Saudi Arabia would hold to a 5% increase in oil prices in order to contribute to the prosperity of the international community.[40]

According to the *London Times* (21 February), American arms sales to Saudi Arabia amounted to \$600m between 1950–73, and then soared to \$14,600m during the first 20 months after the October 1973 war. The paper speculated about the "special relationship" between the two countries "turning into a political alliance . . . The Five-Year \$142,000m Development Plan (announced in mid-1975) was drawn up by Stanford experts; American expertise and technology will take the lion's share; the Bendix Corporation keeps the regular army in business; the Vinnel Corporation is building a new National Guard; Avco Corporation trains the coast guard; TWA keeps the national airline flying; and Lockheed and Raytheon are indispensable for the air defence of the Kingdom." The Planning Minister, Dr Hishām Muḥyī al-Dīn Nāzir, was quoted by the *Times* as saying the Saudi "position is unique . . . We are under-developed and yet we have perhaps more money than we can spend . . . The building of modern Saudi Arabia is not programmed and computerized. Our interests lie with the West and your interests lie with us. It is a two-way street."

At the beginning of March 1977—two weeks after President Carter announced that Israel would not be supplied with American-made concussion bombs—the US Administration was reported to be reviewing both the sale of the 650 *Maverick* missiles, and Raytheon Corporation's previously approved commercial deal worth \$1,400m for the sale of 580 *Hawk* missiles.[41]

Saudi-American relations passed through a sensitive phase early in 1977. Displeased with US policies on the Middle East and feeling that Washington was refusing to put pressure on Israel to reach a peace settlement,[42] Riyadh proceeded with plans to blockade Israel's port of Eilat in the event of a new war. Early in March 1977, President Carter "approved \$500m in contract construction" for Saudi Arabia.[43] At the beginning of April, however, Fahd again warned that Saudi Arabia would not continue its moderate stand on oil prices if it failed to obtain a political return;[44] however his attempt to link oil with a political settlement was promptly disavowed by King Khālid (see essay on "Oil in the Middle East Context").

At the same time, an official Arab source warned that Saudi Arabia might not continue to satisfy growing US oil demands if the political atmosphere was not sufficiently positive.[45] This spokesman also warned that if Congress prevented US companies from doing business in Saudi Arabia, the Saudis might shift their purchases to Western Europe and Japan. In late April 1977, President Carter was reported to have approved the commercial sale by Raytheon of *Hawk* missiles to Saudi Arabia.[46]

A new phase in US-Saudi relations began in late May with Prince Fahd's arrival in Washington during a tour of the US, Britain, Switzerland, France, Spain and Morocco. Asked whether his talks in the US would be conducted in the name of all the Arab states, Fahd said: "Any of those Arab states which are in agreement and solidarity and which follow a common line can speak in the name of its sisters." Referring to the US Congressional legislation against American companies complying with the Arab boycott, he said: "There is no doubt that the development and reconstruction programmes in Saudi Arabia will be affected by this legislation. However, these companies will consequently be the losers like us, and American citizens [in Saudi Arabia] could lose even more. We have declared in public and privately that we will neither accept nor submit to pressure. Pressure will not help, because we will not agree to remove Arab boycott restrictions, which are one of our rights just as it is the right of every state and people.''[47]

Prince Fahd's talks with the Carter Administration on 24-25 May left no doubt as to the new importance of Saudi Arabia as an Arab world spokesman. His reception also showed that the US regarded Saudi Arabia not only as a supplier of oil and petrodollars, and a customer for arms and technology; but also as a very important political ally. The discussions covered the whole question of a possible Middle East settlement; a homeland for the Palestinians and their representation in the projected Geneva conference;[48] a possible oil embargo by Saudi Arabia (Fahd was said to have assured the Administration that oil would not be used as a political weapon); the sale of advanced aircraft (Fahd reportedly asked for 50 F-15s,[49] as well as F-16 fighter bombers); economic co-operation;[50] and problems of the Horn of Africa. Fahd was also reported to have said that his country was ready to prevent Soviet-Cuban penetration in the region, and suggested that the Saudis would pay part of the cost of arms to Somalia if the US agreed to supply them.[51]

The Carter-Fahd meetings set off a wave of rumours about "deals" that had been made.[52] According to one Arab report, a "secret treaty" was signed in which Carter reaffirmed an agreement reached by the Ford Administration.[53] On their side, the Saudis were supposed to have promised to place half of their long-term investments in the US, to restrict any increase in oil prices to a rate of 5% a year until 1984, and to resist using the "oil weapon." In return, the US promised to use its full political, military and economic resources to assist Saudi Arabia in any way that might prove necessary in the light of developing circumstances. However, senior American and Saudi officials both categorically denied such reports. As late as September, the Saudis again twice officially denied the existence of a secret treaty. In an interview published in Beirut on 19 September, the Saudi Arabian Finance Minister and Chairman of the US-Saudi Joint Commission for Economic Co-operation repeated an earlier denial by Saudi Arabia's Information Minister, and said that "all that has been published about such a treaty is untrue. It is pure fabrication."[54]

Whatever the truth about such a treaty—which seems highly improbable—there was no doubt about the broadening of American involvement in Saudi Arabia: the American community was approaching a figure of 100,000 technicians, engineers and workers operating at every level of Saudi economic and military development.[55] "The significance of such a large American involvement extends far beyond plans for Saudi Arabia's economic development . . . It is apparently implicitly understood that the vast American presence [and the American commitment to Saudi Arabia] will act as a political and military guarantee to Saudi Arabia of American support in case of external aggression. Senior Saudi circles have been displaying much concern in recent months at the Kingdom's potential vulnerability to interference from outside hostile forces. Not the least suspect of these is Israel. By establishing a close link with the US, the Saudis are understood to feel that Israel could be effectively restrained from any military operations she might contemplate against Saudi Arabia's Red Sea Coast."[56]

In July 1977, the Carter Administration was said to be seriously considering the sale to Saudi Arabia of 60 advanced F-15 fighter bombers, which Carter himself "approved in principle."[57] The report added that the Saudis had not specifically pressed for the F-15s, but had listed several planes of interest—the F-14, the F-15, the F-16 and the F-18L. "Only the F-15 was offered by the Pentagon . . . The Air Force is seeking to sell the F-15 to the Saudis because a major sale would accelerate production and help reduce costs."[58] At the beginning of August 1977, it was reported that a decision on the 60 F-15s had been temporarily delayed because of expected widespread opposition.[59] However, on 10 August 1977, the Egyptian *Ākhar Sā'a* reported that an advanced arms deal was signed between the US and Saudi Arabia, which included 60 F-15 fighter bombers. Quoting American sources, the report added that military co-operation between the two countries over the next five years would reach $5,000m, and would include the supply of 14 *Hawk* missile batteries, 500 M-50 tanks, 150 fighter planes, and transport planes capable of carrying armoured cars and artillery. American experts would train the Saudi Arabian army in the use of the new arms and would also participate in the building of air fields.

At the end of August, the Pentagon was said to be quietly urging the Administration to sell the 60 F-15s to the Saudis; to strengthen US ties with Saudi Arabia "which is sure to have a key role in any Middle East peace negotiations;" and to replace the ageing fleet of British *Lightning* jets, which have been experiencing metal fatigue.[60] At the beginning of September 1977, Saudi Arabia was reported to have requested missile-carrying reconnaissance boats from the US to strengthen the Saudi naval capability in the Red Sea.[61]

However, in mid-October 1977, there was apparently a "re-evaluation of the [proposed] sale of F-15s to Saudi Arabia."[62] Although the Defence Secretary recommended the sale, the Administration was said to have asked the Pentagon to review the deal because of growing Congressional opposition. It was "seriously questioning the sale" and considering, instead, an offer of the less sophisticated F-16 jet fighters.

RELATIONS WITH FRANCE

Saudi-French relations in 1976–77 focused mainly on the question of French participation in the Arab Military Industries' Organization,[63] mutual interests in the Red Sea, and economic co-operation. The visits of the French Defence Minister, Yvon Bourges, in November 1976 and of President Valéry Giscard d'Estaing (22–25 January 1977) were both connected with these issues.

In a joint statement on 25 January 1977, the French and Saudi leaders called for initiatives in the search for "a comprehensive, just and durable solution of the [ME] crisis." They agreed that respect for the independence of the Red Sea region in the future was "a basic condition for safeguarding peace and stability in this area of the world." The two sides also affirmed their determination to work for the establishment of "a new international economic system that will be more just, wiser and more effective for peace and stability in the world." They emphasized the importance of continuing the International Economic Co-operation Conference (North/South Dialogue) which both had strongly supported. The French side praised the Saudis' moderate stand over oil prices, which stemmed from "Saudi Arabia's balanced understanding of the world economic situation." They agreed on the importance of the "political, economic and cultural aspects of the dialogue between the Arab world and Europe, as representing two integrated cultural centres." They also affirmed their determination to go on exerting efforts so that "this dialogue will include all aspects." Finally, they expressed the view that the Saudi development plan would "open new horizons" for bilateral and international co-operation in the fields of desalination, the assessment of water resources, electricity, transport, telecommunications, housing, supply and utilization of natural and mineral resources, as well as joint industrial projects. They expressed interest in a formula to secure participation by both Saudi and French corporations (private and public) in these various economic and social development projects.[64]

The Saudi Minister of Information, Muḥammad 'Abduh al-Yamānī, visited Paris in April 1977 for talks on co-operation in the development of Saudi television. At the end of April, a Saudi military delegation visited military installations in France. Prince Fahd arrived in Paris on 30 May on his return from the US for discussions with the French President on a possible Middle East peace settlement; the situation in the Horn of Africa; Djibouti's forthcoming independence, and possible Saudi aid to the new state; as well as energy and economic problems. One report suggested that Fahd had promised the French President economic assistance to bolster his Government which was increasingly under challenge by the Left.[65] At the end of June, France won a bid for a two-year $113m contract to prospect for minerals in the central and western region of the Kingdom.

RELATIONS WITH THE UK

The Saudi Defence and Aviation Minister and General Inspector of the Army, Prince Sultān b. 'Abd al-'Azīz, visited Britain from 8–13 November 1976 and negotiated a four-year extension of the British Aircraft Corporation (BAC) contract worth $1,240m, for servicing and maintaining the Saudi Air Force as well as operating the Air Academy and Technical Training Institute.

The British Foreign Secretary, Dr David Owen, visited Saudi Arabia on 12 May 1977 for discussions on economic relations and the Middle East. Prince Fahd visited London on his way to the US, from 20–23 May 1977. In September 1977, a £500m contract for the development and maintenance of the Saudi Air Force was signed in Tā'if, according to which Britain would supply a wide range of items, from household goods and foodstuffs to engine spare parts.[66]

Saudi relations with other West European countries and Japan concentrated on routine economic and industrial assistance and trade.

SAUDI ARABIA AND THE ARAB-ISRAELI CONFLICT

The Arab-Israeli conflict was a major Saudi Arabian concern—ideologically as well as politically—in 1976–77, but it was not an overriding consideration in Saudi foreign policy. There seemed a basic dichotomy in the Saudi approach—as between its attitude to Israel as a sovereign state embodying Zionism; and its view of the Arab-Israeli conflict as a complex confrontation of military, political, economic and other dimensions. Publicly, it condemned the Jewish state as an alien, hostile, and fundamentally unacceptable political entity. In May 1977, for instance, after the elections in Israel, Prince Fahd said: "All Israeli and Zionist blocs, whether extremist or moderate, constitute a common enemy of the Arabs." As to the possibility of a peaceful settlement in the Middle East, his view was: "Israel has no desire to arrive at peace with the Arabs . . . Israel is now making serious calculations in regard to war."[67]

The fact that Saudi Arabia does not border directly on Israel has enabled its leaders to view the politico-military aspects of the confrontation as a major—though not exclusive—element in a complex web of issues and problems. Ever since Saudi relations with Syria and Egypt began to improve in the 1970s, and especially since October 1973, its leaders have utilized their special relationship with the US, their position as mediators between rival Arab states, and their ability to extend financial support to promote their own standing as a leading force in regional affairs. Knowing that Egypt, Syria and Jordan—singly or together—needed extensive Saudi assistance (particularly in the event of a future war), the leadership manoeuvred between grand declarations of Arab fraternal co-operation and generous promises on one hand, and only limited financial assistance on the other. None of the "confrontation states" could entirely ignore its dependence, in one form or another, on Saudi Arabia—a condition which suited

Riyadh's own role and interests.

Saudi demands for a settlement with Israel focued on three major points: 1) Israel's withdrawal to the frontiers of 4 June 1967; 2) the return of the holy places in Jerusalem to Muslim custody; and 3) the restoration of the legitimate rights of the Palestinians, who are "not just a group of refugees as was implied in Resolution 242."[68] The last two demands were given increased emphasis in 1977.

In a major speech traditionally delivered in Mecca during the annual pilgrimage ceremonies, King Khālid called for the "regaining of the third holiest mosque (Aqsā) in Jerusalem and noble Jerusalem itself, and for cleansing them of all the impurities that have been attached to them."[69] In May 1977, the Saudi Foreign Minister stated that Zionism was trying to transform the "Jerusalem problem from a religious to a political one." He expressed his country's opposition "to any kind of internationalization of Jerusalem."[70] As in previous years, the issue of Jerusalem was presented and utilized by Saudi leaders within an all-Islamic rather than merely an Arab context.

From the beginning of 1977, the Saudis began to be more specific on the Palestinian issue. They insisted that the Palestinians should regain "all their legitimate rights, including the setting up of their state (*dawla*) to be decided by the representatives of the Palestinian people."[71] The Palestinians' right "to establish a nation on their land is the correct way for peace and for restoring security and stability to the region."[72] The Information Minister, Dr Muḥammad 'Abduh al-Yamānī, reaffirmed in September that the Saudi position on the Palestine question was "firm, unshakeable, unchangeable and accepts no bargaining." He added that all Palestinian demands must be taken into consideration "including their return to their country and having an independent homeland."[73] All these declarations stopped short of specifying the borders of the future Palestinian state. The Saudis also insisted that the Palestinians could not be ignored in any deliberations at a future Geneva conference since this conference was a "framework for a settlement."[74] In October 1977, the Saudi Foreign Minister, Sa'ūd al-Faysal, said that contacts between the US, the USSR and the parties concerned with the Middle East problem were continuing in order to convene the Geneva conference "with the presence of all the parties."[75]

Riyadh's main support was for Yāsir 'Arafāt and al-Fatḥ (see essay on the PLO). Its attitude to the *fidā'iyyūn* organizations was selective and determined by the political orientation and ideological concept of each. Those considered Leftist, such as the organizations led by George Ḥabash and Na'if Ḥawātima, were identified in Saudi eyes with radicalism, communism and hostility to Islam. Therefore, as far as was known, they were not supported financially. But al-Fatḥ, regarded as relatively conservative and in keeping with Saudi norms, did receive official financial support. Typically in 1977, 'Arafāt visited Saudi Arabia in March, May, June and July. The fact that he met Fahd and other high-ranking officials during each visit was indicative of his standing with the regime. However, the Palestinian community resident in Saudi Arabia—a vital element in the country's development—was subject to very strict supervision by the security authorities and, along with everybody else, denied the right of independent political activity.

The oil issue quite naturally was raised in the context of Saudi policy on the Arab-Israeli conflict (see essay, "Oil in the Middle East Context"). Statements relating to the use of oil as a political weapon were often contradictory or ambiguous, as exemplified in Prince Fahd's statement in May 1977: "We will not use [oil] for blackmail. However, our oil belongs to us and is subject to our wishes and decisions and to our national and pan-Arab interests . . . [We] hope that we will not be forced to use this weapon as [a] method of pressure to achieve peace. We have the ability to increase petroleum production to a level which would gradually help the US to secure a six-month supply of oil reserves . . . But we have some demands in return, foremost of which is that the US put all its weight behind efforts to achieve a just solution to the ME question. We will not lay down the weapon of the boycott before the occupied territory is liberated and the Palestinian people's rights are guaranteed. Perhaps the Americans will realize that the American companies can be replaced, but that there is no replacement for the developing and continuously expanding Arab markets in the world."[76]

ECONOMIC AFFAIRS ($1 = 3.52 Saudi riyals; £1 = 6.5 SR)

For a comprehensive account of Saudi Arabia's recent economic development and performance during the period under review, see essay entitled "Major Trends in Middle East Economic Development."

1975–80 PLAN EXPENDITURES (million Saudi riyals)

Water and Desalination	34,065
Agriculture	4,685
Electricity	6,240
Manufacturing and Minerals	45,058
Education	74,161
Health	17,302
Social Programmes and Youth Welfare	14,649
Roads, Ports and Railroads	21,283
Civil Aviation	14,845
Telecommunications and Post	4,225
Municipalities	53,328
Housing	14,263
Holy Cities and the Hajj	5,000
Other	9,312
Sub-total Development	**318,416**
Defence	78,157
General Administration	38,179
Fund	63,478
Total Plan	**498,230**

Source: Financial Times, 27 March 1977.

GOVERNMENT BUDGETS (million Saudi riyals)

	1973-74	*1974-75*	*1975-76*
A. Revenue			
Oil Revenues	39,285	94,190	95,040
Other Revenues	2,420	5,913	6,138
Total	**41,705**	**100,103**	**101,178**
B. Expenditure			
1. Recurring expenditure:			
Salaries and Allowances	(3,158)	(4,453)	
Supplies and Services	(1,271)	(1,785)	
Transfers, Subsidies, Foreign Aid	(4,041)	(8,969)	
Sub-total	8,470	15,207	32,982*
2. Non-recurring expenditure projects	10,125	19,832	44,507
General Total	**18,595**	**35,039**	**77,489**

* Includes transfers of SR 13,960m to government-sponsored credit institutions.
Source: Saudi Arabia Monetary Agency.

BALANCE OF PAYMENTS (millions of SDRs)*

	1973	*1974*	*1975*
A. Goods, Services and Unrequited Transfers	1,790	18,519	13,466
Merchandise, exports fob	7,179	28,200	23,190
Merchandise, imports fob	-1,764	-3,087	-5,384
Services: credit	641	2,125	3,101
Services: debit	-3,621	-7,584	-6,179
Private Unrequited Transfers, net	-329	-431	-642
Government Unrequited Transfers, net	-316	-704	-620
B. Long-term Capital	-529	-3,138	1,412
C. Short-term Capital	109	-512	-1,358
Total, A through C	**1,370**	**14,869**	**13,520**
D. Monetary Changes	-1,370	-14,869	-13,520

* Dollars per SDR: 1973 = 1.206; 1974 = 1.224; 1975 =1.170
Source: IMF, *Balance of Payments Yearbook*, December 1976.

IMPORTS FROM MAJOR INDUSTRIAL COUNTRIES (millions of Dollars)

	Jan-Sept 1975	*Jan-Sept 1976*
United States	984	1,942
Japan	994	1,430
West Germany	402	810
United Kingdom	329	486
Italy	196	388
France	139	237
Netherlands	98	175
Switzerland	66	171
Belgium	86	121
Total	**3,294**	**5,760**

Source: Saudi Arabia Monetary Agency, *Statistical Summary*, First Issue, 1397 (1977).

NOTES

1. For a table of new salaries, see *'Ukkāz*, 8 March 1977.
2. *Arabia and the Gulf*, London; 4 and 11 April 1977.
3. *Al-Siyāsa*, Kuwait; 16 April 1977.
4. *The Saudi Gazette*, 4 May 1977.
5. Some years ago, the eldest Prince Muḥammad reportedly conceded the throne in favour of King Faysal, provided that Prince 'Abdallah, to whom he was close, remained in the direct line of succession.
6. *The Financial Times* (*FT*), London; 28 June 1977, quoting sources in Beirut connected with "the hierarchy in Riyadh."
7. *Ibid*, 21 June 1977.
8. *Ibid*, 30 June 1977.
9. *Arabia and the Gulf*, 4 July 1977.
10. Saudi News Agency (SNA), 10 September—Daily Report (DR), 12 September 1977.
11. *FT*, 28 March 1977.
12. *The Guardian*, London; 18 June 1977.
13. According to *Arabia and the Gulf* (27 June 1977), a massive expansion in Saudi-US economic and military co-operation was launched after the Fahd-Carter talks in May. This involved increasing the number of American technicians and advisers working in Saudi Arabia in oil exploitation, oil-based industries, engineering and armed forces to almost 100,000. 2,000 BAC workers were reported to be in Saudi Arabia in September (*Jerusalem Post*, 20 September 1977).
14. *Events*, Beirut; 22 April 1977.
15. *Al-Bilād*, Jidda; 2 May 1976.
16. *Al-Siyāsa*, 16 April 1977.
17. *Al-Anwār*, Beirut; 27 May 1977.
18. *The Military Balance 1977-78* (London: International Institute for Strategic Studies).

19. *Al-Siyāsa*, 16 April 1977.
20. *Events*, 22 April 1977.
21. *The Observer,* London; *The New York Times (NYT)*, 17 July 1977.
22. *Al-Ba'th*, Damascus; 20 February 1977.
23. *Al-'Amal*, Tunis; 4 June 1977. *Arabia and the Gulf*, 11 July 1977.
24. *Al-Thawra*, Damascus; 22 July 1977.
25. *Al-Muḥarrir*, Beirut; 13 January 1976.
26. For the improvements of relations with South Yemen, see chapter on South Yemen.
27. Qatar News Agency (QNA), 19 June—British Broadcasting Corporation, Summary of World Broadcasts, the ME and Africa (BBC), 21 June 1977.
28. In December 1969, Saudi Arabia and Kuwait signed an agreement on a partition line dividing the 5,000-km Neutral Zone which had been jointly administrated since 1922. The agreement delineated the mainland boundary, giving the northern part of the zone to Kuwait and the southern part to Saudi Arabia. It did not demarcate the offshore boundary, including the continental shelf.
29. Deutsche Presse Agentur (DPA), 10 August—DR, 11 August 1977.
30. *Newsweek*, New York; 4 April 1977.
31. *Arabia and the Gulf*, 4 July 1977.
32. *Al-Anwār*, 21 May 1977—DR, 23 May 1977.
33. R Amman, 2 July 1977.
34. *Al-Mustaqbal*, Paris; 21 May 1977.
35. DPA, 27 August 1977.
36. Middle East News Agency (MENA), 26 September 1976. Since the end of 1975 and throughout 1976, the issue of American companies' submission to the Arab boycott of Israel was discussed in Congress. These deliberations produced strong Saudi reactions.
37. *International Herald Tribune* (*IHT*), Paris; 28 September 1976.
38. *Daily Telegraph* (*DT*), London; 30 September 1976.
39. President Carter's message was brought to Riyadh by Saudi Arabia's Ambassador to Washington, 'Abdallah 'Ali Riza, on 13 February 1977. *'Ukkāz*, 10 February—DR, 12 February 1977.
40. The OPEC conference held in Qatar in mid-December 1976 ended in disagreement. Eleven OPEC members decided to raise their oil prices by 10%, while Saudi Arabia and the United Arab Emirates conceded to 5% only until July 1977.
41. *Jerusalem Post*, 4 March 1977. An agreement for the commercial sale of *Improved Hawk* missiles was signed in June 1976 by the Raytheon Corporation. The US agreement to sell the *Maverick* and *Hawk* missiles worried a number of Congressmen who asked for the sale to be banned. Prominent among them was a New York representative, Benjamin Rosenthal who, in a letter to Vance on 1 March 1977, wrote that the deals posed "serious threats to the strategic balance in the region." He argued that if the sale of 580 *Hawk* missiles was allowed, Saudi Arabia would have nearly 1,200 *Hawk* missiles (*Ma'ariv*, 3 March 1977).
42. *Al-Qabas*, Kuwait; 15 March 1977.
43. *Washington Post*, 29 March 1977.
44. *Sunday Times*, London; 3 April 1977.
45. *IHT*, 3 April 1977.
46. *Washington Post*, 27 April 1977.
47. *Al-Anwār*, 21 May—DR, 23 May 1977.
48. *NYT*, 26 May 1977. *IHT*, 26 May 1977.
49. Agence France Presse (AFP), Reuter, 26 May 1977. *Jerusalem Post*, 26 May 1977.
50. MENA, 27 May 1977.
51. *Le Monde*, Paris; 8 June 1977.
52. *Arabia and the Gulf*, 13, 27 June 1977.
53. The alleged "secret treaty" was published in London by *al-Dustūr*, 8-14 August 1977, pp. 12-13.
54. *IHT*, 20 September 1977.
55. *Arabia and the Gulf*, 27 June 1977.
56. *Ibid.*
57. *NYT*, 20 July 1977.
58. The proposed F-15 sale was worth about $1,500m (*Washington Post*, 3 September 1977).
59. *Jerusalem Post*, 3 August 1977.
60. *NYT*, 31 August 1977. *IHT*, 1 September 1977.
61. DPA, 8 September 1977.
62. *IHT*, 19 October 1977.
63. Decided upon in mid-1975 by Saudi Arabia, the United Arab Emirates, Qatar and Egypt.
64. R Riyadh, 25 January—DR, 25 January 1977.

65. *Arabia and the Gulf*, 13 June 1977.
66. *FT*, 22, 23 September 1977.
67. *Al-Anwār*, 21 May—DR, 23 May 1977.
68. Prince Fahd in an interview, *Al-Ḥawādith*, Beirut; 14 April 1977.
69. R Riyadh, 27 November—DR, 1 December 1976.
70. Iraqi News Agency (INA), 31 May 1977.
71. *'Ukkāz*, 7 February 1977.
72. Saudi press statement following Carter-Fahd discussions on 24-25 May in Washington (SNA, 27 May 1977).
73. SNA, 7 September—DR, 8 September 1977.
74. *Al-Ḥawādith*, 14 April 1977.
75. In an interview to R Riyadh, 2 October 1977.
76. *Al-Anwār*, 21 May—DR, 23 May 1977.

The Democratic Republic of Sudan

(Jumhūriyyat al-Sūdān al-Dimuqrātiyya)

HAIM SHAKED and YEHUDIT RONEN

The abortive coup of 2 July 1976 was the most serious threat to the Numayrī regime since the military coup attempt of 1971, and may be regarded as a turning point in Sudan's domestic and foreign affairs. From that point on, Numayrī's regime began an intensive process of administrative and political reorganization, and pursued a more clear-cut foreign policy. More than ever before, Numayrī came to regard the ruling Sudanese Socialist Union (SSU) as essential to mobilizing mass support for his regime. This emerged clearly at the Second General Congress of the SSU, convened at the beginning of 1977.

General Muḥammad Ja'far al-Numayrī's re-election to the Presidency, in the spring of 1977, gave him the confidence he needed to initiate moves for reconciliation with the National Front—an umbrella name for the outlawed coalition of Sudanese right-wing parties which were involved in the July 1976 coup attempt. An amnesty law, announced in August 1977, facilitated this initiative. The leader of the Front and former Prime Minister, al-Sādiq al-Mahdī, had the sentence of death (passed on him after the July coup) quietly removed, and received a warm public welcome on his return from exile in late September 1977. The Numayrī regime's position was strengthened by this act of reconciliation, and its standing rose in the Arab world.

During the period under review (July 1976 to October 1977), Sudan's foreign policy moved more strongly towards the West, at the same time consolidating relations with China. However, its stance towards the USSR became violently hostile. In alliance with Egypt and Saudi Arabia, Sudan formed part of a triumvirate of Arab states strongly antipathetic to the developing Soviet-Libyan-Ethiopian axis and strongly resistant to Moscow's policies in the Red Sea area in particular.

POLITICAL AFFAIRS

THE ABORTIVE COUP OF JULY 1976

At five o'clock on the morning of 2 July 1976, shooting broke out at Khartoum airport, just minutes after President Numayrī's return from a three-week visit to the US and France. After he was whisked from the airport, it was immediately occupied by rebels dressed in civilian clothes and equipped with modern weapons. Telecommunications were suspended and Radio Omdurman went off the air. Heavy fighting went on for much of the day—mainly at the headquarters of the Armed Forces General Command, the Presidential Palace, the armoured forces garrison at Shajara (30 km south-west of Khartoum), and around the broadcasting station. But before evening, the government forces succeeded in getting the upper hand, and by the following day it was clear that Numayrī had won yet another round in his seven-year fight for political survival. (Within ten days the Kuwaiti newspaper *al-Siyāsa*, reported that another attempted coup on 10 July had been foiled, although Government sources strongly denied this report.) Yet the curfew was not lifted until the end of July. Altogether the fighting cost 700 lives, with serious loss of property.

Reprisals were heavy—98 executions and a large number of life sentences. Among those sentenced to death *in absentia* was al-Sādiq al-Mahdī.

The attempt was one of the most serious threats to the Numayrī regime since it came to power through a military coup in May 1969. The quick success in crushing it was due to a combination of factors: the unexpected early arrival home of Numayrī, which took the rebels by surprise; the loyalty of the Sudanese army; and Egypt's immediate aid. There were also serious weaknesses on the rebel side—lack of communications; failure to establish contact with the exile leaders (who were airborne in a Libyan plane); failure to operate the national radio after capturing it; and the absence from the streets of the expected public demonstration of support. While Radio Omdurman was off the air, Radio Juba, located in Southern Sudan, continued to broadcast support for the regime.

Numayrī at first described the abortive coup as "a treacherous foreign invasion for which thousands of people of various nationalities were recruited. Some Sudanese, from among the weak-minded, were added to them."[1] The accusations later became more specific and claimed that the participants in the coup belonged to the National Front, were financed and trained by Libya, which itself was a "tool in the hands of a major strategy."[2] Alongside Libya, Ethiopia was also accused of sheltering and training Sudanese opponents. However, it was only in September 1976 that Numayrī named the USSR as the initiator of "the major strategy." All four—Libya, Ethiopia, the USSR and the National Front—shared a history of tension with Numayrī's regime, but by the end of the summer of 1976 they were openly branded as its enemies. The abortive coup of mid-1971 had produced an open breach with the USSR. Sudan's relations with Libya had deteriorated since 1974-5; and with Ethiopia since the beginning of 1976.

Domestically, the National Front (*al-jabha al-wataniyya*) was a coalition of the right-wing, traditionalist political parties which had been removed from the political arena by Numayrī after he had seized power. It consisted of: 1) the *Umma* party—the political organ of the *Anṣār* (followers of al-Mahdī); 2) the National Unionist Party (*al-ḥizb al-waṭanī al-ittiḥādī*); and 3) the Islamic Charter Front (*jabhat al-mīthāq al-islāmī*) composed mainly of the Muslim Brethren. These political bodies had grouped together at the end of 1972, in an attempt to overthrow the Numayrī regime. Their platform had two major aims: the revival of Islam in a modern, progressive state; and the guarantee of democratic rights to the people. The National Front was not in favour of close relations with Egypt. Its leadership was held responsible by Numayrī's regime for a number of subversive actions, including an abortive coup in September 1975.

As the picture of the abortive coup was unfolding, two major trends in its presentation and interpretation could be discerned. One trend—of which the National Front leader, former PM al-Sādiq al-Mahdī (in exile during July 1976) was a main exponent—emphasized the domestic Sudanese nature of the attempted coup. He described it as "a purely Sudanese affair."[3] On the other hand, the regime portrayed the coup as a "foreign invasion" which was unable to secure more than meagre Sudanese support.

Both images were equally inaccurate. Al-Mahdī's emphasis on the local character of the coup could not provide a convincing explanation for the sophisticated weaponry used by the rebels, the advance planning and training necessary for its staging, as well as the complicated arrangements activated on 2 July. By contrast, Numayrī's actions in the wake of the coup, as well as the fact that it became a turning point in his regime's foreign and domestic policies, shows that he did indeed attach significance to the participation in it of local opposition forces. After devoting the month of July to reasserting the Government's control over Sudanese public life, the Numayrī regime began to reorganize and reorient its governmental base, hoping to revitalize the SSU as a means for mobilizing public support.

SSU MOBILIZED: GOVERNMENT RESTRUCTURED AND RESHUFFLED

The SSU (*al-ittiḥād al-ishtirākī al-sudānī*)—the sole political organization permitted in Sudan—was established in October 1971. Since then many efforts have been made to widen and strengthen its mass support, but with only limited success. When the SSU First National Congress was convened in January 1974, its total membership was officially estimated at 2.25m, compared to the 4m announced in January 1977. In his dual capacity as President and Secretary-General of the SSU, Numayrī has constantly tried to create for the organization the image of a governing body rather than just a government organ. However, the SSU has remained largely an instrument of the regime. As such, it was not in a position to initiate independent political action or programmatic activities, but was rather relied upon to provide the regime with the trappings of broad public support whenever necessary.

Requiring a demonstration of popular support after the abortive July coup, Numayrī issued a presidential order on 31 July 1976, calling for conferences and elections at the levels of village units, divisions, areas and provinces, in preparation for the Second General Congress of the SSU. Numayrī followed up this new initiative on 9 August 1976 by substantial changes in his personal administrative role. He relinquished the key posts of Prime Minister (held since October 1969); Defence Minister (held off and on between 1969 and 1970, and continuously from November 1974); Secretary-General of the SSU (held from October 1972), and Commander-in-Chief (held off and on between 1969 and 1970, and continuously from November 1974). Simultaneously, he appointed al-Rashīd al-Ṭāhir Bakr as Prime Minister and to the newly-created post of second Vice-President (in addition to Abel Alier, a Southerner, first appointed in 1971).

The new Prime Minister, formerly speaker of the People's Assembly, was a civilian, and a lawyer by profession. Two weeks after this appointment, Numayrī announced that he had decided to invest the Prime Minister with additional powers by giving him full responsibility over government ministers, although he himself would retain authority over appointments and dismissals. The new Prime Minister was also appointed to the National Defence Council and the National Security Council (the former in charge of military affairs, and the latter of internal security).

Lt-Gen (*farīq*) Bashīr Muḥammad 'Alī, hitherto Chief-of-Staff, was appointed Defence Minister and C-in-C of the Sudanese Army on 9 August 1976. As the new Chief of Staff, Maj-Gen (*liwā*) Muḥammad 'Uthmān Hāshim was promoted to the rank of Lt-Gen (*farīq*). Major (*rā'id*) Abū al-Qāsim Muḥammad Ibrāhīm, was promoted to Secretary-General of the SSU and Governor of Khartoum Province. Four other new ministers were appointed at the same time (see Government list, below).

Another significant change, announced by Numayrī on 30 August, was the establishment of a new Presidential Advisory Body (*al-jihāz al-idārī li-ri'āsat al-jumhūriyya*) to carry out the functions of a General Secretariat of the Presidency. Dr Manṣūr Khālid was appointed its supervisor as well as Presidential Adviser for Co-ordination and Foreign Affairs. A close friend of Numayrī, Khālid had served as Foreign Minister from 1971 to 1975, but was abruptly transferred to the Ministry of Education in January 1975. His return to the centre of Sudanese politics was in keeping with Numayrī's system of removing and then reinstating political figures, either to prevent the growth of new centres of power or to make scapegoats for the regime's failures. Immediately after the changes of 9 August, Numayrī promised to make "radical ministerial changes" early in 1977, after the

SSU Second General Congress.[4]

Numayrī's decision to reduce his own role in the running of the government was explained by him in the following terms: "Until now everything has been on my shoulders, but I felt it would be a good idea to spread things out . . . to let more people participate in the leadership at the highest level."[5] However, there was no meaningful decrease in Numayrī's political power since he continued to control all major political institutions—the government, the military and the SSU.

Three years after the first General Congress of the SSU, the Second General Congress opened in Khartoum on 25 January 1977. Until its final session on 6 February, it was a colourful and festive occasion, serving mainly to endorse the leader's proposals and ideas. It reaffirmed the regime's domestic and foreign policy, and re-nominated Numayrī (unopposed) for a second term as President of the Republic. It also re-elected the SSU Central Committee (*al-lajna al-markaziyya*), which in turn elected a 24-member Executive Bureau (*al-maktab al-tanfīdhī*), with Numayrī as its chairman. On 8 February, Numayrī issued a decree appointing the political supervisors of the provinces from among the members of the SSU Executive Bureau. That the Executive Bureau and the SSU Central Committee were filled with Cabinet and RCC members demonstrated how Numayrī retained full control over the ruling party. His idiosyncratic system was characterized by the continuous shifting of political and military figures from the Cabinet to the SSU Executive Bureau, or vice versa—from positions of real political influence to posts of mere prestige.

THE JUBA AFFAIR

News of unrest in Juba (the capital of Southern Sudan) reached Khartoum while the SSU congress was still in session. On the morning of 2 February 1977, rebel members of the Sudanese Air Force (probably Southerners) occupied Juba airport for seven hours before being overpowered. Nine Sudanese soldiers were killed and others injured. According to the Sudanese newspaper *al-Saḥāfa*,[6] Israeli elements had instigated the Juba plot in collusion with a Sudanese politician in exile, Philip 'Abbās Ghabbūsh. He had previously been accused by Numayrī of organizing a plot in July 1969, which was referred to by the Sudanese authorities at the time as "the racial conspiracy."

Of Nubian origin, Philip 'Abbās Ghabbūsh was a parliamentary deputy and—before the 1969 takeover by Numayrī—head of the Free Negro Organization (renamed the Front for the Liberation of African Sudan in April 1969). Its major aims, as reported by *al-Ahrām*,[7] were the liberation of the Sudanese blacks from persecution and the ending of the religious dispute between Sudan's Muslims and Christians.

Information relayed about the Juba affair in the Sudanese media was confused. According to the official version, the Juba plotters aimed at eliminating the entire regional leadership of the South. Radio Omdurman broadcast that the rebels wanted to use Juba as a base for striking at Khartoum and the rest of Sudan, adding that the rebels were led both by Philip 'Abbās Ghabbūsh and by al-Sādiq al-Mahdī.[8] The media only carried news of the affair for a few days however, and further diminished its importance by describing it as a local disturbance. Maj-Gen (liwā) Joseph Lagu[9] also minimized the affair as "a minor disturbance" by "a few short-minded people."[10] The Vice-President and Chairman of the High Executive Council of the South, Abel Alier, said that "the plot was manipulated by unspecified foreign hands", although Reuter reported that eye-witnesses had not seen any sign of foreign participation.[11]

The event was significant in that more than half of those involved were soldiers and police. The rebels were severely punished, and strict security measures were adopted in the South. While it is not yet possible to provide an accurate explanation for what happened, there seems little reason to doubt that it was another manifestation of dissatisfaction among certain Southern elements. However, since the end of the civil war and the signing of the Addis Ababa agreement of February 1972, the bulk of Southerners have repeatedly shown that they are loyal to Numayrī.

GOVERNMENT RESHUFFLES

Numayrī formed his new government on 11 February 1977, with extensive reshuffling of portfolios. Seven new Ministers of State were named; five Ministers left the Cabinet and seven new Ministers joined. The most significant appointment was that of Dr Mansūr Khālid as Foreign Minister and Assistant to the President for Coordination. (Khālid's known pro-American stance was an indication of Numayrī's own changing orientation.) While the August 1976 changes in government and personnel had been limited in scope but significant in substance, the February 1977 reshuffle was almost reverse—extensive in scope but less important as a political turning point. In Numayrī's own words: "The new Cabinet represented new methods but the same goals."[12]

Numayrī announced another minor government change on 29 May 1977—the abolition of the Ministry of Local Popular Government, established in 1971. Its Minister, Major (*rā'id*) Ma'mūn 'Awad Abū Zayd, was appointed to the newly-created post of Energy and Mining. (Abū Zayd was one of the original RCC members; from October 1971 to January 1972, he served as the first Secretary-General of the SSU, and was known to be a radical pan-Arabist and socialist. Following a period of political "freeze", he was appointed Presidential Adviser on Arab affairs in February 1976.)

On the same day, a Presidential decree regarding the appointment of Vice-Presidents was announced: First Vice-President, Maj-Gen (*liwā*) Muḥammad al-Bāqir Aḥmad; Vice-President, Abel Alier; Vice-President, al-Rashīd al-Tāhir Bakr.

NUMAYRI ELECTED PRESIDENT FOR SECOND TERM

Numayrī was re-elected President of Sudan for a second six-year term in May, receiving 99.1% of the votes (with a 98.3% turnout of voters).[13] When taking the oath of office on 24 May 1977, Numayrī reviewed the achievements of his first term and outlined his proposals for the second. On domestic policy, he said he would soon be issuing decisions "to end the centralized domination and speed up the transfer of authority to the local executive councils and the other local popular councils. Perhaps the first step in this field is the abolition of the Local People's Government Ministry, which will be replaced by a centralized administrative unit under the Presidency of the Republic." Numayrī added that he would be reviewing the duties of the Vice-Presidents and their authority. He also hinted at a possible change of heart concerning the National Front (see below).

He went on to describe the Soviets in Ethiopia as a "foreign presence" which "must attract a counter-presence in the region and around it." Such a development, he warned, was a danger for Sudan. "This is due to the fact that the major strategic conflicts, within the nuclear balance and the framework of *détente*, are using the small international entities as tools to settle their account and to achieve their aims, at the expense of those entities' security, stability and progress . . . The Sudan is capable of resisting all the winds of danger whipped up by the ambitions of the major [power of] socialism (i.e. the USSR)."

NUMAYRI'S ATTEMPTS "TO OPEN A NEW PAGE" WITH THE NATIONAL FRONT

In the spring of 1977, circumstances created an atmosphere conducive to a *rapprochement* with the National Front. Externally, the attitude of Libya and the threat implicit in Ethiopia's upheavals—especially the Addis Ababa regime's closer ties with the USSR—were construed by Numayrī as a potential threat to Sudan. There was also reason to believe that Saudi Arabia, a major supporter of Sudan since mid-1971, would be favourably disposed towards an alliance of Numayrī's forces with the traditionalist, Islamic-oriented National Front. Domestically, while the coup attempt of July 1976 had turned out a fiasco, it still served as a reminder of the strength and vitality of the socio-political forces grouped together under the National Front banner. Furthermore, security troubles in Western Sudan in July 1976 and January 1977 continued to concern Numayrī, more especially since these areas—Darfur and Kordofan—are traditional strongholds of the pro-Mahdist *Ansār*.

A major declarative move in what became a series of conciliatory steps towards the National Front was made by Numayrī in his Presidential speech of 24 May. He promised "all compatriots who contacted me . . . that, on the threshold of my second term, I will not close the doors of the homeland and will not stand in the way of those of goodwill. I will give an opportunity to open a new page to those who wish to take their place again among the people, to contribute to the reconstruction of the Sudanese nation."[14]

Soon afterwards, on 19 July, it was disclosed that Numayrī and al-Sādiq al-Mahdī had met some days earlier in Port Sudan. On 30 July, Numayrī stated that "he had voluntarily declared together with the competent revolutionary organs to release the political detainees . . . in order to entrench national unity."[15] At a time when there were strong rumours that Saudi Arabia was instrumental in Numayrī's decision to release political detainees and to appease the National Front, Numayrī emphasized that he was attempting reconciliation in order to consolidate national unity: "I am willing to meet the devil himself, if it is in the interests of my country."[16] Simultaneously, 900 political detainees were released (leaving c. 1,000 others still in prison).[17]

A week later, on 7 August 1977, a law was officially announced granting amnesty to "any Sudanese who, on or after 25 May 1969, committed an illegal act inside or outside Sudan, or has illegally refused to carry out a task, and that task and refusal were connected with mutiny, disobedience, sedition, waging war against the state, undermining the Constitution, or committing any other crime punishable under the state security laws, provided that the person concerned has willingly agreed to abide by the Constitution . . . and also provided that he agrees to return to Sudan if he is residing abroad."[18] During the months of August and September 1977, more political prisoners were released.

Several Sudanese communist leaders were also released in August in accordance with the amnesty law.[19] They included Muḥammad Ibrāhīm Nuqud who, in 1971, had become the Secretary-General of the Communist Party (CP) following the execution of 'Abd al-Khāliq Maḥjūb; and Tijānī al-Tayyib, head of the CP's Khartoum branch in 1971. Both had been jailed for their role in the abortive Leftist coup of July 1971. During the period under review, there were two waves of arrests of Sudanese communists—in January and June 1977.[20]

Numayrī's moves did not apparently meet with the complete approval of all his RCC colleagues. There were rumours that the amnesty decision was criticized by personalities such as Abū al-Qāsim Muḥammad Ibrāhīm and Muḥammad al-Bāqir Aḥmad. These rumours were categorically denied by Numayrī. He also denied that the amnesty had been "occasioned by a condition imposed by oil prospects."

COMPOSITION OF SUDANESE CABINETS
(9 August 1976 - 10 September 1977)

Cabinet Ministers

Portfolio	9 August 1976	11 February 1977	29 May 1977	10 September 1977
Prime Minister	Al-Rashīd al-Tāhir Bakr†	Al-Rashīd al-Tāhir Bakr	Al-Rashīd al-Tāhir Bakr	Ja'far al-Numayrī†
Foreign Affairs	Makkāwī Mahjūb	Mansūr Khālid†	Mansūr Khālid	Al-Rashīd al-Tāhir Bakr
Defence and C-in-C of Armed Forces	Lt-Gen Bashīr Muḥammad 'Alī†	Gen Bashīr Muḥammad 'Alī	Gen Bashīr Muḥammad 'Alī	Gen Bashīr Muḥammad 'Alī
Interior[1]	Maj Ma'mūn 'Awad Abū Zayd	'Abd al-Wahhāb Ibrāhīm†	'Abd al-Wahhāb Ibrāhīm	'Abd al-Wahhāb Ibrāhīm
Finance, Planning and National Economy[2]	Ma'mūn Buḥayrī	Al-Sharīf al-Khātim Muhammad	Al-Sharīf al-Khātim Muhammad	Ja'far al-Numayrī†
		Maj-Gen Nasir al-Dīn Mustafā	Maj-Gen Nasir al-Dīn Mustafā	
Education	Daf'allah al-Ḥājj Yūsuf†	Daf'allah al-Ḥājj Yūsuf	Daf'allah al-Ḥājj Yūsuf	Daf'allah al-Ḥājj Yūsuf
Culture and Information	Buna Malwāl	Buna Malwāl	Buna Malwāl	Buna Malwāl
Health	Maj-Gen Khālid Ḥasan 'Abbās	Maj-Gen Khālid Ḥasan 'Abbās	Maj-Gen Khālid Ḥasan 'Abbās	Maj-Gen Khālid Ḥasan 'Abbās
Trade and Supply	Hārūn al-'Awad	Hārūn al-'Awad	Hārūn al-'Awad	Hārūn al-'Awad
Industry[3]	Badr al-Dīn Sulaymān	'Abd al-Raḥman 'Abdallah	'Abd al-Raḥman 'Abdallah	Bashīr 'Abbādī
			Maj Ma'mūn 'Awad Abū Zayd	
Agriculture, Food and National Resources	'Abbās 'Abd al-Mājid	'Abdallah Aḥmad 'Abdallah†	'Abdallah Aḥmad 'Abdallah	'Abdallah Aḥmad 'Abdallah
Transport and Communications[4]	Bashīr 'Abbādī	Bashīr 'Abbādī	Bashīr 'Abbādī	'Abd al-Raḥman 'Abdallah
Public Services and Administrative Reform	'Abd al-Raḥman 'Abdallah	Karamallah al-'Awad†	Karamallah al-'Awad	Karamallah al-'Awad
Construction and Public Works	Maj-Gen Mustafā 'Uthmān Ḥasan	Maj-Gen Mustafā 'Uthmān Ḥasan	Maj-Gen Mustafā 'Uthmān Ḥasan	Mu'āwiya Abū Bakr†
Local Popular Government.[5]	Al-Sharīf al-Khātim Muhammad	Maj Ma'mūn 'Awad Abū Zayd		—
Youth and Sports	Maj Zayn al-'Ābidīn Muḥammad Aḥmad	Maj Zayn al-'Ābidīn Muḥammad Aḥmad	Maj Zayn al-'Ābidīn Muḥammad Aḥmad	Maj Zayn al-'Ābidīn Muḥammad Aḥmad
Social Affairs	Fātima 'Abd al-Maḥmūd	Fātima 'Abd al-Maḥmūd	Fātima 'Abd al-Maḥmūd	Fātima 'Abd al-Maḥmūd
Waqfs and Religious Affairs	'Awn al-Sharīf Qāsim	'Awn al-Sharīf Qāsim	'Awn al-Sharīf Qāsim	
Attorney-General	Zakī 'Abd al-Raḥman	Ḥasan 'Umar†	Ḥasan 'Umar	Ḥasan 'Umar
Irrigation and Hydroelectric Power	—	Sughayrūn al-Zayn†	Sughayrūn al-Zayn	Yaḥyā 'Abd al-Majīd†
Co-operation	—	Muḥammad Hāshim 'Awad†	Muḥammad Hāshim 'Awad	Muḥammad Hāshim 'Awad

Ministers of State

Portfolio	9 August 1976	11 February 1977	29 May 1977	10 September 1977
Presidency	'Izz al-Dīn Ḥāmid	Ḥasan 'Ābidīn†	Ḥasan 'Ābidīn; Khālid al-Khayr 'Umar†	Khālid al-Khayr 'Umar
Prime Minister's Office	Bahā' al-Dīn Muḥammad Idrīs	Muḥammad Ṭāhir;† Maḥmūd Bashīr Jammā'†	Muḥammad Ṭāhir; Maḥmūd Bashīr Jammā'	*
Economy[6]	'Uthmān Hāshim 'Abd al-Salām	'Uthmān Hāshim 'Abd al-Salām	'Uthmān Hāshim 'Abd al-Salām	'Uthmān Hāshim 'Abd al-Salām
Finance[7]	Bashīr Ibrāhīm 'Uthman			
Education	'Izz al-Dīn al-Ḥāfiẓ	Ḥasan Aḥmad Yūsuf†	Ḥasan Aḥmad Yūsuf	Ḥasan Aḥmad Yūsuf
Culture and Information	Ismā'īl al-Ḥājj Mūsā	Ismā'īl al-Ḥājj Mūsā	Ismā'īl al-Ḥājj Mūsā	Ismā'īl al-Ḥājj Mūsā
Planning	Maj-Gen Nāṣir al-Dīn Mustafā			
Foreign Affairs	Francis Deng	Francis Deng	Francis Deng	Francis Deng
Irrigation	Yaḥyā 'Abd al-Majīd	Amīn Abū Snayna;†	Amīn Abū Snayna;	
Agricultural Research[8]	Ḥusayn Idrīs	'Abd al-Raḥīm Makkī;† Muḥammad al-Shazlī 'Uthmān†	'Abd al-Raḥīm Makkī; Muḥammad al-Shazlī 'Uthmān	
Youth and Sports	'Alī Shummū†	'Alī Shummū	'Alī Shummū	'Alī Shummū
Transport and Communications[9]		Aḥmad 'Abd al-Karīm Badrī†	Aḥmad 'Abd al-Karīm Badrī	Aḥmad 'Abd al-Karīm Badrī

† Newly appointed.
* No details available.
1 Changed to *Interior and Head of Public Security* on 11 February 1977.
2 Split into *Finance and Economy* (1), and *Planning* (2), on 11 February 1977.
3 Became *Industry and Mines* on 11 February 1977. Split into *Industry* (1), and *Energy and Mining* (2), on 29 May 1977.
4 Became *Transport* only on 29 May 1977.
5 Portfolio abolished on 29 May 1977.
6 Became *Economy and Finance* on 11 February 1977.
7 Portfolio merged with *Economy* on 11 February 1977.
8 Became *Agriculture, Nutrition and Natural Resources* on 11 February 1977.
9 Became *Communications* only on 29 February 1977.

Without mentioning any Arab oil state specifically, he said: "We do not accept a situation in which strangers can impose conditions on us."[21] The rumours seemed to gain some validity, however, when Numayrī announced the resignation of Muḥammad al-Bāqir Aḥmad as First Vice-President on 15 August because of "poor health." He was replaced by Abū al-Qāsim Muḥammad Ibrāhīm, an original RCC member, who had held important positions continuously since May 1969, and retained his post as Secretary-General of the SSU. These developments confirmed that there were indeed disagreements and resentments within the regime over Numayrī's policy of reconciliation. Abū al-Qāsim Muḥammad Ibrāhīm's appointment as First Vice-President also set the scene for the reinstatement of other veteran members of the original RCC (such as Ma'mūn 'Awad Abū Zayd and 'Uthmān Abū al-Qāsim Hāshim) back into the centre of political power.

On 10 September 1977, Numayrī undertook yet another government reshuffle which was probably connected with the process of reconciliation. This time Numayrī assumed the office of Prime Minister (which he had relinquished in August 1976), as well as the portfolio of Finance and National Economy. Al-Rashīd al-Tāhir Bakr was moved from the Premiership to become Foreign Minister, while still retaining his post as Vice-President. Mansūr Khālid was ousted from the government altogether. The significance of this latest twist in Khālid's checkered career is not yet clear. According to one assessment of the reshuffle, Numayrī's intention of temporarily assuming the posts of Prime Minister and Finance Minister was to enable him to later transfer them to the National Front's leaders, al-Sādiq al-Mahdī and Sharīf al Hindī.[22]

The moves towards reconciliation between Numayrī and the National Front leaders did not only raise problems for hard-core RCC members, but also for three other important centres of opinion. First, with the secularists among Khartoum's sophisticated political intelligentsia, who strongly oppose the Islamic tinge of al-Sādiq al-Mahdī's political ideas. Second, with the Southerners who remain deeply suspicious of any move towards strengthening the Islamic character of the state, and whose leaders have unpleasant memories of the former political role played by men like Sharīf al-Hindī. However, al-Sādiq's own policies towards Southerners while he was Prime Minister won him friends among their old leaders. Third, with the communists who see the National Front leaders as arch-enemies of all progressive policies. The moves towards reconciliation also raised the major question of the future role of a strong young leader like al-Sādiq. None of these questions was clarified by the time the 42-year old Oxford-educated Mahdī returned from exile in England to Khartoum on 27 September 1977. Numayrī encouraged a spectacular homecoming for his rival who, just a year before, he had sentenced to death.

Now that the reconciliation had been effected, the question still to be answered was how it would be consummated. Al-Sādiq did not accept any official post; nor did any of his National Front colleagues join the government when they also returned from abroad during October 1977. Al-Mahdī described the role he wished to play as one of political and constitutional adviser to the President in devising a new political system for the country, flexible enough to allow the regime and its political opponents to coexist without either side having to resort to political violence to assert its rights. He insisted that the reconciliation had been produced entirely by the Sudanese themselves who, after the July coup attempt and its bloody aftermath, found it intolerable to live in an atmosphere of violence and internecine family conflict—more especially when they felt threatened by events in Ethiopia and the expanding Soviet role in the region.

According to al-Mahdī, the July coup attempt taught both his National Front and Numayrī's SSU several important lessons. First, it taught the Front that Numayrī could not be toppled as easily as they had assumed; and it taught Numayrī that the opposition forces were stronger than he had allowed for. Second, both sides realized that their policies of violent confrontation could be continued only by attracting outside support (Libya behind the National Front and Egypt behind the regime), which strengthened foreign involvement in Sudanese affairs. Third, it taught all Sudanese that a society like theirs could prosper only under a system that allowed for adequate democratic participation by all the major political forces in the country. Thus, he argued, the time had come for the Sudan to develop a new political system which would allow for non-violent political change. Al-Mahdī was also keen to dispel the idea that he shared the aspirations of the Muslim Brethren (led by his brother-in-law in the Sudan, Dr Ḥasan Turabī), and that he himself strongly rejected the notion of a theological state.

ARMED FORCES

Total armed forces number 52,100. Defence expenditure in 1975–76 was £S 46m ($131.4m). Military service is voluntary. The Army numbers 50,000 and formations consist of two armoured brigades; seven infantry brigades; one parachute brigade; three artillery regiments; three air defence artillery regiments and one engineer regiment. Equipment consists of 70 T-54 and 60 T-55 medium tanks; 30 T-62 light tanks (Chinese); 50 *Saladin* and 45 *Commando* armoured cars; 60 *Ferret* scout cars; 100 BTR-40/-50/-152, 60 OT-64 and 49 *Saracen* armoured personnel carriers; 55 25-pounder, 40 100mm, 20 105mm and 18 122mm guns and howitzers; 30 120mm mortars; 30 85mm anti-tank guns; 80 Bofors 40mm, 80 Soviet 37mm, 85mm anti-aircraft guns. (AMX-10 armoured personnel carriers on order.) 1,000 men are deployed in Lebanon in the Arab Peacekeeping Force. The 600-strong Navy is equipped with three patrol boats (ex-Iranian); six large patrol boats; six small patrol craft (ex-Yugoslav) and two landing craft. The Air Force numbers 1,500 and is equipped with 27 combat aircraft. Formations consist of one interceptor squadron with ten MiG-21MF; one ground-attack fighter squadron with 17 MiG-17 (ex-Chinese); five BAC-145 and six *Jet Provost* Mk 55, and three *Pembroke* (in storage); one transport squadron with five An-24, four F-27 and one DHC-6 and one helicopter squadron with ten Mi-8. (15 *Mirage* fighters, six C-130H, four DHC-5D transports and ten *Puma* helicopters on order.) Paramilitary forces number 3,500: 500 in the National Guard; 500 in the Republican Guard and 2,500 Border Guard.[23]

FOREIGN AFFAIRS

RELATIONS WITH THE MAJOR POWERS

Sudan's foreign policy in the period under review shifted much closer toward the West, and even further away from the USSR, thus crystallizing a gradual process that had begun after the abortive Leftist coup of 1971. Until mid-1976, Numayrī tried to balance relations with both West and East, paying particular importance to his alliance with Peking. However, the July 1976 abortive coup led to a rapid deterioration in Sudanese-Soviet relations—further accelerated by Soviet policy in the Horn of Africa. At first, Numayrī only implicitly identified the Soviet Union as the power behind the coup. In August 1976, he still suggested that Soviet involvement was only indirect—through its support for Libya. It was not until September 1976 that Numayrī explicitly named the Soviet Union as the major force behind the July coup attempt.[24]

Explaining the USSR's motivation for its "subversive activity" against Sudan, Numayrī said: "We in the Sudan feel that the defeat of the communists in our country [in July 1971] and then the success of the Sudanese government . . . is seen as a threat to communist ideas in the world."[25] These accusations were categorically denied by the Soviet Union.

During the summer and autumn of 1976, Numayrī's main efforts in foreign policy were concentrated on developing Sudan's relations with Saudi Arabia and Egypt. At the same time, the Red Sea area was rapidly becoming a cockpit of international conflict. The "defence of the Red Sea" naturally became a focal point of Sudanese foreign policy. Khartoum adopted the Egyptian and Saudi Arabian aim of turning the Red Sea into a "neutral zone" and an "Arab lake" by removing the influence of the Soviets and non-Arab powers from the area. (See essays, "Inter-Arab Relations" and "The Middle East, the Red Sea and Africa.")

Sudan's concern about Soviet policies in the Horn of Africa established a common interest with the Western community and brought them closer together. Its attitude also appealed to the other anti-Soviet great power, China.

In the Arab world, Sudan's backing of Sadat's policy—and especially its support for the Sinai agreement of September 1975—put the Numayrī regime in the camp with Egypt and Saudi Arabia, and on the side of American-oriented policies in the Middle East. It was therefore no surprise that on 17 November 1976, President Ford announced that Sudan would be allowed to buy American arms. Selling "defence articles" to Sudan, he explained, "will strengthen the security of the US and promote world peace."[26] Sudan's Foreign Minister, Dr Khālid, visited the US on 14 April 1977, to start talks for the purchase of US military equipment. On 29 April, the US announced the sale of six C-130 Hercules (civilian-military) transport aircraft.

Sudan also improved her relations with France. Numayrī's praise of French aid to Zaïre to repulse an armed attack from across the Angolan border in the spring of 1977 was a significant indicator of this closer French-Sudanese relationship. Numayrī paid an official visit to France from 16–19 May 1977, accompanied by his Foreign and Defence Ministers. While in Paris he referred to the USSR's supply of arms and military exports to the Red Sea states as a "new form of colonialism."[27] A joint communiqué issued on 19 May expressed the agreement of both sides on major foreign policy issues, including the "need to safeguard the unity and sovereignty of African states." Referring to the Red Sea region and East Africa, the communiqué stressed "the need to keep the area free of danger of foreign interference to ensure that it remained a zone of security and peace." In the field of bilateral economic relations, the two countries agreed on Sudan's "suitability for investment and the need to protect investors' rights."[28] France also agreed to supply arms to Sudan.

On 18 May 1977—while Numayrī was still in France—the Sudanese News Agency (SUNA) announced that Sudan had decided to "terminate the contracts of Soviet military experts working with the Sudanese army."[29] It also reported that the Russian experts had been given one week to leave the country. At the same time, Sudan asked the Soviet Union to reduce its embassy staff in Khartoum by half. This request was met at the beginning of June.

Numayrī's next state visit, to China from 6–16 June 1977, provided another opportunity for him to attack Moscow's policies. He called the USSR "a merchant of death selling munitions at exorbitant prices."[30] In an interview, Numayrī said that "the Chinese and Sudanese stands are identical on the need to maintain the neutrality of the Red Sea, to keep it free from international disputes and to support the stands of Sudan, Egypt, Morocco . . . on what happened in Zaïre."[31] After the visit Khartoum announced that "China backs Sudan militantly."[32] Both countries also agreed to strengthen their bilateral economic relations.

Numayrī's anti-Soviet attacks continued unabated for the remainder of 1977.

RELATIONS WITH EGYPT AND SAUDI ARABIA

Just 11 days after the coup had been put down, on 13 July 1976, Numayri visited Egypt. Six days later, Sādāt and Numayrī arrived together in Jidda for a tripartite summit meeting with Saudi Arabia's King Khālid. On the same day, Egypt and Sudan announced that on 15 July they had signed a 25-year Joint Defence Agreement[33] whereby an armed attack on either country or on its armed forces would be considered an attack on both. The agreement, which provided for the establishment of a Joint Defence Council and a Joint Staff, was formally ratified on 15 January 1977. On 28 February, Sudan joined the Syrian-Egyptian Command, which had been established in December 1976 (see essay on Inter-Arab Relations).

Economic relations between Egypt and Sudan continued to improve, based on an integration agreement signed in February 1974.

Sudan's position in the Red Sea was clearly stated by Numayrī in May 1977: "It must not be allowed to become an arena for super-power conflict—it must be a sea of peace."[34] Sudan's Prime Minister, al-Rashīd al-Tāhir Bakr, declared his country's interest in the Red Sea as "a vital artery linking the Mediterranean with the [Persian] Gulf and the Indian Ocean." Therefore the states bordering the Red Sea "should co-ordinate stands . . . so the Red Sea remains an Arab lake."[35]

Sudan's cordial relationship with Saudi Arabia was another reflection of the change in Sudan's Arab policy and of its growing concern about the Red Sea. Saudi Arabia was interested in strengthening the Numayrī regime because of its anti-communist, anti-Soviet attitudes, as well as its willingness to adhere to the Egyptian-Saudi axis. Jidda therefore helped Sudan finance her arms deals as well as providing her with military training aid. "Injections" of Saudi capital, though not yet by any means substantial, are expected to play a vital role in Sudan's ailing economy (although in terms of capital investment, the Gulf states actually contribute more).

Numayri pursued his activist policy in the Arab world with an extensive tour in March 1977 which included Oman, South and North Yemen as well as Somalia. During the tour, he attended the Ta'izz (North Yemen) quadripartite summit conference (22-23 March) in which YAR, PDRY and Somalia also participated. According to Numayrī, this conference aimed at achieving co-operation in economic and industrial development among the participating countries. He added that the security of the Red Sea also figured prominently in the conference.[36] (See essay on Inter-Arab Relations.)

RELATIONS WITH LIBYA

Relations between Khartoum and Tripoli, which began to decline in 1972, reached a low ebb after September 1975, and descended to their nadir after the coup attempt of 2 July 1976—which the Sudanese called "the Libyan invasion." Only four days after the "invasion", Numayrī severed diplomatic relations with Libya; all bilateral economic projects and agreements were cancelled. Despite this state of hostility, Numayrī tried to alter the bleak picture towards the end of the summer of 1977 by cautiously exploring the possibility of improving relations.

RELATIONS WITH ETHIOPIA AND SOMALIA

Sudan formally accused Ethiopia in July 1976 of complicity in the abortive coup. By January 1977, and following the ratification of the Egyptian-Sudanese Joint Defence Agreement, relations with Addis Ababa underwent a marked deterioration, probably by Sudan's initiative. Ethiopia's increasing efforts in that month to crush the Eritrean rebels, who were supported by Sudan, probably served as a catalyst for this deterioration. Both sides recalled their ambassadors and accused each other of border violations. As tension along the common border mounted, Sudan declared a state of alert on 2 January 1977. On the previous day Numayrī openly threatened Ethiopia by saying that Sudan could deal with its "hostility and aggression" in one of three ways "in our own capacity to deter; in the possible use of hundreds of thousands of Ethiopians and Eritreans living in our country . . . and closure of our borders with Ethiopia."[37] In reaction, Ethiopia accused Sudan of supporting and assisting the Eritrean rebels, as well as the Ethiopian Democratic Union (EDU) which operates along Sudan's eastern frontier with Tigre, Begemder and Simien. This state of mutual suspicion and hostility reached a new pitch in April 1977. Both countries delivered formal protests to the Organization of African Unity (OAU). Sudan "totally and categorically rejected Ethiopian allegations of Sudanese military intervention in the civil war in Ethiopia."[38] In May, *al-Ra'y al-'Āmm* wrote of an "undeclared war" between the two neighbours. The paper also claimed that Egyptian generals were active in Sudan in fulfilment of the Joint Defence Agreement.[39] Two months later, in June 1977, Sudanese troops were accused by Addis Ababa of having crossed the Ethiopian border and occupied the town of Begi (c. 20 miles within Ethiopian territory). *Arabia and the Gulf* reported that this Sudanese incursion was aimed against anti-Numayrī exiles belonging to the Mahdist *Ansār* sect.[40] On 5 July 1977, the Sudanese *al-Saḥāfa* reported that the OAU had decided to set up a committee to try to resolve the Ethiopian-Sudanese dispute; but nothing came of it.

Simultaneously while Sudan's relations with Ethiopia deteriorated, those with Somalia improved. Following a visit by Numayrī to Somalia from 17-20 March 1977, a joint communiqué declared the necessity of these two "African-Arab countries . . . to co-ordinate between themselves" on the following: the security of the Red Sea; the Palestinian issue; and support for the people of Djibouti in their struggle for independence.[41]

ECONOMIC AFFAIRS ($1 = 0.348 Sudanese pounds; £1 sterling = 0.617 £S)

In 1976, the Sudan suffered a serious foreign trade deficit for the fourth straight year. Since 1972, when Sudan last enjoyed a positive balance of trade imports have outraced exports by a 2–1 ratio. Both imports and exports hovered near the $350m mark in 1972, but by 1976 imports had grown to nearly double the value of exports.

The rising cost of imported oil only partially explains this deficit. From 1972 to 1976, imports from OPEC states grew by $110m, from $4m to $114m. For the same period, however, imports from the industrialized countries jumped nearly $400m, from $153m to $641m. Of this increase, imports of machinery, spare parts and transport equipment accounted for the biggest share—$357m—rising from $84m in 1972 to $441m four years later.

Sudan's exports increased at the same time, though at a much slower rate. Although the volume of its chief export—cotton—fell by one-third between 1972 and 1976, the value of cotton sales rose from £S 72.8m (c. $209m) to £S 97.8m (c. $281m), largely because the price doubled during this period. Sales of its second most valuable export—groundnuts—jumped nearly four-fold from £S 9.7m (c. $27.8m) in 1972 to £S 39.0m (c. $112m) in 1976. However, compared to the overall increase in the cost of imports, Sudan's exports have lagged seriously.

AGRICULTURE

While cotton production fell by nearly one-half in 1975-76, output of groundnuts, dura (millet) and wheat all increased. Production of two other important export crops—sesame and gum arabic—also declined. Sudan's efforts towards self-sufficiency in some agricultural commodities received a setback in May 1977, when the London-based multinational, Lonhro, had its management contract for the large-scale Kenana sugar project cancelled. Since 1974, the estimated cost of the project had risen from $180m to over $500m, and the completion date had been postponed successively from late 1977 to the early 1980s.[42]

INDUSTRIAL PRODUCTION

In 1974-75, manufacturing and handicrafts increased by 35% over the previous year to £S 95.7m (c. $275m). Higher production of flour (16.5%), cigarettes (74%) and shoes (8.3%) contributed to the overall increase. On the other hand, production declined in cement (−27.4%) and sugar (−11.5%).

In early 1977, Sudan joined the Arab Common Market. However, the impact of membership in Sudan's industrial sector will not be evident for another few years.

DEVELOPMENT

1977-78 marks the beginning of Sudan's Six-Year Development Plan—the first third of an 18-year Long-Term Plan (1977-78/1994-95). The principal objectives of the Long-Term Plan are: 1) to propel the economy "into the take-off stage and then into self-sustained growth;" 2) to increase per capita income from the present £S 110 (c. $315) to £S 310 (c. $890) by 1994-95; and 3) to improve the "balance of payments position."[43]

The shorter-range goals of the first Six-Year Plan (1977-78/1982-83) include: 1) an annual overall growth rate of 7.5%; 2) development and modernization of agriculture leading to self-sufficiency in some commodities; 3) creation of more jobs; and 4) improvement of the balance of payments. The first plan is to be financed from both local (48%) and foreign (52%) sources. The public sector is to contribute £S 1,560m ($4,480m), and the private sector £S 1,100m (c. $3,160m), for a total investment of £S 2,660m (c. $7,640m). Agriculture is to be the largest recipient sector, beginning with 39% in 1977-78.

AID

In the first half of 1977, Sudan received loans and/or credits from the World Bank ($12m), the Islamic Development Bank ($8.5m), the Arab Fund for Economic and Social Development ($37m) and the Kuwait Fund for Arab Economic Development ($33m) to help finance transportation development alone.

(Economic Section by Ira E. Hoffman)

GOVERNMENT FINANCE (million Sudanese pounds)

	1974-75	*1975-76*
Central government revenue	278.8	332.0
Central government expenditure	264.0	303.2
Surplus	**+23.8**	**+28.8**
Development expenditure	-102.4	-113.1
Public entities	-43.9	-12.3
Other public sector operations	-40.1	-33.7
Public sector overall deficit	**-162.6**	**-130.3**
Financing of the deficit	162.6	130.3
External loans (net)	103.6	22.5
Bank financing (net)	59.0	107.8

NATIONAL ACCOUNTS (million Sudanese pounds; Year beginning 1 July)

	1972	*1973*	*1974*
Exports	151.3	167.1	183.5
Government consumption	168.5	180.5	207.8
Gross fixed capital formation	95.2	140.2	214.4
Increase in stocks	10.0	89.1	50.6
Private consumption	611.0	846.0	1,170.7
Less: Imports	*-136.2*	*-176.7*	*-316.2*
Gross Domestic Product	986.8	1,246.2	1,510.8
Less: Net factor payments abroad	*-10.1*	*-9.8*	*-15.7*
Gross National Expenditure = GNP	976.7	1,236.4	1,495.1
National Income at market prices	832.7	1,136.9	1,379.7

Source: IMF, *International Financial Statistics.*

SUDAN'S GROSS DOMESTIC PRODUCT AT FACTOR COST BY ECONOMIC ACTIVITY IN CURRENT PRICES (million Sudanese pounds)

	1971–72	*1972–73*	*1973–74*	*1974–75*
Agriculture	321.0	342.2	511.7	580.1
Mining and quarrying	3.0	3.4	4.1	4.6
Manufacturing and handicrafts	48.8	54.5	70.6	95.7
Electricity and water	16.8	17.5	18.6	20.9
Construction and public works	25.6	30.5	59.9	63.8
Commerce and hotels, etc.	103.7	107.9	142.0	214.0
Transport and communications	50.8	60.8	73.9	88.4
Finance, real estate, etc.	42.1	48.5	95.0	110.5
Community, social and personal services	7.3	15.3	15.4	16.6
Nominal financial institutions	-10.7	-10.4	-15.5	-19.0
Total sectors	**608.4**	**670.2**	**975.7**	**1,175.6**
Government services	98.2	104.8	127.9	153.5
Non-profit services	6.1	11.5	12.1	12.9
GDP at factor cost	**712.7**	**786.5**	**1,115.7**	**1,342.0**

Source: Bank of Sudan, *Seventeenth Annual Report, 1976.*

SUDAN'S FOREIGN TRADE

	1972	*1973*	*1974*	*1975*	*1976*
Exports (US$ millions)	357.9	436.7	350.4	439.4	554.2
Annual growth rate (1972 = 100)	100	122	98	123	155
Imports (US$ millions)	338.6	436.1	710.7	1,033.4	980.3
Annual growth	100	129	210	305	290
Trade balance (exports-imports)	**+19.3**	**-0.6**	**-360.3**	**-594.0**	**-426.1**

Source: International Monetary Fund, *Direction of Trade.*

MAJOR EXPORTS (million Sudanese pounds)

	1972	*1973*	*1974*	*1975*	*1976*
Cotton	72.8	84.3	43.3	70.2	97.8 (50.7%)
Groundnuts	9.7	12.9	18.2	34.4	39.0 (20.2%)
Sesame	9.2	10.7	16.5	11.9	17.4 (9.0%)
Gum Arabic	9.1	7.5	14.3	7.6	11.2 (5.8%)
Cake and meal	4.4	7.9	2.2	4.1	5.0 (2.6%)
Others	19.2	28.9	27.5	24.3	22.6 (11.7%)
Total	**124.4**	**152.2**	**122.0**	**152.5**	**193.0**

Source: Bank of Sudan, *Seventeenth Annual Report, 1976.*

PRINCIPAL IMPORTS (million Sudanese pounds)

	1972	*1973*	*1974*	*1975*	*1976*
Machinery and spare parts	15.7	20.0	30.2	59.0	110.6
Transport equipment	13.4	25.4	33.7	64.4	43.0
Chemical and pharmaceutical products	14.3	19.0	27.2	40.3	33.5
Crude materials	1.5	1.5	33.9	28.1	31.8
Textiles	17.0	16.2	24.0	43.2	21.8
Sugar	10.3	14.7	33.4	39.6	21.8
Other foodstuffs	10.0	12.1	14.1	14.4	17.4
Others	35.7	42.9	51.0	70.9	61.5
Total	**117.9**	**151.8**	**247.5**	**359.9**	**341.4**

Source: Bank of Sudan, *Seventeenth Annual Report, 1976.*

SUDAN'S DIRECTION OF TRADE by value (US$ millions)

Suppliers	*1972*	*1973*	*1974*	*1975*	*1976*
EEC	115.6	163.9	215.0	388.4	450.8
of which:					
UK	*61.7*	*78.6*	*81.9*	*158.1*	*199.5*
W. Germany	*22.5*	*28.5*	*46.4*	*87.8*	*82.9*
Italy	*7.6*	*15.3*	*32.6*	*67.3*	*75.9*
France	*12.0*	*18.3*	*27.8*	*24.3*	*36.2*
USA	13.8	33.2	63.6	88.2	92.1
Iraq	—	—	0.3	50.5	75.5
Other Europe	35.7	43.4	48.1	82.0	70.6
Japan	13.6	26.1	37.5	104.8	64.1
India	—	—	—	—	54.8
Kuwait	2.0	9.7	20.5	24.9	37.6
P.R. of China	25.3	29.4	64.8	46.5	27.8
Other Middle East	21.3	18.9	123.4	52.6	26.0
USSR	15.3	26.0	6.9	4.6	18.1
Others	96.0	85.5	130.6	190.9	62.9
Total	**338.6**	**436.1**	**710.7**	**1,033.4**	**980.3**
Customers	*1972*	*1973*	*1974*	*1975*	*1976*
EEC	117.0	158.5	138.2	180.4	235.2
of which:					
Italy	*33.3*	*48.4*	*44.5*	*57.6*	*109.0*
France	*13.0*	*26.6*	*36.3*	*55.3*	*36.8*
W. Germany	*33.2*	*39.8*	*23.4*	*27.0*	*36.5*
UK	*13.5*	*15.7*	*12.0*	*15.9*	*15.8*
Other Europe	34.2	40.4	25.7	45.8	52.9
Japan	29.0	48.5	12.4	18.7	41.6
Yugoslavia	7.0	2.7	2.6	20.2	30.1
P.R. of China	35.8	65.3	33.9	37.5	24.2
India	65.8	25.5	13.1	6.5	23.6
OPEC states	11.8	23.6	40.2	31.7	22.1
USA	10.6	8.4	19.8	9.6	21.7
Egypt	20.2	16.6	10.7	30.6	18.8
USSR	1.4	—	4.7	10.5	18.0
Others	25.1	47.2	49.1	47.9	66.0
Total	**357.9**	**436.7**	**350.4**	**439.4**	**554.2**

Source: IMF, Direction of Trade.

CONSUMER PRICE INDEX (1972 = 100)

1972	*1973*	*1974*	*1975*	*1976*
100	115	145	180	183

Source: *IMF, International Financial Statistics.*

INDUSTRIAL PRODUCTION

		1971-72	*1972-73*	*1973-74*	*1974-75*	*1975-76*	
Cement	'000 tons	200.6	201.2	209.1	217.1	157.1	−27.4%
Flour	'000 tons	191.3	198.2	190.1	220.9	257.3	+16.5%
Sugar	'000 tons	91.2	112.6	120.6	128.7	113.9	−11.5%
Wine	'000 litres	2,955.6	3,378.4	4,307.7	4,592.9	4,607.1	+ 0.3%
Beer	'000 litres	7,713.7	8,697.7	8,579.4	9,634.3	9,579.1	− 0.7%
Cigarettes	'000 kilos	522.4	489.7	567.9	514.3	894.9	+74.0%
Shoes	million pairs	14.7	17.7	12.1	13.3	14.4	+ 8.3%

CENTRAL GOVERNMENT DEVELOPMENT EXPENDITURE

	Estimates 1975-76		*Actual 1975-76*		*Estimates 1976-77*	
	£Sm	*%*	*£Sm*	*%*	*£Sm*	*%*
Agriculture	33.4	25.4	31.5	27.9	73.6	29.0
Industry	44.2	33.6	35.7	31.6	78.1	30.7
Transport and Communications	35.7	27.1	27.9	24.6	50.1	19.7
Services	10.1	7.7	9.7	8.6	23.9	9.4
Others (including reserves)	8.2	6.2	8.3	7.3	28.5	11.2
Total	**131.6**	**100.0**	**113.1**	**100.0**	**254.2**	**100.0**
of which						
Foreign currencies	*76.6*		*Not available*		*135.9*	
Local currencies	*55.0*		*Not available*		*118.3*	

SECTORAL DISTRIBUTION OF PUBLIC INVESTMENT FOR 6-YEAR PLAN, 1977-78/1982-83 (in million Sudanese pounds)

	Continued projects	*New projects*	*Total*
Agriculture and immigration	90	335	425
Industry, mining, power and tourism	160	175	335
Transport and communications	90	230	320
Social services, housing and general administration	30	225	255
Reserves	—	225	225
Total	**370**	**1,190**	**1,560**

Source (of three preceding tables): Bank of Sudan, *Seventeenth Annual Report, 1976.*

NOTES

1. R Omdurman, 4 July—British Broadcasting Corporation, Summary of World Broadcasts: the ME and Africa (BBC), 6 July 1976.
2. R Omdurman, 15 July—BBC, 17 July 1976.
3. Arab Revolutionary News Agency (ARNA), 10 July—BBC, 12 July 1976.
4. Radio Cairo, 10 August—BBC, 11 August 1976.
5. Interview in *Daily Telegraph*, London; 11 August 1976.
6. Al-*Saḥāfa*, Sudan; 6 February 1977.
7. *Al-Ahrām*, Cairo; 14 October 1969.
8. R Omdurman, 6 February—Daily Report (DR), 7 February 1977.
9. Maj-Gen Joseph Lagu had been a major leader of the Anya-nya. Following the Addis Ababa agreement in 1972, which he negotiated on behalf of the South, he became a member of the SSU Executive Bureau, and the commander of the Sudanese Army's 1st Division which was made up mainly of Southerners.
10. *Washington Post*, 10 March 1977.
11. Alier quoted by R Omdurman, 6 February—DR, 7 February 1977. Reuter, 2 February 1977.
12. *The Times*, London; 12 February 1977.
13. On assuming power in May 1969, Numayrī became the Chairman of the Revolutionary Command Council. In October 1971, following the abortive July 1971 coup, he was formally elected President in a general referendum.
14. R Omdurman, 24 May—BBC, 26 May 1977.
15. Sudanese News Agency (SUNA), 30 July—BBC, 1 August 1977.

16. *Arabia and the Gulf*, London; 25 July 1977.
17. *Ibid.* For an assessment of Saudi Arabia's role in the release of detainees and national reconciliation in Sudan, see *Mustaqbal*, Paris; 30 July 1977.
18. *Ayyām*, 8 August 1977.
19. *Al-Siyāsa*, Kuwait; 16 August 1977.
20. The Sudanese Communist Party had been driven underground after the abortive July 1971 coup. In 1977, it had an estimated membership of between 3,000 and 5,000, but its real influence on Sudanese politics is difficult to estimate.
21. Middle East News Agency (MENA), 15 August—BBC, 18 August 1977.
22. *Arabia and the Gulf*, 19 September 1977.
23. *The Military Balance 1977-78* (London: International Institute for Strategic Studies).
24. R Cairo, 14 September—BBC, 17 September 1976.
25. *The Guardian*, London; 10 August 1976.
26. *The Times*, 18 November 1976.
27. *Arab Report and Record*, London; 16-31 May 1977, p. 410.
28. R. Omdurman, 19 May—BBC, 21 May 1977.
29. *Al-Saḥāfa*, 19 May 1977.
30. *Arab Report and Record*, 1-15 June 1977, p. 458.
31. *Al-Akhbār*, Cairo; 20 June—DR, 22 June 1977.
32. R Omdurman, 18 June—BBC, 20 June 1977.
33. For the text of this Joint Defence Agreement, see *Arab Report and Record*, 16-31 July 1976, p. 472.
34. *Events*, 20 May 1977.
35. Qatari News Agency (QNA), 15 May—DR, 18 May 1977.
36. MENA, 23 March—DR, 24 March 1977.
37. R Omdurman, 1 January—BBC, 1 January 1977.
38. R Omdurman, 13 April—BBC, 15 April 1977. *Arabia and the Gulf*, 11 July 1977.
39. *Al-Ra'y al-'Āmm,* Kuwait; 14 May 1977.
40. *Arabia and the Gulf*, 11 July 1977.
41. R Omdurman, 19, 20 March—BBC, 21, 22 March 1977.
42. See *Arab Report and Record*, 16-31 May 1977.
43. Bank of Sudan, *Seventeenth Annual Report, 1976* (Khartoum, April 1977).

Syria

(Al-Jumhūriyya al-ʻArabiyya al-Sūriyya)

ITAMAR RABINOVICH

President Ḥāfiz al-Asad's Baʻth regime celebrated its seventh anniversary in November 1977—a tenure of power unprecedented in the history of the Syrian Republic. Indeed, the emergence of a comparatively stable and effective regime marked a turning point in the country's history, and provided the basis for domestic political and foreign policy developments in the 1970s. Still, the Baʻth regime remained beset by inherent problems and weaknesses, symptoms of which became increasingly manifest throughout 1977.

POLITICAL AFFAIRS

THE NATURE OF THE BAʻTH REGIME

When he seized full power in Syria in November 1970, Asad inherited from the ousted Baʻth leadership (in which he himself had been a major partner) a peculiar working arrangement combining a military oligarchy with a subservient party organization. Such an arrangement could provide an excellent formula for regulating military control of an apparently civilian regime. But in the years preceding 1970, the Baʻth regime had failed to overcome two major difficulties. The first was recurring conflicts within the Baʻth ruling group, the most recent being between Salaḥ Jadīd and Ḥāfiz Asad which led to the "corrective coup" of November 1970. The second was the refusal of Syria's urban Sunnī (orthodox Muslim) population to accept the legitimacy of a regime most of whose leaders originated in rural and minority communities.

Asad's prospects of overcoming the first problem were good. Unlike previous coup authors, he did not seize power as the leader of a heterogeneous coalition, but rather as the undisputed leader of his own coterie. The process of his coming to power was slow, gradual and well-prepared. There was much less that he could do about the second difficulty. Asad himself, and several of his close associates were members of the ʻAlawī minority, and Asad was not willing to risk the coherence and stability of his regime by diversifying the sources of power. Such a policy entailed great risk, while the prospect of making the Baʻth regime acceptable to its critics appeared negligible.

Faced with this dilemma, Asad opted for the intermediary solution of organizing the new regime on a dualistic basis. The core of the regime consisted of Asad and his coterie, army officers and party functionaries. But this core was to operate through a series of institutions and organizations that would endow the regime with a constitutional and non-partisan appearance. This dualistic nature of Ḥāfiz al-Asad's regime is an important key to understanding both its strength and points of weakness. Asad himself was to be the central figure in both systems, and by exercising personal leadership in a style previously unknown in Baʻth politics, his aim was to try and create a direct link between regime and populace. This change in the style of leadership was explicitly acknowledged and publicized by the regime. Its organs underscored the significance of Asad's personal leadership, and contrasted it with the drawbacks of collective leadership which had been a hallmark of Baʻthi politics in previous years.[1]

During its first years in power, Asad's regime set about implementing this domestic strategy. Its initial successes were swift and impressive. Syria, a closed and grim country during the latter part of the 1960s, came to be characterized by a more benign public atmosphere. Within two and a half years, Asad completed a series of constitutional and political reforms: Asad himself was elected President in a referendum and relinquished his formal military position; a "national progressive front" (a nominal coalition of the Ba'th with other "progressive" parties) was formed; a new constitution was drafted and adopted by a plebiscite in 1973, and a Legislative Assembly was elected in accordance with it.

Asad's reforms created the formal structure within which Syrian politics have been conducted since 1973. It comprises several institutions and organizations:

1) The Presidency (given vast powers by the constitution).

2) The Cabinet, whose ministers represent the Ba'th and the other partners to the National Progressive Front.

3) The Ba'th Party, explicitly mentioned in the constitution as the source of authority and defined as "the leading party in the society and the state. It leads a national progressive front, seeking to unite the energies of the masses."

4) The central leadership of the National Progressive Front. Of its 17 members, nine including the chairman represent the Ba'th Party.

5) The People's Council (the Legislative Assembly), elected in July 1973. Of its 195 members, at least half were to be representatives of the workers and peasants.

6) The "Popular Organizations"—the party and state-controlled trade unions, professional associations, youth movement and other similar organizations.

In actual fact, however, power in Syria is exercised by the inner core of the regime: the President's informal circle and the network attached to it. This group performs three major functions: 1) it controls the army and the party and guarantees the survival of the regime; 2) together with the President, it makes all the important decisions; and 3) it controls the functioning of the formal structure of the Ba'th regime. Some members of the group, like the army's Chief of Staff, hold formal positions commensurate with their actual power. In other cases—most notably that of the President's brother, Rif'at—there is a clear discrepancy between their respective positions in the regime's formal and informal hierarchies.

This is the most sensitive and delicate area of Syrian politics and, due to the secretive nature of Ba'thi affairs, little is known about it. But in exceptional circumstances, such as those created by Syria's involvement in the Lebanese civil war, the dualistic nature of the country's politics has been more clearly revealed. Thus, on several occasions during 1976, members of the President's immediate circle performed missions that had little to do with their formal role in the military or civilian bureaucracies. The most notable—and controversial—member of the President's coterie is his brother Rif'at who commands a large and well-equipped praetorian guard known as "The Defence Detachments." Other members of the group seem to be Nājī Jamīl (Deputy Minister of Defence and Commander of the Air Force); Ḥikmat Shihābī (the Chief of Staff); 'Adnān Dabbāgh (Minister of the Interior), and such intelligence officers as 'Alī Dūbā and Muḥammad al-Khūlī.[2]

As a rule, this dualistic system has worked very well, but it has faced two major problems:

1) The Syrian urban population is well aware of the locus of real power in the regime, and remains unreconciled to the fact that it is ruled by what it regards as a minority group. The more liberal atmosphere inaugurated by the Asad regime had been well accepted in 1971–2, but was later exploited by critics in order to

express their rejection of the regime. This occurred most significantly in February 1973 when large demonstrations were held against the proposed draft of the new permanent constitution.

2) Despite the unusual cohesiveness of the ruling group, it has not been entirely free from rivalries and disagreements. Gen Muḥammad ʻUmrān, a former Minister of Defence who was assassinated in Lebanon in 1972, was said to have been plotting with ʻAlawī army officers. In 1975, Asad also had to contend with the strong opposition of radical and pro-Iraqi elements in the Syrian Baʻth party organization.

THE DOMESTIC IMPACT OF SYRIA'S INTERVENTION IN THE LEBANESE CIVIL WAR

The difficulties inherent in the dualistic system had been apparent during the early 1970s, but it was only in 1976 that a number of developments combined to affect the regime's overall performance and thus magnify the impact of such problems. Syria's intervention in the Lebanese civil war, which began in January 1976, served as a catalyst for these developments (see survey on Lebanon). The intervention, which began in an indirect and limited fashion on the side of the anti-establishment coalition, grew in size, became direct and, in the spring of 1976, was turned against Syria's traditional allies in Lebanon—the Palestinians, the Leftists and the Muslim militias.

This policy generated strong criticism inside Syria, as well as elsewhere in the Arab world. While Asad and his associates insisted that their action in Lebanon was fully consonant with Syria's fundamental and immediate interests, they failed to convince either their Baʻthi constituents or the general Syrian public. The former were primarily bewildered and puzzled by the ideological implications of the regime's change of line, as traditional foes and allies exchanged roles within a short span of time. The Syrian public appeared to have been primarily affected by the confessional aspects of Asad's Lebanese policy. Sunnī critics of the regime—who had already regarded it as sectarian ʻAlawī rule—tended to interpret the change in Syrian policy as an ʻAlawī-Christian alignment against the Muslim element in Lebanon.

Criticism intensified after Syria's unsuccessful military offensive in June 1976, the scope and nature of Syria's involvement being altered by its resort to large-scale and violent attacks on Muslim and Palestinian units. The failure of the offensive exacerbated the situation by portraying the regime as inefficient, and by breeding internecine squabbling over responsibility for the poor military performance. Furthermore, Syria's offensive was launched on the eve of Soviet Premier Aleksei Kosygin's visit to Damascus, and confronted him with a *fait accompli*. It thus generated further tension in Syria's relations with Moscow and promoted additional criticism from radical Baʻthis who resented the drift away from the Soviet Union.

Of no lesser importance to the general Syrian public were the economic and other dislocations brought about by the Lebanese civil war. The Syrian economy had suffered from "stagflation" since 1974, and the cost of maintaining a large expeditionary force was a further aggravation. A large number of refugees (many of them Syrians who had been employed in Lebanon) arrived in the country and had to be accommodated. The Syrian bureaucracy, already the subject of many complaints, was hard pressed to cope with this new problem.

The severity of public criticism, and the seriousness with which it was received by the regime, were attested to by a lengthy and detailed speech Asad delivered on 20 July 1976. Addressing himself to the major grievances and controversial issues associated with Syria's Lebanese policy, Asad sought to mollify the Syrian public by making it privy to presidential considerations and to his version of the sequence of events. As such, the speech had no precedent in Ba'thi Syria.

THE FORMATION OF A NEW CABINET

In an attempt to soothe the public and improve the performance of the Syrian government, President Asad's speech was followed by a more concrete measure. On 1 August 1976, Prime Minister Maḥmūd al-Ayyūbī tendered his resignation and 'Abd al-Rahmān Khulayfāwī was nominated to succeed him. Khulayfāwī was 49 at the time, a retired General who had been Minister of Defence in 1970–1 and Prime Minister in 1971–2. He was known to be a close associate of the President and was reputed to have great strength of character, his resignation in 1972 having been due to genuine health reasons. Khulayfāwī's new 36-member Cabinet was formally formed on 7 August.

Khulayfāwī's mandate was explicit and widely publicized by the Syrian media: to improve the economic situation, cleanse bureaucracy of corruption and inefficiency, and make it more open and responsive to the wishes of the public. At the same time, the press opened a campaign against members of Syria's "new class"—employees of the state bureaucracy and the nationalized sector of the economy, accusing them of corruption, nepotism, conspicuous consumption and domineering attitudes—all exercised at the expense of the simple Syrian citizen. The campaign did not spare the new Cabinet; the regime's official mouthpiece, *Tishrīn*, also poked fun at its exaggerated size. The President's directives to his new Cabinet, publicized by the new Minister of Culture, included an admonition not to bow to pressure and to insist on the application of regular procedures and policies. All these were indications that the formation and operation of the Cabinet had become subject to internecine political conflict—a clear departure from the monolithic nature of Asad's regime in earlier years.

DOMESTIC POLITICS AFTER AUGUST 1976

As a measure designed to solve the regime's domestic problems, the formation of Khulayfāwī's Cabinet proved a failure. During its first twelve months in office, the President and his government were beset by increasingly serious domestic problems, which fell into four major categories.

1) *Relations within the ruling élite*. Repeated reports suggested that civilian and military members ot the Ba'th continued to censure the President's brother, Rif'at. On two occasions, foreign sources not usually hostile to the regime (as distinct from the Iraqi press, for instance) reported the arrest of army officers critical of Rif'at Asad's conduct and of the regime's Lebanese policy. As part of a broader change, Rif'at Asad was assigned a new formal position in the Ba'th party in January 1977: instead of being responsible for higher education he was put in charge of the Youth Bureau.

The malfunctioning of the Khulayfāwī Cabinet and the bureaucracy was an additional source of friction within the upper echelons of the Ba'th regime. Khulayfāwī appears to have charged several of his Cabinet colleagues—some of whom were directly linked to Asad—with responsibility for the failure of his own policies. In June 1977, he threatened to resign, thus presenting Asad with two major problems: (a) to replace a Prime Minister twice within ten months would have indicated something fundamentally wrong with the Asad regime; (b) to pick an effective successor from among the regime's leading figures would be difficult without upsetting the delicate balance within Syria's ruling group. Khulayfāwī was

CABINET OF 7 AUGUST 1976

	Incumbent	Party	Community
Prime Minister	Maj-Gen ‘Abd al-Raḥmān al-Khulayfāwī	Ba‘th	Sunnī
Deputy Prime Minister and Foreign Minister	‘Abd al-Halīm Khaddām +	Ba‘th	Sunnī
Deputy Prime Minister for Economic Affairs	Kamīl Shayā	Ba‘th	Druze
Deputy Prime Minister for Public Services	Fahmī al-Yūsufī	Ba‘th	Sunnī
Ministers			
Defence	Maj-Gen Mustafā Talās +	Ba‘th	Sunnī
Interior	Brig ‘Adnān Dabbāgh	Ba‘th	Sunnī
Local Administration	Taha al-Khayrāt	Ba‘th	Sunnī
Public Works and Water Resources	Nāzim Qaddūr	Arab Socialists	n.a.
Euphrates Dam	Subḥī Kaḥḥāla +	Communist	Sunnī
Education	Shākir al-Faḥḥām +	Ba‘th	Sunnī
Culture and National Guidance	Najāḥ ‘Attār	Independent	n.a.
Justice	Adīb al-Nahawī +	Arab Socialist Union	n.a.
Communications	‘Umar as-Sibā‘ī +	Communist	Sunnī
Waqf	‘Abd al-Sattār, al-Sayyid +	Independent	Sunnī
Supply and Internal Trade	Muḥammad Ghubāsh	Ba‘th	Sunnī
Economy and Foreign Trade	Muḥammad al-‘Imādī +	Independent	‘Alawī(?)
Social Affairs and Labour	Anwar Ḥamāda +	Arab Socialist Union	n.a.
Health	Madanī al-Khiyamī +	Independent	n.a.
Tourism	Ghassān Shlahūb	Ba‘th	Christian
Higher Education	Muḥammad ‘Alī Hāshim +	Ba‘th (formerly Socialist Unionists)	n.a.
Housing and Utilities	Muḥarram Tayyāra	Ba‘th	Sunnī
Industry	Shatwawi Sayfū +	Ba‘th	Ismā‘īlī
Transport	Nu‘mān al-Zayn +	Independent	Christian (?)
Power	Aḥmad ‘Umar Yūsuf	Independent	Sunnī
Finance	Sādiq al-Ayyūbī	Independent	Sunnī, Kurd
Information	Aḥmad Iskandar Aḥmad +	Ba‘th	n.a.
Agriculture and Agrarian Reform	Aḥmad Qablān +	Ba‘th	Druze
Oil and Mineral Resources	‘Isā Darwīsh	Ba‘th	Christian (?)
Ministers of State			
Presidential Affairs	Adīb Milḥim +	Ba‘th	Sunnī
Cabinet Affairs	Ḥusayn Aḥmad Kuwaydir +	Ba‘th	n.a.
Foreign Affairs	‘Abd al-Karīm ‘Addī	Ba‘th	Sunnī
Planning Affairs	George Ḥūrāniyya	n.a.	n.a.
Other	Sharīf Kūsh	Ba‘th (formerly Socialist Unionists)	n.a.
	Diyā’ Mallūḥī	Ba‘th (formerly Socialist Unionists)	n.a.
	Zuhayr ‘Abd al-Samad +	Communist	n.a.
	Yūsuf Ja‘īdānī	Arab Socialist Union	n.a.

+ Served in former cabinet
n.a. = not available

prevailed upon to stay in office but, as will be seen below, no radical solution was found for the problems he had raised.

2) *The Performance of the Cabinet and Government Bureaucracy.* Most of Syria's economic problems stemmed from factors beyond the government's control, such as the cost of the Syrian forces in Lebanon, the loss of revenue from Iraqi oil diverted to a new pipeline laid in Turkish territory, and a decline in development investment. Money expected from Saudi Arabia to support the Syrian forces in Lebanon failed, or was slow, to arrive; and investment by Persian Gulf states proved to be smaller than anticipated. For these various reasons, Khulayfāwī was unable to accomplish the tasks he was assigned in August 1976.

More visible to the public, however, were continued inflation, scarcity of consumer goods and deteriorating services, whose impact was magnified by bureaucratic inefficiency, corruption and arrogance. Resentment simmered against the luxurious life-style of a small but highly visible élite, composed of party and military functionaries and members of mercantile families whose fortunes were revived by the Asad regime's liberalization policy.

Khulayfāwī himself minced no words in an effort to stir the government machinery. In an interesting interview with *Tishrīn*, he stated that numerous bureaucrats did not function properly and invited the public to complain against laxness and corruption.[3] But the Prime Minister's efforts, as well as several press campaigns, failed to improve the bureaucracy's performance or to allay public criticism of it or of the regime itself.

3) *Terrorist Challenge to the Regime.* The Syrian regime came to face a new challenge after September 1976: a sustained campaign of terrorist attacks directed against individuals representing the Ba'th regime and seeking to undermine public order in Syria.

A Palestinian group staged an attack on 26 September on the Semiramis hotel in Damascus. On 7 October, Col 'Alī Ḥaydar, Commander of the Ḥamāh Region, was assassinated in Ḥamāh together with two government officials. On 1 December, an unsuccessful attempt was made on the life of 'Abd al-Ḥalīm Khaddām, the Minister of Foreign Affairs. On 22 February 1977, Muḥammad Fāḍil—President of the University of Damascus, a prominent member of the 'Alawī community and a close adviser to Asad—was killed in Damascus. On 19 June, Col 'Abdal Ḥamīd Razzūq, the commander of Syria's missile regiment, was killed near his home in Damascus, and on 4 July, six people were killed when a car filled with explosives was detonated near the headquarters of Syria's air defence in Damascus. Iraqi and other hostile sources reported several additional acts of sabotage which allegedly took place during this period.

The partial success of the Syrian security forces, extended to deal with the terrorist attacks, resulted in a series of public hangings in Damascus between September 1976 and June 1977. These added a grim feature to Syria's public life; but they could not hide the fact that, despite its authoritarian nature, the Ba'th regime was unable to eradicate such novel and violent opposition. The political repercussions of the terrorist attacks were magnified by the sustained nature of the challenge. The early attacks, in the late summer of 1976, were clearly inspired by the Lebanese civil war and were staged primarily by Palestinians who had infiltrated across the border from Lebanon, possibly with Iraqi help. From the outset, the Syrian Ba'th tried to present the attacks against itself as a fresh form of Iraqi hostility, a line pursued by the Syrian media and the courts. There was probably a considerable measure of truth in the Syrian charges, but the political significance of the attacks extended far beyond Syrian-Iraqi rivalry.

a) They shook the regime's nerve and cast doubts on its effectiveness.

b) The sustained nature of the anti-Ba'thi campaign and the fact that several attacks took place in areas traditionally opposed to the Ba'th (such as Ḥamāh) lent credence to the theory that rather than isolated terrorist attacks inspired from abroad, the regime was being confronted with serious domestic opposition.

c) Confessional tensions were exacerbated. That some of the assassination victims were 'Alawīs was a manifestation of anti-'Alawī sentiment which also underscored the regime's sectarian orientation.

4) *Erosion of Public Support*. An improvement of the regime's relationship with the urban community had been one of Asad's early and important achievements. His ability to attract public support, or at least neutralize entrenched opposition, served as a legitimizing and consolidating factor. From this perspective, mounting criticism and apparent disenchantment were alarming developments. The regime's awareness of the serious nature of the public's mood was indicated by the change of government in August 1976 and by the manner in which this and other measures were presented to the public.

The regime's sensitivity to the public's actual and potential reaction was demonstrated during the first few weeks of 1977. The government had reportedly planned to raise the price of basic commodities, but was deterred by the riots which broke out in Cairo in January 1977 after a similar measure had been taken by the Egyptian government. When Prime Minister Khulayfāwī met with representatives of the media on 15 February 1977, he devoted most of his talk to the price of bread.

Equally disconcerting was the resurgence of sectarian tensions, and spokesmen for the regime warned that Syria had started on a dangerous path. Thus, on 21 May 1977, the editor of the government newspaper *al-Thawra*, 'Alī Sulaymān, warned against subversion and domestic dangers. The enemy, he explained, was employing a dual strategy of seeking to keep Syria preoccupied with external problems while eroding it from within. Syria's enemies acted in indirect ways in order "to inject into our country part of what had happened in Lebanon." The external enemies found domestic allies who tried to subvert the public sector, foment dissension and fan "primitive instincts" (a code word for confessional loyalties).[4]

Although the regime's efforts to mollify the public continued during the spring and early summer of 1977, their failure was demonstrated by the elections for the new People's Council, held on 1 August. Of its 195 members, 125 were elected to represent the Ba'th Party, and 24 for its partners in the National Progressive Front: the Socialist Unionists (2), the Nasserite Socialist Union (8), the Arab Socialists (8) and the Communists (6). Two aspects of the elections were alarming from the regime's point of view. First, the very low level of participation, estimated by foreign observers to have varied from 5% to 30% in different areas.[5] These figures were well below the legal minimum of 51% and a second polling day had to be added. Second, the tendency in the provinces to vote for traditionalist local leaders, members of families that had been affiliated with the conservative parties of the pre-Ba'th parliamentary regimes. This was reminiscent of the outcome of the Asad regime's experimentation with liberalism during the elections for provincial councils in 1972, which had ended with defeat for Ba'thi candidates in the face of opposition from traditional leaders.

The elections thus served to demonstrate the public's disenchantment with the Ba'th regime and that regime's tenuous hold on the country. As such, they seem to have prompted Asad to launch his "anti-corruption campaign" of August and September 1977.

THE ANTI-CORRUPTION CAMPAIGN

The Ba'th regime's anti-corruption campaign seems to have been calculated to achieve three goals: to clean out pockets of corruption and inefficiency in the government, to persuade the public that something radical was being done and, at the same time, to settle some political scores without jeopardizing the regime's stability. The campaign began on 9 August when the President published a legislative decree which modified the law of economic transgressions and penalties. On 10 August, the establishment of economic security courts in Damascus, Aleppo and Ḥoms was announced. These measures, reinforced by an exceptionally vitriolic editorial in *al-Ba'th*, served as a prelude to the speech delivered by President Asad on 18 August at the opening session of the new People's Council.[6]

The President began by encouraging the new Council members to discharge their supervisory responsibility over the executive branch of the government. This could be done through the formation of investigative committees which could—indeed, should—interrogate bureaucrats and ministers, discover instances of malfeasance or inefficiency and see that those responsible were punished. But the President was careful to indicate that criticism of the Government should not exceed the boundaries defined by the regime. He stated that "some of what is being written in our papers is not devoid of exaggeration and needs to be more specific"; he explained that "the exercise of freedom means the responsible exercise of freedom."

This was the framework within which the President introduced a novel element—"The Committee for the Investigation of Illegal Profits," which was given very wide powers. It was authorized to review both civilian and military institutions, to issue warrants for arrest and detention, to investigate and prosecute. A special effort was made to persuade the public that popular elements were indeed authorized to investigate "the high and mighty." Most of the committee members were judges or representatives of "popular" organizations. The President announced—and similar statements by the members of the Regional Command followed—that he was transferring a house and a small piece of land from his private possession to the state. At the same time, however, it was also evident that precautions were being taken to ensure that the Committee work did not get out of hand. Aḥmad Diyāb, a member of the Ba'th Party's RC and a confidant of the Asad brothers, was named its chairman. Rif'at Asad, who in the popular mind was the chief culprit as far as excesses and irregularities were concerned, came out in strong support of the Committee and its work.

However, the Committee failed to achieve the desired results, and in a sense the strategy seems to have misfired. The Committee's most publicized measure was the arrest of some 27 persons. The names of 16 were known and included several successful businessmen and government employees who were said to have co-operated in cheating the government and the public. This was widely believed to have been true, but the Committee's work drew heavy criticism from two sources. On the one hand, the regime's critics charged that these were half measures, that members of the political élite remained untouched despite their implication in the same or similar acts of corruption. On the other hand, members of the élite, either in order to protect themselves or out of genuine irritation, protested at the Committee's meddling in the affairs of their civilian and military departments.

The persistent nature of the opposition to the Ba'th regime was again demonstrated when 'Alī Ibn 'Ābid al-'Alī, a Professor of Agriculture at the University of Aleppo, was assassinated on 1 November 1977. Like earlier assassination victims, he was a member of the 'Alawī community and like Fāḍil, personally close to Asad—indeed, a distant relative.

In August 1977, when the Syrian media were preparing the ground for the formation of the "anti-corruption committee," they warned that domestic failures threatened "to destroy all the achievements of our foreign policy." This reflected a feeling current in Syria in the spring of 1977 that external successes were the regime's most important asset. But towards the end of the year, the value of that asset also became questionable.

ARMED FORCES

Total armed forces number 227,500. Defence expenditure for 1977 was £S 3.93 bn ($1.07 bn). Military service is compulsory for 30 months. The Army numbers 200,000, including an Air Defence Command, and consists of two armoured divisions (each with two armoured and one mechanized brigades); three mechanized divisions (each with one armoured and two mechanized brigades); three armoured brigades; one mechanized brigade; three infantry brigades; two artillery brigades; six commando and four parachute battalions; one surface-to-surface missile battalion with *Scud* and two batteries with *FROG*, and 48 surface-to-air missile batteries with SA-2/-3/-6. Equipment consists of 200 T-34, 1,500 T-54/-55, 800 T-62 medium and 100 PT-76 light tanks; 1,600 BTR-40/-50/-60/-152, BMP, OT-64 armoured personnel carriers; 800 122mm, 130mm, 152mm and 180mm guns/howitzers; ISU-122/-152, 75 SU-100 self-propelled guns, 140mm and 240mm rocket launchers; 30 *FROG*-7 and 36 *Scud* surface-to surface missiles; 120mm, 160mm mortars; 85mm, 10mm anti-tank guns; *Snapper, Sagger, Swatter* anti-tank guided weapons; 23mm, 37mm, 57mm, 85mm, 100mm towed, ZSU-23-4, ZSU-57-2 self-propelled anti-aircraft guns and SA-2/-3/-6/-7/-9 surface-to-air missiles. (*Milan* anti-tank guided weapons and *Gazelle* helicopters on order.) 30,000 men are deployed in the Arab Peacekeeping Force in the Lebanon, and there are 100,000 reserves. The Air Defence Command, which is under Army Command with Army and Air Force manpower, consists of 24 surface-to-air missile batteries with SA-2/-3, 14 with SA-6; anti-aircraft artillery; interceptor aircraft and radar.

The 2,500-strong Navy is equipped with two *Petya*-class frigates; six *Komar* and six *Osa*-class guided-missile fast patrol boats with *Styx* surface-to-surface missiles; one T-43-class and two coastal minesweepers and eight motor torpedo boats (ex-Soviet P-4). There are 2,500 reserves.

The Air Force numbers 25,000 and is equipped with about 395 combat aircraft, some believed to be in storage. It is equipped with four ground-attack fighter squadrons with 80 MiG-17; three ground-attack fighter squadrons with 50 Su-7; two ground-attack fighter squadrons with 45 MiG-23 and about 220 MiG-21 interceptors. Transports include eight Il-14, two An-24 and four An-26; trainers include Yak-11/-18, L-29, MiG-15UTI and 32 MBB 223 *Flamingo*; and helicopters include four Mi-2, eight Mi-4, 50 Mi-8 and nine Ka-25. (There are 15 *Super Frelon* and six CH-47C helicopters on order.) Paramilitary forces number 9,500 and consist of 8,000 Gendarmerie and 1,500 Desert Guard (Frontier Force).[7]

FOREIGN AFFAIRS

1976 and 1977 marked an active period for Syria's foreign policy, during which the country's regional and international policies were primarily shaped by the impact of three inter-related processes.

1) the "political process"—the efforts to arrive at a political settlement of the Arab-Israeli conflict.

2) Syria's pursuit of a more ambitious regional policy in an attempt to build an autonomous power position in its immediate Arab environment.

3) Syria's gradual drift from the Soviet orbit to a more balanced orientation between Moscow and Washington.

SYRIA AND THE "POLITICAL PROCESS"

Syria became a partner to the "political process" immediately after the October war when it accepted a ceasefire on the basis of Security Council Resolution 338. It then negotiated a disengagement agreement with Israel through American mediation, and was not opposed to a continuation of "step-by-step" diplomacy as long as its particular outlook and interests were respected. But Syria was distrustful of the US and Egypt, and objected to the modality pursued by Secretary of State Kissinger after the signing of the Syrian-Israeli disengagement agreement in June 1974. It took another year before Syria's participation in the "political process" could be sufficiently reconciled with Asad's reservations (about its essence and conduct and his desire to make a distinctive contribution to the Arab cause) for a formal policy statement to emerge.

Such a policy document was drafted and approved by the 12th National Congress of the Ba'th Party, which met in Damascus in July 1975. The full text of the resolutions adopted by the Congress has yet to be published, but their general drift was indicated by a short statement released in August 1975.[8] The ultimate goal of Syria's policy remained unchanged—"the liberation of all Palestinian soil." But an element of tactical flexibility was introduced when "interim targets" for Syria's policy in the Arab-Israeli conflict were defined, a new departure legitimized by the principle of "revolutionary realism." According to the statements the newly-defined interim targets, including the "establishment of an independent national authority in the liberated parts of Palestine," could be achieved through interim and partial settlements. But the acceptance of interim goals should in no way affect the struggle for the final goal: Syria thus endorsed the Arab consensus arrived at during the Algiers and Rabat Arab summit conferences. But special care was taken to express reservations with regard to Egypt's policy, and to emphasize the distinctive features of Syria's own approach.

The resolutions of the 12th Congress remained the general guiding lines of Syrian policy during 1976 and 1977, and were often mentioned as such in the Syrian media. In practical and specific terms, however, the issue of a second settlement with Israel did not figure prominently in Syria's policy after July 1975. Syria vehemently denounced the 1975 Sinai Agreement and was not interested in the type of settlement which the US proposed at the time. During most of 1976, Syria was preoccupied with the Lebanese civil war; not until November 1977, did the continuation of the "political process" once again became the cardinal issue of Middle Eastern regional politics. But Syria, like the other participants in this process, dealt with the fundamental principles of a potential Arab-Israeli settlement, rather than with the specific problems of Syrian-Israeli relations.

TRANSITION TO A NEW REGIONAL POLICY

During the spring of 1975, it became apparent that Damascus had embarked on a new regional policy which sought to build a power position from which Syria could play a more autonomous role. This was to rest on its influence in Lebanon and Jordan and over the Palestinians; on its increased military power; and on its ability to conduct diversified Arab and international policies.

The background to this development was the vacuum created by the decline of Egypt's regional position which had been an important feature of inter-Arab politics since the late 1960s, but which Syria had not then been in a position to exploit. It was only in the mid-1970s, having for the first time enjoyed a few years of relatively stable and effective government, that Syria could venture upon a more ambitious foreign policy. Between 1970 and 1973, Syria primarily sought to emerge out of the state of isolation which had characterized its position in Arab politics for more than a decade.

But the experience of 1973 and 1974 prompted Syria to redefine its goals. This experience had underlined the importance of the American and Saudi positions in the Middle East, and the unreliability of the Egyptian alliance. During 1975, Syria continued to develop its alliance with Jordan which it began to formalize in a series of agreements. It also proposed to the PLO a unification of political and military commands; but this offer was rejected by the Palestinians who feared Syrian domination. In Lebanon, Syria had gradually built up its influence over the government as well as over a variety of political leaders and political forces so that by 1975, it had achieved a virtual veto power over major decisions in the Lebanese political system.

Syria's new position was tested and demonstrated in the late summer of 1975. When Egypt signed the Sinai Agreement with Israel, Syria mobilized considerable Arab support and was able to isolate Cairo, at least temporarily, in the Arab world. This was not merely retaliation for Egypt's conduct, but also an attempt to show the futility of an American policy which sought to radiate influence in the Arab world through Egypt. And, indeed, Syria's leaders could note with satisfaction that by the end of 1975, Washington had come to recognize Syria's autonomous standing. When Syria initiated a discussion of the Palestinian issue at the Security Council, the US tacitly helped it succeed at the expense of both Egypt and Israel.

Syria's enhanced stature and its actual (albeit undeclared) co-operation with the US were clearly reflected by events in the Lebanese civil war and Syria's role in it in 1976. (The evolution of Syria's policy in the civil war is described in the chapter on Lebanon and in the essay on Inter-Arab Relations.) What cannot be overemphasized was the crucial nature of Syria's involvement in Lebanon, which presented it with great opportunities and risks. Success meant a consolidation of Syria's newly acquired regional position, an improved posture *vis-à-vis* Israel, a bargaining asset in international politics and important dividends at home. Failure meant more than a denial of all that. It would jeopardize the whole structure of Syria's foreign policy and the regime's very existence.

Between January and October 1976, Syria's policy in all domains was focused entirely on the Lebanese civil war. In the Arab world, Syria's role in Lebanon exacerbated its relations with the PLO, Egypt, Iraq and Libya; Jordan alone proffered consistent and unequivocal support. Syria's policy in the Arab-Israeli conflict was affected in two major ways: by a suspension of the "political process"; and by the need to arrive at an understanding with Israel, through American mediation, so as to avoid an uncontrolled deterioration into war due to a conflict of interests in Lebanon. The domestic repercussions of Asad's Lebanese policy have been described above; its impact on Syria's relations with the Soviet Union is discussed below.

RELATIONS WITH THE SOVIET UNION

The October war and its political consequences gave further impetus to existing trends in Syria's relationship with Moscow. As had been the case in Egypt, criticism of Soviet influence and disappointment with its failure to produce Israeli concessions bred tensions between Damascus and Moscow (though these were far less significant than the ones which had led to the expulsion of Soviet advisers from Egypt in 1972). But the course of the October war and the inauguration of the "political process" in its aftermath persuaded Syria first of all that it needed more leverage and autonomy *vis-à-vis* the Soviet Union; and secondly, that in view of the new role acquired by the US and Saudi Arabia in the Middle East, it needed to develop a direct relationship with Washington and Riyadh, rather than depend on Egypt—which Syria came to regard as unreliable.

These conclusions formed the basis of a policy which sought to terminate Syria's exclusive dependence on the Soviet Union, diversify its foreign relations and open a Syrian-American dialogue. However, the policy was pursued with caution due to three major considerations. First, Egypt's experience showed that an actual rift with the Soviet Union narrowed a country's options. Second, a too radical departure from previous policies was precluded by the Ba'th regime's projected and self-image, as well as by its sensitivity to radical domestic and external opposition. Third, Soviet arms supplies and economic aid were vital for the country's military build-up and, to some extent, for its economic development. A strong military posture was an essential feature of Asad's autonomous power base.

The cautiousness which characterized Syria's international policies seemed to disappear early in 1976, largely as a result of the Lebanese civil war. Syria's role there brought it closer to the US and worried the Soviets, who were not only critical of Syria's Lebanese policy, but also resented the fact that it brought Damascus into a sharp conflict with other of the USSR's Arab allies. Matters came to a head following Syria's major offensive in June, which was mounted despite explicit Soviet admonitions, and was presented as a *fait accompli* to Aleksei Kosygin when he arrived for a visit (see above).

The tension which resulted from these developments lasted until the end of 1976. Soviet criticism of Syria's conduct became more explicit,although Syria refrained from responding in kind. Soviet arms supplies to Syria were reported to have slowed down; Syria in turn was said to have considered cancelling port services to the Soviet navy in Tartūs.

RELATIONS WITH OTHER ARAB STATES

The 13 months which separated the Riyadh conference of October 1976 from President Sādāt's decision to visit Jersualem in November 1977 saw a dramatic shift in the direction and fortunes of Syria's foreign policy. Syria could view the outcome of the Riyadh conference as very satisfactory from its point of view: its predominant position in Lebanon was implicitly acknowledged by the major Arab states, and its massive military presence was legitimized by their formal acceptance of Syria as the mainstay of the Arab Deterrent Force. In addition, it was agreed that the expenses of keeping the Syrian troops in Lebanon were to be paid by Persian Gulf oil-producing states. Finally, the stalemate in the "political process" was expected to be broken and joint Arab pressures to be exercised on Washington.

Nevertheless, there were other aspects to the situation as well. Syria had to finally subordinate the PLO in Lebanon and remove Yāsir 'Arafāt from the leadership. Nor were Syria's relations with Saudi Arabia and Egypt free from problems. Syria's leaders must have realized that, appearances apart, the Saudis could exert powerful pressure on Syria to come to Riyadh and adopt what they regarded as an appropriate line. Damascus also had misgivings about co-operation with Egypt. As in earlier years, Syria's outlook on the goals and modalities of the "political process" was different from Egypt's, and the Syrian leadership distrusted Sādāt and his entourage. However, these problems seemed to be clearly outweighed by the advantages of the settlement reached in Riyadh.

During the next few months, the Syrian leadership remained confident of its ability to cope with the problems it faced and accomplish its policy aims. Syria's strategy was to rest on three foundations: 1) co-operation with Egypt and Saudi Arabia (marked, though, by uncertainty and ambiguity) in the implementation of a joint Arab strategy; 2) a consolidation of Syria's position in Lebanon of its relationship with Jordan and hegemony over the PLO; and 3) development of new relations with the two super-powers.

Presidents Asad and Sādāt met for the first time in December 1976 after a year of dispute and acrimony. They decided to form a "united political command," formulate a "joint course of action," and even prepare the ground for a future Syro-Egyptian union. Early in February 1977, the composition of the "united political command" was announced, but no date was set for the "command's" first meeting—evidently its formation and operation were to continue at the same slow pace.

Syria was more energetic in its efforts to bring the PLO into line. It was disappointed with the outcome of the PLO's Central Council meeting in Damascus on 22 January, and expressed its displeasure publicly in such Ba'thi publications as *al-Sā'iqa* and *al-Munādil*, the Ba'th Party's internal organ which was quoted extensively in *al-Ba'th*, the official government newspaper.[9] The PLO was urged to participate in a future Geneva conference in line with the Syro-Egyptian joint strategy. It was strongly reprimanded for its conduct in the past, and there was an implied threat about the need to restructure its ruling bodies. In more specific terms, the Palestinian National Council, due to meet on 12 March 1977, was advised to adopt the necessary changes that would enable it to co-operate with the "theory of stages."

Even while advocating these ideas, however, Syria continued to allude to a different solution to the "Palestinian problem"—inspired and managed by itself. The Syrian Ba'th challenged the validity of the formula adopted by the Palestine National Council in June 1974, recommending instead that the PLO consider various forms of an "entity" linked to Jordan, or to Jordan and other "Confrontation states." Such an entity was obviously meant to be part and parcel of the group of states dominated by Damascus, which Syria had been trying to form since 1975.

These ideas were spelt out in a bolder and more explicit fashion in a most revealing interview which Asad granted to the British journalist, Patrick Seale, early in March 1977.[10] In it, he described Syria's policy as "two-pronged." One prong was "directed at Egypt" and sought to exploit its weakness. More important, however, Seale observed that Asad saw "Syria's immediate neighbours, Lebanon and Jordan, as a natural extension of its territory vital to its defence. This three-nation grouping is already a *fait accompli* although, in the low-key Asad manner, without fanfare. Asad now rules by proxy in Lebanon, while the progressive integration with Jordan is well advanced. If the Palestinians ever recover a West Bank homeland, they too will inevitably join this complex."

Asad also outlined to Seale his international strategy: "It is to forge an Arab bloc strong enough to become a regional power able to stand up to pressure from either of the super-powers." In the spring of 1977, it seemed for a while that Asad might be able to accomplish just that. The termination of the Lebanese civil war facilitated a *rapprochement* with the Soviet Union, and a satisfactory, though not cordial, working relationship was restored. An additional factor was the conviction of the Carter Administration that it was important for American interests and essential for the success of the "political process" to gratify Asad. As a result, Syria was the only Middle East country capable of playing one super-power off against the other in a style that seemed to have disappeared in the mid-1960s.

Thus, within three weeks, Asad met with both the Soviet and American leaders, and did so in a most satisfactory way—from Syria's point of view. Between 18 and 22 April, Asad visited Moscow, and on 9 May met with President Carter in Geneva. (The Syrians later leaked a report to the effect that Asad had rejected a Soviet suggestion to postpone his visit to Moscow until after his meeting with Carter.) During their meeting, Carter made several gestures which were clearly meant to please Asad and enhance his stature.

While May 1977 marked the zenith of Syria's foreign policy, there were signs that this policy would soon run into trouble, although these were not heeded at the time: Syria was now beginning to face difficulties with the two countries forming its "natural extension" (in Seale's words), as well as with the PLO.[11] Although Syria's position in Lebanon was not challenged as such, it soon became clear that the process of effectively securing its influence there would be a lengthy and costly one. A sizeable Syrian force remained stationed in Lebanon, but a stable settlement that would enable an indirect and effective exercise of Syrian influence was not within sight. While no real problems developed with Jordan, neither was there any significant further progress within the limits placed by both regimes on the development of their relationship. The Palestinians in Lebanon were curtailed by Syria, but Syria was unable to dictate political moves to the PLO, as that organization could draw on Egypt, Saudi Arabia and other Arab states for support against Syrian efforts to subordinate it.

Indications of Syrian resentment against Saudi Arabia and other oil-producing Arab states over inadequate financial aid had already appeared in February 1977. The slow flow of this aid was painful not only because it affected Syria's economic situation and contributed to domestic ferment, which became a significant political factor in 1977. But the Syrian leadership also suspected that Saudi reluctance had political overtones—displeasure with Syria's aggrandizement, and an attempt to curtail it. Tension between Syria and the Gulf states also continued during March. On 31 March, the Kuwaiti newspaper *al-Ra'y al-'Āmm* published an evidently Syrian-inspired article that was reproduced the next day by the Syrian *Tishrīn*. The article contained a thinly-veiled threat that failure to extend the necessary financial support to Syria could destroy the country's domestic stability, which could endanger Arab stability in general and particularly affect the Arab states in the Gulf area. This acrimony disappeared in later months, but Syria still remained dissatisfied with Saudi Arabia's financial aid and retained the feeling that the Saudis were trying to cut the Asad regime down to size.

During the spring of 1977, an important though subtle change took place in Syria's conflict with Iraq: while its intensity continued unabated, the Iraqis seemed to be gaining the upper hand. Syria's domestic problems weakened its posture *vis-à-vis* the rival Iraqi regime, while the latter's completion of an oil pipeline to the Mediterranean via Turkey had a similar effect, reducing Iraq's dependence on Syria and depriving it of an important source of income. (See essay, "Middle East Oil Developments" and surveys of Iraq and Turkey.) In June, several articles appeared in the Syrian media which revealed a desire to improve relations with Iraq. The message was conveyed in indirect ways, in calls for clearing the atmosphere in the Arab world and overcoming the causes of disunity in inter-Arab relations. It is not known what the tenor of unpublicized Syrian-Iraqi talks may have been, but public Iraqi pronouncements reflected a confident feeling. Iraq's position was that reconciliation had to be preceded by a "fundamental change" in Syria—a precondition unacceptable to the Syrian Ba'th.

Nor was Syria satisfied with the development of its relations with the US and Egypt during the summer and autumn of 1977. The euphoric atmosphere of the Asad-Carter meeting in May was not followed by concrete measures in the direction expected by Syria. By the end of June, when it appeared that a good working relationship had been established between the Carter Administration and the new Israeli government, Syria was already indicating its disillusionment with the US and its policies; this did not change later in the year when American-Israeli relations were beset by friction and tension. Some aspects of the situation were undoubtedly satisfactory to Syria: the American-Israel divergence; the actual positions adopted by the Carter Administration on various issues pertaining to the Arab-Israeli conflict, and the evident American concern with and consideration of Syria's particular outlook. But Syria remained sceptical about America's willingness and ability to force Israel into making far-reaching concessions, and suspicious of Egypt's conduct and motives. Indeed, Egypt and Syria's mutual suspicions were apparent throughout this period, beginning with Secretary of State Vance's visit to the Middle East in August, and continuing through the various compromise formulas tried by the US in order to facilitate the convening of the Geneva conference. (See essay, "Chronology and Commentary on Political Developments in the Middle East.")

It is against this background that Syria's response to Sādāt's visit to Jerusalem should be seen. Once the initial shock was over, two fundamental facts became apparent to the Syrian leaders.

1) The transition to a novel Egyptian policy created a new situation in the Middle East with which Syria was hard put to contend. Sādāt's willingness to enter into a dialogue with Israel and break a series of taboos (which were ideological and political cornerstones of the Arab position in the conflict with Israel) were unacceptable to the Syrian Ba'th. They also realized that Egypt now reoccupied the centre of the stage in inter-Arab relations, to the detriment of Syria's own ambitions. Finally, distrustful of President Sādāt, the Syrian leadership suspected that he might opt, deliberately or inadvertently, for a separate settlement with Israel.

2) At the same time, there was not much that Syria could do. Its relations with Iraq and the PLO remained problematic; those with Libya were not so bad, but Asad did not regard Qadhdhāfī as a reliable partner. Jordan did not abandon Syria completely, but indicated that it might under certain conditions endorse the Egyptian policy. Even Syria's client, the Sarkīs Administration in Lebanon, did not provide the Syrian government with solid support.

The conclusion to be drawn from this situation was that while it behoved Syria to denounce Egypt's conduct vehemently, all practical options were kept open—a line pursued until the beginning of December 1977 when the potential members of an anti-Egyptian coalition met in Tripoli. Syria's dilemma was demonstrated when Iraq demanded that all participants renounce the "political process." In practical terms the demand was directed at Syria, the only participant which had accepted, albeit conditionally, Resolutions 242 and 338. Syria refused to endorse this demand, which not only revealed its current predicament, but also an inherent ambivalence in the very foundations of its policy.

ECONOMIC AFFAIRS (3.925 Syrian pounds = US$1; 6.6 £S = £1 sterling)

For a comprehensive account of recent economic developments in Syria, and performance in 1976–7, see essay entitled, "Major Trends in Middle East Economic Developments."

BALANCE OF PAYMENTS SUMMARY (SDRs m)

	1973	*1974*	*1975*	*1976**
Goods and services	- 58.4	244.6	- 504.9	- 1,062.3
Exports (fob)	294.0	650.9	765.9	922.6
Imports (cif)	- 514.0	- 932.8	- 1,268.1	- 1,966.4†
Trade balance	- 220.0	- 281.9	- 502.2	- 1,043.8
Receipts from services	226.8	298.9	316.1	272.7
Payments for services	- 65.4	- 261.6	- 318.8	- 291.2
Net services	161.4	37.3	- 2.7	- 18.5
Transfer payments (net)	330.6	382.9	581.4	393.5
Private	30.7	37.3	43.4	45.7
Official	299.9	345.6	538.0	347.8
Non-monetary capital (net)	20.9	- 0.5	- 7.8	233.5
Private	- 21.7	14.0	15.1	62.4
Official	42.6	- 14.5	- 22.9	171.1
Net-errors and omissions	- 40.6	- 6.0	- 4.2	11.1
Overall surplus or deficit (–)	**252.5**	**131.8**	**64.5**	**- 424.2**
Monetary movements (increase in assets –)	**- 252.5**	**- 131.8**	**- 64.5**	**424.2**
Conversion rates (£S per SDR)	**4.5549**	**4.4768**	**4.4924**	**4.4882**

* Preliminary.
† Including imports of non-monetary gold valued at SDR 328 m.
Source: Central Bank of Syria.

GROSS DOMESTIC PRODUCT
(£Sm at current market prices)

	1970	*1971*	*1972*	*1973*	*1974*	*1975*	*1976*
Agriculture*	1,380	1,627	2,352	1,709	3,045	3,623	4,428
Industry†	1,264	1,450	1,729	1,942	3,758	4,334	5,134
Construction	225	297	331	395	704	1,148	1,948
Transport and Communication	639	812	704	1,045	1,003	1,383	1,160
Trade	1,172	1,325	1,642	1,719	3,089	3,488	4,424
Finance and Insurance	120	131	157	161	186	122	135
Rents	498	534	556	578	613	668	737
Government	711	816	919	1,198	1,606	2,510	2,810
Other services	424	456	501	666	865	1,119	1,392
Total GDP	**6,433**	**7,448**	**8,891**	**9,413**	**14,869**	**18,395**	**22,168**

*Includes forestry and fisheries.
†Manufacturing, mining, electricity, gas and water.
Source: Central Bureau of Statistics.

OIL PRODUCTION AND EARNINGS

	Production ('000 barrels/day)	*Exports* ('000 barrels/day)	*Value of Exports (£S'000)*	*Percentage of Exports*
1968	20,660	16,800	30.0	4.5
1969	52,400	46,600	83.2	10.5
1970	84,840	71,300	128.7	16.6
1971	105,780	69,600	176.1	22.3
1972	117,240	77,100	200.1	17.6
1973	110,420	82,700	291.3	21.7
1974	130,700	117,300	1,607.5	55.2
1975	192,740	189,400	2,376.6	69.1
1976	195,200	183,300	2,585.7	62.4

Source: Financial Times, 16 November 1977.

MAIN TRADE PARTNERS (millions of Dollars)

	1974	*1975*	*1976*
Exports to:			
Italy	24	168	200
Federal Germany	119	94	109
USSR	111	55	85
Belgium	16	98	81
France	6	4	75
Yugoslavia	33	53	60
United Kingdom	76	75	52
Netherlands	—	2	50
Saudi Arabia	14	23	45
China	42	23	31
Czechoslovakia	20	10	10
Switzerland	2	2	26
Egypt	7	10	22
Jordan	11	13	21
Turkey	8	4	20
Total (including others)	**784**	**930**	**1,045**
Imports from:			
Switzerland	22	65	383
Federal Germany	147	215	318
Italy	110	154	202
France	107	126	179
Japan	40	77	160
United States	36	109	130
United Kingdom	38	71	87
Belgium	41	34	77
Netherlands	28	47	52
Czechoslovakia	41	48	52
Lebanon	96	67	47
USSR	47	52	45
China	51	45	42
Turkey	32	24	38
Total (including others)	**1,230**	**1,685**	**2,428**

Source: IMF, *Direction of Trade, 1970–76.*

STATE BUDGET EXPENDITURE (£Sm)

	1975	*1976*
Justice and Public Administration	768	1,302
National Security	3,344	3,690
Culture and Information	1,056	1,640
Social Welfare	97	144
Economy and Finance	842	1,100
Agriculture and Land Reclamation	1,270	1,416
Industry and Mining	3,188	4,646
Communication, Utilities and Public Works	1,253	2,005
Other Expenditure	605	606
Total	**12,242**	**16,549**

Source: Statistical abstract, 1976.

INVESTMENT FOR THE FOURTH FIVE-YEAR PLAN, 1976–80 (£Sm)

	Public Sector	*Private and Mixed Sector*	*Total*
Euphrates Dam Project	7,439	—	7,439
Irrigation*	1,095	2,500	5,499
Agriculture†	1,904	2,500	5,499
Industry‡	9,889	1,400	11,289
Energy and Fuels	7,986	—	7,986
Transport and Communication	5,136	500	5,636
Trade and Commerce	944	200	1,144
Housing and Public Utilities	3,997	4,089	8,086
Services	5,194	700	5,894
Administration	1,034	—	1,034
Popular Work	160	—	160
Total	**44,777**	**9,389**	**54,166**

*Includes land reclamation.
†Includes forestry and fisheries.
‡Includes manufacturing, mining, electricity, water and gas.
Source: State Planning Commission.

NOTES

1. *Al-Ba'th*, Damascus; 8 March 1971.
2. Cf *Al-Watan al-'Arabī*, Paris; 23 September 1977.
3. *Tishrīn*, Damascus, 12 March 1977.
4. *Al-Thawra*, Damascus; 21 May 1977.
5. *Arabia and the Gulf*, London; 15 August 1977.
6. R Damascus, 18 August 1977.
7. *The Military Balance 1977–78* (London: International Institute for Strategic Studies).
8. R Damascus, 4 August 1975.
9. *Al-Ba'th*, 1 February 1977.
10. *The Observer*, London; 6 March 1977.
11. These issues are treated in detail in the essay, "Inter-Arab Relations," and in the relevant country chapters.

Turkey

Türkiye Cumhuriyeti

ARYEH SHMUELEVITZ and ESTHER LIDZBARSKI-TAL

The background to the crucial developments in Turkey in 1977 was established in 1973 when the army withdrew from the political scene and a period of instability under shaky coalition or caretaker governments ensued. The general elections were held on 5 June amid grave domestic and international problems which the divided government proved incapable of tackling. The main domestic problems were the deterioration of internal security and of the economy. In foreign affairs, the problem created on Cyprus when the Turkish army took over 40% of the island in July 1974 remained unsettled; so did the conflict with Greece over the control of air space and the continental shelf in the Aegean Sea. The failure to make progress over Cyprus led to a deterioration in Turkey's relations with the US, while relations with the EEC were strained over an association agreement.

The crucial general elections in 1977 succeeded in moving the country closer to a two-party system, but failed to produce a decisive result that could have brought a strong and effective government to power. This left the country facing a further period of coalition government. The new coalition was comprised of virtually the same combination of parties as the outgoing one, but with more power residing in the hands of the small extreme Rightist member parties. It was no surprise, therefore, when this coalition collapsed and Bülent Ecevit appointed a new government at the beginning of 1978.

POLITICAL AFFAIRS

THE SITUATION BEFORE THE ELECTIONS ON 5 JUNE 1977

From 31 March 1975 until the general election of June 1977, Süleyman Demirel's Nationalist Front (*Milliyetçi Cephe*) led a coalition government comprised of four rival conservative parties under the slogan "a Rightist Front against the Left" (*sola karşı sağ cephe*). The largest party in the coalition was Demirel's right-of-centre conservative Justice Party (*Adalet Partisi* or JP) with 165 seats in the 450-seat National Assembly (NA). Its main partner was Necmettin Erbakan's Muslim fundamentalist, though to some extent socialist, National Salvation Party (*Milli Selâmet Partisi* or NSP) with 48 seats. The two minor partners were Alparslan Türkeş' ultra-rightist Nationalist Action Party (*Milliyetçi Hareket Partisi* or NAP) with three seats, and Turhan Feyzioğlu's Republican Reliance Party (*Cumhuriyetçi Güven Partisi* or RRP), a right-of-centre liberal party with ten seats. The leaders of the three smaller parties served as Deputy Prime Ministers.

As the election approached, the perennial frictions within the coalition escalated as each party competed for votes from almost the same social stratum. At the same time, tension mounted between the government and the opposition, particularly the social-democratic Republican People's Party (*Cumhuriyet Halk Partisi* or RPP) whose 189 seats made it the largest party in the Assembly. The RPP used its power to defeat or obstruct legislation contrary to its own policies, its methods virtually paralysing the Assembly. Its leader, Bülent Ecevit, continued to be one of the most popular men in the country. These political conflicts were sharpened by a rise in political violence and by the deepening economic crisis.

The coalition Government's authority was undermined by the strenuous rivalries of its constituent parties in trying to implement their own programmes and promises. Demirel had little control over his deputy Prime Ministers, particularly Erbakan (NSP), whose support was vital to the Government's survival. Erbakan fully exploited his position over domestic and foreign issues, advocating hawkish views on Cyprus and a strongly nationalist line *vis-à-vis* the US, the EEC and Greece. He was opposed to making any concessions on Cyprus, and urged that the Turkish zone declare its independence. Contrary to this view, Government policy favoured a federal bi-zonal independent state for Cyprus. Furthermore, this occurred at the time when the Turkish-US defence agreement was stalled in Congress pending progress over Cyprus. Erbakan also insisted on severance of Turkey's ties with the West in favour of alignment with the Islamic East. At a time when Demirel was also attempting to overcome problems of the association agreement with the EEC, Erbakan criticized the previous agreement and literally brought negotiations to a standstill.

Domestically, Erbakan agreed to sign the 1977 national budget only after Demirel had allocated c. $1,000m to industrial projects favoured by his party. During the budget debates, which began on 3 February 1977, Erbakan's NSP cooperated with the main opposition party, the RPP, to increase the civil servants' coefficient from 9 to 12. They thus succeeded in defeating the Government's own budget proposal for a coefficient of only ten. Erbakan defended himself from JP attacks by stressing that the joint Budget Committee (in which the JP had a majority) had increased the appropriation of departments under JP control by TL 13,000m.

Another source of tension and competition with Demirel was Erbakan's campaign for the immediate development of a national programme of heavy industry which, he claimed, would place Turkey among the top industrial countries within seven years. On 26 July 1976, Erbakan had outlined a quite unrealistic programme for 383 industrial projects, which would have required skilled technical personnel and finance on a scale hardly possible for Turkey. In contrast, Demirel advocated economic diversification and gradual industrialization. Another source of disagreement was over the location of industrial projects. While Erbakan called for the construction of plants and factories all over Anatolia, Demirel advocated their concentration in western Turkey. In an attempt to win votes, both party leaders criss-crossed the country to lay cornerstones at every new major industrial project.

The NSP's political platform explicitly appealed for the restoration of Islam at a time when Turkey's constitution forbade the exploitation of religion for political purposes. The NSP's initiative to host the International Religious Conference on Islamic Law (*sheriat-i-nebi*) in Istanbul during March 1977 was taken without first consulting the JP-controlled Foreign Ministry, which opposed it. The RRP also objected that the very nature of the conference was contrary to Turkey's principle of secularism. The NSP argued that the conference would simply make recommendations: when it finally began on 10 June, only NSP members participated.

Rivalry among the coalition partners was also reflected in relations between the ministries under their control. At the beginning of January 1977, the Ministries of Finance (JP) and Industry (NSP) were at odds over the former's attempt to take back bonuses distributed at the New Year to 19 state enterprises under the latter's control. The Finance Ministry claimed that the money had been earmarked as bonuses for civil servants in all state enterprises which had rendered exceptional service during 1976. The Ministry of Industry also embroiled the Government in a dispute on import policy, over which it eventually won more authority at the expense of the Ministry of Commerce (JP).

These frequent disagreements and chronic rivalries led to threats on 31 January by Feyzioğlu, chairman of the moderate RRP, to pull his party out of the coalition unless the government's performance improved, the constant concessions to the NSP ceased, and the coalition protocol was fully implemented. The RRP stopped attending cabinet meetings; it decided to return on 11 March only after receiving assurances from Demirel concerning the coalition protocol. Thus, although the coalition was deeply split, it was united in its determination to remain in power and to enter the election campaign from a position of strength.

THE ECONOMIC CRISIS

Turkey's economy seemed on the verge of bankruptcy in 1976–7: inflation averaged 25% (due mainly to wage increases) and unemployment exceeded 13%. Owing to dwindling gold and foreign currency reserves (and an estimated $2,000m in short-term loans due for repayment at the end of 1977), from February the Turkish Central Bank had only transferred money for "emergency and strategic" imports. Banks in Tokyo, Geneva and London stopped honouring cheques from the Turkish Central Bank.[1] The Finance Minister claimed that these cheques were not honoured not for lack of funds, but due to exaggerated reports about the Bank's difficulties. The economic crisis was deepened mainly by the Government's reluctance to impose unpopular austerity measures in an election year. Echoing RPP criticisms, a columnist claimed that "the Administration . . . in order to have everything in the market, has squandered the resources of the country to such an extent that the burden of external debt has reached unbearable magnitude."[2]

INTERNAL SECURITY

Clashes between Left and Right-wing groups, as well as between rival factions within these groups, claimed 200 lives and 2,438 non-fatal casualties during the Government's term of office. Most of the violence took place in or near the universities and student hostels, and the majority of victims were university students. The clashes were mostly ideological in origin, although the students' main aim was to obtain control over university departments and hostels in order to prevent opponents from attending classes or using accommodation facilities. Most of the violence was probably provoked by the extreme Rightists in a possible attempt to prevent the RPP winning the elections by forcing the Government to declare martial law. Many faculties were closed down during a major part of 1977 to avoid clashes, and higher education came to a virtual standstill. However, students were not the only participants in the disruptions. They were joined by some radical trade union groups, including the Teachers' Unity and Solidarity Organization, the Civil Servants' Unity and Solidarity Organization and the United Technicians' Association.

The extreme Left was split into various factions ranging from Leninists to Maoists. The extreme Right was consolidated into two groups: the NAP Youth Organization, the "Idealist Club Association" (*Ülkü Ocaklari Birliği*), which included a military arm—the "commandos" or "Grey Wolves" (*Bozkurtlar*); and the "Vanguard Association" (*Akıncılar*),[4] a youth organization affiliated with the NSP National Student Organization. "Vanguard" was not mentioned as participating in any of the clashes in 1977, except for a single confrontation with the "Idealists."

The Government proved unable to deal with political violence, despite widespread searches for arms and arrests, mainly among the Leftists. Replying to opposition charges of weakness, the Interior Minister, Oğuzhan Asiltürk, claimed that while 40,000 policemen had been mobilized to deal with the situation, it was impractical to assume that a policeman could be assigned to every citizen. Demirel blamed the opposition for impeding legislation on public order, citing the prevention by the RPP of the re-establishment of State Security Courts. In contrast, the opposition, as well as the local and foreign press, accused Türkeş (NAP) of instigating Right-wing violence—with the tacit consent of Demirel—through his party's youth movement.[5] Demirel rejected these accusations and claimed that the violence, caused mainly by fighting between Leninists and Maoists, was a "communist plot." He singled out Ecevit as the one who had freed the trouble-makers.[6]

In February 1977, the University Board of Trustees forced Ilgaz Alyanak to resign as Rector of the Middle East Technical University (METU) in Ankara. The appointment of his successor, Prof Hasan Tan—said to be pro-NAP—prompted the opposition to accuse the Government of attempting to gain control over the educational system and, by so doing, to provoke violence. Until Prof Tan's appointment, METU had been able to hold regular classes with a minimum of incidents. Subsequently, however, students and staff began to demonstrate against him and ultimately clashed with the gendarmerie. Refusing to resign, Prof Tan decided to suspend classes for 15 days and evacuated the student hostels on security grounds. This precipitated further clashes, and a number of faculty members either resigned or announced their refusal to co-operate with Prof Tan. When the issue was brought before the Council of State on 3 March, it ordered the university to be reopened, but clashes continued nevertheless. On 23 June, Prof Tan resigned.

On 6 January 1977, a joint meeting of government members and university rectors had decided to cut scholarships to those students who became involved in illegal activities. They also recommended (a) that organizations should be made to pay for damage caused by their members; (b) that the expulsion from university of militant activists and students who destroyed public property should be strictly enforced; (c) that disciplinary action should be taken by the university independently of judicial procedures.[7] At a cabinet meeting on 11 February, Türkeş and Feyzioğlu demanded that martial law be proclaimed, but this was rejected by JP and NSP ministers on the grounds that the armed forces would object to such a move.

President Fahri Korutürk, initiating a meeting with university rectors and officials from the High Court to discuss measures against anarchy, denounced both Left and Right-wing militants. Public order was also regularly discussed during National Security Council (NSC) meetings in the first three months of 1977. On 26 February and 22 March, the Council decided to reinforce measures against arms smuggling and Left-wing activities, as well as to take steps against Right-wing and reactionary organizations.

These measures proved to be ineffective, however, and speculation grew about the possibility of another military intervention. But the Turkish military command was reluctant to interfere for a number of reasons, including the consequences of the US arms embargo; the foreign exchange problem; the army's bitter experience of 1971–3 when it exercised political control; and in addition its failure in March 1973 to impose its candidate for the presidency on Parliament. The Chief of Staff, General Semih Sancar, was himself a strong opponent of army intervention in politics. He was reported to have close ties with Demirel,[8] and was satisfied with being able to influence domestic politics through the National Security Council and the Presidency.

However, on 11 February, an Air Force General and member of the Supreme Military Council, Irfan Özaydınlı, handed Demirel a "memorandum" sharply criticizing his Administration, in particular condemning the political violence. A similar memorandum from army commanders had preceded the military intervention in March 1971; but on this occasion, Özaydınlı's move did not have the backing of the army as a whole. Demirel persisted in denying that a memorandum had been presented to him; the General Staff remained silent.[9]

PROPOSALS FOR EARLY ELECTIONS

The deepening political crisis led many labour leaders, businessmen, industrialists, university professors and leading newspapers to urge that the general election, originally scheduled for 12 October, should be brought forward.[10] The hope that elections would produce a stronger government was supported by the evidence of the 1975 partial elections, which indicated that voters were tending to favour the two major parties. Others supported the move because they believed that an RPP victory would lead to greater success in overcoming political violence.

Although Demirel had voiced his support for early elections at the end of 1976, he put off any decision until after the 1977 budget had been ratified.[11] By this time, he was thoroughly exasperated by the behaviour of the coalition partners, principally Erbakan. The coalition as a whole was steadily losing popularity. Furthermore, Demirel was about to come under investigation by two parliamentary commissions: one into allegations that he was involved in payoffs by the Lockheed Aircraft Corporation, and the other to investigate irregularities in furniture exports. Demirel concluded that, in the interest of his party, earlier elections would be advantageous, especially as the date originally scheduled meant that the election campaign would coincide with Ramadan, thereby giving Erbakan an important advantage. On 20 March, the JP also issued an official statement supporting elections in June as "the most effective answer to an opposition which instigates divisiveness and destruction daily . . . and which does not refrain from causing state agitation with the aim of wearing out the Government . . . The strongest measure against the enemies [the Left] . . . to our . . . national existence is for the JP to come to power alone."[12] On 24 March, the RPP decided to support early elections since the sooner the elections took place the greater the RPP's prospects were of winning, for Ecevit's prestige as the Cyprus hero had been steadily declining since 1974. Furthermore, the RPP announced that early elections would save the country "from greater crises, the people and youth from the murderers and guerrillas who were encouraged and incited by the JP."[13]

Erbakan opposed early elections because he wanted to achieve some progress in the construction of factories that had been publicized over a period of time. He was also counting on exploiting religious sentiment during the month of Ramadan. Erbakan argued that early elections would be destructive to the development of industry, and criticized the JP for wishing to undermine the NSP's efforts in this direction. He accused both the JP and RPP of acting under external influence (i.e. the US) and against Turkey's national interest. To prevent early elections, Erbakan was even prepared to abandon the coalition and form a new government with the Democratik Parti (DP), with the participation or backing of the RPP. However, factions within the NSP opposed any co-operation with the RPP, and Erbakan himself feared that such a move might be unfavourably interpreted by the electorate.

As a result of co-operation between the JP and the RPP, a motion for early elections was passed on 4 April, despite an attempted filibuster by the NSP. The elections were thus scheduled for 5 June.

THE GENERAL ELECTIONS

The High Electoral Council (HEC) announced on 5 April that eight parties, as well as independent candidates, would participate in the elections for the entire National Assembly and for the renewal of one-third of the Senate seats: the JP, RPP, NAP, NSP, RRP, DP, the Unity Party of Turkey (*Türkiye Birlik Partisi* or UPT, a Leftist group supported by Muslim minorities), and the pro-Marxist Labour Party of Turkey (*Türkiye Işçi Partisi* or LPT).[14]

The various parties began exploring common ground in order to form unified fronts, seeking co-operation from outside groups as well. On 24 February, Turkey's second largest trade union confederation, the radical DISK (*Devrimci İsci Sendikaları Konfederasyonu* or Revolutionary Trade Union Confederation) announced its support for the RPP in the elections. Unlike DISK, the largest labour union confederation, Türk-İş (*Türkiye İşçi Sendikaları Konfederasyonu* or Trade Union Confederation of Turkey), had consistently stood apart from politics; but in April 1976, a draft resolution (supported by Halil Tunç, the President of Türk-Iş) committed it to future political involvement, but without mentioning any particular party. Consequently, on 11 April 1977, the General Executive Board held an emergency meeting to decide which party to support. Although the affiliated unions generally favoured the RPP, none of the parties received the two-third majority required, mainly due to efforts by pro-JP members. Instead, on 14 April, the General Executive Board presented to the two major parties a list of "unacceptable conditions" in return for its support. For example, it demanded that the RPP abandon any relations with other labour organizations (referring to DISK), and required a bloc of 38 seats from the RPP and 32 from the JP. When both parties rejected these conditions, Tunç announced that all member unions would be free to decide for themselves which party to support.

In March, Ecevit held several meetings with Behice Boran, chairman of the re-established LPT, and with Mustafa Timisi, chairman of the UPT. It was reported that the three party leaders planned to merge and form a united leftist front for the elections. JP and NAP at once accused the RPP of moving further to the Left. Ecevit denied on 19 March that the RPP was planning to merge with the LPT. On the same day, Timisi said that the UPT had decided to reject the RPP's offer. The merger therefore did not take place, probably because the parties could not agree on the number of candidates each was to have on the RPP's list. Also, the RPP probably concluded that radical elements might do the party more harm than good in the elections.

At the end of March, negotiations were held between the JP and NAP, who decided not to stand together on an electoral list, but only to co-operate in order "to ensure the safety of the ballot box." Ex-president and former Democrat Party leader, Celâl Bayar, turned down a JP request to include him in its Istanbul list, but agreed to take part in JP's election campaign. Bayar's support brought to the JP's list a number of Democrat Party veterans, such as Sebati Ataman (former Minister of Co-ordination and of Industry), and Mükerrem Sarol (former Minister of State). It also led to the defection of deputies like Bahri Dağdaş from the present Democratic Party.

Before the primary elections on 24 April, the RPP administration vetoed the candidacy of 89 members, most of whom were known to advocate a line more radical than the "democratic left" of the party. Some of the rejected candidates decided to work for the RPP in the elections despite the veto. Others, like deputies Nurettin Yılmaz (Mardin), Cemil Erham (Ağri) and Abdülkerim Zilan (Siirt), resigned from the party and stood as independents.

In the RRP, the "Republicans" decided to leave the party.[15] From among the founders of the group, Health Minister Kemal Demir resigned on 16 April, as did the chairman of the RRP Council, Kemal Satır, and Ali Ihsan Göğüs two days later. All denied rumours that they intended to join the JP after the elections.

On 21 April, 13 NSP members of parliament announced that they would not become candidates; followers of the Nurist sect were also expected to resign from the party. A few days before the election, some of the ten deputies (including leading figures like ex-Labour Minister Ahmet Tevfik Paksu and the former Secretary-General, Gunduz Sevilgen) left the party.[16] Paksu claimed that the resignations were due to the party's "drift towards its own brand of [Erbakan] dictatorship."[17]

The primary elections resulted in the defeat of many JP and even more RPP parliamentarians. This was interpreted as a reaction against the fact that the 1973–7 parliament had been unable to pass bills concerning local development, and that members had generally failed to realize various promises to their constituents.[18]

THE ELECTION CAMPAIGN

The election campaign officially started on 5 May (when the parties submitted lists of final candidates to the HEC), the major issues being the economic crisis and the breakdown of law and order. However, debate between the two principal parties rarely rose above the level of hurling charges of "communist" and "fascist" at one another. Ecevit pleaded with the people to vote for his party in order to save their children from violence incited by the JP; Demirel described Ecevit as an architect of anarchy. The JP stressed that they had saved the Republic from disintegrating into chaos in March 1975, and had served the country loyally in spite of a destructive opposition as well as difficulties with the NSP, whom they attacked fiercely. The RPP laid responsibility for Turkey's inflation and balance of payment's deficit at the door of the NF Government and promised to improve the country's economy—not at the expense of the "workers," but of those who exploit them. Both the RPP and the JP emphasized the advantages of one-party majority government. The JP appealed to the religious population by insisting that though the NSP claimed a monopoly on Islam, the JP had opened the path of religion into politics. To underscore this point, Demirel conspicuously kissed the *Kur'an* at every public rally.

None of the parties placed much emphasis on foreign affairs, except the NSP, primarily because there was no fundamental difference between the major parties. Erbakan stated, however, that he would not honour the agreements signed with the EEC because they were incompatible with Turkey's sovereign rights; that he would proclaim the independence of the Turkish federated state of Cyprus on 29 October 1977; and that he would dismantle the illegal Greek fortifications in the Aegean Sea. He vowed that he would speed up the Republic's industrial drive and further promised to build a mosque in every village.

For the first time in the history of modern Turkey, there was considerable violence and bloodshed in the election campaign, despite special security measures and warnings by the President and Gen Sancar to maintain public order. Armed clashes occurred daily, and explosives were thrown at party headquarters and provincial offices. Three assassination attempts were made on Ecevit's life: in Niksar on 26 April; in Şiran on 27 April, when he and his companions were attacked by alleged Right-wing extremists; and at Izmir airport on 29 May, when he was fired on by a policeman. It appeared that other police, including senior officers, were involved in this last plot.

The daily violence culminated in what was described by the press as a "May Day Massacre." During a DISK rally of c. 150,000 supporters in Istanbul's Taksim

Square, 38 people were killed and about 200 wounded when shots were fired into the crowd causing great confusion and panic. The official and general view was that Maoists were responsible, especially considering their earlier rejection of DISK support of the RPP. The chairman of DISK, Kemal Türkler, admitted that the Maoists caused the violence, but claimed that they were acting on behalf of the CIA and the NF Government. The Maoists themselves were divided: one faction blamed the other.

Election day was unexpectedly quiet, although over 75% of the electorate voted. None of the parties obtained a clear mandate however. The RPP total was 13 short of the 226 seats required for an absolute majority. The most dramatic gains were made by NAP, and the most dramatic losses by the DP and the RRP.

ELECTION RESULTS

	1977		*1973*	
	Seats Won	*% of Vote*	*Seats Won*	*% of Vote*
RPP	213	41.38	185	33.4
JP	189	36.87	149	29.8
NAP	16	6.42	3	3.4
NSP	24	8.6	48	11.8
RRP	3	2.0	13	5.3
DP	1	1.8	45	11.9
UPT	0	0.4	1	1.08
LPT	0	0.1		(did not stand)
Independents	4	2.5	6	2.8

In the Senate partial elections, the RPP won 28 of the 50 seats (42.3%); the JP, 21 seats (38.25%); and the NSP, 1 seat (8.53%). Thus the number of RPP seats increased to 75; JP ended up with 64 seats; and NSP with six seats. (In the 1975 partial elections, the RPP won 25 seats—49.9%; the JP, 22 seats—41.29%; the NSP two seats—8.86%; and the NAP, one seat.)

The RPP's majority was due to major gains in the big cities: in Ankara, Istanbul and İzmir, it received more than 50% of votes cast.[19] In nearly all other places, RPP and JP were almost even. The population clearly displayed a wish for stability by supporting the two major parties, who received 80% of the total vote. This confirmed that there was indeed a shift, noted in the 1975 election, towards a two-party system.

Erbakan blamed his party's setback on 2.5m votes which he claimed were improperly cast. However, the High Electoral Council rejected his claim as undocumented and unproven. The NSP setback was probably due mainly to intraparty rivalry, which precipitated the defection of the Paksu faction. Most of the NSP votes were lost to the NAP and the JP. The NAP was perhaps more successful in this election because of its efficient organization and relatively minor internal rifts and struggles. The main reason for the collapse of the RRP and the DP was that many leading personalities had left those parties and joined other Right-wing parties—mainly the JP—or left political life altogether.

THE RPP GOVERNMENT

The new Turkish Grand National Assembly (*Büyük Millet Meclisi*) convened on 13 June. Demirel submitted his Government's resignation, and on 14 June, Ecevit was asked by the President to form a government. To ensure freedom of action in tackling the country's problems, Ecevit chose to form a one-party minority government instead of being shackled by a coalition. He looked for support from Independent MPs and hoped to induce members of other parties to cross the floor. He voiced readiness to discuss conditions for co-operation with any party except the

JP and the NAP, and promised reconciliation and reciprocity to those who supported him. On 17 June, Deputy Eşref Cengiz (independent-Diyarbakır) joined the RPP, and DP Deputy Faruk Sükan also announced his support for Ecevit. The RRP stated that it would not take part in any government, and that it would oppose any government that included the NSP. RRP's chairman Feyzioğlu called on the two main parties to form a grand coalition. In the Senate, the group of Presidential quota Senators announced support for Ecevit's Government. Outside the National Assembly, support was promised by the President of the Union of Chambers of Industry, Şakip Sabancı; President of DISK, Kemal Türkler; and President of Türk-İş Halil Tunç. On 20 June, Ecevit had a meeting with Demirel, at the President's request, but nothing came of it.

Despite its electoral setback, the NSP still held the balance of power. On 8 June, Erbakan said that he would only support a Government which accepted his ten conditions, including hardline policies on Cyprus and the EEC. He wanted seven ministries for the NSP, including the Ministry of Industry, as well as the NA Speaker. Other conditions were: nationalization of education and assignment of teachers to religious schools by a joint committee; foreign policy decisions to be taken by a committee composed of ministers from the coalition parties; a committee on economic policy to be headed by himself; abolition of Article 163 of the Penal Code concerning crimes against secularism; abolition of interest in banking, and revision of the fiscal system. Three factions were reported to exist in the NSP.[20] One, which included ex-Agriculture Minister Korkut Özal, demanded co-operation with the RPP; the second insisted on co-operation with the JP-NAP; while the third—centred on Erbakan—was willing to work with whomever would give the NSP the most advantageous conditions.

However, after Ecevit's meeting with Erbakan on 24 June, the NSP group unanimously decided to vote against the Government. JP, NAP and NSP claimed that Ecevit's move to form a minority government was unconstitutional. (The Constitution states that the leader of the largest party should be invited to form a government. It does not state that the government must command a majority in the National Assembly.) Demirel and Türkeş declared that the factors that had brought the nationalist parties together in 1975 still existed, and they asked that the Front be re-established. They also claimed that the 58.82% vote gained by the Right-wing parties in the elections proved that they were more popular than the Left.

The President approved the cabinet list submitted by Ecevit on 21 June, overriding opposition and criticism by Demirel, Erbakan and Türkeş. During its brief tenure, Ecevit's Government made no major policy decisions except—on its last day in power—to reopen Maraş (Varosha) to settlement, a move interpreted as a final attempt to cause difficulties to the Nationalist Front Government over the Cyprus issue. This Ecevit denied. He also took steps to end campus and street violence: one of the Government's first acts was to set up a committee, under Deputy Premier Orhan Eyüboğlu, to fight anarchy.

Ecevit rejected charges made by NAP officials that acts of violence had intensified since he took office. According to press reports, although the atmosphere remained tense, there were fewer incidents than before the elections. The Government's first change in personnel was to remove the Director-General of Turkish Radio and Television, Prof Şaban Karataş, whose appointment on 19 January 1976 had provoked an outcry from the TRT and opposition parties, and was even delayed by the President himself. The JP was charged with making a political appointment in violation of the 1961 Constitution, which states that the media should remain nonpartisan. On 1 July 1977, the President approved a decree

THE GOVERNMENT (JANUARY 1977—SEPTEMBER 1977)

Portfolio	The First NF Government 1 January 1977[1]	RPP Minority Government 21 June 1977[2]	The second NF Government 21 July 1977
Prime Minister	Süleyman Demirel (JP)	Bülent Ecevit	Süleyman Demirel (JP)
Deputy Prime Ministers	Prof Necmettin Erbakan (NSP), Turhan Feyzioğlu (RRP), Alparslan Türkeş (NAP)	Orhan Eyüboğlu, Turan Güneş	Necmettin Erbakan (NSP), Alparslan Türkeş (NAP)
Ministers of State	Seyfi Öztürk (JP), Hassan Akay (NSP), Mustafa Kemal Erkovan (NAP), Giyasettin Karaça (JP)	Dr Lutfü Doğan, Prof Kenan Bulutoğlu	Seyfi Öztürk (JP), Süleyman Arif Emre (NSP), Sadi Somuncuoğlu (NAP), Ali Şevki Erek (JP)
Justice	İsmail Müftüğlü (NSP)	Selçuk Erverdi	Necmettin Cevheri (JP)
National Defence	Ferit Melen (RRP)	Hasan Esat Işık	Sadettin Bilgiç (JP)
Interior	Oğuzhan Asiltürk (NSP)	Necdet Uğur	Korkut Özal (NSP)
Foreign Affairs	Ihsan Sabri Çağlayangil (JP)	Prof Gündüz Ökçün	İhsan Sabri Çağlayangil (JP)
Finance	Yılmaz Ergenekon (JP)	Prof Besim Üstünel	Cihat Bilgehan (JP)
National Education	Ali Naili Erdem (JP)	Dr Mustafa Üstündağ	Nahit Menteşe (JP)
Public Works	Fehim Adak (NSP)	Abdülkerim Zilan (Independent)	Selahâttin Kılıç (JP)
Commerce	Halil Başol (JP)	Ziya Müezzinoğlu	Ağah Oktay Güner (NAP)
Health and Social Welfare	Dr Kemal Demir (RRP)[3]	Prof Celal Ertüğ	Cengiz Gökçek (NAP)
Customs and Monopolies	Orhan Öztrak (RRP)	Mehmet Can	Gün Sazak (NAP)
Food, Agriculture and Husbandry	Prof Korkut Özal (NSP)	Fikret Gündoğan	Fehim Adak (NSP)
Communications	Nahit Menteşe (JP)	Erol Çevikçe	Yılmaz Ergenekon (JP)
Labour	Şevket Kazan (NSP)	Bahir Ersoy	Fehmi Cumalioğlu (NSP)
Industry and Technology	Abdülkerim Doğru (NSP)	Tarhan Erdem	Oğuzhan Asiltürk (NSP)
Energy and National Resources	Selâhattin Kılıç (JP)	Neşet Akmandor	Kâmran İnan (JP)
Tourism and Information	Lütfü Tokoğlu (JP)	Altan Öymen	İskender Cenap Ege (JP)
Housing and Reconstruction	Nurettin Ok (JP)	Erol Tuncer	Recai Kutan (NSP)
Rural Affairs and Co-operatives	Vefa Poyraz (JP)	Ali Topuz	Turgut Yücel (JP)
Forestry	Turhan Kapanlı (JP)	Vecdi Ilhan	Sabahattin Savci (NSP)
Youth and Sport	Ali Şevkei Erek (JP)	Yüksel Çakmur	Önal Şakar (JP)
Culture	Rifki Danişman (JP)	Dr Mustafa Üstüdağ	Avni Akyol (JP)
Social Security	Ahmet Mahir Ablum (JP)	Hayrettin Uysal	Turhan Kapanlı (JP)

[1] Traditionally, a few weeks before the elections, certain key ministers are changed to become non-partisan. In this case, prior to the elections, on 11 April, the following changes took place: Zeyyat Baykara replaced İsmail Müftüğlü (Justice); Sebahattin Özbek replaced Oğuzhan Asiltürk (Interior); İbrahim Aysoy replaced Nahit Menteşe (Communications); and Nahit Nenteşe replaced Lütfü Tokoğlu (Tourism and Information). Tokoglu resigned at Demirel's request.

[2] All members in Ecevit's minority government were RPP.

[3] Resigned on 16 April and succeeded by Vefa Tanir.

appointing Dr Cengiz Taşer as acting TRT Director-General.

The Government's programme, prepared by a committee under Deputy Premier Turan Güneş, was outlined by Ecevit on 28 June.[21] Right-wing opposition members walked out of the House, as Ecevit accused the previous Government of turning Turkey into "a country of chaos, conflict and political murders." In fact, Ecevit's programme was much milder on certain issues than the RPP election manifesto: despite the opposition's boycott, he hoped to obtain the backing of a few conservative deputies for the confidence vote the following week. This was probably why there was no mention of repealing Articles 141–142 of the Penal Code, which prohibited the establishment of extreme organizations (used mainly against the Left). Also not mentioned were self-management in state economic enterprises and the abolition of lockouts. On the other hand, a large part of the programme was devoted to social security problems, including measures affecting seasonal and temporary labour. Also outlined were ways of reviving the country's economy—mainly by using outside resources and securing long-term, low-interest loans to pay the debts left by the previous Government.

Foreign policy was discussed only in very general terms. The programme stressed the importance of maintaining friendly relations with all countries; the need to protect the rights of the Turkish Cypriots; the need to find a rapid solution to the problems of Cyprus and the Aegean Sea; and the importance of breaking the deadlock between Turkey and the EEC. While the programme expressed a commitment to existing alliances (NATO and CENTO) and communities (EEC), the Government also intended to "broaden its friendships and international relations without taking into consideration their domestic regimes" (i.e. the Soviet bloc). This was mainly in order to avoid dependence for national security on a single external source—the US. At the same time, the programme stated that Turkey should develop her own arms industry.

On 3 July, the Ecevit Cabinet fell when Right-wing parties united behind a vote of no confidence. The NSP, NAP, JP and one independent (Ali Riza Septikaoğlu) won 299 votes against the 217 of the RPP, DP and two independents (Abülkerim Zilan and Nurettin Yilmaz).[22] RRP's three deputies abstained. On the same day, Ecevit tendered his resignation.

THE SECOND NF COALITION GOVERNMENT

The President asked Demirel to form a government on 5 July; on the same day, Demirel began negotiations with Erbakan and Türkeş. In an attempt to keep the smaller extremist parties out of power, a proposal to form a "grand coalition" between the JP and the RPP was endorsed by the President, army officers, trade unions, big business and the universities. Before the elections, both Ecevit and Demirel had claimed that there could never be a RPP-JP coalition; after the elections, Ecevit announced that the RPP would co-operate with every party except the JP and NAP. However, on 9 July, after a meeting of the RPP's Joint Executive Board, Ecevit offered Demirel a RPP-JP coalition with himself or an independent deputy as premier, in order to avoid a second NF Government. Demirel rejected the offer on the grounds that he was already working on a coalition formula with NAP and NSP.

Demirel presented his new Government on 21 July, with the JP holding 16 seats in the Cabinet, the NSP eight seats, and the NAP five seats. However, serious differences had arisen over the distribution of these 29 ministries. The NSP and NAP had both held out for the Education and Interior; at least each wanted to prevent these posts going to the other. There was also dissension within the JP over the number of concessions being made to the other parties. One JP deputy, Orhan Alp, declared that his conscience would not allow him to vote for the Government; he accused Demirel of surrounding himself with "a sectarian junta." At first there were also objections from the JP deputies for Ankara and from İzmir, Oğuz Aygün and Cemal Tercan, as well as from some of the veteran Democrats; but they were all won over in the end by Demirel and Bayar and voted for the Government. Kâmran Inan (JP) intially refused to accept the Ministry of Power—a post, he claimed, that was assigned to him without his knowledge and which lay outside his competence.[23] He had apparently hoped to get the Foreign Ministry, but was finally persuaded to accept the original appointment.[24]

After debating its programme, the National Assembly gave the new Government a vote of confidence of 229 votes against 219 on 1 August. Nevertheless, the considerable concessions given to Erbakan brought strong criticism from JP members who objected to the agreement that "ethics" courses be given in public schools, and to the right of graduates from religious schools to enter universities on the same basis as high school graduates. These two concessions seriously weakened the principle of secularism enshrined in the Constitution. Another of the concessions pledged the abolition of Article 163 of the Penal Code relating to crimes against secularism.[25] Erbakan also achieved an additional domestic goal: an ambitious industrialization programme which included projects to build up heavy industry, armaments and infrastructure.

The Government's foreign policy pledged loyalty to the country's existing commitments, but at the same time promised to defend its legal rights and national interests without making any concessions. Erbakan succeeded in his demand that relations with the EEC be revised to secure national interests, mainly in protecting industry. The programme called for closer co-operation with the Muslim world, especially in the fields of industry and technology. National security was to be assured by no longer depending on the US as the single source of arms; in addition to diversifying arms purchases, a national arms industry was to be established. On Cyprus, the NSP failed to get its way: the Government promised to stand by the previous commitment to preserve Turkish-Cypriot rights; it continued to support the need for a negotiated settlement with the aim of establishing a bi-zonal independent state. Nothing was said about territorial concessions—which Erbakan had opposed. Although the Ministry of Foreign Affairs came under the JP's Control, Erbakan won his demand that foreign policy be decided by a special council on which all three party leaders would have a say. The JP and NAP probably acceded to this point in order that the NSP should share responsibility for foreign policy decisions and so avoid a repetition of the contradictory statements which had embarrassed the previous National Front Government. Türkeş wanted this collective responsibility to extend to the opposition as well, by inviting the RPP to participate in the Foreign Security Council; but the RPP declined.

The Government's economic programme pledged to fight inflation and unemployment, and to improve the balance of payments. It included Erbakan's proposal for an interest-free loan system. Foreign capital was to be accepted only on condition that it helped to develop advanced technology, accelerate industrialization, was export-oriented, and made "a positive contribution" towards the balance of payments.

On internal security, the programme pledged to restore public order by fighting anarchy "fostered from abroad by international communism." The Nationalist Front declared itself against "communism, fascism and other concepts based on materialism . . . which destroy material and spiritual values."[26]

Demirel's new Government faced stiff opposition in the Grand National Assembly. The RPP had 214 deputies in the NA, and enjoyed an absolute majority in the Senate, which gave it an overall majority whenever both Houses met to debate issues of exceptional importance. The RPP therefore had the power to delay or even prevent legislation. In a speech on 7 July, Ecevit reminded the Nationalist Front that it could not function effectively without RPP support. He also implied that the Senate and the National Assembly could together bring Demirel before the Supreme Court, if accusations made against him about alleged distribution of Lockheed bribes and misuse of office to enrich members of his family were ever brought before the two Houses.

The National Assembly could not function as a legislative body, however, until a Speaker and a Chairmanship Council were elected. Under a gentlemen's agreement of 1961, the Speaker was to be elected from the largest party in the House: in the present situation, the RPP. Although the RPP had been demanding the election of a Speaker since 13 June, Demirel ensured that no quorum was ever available. The National Assembly was thus virtually recessed from August to November 1977. This enabled Demirel to consolidate his Government's power without interference from Parliament, and especially from the Senate, with its RPP majority. He quietly prepared for the election of a Speaker with his coalition partners, hoping that the President's new nominations to the Senate, due in October, might change the balance of power there.

Meanwhile, the Government also had to deal with extra-parliamentary opposition. On 12 July, the President of Türk-İş, Haili Tunç (who is also a Senator), threatened a general strike if Demirel obtained a vote of confidence. Tunç had supported the Ecevit Government and, when it was defeated, favoured a JP-RPP coalition. He was totally opposed to any government which included the NSP, which was attempting to undermine the Republic's fundamental principles. Tunç's stand was supported both by the Left-wing press and pro-RPP unions, inside and outside Türk-İş. On 26 July, DISK's Executive Council offered to co-operate in any strike action. But Tunç was criticized by pro-JP unions in Türk-İş, and by the two small recently-established extreme Right-wing confederations: the NAP-affiliated MISK (*Milliyetçi Işçi Sendiklar Konfederasyonu* or Nationalist Trade Union Confederation); and the NSP-sponsored Hak İş. Both claimed that strike action against a Government was contrary to the Confederation's principles. The President of the Turkish Employers' Confederation, Rafet İbrahimoğlu, supported this view, asserting that the right to strike was intended exclusively for the purpose of improving workers' conditions.

Tunç introduced the general strike motion to Türk-İş's Executive Board on 10 August, but when his proposals were rejected, he was forced to abandon this line of action. The sharpest reaction to Halil Tunç's declaration came from the army. On 13 July, General Sancar issued a warning against attempts to provoke the armed forces, threatening legal action against those responsible. Sancar's warning came the day after Tunç had called on all those who accepted Atatürk's principles to accept their duty to protect them—including the army. He demanded that a stand be made against the re-establishment of the Nationalist Front Government. The Military Prosecutor's office opened a preliminary investigation against Tunç on 15 July, demanding his punishment under Article 58 of the Penal Code, which deals with inciting soldiers to disobey laws and break their oaths. On 22 September, the Military Prosecutor demanded that the Defence Minister waive Tunç's immunity as a Senator to allow him to stand trial (but there were no further developments on this issue in the period under review).

There was a resurgence of violence immediately following the vote of confidence in the new Government at the beginning of August. Explosives were thrown into buildings occupied by the JP and especially the NAP. Members of the "Idealist

Club," NAP workers, and policemen were ambushed and killed. NAP deputies appealed to the RPP to denounce the violence, and at the same time tried to pacify their own youth organizations. This might be explained as a NAP attempt to gain respectability. The Council of Ministers announced on 25 August that any attack against security force members would be considered an attack against the state. A week later, on 2 September, the Minister of Interior, Korkut Özal (NSP), announced new measures to "combat anarchy." The police force was to be modernized and strengthened by 5,000. Promises were given about steps to ensure police impartiality. The Government also decided to co-operate closely with the universities and control student hostels more strictly. Students involved in violence would have their scholarships revoked, face suspension or expulsion from school, or be conscripted into the army.[27]

THE NEW RPP GOVERNMENT

The Demirel Government was replaced by a new coalition government, headed by Bülent Ecevit, on 5 January 1978. It obtained a vote of confidence by 229 votes to 218 in the National Assembly on 17 January.

THE GOVERNMENT, AS AT 5 JANUARY 1978

Prime Minister	Bülent Ecevit
Deputy Prime Ministers	Orhan Eyüboğlu
	Turhan Feyzioğlu
	Faruk Sükan
Ministers of State	Enver Akova
	Salih Yıldız
	Lütfü Doğan
	Ali Riza Septioğlu
	Mustafa Kılıç
	Ahmet Şener
	Hikmet Çetin
Ministers:	
Justice	Mehmet Can
National Defence	Hasan Esat Işık
Interior	Irfan Özaydınlı
Foreign Affairs	Gündüz Ökçün
Finance	Ziya Müezzinoğlu
National Education	Necdet Uğur
Public Works	Şerafettin Elici
Commerce	Teoman Küprülüler
Health and Social Aids	Mete Tan
Customs and Monopolies	Tuncay Matarci
Communications	Güneş Öngüt
Agriculture and Animal Husbandry	Mehmet Üceler
Labour	Bahir Ersoy
Industry and Technology	Orphan Alp
Economic Management	Kenan Bulutoglu
Energy and Natural Resources	Deniz Baykal
Tourism and Information	Alev Coşkun
Housing and Public Works	Ahmet Karaaslan
Rural Affairs and Cooperatives	Ali Topuz
Forestry	Vecdi İlhan
Youth and Sports	Yüksel Çakmur
Social Security	Hilmi İşgüzar
Culture	Ahmet Taner Kışlalı
Local Administration	Mahmut Özdemir

DEFENCE AND SECURITY

The Government decided on 17 February 1977 to extend the term of the Army Commander, Gen Sancar, for another year, beginning on 7 March. When discussed at the Council of Ministers earlier in the year, the NSP was reported to have proposed a different candidate—the Ground Forces Commander, Gen Namık Kemal Ersun—whom Demirel rejected. (NSP officials subsequently denied these reports.)[28] However, the retirement of Gen Ersun on 2 June without explanation and only a few days before the general elections naturally caused speculation: some claimed that Ersun was a NAP sympathizer, but no one could explain the unusual timing. Two days later, on 4 June, Demirel warned Ecevit to cancel an election rally, because he had received information about a possible terrorist attack (Ecevit nevertheless took part). On 12 June, the daily *Hürriyet* reported the discovery of a military coup attempt, supposedly planned by some 200 Right-wing officers, including Gen Ersun and the ninth corps commander Lt-Gen Musa Oğun, who had established a "counter-guerrilla" organization in order to prevent the expected RPP election victory. The 200 officers were subsequently arrested.

On 20 June, Gen Ersun appealed to the High Military Administrative Court against his retirement in order to clear himself, as well as to prove that he had not been a member of a political party. He claimed that the real reason for his retirement was the disciplinary action he had taken against the Third Army commander, Gen Ali Fethi Esener, who had awarded Demirel a military medal in violation of military regulations. Lt-Gen Musa Oğun also applied to the prosecutor of the General Staff on 19 August demanding that Gen Sancar be brought to court because he had not reacted to the rumoured coup attempt, and had not refuted press reports concerning the detention of some officers including himself. Oğun claimed that because of the rumours, he was being forced to retire on 30 August, despite his exemplary military record.

Army tradition required that the next most senior officer, First Army Commander Gen Adnan Ersöz should succeed Gen Ersun. However, Gen Sancar continued to act as the Commander of the Ground Forces until 17 July, when Gen Ersöz was temporarily assigned as Acting Commander. No final decision could be made because of a disagreement between the President and Demirel, who broke with tradition in making his own nomination to the President—that of Gen Esener, reportedly a very religious soldier, whose appointment was probably also supported by the NSP. The President refused to sign the decree because Gen Ersöz was the most senior Ground Forces officer. In nominating Esener, the RPP accused the Government of attempting to politicize the army and of thus violating the tradition of the Turkish army and Turkish law.

Demirel insisted that the procedure he had followed in making the appointment was in accordance with legal requirements. On 8 August, the Supreme Military Council decided that several Army commanders—including Gen Ersöz and Gen Esener—would be required to retire on 30 August. Nevertheless, Demirel continued to insist on Esener's appointment. It was reported that as a result of Demirel's attitude, the President refused to receive him on his weekly visits, and again on the traditional Army Day, 30 August when, as a "protest," the President stayed in Istanbul. Another act of protest—this time against the President—was made by Gen Esener, who resigned a day before he was due to retire. After both Esener and Ersöz left the army, Gen Sancar was free to appoint the most senior general, the Commander of the Aegean Army, Gen Kenan Evren as Ground Forces Commander (approved of by both Demirel and the President).

ARMED FORCES

Total armed forces number 465,000, including 310,000 conscripts. Defence expenditure in 1977–8 was TL 46.42 bn ($2.65 bn). Military service is compulsory for 20 months. The Army numbers 375,000, including 250,000 conscripts (about half the divisions and brigades are below strength). Formations consist of one armoured division; two mechanized infantry divisions; 14 infantry divisions, five armoured brigades; four mechanized infantry brigades; five infantry brigades; one parachute brigade; one commando brigade; four surface-to-surface missile battalions with *Honest John*. Equipment consists of 2,800 M-47 and M-48 medium tanks; 1,650 M-113, M-59, *Commando* armoured personnel carriers; 1,500 75mm, 105mm, 155mm and 203mm howitzers; 265 105mm, 190 155mm and 36 175mm self-propelled guns; 1,750 60mm, 81mm and 4.2-in mortars; 18 *Honest John* surface-to-surface missiles; 1,200 57mm, 390 75mm, 800 106mm recoilless rifles; 85 *Cobra* anti-tank guided weapons; 900 40mm anti-aircraft guns; ten *Beaver*, 95 U-17, three Cessna 421, seven Do-27, 18 Do-28 D-1, 20 Beech *Baron* aircraft; 100 AB-205/-206 20 Bell 47G, 48 UH-1D helicopters. (193 *Leopard* tanks; *TOW, Milan* anti-tank guided weapons; 56 AB-205 helicopters on order.) Two infantry divisions are deployed in Cyprus; reserves number 700,000.

The Navy numbers 43,000, including 31,000 conscripts. It is equipped with 14 submarines (two on order); 12 destroyers (five ex-US *Gearing*, five *Fletcher*, one *Sumner*, one RH *Smith*-class); two frigates (with one helicopter); 14 fast patrol boats (14 on order), six guided-missile fast patrol boats (three on order); 41 large and four coastal patrol craft; 21 coastal and four inshore minesweepers; nine minelayers (six coastal); two tank landing ships, 20 tank landing craft and 36 landing craft; one maritime reconnaissance squadron with ten S-2E *Tracker* (two trainers); three AB-205 and 12 AB-212 anti-submarine warfare helicopters. (Six AB-212 helicopters and 33 *Harpoon* surface-to-surface missiles are on order.) Reserves number 25,000.

The Air Force numbers 47,000 (including 29,000 conscripts) and has 319 combat aircraft; 14 ground-attack fighter squadrons; two with 40 F-4E, four with 70 F-5A, two with 34 F-104G, two with 40 F-104S, three with 54 F-100D/F and one with 20 F-100C; one interceptor squadron with 25 F/TF-102A; two reconnaissance squadrons with 36 RF-5A; four transport squadrons with seven C-130E, 20 Transall C-160, 30 C-47, three C-54, three *Viscount* 794 and two *Islander*. Helicopters include ten AB-204, ten UH-1D and ten H-19. There are eight surface-to-air missile squadrons with *Nike Ajax/Hercules*. Trainers include 20 T-33A, 35 T-37, 18 T-34, 25 T-41, 35 F-100C, 13 F-5B, TF-102A, TF-104G, Beech AT-11 and Cessna 421B. (56 *AlphaJet* trainers on order.) Paramilitary forces consist of 75,000 gendarmerie, including three mobile brigades.[29]

FOREIGN AFFAIRS

Since the mid-1960s Turkey's foreign policy has gradually shifted away from an almost exclusive US orientation in the direction of a more diversified and flexible approach. While the main component of the shift was its European orientation, another major trend involved forging new links with the Soviet bloc and Arab and Islamic states. Two major factors contributed to these developments: the Cyprus problem, and resulting relations with Greece and the US; and the energy crisis, which has had grave economic consequences for Turkey.

RELATIONS WITH GREECE AND CYPRUS

Turkish foreign relations have been dominated by the problem of Cyprus ever since its army landed on the Island on 20 July 1974, in response to the Greek Junta's attempt to overthrow President Makarios and declare "Enosis." Turkey claimed that the coup was not an internal affair and that it was exercising its right to intervene under the Zürich and London Agreements (1959) as a guarantor power required to defend the Republic's independent status and the Turkish community.[30] Since 1974, successive Turkish Governments have given broad support to the aim of a federal republic, with autonomy for the Greek and Turkish communities.

Turkey helped the Turkish Cypriots establish their authority over the northern 40% of the island, and gave vital economic assistance. The Turkish Federated State of Cyprus (TFSC) was founded on 13 February 1976; elections held in the Turkish Zone on 20 June were won by Rauf Denktaş' National Unity Party. A Government, parliament, and local army were established. However, efforts to reach agreement on a federal solution have remained deadlocked since February 1976.

Turkey's intervention in Cyprus profoundly affected its relations with Greece, Western Europe, and especially the US. It led to the Greeks withdrawing from NATO's military command (accusing the Ford Administration of indifference to Turkish aggression), and to the US Congress imposing an arms embargo on Turkey on 5 February 1975, partially lifted in October 1975. Total repeal was conditional on progress being made towards a settlement on Cyprus, as well as ratification of a new Defence Co-operation Agreement (DCA), signed in March 1976. In response to the embargo, Turkey closed down 26 US bases on her soil. Despite pressure from Congress, Turkey remained intransigent on this issue (see below).

The Cyprus crisis raised new issues and deepened existing tension between Turkey and Greece, for instance in the dispute over control of the continental shelf in the Aegean Sea. This began in March 1974 when Greece struck oil, which was badly needed by both countries. Greece cited the 1958 Geneva Convention in support of its claim that each island had its own continental-shelf rights. Turkey, which has not signed the Convention, insisted that the Aegean was a special case: although each state had an almost equal extent of coastline, Greece controlled all the islands in the sea between. It further claimed that the continental shelf was the natural extension of Anatolia.

Immediately following Turkey's intervention in Cyprus, Greece claimed that it too might face invasion and transferred army units to its islands off Turkey's coast, in contravention of the Treaty of Lausanne (1923). Turkey reacted by founding the "Aegean Army," based on the coast facing the islands. Yet another dispute concerned the limits of the air traffic control zones over the Aegean. Greece had closed the region to international flights in response to Turkish demands after the Cyprus crisis for early advance notification of eastbound flights.

While Greece wished to settle these disputes through international arbitration, it agreed to the Turkish proposal for bilateral negotiations, with only final outstanding problems being referred to such bodies as the UN, the Civil Aviation Organization or the International Court of Justice. However, bilateral negotiations over the Aegean dispute became deadlocked, and war nearly ensued in the summer of 1976 when Turkey sent a seismic survey ship into the Aegean. Tension eased after the two countries agreed in November 1976 to resolve their differences through peaceful and secret negotiations, and to refrain meanwhile from any activities that might impede a settlement.

While Demirel was ready to negotiate seriously with Greece, his hands were virtually tied by Erbakan's hawkish attitude. Furthermore, even the modest

November 1976 agreement—which meant keeping Sismik I out of the disputed waters—was attacked by Ecevit who accused Demirel of "giving in" to Greece. In view of the Government's weakness in the National Assembly and Demirel's own weakness within the coalition, the Greeks felt that any agreement would depend on the 1977 elections producing a strong Government—a hope not fulfilled by the final emergence of the new National Front. Turkey for its part accused Greece of continuing indecision on key issues.

CYPRUS NEGOTIATIONS

On 27 January 1977, the Turkish-Cypriot leader, Rauf Denktaş, took the initiative to open talks with President Makarios—their first in 13 years. Some sources attributed the meeting to Western diplomatic moves;[31] others suggested that the Turkish Government was attempting to prove its "goodwill" in anticipation of a visit by President Carter's special envoy, Clark Clifford, in February.[32] Three days before the meeting, Turkey made an additional gesture by withdrawing 1,000 of its soldiers from Cyprus. Of major significance was the fact that Makarios for the first time publicly discussed the possibility of a federation. At a second session, on 13 February, it was agreed to reopen communal talks (stalled for a year) in Vienna at the end of March.

The second round of talks in Vienna, held from 31 March–7 April, ended without concrete results: irreconcilable differences persisted both over territorial and constitutional issues. The increase in tension between Turkey and Greece over the Aegean in the same period probably influenced the Vienna talks' failure.[33] The two sides met again in Nicosia from 20–26 May, for the sole purpose of getting the Greek economic blockade lifted against the Turkish Cypriots. After apparently succeeding in this, a further meeting was held on 3 June, but only to agree to postpone further negotiations until after the Turkish general election.

In an interview before the elections, Ecevit said that the situation in Cyprus had hardened since he left office and that the formula he had in mind at the end of 1974 might not be easily applicable now. "However, the basic principle—that is that the island must be allowed to continue as an independent state within a federal framework—should be upheld."[34] Although Ecevit, the man who sanctioned the intervention in Cyprus, was considered by the Greeks and Greek Cypriots as most able to make territorial concessions and yet survive politically, he refrained from taking any positive step towards a settlement in Cyprus during his brief period in office—except to announce the Government's decision to reopen the Magosa's (Famagusta's) Maraş (Varosha) tourism district for settlement.[35]

Amid Greek and Greek-Cypriot protests over Denktaş' initiatives to implement this decision on Famagusta (especially without reciprocal land concessions), President Makarios died on 3 August. Two days later, Turkish Foreign Minister Çağlayangil announced that as before the Turkish Government would not accept a new Greek-Cypriot leader as President of the whole island. He said that until a bi-regional, bi-national, independent and non-aligned state was established, the island would be governed by two autonomous administrations equal in all respects. Ecevit was the only leading Turkish politician to extend condolences to the Greek-Cypriot community for its loss in the death of Makarios.

The Greek-Cypriot Government called for an urgent session of the UN Security Council on 27 August to discuss Turkey's "continued violations" of UN resolutions and the resettlement of Maraş.[36] Çağlayangil suggested that the Greek-Cypriot complaints would only make the resumption of intercommunal talks more difficult. He insisted that the Maraş district was no different from any other region in the TFSC. During the UN debates at the beginning of September, the Turkish

Ambassador, Ilter Türken, claimed that the Greek-Cypriot administration had no right to interfere in what was happening in the Turkish sector of the island. The Greek Ambassador, George Papulias, replied that Maraş was an extremely important issue in the intercommunal talks and that the Turkish "colonization" of Famagusta would jeopardize their future. During the debate, on 6 September, Denktaş arrived in Ankara; he stated that if the Greek-Cypriot Government continued to be so intransigent, the only solution would be a declaration of independence, after which the two states could easily work out a formula for federation. However, in spite of Western recognition of the newly-elected Greek-Cypriot leader, Spiros Kiprianou, as President of Cyprus, the Turkish Government is believed to have told Denktaş to refrain from taking action that might prejudice the intercommunal talks.[37] (While the Greek Government's influence on Makarios had been negligible, there was no doubt about Denktaş's dependence on Ankara for both military and economic support.)

The Security Council resolution, adopted on 15 September, called on the Cypriot communities to resume the talks and summoned both sides to refrain from unilateral action. The resolution also expressed concern over Turkey's attempt to resettle Maraş. Despite the mild nature of the resolution, Turkey rejected it, claiming that it constituted interference in the internal affairs of the TFSC.

NEGOTIATIONS WITH GREECE

The first two months of 1977 were marked by such positive developments as the Çağlayangil-Bitsios meeting on 28 January, the resumption of negotiations over air traffic control,[38] and talks over the continental shelf on 31 January–6 February in London. But by March, the negotiations were once again deadlocked. Even the simplest issue—the reopening of Aegean airspace to international flights—ran into difficulties. RPP accusations that the Government had made a "secret agreement" with Greece in order to please the US were promptly denied.

Responsibility for the lack of progress was laid at the door of the National Security Council (NSC),[39] and especially its army commanders, who had recommended a "tough line" on Cyprus and the Aegean following Bitsios' rejection of the Turkish proposal for joint oil exploration. Greece's intention was ultimately to extend its territorial waters to 12 miles, although for the time being it was ready to agree to six miles, provided that a ten-mile airspace control zone over the islands was recognized. It proposed that Turkey give Greece ten minutes advance notice of aircraft flying west, while Greece would inform Turkey of eastward flights only four minutes in advance.[40] The NSC response was to stage air and naval exercises in the Aegean between 21–27 March, which evoked strong Greek protests and further intensified tensions between the two countries. The NSC insisted that the exercises were "routine" and that the Aegean was not a "Greek sea."[41] Much verbal wrangling ensued, with Greece deciding to hold military manoeuvres at the same time.

After what was described as an "imposed meeting" between Çağlayangil and Bitsios in Strasbourg on 28 April,[42] negotiations on the continental shelf resumed on 31 May in Paris; and on airspace through diplomatic channels. The agenda provided for discussions: 1) on the establishment in principle of a special committee to start substantive talks on the continental shelf and on the airspace issue; and 2) on Turkey's proposals submitted at the beginning of March (including its consent to the continental shelf concept, provided that Greece did not increase its territorial waters to 12 miles and agreed to equal demarcation of the Aegean Sea).[43] As a prerequisite to any agreement, Turkey also insisted that the Aegean islands be demilitarized. Talks on the continental shelf ended on 3 June with no visible progress.[44]

Relations again deteriorated after the elections, probably due to Greece's disappointment with the resurrection of the Nationalist Front; developments in Cyprus; and further Turkish naval and air manoeuvres in the Aegean, which led to the reinforcement of Greek forces in the Aegean islands on 30 July. Negotiations were not resumed until 2 October.

Another complicating factor had been introduced at the beginning of January when the world press published a confidential report, prepared for the European Commission of Human Rights, in which Turkey was indicted for consistently violating six articles of the European Convention on Human Rights in Cyprus. The report, submitted to the Council of Europe in August 1976, had been kept secret because of pressure by EEC and NATO countries who feared that it would lead to Turkey's withdrawal or expulsion from the European Council. In fact, the report was probably "leaked" by Greece. Turkey described the report as "unfair and incomplete" as it embraced only a short period following the 1974 "peace operation" in Cyprus, and did not cover either the period between Christmas 1963 and July 1974 (during which "Greek Cypriots committed numerous atrocities against the Turkish Cypriots), or the atrocities committed against Turkish Cypriots by the Greeks after the war."[45]

The publication of the report also aggravated the problem of the Turkish minority in western Thrace. Turkish Government and opposition members both accused Greece of oppressing the Turkish minority, in violation of the 1923 Lausanne Treaty. The opposition also accused the Government of remaining indifferent to the suffering of the Turks in western Thrace, and demanded a forceful stand. Greece refuted the charges and claimed that it was Turkey who was violating the Lausanne Treaty by systematically discriminating against the Greek minority in Turkey. After the elections, both the Ecevit and the Demirel Governments promised that the rights of this Turkish minority would be safeguarded.

THE US AND NATO

Turkish-US relations, strained since the Turkish intervention in Cyprus, remained unchanged during 1976–7. The ban on arms supplies imposed by Congress on 5 February 1975 was only partially lifted on 2 October 1975, and the Defence Cooperation Agreement (DCA) was still stalled in Congress.[46] Both restrictions were intended to encourage the Turkish Government to negotiate a settlement over Cyprus. Nevertheless, Turkish politicians insisted that defence relations with the US were based on their mutual membership in NATO; that the Cyprus issue concerned only Turkey and Greece and the two Cypriot communities; and that they would not make concessions under pressure. The US attitude was seen as unilateral hostility by one NATO member against another. It seemed unreasonable to Ankara that the US should withhold arms supplies to its NATO partner, while providing military equipment to some 90 other countries, including communist Yugoslavia.

The US embargo and failure to ratify the DCA undoubtedly affected the Turkish army. Gen Sancar admitted in an interview in January that the army was having difficulties in maintaining NATO's strategic requirements.[47] NATO's supreme commander, Gen Alexander Haig, appealed in March for the embargo to be lifted, as Turkey's military strength was being reduced by 50% while Soviet military power increased.[48] Without US aid, there were doubts about Turkey's ability to protect the alliance's south-east flank. Having to pay for armaments from other sources, the embargo also put a strain on Turkey's already-low foreign exchange reserves.

Carter's election aroused disappointment in Turkey. Unlike Ford and Kissinger, who had argued that the crucial factor in the two countries' relations was Turkey's strategic value, Carter and Vance maintained that ratification of the DCA should be linked to progress on the Cyprus dispute. The Carter Administration's first decision did little to allay Turkish anxiety of a new pro-Greek policy in Washington. On 19 January, the Carter Administration decided to postpone any action on ratification of the DCA until a general survey of foreign policy in the region had been made. This decision renewed demands among some Turkish politicians for a revision of the country's military and political orientation, since the Americans appeared to be favouring the Greek cause. The Supreme Military Council, at its meeting on 8 February, noted that it had been a mistake to depend solely on NATO for armaments and war preparations. However, most Government members including Demirel, though severely critical of the US, stressed Turkey's commitment to the West.

President Carter's special envoy, Clark Clifford, began his "fact-finding" visit to Greece, Turkey and Cyprus in February, but failed to bridge the main differences between the US and Turkey. Demirel refuted Greek claims that Turkey was following an expansionist policy, and declared that unless the US was impartial, repealed the arms embargo and ratified the DCA, no Government would be able to prevent the liquidation of the US bases in Turkey due to strong anti-American sentiment. Relations would then be irreparably harmed, and the Government would have to reconsider its place in NATO.[49] Demirel admitted that he could not make concessions in a crucial election year, as this might indicate that he was bending under American pressure besides being saddled with Erbakan.[50] He insisted again that the Aegean and Cyprus disputes should be resolved by the parties directly involved.

After taking a month to consider Clifford's report, the US Government decided to endorse the DCA on 20 April, but recommended Congress to act at a "later date"—presumably after progress was made on Cyprus.[51] However, as interim measures, Congress was asked to increase the ceiling on credit for arms sales to Turkey—from $125m in 1977 to $175m in 1978—and to allow the purchase of 40 F-4 Phantoms on a government-to-government basis. (Greece also received Phantoms, as well as a quantity of arms.) Carter's attempt to maintain credibility with both Turkey and Greece pleased neither side. Under pressure from the Greek lobby in the US, the sale of Phantoms was dropped from the plan, and Ankara rejected the alternative proposal to buy them through commercial channels.

Throughout the Turkish election campaign (see above), US officials expressed the hope that either Demirel or Ecevit would win an overall majority and thus be in a position to act decisively. The two party leaders held the same attitude towards the US: both appreciated the importance of friendly relations, but at the same time insisted that continuation of the embargo might cause Turkey to revise its relations with NATO as well as with the US.[52]

Carter and Demirel met in London on 10 May during the NATO conference; but their talk did not produce any concrete results, despite the President's statement that military aid to Turkey should be separated from the Cyprus problem. Demirel insisted that Turkish-US relations should not impinge upon the Cyprus problem, and that no Turkish Government would make concessions against the wishes of the nation. He again hinted that unless the embargo was lifted, public opinion might force the Government to leave NATO; in any case, without arms, Turkey could not fulfil its commitments. NATO's secretary-general, Joseph Luns, confirmed that the rift between Turkey and Greece was a major threat to the alliance.

Finally, on 21 July, the US Congress approved $175m in military aid for Turkey (the $75m grant conditional on progress on the Cyprus issue was deleted from the bill). But this did not satisfy Turkey: Demirel repeated that as long as the US was using arms to pressure Turkey to settle the Cyprus issue, no progress was possible.

The tension in Turkish-US relations continued throughout Çağlayangil's talks in

Washington at the end of September. The Americans were reported to have demanded a written assurance about Turkey's readiness to make concessions on Cyprus, including territorial concessions; but this was refused by Çağlayangil. Reported difficulty in obtaining a US bank loan aroused suspicions that the US Administration was also planning to impose an economic embargo—as claimed by Ecevit. This was denied by US officials.

RELATIONS WITH THE EUROPEAN ECONOMIC COMMUNITY (EEC)

Turkey's application for EEC membership in 1959 (within two years of the Community's foundation) as well as its participation in NATO, had symbolized its commitment to the West. A pre-association agreement signed in June 1963 provided for a transition period of 12 years during which Turkey was gradually to withdraw protective legislation and place its economy on a competition footing *vis-à-vis* the EEC countries.

Most of the difficulties between the EEC and Turkey over the association agreement during 1976-7 stemmed from the additional protocol signed in 1970 which became operative in 1973. The EEC's refusal to permit a total revision of the protocol embittered relations. Turkey demanded better access for its agricultural products and complained that other Mediterranean countries which had subsequently signed agreements with the EEC obtained more favourable preferences than Ankara. It also demanded special concessions to protect its developing industry, and insisted that its trade deficit with the EEC—which in 1976 reached $1,400m—proved that the agreement was one-sided. However, the major problem concerned Article 36 of the additional protocol which called for complete freedom of movement for Turkish workers in EEC countries by 1986, to be gradually implemented. The EEC Commission wanted this to start in December 1976, but the EEC Council of Ministers failed to agree because of serious unemployment within EEC countries. In response, Turkey threatened to freeze the association agreement until the Community fulfilled its obligations.

Turkish workers in Europe are of great economic and social importance for the country. During the period under review, the official unemployment rate in Turkey was 2m, but unofficially much higher. The situation could become even more acute because of the large numbers joining the labour market, and eventually result in a serious social crisis. Even though workers' remittances had declined from $1,300m in 1975 to $1,150m in 1976, they still remained an important source of badly-needed hard currency.

The EEC agreed to provide some agricultural facilities and a loan of $385m to finance agricultural and industrial projects, but no progress was made over any of the major issues. Turkey reacted by excluding the EEC from its import quotas in January 1977. Relations were further strained when the EEC decided to reduce textile imports from Turkey by 50%; at the end of September 1977, the Community was reported to be planning to curtail these imports altogether.[53] An additional difficulty was the prospect of Greece becoming a full EEC member. This was strongly opposed by Turkey which feared that Greece might exploit its position and try to keep Turkey out of the Community.

The EEC's reluctance to concede to Turkish demands weakened the JP's stand within the Government. Erbakan became more insistent on severing all ties with the West and turning to the Islamic East. He claimed that the EEC was treating Turkey as a second-rate nation, and that the country's economy and industry could survive competition from the Arab world but not from Western Europe. The JP could hardly make any concessions to the EEC before the election as these would have been exploited by the party's opponents during the campaign; nor could it make any concessions afterwards because it needed NSP co-operation in the new coalition government.

Turkey continued to purchase weapons and military equipment from West Germany, including *Leopard* tanks. It also received financial aid from Bonn. Two agreements were signed with Italy: one for $1,000m to promote economic relations, and one to build a "maritime bridge" between the two countries.

RELATIONS WITH THE MIDDLE EAST AND ISLAMIC WORLD

Since the 1964 Cyprus crisis, Turkey has attempted to improve its relations with the non-aligned nations, particularly some of the Arab and non-Arab Muslim states. This trend was further strengthened after the Turkish intervention in Cyprus in July 1974, when it sought support in the Islamic world which the West failed to provide. Turkey considered itself the most economically developed of the Muslim countries, and therefore hoped to find export markets for its consumer goods. It also hoped to raise petrodollars from oil-rich Arab countries for investment in industrial and other development projects, as well as purchase oil at prices lower than those fixed by OPEC. Although NSP pressure on the Government to reorient its foreign policy had some influence, its demand for an Islamic common market was not taken seriously.[54]

These new links with Arab states were marked by the convening of the seventh Conference of Islamic Foreign Ministers in Istanbul in May 1976, a particularly significant development in view of Turkey's constitutionalized secularism. Ankara made two gestures towards the Arab world. First, it announced its intention of becoming a full member of the conference and ratified its charter—a step it had been reluctant to take before. Second, it announced that it would allow the PLO to open an office in Turkey, a move it had also previously refused, possibly because of co-operation between extreme Leftist groups inside the country and Palestinian organizations. However, no step towards opening a PLO office had been taken by late 1977—supposedly because of the war in Lebanon.[55] Although Turkey in turn won conference approval for its stand on Cyprus, the Muslim countries failed to support Ankara on the same issue at the Non-Aligned Conference in Colombo in August 1976.

The eighth Islamic Conference, held from 16–23 May 1977 in Tripoli, affirmed the "political equality" of the two communities in a Cypriot federal state, and called for economic support for the TFSC. Syria and Lebanon opposed the Turkish draft resolution on Cyprus at committee-level, declaring their support for the Non-Aligned Conference resolution. However, they were reported to have made no reservations at the plenary meeting. The conference endorsed an economic, technical and commercial co-operation agreement, which laid down principles for the expansion of trade, encouragement of mutual investment and capital movements, and priority in labour exchange among member-countries. The resolution's acceptance was largely due to Turkey's efforts and stood to benefit her greatly.

There was also a shift away from Turkey's traditional neutrality in the Arab-Israeli conflict to a more pro-Arab position. Turkey supported Arab resolutions in the UN, including the one against Zionism. The Government also called for Israeli withdrawal from the occupied territories, and for recognition of the "legitimate rights of the Palestinians."[56] In a message to the Egyptian Foreign Minister on 28 August, Çağlayangil expressed anxiety over the establishment of new Israeli settlements on the West Bank.

The programmes of Ecevit and Demirel both called for strengthened relations with Muslim countries; the Demirel government further emphasized that a solution to the Arab-Israeli conflict would be possible only if Israel withdrew to the pre-1967 borders and recognized the legitimate rights of the Palestinian people. However, despite Arab pressure, Turkey was reluctant to impose an economic embargo on Israel or to break its diplomatic ties. (Israel participated in the İzmir International Fair in August 1977.)

The Demirel government fostered special links with radical Iraq and Libya. The latter in particular responded favourably to the new pro-Islamic trend in Turkey, providing unconditional support during and after the intervention in Cyprus. Libya also supplied one-quarter of Turkey's oil imports in 1976–7—3m out of a total of 12m tons—and agreed on 29 August 1977 to sell its oil on privileged terms. In addition, over the last two years Libya has become the main importer of Turkish labour: as of 10 August 1977, Libya employed 20,000 Turkish workers. (Saudi Arabia also supplies 3m tons of oil per year and employs Turkish workers, though not on as large a scale as Libya.)

A number of economic co-operation agreements were signed between Libya and Turkey in 1976–7, including a major road construction programme in Libya; a joint maritime transportation company; and a joint shipbuilding and repair company. On 5 April 1977, an Arab-Turkish bank was formed with a capital of $15m to which Turkey and Libya each contributed 40% and Kuwait 20%. Its main purpose was to help the three countries in investment and foreign trade.

Iraqi-Turkish co-operation was marked by the opening of the Kirkuk-Yumurtalık oil pipeline on 3–4 January 1977, thus ensuring a constant flow of crude oil through Turkey which is expected to earn c. $100m a year in transit fees. Iraq stopped pumping oil into the pipeline at the beginning of March over a disagreement on prices, but on 13 April this was resolved. Water was also an important element in economic co-operation: Iraq needed Turkey's support in any future agreement between themselves and Syria over the division of the Euphrates waters. Both relatively isolated politically, the two countries also co-operated in such fields as tourism and communications, operating several joint projects including the expansion of the İskenderun port and the building of a motorway to link İskenderun to Iraq. A loan of $1,200m was also promised by Iraq in May; an agricultural co-operation agreement was signed in March.

Turkey's relations with Egypt have remained relatively cool, due primarily to Cairo's unconditional support for Makarios. A visit by Çaglayangil to Egypt was postponed several times.

For relations with Iran and membership in CENTO, see Iran—Foreign Relations.

THE COMMUNIST BLOC

Turkey's northern neighbour has been its traditional enemy since the Ottoman period, and subsequently fears of the USSR have always dominated Ankara's foreign relations. Nevertheless, since the beginning of the Cyprus crisis in 1964 when relations with the US began to turn sour—and especially after the 1967 crisis—Turkey began mending fences with Moscow. The US arms embargo accelerated the change, although economic co-operation had already developed considerably. This trend culminated with the announcement by Demirel and Kosygin (during the latter's visit to Ankara in January 1976) that the two countries would sign a "political document" on friendship and co-operation: this fell short of the Soviet wish to sign a non-aggression treaty. Nevertheless, the proposed agreement symbolized a profound improvement in relations between the two countries. A joint communiqué issued at the end of Çağlayangil's visit to Moscow (14–19 March 1977) disclosed that the "political document" would be signed during future high-level discussions.[57] However, Demirel's planned visit to the USSR did not take place in 1977. Both major Turkish parties made it clear that although Turkey would not withdraw from NATO, they are pledged to promote closer relations with Moscow. the Soviet attitude towards the Cyprus issue has contributed to this positive response.

Soviet-Turkish economic ties are particularly significant as the USSR now became Turkey's principal source of investment capital. An agreement was signed on 15 March 1977 by which Moscow will provide credit of $1,200m over a period of ten years for industrial projects.[58] It also covered scientific technical and cultural co-operation. On 9 August, the two countries reached an agreement in principle for electricity networks to be implemented in 1978. A confidential study by the Rand Corporation stated that "the Soviets will probably make a quiet breakthrough—already well prepared—in Turkey, the recipient of the largest amount of Soviet aid last year, which will eventually lead to a fundamental change in the balance of power in the Mediterranean."[59]

Turkey also developed close economic relations with East European countries, principally Hungary, Romania and Bulgaria. Agreements were signed on production and marketing of agricultural goods, transport, oil and coal exploitation, and electric power to be supplied to Turkey by Bulgaria.

ECONOMIC AFFAIRS (1 US$ = 17.67 Turkish lira; £1 sterling = TL 34.28)
Measures to tackle Turkey's economic crisis were delayed until after the general elections. Finally, on 8 September 1977, Demirel announced a programme of economic austerity measures designed to cope with inflation and the foreign exchange crisis. (Gold and foreign exchange reserves had dropped to $570m on 30 August from $630m on 5 August.) Price increases were allowed on basic commodities and services; for example, the price of petrol, previously subsidized, went up by over 96%. The new measures were mainly designed to increase exports and decrease the trade deficit. Exports were $884m from January-June 1977, 24% lower than in 1976. The trade deficit was $3,079m in the same period, 74% higher than in 1976. "Luxury" imports were restricted, including expensive cars; spending by Turkish tourists abroad was curtailed. The long-expected devaluation was announced only on 21 September, when the Turkish lira was devalued 10% against the dollar—only half the rate Turkish and foreign bankers had thought necessary. This move followed a visit by an IMF delegation from which the Government sought a $400m credit.

GROSS NATIONAL PRODUCT
In real terms, GNP increased by 8.1% in 1976, slightly more than the 8% real growth achieved in 1975. It is estimated that (on the basis of 1968 prices), 23% of total resources were allocated for investments and 77% for consumption in 1976, as in 1975. Likewise, compared with 1975, investment expenditure rose by 7.4% and consumption by 6.4%, against the respective rates of increase of 18.6% and 6.3% in 1975 over 1974.

AGRICULTURE
According to the preliminary estimates, agricultural product in 1976 increased by 9.2% at constant prices over 1975 (cf an increase of 10.9% in 1975), the fairly high agricultural output in 1975 being mainly due to favourable weather conditions. In 1976, harvests were smaller in rye, chick peas, cotton, sultanas and pistachios, although substantial increases were expected in wheat, tobacco, lentils and olives.

INDUSTRY
Industrial product registered a real growth of 10.3% in 1976 (cf the 9% increase

attained in 1975). Despite various adverse factors, manufacturing industries showed a faster rate of real growth in 1976 than in 1975, due to new plants becoming operational, expansions, and increased capacity utilization spurred on by keener demand. The fastest increases were realized in the tobacco, glass, non-ferrous metals and printing industries, but especially in petro-chemicals, commercial fertilizers and shipbuilding.

BALANCE OF TRADE

The trade deficit amounted to $3,169m in 1976, a decrease of 5% from 1975. The pronounced increase in exports (+40%) during 1976 resulted largely from growth in Turkey's traditional exports, as well as from increased exports in industrial products. The slowdown in imports (an increase of 8% in 1976 as against 25% in 1975) can be mainly imputed to Government restrictions (see above).

West Germany was the most important market for Turkish exports (19%), followed by the US (10%), Switzerland and Italy (9% each) and the UK (7%). West Germany also remained the major supplier of Turkish imports (18%), followed by Iraq (12%), the US and UK (8% each) and Italy (5.5%).

BALANCE OF PAYMENTS

The deficit in the overall balance of payments in 1976 increased to $1,751m (cf a deficit of $1,360m in 1975). This was financed by a decrease of $112m in reserves, by IMF loans (utilization of SDRs) amounting to $149m, and by an inflow of short-term capital totalling $1,520m. Thus the deficit in the balance of current account grew from $1,880m in 1975 to $2,286m in 1976. The pronounced decrease in net income from invisibles was caused mainly by the decline in workers' remittances, which dropped from $1,312m in 1975 to $983m in 1976. An analysis of the capital account (comparing 1975 to 1976) indicates that the influx of foreign private capital dropped from $153m to $27m, whilst repayments of external debt increased from $118m to $119m, project loans from $381m to $485m, imports with waivers from $98m to $136m. As a result, the favourable balance on the capital account rose from $520m to $535m in 1976.

GENERAL BUDGET

The consolidated budget in 1976 showed revenues at TL 154,247m, an increase of more than 36% over 1975. This increase was mainly due to increases in tax revenue and domestic borrowing by the Government. As projected, expenditure will amount to TL 153,440m, permitting a surplus of TL 807m (cf a surplus of TL 644m in 1975).

INVESTMENTS AND DEVELOPMENT PLAN

According to estimates by the State Planning Organization, fixed capital investment at 1976 prices increased by TL 16,743m (13%) in 1976 over 1975, reaching a total of TL 144,486m. In 1976, whereas fixed capital investment in the public sector fell short of the Development Plan target, that in the private sector exceeded the target. In both sectors, however, fixed capital investment was estimated to have risen more slowly in 1976 than in 1975. The allocations to manufacturing industries and housing in the total fixed capital investment declined; those to tourism and education remained unchanged; but in the case of agriculture, mining, energy and transport, increases were pronounced. As a result, the volume of employment in non-agricultural sectors is estimated to have grown by 327,000 to 5,806,000 in 1976, an increase of 6% over 1975, when growth was only by 5.3%. However, these achievements are slight compared with the targets fixed in the Annual Programme of the Third Five-Year Development Plan.

(Economic section by Moshe Efrat)

BALANCE OF PAYMENTS (million Dollars)

	1974	1975	1976
Current Account			
Foreign Trade:			
Exports (fob)	1,532	1,401	1,960
Imports (cif)	-3,778	-4,739	-5,129
Trade balance	-2,246	-3,338	-3,169
Invisible transactions (net)	1,500	1,435	868
Infrastructure and Offshore	27	23	15
Balance of current account	*-719*	*-1,880*	*-2,286*
Capital transactions:			
External debts repayments	-126	-118	-119
Private foreign capital	88	154	27
Project credits	269	381	485
Imports with waivers	58	98	136
Programme credits	2	5	6
Balance on capital transactions	*291*	*520*	*535*
Overall Balance	**-428**	**-1,360**	**-1,751**
Reserve movements (+ = decrease)	431	417	112
Special drawings rights	-8	301	149
Short-term capital movements	60	666	1,520
Net errors and omissions	-55	-24	-30

Source: Bank of Turkey, *Economic Indicators 1972–76*; Economic Research Department, Ankara.

PUBLIC FINANCE (million TL)

	1974	1975	1976
A. Revenue—Consolidated budget	74,997	113,697	154,247
Tax Revenues	64,678	93,481	126,949
Direct Taxes	29,774	44,049	
Indirect Taxes	34,904	49,432	
Revenues other than Taxes	3,783	9,745	10,494
Special Revenues and Funds	1,317	990	2,819
Domestic Borrowing	3,603	7,428	10,974
Net Revenues from Annexed Budgets	1,616	2,053	3,011
B. Expenditure	76,170	113,053	153,440
Balance Deficit (-) or Surplus (+)	**-1,173**	**+664**	**+807**

Source: Bank of Turkey; *Economic Indicators 1972–76.*

MAIN TRADE PARTNERS (millions Dollars)

Exports to:	1974	1975	1976
Federal Germany	343.0	304.9	376.7
United States	144.2	147.1	191.4
Switzerland	94.2	95.8	179.6
Italy	90.3	82.1	171.5
United Kingdom	81.6	70.1	137.6
France	66.6	61.9	108.4
Belgium	67.6	30.3	85.9
Netherlands	52.4	50.8	63.8
Lebanon	109.7	66.5	55.4
Iraq	30.2	45.2	41.1
Japan	18.1	28.7	36.0
Iran	15.1	37.1	33.6
Syria	29.7	25.1	32.3
Romania	6.0	6.6	30.6
Portugal	4.5	10.6	29.9
Total (including others)	**1,532.0**	**1,400.9**	**1,960.2**

Imports from:			
Federal Germany	680.9	1,057.7	945.6
Iraq	327.4	504.2	644.4
United States	350.4	425.8	438.2
Italy	270.8	357.9	386.1
United Kingdom	266.9	344.3	409.9
France	244.9	278.7	308.7
Switzerland	210.9	281.3	280.4
Libya	5.7	78.0	233.7
Japan	199.2	211.4	227.8
Netherlands	116.2	138.9	168.0
Iran	42.3	26.1	109.3
Belgium	106.7	129.3	103.3
Romania	78.0	59.7	90.0
Austria	55.3	60.2	61.0
Canada	49.6	58.8	55.0
Total (including others)	**3,776.8**	**4,737.8**	**5,129.9**

Source: IMF Direction of Trade 1970–76.

NOTES

1. *Milliyet*, Istanbul; and *Cumhuriyet*, Istanbul; 17 May 1977. Both printed telegrams of complaint to this effect, which had been sent to the Foreign Ministry by the ambassador to Tokyo and the consul-general in Geneval.
2. *Milliyet*, 24 April 1977.
3. Named after the legendary wolf which is supposed to have led the Turks from Central Asia to Asia Minor.
4. Named after the corps of light cavalry in the Ottoman Empire.
5. *The Guardian*, London; 28 February 1977. *International Herald Tribune (IHT)*, Paris; 25 May 1977. *Milliyet*, 4 January 1977, *Amnesty International Report*, May 1977.
6. Demirel referred to the pardon given by the Ecevit government to Leftists in May 1974.
7. *Pulse*, Ankara; 6 January 1977.
8. *Financial Times* (*FT*), London; 14 July 1977.
9. In 1976, Özaydınlı's candidacy for Commander of the Air Force was vetoed by Erbakan. He resigned from the army on 6 April, and on 5 June was elected RPP Senator.
10. *Milliyet*, 11 February 1977; *Outlook*, Ankara; 2 March 1977.
11. The budget vote is traditionally considered a vote of confidence, though the constitution is not explicit about it.
12. R Ankara, 20 March 1977—BBC Summary of World Broadcasts, the Middle East and Africa (BBC), 22 March 1977.
13. *Pulse*, 24 March 1977.
14. The party had been closed down in 1971, but it was re-established in May 1975, after the general amnesty.
15. The founders of the "Republican Party" founded by RPP members who defected after Ecevit had become chairman in May 1972. The Republicans merged with Feyzioğlu's National Reliance Party.
16. On 27 October 1976, Paksu resigned both from his position as Minister of Labour and from the Party's General Executive Board after inter-party strife had come to a head at the Board election two days earlier, when a group of dissidents close to Paksu were purged from the party's executive.
17. *Outlook*, 15 June 1977, p. 17.
18. *Ibid*, 8 May 1977, p. 15.
19. For a detailed record of results throughout the country, see *Diplomat*, Ankara; 22 June 1977, pp. 4-5.
20. *Cumhuriyet*, 8 June; *Milliyet*, 9 August 1977.
21. For the Government's programme, see *Cumhuriyet*, 29 June 1977.
22. Both were previously members of the RPP, but were rejected by the party's administration because of their radical views.
23. *Milliyet*, 21 July 1977.
24. *Diplomat*, 10 August 1977.
25. Erbakan's former Order Party (*Nizam Partisi*) was banned under this law in 1971.
26. R Ankara, 23 July—BBC, 26 July 1977. For further details on the programme, see *Cumhuriyet*, 28 July 1977.

27. In accordance with his demands on 26 August, Erbakan was appointed chairman of the interministerial Economic Council and the Turkish Scientific and Technical Research Institution.
28. *Outlook*, 9 March 1977, p. 7; *Pulse*, 22 January 1977.
29. *The Military Balance 1977-78* (London: International Institute of Strategic Studies).
30. For details, see Suat Bilge, "The Cyprus Conflict and Turkey" in Kemal H Karpat, *Turkey's Foreign Policy 1950-75* (Leiden, 1975), 135-85.
31. *Christian Science Monitor*, Boston; 27 January 1977. *The Guardian*, 27 January 1977.
32. *FT*, 18 February 1977. See also, *Washington Post*, 11 February 1977 and *The Times*, London; 26 February 1977.
33. See also, *Milliyet*, 10 April 1977 and *Tercüman*, Istanbul; 8 April 1977.
34. *IHT*, 23 May 1977.
35. Since 1974, Magosa had remained in the military zone and was considered an important bargaining counter for the resettlement of 40,000 Greek refugees, and thus a means of at least partially solving the refugee problem.
36. *The Guardian*, 30 August 1977. The UN resolution of 14 November 1974, which was accepted by Turkey, called on all parties involved to respect the sovereignty, independence and territorial integrity of Cyprus, to withdraw all foreign forces and to allow for the return of refugees to their homes.
37. *Milliyet*, 8 September 1977.
38. *Tercüman*, 31 January 1977.
39. *Cumhuriyet*, 1 March 1977.
40. *Ibid.*
41. *Ibid*, 17 March 1977; *Milliyet*, 17 March 1977.
42. *Milliyet*, 29 April 1977.
43. *Ibid.*
44. There was no definite information about the talks concerning airspace.
45. *The Guardian*, 20 January 1977.
46. Demirel's Government responded to the arms embargo by stopping operational activities in all 27 US bases in Turkey, except İncirlik—reportedly the most important one. For details on DCA, see *The Middle East*, London; May 1976.
47. *Outlook*, 26 January 1977.
48. *Pulse*, 3 March 1977.
49. *Milliyet*, 23 February 1977.
50. *FT*, 22 February 1977.
51. *Milliyet*, 14 and 23 April 1977. *Outlook*, 4 and 25 May 1977. R Ankara, 22 April 1977.
52. For reactions to Carter's policy, see interview with Demirel and Ecevit in *IHT*, 23 May; *Milliyet*, 27 May; and *Washington Post*, 22 April 1977.
53. *Milliyet*, 27 September 1977.
54. *Outlook*, 28 September 1977, pp. 7-8.
55. *Pulse*, 2 May 1977.
56. Demirel, on 23 February 1977, at a dinner party organized by ambassadors from Arab countries. Çağlayangil, during his visit to Saudi Arabia and the UAE in March. In a joint communiqué released after Saddam Ḥusayn's visit to Turkey in February.
57. For claims that the USSR pressed Çağlayangil to commit Turkey to political "consultation" in advance of any military operation, see *IHT*, 27 April 1977; *Milliyet*, 15 March 1977.
58. These included iron and steel, aluminium, thermal power, generator and turbine projects.
59. *IHT*, 27 April 1977.

The Yemeni Arab Republic

Al-Jumhūriyya al-'Arabiyya Al-Yamaniyya

TAMAR YEGNES

The assassination of the Chairman of the Military Command Council, Ibrāhīm al-Ḥamdī, in October 1977 followed a period of severe internal disturbances and disputes in North Yemen. During his three-year tenure of office, Ḥamdī had attempted—for the most part unsuccessfully—to manoeuvre between two conflicting and hostile forces. The first was the northern tribal chiefs headed by the powerful leader of the Ḥāshid tribal confederation, 'Abdallah al-Aḥmar, who had strong connections with Saudi Arabia. The second was the National Democratic Front, composed of six small Leftist organizations and backed, morally and in other ways, by the People's Democratic Republic of Yemen (PDRY or South Yemen). Ḥamdī's attempt to balance these two forces had repercussions on the country's foreign policy, which wavered between a strong Saudi orientation (encouraged by Saudi financial assistance) and a tentative movement towards South Yemen in line with traditional aspirations for unification. This situation was compounded by religious differences: most of the tribes belong to the Zaydī sect of the Shi'ī branch of Islam, whereas most of the townspeople and inhabitants of the coastal plain are Sunnīs of the Shāfi'ī school.

POLITICAL AFFAIRS

THE ROLE OF IBRĀHĪM AL-ḤAMDĪ (1974–76)

Since the reconciliation agreement between the Republicans and the Royalists reached under Saudi auspices in mid-1970, the most outstanding event in Yemeni politics was undoubtedly the "corrective movement" (*ḥaraka tasḥīḥiyya*) of 13 June 1974. This was led by Col Ibrāhīm Muḥammad al-Ḥamdī who, at the age of 35, was already regarded as an experienced military commander. Two years earlier, he had been appointed the Deputy Commander-in-Chief to 'Abd al-Raḥmān al-Iryānī, Chairman of the Republican Council. Following almost four years of frequent political upheavals and serious economic and social problems, Ḥamdī seized power in an apparently bloodless coup, assisted mainly by several senior military officers. He abolished the Republican Council, the Consultative Council and the Permanent Constitution,[1] and in their place established a seven-member Military Command Council (MCC), with himself as chairman as well as Commander-in-Chief of the armed forces.

The Military Commanders formed the mainstay of Ḥamdī's power base—two in particular. The first was Ḥamdī's brother, 'Abdallah, who commanded the 'Amāliqa (Giants) Brigade, which was composed of 13,000 soldiers, equipped with modern arms, with its headquarters in the Dhamār area (between San'ā and Ta'izz). The second was Maj 'Abdallah 'Abd al-'Ālim, an MCC member and commander of the Paratroops Brigade. These two brigades were the ones usually called upon to suppress periodic tribal rebellions.

One of Ḥamdī's first measures was to abolish the Consultative Council (*majlis shūrā*)—the supreme legislative body which was responsible for supervising the Executive authority and was headed by the powerful chief of the northern Ḥāshid tribal confederation, 'Abdallah al-Aḥmar, who was then restricted to his tribal stronghold in the Khamir area. By abolishing the Consultative Council, Hamdī deprived the tribal chiefs of one of their major sources of power. Over the previous eight years, however, the tribal chiefs had also received official and unofficial allocations of arms as a means of securing their loyalty, and had thus strengthened their position in the Consultative Council, to the extent that they exercised a virtual veto power over any decisions regarded as detrimental to their interests.

In pursuit of his declared policy of thoroughly centralizing administrative and economic activity, Ḥamdī considerably reduced the unofficial allocations to the tribal chiefs, which further curtailed their power. At the same time, the central authority in San'ā tried unsuccessfully to persuade them to hand over their heavy weapons—a measure vehemently opposed by the tribes who, throughout Hamdī's tenure, waged a campaign of harassment and obstruction which led to sporadic armed clashes. These activities had the covert support—primarily in arms and gold—of the Saudis, who used the tribal chiefs as a counterweight to the central authority in San'ā, and as such as one of its main vehicles for influencing Yemen's internal affairs. The chiefs were also regarded by Saudi Arabia as a restraint upon Leftist elements in Yemen which had strong links with Aden and were seen to spearhead the penetration of Communist ideas into the region—ideas considered dangerous to the traditional tribal power system throughout the entire Arabian Peninsula.

In an effort to further consolidate his power, Hamdī dismissed his strong-willed Prime Minister, Muḥsin al-'Aynī (suspected of having links with Ba'thist and Leftist elements) in January 1975, apparently with Saudi backing. He appointed in his place 'Abd al-'Azīz 'Abd al-Ghanī, a technocrat and former Minister of the Economy in 1968. Between April and June 1975, Ḥamdī dismissed three further MCC members who were considered sympathetic to the tribes: Mujāhid Abū Shawārib, one of the officers who had helped Hamdī seize power and a brother-in-law of 'Abdallah al-Aḥmar; also Dirham and 'Alī Abū Luḥūm, sons of the shrewd and influential leader of the Nahm tribe and Governor of Hodeida Province, Shaykh Sinān Abū Luḥūm. This left in the MCC, Ḥamdī (as Chairman); 'Abd al-'Azīz 'Abd al-Ghanī (Prime Minister); Lt-Col Aḥmad al-Ghashmī (Deputy Commander-in-Chief and Chief of Staff); and Maj 'Abdallah 'Abd al-'Alim (paratroop commander). Seeing these dismissals as a further threat to their position, the tribes greatly intensified their conflict against Hamdī. In the latter part of 1975 and the beginning of 1976, several prominent tribal leaders, including Aḥmad, reportedly convened "secret meetings" and escalated tribal resistance in an attempt to overthrow the regime.

The regime had not only to contend with civil disturbances caused by the Zaydī tribal chiefs of the north, but also with the persistent and traditional rivalry between the Zaydī's and the relatively more advanced urban Shāfi'ī population of the Tihāma coastal plain and the south. Shāfi'ī officers and civil leaders had gained high military and civil posts during and immediately after the civil war, thereby reducing Zaydī influence over the central authority. Considered to be mainly radical Leftists, their links were with the regime in Aden—another source of tension since the Zaydī tribes, assisted by the Saudis, opposed any meaningful *rapprochement* with the pro-Communist regime of the South. The constant fear of the Shāfi'īs was of losing their recently-gained political and social achievements; Shāfi'ī officers were a volatile element at this time, and several foiled coups were attributed to them. Even the exclusion of the Zaydī Royalist Hamıd al-Dīn family from the 1970 reconciliation agreement between Republicans and Royalists, did little to reduce the deep suspicion among Shāfi'ī leaders of the possible revival of Zaydī power. The latter's close relations with Saudi Arabia since mid-1970 only deepened this suspicion, with Shāfi'i leaders often claiming that the September 1962 revolution in Yemen had done no more than establish a "Zaydī Republic" instead of a "Zaydī Imamate."

After coming to power, Ḥamdī allowed the Shāfi'īs relative political freedom, presumably to channel their grievances in a non-violent way. As a result, six main small radical Leftist organizations came into being.

1) The Yemeni Revolution Democratic Party (*al-ḥizb al-dīmuqrāṭī al-thawrī al-yamanī*)
2) The Democratic People's Union (*ittiḥād al-sha'b al-dīmuqrāṭī*)
3) The Vanguard Popular Party (*ḥizb al-ṭalī'a al-sha'bī*)
4) The Yemeni Labour Party (*ḥizb al-'amal al-yamanī*)
5) The Revolutionary Resistance Party (*ḥizb al-muqāwamīn al-thawriyyīn*)
6) The pro-Iraqi Ba'th Party (*ḥizb al-ba'th al-mu'ayyad lil-Iraq*)

In order to mobilize their influence on the central authority in San'ā and to stand more firmly against "tribalism" (as represented by Aḥmar and his followers), these organizations formed the National Democratic Front (*al-jabha al-waṭaniyya al-dīmuqrāṭiyya*) in 1976.

INTERNAL STRUGGLES (AUGUST 1976–MARCH 1977)

Continuing conflict between the various groups, as well as the struggle for power of each of them *vis-à-vis* the central authority compelled Ḥamdī to devote most of his energies to contending with these forces. He was largely unsuccessful, however, and his tenure was marked by smouldering resentment, resistance and intermittent outbreaks of armed clashes.

A minor Cabinet reshuffle on 24 August 1976—the fourth of that year—was caused by the internal power struggle in which Ḥamdī tried to satisfy the demands of both rival groupings. For example, Education Minister Ḥusayn 'Abdallah al-Maqdamī, known to be sympathetic towards the tribes, was appointed Secretary-General of the Supreme Committee for Administrative and Financial Reform, an important and highly sensitive post which determined tribal allocations. He replaced Aḥmad Qāsim Dahamsh, whom the tribes had regarded as hostile. Dahamsh was appointed Minister of Social, Labour and Youth Affairs. (For composition of the Government, see Table.)

In the following two months, there were reports of sporadic local tribal insurgencies, mainly in the north. Probably in an attempt to calm the tribes, Ḥamdī, announced towards the end of 1976 that a Supreme Committee was working on preparations for free general elections. It was headed by the prestigious 65-year old conservative qādī, Deputy Chief Justice of the Supreme Court, 'Abdallah al-Ḥajrī (who had been Prime Minister from the end of 1972 until autumn 1973, see below). As part of this process, a Consultative Council, representing the tribes, merchants and youth was to be established. At the same time, a new Supreme Committee for Administrative and Financial Reform was set up, one of its main tasks being to "purge corruption"; namely, to supervise the allocations given to the tribes. This new committee was regarded by the tribal leaders as another step towards restricting their influence, since the central authority in San'ā ordered that official payments be given through the committee and government officials, not directly through the tribal leaders. In this way, the authorities tried to circumvent one of the key channels through which the tribal chiefs gained and exercised their power. Meanwhile, probably as a veiled threat to the tribes, Ḥamdī was allowing Leftist officers in exile in South Yemen to return to San'ā, although he did not allow them to join the security forces.

NORTH YEMENI GOVERNMENT (as of August 1976)

Prime Minister	ʻAbd al-ʻAzīz ʻAbd al-Ghanī
Deputy Prime Minister for Foreign and Economic Affairs	Yaḥyā Jughmān
Deputy Prime Minister for Internal Affairs	ʻAbd al-Laṭīf Dayfallah
Interior	Lt-Col Muḥsin al-Yūsufī
Communications	Lt-Col Ḥusayn al-Ghaffārī
Finance	Muḥammad Aḥmad al-Junayd
Local Administration	ʻAbd al-Mālik al-Tayyib
Economy	ʻAlī Luṭf al-Thaur
Foreign Affairs	ʻAbdallah ʻAbd al-Majīd al-Asnaj
Information	Yaḥyā al-ʻArashī
Development and Planning[1]	ʻAbd al-Karīm al-Iryānī
Justice	ʻAlī al-Sammān
Waqf	Muḥammad Lutfī al-Sabbāḥī
Supply	Muḥammad ʻAbd al-Mālik
Social, Labour and Youth Affairs[2]	Aḥmad Qāsim Dahamsh
Health	ʻAbd al-Mālik Muhammad ʻAbdallah
Agriculture	Muḥammad ʻAbd al-Khādim al-Wajīh
Works and Municipalities	ʻAbdallah al-Kurshumī
Ministers of State[3]	Aḥmad ʻAbduh Saʻīd
	ʻAbd al-Karīm al-ʻAnsī
	Salāḥ al-Masrī
	Amīn Ḥasan Abū Ra's

[1] On 19 April 1972, Muḥammad Sālim Basinduh was appointed Minister of Development and also Chairman of the Central Planning Authority.
[2] On 10 October 1977, the Finance Deputy Minister, ʻAbd al-Salām Muḥammad al-Muqbil, was appointed Minister of Social, Labour and Youth Affairs, replacing Aḥmad Qāsim Dahamsh.
[3] At the beginning of October 1977, the Yemeni Ambassador to Federal Republic of Germany, Aḥmad Qā'id Barakāt, was appointed Minister of State and Director of the Mineral Resources Authority.

On 3 January 1977, several tribal chiefs convened a "secret meeting" near Sanʻā in which they called Ḥamdī's regime "communist and atheist" and declared a "holy war" against it. They also formed an Information and Mobilization Committee to rally tribal forces to rebel against Ḥamdī's regime.

Apparently in response to these developments, Ḥamdī held several meetings with the National Democratic Front, which led to the adoption of the following recommendations: 1) "a central state extending its authority to the entire Yemeni area; 2) a strong national army; 3) an end to foreign interference in Yemen's affairs; and 4) an end to and liquidation of the tribal influence." The National Democratic Front wanted to include another resolution calling for a sharp reduction of co-operation with Saudi Arabia, but Ḥamdī rejected this suggestion as nothing but "light-headedness."

In the following months, both Ḥamdī and Prime Minister ʻAbd al-ʻAzīz ʻAbd al-Ghanī denied reports of tribal rebellions on a number of occasions. However, both said that the tribes were still trying to prevent any administrative or financial reform. They also insisted that the time was not yet ripe for a representative (i.e. consultative) council as long as Yemen had "to concentrate on the elimination of the remnants of reaction." [2]

THE ASSASSINATION OF ʻABDALLAH AL-ḤAJRĪ

Qāḍī ʻAbdallah al-Ḥajrī, his wife and a senior Yemeni embassy official were assassinated in London by an unidentified assailant on 10 April 1977.[3] Ḥajrī—who had come specially to England to visit King Khālid of Saudi Arabia, then in a London hospital—was regarded as a zealous supporter of the pro-Saudi orientation. During his tenure as Prime Minister, he had restricted the movements of Leftist elements and opposed all efforts to unify the two Yemens.

Statements made by Yemeni officials and various political groupings shed more light on the country's internal political conflict than on the motivation behind the assassination. The Yemeni Ambassador to London, Muḥammad 'Abdallah al-Iryānī, believed it was "politically motivated," although he said he had no idea who was responsible. Arab and foreign papers commenting on the incident claimed that Ḥajrī was killed by Yemeni Leftists who opposed his pro-Saudi orientation and his connections with the exiled Imam Muḥammad al-Badr, who has lived in London since 1970. Other commentators said it was either revenge by Leftist elements for the arrests and executions that had occurred during Ḥajrī's tenure as Prime Minister, or that it was the work of Yemenis who favoured a union with South Yemen and opposed the inclusion of ex-Royalists in the government and administration. Several reports said the assassination was a result of Palestinian-Yemeni co-operation, a claim categorically denied by the Voice of Palestine which denounced these reports as an attempt "to harm the Palestine Revolution and the Palestinians."[4]

Reports in the Egyptian press attributed the assassination to the internal leadership struggle. According to these reports, the murder was committed by followers of the former Prime Minister, Muḥsin al-'Aynī (who had lived in Cairo and other Arab capitals since his dismissal by Ḥamdī in early 1975),[5] and was carried out in co-operation with the Libyan Criminal Investigation Department in order "to injure the current Yemeni regime which refuses to be a willing tool moving in Libya's orbit."[6] One source even sought to implicate Ḥamdī in the assassination, alleging that in spite of prior information, he had not acted to prevent it.[7]

ESCALATION AND RECONCILIATION

In May and June 1977, there were reports of relations deteriorating further between Ḥamdī and the northern tribes who, from a campaign of harassment, had expanded their activities to include attacks on army convoys, laying mines and setting up roadblocks on the main roads leading from San'ā to the north.

In July 1977, while the Saudis were reportedly trying to mediate between Ḥamdī and Aḥmar, Ḥamdī issued an inflammatory statement on the subject of union with South Yemen. This prompted Aḥmar to mobilize c. 40,000 tribal fighters—often called "Aḥmar's private army"—to launch an attack on the towns of Khamir and Sa'da (a chief Royalist stronghold in the civil war, c. 60 km from the Saudi border). Aḥmar's force succeeded in occupying the two towns and the surrounding mountainous area, but his call did not stir up the tribes of the centre and of the Tihāma coastal plain. However, this occupation lasted only a few days. Using the air force, Ḥamdī launched a swift counter-attack, and drove the rebels back to the Royalists' traditional strongholds in the north-eastern part of the country.

The success of the counter-attack increased Ḥamdī's authority, and represented a severe defeat for Aḥmar. It was also an indication that the Saudis had by then come to regard Ḥamdī as sufficiently reliable for them to reduce their support in money and arms to the tribes. In fact, the tribal leaders had come to be seen as more of a liability than an asset to the Saudis. This was because they had sabotaged Ḥamdī's attempts to bring about social and economic change and thereby endangered joint Saudi-Yemeni economic projects (see below); they also constituted a threat to the stability of Saudi Arabia's borders. Although still hinting at the possibility of renewing direct assistance to the tribes, the Saudis gradually shifted their support to the central authority.

In August 1977, Ḥamdī declared that fighting with the tribes had "caused deep wounds which have endangered the national equilibrium. . . . The tribal structure remains strong, but the republican structure has been strengthened and it continues its work of pacification of the masses." [8] Despite their defeat, the northern tribal forces continued to challenge the central authority; but since mid-1977, it became clear to both Ḥamdī and Aḥmar that neither side could achieve a decisive victory, and they therefore both began to seek reconciliation.

At the beginning of September 1977, it was reported that a "political reconciliation" had been reached between Ḥamdī and Aḥmar to end the "hostilities which broke out in recent months." [9] According to the agreement, Ḥamdī would appoint 'Abdallah al-Aḥmar as MCC Deputy-Chairman for Tribal Affairs; Sinān Abū Luḥūm as MCC Deputy-Chairman for Economic Affairs; and Mujāhid Abū Shawārib as an MCC member. Ḥamdī also agreed to hold general elections for the Consultative Council (although no date was mentioned), and form a 3,000-man "popular army" from among the tribesmen, who would be armed and financed by the government and placed under the command of Mujāhid Abū Shawārib. He further agreed to allow the return of tribal chiefs to their posts in the government, and allow them free movement in the country with their arms and bodyguards; to reshuffle the Cabinet; and to replace the Prime Minister, 'Abd al-'Azīz 'Abd al-Ghanī, with someone more acceptable to the tribal chiefs. The tribal leaders, for their part, agreed to surrender their heavy weapons and withdraw their armed forces from the combat zones (i.e. from the north-eastern areas which were still under the tribes' control). [10]

Following the agreement, Aḥmar left his stronghold in the north with c. 300,000 "heavily armed tribal fighters," and tried to enter the capital to participate in the 15th anniversary celebrations of the 26 September (1962) Revolution, possibly intending this as a demonstration of loyalty. But apprehensive of such an armed tribal force in San'ā, Ḥamdī refused to allow Aḥmar's fighters entry, claiming that their appearance would create an "impression of power and a threat." [11] Arab commentators tended to regard this incident as the first sign that the agreement had failed.

In his anniversary address, Ḥamdī made no direct references to the agreement; instead, he stressed the need to rebuild the armed and security forces. He recalled that the armed forces and security forces "had . . . become an arena for . . . the power centres to win the loyalty of some of these, and to make them protect personal interests. . . . The 13 June Corrective Movement has placed the security forces and armed forces in their natural place. Today they belong to the people and are an obedient instrument in the hands of the people . . . in order to protect the gains, the discipline and the principle of the revolution." [12]

The agreement between Ḥamdī and Aḥmar aroused the opposition of those elements within the government who refused to grant the tribal leaders any political power. Arab sources, which reported a split in the Yemeni leadership, said that the Social, Labour and Youth Affairs Minister, Aḥmad Qāsim Dahamsh, had rejected the line taken by Ḥamdī. At the beginning of October 1977, Dahamsh issued a statement declaring that he opposed the return of the tribal leaders to power "after four years of correction and the reduction of tribal influence." [13] Shortly after this statement, Dahamsh left San'ā for his birthplace in the Khawlān tribal area, east of the city. Although no official statement was issued on Dahamsh's departure, several Arab sources claimed that he had been dismissed. On 10 October, after a week of rumours of Cabinet changes, the Deputy Minister for Financial Affairs, 'Abd al-Salām Muḥammad al-Muqbil, was appointed to the post previously held by Dahamsh. The National Democratic Front issued a statement in support of

Dahamsh, describing him as a friend of the Left.

THE ASSASSINATION OF HAMDĪ

Ḥamdī and his brother, Lt-Col ʻAbdallah al-Ḥamdī, were assassinated on 11 October 1977. The official announcement over R Sanʻā carried at 2100 GMT of the same day provided no details of the assassination; nor did it name any individuals or groups which might be responsible for it. The statement simply declared that "criminal hands, which have betrayed their people and homeland, took the life of the leader . . . whom our entire people had known as a devout leader, a unique struggler and a faithful leader." [14]

Later that day, the MCC met and appointed MCC member Lt-Col Ahmad Ḥusayn al-Ghashmī as Chairman and Commander-in-Chief of the armed forces. The Prime Minister, ʻAbd al-ʻAzīz ʻAbd al-Ghanī, and the Paratroops Commander, ʻAbdallah ʻAbd al-ʻĀlim, continued as members. On 12 October, the MCC announced that the Cabinet would continue in office. The new MCC Chairman set up a commission of inquiry to investigate the assassination, which included the following as members: the Deputy Chief of Staff, Lt-Col ʻAlī Shayba (Chairman); the Interior Minister, Lt-Col Muḥsin al-Yūsufī; and the Head of the Central National Security Organization (referred to by several sources as the Director of the Military Intelligence), Lt-Col Muḥammad al-Khamīs. [15]

The regime treated the assassination as a political and an internal matter. The Foreign Ministry told the heads of diplomatic missions in Sanʻā that there was no need to send delegates to Ibrāhīm al-Ḥamdī's funeral, held on 13 October 1977. Nonetheless, South Yemen's President, Sālim ʻAlī Rubay', chose to attend (see below). The Foreign Minister also issued a statement declaring that there would be no change in Yemen's internal and foreign policies, and confirmed Yemen's commitment to the UN and Arab League Charters. [16]

An announcement over R Sanʻā which followed the statement of the Foreign Ministry, said that the Corrective Movement would continue and that the Armed Forces pledged its allegiance, declaring that "the armed and security forces remain to protect the revolution and its principles and will continue to protect the revolution under all circumstances." [17]

There were conflicting reports on the security situation in the aftermath of the assassination. Several Arab sources stated that on 11 and 12 October, the situation in Sanʻā was tense and that armoured vehicles and paratroops were deployed at the radio station and at the Armed Forces Headquarters. A number of officers were reported to have been arrested. Others said that the situation was calm; still others reported demonstrations in Sanʻā calling for revenge. One correspondent, commenting on the absence of any reference to the assassination in the Yemeni press of 12 October 1977, said that "it seems the papers were taken by surprise." [18]

INTERPRETATIONS OF ḤAMDĪ'S ASSASSINATION

The various motives given for the assassination tended to reflect the political climate rather than throw much light on the facts themselves. The official account was not given until five days after the assassination. By this time, a number of embarrassing details and unfavourable interpretations had appeared in the Arab press (see below). The official statement read over R Sanʻā said that on 11 October 1977, Ḥamdī had left his house for the "humble home" which was rented by his brother ʻAbdallah, who had "turned [it] into a sort of rest house for relaxation from the strain of work. Ḥamdī used to spend time here whenever the need arose, or there was an opportunity to do so." ʻAbdallah preceded Ḥamdī to his house, and "some spiteful and mercenary enemies of the regime, who had previously been convicted of murder and other crimes, took advantage of the opportunity. They sneaked into the house where they fired the bullets . . . at the great deceased and his brother, and did not leave them until they were stiff corpses." The statement noted that it was Ḥamdī's custom "to spend some days alone by himself away from his office and home, so that he could have time to study various issues and cases." When he was alone, he preferred not to be accompanied by guards "as it was his nature to be modest and simple and he disliked the controls of ceremonies and formalities."[19]

On the other hand, Arab sources quoted the Yemeni Ambassador to Cairo, Ḥasan al-Suḥūlī, as saying that the two brothers were assassinated while driving a car near San'ā, and that the target of the murderers was really Ḥamdī's brother, 'Abdallah.[20]

According to *al-Ahrām*, the assassination was part of a very carefully planned plot, involving "three groups of criminals" who were instructed to carry out assassinations in three different places at the same time. 1) The Ḥamdī brothers were killed in 'Abdallah's home while chewing *qāt* (a narcotic leaf popular in both Yemens) by a group of men disguised in women's clothing who thus passed by the guards unchallenged. 2) Reserve Forces Commander Maj 'Alī Qannāf Zahra (referred to by other sources as the Commander of the Seventh Armoured Brigade), a relative of Ḥamdī, was killed at his headquarters in San'ā. 3) The third group was to assassinate Commander of the Sixth Armoured Brigade Maj Aḥmad Faraḥ in his home, but inadvertently killed his brother. The three groups were able to flee after carrying out the assassinations despite the heavy guard in all three areas.[21]

Sources in Abū Dhabī maintained that the assassination of the Ḥamdī brothers did not take place inside 'Abdallah's house, but outside—a few metres away from the General Command Headquarters in San'ā, and that at least four of their aides were killed.

The Kuwaiti *al-Watan* claimed that the Ḥamdī brothers were murdered in 'Abdallah's house—while "occupied" with two young Frenchwomen. It named the assassins as Qannāf Zahra and the Head of Ḥamdī's Special Intelligence, 'Abdallah al-Shamsī, in what was regarded as a signal for the execution of a military coup. But the coup misfired because several hours prior to the planned assassination, the army commanders had been assembled by Ghashmī for a lecture on Yemen's attitude towards South Yemen. The paper went on to say that there was a gunfight between the conspirators and Ḥamdī's guards, in which four guards were killed. However, one of them alerted the Paratroop Commander, 'Abd al-'Ālim, who had 'Abdallah's house surrounded and killed Zahra and Shamsī, along with several of their followers. During the fighting, the two French girls were also killed.[22]

In the version given by the pro-Iraqi *al-Dustūr*, Ghashmī himself was implicated along with the Head of Military Intelligence, Muḥammad al-Khamīs; the Interior Minister, Muḥsin al-Yūsufī; the Military Commander of the Ta'izz Province, Maj 'Alī 'Abdallah Sāliḥ and several other high-ranking officers. It described the killing as a well-planned conspiracy aimed at seizing power. In this version, the assassination took place in Ghashmī's house where the two Frenchwomen were brought for the purpose of "funmaking" to make it appear a "moral crime." The paper added that it was a former Royalist officer who killed Ḥamdī, and that it was not clear whether Zahra was killed or wounded.[23]

A number of Arab and foreign observers connected the assassination with the tribal rebellion of July 1977. According to this view, Ḥamdī's efforts to patch up the quarrel with South Yemen and give support to the National Democratic Front were said to have contributed to tension with the tribal chiefs. Ḥamdī had been scheduled to visit Aden between 13–15 October—two days after the assassination—

where he was expected to discuss unity and the improvement of relations. This possibility was regarded by the tribal chiefs as another threat to their positions.[24] *Al-Dustūr* suggested that the Saudis had come to the conclusion that the preferred way to calm the tribes was to get rid of Ḥamdī and thus also prevent a further *rapprochement* with South Yemen.[25]

In contrast, *Arabia and the Gulf*—quoting "informed Gulf sources"—said that there was strong evidence that the leaders of the refractory tribes of the north had nothing to do with the assassination, since it was unlikely that they would choose to sabotage the agreement reached between them and Ḥamdī so quickly. The paper quoted a diplomatic source in Beirut as claiming that Palestinians were involved in the affair, on the grounds that Ḥamdī had imposed severe restrictions on the Palestinians in Yemen.[26] Yet another version was that Ḥamdī was assassinated in revenge for Ḥajrī's death several months before.[27]

ATTEMPT TO ASSASSINATE GHASHMĪ

An assassination attempt on Ghashmī was reported on 16 October 1977, allegedly the work of Lt-Col Zayd al-Kabsī, a division commander in the Giants Brigade, who was loyal to Ḥamdī. Kabsī supposedly infiltrated a group of religious leaders seeking to convey to Ghashmī their condolences over Ḥamdī's death, tried to shoot him but failed in the attempt. Kabsī was executed on the same day on charges of mutiny against the Army General Command.[28]

Towards the end of October, Ghashmī said he would not allow any tribal loyalty among the Armed Forces; the Army should be loyal to the central authority only.[29]

ARMED FORCES

Total armed forces number 39,850. Defence expenditure in 1975–6 was 261.7m riyals ($60m). Military service is compulsory for three years. The Army numbers 37,600 in three infantry divisions (ten infantry brigades including three reserve); one parachute brigade; three commando brigades; two armoured battalions; two artillery battalions and one anti-aircraft artillery battalion. Equipment consists of 30 T-34, T-54 medium tanks; 30 *Saladin* armoured, *Ferret* scout cars; 120 BTR-40/-152, *Walid* armoured personnel carriers; 50 76mm and some 122mm guns; 50 SU-100 self-propelled guns; 82mm, 120mm mortars; 75mm recoilless rifles; *Vigilant* anti-tank guided weapons and 37mm guns. (Howitzers and anti-aircraft guns on order.) 500 men are deployed in the Lebanon with the Arab Peacekeeping Force. The Navy numbers 750 and has five large patrol craft (ex-Soviet *Poluchat*-class) and three motor torpedo boats (ex-Soviet P-4 class). The 1,500-strong Air Force has c. 22 combat aircraft (some believed to be in storage); one light bomber squadron with 14 Il-28; one fighter squadron with eight MiG-17 and some MiG-21; C-47, two *Skyvan* and some Il-14 transports; four MiG-15UTI and 18 Yak-11 trainers; Mi-4 and AB-205 helicopters. Paramilitary forces consist of 20,000 tribal levies.[30]

FOREIGN AFFAIRS

RELATIONS WITH SAUDI ARABIA

Relations with Riyadh began to improve after official Saudi recognition of the Yemeni Arab Republic in July 1970; by mid-1976, the Yemen had been drawn closely into the Saudi orbit. This relationship developed out of the gradually deepening, albeit covert, Saudi involvement in Yemen's internal affairs, particularly in extending its influence over the tribal chiefs of the northern region (see above); it was further determined by Yemen's bleak economic position which stood to gain from a closer Saudi connection. Accordingly, Yemen's relations within the

Arabian Peninsula, with other Arab countries and in the international sphere all bore the mark of Saudi influence.

A Joint Yemeni-Saudi Co-ordination Committee met in Riyadh in January 1977 under the chairmanship of the Saudi Defence and Aviation Minister, Sulṭān b. ʻAbd al-ʻAzīz. The Committee, first established in 1970, was responsible for channelling Saudi funds and for supervising and directing social, economic and military projects financed by them. A joint communiqué issued at the end of the January meetings reaffirmed the importance of "strengthening the cordial, fraternal and co-operative relations" between the two countries.[31] Resolutions approved by the committee provided for education, agriculture and communication projects to be financed by the Saudi Development Fund. The grant given to cover the Yemeni deficit was also raised to $99m. At the beginning of February, R Sanʻā announced that Saudi Arabia would give Yemen $140m for the purchase of American arms in order to facilitate the "process of modernization of the Yemeni army."[32] Over the following months, several economic agreements were signed in accordance with these resolutions.

Ḥamdī arrived in Riyadh for a two-day visit at the beginning of July 1977 on his way to Paris (see below). He described his discussions with King Khālid and Crown Prince Fahd, which reportedly concentrated on Saudi financial aid and the situation in the Red Sea area, as "successful and positive."

Following Ḥamdī's assassination on 11 October 1977, the Saudi government issued a statement strongly condemning "the treacherous aggression" and affirmed that the Saudis would stand by the Yemeni people, whom they hoped would "rally around" their new leadership.[33]

RELATIONS WITH SOUTH YEMEN

Since South Yemen's independence in late 1967, relations between the two Yemens have fluctuated between extremes of friendship and hostility, intermittent calls for unity being interspersed with sporadic outbreaks of fierce border clashes. This ambivalent relationship was the result of a number of complex factors ranging from internal rivalries both in Sanʻā and in Aden, to relations of the two Yemens with Saudi Arabia, and to the influence of Arab and international interests in the region.

The traditional and mutual call for union between North and South Yemen—as formulated in the unification agreement signed in Cairo in October 1972, after Arab League mediation—remained in practice a dead letter, mainly because of Saudi obstruction. However, the gradual improvement in relations between Saudi Arabia and South Yemen after they established diplomatic relations in March 1976 (see survey of South Yemen), also contributed to the improvement of relations between the two Yemens.

At the end of 1976, both Ḥamdī and the Republican Council Chairman Sālim ʻAlī Rubayʻ referred to ties of common interest between their countries and Saudi Arabia, and expressed the hope that "rapid measures would be taken to unify the two parts of Yemen as a natural and necessary step . . . and as a strategic issue important to both countries."[34] Ḥamdī and Rubayʻ agreed that a unified delegation should represent both Yemens in international conferences and that their embassies should look after each other's interests in countries where only one of them had diplomatic representation.

In mid-February 1977, the two leaders arrived in Qaʻtaba, a little town on the border, for what was described as an "amicable and historic meeting." A joint communiqué issued afterwards announced the setting up of a Joint Council composed of the two leaders and their respective Ministers of Defence, Foreign Affairs, Economy, Trade and Planning. The Council was scheduled to meet every six months alternatively in Aden and San'ā "to discuss and follow up issues which concern the Yemeni people." A joint economic, trade and planning sub-committee was also planned to survey, study and follow up development and economic projects.[35] At the same time, a joint delegation represented by the North Yemeni Minister of State, Aḥmad 'Abduh Sa'īd, and the South Yemeni Minister of Industry and Planning, 'Abd al-'Azīz 'Abd al-Wālī Nāshir, began a tour of Saudi Arabia and the Gulf states to explain their economic difficulties.

On several occasions in the following four months, both Ḥamdī and Rubay' declared their intention to move towards unification.[36] Nonetheless, reports continued to circulate of an unpublicized dispute between them over control of Perim Island in the strategic Bāb al-Mandūb Straits, held by South Yemen since 1967. These reports were emphatically denied by Ḥamdī. However, the two Yemens did pursue divergent policies towards Ethiopia and Somalia in the Red Sea conflict.

The leaders of the two Yemens met again in San'ā from 13–15 August 1977. Afterwards, Rubay' said that his visit, which came "within the framework of continued contacts . . . has given us the opportunity to review the affairs of our Yemeni people in both parts . . . [and] to exchange views on the Arab and international situations."[37]

There were vague and general reports throughout September 1977, that Ḥamdī was accelerating the pace, if not towards early unification, at least towards strengthening the two countries' relations. Simultaneously, there were more substantial reports of internal—apparently tribal—opposition to this move. Ḥamdī was due to visit Aden from 13–15 October 1977 where he was expected to pursue unification talks. That his assassination came two days before the scheduled visit gave credence to speculation that the deed was instigated by those opposed to any significant *rapprochement* between the two Yemens.

A statement issued by the South Yemeni Presidential Council on 12 October 1977, described the assassination as a "despicable conspiracy [which] was part of an imperialist plot hatched long ago to harm the struggle of the sons of the Yemeni people."[38] The South Yemenis announced a 40-day official mourning period, cancelling the 14th anniversary celebrations scheduled for 14 October, (which marked the beginning of the armed struggle against the British in 1963). The South Yemeni Minister of Interior, Qāsim Sāliḥ Musliḥ, said in San'ā on 12 October that Ḥamdī's death would not "affect the attempts at unification of the territory and people."[39] The South Yemeni Chairman, Sālim 'Alī Rubay', attended Ḥamdī's funeral despite San'ā's declared wish that no foreign dignatories be present (see above).

RELATIONS WITH OTHER ARAB COUNTRIES

The official and frequently-repeated Yemeni position with regard to inter-Arab affairs was to promote fraternal relations with all Arab countries irrespective of their regimes, and to co-ordinate a collective stand on the Arab-Israeli conflict and other international problems. However, visits of high-ranking Yemeni officials to Arab capitals were mainly to solicit economic aid. Assistance in the fields of economy, agriculture, information, communication, health and education was given by Kuwait, the United Arab Emirates, Iran, Egypt, Iraq, Syria and Libya. A group of Jordanian officers, including pilots, was reported to have helped train the Yemeni army under an agreement reached with Saudi help.[40]

Following Ḥamdī's assassination, the Foreign Minister, 'Abdallah al-Asnaj, declared that his country would continue its policy of close co-operation with all Arab countries, and that there would be no change in the foreign policy, principles and objectives laid down by Ḥamdī.[41]

INTERNATIONAL RELATIONS

The regime's pro-Saudi orientation undoubtedly influenced its attitude towards international affairs. While reaffirming its nonaligned commitments, Yemen's policy has undergone a decided, although gradual, shift towards the West since 1976. At the same time, its relations with the USSR progressively worsened, as manifested by the reported ending of Soviet military aid in 1976. The Russian navy also ceased to use the facilities it had previously enjoyed in Hodeida.

San'ā reiterated its intention "to diversify its sources of arms because dependence on the one source is no longer practical, considering the current international political changes."[42] The visit of an American military delegation to San'ā in March 1976, and of a Yemeni military delegation to France in June 1976, laid the foundation for arms agreements, to be financed mainly by Saudi Arabia.

Foreign Minister 'Abdallah al-Asnaj paid an official visit to France in February 1977, to discuss French technological assistance for the development of Yemen's agriculture, tourism and telecommunications—to be financed by the Saudis and other Gulf states. Four months later, between 4 and 7 July 1977, Ḥamdī and a large ministerial delegation paid a second visit to France during which a series of five-year agreements were signed covering economic, trade and communications co-operation. Arab sources reported that Ḥamdī had also asked for French arms. In October 1977, an agreement was signed with France for a loan of FF 120m.[43]

Throughout the first half of 1977, reports on relations with the USSR were vague and conflicting. According to some sources, Yemen finally severed its "military relations" with the USSR in June 1977;[44] others claimed that Soviet arms shipments were still continuing. At the beginning of August 1977, Tass reported that Yemen had expelled its correspondent in San'ā. No reason had been given, but it was "probably caused by the pressure of forces which would like to damage Yemen-Soviet relations."[45]

ECONOMIC AFFAIRS (4.56 Yemeni riyals = US$1; YR 8.65 = £1 sterling)

North Yemen is one of the poorest countries in the world, with *per capita* GNP at no more than $300 in 1977.[46] However, GDP increased by 7% in 1975–6, as in the previous two years.

The first significant attempt to create a basis for economic development was announced in mid-1977, when the Government launched a Five-Year Development Plan (1977/8–1981/2) of YR 16.5 bn ($3.6 bn), two-thirds to be financed from internal sources and one-third from foreign capital. The public sector is expected to provide c. 40% of total investment; the private, mixed and co-operative sectors the remainder. The Plan's aim is to work towards economic self-sufficiency based on agriculture and industry. Proposed allocations include 25% to industry, electricity and drinking water; 14% to agriculture; another 25% to transport and communications, and 12% to services.[47] During the period of the Plan, GDP is expected to increase yearly by 8%. However, some observers regarded the Plan as overly-ambitious, as most of the funds will be required to develop industrial infrastructure. A conference, attended by experts from Arab countries, Europe and the US, was held in San'ā in the latter part of November 1977 to discuss economic problems, mainly the new Development Plan.

Yemen continues to suffer from a serious shortage of skilled manpower, and has to rely for funds and personnel on Saudi Arabia, Kuwait, UAE, Egypt and Iraq. The UN also provides experts to work with various ministries under the joint co-ordination of the UN Development Programme and the Yemeni Central Planning Organization.[48]

Development in the industrial sector (which contributes only 3% of GDP) was mainly reflected by decreased production in the cotton textile industry (-17%), due to the shortage of skilled labour; increased electricity production (+10%), as a result of the installation of new generators in San'ā and Ta'izz; and increased cement production (+14%), reflecting the boom in building and construction activities.

Agriculture, which contributes more than 50% of GDP, was affected by excessive rains in 1975-6, causing a reduction of 10% in total production (cereals by -14% and cotton by -5%) from 1974-5.

In 1975-6, total current expenditure amounted to YR 819m, an increase of c. 36% over 1974-5. As in the past, c. 50% of this was allocated to defence. Internal revenues, amounting to YR 805m, were allowed only a small deficit of YR 15m—2% of total current expenditure.

The Yemeni budget for 1977-8 was fixed at $452m, with a deficit of $111m.[49] Yemen's exports—of which cotton, hides and skins, and coffee are the main products—showed a decline from YR 55.3m in 1973-4 to YR 50.5m in 1976-7. Imports, on the other hand, grew from YR 744.9m in 1973-4 to YR 3.03 bn in 1976-7.

The balance of trade deficit increased to YR 1,666m in 1975-6 (cf YR 1,105m in 1974-5), mainly because of the high increase in imports (+48%). Already negligible, exports decreased further (-5%), mainly due to reduced cotton exports.

China remained the most important market for Yemeni exports (c. 50% of the total), followed by South Yemen, 17%; Italy, 16%; and Saudi Arabia, 9%. Japan continued to be the most important supplier of imports, with 14% of the total; followed by India, 9%; and Australia and China, 8% each.

In spite of the large deficit in the balance of trade, the balance of payments was in surplus in 1975-6 by more than YR 1,424m (cf c. YR 492m in 1974-5). This was mainly due to higher remittances from workers abroad, which amounted to YR 2,363m in 1975-6 (cf YR 1,013m in 1974-5). Foreign economic loans were less important, contributing only YR 213m (cf YR 164m in 1974-5).

(Economic Section by Moshe Efrat

MAIN TRADE PARTNERS (millions of Riyals)

	1973-74	*1974-75*	*1975-76*
EXPORTS TO:			
China	3.0	22.1	24.6
Italy	4.9	4.3	8.7
South Yemen	3.8	6.3	8.4
Saudi Arabia	3.6	2.5	4.6
France	2.8	0.3	0.7
United States	0.3	0.3	0.6
Djibouti	0.5	0.4	0.5
United Kingdom	0.1	0.1	0.5
Netherlands	0.1	0.8	0.4
West Germany	0.1	1.3	0.3
Japan	30.0	7.2	0.1
Singapore	5.9	0.5	0.1
Total (including others)	**55.4**	**53.0**	**50.0**

IMPORTS FROM:			
Japan	96.7	170.7	239.6
India	15.1	27.1	147.0
China	30.9	114.1	139.3
Australia	29.6	44.2	133.3
Saudi Arabia	36.3	56.7	118.8
Netherlands	35.9	37.4	105.8
United Kingdom	26.7	49.7	90.0
South Yemen	42.4	47.2	84.3
West Germany	38.5	59.4	80.2
Djibouti	39.5	28.2	77.1
Singapore	22.3	26.1	57.8
France	49.6	29.6	56.1
Total (including others)	**745.0**	**981.0**	**1,706.8**

Source: Central Bank of Yemen, *Annual Report 1975–76.*

BALANCE OF PAYMENTS (millions of Riyals)

	1973–74	*1974–75*	*1975–76*
Current Accounts	− 83.7	306.7	1,100.4
Imports	− 873.3	− 1,163.4	− 1,721.3
Exports	61.9	58.5	55.3
Balance of Trade	*− 811.4*	*− 1,104.9*	*− 1,666.0*
Services:			
Government receipts (incl workers' remittances)	875.7	1,655.5	3,219.3
Government payments	− 148.0	− 243.4	− 452.9
Net visible account	727.7	1,412.1	2,766.4
Capital accounts:			
Government receipts (commodities and cash loans)	144.4	164.3	213.1
Government payments (loan statements)	− 15.1	− 16.9	− 14.1
Net capital accounts	129.3	147.4	199.0
Private investment, errors and omissions (net)	+ 37.4	+ 37.5	+ 123.0
Balance of Payments	**+ 83.0**	**+ 491.6**	**+ 1,422.4**

Sources: Middle East Annual Review 1977. The Economist Intelligence Unit. Central Bank Yemen, *Financial Statistical Bulletin*, January– March 1977.

GOVERNMENT BUDGETS (millions of Riyals)

	1975–76	*1976–77*
A) REVENUE		
Direct Taxes	45.0	47.4
Taxes on Income and Profits	24.0	23.4
Taxes on Foreign Trade	394.0	496.1
Taxes on Goods and Services	59.3	94.2
Non-tax Revenue	66.2	143.5
Total	**588.5**	**804.6**
B) EXPENDITURE		
General Public Services	184.8	231.8
Defence	298.0	385.9
Education	46.6	74.5
Health	22.6	32.8
Social Services	14.5	23.3
Economic Services	34.0	61.2
Unallocated and other purposes	3.5	10.3
Total	**603.5**	**819.8**

Source: Central Bank of Yemen, *Fifth Annual Report 1975–76.*

ANNUAL AVERAGE RATE OF GROWTH OF REAL GDP

	69/70–75/76 actual %	72/73–75/76 actual %	76/77–80/81 planned %	GDP at Constant Prices of Base Year: Base year 75/76 Mill. YR	%	80/81 Mill. YR	%
Agriculture	6.6	4.9	5.5	2,305	44.5	3,010	39.2
Industry	11.8	8.6	11.7	302	5.8	526	6.8
Building and Construction	8.0	5.2	14.4	227	4.4	445	5.8
Transport and Communication	12.0	8.0	11.3	151	2.9	258	3.4
Trade	70.0	10.4	10.1	1,220	23.6	1,970	25.7
Finance	29.9	35.4	9.5	141	2.7	222	2.9
Real Estate	3.2	3.0	3.6	199	3.8	238	3.1
Government Services	10.5	11.0	10.0	509	9.8	820	10.7
Other Services	7.1	7.1	7.5	127	2.5	182	2.4
Total	**7.7**	**7.0**	**8.2**	**5,181**	**100**	**7,671**	**100**

Source: The Times, London; 17 November 1977.

FINANCIAL RESOURCES OF FIXED CAPITAL FORMATION

Socio-economic Sectors/ Financial Resources	*Government Sector*	*Existing public & mixed sector*	*Co-operative Sector*	*New mixed Sector*	*Private Sector*	*Total*
Government	1,750	250	268	381	—	2,649
Self-financing	25	375	411	225	73	1,109
Citizens	25	25	402	900	4,005	5,357
Commercial Banks	—	50	—	90	110	250
Subtotal: Internal Resources	*1,800*	*700*	*1,081*	*1,596*	*4,188*	*9,365*
External loans, committed	700	900	—	16	—	1,616
External loans under negotiation	1,100	300	—	123	—	1,523
Foreign aids committed	790	10	—	3	—	803
Foreign Aids under negotiation	360	40	—	—	—	400
Loans and aids needed	650	650	20	205	100	1,625
Equity	—	6	—	400	233	639
Subtotal: External Resources	*3,600*	*1,906*	*20*	*747*	*333*	*6,606*
Grand Total	**5,400**	**2,606**	**1,101**	**2,343**	**4,521**	**15,975**

Source: The Times, 17 November 1977.

NOTES

1. The Permanent Constitution was proclaimed at the end of 1970. See *Middle East Record 1969–70* (Jerusalem: Israel Universities Press, 1977), pp. 1332–4.
2. *Al-Qabas*, Kuwait; 12, 13, 18 January. *Rūz al-Yūsuf*, Cairo; 28 March. *Al-Ahrām*, Cairo; 13 April 1977.
3. The suspected assassin, later identified by British police as PLO member Zuhayr Yūsuf 'Akkāsh, remained at large. His name was mentioned again in October 1977 in connection with the hijacking of the Lufthansa plane.
4. Voice of Palestine, 20 April—BBC Summary of World Broadcasts (BBC), 22 April 1977.
5. *Al-Ahrām*, *Al-Akhbār*, Cairo; 26 April 1977.
6. Middle East News Agency (MENA), 26 April—BBC, 29 April 1977.
7. *Al-Mustaqbal*, Paris; 29 October 1977.
8. *The Middle East*, London; August 1977.
9. *Rūz al-Yūsuf*, 5 September 1977.
10. *Al-Siyāsa*, Kuwait; 25 September, 13 October 1977.
11. *Ibid*, 6 October 1977.

12. R San'ā, 25 September—Daily Report (DR), 27 September 1977.
13. *Al-Siyāsa*, 6 October 1977.
14. R San'ā, 11 October—DR, 12 October 1977.
15. R San'ā, 13 October—BBC, 15 October 1977.
16. Iraqi News Agency (INA), 12 October—BBC, 15 October 1977.
17. R San'ā, 13 October—BBC, 15 October 1977.
18. INA, 12 October 1977.
19. R San'ā, 16 October—BBC, 18 October 1977.
20. Qatari News Agency (QNA), 13 October—BBC, 15 October 1977.
21. *Al-Ahrām*, 14 October 1977.
22. *Al-Watan*, Kuwait; 22 October 1977.
23. *Al-Dustūr*, London; 21–27 November 1977.
24. *The Guardian*, London; 13 October. *Al-Ahrām*, 14 October. *Financial Times (FT)*, London; 13, 15 October 1977.
25. *Al-Dustūr*, London; 21–27 November 1977.
26. *Arabia and the Gulf*, London; 24 October 1977.
27. *Al-Mustaqbal*, 29 October 1977.
28. INA, 20 October—DR, 20 October; *Al-Ahrām*, 20 October 1977.
29. *Rūz al-Yūsuf*, 24 October 1977.
30. *The Military Balance 1977–78* (London: International Institute for Strategic Studies).
31. R Riyadh, 30 January—BBC, 1 February 1977.
32. MENA, 4 February 1977.
33. R Riyadh, 12 October—BBC, 14 October 1977.
34. *Rūz al-Yūsuf*, 6 December 1976.
35. R San'ā, 16 February—BBC, 18 February 1977.
36. *Rūz al-Yūsuf*, 28 March; *al-Yaqza*, Kuwait; 4 July 1977.
37. R San'ā, 15 August—BBC, 17 August 1977.
38. R Aden, 12 October—BBC, 14 October 1977.
39. *Ibid.*
40. QNA, 18 September—DR, 20 September 1977.
41. R San'ā, 18 October—BBC, 20 October 1977.
42. MENA, 17 May—DR, 20 May 1976.
43. R San'ā, 15 October—BBC, 25 October 1977.
44. *Daily Telegraph*, London; 8 June 1977.
45. *Tass*, 6 August; *New York Times*, 7 August 1977.
46. *Jordan Times (JT)*, Amman; 10 September 1977.
47. *FT*, 7 December 1977.
48. *JT*, 10 September 1977.
49. Deutsche Presse Agentur, 30 August 1977.

Index

NOTE

The definite article al- has been dropped from many Arabic names listed in the index. Wherever retained, it has been disregarded in the alphabetical order of entries. Similarly, honorific titles, when given before the name of the bearer, are disregarded in the arrangement. Names enclosed in quotation marks are code names used by members of fidā'iyyūn organizations. The names included in Government lists are not indexed, only those mentioned in the text.

Most political parties, organizations, public bodies and institutions have been indexed by name and not according to country, which appears in parentheses at the end of the entry.

Page numbers in bold type indicate principal references. The alphabetical order is word-by-word.

IRA E. HOFFMAN

430, 437–40, 442–3, 449, 451, 453–63, 466, 470, 482
Beirut, 7, 115–17, 127, 136, 147, 162, 185–6, 194–5, 218, 238, 240, 293, 411, 459, 462, 494–8, 502–11 *passim*, 574, 578, 583, 659
Beirut Chamber of Commerce and Industry, 522
Beit-El, 443
Beit Homotayim (Dotan), 443
Beit Shean, 435
Beit Yisrael (House of Israel—Yemenites), 425
Belgium, 378, 400, 417, 420, 525, 546, 583
Belgrade Conference on Human Rights, 465
Bendix Corporation, 577
Ben-Elisar, Eliahu, 439
Ben Yisrael, Gideon, 469
Benevolent Society for the Welfare of the Gaza Strip Inhabitants, 221
Benghazi, 167, 536, 538
Benghazi University, 533
Ben-Gurion, David, 424
Ben-Porat, Mordecai, 425, 427
Bension, Yehoshua, 448–9
Berbera, 47, 60, 62–4, 69, 173
Berlin, 131
Bethlehem, 209, 211, 214, 460, 484
Bhutto, Zulfiqar 'Ali, 45, 395
Bint Jubayl, 519
Biqa', 509
Bīr Zayt, 209, 214
Bīra al-, 209
Bir'am, 446
Bitsios, Demitrius, 640
"Black June Organization", 161, 474
Black Panthers (Israel), 425, 444
Black Sea, 67, 71, 73, 345
"Black September", 463
Bnei Braq, 451
Bochner, Michael, 449
Bombay, 464
Bonn, 266, 377
Boran, Behice, 627
Bosporus, 71–2
Boston, 466
Boumedienne, Houari, 169, 171, 537, 539
Bourges, Yvon, 600
Bouteflika, 'Abd al-'Azīz, 171
Brandt, Willy, 274, 462
Brazil, 418, 420
Brezhnev, Leonid, 35–6, 199, 308, 559
British Aircraft Corporation (BAC), 580
British Broadcasting Corporation (BBC), 378
British Petroleum (BP), 254–5, 558, 561
Brookings Institution, 53, 126, 272
"Brookings Report" (*Towards Peace in the Middle East*), 25, 101, 126
Brussels, 51, 53, 270, 455, 488
Brzezinski, Zbigniew, 22, 25, 101, 126, 129, 131, 456, 487
Būbīyān, 344–6, 394, 413
Budayrī, Misbāh, 480
Bugurgan-Abu Ghurayb, 417
Bulgaria, 377, 416, 489, 646
Buraimi, 363
Burg, Yosef, 424, 449, 451, 466
Burhan Shahidi (Pao Erh-han), 47
Burma, 464
Būshehr, 387
Business Week, 269, 272
Bustānī, Jūll, 508

Çağlayangil, İhsan Sabri, 639–40, 642–5
Cairo, 3, 8, 14, 33, 36, 52, 89, 98, 112, 114, 123–5, 127, 129, 148–9, 151, 154–9, 165–7, 171, 176, 183, 197, 200–1, 211, 217, 221, 233–4, 274, 289–91, 295, 298, 306, 310, 312–16, 319, 412, 456–7, 460, 480, 526, 531, 533, 536, 543, 554–5, 609, 614, 645, 655, 658, 660
Cairo agreement (November 1969), 117, 193–4, 196, 504, 507–9, 511, 513, 520, 573
Cairo conference (December 1977) (Egypt-Israel), 3, 7
Cairo Criminal Court, 287
Cairo summit (October 1976), 86, 123, 149, 160, 162, 171, 175–6, 183, 193–5, 198, 412, 479, 486, 492, 496, 505–6, 509, 513, 518
Callaghan, James, 268
Canada, 54, 255, 400, 420
Canberra, 44
Capucci, Hilarion, 451
Carter, Jimmy or Carter Administration, 9–10, **21–31**, 52, 54, 65, 68, 87, 91–101, 103–9, 120, 123–41, 152, 156, 162, 199–201, 215, 256, 270, 309–10, 319–22, 378, 387, 389–91, 421, 438, 442, 452–7, 487–8, 542, 576–8, 583–5, 616–18, 639, 641–2
Carthage, 542
Caspian Sea, 391
Castro, Fidel, 63, 351, 541, 557, 560, 575
Ceausescu, Nicolae, 33, 463
Cengiz, Eşref, 630
Central Treaty Organization (CENTO), 378, 389, 391, 394, 632
Chad, 168, 536, 540
Chah Bahar naval base, 393
Chamoun, Camille, 496–7, 506, 508–9, 512, 519
Chamoun, Dany, 497
Chamoun, Dori, 497
Chiang Kai-shek, 40, 42–3, 46
Chiao Kuan-hua, 44
Chicago, 377
China (People's Republic) (PRC), 39–48, 65–7, 310, 349, 387, 416, 420, 489, 547, 586, 595–6, 601, 663
  Communist Party National Congress, 40
  Constitution, 40
  National People's Congress (NPC), 45, 47
  Politburo, 39–40, 47
Chi Teng-kuei, 45
Chou En-lai, 39
Christian Highlands of Ethiopia, 57
Citizens' Rights Movement (CRM) (Israel), 425, 432, 435–6, 441
Clifford, Clark, 639, 642
Clinton, Massachusetts, 22
Coexistence with Justice (Arab list) (Israel), 425
Cohen, Menahem, 435
Cohen, Shalom, 425
Colombo, 390, 644
Columbia Broadcasting System (CBS), 131
Comecon (Council for Mutual Economic Assistance) (CMEA), 33, 38, 416
Communist Labour Organization (Lebanon), 501
Communist Labour Party (Egypt), 291
Communist Party (China), 40–1, 45, 47
Communist Party (Cuba), 560
Communist Party (Iraq), 403, 405, 408
Communist Party (Italy), 377
Communist Party (Jordan), 223
Communist Party (Lebanon), 500, 511
Communist Party of the Soviet Union (CPSU), 29
  Politbureau, 29
Communist Party (Sudan), 591, 603
Communist Party (Syria), 610
Communists, 288, 291–2, 294–5, 415
Compagnie Française des Pétroles (CFP), 355, 365
Complete Land of Israel Movement, 424, 441
Confederation of Iranian Students Abroad (CISA), 377–8
Conference on International Economic Co-operation (CIEC) ("North-South dialogue"), 49, 53, 253, 257, 267, 269, 579
Conference of Islamic Foreign Ministers (Eighth), 438, 536, 540
Conference of Presidents of Major Jewish Organizations in the US, 466
Conference of Socialist and Progressive Parties (second, 1977), 412
Coptic community in Egypt, 14, 298, 300,
Coptic Holy Synod (Egypt), 298
COREDIF, 386
Costa Rica, 464
Council of Europe, 641
Crete, 71
Cuba, 47, 58–9, 61–4, 174, 332, 349, 351, 377, 394, 464, 541, 551, 554, 559–60
Cultural Revolution (China), 39, 47
Cyrenaica, 537
Cyprus, 33, 38, 55, 71–3, 622–3, 626, 628, 630, 632–3, 637–46
Czechoslovakia, 33, 273–4, 307, 392, 416, 420, 490, 554